Malcolm E. Stacey

AUSTRALIA
LBC Information Services
Sydney

CANADA and USA
Carswell
Toronto

NEW ZEALAND
Brooker's
Auckland

SINGAPORE and MALAYSIA
Sweet and Maxwell Asia
Singapore and Kuala Lumpur

DATA PRO

LAW AND

DATA PROTECTION

LAW AND PRACTICE

by

Rosemary Jay

London
Sweet & Maxwell
2007

Second Edition 2003

Published in 2007 by
Sweet & Maxwell Limited of
100 Avenue Road, Swiss Cottage, London NW3 3PF
www.sweetandmaxwell.co.uk

Typeset by Servis Filmsetting Ltd
Printed and bound in Great Britain by
William Clowes Ltd, Beccles, Suffolk

No natural forests were destroyed to make this product;
only farmed timber was used and replanted

A CIP catalogue record for this book
is available from the British Library

ISBN 9780421954700

©
Sweet & Maxwell
2007

Preface

Data protection lives in the real world. It is about people and what happens to information about them. It should be seen as neither an esoteric concept, nor a set of burdensome rules. With parallel increases in the power of technology and the ambitions of government and businesses to collect information about all of us, the Data Protection Principles have never been more important. They go to the heart of personal autonomy and human dignity. The law which brings the principles to life provides the regulatory framework and vital safeguards, but it also makes good business sense. It needs to be understood and followed by data controllers in ways which inspire trust and confidence. When processing personal information they need to meet reasonable expectations of integrity, security, and fairness.

Individuals also need to understand how their information is used, be aware of their rights, and be confident in using them. At the heart of my office's role is "strengthening public confidence in data protection by taking a practical down to earth approach, simplifying and making it easier for the majority of organisations who seek to handle personal information well and tougher for the minority who do not."

The law, with the Data Protection Act at its heart, is the main tool to minimise data protection risk for both individuals and society. This new edition of "Data Protection Law and Practice" provides a welcome and up-to-date contribution to understanding legal provisions which have an unwelcome reputation for opacity. Even where there is doubt on particular points, there needs to be full analysis and discussion. I am confident that this book will promote compliance and good practice, will aid debate and ultimately will help contribute to strengthened public confidence.

Richard Thomas
Information Commissioner
September 2007

Acknowledgments

By the time a book reaches its third edition it has inevitably built up a vast level of indebtedness to those who have assisted, whether by contributing material, reading and commenting, suggesting new sources or pointing to relevant materials. In the two previous editions I had the benefit of working with a co-author, Angus Hamilton. Since the last edition Angus's changed role has left him with insufficient time to contribute. However, this edition still contains important contributions made by Angus. Thanks are due to him as well for his helpful comments on the chapter on prosecution and enforcement in this edition.

I will not repeat the names of all those who helped by reviewing chapters in previous editions but acknowledge their contributions. This work builds on the previous editions and I remain beholden to them. Thanks are also due to Jon Fell who contributed his expertise to the chapter on electronic communications. The hard work and dedication of a number of trainees in the Manchester office, Liam Fitzgerald, Sarah Mather, Danielle Ingham, Jenna Clarke and Amie Norris who kindly assisted with initial research into some of the more obscure statutory provisions deserves a special mention.

In finalising this edition I have been indebted to a wide range of people. The data protection regulators from Jersey, Guernsey and the Isle of Man, that is Emma Martins, Peter Harris and Iain McDonald, kindly commented on the new chapter on the data protection regimes in the islands. Partners and colleagues from PinsentMasons, David Barker, Susan Biddle, Sue Cullen, Richard Ives, William Malcolm, Iain Monaghan, Louise Townsend, Chris Pounder, Vicki Southern and Struan Robertson, have been most generous in spending time reviewing chapters. Grateful thanks are also due to David Smith of the Information Commissioner's Office who kindly commented on two chapters and Sian Rudgard who reviewed the material on Binding Corporate Rules. Thanks are also due to Paul Taylor of Education Leeds and a member of the Information Tribunal and Chris Brogan of Security International for chapter reviewing. The work has been improved by all their comments and contributions but any mistakes or infelicities remain my responsibility.

As the field of law has grown a work the text takes ever longer to revise. The content is generally up to date as at June 2007. In some areas I have managed to add slightly later materials, but even since handing over the text to the publishers there have been further developments including the publication of a long-awaited piece on the meaning of the term "personal data" from the Article 29 Working Group. It is inevitable that a work of this size cannot quite keep pace in a fast-changing environment, but I hope that it has captured all the important changes since the last edition in 2003.

The editors from Sweet and Maxwell have made their usual invaluable contribution, amending, suggesting and supporting. In particular, Julian Chase has encouraged me to include a set of Navigation Charts which it is hoped will prove an invaluable aid for the new user. Those who have had previous editions will recognise that there has only been limited updating of the case studies. Time simply did not permit re-drawing them. I hope that they remain relevant and promise to provide a new set for the next edition.

Thanks are also due to Janet Aston my secretary for her valiant contribution in typing and sorting out footnotes and, as ever, to my family for putting up with the work which yet another edition entails.

Rosemary Jay
September 2007

Table of Contents

CHAPTER 3

Interpretation of the Act and Key Definitions, including Territorial Application

CHAPTER 4

Data Protection and Rights of Access under the Freedom of Information Act 2000 and the Environmental Information Regulations 2004

CHAPTER 5

The Principles

CHAPTER 6

Legitimate Processing

CHAPTER 7

Sensitive Data

CHAPTER 8

Overseas or Cross-border Transfers of Personal Data

CHAPTER 9

Notification

CHAPTER 10

Individual Rights—General Points

CHAPTER 11

Subject Access

CHAPTER 12

Rights to Prevent Processing

CHAPTER 13

Rights Relating to Automated Decisions

CHAPTER 14

Compensation and Other Individual Remedies (including the Assessment of Claims by the Commissioner)

CHAPTER 15

Exemptions for Regulation, National Security, Crime Control and Taxation

CHAPTER 16

Exemptions for the Protection of the Individual: Family, Employers, Health, Social Work and Schools Information

CHAPTER 17

Exemptions for the Special Purposes: Journalistic, Literary and Artistic

CHAPTER 18

Research

CHAPTER 19

Miscellaneous Exemptions

CHAPTER 20

Enforcement and Prosecution

CHAPTER 21

Access to Criminal Records and Enforced Subject Access

CHAPTER 22

Electronic Communications and the Privacy and Electronic Communications (EC Directive) Regulations 2003

CHAPTER 23

Monitoring of Communications and Data Retention

CHAPTER 24

**Data Protection Supervision of EU Co-operation in Immigration,
Asylum, Customs, Policing and Judicial Matters, Role of the
European Supervisor and the Information Commissioner**

CHAPTER 25

The Commissioner

CHAPTER 26

Information Tribunal

CHAPTER 27

Data Protection Law in Jersey, Guernsey and the Isle of Man

APPENDICES

Topic Navigation Charts

Introduction
The charts are intended to be used as a tool to indicate issues of particular significance in dealing with specific areas. They are intended as a starting point and not an exhaustive guide. A practitioner faced with a problem in a particular area will probably need to read more widely; the chart is a starting point tool. Where a topic is already covered in a dedicated chapter (journalism and research), it is not covered here.

How to use this section
The first Navigation Chart is intended for the first-time adviser and indicates the core topics and introductory paragraph numbers for each topic. Under the subsequent headings the topics of particular relevance to the issue and the corresponding paragraph references are listed.

GENERAL—GUIDE TO RESPONSIBILITIES OF A DATA CONTROLLER

Topics

BUSINESS COMMERCIAL ISSUES

In this we indicate those points where there is an intersection of business agreements or commercial relationships with data protection requirements.

CCTV

CHARITIES

FRAUD INVESTIGATION OR ASSESSMENT

JOURNALISM—This is covered in Chapter 17

MARKETING

ON–LINE ACTIVITIES

RESEARCH—This is covered in Chapter 18

Table of Cases

(All references are to paragraph numbers)

Sweden

France

Table of Statutes

(All references are to paragraph numbers)

Table of Statutory Instruments

(All references are to paragraph numbers)

Table of European Legislation

(All references are to paragraph numbers)

Background, History and Context

INTRODUCTION

1–01 In the late 1970s and early 1980s there was an explosion of information power brought about by computing. Fears that the use of the new machines might weaken or undermine individual human rights surfaced early on in mainland Europe. Europe had only established its Human Rights Commission in the 1950s after the European Convention for the Protection of Rights and Fundamental Freedoms was adopted in 1950. The suggestion that data movements might be curtailed or controlled on human rights grounds gave rise, in its turn, to fears of a different kind; fears that trade would be fettered if information could not flow freely. The development of standards for the use and dissemination of personal data, or data protection standards, proved to be the response to these fears. The standards are now embodied in enforceable laws throughout Europe and in many other parts of the world.

1–02 Since the first edition of this text was published in 1999 information law has come of age. In the last edition in 2003 we commented:

> "While data protection instruments, at both international and national level, were probably the earliest legislative responses to the information age, since then the field of information law has matured. There is a host of European legislation either in force or in preparation dealing with what can broadly be described as information law issues; numerous UK statutes cover or include information provisions and the courts are increasingly called on to decide cases concerned with information."

Now, in 2007, the law dealing with information has developed significantly.[1] Within that area the law affecting personal information has become a field in its own right. Practitioners can no longer consider data protection, privacy or rights of access as being specialist or niche areas; as information has become ever more necessary to commercial and public life the laws governing its use have become equally significant.

---

[1] For an overview of the European position see *http://www.europa.eu/en/information society* [Accessed on 2 September 2007] and the range of developments and legal initiatives completed or underway ranging from the regulatory framework for electronic communications to eSafety and payment systems.

There appears to be no end to the development of the area. The introduction of identity cards, the growth of the national DNA database, the development of the right of privacy by the courts using the Human Rights Act 1998, the move to legislate for increased data-sharing by Government are just examples of continued expansion in the UK alone. In Europe the programme of legal development continues with the aim of ensuring that Europe becomes an area of justice, freedom and security and at the same time remains competitive in the electronic world with the benefits of such a world becoming available to all its citizens.[2] When the law is moving and developing so fast it can be tempting to focus only on the present, however sometimes a longer perspective can be useful. In this chapter we look at the 1998 Data Protection Act in its national and international context. This is not however merely a historical exercise; the older instruments may still impact on interpretation or approach, for example Treaty 108 of the Council of Europe continues to bind the UK.

THE NATURE OF INFORMATIONAL PRIVACY

1–03   In addressing the background to the data protection regime the broader context of privacy rights cannot be ignored. Data protection was developed to protect personal information held primarily in electronic form and yet sometimes its relationship with privacy is not recognised. That relationship and privacy rights themselves are still being developed in UK law. There is a growing recognition of the centrality of privacy to individual. As Lord Nicholls commented in *Campbell v MGM*:

> "The importance of freedom of expression has been stressed often and eloquently, the importance of privacy less so. But it too lies at the heart of liberty in a modern state. A proper degree of privacy is essential for the well-being and development of an individual. And restraints imposed on government to pry into the lives of the citizen go to the essence of a democratic state."[3]

It must be remarked however that the nature of privacy, the extent of protection to which individuals are entitled and the relationship with data protection are still matters of debate. In a very recent case the Court of Appeal took a narrow view of data protection describing the purpose of the Act as being to give the individual right to control the flow of information about himself, ensure that all information is handled properly.[4] There is a similar absence of agreement on the level of protection or freedom from intrusion to which individuals may be entitled in their day-to-day lives, their work places and in cyberspace as well as the most appropriate tools for achieving such protection.[5]

Despite the absence of an agreed common definition of, or an approach to, privacy there has been a significant increase in the number of privacy or data protection laws throughout the world. However, not all commentators would agree that the development of law has meant an increased protection from intrusion. Privacy International, a specialist pressure group in the privacy domain, has carried out an annual global

---

[2] See the i2010 programme *A European Information Society for growth and employment* COM (2005) 229 final as an example.
[3] Lord Nicholls, para.12.
[4] *Johnson v Medical Defence Union* [2007] 1 All E.R. 464 (Mar).
[5] See Ch.2 for an analysis of the developing case law on privacy.

review of the state of privacy since 2003. In the 2006 report they described some 70 countries as having some form of privacy protection and assessed those countries for their comparative privacy status, with the lowest level of privacy meriting a black mark and the highest a blue one.[6] They assessed the UK as being below the US as well as other EU countries. One of the issues which weighed strongly against the UK was the prevalence of CCTV cameras, leading to the "surveillance society" accusation. This issue has also been raised by the Information Commissioner. In the same vein the Article 29 Working Party has continued to take a strong view of the protection of informational privacy rights and has criticised the response of governments to sanction more and more intrusion in the name of law enforcement.[7] However there are other perspectives, on the other hand the development of case law restricting the media from publishing information about individuals without consent has been described in colourful terms as an attack on press freedoms[8] or "privacy gone mad".

1–04 The picture is made even more complex by the international nature of the issues. Historically there has been a difference between the US approach to privacy and the European one.[9] In the broadest terms the US approach has been that the right to privacy is an aspect of individual self-determinism, the right of the individual to do what he or she wants as long as it does not harm others[10]; whereas the European approach linked to Art.8 includes consideration of the individual's rights to exist in or be accepted by the community.[11] Americans have tended to reject overarching regulation in favour of a self-regulatory or mixed approach.[12] Rather than rely on regulation they have looked more to the market to develop privacy solutions; for this reason American companies have espoused the technical approach to solving privacy issues such as anonymisation technologies or the use of intelligent agents. Since September 2001 the US has been more accepting of State surveillance and data capture with the aim of dealing with security threats. Interestingly over the same period there seems to have been a gradual change in US attitudes towards protecting privacy resulting in the development of specific types of legal instrument, for example it was reported in January 2007 that more than half of the US States have enacted laws requiring customers to be notified where there is a data security breach.[13] Other cultures have other approaches. There is a move towards convergence but there is still a long way to go and in the course of the journey the differences have spawned a host of privacy specialists, a "conference rich environment" and a vast range of books, articles, discussion sites, working groups and initiatives.

---

[6] *www.privacyinternational.org* [Accessed on 2 September 2007].
[7] See Ch.24 for a detailed examination of the international stresses and tensions in this important debate.
[8] See Ch.2 for an analysis of the developing case law on privacy.
[9] Although commentators from both sides of the Atlantic pay homage to the effect of the US article in 1890 by Samuel Warren and Louis Brandeis, "The right to Privacy" (1890) 4 Harvard L.R. 194 the development of approaches to privacy has been different in the two jurisdictions.
[10] See for example papers from *Computers, Freedom and Privacy* (US Annual Conference) 1995 onwards. The *Report of the Initiative for Privacy Standardisation in Europe (IPSE)* (February 2002) produced by the European Committee for Standardisation (CEN) covers the difference between the approaches.
[11] *Niemietz v Germany* (1992) 16 E.H.R.R. 97 "Respect for private life must also comprise to a certain degree the right to establish and develop relationships with other human beings".
[12] See debate on Safe Harbor in context of overseas transfers. The paper is available at *http://www.europa. eu/international_market/dataprotection* [Accessed on 2 September 2007].
[13] Perkins Coie, *Data Breach Notification Chart* (December 21, 2006) online and other sources referenced at p.9 in the White Paper *Approaches to security Breach Notification* published by Canadian Internet Policy and Public Interest Clinic January 2007.

UNITED KINGDOM DEVELOPMENTS BETWEEN 1960 AND 1972

1–05   In the United Kingdom, the late 1960s and early 1970s saw a commitment to individual rights which resulted in the passage of the Sex Discrimination Act 1975 and the Race Relations Act 1968. It also manifested itself in a concern for personal privacy. The Consumer Credit Act 1974 included provisions to allow individuals to have sight of their credit "files"[14] together with a mechanism for inserting Notices of Correction on those files where the individual disagreed with the information recorded by the credit reference agency. Various privacy Bills were introduced into Parliament during the 1960s and early 1970s.[15] Although the Bills had no real hope of success they had produced sufficient impetus by May 1970 to persuade the then Labour Government to appoint Kenneth Younger to chair a Committee on Privacy which reported in 1972.[16] As part of its work the Younger Committee undertook a survey of public attitudes to privacy which highlighted a high level of concern regarding the possibility of widespread availability via computers of information about individuals. Younger looked at both physical privacy, that is freedom from intrusion in ones home and family life, and informational privacy. It is in the latter area that his report impacted on subsequent data protection developments.

The Younger Report

1–06   The *Report of the Committee on Privacy* (the *"Younger Report"*) was restricted to considering computing in the private sector. It formulated 10 principles which it recommended should apply in the handling of personal information where computers are used. Many of these principles have a familiar ring today and were largely embodied in the legislation in 1984. It is interesting to note that they concentrate particularly on security and access to data rather than issues arising from dissemination of information. This is not surprising given the nature of computing at the time, when communication between computers had yet to become a significant feature of ordinary computing.

The Younger principles were:

(a) The purpose of holding data should be specified.

(b) There should be authorised access only to data.

(c) There should be minimum holdings of data for specified purposes.

(d) Persons in statistical surveys should not be identified.

(e) Subject access to data should be given.

(f) There should be security precautions for data.

(g) There should be security procedures for personal data.

(h) Data should only be held for limited relevant periods.

---

[14] Consumer Credit Act 1974, ss.158 and 159.
[15] 1967: Mr Lyon; 1969: Mr Walden; 1968: Kenneth Baker; 1969: Mr Huckfield; 1971: Lord Manocroft.
[16] Cmnd.5012, July 1972.

(i) Data should be accurate and up-to-date.

(j) Any value judgments should be coded.

Younger recommended that these principles should form the basis of a voluntary code of practice which could be adopted by computer users. Younger also recommended the setting up of a Standing Committee to consider the use of computers and their impact on individuals.

Three years after the *Younger Report* the Government published two White Papers, one entitled *Computers and Privacy*[17] in which it announced its intention to consider legislation, and the other, *Computers: Safeguards for Privacy*,[18] which dealt with computer use in the public sector. Following the publication of these two White Papers in December 1975, the Government announced the setting up of a Data Protection Committee under the chairmanship of Sir Norman Lindop in July 1976.

The Lindop Report

1–07   The Lindop Committee's remit was to advise the Government on the best way forward, following the *Younger Report's* recommendations, to ensure appropriate privacy safeguards in the operation of computers in both the public and private sectors and to look for the establishment of such safeguards in some permanent form.

Lindop reported in December 1978. In his *Report of the Committee on Data Protection*,[19] he recommended legislation covering both public and private sectors. He further recommended that the legislation should be supervised by an independent data protection authority. The report proposed that principles for information use be adopted, as articulated by the *Younger Report*, covering broadly the same areas and in particular:

(1) In the interests of data subjects:

    (a) data subjects should know what personal data relating to them are handled, why those data are needed, how they will be used, who will use them, for what purpose, and for how long;

    (b) personal data should be handled only to the extent and for the purposes made known when they are obtained, or subsequently authorised;

    (c) personal data handled should be accurate and complete, and relevant and timely for the purpose for which they are used;

    (d) no more personal data should be handled than are necessary for the purposes made known or authorised;

    (e) data subjects should be able to verify compliance with these principles.

(2) In the interest of users:

    (a) users should be able to handle personal data in the pursuit of their lawful interests or duties to the extent and for the purposes made known or authorised without undue extra cost in money or other resources.

---

[17] Cmnd.6353.
[18] Cmnd.6354.
[19] Cmnd.7341.

(3) In the interests of the community at large:

    (a) the community at large should enjoy any benefits, and be protected from any prejudice, which may flow from the handling of personal data.

Lindop further recommended mandatory registration for computer users and the development and adoption of codes of practice to develop compliance with these principles. Such codes of practice would have the force of law. This concept was not adopted in the United Kingdom although it did form the basis of the law passed by the Netherlands. Nevertheless, codes, and other types of "soft" law, have proved to be an enduring mechanism in data protection regimes and continue to have an important place. Several different kinds of codes can be produced under the Directive and the 1998 Act, although none of them have the force of law.

It was several years before the *Lindop Report's* recommendations were taken further. However, in the interim there were also developments on the international front.

INTERNATIONAL DEVELOPMENTS—1978–1982

1–08   Over the period in which the United Kingdom was commissioning and considering national reports the interrelationships of computers, freedom, privacy and trade were also topics of concern among international organisations. The right to a private domain was recognised in Art.12 of the Universal Declaration of Human Rights adopted by the United Nations in 1948 and the right to private and family life is one of the fundamental rights guaranteed by the Human Rights Convention adopted in 1950 by the Council of Europe. Work carried out during the 1970s by the Organisation for Economic Co-operation and Development (OECD) and the Council of Europe came to fruition in two significant international instruments. On September 23, 1980 the OECD adopted guidelines governing the protection of privacy and transborder flows of personal data and on January 28, 1981 the Council of Europe opened Treaty 108 for signature, that is, the Convention for the Protection of Individuals with regard to Automatic Processing of Personal Data. Both instruments remain applicable today and may, in some instances, be relevant to assist in understanding or even interpreting the law. For that reason they are described in some detail in this chapter.

While the impetus at national level for law in the area of computerised information was concern for personal freedom and privacy, an equally important impetus for the international instruments was concern for the maintenance of free trade.

Concern for the maintenance of that right in an automated society had led to the passage of data protection laws in some European countries. There were rumblings from some of those states which had adopted data protection controls in the 1970s which suggested that they might seek to restrict the movement of data about their citizens, to ensure that such data remained within jurisdictions in which the legal systems provided protection for their subjects' "informational freedoms". While the threats envisaged to the liberties of their subjects by the transfer of data might not have been completely clear the rhetoric was chilling enough to be treated seriously. In a world where global trade was coming to depend on the use of computers and where the movement and manipulation of information was necessary for the healthy expansion of the global economy, threats to restrict data exchange on the grounds of concern for personal privacy were taken extremely seriously. International organisations moved to deal with these problems and develop instruments designed to reconcile the twin aims of respect for personal privacy and the need to ensure free trade between nations.

OECD GUIDELINES 1980

Summary of content

1–09   The OECD is an international organisation, two of whose primary aims are to foster economic stability and encourage trade and development. Like the Council of Europe it owes its existence to the vision of a post-war Europe rebuilt on a new model. It originated in 1948 as the Organisation for European Economic Co-operation, with the aim of co-ordinating national economic policies in Europe and liberalising European trade. In 1961, as other European institutions took responsibility for co-operation in economic and trading areas, it metamorphosed into its present being as the OECD. It adopted a new Convention and refocused its activities, working to foster economic stability and trade. It has 30 Member States including the founding Western European countries, Canada and the United States plus Japan, Australia, New Zealand, Finland, Mexico and now a number of former Communist bloc States.[20] The OECD is therefore an international body, not a European one. The membership of the United States and its contribution to its working gives the OECD a powerfully persuasive voice. In 1978, it drew up Recommendations and Guidelines in relation to data protection which were adopted by the Council of the OECD in 1980. The preamble to those Recommendations emphasises the concern that the moves to protect privacy might create unjustified obstacles to trade and recommends that Member States take account of the Guidelines in their domestic legislation in order to overcome the possibility of the growth of trade barriers. The Guidelines apply to data held in both public and private sectors:

> "which, because of the manner in which they are processed, or because of their nature or the context in which they are used, pose a danger to privacy and individual liberties."

Exceptions are provided for where appropriate and a list of governing principles with which data processors should comply are set out. They are:

(a) personal data should be collected fairly and lawfully;

(b) personal data should be relevant, and kept up-to-date;

(c) personal data should be used only for purposes specified at the time of collection or compatible purposes unless under legal authority or with the consent of the individual;

(d) personal data should be protected by adequate security;

(e) there should be transparency in personal data use;

(f) there should be subject access to personal data.

---

[20] Czech Republic, Hungary, Poland and the Slovak Republic. Source: *http://www.oecd.org* [Accessed March 2007].

They recommend that transborder data flows should not be restricted to other Member countries. There is no formal process for Member States to ratify or adopt OECD guidelines. On adoption the Australian, Canadian, Irish, Turkish and UK Governments abstained. However the guidelines were accepted by the United States which did not abstain. Since the adoption of the Guidelines the OECD has continued to work in the area of data privacy and information security. Among its achievements is the development of a Privacy Policy Generator for websites which can be used as a basis for conducting a privacy review and producing a Privacy Policy. The Generator is available on its website which is a valuable source of privacy-related materials: for example in 1999, it carried out a review of privacy instruments relating to privacy on global networks which was updated in January 2003.[21] The relevance of OECD material in interpreting the Data Protection Act 1998 is covered in Ch.3, below.

Council of Europe Convention 1981

Summary of content

1–10   The Council of Europe is a pan-European intergovernmental organisation. Like the OECD it developed from the post-war vision of a reconstructed and peaceful Europe. It was formed in 1949 with the aim of bringing political co-operation for the advancement and protection of individual rights and freedoms throughout Europe. It is responsible for the European Convention for the Protection of Human Rights and Fundamental Freedoms (the Human Rights Convention) and for administering the Court of Human Rights at Strasbourg. Unlike the OECD, the Council of Europe has a formal mechanism for adoption of its instruments.

In 1973 and 1974 the Council issued two early Resolutions concerning data privacy issues[22] which it followed up by work on a more substantial legal instrument.

Spurred on by concerns for trading freedoms and individual rights similar to those that motivated the OECD, the Council of Europe drew up the Convention for the Protection of Individuals with regard to automatic processing of personal data (Treaty 108) over the same timescale.

In 1981, the Council of Europe opened the Treaty for signature. The preamble makes it clear that its aim is to reconcile the need for privacy embodied in the Human Rights Convention right to private life with free trade as follows:

> "Recognising it is necessary to reconcile the fundamental values of respect for privacy and the free flow of information between peoples."

Treaty 108 covers both public and private sectors and allows for exemptions. Like the OECD Guidelines, it contains a set of principles to govern data processing. Its main principles are as follows:

(a) fair and lawful obtaining and processing of personal data;

---

[21] Inventory of instruments and mechanisms contributing to the implementation and enforcement of the OECD privacy guidelines on global networks.

[22] Resolution (73)22 on the protection of privacy of individuals vis-à-vis electronic databanks in the private sector and Resolution (74)29 on the protection of individual vis-à-vis electronic databanks in the public sector.

(b) storage of data only for specified purposes;

(c) personal data should not be used in ways incompatible with those specified purposes;

(d) personal data should be adequate, relevant and not excessive in relation to the purposes to which the data are stored;

(e) personal data should be accurate and where necessary kept up-to-date;

(f) personal data should be preserved in identifiable form for no longer than is necessary;

(g) there should be adequate security for personal data;

(h) personal data should be available to be accessed by individuals who have rights of rectification and erasure.

States should not restrict transborder data flows to other States which have accepted these standards and signed the Treaty. States may not sign the Treaty until they have national law in place guaranteeing compliance with the standards set out in it. Until States can give such guarantees they run the risk of trade barriers being erected against them or alternatively of becoming "data havens" for those who wish to avoid control of data processing.

While concern about personal privacy might not have been sufficient to produce domestic legislation from a UK government (of whatever political persuasion), the threat of trade barriers galvanised the Government of the day into action. In 1984, the United Kingdom passed the Data Protection Act. In 1985, it signed Treaty 108 which entered into force, as far as the United Kingdom was concerned, in January 1985.[23]

Council of Europe conventions are binding on States which become signatory to them. Adherence to a convention may have different effect in different States' legal systems. In some cases the convention itself maybe self-executing, that is "absorbed", into the national law. This is not the case in the United Kingdom. A convention will be of interpretative force and the UK courts will be bound to seek to interpret any national instrument passed in order to apply the convention in conformity with it.[24]

Following adoption of Treaty 108, the Council of Europe set up a Committee of Experts on Data Protection which has worked on a number of recommendations to Member States on various aspects of data protection. Those recommendations have been adopted by the Council. A list of the published recommendations is to be found at the end of Ch.3. These are advisory only but may give useful policy background in particular areas.[25]

---

[23] In 2001 the Treaty was amended to bring its provisions into line with Dir. 95/46 ([2005] O.J. l281/31).

[24] *Garland v British Railway Engineering Ltd* [1982] 2 All E.R. 405; *R v Secretary of State for the Home Department Ex p. Bring* [1991] A.C. 696.

[25] It should be noted however that there has been a tendency to look to the Recommendations by the courts when deciding cases on difficult issues of policy. The ECtHR did this in *Z v Finland* (1998) 25 E.H.R.R. 371. In another use of soft law the High Court in *Naomi Campbell v Mirror Group Newspapers* [2002] EWCA Admin 499 referred to Recommendations 1/97 of the Article 29 Working Group on Data Protection and the Media.

Amendments to Treaty 108

1–11   Amendments adopted in June 1999 provide for the European Communities to accede to the Convention. The amendments also allow the Committee of Ministers to invite non-Member States of the Council of Europe to accede to the Treaty, however, such an invitation will require a unanimous vote of the Committee. There are associated provisions dealing with territorial coverage and voting rights. Where Member States have transferred their competencies to the European Communities in the field concerned the European Communities will exercise the right to vote.[26] The amendment provides for States to apply the Convention to non-automated data and to records relating to legal persons as well as living individuals. States may also disapply the Convention but not to files which would be covered by national data protection laws.[27]

The European Communities have not yet acceded to the Treaty.

Additional Protocol to the Convention

1–12   An additional protocol was agreed on November 8, 2001 which explicitly requires:

- The creation of independent supervisory authorities with powers of investigation and power to bring legal proceedings.

- That personal data shall not be transferred to States which are not party to the Convention unless the State affords an adequate level of protection for the intended data transfer.

The latter provision alters the burden in relation to transborder data flows from that originally included in the Treaty and is an example of the strengthening of data protection rules since the inception of Treaty 108. The new provisions are to be regarded as additional articles to the Convention and are opened for separate accession.

DATA PROTECTION ACT 1984

Summary of content

1–13   In April 1982, the Government produced a White Paper on data protection *The Government's proposals for legislation*.[28] This was followed by the Data Protection Bill in December 1982. The Bill was introduced into the House of Lords but its passage was brought to an end by the 1983 General Election. In July 1983, a further Bill was introduced in the House of Lords which was to become the Data Protection Act 1984.

The 1984 Act drew on both the OECD and Council of Europe principles and the earlier work carried out by Younger and Lindop. It set out eight principles for data handling, largely drawn from the two international instruments. To the *Lindop Report* it was indebted for the concept of mandatory registration of data users. It also provided

---

[26] Arts 2 to 5 inclusive.
[27] Art.1 amending paras 2, 3 and 6 of Art.3 of the Convention.
[28] Cmnd.8539.

for appropriate exemptions from the rigours of regulatory control but did so largely by an unwieldy amalgam of registration and the duty to comply with the requirements of the Principles. The scheme of the Act was to require those data users who were not exempt to register with the Data Protection Registrar and only those data users who actually registered were then subject to the Principles.

This had the curious effect that users who failed to register, and it was estimated that many thousands who should have done so did not do so, could not be required to comply with the Principles.

The Data Protection Principles were taken almost directly from the Council of Europe Convention 108. They required that:

(a) personal data shall be obtained and processed fairly and lawfully;

(b) personal data shall be held only for specified and lawful purposes;

(c) personal data shall not be used or disclosed in a manner incompatible with those purposes;

(d) personal data shall be adequate, relevant and not excessive in relation to those purposes;

(e) personal data shall be accurate and where necessary kept up-to-date;

(f) personal data held for any purpose or purposes shall not be kept for longer than necessary for that purpose or those purposes;

(g) an individual shall be entitled to subject access;

(h) there shall be appropriate security measures for personal data.

In one significant aspect the 1984 Act turned its back on its roots. Although the *Younger* and *Lindop Reports* were fuelled by concerns over the loss of personal privacy in the computer age, and although both the OECD Guidelines and Treaty 108 specifically relate to the importance of privacy protection, basing their position on the right to private life in the Human Rights Convention, the 1984 Act remained resolutely silent on the point. On the contrary, it pointedly ignored any questions of privacy. The long title of the 1984 Act was:

"An Act to regulate the use of automatically processed information relating to individuals and the provision of services in respect of such information."

This had the curious effect of removing considerations of individual privacy from the interpretation of the 1984 Act except insofar as its genesis via Treaty 108 could be prayed in aid. A similarly obscure refusal to acknowledge its privacy roots can be seen in the 1998 Act which, despite the clear provisions of the Directive relating to private life, equally refuses to acknowledge it.

The long title of the 1998 Act is:

"An Act to make new provision for the regulation of the processing of information relating to individuals, including the obtaining, holding, use or disclosure of such information."

Directive 95/46 of the European Parliament and of the Council of 24 October 1995 on the protection of individuals with regard to the processing of personal data and on the free movement of such data ("the Directive") ("Directive 95/46/EC")

Background

1–14   Data protection laws had already spread through Europe before 1981. After the adoption of Treaty 108 they became even more widespread. However, although these laws had a common root, they did not follow the same pattern. The generality of the standards set by Treaty 108 allowed for considerable divergence within the Convention norms. This provoked concern at Community level, resurrecting fears of the erection of trade barriers based on differential privacy protection in Member States. Although the European Commission had earlier hoped that questions of harmonisation of personal privacy protection could be addressed by ratification of the Convention by Member States, and in 1981 issued a recommendation to Member States to ratify Treaty 108,[29] the divergence of the laws adopted by different countries coupled with the failure of some States to legislate at all prompted the Commission in 1990 to address the issue of data protection with the aim of harmonising Community law in this area. In 1990, the Commission issued a number of related draft measures covering this area including:

(a) a Directive on the protection of individuals with regard to the processing of personal data and on the free movement of such data (to become the general Directive 95/46);

(b) a Directive concerning the processing of personal data and the protection of privacy in the telecommunications sector (to become the Telecommunication Directive 97/66);

(c) a proposal that the Commission adopt a data protection policy;

(d) a proposal for a Framework Convention on all Title VI agreements (e.g. police activities).

Out of these, the first two have had legislative impact in the United Kingdom. The Telecommunication Directive imposed an additional regulatory regime on providers of public telecommunications services. It was implemented in the United Kingdom by Regulations made under the European Communities Act 1972 and came fully into force with the Telecommunications (Data Protection and Privacy) Regulations 1999. It was subsequently repealed and replaced by Directive 2002/58 concerning the processing of Personal Data and the Protection of Privacy in the Electronic Communications Sector. The regulations implementing Directive 2002/58[30] are the Privacy and Electronic Communications (EC Directive) Regulations 2003, made under s.2(2) of the European Communities Act 1972. They came into effect on December 11, 2003. The Regulations are covered in Ch.22, below.

---

[29] Commission Recommendation 81/679.
[30] SI 2003/2426.

The Commission proposed a Regulation to protect personal data within EU institutions and bodies in July 1999. This was required by new Art.286 introduced into the EU Treaty post Amsterdam. This took effect by virtue of Regulation No.45/2001 on the protection of individuals with regard to the processing of personal data by the Community institutions and bodies and on the free movement of such data. The instrument requires the Community institutions to comply with data protection principles and establishes the post of European Data Protection Authority with supervisory powers over Community institutions in the same way as national supervisory authorities. The proceedings of the Committee set up under Art.31 of the Directive became subject to amended Conciliation Procedure under Art.251 of the Treaty from November 20, 2003.[31]

The last proposal in the list, for a Framework Convention, has not materialised although a draft instrument has been produced and has been referred to in subsequent documents. There remain a number of significant separate conventions on Title VI matters. These conventions and the European background to them are explained and described in detail in Ch.24, below.

1–15 The first draft of the general Directive appeared in 1990, followed by second and third drafts in 1992 and 1993. Intense negotiations over the terms took place. The UK Government, intent upon following a deregulatory strategy, did not see the need for a data protection Directive at all and opposed the initiative throughout its European progress. Their opposition succeeded in bringing a number of changes to the detail of the draft but not in defeating the move to adopt a Directive, and finally a common position was reached by the Council in February 1995 with the Directive being adopted in October 1995. Significant amendments were made to the Directive as it moved through the agreement process. The Directive is reproduced in full at Appendix B and in each Chapter reference is made to the relevant Articles and paragraphs of the Recital.

The focus of the Directive is on reconciling privacy protection with the free flow of trade. Article 1 sets out the object of the Directive as follows:

"In accordance with this Directive Member States shall protect the fundamental rights and freedoms of natural persons, and in particular their right to privacy with respect to the processing of personal data.

Member States shall neither restrict nor prohibit the free flow of personal data between Member States for reasons connected with the protection afforded under paragraph 1".

The Directive marks a step forward from the earlier thinking on personal data and privacy. It has a number of significant features which separate it from the previous UK law and from some of the other earlier instruments as follows:

(i) it applies to some manual files;

---

[31] Regulation No.1882/2003 of the European Parliament and of the Council of 29 September 2003 adapting to Council Decision 1999/468 the provisions relating to committees which assist the Commission in the exercise of its implementing powers laid down in instruments subject to the procedure referred to in Article 251 of the EC Treaty ([2003] O.J. L284/1).

(ii) it sets out requirements for the legitimacy of processing as threshold requirements;

(iii) it requires that specific controls be afforded to sensitive data;

(iv) it provides for extensive individual rights, not only the rights of access and rectification;

(v) it restricts transborder data flows outside the Community to those States without adequate protection;

(vi) it provides exemptions for journalistic, literary and artistic purposes;

(vii) it significantly strengthens the security requirements for processing.

In other aspects, the Directive reproduces features of earlier instruments, providing for notification of processing on public registers and re-affirming the core Data Protection Principles.

SCOPE AND APPLICATION OF DIRECTIVE 95/46

1–16   The Community background is set out in more detail in Chapter 24, below, but the fact that Directive 95/46 is a harmonisation measure affects how the Directive applies to actions carried out by both Member States and institutions of the Community. In this section that issue is examined further. The Directive is part of the Community's internal market legislation under Art.100A of the Treaty of Rome (after amendment, Art.95 EC). A Directive is a secondary method of Community legislation. Authority for a Directive must be found within the Treaties. It goes without saying that a Directive, as with any other legislative act of the Community, can only cover those matters within Community competence. In Chapter 24, below the changing borders of Community competence are explored in more detail but in broad terms at present the areas of policing and security remain outside Community competence. The boundaries of those areas which are within and without such competence can be difficult to ascertain. In Directive 95/46 the exclusion of those areas outside competence is made explicit in Art.3(2) which provides that the Directive shall not apply to the processing of personal data:

"in the course of an activity which falls outside the scope of Community law, such as those provided for by Titles V and VI of the Treaty on European Union and in any case to processing operations concerning public security, defence, State security (including the economic well-being of the State when the processing operation relates to State security matters) and the activities of the State in the area of criminal law."

Directive 95/46 is firmly established as an internal market measure under Art.95.[32] Article 95 provides that, in order to achieve the objectives set out in Art.14, that is to create an area without internal frontiers in which the free movement of goods, persons, services and capital is ensured, the Council may adopt measures:

---

[32] The basis of the Directive was specifically accepted in the Opinion of the Advocate General in cases C-317/04 and C-318/04 at paras 185–187.

". . . for the approximation of the provisions laid down by law, regulation or administrative action in Member States, which have as their object the establishment and functioning of the internal market."[33]

Case law

1–17 The basis of a Directive may impact on the powers of Member States in the implementation of a Directive and on powers of the institutions of the Community to take action under it. In respect of Member States a Directive in European law imposes a requirement on Member States to pass national law in conformity with it. The impact of this has been considered in two cases; in *Lindqvist*[34] the European Court held that there is nothing to stop Member States from extending the scope of the national provisions to include areas not within the scope of the Treaty as long as no other provisions forbid this[35]; in *Österreichischer Rundfunk*[36] and in *Lindqvist* the European Court has held that the legal basis of the Directive as an internal market measure does not mean that there must be an actual link with free movement in every situation governed by the resulting Directive.

Passenger Name Records

1–18 In respect of the powers of the institutions of the Community the basis of the Directive was considered in the ruling of the European Court of Justice on the transmission of Passenger Name Records to the United States in May 2006.[37] The background to the case is set out in the Opinion of the Advocate General delivered on November 22, 2005 as follows:

> "Soon after the terrorist attacks on 11 September 2001, the Unites States passed legislation providing that air carriers operating flights to, from or through the United States territory must provide the United States customs authorities with electronic access to that data contained in their automatic reservation and departure control systems, known as Passenger Name Records ('PNR'). While acknowledging the legitimacy of the security interests at stake, the Commission of the European Communities informed the United States authorities, from June 2002, that those provisions might come into conflict with Community and Member States legislation on the protection of personal data, as well as certain provisions of the regulation on the use of computerised reservation systems (CRSs). The United States authorities postponed the entry into force of the new provisions but refused to waive the right to impose sanctions on airlines failing to comply with those provisions after March 2003."

This ruling would affect all European air carriers. The Directive forbids the transfer of personal data outside the EEA unless it is adequately protected by law or other

---

[33] Article 95 Title VI Common Rules on Competition, Taxation and Approximation of Laws, Chapter 3 Consolidated Treaty on European Union.
[34] See Ch.3, below for a full description of the case.
[35] See n.32 above, para.98.
[36] Joined Cases C-465/00, C-138/01 and C-139/01.
[37] Joined Cases C-317/04 and C-318/04.

adequate protection is provided in the receiving country. There are various ways of dealing with this, which are considered in depth in Chapter 8, below, but all except one would be difficult and burdensome for the European air carriers. The one mechanism that could be used was for the European Commission to use its powers under Art.26(6) of Directive 95/46 to determine that any personal data transferred to the Bureau of Customs and Border Protection ("CBP") of the Department of Homeland Security would be adequately protected. Accordingly that is what the Commission did.

The Commission entered into negotiations with the US administration which resulted in an agreement with the US Administration in relation to the transfer of PNR and the treatment of such data by the CBP of the Department of Homeland Security. The mechanism to reach the agreement was for the Commission to make a finding under Art.26(6) of Directive 95/46 that the transfer of the PNR to the CBP on the terms agreed between the Council and the US would provide an adequate level of protection for the personal data (which it did on May 14, 2004) followed swiftly, only days later on May 17, by a Decision by the Council using its powers under Art.95 of the Treaty which had the effect of implementing the terms of the agreement.[38]

1–19   As will be realised from the discussion above, given the legal basis of the Directive as an internal market measure, and the scope of the Directive as set out in Art.3(2), this mechanism had an element of the fig leaf, if not the Emperor's clothes, about it and its success depended on the acceptance by all those affected that:

(i) the Agreement with the CBP was related to the functioning of the internal market and could thus be made as an internal market measure by the Council within Art.95; and

(ii) the processing involved, being the transfer of the PNR data to the US, was within the scope of the Directive so that the Commission was entitled to make a finding of adequacy in relation to its transfer under Article 25.

Unfortunately for the Council and the Commission neither the European Parliament nor the European Data Protection Supervisor were willing to accept the view of the Council or the Commission as to the extent of their authority in this area. Neither response came as a surprise; the agreement had been reached in the teeth of opposition from the European Parliament. The Parliament immediately issued proceedings before the European Court of Justice for annulment of the decisions. The European Supervisor was given leave to join the proceedings, broadly supporting the Parliament, and the UK weighed in on the side of the Council and Commission.

1–20   The Court dealt with the cases as joined. The Opinion of the Advocate General was given in November 2005 followed by the judgment of the Court in May 2006 annulling the two instruments. In essence the Court ruled that the Agreement was outside the scope of Art.95, thus the Council's purported Decision was a nullity. In the judgment it stated that Art.95 EC, read in conjunction with Art.25 of the Directive, "cannot justify Community competence to conclude the Agreement".

The Agreement related to the transfer of data for the purposes of preventing and combating terrorism and other serious crimes. As such the processing operations were

---

[38] See n.33 above.

excluded from the scope of the Directive and the Decision could not have been validly adopted on the basis of Art.95 EC.

Secondly the transfer of personal data for the purposes of security was not covered by Directive 95/46 and thus the Commission had no power to make a finding of adequacy in respect of it. The Court found that the processing of personal data in the course of an activity which falls outside the scope of Community law was excluded from the Directive. As the decision on adequacy concerned only PNR data transferred to the CBP which was to be used strictly for purposes of preventing and combating terrorism and related crimes, other serious crimes, including organised crime, that are transnational in nature, and flight from warrants or custody for those crimes, it followed that the transfer of PNR data to the CBP constituted processing operations concerning public security and the activities of the State in areas of criminal law.

While the Court accepted that PNR data are initially collected by airlines in the course of an activity which falls within the scope of Community law, namely the sale of an aeroplane ticket which provides entitlement to a supply of services, it took the view that the data processing taken into account in the decision on adequacy was quite different in nature. The data processing in question was not necessary for a supply of commercial services, but data processing regarded as necessary for safeguarding public security and for law enforcement purposes.

The Court distinguished the finding in para.43 of *Lindqvist*, which was relied upon by the Commission in its defence, that the activities mentioned by way of example in the first indent of Art.3(2) of the Directive must be activities of the State or of State authorities and unrelated to the fields of activity of individuals, explaining that this does not mean that, because the PNR data have been collected by private operators for commercial purposes and it is they who arrange for their transfer to a third country, the transfer in question is not an activity of the State. In the Court's view the transfer fell within a framework established by the public authorities that relates to public security.

It followed therefore that the decision on adequacy concerning processing of personal data did not fall within the scope of the Directive and must consequently be annulled. In view of this finding the Court did not find it necessary to consider the other matters relied upon by the Parliament.

The Court did not immediately nullify the adequacy finding but preserved it for a period of 90 days, until September 30, 2006. The 90-day period was selected as the termination period allowed for in the Agreement. It pointed out that the Community could not pray in aid its own breach of its own laws as a reason for terminating the Agreement but would have to take action under the relevant provision which allowed either party to terminate the Agreement at any time, with the termination taking effect 90 days from the date of notification to the other party.

1–21 On October 16, 2006 the European Union entered into a replacement interim agreement with the United States Government on the basis of a Decision of the Council based on Arts 24 and 38 of the Treaty.[39] Article 38 provides that agreements between the EU and States outside the EU may be made for the purpose of police and judicial co-operation in criminal matters. Article 24 allows the Council, acting

---

[39] Agreement—[2006] O.J. L298/29 and Council Decision 2006/729/CFSP/JHA of October 16, 2006.

unanimously, to conclude agreements with other States. Such an agreement will not be binding on a Member State where its own constitution would be breached. The agreement reached allowed the US to continue to access PNR data until July 31, 2007 when the agreement expired. It has been replaced by a further agreement which will apply from July 2007 for a period of seven years.

In the Opinion of the Advocate General, in which the surrounding and associated issues were explored far more fully than in the decision of the Court, he set out his view that transfer would not breach Art.8 of the Convention Rights, which enabled the Council to assert that the protection in the US would be adequate and paved the way for the subsequent decision and agreement. In February 2007 the Article 29 Working Party issued an Opinion which emphasised that the air carriers remain subject to Directive 95/46 and must provide appropriate notices to the data subjects.[40]

Whereas the judgment deals only with the central issues the Opinion includes some interesting comments on issues such as the nature of a transfer, proportionality in retention periods, and privacy protection.

The scope and basis of the Directive has also been an issue in the agreement of Directive 2006/24 referred to in para.1.23, below.

Directive 2002/58 concerning the processing of personal data and the protection of privacy in the electronic communications sector

1–22   Directive 2002/58 replaced Directive 97/66 concerning the processing of personal data and the protection of privacy in the telecommunications sector. The 1997 Directive was part of the package referred to in para.1–14, above. It applied to personal data processed in telecommunications systems. A Common Position was agreed on Directive 97/66 in December 1997 and national implementing legislation should have come into effect at the same time as for the general Directive by October 1998. It did not do so in the UK. The implementing legislation came in three stages. Some provisions, those dealing with direct marketing, came into effect in May 1999 in the Telecommunications (Data Protection and Privacy) (Direct Marketing) Regulations 1998.[41] These Regulations were then repealed and replaced by others which implemented all the requirements of the Directive bar Art.5. The replacement regulations were the Telecommunications (Data Protection and Privacy) Regulations 1999 which came into effect in March 2000 with the main Act. Article 5, which covers security of communication and intercepts of telecommunications, was implemented by the Regulation of Investigatory Powers Act 2000 and regulations made under it, the Telecommunications (Lawful Business Practice) (Interception of Communications) Regulations 2000.[42]

Directive 97/66 was subsequently reviewed and replaced by Directive 2002/58. The new Directive was required in order to deal with the never-ending increase in communications technologies including developments in digital mobile networks and email and deal with inconsistencies of interpretation of Directive 97/66 in

---

[40] Opinion 2/2007 on information to passengers about transfer of PNR data to US authorities Adopted on February 15, 2007.
[41] SI 1998/3170.
[42] SI 2000/2699.

different Member States. It was implemented in the UK by the Privacy and Electronic Communications (EC Directive) Regulations 2003 which came into force on December 11, 2003, just a few weeks later than the required implementation date of October 31, 2003.[43]

Directive 2006/24 on the retention of data generated or processed in connection with the provision of publicly available electronic communications services or of public communications networks and amending Directive 2002/58

1–23   The details of this provision are dealt with in Chapter 23, below. It amends Arts 5, 6 and 9 of Directive 2002/58 which cover the privacy of communications and retention of traffic and location data to require Member States to ensure that providers of publicly available electronic communication services retain certain categories of data and allow access to such retained data by competent national authorities. The Directive has not been implemented at the time of writing.

Directive 2006/24 is a further example of the fine lines that have to be observed in producing Community legislation dealing with data protection and law enforcement matters. The political reality is that a number of governments have wished to enforce the retention of communications data by service providers and to have access to it by law enforcement agencies since September 11, 2001 and earlier. However the retention was forbidden by Directive 1999/67 and then Directive 2002/96, which required the erasure of communications data once it was no longer needed for the purpose of the services. In any event the provision of access to the data would be outwith Community competence. The position has finally been dealt with in Directive 2006/24.

As we have seen above no Directive can cover matters outside Community competence and Directive 2006/24 explicitly states (Recital 25) that issues of **access** by law enforcement agencies to data retained pursuant to implementing national provisions are outside the scope of Community law, and hence the Directive, although they may be covered by national law or action under Title VI of the Treaty.[44] Directive 2006/24 is stated to be made under Art.95 of the Treaty as a single market measure on the basis that a number of Member States have exercised powers under Art.15(1) of Directive 2002/58, which allows Member States to provide derogations from the rights in Arts 5, 6, 8 and 9 of Directive 2002/58, to require service providers to retain data for the purposes of law enforcement. It goes on to explain that:

> "The legal and technical differences between national provisions concerning the retention of data for the purpose of the prevention, investigation, detection and prosecution of criminal offences present obstacles to the internal market for electronic communications, since service providers are faced with different requirements regarding the types of traffic and location data to be retained and the conditions and periods for retention."[45]

---

[43] See Ch.22, below for a full discussion of these provisions.
[44] For an explanation of Title VI and Third Pillar areas see Chapter 24, below.
[45] Recital 5.

Accordingly the retention of data under the Directive is justifiable as a single market measure and can be brought within Art.95 of the Treaty. The Directive is applicable to the data retained by service providers as they are not part of the State or acting for the State in the retention following *Lindqvist*. This would appear to be an arguable, if bold, position although one has to wonder what justification could have been found if there had been no contradictory national law to pray in aid. However the Directive also deals with ensuring that the retained data are ". . . available for the purpose of the investigation, detection and prosecution of serious crime". It would be difficult to justify this as a single market measure (to put it mildly) and the justification is not at all clear (at least to this commentator). Recital 9 states that the Directive is necessary to provide a lawful basis for the retention given the requirements of Art.8 ECHR but does not set out the single market justification. A challenge has been mounted to Directive 2006/24 in the European Court by Ireland and Slovakia. Implementation in the UK is the subject of a consultation which is covered in Chapter 23, below.

CHARTER OF FUNDAMENTAL RIGHTS

1–24   The Charter has not been adopted by the EU as it is part of the constitution which was rejected in the referenda of a number of Member States, nevertheless it is referred to in various instruments and a number of cases and may be argued to have, as the Commission website describes it, "declaratory effect" or a persuasive value. It was signed at Nice in December 2000 and was then integrated into the draft Constitutional Treaty in 2003. It includes rights to the protection of personal data in Part II—Freedoms, in the following terms:

> "1. Everyone has the right to the protection of personal data concerning him or her
> 2. Such data must be processed fairly for specified purposes and on the basis of the consent of the person concerned or some other legitimate basis laid down by law. Everyone has the right of access to data which has been collected concerning him or her, and the right to have it rectified.
> 3. Compliance with these rules shall be subject to control by an independent authority."

The current situation is not clear; there is a view in many Member States that the adoption of a constitution or new Treaty is inevitable and the reluctance of a few should not stand in its way. However it is also possible that a more timid instrument will eventually be adopted. Whether the data protection provisions will remain in any final instrument is not known. If they did remain, however, they would be a useful tool with which to address the tendency of the UK courts to regard data protection as wholly coterminous with conventional privacy rights and their refusal to countenance the wider issues of informational self-determination which the scope of data protection legislation more properly addresses.[46]

---

[46] See *Johnson v Medical Defence Union* [2007] 1 All E.R. 467.

European Data Protection Supervisor

1–25 Regulation 45/2001 established the European Data Protection Supervisor as an independent supervisory authority with three main tasks:

- to monitor the EU administration's processing of personal data;

- to advise on policies and legislation that affect privacy; and

- to co-operate with other similar authorities to ensure consistent data protection.

Peter Hustinx, who was previously the Commissioner for the Netherlands Supervisory Authority, was appointed for a five-year term as of January 2004. In applying the requirements of Directive 95/46 and Regulation 45/2001 to the institutions of the Community, each institution and body must appoint an internal Data Protection Officer responsible for maintaining a register of processing operations. Systems which pose a special risk are notified to the Supervisor for prior assessment. The Supervisor also deals with complaints and conducts enquiries. The Supervisor is responsible for the data protection supervision of Eurodac, the database of fingerprints of illegal immigrants and asylum seekers in the EU.[47] In addition he carries out Privacy Impact Assessments on new or proposed legislation and delivers formal Opinions on significant issues. Among the Opinions issued over the last three years are a number of important ones on police and judicial co-operation and visa and immigration policy issues. These are referred to in Chapter 24, below. In all the Supervisor has issued 21 formal Opinions to the end of March 2007. They are an excellent reference source on the topics covered.

Implementation of Directive 95/46 in the United Kingdom

Introduction in the United Kingdom

1–26 While the Directive allows Member States some room for manoeuvre in certain areas it requires harmonisation of national laws at a high level. The Home Office published a consultation paper in March 1996 setting out a number of questions as to how the Directive should be implemented in the United Kingdom. The consultation paper called for responses by July 1996. Although that document was published and responses to it were received under the Conservative Government the Data Protection Bill which followed did not see the light of day until some nine months after the May 1997 elections, which had returned a substantial Labour majority.

The general approach to the implementation of the Directive had been set out under the Conservative Government and is summarised in Ch.1 of the Consultation Paper as follows:

"Over-elaborate data protection threatens competitiveness and does not necessarily bring additional benefit for individuals. It follows that the Government intends to go no further in implementing the Directive than is absolutely necessary to

---

[47] See Ch.24 for a full assessment of Eurodac and the other instruments dealing with issues of justice and policing under the Third Pillar.

satisfy the U.K.'s obligations in European law. It will also consider whether any additional changes to the current data protection regime are needed so as to ensure that it does not go beyond what is required by the Directive and the Council of Europe Convention."[48]

This approach to implementation remained a starting point for the legislation despite the change of government between consultation and introduction of the Bill. However, as the Bill moved through Parliament the Labour Government indicated a willingness to alter its position and provide some stronger regulatory protection for individuals than appeared in the first draft. In particular, it accepted the inclusion of an offence provision outlawing the practice of enforced subject access.

Following the consultation, the Government decided to implement the Directive by primary legislation. This had not been a foregone conclusion. It might have been possible to implement it by regulations under the European Communities Act 1972. However, this possibility was the cause of considerable concern among those potentially affected by the Directive. There were worries that it would give rise to two parallel legal regimes governing the use of personal data in the United Kingdom with concomitant difficulties for data users in deciding which regime applied to particular data used for particular functions. There was considerable lobbying by those concerned to persuade the Government to proceed by primary legislation and the decision to do so was generally welcomed. It also provided the Government with an opportunity to deal with some outstanding matters of concern which did not arise directly from the Directive and which could therefore not have been dealt with under the European Community regulations.

Passage of the Act through Parliament

1–27　At the end of each chapter reference is made to relevant *Hansard* materials to enable practitioners to consider material which may be admissible under the rules in *Pepper v Hart*.[49] It is not intended to repeat those references here, although it may be worth noting that on some occasions, particularly as the Bill neared its final stages, a conscious attempt to insert *Pepper v Hart* materials appears to have been made. A brief outline of the passage of the Bill through Parliament focusing on the main debates in those proceedings can be found in the Additional Material section at the end of this chapter.

It was treated by all parties as a technical piece of legislation. When it was first introduced it was missing some important provisions which were added in as it progressed through both Houses.

The Bill was introduced to the House of Lords on January 14, 1998 and Second Reading took place on February 2. It was considered in Standing Committee D on February 23, 24 and 25 and went to Report on March 16 with Third Reading in the Lords on March 24. It went through the House of Commons between April 20 and July 2 with Committee Stages on May 5, 12, 14, 19 and 21 and June 2 and 4. The Commons amendments were considered and agreed in the Lords on July 10 with Royal Assent following on July 16, 1998. A full review of the passage of the Bill through Parliament will be found at paragraph 1.73 onwards.

---

[48]　Ch.1/para.1.2.
[49]　[1993] A.C. 593. See Ch.3 for the role of *Hansard* material.

Implementation timetable

1–28   Some technical measures to allow preparatory work for the full introduction of the Act came into force on Royal Assent being:

(a) s.75 (commencement);

(b) ss.1–3 (definitions of data, data controller, data processor, data subject, personal data, processing, relevant filing system, sensitive data and special purposes);

(c) s.25(1) and (4) (provisions for submission of proposals for a notification scheme by the Commissioner to the Secretary of State and duty on the Secretary of State to consider any such proposals after consultation of the Commissioner);

(d) s.26 (fees regulations, provision for different fees to be prescribed for different types of notification cases and those matters to which the Secretary of State must have regard in making fees regulations);

(e) ss.67–71 (s.67 contains the order making powers, ss.68, 69, 70 and 71 further definitions and a table of defined terms);

(f) s.75(2)(g) (powers to make subordinate legislation).

There was some delay before implementation of the substantive provisions. This was announced in the House of Commons by George Howarth, the Minister of State in the Home Office, on July 3, 1998. In the event the Act, together with supporting secondary legislation, but excluding the provisions dealing with enforced subject access, did not come into force until March 1, 2000. The delay meant that the Government did not implement by October 24, 1998 in accordance with the requirements of the Directive. However the UK implementation was earlier than a number of other EU countries. A chart showing the implementing legislation and date of implementation is available on the Commission website at *http://www.europa.eu.justice-home/fsj/ privacy/law/implementation-en.htm* [Accessed on 1 September 2007]. In December 1999 the Commission decided to take France, Germany, Ireland, Luxembourg and the Netherlands to the European Court of Justice for failure to notify all the necessary measures to implement the Directive. However all Member States successfully implemented by 2003. Countries which apply for accession to the Community must commit to transposing the Directive by the time of accession. The Commission Report of May 2003[50] reported that the ten countries which joined the Community in 2004 have legislation in place which incorporates most of the key elements of the Directive, but legislation in those countries is not yet fully compliant with Directive standards. It has not yet reported on the position of the further two accession States which joined in January 2007, Bulgaria and Rumania.

A Directive is binding on Member States as to the results to be achieved but leaves the form and method by which it is achieved to national authorities.[51] The obligation

---

[50] COM (2003) 265 Final.
[51] Art.189(3) of the Treaty.

of the Member State is to transpose the Directive into national law. As the United Kingdom had not implemented the Directive by October 24, 1998, there was some risk of direct effect actions against public bodies on this basis, however none materialised.

Subject access offence

1–29   The only remaining provision from the 1998 Act not in force at the time of writing is the enforced subject access offence in s.56. Section 75(4) provides that it must not be earlier than the day on which ss.112, 113 and 115 of the Police Act 1997 come into force. The provisions in the Police Act set out a mechanism for employers and others to obtain information about the criminal convictions of applicants legitimately. However, as the certification provisions are still being brought into effect the problem of enforced subject access is deferred until employers are able to procure all levels of certificate under the Police Act 1997. The Criminal Records Bureau is charged with implementing the arrangements for the issue of criminal records certificates. It issues standard and enhanced disclosure certificates but there is, as yet, no sign of the basic level certificates.

Implementation of other instruments

1–30   The implementation of Directive 2002/58 is covered in Ch.22, below and the implementation of Directive 2006/24 in Ch.23, below.

Statutory instruments

1–31   There is a significant amount of secondary legislation made under the Act, much of it containing important provisions. The secondary legislation is listed at the end of this chapter. It is dealt with in the text under the substantive topic as necessary. Section 67 sets out the powers of the Secretary of State to make secondary legislation. The Secretary of State is under a duty to consult the Commissioner before making any secondary legislation except in the case of commencement orders or notification regulations. Although it is not made explicit, an obligation to consult implies an obligation to take note of the comments made in the consultation.

Commencement orders remain within the sole control of the Secretary of State. The provisions for notification consultation are set out in s.25. Under s.25(1) the Commissioner must submit proposals on the content of the first notification regulations to the Secretary of State as soon as practicable after the Act has been passed. The Secretary of State has an obligation to make the regulations but before doing so must consider the Commissioners' proposals and consult with the Commissioner on them (s.25(4)).

The Commissioner has a continuing duty to keep the working of the notification regulations under review and submit proposals as to amendments from time to time. The Secretary of State has a further power to require the Commissioner to consider matters relating to the notification regulations and submit proposals for amendments. The obligation to consult the Commissioner before making any regulations applies equally to the making of amendments.

Types of statutory instruments

1–32 Nine of the instruments which may be made under the Act require the positive approval of Parliament. The draft instrument must be laid before each House of Parliament and approved by positive resolution of each House. The instruments subject to this procedure are primarily those which deal with exemptions; prior checking and the extension of the enforced subject access offence to further organisations would also require affirmative resolution.

Most orders are subject to negative resolution, that is they require laying before Parliament subject to annulment in pursuance of resolution of either House. It should be noted that if an instrument contains a mixture of provisions, some of which would require positive and some simply negative procedure, they must be treated as requiring positive affirmation.

Orders which prescribe fees for the purposes of the Data Protection Act 1998 or of the Consumer Credit Act 1974 need only follow the procedure for laying before Parliament after being made in order to be valid.

Consultation on subordinate legislation

1–33 In August 1998 the Home Office published a Consultation Paper on subordinate legislation inviting comments by the end of September 1998. A number of orders were proposed for initial implementation. In the event, implementation was delayed in order to allow for the orders to be ready. In all cases, except the proposals in respect of prior checking, the consultation resulted in the passage of the appropriate secondary legislation and is dealt with in the text. The proposal for prior checking has not been taken further to date and there is no indication that it will be.

Prior checking

1–34 This term is used in the Directive but in the Act it has become "preliminary assessment". A number of categories of processing were proposed to be subject to preliminary assessment in the White Paper in July 1997. They covered data matching, processing involving genetic data, processing by private investigators and the processing of sensitive data. However no orders dealing with preliminary assessment have been forthcoming and it is understood that at the time of writing none are under consideration.

Repeals

1–35 These are set out in s.74(2) and Sch.15, Pt I. The Data Protection Act 1984 has been repealed in its entirety, as has the Access to Personal Files Act 1987 and most of the Access to Health Records Act 1990 in order to subsume the rights of access into the subject access right. The remainder of repeals in the Schedule consists largely of technical amendments to tidy up the legal provisions where the old provision has been replaced by one in the 1998 Act.

Revocations

1–36 These are found in Pt II of Sch.15. Revocations apply to statutory instruments and regulations. Only one statutory instrument was revoked in whole, the Data

Protection Registration Fees Order 1991. Other orders made under the Data Protection Act 1984 simply died with the repeal of the 1984 Act. The other orders listed in this part of the Schedule are those made under other legislation which have been revoked in part where the relevant provisions in the order have now been covered by the new law.

Consequential amendments

1–37   These are set out in Sch.14, under s.74(1). Amendments have been made to 10 pieces of primary legislation and two statutory instruments. The amendments in paras 1, 2, 3, 4, 5, 6, 7, 9, 10, 14, 16 and 18 simply reproduce the same legal effect as the current law by replacing references to the 1984 Act and associated elements, such as replacing the Registrar with references to the Commissioner. The others substitute the definitions of health professional in the new Act for the one found in earlier Acts or make consequential changes to the access to health information provisions.

TRANSITION

1–38   The Data Protection Act 1984 was repealed in full when the 1998 Act came into force (Sch.16) and most of the 1998 Act took effect immediately, however, some require-ments were delayed by "transitional relief". The rules governing the application of tran-sitional relief were complex. This complexity reflected the constraints imposed by the Directive itself and the Government's commitment to adopt an approach which would make the burden of compliance with the new requirements the least onerous possible. The Act also contains savings provisions to deal with those cases where actions were started under the 1984 Act but not completed before repeal. The aim of the transitional provisions was to allow for a smooth and gradual movement from the 1984 regime to the 1998 one. The transitional period has now expired for all automated and most manual data with only the transitional exemptions for some manual data remaining in effect until October 2007. In earlier editions of this book the transitional provisions were covered in full but these have been omitted from this edition as they are now of histori-cal interest only. The remaining transitional derogation for manual processing is only partial and only applies to manual data actually held in personal data filing systems as at October 24, 1998. Even where manual data are exempt until 2007, controllers have been obliged to comply with a number of the individual rights since October 2001.

In view of the limited amount of data subject to the remaining exemption and the restricted nature of the exemption itself, the final ending of the transitional provisions is likely to have minimal impact. However the remaining provisions are covered here for completeness and because they may have some continuing impact on the Channel Islands.

Manual data

1–39   Manual data became subject to the 1998 Act if:

(a) they were previously open to individual scrutiny under the Consumer Credit Act 1974, the Education (School Records) Regulations 1989, the Access to Medical Records Act 1990 or the Access to Personal Files Act 1987 (accessi-ble records); or

(b) they consisted of other manual data falling within the definition of a "relevant filing system".

Different transitional arrangements applied to the two categories.

Accessible records

1–40 Manual data in respect of which access and other rights were previously given under other legislation was made subject to analogous rights under the data protection regime. Thus such data became subject to some requirements of the new Act, in particular rights of access and compensation for inaccuracy, from the date of commencement. The transferred access rights and the arrangements for transition in respect of such data are covered in Ch.11, below.

Other manual data

1–41 Manual data which:

(a) fall within the definition of a "relevant filing system";

(b) were not records to which access rights were previously available under the other legislation listed above; and

(c) were subject to processing which was already underway immediately before October 24, 1998;

were not affected by the 1998 Act until October 2001 and can claim the benefit of the remaining exemption until October 2007.

Manual data—exemptions from October 2001 to October 2007

1–42 These are dealt with at para.14 of Sch.8. There are special provisions for data held for research purposes after 2001. These are covered in Ch.18, below which deals with the exemptions affecting personal data used for research.

Leaving aside the specific exemptions for research purposes, the exemptions for manual data available up to October 2007 cover:

"(a) the first data protection principle except to the extent to which it requires compliance with paragraph 2 of Part II of Schedule I;
(b) the second, third, fourth and fifth data protection principles; and
(c) section 14(1) to (3)."

This means that the data are not subject to: the requirements for legitimate processing in Sch.2; the sensitive data controls in Sch.3; or the general requirement that personal data shall be processed fairly and lawfully. However, they are subject to the specific requirements governing fair obtaining and processing, referred to as the "fair obtaining and processing code" in this book and described in Ch.5, below.

They are also exempt from the requirements that:

(a) personal data shall be obtained only for specified and lawful purposes and not further processed in any manner incompatible with that purpose or those purposes (Second Principle);

(b) personal data shall be adequate, relevant and not excessive in relation to the purpose or process to which they are processed (Third Principle);

(c) personal data shall be accurate and where necessary kept up to date (Fourth Principle);

(d) personal data processed for any purpose or purposes shall not be kept for longer than is necessary for that purpose or those purposes (Fifth Principle);

(e) s.14 of the Act, which deals with the rights of individuals to ensure rectification, blocking, erasure and destruction of inaccurate data.

However, although para.14 of Sch.8 gives this widespread exemption, it should be noted that Sch.13 re-imposes a set of provisions dealing with accuracy of data and orders relating to accuracy. The result is that the transitional exemptions are limited in effect.

Which data can claim these exemptions up to 2007?

1–43   The data for which this exemption can be claimed are defined in para.14 of Sch.8 as:

"(a) eligible manual data which were held immediately before October 24, 1998; and
(b) personal data which fall within paragraph (d) of the definition of 'data' in section 1(1) but do not fall within paragraph (a) of this sub-paragraph
but does not apply to eligible manual data to which the exemption in paragraph 16 applies."

The proviso thus excludes manual data held for research purposes but not information relating to the financial standing of an individual.

Sub-paragraph 14(a) applies the exemption to manual records in relevant filing systems where the records were in existence before October 24, 1998. It applies to the actual records, not the type of records. It does not require that the record was held by the controller who claims the exemption so the fact that a file has changed hands since October 1998 will not be a bar to claiming the exemption. The term "held" is not a defined term. In the 1984 Act the term "held" had a defined legal meaning, but there is no reason to attribute that definition to it in this context and it should be given its ordinary meaning of "being in possession of".

The second category of information which can claim the exemption covers those parts of "accessible records" which are neither held on automated systems, nor manual files covered by the Act. Controllers who deal with "accessible records" will note that this exemption applies to all accessible records which fall within the definition, irrespective of when the record was generated. If the record was generated on October 22, 2001 or October 18, 2007 or any time before or between, up to October 24, 2007 this exemption can be claimed.

What is eligible data?

1–44   The relevant definition is found in Sch.8, para.1(1):

"For the purposes of this Schedule, personal data are 'eligible data' at any time if, and to the extent that, they are at that time subject to processing which was already under way immediately before October 24, 1998."

This applies to the remaining manual data.

The term "processing underway" and the timescale involved in being "immediately before" October 1998 was litigated in the case of *Michael Douglas, Catherine Zeta-Jones and Northern Shell Plc v Hello!*.[52] The main issues are described below.

Processing under way

1–45 Processing is defined in s.1(1) in relation to information or data and the definition is extremely wide, covering obtaining, recording or holding information or carrying out any operation or set of operations on the information, which includes organising or adapting the information, retrieving or using the data, disclosure or blocking, destruction or erasure. Reference to the definition itself, therefore, does not resolve the ambiguity because the definition includes both the general term, "carrying out an operation or set of operations" and the particular terms, "retrieving, blocking etc".

Recital 69 of the Directive deals with implementation of the Directive as follows:

"Whereas Member States should be allowed a period of not more than three years from the entry into force of the national measures transposing this Directive in which to apply such new national rules progressively to all processing operations already under way; whereas in order to facilitate their cost effective implementation, a further period expiring twelve years after the date on which this Directive is adopted will be allowed to Member States to ensure the conformity of existing manual filing systems with certain of the Directive's provisions; whereas, where data contained in such filing systems are manually processed during this extended transition period those systems must be brought into conformity with these provisions at the time of such processing."

There was much debate about whether a generous or a tight approach to the term "processing already underway" should be taken. If the generous meaning of the term were adopted it could be argued that any set of processing operations already carried out at the material time provided the basis for the exemption. On this basis, if a data controller already made disclosures then all disclosures would be exempt. If a controller held personal data all data holding would be exempt during the transitional period. The only data controllers who would be unable to claim the transitional relief would be those who started processing for the first time after October 1998.

This approach had the attraction of certainty and "light regulation", however, it came uncomfortably close to giving existing controllers a three-year sabbatical from data protection controls.

1–46 When the provision was considered by the judge in *Douglas, Zeta-Jones and Northern Shell v Hello!*, a narrower approached emerged. It was held that the

---

[52] [2001] 2 All E.R. 289.

transmission of photographs of the wedding from California to London via Madrid and their subsequent publication was not covered by the transitional relief. It was not "processing underway" as, although there had been processing of photographs of celebrities on a continuing basis, these had been separate individual acts of processing. There had not been a continuous process running, as for example running a bank account (paras 231–234).

Immediately before October 1998

1–47   Transitional relief can only be claimed for data which were subject to processing which was underway "immediately before October 24, 1998". Again there is no definition of this important provision. It is not clear how immediately before the cut-off date the processing must have taken place. The intention appears to be to provide the exemption only for live processing systems and not to allow a controller to claim the benefit of the transitional exemptions for processing which he has not undertaken for a considerable length of time.

It is suggested that the issue is a question of fact in relation to the particular processing system. If a system, when working, is only employed every two months then if it has been employed regularly during the previous 12 months or so it is suggested that two months should count as being in the period immediately before October 24, even though the same would not apply to a system which is designed to be used every day.

The general effect of applying these approaches to the remaining transitional exemption for manual data is that only existing business systems which have continued to use the manual data held as at October 1998 on a day-to-day basis have been able to claim the benefit of the transitional provisions. Even so they have still been subject to significant specific rules.

Rights which will apply

1–48   As noted above, although an exemption is given by para.14 for manual data, after 2001 the data has been subject to a specific set of rights which are set out in Sch.13. The Sch.13 provisions apply to manual data between October 24, 2001 and October 24, 2007. In effect this gives individuals limited rights over manual data part way though the transitional period. Rather confusingly, however, these rights are expressed in somewhat different terms to those used in the remainder of the Act, so there exists a specific set of rights in respect of manual data which has only applied between 2001 and 2007. This apparently complex arrangement, of providing for extensive transitional exemptions for manual data on the one hand, but then introducing specific duties in relation to individual rights in manual data, derives from Art.32.2 of the Directive under which Member States may delay implementation of various Articles of the Directive for manual data already processed until 2007 but: "shall, however, grant the data subject the right to obtain, at his request and in particular at the time of exercising his right of access, the rectification, erasure or blocking of data which are incomplete, inaccurate or stored in a way incompatible with the legitimate purposes pursued by the controller".

To recap, this specific set of rights (the s.12A rights) applies:

(a) between commencement and 2007 to accessible records and credit reference records;

(b) between 2001 and 2007 to manual data that were held as at October 24, 1998.

Section 12A rights

1–49   These apply where data are:

(a) inaccurate;

(b) incomplete; or

(c) held in a way incompatible with the legitimate purposes pursued by the data controller.

Inaccurate

1–50   The partial protection for "received" data provided by para.7 of Pt II of Sch.I does not apply to s.12A. The term inaccurate is defined in s.70(2):

> "For the purposes of this Act data are inaccurate if they are incorrect or misleading as to any matter of fact."

Incomplete

1–51   Section 12A(5) provides that:

> "for the purposes of this section personal data are incomplete if, and only if, the data, although not inaccurate, are such that their incompleteness would constitute a contravention of the third or fourth data protection principles, if those principles applied to the data."

Principles 3 and 4 require that personal data "shall be adequate, relevant or not excessive in relation to the purpose or purposes for which they are processed, and that personal data shall be accurate and, where necessary, kept up to date". The net effect of these provisions appears to be to re-apply Principles 3 and 4 to such data. The remaining requirement is similar to the second limb of Principle 2.

Holding incompatible with legitimate purposes

1–52   This is the third circumstance in which the s.12A rights will apply. The term "holding" is not defined. In ordinary terms it would cover retaining a copy of, or having a record of data in the controller's possession. It suggests a more permanent relationship with the relevant data than is necessarily incurred by simply processing the data. The word "incompatible" is not defined. It appears to require quite a high level of incongruity or mismatch before purposes are regarded as incompatible. Again, the interpretative provisions which apply to the Principles are not applied to this section. It is the holding of the data which must be incompatible, not the processing.

The nature of the rights

1–53   Where one of these applies the data subject is entitled to serve notice in writing on the controller setting out his grounds for believing the data to be in contravention of these rights and requiring the data controller to put it right. Where the subject alleges that the data are inaccurate or incomplete he can require the controller to rectify, block, erase or destroy the data.

Where he alleges the data are held in a way incompatible with the legitimate purposes pursued by the data controller he can require the controller to cease holding it in such a way. The section does not in fact limit the subject's right to object to data held about himself but is wide enough to apply to any eligible manual data. It seems unlikely, however, that the courts will be inclined to construe it otherwise than as relating to data held about the individual. The remedy for failure to act on the notice is an application to the court. The subject must state in the notice his reason for believing the data to be inaccurate or incomplete or held in a way incompatible with the legitimate purposes of the controller. The phrase "held in a way" incompatible seems to go to the nature of physical storage rather than the content of the data. It is possible this provision could be used to deal with security issues.

If a court is satisfied that a controller has failed to comply with a justified notice it may order the controller to take steps to comply with it in whole or in part. The application goes to the same courts which will hear applications under the individual rights provisions described in Ch.14, below.

The remainder of s.12A contains minor amendments to ensure that where data are exempt from the other accuracy rights they are also exempt from s.12A. Given the limited amount of data to which the remaining transitional exemption applies and the extent of the existing obligations under s.12A it is not anticipated that the expiry of the final transitional provision will have any noticeable impact on data controllers.

Data Protection Act 1998 Post-Implementation Appraisal

UK appraisal

1–54   The Data Protection Act 1998 (DPA) came into force in March 2000. At implementation the Data Protection Registrar became the Data Protection Commissioner, a title that was to exist for only nine months until it was replaced by the title Information Commissioner in January 2001 under the Freedom of Information Act 2000.[53] Under the DPA the transitional exemptions for data subject to processing already underway and most manual data lasted until October 2001. However, in autumn 2000, even before the first transitional exemptions had expired, the Home Office undertook a post-implementation appraisal. This was partly in order to allow the United Kingdom to contribute to the European Union review required by Art.33 of the Directive. Article 33 requires the Commission to report on the

---

[53] For the impact of the Freedom of Information Act 2000 and changes brought to the Data Protection Act 1998, see Ch.4, below.

implementation of the Directive to the Council and the Parliament at regular intervals starting not later than three years after October 1998.[54] The post-implementation appraisal was stated to be undertaken:

> "to assess the new regime's immediate effect, focussing in particular on those provisions which are new to UK data protection law."

The specific issues covered in the document and on which comments were invited covered:

- definitions of controller and processor and scope of manual records covered;
- conditions for processing and collection notices;
- sensitive data;
- arrangements for subject access and exemptions from it;
- revised notification scheme, particularly the exemptions;
- international transfers; and
- new technology.

After the appraisal letter was issued responsibility for data protection and freedom of information was transferred from the Home Office to the Lord Chancellor's Department. On June 12, 2003 the Department of Constitutional Affairs was created, replacing the Lord Chancellor's Department. On May 9, 2007 the Ministry of Justice took over responsibility for data protection.

Response of the Information Commissioner

1–55   In the Response dated December 20, 2000 the Information Commissioner, Elizabeth France, reviewed separately matters arising from the Directive and those arising from the United Kingdom's method of implementation. In relation to the Directive she expressed concerns over the blanket coverage of data falling in the sensitive categories, irrespective of the use to which such data are put, the requirement for formal contracts where processors are used, the burden of notification and the prescriptive nature of the ban on overseas transfers. In considering implementation in the United Kingdom she expressed concerns over a number of the exemptions, particularly those for domestic and recreational purposes and over public registers, the fact that a data controller must consent before the Commissioner can exercise her audit powers, the criminal penalties imposed for disclosures by her staff outside the remit of the Act and the limitations on the processing of sensitive personal data which create problems for a number of innocuous uses of such data.

Other responses

1–56   There were about 100 responses. As would be expected they raised many different points. The concerns expressed included particularly the cost of complying with

---

[54] Arts 33 and 32(1).

subject access requests and the difficulties in providing collection notices in all cases. There was general agreement that the new notification system is satisfactory.

Review of Directive—European Commission

1–57 The European Commission also embarked upon a review of the implementation in 2002. In its Report following the review it explained that it had not only carried out the review of implementation but conducted an open public debate on the area, which was justified not only by the nature of the Directive but the rapid pace of technological change and other international developments since the Directive was finalised in 1995. In carrying out the review the Commission issued a general invitation to submit views. It sent questionnaires to Member State governments and separately to supervisory authorities. It commissioned two studies by academic experts. In June 2002 it issued two consultation documents, one for citizens and another for data controllers, seeking views on data protection and privacy. It held a major conference in Brussels in October 2002 at which the responses were considered with a view to the preparation of the report on the Directive, possibly including views on how it could be improved.

Controller consultation

1–58 The controller questionnaire posed queries about the use of anonymous data, the nature of consent, collection of data over the internet, subject access, notification, free movement of data, consumer awareness, web privacy seals, codes of conduct and advice from supervisory authorities.

Citizen consultation

1–59 The citizen questionnaire covered citizen awareness, buying online, subject access and employee monitoring of emails.

Submissions by Austria, Finland, Sweden and the United Kingdom

1–60 A joint proposal for amendment of Directive 95/46 was made by these four Member States and the paper remains available on the Department for Constitutional Affairs (DCA) website. The approach taken in the paper contrasts with some of the more expansionist interpretations adopted by the national regulators and the Article 29 Working Party. In summary they proposed that:

- the definitions of personal data and personal data filing system should be reviewed and made more precise;

- the definition of processing should be clarified and made more specific;

- consideration should be given to narrowing the scope of the processing covered by the Directive to that carried out by reference to the data subject;

- the territorial provisions in Art.4 should be reviewed with a view to achieving uniform application throughout the Union and avoiding extra-territorial effect;

- the imposition of special rules for sensitive data should be reviewed;

- the subject access rights should be reviewed in the light of the burdens that they cast upon data controllers as a result of technological developments;

- the prohibition on overseas transfers should be reviewed and a more flexible regime developed;

- the need for organisations to notify in more than one Member State should be reviewed;

- in relation to processors:

  - the Commission should review the requirement to have written contracts with all processors; and
  - the terms of Art.17 of the Directive, which provides that processors should comply with the security requirements of the Member State in which they are situated, should be reviewed.

Commission position

1–61 Summing up at the end of the Consultation Conference in October 2002 Commissioner Bolkestein stated that the Commission would be reporting on the Directive taking account of three matters:

- It wishes to see a high but effective standard of privacy taking account of technological developments.

- It wishes to see a more consistent application of the Directive which assists the free movement of personal data around Europe.

- It would like to achieve legal clarity and alleviate administrative burdens on data controllers.

The Commission issued its Report in May 2003.[55] It concluded that it was not appropriate to make amendments to the Directive in the immediate future because:

- The delay in implementation meant that there was inadequate experience of the current Directive on which to make sound decisions.

- It considered that many of the difficulties which had been identified in the review could be resolved without amendment as they arose because of the implementation by Member States or the application of the margin of appreciation rather than the requirements of the Directive.

- Some proposals for amendment, which were aimed at reducing the burdens of compliance for controllers, would have the effect of reducing the protection of individuals. This would not be possible as those protections are guaranteed by other binding legal instruments such as Treaty 108.

---

[55] Report from the Commission, *First report on the implementation of the Data Protection Directive (95/46/EC)*, Brussels, May 15, 2003, COM (2003) 265 Final.

However the Report makes clear that there is still work to be done, in particular it expressed concerns at the divergence between the legislation in Member States, particularly on the rules relating to transfers to third countries, and at the problems with weak enforcement, low levels of awareness of rights among data subjects and patchy compliance by data controllers. The failure of convergence between Member States is attributed to a range of factors. In some cases Member States have gone beyond the requirements of the Directive, in some cases implementation has fallen short. The Commission indicated that it would be prepared to use its powers under Art.226 of the Treaty to enforce compliance but would prefer to proceed by discussion with Member States. In other cases the divergence is the result of legitimate exercise of national discretion but still raises concern that the divergence may impede the working of the Internal Market or create unjustified burdens for controllers.

As a result of the review the Commission set out a work programme to address the perceived problems. The Report lists 10 Action points. The first seven are actions for the Commission itself and the remaining three involve a broader constituency. The action points address the issues of concern.

In 2007 the Commission published a report on the follow-up of the Work Programme[56] which set out progress to date. The Action Points from the earlier report are set out below together with a short explanation of the perceived problem giving rise to the need for the action point and a commentary on progress since 2003 and the follow-up Report.

Commission's initiatives

1–62   Action 1: Discussion with Member States and Data Protection Authorities

This was to address any changes needed to national legislation to bring it fully into line with the Directive; to consider strengthening enforcement and discuss improving resources where necessary. Work would also include discussions by the Article 29 and 31 Working Parties and discussions at other meetings with Member Sates. In 2007 the Commission simply reported that a "structured dialogue" had been in process with Member States with the aim of bringing all the national legislation fully into compliance.

Action 2: Association of the candidate countries with efforts to achieve a better and more uniform implementation of the Directive

The Commission committed to bilateral discussions and possibly peer review to continue up to and beyond accession to ensure alignment of the laws of the accession countries with the Directive. On this the 2007 Report stated that the Commission has been working closely with Authorities to ensure proper alignment with the acquis.

Action 3: Improving the notification of all legal acts transposing the Directive and notifications of authorisations granted under Article 26(2) of the Directive

---

[56] COM (2007) 87 Final.

The Commission determined to continue to collect data on implementation and exhorted Member States to notify national authorisations for transfer granted under Art.26(2). It committed to the creation of a new web page on work progress on the work plan. In 2007 it reported that there had been an increase in notifications from some Member States and some key national papers, policies and other documents had been put onto the Commission's website.

Action 4: Enforcement

The Article 29 Working Party was asked to consider enforcement practices and compliance guidance for sectors. In 2007 it reported on a Declaration on Enforcement in which the Article 29 Working Party agreed on the criteria for identifying issues for EU-wide investigations. In March 2006 the Data Protection Authorities launched a joint investigation on the processing of personal data in the health insurance sector.

Action 5: Notification and publicising of processing operations

There was criticism of divergent notification requirements and the Article 29 Working Party was asked to put forward proposals for simplification and co-operation mechanisms. In 2007 the Commission reported that the Working Party had produced the Report requested and made similar recommendations to those made by the Commission.

Action 6: More harmonised information provisions

This addressed the "fair processing notice" requirements which vary from State to State. The Commission proposed to address this with Member States insofar as it results from inadequate transposition and also called on the Article 29 Working Party to search for a more uniform interpretation. The 2007 Report referred to the work of the Article 29 Working Party and the guidance on multi-layered privacy notices as well as the PNR data notice guidance.

Action 7: Simplification of the requirements for international transfers

This was perhaps the most forceful action point. The Article 29 Working Party was asked to raise discussions about simplification and harmonisation of practices. The Commission stated its intention to make use of the powers under Arts 25(6) and 26(4) to make further findings of adequacy or settle agreed contractual clauses respectively; to work on the development of binding corporate rules and seek a more uniform approach nationally to Art.26(1) on adequacy. In the 2007 Report it refers to its further findings on adequacy, the Safe Harbor review, the increase in transfer clauses, Binding Corporate Rules and the Opinion of the Working Party on Art.26.[57]

---

[57] See Ch.8, below for a full exposition of the rules governing transfers of personal data outside the EEA.

Other initiatives

1–63   Action 8: Promotion of Privacy Enhancing Technologies (PETS)

The Commission reports on its existing work in this area and commits to further work and consideration of the promotion of PETS by mechanisms such as seals or certification systems. The 2007 Report promises a forthcoming Commission Communication on this.

Action 9: Promotion of self-regulation and European Codes of Conducts

The Commission expressed disappointment at the dearth of Community Codes presented by industry groups. It encouraged the development of such codes. It voiced a hope that an EU instrument on employment and personal data would be possible. The Report in 2007 welcomed the acceptance of the FEDMA code[58] and regretted that it had not been possible to reach agreement on the employment code.

Action 10: Awareness raising

The Commission announced its intention to launch a Eurobarometer survey along the lines of the 2002 consultation. The 2007 Report stated that the survey had been conducted and had shown "that people are concerned about privacy issues, but not sufficiently aware of the existing rules and mechanisms to protect their rights".

In its Overview to the 2007 report the Commission accepted that Member States have now transposed the Directive but there are still some concerns at incoherent or inadequate transposition. Nevertheless the Directive has succeeded in its aims and does not require amendment. It does however raise the continuing problems arising because of the separation of Third Pillar matters and the need to address that.[59] It concludes that the Commission will keep the Directive under review and continue to work with Member States to achieve better harmonisation.

UK DEVELOPMENTS

Action against the UK

1–64   Apart from the discussions which arose between the Commission and the UK as a result of the review the UK is subject to possible action for non-compliance with the Directive as a result of the decision of the Court of Appeal and the resulting Guidance issued by the Information Commission in the case of *Durant v FSA*.[60] It has been suggested that the effect of the decision is that the UK offers a lower level of protection as the case adopts a narrow approach to the definition of personal data, which has been, in effect, accepted by the Commissioner. There has been correspondence between the UK and the Commission but the details are not known, despite repeated

---

[58] Federation of European Direct Marketing Associations.
[59] See Ch.24, below for an analysis of the issues in relation to the Third Pillar.
[60] [2003] EWCA Civ 1746.

applications to all the parties for disclosure under the Freedom of Information Act 2000 by the indefatigable Dr Chris Pounder.

Transfer of responsibility for data protection

1–65 After the passing of the 1984 Act data protection remained the responsibility of the Home Secretary, latterly as part of the (unlikely sounding) Liquor, Gambling and Data Protection Directorate. In preparation for the implementation of Freedom of Information, responsibility was transferred to the Lord Chancellor's Department in autumn 2001.[61] Responsibility remained with the Department when it was renamed the Department for Constitutional Affairs in June 2003 and data protection remained within its remit until May 2007 when it passed to the new Ministry of Justice.[62]

Amendments to the Act post October 1998 and related legislation

1–66 There is a growing body of law dealing with information, and personal information in particular. Increasingly specific data protection provisions appear in legislation or other provisions affect how the DPA applies in particular cases. The only statute which makes major amends to the DPA is the Freedom of Information Act 2000 (FOIA) and the interface between FOIA and the DPA and the amends made to the DPA are covered in detail in Ch.4, below. However there are numerous related legal developments that, for reasons of space, it is not possible to detail in this book. We have tried to refer to a number of such amendments and developments where they are not referred to elsewhere in the book where relevant but we do not guarantee that this provides exhaustive coverage. Anyone researching a specific topic should check for developments in related areas.

Under the Scotland Act 1998, Sch.5 Pt II B2, the DPA is a reserved matter: that is it is a matter which it is not within the power of the Scottish Act to influence or affect. It is also a reserved matter under the Northern Ireland Act 1998, Sch.3 para.40.

Amendments made by the Freedom of Information Act 2000 (FOIA)

1–67 The relation between the two pieces of legislation is covered in Chapter 4, below. The FOIA came fully into force by January 2005. In summary:

- The period for registration was extended so that old register entries do not expire until three years after they were first entered on the register.

- The responsibilities of the parties where data controllers receive a subject access request but need more information to find the information the subject seeks was clarified.

- The definition of personal data was extended in relation to information held by public authorities. Personal data falling in the extended definition became open to subject access and the remedies for inaccurate data but not the other data protection principles.

---

[61] The Transfer of Functions (Miscellaneous) Order 2001 (SI 2001/3500) made under the Ministers of the Crown Act 1975 came into effect on November 26, 2001.
[62] The Secretary of State for Constitutional Affairs Order 2003 (SI 2003/1887).

- Personnel records falling within the extended definition became eligible for a new exemption from subject access.

- Public authorities were required to include a statement in their notification to the effect that they are public authorities subject to the FOIA.

- A new offence of destroying records, in respect of which an access request has been made, is created. This applies whether the access request was made under the DPA or the FOIA.

Most of the above provisions apply in Scotland by virtue of regulations made under the Scottish Act 1998.

Codes of Practice

1–68   The Employment Practices Code has been issued by the Information Commissioner under the DPA but relevant codes are also to be found under other legislation. The codes issued under the Regulation of Investigatory Powers Act 2000 (RIPA) are referred to above. Relevant aspects of RIPA and related codes are covered in Ch.23, below. The Code of Practice on the Management of Police Information issued under following the recommendations of the Bichard Enquiry is referred to in Ch.21, below. However there are many other relevant Codes of Practice and when advising on informational issues it is always prudent to review the existence of soft law surrounding the relevant area.

Comment

1–69   The aim of this chapter is to provide a context for the UK Act. However the instruments and developments covered here are only part of a wider set of developments. International work on individual rights, in which the importance of personal privacy is acknowledged, continues to develop. There is so much debate that it is not possible to do much other than alert the reader to its existence. International initiatives continued to develop after Treaty 108 and the OECD Guidelines were settled. In 1990, the United Nations adopted Guidelines for the Regulation of Computerised Data Files. The Charter of Fundamental Rights of the European Union includes recognition of the right to the protection of personal data and access to data as well as respect for private and family life.

European initiatives on data protection have not halted with the promulgation of the Directive. Indeed, post-Directive, the possible impact of European bans on transborder data flows outside areas having "adequate protection" gave them extra strength and momentum. In relation to North America there was considerable discussion between Europe and the Federal Trade Commission representing the US Government on privacy regulation. In the United States despite European pressures self-regulation remains the basis for the "safe harbor" arrangements.[63] However there appears to be an increased move towards the acceptance in the US by some organisations of the need for privacy protection. There are a growing number of privacy laws and regulation at State level in the US. The Canadian Standards Institute issued a set of data protection standards for

---

[63] See Ch.8, below for a full discussion of the Safe Harbor provisions.

voluntary adoption followed by the Canadian Personal Information and Electronic Documents Act 2001 at federal level and its provincial equivalents in Alberta, British Columbia and Quebec. There is also State legislation in Ontario. The European Commission issued a decision recognising the adequacy of the Canadian law for the purposes of overseas transfers in December 2001. The Asian Pacific countries have an increasingly strong privacy interest; Japan has adopted a privacy law and Privacy International in 2006 commented that over 70 countries have some form of privacy law.

ADDITIONAL INFORMATION

1–70   Material on the interpretation of the Act will be found in Ch.3, below.

Websites

1–71   Throughout the text relevant website addresses are given in footnotes (all accessed on 2 September 2007). There are now a mass of sites which provide information on data protection and privacy. The author's law firm maintains two sites; *http://www.pinsentmasons.com* and *http://www.OUT-LAW.com*. The latter specialises in e-commerce and related areas. It also provides weekly free email bulletins on selected topics which include data protection. Other data protection and freedom of information material is on the *http://www.pinsentmasons.com* website. The Joint Information Services for the higher education sector (JISC) runs a mailbase for data protection.

The sites maintained by regulatory organisations or government bodies are as follows:

- The Department of Constitutional Affairs is *http://www.dac.gov.uk* and data protection is found under People's Rights. There is a separate (and most useful) section on data-sharing.

- The Information Commissioner's site is *http://www.ico.gov.uk*. It contains Annual Reports and the Commissioner's published guidance. The register can be accessed from the site. It also has a useful index of other links and sites.

- The European Union site is at *http://www.europa.eu*. Data protection information is found under Information Society although much information will also be found under Justice, Freedom and Security. The entry includes references to other useful European sites including the European Data Supervisor.

- Recent UK case law is available on *http://www.courtservice.gov.uk*.

- Information on Safe Habor is available at the US Department of Commerce site *http://www.ita.doc.gov*.

- Council of Europe: *http://www.coe.int* where data protection will be found under the Legal Affairs section.

- The Criminal Records Bureau is at *http://www.crb.gov.uk*.

- European Court of Human Rights: *http://www.echr.we.int*. This site includes judgments on cases on the Art.8 right to private life and other convention rights.

- Legislation is found at *http://www.opsi.gov.uk*. This site includes the Data Protection Act and the statutory instruments.

- OECD: *http://www.oecd.org*. This site contains material generated by the OECD.

The *Encyclopaedia of Data Protection* (Sweet & Maxwell) contains a wealth of source materials and background papers.

Statutory instruments

1–72   The bulk of the statutory instruments made under the Act came into effect on commencement on March 1, 2000. The commencement order for the Act was made in January 31, 2000. Amendment order 1865 came into effect in July 2000.

- SI 2000/183: The Data Protection (Commencement) Order;

- SI 2000/184: The Data Protection (Corporate Finance Exemption) Order;

- SI 2000/185: The Data Protection (Conditions under paragraph 3 of Part II of Schedule 1) Order;

- SI 2000/186: The Data Protection (Functions of Designated Authorities) Order;

- SI 2000/187: The Data Protection (Fees under section 19(7)) Regulations;

- SI 2000/188: The Data Protection (Notification and Notification Fees) Regulations;

- SI 2000/190: The Data Protection (International Cooperation) Order;

- SI 2000/191: The Data Protection (Subject Access) (Fees and Miscellaneous Provisions) Regulations;

- SI 2000/206: The Data Protection (National Security Appeals) Regulations;

- SI 2000/413: The Data Protection (Subject Access Modification) (Health) Order;

- SI 2000/414: The Data Protection (Subject Access Modification) (Education) Order;

- SI 2000/415: The Data Protection (Subject Access Modification) (Social Work) Order;

- SI 2000/416: The Data Protection (Crown Appointments) Order;

- SI 2000/417: The Data Protection (Processing of Sensitive Personal Data) Order;

- SI 2000/418: revoked by SI 2000/1864;

- SI 2000/419: The Data Protection (Miscellaneous Subject Access Exemptions) Order;

- SI 2000/1864: The Data Protection (Designated Codes of Practice) (No. 2) Order;

- SI 2000/1865: The Data Protection (Miscellaneous Subject Access Exemptions) (Amendment) Order;

- SI 2002/2905: The Data Protection (Processing of Sensitive Personal Data) (Elected Representatives) Order 2002;

- SI 2005/467: The Data Protection (Subject Access Modification) (Social Work)(Amendment) Order 2005;

- SI 2006/2068: The Data Protection (Processing of Sensitive Personal Data) Order 2006;

- SI 2005/14: The Information Tribunal (Enforcement Appeals) Rules 2005 [revokes SI 2000/189 and 2002/2002];

- SI 2005/13: The Information Tribunal (National Security Appeals) Rules 2005 [revokes SI 2000/206];

- SI 2005/450: The Information Tribunal (Enforcement Appeals) (Amendment) Rules 2005;

- SI 2001/3500: Transfer of Functions (Miscellaneous) Order 2001;

- SI 2003/1887: Secretary of State for Constitutional Affairs Order 2003.

Passage of the Act through Parliament

1–73 In order to ensure that the summary makes sense without having to go back to early versions of the Bill, the clause references used are those to the clauses as they appear in the final version, even if the clause had a different number at the time of the debate.

Overview

1–74 The Bill was treated by both parties as a technical and largely non-partisan matter. The Government was under pressure to have the Act implementing the main Directive on the statute book by the October 24, 1998. To achieve that end, it had to receive Royal Assent by the end of the summer session 1998. Pressure of time to get it before the House meant that it was still missing some important elements when it was introduced into the Lords in February 1998. These were gradually added as the Bill progressed. However, even with the addition of further provisions, some important matters were left to be dealt with in regulations, notably the detail of the notification scheme.

Speeches in the main debates on the Bill tended to focus on a number of particular elements:

(a) the exemption for journalistic, literary and artistic purposes;

(b) the coverage of manual records;

(c) the powers of the Commissioner to conduct audits and serve notices;

(d) the exemptions available to the Inland Revenue and others;

(e) the effect of the enhanced individual rights on those dealing with automated decision-making;

(f) the control of data matching by government departments;

(g) the effect of the Bill on overseas transfers of personal data;

(h) the prohibition on the processing of sensitive personal data; and

(i) the replacement of registration with a simplified form of notification.

House of Lords

1–75 *Second Reading.* The Data Protection Bill was introduced in the House of Lords on January 14, 1998. The Second Reading in the Lords took place on February 2, 1998 when it was introduced by Lord Williams for the Government in the following terms:

> "I recognise that data protection does not sound like a subject to attract obsessive interest; witness the general exodus from your Lordship's House as I start to introduce this Second Reading. Data protection is redolent in many ways of computers and electronic processing; necessary but essentially technical providers of services. In fact it affects our well-being in a much more general way. It shares common ground to that extent with the Human Rights Bill. That Bill will improve the position of citizens of this country by enabling them to rely on the wide range of civil and political rights contained in the European Convention on Human Rights. Those rights include the right to respect for private and family life. The Data Protection Bill also concerns privacy, albeit a specific form of privacy: personal information privacy. The subject matter of the Bill is, therefore, inherently important to our general social welfare."[64]

During Lord Williams' brief tour of the main provisions he referred particularly to some of the exemptions, including that for journalistic, artistic and literary purposes:

> "It is not the intention of the Government for the Directive to be used to inhibit programme makers from making the programmes they have up to now. The Government believes that both privacy and freedom of expression are important rights and that the directive is not intended to alter the balance, which is a fine one and always should be, that currently exist between these rights and responsibilities. I believe that the Bill does strike the right note in that respect. It was not until after a great deal of consultation and discussion, and perhaps cross-fertilisation of ideas, that we came to our conclusion."

He also referred to the new powers of the Commissioner and the rules for overseas transfers.

Viscount Astor, speaking for the Opposition, raised concerns about the cost of implementing the Directive and the possible burdens for business. He highlighted concerns brought to him by the CBI about the restrictions on the holding of sensitive data and the problems those could cause for employers who might find it necessary to hold criminal records. He queried the application of the new law to the internet and its

---

[64] *Hansard*, HL Vol.585, No.95, col.436.

effects on the use of processors based overseas, as well as raising the interface with freedom of information. Other contributors to the debate were Baroness Nicholson of Winterbourne, who took a wide-ranging overview of the Bill, and Lord Wakeham, who dealt exclusively with the media exemption in cl.32 which he welcomed warmly. Lord Norton raised some detailed points on the effect on fraud prevention, in which he expressed an interest, and a number of points on the individual rights. Some criticisms were made by the Earl of Northesk who described the Bill as being "almost a quarter of a century past its sell-by date" and highlighted the absence of a code to deal with data matching.

The Bill was referred to the Grand Committee for consideration by motion of February 19. It was considered by Standing Committee D on February 23, 24 and 25. The motion for consideration of the amendments tabled for Report stage was moved on March 11 and Report took place on March 16.

1–76 *Report Stage.* At Report, Lord Williams explained the Government's position on the nature and extent of the manual records covered by the definition of the term "relevant filing system". Soon after publication of the Bill, the Registrar issued a statement setting out her opinion that the definition of "relevant filing system" as it appeared in the Bill did not achieve the Government's stated intention to exclude personnel records. At Second Reading, Lord Williams had made clear the Government's intention to focus the definition on highly structured files and by amendment at Report altered the word "particular" to "specific" in the definition. Lord Williams spoke to the effect of the amendment in the following terms:

> "We intend that 'particular' information should mean 'specific' information.
> That is what our amendment provides. The search for unambiguous language can
> sometimes be exhausting. I do not say that 'specific' admits of no shades of
> meaning; it does. Information may be more or less specific in different degrees of
> detail. Very much may depend on context. But if there is any significant ambigu-
> ity in the introduction of 'specific' into the definition of 'relevant filing system', it
> is not capable of admitting into that definition the sort of general, unindexed per-
> sonnel files that we have been talking about. All the information in those files
> may conceivably be though 'particular' but not 'specific'. 'Specific' information is
> intended to mean and does mean distinct information within the file which can be
> distinguished from other information in the file and separately accessed. It means
> information of a distinct identity which sets it apart from the rest of the general-
> ity of personal information held. That is what our amendment intends to pin
> down."

Viscount Astor returned to the potential problems caused to business by the rules governing overseas transfers, especially in relation to trade with the United States. Lord Dholakia moved an amendment to include the purpose of ethnic monitoring among the categories of permitted processing of sensitive data which was sympathetically received by the Government and subsequently incorporated into Sch.3.

The provisions bringing the rights of access to consumer credit reference files, previously exercised under the Consumer Credit Act 1974, into the Bill were inserted by Government amendment and gave rise to some expressions of concern that this might affect the position of third-party credit information on an individual's credit file, a concern which the Government dismissed. Credit industry concerns were also aired in discussions on the meaning of the term "trade secret" in relation to automated decision-making and whether it was wide enough to cover all the interests which would merit protection. The Government was firm in the view that it would.

An amendment originally proposed by Lord Norton in Committee to require controllers who receive individual rights notices to respond to them and in writing was moved by the Government (although this was later removed in the case of the direct marketing notices). The Government also put forward a complete re-draft of cl.12 dealing with the right to object to automated decision-making. In the new formulation, the individual must activate the objection rather than there being an outright ban on such processing.

Other government amendments were used to introduce the first elements of the transitional relief provisions. Amendment was also made allowing the Commissioner to assist her opposite number in a colony, altering the confidentiality clause binding the Commissioner and making the provision for consultation on Codes of Practice mandatory.

Lord Norton argued that the term "substantial damage and distress" as used in cl.10 to describe the basis on which an individual could object to the processing of personal data about him should be replaced by the words of the Directive, "compelling legitimate grounds", but his argument was not accepted.

In relation to the Commissioner's power, Lord Norton spoke for giving the Commissioner stronger audit powers to carry out audits without the consent of the controller. Lord Astor suggested procedural restrictions on the exercise of the Commissioner's powers under which she would be bound to try to resolve matters by informal methods before moving to formal action. Neither proposal found favour with the Government.

There was further debate on the need to control data matching by imposition of a statutory code but expressions of concern were met by resolute Government refusal to move on the issue.

1–77 *Third Reading.* The Third Reading took place in the Lords on March 24 and saw the only division forced during the Bill's passage through Parliament. The division resulted in a Government defeat on cl.28(4). This clause would have given the Secretary of State wide ranging powers to allow exemptions for the purposes of tax collection. The provision had been inserted, explained Lord Falconer, speaking for the Government, to deal with particular problems faced by the Inland Revenue:

> "I remind the House that without the clause 28(4) general exemption, as opposed to case by case exemptions, the Inland Revenue and hence honest taxpayers would suffer losses with information being revealed to suspect taxpayers about the nature and origin of material passed to the Inland revenue by third parties such as banks and retail businesses and about the revenue's risk rules and scores under the new self assessment tax system."[65]

---

[65] *Hansard*, HL Vol.587, col.1101 (March 24, 1998).

The clause allowed for class exemptions whereas other exemptions in the Bill were to be applied on a case-by-case basis. The clause had already been criticised by the Delegated Powers and Deregulation Select Committee in its consideration of the Bill on February 4 in the following terms:

"Of far greater concern is the wide ranging power under clause 28(4) to grant exemptions from the requirement to process personal data fairly and lawfully (the first data protection principle). This principle goes to the heart of the Bill and the Committee views with the greatest concern the scope of this provision. If the power remains in the Bill as it is currently drafted, there will be no limits to the inroads which could be made into the fundamental requirement that personal data be processed fairly and lawfully—a power which in the Committee's view it would be impossible to justify. The House will no doubt wish to consider these issues with the greatest care during the Bill's subsequent passage and may wish to amend the Bill to remove the general power to grant exemption from the first data protection principle."[66]

Despite attempts by the Government to head off the division by expressing a willingness to hold further talks with the Registrar over the issue it was moved and the Government defeated. In the Commons the Government returned with a limited exemption related specifically to the risk assessment system adopted by the Revenue. In respect of which Lord Falconer subsequently said in the Lords' closing debate:

". . . we have decided not to pursue further in this Bill the non-disclosure exemption. On reflection we accept that, where systematic disclosure of information to government departments is appropriate, we should seek specific statutory powers within the relevant departmental legislation. On risk assessment we have concluded that we can deal with this on the face of the Bill in a way that should reassure the House about our intentions."[67]

1–78 Government amendments were moved to alter the category of those able to claim compensation for breaches of the law to "individuals" rather than "persons" as the latter term would have covered companies and other legal entities; to extend the powers of the Commissioner; to serve information notices in those cases where information is required to determine if there has been a breach of principle; and to deal with a number of technical and drafting points, particularly on transition.

The other amendments moved and defeated related to cl.32. Lord Lester argued that the clause as it stood did not comply with the ECHR. It did not provide for the appropriate balance to be struck between the rights to private life and freedom of expression in particular cases, nor did it import the tests of proportionality or necessity but simply required that the journalist should hold a reasonable belief that the technical grounds to claim the exemption were made out. When it became clear that a wider attempt to amend the clause was going to be resisted by the Government he proposed a more modest amendment. His proposal was to insert the word "necessary" in relation to the

---

[66] Select Committee on Delegated Powers and Deregulation (1997–98 HL 66) para.8.
[67] *Hansard*, HL Vol.591, No.184, col.1494.

public interest, so the journalist would not only have to show that publication was in the public interest but it was "necessary" in the public interest, saying:

> "in other words, the amendment requires the data controller to have a reasonable belief that the obtaining, storing or publishing of personal data is necessary in the interests of free expression and does not involve a disproportionate interference in the right to private life".[68]

He also commented on the unsatisfactory nature of the discretionary power given to the courts to consider codes of practice under this clause, arguing that, in the interests of legal certainty, such reference should be mandatory.

The refusal of the Government to heed neither the proposed amendment nor the comments on the role of the codes of practice led Lord Lester to prophesy a litigious future for cl.32.[69]

Commons Stages

1–79   Second Reading.   In the Commons, the Bill had its Second Reading on April 20 when it was introduced by the Home Secretary Jack Straw. He drew attention to the limitation of the coverage of manual records to structured records; the approach being taken to deal with adequacy requirements for overseas transfers; the continuing commitment of the Government to deal with the problems of enforced subject access; the amendments made in the Lords to cl.28 and the resolution of the concerns of the media in cl.32.

The Conservative spokesman supported the aims of the Directive but vented concerns that the Bill should implement at the minimum level necessary to achieve compliance and raised the question of the suggested costs of compliance to business. There were also queries over the controls on sensitive data and the regulatory powers of the supervisory body.

The Liberal Democrats generally welcomed the Bill but raised the absence of provisions to deal with enforced subject access, to allow for the holding of sensitive data for ethnic monitoring purposes or to control data matching by government departments. Concerns about the interrelationship of cl.32 and the Human Rights Bill were also raised. The other main issue of concern to the House was the removal of cl.28(4) and the question of whether it should be replaced and if so by what, a point which the Government was still considering at that stage.

1–80   Committee Stages.   The Bill went to Standing Committee D and was considered on May 5, 12, 14, 19 and 21 and June 2 and 4. Government amendments continued to be added as the Bill passed through the Committee Stage. As well as dealing with a considerable number of drafting and technical points, many of them revising the detail of notification. Government amendments during the passage through the Commons covered:

---

[68] *Hansard*, HL Vol.587, No.127, col.1114.
[69] A prophecy only partially fulfilled so far in the case of *Naomi Campbell v Mirror Group Newspapers* above.

- the introduction of the access rights given under other legislation (the Access to Personal Files Act 1987, the Access to Health Records Act 1990 and the Education (School Records) Regulations 1989 and corresponding Northern Ireland and Scotland provisions) to the DPA in order to consolidate the rights and incorporate the *Gaskin* ECHR ruling;

- the removal of the requirement (which had been inserted during the passage through the Lords) for direct marketers who received notice of objection to respond to individuals in writing;

- provision for individuals serving notices under the Act to do so electronically;

- insertion of the court's power to require notification to third parties of a finding of inaccuracy;

- the insertion of the offence provisions in respect of enforced subject access;

- the addition of ethnic monitoring as a ground for holding sensitive personal data;

- the addition of the exemption for corporate finance from the subject information provisions;

- the insertion of a number of the transitional provisions;

- the replacement of a revised cl.28(4) containing a limited exemption.

1–81 *Third Reading.* It was read for the third time in the Commons on July 2. In contrast to the Third Reading in the Lords, which had dwelt on issues of principle, the debate was largely on technical points. Government amendments were still being inserted. The Government deleted provisions which had been included to deal with the geographical scope of the Bill and clarify what amounted to a transfer of data. The provisions had been much criticised and the Government decided to withdraw them. There were various drafting amends, for example to tidy up the provisions dealing with prior checking, and to allow exemptions to the rights of subject access to educational records.

Mr Harry Cohen moved several amendments aimed at strengthening the protection given by the Bill, none of which were successful. He sought to reduce the breadth of the exemption for national security purposes and "introduce some element of accountability to the processing of personal data for the purpose of national security"[70] by making some aspects subject to external review. He pressed for some restrictions to be introduced on the potential uses of information available on public registers, such as registers of shareholders. He asked for the definition of "relevant filing system" to be extended to ensure that private bodies like the Economic League could not use paper files to remain outside the scope of the data protection regime. In response, Mr Hoon reiterated the Government's determination to cover manual records to the extent required by the Directive but not an iota more.

An amendment was unsuccessfully sought to allow third-party credit reference information to be kept confidential.

---

[70] *Hansard*, HC Vol.315, No.198, col.583.

Mr Greenway asked the Government to extend the reach of the crime prevention exemption by adding the term "investigation of crime" to the list of activities, and the phrase "safeguarding public security" to the list of purposes, for which the exemption could be claimed. He explained the particular aim was to enable information sharing between the police and other concerned parties about football hooligans. In response, the Government spokesman explained that the problems encountered in making disclosures relating to convictions of football supporters was not attributable to data protection problems but to the general law and practical problems of correct identification.

Mr Richard Shephard proposed that the Commissioner should be enabled to keep a register of enforcement action taken and that the restrictions on disclosure of information by her should be lessened. This was met by some easing of the position on both points by the Government in the form of allowing for notification regulations to include additional information on the register and slightly widening the grounds for disclosure by the Commissioner.

Another proposed amendment which met with some sympathy from the Government was one to include political canvassing in the list of permitted activities for which sensitive data could be held without individual consent. The preference of the Government, however, was to deal with it by subordinate legislation which they undertook to do.

An amendment aimed at making millennium compliance a specific statutory obligation for data controllers met with less success and was rejected.

In summing up spokesman on all sides (as well as expressing relief at having concluded work on the Bill), expressed some satisfaction with the changes made during its passage through the House. Although Mr Greenway concluded with some lingering concerns at the failure to revisit cl.32 and to tackle the potential problems which the Lords had described.

At the conclusion of the debate Mr Howarth announced that implementation would not be possible by October 24, 1998 in view of the substantial amounts of secondary legislation still to be put into place.

Final Stages

1–82   The Bill returned to the Lords where the Commons amendments were considered and agreed on July 10. The Lords consideration gave rise to some final efforts to insert potential *Pepper v Hart* material. On the incorporation of the access rights to some kinds of manual information Lord Williams said:

> "*Gaskin* is to do with refusal of subject access. It says that where access is refused because of the risk of identifying third parties who have not consented there must be a mechanism for independent review of that refusal. The Bill deals with this in two ways. Where access has been refused data subjects may seek a court order requiring access to be given or they may request an assessment to be made by the data protection commissioner who has the power to take the necessary enforcement action."[71]

---

[71] *Hansard*, HL Vol.591, No.184, col.1477 (July 10, 1998).

There was also discussion on the meaning of the term "trade secret" in cl.8(5) in which Lord Williams expressed the Government view that the term carried its ordinary meaning but was probably wide enough to allow the withholding of algorithms:

> "which some organisations use to determine whether to meet individual's requests for a service of some kind; for instance a credit scoring system used to determine whether or not to give people credit."[72]

Baroness Nicholson of Winterbourne asked a final question of the Government on cl.32:

> "Will the Minister confirm that as his Written Answer of April 8 to my noble friend Lord Lester of Herne Hill indicates, the Data Protection Bill interpretation of clause 31 will be applied by the courts and interpreted in accordance with the European legal principles of proportionality and legal certainty."

The response Lord Williams for the Government was:

> "The noble Baroness gave me notice of this matter and I affirm that what I said in the Written Answer remains correct."[73]

The written answer was:

> "Yes: According to the consistent case law of the European Court of Justice, in the application of Community law the guiding principles, which include proportionality and legal certainty, must be observed by the courts."

---

[72] *Hansard*, HL Vol.591, No.184, col.1482 (July 10, 1998).
[73] *Hansard*, HL Vol.591, No.184, col.1499.

CHAPTER 2

Privacy Rights and the Misuse of Private Information

INTRODUCTION

2–01 Since the implementation of the Human Rights Act 1998 (HRA) the courts have moved gradually to recognise a right to personal informational privacy in the United Kingdom, as a species of confidentiality independent of the rights guaranteed by the Data Protection Act 1998 (DPA). In these cases the courts have looked at informational privacy in a broad legal context. The essence of the development of the law in this area was captured by Lord Hoffman in *Naomi Campbell v MGN Ltd*[1] explaining where the law now stands as well as looking forward to the questions yet to be addressed:

> "In recent years there have been two developments of the law of confidence. . . . One has been an acknowledgement of the artificiality of distinguishing between confidential information obtained through the violation of a confidential relationship and similar information obtained in some other way. The second . . . . . . has been the acceptance of the privacy of personal information as something worthy of protection in its own right."

> "What human rights law has done is to identify private information as something worth protecting as an aspect of human autonomy and dignity. And this recognition has raised inescapably the question of why it should be worth protecting against the state but not against a private person . . . . I can see no logical ground for saying that a person should have less protection against a private individual than he would have against the state for the publication of personal information for which there is no justification."

> "The result of these developments has been a shift in the centre of gravity of the action for breaches of confidence when it is used as a remedy for the unjustified publication of personal information . . . . Instead of the cause of action being based upon the duty of good faith applicable to confidential personal information and trade secrets alike, it focuses upon the protection of human autonomy and dignity—the right to control the dissemination of information about one's private life and the right to the esteem and respect of other people."

---

[1] [2004] UKHL 22.

"These changes have implications for the future development of the law. They must influence the approach of the courts to the kind of information which is regarded as entitled to protection, the extent and form of publication which attracts a remedy and the circumstances in which publication can be justified."

Anyone advising on data protection needs to be aware of this broader context.

This chapter describes the development of the law of confidence in the UK, the effect of the HRA, case law from the European Court of Human Rights (ECtHR) at Strasbourg on Art.8 of the European Convention on Human Rights and Fundamental Freedoms (the Convention), the impact of Convention Rights on the interpretation of the data protection Directives and analyses the development of the tort of misuse of private information in the case law on informational privacy and data protection in the UK since the implementation of the HRA.

Although the context and related UK cases before and after the HRA are reviewed, the chapter does not even try to offer more than the scantest reference to the wider topic of privacy. There is a mass of writing on privacy from different perspectives, from the sociological or philosophical through to the technical. Much of it is the result of US scholarship.[2] This includes a body of material on the legal issues related to privacy.[3] Here it is not possible to do more than acknowledge its existence.

Protection of privacy

2–02   It should be recognised that the case law has not developed a general law of privacy. Indeed the House of Lords decided in *Wainwright v Home Office*[4] that English law knows no general tort of the invasion of privacy. The cases examined in this chapter examine only the area of informational privacy. Other laws such as protection from harassment or anti-discrimination legislation provide some protection but we are still a long way from a general privacy right. Even in the area of information privacy for the 21st century is still a concept under construction. In the cases that have come before the courts after October 2000 judges have acknowledged the difficulties of definition. In *A v B & C*[5] Lord Woolf took a pragmatic approach:

"... the question of whether there is an interest capable of being the subject of a claim for privacy should not be allowed to be the subject of detailed argument ... In those cases in which the answer is not obvious, an answer will often be unnecessary."

The courts seem to be moving towards an acceptance that privacy is not a "one size fits all" right and that the scope and nature of the areas which individuals may legitimately regard as private will vary from case to case.[6]

---

[2] It is difficult to single out any one contributor but for example Paul Schwartz, Alan Westin, Colin Bennett, David Flaherty.
[3] For example Lord Bingham of Cornhill, "Should there be a law of personal privacy?" (1996) 5 E.H.R.I.R. 451.
[4] [2003] W.L.R. 1137.
[5] [2002] 3 W.L.R. 542.
[6] See *Ash v McKennitt* [2006] EWCA Civ 1714.

Summary of Main Points

2–03   (a) There is no over-arching cause of action in English law for breach of privacy.

(b) The wrongful disclosure of private information will give rise to a remedy before the courts in certain circumstances. This is equally applicable between private parties. In applying this right the courts will apply Art.8 of the Convention rights.

(c) Personal information can be protected where the person had a reasonable expectation of privacy in respect of the information. There is no need for the parties to have been in a prior relationship.

(d) The categories of the information that may be protected are not closed but the essence is that the action protects the dignity and autonomy of the individual. Thus the information may be related to behaviour in public places or information which is known to a limited number of people. Those who are in the public eye or have a public role are as entitled to have their privacy protected as anyone else.

(e) The right of free speech is an important human right but it is not paramount. Neither privacy nor freedom of speech are absolute rights nor is one superior to the other.

(f) Where the person who wishes to publish personal information which would affect the privacy of another invokes the right of freedom of speech the courts must carry out a balancing act between the two rights set out in Arts 8 and 10 applying considerations of proportionality.

(g) The right of free speech is one of the most important rights in a democracy and must be fiercely guarded but not all speech has the same value. The right to free political speech is much more important than the right to repeat trivial gossip.

(h) Where the information concerns two parties careful scrutiny will be required to ensure that the Art.10 rights of the would-be discloser are considered but again these will be balanced against the privacy rights of the subject applying considerations of proportionality.

(i) Where the disclosure is justified in the public interest, for example to "set the record straight" then it must still be proportionate.

(j) The remedies provided by the courts may cover injunctions or damages.

Exploitation of Image

2–04   The United Kingdom has lagged behind the United States in providing a right to prevent the commercial exploitation of the image of the individual. In the United States the right of individuals to control and exploit their own images has developed as a sub-set of the right of privacy.[7] Actions may be brought where the commercial use

---

[7] See M. Henry, ed., *International Privacy, Personality and Publicity Laws* (Butterworths, 2001) Ch.30.

merely evokes the identity of the individual. In the absence of such a right in the United Kingdom the courts have sometimes afforded protection for commercial interests under the name of personal confidentiality. Thus photographs resulting from a photo shoot which had been opened to fans to view were protected on the grounds of confidentiality in *Creation Records v News Group Newspapers Ltd*.[8] A court has been persuaded to grant an injunction to restrain the publication of an unauthorised photograph of the survivor of the Maltese conjoined twins, apparently on the grounds that the sale of the rights to the image would be a source of much-needed income for the family[9] and, in making an order to restrain the publication of pictures of a house purchased by a celebrity couple, has acknowledged that the couple had an interest not only in protecting their privacy but in the possibility of selling an "exclusive" set of pictures of the property to a magazine.[10]

The protection of commercial interests in images from unfair exploitation has tended to blur the distinction between commercial confidentiality and the protection of privacy and obscure the principled basis of the privacy right. However, in developments, which may prove to be of long-term significance in separating commercial interests in identity from privacy interests per se, a recognition of the commercial aspect of protection of personal images have appeared in the United Kingdom with two decisions. In *Douglas v Hello! (No. 6)*,[11] it was accepted that a couple were entitled to protect the exclusive photographic rights to official pictures of their celebrity wedding, to which over 300 guests had been invited, to the extent that they had a legitimate commercial interest in the exploitation of the pictures. In the Court of Appeal it was held that this was a species of property right that could not be passed on to another and hence *OK!* were unable to benefit. However on appeal to the House of Lords *OK!* succeeded in establishing that the arrangements entered into for the security of the wedding had created a form of confidentiality which protected its interests as well as that of the protagonists in the event and were entitled to succeed in their action for a breach of their confidentiality by *Hello!* magazine. In *Edmund Irvine Tidswell Ltd v Talksport Ltd*[12] a Formula 1 driver was photographed holding a mobile telephone. The image was manipulated so that he looked as though he was listening to a portable radio, which had the words "Talk Radio" on it. The judge held that the photograph amounted to passing-off and acknowledged that celebrities have a property right in their image which is capable of protection. More recently the runner, David Bedford, succeeded in a complaint to Ofcom about an advertisement for a directory enquiry service which used "look alikes". He complained of breach of the Advertising Standards Code, r.6.3 of which provides that living persons must not be portrayed, caricatured or referred to in advertisements without their permission. The advertisements however were not banned, despite the finding in David Bedford's favour. In another case of a "look alike" a claimant failed in an action for defamation against a pornographic website on which a woman who was, apparently, identical to the claimant was

---

[8] [1997] E.M.L.R. 444. Case concerned the Oasis photoshoot for a record album cover. A Rolls Royce was put into a swimming pool. Fans were allowed to watch but when one took a photograph and offered it for publication in a newspaper the record company succeeded in restraining the use of the photograph.
[9] Reported in the *Manchester Evening News*.
[10] *Beckham v MGM*, unreported, June 28, 2001, QBD.
[11] [2005] EWCA Civ 595, CA: *OBG Ltd v Allan* [2007] UKHL 21
[12] [2002] EWHC 367.

portrayed. The claimant argued that the website was defamatory of her. The court rejected the claim as having no realistic prospect of success.[13] Although the full extent of the protection, and its relation with the law of confidence described later in the chapter, remains unclear these decisions mark an acknowledgment of a range of interests in personal images and information, some related to privacy and some to commercial interests which are likely to future development.[14]

BACKGROUND—PRIVACY RIGHTS

2–05   As has been explained in Ch.1, above the immediate predecessors of Directive 95/46 were Treaty 108 and the OECD Guidelines. Those instruments themselves owed their existence to the acknowledgement of the right to private and family life in Art.8 of the Convention. While those interpreting the 1984 Data Protection Act tended to look back primarily to its immediate predecessors, particularly Treaty 108,[15] over the last few years there has been, and continues to be, an increasing tendency for those interpreting the 1998 Act and the Directive to look to Art.8 directly.[16] At EU level this reflects the development of case law to the effect that fundamental rights form part of the general principles of law which are applied b the European Court[17] and that the Treaty of Amsterdam strengthened the commitment of the Union to regard Convention rights as a fundamental aspect of EU law. Article 6 of the EU Treaty provides:

> "1. The Union is founded on the principles of liberty, democracy, respect for human rights and fundamental freedoms, and the rule of law, principles which are common to the Member States.
> 2. The Union shall respect fundamental rights, as guaranteed by the European Convention for the Protection of Human Rights and Fundamental Freedoms signed in Rome on 4 November 1950 and as they result from the constitutional traditions common to Member States, as general principles of Community law."

Moreover the importance of privacy has been emphasised by the inclusion in the Charter of fundamental rights of the European Union of Art.8 which specifically covers personal data protection:

> "1. Everyone has the right to the protection of personal data concerning him or her.
> 2. Such data must be processed fairly for specified purposes and on the basis of the consent of the person concerned or some other legitimate

---

[13] *O'Shea v MGN Ltd* [2001] E.M.L.R. 40, QBD.
[14] Earlier cases had not accepted this right: *Mirage Studios v Counter-Feat Clothing Co.* [1991] F.S.R. 145. The estate of Princess Diana was not able to restrain use of her image.
[15] See the judgments of the Data Protection Tribunal (as it was then) in the cases of *Data Protection Registrar v Equifax 1991*, reported in the Encyclopaedia of Data Protection.
[16] See *Brian Robertson Reid v Secretary of State for the Home Department* [2001] EWCA Admin 915.
[17] Case 29/69 *Stauder* [1969] E.C.R. 419; Case 4/73 *Nold v Commission* [1974] E.C.R. 491; Case C-274/99 P *Connolly v Commission* [2001] E.C.R. I-1611; Case 136/79 *National Panasonic v Commission* [1980] E.C.R. 2033; Case C-62/90 *Commission v Germany* [1992] E.C.R. I –2575; Case C-404/92 P *X v Commission* [1994] E.C.R. I-4737

basis laid down by law. Everyone has the right of access to data which has been collected concerning him or her, and the right to have it rectified.

3. Compliance with these rules shall be subject to control by an independent authority."

Although the Charter has not yet entered into force the Court of First Instance has commented:

"although [the Charter] does not have legally binding force, it does show the importance of the rights it sets out in the Community legal order."[18]

Directive 95/46 refers directly to Art.8 as its basis. Article I of Directive 95/46 states that one of the objects of the Directive is the protection of:

". . . the fundamental rights and freedoms of natural persons, and in particular their right to privacy with respect to the processing of personal data."

In the UK the implementation of the Convention rights in the Human Rights Act has brought an increased familiarity and ease with the application of the Art.8 right which is increasingly reflected in the case law. That case law has gradually moved the UK towards the development of a privacy right which would have been unthinkable only a few years ago.

UK background—meaning of privacy

2–06   The Younger Committee discussed the idea of privacy in its report[19] in 1972 and reviewed the various efforts over the years to define it. David Calcutt Q.C. in the *Report of the Committee on Privacy and Related Matters* in 1990,[20] after rehearsing the difficulties in coming to a satisfactory definition, posited a working one as:

"the right of the individual to be protected against intrusion into his personal life or affairs, or those of his family, by direct physical means or by publication of information."

and concluded that:

"a natural person's privacy shall be taken to include matters appertaining to his health, personal communications and family, personal relationships and a right to be free from harassment or molestation."

Other analyses echo the themes of the right to choose to be alone or seek companions of one's choice, to control the information publicly known about oneself, to seek seclusion and to be free from outside interference in one's own domain.[21] In the

---

[18] *Philip Morris International v Commission* [2003] E.C.R. II-I para.122 cited in the Opinion of the Advocate General in the PNR cases C-317/04 and C-318/04 at para.23.
[19] *The Younger Committee Report*, Cmnd.5012 (July 1972).
[20] Cm.5012.
[21] See Westin and others referred to in n.2 above.

context of the Convention, it is part of a package of rights which overlap and intersect, but all of which support the same core values to assert and protect the dignity of each human being.

The Younger Committee did not consider that there should be a general protection afforded to private life but recommended some new remedies to deal with areas of specific mischief. It also commented on the development of the law of confidence, which it thought provided a basis for developing privacy protection. It recommended that the Law Commission should reconsider the action for breach of confidence.[22]

CONFIDENTIALITY—BEFORE OCTOBER 2000

2–07   There are different views on whether a right to privacy should be developed through case law. Judges have expressed their concerns and reservations both in extra-judicial writings[23] and in a number of judgments.[24] More recently Buxton L.J. set out the extent of judicial reservations in *Wainwright v Home Office*[25]:

> "Since however the protection of privacy has been seen by some as nonetheless a proper field for the exercise of judicial activism, I venture to go further and draw attention to some difficulties that stand in our way.
>
> 'Privacy' covers a very wide range of cases, which are affected by a very wide range of policy consideration. What occurred in our case is perhaps one of the simpler examples. The right not to have another stare at one's naked body, save by consent or in clearly defined situations of necessity, would be unambiguously regarded as a matter of privacy. But what of the obtaining of information that (on the assumptions made to justify the extension of the law of tort into new situations of privacy) is not covered by the law of confidence? What of the maker of true statements about others, hitherto rigorously excluded from the law of defamation? What of the whistle blower? And, indeed, what of a preference to have photographs of your wedding in one publication rather than another?
>
> As is well accepted, in none of these cases can a right to privacy be absolute. But that is only the start. What needs to be worked out is the delicate balance, particularly in the area of publication of information, between the interests on the one hand of the subject and on the other of someone entering his private space, or that of the publisher and the latter's audience . . .
>
> All these considerations indicate that not only is the problem a difficult one, but also that on grounds not merely of rationality but also of democracy the difficult social balance that the tort involves should be struck by Parliament and not by the judges."[26]

Not all judges share these reservations[27] but over the decade before the Human Rights Act came into force even the keenest proponents of judicial activism in this area

---

[22] See Toulson and Phipps, *Breach of Confidence* (Sweet and Maxwell, 1996), p.112, para.9.01.

[23] See the article by Lord Bingham at n.3 above.

[24] See the comments of Megarry V.C. in *Malone v Commissioner of the Metropolitan Police (No. 2)* [1979] 2 All E.R. 620.

[25] [2001] EWCA Civ 208; [2002] 3 W.L.R. 405.

[26] Text extracted from paras 108 to 111.

[27] See comments of Sedley L.J. in *Douglas v Hello* cited later at para.2.

faced difficulties in seeking to develop a more general right of privacy because of the chilling effect of the decision in the case of *Kaye v Robertson*.[28] In this case the subject had been in an accident, which had resulted in severe injuries. A journalist entered his hospital room without permission and photographed him. The photograph was published. The action was taken against the photographer. Although the entry was wrongful, being a trespass, and the Court of Appeal acknowledged that the publication was an appalling invasion of his privacy, it refused to grant an injunction restraining publication. As a number of commentators have subsequently pointed out, the Court was not referred to the developing cases on confidentiality, presumably because the intrusion was by a stranger. It must also be borne in mind that the case was decided at a time when possible legislation restricting freedom of the press was a live issue.[29] The Court, recognising that a decision to protect the actor's privacy would be going beyond the boundaries of the law of confidence and, presumably, the wider political context, reaffirmed that the UK law knew no right of privacy and that it was a matter for Parliament, not the courts, to develop one. If the Court hoped that this principled abstention from developing the law would stir Parliament into action over press excesses it was to be disappointed. However, the clarity of the judgment was to prove a setback for those who advocated the development of a judge-made right to personal privacy for nearly a decade.

Other areas of law related to privacy protection, as well as trespass, are nuisance, action for harassment, or defamation. However, the pre-existing area of jurisprudence which is most akin to a privacy right, and has been used by the courts to develop one, is the law of confidence. As has been noted above the concept of confidentiality was not argued in *Kaye v Robertson*.

In *A v B & C*[30] which is described below, Lord Woolf L.C.J. said that, in cases on Art.8, citation of authorities which relate to the action for breach of confidence prior to the coming into force of the 1998 Act "are largely of historic interest only". Nevertheless anyone advising in this area will find it important to understand the evolution of the current cases.[31]

Development of jurisprudence on confidentiality

2–08　The case usually cited as the first major case in the area of personal confidentiality is *Prince Albert v Strange*.[32] When the facts are considered it seems but a short distance to *A v B & C* and surprising that it took 153 years to make the journey (*A v B & C* was decided by the Court of Appeal in March 2002). In the former case Prince Albert had made some private etchings which he wished to have copied. He placed them with a printer in Windsor to have copies made. An enterprising employee took extra copies which were then offered for sale to the public via a sale catalogue, in which they were described, not pictured, and which gave the impression that they were being published with consent. The Prince took Mr Strange, the publisher of

---

[28] [1991] F.S.R. 62.
[29] See discussion in Ch.17, below on the exemption for journalism.
[30] [2002] EWCA 337.
[31] For the material in the following section I am much indebted to Toulson and Phipps, above and Francis Gurry, *Breach of Confidence* (Clarendon Press, 1984).
[32] (1849) 1 Mac. & G. 25.

the catalogue, to court to stop publication and succeeded.[33] The Prince had no pre-existing relationship with Mr Strange. There was no contract between them. The Court held that there was an infringement of the Prince's rights in the material and that there had been some breach of trust. It was suggested in the judgment that the breach of trust or confidence in itself entitled the Prince to a remedy.

The textbooks report relatively few cases in the same area over the next 100 years. The courts seem to have been little troubled by cases claiming breach of confidence in personal matters although there seems to have been a gradual recognition of confidentiality in those relationships where sensitive information most commonly passed between two people.[34] The relationships of bankers, doctors, lawyers, clergy or other counsellors as well as other professionals with their clients are all regarded as confidential.

An extra-judicial development worthy of mention is be the article published in the *Harvard Law Review* in 1890 in which the authors, Samuel Warren and Louis Brandeis, argued vigorously for a law of privacy to restrain the intrusions of the press. It has been much cited since.

The next significant case was *Saltman Engineering Co Ltd v Campbell Engineering Co Ltd*.[35] Although this did not concern personal relationships it confirmed two features of the action for breach of confidence which were essential for its future vigorous development: there did not have to be a contractual relationship between the parties before breach of confidence could be claimed; and, where there was no contract, the action could be used to protect a wide range of subject-matter as long as it was not "public property or public knowledge". The generous approach taken to both the relationships and subject-matter capable of being protected meant that confidentiality could be invoked in a range of situations.

2–09   As the action for breach of confidence developed over the next 20 years, most of the reported cases concerned commercial or employment cases. However in *Argyll v Argyll*[36] the Duchess of Argyll was successful in stopping her husband from disclosing information about the marital relationship. In that case the court confirmed that the doctrine could be applied in personal matters; rejected the argument that confidentiality could only be argued in a limited class of (primarily commercial) cases; and reiterated that this was a broad jurisdiction.

In 1981, the Law Commission produced a *Report on Breach of Confidence*.[37] The report reviewed the development of the law in this area. The review was no easy task. The body of case law on breach of confidence had grown organically. It had taken and used ideas from other areas. It had provided remedies where it thought they were needed. It had been messy, patchy, haphazard, vigorous and unplanned. There was no agreement on the legal basis of the right (a property right, contract, equity)[38]; the nature of the exemptions (are they exceptions to the obligation or defences to a breach?)[39]; the availability of damages (are they available or can only an injunction

---

[33] For a discussion of the historical basis of the action and this case in particular see Toulson and Phipps.
[34] Gurry, above at pp.143 onwards.
[35] (1948) 65 R.P.C. 203.
[36] [1967] Ch. 302.
[37] Cmnd.8388 (1981).
[38] Gurry, above, Ch.2.
[39] *ibid.*, Chs 15 and 16.

be issued?)[40]; the effect on third parties (in what circumstances could they be bound if they came into possession of the confidential material?).[41] Not surprisingly the Law Commission proposed that these uncertainties and anomalies should be tidied up and the action for breach of confidence put on to a statutory footing. The report was never acted upon. If it had been the recent privacy jurisprudence might not have been possible.

The publication of personal information which has been unfairly obtained was considered in a number of cases over the following years. In *Stephens v Avery*[42] the defendant had betrayed her friendship with the plaintiff by providing a newspaper with details of the plaintiff's sexual life. The plaintiff claimed damages for breach of confidence. In *Francome v Mirror Group Newspapers*[43] a home telephone was bugged and the conversations over it taped by strangers. The resulting information was sent to the newspaper. In restraining publication before the trial the Court of Appeal recognised that the conversations were confidential. On the other hand, some judges were reluctant to protect information about those whose lives were in the public domain. Plaintiffs failed in *Woodward v Hutchins*[44] and *Lennon v News Group Newspapers Ltd*.[45] In the first case the *Daily Mirror* wanted to publish material about a number of pop stars and the court refused to restrain the publication as it said that they had already put their lives in the public domain. In the second, the *News of the World* wanted to publish material about John Lennon's first marriage. The Court of Appeal said that the relationship had ceased to be private and refused to stop publication. The two cases have been distinguished in latter cases and can no longer be regarded as sound authority.

In *Attorney-General v Guardian Newspapers Ltd (No. 2)*,[46] the *Spycatcher* case, the judges expressed a range of views on the action for breach of confidence and its application to personal information which have been much cited in later cases. A former member of the security services had published a book of memoirs of his time with the service. The Government tried to restrain publication of material from the book in *The Guardian* newspaper, even though it had been published outside the United Kingdom and the UK Government had been unable to restrict its publication abroad. The Government claimed that the disclosure of information by the individual was a breach of confidence. Lord Goff in his judgment described the position that the law of confidence had reached at the end of the last century, although he disclaimed any intention to produce a definitive description of the area (ineffectually as every text book cites it).

Lord Goff said that a duty of confidence arises when:

> "confidential information comes to the knowledge of a person (the confidant) in circumstances where he has notice, or is held to have agreed, that the information is confidential, with the effect that it would be just in all the circumstances that he should be precluded from disclosing the information to others."

[40] *ibid.*, Ch.23.
[41] *ibid.*, Ch.13.
[42] [1988] 1 Ch.419.
[43] [1984] 1 W.L.R. 892.
[44] [1977] 1 W.L.R. 760.
[45] [1978] F.S.R. 573.
[46] [1990] 1 A.C. 109.

2–10   There can be no confidentiality unless the information is "confidential", that is it has not entered the public domain; the duty does not apply to information which is trivial or useless and confidentiality can, in some circumstances, be negated by public interest.

In the same case, Lord Keith signalled a green light for future privacy cases by accepting that privacy was a right capable of protection by the law of confidence.[47]

It might have been thought that after such encouraging dicta the courts would have moved forward to develop the action for breach of confidence into one which offered a more general protection for personal privacy. However the decision in *Kaye v Robertson* the following year proved a setback and, although the decision was later criticised by some, it continued to be applied. In *R. v Khan*,[48] a case which was later considered by the ECtHR,[49] the House of Lords reiterated that in the United Kingdom there was nothing unlawful about a breach of privacy.

Development continued in related areas and in *Hellewell v Chief Constable of Derby*[50] the court considered the disclosure of personal information which had been obtained under compulsion by a public body. This was partly a response to a wider development of information sharing by the public sector with increased privatisation, moves to partnership workings with the private sector and the disclosure of information between government departments and other public bodies, for example via data matching initiatives. Concern had previously been expressed at such developments and the limitations on the powers of public bodies to use and disclose personal information was emphasised in *Marcel v Commissioner of Police for the Metropolis*[51] by the Vice Chancellor who had memorably commented that:

" . . . the dossier of personal information is the hallmark of the totalitarian state".

In a number of cases the courts held that personal information obtained under compulsion would be subject to an obligation of confidence in the hands of the public body.[52] In *Hellewell* the local police force had provided shopkeepers with photographs of a known shoplifter. The photographs had been taken under compulsion when the individual was in custody. The individual complained of breach of confidence. It was held that there was an obligation of confidence owed to the individual as the information had been extracted under compulsory powers and the police were limited in the uses they could make of the information. In the particular case the disclosure of the photograph was justified in the public interest. More importantly for the purposes of the development of a more general privacy right, the judge commented that the law of confidence would be able to protect someone from an invasion of privacy caused by being photographed without consent from a distance.

2–11   The comment was *obiter* and was not followed in *R. v Brentwood BC Ex p. Peck*.[53] In that case the court dismissed a claim that the local council had acted

---

[47] *ibid.*, at 255.
[48] [1997] A.C. 558.
[49] ECtHR report, *The Times*, May 23, 2000.
[50] [1995] 1 W.L.R. 804.
[51] [1991] All E.R. 845; [1992] 1 All E.R. 72, CA.
[52] *Alfred Crompton Amusement Machines v Commissioner for Customs and Excise (No.2)* [1973] 2 All E.R. 1169.
[53] [1998] E.M.L.R. 697; *The Times*, December 18, 1997, QBD.

unlawfully in giving the media copies of a CCTV recording of Mr Peck engaged in a suicide bid in a public place. It should be noted however that Mr Peck was later successful in his action against the UK in the ECtHR at Strasbourg (*Peck v UK*). He succeeded not only on Art.8 but also Art.13 as the Court held that he had no effective legal remedy in the UK in relation to the violation of his right to respect for private life.

In *R. v Chief Constable of the North Wales Police Ex p. Thorpe*[54] the disclosure of information about an individual's previous criminal history of offences against children by a public authority was considered by the court and held to be justified in the circumstances.

Thus, despite the uneven growth of authority in this area, by the time the HRA came into effect the law of confidence had developed significantly in the United Kingdom and there were persuasive dicta that an action for breach of confidence might be employed to protect personal privacy.

The action for breach of confidence offers a useful starting point for the development of a privacy right. There is no absolute right to confidentiality. Confidentiality may be breached where an opposing interest outweighs the obligation. Thus confidentiality will give way to an order of the court, legal compulsion, or a greater public interest in the disclosure. As such it incorporates a balancing test that makes it a malleable tool to apply where balances have to be struck, particularly between Art.8 and other rights.

2–12 The European Court has recognised the development of the law of confidence in the United Kingdom and its growing potential to protect personal privacy over the last 20 years. The two cases usually cited to support this statement are *Winner v United Kingdom*[55] and *Earl and Countess Spencer v United Kingdom*.[56] In both cases the applicants chose to bring cases in Strasbourg on the grounds that the United Kingdom did not offer the remedies they needed to protect their privacy rather than try to bring actions in the UK courts. In the *Winner* case various statements had been made about the plaintiff's relations with his wife, not all of which were true. The court held that the UK law afforded sufficient remedies to protect his reputation (including libel, in respect of which he already had obtained a settlement), but said the failure to take action for breach of confidence did not amount to a failure to exhaust his remedies in the United Kingdom due to the uncertainty and lack of clarity in the jurisdiction. In the *Spencer* case, the Earl and his wife had been subject to articles in the newspapers about their marriage and about her health problems and photographs had been taken without consent. To that extent it was not dissimilar to the situation in which Naomi Campbell later found herself. The Commission declared the complaint to the court inadmissible as the applicants had not exhausted their domestic remedies and the extension and development of the law of confidence by the courts meant that they were likely to have found a remedy in the UK courts.

Regulation of the press

2–13 Between 1989 and 2003 a series of Committees considered whether the United Kingdom should regulate the press to protect the privacy of individuals and

---

[54] [1999] Q.B. 396.
[55] Application 1087/84 (1986) 48 D.R. 154, EComHR.
[56] Application 28851/95 (1998) 25 E.H.R.R. CD105.

issued a number of reports. The history is set out in Ch.17, below on the exemptions for the special purposes. To an extent, the considerations of the Calcutt Committee and its reports played their part in the development of this area. They may have been an added reason for the exercise of judicial restraint in the case of *Kaye v Robertson* and were instrumental in bringing about the Press Complaints Commission (PCC) Code of Practice. Although decisions of the Commission have been criticised the Code has been a mechanism for bringing some degree of regulation to bear on the behaviour of the press. It might have been harder for the courts to develop the case law dealing with media restriction post October 2000 had the Code not been in force for several years beforehand. (For a detailed analysis of the moves to press regulation see Ch.17, below on the special purposes.) The Code, together with the other self-regulatory codes for the media, has a role in the legal framework as both the HRA and the DPA require courts to take them into account when considering actions which may restrict freedom of expression. The PCC Code is described below.

HUMAN RIGHTS ACT 1998 (HRA)

2–14 The European Convention for the Protection of Human Rights and Fundamental Freedoms (the Convention) was adopted by the Council of Europe on November 4, 1950 and ratified by the United Kingdom in 1951. The United Kingdom did not incorporate the Convention into domestic law on ratification. The Convention guarantees civil liberties which include the right to life, freedom from torture, freedom from inhuman and degrading treatment, the right to a fair trial, freedom of religion, expression and assembly. The Convention binds the State and is enforceable against the State. Individuals have been able to take legal action against the United Kingdom in the European Court of Human Rights at Strasbourg in reliance on the Convention since 1966, but its application in the UK courts used to be limited. It could be looked at as an aid to interpretation in the case of ambiguity, as in *R. v Secretary of State for the Home Department Ex p. Brind*[57] or to influence judicial decisions where there was an element of discretion as in *Attorney General v Guardian Newspapers (No. 2)*.[58] However, individuals have not been able to rely on Convention rights directly in the UK courts. The incorporation of the Convention rights into UK law was the central vehicle in the Labour Government's policy commitment to "Bring Rights Home". The HRA did this by imposing specific obligations on courts and public bodies to take account of and apply Convention rights.

Interpreting legislation

2–15 Section 3(1) of the Human Rights Act provides that, so far as it is possible to do so, primary and subordinate legislation must be "read and given effect in a way which is compatible with the Convention rights". This provision applies to all primary and subordinate legislation whenever enacted.

---

[57] [1991] A.C. 696.
[58] [1987] 3 All E.R. 316.

Court rulings

2–16 Under s.2(1), "a Court or Tribunal determining a question which has arisen in connection with a Convention right must take into account" any judgment, decision or ruling of the European Court of Human Rights or any opinion of the Human Rights Commission or other authoritative precedent material insofar as that is relevant to the proceedings. This imposes a duty to consider the Strasbourg jurisprudence on courts and tribunals, although courts are not bound to follow the case law as they would be if these cases were treated as strict precedents. The Information Tribunal, in deciding any appeal heard from the decision of the Commissioner, is bound to take account of such jurisprudence because of this provision.

Incompatibility

2–17 By s.4(1), where a court determines in any proceedings that a provision of primary legislation is not compatible with a Convention right, it may make a declaration of incompatibility. Similar declarations may be made in respect of secondary legislation. Section 10 provides for a speedy procedure whereby Parliament can make appropriate amendments to the law.

Acts of public authorities

2–18 Under s.6(1) a public authority is bound to act in a way compatible with the Convention rights. If a public authority acts in a way incompatible with the Convention rights the authority will be acting unlawfully unless the governing primary legislation leaves the authority with no choice in the matter. Where there is an unlawful act a person who is a "victim" of the act may use the Convention rights as either a sword or a shield in the proceedings. That is they may either bring proceedings against the authority "in the appropriate court or tribunal" or rely on the Convention rights concerned in any legal proceedings against them. This remedy is only available to a "victim" of the unlawful act. A person will only be regarded as a victim if he "would be a victim for the purposes of Article 34 of the Convention".

Where an act by a public authority is unlawful under this provision the court has a wide jurisdiction to grant relief under s.8. The defence of unlawful behaviour by a public authority applies under s.7(1)(b) to any proceedings "brought by or at the instigation of a public authority".

Victims

2–19 Under s.7(1) a person may only bring proceedings against a public authority or rely on a Convention right in any proceedings brought against him if he "is (or would be) a victim of the unlawful act". The limitation applies to all proceedings, including judicial review in connection with an unlawful act. Under s.7(7):

"For the purposes of this section a person is a victim of an unlawful act only if he would be a victim for the purposes of Article 34 of the Convention if proceedings were brought in the European Court of Human Rights in respect of that Act".

Accordingly one has to look to the Strasbourg case law to establish the meaning of the term victim. A victim must be affected by the act or omission that is the subject of the complaint. An interest group or public defender cannot take action. The person need not actually have suffered in order to take action. It will be enough if the person is at risk of being directly affected.[59]

Effect on approach to interpretation

2–20   When interpreting any matter that involves the Convention rights the courts must take account of those rights. This impacts on the Commissioner's advice and supervisory actions, both criminal and civil actions. The Commissioner is under a duty to interpret the DPA in a manner compatible with the Convention rights. The same obligation applies to any court or tribunal which is called upon to interpret any provision in proceedings before it. The provisions of the HRA Act have affected the way that the Commissioner approaches the DPA. In the introduction to the *Guidance* issued on October 28, 2001 the Commissioner said:

> "As I am required to do, I have sought to interpret the Act in the light of the provisions of the Human Rights Act 1998, which came into force on 20 October 2000. This will need to be kept under review. The full effect of the Human Rights Act on our legal system, and on society as a whole, has yet to be felt. It is however, clear that the role of information in our society makes it increasingly important to develop respect among data controllers for the private lives of individuals and to ensure good information handling practice. The Human Rights Act, and in particular Articles 8 and 10 of the European Convention on Human Rights provide the legal framework within which interpretation of the Act, and the Data Protection Principles which underpin it, can be developed."

The obligation to comply with the Convention affects the actions of the Commissioner as a public authority in taking enforcement and other actions.

THE APPLICATION OF THE CONVENTION RIGHTS

2–21   The rights are referred to in the HRA as the Convention rights. Some Convention rights are absolute: for example freedom from torture is an absolute right. The provisions of the Convention which are most obviously relevant to the DPA are Arts 8 and 10—the right to respect for private and family life, home and correspondence and the right to freedom of expression respectively. However, before considering those two rights in more detail, it must be emphasised that the HRA cannot be read selectively. The qualifications have to be read with the rights[60] and all the Convention rights have to be read as a whole. There are tensions between some of the rights. Where there are conflicts the absolute rights will take precedence over qualified rights[61] and where two or more qualified rights come into opposition the courts have to take account of both. Where Art.10 is concerned the HRA contains special provisions

---

[59] *Norris v Ireland* (1998) 13 E.H.R.R. 186.
[60] See comments in *Douglas v Hello!* [2001] 2 All E.R. 289.
[61] *Venables v News Group newspapers* [2001] 1 All E.R. 908.

requiring the UK courts to weight the issues with particular care before acting to prevent publication of materials.[62]

Personal informational privacy, which is used here to mean the control or restriction, of the collection, availability or use of information about an individual, is a narrower concept than the Art.8 right which requires respect for private and family life, home and correspondence. The ECtHR has considered many cases on Art.8 but comparatively few concern the use of information.

Application to private bodies or persons

2–22   The Convention rights are primarily the rights of individuals in relation to the State. However, they may affect the relations between private parties in a number of ways:

- In some cases the State has an obligation to step between two (or more) private parties and protect one against another. As an example, Art.3 guarantees the right not to be subject to inhuman or degrading treatment. In order to comply with this right the State must not only restrain from the prohibited acts but it must also protect its citizens from such treatment by any other person. This obligation applies to Art.8: *Stjerna v Finland*.[63] In that case, the court said that the boundaries between the State's positive and negative obligations do not lend themselves to precise definition. This aspect of Art.8 is important in that it allows for the extension of the Convention right as between private parties and has been relied on by the courts to do so. In the *Hello!* case[64] Brooke L.J. reviewed the Strasbourg cases on this aspect of the Convention rights (in paras 83 to 86). In doing so he quoted *X v The Netherlands*[65]:

"these [positive] obligations may involve the adoption of measures designed to secure respect for private life even in the sphere of the relations of individuals between themselves."

He then applied it to the facts of the case to decide that he was able to apply the Art.in the action between the two competing private parties.

- The courts themselves are public authorities for the purposes of the HRA. As such they may be obliged to interpret any law that they apply so as to conform to the Convention rights. This obligation and its effect on interpretation was recognised by Lord Woolf in *A v B & C*[66] and has been applied by the courts in subsequent cases.

- The courts must interpret the law to comply with the Convention when adjudicating in cases concerning public bodies. They will not want to have the

---

[62] HRA s.12.
[63] (1994) 24 E.H.R.R. 195.
[64] See paras 2–45 onwards.
[65] (1986) 8 E.H.R.R. 235.
[66] [2002] 3 W.L.R. 542.

same legal provisions interpreted one way for the private sector and another for the public sector. By the same logic any regulator or public authority charged with exercising legal powers must interpret the law in accordance with Convention rights. It would be unrealistic to have different interpretations of the law.

The nature of qualified rights

2–23   Absolute rights cannot be interfered with by the State. Qualified rights can be interfered with by the State but any interference must conform to the following norms:

- The interference must be "in accordance with" or "prescribed by" law. That means that the State must have a legal basis for the interference. The law must be accessible, predictable and not arbitrary[67];

- The interference must be carried out for one of the prescribed purposes set out in the second part of the relevant article. The list of the prescribed purposes is specific to each Article. The list is exhaustive in each case. As with all exemptions or restrictions it will be narrowly construed compared to the right[68];

- The interference must be "necessary in a democratic society": that is it must be a reasonable and proportionate response to the threat which justified the interference. The State must not use "a sledgehammer to crack a nut".[69]

When considering the application of a right the first question is whether the right comes into play or is "engaged" by the facts of the case. A minor invasion might not justify engagement.[70] If the right is engaged the next question is whether the right has been breached by the action complained of. If the right is breached the court will consider whether the breach has been carried out with a proper legal basis, is in one of the specified interests and was a proportionate response to the problem. Where the interference is an interference by another private party the courts have not considered the lawfulness of the actions of party in the cases heard to date. It appears to have been accepted by the courts that a private person may carry out any action as long as it is not forbidden by the law. The cases have instead focused on the questions of justification and proportionality.

Article 8

2–24   This has proved to be a flexible right and has lent itself to cover a wide range of issues in the Strasbourg jurisprudence.[71] It reads:

---

[67] In *Malone v UK* (1984) E.H.R.R. 14 it was held that unpublished administrative arrangements governing telephone tapping in the UK we not sufficient to qualify; *Khan v UK, The Times*, May 23, 2000.
[68] *Sunday Times v UK* (1979) 2 E.H.R.R. 245 at 281.
[69] *Handyside v UK* (1979–80) 1 E.H.R.R. 737.
[70] In *Costello-Roberts v United Kingdom* (1995) 19 E.H.R.R. 112 the court held that the corporal punishment involved was not sufficiently serious to bring it within Art.8.
[71] See Lord Lester of Herne Hill and David Pannick Q.C., ed., *Human Rights Law and Practice* (Butterworths 1999).

"(1) Everyone has the right to respect for his private and family life, his home and his correspondence.

(2) There shall be no interference by a public authority with the exercise of this right except such as is in accordance with the law and is necessary in a democratic society in the interests of national security, public safety or the economic well-being of the country, for the prevention of disorder or crime, for the protection of health or morals, or for the protection of the rights and freedoms of others."

Strasbourg cases on the right to private life and information uses

2–25 Article 8 offers protection primarily to individuals, not to legal persons. Limited companies cannot have a family life, nor can government departments. This approach is similar to that taken in the UK in relation to the reputation of public bodies, where such bodies cannot sue for attacks on reputation. In *Derbyshire County Council v The Times Newspapers*[72] the Council sued *The Times* for libel and the House of Lords held that a local authority cannot sue for attacks on its reputation. Apart from that limitation, however, it has proved to be a wide and elastic right. It covers more than personal privacy. It has been used for purposes as diverse as restricting night flights over Heathrow Airport to mandating the provision of legal support for a woman who needed to escape from a violent relationship.[73] In its judgment in the case of *Pretty v United Kingdom*[74] the court accepted that Art.8 encompassed the right to determine when the quality of life had become insupportable and chose to leave it, although they went on to decide that the State's interference with that right was justified and proportionate. It has been used to protect personal informational privacy in a number of cases.

Strasbourg jurisprudence

2–26 It is not always easy to distinguish between informational and other aspects of private life but in this section we have tried to pick out Strasbourg cases that concern the obtaining, use or disclosure of information about living individuals. When considering the cases there are obviously overlaps with the protection of home and family life.

Consent as a basis for interference

2–27 Article 8 requires "respect" for private life. Not every interference with private life will be a breach of Art.8. Importantly, what might otherwise be an unwarranted interference will not be a breach if the act has the consent of the individual. The consent must be true and freely given. Where genuine consent is given it is implicit that sufficient respect has been accorded to the rights of the individual by the provision of choice. It has been held that there was no interference with the Art.10 right where the individual had agreed or contracted to limit his freedom of expression.[75] In another case an individual was offered a new contract of employment which entailed working on a Sunday. The applicant claimed that it interfered with her right to practice religion and took action under Art.9. The court held that the applicant had a free choice in

---

[72] [1993] A.C. 534.
[73] *Airey v Ireland* (1979) E.H.R.R. 305.
[74] *R (On the Application of Pretty) v DPP* [2002] All E.R. 1.
[75] *Vereiging Rechtswinkels Utrecht v Netherlands* 46 D.R. 1986, EcomHR.

employment, could have taken another job and thus the right was not engaged.[76] Although the law can be stated simply there are difficulties in applying it. The Article 29 Working Group[77] in a paper on the use of personal data in the employment sphere, have suggested that true consent can never be given in the employment context because of the imbalance of power between the parties and inevitable pressure that this brings to bear on individuals[78]:

> "An area of difficulty is where the giving of consent is a condition of employment. The worker is in theory able to refuse consent but the consequence may be the loss of a job opportunity. In such circumstances consent is not freely given and is therefore not valid. The situation is even clearer cut where, as is often the case, all employers impose the same or a similar condition of employment."

It is suggested that this goes too far. Consent may be reluctant but still valid. Individuals can waive their rights under the Convention. The question of whether a consent is valid will be a question of fact in all the circumstances.

Relationship between the case law and directive 95/46

2–28   Article 1 states that the object of the Directive is the protection of:

> ". . . the fundamental rights and freedoms of natural persons, and in particular their right to privacy with respect to the processing of personal data."

The Directive is not a codification of the case law on informational privacy as developed by the court at Strasbourg. Rather the Directive is a completion and working out of the rules governing informational privacy. Some of the Strasbourg cases cover areas covered by the Directive but the match between the two is incomplete. Where there is relevant case law it is likely to influence the development of the DPA either directly, possibly by resolving ambiguities in the Act, or indirectly by influencing the case law under the HRA. For that reason an outline of the Strasbourg cases on personal information is provided below.[79]

ECtHR cases on personal information

2–29   The cases mentioned in this section have been decided over nearly 30 years from *Klass v Federal Republic of Germany*[80] in 1978, and over that period the Court

---

[76] *Stedman v UK* (1997) 23 E.H.R.R. CD168.
[77] The representative group of data commissioners set up under the Directive; see Ch.25, below for an analysis of the work of the group.
[78] Opinion 8/2001 on the processing of personal data in the employment context: see at *http://ec.europa. eu/justice_home/fsj/privacy*.
[79] In producing the summary I am indebted to Lee A. Bygrave, "Data Protection Pursuant to the Right to Privacy in Human Rights Treaties", *International Journal of Law and Information Technology*, Vol. 6; Lord Lester and David Pannick, ed., *Human Rights Law and Practice* (Butterworths, 1999); Helen Mountfield and John Wadhad, *Human Rights Act 1998* (Blackstones, 1999); Keir Strumer, *European Human Rights Law* (LAG, 1999); and essays published in *Freedom of Expression and Freedom of Information* (Oxford University Press, 2000), particularly those by Michael J. Beloff Q.C. and Professor David Feldman.
[80] (1978) 2 E.H.R.R. 214.

has become more willing to protect individuals against breaches of informational privacy both by extending the category of circumstances in which it will hold that the right is engaged and by subjecting the State's claim to justification to more stringent scrutiny. However the Court has proved itself more minded to allow for a wider margin of appreciation, or area of discretion to the State, in cases where the intrusion is justified on the grounds of combating terrorism or serious crime (see the later section for cases in this area).

Collection of information

2–30 The collection of personal information without consent, whether under compulsion or from third parties will be a breach. In *McVeigh v UK*[81] the taking of fingerprints without consent was held to be a breach but a justifiable one, as it was in *Murray v UK*.[82] However in *Kinnuen v Finland*[83] the Commission held that retention of fingerprints did not constitute an interference. While in the later case of *Van Der Velden v the Netherlands*[84] the Court decided that both the taking and retention of DNA samples from a person convicted of serious offences breached Art.8.1 but was justified and proportionate. Even where the authority has a legal power to collect information it should not do so in covert ways unless there is a legal basis for the secret collection and the secrecy is justifiable. The collection of a dossier of information about an individual by a public body without the knowledge or consent of the individual will be a breach of Art.8, although it may be justified under Art.8(2). In *Hilton v UK*[85] information was collected without the individual's knowledge as part of a security check and the secret collection was held to be a breach. Covert surveillance has been found to be a breach and the collection of personal information by covert methods will be a breach, even if no record is retained. These cases have usually occured in the context of police investigations into criminal activity as in *Klass v Federal Republic of Germany*.[86]

It follows that the use of covert and intrusive methods of obtaining of information will be a breach, including telephone tapping and covert listening devices. These areas have given rise to particular problems for the United Kingdom given the UK's previous persistent reliance on non-statutory powers in these areas. The United Kingdom was found to be in breach of Art.8 in *Malone v UK*[87] because the police had an insufficient legal basis for tapping telephones. This was remedied by the Interception of Communications Act 1985 which provided for the interception of calls made on public lines. However, it did not cover interception on private lines nor did it cover the use of listening devices, which continued to be used after 1985 on a non-statutory basis. In *Halford v United Kingdom*[88] the court found the United Kingdom in breach of Art.8 again because the police had intercepted calls on a line which had been provided for private use and the UK had no legal basis on which the interception of private lines

---

[81] (1983) 5 E.H.R.R. 71.
[82] (1995) 19 E.H.R.R. 193.
[83] Application No. 24950/94.
[84] Application No. 29514/05.
[85] (1981) 3 E.H.R.R. 104.
[86] (1979–80) 2 E.H.R.R. 214.
[87] (1985) 7 E.H.R.R. 14.
[88] (1997) 24 E.H.R.R. 523.

could be authorised. In *Copland v United Kingdom*[89] the Court held that there was a violation of the Art.8 rights of an employee of a further education college where her work emails, telephone calls from work and internet usage were monitored without being given warning that such monitoring would take place. This applied equally to the monitoring of the communication data arising from the calls.[90]

This has now been dealt with, at least partially, although the UK has not yet dealt with the issue of communication data, under the Regulation of Investigatory Powers Act 2000 (RIPA). In *Govell v UK*[91] a hole had been drilled into the wall of a living room from the house next door to enable the police to listen in to the conversations in the room. The only regulation of covert listening devices and visual surveillance at the time was in Home Office Guidelines and again the United Kingdom was found in breach of Art.8 on the ground that there was no legal basis for the activity. In *Khan v UK*[92] and *Schenk v Switzerland*[93] the same rule applied to surreptitiously obtained recordings by police. The court has also found that the collection and use of communications data, for example the maintenance of a register of the numbers called from a particular telephone or their disclosure to the police, for purposes other than the necessary provision of a telecommunications service, is a breach.[94]

The interception and opening of private mail was an interference with correspondence and also an interference with private life in *Hewitt and Harman v UK*.[95]

Article 8 has been raised in cases where personal information was obtained via samples taken under compulsion. In *X v Austria*[96] the court considered the taking of a blood test under compulsion in paternity proceedings and held that there was a breach but that it was justified. In *Peters v Netherlands*[97] it considered the compulsory random drug testing of prisoner's urine and held this was a breach but fell within Art.8(2).

Maintenance of records

2–31   It now appears that the court will treat the maintenance of any dossier or record on an individual by a public body as amounting to a prima facie interference with the Art.8 right, even if the record is not particularly sensitive. In *Amman v Switzerland*[98] both the interception of telephone calls and the maintenance of a record relating to the individual by an authority of the State amounted to an interference. A public body must therefore be able to justify the retention of any record under Art.8(2). It must be able to point to a specific legal basis empowering it to maintain the record, the record must be justified in one of the specified interests and it must be proportionate to the interest to be protected to retain the record. In *Chare v France*[99] a record was

---

[89] Application No. 6217/00 (2006) 43 E.H.R.R. SE5.
[90] See Ch.23, below for a detailed analysis of the law relating to the monitoring of electronic communications.
[91] (1998) E.H.R.L.R. 121.
[92] *ibid.*, n.19.
[93] (1988) 13 E.H.R.R. 242.
[94] *Malone v UK* (1985) 7 E.H.R.R. 14.
[95] (1992) 14 E.H.R.R. 657.
[96] *X v Austria* (1979) 18 D.R. 1549 (blood test pursuant to court order).
[97] 1994 77 A D.R. 75.
[98] February 16, 2000, ECtHR.
[99] (1991) 71 D.R. 141.

maintained of the fact that an individual had had psychiatric medical treatment. The individual wished to have the record expunged but the court held that the continued registration was justified. This approach to retention was confirmed in the United Kingdom by the House of Lords in the decision in *R. (on the application of Marper) v Chief Constable of South Yorkshire and Secretary of State for the Home Department.*[100] In that case the House held that mere retention of DNA samples did not constitute an interference, but even if that were not the case any interference would be justified under Art.8(2). In *Marper* the applicants had not been the subject of criminal proceedings. The case is being appealed to Strasbourg at the time of writing. In *Van der Velden v Netherlands*[101] the applicant was convicted of serious offences and his DNA taken and stored. He complained that the retention of the DNA was in breach of Art.8 as the DNA had had no part in his conviction. The Court held that while the view had previously been taken that the retention of fingerprints did not engage Art.8[102] given the use to which cellular material could be put in the future the retention did constitute an interference but was justified and proportionate. In *Leander v Sweden*[103] the court held that the maintenance of a dossier by the security service was a breach but the applicant was not entitled to access the information complained of. This illuminates another aspect of Art.8—the right to access personal information.

Access to information

2–32   In some limited cases the right to private life may entail the disclosure of information about an individual's past life by the state. In *Gaskin v United Kingdom*[104] the court held that the right to private life could require a public authority to open its files and provide information to an individual about his past, subject to having a method of making proper decisions to balance this right with the expectations of, and public interest in privacy, of others. This may also apply where the disclosure of information is necessary for an individual to protect his family as in *Guerra v Italy*[105] where the court held that the individual had the right to find out about an environmental hazard. The same approach was applied in *McGinley and Egan v UK*[106] where the court held that ex-servicemen were entitled to know of the levels of radioactivity to which they had been exposed. However there is no general right to access public information under Art.8.

Photography

2–33   A number of cases have concerned the use of cameras and the taking of photographs by public authorities, not all of them covert. In *Murray v UK* the police in Northern Ireland took photographs and fingerprints at the police station without consent in anti-terrorist operations. It was held to be a breach. In *Friel v Austria*[107] the

---

[100] [2004] 1 W.L.R. 2196.
[101] Application No. 29514/05.
[102] *Kinnuen v Finland* No. 24950/94, Commission Decision of May 15, 1996
[103] (1987) 9 E.H.R.R. 433.
[104] (1989) 12 E.H.R.R. 36.
[105] (1998) 26 E.H.R.R. 357.
[106] (1999) 27 E.H.R.R. 1.
[107] (1995) 21 E.H.R.R. 83.

applicant was photographed taking part in a demonstration. The court held that no breach of his right to private life was involved either in the taking of the photograph or its retention. However, in this case the individual was not identified by name with the photographic record and the photograph had been taken of a public activity in a public place. In later cases the Court has addressed the protection which should be afforded to private activity in a public space or a "semi private space" such as a restaurant and held that there is a zone of interaction with others which falls within the scope of private life, even where the action takes place in a private place. The question arose in *Von Hannover*[108] and in *Peck v United Kingdom*.[109] The *Von Hannover* case concerned Princess Caroline of Monaco, the eldest daughter of Prince Ranier of Monaco. Despite having no formal public role she has been of great interest to the tabloid press in a number of European countries. In 1993 and onward several German magazines and newspapers had published articles of her, without her consent, engaged in private activities with her family and friends, such as dining in restaurants, shopping, riding or playing tennis. She objected to the publications but the German courts refused to grant her relief because she was regarded as a figure of contemporary society, *Person der Zeitgeschichte*, in the relevant German provisions, and therefore her right to privacy was limited. She was entitled to privacy where her activities were in a "secluded place", that is somewhere clearly meant to be private, but not otherwise. She was partially successful in her appeal through the German courts and succeeded in restricting the publication of photographs of her children but not other photographs. She complained to the Court of Human Rights that the German law did not protect her Art.8 rights. The Court held that:

- Article 8 has horizontal effect therefore the State has positive obligations to protect the individual from other private parties;

- the protection of private life has to be balanced against the Art.10 right of freedom of expression;

- a fundamental distinction must be made between those matters capable of contributing to debate in a democratic society and those merely satisfying the curiosity of readers about individuals' private lives;

- the protection of private life extends beyond the family circle and applies to activities which are private and personal but which are conducted in public places;

- there is a particular interest in protecting private life to contend with the new technologies which make it possible to take surreptitious or long distance photographs and make them widely available.

The judgment in *Von Hannover* was referred to in the UK case of *Niema Ash v Loreena McKennit*.[110] In the case of *Peck* the Court had held that the dissemination of the photographs of Mr Peck taken in a public place breached his Art.8 rights.

---

[108] Application No. 59320/00 *Von Hannover v Germany* (2005) 40 E.H.R.R. 1.
[109] *Peck v United Kingdom* No. 44647/98 (2003) 36 E.H.R.R..
[110] See below for a discussion of UK cases.

Disclosure of information

2–34 The disclosure, as well as the collection and retention, of personal information has been raised before the court. In at least two cases applicants have complained about the disclosure of sensitive medical information about them. In *Z v Finland*[111] the fact that a woman was HIV positive was disclosed in court proceedings and her identity was also disclosed in the court judgment. It was held that the disclosure of the HIV information was necessary for the court case but was not required in the record of the judgment. In *TV v Finland*[112] the court held that the disclosure that a prisoner was HIV positive was necessary to protect prison staff.

In *MS v Sweden*[113] the disclosure of medical records to a Social Insurance Office for the purpose of compensation assessment was held to be a breach but was justified. It was proportionate as the recipients were only entitled to make a limited use of the data. In *Peck v United Kingdom*[114] a local authority which disclosed film of an individual who had been caught on CCTV carrying a knife (the individual had used it to try to commit suicide not to harm others) was held to be in breach of Art.8. The film was released as an example of the usefulness of CCTV, unfortunately the identifying details had not been properly disguised so the individual could be recognised. The Court accepted that the actions of the local authority were lawful and the disclosure of the film was in support of a legitimate purpose but held that the disclosure was disproportionate and hence a breach.

Sensitive data

2–35 There has also been confirmation from the court that the retention of personal data in the sensitive data categories requires particularly strong justification, as in *Lustig-Prean v UK*[115] where the information related to sexual life.

Relation with Directive 95/46

2–36 Not every aspect of the Directive has been reflected in the cases heard before the ECtHR but, as the analysis above shows, a number have. In particular the cases mirror the requirement to have grounds for processing any personal data and the transparency requirements of the Directive. The Court has referred to data protection guidance produced by the Council of Europe (the influence of which is discussed in Ch.3, below) in *Z v Finland* when considering a case on information about someone who was HIV positive.

ARTICLE 10

2–37 When considering the use and dissemination of information, Art.8 cannot be considered in isolation and account must be taken of the Art.10 right to freedom of expression. The balance between the two rights has featured in a number of the privacy cases heard by the UK courts since October 2000. One man's right to freedom of

---

[111] (1998) 25 E.H.R.R. 371.
[112] (1994) 776 A DR 140.
[113] (1997) 1 B.H.R.C. 248.
[114] Unreported, January 2003.
[115] (1999) 23 E.H.R.R. 548.

expression may have to give way to another's right to privacy, whether as protected by Art.8 or by the specific rights and protections offered by the DPA.

Article 10 provides:

"(1) Everyone has the right to freedom of expression. This right shall include freedom to hold opinions and to receive and impart information and ideas without interference by public authority and regardless of frontiers. This Art.shall not prevent States from requiring the licensing of broadcasting, television or cinema enterprises.

(2) The exercise of these freedoms, since it carries with it duties and responsibilities may be subject to such formalities, conditions, restrictions or penalties as are prescribed by law and are necessary in a democratic society, in the interests of national security, territorial integrity or public safety, for the prevention of disorder or crime, for the protection of health or morals, for the protection of the reputation or rights of others, for preventing the disclosure of information received in confidence, or for maintaining the authority and impartiality of the judiciary."

Like Art.8 this is a qualified right but the ECtHR seems to set a higher threshold to justify interference with Art.10 than with Art.8, at least in respect of political speech. In the United Kingdom the freedom of the press was already protected before October 2000. See the comments of Lord Denning in *Schering Chemicals Ltd v Falkman Ltd and Elstein* referred to in Ch.17, below.

Article 10 covers the right to hold opinions, to receive information and to pass it on. It does not give a right to obtain information that another party is not willing to disclose. Thus it cannot be used as the basis of a right to freedom of information.[116] The Court has expressly rejected such a development of the Convention rights to date. The UK courts have followed this line in recent cases.[117] The term "expression" extends to words, pictures or images to express an idea or convey information. All are protected. There is clearly an overlap with the respect for personal correspondence under Art.8 but the Court does not seem to have been asked to consider freedom of expression in relation to personal communication under Art.10; that has been dealt with under Art.8. The Court has considered freedom of expression in relation to political and journalistic materials, artistic expression and commercial communications. All are capable of protection.

Political and journalistic materials

2–38   The right to express political opinions will require a strong countervailing interest to displace it. To that extent it is the most strongly protected form of expression. Freedom of political speech is regarded by the Court as a core right in a democracy. In *Bowman v UK*[118] the Court held that the penalty enforcing the restriction on spending by candidates imposed by the Representation of the People Act 1983 was disproportionate to the legitimate aim pursued by the section. In *Handyside v UK*[119] the banning of a book of political thought was found to be a breach. The rights of

---

[116] *Leander v Sweden* (1987) 9 E.H.R.R. 433.
[117] *Howard and Wight Hogland v Secretary of State for Health* [2002] EWHC Admin 3996.
[118] (1998) 26 E.H.R.R. 1, 121; *Murray v UK* (1995) 19 E.H.R.R. 193.
[119] (1979–80) 1 E.H.R.R. 737.

the press and the right of journalists to report freely and comment freely are accorded a similar weight in *Jersild v Denmark*.[120] In several cases the Court has considered the balance between rights of privacy and freedom of expression. Where the publication of private information has merely been for the purposes of amusement and gossip the Court has held that the privacy right was not outweighted by the Art.10 rights, however where the publication of private information served a valid public interest debate the Court has found a breach of Art.10.[121] In *Mersey Care Health Trust v Ackroyd (No. 2)*[122] the UK Court of Appeal protected the source of information about medical records of Ian Brady under Art.10 even though the disclosure of those records had breached his privacy:

- Artistic works are protected by the Court but the right to express artistic impulses may be more easily outweighted by other interests, for example those connected with taste and decency (*Wingrove v UK*).[123]

- Commercial speech will also be protected. It follows that the Art.10 right applies to legal persons as well as to individuals. As might be expected, in the hierarchy of protection, the right to commercial freedom of speech is more easily displaced than the others (*Colman v UK*).[124]

The Court will not only protect freedom of expression from pre-publication restraint but will also have regard to the possible sanctions imposed post-publication. If those are disproportionate then there will be also be a breach. In *Tolstoy Miloslavsky v UK*[125] libel damages of £1.5 million were too high and interfered with freedom of speech.

The Court has looked at collateral issues such as the protection of sources for journalists. In *Goodwin v UK*[126] the Court considered the effect of the Contempt of Court Act 1981 s.10. This allows the UK courts to order journalists to hand over information about their sources if the disclosure is necessary to allow wrongdoing to be traced. In *Goodwin* it was held that the requirement to hand over information about a disloyal employee was not justified. However, s.10 was still valid.[127]

Freedom of expression

2–39 In addition to the *Campbell, Theakston* and *A v B* cases described below, the courts have heard a number of other cases in which Art.10 has been raised and in which the importance of the right, particularly where political speech is concerned, has been asserted. However, the cases have recognised that freedom of expression must give way to other rights, such as the right to life and security of the person, as well as to

---

[120] (1995) 19 E.H.R.R. 193.
[121] See *Von Hannover* and contrast *Plon (Societe) v France No.58148/00* (2006) 42 E.H.R.R. 36 in which the Court found that the restriction of the publication of a book about President Mitterand's health during his terms in offices was a breach of Art.10.
[122] Court of Appeal, February 2007.
[123] (1997) 24 E.H.R.R. 1.
[124] (1997) 18 E.H.R.R. 119.
[125] (1995) 20 E.H.R.R. 442.
[126] (1996) 22 E.H.R.R. 123.
[127] For comment on cases on Art.10 in the UK courts other than those which have dealt with personal privacy, see Ch.4, below on Freedom of Information.

accommodate privacy rights. In *Venables and Thompson v News Group Newspapers Ltd*[128] an injunction was granted against the whole world restraining the disclosure of any information that could lead to the identification of the murderers of Jamie Bulger after their release from prison. Dame Elizabeth Butler-Sloss held that the law of confidence could cover the information and the possibly fatal consequences for the individuals concerned, who had been the subject of death threats, outweighed the rights of freedom of expression of the press. The UK courts have also maintained the position taken in Strasbourg that the Art.does not give any right to access to information.[129] The general approach of the courts to freedom of speech is dealt with in Ch.17, below. There is also reference to the relation between Freedom of Information and Art.10 in Ch.4, below.

Procedure

2–40 The way the Convention was inserted into United Kingdom law did not give individuals a direct right to take action in the courts for a breach of their privacy under the HRA. The HRA created no equivalent to a statutory tort of infringement of privacy enforceable against the world at large. Consideration was given to the introduction of such a tort in the Law Commission Report in 1981 but the Government of the time rejected the proposal. So far the courts have rejected the creation of such a general cause of action. If an action of the State infringes the individual's right to private life the individual will have a cause of action against the arm of the State or a defence based on the same right if action is taken against him. But if the right to private life is infringed by a private party, such as a newspaper, the individual cannot bring an action based directly on Art.8. Litigants since October 2000 have dealt with this by bringing actions for breach of confidence and the courts have responded by gradually aligning breach of confidence with breach of Art.8. In the following section the development of this approach post October 2000 can be seen in the case law. In the last edition of this text we commented:

> "it cannot be certain that every breach of Art.8 will be treated as a breach of confidence and it may not always be easy to find a way of bringing an action to enforce the Art.8 right."

In the cases since then the Courts have shown that they will not let procedural difficulties stand in the way of valid claims and proved flexible in their ability to allow individuals to bring Art.8 claims.

The UK cases post-October 2000 are covered in some detail below. In considering the cases the courts have taken into account the development of the law of confidence, the effect of the Human Rights Act 1998 and, to a far lesser extent the impact of the Data Protection Act 1998. Regrettably there has been a tendency for the courts to regard Art.8 and Data Protection as coterminous and focus only on Art.8, even in cases where the Data Protection Act may have been able to contribute to a robust solution. Where the cases have involved the balance between freedom of expression the

---

[128] [2001] Fam. 430.
[129] *R. (Persey) v Secretary of State for the Environment, Food and Rural Affairs* [2002] EWHC 371; *R. (Howard) v Secretary of State for Health* [2002] EWHC 396.

courts have also had regard to the Press Complaints Code of Practice as required by s.12 of the HRA.

Human Rights Act 1998 s.12

2–41 This section applies if a court is considering whether to grant any relief which, if granted, might affect the Convention right to freedom of expression. In the bulk of cases concerned with freedom of expression and privacy the applicant will be seeking an order that material should not be published and accordingly s.12 will come into play.

The respondent must be given an opportunity to be present and to speak. The court is not to grant relief unless it is satisfied that the applicant has taken all practicable steps to notify the respondent or that there are compelling reasons why he should not be notified.

The court must not restrain publication before trial unless it "is satisfied that the applicant is likely to establish that publication should not be allowed". There has been considerable discussion as to the impact of this test and the burden it imposes.

In reaching its decision the court must have "particular regard" to the importance of the Convention right to freedom of expression and, where the proceedings relate to material which is journalistic, literary or artistic, the section specifies a number of matters which must be considered. It will be noted that the same terms for the special purposes are used as in the DPA. The terms are discussed in Ch.17, below. As in the DPA they are used without any further definition. The matters to be considered are:

- the extent to which the material is already or is about to become available to the public;
- the extent to which publication would be in the public interest; and
- "any relevant privacy code".

The codes are not specified by order as they are in the DPA but it would be reasonable to expect a court to look at the same codes.[130] In cases since October 2000 advocates have cited decisions of the Press Complaints Commission under the Press Complaints Commission Code of Practice.

Section 12 was inserted into the HRA at the pressing of the press lobby to bolster the right to freedom of expression in the face of the potential for the courts to create a right to privacy using Art.8. However, the courts have pointed out that, in considering the impact of the section, consideration of Art.10 must entail the reservations in Art.10(2) as well as the right itself and thus the need to weight competing rights and interests. Regarded in this way it has not proved a dampener on the development of the privacy right. On the contrary it has been used to justify consideration of Art.8 in cases between private persons.

---

[130] See Ch.17, below.

Press Complaints Commission Editors' Code of Practice and others

2–42   There are several self-regulatory codes in the media area of which the Press Complaints Commission ("PCC") Editors' Code is one. It covers accuracy; opportunity to reply; privacy; harassment; intrusion into grief or shock; children; children in sex cases; hospitals; reporting of crime; clandestine devices and subterfuge; victims of sexual assault; discrimination; financial journalism; confidential sources; witness payments in criminal trials; and payment to criminals.[131] Out of these several are related to privacy and data protection rights. Several provisions are subject to a public interest test. It applies to editorial content in newspapers and magazines. The Commission will consider complaints of breach of the code from members of the public, either individuals or organisations directly affected by the content complained of. It adjudicates on the complaint and may require a publication to carry a note of rectification or apology but has no power to order compensation. The PCC was established in 1991 following the concerns expressed by the Calcutt Committee. It has been amended several times since then.

The Code is admirably short. The section dealing with privacy reads:

> "i)   Everyone is entitled to respect for his or her private and family life, home health and correspondence including digital communications. Editors will be expected to justify intrusions into any individual's private life without consent.
>
> ii)   It is unacceptable to photograph individuals in a private place without their consent
>
> Note—Private places are public or private property where there is a reasonable expectation of privacy."

The areas which most intersect with the standards and requirements of data protection are:

- accuracy of information;

- a ban on unfair collection by the use of clandestine listening devices or intercepting private telephone calls;

- restrictions on the use of data in some of the sensitive categories—sex cases, particularly those involving children, and information gathered in hospitals.

It accepts that members may derogate from privacy standards and some of the other standards, where it is in the public interest to do so. Public interest is not exhaustively defined but "includes":

1. "i)   detecting or exposing crime or serious impropriety;
   ii)   protecting public health and safety;
   iii)   preventing the public being misled by some statement or action of an individual or organisation."

---

[131] As ratified by the PCC August 2006.

2. There is a public interest in freedom of expression itself.

3. Whenever the public interst is invoked the PCC will require editors to demonstrate fully how the public interest was served.

4. The PCC will consider the extent to which material is already in the public domain, or will become so.

5. In cases involving children under 16, editors must demonstrate an exceptional public intersest to override the normally paramount interest of the child.

The Code was considered relevant in the case brought by the model, Naomi Campbell, which is described later. Cases decided on the Code are published on the website of the PCC which also publishes Guidance Notes on issues including data protection.[132]

UK cases on private life post HRA

2–43 Since October 2000 the courts have been called on to consider the application of Art.8 in a wide range of cases from those concerned with flooding to any number of asylum and immigration cases. In this section a number of the most significant cases in which informational privacy has been considered by the courts since October 2000 are reviewed. In all cases the events giving rise to the case took place after October 2000. While the courts have been responsive to the changes bought about by the HRA they have not been prepared to change the law retrospectively. In *Home Office v Wainwright*[133] the Court of Appeal restated the position that there is no common law tort of invasion of privacy and the Human Rights Act could not change the law by retrospectively introducing a right of privacy at common law. In that case the events complained of had occurred in 1997. The claimants had visited prison and had been searched for drugs. One claimant brought an action for breach of privacy. The Court of Appeal rejected the claim on appeal but commented that the position would have been different had the searching occurred after October 2000 as Art.8 would have impacted on their judgment.

Many of the most celebrated cases on personal information since October 2000 have been between media organisations and individuals, and have concerned the publication of private material, but not all.

2–44 In *Brian Robertson v Wakefield District Council and the Secretary of State for the Home Department*[134] the High Court was asked to consider whether the sale of names and addresses from the electoral roll breaches s.11 of the DPA, Art.8 and Art.3 of Protocol 1 in the HRA. It is dealt with in this chapter as it involves the Convention rights, rather than Ch.3.

In order to vote in the United Kingdom citizens must be registered on the electoral roll. Registration forms are sent out annually. It is an offence to fail to return the form duly completed. Electoral Registration Officers (EROs) had an obligation to sell copies of the electoral register to any person who wished to purchase a copy, subject to the ERO having sufficient copies available for sale.[135]

---

[132] *http://www.pcc.org.uk.*
[133] [2002] 3 W.L.R. 405, CA.
[134] [2001] EWCA Civ 2081.
[135] CO/284/2001.

Copies of the electoral register are sold to many organisations as the basis of various commercial products. The commercial products include the sale of data for direct marketing. Mr Robertson objected to the sale of the electoral register, for which he had been forced to provide his name and address for electoral purposes, for uses which might include the sending of unsolicited mail.

The unrestricted sale of the electoral registers and their commercial use, especially for marketing, had been a point of public concern for some time. In 1999, the *Final Report of the Working Party on Electoral Procedures* had dealt with the sale of the registers and noted that the supply of the electoral registers for commercial use had been a source of complaint.

2–45 After the HRA came into force in October 2000, Mr Robertson objected to the sale of his name on the electoral roll. The ERO refused to omit his name from the roll, on the basis that the ERO had a statutory obligation to sell the register imposed by the Regulations. Mr Robertson took an action for judicial review of the ERO's decision.

The claimant relied on three grounds:

 a) that there was a breach of his Art.8 right by the sale of his name and address, by the ERO;

 b) that, as the ERO knew that the register was purchased for commercial purposes which included direct marketing, the ERO was processing his personal data for the purposes of direct marketing, and therefore had an obligation under s.11 of the DPA to stop processing for that purpose on service of a notice by claimant; and

 c) that the sale breached his right to free elections under Art.3 of the First Protocol to the Convention as it imposed an unjustifiable restriction by making his right to vote conditional upon the use of his name by commercial organisations.

The Secretary of State for the Home Department, at that time responsible for the Regulations, was joined as a defendant and had the conduct of the case; the ERO taking no further part in the action.

After the proceedings had started the governing law changed. The Representation of the People Act 2000 replaced the 1983 Act. It contained new regulation-making powers which provided for the making of regulations which would enable voters to chose to have their names and address omitted from the copies of the register provided for sale. Although the power to make such regulations was included in the primary legislation, the regulations[136] did not include an "opt-out" provision. They continued to impose an obligation on the ERO to supply a copy or copies of the register to any person on payment of a fee. The primary legislation did not mandate the inclusion of the requirement to sell the registers in the Regulations.

The claimant succeeded in his claim on all grounds. The judge found breaches of Art.8 and Protocol 1 by the sale of the registers without a right of objection to sale for

---

[136] Representation of the People Regulations 1986, made under s.53 of and Sch.2 to the Representation of the People Act 1983.

commercial purposes. The judge interpreted s.11 of the DPA so as to accord with his view of the impact of Art.14 of the Directive. He held that the EROs did "process the personal data on the register for the purposes of direct marketing" when they sold them to commercial organisations knowing that the data would be likely to be put to such a use and were therefore obliged to respond to objections to the use for marketing. He went on to find that the EROs had not been complying with the DPA because they had failed to take account of objections raised with them over subsequent uses for direct marketing. He considered the requirement under the Directive. Article 14(b) provides for the Member State to grant the data subject the right "to object . . . to the processing of personal data relating to him which the controller anticipates being processed for the purposes of direct marketing". This is implemented in the United Kingdom by s.11 which provides individuals with the right to: "require the data controller at the end of such a period as is reasonable in the circumstances to cease, or not to begin, processing for the purposes of direct marketing personal data in respect of which he is the data subject".

2–46　It was argued that the ERO did not process the personal data for the purposes of marketing and that the mere fact that the ERO knew that others intended to do so after they purchased the data did not amount to processing for the purpose. The judge considered that he was under an obligation to interpret the Act so as to conform to the Directive as far as possible citing *Litster v Forth Dry Dock Co Ltd*.[137] This could be done by taking a wide construction:

> "I therefore find that EROs inevitably anticipate that the personal data will be processed by commercial concerns for the purposes of direct marketing."

The judge also found in favour of the claimant on Art.3 of Protocol 1. This is expressed in general terms as:

> "[States] undertake to hold free elections at reasonable intervals by secret ballot, under conditions which will ensure the free expression of the opinion of the people in the choice of the legislature."

The judge held that the act of making the right to vote conditional upon the provision of the information to commercial organisations, with no right to object, was an unjustified and disproportionate restriction on the right to vote.

In relation to the Art.8 claim he found that the Article was engaged in the matter despite the limited and harmless nature of the information.[138] It consisted of name and address only. Although in the judgment he posited the possibility that a list of the names and addresses of those known to be in a specific group might involve information which merits protection, a proposition with which few would disagree, on the facts of the case the relevant information did not fall into such a category. It consisted of name and address on the public register and involved no further information. Name and address alone do not appear to have been considered confidential in any ECHR or UK cases to date. In a decision on Art.8 of the HRA made earlier in 2001, the High

---

[137] The Representation of the People (England and Wales) Regulations 2001.
[138] [1990] 1 A.C. 546.

Court had declined to protect the address of Heather Mills, then the girlfriend of Paul McCartney, as private or confidential despite the fact that the publication of her address exposed her to detrimental press attention and potential risk simply because of her celebrity status; neither consequences likely to inconvenience Mr Robertson. In the decision of the Data Protection Tribunal in the case brought, in 1998, by the Data Protection Registrar over the use of name and address of customers of British Gas Trading Limited, the Tribunal made clear that it did not regard customer name and address, without more, as being confidential. Nevertheless, the judge decided that the dissemination of name and address from the electoral register could be protected by Art.8. Thus the judgment offers significantly more extensive protection to non-sensitive data than has ever been afforded by the UK courts or the Court at Strasbourg under Art.8. In none of the cases before the ECtHR have name and address alone been protected. The judge was aware that he was affording a higher level of protection than had been afforded to such information before:

> ". . . I am being invited to go further than the courts have gone before by holding that the sale of the register engages article 8. . ."

He nevertheless went on to find that the Article was engaged.

Having held that the right was engaged by the sale of name and address from the register the judge considered whether it was justified under Art.8(2) and if so whether the restriction was proportionate. In considering Art.8(2) he decided that there was a legitimate interest in the commercial uses of the register but that the failure to provide an opt-out was disproportionate.

In *R. v Law Society Ex p. Barry Francis Pamplin* (2001) the High Court held that employment, which is part of a lawyer's public life, would not be protected by Art.8 to the degree that an individual's private, that is family or home, life would be.

Cases on policing and security

2–47   In *R. (on the application of S) v Chief Constable of South Yorkshire and the Secretary of State for the Home Department* and *R. (on the application of Mr Marper) v Chief Constable of Yorkshire and the Secretary of State for the Home Department*[139] the House of Lords was divided on whether the retention of fingerprints, samples, photographs and DNA profiles obtained in connection with the investigation of an offence, from a person who was never convicted, engaged Art.8 but held that if it was such an interference it was "very modest indeed" and was a justifiable and proportionate breach.

The applicants argued that a provision in the Criminal Justice and Police Act 2001 which permits the retention of fingerprints and DNA samples, even if the person from whom the samples were taken is found not guilty of any offence or is never charged, was incompatible with the Convention. Alternatively they complained that the Chief Constable had acted unlawfully by adopting a general policy of retention, subject only to exceptions where specific grounds could be made out. The DPA does not appear to have been mentioned in this case.

---

[139] [2004] UKHL 39.

The legislative background is complex but in summary the rules used to be that such materials had to be destroyed if taken from individuals who were subsequently cleared of any offence. There had been cases where such material had not been destroyed. The police had tried and failed to introduce it into evidence, so the provision had amended the rules and allowed the retention of samples which should have been destroyed.

The section provides that where fingerprints or other samples are taken in the course of an investigation into a crime they may be retained but may only be used in the future for purposes related to the prevention or detection of crime, investigation of an offence or the conduct of a prosecution. The only cases in which the fingerprints or samples must be destroyed are if fingerprints or samples are taken from a person who is not suspected of an offence, in the course of an investigation of an offence, and there is no conviction following that investigation (see s.64 of the Police and Criminal Evidence Act 1984 as amended by s.82 of the Criminal Justice and Police Act 2001). Otherwise it is up to the Chief Constable to decide whether to retain the materials. The two claimants, S and M, were both of previous good character and were arrested for unconnected offences. Neither was charged and both subsequently requested the destruction of the fingerprints and other materials relating to them. The Chief Constable refused to destroy the material. It was also argued by the appellants that the Chief Constable should consider each case on its merits and the policy of retaining all materials was flawed. The House of Lords did not accept this and upheld the policy as lawful.

Passenger Name Records (PNR)

2–48   In the PNR cases before the European Court[140] the Advocate General's Opinion covered the question of whether the Agreement with the US Government for the transfer of PNR to the US Bureau of Customs and Border Protection (part of the Department of Homeland Security) was in breach of Art.8 on the basis that it was neither accessible nor foreseeable nor was it proportionate to the objective pursued in view of the significant number of data elements transferred on every passenger and the length of time for which the data were retained. The Advocate took the view that the entire Agreement and linked provisions should be examined together. While he agreed that there was an interference with private life by reason of the transfer he considered that the legal basis was made out and was sufficiently accessible to those affected. He was clear that the transfer pursued a legitimate aim and went on to deal with the question of the margin of appreciation "the scope of which will depend not only on the nature of the legitimate aim pursued but also on the particular nature of the interference involved"[141]:

> "The review of proportionality by the European Court of Human Rights varies according to parameters such as the nature of the right and activities at issue, the aim of the interference and the possible presence of a common denominator in the States' legal systems.
>
> As regards the nature and activities of the rights at issue, where the right is one which intimately affects the individual's private sphere, such as the right to

---

[140] Cases C-317/04 and C-318/04 [2007] All E.R. (EC) 278 of the European Court of Justice.
[141] *Ibid.*, para.26 citing *Leander v Sweden* ECt HR.

confidentiality of health-related personal data the European Court of Human Rights seems to take the view that the State's margin of appreciation is more limited and its own judicial review must be stricter.

However where the aim of the interference is to maintain national security or to combat terrorism the European Court of Human Rights tends to allow States a wider margin of appreciation."[142]

He went on to suggest that the margin of appreciation should be limited to determining whether there was any manifest error of assessment in making the decision. On the facts of the case he did not regard the number of data items required or the retention time as manifestly unreasonable.

2–49 In *R. (on the application of Morgan Grenfell & Co Ltd) v Special Commissioner of Income Tax*[143] the House of Lords considered the relation between legal professional privilege and Art.8. The House held that the privilege is an important component of the Art.8 right. The bulk of the cases which have been brought on privacy and intrusion have inevitably arisen as a result of celebrities seeking to restrain the activities of the press and it those cases that are examined in the next section.

Cases dealing with privacy and the press

Michael Douglas, Catherine Zeta-Jones, Northern & Shell Plc v Hello! Ltd

2–50 The first two claimants are a celebrity couple and the third are the owners of *OK!* Magazine. The first two claimants had agreed an exclusive licence to *OK!* for a nine-month period to publish authorised photographs of their wedding in New York. The wedding was a splendid affair with many guests but throughout the couple had made every effort to preserve the exclusivity of the pictures, banning cameras and requiring guests to sign an agreement that they would not take photographs. Nevertheless, the rival magazine *Hello!* managed to obtain pictures of the event from a paparrazi photographer who had infiltrated the event and took steps to publish them as a "spoiler", that is before *OK!* published the official photographs. Action was taken by *OK!* to stop *Hello!* selling the issue with the photographs. *OK!* were intially successful in obtaining a injunction but on appeal to the Court of Appeal *Hello!* were successful in overturning the injunction. The judges agreed that the remedy, if remedy there was to be, would issue in damages. In the High Court a total of £14,600 damages were awarded to the first two claimants, being £7,000 for the inconvenience they incurred in having to expedite the choice of official photographs and £3,750 each for breach of their privacy. *OK!* were awarded £1,033,156 for interference with their contractual rights. The decision was appealed and cross appealed to the Court of Appeal which held that there had been a breach of the Douglases' right to privacy and the award to them should stand but overturned the judgment in favour of *OK!*.[144] On the further appeal to the House of Lords by *OK!*, in which the Douglases' took no part, the Lords reinstated the award to *OK!*, holding that there was no reason they should not benefit from the rights of confidentiality in the event.

---

[142] *ibid.* paras 228–230 citing cases *Z v Finland, Leander* and *Murray v UK.*
[143] [2001] UKHL 21.
[144] [2005] EWCA Civ 595.

2–51 The judgments from the interlocutory judgment of the Court of Appeal through to the Court of Appeal hearing on liability and quantum almost chart the development of the law in this area.

At the first Court of Appeal hearing Brooke L.J. took the view that the Court had to weight the competing elements of freedom of expression on the one hand and privacy on the other, and, as far as privacy was concerned the claimants' case was not a particularly strong one. If they had an action it was in confidence. In any event this was essentially a commercial dispute between two magazines and there should be no injunctive relief to restrain publication. If there was to be a remedy for the claimants it would be sufficient to leave it to damages for the loss of profit on the exclusive photographs.

Sedley L.J. took a bolder line, saying:

". . . we have reached a point at which it can be said with confidence that the law recognises and will appropriately protect a right of personal privacy."

He took the view that if the photographer was an intruder with whom no relationship of trust had been established then there could be no action in confidence. However, the law should now move beyond the concept of confidence:

"the law no longer needs to construct an artificial relationship of confidentiality between intruder and victim; it can recognise privacy itself as a legal principle drawn from the fundamental value of personal autonomy."

In common with Brooke L.J. he cited s.12 of the HRA as requiring the court to consider the Convention right to freedom of expression in all cases, not merely where one party to the litigation is a public authority. The section requires the court to have regard to Art.10, including the qualifications. The court must therefore carry out a balancing test taking account of all the relevant aspects.

In relation to the appropriate remedy in the case it was his view that the claimants had sold their privacy and concurred with the others in the view that they would only be entitled to a remedy in damages.

Keene L.J. agreed with his fellows that the law of confidence was nearly developed enough to cover the case even if the unauthorised photographs had been taken by someone without a pre-existing relationship who could be regarded as bound by an obligation. However, while he agreed that the courts were bound to have regard to the Convention when interpreting the common law and equity, he was less persuaded that the wedding was a private occasion or that confidentiality could attach to photographs or other records of it. In any event he agreed that if there was to be a remedy the claimants could be compensated in damages.

2–52 By the date of the full hearing in the High Court in February 2003 the particulars of claim had been re-amended several times to include claims for conspiracy by various parties with the intent of injuring the claimants, breach of the Data Protection Act 1998, breach of confidence, breach of privacy, breach of commercial confidence, infringement of rights under Spanish law (*Hello!* being in Spanish ownership and the decisions as to publication of material made in that jurisdiction), unlawful interference with the business or rights of the claimants and claims for aggravated and exemplary damages. Judgment was delivered in April.[145] The judge dismissed the conspiracy claims after extensive consideration of the available evidence as to how the photographs had come into the possession of *Hello!* magazine. He held that the Douglases succeeded in their confidentiality claim on the basis that the wedding reception was a private event and *OK!* also succeeded in their claim for a form of commercial confidentiality as being a:

> "case . . . of either commercial confidence or of a hybrid kind in which, by reason of it having become a commodity, elements that would otherwise have been merely private become confidential."

The arrangements for the security at the wedding were such that all those attending would know that they were intended to be confidential in nature. The proprietor and others at *Hello!* knew of the confidentiality of the event and were thus (applying the dicta in *A v B*, see later) bound by an obligation of confidence in respect of the material. The publication of the pictures as a "spoiler" was to the detriment of both the celebrity couple and *OK!* magazine. He held that the Data Protection Act applied and that all three defendants were data controllers. He followed the *Campbell* decision in holding that the publication of the material in the UK amounted to processing and therefore fell under the Act. The transitional exemptions did not apply to the relevant processing and there had been breaches of the Act in that the processing was both unfair and unlawful as being without justification under Sch.2. However he only awarded nominal damages under that head on the ground that the damage and distress to the Douglases was not caused by the breach of the Act. The reasoning behind this last part of the decision (para.239) is not easy to follow. *OK!* had also claimed against *Hello!* on the basis of economic torts but these claims were dismissed.

2–53   In the Court of Appeal hearing in 2005 the Court was able to take account of the development of the Strasbourg case law in *Von Hannover* and *Peck*[146] as well as the more recent United Kingdom cases. The lengthy judgment covers both the claims in privacy and those related to the torts of economic loss but in this commentary we only describe the privacy issues. For the most part the judgment reflects the growing consensus of the case law in this area but it includes two element which are particularly interesting; one deals with the commercial interest of the Douglases in their private information and the other the actions which should have been taken at the early stage of the case.

The Court accepted that Art.8 has a horizontal effect and in cases such as these must be applied so as to protect one person's right of privacy from the intrusion of another private party. The Court also confirmed that information does not have to be "confided" for the obligation to apply and will be eligible for protection where information which is obviously private comes into the possession of a third party. One of the points raised by *Hello!* was that any intrusion took place in New York and if the photographs could be lawfully published there the law in the UK should not penalise publication

---

[145] *Douglas v Hello! (No. 6)* [2003] EWHC 786 (Ch).
[146] *Von Hannover v Germany* Application (No. 59320/00) [2004] E.M.L.R. 21; and *Peck v UK* (Application No. 44647/98) [2003] E.M.L.R. 15 and see para.2–33, above.

here. The Court did not accept that. It ruled that as long as the Douglases were entitled to hold their wedding in private in New York, which they were, then the publication of unauthorised photographs of that wedding in the UK would be considered under UK law.

2–54 *Hello!* further argued that once the Douglases had agreed with *OK!* to publish some photographs of the wedding they could not claim that other photographs were private or confidential. The Court accepted that once information is in the public domain it can no longer be regarded as confidential but pointed out that care must be taken in determining whether this is the case, for example the re-publication of a private photograph will be a fresh intrusion and it will be no defence to a re-publication which breaches privacy to say that the photograph has been published before. This was another "important distinction between the law relating to private information and that relating ot other types of confidential information".[147] Moreover the photographs were not all of the same nature. In this case the Douglases had chosen those official pictures which they wished to disclose and thereby kept the remainder of the wedding as a private affair out of the public gaze. It followed that this argument was not accepted.

On the question of the extent of the commercial interest that the Douglases were exercising in the exploitation of the private occasion Lord Phillips answered the question posed *Did the law of confidence protect the Douglases commercial interest in information about their wedding?* with a positive but restrictive response. The question raised the possibility of a right in image or personality which is not recognised in UK law, however there are cases in the UK which have protected secrets in not dissimilar circumstances; *Creation Records v News Group Newspapers Co Ltd* and *Gilbert v Star* were cited. The Court dealt with the position thus:

> "Where an individual ('the owner') has at his disposal information which he has created or which is personal or private and to which he can properly deny access to third parties, and he reasonably intends to profit commercially by using or publishing that information, then a third party who is, or ought to be, aware of these matters and who has knowingly obtained the information without authority, will be in breach of duty if he uses or publishes the information to the detriment of the owner. We have used the term 'the owner' loosely.
>
> We have concluded that confidential or private information which is capable of commercial exploitation but which is only protected by the law of confidence, does not fall to be treated as property that can be owned and transferred."

With the last part of the decisions the Court put paid to the claims of *OK!* for damages for the loss to them. They took the view that while the Douglases could have a commercial interest in the privacy of their wedding they could not transfer that to a third party. It followed that *OK!* had no legal interest which was breached by the taking of the paparazzi pictures or their publication.

The other noteworthy point was the clear message that the Douglases should have succeeded in obtaining their injunction against publication with the clear message that similar claimants should receive such relief in the future.

---

[147] para.105, Lord Phillips.
[148] [2007] UKHL 21.

2–55   The House of Lords judgment delivered in April 2007[148] did not disturb the findings in relation to the Douglases, who had taken no part in the appeal, but reinstated the judgment in favour of *OK!*. By a margin of 3 to 2 the House held that *OK!* could benefit from the confidentiality which had been created in the occasion and there was no reason that exclusive coverage of a "spectacle", as the happy event was described in one judgment, could not benefit from the protection of the law of confidence where the parties had deliberately created that in order to protect its commercial value.

Theakston v MGN Ltd[149]

2–56   This case was considered by the High Court before the Court of Appeal had issued its guidance in *A v B*. The claimant was a television personality who had visited a brothel after a night out drinking. The prostitutes involved wanted to sell the story and photographs which had been taken without the claimant's knowledge to the newsaper. The judge held that the fact that the claimant had visited prostitutes for sexual activity could not be regarded as intrinsically confidential, particularly as one of the prostitutes was eager to tell the tale to the newspapers and therefore her right to freedom of expression was engaged. However he ruled that photographs taken in the brothel could not be published as they were taken without his consent and photographs were particularly intrusive. The judge held that not every sexual relation should be regarded as confidential; confidentiality would depend on the circumstances of the case.

A v B[150]

2–57   There were two aspects to this appeal from the High Court: a procedural one and a substantive one. The procedural aspects are not dealt with here. The facts were: A was a footballer with a club in the premier division football league. He was a married man with children. He had affairs with two women, refered to as C and D. C had wished to sell her story of the affairs to a newspaper, B. D took no part in the proceedings.

In September 2001, the judge in the High Court confirmed an interim injunction restraining publication of the "kiss and tell" story. The order restrained the newspaper from publishing anything about the sexual relationships and restrained C from making any disclosure to the media, although she was free to tell others, for example A's wife, should she so chose. The newspaper and C appealed to the Court of Appeal. Before dealing with the facts of the presenting case Lord Woolf set out a set of Guidelines for dealing with actions in which injunctions are sought to protect claimants from the publication of material on the grounds that the publication of confidential material would infringe their privacy.

His starting point was to accept that the court, as a public authority, has an obligation not to act "in a way which is incompatible with a Convention right". When deciding any case, irrespective of whether the parties are public or private bodies, the court must take account of the Convention rights. Thus the court can deal with a claim that privacy has been infringed by "absorbing the rights which Arts 8 and 10 protect into the

---

[149] [2002] EWHC 137, QB.
[150] [2002] EWCA Civ 337.

long-established action for breach of confidence". The HRA does not give a basis for introducing new torts but, in any event, in the case of privacy protection, there is no need to do so as confidentiality can be, (and was), grown to fit the case. There is no need to cite massive amounts of previous authority and cases on confidence pre-October 2000 are largely of historic interest only. He reviewed the equitable (and elastic) history of the law of confidence to reinforce this position and then set out a series of Guidelines for dealing with such cases in the future. The Guidelines strike a blow against the development of a rule-bound and legalistic approach to privacy. It brings the action back to the equitable roots of action for breach of confidence. This marries well with the purposive and contemporary approach to the interpretation of the Convention rights.

The Guidelines

2–58 • An interim injunction is a discretionary remedy and the judge must exercise his discretion properly, only granting it if it is likely that one would be granted after a substantive hearing.

• The judge must recognise that the interests to be weighted are both significant ones: if the claimant does not obtain his injunction he may be deprived of the only remedy which is of value to him; but granting an injunction will interfere with the defendant's right to freedom of expression whose importance has been enhanced by the effect of s.12 of the HRA.

• "Likely" means little more than that there should be a real prospect of success and the *American Cyanamid*[150a] test remains the relevant test in deciding whether to grant an injunction, although likelihood is a shade stronger and the possibility of borderline cases was preserved. Section 12(3) of the HRA and the Convention are compatible.

• If the grant of an injunction will interfere with press freedom that is a matter of particular importance. The existence of the freedom of the press in itself is desirable and any interference with it has to be justified.

• The burden is not on the press to show that the publication of the material is in the public interest. There is an interest in press freedom itself beyond the material published in the specific case.

• Where privacy merits protection an action for breach of confidence should be capable of providing that protection so there is no need to tackle the question of whether a new tort should be developed.

• In cases where privacy is being weighted against freedom of expression there will not usually be much scope for detailed arguments about whether the subject-matter is private and worthy of protection. Whether there is a breach of privacy will be a matter of common sense, not fine analysis of previous cases.

• Where there is a public interest in the publication of material it strengthens the case against granting an injunction. Whether there is a public interest will also

---

[150a] *American Cyanamid v Ethicon Ltd* (1975) 2 W.L.R. 316.

usually be a matter of common sense and the citation of authority is not likely to be helpful.

- The legal basis of an obligation of confidence is elastic enough to offer privacy protection, if such protection is merited on the facts. An obligation can be implied/applied wherever the subject can reasonably expect his privacy to be protected.

- The factual basis is simple. "If there is an intrusion in a situation where a person can reasonably expect his privacy to be respected then that intrusion will be capable of giving rise to liability in an action for breach of confidence unless the intrusion can be justified". However, it should not be taken for granted that obtaining information by unlawful means give an automatic right to an injunction, although obviously the other party will then not be coming with clean hands and it will weight heavily.

- Where there is no intrusion (and presumably no contract to maintain confidence) but one party to a relationship wants to talk about the other, the Art.10 rights of that party have to be taken into account. Where the parties are or have been married one can restrain the other from disclosing private material but other relations, including sexual ones, have different degrees of privacy. These have to be considered on their facts but there is no assumption that one party to any kind of relationship can gag the other about it.

- People who are public figures have to be realistic in their expectations as to how far their privacy can and will be protected by the courts. They do have a right to privacy but in a society with a free press they will be the subject of legitimate interest and reporting. The higher the profile the more they are likely to be interesting to the press. If someone has courted publicity then they will have less ground to object to intrusion which may follow. It should be noted that this has been much doubted in subsequent cases and probably does not represent the current consensus.

- In balancing the competing interests the courts should stick strictly to the core question of whether publication should be restrained. They should not be influenced by disapproval of possibly lurid presentations by the press.

- Section 12(4) requires the court deciding a case to consider any "relevant privacy code" and the Press Complaints Commission Code of Practice has helpful material on privacy and harassment to which attention is drawn. Such material has to be considered in full and a court can also take into account that there has been a breach of the Code.

- Although the Code is relevant individual decisions of the Press Commission are not and should not be cited.

2–59 On the specific case the court ruled that A did not have any special rights to confidentiality in his relations with C and D. The mere fact of a sexual relation did not, outside marriage, make the relation a confidential one. Regard had to be had to the nature of the engagement. The judge quoted the dicta of the court in *Theakston v*

MGM Limited with approval on this point (see above). Further the fact that C and D did not regard the relationship as confidential and were happy to talk about it was relevant. The rights of C and D to freedom of expression came into play. The judge at the High Court had assumed that the ban was to the benefit of A's wife despite the fact that she was not a party to the proceedings and had not had a say. The court said that it was not for the court to decide what was or was not to her benefit. The question of a public interest in the publication was a difficult issue for the court to come to a view on and the possibility of there being a public interest should not have been rejected. It was possible that there was some aspect of it. Overall therefore the court would not approve the injunction.

Campbell v Mirror Group Newspapers

2–60   The next case gained popular coverage, Naomi Campbell is a well-known fashion model who has, in the past, denied taking drugs. At the beginning of 2001 she was surreptitiously photographed leaving a London clinic where she had been having treatment for addiction. The *Mirror* published the picture and information about her therapy. After she complained about the disclosures the *Mirror* published criticisms of her complaint and claim for breach of privacy. She took action against them claiming damages for breach of confidentiality and compensation under s.13 of the DPA. When the case was heard in the High Court[151] Ms Campbell was successful in her claim for breach of confidence and breach of the Data Protection Act, and was awarded damages amounting to £3,500 for distress and hurt feelings. The *Mirror* then appealed to the Court of Appeal and was successful in overturning the award. Miss Campbell in turn went to the House of Lords and emerged the victor in the end.

High Court judgment

2–61   Ms Campbell had accepted that the paper was entitled to publish the basic fact that she was addicted to drugs and was having therapy, but claimed that it was not entitled to use photographs of her or give detail of the therapy or from whom she was receiving it. The judge ruled that the details of her attendance at Narcotics Anonymous had the necessary quality of confidence to attract protection and the information giving details of her attendance must have been imparted in circumstances importing an obligation of confidence, even though it was never shown who had provided them. He held that the publication of the details was detrimental to her and applied the Guidelines set out by Lord Woolf in *A v B*. He held that as Ms Campbell was a role model and had made public statements that she was not addicted, the *Mirror* was entitled to disclose that she had lied and did have drug addiction problems. There was a public interest in revealing that she had lied. However, the newspaper was not entitled to go beyond that into material which she had not put into the public domain. The details which were revealed about her treatment amounted to an invasion of her privacy which was not justified by any public interest.

In relation to the Data Protection Act the *Mirror* had argued that the exemption in s.32 of the DPA. applied to the publication and moreover that they not only had the

---

[151] [2002] EWCA Civ 1373.

benefit of the substantive exemption once the material complained of had been published but the procedural exemption in s.32(4) continued to apply after publication. Thus the court was precluded from hearing the case until the Commissioner had made a determination under s.45.[152] The court rejected the contention that the procedural provision applied post-publication and went on to consider the application of the substantive exemption. The judge's ruling on the substantive exemption is not wholly clear. He held that the *Mirror* had not complied with the requirements of the Data Protection Act 1998. It had not obtained the photographs fairly and had no grounds on which to justify the holding of the sensitive data. He then considered whether the *Mirror* could claim the benefit of the substantive exemption in s.32. Unfortunately the judgment appeared to suggest that the substantive exemption itself ceased to apply after publication of the material.[153] Nevertheless, he went on to consider the terms of the exemption and decided that as the *Mirror* could not claim that the publication of the photographs and other detailed material was justified in the public interest they did not fall within the exemption. He considered the effect of s.13 and agreed that where the special purposes were concerned the applicant did not have to show actual damage. He awarded damages of £3,000 for distress plus a further £1,000 for aggravated damages arising from the response of the *Mirror* after Ms Campbell's initial complaint.

Court of Appeal[154]

2–62   It was accepted by Ms Campbell that the publication of the fact that she had a drug problem and was receiving treatment for addiction was justified.

The *Mirror* accepted that the material published on the whole disclosed confidential information but argued that public interest justified the publication of all the material.

Lord Phillips M.R. held that the fact that Ms Campbell was receiving treatment from Narcotics Anonymous (NA) could not be equated with disclosure of clinical details of medical treatment and, given that it was legitimate for the *Mirror* to publish the fact that she was receiving treatment it did not seem significant that the treatment consisted of attending meetings of NA. The publication of the additional details was not sufficient to amount to a breach of an obligation of confidence.

The court considered that the detail that was provided in the story and the photographs were a legitimate, if not essential, part of the journalistic package putting out the story:

> "Provided that the publication of particular confidential information is justifiable in the public interest, the journalist must be given reasonable latitude as to the manner in which that information is conveyed to the public or his Article 10 right to freedom of expression will be unnecessarily inhibited."

---

[152] See Ch.17, below for a full description of the exemption for the special purposes.

[153] On this point, the judge referred, among other material, to the relevant chapter in the first edition of this textbook. It was never intended to suggest in that chapter that the substantive exemption ceases to apply after publication, and I did not think I had done so. (It's a bit discouraging to a text book writer to be cited in a judgment in support of something they did not intend to say.)

[154] [2002] EWCA Civ 1373.

The court dismissed an argument that a publisher of information had to act dishonestly before he could be liable for breach of confidence in the case of personal privacy.

In relation to the Data Protection Act, the arguments took on the labyrinthine nature that seems to afflict nearly all judgments on the DPA. In considering the Act they held that MGM was the data controller and had acted through Mr Morgan the editor who had taken the decisions in respect of the publication. It was common ground that, unless the actions of the *Mirror* fell within the s.32 exemption, they would be in breach of the DPA.

2–63   The court held that there were three questions for decision:

1. Does the DPA apply to publication of newspapers and other hard copies containing information that has been subjected to data processing?

2. Does the s.32 (substantive) exemption only apply up to the moment of publication?

3. Does the s.32 (substantive) exemption apply to publication, insofar as this falls within the scope of the Act?

On question 1 they held that the definition of "processing" covers publication:

"Accordingly we conclude that, where the data controller is responsible for the publication of hard copies that reproduce data that has previously been processed by means of equipment operating automatically, the publication forms part of the processing and falls within the scope of the Act."

On question 2 they agreed that the subss.(4) and (5) are purely procedural and are exhausted on publication. They then considered subss.(1) to (3) and took the view that they apply both after and before publication.

On question 3 they held that as the processing of the data fell within the Act the exemption would also apply to it and therefore the *Mirror* was entitled to invoke the protection of the substantive s.32 exemption in answer to Ms Campbell's claim.

They went on to consider how the s.32 exemption applied to the facts of the case. It was accepted by all parties that the publication was for the purpose of journalism. The court held that the data controller did reasonably believe that the publication was in the public interest and would not have been able to publish had they sought to comply with the DPA. Accordingly the exemption was made out. Ms Campbell lost the appeal. The judgment on the DPA suggests that the Court thought that the exemption from s.32 would be of wide application to the press and other daily media, saying:

". . . the definition of processing is so wide that it embraces the relatively ephemeral operations that will normally be carried out by way of the day-to-day tasks, involving the use of electronic equipment such as the lap-top and the modern printing press, in translating information into the printed newspaper. The speed with which these operations have to be carried out if a newspaper is to publish news renders it impracticable to comply with many of the data processing principles and the conditions in Schedules 2 and 3, including the requirement that the data subject give his consent to the processing.

Furthermore the requirements of the Act, in the absence of section 32, would impose restrictions on the media which would radically restrict the freedom of the press." (paras 123 and 124)

House of Lords[155]

2–64   The House of Lords was split on the decision on the facts but unanimous on the approach to be taken to the case. The House overruled the Court of Appeal by 3 to 2. It held that the publication of the three disputed items of information: (1) the fact that Naomi Campbell was receiving treatment at Narcotics Anonymous; (2) the details of the treatment—how long she had been attending meetings, how often she went and associated matters; and (3) the photographs of her leaving the meeting with other addicts amounted to a misuse of her private information. On behalf of Ms Campbell it had been accepted that the Mirror was entitled to publish the fact that she was addicted and was receiving treatment in view of her earlier public assertions in relation to drug use. There were no findings in the Data Protection Act in the judgments of the Lords. It had been accepted that the DPA case stood or fell with the action for misuse of private information. The basis for this is not explained but it is assumed that the court considered that if it was decided that the publication of the three disputed items was justified and proportionate then the public interest test in s.32(1)(b) would be made out and the exemption for the special purposes would apply to the publication. In the final analysis the House held that the photographs should not have been published and Miss Campbell's determination to protect her privacy was vindicated. In the section below we have analysed the case and two other important similar cases in more detail but it must be recognised that the privacy cases are very fact-sensitive. In the case of *Re S (A Child) (Appellant)*[156] later in 2004 a very different decision was reached in considering what might be regarded as a more serious privacy issue.

Re S (A Child) (Appellant)

2–65   In the judgment the House of Lords reiterated its view on the proper way to approach cases where the rights of privacy and freedom of speech are to be balanced but on the facts of the case came to a different view on the balance to be struck. The judgement was given by Lord Steyn who summarised the position following *Campbell* in four propositions:

> "Firstly, neither article *as such* has precedence over the other. Secondly, where the values under the two articles are in conflict, an intense focus on the comparative importance of the specific rights being claimed in the individual case is necessary. Thirdly, the justification for interfering with or restricting each right must be taken into account. Finally, the proportionality test must be applied to each. For convenience I will call this the ultimate balancing test."[157]

---

[155] [2004] UK HL 22.
[156] [2004] UKHL 47.
[157] para.17.

In the particular case there had been a question of whether the identity of a child who was not the subject of proceedings or concerned in any proceedings could be protected by the imposition of an order that a criminal case against his mother be subject to reporting restrictions. The mother was accused of killing the child's brother. Those responsible for the care of the child had raised concerns that the publicity associated with the case would have a detrimental impact on the child and sought the order to shield him from it. The effect of the order prohibiting the press from publishing any information about the criminal proceedings which might lead to the identification of the child would be to prevent the reporting of the case against the mother.

The court recognised that Art.6 sets a strong prima facie rule in favour of open hearings in criminal trials but the real tension lay between Arts 8 and 10. The House was in no doubt that the courts had the jurisdiction to restrain publicity on the basis of the appliation of the convention rights but declined to exercise it powers. As Lord Steyn put it:

> "The glare of contemporaneous publicity ensures that trials are properly conducted. It is a valuable check on the criminal process."[158]

The inevitable consequences of the grant of an injunction in this case, leading to further restrictions and restricting reporting and debate, were recognised and the impact that such restrictions would have on regional and local as well as national press. For all those reasons the appeal was dismissed.

2–66   In the cases charted above the issues of law which have emerged in this area can be seen as follows:

- the application of Art.8 rights between private parties;
- whether a pre-existing relationship of confidence is required;
- the extent of Art.8 rights;
- the concept of control of private information;
- the Art.10 rights of the confidant;
- the privacy rights of public figures;
- photographs taken of behaviour in public places;
- the balance between Arts 8 and 10;
- the extent and nature of the public interest override;
- the public interest in the preservation of the press;
- The publication of false private information.

In the next section therefore we have examined the judgment of the House of Lords in the cases of *Campbell* and the judgments of the Court of Appeal in *Niema Ash v*

---

[158] para.30.

Loreena McKennitt[159] and *Associated Newspapers Limited v His Royal Highness the of Wales* [160] under those headings to illustrate the way that case law has developed and a consensus has emerged.

Campbell v MGM

The application of Art.8 rights between private parties

2–67   All of the Law Lords accepted that the rights given by Art.8 were applicable between the two private parties and the court was obliged to take them into account in determining the case.[161]

Whether a pre-existing relationship of confidence is required

2–68   There was unanimous confirmation that in the case of personal information no requirement for a pre-existing relationship applies.[162] This confirmed the dicta of Lord Goff in *Attorney General v Guardian Newspapers Ltd (No. 2)*.[163] It follows that in future cases a distinction must be drawn between cases of commercial confidentiality where the information must still be disclosed by a party for the obligation to bite and those concerning personal private information.

The extent of the right to privacy under Art.8

2–69   There was significant debate about the extent of the right to privacy and how the right should be defined. There was agreement that the test of a "reasonable expectation of privacy" was the threshold which should bring the right into play as per Baroness Hale at para.137, Lord Nicholls at para.21.

In a recent Australian case the courts have used the formulation drawn from the US Restatement of Torts[164] that the courts should restrain the publication of information which would be "highly offensive to a reasonable person". Lord Nicholls regarded this as setting the bar too high and preferred the formulation of the individual having a "reasonable expectation of privacy" in relation to the information.[165] Lord Hope referred to the formulation used in *A v B* by Lord Woolf that the disclosure of information in that nature would give "substantial offence" to the individual, assuming that the individual was one of ordinary sensibilities. He also referred to the US formulation and quoted William L Prosser that:

> "the matter made public must be one which would be offensive and objectionable to a reasonable man of ordinary sensibilities, who must expect some reporting of his daily activities. The law of privacy is not intended for the protection of the unduly sensitive."[166]

---

[159] [2006] EWCA Civ 1714.
[160] [2006] EWCA Civ 1776.
[161] paras 17, 50, 86, 132, 167 as per Lords Nicholls, Hoffman, Hope, Hale and Carswell.
[162] paras 14, 48, 85, 134, 166 as per Lords Nicholls, Hoffman, Hope, Hale and Carswell.
[163] [1990] 1 A.C. 109 at 281.
[164] *Australian Broadcasting Corporation v Lenah Game Meats Pty Ltd* (2001) 185 A.L.R. 1, at 13.
[165] para.22.
[166] para.94.

In relation to Miss Campbell the court had to consider the disclosure of the photographs from her perspective with her vulnerabilities. This approach was also adopted by Baroness Hale who placed a high premium on the nature of the information and its relation to an individual's health and well-being:

"... the information was of exactly the same kind as that which would be recorded by a doctor on those [medical] notes" [167]

"... People trying to recover from drug addiction need considerable dedication and commitment, along with constant reinforcement from those around them." [168]

The concept of control of private information

2–70 The specific question of control was not addressed in terms although the judgments explore the nature of privacy as described above.

Article 10 rights of the press or a confidant

2–71 In this case there was no confidant to claim a right to freedom of expression but the rights of the press and the importance of freedom of speech were considered at length.[169] The importance of the freedom of political speech was emphasised by Baroness Hale but the focus was on the particular facts and it was emphasised that the issue under consideration was the balance and proportionality involved:

"There are undoubtedly different types of speech just as there are different types of private information, some of which are more deserving of protection in a democratic society than others. Top of the list is political speech. The free exchange of information and ideas on matters relevant to the organisation of the economic, social and political life of the country is crucial to any democracy."

However she distinguished the particular material under consideration taking the view that the information was highly invasive of her privacy with no corresponding justification for publication.[170]

Privacy rights of public figures

2–72 There was unanimity that the mere fact that an individual is in the public eye for other reasons or as part of that person's role, even where the individual has courted and lives by publicity does not deprive the individual of the right to a proper protection of privacy.[171]

Photographs or behaviour taken in public places

2–73 In this case the complaint was made of the publication of the photographs and not the taking of them. It was accepted that the mere taking of a photograph of

---

[167] para.146.
[168] para.157.
[169] paras 61–66 Lord Hoffman, 108 Lord Hope, 140 Baroness Hale.
[170] paras 148 onwards.
[171] paras 28, 57 and 67, 81, 144 and 157, per Lord Nicholls, Hoffman, Hope and Hale.

an individual in the street or another public place was not a breach of privacy. The matter would be different if the person were engaged in a private activity but there was a disagreement of fact as to whether the particular circumstances were sufficiently private to render the publication of the photographs a breach. This case was decided before *Von Hannover*.

In Lord Nicholl's view the photographs:

> ". . . conveyed no private information beyond that discussed in the article. The group photograph showed Miss Campbell in the street exchanging warm greetings with others on the doorstep of a building. There was nothing undignified or distrait about her appearance."[172]

Lord Hoffman agreed that the mere taking of the photographs without consent was no breach:

> "The famous and even the not so famous who go out in public must accept that they may be photographed without their consent just as they may be observed by others without their consent."[173]

However he drew the distinction between the taking of the photograph and the publication so that the widespread publication of a photograph which shows someone in a position of humiliation or severe embarrassment may be a infringement of personal information as may the taking of a photograph in a private place with a long range lens. In the present case as there was nothing humiliating about the photograph it was not an infringement of Miss Campbell's right to privacy.

Lord Hope in his analysis agreed that the risk of being photographed in a public place was a hazard of living in society but drew a distinction between the incidental inclusion on a photograph and the deliberate taking of the photographs in this case:

> "Miss Campbell could not have complained if the photographs had been taken to show the scene in the street by a passer-by and later published simply as street scenes. But these were not just pictures of a street scene where she happened to be when the photographs were taken. They were taken deliberately in secret and with a view to their publication in conjunction with the article. The zoom lens was directed at the doorway of the place where the meeting had been taking place."[174]

He agreed that the publication of photographs could raise breaches of the right of privacy and referred to the case of *Peck*.

Baroness Hale took the same view, that a photograph, even a covert photograph, does not make the information in it confidential, the activity photographed must be private in nature. In this case she considered that the activity photographed was private in nature.[175]

---

[172] para.31.
[173] para.73.
[174] para.123.
[175] paras 154 and 155.

Balance between Arts 8 and 10

2–74   Lords Nicholls and Hoffman took the view that the Art.8 rights of Miss Campbell should not weight sufficiently heavily to outweight the Art.10 rights of the press in the circumstances. They agreed with the Court of Appeal that too nice a line cannot be drawn between the different types of information. Lords Hope and Carswell and Baroness Hale came down on the other side on the facts and it was this difference that swung the case in favour of Miss Campbell. However the **approach** of the judges to the assessment of the balance was the same. As Lord Hoffman said:

> "The importance of this case lies in the statements of general principle on the way in which the law should strike a balance between the right to privacy and the right to freedom of expression, on which the House in unanimous."[176]

There is no presumption in favour of one right or another. The question is how far it is necessary to qualify one right in order to protect the other.[177] The main analysis is set out by Lord Hope in paras 105 to 113. Of particular importance will be the nature of the freedom of expression which is to be protected. The fact that there are different types of freedom of expression is echoed in the judgment of Baroness Hale.

Public interest override

2–75   There was agreement that the right of privacy could be overridden by a disclosure made in the public interest and it was common ground in this case that the fact that Miss Campbell had carried through a public deception justified the press in "putting the record straight".[178]

Public interest in the preservation of the press

2–76   In *A v B* Lord Woolf had acknowledged the importance of the preservation of a vigorous press in a democracy. The point was pursued in only one of the judgments by Baroness Hale who acknowledged the importance of the press as a commercial sector, in addition to the right of freedom of speech:

> "One reason why press freedom is so important is that we need newspapers to sell in order to ensure that we still have newspapers at all."[179]

However she did not consider that this could justify the intrusion into the particular area of personal privacy in this case which involved running the piece without the cooperation of Miss Campbell.

---

[176] para.36.
[177] paras 20, 55, 105–113, 139, 167 per Lords Nicholls, Hoffman, Hope, Hale and Carswell.
[178] paras 24, 58, 82, 129 and 151, 163 per Lords Nicholls, Hoffman, Hope, Hale and Carswell.
[179] Baroness Hale at para.143.

Publication of false private information

2–77 In the articles published by the *Mirror* there were a number of inaccuracies but it was held that in all the circumstances of this case the inaccuracies were unimportant and made no difference to the privacy claim:

> ". . . there is a vital difference between inaccuracies that deprive the information of its intrusive quality and inaccuracies that do not. The inaccuracies that were relied on here fall into the latter category."[180]

Niema Ash v Loreena McKennitt[181]

2–78 This case was heard by the Court of Appeal on an appeal from a judgment of Mr Justice Eady in which he had found in favour of the folk singer, Ms McKennitt.[182] Ms Ash, a former friend and confidant of Ms McKennitt, had written a book about the singer which revealed various material about the singer's life which she regarded as private. Ms McKennitt had taken action to restrain the publication of the book and had succeeded before Mr Justice Eady. If she had hoped that the Court of Appeal would take a more kindly view of her case she was sadly disappointed. The judgment of the Court was delivered by Lord Justice Buxton. In this case there was no doubt but that Ms Ash had been a confidant in the traditional sense of the terms as used in actions for breach of confidence so the Court did not have to consider the situation of the stranger who comes into possession of information.

The importance of the case in the development of this area can be gauged by the interest of the media. A number of media organisations including the BBC and Times Warner sought permission to intervene despite the fact that these were private proceedings and the would-be intervenors had no public interest role. The Court dealt with the difficulty adroitly by taking note of the submissions made but did not allow formal intervention.

The application of Article 8 rights between private parties

2–79 While generally Convention rights do not create rights between private bodies, Art.8 is different. It has long been accepted that an individual can complain to the State about the behaviour of others which impacts on his private life.[183] As between private parties it is authority that ss.6(1) and (3) of the Human Rights Act 1998 place an obligation on the court as a public authority to take account of Art.8 and 10 in deciding cases for breach of confidence (or as it now known misuse of private information).[184]

Whether a pre-existing relationship of confidence is required

2–80 It is now clear from the case law that no pre-existing relationship is required.[185] However in this case the parties were clearly in a relationship of confidentiality.

---

[180] Lord Hope paragraph 102.
[181] [2006] EWCA Civ 1714.
[182] [2005] EWHC 3003 (QB).
[183] *Marckx v Belgiul* (1979) 2 E.H.R.R. 330; and *X and Y v Netherlands* (1985) 8 E.H.R.R. 235.
[184] See paras 9 –11 of *McKennit* and the cases cited therein.
[185] *Campbell v MGM* [2004] 2 A.C. 457.

The extent of the Art.8 rights—personal life and home

2–81   The touchstone of whether there is an action is whether the information is private and falls to be protected under Art.8. The Court confirmed the view taken in *Campbell* that the test is a broad one. Quoting the speech of Lord Nicholls in *Campbell*:

> "in deciding what was the ambit of an individual's "private life" in particular circumstances courts need to be on guard against using as a touchstone a test which should more properly be considered at the later stages of proportionality. Essentially the touchstone of private life is whether in respect of the disclosed acts the person in question had a reasonable expectation of privacy."

In particular the book contained information about a property which Ms McKennitt owned. The High Court had held that there was a reasonable expectation of privacy in relation to its nature and domestic arrangements. Even trivial details could be protected under this approach. This was confirmed by the Court of Appeal. While it accepted that whereas Strasbourg cases have tended to be concerned with the security or stability of the home, information about an individual's home could still raise a privacy issue.

Control of personal information

2–82   The Court found that Ms McKennitt was unusual among stars in the entertainment business in that she guarded her privacy carefully and controlled the information about her which was published. It was accepted that she only released information that she "felt comfortable with" and that some of that information, which was of a private nature, was only released as part of her work for a charity to campaign for water safety after she had suffered personal loss. The appellant argued that once Ms McKennitt had disclosed some information about her loss she had thereby opened up all of that area of her life for public scrutiny. The Court did not accept this argument and took the view that Ms McKennitt was entitled to limit publication of information about herself to that which she wished to be published. This was clearly on the basis that there was no other public interest in publication of information. Lord Justice Buxton stated:

> "If information is my private property, it is for me to decide how much of it should be published."[186]

Article 10 rights of the confidant

2–83   One of the arguments for Ms Ash was based on the arguments which prevailed in *Woodward and Hutchins*[187] and to some extent in *A v B Plc*[188] that Ms Ash was entitled to tell her own story and the restriction upon her was a breach of her own rights to freedom of speech. The Court however distinguished the cases pointing out

---

[186] *ibid.* paras 6 and 55.
[187] [1997] 1 W.L.R. 760.
[188] [2002] EWCA Civ 337.

that Ms Ash's story was not about herself but was "largely parasitic". In *A v B plc* there was no relationship that could be characterised as one of mutual confidence. Dealing with *Woodward and Hutchins* Lord Justice Buxton pointed out that this was a case prior to the coming into force of the Human Rights Act and therefore had to be treated with caution but in any event it concerned singers who had sought and welcomed publicity to the extent that the material which they wished to protect no longer enjoyed the protection of confidentiality in the first place.

Rights of public figures

2–84   The Court considered the ruling in *Von Hannover* and whether Ms McKennitt is a public figure. It repeated the distinction made in that case between matters of legitimate democratic debate and mere trivial interest in the behaviour of those who are in the public eye. In the latter case the individual is entitled to respect for privacy unless there is some circumstance which makes the behaviour of the person a matter of legitimate debate. In this case it held that there were no special circumstances which would warrant public interest in Ms McKennitt. It then considered the comments made by Lord Woolf on *A v B plc* to the effect that mere celebrity would lessen the extent of the private domain to which an individual was entitled it acknowledged that this approach conflicted with the view taken in *Von Hannover*. It further noted, as was urged on behalf of the appellant, that the court is bound to apply the Convention rights as interpreted in the UK law in a previous UK case in preference to Strasbourg jurisprudence on the same point right.[189] At this stage of the judgment it seemed all might have been lost until Lord Justice Buxton pointed out that the court had not ruled on Art.10 in *A v B plc* and therefore he was at liberty to apply *Von Hannover* and did.

Photographs or information about behaviour in public places

2–85   The case of *Von Hannover v Germany*[190] as well as *Campbell* was considered and the court accepted that *Von Hannover* had extended the reach of Art.8. In *Von Hannover*, as we have seen earlier, the Court of Human Rights held that the German courts had failed to protect the privacy of Princess Caroline of Monaco by allowing the publication of photographs of her in public places. The Strasbourg court had held that she was entitled to a degree of privacy for her actions even in public places as:

> "There is ..a zone of interaction of a person with others, even in a public context, which may fall within the scope of 'private life'."

The appellant advanced the argument that the judgment in *Von Hannover* was fact-specific and should not be the basis of a wider application. It was necessary that media intrusion into the Princess's privacy was restrained because of the intrusive nature of the interest shown by the press into her activities and had this not been the case the photography would have been held harmless.[191] However this argument was not accepted by the Court.

---

[189] Applying the judgment in *Kay v Lambeth LBC* [2006] 2 W.L.R. 570.
[190] (2005) 40 E.H.R.R. 1.
[191] para.41.

Balance between Arts 8 and 10

2–86   As had been accepted in other cases the rights of individuals under the two articles must be balanced with neither having precedence over the other.[192] The approach of Mr Justice Eady was endorsed as follows:

(i)   Neither article as such has precedence over the other.

(ii)   Where conflict arises between the values under Arts 8 and 10 an "intense focus" is necessary upon the comparative importance of the specific rights being claimed in the individual case.

(iii)   The court must take into account the justifications for interfering with or restricting each right.

(iv)   So too the proportionality test must be applied to each.

Public interest override

2–87   One of the arguments advanced by the appellant was that there was a public interest in the disclosure of the information as it showed Ms McKennitt to be a hypocrite. The court accepted the there is a public interest override to an obligation of confidence or a claim in Art.8 but accepted the finding of the High Court that it did not apply in this case.

Public interest in the preservation of the press

2–88   The court recognised the difficult (and occasionally criticised) comments of Lord Woolf in *A v B*, that weight must be given to the commercial interests of the press, but was able to bypass them and pointed out that this had no significant impact on the present case.[193]

Disclosure of "false" private information

2–89   Under this point the appellant claimed that there could be no restriction of the publication of information on privacy grounds where the court has found that the statements were false. On the face of it a strong, if distasteful, argument. Lord Justice Buxton dismissed the argument on the basis that such information could still infringe privacy depending on the facts of the matter.

Associated Newspapers Limited v His Royal Highness the Prince of Wales[194]

2–90   This case followed close on the *McKennitt* case. The facts were simple. Prince Charles has for many years been in the habit of producing handwritten journals setting out his thoughts and impressions after overseas visits. On his return to the UK he would have these copied and sent to a list of individual recipients with a signed letter. The envelope was marked "Private and Confidential". The recipients were friends from

---

[192] *Re S (FC) (A child)* [2005] 1 A.C. 593.
[193] para.66.
[194] [2006] EWCA Civ 1776.

different walks of life. Ms Sarah Goodall worked in the Prince's private office between May 1988 and December 2000. She had signed undertakings as to confidentiality on entering her employment. In May 2005 she supplied the *Mail on Sunday* with copies of eight of the journals via an intermediary. In October 2005 she appears to have had a change of mind and confessed her actions to one of her superiors and also approached the *Mail on Sunday* to ask for the copies back. Although the set was returned the newspaper retained a copy. Despite threats from the Princes' lawyers the *Mail on Sunday* went ahead and published substantial extracts from the journals on November 13, 2005. The Prince's lawyers then succeeded in obtaining an interlocutory order to stop the newspaper printing any more of the material. The substantive issues were reserved for the later hearing.

There were some differences of fact between the newspaper and the Prince (as to how many copies of the journal were circulated, how securely they were held and whether, on a previous occasion a journalist writing an authorised biography had been given access to them). In order to avoid a trial on the facts counsel for the Prince invited the court to proceed on the basis that the facts were those least advantageous to the Prince. The court did so and even on that basis found against the Mail on Sunday all counts. We have examined the case under the same headings as those used for the *McKennitt* case described above, although not all are relevant to this case. Lord Phillips, the Chief Justice, delivered the judgment.

Article 8 rights and private parties

2–91   The obligation of the courts to give effect to the Art.8 rights was accepted.[195]

Whether a pre-existing relationship is required

2–92   It was accepted that no pre-existing relationship is now required for the action for misuse of private information to be established. However the court took the view that the existence of a relationship of confidence remains a relevant issue in the new action. The new action is still built on and reflects the old law of breach of confidence. The court may therefore need to distinguish those cases where the information itself is not obviously such as to engage Art.8 but has been received in confidence and points out that Art.10 rights may well have to give way to confidentiality even where the confidentiality does not protect personal privacy.[196] In this case the court gave weight to the fact that the information was disclosed in breach of a well-recognised relationship of confidence, that which exists between master and servant and in breach of a contractual obligation.

Extent of Art.8 rights—home and correspondence

2–93   The court was in no doubt that the material was confidential, describing the journals as "paradigm examples of confidential documents".[197] In relation to deciding how the right to protection is to be established Lord Phillips comments:

---

[195] See paras 24 and 25.
[196] See paras 28 and 29.
[197] See para.35.

"It is not easy in this case, as in many others, when concluding that information is private, to identify the extent to which this is because of the nature of the information, the form in which it is conveyed and the fact that the person disclosing it was in confidential relationship with the person to whom it relates. Usually as here, these factors form an interdependent amalgam of circumstances."

On behalf of the *Mail on Sunday* it had been argued that as the subject of the journals was in the public domain and there was a circulation of the journals then the Prince, being himself a public figure who used the media to further his views, could have no reasonable expectation of privacy in them. This submission received short shrift. Lord Phillips pointed out that the question of whether the Prince had forfeited any right of privacy was a separate one from whether the right existed in the first place. He was in no doubt that it did.

Control of personal information

2–94   The right of the Prince to control his own material and private writings was accepted by the court but one of the most interesting comments was in relation to the extent of privacy to which the Prince, as a public figure, might be entitled.

Rights of public figures

2–95   The *Mail on Sunday* the familiar argument that those whose activities and role are in the public domain can have less expectation of privacy to be met by the endorsement of a view expressed by the judge at first instance and quoted with approval that:

"Not the least of the considerations that must be weighted in the scales is the claimant's countervailing claim to what was described in argument as 'his private space'; the right to be able to commit his private thoughts to writing and keep them private, the more so as he is inescapably as public figure who is subject to constant and intense media interest . . . . The claimant is as much entitled to enjoy confidentiality for his private thoughts as an aspect of his own 'human autonomy and dignity' as is any other."[198]

This seems to suggest that, far from public figures being entitled to less privacy than the ordinary person, they may be entitled to more, or at least to strong protection for that area which is regarded as legitimately private.

Information or pictures about behaviour in public places

2–96   This issue was not considered, save insofar as the argument was that the matters written about were in the public domain, however as the nub of the case was the actual journal, this made no difference

---

[198] para.70.

Balance of Arts 8 and 10

2–97   Here the court stressed the importance of freedom of expression in a democratic society and considered those cases where the public interest in freedom of expression has prevailed over privacy rights. It treated the balance in this case as a question of whether the Art.10 right represented a public interest argument that could override the right of confidentiality.

The public interest override

2–98   The weight that should be given to the rights of confidentiality and the relation between the public interest test for breach of confidence and the application of Art.8(2) is canvassed at length in paras 50–69. Lord Phillips concluded that the test for the public interest override has changed:

> "Before the Human Rights Act came into force the circumstances in which the public interest in publication overrode a duty of confidence were very limited. The issue was whether exceptional circumstances justifying disregarding the confidentiality that would otherwise prevail. Today the test is different. It is whether a fetter of the right of freedom of expression is, in the particular circumstances 'necessary in a democratic society'. It is a test of proportionality. But a significant element to be weighted in the balance is the importance in a democratic society of upholding duties of confidentiality that are created between individuals. It is not enough to justify publication that the information is a matter of public interest . . . . . . The test to be applied . . . . is whether in all the circumstances it is in the public interest that the duty of confidence should be breached."

The public interest in the preservation of the press

2–99   This issue was not considered.

Disclosure of false " private" information

2–100   This issue was not considered.

2–101   One might have thought that with those cases the ground rules had been laid out and the courts would be able to turn their attention to some other topic but there have been one or two cases in the area that merit a mention. In the splendidly titled case of *X & Y v Persons Unknown*[199] Mr Justice Eady in the High Court granted the claimants an injunction to restrain the publication of information about the claimants' marriage. The initial injunction was granted at short notice and in wide terms as the claimants did not know who was peddling the story about their marriage to the press. At the full hearing the judge provided guidance on the approach that should be taken when deciding to grant injunctions in such circumstances. The court will take into account what the parties have put into the public domain. The fact that some material has been put into the public domain does not make all material "fair game" for the press. He drew a distinction between a couple who allow the publication of wedding or honeymoon photographs (as the couple in question had done) and

---

[199] [2006] EWHC 2783, QB.

those who speak to the media about the details of their married lives. In a similar way he distinguished between someone being "in the public eye" and being a "publicity seeker". One of the parties in the case was a model who was, of necessity, in the public eye and who had a contractual obligation to give a number of interviews. He drew a distinction between matters which are naturally accessible to outsiders, such as the fact that a couple are living apart, and matters which are private between the parties only. He acknowledged the difficulty for a third party, such as a newspaper, faced with an order not to disclose private information, in deciding what was private and knowing what might have reached the public domain. The solution adopted in the case was to attach to the order a confidential schedule containing the specific allegations which there is reason to suppose may be made public in the absence of an order banning the publication.

CC v AB[200]

2–102   In this case the defendant wished to tell the press about an affair between his wife and the claimant. The claimant wished to restrain the disclosures in order to protect the claimant's wife, himself and his own wife and children from the stress and strain of press intrusion. The defendant was motivated by a mixture of greed and a wish for revenge. The court recognised that it had to apply the competing rights between the parties and accepted that there is a powerful argument that the conduct of an intimate sexual relationship is one in which the parties would have a legitimate expectation of privacy. The court did not distinguish here between a marital or other relationship, although the judge acknowledged that a "fleeting one night encounter" might well attract less protection that a genuine relationship. Despite being urged to refuse the protection of confidentiality to an adulterous relationship the judge refused to do so, emphasising that it was not for a judge to take a personal moral view when applying the Convention rights which he described as a "secular code". In deciding the application of the rights the judge referred to the observations made in *A Local Authority v W*[201] on the proper approach to be adopted when competing Convention rights are in issue. The starting point is one of "presumptive parity" as neither right takes precedence over the other. The justification for interfering with each and the issue of proportionality is to be considered for each.

The judge considered the extent to which the court should restrict the freedom of the defendant to disclose the information and accepted that there existed a range of disclosures which could not be restricted as to his family, lawyer and others of a similar relationship, however selling the story to the tabloid press was another matter. There was no genuine public interest in the disclosure. It was argued that, as the adulterous couple had stayed in hotels together and been seen in public, although never recognised, that they had put the affair into the public domain but the argument was not accepted, particularly in the light of the decision in *Von Hannover*. The claimant succeeded in obtaining an injunction to prevent the defendant from communicating with the media or on the internet about the former relationship.

---

[200] [2006] EWHC 3083 (QB).
[201] [2005] EWHC 1564 (Fam).

Conclusions

2–103 It may seem from the cases described that privacy issues are only being raised in relation to the actions of the press and certainly the clear message from these most recent cases is that the courts are determinedly doing their best to restrain the excesses of tabloid intrusion. Privacy rights have however also been protected in other circumstances. In *London Borough of Brent v N and P* [202] the court held that the local authority had no duty to inform natural parent's of a foster parents HIV positive status as this would be an unnecessary disclosure which would have a significant impact on the private and family life of the foster parent. The Court also seem to become less sympathetic to those who fail to heed the guidance the courts have established. Ms Ash had her application to appeal to the Court of Appeal repeatedly refused and only succeeded on her third application. It should not be assumed however that privacy rights are being given precedence over other rights.

2–104 In *Michael Stone v S.E. Coast Strategic Health Authority*[203] the Court held that the public interest in the publication of a report into the case, treatment and supervision of a man convicted of murder which included extensive citation from his medical and psychiatric records overrides the Art.8 rights of the individual and involved no breach of the DPA. Mr Stone had co-operated with the inquiry which produced the report and originally consented to its publication. In 2005 he withdrew his consent. It was accepted that he was entitled to withdraw consent and the question facing the Court was whether to sanction publication in the absence of consent. The court applied *Campbell* and *Re S* in seeking the proper balance in the case. On the Art.8 and the confidentiality arguments it determined that Art.8(2) was properly applied and Mr Stone's rights of confidentiality must give way to a greater public interest in publication. In relation to the DPA however the judgment was less satisfactory and did not address issues of either in fairness or compatibility, which might reasonably have been regarded as significant issues. It focused solely on the ground for the processing under Schs 2 and 3. It followed *Campbell* in holding that the publication would involve processing. In relation to Sch.3 the Court held, not unsurprisingly, that in the circumstances ground 7 applied in that the publication was necessary for the exercise of the functions of the health authority, accepting that the term "necessary" imports a balance reflecting the concepts of proportionality and public interest.

The wholly unexpected, and it is respectfully submitted wholly onerous, finding was that ground 8 could be applied, that is, the publication was "necessary" for medical purposes. The judgment is examined in more details in Ch.7, below but strengthens the concern that, while the courts have clearly taken on board considerations of privacy and human rights in terms of Art.8 there is still some way to go before DPA rights and constraints are recognised.

OVERVIEW

2–105 Until the coming into force of the Human Rights Act data protection had tended to be seen as a "stand alone" area of law but, in the cases that have come before

---

[202] [2005] EWHC 1676.
[203] [2003] EWHC 1668 (Admin).

the courts since October 2000, judges have increasingly taken a holistic view of personal information, bringing together concepts from the cases on breach of confidence, Arts 8 and 10 of the Convention and the self-regulatory regime governing the media and, although regrettably to a lesser extent so far, data protection standards. In this chapter we have considered the sources and examined the material which is now converging.

The convergence is nowhere near complete. In particular the courts have yet to explore the relationship between privacy and data protection in any depth.

So far the courts have moved to offer protection of privacy against press intrusion while maintaining the protection given to freedom of speech. In the process there has been a radical development in the law of confidence, comparable to the developments in *Prince Albert v Strange* and *Saltman*. This received a full exposition in the statement by Lord Woolf in *A v B* that an obligation does not depend for its creation on the relationship between two persons or whether information was confided but rather the nature of the information and the circumstances. It has now been confirmed that this will not be taken to apply to all types of confidentiality or only in relation to personal privacy. Even limited to the area of personal privacy it is a radical re-configuring of the law of confidence. It frees it from the constraints of being a right created by the relationship between two parties in the particular case, and changes it to being an obligation which could bind anyone who intrudes on information of a personal nature. In doing so it opens the doors to allow the development of a specific action to protect personal privacy in a range of circumstances.

In the cases the courts are gradually teasing out the various aspects of privacy protection and placing them into perspective. However, so far the courts have not tackled the difficult issues of State intrusion into personal privacy. In *Marper* they have followed the ECtHR in accepting a high margin of appreciation for the State in the areas of policing and national security. There is a view among many who work in the privacy domain that for most of us personal privacy and liberty are more at risk from State surveillance and intrusion than the attentions of the press but we have yet to see how far or how boldly the courts will be prepared to venture into that terrain.

CHAPTER 3

Interpretation of the Act and Key Definitions, Including Territorial Application

INTRODUCTION

3–01   The background to, and the wider context of, the Data Protection Act 1998 (DPA) (the Act) have a continued relevance in interpreting its provisions. In Chapters 1 and 2, above the wider background and legal context were considered. This chapter examines the approach to the interpretation of the Act, major cases on interpretation since 2001 and reviews the main definitions.

SUMMARY OF MAIN POINTS

3–02   (a)   The most important influences on the interpretation of the Act are Directive 95/46 (the Directive) and the Convention rights (incorporated in the United Kingdom by the Human Rights Act 1998) together with rulings of the European Court of Justice, the European Court of Human Rights and the UK courts.

(b)   When considering the interpretation of the Privacy and Electronic Communications (EC Directive) Regulations 2003[1] Directive 2002/58/ is also a primary influence on interpretation.

(c)   Of secondary importance are decisions of the Information Tribunal, other instruments, cases from other areas and previous court or tribunal decisions on the 1984 Data Protection Act.

(d)   There are a number of key definitions in the Act. The most significant are:

- "data controller", this is the person who determines the manner and purposes of the processing;
- "data", this definition is important in establishing the scope of the Act. The definition has a wider scope in relation to information held by public

---

[1] SI 2003/2426.

authorities than it has for data controllers in the private sector. The definition includes data which are part of a "relevant filing system";

- "personal data" , this definition delineates the scope of the data about a living individual which will be subject to the Act;
- "processing", this definition ensures that all use and manipulation of personal data is covered by the law.

(e) The Act applies to all controllers who are established in the United Kingdom and process in the context of that establishment.

(f) Those who have data processed in the United Kingdom but who are not established in an EEA State must nominate a UK representative for the purposes of the Act.

APPROACH TO INTERPRETATION

Impact of Directive 95/46

3–03 A directive is binding on Member States as to the results to be achieved but leaves the form and method by which it is achieved to national authorities.[2] The obligation of the Member State is to transpose a directive into national law. This obligation informs the actions of every public organisation that deals with a directive. The courts, when construing statutes based on a directive, must seek to construe them in accord with the directive.

The approach to construction is to be purposive, not literal: that is it must seek to give effect to the objects and purpose of the directive. In the case of *Von Colson*,[3] the European Court laid down that there is an obligation on authorities of Member States and their courts to produce consistent interpretation and to interpret national laws designed to implement a directive in accordance with the terms and the purpose of the directive. Even when a directive is adequately transposed into national law, therefore, it remains relevant as a standard for interpreting the implementing measure. Not only must the national courts apply consistent interpretation to ensure that the directive is complied with, but they must construe the national provisions in the light of the objectives of the directive.

This was applied by the House of Lords in *Campbell v MGN Ltd*[4] where Lord Philip Worth of Matravers said:

"In interpreting the Act it is appropriate to look to the Directive for assistance. The Act should, if possible, be interpreted in a manner that is consistent with the Directive. Furthermore, because the Act has, in large measure, adopted the wording of the Directive, it is not appropriate to look for the precision in the use of language that is usually expected from the parliamentary draftsman. A purposive approach to making sense of the provisions is called for."

---

[2] Art.189(3) of the Treaty.
[3] Case 14/83 [1984] E.C.R. 1891.
[4] [2002] EWCA Civ 1373; [2003] 2 W.L.R. 80 at para.[96].

The interpretative approach can only be adopted within the confines of the national provisions and therefore applies "as far as possible". The UK courts have considered Directive 46/95 in a number of cases including *Campbell*[5] and *R (on the application of Alan Lord) v the Secretary of State for the Home Department*.[6] The clearest application of a purposive approach to date is probably to be seen in *Brian Reid Robertson v City of Wakefield Metropolitan Council and Secretary of State for the Home Department*[7] in which the High Court applied a purposive approach to the interpretation of s.11 based on Art.14.

3–04   In order to look at the purpose of a directive the recitals may be relevant. The other background papers which may be of interpretative relevance are the *travaux preparatoire*. These are usually referred to in the opening provisions of a directive. The papers referred to in Directive 95/46 are the original proposal from the European Commission of 1990 and the opinion of the Economic and Social Committee of 1991. The relation between the Directive and the requirements of Art.8 of the Human Rights Convention is relevant in this context. This relationship has been considered in a number of cases. As is explained in Ch.2, above, the Directive is a "working out" of the Art.8 right in the area of information and in many areas it goes beyond the relatively limited range of ECtHR cases on informational privacy. Regrettably however there has been a tendency in some cases in the UK to treat the requirements of the Act as co-terminous with Art.8. The court or Tribunal has assumed that as long as Art.8 is satisfied there will be no breach of the Act. It is submitted that this approach, although it has the effect of simplifying issues, is misconceived and potentially undermines the protection provided to individuals.[8]

Article 8 is a qualified right. The interpretation of directives must take account of all the Convention rights and of the fundamental concepts of Community law: equality, legal certainty, proportionality, natural justice, fundamental rights and the protection of legitimate expectations. The rights and interests guaranteed by the Convention constitute general principles of Community law, e.g. *Nold*[9] and Art.6(2) of the Treaty on European Union. In the *Rundfunk* case (described in more detail below) the European Court said:

> ". . .the provisions of Directive 95/46, in so far as they govern the processing of personal data liable to infringe fundamental freedoms, in particular the right to privacy, must necessarily be interpreted in the light of fundamental rights, which according to settled case law, form an integral part of the general principles of law whose observance the Court ensures."[10]

3–05   In *Lindqvist*[11] the European Court held that the authorities and courts of the Member States must interpret their national law in a manner consistent with the

---

[5] *ibid.*
[6] [2003] EWHC 2073 (Admin).
[7] [2001] EWCH Admin 915, November 2001; see paras 2–40 onwards for a full discussion of the case. See also the decision of the Court of Appeal in *Naomi Campbell v MGN* [2002] EWCA Civ 1373.
[8] See for example, *the Chief Constables of West Yorkshire, South Yorkshire and North Wales Police v the Information Commissioner, Decision of the Information Tribunal*, 2006.
[9] Case 4/73 [1974] E.C.R. 491.
[10] para.66.
[11] See paras 3–12 onward, below for a full analysis of the facts.

Directive but also make sure that they do not rely on an interpretation which would conflict with the fundamental rights protected by the Community legal order or with the other general principles of Community such as the principle of proportionality. It would follow therefore that where there is ambiguity in the Directive it should not be assumed that Art.8 will be the only influence on its interpretation or even that, in any particular case, it will be the predominant influence. Other Convention rights will also have to be considered. For example in *Lindqvist* the Court held that the provisions of the Directive do not in themselves bring about a restriction which conflicts with the general principles of freedom of expression or other rights and it is for national authorities implementing the Directive to ensure that a fair balance is achieved when applying the national implementing legislation.

3–06 The European Court of Justice has developed the doctrine of direct effect as a tool to employ where Member States have either failed to implement a directive or failed to implement one properly. This doctrine allows a claimant to rely directly on the terms of a directive rather than on national law where the national law has not properly transposed the directive. As the United Kingdom had not implemented Directive 95/46 by October 24, 1998, there was some risk of direct effect actions against public bodies on this basis; however, none materialised. There was a further risk in relation to Directive 2002/58 but the UK escaped action. The claimant can only rely on a directive as against organisations or bodies treated as part of the State, not against private sector organisations. The provision in the directive must be clear and must confer an individual right which is capable of being enforced without further elucidation.[12]

The State may also be liable to pay compensation where a claimant suffers damage because of the non-implementation, or insufficient implementation, of a directive. This occurred in the case of *Francovitch*.[13] Compensation can be recoverable in *Francovitch* type cases where:

(a) the result prescribed by the directive entails the grant of rights to the person;

(b) it is possible to identify the content of those rights from the directive;

(c) there is a causal link between the breach of the State's obligation and the loss and damage suffered by the injured party.

Directive 2002/58 and the Privacy and Electronic Communications (EC Directive) Regulations 2003

3–07 These Regulations and the related Regulations which govern the surveillance and interception of communications are dealt with in Chs 22 and 23, below. The relationship between these provisions and EC law is complex because the UK provisions cover some areas which fall outside Community competence. A further discussion of the relationship between data protection instruments and Community competence is found in Ch.23. This relationship was also the root of the decision of the European Court in the case which considered the "agreement" by the EU Commission to permit

---

[12] Case C152/84 *Marshall and Southampton* [1986] E.C.R. 723.
[13] Case 9/90 [1991] E.C.R. 1–5357.

the transfer of passenger name data to the US. The Court decided that the purported agreement was invalid as the basis of the transfer was for purposes falling outside Community competence. For a discussion of this case see Ch.1, above.

Relation with the European Convention on Human Rights and Fundamental Freedoms (the Convention)

3–08   The DPA and the Convention rights interface in three ways:

- the Convention Rights are regarded as being a part of fundamental Community law and thus may be used to assist in the interpretation of the Directive itself;

- Directive 95/46 is stated to be the working out of the application of the right to respect for private and family life in the informational arena and thus the Art.8 right will be relevant to the interpretation of the Directive[14];

- the interpretation of the Act will be affected by the application of the Human Rights Act 1998 in the United Kingdom. The influence of the Convention rights and the development of case law on privacy has been covered in Ch.2, above and is not dealt with here.

European Court of Justice Case Law—Overview

3–09   National courts refer cases to the European Court of Justice (ECJ) for rulings under Art.234 where the national provisions adopted to comply with a Directive are argued to be impossible to reconcile with the fundamental principles of Community law. This has occurred in two cases concerned with data protection so far. These are the cases of *Rundfunk*[15] and *Lindqvist*[16] described below. The ECJ may also be asked to rule upon the legality of acts adopted by the Council or other institution under Art.230. This occurred when the Court was asked to rule on the legality of the agreement with the United States over the transfer of Passenger Name Records (PNR data) which is referred to briefly here but covered in Ch.1, above. ECJ cases are of prime importance in interpreting the national law arising from a directive. Out of the three cases which have been referred to the ECJ to date *Lindqvist* is probably the most useful to ordinary data controllers.

Overview of case decisions

3–10   In *Rundfunk* the Court was asked to consider the boundary between rights of informational privacy for those employed by the State and the disclosure of information about their emoluments as a matter of public interest. The Court refused to make a substantive decision on the proposed disclosure but confirmed that the relevant information should be regarded as personal data, albeit generated in the course of employment and related to the employment of the individuals rather than their private

---

[14] See Ch.2, above, for an analysis of the impact of Art.8.
[15] Cases C465/00, C138/01 and C39/01.
[16] Case C–101/01 [2003] ECR-I-12971.

life, but that the question of mandatory disclosure was for the State to decide. The State had to be satisfied that the disclosure would serve a proper public interest and apply proper principles of proportionality. The case seems to have been little regarded in the UK. In the *Lindqvist* case it was argued that, as the Directive was passed to harmonise data protection regimes in order to ensure the functioning of the internal market, national laws based on it are not applicable to activities which are not directly related to support the internal market. The ECJ took a robust approach pointing out that recourse to Art.100a of the Treaty as a legal basis "does not presume the existence of an actual link with free movement between Member States in every situation referred to by the measure founded on that basis . . . what matters is that the measure adopted on that basis must actually be intended to improve the conditions for the establishment and functioning of the internal market".[17] In both cases the ECJ ruled that the Directive is compatible with the Convention rights and that the national provisions adopted by the Member State could be interpreted in a manner which was also compatible. The ruling in *Lindqvist* has been considered and applied (in theory at least) by UK courts.

In the *PNR* case the European Court of Justice was asked to rule on whether actions of the Council and the Commission were compatible with Community powers. The Court held that the actions of the Commission (making a finding of adequacy and an Agreement with the US to allow the transfer of Passenger Name Records to the US for security purposes) were not compatible and in doing so distinguished the actions of a non-State body from activities of the State.[18]

Joined Cases C-465/00 Rechnugshof and Osterreichischer Rundfunk and C-138/01 Christa Neukomn and Osterreichischer Rundfunk and C-139/01 Joseph Lauermann and Osterreichischer Rundfunk[19]

3–11 Austrian legislation required public bodies subject to the oversight of the Austrian State audit body (the Rechnungshof) to provide it with the names and payments details of those who received salaries or pensions of over a specified value. This information was included in an annual report (the Report) which was sent to the upper and lower chambers of the Federal Parliament and the provincial assemblies and subsequently made available to the public. The legislation itself did not specify that the names of the persons concerned and the amount of annual remuneration received must be included in the Report.

The first case arose because there was a dispute between the Rechnungshof and various public bodies under its supervision as to whether personal data were required to be disclosed by the legislation. Several of these bodies supplied the information in anonymised form and refused to co-operate in providing access to the original documentation on the payments. Proceedings were brought before the Austrian constitutional court seeking a ruling on the interpretation of the provision. The Austrian court in turn referred the point to the ECJ.

The two individual cases arose from proceedings brought in the Austrian courts by individual employees of the Austrian State broadcasting organisation seeking

---

[17] para.41 of case C-465/00.
[18] See Ch.1, above for a full analysis of this aspect of the case.
[19] [2003] E.C.R. I-4989.

orders preventing their employer from disclosing information about them to the Rechnungshof.

The same questions were referred to the ECJ namely:

"1. Are the provisions of Community law, in particular those on data protection, to be interpreted as precluding national legislation which requires a State body to collect and transmit data on income for the purpose of publishing the names and income of employees of:

    (a) a regional or local authority,
    (b) a broadcasting organisation governed by public law,
    (c) a national central bank,
    (d) a statutory representative body,
    (e) a partially State-controller undertaking which is operated for profit?

2. If the answer to at least part of the above question is in the affirmative

Are the provisions precluding such national legislation directly applicable, in the sense that the persons obliged to make disclosure may rely on them to prevent the application of contrary national provisions?"[20]

The question clearly has significance for any jurisdiction which is subject to a statutory access regime.

The Court dealt with the applicability of the Directive (referred to in para.3–10, above) as a preliminary issue. It pointed out that Art.3(1) defines scope in very broad terms. It would follow that any processing of personal data other than that which is outside scope because it falls under the exceptions in Art.3(2) will be covered by the Directive. It went on to hold that the provisions were not necessarily in breach but the question depended on the justification for them. If the disclosures were not proportionate then the national legislation would be incompatible with both the Convention rights and the Directive. As Arts 6(1)(c) and (2)(c) and (e) apply unconditional obligations on Member States and are sufficiently precise to be applied by national courts they can be relied upon by the national courts to oust national rules which are not compatible with them.

The Court held that the information about the payments to named individuals relates to identified or identifiable natural persons and is therefore personal data. There is no reason to justify excluding activities of a professional nature from the scope of personal data.

While the retention of such data by the employer is not an infringement of Art.8 rights the communication of such data to third parties amounts to an interference, irrespective of whether the information would amount to sensitive personal data.

The provisions of the Directive must be interpreted in the light of Convention rights. Thus, where the Directive permits derogations from rights it provides, and actions carried out in reliance on those derogations would amount to an interference with the Art.8 right, the actions must have a legal basis and the interference must be justified and proportionate. This includes the requirement that the law must be sufficiently precise and foreseeable.

---

[20] para.23—this is the question as phrased on Case C 465/00; the questions as phrased by the other cases were essentially the same (para.30).

Legal commentators in Austria had deduced in the light of the relevant *travaux preparatoires* that the legislation required the disclosure of specific names and payments. It was for the national court to determine whether the provisions met the test of forseeability.

The objective of exerting pressure on public bodies to keep salaries within reasonable limits was a legitimate aim which would be capable of justifying interference with Art.8.

National authorities enjoy a margin of appreciation in determining the balance between the social needs and the interference with private life in issue. It is for the national courts to ascertain whether the interference is proportional and it could only be satisfied on this point if the wide disclosure of names and income is necessary for and appropriate to the aim of keeping salaries within reasonable limits.

Where the provisions of a directive are unconditional and sufficiently precise they may be relied upon directly by individuals and applied by national courts. The provisions of Art.6(1)(c) under which personal data must be adequate, relevant and not excessive in relation to the purposes of the processing; and Art.7(2)(c) and (e) which set out the grounds for processing applicable to the public sector, fall into that category and may therefore be relied upon before the national courts to oust the application of national rules which are contrary to those provisions.

Case C-101/01 Bodil Lindqvist v Aklagarkammaren i Jonkoping[21]

3–12 The first case on Directive 95/46 considered by the European Court of Justice involved a Swedish defendant who had been prosecuted for posting information about members of a church congregation on a website. It was referred to the ECJ from the Swedish Court of Appeal for a preliminary ruling under Art.234 on seven questions on the interpretation of the Directive. The two preliminary questions deal with the definition of personal data and the scope of the Directive. The preliminary questions were:

"(1) Is the mention of a person—by name or with name and telephone number—on an internet home page an action which falls within the scope of the Directive. Does it constitute the processing of personal data wholly or partly by automatic means to list on a self-made internet home page a number of persons with comments and statements about their jobs and hobbies etc . . .

(2) If the answer to the first question is no, can the act of setting up on an internet home page separate pages for about 15 people with links between the pages which make it possible to search by first name be considered to constitute the processing otherwise than by automatic means of personal data which form part of a relevant filing system."

The Court was quite clear in answering yes to the first question in the following terms:

"The term personal data used in Article 3(1) of Directive 95/46 covers, according to the definition in Article 2(a) thereof, any information relating to an identified

---

[21] [2003] E.C.R. I-1297.

or identifiable natural person. The term undoubtedly covers the name of a person in conjunction with his telephone coordinates or information about his working conditions or hobbies."

This response reinforces the widely accepted view that the term "personal data" is intended to have and indeed has a wide ambit. As the question was answered in the affirmative the Court did not go on to consider the second question. The further questions posed for the Court covered the following points:

(3) Could the act of loading the information to the web page be covered by any of the exceptions?[22]

(4) Was the information about a colleague who had injured her foot sensitive personal data?[23]

(5) Could the loading of the data on to a web page hosted in Sweden be a transfer of personal data?[24]

(6) In a case such as this does the restriction in the Directive conflict with the Art.10 Convention rights?

(7) Can a Member State provide a higher level of protection or extend the scope of the Directive on the issues canvassed here?

The Court answered as follows:

(3) No. The processing was neither outside the scope of Community law nor carried on only in the course of the private or family life of the individual.

(4) Yes. The information constituted information about health and was therefore sensitive personal data.

(5) No. Mrs Lindqvist's actions did not constitute a transfer of personal data. The transfer only took place when it was accessed from a third country.

(6) No. Nevertheless the national courts applying the Directive must ensure that restrictions are applied in a proportionate manner.

(7) No. The Directive is a harmonising measure and must be applied in that way, nevertheless the Directive allows Member States a margin for manoeuvre in certain areas. Further, nothing in the Directive prevents Member States from extending the scope of national legislation to areas not otherwise within scope.

The judgment is useful in a number of significant areas. However in the UK it appears not to have been followed in the important case of *Durant v FSA*, considered later in the chapter.

---

[22] See Ch.16, below for exemptions for private use.
[23] See Ch.7, below for sensitive data.
[24] The judgment of the Court on this point is considered further in Ch.8, below on overseas transfers.

Law of other Member States as an interpretative tool

3–13   There is a practical difficulty for data controllers and those advising them in even trying to be aware of decisions made by the courts in other Member States but it is a possibility that the law of other States may be directly relevant even without a ruling by the ECJ. This may occur in two circumstances:

(a)   Where a provision derives directly from a previous provision in the law of a Member State and was incorporated expressly to preserve it. Such decisions are of persuasive value only. In *Pioneer Electronics Capital Inc v Warner Music Manufacturing Europe GmbH*,[25] a section in the Patents Act 1977 had its origin in an article of the European Patent Convention which in turn was based on a provision in German law. The judge took into account of how a term derived from it had been applied by the German courts. This approach had some relevance in the interpretation of the term "relevant filing system" by the Court of Appeal in *Durant* when the German law provision which was a predecessor of the term in Directive 95/46 was considered. However such examples are likely to be extremely rare.

(b)   Where a court in a Member State rules on a provision common to the laws of the two states both of which derive from a requirement of the Directive. Such decisions will be of persuasive value only and care must be taken in applying them. In *Wagamama Ltd v City Centre Restaurants Plc*,[26] Laddie J. said:

> "In any event the obligation of the English court is to decide what the proper construction is . . . it would not be right for an English Court to follow the route adopted by the courts of another Member State if it is firmly of a different view simply because the other court expressed a view first. The scope of European legislation is too important to be decided on a first past the post basis."

There are a number of reported cases from other countries which may give guidance to the UK courts should similar issues ever arise here, although these do not appear to have been cited in or relied upon in judgments of the UK courts to date.

Case No. B 293–00, June 12, 2001, Swedish Supreme Court[27]

3–14   The Swedish Data Act 1973 was amended by the Protection of Data Act 1997 in order to implement Directive 95/46. The actions complained of—the posting by the defendant of material about individual employees and directors of banks on a website—took place before the law was amended. However, under Swedish law a defendant has the benefit of any change in the law between the time the act complained of is done and the trial. Accordingly the defendant was able to rely on the exemption for journalistic material in s.7 of the Protection of Data Act 1997 which implements Art.9 of the Directive. The court considered the provision in the light of both Art.9 of

---

[25] [1995] R.P.C. 487.
[26] [1995] F.S.R. 713.
[27] Reported in *Electronic Business Law* (October 2001).

the Directive and Arts 8 and 10 of the Human Rights Convention. It considered how far the term "journalism" extended, the importance of freedom of speech and the distinction between private and public life in relation to free speech. It held that the publication was covered by the journalistic exemption which was applied to the activity of generating comments by the publication of material, rather than merely to formal journalistic material.

Societe Nikon France Sa v M. Frederic,[28] Cour de Cassation Chambre Sociale

3–15   An employee of Nikon France had made personal use of the email system despite the employer's policy stating that this was not acceptable. The employer gained access to the private emails and used them as evidence that he had breached company policy. They dismissed M. Frederic for gross misconduct. M. Frederic actually took action against Nikon to contest a confidentiality agreement which applied to him after his employment but the Court also considered the interception. They held that there was a breach of his privacy in the interception of the emails even though the employer had a policy that they were only to be used for work-related purposes.

The ruling would be unlikely to have an effect in the United Kingdom because the issue of interception in the workplace has been covered in the Telecommunications (Lawful Business Practice)(Interception of Communications) Regulations 2000.[29]

CE Effia Servs & Syndicate Sud Rail v Effia Servs (Paris High Court, April 19, 2005 reported by Privacy and Data Protection)

3–16   The mandatory use of biometric identity cards to control access to a work site and monitor the activity of employees was unlawful under French data protection law as it was disproportionate to the business need.

3–17   The magazines have also reported a case in the Spanish High Court in which the Spanish Commissioner's practice of requiring additional safeguards to the standard for model transfer contracts to be provided to his authority before transfers would be permitted was successfully challenged which might be useful in other jurisdictions.

Other international instruments

Interpretative Relevance of the Council of Europe Convention for the Protection of Individuals with regard to Automatic Processing of Personal Data (Treaty 108)[30]

3–18   Conventions are binding on States which become signatory to them. Adherence to a convention may have different effect in different States' legal systems. In some cases the convention itself may be "self-executing" or "absorbed" into the national law. This is not the case in the United Kingdom. A convention will be of interpretative force and the UK courts will be bound to seek to interpret any national instrument passed in order to apply the Convention in conformity with it.[31]

---

[28] Publication date October 10, 2001. Reported on Butterworth Tolley.
[29] SI 2000/699.
[30] See Ch.1, above for contents of the Treaty.
[31] *Garland v British Railway Engineering Ltd* [1982] 2 All E.R. 405; *R. v Secretary of State for the Home Department Ex p. Brind* [1991] A.C. 696.

In the United Kingdom, Treaty 108 fulfilled this function on two occasions when the 1984 Act was under consideration. In *CCN Credit Systems Ltd v The Data Protection Registrar*,[32] decided in February 1991, the Data Protection Tribunal considered Treaty 108 in order to assist in elucidating the meaning of the term "unfairly" in Principle 1. The House of Lords in *R. v Brown*[33] sought assistance from it to decide on the difference between "processing" and "use". In both judgments the background of Treaty 108 and its roots in a concern for the right to private life were acknowledged.

The Treaty remains relevant as the United Kingdom is still a signatory, although it has been replaced in importance by the Directive. The Treaty has also been amended to require the same standards as the Directive.[34]

Recommendations

3–19 Following adoption of Treaty 108, the Council of Europe set up a Committee of Experts on Data Protection which has worked on a number of Recommendations to Member States on various aspects of data protection. Those Recommendations have been adopted by the Council. A list of the published Recommendations is at para.3–59 of this chapter. These are advisory only but may give useful policy background in particular areas.[35]

Interpretative Relevance of the OECD Guidelines[36]

3–20 In UK law, the Guidelines are the least influential of the various instruments covered in this chapter. However, in policy and political terms they may be of assistance in elucidating the intention of or approach to specific provisions. They can best be described as having advisory rather than persuasive effect. In data protection terms, the OECD has its main importance as a forum for discussion of data protection issues among the international community. This is derived from the presence of the United States and other non-European members who come together in regular working groups on privacy and data protection issues. The OECD also issues advisory papers, reports and expert materials. A list of recent OECD papers is included in the Additional Materials at the end of this chapter and can provide useful assistance.

Decisions of UK Courts and Tribunals

Previous decisions on the Data Protection Act 1984

3–21 There is relatively little case law under the 1984 Act. It only figured in one House of Lords case[37] and four High Court cases.[38] Even then it was regarded as a

---

[32] Reported in the *Encyclopaedia of Data Protection*, published by Sweet and Maxwell.
[33] [1996] All E.R. 545.
[34] See Ch.1, above.
[35] It should be noted that occasionally the courts have looked at the relevant Recommendations when deciding cases on difficult issues of policy. The ECtHR did this in *Z v Finland* (1997) 25 E.H.R.R. 371. In another use if soft law the High Court considered Recommendation 1/97 of the Article 29 Working Group on Data Protection and the Media in the case of *Naomi Campbell v Mirror Group Newspapers* [2002] EWCA Civ 1373.
[36] See Ch.1, above for an explanation of the role of the Guidelines.
[37] *R v Brown* [1996] All E.R. 545.
[38] Listed at the end of this chapter.

difficult statue. As Woolf L.J. (as he was then) opined in the case of *Rowley v Liverpool City Council*[39]:

> "Before the learned judge [counsel] also relied upon the provisions of the Data Protection Act 1984 and it is right to say straightaway that that Act is a complex enactment in which it is difficult to find your way about unless you are very familiar with it indeed."

Not all of those reached the law reports, although all are available in the *Encyclopaedia of Data Protection.*

In approaching interpretation where previous statutes cover the same ground a distinction is drawn between codifying and consolidating statutes. Consolidating statutes are more likely to be interpreted in line with previously decided questions on the same words. However, Bennion[40] states that the distinction between the two has a purposive base. It is prima facie presumed that a consolidating statute did not intend to change the law whereas there is no such presumption for a codifying statute. The issue is whether the new provision is intended to achieve the same end in the same way. The 1998 Act is not a consolidating statute and there is no presumption that the law was intended to remain the same as in the 1984 Act. In considering the relevance of decisions on the 1984 Act to the meaning of the 1998 Act, regard must be had to the provenance of the particular provision. The Data Protection Principles are largely unchanging in wording from the 1984 Act. In some cases, expanded interpretations have been provided, in particular by way of additional interpretative provisions and further Schedules adding to the coverage of Principle 1, but these may be regarded as extensions rather than changes to the meaning of the core terms "fair and lawful processing and obtaining". Given the common root of the 1984 Act and Directive 95/46 in Treaty 108 and the use of common terms throughout, and given that a number of the decisions on the Principles in the 1984 Act are expressed to be intended to respect and apply rights drawn from Treaty 108, it is reasonable to regard the case law on those provisions as having a continuing persuasive relevance. This appears to have been accepted by the Court in *Lord*[41] in which the Court was directed to the decision of the Data Protection Tribunal in the case of *Equifax v Data Protection Registrar*[42] when considering the application of one of the exemptions. The Court was considering provisions which were "materially indistinguishable" from those which had been considered in the *Equifax* case and took into account the ruling in the earlier case.

However, it must be recognised that there was no binding case law on the Principles under the 1984 Act. There were nine decisions on the Principles adjudicated by the Data Protection Tribunal whose decisions are, in any event, of persuasive force only. Decisions of the Tribunal under the 1984 Act were put forward by the applicant in *David Paul Johnson v The Medical Defence Union.*[43] The court appears to have accepted that they could be considered and cited with approval the view of the Tribunal in relation to fairness.

---

[39] *The Times*, October 26, 1987.
[40] Bennion, *Statutory Interpretation* (3rd ed., 1997), p.463.
[41] [2003] EWHC 2073 (Admin).
[42] Case DA/90 25/49/7 reported in the *Encyclopaedia of Data Protection.*
[43] [2006] EWHC 321, paras 116 to 123.

Decisions on the 1998 Act

3–22 There have been very few cases on data protection before the Information Tribunal. This contrasts with the large number brought under the Freedom of Information Act 2000. The Commissioner has brought action against a number of data controllers for sending unsolicited faxes contrary to the Telecommunications (Data Protection and Privacy) Regulations 2000 but appeals against the notices in these cases were settled and, although there has been an agreed order, gave rise to no judgments. In the case of *The Chief Constables of West Yorkshire and South Yorkshire and North Wales Police v The Information Commissioner*[44] the Tribunal declined to give any general guidance on the third and fifth principles. In the recent case of *The Scottish National Party v The Information Commissioner*[45] the Tribunal agreed with the Commissioner's view of the prohibition on marketing without consent.

In the courts the Directive or the 1998 Act has been considered or referred to in a number of cases which have given some guidance on different parts of the Act. The decisions which have had a bearing on the core definitions are the Court of Appeal judgment in the *Campbell* case and *Johnson*[46] on the definition of the term "processing" and *Durant* on the terms "personal data" and "relevant filing system". As we have seen in the previous chapter, when considering privacy cases the courts have tended to turn to the law of confidence and the Art.8 rights rather than data protection. This development has left data protection in a surprisingly undeveloped state considering that it has been on the statute books for nearly a decade.

In the case of *Norman Baker MP v The Secretary of State for the Home Department*[47] a national security certificate under s.28 drawn in very general terms was successfully challenged and the Secretary of State had to re-issue it in more limited terms. It does not offer any general guidance on the DPA.

Hansard references and Explanatory Notes as aids to interpretation

3–23 Although a Directive will be the governing instrument as far as results to be achieved are concerned, there may remain some leeway, within the transposition of a Directive, for national approaches. In some areas the Directive leaves the choice of how matters are handled to the discretion of Member States. Moreover, in other areas the national legislation may cover issues not dealt with by the Directive. Where there is ambiguity in such provisions, the doctrine in *Pepper v Hart* will allow recourse to be had to the *Hansard* record of parliamentary material in appropriate circumstances.

In *Pepper (Inspector of Taxes) v Hart*,[48] the Court held that parliamentary material could be looked at in limited circumstances. Where a statutory provision is ambiguous or obscure or where the literal meaning would be absurd, and it can be elucidated by reference to clear parliamentary material emanating from the Minister which sets out why that provision was enacted and the purpose it was meant to achieve: such

---

[44] 2005. Reported on the website of the Information Tribunal at *www.informationtribunal.gov.uk* [Accessed on 2 September 2007].
[45] 2006. Reported as above.
[46] [2007] 1 All E.R. 467.
[47] October 1, 2001 reported in Commissioner's *Annual Report* (July 2002) and *Data Protection and Privacy Practice*.
[48] [1993] A.C. 593.

material may be examined and taken into account in determining the proper meaning of the provisions.

The limits of *Hansard* material should be borne in mind. In resolving ambiguities the courts now look more frequently towards Brussels or Strasbourg than towards Westminster. It has already been noted that where a statutory provision arises from a requirement of a directive, the directive will be the governing instrument. Further, where a provision is derived from or affected by a Convention right, the court will look to the Strasbourg jurisprudence on that right rather than to the views of Parliament. This shift in emphasis was already underway before the Human Rights Act 1998 (HRA) came into force; see *R. v Broadcasting Complaints Commission Ex p. Barclay*[49] in which the court declined to give *Hansard* preference over matters deriving from the ECHR, and has been mandatory since October 2000 when the HRA came into effect.

Nevertheless *Hansard* material may be relevant in some cases. The range of material can be wide. In *Callery v Gray*[50] the Court of Appeal accepted that explanatory notes produced by the Department sponsoring the Act in question constitute "parliamentary material" for the purposes of *Pepper v Hart* and accordingly can be used to interpret an ambiguous provision. However, the courts have tended to limit the occasions when it can be used to cases falling strictly within the test in *Pepper v Hart*; that is where the ambiguity is in a statutory expression, not a statutory power, and where it is not possible to resolve the ambiguity by any other means.[51] In cases under the 1998 Act *Hansard* material was considered to resolve ambiguity in the definition of a relevant filing system in *Durant*.[52]

Since 1999 Explanatory Notes have been introduced to accompany Bills through their Parliamentary progress. Insofar as they cast light on the setting of a statute and the mischief at which it is aimed they are admissible in the construction of a statute.[53] The Act pre-dates the system but such Notes have been referred to in cases on legislation in the same area such as *Marper* case on the retention of DNA under the Criminal Justice and Police Act 2001.

Rules of statutory interpretation—general

3–24   As can be seen from this chapter, the topic of statutory interpretation is a large one. The emphasis placed on particular aspects of it in this chapter should not be taken to imply that the usual rules for approaching the meaning of statutes in English law do not apply; they will do so in appropriate cases. For example, the rules that exemptions will be construed narrowly,[54] or that ambiguities in criminal provisions must be resolved in favour of the defendant,[55] continue to apply. However, they

---

[49] [1997] Admin L.R. 256.
[50] *Callery v Gray* [2001] 1 W.L.R. 2112.
[51] See *R v Secretary of State for the Environment, Transport and the Regions Ex p. Spath Holme Ltd* [2001] 1 All E.R. 195; *R. v Mullen* [2000] Q.B. 520; *Stevenson v Rogers* [1999] Q.B. 1028.
[52] [2003] EWCA 1746.
[53] *R v Chief Constable of South Yorkshire Police Ex p. LS R v Chief Constable of South Yorkshire Police Ex p. Marper* [2004] UKHL 39, Lord Steyn, para.4.
[54] The principle "expression unius est exclusion alreius". According to *Bennion* "*Where an Act contains specific exceptions, it is presumed that these are the only exceptions of the kind intended*".
[55] According to *Bennion* the principle applies to any form of detriment although often referred to as though limited to criminal statutes. It was applied in *R. v Bristol Magistrates Court Ex p. E* [1998] 9 All E.R. 798

have to be applied in the context of an Act intended to give effect to a directive. While the hope must be that the rules applied by English law and the purposive approach of Community interpretation will lead to the same end, and indeed draw strength from one another, the possibility of the two approaches producing conflicting results must be acknowledged. Where there is a conflict resulting from the two approaches to statutory interpretation, the Community approach must be preferred and adopted by the court if possible; but if the conflict raises doubts as to the principle of community law to be applied, the court must consider a reference to the European Court for guidance.[56]

Guidance from the Information Commissioner

3–25   The Office of the Information Commissioner (ICO) is active in issuing guidance to the Act and its application in specific areas. The website lists the guidance material available in three categories: introductory; practical application; and detailed specialist guides. The Office has shifted focus in the last few years to issue more practical materials. As a result there are about 80 guidance documents listed under the data protection section of the website; some are very brief, practical and specific and others longer or more general. The Legal Guidance, "Data Protection Act 1998—Legal Guidance" was issued in October 2001 to coincide with the ending of the first transitional period and remains the core guidance material. It must however be treated with some caution, as the Commissioner states in the introduction to the current text on the website,

> "It is my intention to continue to develop this guidance, increasing its detail and authority as my Office gains practical experience of applying the Act. It is important that data controllers should be aware that my advice may develop in certain areas in the light, for example, of decisions taken on particular cases or other relevant case law. As such changes become necessary we shall amend the web version. Those familiar with the introductory guidance will notice some area where the thinking of my Office has already evolved, such as the definitions of personal data and data controller and the practical application of the conditions for processing in Schedules 1 and 2."

Unfortunately the date of the latest revision is not shown on the web version which simply shows "Version as print date" nor is it possible to chart what has altered and when. In this text we only refer to the general legal guidance on the Act, and a few of the specific guidance documents, such as overseas transfers. However for those advising on the Act it is always worth reviewing the website to check for additional specific materials. It is always useful to consider the view taken by the OIC on any topic, however, there are two points should be borne in mind:

- The Commissioner will always reserve the right to amend or develop guidance. Where an area of particular volatility or uncertainty is in question

---

at 804 per Simon Brown L.J. "It's a principle of legal policy that a person shall not be penalized except under clear law".

[56] *Rosgill Group Ltd v Customs and Excise Commissioners* [1997] 3 All E.R. 1012.

therefore it is generally worth checking the most recent advice on the website or speaking to the office.

- The guidance is not authoritative. The Commissioner habitually prefaces publications with the statement that definitive guidance can only be provided by the courts. In none of the decisions in cases before the courts since implementation does the Commissioner's guidance appear to have been referred to.

It should also be noted that the Commissioner, quite properly, is keen to advocate good practice, which may go beyond the strict requirements of the law and that, where there is any possible ambiguity, the interpretation favoured by the Commissioner is generally the one which takes a broader view of the boundaries of the Act, the protection of privacy and the impact of Art.8. However, as noted above, this may not be the only legitimate approach as other Convention rights may be relevant, and in some cases in this chapter a slightly different approach to the one taken by the Commissioner is suggested.

Article 29 Working Party

3–26   The Article 29 Working Party ("WP") produces a significant amount of material which provides useful background, however the WP generally tends to a stricter application of the Directive than has found favor in the UK courts. Article 29 documents tend to be advisory at the most.

Codes of Practice

3–27   The Act and Directive provide for the preparation and adoption of Codes of Practice, under s.51 and Art.27. These have no formal interpretive status but are likely to be persuasive.

DEFINITIONS

Introduction

3–28   The Consultation Paper issued by the Home Office in March 1996 on the implementation of the Directive raised the question as to how the definitions should be tackled. In the summary of responses, published in March 1997, it was reported that a majority of respondents had made clear their preference for precise definitions. There were, however, two views on how those should be approached. Many had suggested that the new legislation should resemble the 1984 Act as far as possible, because users were familiar with that pattern. Others, however, advocated taking definitions from the Directive to ensure that there was no possibility of conflict between the national law and the Directive.

In the 1998 Act an attempt appears to have been made to please both parties. The definitions are a hybrid owing much to both the 1984 Act and to the Directive. This creates some strains, as it is not always apparent how the definitions map on to the Directive. Where there is ambiguity this is pointed out and where possible an interpretation which resolves the strain is suggested. In view of the importance of the core definitions in some cases, the provisions of the Directive are reproduced in the body of the text to compare and assist in elucidating the position.

There is a difference in approach between the Act and the Directive. The Directive sets out a list of definitions then describes the scope of the Directive (in Art.3(1)). In the Act, the two are rather more entwined. "Relevant filing system" feeds into "data" which feeds into "personal data" which feeds into "data controller". The data controller carries the core obligations set out at s.4(4). Aspects of scope are, therefore, dealt with by definitions. An example of this is the way the concept of data being "processed wholly or partly by automatic means" has been dealt with by inclusion in the definition of data. The use of this technique makes it more difficult than it might otherwise have been to map the Act on to the Directive and be content that the two are mutually coherent.

In considering definitions, one must distinguish between questions of fact and law. Many of the questions which practitioners will be faced concerning the definitions will be questions of fact. This chapter seeks to provide an explanation of the meaning of the main defined terms as a matter of law.

As noted above, even where definitions owe something to the 1984 Act, the primary reference point for their interpretation is the Directive. It must not be assumed they are transposable from the 1984 Act, although there are some similarities. Regrettably, there are also some outstanding ambiguities, and one of the Directive's core terms, "consent", is not defined in the Act.

This chapter does not cover all the defined terms. Section 71 of the Act lists a table of defined terms and the relevant section of the Act in which they are defined or explained. This chapter covers the basic interpretative provisions which are set out in s.1 of the Act. In addition, it deals with three terms which are not included in s.1 but which were included in the key interpretative provisions in Art.2 of the Directive. They are "third party", "recipient" and "consent". The territorial application of the Act is also dealt with.

Note: The definitions in this chapter do not follow the alphabetical order in s.1 of the Act.

Personal data

3–29   This definition derives from Art.2a of the Directive. Article 2a reads:

> "Personal data shall mean any information relating to an identified or identifiable natural person (data subject); an identifiable person is one who can be identified, directly or indirectly, in particular by reference to an identification number or to one or more factors specific to his physical, physiological, mental, economic, cultural or social identity."

The definition in the Directive gives considerable weight to the concept of an "identifiable person". This is reinforced in Recitals to the Directive. Recital 26 reads:

> "Whereas the principles of protection must apply to any information concerning an identified or identifiable person. To determine whether a person is identifiable account should be taken of all the means likely reasonably to be used either by the controller or by any other person to identify such person; . . . whereas the principles of protection shall not apply to data rendered anonymous . . ."

This core definition from the Directive has been rendered in s.1(1) as:

"Personal data means data which relate to a living individual who can be identified

(a) from those data; or

(b) from those data and other information which is in the possession of or is likely to come into the possession of the data controller,

and includes any expression or opinion about the individual and any indication of the intentions of the data controller or any other person in respect of the individual."

The term has been considered by the European Court of Justice in *Lindqvist*[57] and by the UK Court of Appeal in the case of *Michael John Durant v Financial Services Authority*[58] and Lord[59] The decision in *Durant* has been followed in the further case of *Johnson v Medical Defence Union*.[60] Before the judgments in *Durant* and *Johnson* it was generally accepted that the concept of data "relating" to an individual embraced a wide range of data. Post *Durant* the position in the UK is uncertain. It remains the case that the question of whether or not particular data relate to a particular individual will be a question of fact, dependent largely on an assessment of the proximity of the data and the relevance of the data to him. It is possible however that the information must be more proximate than was previously thought as *Durant* has given rise to a new test. This poses significant problems for data controllers who are uncertain as to where to draw the line, particularly when dealing with subject access requests.

Following the decision of the Court of Appeal in *Durant* the Information Commissioner issued guidance on the application of the judgment. Both the decision and the subsequent guidance have been the subject of criticism from a number of sources, most importantly the European Commission, as being incompatible with the Directive. In view of the significance of the judgment it is covered in some depth.

Michael John Durant v Financial Services Authority[61]

3–30   Mr Durant had made a subject access request to the Financial Services Authority (the "FSA") under s.7 of the Act. The FSA held information on Mr Durant because it had investigated a complaint which Mr Durant had made against Barclay's Bank. The Court considered whether the information sought was personal data within the meaning of the Act. The information which Mr Durant wanted was held in four types of files and covered:

- documents relating to part of the complaint about the systems and controls which Barclay's bank was obliged to maintain;

---

[57] para.3–12, above, Case C-101/01.
[58] [2003] EWCA Civ 1746.
[59] [2003] EWHC 2073.
[60] [2004] EWHC 347.
[61] [2003] EWCA Civ 1746.

- documents relating to his complaint held on a file containing complaints received from customers on Barclay's bank. These were behind a divider marked with his name;

- documents relating to his complaint on a file relating to issues or cases concerning Barclay's Bank;

- a sheaf of papers held by the Company Secretariat of the FSA relating to Mr Durant's complaint about the FSA's refusal to disclose information about its investigation of his complaint about Barclay's Bank.

"The FSA has acknowledged in correspondence that each of the files in question contains information in which Mr Durant features, that some of them identify him by reference to specific dividers in the file and that they contain documents such as: copies of telephone attendance notes, a report of forensic examination of documents, transcripts of judgments, hand-written notes, internal memoranda, correspondence with Barclay's Bank, correspondence with other individuals and correspondence between the FSA and him."

Delivering judgment Auld L.J. held that none of the information was personal data which related to Mr Durant, rather it was information about his complaint and the objects of them, the Bank and the FSA. Auld L.J. acknowledged this to be a narrow interpretation of the term personal data.[62] He stated that he drew support for the interpretation from the way it is applied in s.7, that there is an entitlement to personal data "of which . . ..[he]is the data subject". However s.7 offers no support as the point is circular; a data subject is simply someone who is the subject of personal data. More tellingly he relied upon the express inclusion in the definition of personal data of expressions of opinion or intention, pointing out that, if the term had been intended as a broader one such provision would have been otiose.[63]

The alternative view is that the words were indeed mere surplusage, having been included because expressions of intention were excluded explicitly from the 1984 Act definitions.

Auld L.J.'s reasoning and explanation were the basis of the subsequent guidance from the Commissioner and therefore we set them out in full:

"It follows from what I have said that not all information retrieved from a computer search against an individual's name or unique identifier is personal data within the Act. Mere mention of the data subject in a document held by a data controller does not necessarily amount to his personal data. Whether it does so in any particular instance depends on where it falls in a continuum of relevance or proximity to the data subject as distinct, say, from transactions or matters which he may have been involved in to a greater or lesser degree. It seems to me that there are two notions which may be of assistance. The first is whether the information is biographical in any significant sense, that is, going beyond the recording of the putative data subject's involvement in a matter or an event which

---

[62] para.29.
[63] para.29.

has no personal connotations, a life event in respect of which his privacy cannot be said the be compromised. The second is one of focus. The information should have the putative data subject as its focus rather than some other person with whom he may have been involved or some transaction or event in which he may have figured or had an interest, for example, as in this case, an investigation into some other person's or body's conduct that he may have instigated. In short it is information that affects his privacy, whether in his personal or family life, business or professional capacity."[64]

The approach of the Court of Appeal can be criticised for failing to take account of the scope of the provision in the Directive on which the definition in the UK Act is based despite the fact that in the judgment the Court expressly acknowledges that it is bound to interpret the law in accord with the Directive[65] and states that is applying *Lindqvist*.[66]

3–31 The Information Commissioner issued guidance following the judgment which was re-issued in February 2006. The preface states that it is intended to be replaced with more general guidance taking account of work of the Article 29 Working Party. The more general guidance has not been forthcoming to date but practitioners will wish to take it into consideration in due course. In the guidance the Commissioner explains that the test of relationship depends on whether the information affects the privacy and states that:

"This [the terms of the judgment] suggests to the Commissioner that in cases where it is not clear whether information relates to an individual you should take into account whether or not the information in question is capable of having an adverse impact on the individual."

It goes on to describe the "notions" referred to in the Court of Appeal and the issue of whether a name amounts to personal data:

"Where an individual's name appears in information the name will only be personal data where its inclusion in the information affects the individual's privacy."

"It is more likely that an individual's name will be personal data where the name appears together with other information about the named individual such as address, telephone number or information regarding his hobbies." (footnotes omitted)

It confirms the Commissioner's view that marketing lists which include contact details such as email addresses will be personal data. Although it follows Auld L.J.'s approach that information such as a house survey will not be personal data where the individual is not the focus of the data it points out that there are cases where such information is directly linked to the individual and therefore will be personal data and gives the example of a car photographed by a speed camera where the details are used to direct a notice of intention to prosecute to the registered keeper of the vehicle.

---

[64] para.28.
[65] para.3.
[66] para.28.

The current position in respect of personal data is, therefore, confusing for both data controllers and data subjects. The "tests" suggested by the Court in *Durant* are difficult to apply in practice.

The application of the ruling in Durant

3–32 The ruling by the Court of Appeal on the scope of the term personal data has caused a number of problems for data controllers because it is difficult to apply. Most of the information which data controllers hold about other individuals is concerned with the minutae of day-to-day transactions. Moreover it tends to be mingled with other information, in emails, letters, references in reports and so on. Deciding whether such information should be regarded as "biographically significant" on each occasion can be both difficult and time-consuming. There is the additional problem for public sector data controllers that if a narrow view of personal data is taken then more information about individuals will often have to be disclosed under the Freedom of Information Act as, unless another exemption applies, it can only be withheld if it falls within the definition of personal data. They are also difficult to square with *Lindqvist* and the Directive. There does not however appear to be any foreseeable resolution to the uncertainty of the current position. We would suggest that data controllers take the wider view of the term personal data applying the Directive as explained in *Lindqvist*.

In the case of *Lord*[67] the judge appears to have accepted that, even though taken individually items of information would not amount to personal data within the definition as expounded in *Durant,* in the particular case the sum total of the information was such that it amounted to personal data and should be provided to the applicant.

In the case of *Terence William Smith v Lloyds TSB*[68] the applicant who wished to obtain sight of information about himself argued that documents which had been produced by computer fall within the definition of personal data even when no longer held in that manner. In that case it was not disputed that a number of records were held on manual files which would not fall within the definition of a relevant filing system but it was argued that a document which had *at any time* been recorded in electronic form, for example by being produced on a computer, should be treated as a electronic records even though it was no longer held as such. The Court rejected this contention.

Infringement proceedings

3–33 Since the judgment the European Commission has raised questions with the UK government as to whether the UK law now meets the definition in the Directive. It is understood that the position of the UK is that the judgment can be read in such a way as to accord with the Directive. However these submissions do not deal with the fact that the judgment has been followed in the case of *Paul Johnson v Medical Defence Union*.[69]

Infringement proceedings may be brought by the European Commission under Art.226 if the Member State does not fulfil its obligations within a period laid

---

[67] See Ch.11 on subject access.
[68] [2005] EWHC 246 (Ch).
[69] [2004] EWHC 347.

down by the Commission. Before commencing such proceedings before the ECJ the Commission must deliver a reasoned opinion to the State in question and give it an opportunity to submit its observations. It has not proved possible to obtain copies of the correspondence with the Commission however there does not appear to be any possibility of imminent action against the UK.

Data relating to more than one person

3–34   Data can of course relate to more than one person; data on a joint bank account for example, will relate to two persons. There is no necessary exclusivity about data. Personal data are not limited to private or family data nor is there any particular way in which the data must relate to an individual. It might be in any aspect of their lives, whether their business lives, professional lives or private lives. If an individual is a sole trader then information about his business is likely to relate to him. If he is a partner then partnership data might relate to him, although this may depend upon the size and complexity of the partnership. The requirement that data relate to the individual is no different from the definition in the 1984 Act. There is, however, a difficult issue as between the 1998 Act and the Directive over the concept of identification.

3–35   Both the Act and the Directive appear to cover what are broadly two concepts. The first is the concept of being identifiable; the second is of being identified. An identifiable person appears to be one whose separate identity is ascertainable but who is not necessarily known in person. He or she may be traceable by virtue of the list of factors set out in Art.2A, that is by identification number or factors specific to the person's physical, physiological or other aspects of his identity. An identified person appears to be one who is known in the physical world. It is suggested that someone is *identifiable* where there is sufficient information available to distinguish the separate fact of his existence, his being as a unique person, and then becomes *identified* where there is sufficient information either to contact him or to recognise him by picking him out in some way from others. In everyday terms, the latter is usually achieved by knowing a name and address. In the context of the Directive, information about both identifiable and identified persons is personal data. Whether someone is identifiable will be a matter for assessment and the Recital is of assistance in explaining how identifiability is to be assessed. Someone is identifiable if their identity can be ascertained from the information held plus the results of reasonable inquiries, whether made by the controller or another.

For example, if an individual's sex, height and fingerprints are held by a store detective on a file, the question of whether that person can be identified may depend upon whether police records show those fingerprints and other identifiable particulars, including possibly a name, address and description. The question of whether the data in the hands of the store detective are personal data does not depend on the knowledge of the store detective or of the likelihood of disclosure by the police. In the Directive, the question of identification is left at large. In the UK Act, however, it has been tied either to the data itself or to the knowledge or likely knowledge of the data controller. It is not at all clear why this limitation on the Directive has been adopted.

3–36   Unfortunately the OIC Legal Guidance is somewhat confusing on the question of identification. It is difficult to discern whether the OIC is applying an interpretation consistent with the Directive or one restricted to the narrower approach taken by the UK Act. In the Legal Guidance it is accepted that an individual may be "identified" without the data controller necessarily knowing the name and address of the individual, an approach which accords with the Directive, however, it goes on to state:

> "The Commissioner's view is that it is sufficient if the data are capable of being processed by the data controller to enable the data controller to distinguish the data subject from any other individual. This would be the case if a data subject could be treated differently from other individuals."[70]

This appears to be conflating two different issues: the ability to distinguish an individual uniquely and the ability to affect an individual. For the reasons set out above it is suggested that, if it is possible to identify a unique individual from the data, there is no further requirement that the data controller should be able to affect the individual. It could be argued that the consideration of whether an individual can be affected by processing is the application of a purposive approach, however, it is suggested that is not necessary. The Directive is quite clear on the issue of identifiability (see the reference to the definition and Recital above); any ambiguity in the UK Act can be resolved by applying the definition in the Directive. The purported application of a purposive approach in this context appears to be an attempt to widen the scope of the Directive; becoming what has been referred to as "divination" rather than "interpretation".[71]

The guidance then confuses the position further by giving examples of data which may be personal data. In relation to CCTV images it states:

> "The capture of an image of an individual by a CCTV camera may be done in such a way that distinguishable features of that individual are processed and identified from the captured images. However, in order to be able to identify that individual it will be necessary to match the image to a photograph, a physical description or a physical person. If this can be done the CCTV footage will be personal data."

However, if the captured image is sufficient to show a unique human being then it will be personal data in that it is identifiable in terms of the Directive definition as long as it can be matched with other information, irrespective of whether it is so matched.

In the second example, however, the Guidance appears to suggest that data may be personal data even where the controller cannot be sure that they relate to a unique individual. The example concerns the position of internet companies who can trace the computer used but not necessarily the unique user, which may have:

> ". . . Information about a particular web-user, but there might not be any intention of linking it to a name and address or e-mail address. There might merely be an intention to target that particular user with advertising, ...The Commissioner takes the view that such information is nevertheless personal data. In the context of the on-line world the information that identifies an individual is that which uniquely locates him in that world, by distinguishing him from others."

This addresses the ability of those who deliver advertising on web pages to modify the advertising shown in the advertising boxes showing particular products on web

---

[70] Legal guidance, p.11.
[71] *Levi Strauss v Tesco* [2002] 2 W.L.R. 321.

pages for different computers. The technique is not dissimilar to sending specific offers by terrestrial mail to specific postcodes. It is not "targeted" in the sense of aiming at known individuals. The problem here is that, in the absence of user-specific information, there can be no certainty that information generated by web use relates to one individual. It may relate to a particular computer but, whereas it can be said with certainty that the footage on the CCTV film relates to one person, it is often not possible to say that with certainty about computer use. The issue is a simple one; while several people can share a computer they cannot share a face.

Processing

3–37   As with the term personal data, the definition of "processing" was not directly transposed from the Directive although again the reasoning behind the decision here is obscure. The definition in the Directive in Art.2 starts with a broad inclusive definition of processing:

> "Processing of personal data shall mean any operation or set of operations which is performed upon personal data, whether or not by automatic means, such as collection, recording, organisation, storage, adaptation or alteration, retrieval, consultation, use, disclosure by transmission, dissemination or otherwise making available, alignment or combination, blocking, erasure or destruction."

However, in the Act the definition specifies three particular processing operations and separates them from the concept of carrying out operations.

In s.1(1) the definition reads:

> "'Processing', in relation to information or data, means obtaining, recording or holding the information or data or carrying out any operation or set of operations on the information or data, including:
>
> (a) retrieval, consultation or use of the information or data;
> (b) disclosure of the information or data by transmission dissemination or otherwise making available; or
> (c) alignment, combination, blocking, erasure or destruction of the information or data."

The definition is extremely wide. All manipulation of data is covered by the definition. In particular capturing of information and dissemination or disclosure of information are included in processing. There are further changes between the wording of the Directive and the UK Act. "Collection" has been changed to "obtaining" and "storage" has been changed to "holding". Throughout the definition in the national legislation "processing" is applied both to data and to information contained in the data. This is explicit in the definition of processing and there is a separate provision in s.1(2) in relation to obtaining, recording, using and disclosing which provide that any of those actions include the same action in relation to the information contained in the data.

3–38   In the 1984 Act only personal data "processed by reference to" the individual was caught by the Act. This restricted the scope of the personal data covered by the 1984 Act. However, the term was widely construed under the 1984 Act and the extension of the definition has not had as radical an effect as it might otherwise have done.[72] In the case of *Campbell v MGN*[73] the Court of Appeal held that the publication of material in hard copy, where it had previously been automatically processed, was processing which fell within the Act. Per Lord Worth of Maltravers M.R.:

> "101 The definition of 'processing' in the Directive and the Act alike is very wide.
> 103. The Directive and the Act define processing as 'any operation or set of operations'. At one end of the process 'obtaining the information' is included, and at the other end 'using the information'. While neither activity in itself may sensibly amount to processing, if that activity is carried on by, or at the instigation of, a 'data controller', as defined, and is linked to automatic processing of the data, we can see no reason why the entire set of operations should not fall within the scope of the legislation. On the contrary we consider there are good reasons why it should."

3–39   In *Johnson*[74] the Court of Appeal overruled a finding at first instance that the selection of material from both computerised files and various manual and microfiche files, which it was accepted were not themselves covered by the Act, and their inputting into a computer amounted to processing within the Act. The was however a strong dissenting judgment from Lady Justice Arden.

The main judgment was given by Buxton L.J. The facts were that Mr Johnson had been a member of the Medical Defence Union (MDU) until his membership was terminated. He brought an action against the MDU on the basis that the MDU had unfairly processed personal data relating to him in making the decisions to terminate his membership. The MDU had a system in which they retained records on every complaint or reference about a member. They assessed the risk of a member having a claim against them by reference to the number of records. Where a member was a high risk they might terminate the membership. The records held by the MDU consisted of three files held on computer, 14 hard copy files (not falling within the definition of a relevant filing system) and a summary of each file held on computer. The activity which Mr Johnson asserted amounted to unfair processing was the extraction of the information, the completion of summaries of each record, the addition of observations, and the allocation of scores by an assessor. The process was not automated and there was no automatic decision-taking involved. The information was evaluated by the assessor addressing her mind to the materials. She then captured her assessment on another data set on the computer and it was transmitted to the decision-making committee in electronic form. The Court of Appeal was asked:

1. Whether this involved the processing of personal data within the Act?

2. If so was there any unfairness in the processing?

3. If the processing was unfair was the unfairness responsible for the MDU's decision?

4. If the processing was unfair and that unfairness affected the MDU's decision what, if any compensation, would Mr Johnson be entitled to?

---

[72] See guidelines on the 1984 Act published by the Data Protection registrar, p.19 (November 1994).
[73] [2003] Q.B. 633.
[74] [2007] 1All E.R. 464.

At the first instance the judge had decided that there was processing and some unfairness, in that Mr Johnson had not received a fair processing notice in respect of some of the data held. On the question of whether there was processing within the definition the Court of Appeal had to decide whether the selection, analysis and decision as to what went into the final summary fell into the definition. The Court considered the definition of processing both in the Act and the Directive, together with the relevant recitals and the *Lindqvist* case. The appellant had pointed in particular to the provision in Art.2b of the Directive, that the Directive covers the processing of personal data "whether or not by automatic means" and argued that the Court should have regard to the entire operation which resulted in the decision impacting on the appellant. The appellant also relied upon *Campbell* as authority for the proposition that the term could, and properly did, cover the product of processing as well as the automated sequence. Buxton L.J. decided that the activities did not amount to processing. He distinguished the decision in *Campbell*,[75] expressed concern at the possible reach of the Data Protection Act if the wider view was taken[76] and decided that the relevant activities were conducted wholly by the human agent and involved no processing at all which involved automatic means. On this point Longmore L.J. agreed with him but Lady Justice Arden took the contrary view arguing that manual selection and presenting into automated form was covered as processing includes collection and obtaining of information and rendering it into automated data.[77] She drew attention to the Strasbourg jurisprudence to the effect that the creation and maintenance of a record engages the Art.8 right[78] and cited in support the decision in *Campbell*.

Buxton L.J. approached the case with a focus on the privacy of the data subject and commented that this case did not involve Mr Johnson's privacy, rather how he had been treated by the MDU. He went on to consider the remaining questions answering them with the robust response of No, No and "Not as much as the judge at first instance would considered appropriate". These other aspects of the judgment are considered in the relevant chapters. Of particular interest are the discussions on compensation and Lady Justice Arden's consideration of the relationship between fairness and contractual obligations.

Comment

3–40   It seems unlikely that this decision will make a difference to the position of many data controllers. The MDU system was an unusual one with an individual taking a central role in the process rather than it being automated. The case does illustrate the slant that is being given to the Act by the focus on its relation with Art.8. In the US equivalent legislation is often referred to as Fair Information Practices legislation and that captures the fact that the regulatory aim of the regime covers more than privacy alone. The appellant in this case complained that he lost his cover because the way in which the respondent dealt with the information relating to him was unfair. However he was denied the opportunity to actually make that argument because he had to first bring himself within the technical definitions which he failed to do.

---

[75] paras 38–43.
[76] paras 44–48.
[77] See in particular para.128.
[78] para.97, *Amman v Switzerland* No.27798/95. See Ch.2, above for a discussion of the relevant case law.

Data

3–41   A definition of data does not appear in the Directive. The inclusion of it in the 1998 Act appears to derive partly from the 1984 Act and partly as a method of setting out the scope of the Act. The Directive applies to "the processing of personal data wholly or partly by automatic means . . .".

This is not reproduced in terms in the Act but a definition of data is inserted. The definition has five limbs. The fifth limb was added by the Freedom of Information Act 2000 which came into force in January 2000. The additional category covered is all recorded information held by a public authority.[79] Such data are however only subject to limited aspects of the Act. The definition covers information held in any of five different forms:

> "(a) [which is] being processed by means of equipment operating automatically in response to instructions given for that purpose."

This definition is very similar to the one in the 1984 Act. The extent of automatic processing[80] means it will apply to all forms of computerised data. The definition is not technology specific and the use of any form of equipment will be covered:

> "(b) [which is] recorded with the intention that it should be processed by means of such equipment."

The record need not be an automated record. The information could be manually recorded as long as it is intended it should be automatically processed. It appears the intention to so process must exist at the time of the recording. It does not appear that the person who recorded it must also process it. It would, therefore, be possible for one person to record information as long as there was a present intention that it should be processed subsequently by automatic means. The record could be manual data even though it does not fall into the definition of a "relevant filing system". This provision could possibly catch written documents intended for document image processing:

> "(c) [which is] recorded as part of a relevant filing system or with the intention that it should form part of a relevant filing system."

The term "relevant filing system" is a core definition incorporating the manual data provisions. Again, this appears to apply only where an intention to add information to a relevant filing system is present at the time of recording. This interpretation would have the odd effect that unless information is recorded as part of a relevant filing system or with such an intention at the time of the recording, it will not be data within the terms of the definition. On this basis, it could be suggested that if information is first recorded wholly outside the system with no intention of it becoming part of a relevant filing system, for example on a separate sheet, but is later incorporated into a relevant filing system, such information would not be covered by the definition of data.

---

[79] See Ch.4, below for the changes brought by the Freedom of Information Act.
[80] See the definition of processing, above.

This view appears to have been espoused by the Minister speaking in Committee in the Commons on May 12, 1998 but it is suggested that it is not the correct approach. It does not appear to be compliant with Art.3 of the Directive which reads:

> "(1) This Directive shall apply to the processing of personal data wholly or partly by automatic means and to the processing otherwise than by automatic means of personal data which form part of a filing system or are intended to form part of a filing system."

From that, it appears that it is intended by the Directive that data should be covered as long as it forms part of a relevant filing system irrespective of how it was first acquired. One must therefore construe it so as to comply with the Directive, despite the fact that this places some strain upon the words[81]:

> "(d) [which] does not fall within paragraph (a) (b) or (c) but forms part of an accessible record as defined by Section 68."

This part of the definition covers manual information on personal files held for specific functions. Such information was not immediately subject to all the rigours of the Act. (e) recorded information held by a public authority which does not fall into any of the categories (a) to (d). This is further sub-divided into structured and unstructured files. It only applies however to public authorities under the Freedom of Information Act.

Relevant filing system

3–42   This term was considered by the Court of Appeal in *Durant*[82]:

> " 'Relevant filing system' means any set of information relating to individuals to the extent that, although the information is not processed by means of equipment operating automatically in response to instructions given for that purpose, the set is structured either by reference to individuals or by reference to criteria relating to individuals, in such a way that specific information relating to a particular individual is readily accessible."

In the Directive, personal data filing system (filing system) means:

> "Any structured set of personal data which are accessible according to specific criteria, whether centralised, de-centralised or dispersed on a functional or geographical basis."

Such files are not subject to the requirement that they must be processed automatically. Again, the definition adopted in the national legislation is not the same as that in the Directive. In particular, the words "Whether centralised, de-centralised or dispersed on a functional or geographical basis" have been omitted and attempts to have them reinserted during the passage of the Bill failed.

---

[81] See discussion of this approach in para.3–02, above.
[82] [2003] EWCA Civ 1746.

Since this appears to have been an avoidance of doubt provision in the Directive, it may not be a core omission. However, the words should be borne in mind where any question arises on the application of the Act to dispersed data sets.

There must be a set of information relating to individuals. The use of the term set suggests some degree of coherence in content rather than random groupings of information but could be of any size. In the Interpretation Act 1889, the singular includes the plural and vice versa unless the contrary appears from the legislation. There is nothing to suggest other than the usual rule, so it could cover a set of information about *one person*.

Further the set must be structured, by one of two possible methods, so as to produce a particular result. That result is that specific information relating to a particular individual is readily accessible. This potentially covers a broad scope and it was this ambiguity which gave rise to the arguments canvassed in *Durant*. The concept of reference to individuals, or criteria relating to them, could be given either a broad or a narrow meaning. The relevant parts of the Directive are Art.2(c) and Recital 27:

> "2(c) personal data filing system ('filing system') shall mean any structured set of personal data which are accessible according to specific criteria, whether centralised, decentralised or dispersed on a functional basis."

are no less ambiguous than the UK provision, although considerably (and one might say commendably) briefer. However, further assistance is to be found in the Preamble. Recital 27 reads, inter alia:

> "Whereas . . . nonetheless, as regards manual processing, this Directive covers only filing systems, not unstructured files, whereas in particular, the content of a filing system must be structured according to specific criteria relating to individuals allowing easy access to personal data; whereas in line with the definition in Article 2c the different criteria for determining the constituents of a structured set of personal data, and the different criteria governing access to such a set, may be laid down by each Member State; whereas files or sets of files as well as their cover pages, which are not structured according to specific criteria, shall under no circumstances fall within the scope of this Directive."

The preamble can be viewed as containing four separate aspects of guidance, each starting with "whereas". The first makes it clear that it is not intended to cover all manual records. "Unstructured" files are excluded, so we are looking for an approach that achieves the aim of exclusion of some manual records. The second "whereas" reinforces the approach that the structure mechanism is intended to be a clear set of criteria, so a date may not be acceptable. The third "whereas" makes clear the state has a discretion in this area to set out two criteria, for organisation and for access; the fourth "whereas" reinforces the message that only some manual files are intended to be covered.

3–43 Further assistance, persuasive only, might be found by looking at the provenance of this aspect of the Directive. It comes from the German Federal Data Protection Act under which some manual files are covered, for example structured sets of data such as card indexes, forms and questionnaires or sortable microfiche.

In the Bundesdatenschutzgesetz (BDSG) Federal Data Protection Act 1993, "Data file" means:

"(a) set of personal data which can be evaluated according to specific character-istics by means of automated procedures (automated data file); or

(b) any other set of personal data which is similarly structured and can be arranged, rearranged and evaluated according to specific characteristics (non-automated data file).

This shall not include records and sets of records, unless they can be rearranged and evaluated by means of automated procedures.

File means any other document serving official purposes; this shall include image and sound recording media. It shall not include drafts and notes that are not intended to form part of a record."

In the Hessian Data Protection Act (1986), "Data file" means:

"(a) any set of data of which use can be made by means of automated procedures (automated file); or

(b) any similarly structured set of data which can be organised and used accord-ing to specific criteria (non-automated file)."

Record means any document serving an official purpose.

As there is a degree of leeway open to the Member State on this issue and there is an ambiguity in the definition it may be relevant to consider the parliamentary debates and here the issue of the coverage of manual data was canvassed.

Speaking in the debate on the Third Reading in the House of Lords in February 1998, Lord Williams made clear that it was the Government's intention that the defin-ition should be restricted so it covered only highly structured records such as files indexed by sections. The Government introduced an amendment at Report Stage in the House of Lords on March 16, 1998 which altered "particular information" to "specific information" to seek to ensure that the term only covered highly structured files:

". . . The intention of the wording is that it should only catch manual records where the internal content of the record is structured, rather than catching any file simply because it has the name of an individual on the cover. The restrictive meaning would appear to be consistent with the Directive, it is important to realise that it does not have any bearing on the *purpose* of files but simply to their internal organisation."

3–44   In *Durant*[83] the Court of Appeal considered the four files to which the appli-cant sought access:

- Documents relating to part of the complaint about the systems and controls which Barclay's Bank was obliged to maintain which was **arranged in date order.**

- Documents relating to his complaint held on a file containing complaints received from customers on Barclay's Bank. These were behind a divider marked with his name **but the papers were not internally structured.**

---

[83] [2003] EWCA Civ 1746.

- Documents relating to his complaint on a file relating to issues or cases concerning Barclay's Bank. **This contained a sub-file marked with his name and including documents relating to his complaint but neither the file nor the sub-file was indexed in any way save that his name was on the sub-file.**

- A sheaf of papers held by the Company Secretariat of the FSA relating to Mr Durant's complaint about the FSA's refusal to disclose information about its investigation of his complaint about Barclay's Bank. **This was not organised by date or any other criteria.**

The Court considered the provenance of the definition, referring to Article 2(c) and Recital 27 (see para.3–42, above). The Court also referred to Recitals 11 and 15 as support for a narrow meaning of the term. This may be doubtful as Recital 11 merely reflects the provenance of the Directive as having its roots in the 1981 Convention and it is suggested that the judicial attempt to narrow the scope of the Directive to the scope of material covered by the Convention was misconceived. Moreover the natural reading of Recital 15 would limit it to sound and image data on identifiable persons.

Accordingly the Court concluded:

"that 'a relevant filing system' for the purpose of the Act, is limited to a system:

1) in which the files forming part of it are structured or referenced in such a way as clearly to indicate at the outset of the search whether specific information capable of amounting to personal data of an individual requesting it under section 7 is held within the system and, if so, in which file or files is it held; and

2) which has as part of its own structure or referencing mechanism, a sufficiently sophisticated and detailed means of readily indicating whether and where in an individual file or files specific criteria or information about the applicant can be readily located."

None of the files which Mr Durant sought would be covered by the definition.

In reviewing his conclusion Auld L.J. referred to the analysis in the earlier edition of this text.

The guidance published by the Information Commissioner originally tended to a more expansive view but was subsequently amended to reflect the decision of the Court of Appeal. The guidance[84] advises that following the *Durant* judgment it is likely that very few manual files will be covered by the Act and gives examples of those that are likely to be and those that are not.

Category (e) data

3–45 This is the new aspect of the defintion inserted by the Freedom of Information Act 2000 (FOIA) and covers recorded information held by a public authority and does not fall within any of paras (a) to (d). Public authority has the same meaning in the DPA as in the FOIA.

---

[84] Technical Guidance Note: The Durant Guidance and its impact on the interpretation of the Data Protection Act 1998 version February 2006.

Prima facie the amendment makes a massive extension to the personal information covered by the DPA where public authorities are concerned. As long as the information is reduced to some recorded form (s.84 of the FOIA defines "information" for this purpose as "information recorded in any form") then, if it relates to a living individual who can be identified by that data or that and other information in the hands of the data controller, it is covered by the DPA. However the data is exempt from the impact of all the Principles and the remainder of the Act's provisions other than those covering subject access, obligations in respect of accuracy and rights to rectification and compensation.

Data held by the authority

3–46   The new category of information must be "held" by the public authority, whereas for other data within the definition it must be "processed". Although a different term is used there does not appear to be a material difference between the two.

The section provides that the term "held" shall be construed in accordance with s.3(2) of the FOIA. This does not assist as it merely provides that information is held by a public authority if it is held otherwise than on behalf of another person or is held by another on behalf of the authority. It is included to make clear that it is control of and rights to the information that are decisive, not mere custody.

Structured manual data

3–47   Section 69 of the FOIA adds a new s.9A to the DPA which contains special provisions for the exercise of the right of subject access to the new category of information. The intention is to restrict the obligation on public authorities to giving access to that data which can be found with resonable endeavours. Otherwise the general extension of the definition in para.(e) would have meant that on a subject access request the authority would have to find every single piece of paper on which the individual had ever written, every old letter in which he/she was mentioned or which was copied to him or her, every tattle of information about him or her. The volume of information with an individual's "fingerprints" on it in an organisation where a person has worked for any length of time is inevitably enormous. The public authority would prima facie be required to find and deliver it all. The problem is tackled by:

- introducing a further sub-division into the new category which divides it into structured and unstructured information; and

- restricting access to the unstructured information to that which is described by the data subject and falls within the costs limits as prescribed by the Secretary of State.

Somewhat confusingly s.9A(1) introduces this further division into the categories of personal data by defining "unstructured personal data". It defines "unstructured personal data" by exclusion as:

"any personal data falling within paragraph (e) of the definition of 'data' in section 1(1), other than information which is recorded as part of, or with the intention that it should form part of, any set of information relating to individuals to the extent that the set is structured by reference to individuals or by reference to criteria relating to individuals."

Thus the definition repeats material parts of the definition of "relevant filing system" in s.1(1). That definition has been discussed above. A relevant filing system is ". . . any . . . set of information [which] is structured, either by reference to individuals or by reference to criteria relating to individuals, *in such a way that specific information relating to a particular individual is readily accessible*" (emphasis added).

3–48   In effect therefore the amendment introduces a new definition of "structured manual data". For personal data to fall into this definition there must be a set of information and thus something coherent or defining about the nature of the data in order to regard it as a set. The information set must relate to living individuals. The set must have an internal structure and that internal structure must be dictated by reference to individuals or criteria relating to them. To that extent it is the same as the definition of a relevant filing system, however there is no requirement that the specific information must be "readily accessible". Thus a file arranged in date order would be covered as long as it had the name of the individual on the cover or was referenced by some criteria relating to that individual.

Data controller

3–49   This definition is divided into two parts. The first part in s.1(1) is:

"A person who (either alone or jointly or in common with other persons) determines the purposes for which and the manner in which any personal data are, or are to be processed."

The second part is found in s.1(4) and provides that where personal data are processed only for purposes for which they are required by or under any enactment to be processed, the person on whom the obligation to process the data is imposed by or under that enactment is for the purposes of this Act the data controller.

Note that the second part of the definition does not require a specific clause in a statute referring to the technical nature of processing data, but it will apply where the statute or regulation imposes an obligation which involves the use of information which is then processed as data. The obligation may be imposed on either a public or a private body, for example an employer may be required to keep records of employees' tax and national insurance by a statutory provision and this provision would cover such data.

The term "jointly" has come from both the Directive and the 1984 definition of data user. However, the term "in common" does not appear in the Directive and appears to have been derived from the 1984 Act. In the Legal Guidance in dealing with the terms jointly or in common, it is said (at p.16):

"The determination of the purposes for which and the manner in which any personal data are, or are to be, processed does not need to be exclusive to one data controller. Such determination may be shared by others. It may be shared jointly or in common. 'Jointly' covers the situation where the determination is exercised by acting together. Determination 'in common' is where data users share a pool of information, each processing it independently of each other."

This echoes very closely the guidance given over the same terms used in the 1984 Act. The point has never been tested but it is difficult to attribute any other meaning to the terms and it is suggested this is an appropriate working definition to apply. The Guidance does not however deal with the issue of split determination, for example where one party decides on the purpose of the processing and the other decides on the manner of the processing. The Commissioner's view, as described below, would appear to suggest that the one who determines the purpose of the processing will be the controller and the other will merely be the processor, but the point is not clear.

3–50   A data controller is not the same as a data user under the 1984 Act, although there are similarities. A data user was defined as one who controlled the contents and use of data. A data controller is one who determines the purposes for which and the manner in which personal data are processed. The concept of determining purposes is relatively straightforward and the same term is used in the Directive. However, the phrase "the manner in which data are processed" is more obscure. In the Directive, the wording used is "controls the means of the processing". One possibility is that the term refers to the person who has authority over the choice of the particular types of processing, for example whether by erasure or disclosure or otherwise. It does not appear to mean that the controller has to exercise that authority in each instance and he may be able to delegate it within a range of possibilities to the data processor. However, the controller will be the person who retains the ultimate power to determine whether data should be, for example, retained or disseminated. This appears to be the view taken by the OIC.

In the Legal Guidance the Commissioner has taken a somewhat unorthodox approach to the interpretation of this provision:

> "The Commissioner's view is that the determination of the purposes for which personal data are to be processed is paramount in deciding whether or not a person is a data controller and that when a person determines the purposes for which personal data are to be processed, a decision as to the manner in which those data are to be processed is often inherent in that decision."

The Commissioner's view appears to be that, as a matter of law, the manner of processing flows from the purpose of the processing. Accordingly one need only look to find the person who determines the purpose to ascertain the data controller. There is no discussion as to what is meant by the phrase the "manner of processing" so it is difficult to ascertain why it is considered dependent on the determination of purpose. It is submitted that the two do not necessarily depend on one another. A public body may decide to hold personal data for the purpose of crime prevention but there is nothing inherent in that decision as to how the data will be held, where it will be held, for how long, to whom disclosed or generally processed. One may follow the other in time but the nature of the processing carried out for the purpose is not inherent in the decision to hold it for that purpose. Moreover there is nothing in the Act or the Directive to support the view that one part of the definition should be given more weight than the other, let alone that one is "paramount". It is submitted that the approach proposed by the Commissioner is not correct and both aspects of the definition have to be fulfilled.

There is also some difficulty in reconciling the statements with the example given. In the example it is suggested that subscribers to the services of credit reference agencies, who have "read-only" access to credit data, become data controllers for such data under the 1998 Act as the subscriber:

> "consults, obtains or retrieves personal data disclosed to it by the agency before using such data, for example to inform a decision on whether to supply the customer. It is the ability to decide these things that makes them data controllers to the extent of the processing undertaken by them."

However, these are relatively minor decisions on how the data should be processed in any particular case. The subscribers do not determine the purpose of the processing. The purpose is determined by the agency which only supplies the data for the purpose of credit reference and which binds the subscriber by contractual undertakings to only use the data for the same purpose.

It might be argued that, within narrow limits the subscribers can determine some aspects of the processing but only within a very narrow range, limited as to whether to search or what category of search to make. The Commissioner's view, implicit in this example, that the relevant processing for which the subscriber is responsible includes the use of the information retrieved has now been overruled by the finding of the Court of Appeal in *Johnson* (see para.3–39, above).

3–51 The extent of control over the purpose and the manner of processing will be relevant in determining whether a body is a controller or a processor. In Opinion 10.2006 on the processing of personal data by the Society for Worldwide Interbank Financial Telecommunications (SWIFT) the Article 29 Working Party considered whether SWIFT should be regarded as a processor or a controller under the Directive. It took the view that SWIFT could not be regarded as a mere processor because SWIFT had "taken on specific responsibilities which go beyond the set of instructions and duties incumbent on a processor". SWIFT decided on the location of its facilities, security levels, services offered and standards or processing. It should be noted that this Opinion of the Article 29 Working Party has no binding effect; it is persuasive only however the Belgium Commissioner took a similar view.

Data processor

3–52 The definition of data processor is in s.1(1) and:

> "in relation to personal data, means any person (other than an employee of the data controller) who processes the data on behalf of the data controller."

The Directive provides that a processor "shall mean a natural or legal person, public authority agency or other body which processes personal data on behalf of the controller". There are some slight changes in the wording in the UK Act but they do not appear to make any material difference. A processor is similar to a computer bureau under the 1984 Act but the 1984 Act covered those who processed "as agent" for the user. This produced a degree of regulatory control over the middleman or broker in information terms. In the 1998 Act only those who either determine the purposes or the manner of processing are covered. List brokers, who were covered by the 1984 Act, are unlikely to be covered. The definition does, however, extend the range of the processor in another area because it includes the person who disseminates information or who collects it. On this basis it might be wide enough to cover electronic publishing and wide enough to cover those who collect information on behalf of another or others. There is no requirement in the definition that a person must have a direct relationship with the controller and it is submitted that where a processor sub-contracts elements of processing to another they will also be a processor for the data controller. The requirements to impose appropriate obligations on such persons are usually dealt with in the agreements between the parties.

Data subject

3–53   There is no definition of data subject in the Directive but one has been included in the Act simply as an individual who is a subject of personal data.

Obtaining, recording, using and disclosing

3–54   Each of these activities comes within the definition of processing. Processing, in relation to information or data, means carrying out any of the processing activities "on the information or data".

Given the breadth of that definition it is not apparent why the additional provision has been included in s.1(2) which reads:

> "In this Act, unless the context otherwise requires:
>
>   (a) 'obtaining' or 'recording' in relation to personal data, includes obtaining or recording the information to be contained in the data, and
>   (b) 'using' or 'disclosing' in relation to personal data, includes using or disclosing the information contained in the data."

Section 1(2) makes clear that the terms include the same actions in relation to information contained in personal data. Possibly this provision was included to ensure that any disclosure *from* personal data would count as a disclosure *of* personal data irrespective of the fact that identifying particulars might not be disclosed. In *Rooney*[85] the Court of Appeal ruled that the disclosure of information contained in personal data did not require that the identity of the individual must be disclosed.

Third party

3–55   A further set of definitions are found in s.70 of the Act. Of these "third party" is a key definition derived from the Directive:

> "In relation to personal data it means any person other than:
>
>   (a) **the data subject;**
>   (b) the data controller or;
>   (c) any data processor or other person authorised to process data for the controller or processor."

---

[85] *R. v Rooney* [2006] EWCA Crim 1841.

Accordingly, an employee or an agent will not be a third party. The term "third party" will only refer to those outside the ambit of the data controllers' authority. The definition is taken, unchanged, from the Directive. It is important in relation to the application of the fair obtaining and processing "code" now incorporated in Sch.I which requires notice to be given to third parties in some circumstances.

Recipient

3–56 The definition of recipient is also found in s.70:

> "In relation to personal data [it] means any person to whom the data are disclosed, including any person (such as an employee or agent of the data controller, a data processor or an employee or agent of a data processor) to whom they are disclosed in the course of processing the data for the data controller, but does not include any person to whom disclosure is or may be made as a result of or with a view to a particular enquiry by or on behalf of that person made in the exercise of any power conferred by law."

A recipient is any person who obtains a disclosure of data and includes employees or agents who would not be regarded as third parties. However, it has an exclusion for those who obtain a disclosure because of legal powers. Recipient is a relevant term in relation to notification. If a person is not a recipient within the terms of the definition the notification need not cover them.

The term comes from the Directive in which "recipient shall mean a natural or legal person, public authority, agency, or any other body to whom data are disclosed, whether a third party or not. However, authorities which may receive data in the framework of a particular enquiry shall not be regarded as recipients".[86]

Consent

3–57 Consent is not defined in the 1998 Act. In Art.2(h) of the Directive, "the data subject's consent" shall mean "any freely given, specific and informed indication of his wishes by which the data subject signifies his agreement to personal data relating to him being processed".

Consent is one of the grounds on which personal data may be processed legitimately under Art.7(a) ("the data subject has unambiguously given his consent"), sensitive data held under Art.8 ("the data subject has given his explicit consent to the processing of those data"), or personal data transferred overseas to a jurisdiction without adequate protection under Art.26(1)(a) (the data subject has given his consent unambiguously to the proposed transfer).

In the Act the provisions of Art.7(a) are enacted in Sch.2 para.1 in relation to the legitimising grounds for processing personal data, as "the data subject has given his consent to the processing". The Art.8 provision in Sch.3 para.1, in relation to sensitive data, is rendered as "the data subject has given his explicit consent to the processing of the personal data". The Art.26 provision is rendered in Sch.4 para.1 in relation to overseas transfers as "the data subject has given his consent to the transfer".

---

[86] Art.2(g).

As the definition in Art.2(h) covers all consent, both for legitimising processing and allowing the processing of sensitive personal data, it is perhaps best approached by regarding the Art.2(h) standard as the threshold requirement for all forms of consent, and examining the further requirement for "explicit" consent in Sch.3 para.1 in the light of that.

Consent is an area in which there is a variety of case law, drawn from different areas of law, particularly contract law, criminal law and confidentiality cases. The following principles have been applied in relation to the question of consent.[87]

No one can consent to something of which he has no knowledge.[88] Consent may be express or inferred from some relevant action (implied consent) but cannot be inferred from silence[89]:

> "Consent involves some affirmative acceptance, not merely a standing by and absence of objection. The affirmative acceptance may be in writing, which is the clearest obviously; it may be oral; it may conceivably even be by conduct, such as nodding the head in a specific way in response to an express request for consent. But it must be something more than merely standing by and not objecting."[90]

The case of *Levi Strauss & Co v Tesco Plc*[91] is authority for the proposition that whilst consent cannot be inferred from silence it could be inferred from conduct.

A person cannot consent to a contract if he was incapable of understanding the nature of the contract.[92] A document may be pleaded as not binding a person under the doctrine "*non est factum*" where he was induced to sign a document containing a contract which is fundamentally different in character from what he contemplated.[93]

3–58 Consent obtained by coercion or duress is not true consent and may be set aside. In relation to a criminal charge duress affords a defence which if proved exonerates the defendant altogether but the cases on duress in criminal matters are not likely to be of much assistance with a data protection case. The pressure of undue influence by another may in some circumstances nullify apparent consent in civil claims. The line between duress or undue influence so as to vitiate consent on the one hand and reluctant but genuine consent on the other is a difficult one. In more recent cases the courts seem to have taken a broader view as to what may vitiate consent. In *The Sibeon*[93a] the Commercial Court took the view that commercial pressure could not vitiate consent, however, later cases have acknowledged that economic pressure can amount to duress so as to vitiate consent. In *Pau On v Lau Yiu Long*[94] a dictum indicates that economic pressure can amount to duress so as to vitiate consent:

---

[87] Some of the cases are taken from the useful discussion of consent in the criminal law in Law Commission Consultation Paper No. 139.

[88] *Re Caughey Ex p. Ford* (1876) 1 Ch. D. 521.

[89] *Attorney General v Jonathan Cape* (the "Crossman Diaries" case) [1975] 3 All E.R. 484.

[90] *Bell v Alfred Franks & Bartlett Co Ltd* [1980] 1 All E.R. 356; applied in *Trustees of the Methodist Secondary School Trust Deed v O'Leary* (1993) 25 H.L.R. 364.

[91] Case C-414/99 [2002] Ch.109.

[92] *Boughton v Knight* (1873) L.R. 3 P.D. 64.

[93] *Lewis v Clay* (1897) 67 L.J.Q.B. 224.

[93a] *The Sibeon and the Subotre* [1976] 1 Lloyd's Rep. 293.

[94] [1980] A.C. 614.

"There is nothing contrary to principle in recognising economic duress as a factor which may render a contract voidable provided always that the basis of such recognition is that it must amount to a coercion of the will, which vitiates consent. It must be shown that the payment made or the contract entered into was not a voluntary act."

3–59 Reluctant consent may be valid consent as long as it is voluntary; relevant factors to consider will be whether the person protested, or had an alternative open to him, or was independently advised. Consent must be distinguished from acquiescence or submission. *Hirani v Hirani*[95] indicates that the courts have been taking a broader view of the circumstances which can vitiate consent. In this case P, the daughter of Hindu parents, had formed an association with a young Indian Muslim. The parents arranged a marriage for the young woman with a man of their own religion whom she had never met. The marriage took place but was never consummated. P, left R, her husband, and petitioned for a nullity on the grounds of duress exercised by her parents, on whom she was wholly dependent and who had threatened to turn her out of home unless she went through with the marriage. The Court of Appeal held that the crucial question was whether the threats or pressures were such as to overbear the will of the individual and destroy the reality of consent. Duress, whatever form it took, was a coercion of the will so as to vitiate consent. This was followed by the factually similar Scottish case of *Mahmood v Mahmood*.[96]

3–60 Drunken consent remains valid as long as the person was capable of knowing what they were doing (although the possibility that data controllers will start plying reticent data subjects with strong drink in order to persuade them to consent to data processing activities, such as overseas transfers of data, seems remote).

As far as capacity to consent applies an individual reaches majority at 18 years of age, and under the Family Law Reform Act 1969 s.1(1), is presumed to have sufficient maturity to consent to any medical treatment or enter into a legal contract for him or herself, unless he or she suffers from mental incapacity. Young persons aged between 16 and 17 can consent to medical treatment to the same extent as someone of full age.[97] Children may exercise some rights or consent to the exercise of such rights as long as they are capable of understanding the import of the relevant matters and a person with parental responsibility for a child may give consent to a lawful activity for the child provided he or she acts in the child's best interests.

An individual may be enabled to exercise choice and consent on behalf of another under an enduring power of attorney under the Enduring Power of Attorneys Act 1985.

3–61 Consent has been considered in some cases brought before the European Court under the Human Rights Convention. The Court has held that individuals are capable of consenting to waive qualified rights under the Convention. In *Stedman v UK*[98] a Christian employee had been required to work on Sundays and had been dismissed for refusing to do so. The Court held that she could not claim breach of her rights under Art.9 (the right to freedom of thought, conscience and religion) where the obligation to

---

[95] (1983) 4 F.L.R. 232.
[96] 1993 S.L.T. 589.
[97] Family Law Reform Act 1969 s.8(1).
[98] [1997] E.H.R.L.R. 545.

work was a contractual obligation and she was free to resign. The Court held that there was no interference as the individual had a choice as to the employment and had chosen that particular job. She had consented to the breach of her rights. Similar reasoning was applied in the case of *X v United Kingdom*.[99] In relation to Art.8 it appears that if true consent is obtained to an action there will be no breach of the right.

Speaking in the debate in the House of Lords in answer to a question as to why no definition of consent had been included in the Bill, Lord Williams responded that it was not considered necessary in view of the existing approach in the law. It is suggested that this is supported by the range and nature of the cases cited above. As noted above, Art.2(h) of the Directive requires that consent must:

(a) be freely given;

(b) be specific;

(c) be informed;

(d) consist of any indication by which he [the data subject] signifies agreement.

Freely given

3–62 While consent may be free even if it is reluctant, consideration should be given to the degree of choice open to the individual. It is suggested that a standard industry practice for information uses which effectively deprive the individual of a choice may be questionable where such uses are not essential for the purposes of the contract. As the cases illustrate consent may be freely given even where the giver would prefer not to have to give it. The Article 29 Working Party has considered the giving of consent in the context of employment and has suggested that consent given to uses of personal data as part of an employment contract is not "freely given". It is suggested that this is going too far. The entire basis of contractual relationships is that the parties give something in order to gain something. Individuals accept the restraints of working life in order to earn money and may consent to data uses within that context. As noted above the ECtHR has confirmed that individuals may chose to consent to waive their rights.

Specific

3–63 It is not clear what this means. It can be argued that it suggests that the consent should be specific to the processing or the purpose. Vague and generalised consent clauses are brought into question by this requirement but it does not mean that consent cannot be obtained to broad purposes or that consent must relate to a short time only. Clauses can be specific in different ways. For example a clause can be specific in terms of duration if it says "two days" or "two years" or "during your lifetime". Each one describes a specific term. It is suggested that consent clauses can be broad as long as they are very clear about all relevant matters.

Informed

3–64 The data subject need not be aware of every detail of the processing but must be aware of the fundamental nature of the processing and any important features

---

[99] [1981] 22 D.R. 27.

which might particularly affect him. The degree of knowledge and understanding necessary to make consent valid was considered by the High Court in *Johnson*[100] and the particular finding does not appear to have been disturbed by the Court of Appeal. Mr Johnson entered into an agreement with the Medical Defence Union for membership by an agreement the consent clause of which included the following words:

> "I agree that by renewing my membership I consent to [ ] processing personal information about me, including sensitive personal data (Personal Data) for administration of my membership, the insurance policy and indemnity claims, risk management, marketing and advisory purposes. . . ."

His membership was not renewed because he was regarded as posing a high risk of making a claim on the funds. He argued that he had not been properly told of the use of his personal data for the purpose of assessing the risk. The Court held that the notification in the clause was sufficient. In doing so it appears to have taken into account the nature and state of knowledge of the individual:

> "I consider that the application of any proper consideration by a doctor to the terms of the processing agreement would or should have informed him sufficiently of the likely ambit of the 'risk management' referred to."[101]

Consist of an indication of agreement

3–65   Mere passive acquiescence with no indication of response will not be enough. This has not so far rung the death-knell of the "opt-out" approach to "consent" but it is always preferable to seek a positive response where possible. "Opt-out" consent is obtained where a data controller notifies the data subject of a use to be made of personal data on some appropriate vehicle (like a reply coupon) which will be returned to the controller and states that if a particular action is not taken, usually a box ticked, the "consent" of the subject will be assumed. In such a case the argument runs that the data subject has impliedly consented by returning the vehicle with the box unchecked. However, because the subject may not have noticed the box or read the material sentence, it can be argued that there is no clear indication of agreement from the subject. The point has not been determined in any proceedings to date. A similar technique is commonly used on internet sites to obtain "consent" to send email or sometimes other forms of marketing. A consent clause is included as part of the standard terms and conditions for the use of the website. The user must accept the terms and conditions by checking a box before he or she can proceed to use the site. A separate check box "opt-out" option appears on the site which the user can complete. The combination of the two provides a consent mechanism. It would of course be a question of fact and degree whether the consent was valid and freely-given in any particular case. Relevant considerations might also be that such "consent" is usually only used for the sending of direct marketing material, and consumers are increasingly aware of the existence of such boxes and tend to look out for them if they have a dislike of such marketing.

---

[100] [2004] EWHC 347.
[101] *ibid.*, para.103.

Unambiguous consent

3–66   This is required by Art.7(a) under which consent is the basis for legitimising processing. In the 1998 Act the relevant provision is found in Sch.2 para.1:

> "The data subject has given his consent to the processing."

It is suggested that the appearance of the adjective "unambiguous" in the equivalent provision in the Directive strengthens the argument that consent must entail a clear indication of the agreement of the individual to the particular processing.

Explicit consent

3–67   This is required by Art.8 where consent is the basis for processing sensitive personal data. In the 1998 Act the relevant provision is found in Sch.3 para.1:

> "The data subject has given his explicit consent to the processing of the personal data."

It is not clear whether the term "explicit" applies to the record of the consent or the nature of the consent itself. It can be argued that it requires a written or other permanent record. In either case, it reinforces the need for any consent for the processing of sensitive personal data to be specific and informed. Furthermore, the existence of appropriate consent will be a matter of fact and degree, to be judged in the light of the particular data, the processing at issue and other relevant facts.

In the Legal Guidance the following advice is offered on the nature of consent by the OIC:

> "The adequacy of any consent or purported consent must be evaluated. For example, a consent which was later found to have been obtained under duress or on the basis of misleading information would not be a valid basis for processing.
> . . . even when consent has been given it will not necessarily endure forever. While in most cases consent will endure for as long as the processing to which it relates continues, data controllers should recognise that, depending on the nature of the consent given and the circumstances of the processing, the individual may be able to withdraw consent.
> Consent must be appropriate to the particular circumstances. For example, if the processing to which it relates is intended to continue indefinitely or after the end of a trading relationship then the consent should cover those circumstances."

On the requirement for explicit consent it comments[102]:

> "The use of the word 'explicit' and the fact that the condition requires explicit consent 'to the processing of personal data' suggests that the consent of the data subject should be absolutely clear. In appropriate cases it should cover the specific detail of the processing, the particular type of data to be processed (or even the specific information), the purposes of the processing and any special aspects of

---

[102] at 10.

the processing which may affect the individual, for example disclosures which may be made of the data."

TERRITORIAL APPLICATION OF THE ACT

3–68   Section 5 sets out the limits of processing covered by the UK Act. In doing so it follows Art.4 of the Directive and Recitals 18–20. The general rule is that a controller who is established in an EEA State must follow the national law applicable to the place in which he is established. If the controller has establishments in more than one EEA State he must follow the relevant national law applicable to each one for the processing attributable to each one. Under Art.17(3) the processor contract required with a data processor must stipulate that the processor shall follow the security obligations required by Art.17(1) as defined in the law of the Member State in which the processor is established. It follows that the concept of establishment is important. Section 5(3) sets out those circumstances in which controllers are to be treated as being established in the United Kingdom.

Establishment

3–69   An individual who is ordinarily resident in the United Kingdom is treated as established here. The concept of ordinary residence is found in other areas of law. A corporate body will be treated as established in the United Kingdom if it is incorporated under UK law. In a similar way a partnership or other unincorporated association formed under UK law will be treated as being established in the United Kingdom. Any other person, which term includes individuals and bodies corporate and unincorporate, who does not fall within one of the three categories referred to above will be treated as established if they maintain a "regular practice" in the United Kingdom, or an office branch or agency through which they carry on any activity.

The concept of a "branch" applies in the rules governing the registration in the United Kingdom of companies incorporated overseas. A "branch" in this sense is not the same as the commonly used term of a branch office. It is a term used in Community law for an organisational sub-division of a company which has some degree of both identity and independence. A branch can consist of more than one office. An office is likely to involve a less substantial presence than a branch and an agency may mean that the controller has no employees in the jurisdiction but merely another who acts on his behalf. It is not clear whether the term "agent" here is used in the sense of one who has the power to enter into a legally binding arrangement on the part of his principal, or the broader general sense of one who acts on behalf of another. It is suggested that the latter is the more likely meaning. The Recitals at 19 deal with the concept of establishment:

> "whereas establishment on the territory of a Member State implies the effective and real exercise of activity through stable arrangements: whereas the legal form of such an establishment, whether simply branch or a subsidiary with a legal personality, is not the determining factor in this respect."

Accordingly, the test is not intended to be one of legal formalism. In each case not only must the controller be established in the United Kingdom but there must be data "processed in the context of that establishment".

The term "in the context of" is not further defined. It is taken directly from Art.4(1)(a). It suggests that the processing is carried out in the course of the activities and within the control of the relevant establishment.

The test of establishment is stated to be the same throughout the EEA. Therefore if a controller is faced with a question of whether another controller is established in another EEA State he should apply the s.5 tests to determine the question.

The High Court considered the territorial scope of the Act in *Douglas v Hello!*[103] This case arose from the dispute between *Hello!* magazine and *OK!* over the publication of the photographs of the wedding of Michael Douglas and Catherine Zeta-Jones. The main judgment is covered at para.2–45, above. Mr Ramey was a New York based photographer who was alleged to have obtained the photographs of the wedding which later appeared in *Hello!* He succeeded in his application to have service on him set aside arguing that he had no joint liability for the publication of the material and that he was not subject to the Data Protection Act 1998 as, even if he was a data controller within the terms of the Act, he was neither established in the United Kingdom nor did he make use of any equipment here so as to bring him within the Act.

Representatives

3–70   In some circumstances, a controller who is not established in the United Kingdom or another EEA State must nominate a representative who is established in the United Kingdom. This obligation falls on a data controller who uses equipment in the United Kingdom for data processing and is not established in any EEA State; in other words, is processing here but is not subject to the Directive. An example would be a US corporation with no office or establishment in the United Kingdom but a server which was serviced by an employee who worked from home. If it purchased marketing lists with the names of United Kingdom consumers and processed those using its server and its own employee in the United Kingdom it would be "using equipment" in the United Kingdom and would have to nominate a representative.[104] The position is not clear where the overseas data controller uses the services of a third party. It can be argued that in such a case they do not "use" equipment in the United Kingdom. They may cause it to be used or it may be used on their behalf but they may not be regarded as using it themselves and thus may not require to nominate a representative, however the contrary interpretation is also arguable. The representative is to be nominated "for the purposes of this Act". The intention appears to be that the nominated representative will be responsible for compliance with the UK Act for the processing which takes place in the United Kingdom. However the section does not in terms impose any such responsibility, and it is not clear how the Commissioner's powers or the individual rights apply to such a representative.

The arrangements set out in s.5 are subject to any additional provisions which may be made under s.54 in respect of actions to be taken by the Commissioner at the request of a supervisory authority in another EEA State. For a discussion of s.54 see Ch.25, below.

A representative may be used by a data controller in the UK.

---

[103] December 3, 2002.
[104] See the discussion of this point and the meaning of the term "using" in para.3–54, above.

ADDITIONAL INFORMATION

Definition	Directive 95/46		1984 Act	1998 Act
	Article	Preamble		
Data		14/15	1(2)	1(1)
Personal Data	2A	26	1(3)	1(1)
Processing	2B		1(7)	1(1)
Relevant filing system	2C	15/27		1(1)
Obtaining				1(1)
Using				1(1)
Disclosing			1(9)	1(2)
Transferring			1(9)	
Data processor	2E		"Data user" 1(5)/computer	1(1) 1(1)
Data controller	2D	32/47	bureau (6)	1(1)
Data subject	2A		1(4)	1(1)
Third party	2F			64
Recipient	2G			64
Consent	2H			

Derivations

3–71   • Directive 95/46 (see App.B).

   • Art.4, Recitals 18, 19, 20 (see also table above).

   • Council of Europe Convention of January 28, 1981 for the Protection of Individuals with regard to automatic processing of Personal Data: Art.2 defines "personal data", "automated data file", "automatic processing", "controller of the file".

   • Data Protection Act 1984: see the table above and ss.38 (application to Government Departments), 39 (data held and services provided outside United Kingdom), 41 (general interpretation).

   • Organisation for Economic Co-operation and Development Guidelines: Annex, Pt One, 1(a) and (b) define "data controller" and "personal data".

Hansard references

3–72   Volume 586, No. 108, col. CWH5, Lords Grand Committee, February 23, 1998 Meaning of data, discussion of CCTV:

"There is no doubt in our mind that 'operating automatically in response to instructions given for that purpose' covers text or image and storage and other processing." (Lord Williams)

ibid., col.CWH8–10
Control of purpose and manner of processing, emails and whether service providers
can be controllers for message content

ibid., col.CWH15
Consent to be a matter for the courts

Vol.587, No.95, col.467, Lords Report, March 16, 1998
Relevant filing system

ibid., col.500
Consent and the use of tick-boxes

ibid., col.625
Withdrawal of consent

> "Any consent given in any part of the Bill may be withdrawn at any time and there
> is nothing to prevent that." (Lord Williams)

Commons Standing Committee D, May 12, 1998, cols 15–19
Personal data and information, meaning of the term information covers encrypted
data; intention of the data controller when data is collected is relevant to the inclusion
of data within a relevant filing system

ibid., cols 25–27
Meaning of establishment and territorial scope

ibid., cols 29–33
Data processor, personal data, processing and relevant filing system

ibid., cols 57–60
Territorial application

Commons Standing Committee D, May 21, 1998
Necessary

> "I shall deal first with the European provenance of the word 'necessary'.
> The Government accepts that the restrictions that it places on privacy in favour
> of freedom of expression must meet the European 'pressing social need' test of
> necessity, which is set out in Articles 8 and 10 of the European Convention of
> Human Rights. We also accept that the test embodies the European legal princi-
> ple of proportionality."

Commons Standing Committee D, June 4, 1998, col.310
On consent and withdrawal of consent

> "Consent that is withdrawn before it is acted on cannot be explicit consent.
> Consent can be explicit only for as long as the person giving it allows."

Vol. 315, No.198, cols 615–616, Commons Third Reading, July 2, 1998
Relevant filing system

"The definition of relevant filing system in clause 1(1) is based on the provisions of the directive. The Government's purpose has been to cover all the manual records that the directive requires Members States to cover, but to go no further than the directive requires."

Case law

3–73 *List of cases decided under Data Protection Act 1984:*

- *Data Protection Registrar v Amnesty International* [1995] Crim. L.R. 633;

- *Dubai Aluminium v Al Alawi* [1999] 1 All E.R. (Comm.) 1;

- *Griffin v Data Protection Registrar* [1994] E.C.C. 369;

- *McConville v Barclays Bank, The Times,* June 30, 1993;

- *McGregor v McGlennan* 1993 S.C.C.R. 852;

- *R. v Brown* [1996] 1 All E.R. 545;

- *R. v Chief Constable of B County Constabulary,* unreported, November 1997;

- *Rowley v Liverpool Corporation, The Times,* October 26, 1987, CA.

Note: The cases which are not reported in law reports can be found in the *Encyclopedia of Data Protection.*

3–74 *List of significant cases decided under the Data Protection Act 1998:*

- *R (on the application of Alan Lord) v Secretary of State* [2003] 2 W.L.R. 80;

- *Norman Baker v Secretary of State* [2001] U.K.H.R.R. 1275;

- *P v Wozencroft* [2002] EWHC 1724 Fam;

- *Johnson v Medical Defence Union* [2004] EWHC 347;

- *Johnson v Medical Defence Union* [2006] EWHC 321; [2007]All E.R. 464;

- *Durant v Financial Services Authority.* [2003]EWCA Civ 1746;

- *Brian Robertson v Secretary of State for the Home Department* [2001] EWHC Admin 915;

- *Lord Ashcroft v AG* [2002] EWHC 1122;

- *Terence William Smith v Lloyds TSB* [2005] EWHC 246;

- *Campbell v MGN* [2003] Q.B. 633; [2004] UKHL 22.

Note: The Act has been referred to in other cases—only those which focus on the Act are listed here.

Data Protection Tribunal Cases 1984 Act

3–75   • *Rhonalda Borough Council v Data Protection Registrar* 1990;

• *Runneymede Borough Council v Data Protection Registrar* 1990;

• *CCN Credit Systems Ltd v Data Protection Registrar* 1991;

• *CCN Systems Ltd v Data Protection Registrar* 1991;

• *Equitax (Europe) Ltd v Data Protection Registrar* 1991;

• *Infolink Ltd v Data Protection Registrar* 1991;

• *Credit & Data Marketing Services Ltd v Data Protection Registrar* 1991;

• *Innovations (Mail Order) Ltd v Data Protection Registrar* 1993;

• *Linguaphone Ltd v Data Protection Registrar* 1993;

• *British Gas Trading Ltd v Data Protection Registrar* 1998;

• *Midlands Electricity Plc v Data Protection Registrar* 1999.

Data Protection Tribunal Cases 1998 Act

• *Chief Constables of West Yorkshire, South Yorkshire and North Wales Police and the Information Commissioner.*

Decisions of the Tribunal are available on the website of the Information Tribunal *http://www.informationtribunal.gov.uk* [Accessed on 2 September 2007].

Council of Europe recommendations

3–76   Recommendations on:

• Automated Medical Data Banks, R (81) 1;

• Users of Computerised Legal Information Services, R (83) 3;

• Personal Data used for Scientific Research and Statistics, R (83) 10;

• Personal Data used for Direct Marketing, R (85) 20;

• Personal Data used for Social Security Purposes, R (86) 1;

• Personal Data in the Police Sector, R (87) 15;

• Personal Data used for Employment Purposes, R (89) 2;

• Personal Data used for Payment and Related Operations, R (90) 19;

• Access to Information held by Public Authorities, R (91) 19;

• Communication of Personal Data held by Public Bodies, R (91) 10;

• Personal Data in the area of Telecommunications, R (95) 4;

- The Protection of Medical Data, R (97) 5;

- Personal Data collected and processed for Statistical Purposes, R (97) 18;

- The Protection of Privacy on the Internet, R (99) 5;

- The Protection of Personal Data collected and processed for Insurance Purposes, R (2002) 9.

Copies of Council of Europe Recommendations are included in the *Encyclopaedia of Data Protection* or available from the website of the Council at *http://www.coe.int* [Accessed on 2 September 2007].

OECD *papers since 2003*

3–77   For additional information:

- Report on the Cross-Border Enforcement of Privacy Laws October 18, 2006;

- Making Privacy Notices Simple: an OECD Report and Recommendations July 24, 2006;

- Radio frequency Identification (RFID): Drivers, Challenges and Public Policy Considerations March 21, 2006;

- The Promotion of a Culture of Security for Information Systems and Networks in OCED Countries December 21, 2005;

- The Use of Authentication Across Borders in OCED Countries December 7, 2005;

- APEC-OECD Workshop on Security of Information Systems and Networks in OCED Countries December 7, 2005;

- Scoping Study for the Management of Trust in the Online Environment December 4, 2005;

- Biometric Based Technologies June 16, 2005;

- OECD Input to the United Nations Working Group On Internet Governance (WGIG) May 24, 2005;

- Summary of responses to the Survey on the Implementation of the 2002 OECD Security Guidelines;

- Report on OCED Forum Session on Privacy-Enhancing Technologies February 16, 2004;

- Privacy Online: Policy and Practical Guidance November 14, 2003.

Copies of OECD papers are available on *http://www.oecd.org* [Accessed on 2 September 2007].

Data Protection and Rights of Access under the Freedom of Information Act 2000 and the Environmental Information Regulations 2004

INTRODUCTION

4–01   The subject access right is covered in Ch.11, below. On its introduction in 1984 it was a radical new right. Since the coming into force of the Freedom of Information Act 2000 (FOIA) and the Environmental Information Regulations 2004 (EIRs) rights of access to other types of information have significantly increased. Since the two pieces of legislation came into force on January 1, 2005 recorded information held in the public sector (and in the case of environmental information some parts of the private sector) has been open to wider public scrutiny, subject only to exemptions and administrative limitations. The two access regimes have a number of differences but both impose obligations on those organisation subject to them to publish information and place them under a duty to provide specific information in response to requests. The obligations relating to publication schemes under the FOIA were introduced between November 2002 and June 2004 through the public sector. The obligation to respond to specific requests for information under both regimes came into effect on January 1, 2005.[1]

The new rules extend to all recorded information, including all recorded information about living individuals. Their impact on data protection practice is not limited to the handling of specific requests for access. Decisions on the retention, organisation and collection of information, as well as record-keeping standards, have been affected.

4–02   This chapter covers the following topics:

- an overview of the FOIA and the EIRs, which are referred to as the access regimes;

---

[1] Commencement Order 15.

- an overview of how subject access to personal information is affected by the access regimes;

- the treatment of requests for access to third party data and the exemptions to the duty to provide information in response to such requests;

- decisions of the Information Tribunal and Courts.

The extension of the definition of personal data and associated amendments to the Data Protection Act 1998 (DPA), the extension of subject access and the new subject access exemption are dealt with briefly but readers should see Ch.3—Definitions, above Chapter 11—Subject Access and Chapter 16—Exemptions, below for a fuller discussion of the respective changes to those areas

SUMMARY OF MAIN POINTS

4–03 (a) There are two separate access rights; subject access under the DPA and a general right of access under the access regimes.

(b) Any access request to a public authority in which an individual asks for information about him or herself should be dealt with under the subject access provisions of the DPA but subject to an additional subject access exemption for personnel information which falls within the extended definition of personal data, that is "unstructured" information.

(c) Any access request made under the general right of access by someone other then the data subject and which covers personal information, *not merely personal data as defined in the DPA*, should be handled so that the disclosure of the personal information is treated in accordance with data protection standards. This is achieved by extending the definition of data, for this and connected purposes only, beyond that in the DPA and making a number of corresponding adjustments to the application of the DPA to such information. In such cases the controller does not have to supply the personal information:

(i) if a subject access exemption under the DPA would apply to the information if it were requested by the data subject;

(ii) unless he can do so without breaching the standards in the data protection principles; or

(iii) in cases where the data or part of the data fall into the definitions in s.1(a) to (d) of the DPA, if the disclosure would contravene an objection under s.10 of the DPA.

The overall effect of these restrictions is to ensure that the public authority does not fall foul of the DPA or Art.8 of the ECHRFF and that personal information is not released in breach of an individual's right to respect for private and family life. However, such considerations do not exhaust the applicable exemptions. Even if the requested information can be supplied without breach of DPA and Art.8 obligations another exemption may still apply.

RELATION BETWEEN THE FOIA AND THE EIRs

4–04   The two access regimes operate side by side. Environmental information is very widely defined and access to any such information will be dealt with under the EIRs, not under the FOIA. Under s.39 of the FOIA information is exempt from the right of access where such access is available under the EIRs or would be available but for the application of an exemption under the EIRs. The EIRs are therefore effectively incorporated into the FOIA. The exemptions in relation to personal data are almost identical in both pieces of legislation.

The FOIA was passed in 2000. At the time the UK was due to implement the rights of access in the Convention on Access to Information, Public Participation in Decision Making and Access to Justice in Environmental Matters of June 25, 1998 (the Aarhus Convention). Accordingly the Secretary of State was empowered to make regulations under s.74 of the FOIA in order to implement the Convention obligations. However the EU dealt with Aarhus by repealing an earlier Directive on public access to environmental information and replacing it with a new Directive which meets the requirements of Aarhus. This is now Directive 2003/4 on public access to environmental information. The Government therefore implemented the Directive using the European Communities Act 1972. The effect was to implement the Convention obligations at the same time.

Privacy and access

4–05   As is explained in Ch.1, above, the Data Protection Act 1998 derives from Directive 95/46 (the Directive). Prima facie, where a conflict occurs between privacy and openness, the right of informational privacy might be expected to carry more weight than the right to access information. The access regimes include an exemption for personal information which provides a detailed code which public authorities must follow. However they cannot finally determine all questions. In some circumstances the Art.8 right to respect for private and family life can be used to support disclosure of information[2]; under the European Convention on Human Rights and Fundamental Freedoms (ECHRFF) the balance between privacy and openness may swing in favour of openness where the freedom of the press is involved and finally, the area of information law is being developed by the courts so that its future direction cannot be foretold with certainty.[3]

OVERVIEW OF THE FREEDOM OF INFORMATION ACT 2000[4]

4–06   The FOIA was brought fully into force on January 1, 2005.

Application of the Act

4–07   The FOIA applies in England, Wales and Northern Ireland. It does not apply to bodies subject to the Scottish Executive. A separate Freedom of Information (Scotland) Act 2002 was passed by the Scottish Parliament on April 24, 2002 and

---

[2] *Gaskin v* UK EHRR (1990) 12 E.H.R.R. 36. See Ch.2, above for a discussion of the *Gaskin* case.
[3] See Ch.2, above for an explanation of the recent cases on privacy.
[4] More information can be found on the website of the Information Commissioner at: *http://www.informationcommissioner.gov.uk* and the Department of Constitutional Affairs site at: *http://www.dca.gov.uk* [Accessed on 2 September 2007].

received Royal Assent on May 28, 2002. There are some differences between the two Acts however they are very similar in structure and general approach. The provisions dealing with personal data are covered below.

Freedom of Information (Scotland) Act 2002 (FOISA)

4–08   The exemptions in relation to personal data are worded slightly differently in the Scottish Act and include two further categories of information.

Section 38 provides that "information is exempt information if it constitutes" data within certain categories. These cover the categories covered by the UK Act (described below) and also:

- personal census information; and

- a deceased person's health records.

Personal census information is defined at s.38(5) by reference to the census legislation.

Who is covered?

4–09   The FOIA applies to public authorities. "Public authority" means a body listed in Sch.1, or designated by order of the Secretary of State under s.5, or a publicly-owned company as defined in s.6.[5] The bodies listed in Sch.1 cover central government, that is all government departments, the Houses of Parliament and National Assemblies and the armed forces with the exception of the special forces; local government; the national health service; maintained schools and other educational establishments; the police; and a host of non-departmental public bodies (NDPBs) listed in Pt VI of the Sch. All recorded information held by or on behalf of a public body is covered.[6] There are provisions to allow for amendment of the Schedule and to allow the Secretary of State to extend coverage to a private body which carries out functions for a public body. Some public bodies are only subject to the FOIA in respect of part of their information.[7] The courts are outside the access regime when exercising their judicial functions.

How requests must be made

4–10   Any person may make a request for information. A request must be in writing, must give the name of the applicant and an address for correspondence and must describe the information requested.[8] Writing includes electronic communication as long as it is legible and is capable of being used for subsequent reference. The applicant does not have to refer to the FOIA or state that the request is made under the Act. It follows that public authorities have to treat any written request for information as an FOIA request unless it is clear that the request is not a FOIA request. Public authorities have an obligation to provide advice and assistance, so far as it would be

---

[5] FOIA s.3.
[6] *ibid*. ss.1 and 84.
[7] *ibid*. s.7.
[8] *ibid*. s.8.

reasonable to expect the authority to do so, to persons who propose to make or have made requests for information to it.[9]

Obligation to respond to requests for information

4–11 Where a valid request is made the public authority is subject to a twofold obligation:

- to be informed in writing by the authority whether or not the authority holds information of the description specified in the request ("the duty to confirm or deny");
- if that is the case, and subject to any applicable exemptions, to have the information communicated to him.[10]

Where an authority releases information under the FOIA it must do so without constraint or conditions. A release is equivalent to placing the information into the public domain. The information will still be subject to any intellectual property rights which can be asserted by the authority so a requester who wishes to make a re-use of the information must also apply for a licence to re-use under the relevant re-use regulations.

Fees

4–12 Public authorities may charge fees for the provision of information in accordance with the statutory scheme. In the Freedom of Information (Fees and Appropriate Limits) Regulations 2004[11] there is no fee for access although the cost of disbursement may be charged. Authorities do not have an open-ended obligation to search for and retrieve information requested. Their obligations are capped by a cost ceiling of £600 for central government bodies and £450 for all others. In assessing whether the appropriate limit has been reached the authority must cost staff time at a maximum notional cost of £25 per hour and may take into account the costs of locating and retrieving the information but not of consulting with third parties or considering the application of exemptions. Where the estimated cost would be above the appropriate limit the authority may impose a charge to reflect the cost of the search based on the same cost basis as the calculation of the appropriate limit. If the authority is going to charge a fee it must let the applicant know by serving a fees notice on him.[12] The applicant has a period of three months in which to decide whether to accept the fees notice and proceed with the request. At the time of writing the Ministry of Justice is consulting on the costs regime. Critics fear that the proposals for alteration to the fees regime will make the Act less useful to journalists and pressure groups.

Time for compliance with requests

4–13 Public authorities must respond to requests within 20 days but a longer period is allowed if they are considering the application of the public interest test to exemptions.

---

[9] *ibid*. s.16.
[10] *ibid*. s.1.
[11] SI 2004/3244.
[12] *ibid*. s.9 and the Fees Regulations.

Exemptions from the obligation to provide information

4–14 The FOIA contains a considerable number of exemptions. Some are similar to subject access exemptions in the DPA. However, where there is an overlap a comparison of the two regimes shows that the FOIA exemption is always wider than the corresponding subject access exemption. The public authority can be exempt from both the duty to confirm and deny that it holds the information and the obligation to provide the information. Some exemptions are "absolute" exemptions. This means that, where one of them applies, the public authority does not have to consider the public interest in disclosure of the information.[13] Other exemptions are non-absolute. This means that, even though the exemption applies, the public authority cannot rely on it without further consideration. The authority must consider whether it should claim the benefit of the exemption weighting whether:

> "in all the circumstances of the case the public interest in maintaining the exemption [or the exclusion of the duty to confirm or deny] outweighs the public interest in disclosing the information".[14]

The absolute exemptions include exemptions for information which is accessible to the requestor by other means, information relating to the security services, personal information, information provided in confidence and information which the authority is barred from disclosing under other legislation or by order of a court.

The non-absolute exemptions include exemptions for information intended for future publication, information the disclosure of which would be prejudicial to international relations or defence, information relating to investigations and proceedings conducted by public authorities, information relating to the formulation of government policy and communications with the Royal Household.

All save one of the exemptions incorporate an exemption from the duty to confirm or deny to some extent; the exception is where the information is accessible by other means. As might be expected, the public interest test is also applied to the duty to confirm or deny. This provision is found in s.2(1).

Where the exemption states that the duty to confirm or deny does not apply to certain information, or in certain circumstances, then where the exemption is also an absolute exemption the authority does not have to consider whether there is a public interest in acknowledging the existence of the information, even if it is not going to be disclosed. In other cases, however, the authority must weight whether the public interest in acknowledging that the requested information exists outweights the public interest in refusing to confirm or deny.

Code of practice issued under s.45 of the Act

4–15 The Secretary of State has an obligation to issue a code of practice providing guidance to public authorities:

---

[13] *ibid*. s.2(1A).
[14] *ibid*. s.2.

"as to the practice which it would, in his opinion, be desirable for them to follow in connection with the discharge of the authority's functions under Part I."[15]

A code was issued in November 2002. It is available on the DCA website. The areas which it must cover are set out in s.45 and include the provision of advice and assistance, the transfer of requests between authorities, consultation with those potentially affected by a disclosure under the Act and procedures for handling complaints.

Obligations in relation to record-keeping

4–16   A further code must be issued by the Secretary of State providing guidance to relevant authorities as to "the practice which it would, in his opinion, be desirable for them to follow in connection with the keeping, management and destruction of their records".[16] A code was issued in November 2002 and is available on the DCA website. The code sets out standards for the handling of records from inception of the record to final destruction or long-term preservation. In a nutshell every public authority must ensure that its record-keeping is effective, well-organised and systematic; that it knows where everything is and can find it. The aim is to reach a situation in which each note, each diary, each minute, each report will be part of a clear, accessible, easily discoverable record of activity in the public sector. As far as historical records are concerned the old rules, which delayed the opening of public records for three decades or more, are swept away. All records, whenever created, are subject to the same obligations of public access. There are no special exemptions for them, and those exemptions that do apply gradually fall away with the years as the records age.[17]

Publication schemes

4–17   Every public authority must set up an effective scheme for opening the information it routinely produces to the public at large. This is achieved by the imposition of an obligation to publish information.[18] Every authority must have a publication scheme in which it sets out the classes of information which it undertakes to publish and must publish in accordance with that scheme. In setting its scheme the authority must have regard to the public interest in allowing public access to information held by the authority and in the publication of reasons for decisions made by the authority.[19] Publication schemes must be approved by the Information Commissioner. The Commissioner may provide or approve model schemes. Where an authority publishes information under its publication scheme the authority is under no obligation to answer specific queries in respect of it; the information is exempt because it is accessible to the public by other means.

Where personal data are included in a publication scheme it may be prudent to inform individuals of that intention.

---

[15] *ibid*. s.45(1).

[16] *ibid*. s.46(1).

[17] *ibid*. Pt VI dealing with historical and public records.

[18] *ibid*. s.19.

[19] *ibid*. s.19(3).

Enforcement

4–18   Unlike the DPA the FOIA does not give applicants any right to apply to the courts. Where a public authority fails to provide access the applicant cannot apply to the court. Each authority should have its own complaints procedure. If this does not satisfy the applicant he may apply to the Information Commissioner who must determine whether the applicant should be given the information requested. The Commissioner has powers to serve information notices and to obtain warrants and can serve either a decision notice or an enforcement notice.[20] Such notices will set out the Commissioner's decision and may order the authority to disclose the information. An authority has a right of appeal to the Information Tribunal against an order to disclose.[21] An applicant also has a right of appeal to the Tribunal against a refusal to order disclosure.

Role of the Information Commissioner

4–19   The Data Protection Commissioner became the Information Commissioner in January 2002 with responsibility for the two pieces of legislation. The Data Protection Tribunal became the Information Tribunal. As well as approving publication schemes and dealing with complaints of non-compliance the Information Commissioner has an obligation to promote the following of good practice by authorities and arrange for the dissemination of information about the Act.[22]

Interface with data protection

4–20   The definition of personal data is extended for public authorities to cover all recorded information which relates to living individuals.[23] Rights of subject access and accuracy apply to all such information. Two new categories covering "structured" or "unstructured" information are created within the definition of personal information. Where requests are made for access to third party personal data (that is personal data about a person other than the applicant) the Act provides extensive exemptions to ensure that there is no breach of privacy in the provision of such information.

OVERVIEW OF THE ENVIRONMENTAL INFORMATION REGULATIONS 2004

Application of the Regulations

4–21   The Regulations apply throughout England, Wales and Northern Ireland. There are separate Regulations for Scotland but there are no real differences between the two, apart from the enforcement provisions. In each set of Regulations the enforcement provisions of the FOIA and FOISA respectively apply and there are some differences between those two enforcement regimes.

---

[20] *ibid.* ss.50 and 52.
[21] *ibid.* s.57.
[22] *ibid.* s.47.
[23] *ibid.* s.68.

Who is covered?

4–22   The Regulations apply to all the organisations covered by the FOIA plus the special forces but excluding those only covered in part by FOIA. In addition any other body or person that carries out functions of public administration or is under the control of a public body and has a public service function in relation to the environment is covered.[24] The boundaries of this definition are not wholly clear but there is no doubt that some private sector bodies are caught. Public authorities acting in a judicial or legislative capacity are excluded as from the FOIA.

What is environmental information?

4–23   The Regulations include a definition of environmental information drawn from Directive 2003/4 and the Aarhus Convention. It covers the state of the environment and all the factors, including decisions and human activities, which will impact upon it. The scope of the definition is wide and all public bodies will hold some environmental information. Information is covered if it is in the possession of the authority and has been produced or received by the authority or is held by another person on behalf of the authority.[25]

How requests must be made

4–24   there are no formalities to follow and requests may be made orally or in writing.

Obligation to respond to requests for information

4–25   There is no explicit obligation to confirm or deny that information is held however the provisions achieve the same result as one of the exemptions is that the information is not held. Where an exemption applies the authority must tell the applicant of the reasons for the refusal. Accordingly if information is not held the authority has an obligation to tell the applicant.[26] The obligation to respond is set out in reg.5 under which a public authority that holds environmental information must make it available in response to a request. Where the information has been published and is easily accessible to the applicant the authority may direct the applicant to the published version.[27] Applicants can express a preference for the form and format in which the information is to be provided which the authority should accommodate if possible.[28] Where the applicant requests it the authority must also direct them to the methods of sampling, analysis and measurement involved in the information.[29]

Fees

4–26   There is no cap on the amount of information that may be requested, although a request may be refused if it is "manifestly unreasonable". Authorities are

---

[24] EIRs reg.2.
[25] EIRs reg.3.
[26] EIRs reg.12(4)(a).
[27] EIRs reg.6(1).
[28] EIRs reg.6.
[29] EIRs reg.5(5).

able to charge a "reasonable amount" for providing information although it may not charge for access to public registers or for mere examination which does not involve the supply of a copy. Schedules of charges must be published as well as the circumstances in which charges may be waived. If an authority wishes to impose a charge it must give a fees notice within 20 working days of the receipt of the request. There is no clear guidance available yet on charges although in *Markinson v Information Commission* the Tribunal ruled that the charges that may be levied for photocopying information may only reflect the cost. DEFRA have suggested that the charging regime in the FOIA be applied by authorities.

Time for compliance with requests

4–27　The time limit is 20 working days with an extension to 40 working days if the request is both complex and voluminous. There is no extension to enable the authority to consider the application of exemptions or the public interest in disclosure.

Exemptions from the obligation to provide information

4–28　Requests can be refused where the information is not held, the request is manifestly unreasonable or the requester has not described the information in a way that enables the authority to answer the request. There are also grounds to refuse where the information is incomplete or it involves "the disclosure of internal communications". This is clearly a wide ground. All the grounds in reg.12 are however subject to the test of public interest.[30] The remaining exemptions only apply if the disclosure would have an "adverse effect" on one of the specified list of interests. The public interest test must also be applied. The exemptions protect broadly the same areas of interest as the FOIA exemptions with the addition of one to protect the environment itself and another to protect the interests of a person who provided information to the public body which they were not obliged to supply and where they have not consented to its disclosure.

Code of practice

4–29　As under the FOIA public authorities are under an obligation to provide advice and assistance to applicants and prospective applicants as far as would be reasonable and to comply with a code of practice for handling requests.

Publication of information

4–30　Under reg.4 the authority is required to progressively make the environmental information which it holds available to the public by electronic means and must take steps to organise the information in a way that makes such information accessible. Where information has been collected before January 1, 2005 it may remain in manual form but information collected after that date must be available electronically.

---

[30] EIRs reg.12(4).

Information quality obligations

4–31   Where information made available by the authority is compiled by the authority it must ensure that it is "up to date, accurate and comparable so far as the public authority reasonably believes".[31]

Enforcement

4–32   The enforcement provisions are the same as for the FOI and the Information Commissioner is the regulator. The internal review process is slightly different as it is statutory and subject to time limits with reviews having to be concluded within 40 working days. The Regulations are silent on the question of whether requesters have any recourse other than to the Information Commissioner. It is submitted that a court would be likely to apply the same restriction as that which is explicit under the FOIA and limit the rights of access to the courts but the point has not yet been considered in any cases.

Interface with data protection

4–33   The interface with data protection is identical to that in the FOIA. If the information requested includes personal data of the applicant it is outside the EIRs.[32] Where a request covers personal data which relates to another individual the exemption in reg.13 applies. This is in almost exactly the same terms as s.40 of the FOIA.

OVERVIEW—HOW PERSONAL INFORMATION IS AFFECTED BY THE ACCESS REGIMES

Exemption for third party personal data—s.40 and reg.13

4–34   The exemptions only apply to information covered by the request for information. Therefore the other obligations under the access regimes continue to apply to information which constitutes personal data. As has been seen in the overview of the Act and the Regulations above these obligations cover record-keeping, the publication or dissemination of information, the provision of advice and assistance to inquirers and the handling of requests for information.

Record-keeping and personal data

4–35   As described above under the FOIA the authority has to establish and maintain a system of record-keeping meeting the standards in the code of practice issued by the Secretary of State. The authority should be in a position to know what information it holds and establish how long it will take to find the request. In view of the extension of the definition of personal data and the fact that, under the subject access right, there is a different charging regime depending on the type of data involved in answering a request, that is whether it is structured or unstructured data, the authority may wish to determine in advance of receiving requests, which of their personal data records they

---

[31] EIRs reg.5(4).
[32] EIRs reg.5(3).

regard as falling within the structured category and which the unstructured category. The question of whether data falls within the definition of personal data is the first issue which the controller has to consider. In the only case decided by the Tribunal at the time of writing and which dealt with MPs expenses, the Tribunal applied the *Durant* test.

Anonymisation of personal data

4–36   The concept of anonymisation is the removal of identifying particulars from personal information so that it is no longer identifiable with a unique individual. In data protection compliance work there is considerable emphasis on the adoption of Privacy Enhancing Technologies, those are technologies which do not focus on individual identities but protect or remove them in different ways. Such technologies rarely achieve complete anonymisation as the data controller can usually reconstitute the data as personal data, however the data may be functionally anonymous as, without the unique information available to the data controller, no third party will be able to reconstitute the data as personal data.

This gives rise to several questions in relation to the access regimes:

- Where data are functionally anonymous should they be disclosed even though technically they are personal data in the hands of the controller?

- Is there any obligation to process data so that identifiers are removed?

- Should this option be offered when a potential applicant seeks advice and assistance?

These issues have been addressed to some extent by the Court of Session in the case of *Common Services Agency v Scottish Information Commissioner*.[33] In that case a requester asked the Common Services Agency (CSA) for information on the incidence of childhood leukaemia in Dumfries and Galloway. The CSA was concerned that the numbers were so low that the release of the numbers could lead to the identification of specific individuals. They therefore declined to release the information. The Scottish Commissioner ordered the release at ward level after barnardisation. This is a technique used to disguise exact small figures by rounding them up or down. The CSA appealled to the Court of Session which held that the barnardised data were not personal data and should be released. The Court held that the barnardised figures were no longer personal data applying the test in *Durant*[34] because the focus was no longer the child but the illness. Lord Mamoch said:

> "I am of the opinion that the statute, whose whole purpose is to secure the release of information should be construed in as liberal a manner as possible, and so long as individual and other private rights are respected and the cost limits are not exceeded, I do not myself see any reason why the Commissioner should not be accorded the widest discretion in deciding the type and form of information which should be released in furtherance of its objectives."

---

[33] 2007 S.L.T. 7.
[34] [2003] EWCA Civ 1746.

Requests for data about the dead

4–37   Information about the dead is not protected by the exemption for personal data as such information falls outside the definition. However it should be borne in mind that such data may also be about those who are still living. The Information Commissioner has however issued a decision notice in relation to the medical data of a deceased person holding that the exemption which protects confidential information obtained from a third party in s.41 of the Act is applicable to the medical records of a deceased person. In this case Epsom & St Helier University NHS Trust withheld access to the medical records of a deceased patient whose parents wished to obtain access. The Commissioner decided that the duty of confidence attached to medical records was able to survive the death of the person to whom the records relate and upheld the decision of the Trust. This is a thoroughly understandable decision; there has been concern at the possible disclosure of sensitive medical or other records after death since the access regimes came into effect, however it is questionable whether the Commissioner's decision is supportable under s.41. Section 41 applies where information is subject to an "enforceable obligation of confidence". The deceased clearly is not in a position to enforce those obligations and the requesters in this case were the parents of the deceased. The alternative argument is that the confidentiality could be enforced in the case of medical records by the those with regulatory functions in relation to doctors. The argument however does not apply to other kinds of information. At the time of writing the case has not been appealed.

Defence against action for defamation

4–38   Section 79 of the FOIA deals with the possibility that the authority may provide information which is defamatory in response to an FOIA application. The authority will have a privilege against action based on such material as long as the material was provided by a third party, that is not generated by the authority itself, and the publication was made without malice. This does not appear in the EIRs.

Disclosures other than under the access regimes

4–39   The disclosure of personal data by public authorities to third parties is not a new phenomenon. Many disclosures are made under statutory obligations, for example by employers to the Inland Revenue. Disclosures are also made under settled arrangements or protocols, or disclosures to provide joint services, for example between Social Services Authorities and Health Trusts. Finally there are voluntary disclosures, for example disclosures of information to the police to assist in the detection of crime.

Disclosures made under existing powers are not affected. This is implicit in the EIRs but explicit in FOIA as s.78 provides that "Nothing in this Act is to be taken to limit the powers of a public authority to disclose information held by it".

Where information would be exempt from the rights of access but the public authority discloses under other powers there is nothing to prevent it from continuing to impose restrictions on the use or further disclosure of the information. However the interface between disclosures under other powers and disclosures under the access regimes needs to be managed clearly and consistently.

Publication schemes and personal data

4–40   As outlined above, s.19 of the FOIA requires every public authority to adopt and maintain a scheme which relates to the publication of information. The scheme must be approved by the Commissioner. The authority is required to specify the classes of information which the authority publishes or intends to publish. Classes are not defined.

Personal information is not exempt per se from inclusion in a publication scheme and may be included. The dissemination obligation under the EIRs does not extend to the dissemination of information that would be exempt from access but otherwise personal data may also be part of the information disseminated under the EIRs.

Applicant's duty to assist authority in locating the data requested

4–41   Under the Data Protection Act 1998, data controllers have obligations to inform data subjects if they require further information to locate the information sought. This point was clarified in the DPA by an amendment made by Sch.6 to the FOIA. This substituted a new subs.7(3) of the DPA 98 as follows:

"(3) re a data controller—

(a) reasonably requires further information in order to satisfy himself as to the identity of the person making a request under this section and to locate the information which that person seeks and

(b) *has informed him of that requirement,*

the data controller is not obliged to comply with the request unless he is supplied with that further information."

In the predecessor provisions which this subsection replaces, there was no obligation on the data controller to inform the data subject of his requirement for further information.

A similar provision is included for handling FOIA requests in s.1(3) of the FOIA where a public authority:

"(a) Reasonably requires further information in order to identify and locate the information requested and

(b) has informed the applicant of that requirement
the authority is not obliged to comply with the request unless it is supplied with the further information."

In reg.9 of the EIRs where a public authority decides that an applicant has formulated a request in too general a manner it shall:

"(a) ask the applicant as soon as possible and in any event no later that 20 working days after the date of receipt of the request, to provide more particulars in relation to the request; and

(b) assist the applicant in providing those particulars."

Where the authority has been through this process and the request is still formulated in too general a manner for the authority to be able to deal with it then the authority may issue a refusal.[35]

Authority's duty to give advice and assistance to applicants

4–42   Public authorities have wide obligations to give assistance before an application is made in the obligation to provide advice and assistance. This contrasts with the DPA under which they have no obligation to assist data subjects with the framing of their subject access requests. As a matter of good practice the Information Commissioner encourages data controllers to be helpful but there is no obligation on them to be so.

Under s.16 of the FOIA, public authorities have a duty to provide advice and assistance, so far as it would be reasonable to expect the authority to do so, to persons who propose to make or have made requests for information to it. The same obligation applies under reg.9(1) of the EIRs. The obligation is not abrogated because the information might be exempt. The obligation applies both when the applicant is making or considering making a request for information and after a request has been made. There is no comparable obligation under the DPA.

Obtaining information and handling requests for personal information

4–43   Much of the recorded information held in public authorities will be information about living individuals, whether public figures, officials or members of the public. Inevitably access will be sought to such information. Moreover, even where the request is not specifically directed at obtaining personal information, the information produced to satisfy the request may often involve such information. Personal and non personal information may be inextricably linked in recorded information, whether in letters, reports, research papers, minutes or other documents. In order to ensure that personal information is not opened to possible disclosure unnecessarily in the future it may be necessary to re-visit the methods of recording any information which may include personal information.

The fact that access may be sought to information is affecting the collection of personal information by public sector data controllers. The fact that disclosure may be made in response to an access request is likely to be relevant information to be notified to individuals at the point of collection; the disclosures themselves will impact on the fairness of processing. As the information open to disclosure under the FOIA and EIRs is wider than that covered by the DPA the data controller should now consider whether it should apply the fair collection rules to all personal information. Where requests for information involve personal information it will often be necessary to notify the individual and consult him or her before making a disclosure.

Organisations only partly covered by the FOIA

4–44   Where a public authority is only covered by the FOIA in relation to information of a specified description, which is provided for in Sch.1, then only personal

---

[35] EIRs reg.12(4)(c).

information that falls within the specified information will be covered. The wording of this provision, in s.68(6), is not completely clear. Schedule 1 provides that four organisations are only covered for information relating to parts of their functions. Three are media organisations and the other is the Bank of England. An example of partial coverage is Channel Four Television Corporation which is only covered by the FOIA in respect of information held for purposes other than those of journalism, art or literature.

The effect is to exempt all information held in respect of journalism, art or literature from the FOIA, so it is possible to obtain videos of your favourite programmes under the FOIA, however, the parameters of the definition are not clear. If a journalist is employed to conduct interviews, film footage of that journalist doing so is personal information about that journalist. Is it held for the purposes of journalism or for other purposes? There is a clear argument that it is held for the purposes of journalism. However, other information about the same journalist may not be so clear cut. How will information about decisions on which journalist to send out on a particular interview be treated? The distinction may not matter so much where the information relates to personnel matters, as the new exemption will protect it, but administrative or management information which includes personal data may be problematic for the relevant bodies. As the organisation is only counted as a public authority for non-journalistic purposes then any personal data held for such purposes would be available (subject to the cost limits). So if the organisation can argue that the data are held for the journalistic purposes they have a narrower obligation of subject access.

Section 34 exemption

4–45   Under s.34 of the DPA information which the data controller is obliged to make available to the public, whether by publishing it or by some other mechanism, is exempt from the right of subject access, the remedies for inaccuracy and prohibitions on disclosure of information. Thus prima facie, this would have meant that where an authority was willing to give access to personal information to the public under the FOIA or the EIRs, e.g. published in its publication scheme or provided under a request for access, the data subject would thereby be deprived both of his individual rights of access and his remedies for wrongful disclosure and inaccuracy. While the former would be of less moment, save where there were disputes about the data covered, as the individual would be able to find the information anyway as a member of the public, the latter would mean that the individual was deprived of one of his rights guaranteed by the Directive. Section 72 of the FOIA deals with this by inserting the words "other than an enactment contained in the Freedom of Information Act" into s.34. As noted in para.4–03 above the EIRs are such an enactment. Accordingly where the information is disclosed under some other legal provision, e.g. an obligation to publish planning applications, the exemption in s.34 will still apply but not otherwise.

EXTENSION OF THE DEFINITION OF PERSONAL DATA AND OTHER AMENDMENTS TO THE DPA

4–46   This section briefly examines the provisions in Pt VII of the FOIA which amend the DPA. As has been explained above the drafting approach adopted is to add a further category to the definition of "data" in s.1 of the DPA for the purposes of requests for access to public authorities.

The amended definition reads as follows:

" 'data' means information which—

(a) is being processed by means of equipment operating automatically in response to instructions given for that purpose,

(b) is recorded with the intention that it should be processed by means of such equipment,

(c) is recorded as part of a relevant filing system or with the intention that it should form part of a relevant filing system,

(d) does not fall within paragraphs (a) (b) or (c) but forms part of an accessible record as defined in section 68, or

(e) is recorded information held by a public authority and does not fall within any of paragraphs (a) to (d)."

It also provides that "public authority" has the same meaning in the DPA as in the FOIA.

Prima facie therefore the amendment makes a massive extension to the personal information covered by the DPA where public authorities are concerned. As long as the information is reduced to some recorded form (s.84 of the FOIA defines "information" for this purpose as "information recorded in any form") then, if it falls within the definition of personal data, that is it relates to a living individual who can be identified by that data or that and other information in the hands of the data controller, it is covered by the DPA.

Effect of the extended definition on the rights of data subjects

4–47 Having brought this new category of data into the ambit of the DPA by adding them to the definition they are then exempted for the purposes of everything but the access and accuracy provisions and supporting provisions. There are also further provisions dealing with the provision of subject access to some of this information.

The new data will be covered only by the following provisions of the DPA:

- all of Pt I, that is preliminary definitions and territorial application;

- of Pt II ss.7, 8 and 9 relating to subject access; s.13 as far as it relates to damage caused by contravention of s.7 or the Fourth Principle and to any distress caused as a result of that damage; s.14 which covers rectification, blocking erasure or destruction and s.15 which covers jurisdiction and procedure;

- Pt VI—all of the exemptions apply to the new sets of data, including the transitional exemptions (for details of which see below);

- Pt V enforcement;

- Pt VI except for s.55 which deals with the unlawful obtaining of personal data. Section 55 is amended so that subs.55(8) will read:

"References in this section to personal data do not include references to personal data which by virtue of section 28 *or 33A* are exempt from this section" (s.70(2) of the FOIA)."

Position of public authorities in relation to the new category of data

4–48   In respect of the new sets of personal data public authorities:

- must ensure that such data are accurate and, where necessary, kept up-to-date. This only applies fully after October 24, 2007 for the newly covered manual records, until then it applies in reduced form as set out in s.12A of the DPA;

- must provide access in accordance with the subject access right (see Ch.11, below for a full discussion of subject access rights);

- have a liability for compensation for any damage caused by inaccuracy (once that obligation is in force) or failure to provide access and for any associated distress (see Ch.14, below for a discussion of this);

- have a liability to comply with rectification, erasure, destruction or blocking orders made under s.14. This only applies fully after October 24, 2007 for the newly covered manual records, until then it applies in a reduced form as set out in s.12A;

- are subject to the jurisdiction of the Commissioner and the Information Tribunal (see Chs 23 and 24, below for these provisions).

EXTENDED RIGHT OF ACCESS IN RESPONSE TO REQUESTS FOR INFORMATION BY THE DATA SUBJECT

4–49   As noted above, where the applicant is the subject of the personal data requested the application is exempt from the FOIA under s.40(1) and the EIRs under reg.5(3). Such applications will fall under the subject access provisions of the DPA. Given the extension in the meaning of the term personal data where public authorites are concerned this is a potentially massive extension of the right of subject access. However the obligations of authorities are curtailed to make the exercise manageable by the introduction of the concepts of "structured" and "unstructured" manual data. The terms are considered in full in Ch.3, above on definitions but, broadly speaking structured data is manual information which is part of a set of information relating to individuals to the extent that the set is structured by reference to individuals or criteria relating to individuals. Everything else then falls into the category of "unstructured" data. The line between structured and unstructured is not merely a legal definition but has a practical impact as unstructured data is subject to cost restrictions under the Fees Regulations. Where the personal information falls into the definition of structured manual data the public authority dealing with the subject access request must provide all of it, subject only to the usual exemptions, for the £10 subject access fee. Where the data fall within the unstructured category the obligation to provide the actual information, although not the obligation to respond to requests and state whether the authority has data of that description, is subject to the appropriate limits.

Under the subject access regime all of the requirements of s.7 of the DPA apply to the information so the public authority must be able to state:

- whether it holds any structured personal information on the individual;

- what information it holds, the purposes for which it holds the data and the recipients or classes of such;

- whether it has any information available on the sources of the data;

as well as to provide access to the data.

Transitional exemptions

4–50   The transitional exemptions from the DPA for automated data have been exhausted. They ended in October 2001. There are still exemptions for manual data. In brief, manual information which was held in a relevant filing system by the public authority immediately before October 24, 1998 and those parts of accessible records which fall outside the rest of the definition of personal data, however long they have been held, are exempt from a number of provisions (see para.14(2)(a) to (c) of Sch.8), until October 24, 2007. However, during that period they are covered by a reduced set of requirements found in s.12A. There is a more extensive, and continuing, exemption for manual data in a relevant filing system which was subject to processing which was already underway immediately before October 24, 1998 where such data are processed for historical research subject to the relevant conditions as set out in s.33 of the DPA.

The further category of data, that is s.1(1)(e) data, except for accessible records and category (e) personal data that can claim the continuing historical research exemption, are exempted from the Fourth Principle and s.14(1) to (3) until October 24, 2007. However they remain subject to the s.12A requirements during that period so the difference may be negligible as far as public authorities are concerned.

Effect of the subject access exemptions under the DPA

4–51   These are to be taken into account in the usual way.

Refusal of FOIA or EIRs request where the requester has the right to make a Data Protection Act request

4–52   Because of the different drafting of the two access regimes there is a difference in the way that the rules apply. Under the EIRs reg.5(3) simply excludes personal data of which the applicant is the data subject from the obligation to make it available under the Regulations. However under the FOIA such data is covered by an exemption. It follows that under the FOIA the authority has to service a refusal notice. Refusal notices are dealt with under s.17 of the FOIA. The authority must respond by a notice in writing which specifies that the authority is claiming an exemption for the information, sets out which exemption(s) apply, why they apply and any reasons in the public interest which have been applied to the decision. Applicants are also entitled to be told of their rights to complain and have an internal review or to apply to the Information Commissioner.

It follows that where a public authority receives a request for information which appears to be a FOIA request, which relates to information about a living individual, and the application is from that individual, the public authority must, within 20 working days, serve on the applicant a notice notifying the individual that it is refusing his request on the grounds that the data are exempt under s.40(1). Although the public authority has to tell the individual of his or her rights to complain and to appeal the decision there is no clear requirement in law for the public authority to tell the individual that he or she is entitled to make a subject access request for the same data.

Under the EIRs there appears to be no statutory requirement to respond at all although in practice authorities sent a refusal notice. In any event it is arguable that the obligation to provide advice and assistance applies. This imposes an obligation on the public authority to inform the applicant of his or her rights under the DPA.

Treating an FOIA/EIR request as a subject access

4–53   If the request is silent as to the legislation under which it is made the authority should consider whether it appears as a matter of fact to be a subject access request. The authority is not able to merely treat an ambiguous request as a subject access request because the requirements are different under the two pieces of legislation. The authority may be unsure about the identity of the applicant. Under the FOIA or the EIR the authority is not entitled to take the identity of the applicant into account whereas under the DPA the authority must ascertain the identity of the applicant before providing subject access. For example an application for personal data could be made in the name of a specific individual but from an address other than the one the data controller has for that data subject. The public authority cannot know whether the application has been made by the data subject or not. The safest course is for the authority to provide only the limited information it would do under an access regime request, refuse the remainder of the request under s.40(1) of the FOIA or reg.5(4) of the EIRs and at the same time invite the applicant to consider making an application for subject access. Relying on its right in s.7(3) of the DPA to ascertain the identity of the applicant for subject access, it can send the applicant an application form to apply for subject access or ask for further identifying particulars. It can also ask for the fee of £10. If the authority refuses a FOIA/EIRs request and does not notify the applicant of his/her rights under subject access then the individual may eventually apply to the Information Commissioner. The Commissioner can serve an enforcement notice under s.40(1) requiring the public authority to comply with its obligation to give the applicant information about his or her rights to subject access and explain how to make a request. However, the Commissioner cannot treat the abortive FOIA/EIRs request as a subject access request unless it complies with the requirements for such a request under s.7 of the DPA. Section 7 requires that the request be in writing and accompanied by a fee of £10.

Applications for Personal Data by Third Parties

4–54   The access regimes provide a right of access to all recorded information held in the public sector. That recorded information will include information about living individuals. Applications for such information may be made to public authorities where the applicant is not the data subject but a third party. The range of data which may be the subject of such requests will be very wide. Moreover, even where the request is not specifically directed at obtaining personal information, the information produced to satisfy the request may often involve such information. The access regimes have a complicated exemption which allows public authorities to withhold access to such information unless satisfied that the disclosure will not interfere with the privacy of the individual.

Exemption from the right of access for third party data

4–55   A public authority is not obliged to release information where the exemption for personal data in s.40(2) to (7) of the FOIA or reg.13 of the EIRs applies. This is a conditional exemption, which only applies where certain conditions are satisfied. The wording is slightly different between the EIRs provision and the FOIA provision. In the EIRs reg.13 states that the a public authority "shall not disclose" the personal data to the extent that the exemption applies. In other ways the terms of the exemptions are identical. To avoid confusion therefore in this section we refer only to the relevant provisions of s.40 but it should be borne in mind that reg.13 works in exactly the same way.

There are, in effect, three possible conditions. One of those conditions gives rise to an absolute exemption but, where the other conditions are invoked, that is in those cases where the data are subject to the DPA, and a s.10 notice would be breached, or the information would not be provided in response to a subject access request, the exemption is non-absolute. Section 40 also incorporates an exemption from the duty to confirm or deny that the information requested exists.

Absolute and non-absolute exemptions

4–56   The difference between absolute and non-absolute exemptions has been explained above. The relevant provisions are set out in s.2 of the FOIA which lists those sections which contain absolute exemptions and those which contain non-absolute exemptions. Where a non-absolute exemption applies the authority is not able to rely on the exemption alone to withhold the information. It must consider whether, despite the exemption, the public interest in maintaining it outweighs the public interest in disclosure of the information. In doing so it must consider all the circumstances of the case. Only if the authority is satisfied that, in all the circumstances of the case, the exemption should be maintained, is the authority exempt from the obligation to disclose the information.

In cases where an absolute exemption applies the authority does not have to undertake such a balancing exercise before deciding to withhold the data. It is sufficient for it to be satisfied that the grounds of the exemption are made out. All of the exemptions in the EIRs apart from parts of reg.13 are non-absolute. Regulation 13 imposes a specific regime which follows that in the FOIA.

Duty to confirm or deny that the authority holds information

4–57   The duty imposed on public authorities by the access regimes is twofold; as well as the obligation to communicate information the authority has an obligation to inform the applicant whether or not it holds information of the nature requested. In the FOIA this is described as the duty to confirm or deny. Just as information can be exempt from the obligation to disclose so it can be exempt from the duty to confirm or deny that the information exists, for example in circumstances where the acknowledgment that information exists would in itself damage the interest protected by the exemption.

Conditions for the application of the s.40(2) exemption

Breach of principle condition

4–58   Section 40(2) states that, where the requester is not the data subject, personal data will be exempt if it fulfils either of two conditions. The first condition varies depending on which category of data the information requested falls into. If the data fall into ss.1(1)(a) to (d) of the DPA they are exempt if the disclosure of information to a member of the public other than under this Act would either contravene any of the data protection principles or s.10 of the DPA. Otherwise, that is if the data fall within s.1(1)(e), the s.10 exemption does not apply and the data will only be exempt if the disclosure would breach the standards in the Data Protection Principles. In other words the data are treated as though the Principles applied to them. As has been explained above most of the provisions of the principles are disapplied to the "new" category of data by new s.33A(1), however, for the purposes of considering third party access the data are treated as though the principles applied. This has the effect of ensuring that the level of protection for all personal information meets the standards in the Data Protection Principles. However, the specific right of objection in s.10 of the DPA is only intended to be applicable to data falling in s.1(1)(a) to (d).

Disclosure of information "otherwise than under this Act"

4–59   The formulation "otherwise than under this Act" was included in both limbs of s.40(3) to make clear that the proposed disclosure has to be considered as though there were no FOIA/EIRs obligation to disclose. Thus all the DPA provisions are to be considered before determining whether to disclose under the access regimes. The access regimes cannot sanction a disclosure in breach of the DPA; if the phrase were not included it might have been suggested that this was the case. The same phrase "otherwise than under this Act" is also employed in s.41 in the context of the exemption for confidential information. This interpretation was endorsed by the Information Tribunal in *House of Commons v Information Commissioner* which referred to the debate in the House of Commons Standing Committee in February 2000 under the rule in *Pepper v Hart*.[36]

Section 10 condition

4–60   This only applies to data covered by s.1(1)(a) to (d) of the DPA and is a non-absolute exemption. Section 10 provides that an individual may require a data

---

[36] [1993] A.C. 593.

controller to cease or not to begin processing his or her personal individual data in a manner likely to cause substantial damage or distress to him or another. It only applies where the data controller is relying on certain limited grounds to carry out his processing and the notice must have been accepted by the public authority. There are various formalities to go through before a notice is accepted. Once accepted by the authority it can be enforced by the Information Commissioner or, where the individual applies to the court, by the court.[37] The application of the exemption and its impact on processes are dealt with in more detail below.

Subject access condition

4–61   The public authority will not have to provide the information if the information would be exempt from subject access by virtue of any provision of Pt IV of the DPA. This is a non-absolute exemption. It should be noted that, as subject access now extends to all recorded information, the exemptions from subject access provided by the new s.33A(2) which brings in the exemption for personnel data, will also apply. However the new s.9A provisions, which affect how access is provided to unstructured data access, do not. These points are examined in more detail below.

Exemption from the duty to confirm or deny

4–62   There is an absolute exemption from the duty to confirm or deny "if and to the extent" that:

- where the information is data falling within s.1(1)(a) to (d) of the DPA the provision of the confirmation or denial would contravene either the Data Protection Principles or s.10 of the Data Protection Act;

- where the information is data falling within s.1(1)(e) of the DPA the provision of the confirmation or denial would contravene the standards set in the Data Protection Principles; or

- the information is exempt under the DPA from the data subject's right to be informed whether personal data about the individual are being processed.

Processing personal data for the purpose of responding to an access request

4–63   If the conditions set out in the exemption apply the data will be exempt from third party access requests. Before examining the conditions in more depth the general application of the DPA to the processing of third party requests is considered.

No correspondence with s.9 of the DPA

4–64   The new s.9A of the DPA sets out the rules for provision of information under a subject access request. As described above this is a two stage process. Information which is held in automated form, is part of a relevant manual filing system or a structured file must all be supplied for the standard fee of £10. As far as the other data are concerned the data subject is under an obligation to describe the unstructured

---

[37] See Ch.12, below for a full discussion of s.10.

data and the public authority is not obliged to comply with the request if the cost of doing so would exceed the appropriate limit.

There is no such two stage process where the request is a third party request for data. The authority will be required to consider all the personal information without differentiation as to how it is held. The cost limit will be assessed on all the information which might be disclosed.

Grounds for processing in response to an access request

4–65 Every data controller must be able to show a basis for processing personal data which falls within one of the grounds set out in Sch.2 to the DPA. This applies as much to the processing to deal with an application under the access legislation as to any other processing.

In the last edition of this text we suggested that grounds for processing would be that the authority has a legal obligation to process the data. The reasons for this approach are set out below however in the only case to be considered by the Tribunal so far on personal data the Tribunal took the view that Ground 6 provided authority for disclosure and no other grounds were considered. In our respectful submission this view is wrong. It is extremely questionable whether any public body can rely on grounds other then Grounds 3 and 5, that is that the body has either a legal obligation to process or is exercising a discretionary power. In the case of *Rundfunk* the European Court referred to the equivalent grounds in the Directive as being the basis for processing by public authorities, The case is considered in detail at paras 4–89 onwards. In any event, applying general principles it is submitted that this is the correct approach as Ground 3 applies. The public authority dealing with an access request is carrying out its statutory obligations under the access regimes. If the disclosure is not exempt then it **must** disclose. To apply Ground 6 is to conflate the need to have an appropriate ground for processing with the application of the test of fairness and compatibility, which is what occurred in the Tribunal case described below.

4–66 The legal basis for an authority's processing of personal data is found in its obligations under the access legislation. Under the access regimes any person making a request to a public authority is entitled to be informed in writing by the public authority whether it holds the information specified and if so to have it communicated to him.

Although neither piece of legislation states in terms that the authority has an obligation to consider every request and determine what to provide or not to provide taking account of relevant considerations, clearly it has an obligation to do so and if it failed could be forced by a mandatory order of the High Court to do so.

In respect of any information which is exempt information the obligation to communicate the information to the applicant does not apply either if there is an absolute exemption or, if there is an non-absolute exemption, to the extent that, "in all the circumstances of the case the public interest in maintaining the exemption out weights the public interest in disclosing the information". The effect of the exemptions have been considered above.

Thus the legal obligation, to disclose information in response to a request, only applies to those cases where the exemptions do not apply. The public body has to decide whether or not an exemption applies and whether it should be claimed and make a decision on that before the legal obligation to disclose sets in.

Schedule 2

4–67 When a request for third party data is received the authority may have to process the personal data to find and consider whether it should be disclosed. This is processing under a legal obligation, as we have seen the authority has an obligation to consider all requests. Applying this logic it is submitted that the basis for the public authority's processing, out of the grounds for processing set out in Sch.2, will be that the processing is necessary for compliance with a legal obligation to which the data controller is subject. At this stage, however, it has no legal obligation to disclose the information. The obligation to disclose only applies after the applicability of the exemption has been determined. The same reasoning would apply to the grounds for processing sensitive personal data under Sch.3 to consider it for release (although it is accepted that the circumstances in which sensitive personal data would be released in response to an access request would be limited).

In the House of Commons case before the Tribunal both parties and the Tribunal agreed that the relevant ground to be considered was Ground 6, that the processing is necessary for the purposes of legitimate interests pursued by the data controller or by the third party or third parties to whom the data are disclosed, except where the processing is unwarranted in any particular case by reason of prejudice to the rights and freedoms or legitimate interests of the data subject. The Tribunal held that the ground involves a balance between competing interests, "broadly comparable, but not identical, to the balance that applies under the public interest test for qualified exemptions", the difference being that the disclosure could only be justified where the legitimate interests to be served by disclosure to the public outweigh the prejudice to the data subject. The Tribunal did not then separately consider the application of the fairness test in Principle 1. It is submitted that in doing so the Tribunal conflated two different issues, the ground for processing and the question of compliance with the substantive principles. The point is dealt with in more detail in the analysis of the case below.

None of the data under consideration was sensitive personal data so the Tribunal did not have to consider which Sch.3 ground might be applicable in the case of sensitive personal data.

Relation with s.35 of the DPA

4–68 Section 35 of the DPA covers disclosures required by law. It provides that personal data are exempt from any prohibition on disclosure imposed by the principles where the disclosure is required by or under any enactment, rule of law or order of the court. However, s.35 is not applicable to a disclosure or proposed disclosure under the access regimes, as the disclosure has to be evaluated as though it were "otherwise than under this Act" that is, as though there was no statutory obligation under the access regimes.[38] Even if this were not provided for it is suggested that, until all the exemptions have been considered, the public authority is under no obligation to make the disclosure under the access regimes. The obligation only applies after all the aspects of the exemption have been considered. Whichever construct is the correct one there is no

---

[38] An interpretation endorsed by the Information Tribunal in *House of Commons v Information Commissioner*, January 2007.

doubt that the public authority has to be able to satisfy the Principles without recourse to the s.35 exemption.

Relation with s.10 of the DPA

4–69 The relation between s.10 notices and the access regimes can be confusing. It is explored in more detail below. A s.10 notice cannot be served to prevent processing which is carried out in compliance with a legal obligation. Thus, prima facie, as the authority will have a legal obligation to process personal data which are the subject of a third party request, the s.10 right would not be applicable to a disclosure made under the access regimes. However the policy is to allow individuals to register appropriate objections and thus s.10 is reapplied.

It could be argued that the provision is not necessary as s.10 applies as one of the individual rights under the Principles in any event and, if a s.10 notice were served before the obligation to disclose crystallised, arguably it would be valid if it came into effect at the stage before the authority has a legal obligation to disclose. However, this is a fairly complex line of argument and one which would leave the matter open to doubt. The provision in the exemption in s.40(3)(a)(ii) makes clear that an individual can serve a s.10 notice seeking to restrict disclosure which must be considered and taken into account in considering a disclosure under the access regimes.

It is not clear whether a s.10 notice could be used to restrict the processing necessary to find information and to review whether it should be disclosed. It is suggested that, as s.40(3) and reg.13 specifically relate to the "disclosure of information" to a member of the public, that only disclosure and not the prior processing to locate and retrieve the relevant data can be restricted by a s.10 notice.

Effect of s.35 of the DPA once a disclosure is made

4–70 Once the conditions attached to the exemption are satisfied the duty to provide the information applies and the public authority has a legal obligation to disclose the data. Is the authority then protected by the provision in s.35? As noted above this protects the data controller, in this case the public authority, by exempting the personal data from the effect of the non-disclosure provisions if the disclosure is required by any enactment, rule of law or order of the court.

If this is the case then it applies to the data in s.1(1)(a) to (d) of the DPA. Thus where the public authority has considered and properly applied the conditions of the exemption and made a true determination then neither the data subject nor the Information Commissioner can restrict the disclosure. Obviously there is still room to argue over whether the exemption was properly applied and the OIC can serve enforcement or decision notices related to such disclosures.

As far as the data in s.1(1)(e) of the DPA are concerned there is no DPA barrier against the disclosure of such information in any event. Section 35 is therefore not needed.

Penalties for wrongful disclosure of personal data under the FOIA

4–71 This leaves open the question of remedies under the DPA for wrongful disclosure, i.e. not justified by the exemption, of data falling within s.1(1)(a) to (d) and remedies under general law for disclosures of data falling within s.1(1)(e). Section 56 of the FOIA provides that the FOIA does not "confer any right of action in any civil proceedings in respect of any failure to comply with any duty imposed by or under this Act". Thus there can be no action for breach of statutory duty under the FOIA but it does not take away the right to bring action under other Acts or for breach of other legal duties. The EIRs do not contain an equivalent explicit prohibition, although, as suggested above the courts would be likely to take the view that the available remedies were limited to those set out in the legislation. Prima facie therefore one might expect that individuals could bring actions under s.13 of the DPA alleging wrongful disclosure of s.1(1)(a) to (d) data. In order to do so they would have to argue that the disclosure was in breach of the principles and not protected by s.35 of the DPA.

This analysis assumes a careful consideration of the application of the exemption and a dispute over how exactly it applies. What is the position where the dispute arises over a disclosure made without due care? There is a limited protection in s.79 against an action for defamation where the information was supplied to the authority by a third person, but other legal actions are not barred. It can be argued that an individual will be able to bring an action for negligence if an authority makes a disclosure without proper care and it causes loss. This could be argued both for the s.1(1)(a) to (d) data and the s.1(1)(e) data. Equally such an action might face the counter-argument that this was merely an action for breach of statutory duty under another name and was thus barred by s.56.

Given the possibility, however, and the clear application of s.10 to part of the data, it supports a strong argument for giving notice to the individual of a proposed disclosure of personal data about them wherever possible and certainly where there seems to be any real risk to the third party.

There must also be a strong possibility that a disclosure of any information, falling into either category, which breached individual privacy, would be open to action by the individual against the public body for breach of Art.8 of the Convention rights. The argument being that the public authority is just as obliged to comply with the Art.8 right to respect for private and family life, home and correspondence in respect of manual information, whether structured or unstructured, as it is for automated data or that held in manual filing systems.

Application of the Principles to proposed disclosures

4–72   As noted above, one of the conditions for disclosure of personal information is that the disclosure must not breach the Data Protection Principles. In this section we consider how a disclosure made under the access regimes might be a breach of the principles. The principles are applied to all types of personal data and information for this purpose.

The interpretation of the principles is dealt with at s.40(7) which provides that the data protection principles referred to in this section means:

"the Principles set out in Part I of Schedule I to the Data Protection Act 1998 as read subject to Part II of that Schedule and section 27(1) of that Act."

Part II contains the interpretation provisions which are referred to where appropriate below. Section 27(1) incorporates into the definition of the principles any exemptions which apply to them. The wording of s.27(1) is:

"References in any of the data protection principles or any provision of Parts II or III to personal data or to the processing of personal data do not include references to data or processing which by virtue of this Part are exempt from that principle or other provision."

In other words the exemptions from the Principles apply as well as the Principles themselves. It might be argued that this means that where a request for personal data is made to a public authority and a non-disclosure exemption applies under the DPA the public authority will have to supply the data, however this is not the case. The non-disclosures exemptions have to be ignored as they all require a consideration of the purpose of the recipient but the access regimes are purpose blind.

Principle 1

4–73   Part I Sch.1:

"Personal data shall be processed fairly and lawfully and, in particular, shall not be processed unless:

(a) at least one of the conditions in Sched.2 is met; and
(b) in the case of sensitive personal data, at least one of the conditions in Sched.3 is also met."

There are then further interpretative provisions for Principle 1 found in Pt II of the Schedule, paras 1 to 4. Together these add up to an entire code by which to consider the disclosure of personal data. The various aspects of the code are considered under the following headings: grounds for processing; fair obtaining; fair processing; disproportionate effort; fairness and lawfulness.

4–74   *Grounds for processing.*   There are two sets of grounds for processing. The first grounds, set out in Sch.2, apply to all personal data. The second grounds, set out in Sch.3, apply only to sensitive personal data. In the last edition of this text we suggested that the processing involved in the handling of access requests could be regarded as two stages: first finding the data and assessing whether to make the disclosure; and secondly, actually making the disclosure, both of which would be carried out under a legal obligation. In the *House of Commons v Information Commissioner*, however, the Tribunal accepted the views of both parties that the relevant ground in that particular case was Ground 6 of Sch.2 and no other grounds were considered. As noted earlier we remain of the view that Ground 6 is not the proper ground.

4–75   *Obtaining fairly.*   There is a specific provision in para.1(1) of Pt II that personal data are treated as obtained fairly if they are supplied by a person who is authorised or required by an enactment to supply. That means if a person who obtains personal data by a request under the access regimes becomes a data controller for the information, the data will have been obtained fairly. They will still however be under an obligation to notify the data subject that they hold the data.

4–76   *Processed fairly.*   Paragraphs 2 and 3 of Pt II of Sch.1 set out formal requirements which must be met before data are processed fairly. They require that the

individual is notified of the potential uses/disclosures of data about him/herself before
they occur. The data controller has to ensure that the data subject has, is provided with
or has made readily available to him, particular information before processing or disclosure. The information is as follows:

- the identity of the data controller or his nominated representative;

- the purpose of purposes for which the data are to be processed; and

- Any further information having regard to the circumstances to enable processing to be fair.

Before disclosing information in response to an access request the authority will have
to consider the collection notice which has been provided to the data subject to whom
the data relate. The public authority should consider whether the notice included a
statement that the data could be disclosed in response to an access request, when the
notice was given, whether it covered all the data considered for disclosure and whether
the data subject was aware that he or she had the right to make a s.10 objection to the
disclosure. It is important to bear in mind that a disclosure is treated as a disclosure to
a member of the public, that is, is equivalent to putting information in the public
domain.

How is an access request to be handled where disclosure under the access regimes has not been included in the collection notice?

4–77   If no notice has been given then the possibility of giving a notice before
disclosure should be considered and the question of whether the provision of
the notice would involve disproportionate effort should be considered. In para.3 of
Pt II of Sch.1 it is provided that the fair processing notice will not apply where,
either, the provision of the information would involve a disproportionate effort or
where:

". . . the disclosure of the data by the data controller is necessary for compliance
with any legal obligation to which the data controller is subject other than an
obligation imposed by a contract."

As with the s.10 objection and the effect of s.35 this provision raises the relation
between the protection of the DPA and the concept of legal obligation to disclose. As
with s.35 and s.10 it does not apply to potential disclosures made under the access
regimes because of the phrase "otherwise than under this Act" in s.40(3)(a). Legal
obligations to disclose under the access regimes are discounted when considering the
application of the Principles to the proposed disclosure.

The combination of the fair processing requirement, the s.10 right and the general
obligation of fairness results in a strong argument that individuals who have not been
given notice of possible disclosures as part of the collection process, and thus have not
been able to raise legitimate objections to such disclosures, should be given notice
before a disclosure is made. This is further strengthened by guidance in the code of
practice on handling requests for information.

4–78 *Fairness.* In addition to the specific rules in the fair processing code the authority must consider the general issue of the fairness of any processing. In this part of the assessment the nature of the data, the identity of the disclosee, the purpose or purposes to which the disclosee intends to put the data and the possible implications for the individual would usually be relevant considerations. Here, however, the authority faces different considerations. Under the access regimes the authority is not to take account of the purpose for which the applicant wishes to have or use the information. The authority can place no limits on the subsequent use or disclosure of information released Section 40(3) states that the relevant standpoint is to consider the disclosure to "a member of the public". The purpose of a disclosure should be regarded as the publication of information under an access regime and any motive of the particular individual applicant must be ignored.

4–79 *Lawfulness.* The disclosure of the personal data must be lawful. Clearly all public authorities will have the *vires* or powers to make disclosures under the FOIA and the EIRs, as public authorities have the obligation to disclose information under the legislation. However, there are a number of legal prohibitions on the disclosure of personal information by public authorities which are considered relevant to the question of whether personal data are being processed lawfully. Thus, if the information is protected by an obligation of confidence or another legal barrier to disclosure, then the disclosure would be prohibited by the operation of the First Principle.

Some information will be subject to obligations of confidence in the hands of the authority. These obligations may derive from the specific arrangements between the individual and the authority, for example undertakings to treat information in confidence may have been given in particular cases. They may also derive from the nature of the relationship or the nature of the data, for example medical information that is disclosed by patients to doctors or statements taken under caution are protected by obligations of confidence.[39] There are also a range of statutory rules which prohibit the disclosure of information, including the Official Secrets Act 1989. It should be noted that the EIRs provides that no prohibition in other statute or rules can restrict disclosure. This poses a difficult issue when considering how the concept of lawfulness applies under Principle 1 of the DPA. The interplay is not clear. It is submitted that the better view is that the prohibitions continue to be relevant to the question of whether disclosure would be lawful processing under the DPA but the point is not free from doubt.

Principle 2

4–80 Personal data shall be obtained only for one or more specified and lawful purposes and shall not be further processed in any manner incompatible with those purposes.

According to the interpretation provision the purposes may be specified in either the register entry on the register of notifications or in the notice to the individual. It is suggested that the purpose be regarded as "a disclosure to the public under the FOIA or the EIRs".

---

[39] See Ch.2, above for the law of confidence.

It is suggested that both collection notices and the register entry should be used to specify the purpose. It is recommended that all public authority information gathering exercises which include personal data should include some form of notice about the possible disclosure of information under publication schemes or in response to access requests in the future.

In determining whether any disclosure is compatible with the purpose or purposes for which the data were obtained the data controller must have regard to the purpose or purposes for which the personal data are intended to be processed by any person to whom they are disclosed. In the context of the access regimes the authority must consider whether putting the information into the public domain is compatible with the purpose specified when the data were obtained. In cases where the information is innocuous and the individual has been notified of the possible disclosure then the answer will probably be yes. If the individual has been notified and consented to the publication the answer will also be yes.

Principles 3 to 5

4–81 The next three Principles deal with data quality. They require that data are kept up-to-date, are adequate and relevant for the purposes for which they are processed and are only retained for as long as is necessary to fulfil the purpose for which they are held. They do not impact on disclosure.

Principle 6

4–82 This provides as follows:

> "Personal data shall be processed in accordance with the rights of data subjects under this Act."

The rights of data subjects for this purpose are specified in the interpretation provision in para.8 of Pt II of Sch.1 which provides that a person is only to be regarded as contravening the sixth Principle if:

> "(a) he contravenes section 7 by failing to supply information in accord with that section;
>
> (b) he contravenes section 10 by failing to comply with a notice given under subsection (1) of that section to the extent that the notice is justified or by failing to give a notice under subsection (3) of that section;
>
> (c) he contravenes section 11 by failing to comply with a notice given under subsection (1) of that section; or
>
> (d) he contravenes section 12 by failing to comply with a notice given under subsection (1) or (2)(b) of that section or failing to give a notification under subsection (2)(a) of that section or a notice under subsection (3) of that section."

Prima facie the application of Principle 6 brings into play the four specified individual rights, however it must be arguable that this was not the intention of the draftsman. This is because, as we have seen the s.10 right to object is specifically applied to data which fall within the DPA, with the implication that only the s.10 right, out of all the individual rights, applies and it only applies to such data. The reason for the specific reapplication of s.10 appears to be that explained above, that as the data are being processed in response to a legal obligation, the s.10 right could be argued not to apply to the disclosure. As s.10 is based on a right in the Directive its disapplication would bring the United Kingdom into non-compliance with its European obligations.

Application of the individual rights to disclosures under the access regimes

4–83   To consider each of these in turn s.7 deals with subject access and is not relevant for these purposes. Section 10 is the right to object to processing and is dealt with above. Section 11 is the right to object to processing for direct marketing. It may be considerer that s.11 has no application as the public authority itself will not use the data for direct marketing. However that does not take account of the decision in the case of *Brian Robertson v Wakefield DC and the Secretary of State for the Home Department.*[40]

The right in s.12 relates to the objection to automated decision-making. It is possible that the delivery of access rights might be by automated means although not likely.

Robertson v Wakefield DC

4–84   The whole area of disclosure of personal data by public authorities to third parties has to be considered in the light of the decision in *Robertson.* In the exemption authorities are specifically required to take account of objections lodged under s.10 of the DPA; no mention is made of s.11. Section 11 provides for individuals to have the right to object to the use of data about them for marketing. In *Robertson* the Court held that any s.11 objection of which the public authority is aware must be honoured. The Court held that the public authority should specifically take account of objections to disclosures of names and addresses from the electoral register where the Electoral Registration Officer knew that the data disclosed would be used for marketing or other commercial uses by others. The decision in *Robertson* is difficult to reconcile with the approach of the FOIA and EIRs because it obliges the public authority, when making a disclosure under a statutory provision, to take account of the intentions of others. If it is applied to areas other than the electoral register it potentially impacts on whole areas of disclosure of information drawn from public sources.

It is arguable that a public authority could be precluded from making any disclosure of personal data that might be used for marketing unless the authority has a method of accepting and honouring opt-out notices which would prevent the authority passing on the data. However the point has not been tested before the Tribunal at the time of writing.

Exemption from the obligation to confirm or deny where to do so would contravene any of the Principles

4–85   The obligation to confirm or deny is a separate legal obligation from the obligation to provide the information. The authority must consider whether to confirm it holds information independently of the substantive decision on disclosure. Any

---

[40] [2001] EWHC Admin 915, see Ch.2, above for a full discussion of the case.

response to confirm or deny that personal data relating to a particular individual are held is likely to amount to a disclosure of information about that individual. However, save in particular circumstances, for example where the mere fact of holding or not holding data necessarily implies some other private information about the individual, disclosure at this level is less likely to be a breach of the Data Protection Principles. Clearly the same considerations as applied to the substantive disclosure apply to the disclosure of the fact that information is held.

Should there be consent or consultation before issuing a confirmation or denial?

4–86   If there is to be consultation with the individual before a decision to disclose is made then the individual can be asked at the same time whether he or she objects to the authority confirming that data are held.

Objections lodged under s.10

4–87   Section 10 is dealt with in detail in Ch.12, below. It provides that an individual is at any time entitled to serve a notice in writing on the data controller to require the controller to cease or not to begin specified processing of personal data of which he is the data subject on the basis that the processing would cause unwarranted substantial damage or distress to him or another. The wording in the exemption relates to a contravention of s.10. This implies that the s.10 notice must be in place, however, there seems no reason why an individual could not lodge a s.10 notice at the time of a proposed disclosure.

A distinction can be made between those cases where the authority is dealing with an objection lodged and accepted prior to the request and those where the individual lodges one in response to the notice of the request and proposed disclosure.

Where a section 10 notice is applicable at the time a request is received the authority must not regard it as a binding obligation as the exemption is a non-absolute exemption. Accordingly the authority has to decide whether it should disclose the information irrespective of the notice. However, if the authority is considering disclosing in contravention of the notice then bearing in mind considerations of natural justice, the individual is arguably entitled to notice of the proposed disclosure so he/she can refresh and revisit the argument. If the authority then proposes to disclose, the individual will have the right to make an application to the court under s.10(4) of the DPA. Where there is no existing s.10 notice the authority should consider not only whether to give the individual notice of the request but also whether to alert him/her to the s.10 right. There is no requirement that the authority has to tell the individual about his/her s.10 rights. However, it is suggested that it would be good practice, wherever the authority decides to consult on proposed disclosure, that the consultation notice should be in a standard form and should alert the individual to his s.10 rights.

Although this is the prudent response it may not be strictly necessary in all cases. However, if an authority decides not to alert individuals to their s.10 rights in every case it is suggested that it should adopt a policy which sets out those cases in which it will do so, perhaps for sensitive personal data.

Duty to confirm or deny where a s.10 notice applies

4–88   There is no duty to confirm or deny where giving such confirmation or denial would contravene a s.10 notice.

Subject access exemptions

4–89   The authority will not have to provide information if the data would not be provided to the data subject had the data subject applied for access to it. The subject access exemptions are covered in Chs 15 to 19, below. There are some similarities between the subject access exemptions and the FOIA/EIRs exemptions but there are also some important differences. In the DPA there is no explicit duty to confirm or deny, although under s.7(1) of the DPA the subject has separate rights to receive:

- a statement as to whether the data controller holds information about the individual;

- a description of the data, its purposes and the recipients;

- communication of the data;

- information about the logic of any relevant automated decision making.

The subject access exemptions apply to the rights contained in s.7 "as far as is necessary" for the purpose of exemption in most cases. There is no separate exemption from the duty to state whether data are held whereas under the access regimes there is a separate exemption from the duty to confirm or deny. The effect however is the same in both cases.

If a subject access exemption would apply the authority may claim an non-absolute exemption. It follows that the authority must consider whether to provide access to the information even if it would refuse access to the individual concerned. It is not easy to envisage cases where this would apply.

Subject access exemptions in the DPA

4–90   For a detailed discussion of each of the exemptions see Chs 15 to 19, below:

- national security—this requires a certificate from the Secretary of State;

- prejudice to the prevention or detection of crime, apprehension or prosecution of offenders, assessment or collection of any tax or duty;

- in the interests of the operation of a classification as part of a risk assessment by a relevant authority;

- prejudice to the physical or mental health of the data subject;

- prejudice to the carrying out of social work;

- certain educational data held by schools;

- prejudice to specified regulatory functions;

- incompatibility with journalism, literature or art where the publication is in the public interest;

- research purposes where the data are not made available in an identifiable manner;

- data made public under any other enactment (not FOIA);

- confidential references in the hands of the data controller;

- prejudice to the effectiveness of the armed forces of the Crown;

- judicial office, honours, QC appointments;

- Crown employment or office;

- personnel information relating to employment by a public authority in relation to s.1(1)(e) data only;

- prejudice to management forecasts or planning;

- price sensitive information;

- prejudice to negotiations with the data subject;

- premature revelation of examination results;

- examination scripts;

- legal professional privilege; and

- privilege against self incrimination.

Guidance on third party disclosures in the code

4–91 Not only must the public authority apply the exemptions but, where a proposed disclosure of personal data is being considered, the requirements of the codes of practice on the handling of requests should also be borne in mind. These provide that, where information about an individual is being considered for disclosure, the authority should review whether to give the individual notice and take account of his/her views.

One of the stated aims of the Code of Practice on the Discharge of the Functions of Public Authorities under Pt I of the FOIA is to:

"ensure that the interests of third parties who may be affected by any decision to disclose information are considered by the authority by setting standards for consultation."

Given the range of considerations which the authority must consider under the exemption the inclusion of additional guidance seems unnecessary but as the Code specifically refers to consultation where disclosure might affect existing legal rights such as "the right to privacy" the guidance should be taken into account.

The Code is issued under s.45 and is a supplement to the legislation, not a substitute for it. Where there is any difference between the Code and the Act, the Act must be preferred.

The Code differentiates between those cases in which the disclosure would affect the legal rights of a third party and those where it would affect interests which do not give rise to legal rights. The right to privacy is approached as a legal right. The right to privacy is not technically exhausted by the DPA protections but in practice the two are likely to be co-terminous. The guidance is specific on the question of consent:

"Where the consent of the third party would enable a disclosure to be made an authority should consult that party prior to reaching a decision, unless it is clear to the authority that the consent would not be forthcoming."

In other cases the authority should consult unless:

- the authority does not intend to disclose anyway;
- the views of the third party can have no effect;
- the cost would be disproportionate;

but should consult where:

- the views of the third party may assist in determining whether an exemption applies;
- the views may assist in determining whether to make a disclosure in the public interest under a non-absolute exemption.

The consultation need not be restricted to the individual who is the subject of the information but may be with others, particularly if they are able to contribute to the decision as to the applicability of relevant exemptions.

Applying the s.40 exemption to the disclosure of personal data—case law

4–92   The European Court considered the balance between privacy and the disclosure of personal data into the public domain in Joined Cases C-465/00 *Rechnugshof and Österreichischer Rundfunk*, C-138/01 *Christa Neukomn and Österreichischer Rundfunk* and C-139/01 *Joseph Lauermann and Österreichischer Rundfunk*.[41] The facts and background as well as a full discussion will be found in Ch.2, above but in brief this concerned the disclosure of the salaries of senior public servants by the Austrian audit authority. The organisations which employed those officials had resisted the public disclosure by the national audit body on the basis that it contravened the privacy rights of the individuals under the Directive. The European Court held that the information about the payments to named individuals related to identified or identifiable natural persons and was therefore personal data. There is no reason to justify excluding activities of a professional nature from the scope of personal data.

While the retention of such data by the employer is not an infringement of Art.8 rights the communication of such data to third parties amounts to an interference, irrespective of whether the information would amount to sensitive personal data.

---

[41] [2003] ECR I–4989.

The provisions of the Directive must be interpreted in the light of Convention rights. Thus, where the Directive permits derogations from the rights which it provides, and actions carried out in reliance on those derogations would amount to an interference with the Art.8 right; the actions must have a legal basis and the interference must be justified and proportionate. This includes the requirement that the law must be sufficiently precise and foreseeable.

Legal commentators in Austria had deduced in the light of the relevant *travaux preparatoires* that the audit legislation required the disclosure of specific names and payments. It was for the national court to determine whether the provisions met the test of proportionality.

The objective of exerting pressure on public bodies to keep salaries within reasonable limits was a legitimate aim which would be capable of justifying interference with Art.8.

Where the provisions of a directive are unconditional and sufficiently precise they may be relied upon directly by individuals and applied by national courts. The provisions of Art.6(1)(c) under which personal data must be adequate, relevant and not excessive in relation to the purposes of the processing and Art.7(2)(c) and (e) which set the grounds for processing applicable to the public sector fall into that category and may therefore be relied upon before the national courts to oust the application of national rules which are contrary to those provisions.

National authorities enjoy a margin of appreciation in determining the balance between the social needs and the interference with private life in issue. It is for the national courts to ascertain whether the interference is proportional and it could only be satisfied on this point if the wide disclosure of names and income was necessary for and appropriate to the aim of keeping salaries within reasonable limits.

The case was therefore remitted to the Austrian courts to determine whether the disclosure was necessary and proportionate.

UK cases

4–93 The Information Tribunal has considered the application of the exemptions for personal data in the case of *The Corporate Officer of the House of Commons v Information Commissioner*, January 2007.[42] The Tribunal heard two consolidated appeals in cases in which applications had been made under the FOIA for the disclosure of information about MPs' travel expenses. The requests were made in similar terms for information:

> "in a format which would show for each MP the amount claimed by mode of travel, and therefore giving specific figures for rail, road, air and bicycle."

The total sum for each allowance which each Member claimed each year was available under the publication scheme of the House of Commons. Members had been given clear notice of the nature and extent of the information so published however the published information did not provide the detailed breakdown requested. The disclosure of the more detailed information sought was refused on the basis that this would

---

[42] See *http://www.informationtribunal.gov.uk* [Accessed on 2 September 2007] for the cases decided by the Tribunal.

breach the data protection principles. There was no dispute that the information was personal data and most of the information was readily available, although some elements such as European travel were not. Family travel was not included in the figures, although it was accepted that some information about means of transport might betray the fact that an MP had family commitments.

The Tribunal set out the provisions of s.40 and confirmed its view that once s.40(2) is engaged the request must be considered under the DPA without further consideration of the FOIA. The Tribunal went on to consider the application of Principles 1 and 2 and the impact of Sch.2. Oddly the Tribunal considered Principle 1 before it considered the grounds for the processing and in considering the processing appears only to have considered the actual disclosure. In our view however as discussed in para.4–62, above there are two sets of processing; processing to carry out the search and consider the application of the exemptions, then processing to disclose. These are two distinct operations. If no exemption applies the authority has a legal duty to make the disclosure.

4–94   In relation to Principle 1 the Tribunal considered three issues:

- whether MPs were provided with the information specified in para.2(3) of Pt II of Sch.1 (the fair processing notice);

- whether first and paramount consideration must be given to the interests of the data subjects, that is the MPs; and

- whether it is correct, as the Commissioner had argued, that a distinction should be drawn between personal data relating to an individual's public and his private life.

On the first point they accepted that no specific notice had been given but pointed out that the requirements of para.2(3) are not absolute and the obligation of the data controller is to "ensure so far as practicable" that the data subject is provided with the information. They pointed out that any finding to the contrary would risk the possibility that a data controller would deliberately fail to provide a proper notice so as to ensure that personal data could not be disclosed. On the second point they had been referred to the cases of *CNN v The Data Protection Registrar* and *Infolink v The Data Protection Registrar* decided by the Tribunal under the 1984 Act in which it was held that the interests of the data subjects are, if not paramount, the most important consideration in determining matters of fairness. The Tribunal pointed out that the cases are not binding on them but in any event considered that they could be distinguished from these cases in which the personal data concerns public officials whose data are being processed for a public function. In doing so the Tribunal dealt with both the second and third points listed above. The Tribunal commented that:

". . . where data subjects carry out public functions, hold elective office or spend public funds they must have the expectation that their public actions will be subject to greater scrutiny than would be the case in respect of their private lives. This principle still applies even where a few aspects of their private lives are intertwined with their public lives but where the vast majority of processing of personal data relates to the data subject's public life."

The Tribunal then turned to the grounds for processing and considered Ground 6. In effect it applied a test of balance and fairness under the guise of applying Ground 6. In considering the application of Ground 6, the Tribunal determined that the balance was broadly similar to the public interest test but that the interests of the public must outweight the possible prejudice to the data subjects in order for the ground to apply. It listed the arguments in favour of a legitimate interest in disclosure and then the possible elements of prejudice to the data subjects and decided that in the particular case the legitimate interests of the members of the public in having the information outweighted any prejudice to the rights and freedoms of MPs. In reaching this determination they took into account that there would be only a very limited invasion of MPs' privacy. In our view these considerations more properly went to the question of fairness of processing and should have been considered under Principle 1.

In relation to the second principle they took into account that the House already publishes the global sums of Members' expenses under the publication scheme. Therefore the data in question was already processed for the purpose and the issue of use or disclosure for a new purpose did not arise.

Decisions under the Scottish legislation

4–95   Under the Scottish Act the Scottish Information Commissioner has held in *Paul Hutcheon, The Sunday Herald and the Scottish Parliamentary Corporate Body* that the expenses of Scottish MPs should be disclosed under the FOISA applying a legal analysis and balancing decisions on all fours with the decisions of the Information Commissioner.[43]

Guidance from the Information Commissioner

4–96   The Commissioner has issued guidance on the application of the exemption for personal data in which he draws a distinction between information relating to an individual in his private capacity and in his public capacity. His advice is that information which is about the private or family life of an individual or relates to him in a personal capacity such as personal finances or personal references, should be regarded as likely to deserve protection. On the other hand information which is about someone acting in an official or work capacity should normally be provided on an access request unless there is some perceived risk to the person from the disclosure. The Guidance also sets out a number of questions which should be addressed when considering the fairness of a possible disclosure as follows:

- Would the disclosure cause unnecessary or unjustified distress or damage to the person to whom the information relates?
- Would that person expect that his or her information might be disclosed to others?
- Had that person been led to believe that his or her information would be kept secret?
- Has that person expressly refused consent to the disclosure of the information?

---

[43] Ref Decisions 033/2005. Cases are reported on the website of the Scottish Information Commissioner: *www.itspublicknowledge.info.*

The guidance appears to have been accepted as the correct approach by the Tribunal in the *House of Commons* case.

The Commissioner's guidance reflects the themes of the guidance published by the European Data Protection Supervisor (EDPS) in July 2005 directed at EU officials faced with requests for access to public documents that contain personal data. The supervisor made clear that the privacy exemption in the relevant EU Regulation could not be treated as a class exemption but had to be applied on a case-by-case basis. The guidance, which is available on the EPS website, includes a useful checklist for officials.

Decisions of the Commissioner

4–97   The Commissioner publishes Decision Notices on his website and several notices deal with the disclosure of personal data. In *Corbay Borough Council*[44] he ordered the amounts paid to a member of staff appointed in a senior capacity on a short term contract be disclosed. In *Calderdale Council*[45] he ordered that the names of social workers who had undertaken a recruitment trip to Australia to persuade Australian social workers to move to Yorkshire be disclosed.

Suggested approach

4–98   Bearing all the points made in this section in mind it is recommended that public authorities approach the disclosure of personal data to third parties by posing the relevant questions in the following sequence:

- Is the information published or otherwise readily accessible to the applicant by other means?

- Is the information environmental information?

- If the FOIA applies do any of the remaining absolute FOIA exemptions apply? If any of these are satisfied the authority will have no requirement to exercise any discretion in relation to a disclosure and may rely on the exemption.

- Do any of the other exemptions which protect public or other interests (rather than the privacy interests of the individual) apply?

- Has the individual given consent?

- If not has the individual been told of the possible disclosure via a collection notice and made aware of his/her right to object?

- Is there an existing s.10 notice in force which should be honoured?

- How do the Data Protection Principles apply? Do they permit disclosure?

- Review the remaining exemptions. In considering the FOIA exemptions the possibility that the authority may be able to confirm that it has the information, even thought it will not disclose it, must be borne in mind.

---

[44] August 25, 2005.
[45] November 24, 2005.

- Address whether the authority has any obligations to consider s.11 objections. This may mean reviewing the possible use of the data for marketing.

It will be noted that we do not consider that the authority needs to be concerned about the grounds for processing. In our view, as described above, the authority is entitled to process in order to consider the request because it has a legal obligation to do so. If no exemptions apply then it has an obligation to make the disclosure and again the authority will be processing in reliance on a legal obligation.

When considering the FOIA and EIRs exemptions regard should be had to the guidance in the Code of Practice and to the possibility of consultation, notifying the individual of the right to exercise a s.10 objection or soliciting consent.

Summary of relevant considerations on disclosure

4–99 It will be noted from the above analysis that there is little by way of a balancing test in this process. In effect the public interest balance between privacy and freedom of access comes into play via the application of the exemptions. If the authority is left with any degree of discretionary choice the deciding factor will be whether the information is such that the publication to any one in the world would be fair or whether the public interest in disclosure would outweigh any detriment to the individual.

Enforced consent

4–100 An area in which difficult judgments may have to be made on requests for personal data by third parties is the area of enforced consent. It is suggested that the fact that an individual has consented to disclosure should not necessarily be taken to mean the disclosure is fair. Enforced subject access is to be outlawed by the DPA but it could easily be replaced under the access regimes with enforced consent to third party access to data.

RELATION BETWEEN RIGHTS OF ACCESS TO INFORMATION AND THE EUROPEAN CONVENTION ON HUMAN RIGHTS AND FUNDAMENTAL FREEDOMS

Background

4–101 The Convention does not include a right of access to information. Article 10 covers the right of freedom of expression:

"(1) Everyone has the right to freedom of expression. The right shall include freedom to hold opinions and to receive and impart information and ideas without interference by public authorities and regardless of frontiers. This article shall not prevent States from requiring the licensing of broadcasting, television or cinema enterprises."

Article 10(2) allows for interference with the right on a list of public interest grounds subject to the usual safeguards. However the freedom to "receive and impart information" has been held by the ECtHR not to extend to a right to obtain information which another party is unwilling to impart. The case most cited is *Leander v Sweden*.[46] An individual sought confidential information from the Government having failed to obtain a job in a shipyard, on security grounds. The Court held that the article did not:

> "confer on an individual a right of access to a register containing information about his personal position nor does it embody an obligation on the Government to impart such information."

Article 10 has been used in the UK since October 2000 in a number of cases. Those dealing specifically with personal privacy and the rights of the media have been covered in Ch.2, above.

In cases in which the Court has decided that applicants do have rights to access information held by the State, the rights have been founded on Art.8 rather than Art.10.[47] The Court has held that individuals may need to have access to information held by the State in order to protect their private or family lives.

Since implementation of the HRA the UK courts have followed the same approach as the ECtHR. In *Persey v Secretary of State for the Environment*[48] the High Court rejected a claim for judicial review of the decision not to hold the various inquiries into the foot and mouth epidemic in public. In *Howard v Secretary of State for Health*[49] an application for hearings in respect of doctors who had been accused of misconduct to be open to the public was also rejected. The same approach has been taken to applications by media organisations to film legal proceedings in the cases concerning the Shipman enquiry and the Lockerbie trial.[50] In only one case has the court accepted that a hearing should be open to the public on Art.10 grounds, the Shipman enquiry.[51] It has been suggested however that this decision is out of line and is unlikely to be followed.[52]

European initiatives in openness

4–102   Although the right of access is not supported by the ECHRFF there have been moves in Europe to enforce greater openness on governments. The Treaty of Amsterdam in 1997 included a provision committing the EU to openness:

> "Article 255
> 1. Any citizen of the Union, and any natural or legal person residing or having its registered office in a Member State, shall have a right of access to European Parliament, Council and Commission documents, subject to the principles and the conditions to be defined in accordance with paragraphs 2 and 3

---

[46] (1987) 9 E.H.R.R. 433.
[47] *Gaskin v United Kingdom* (1989) 12 E.H.R.R. 36; *Guerra v Italy* (1998) 26 E.H.R.R. 357.
[48] *The Times*, March 28, 2002.
[49] [2002] EWHC 396.
[50] *Decision on the Application by Cable News Network*, October 25, 2001; *Petition (No.2) of BBC* [2002] H.R.L.R. 423.
[51] *R (Wagstaffe) v Secretary of State for Health* [2001] 1 W.L.R. 292.
[52] *Privacy versus Freedom of Information: Is there a conflict?* Paper delivered at JUSTICE conference on Privacy in December 2002 by Tim Pitt-Jayne.

    2. General principles and limits on grounds of public or private interest govern-
ing this right of access to documents shall be determined by the Council . . . within
two years of the entry into force of the Treaty of Amsterdam

    3. Each institution referred to above shall elaborate in its own Rules of
Procedure specific provisions regarding access to its documents."

This policy, aimed at making actions and decisions of the Community more transparent, has been applied. It has not been wholly successful as the criticism by the European
Ombudsman that officials are using data protection as a reason not to comply with the
principles of openness evidences. The Commission has enacted a Regulation providing rights of access to commission and institution materials.[53] However, and despite
the admirably liberal regime introduced in relation to access to environmental information, it has to be accepted that there is a long way to go at European level before the
concept of open information becomes a core value of the Community.

---

[53] Regulation (EC) No 1049/2001.

CHAPTER 5

The Principles

INTRODUCTION

5–01   The Data Protection Principles ("the Principles"),[1] found in Sch.1, set out the core standards governing the handling of personal data. All data controllers[2] who process personal data must comply with all the Principles unless a specific exemption applies.[3] The Principles apply irrespective of the notification status of the controller. They derive from the standards originally set out in Treaty 108 in 1981[4] which were the basis of the Data Protection Act 1984 and were strengthened by the requirements of Directive 95/46. Schedule 1 includes extensive interpretation provisions and the Principles are further amplified by three additional Schedules: Sch.2 which deals with the conditions for legitimising processing; Sch.3 which deals with the processing of sensitive personal data and Sch.4 which deals with the conditions for overseas transfers. These are covered in Chs 6, 7 and 8, below respectively. In this chapter the requirements of the Principles themselves are considered.

SUMMARY OF MAIN POINTS

5–02   (a) The first Principle incorporates a detailed set of rules that apply to the obtaining and processing of personal data.

(b) The requirement of lawfulness in the first Principle incorporates considerations of other legal rules and requires data controllers to have regard to other laws in the context of data protection.

(c) Principle 2 incorporates the finality principle and imposes limits on the processing of data for purposes other than those for which they were obtained.

(d) Principle 7 deals with security and sets out detailed requirements for handling personal data.

(e) Data subjects are able to seek compensation for any breach of the Principles which causes them damage however in most instances data subjects tend to

---

[1] It seems to have become accepted practice to capitalise the Principles although the capital is not used in the Act.
[2] See Ch.3, above for the meaning of "data controller", "process" and "personal data".
[3] See s.4(4). Exemptions are covered in Chs 15 to 19, below.
[4] Council of Europe Convention: see Ch.1, above for the backgrounds to the legislation generally.

refer breaches of the Principles to the Commissioner rather than taking action in court.

(f) The Principles apply to the personal data relating to each separate individual who is the subject of the data so may be breached in respect of one person but not of others.

In describing the requirements of the Principles the Legal Guidance given by the Commissioner's Office is referred to where appropriate. At the end of the chapter a description of the Tribunal Decision in the only major case on the Act considered since the Act came into force is provided, together with a selection of case studies drawn from the Commissioner's cases and advice. A number of examples of how the Principles apply in practical situations have also been included. These include a set of precedent clauses for the purposes of Principle 7. The main bulk of the advice provided by the Commissioner's Office is on the application of the Principles but there have been remarkably few cases on them. In considering the application of the Principles in a particular matter the practitioner is recommended to review not only the cases but also any guidance from the Commissioner and from the Article 29 Working Party. In particular sectors there is additional detailed guidance on the application of the Principles and the way in which they relate to other regulatory regimes. In the health sector in particular practitioners must follow the Caldicott principles and the NHS guidance on the uses and disclosures of health information.[5]

Enforcement

5–03   Enforcement of the Principles is principally by the Commissioner serving an enforcement notice. Data subjects' rights under the Act: to see their data[6]; to prevent processing likely to cause damage or distress[7]; to prevent direct marketing—"junk mail"[8]; to object to automated decision-making[9] or to seek compensation[10] can be enforced by the data subject applying for a court order. The Commissioner may also enforce a data subject's rights through enforcement action since Principle 6 requires that personal data be processed in accordance with the data subject's rights. Any breach of those rights thus gives rise to the possibility of enforcement action.[11] In practice, the Commissioner plays a role supporting the actions of data subjects by raising complaints with the relevant data controller in response to a request for an assessment or providing informal advice to the complainant.

THE FIRST PRINCIPLE

5–04   This reflects Arts 10, 11 and 6(1)(a) of the Directive. It requires that personal data shall be processed fairly and lawfully and in particular shall not be processed

---

[5] See Report on the Review of Patient-Identifiable Information by the Caldicott Committee, December 1997 and the Connecting for Health website at *www.connectingforhealth.nhs.net*.
[6] DPA s.7.
[7] DPA s.10.
[8] DPA s.11.
[9] DPA s.12
[10] DPA s.13.
[11] Ch.10, below.

unless at least one of the conditions in Sch.2 is met and, in the case of sensitive personal data, at least one of the conditions in Sch.3 is also met. The Sch.2 and Sch.3 requirements are dealt with in the respective chapters on legitimate processing and sensitive data.[12] The interpretation provision to the Principle lays down a set of rules which apply to the processing of personal data to ensure fairness.

Processing is defined in s.1(1) of the 1998 Act as meaning "obtaining, recording or holding" the data and carrying out various operations with respect to the data including: organising, adapting, altering, retrieving, consulting, using, disclosing, aligning, combining, erasing or blocking the data. The term "processing" is considered in Ch.3, above on the interpretation of the Act. The breadth of the term was confirmed in *Campbell v Mirror Group Newspapers*[13] when the Court of Appeal confirmed that processing covered all handling of personal data up to the moment of publication in hard copy, however the later decision in the case of *Johnson v Medical Defence Union*[14] put a narrower meaning at least as far as the selection of information from computerised records is concerned. The case also went on to consider the question of fairness. This element is explored further below.

Neither "fairly" nor "lawfully" are defined in the legislation and accordingly must be given their normal meaning. The term "fairly" is subject to extensive interpretation in Pt II of Sch.I.

Lawfully

5–05   The meaning of the term "lawfully" has been the subject of some debate in the UK. There is a general acceptance that it must mean in accordance with the terms of the 1998 Act itself and, in particular in accordance with Schs 2 and 3 to the 1998 Act[15] which set out the conditions for legitimate processing. The Recitals to the Directive suggest that "lawfully" could be limited to compliance with the national legislation governing data protection rather than requiring compliance with all relevant legal obligations. Recital 28 commences "Whereas any processing of personal data must be lawful and fair . . .". Recital 30 then continues "Whereas, in order to be lawful, the processing must in addition be . . ." and then sets out most of the Sch.2 conditions. There is an argument therefore that the UK could have complied with the Directive adequately by limiting the meaning of the term "lawfully" to compliance with the requirements of the Act itself. There has also been academic writing which suggests that the current Act can itself be read in that way.[16]

This gives rise to two separate questions:

1. Could the UK have implemented the Directive in a manner which limited the meaning of the term "lawfully" to compliance with the data protection regime itself?

2. Can the current UK Act be read as limiting the meaning of the term "lawfully" to compliance with the Act?

---

[12] Chs 26 and 7, below.
[13] [2002] EWCA Civ 1373.
[14] [2007] EWCA Civ 262.
[15] See Chs 6 and 7, below.
[16] See the arguments put by Professor Liddell, Bio-Science Law Review, Vol.6 Issue 6 2003/2004.

In relation to the first question the stated intent of the Directive was to harmonise data protection at a level which met the best standards of all the previous regimes "harmonization at a high level". The requirement to process personal data lawfully is found in Treaty 108. It also appeared in the 1984 Act in the UK. There must be a presumption that the term had some meaning in Treaty 108 and in the UK's previous legal regime. In the UK the Registrar had already taken the view that the term was of broad application and had been supported in this view by the Data Protection Tribunal. There is a strong argument therefore that the restriction of the term to a self-referential regime would be a reduction of the level of protection both from Treaty 108 and in the UK and from the previous legal regime and therefore not permissible in terms of the Directive.

The answer to the second question follows on inevitably from the answer to the first question in that the UK is obliged to interpret the UK law in accord with the Directive. Moreover such an approach would ignore the wording of Principle 1 itself. Schedule 1 to the 1998 Data Protection Act states that personal data shall be processed fairly and lawfully and in particular, in accordance with the Sch.2 and 3 conditions. The clear implication of the use of the term "in particular" here is that "lawfully" means more than compliance with Schs 2 and 3 alone. It is therefore submitted that the wider meaning of the term "lawful" remains correct.

Relation with the Human Rights Act (HRA)

5–06 Section 3(1) of the HRA provides that, so far as it is possible to do so, primary and subordinate legislation must be "read and given effect in a way which is compatible with the Convention rights".

Article 8 of the Convention provides:

> "(1) Everyone has the right to his private and family life, his home and his correspondence.
> (2) There shall be no interference by a public authority with the exercise of this right except such as is in accordance with the law and is necessary in a democratic society in the interests of national security, public safety or the economic well-being of the country, for the prevention of disorder or crime, for the protection of health or morals, or for the protection of the rights and freedoms of others."

The Art.8 right, however, is neither paramount nor absolute—as cl.(2) makes clear, the State can interfere with the right where other overriding interests require. Furthermore, the right to a private life has to be balanced with other rights specified in the Convention and in particular Art.10—the right to freedom of expression, which provides:

> "(1) Everyone has the right to freedom of expression. This right shall include freedom to hold opinions and to receive and impart information and ideas without interference by public authority and regardless of frontiers. This Article shall not prevent States from requiring the licensing of broadcasting, television or cinema enterprises.
> (2) The exercise of these freedoms, since it carries with it duties and responsibilities may be subject to such formalities, conditions, restrictions or penalties as are prescribed by law and are necessary in a democratic

society, in the interests of national security, territorial integrity or public safety, for the prevention of disorder or crime, for the protection of health or morals, for the protection of the reputation or rights of others, for preventing the disclosure of information received in confidence, or for maintaining the authority and impartiality of the judiciary."

An act which fails to respect an individual's right to be treated lawfully and fairly in the informational sphere is likely to also be regarded as a breach of the Art.8 right. Such an interference must be lawful, justified by reference to one or more of the public interests specified within Art.8 and proportionate. An example might be the disclosure of personal data consisting of medical records without consent or other lawful justification. This would be both a breach of the obligation of confidence and a breach of Art.8 and thus unlawful under Principle 1 as well as being unfair. (Note: The impact of the HRA is discussed in much greater detail in Ch.2, above.)

5–07 Personal data which are processed in breach of any statutory provision or legally enforceable obligation or restriction will be processed unlawfully. "Unlawfulness" may arise when an act is committed in breach of the criminal law, common law (including a breach of confidence or an act which is ultra vires a public authority) or statute. The courts have described the natural meaning of "unlawful" as "something which is contrary to some law or enactment or is done without lawful justification or excuse".[17] In the Legal Guidance the Commissioner singles out four areas as having particular relevance to the first Principle. They are:

- confidentiality arising from the relationship between data controller and data subject[18];
- the rules of law restricting the activities of public bodies to those which are within their statutory or delegated powers;
- the potential effect of the doctrine of legitimate expectation; and
- the effect of Art.8 of the Convention rights in the HRA 1998.[19]

Interestingly the Commissioner does not deal with breaches of the criminal law. Inevitably breaches of the criminal law which involve personal data will entail a breach of the first Principle. The most obvious example being anyone who processes personal data in the course of or as a result of committing an offence of procuring personal data without authority under s.55 of the Act will be processing unlawfully.

5–08 The Registrar's views that the term "lawful" requires the data controller to comply with all relevant laws affecting the data processing received the support of the Data Protection Tribunal explicitly in the case of ultra vires, and implicitly in the case of confidentiality, in the appeal by British Gas Trading Ltd (BGTL)[20] under the equivalent provision of the 1984 Act. The case involved the proposed use by BGTL of the personal data of its gas customers to promote services and supplies unrelated to the

---

[17] *R. v R* [1991] 4 All E.R. 481.
[18] For a full analysis of the law of confidence as it affects personal information see Ch.2, above.
[19] For a full analysis of Art.8 and its relation with data protection see Ch.2.
[20] *British Gas Ltd v Data Protection Registrar*, March 1998.

supply of gas. The Registrar contended that such a use would be unlawful in the sense that in using the data as proposed BGTL was operating outside of its powers and was breaching a duty of confidentiality owed to its customers. Although the Tribunal found that on the facts BGTL was not operating outside of its powers, they agreed that:

> "If we had found that the British Gas Corporation, BGTL's predecessor company, had done acts beyond its statutory powers then we would, for the purpose of deciding if there had been a breach of data protection principles, have regarded such acts as unlawful."

With respect to the duty of confidentiality, the Tribunal held that such a duty did not arise in the particular case:

> "The circumstance that an individual has a supply of piped gas at his home does not appear to us to fall into the category of information that gives rise to a duty of confidence, unless there are special additional features relating to a particular individual or his address."

But the Tribunal did accept that a duty of confidentiality could readily arise between a data subject and a data user and that such a duty may in appropriate situations inhibit use of the personal data as well as disclosure to others.

Breach of the criminal law

5–09   The range of criminal offences that may be committed using personal data is wide. Those offences which focus on the use of personal data, apart from offences under the Act itself and those directly concerned with misrepresentation, would appear to be hacking, identity fraud and pornography. It is perhaps unlikely that action would be taken under the DPA where defendants were being charged with the more serious offences however they are dealt with briefly here.

Hacking

5–10   The act of unauthorised alteration or destruction of computer-based personal data is unlikely to amount to an offence of criminal damage in contravention of the Criminal Damage Act 1971 because there will generally be no physical damage. However such actions may be contrary to the Computer Misuse Act 1990 (CMA) as amended by the Police and Justice Act 2006. The amendments made to the offences by the Police and Justice Act 2006 have not been brought into effect at the time of writing and are themselves subject to proposed amendments in the Serious Crime Bill.

The CMA as amended by the Police and Justice Act 2006 creates four basic offences:

(a) securing unauthorised access to any program or data held on a computer [or enabling such access to be secured] (s.1);

(b) securing or enabling such unauthorised access to a computer with a view to committing or facilitating a serious criminal offence (for example, some form of fraud) (s.2);

(c) carrying out an unauthorised act in relation to a computer which impairs the operation of the computer, any software or the reliability of any data [or enabling any of these to be done] (s.3).

(d) making, supplying or obtaining any articles for use in offences under ss.1 or 3. For these purposes the term "articles" includes any program or data held in electronic form (s.3A).

The words in square brackets were part of the amendments made by the Police and Justice Act 2006 but which are proposed to be repealed by the Serious Crime Bill (cl.55). The effect of the provisions in square brackets would have been to criminalise the actions of assisting or facilitating the substantive offences. The Serious Crime Bill includes a set of broad provisions to deal with encouraging or assisting crime which will be of general application and therefore remove the need for specific provisions in the CMA.

The offences in s.1 (and hence s.2) have to be committed deliberately rather than accidentally. Data or programs on a removable storage medium are also covered. "Securing access" or "enabling such access to be secured" is established if a hacker alters, erases, copies, moves, uses or outputs any program or data or carries out acts which enable another to do this whether by means of a program or by human delivery. The offences in s.3 may be committed where the person is reckless as to whether his actions will have the effect of impairing the operation of any computer, preventing or hindering access to any program or data held in a computer or will impair the operation of any such program or the reliability of any such data. The offence of making or adapting an article for use in the commission of an offence in the new s.3A requires intent, however, for the offence of supplying or offering to supply an article it is sufficient if the person believes it "likely" to be used to commit an offence, a provision that has given rise to some concern.

The Police and Justice Act 2006 also increased the penalties for offences so that all the offences, including the basic offence of securing access or enabling access to be secured, became indictable and punishable by up to two years imprisonment.

The strengthening of the provisions has been the subject of a campaign by *Computer Weekly* magazine and others for several years. The new rules make clear that "denial of service" attacks are caught by the provisions as well as catching those who provide programs which are made available to assist would be hackers over the internet. It is therefore ironic that, when the new provisions were introduced, they sparked fears among security experts that the provisions in s.3A, which make it an offence to supply an article where the person believes there is a likelihood of use in a criminal purpose, could criminalise the distribution of programs used by legitimate IT professionals to check whether a network is secure.[21]

Identity theft and fraud

5–11 This appears to have been a growth area of dishonesty over the last few years. The Regulatory Impact Assessment to the Serious Crime Bill[22] quotes a 2000 report by NERA, an economic consulting firm, which estimated that the total

---

[21] Reported at Out-Law, November 11, 2006.
[22] January 2007.

economic cost of fraud in 1998–1999 was between £6.8bn and £13.8bn. The Fraud Act 2006 which came into effect on the January 1, 2007 is designed to deal with fraud and includes a range of offences which may be committed by those dealing with personal data. These include the offence of failing to disclose information which a person is under a legal duty to disclose[23] and actively misrepresenting the truth.[24] In each case the offence must be committed knowingly or recklessly and the person must be acting dishonestly and with intent to make a gain for himself or another or cause loss to another or expose another to the risk of loss. In dealing with false representation the Act criminalises "phishing" and in ss. 6–8 also criminalises the production and possession of "phishing" kits. Phishing is the act of setting up a website or sending an email to people purporting to come from a financial institution and obtaining the financial details of those individuals to use in fraudulent transactions. It is also an offence to possess the software and tools necessary to launch a phishing attack or to write software knowing that it is designed or adapted for use in connection with fraud.

These changes update the law and address the fact that personal data on a computer does not constitute "intangible property" and is consequently incapable of being stolen. A data thief could only be charged with the theft of a data storage medium. In *Oxford v Moss*,[25] it was held that confidential information per se did not come within the definition of "property" in s.4 of the Theft Act 1968. (A student obtained, read and returned the proof of an examination paper; he was charged with the theft of confidential information but acquitted.)

The Serious Crime Bill will introduce further data-sharing provisions which are covered below.

Obscenity and indecency

5–12 The Protection of Children Act 1978 (PCA) includes provisions which deal with the holding of personal data relating to children and addresses some issues which have a more general application in dealing with personal data. It is an offence to take or distribute indecent photographs or pseudo-photographs of children.[26] The Criminal Justice Act 1988 (CJA) renders mere possession (including on a hard disk) of indecent photographs or pseudo-photographs of a child an offence.[27]

A "pseudo photo" is something that "appears" to be a photo and "appears" to show a child—even if it is not based on a child. This means that electronically manipulated or created images will be caught.[28] In such a case the data will not meet the definition of personal data and there will be no unlawful processing under the DPA. There are two potential defences open to those charged under the legislation—the first being that they did not see the image and had no knowledge or suspicion that the image was indecent, and the second being that there was a legitimate (for example medical) reason for possessing or distributing the image.[29] There are also offences of "making" an

---

[23] Fraud Act 2006 s.3.
[24] Fraud Act 2006 s.2.
[25] (1978) 68 Cr.App.R. 183, DC.
[26] PCA s.1.
[27] CJA s.160.
[28] PCA s.1(7)–(9).
[29] PCA s.1(4).

indecent photo contrary to s.1 of the PCA 1978 and possessing an indecent photo of a child contrary to s.160 of the CJA 1988).

In 2002, the Court of Appeal gave more detailed consideration to what amounts to "possessing" such material in the context of individuals who browse the world wide web and encounter indecent photographs but do not deliberately download the images. There are two parts to the judgment in the case of *R. v Smith*.[30] The first "exonerates" individuals who are not aware of the operation of the internet browser cache and who inadvertently stumble across indecent photos of children whilst browsing, with the result that a copy of the image ends up on his or her hard drive. However, those who cause an indecent photo to appear on their computer screen (even though they do not actively download it) providing they hold the necessary criminal intent or "mens rea" are regarded as being in "possession" of such material. The court defined the required criminal intent as—"the act of making should be a deliberate and intentional act with knowledge that the image made is, or is likely to be an indecent photograph or pseudo-photograph of a child". Not surprisingly the question of whether those persons became data controllers for the data in question did not exercise the Court of Appeal. However, applying the Commissioner's approach to the question of access to credit refernce files it would appear that the Commissioner would take the same view as the Court of Appeal. A similar issue arose in the case of *R v Ross Warwick Porter*[31] as to whether a person who only held the marker to an indecent photograph and had deleted the actual image could be regarded as being in possession of it. The Court held that in the case of a deleted computer image if a person could not gain access to an image or retieve it he no longer had possession of it.

Breach of contract unlawfulness

5–13   Information obtained (or otherwise processed) in breach of an enforceable contractual agreement will be unlawfully obtained (or otherwise processed). This intersects however with the broader question of whether information to which an obligation of confidence applies can be disclosed as most contractual clauses bind the parties to maintain confidentiality in information which qualifies for protection as such. The question is therefore more usually addressed as a matter of confidentiality.

Torts and civil wrongs

5–14   In terms of the common law actions for defamation will involve allegations of the unlawful processing of personal data as might breaches of intellectual property rights. However the area of common law that has been the subject of most attention in its relation to Principle 1 is the law of confidence.

Confidentiality

5–15   The law of confidence is a developing area and where personal information is concerned the relationship between confidentiality and Art.8 of the Convention has given rise to significant recent case law. The cases which develop the aspect of personal privacy are covered in Ch.2, above. The fundamental point however is that where an

---

[30] *R v Smith*, *The Times*, April 23, 2002, CA.
[31] [2006] EWCA Crim 560, CA.

obligation of confidence applies in relation to personal data any breach of the obligation without justification, or in current legal terms, any misuse of the personal information, is likely to amount to unlawful processing in breach of Principle 1. In the cases of *A v B*[32] and *Naomi Campbell v MGN Limited*,[33] the Courts held that a duty of confidence can apply even where information is not "confided" in the traditional manner. The obligation of confidence will now apply in any circumstances where an individual has a reasonable expectation of privacy in relation to the information in question.

There are three grounds which will justify breach of a confidentiality obligation. These are:

(a) consent of the individual;

(b) compulsion of law;

(c) public interest.

Public interest will not necessarily justify widespread publication:

"the obligation to the particular individual may be set aside by reason of an overriding public need. Even when disclosures have been held to be in the public interest this would not permit publication of information to the world, but only to the appropriate authorities who would investigate the matter."[34]

There are a number of cases where the courts have engaged in balancing the obligation of confidence against the wider public interest requiring disclosure.[35] A fuller exposition is found in Ch.2, above. In many of these cases the disclosure proposed is not a disclosure to the world at large. In *Andrew Wakefield v Channel Four Television Corporation*[36] the General Medical Council (GMC) argued that they should not disclose information provided by patients in relation to disciplinary proceedings to Channel 4 to enable it to defend itself against a claim by the applicant, as they had obtained the documents under compulsory powers and were therefore not entitled to use them for another purpose; they had given assurances that the documents would only be used for the purposes for which they were obtained and it would undermine their investigative function if they were required to disclose. The Court held that the GMC should make the disclosure taking into account the fact that the disclosure to the applicant would not result in wider disclosure of the information and that it was necessary to enable the proceedings to be dealt with. It advised that the GMC should ensure that its undertakings of confidentiality were accurate and not overstated.

---

[32] [2002] 3 W.L.R. 542.
[33] [2002] EWCA Civ 337.
[34] Legal Guidance.
[35] See, for example, *Butler v Board of Trade* [1971] 1 Ch.680; *Norwich Pharamacal Co v Commissioners for Customs and Excise* [1973] 2 All E.R. 943; *Alfred Crompton Amusement Machines v Commissioner for Customs and Excise (No.2)* [1973] 2 All E.R. 1169; *Marcel v Commissioner for Police of Metropolis* [1992] 1 All E.R. 72; *Lonrho v Fayed* (No. 4) [1994] 1 All E.R. 870; *Bank of Crete v Koskotos (No.2)* [1993] All E.R. 748; *Hoechst UK Ltd v Chemiculture* [1993] F.S.R. 270; *Hellewell v Chief Constable of Derbyshire* [1993] 4 All E.R. 473; *Melton Medes Ltd v SIB* [1995] 3 All E.R. 880.
[36] [2006] EWHC 3289.

In the *Campbell* case the House of Lords also accepted that there is a public interest in the disclosure of personal information which "sets the record straight" where the subject has misled the public.

The law of confidence applies to public bodies as well as to private persons. The question as to whether a public body will be bound in confidence wherever it obtains information under compulsory powers or only where the information is particularly sensitive is a difficult one and there is no clear authority on the point. Although case law suggests that the former is the case the cases have all concerned information which was sensitive (although not necessarily in terms of the DPA). The approach of the current Government is that non-sensitive data at least should not be regarded as subject to such a prohibition. These issues are covered under the topic of data-sharing below.

Statutory powers or delegated powers

5–16 The public sector does not enjoy the same freedom of action as the private sector. Public bodies are set up and funded for specific purposes, often with restrictions on the ways in which those purposes are achieved. The nature of the way that the restrictions are enforced are different depending on the nature of the public body but whatever the nature of the body the courts have the power to act to ensure that the body acts only within its powers. Where bodies are established under statute, such as local authorities, their powers will be set out in the statute which establishes the body.[37] They have the powers that Parliament granted them in the statute. The body may carry out those things mandated by the statute and those which are reasonably incidental to them.[38] This is called the ultra vires rule as authorities must not act ultra vires or outside their powers. The Crown is different as the Crown has inherent powers and starts with all the powers of a natural person, in other words the Crown can do anything that is not prohibited by the law. However in many areas Parliament has legislated and where there is legislation then the powers of the Crown are limited by that legislation and must be exercised in accord with it.[39] The Crown may also do those things which are reasonably incidental to the relevant functions. However, this does not extend powers. The absence of an express restriction on an activity does not mean that it can be carried out under any ancillary powers.[40]

In carrying out their functions public bodies of any type must not act unreasonably, unfairly or use their powers for the wrong reasons. If they do any of these things, then they may be subject to judicial review.

Legitimate expectation

5–17 The courts have also developed the doctrine of legitimate expectation which may constrain the actions of a public body. The conditions in which a legitimate expectation will arise were explained in *Council of Civil Service Unions v Minister for the*

---

[37] See comment of Lord Neill in *Credit Suisse v Waltham Forest* [1996] 4 All E.R. 176 that statutory powers are conferred on local authorities on trust and can only be used in the ways that Parliament is presumed to have intended.
[38] *AG v Great Eastern Railway* (1880) 5 App. Cas. 473.
[39] *R. v Secretary of State for the Home Department Ex p. Fire Brigades Union* [1995] 2 A.C. 513.
[40] *Credit Suisse v Allderdale BC* [1966] 1 All E.R. 129.

Civil Service.[41] A legitimate expectation may arise either from an express promise given on behalf of a public authority or from the existence of a regular practice. The authority must by its words or its conduct have led someone to expect that it will act in a particular way so that the person affected will receive or retain a benefit. The authority may then be held to its promise or made to abide by its practice (subject to the requirements of public interest) at least until it has heard from the people affected by the proposed change. The concept applies not just to the Crown but also to other public authorities.[42]

5–18 As has been noted above the Human Rights Act also imposes on public authorities the obligation to act only in accord with Convention rights. The intersection of these rules on lawfulness on the use that public bodies can make of the personal data which they obtain or generate as a result of their functions has given rise to a number of uncertainties which have yet to be resolved by the courts. In particular there is a lack of clarity over how far information obtained for one function can legitimately be used for other, unassociated, purposes.

Does unlawful always mean unfair?

5–19 Personal data must be processed both fairly and lawfully. It is difficult, at first, to conceive of "unlawful" processing that might still be considered "fair" however the two may not be co-terminous. Fairness is a concept which is applicable between two or more parties, usually individuals but possibly organisations or statutory bodies. Lawfulness suggests a community-wide set of norms enforceable by the intervention of the state.

An act could be fair between consenting private parties but unlawful by virtue of legal rules, for example, the madam of a brothel who, with the full consent of both her clients and her staff, keeps a computerised list of clients and their particular preferences for the purpose of running the establishment. She might not be acting unfairly in carrying out such processing but might be acting unlawfully.

Data-sharing

5–20 One of the issues which raises the question of lawful processing more that others is the development of data-sharing in the public sector. Guidance was given by the Data Protection Registrar on the impact of the requirement to process personal data lawfully in a publication called *Private Lives and Public Powers* issued in 1997 under the equivalent provision of the 1984 Act which took the view that the public law restrictions on the powers of public authorities and the effect of implicit obligations of confidentiality had a restrictive impact on the uses and disclosures that could be made of personal data in the public sector.

In the Legal Guidance issued by the Commissioner under the 1998 Act the legal analysis set out in *Private Lives and Public Powers* was largely repeated. Since then the increased wish of Government to allow Departments and other parts of the public sector to share information about individuals has led to a focus on this area and a rash of different materials. In April 2003 the Cabinet Office issued a report on privacy and

---

[41] [1984] 3 All E.R. 935.
[42] *R v Devon CC Ex p. Baker* [1995] 1 All E.R. 73; and its joint case: *R. v Durham CC Ex p. Curtis.*

data-sharing which started from the presumption that any disclosures or uses for "new" purposes would be based on the consent of citizens.[43] In November 2003 the Department of Constitutional Affairs (DCA) issued legal guidance which set out a detailed exposition of the legal issues which are involved where information obtained for one purpose is intended to be used for another or disclosed for use by another public body which applied largely the same legal analysis as the Commissioner had done in the earlier guidance materials.[44]

More recently however the Government has flagged its concern at the way that the law restricts the potential sharing of information between public sector bodies and has signaled a policy change in the area. In a document produced by the Department of Constitutional Affairs entitled *A Vision Statement for Data Sharing*, issued in September 2006, it committed Government to achieve more sharing of information between public sector organisations and the public and private sectors. It made clear that there would be some changes to the law to facilitate this but no change to the Data Protection Act. In January 2007 it published the Serious Crime Bill which would enable two kinds of data-sharing: the disclosure of information from the public sector to the private sector for the purpose of preventing fraud[45]; and the extension of the annual data-matching exercise by the Audit Commission by placing it on a statutory basis and giving increased powers to the Audit Commission.[46]

In both cases the Bill will disapply any prohibitions on disclosure which would apply by reason of any obligation of confidence or other legal restriction but leaves the exercise subject to the Data Protection Act. These proposed gateway provisions therefore overcome the possibility that such uses and disclosures might be held to be unlawful.

5–21   The current position of Government appears to have shifted considerably since the publication of the PIU Report and moved to the position that the consent of individuals should **not** be required before their information is shared (apart for some sensitive data categories) and there should be a presumption that information is available for a wide range of public sector uses. This approach has already influenced the enforcement policy of the Commisioner. In December 2006 the Commissoner altered his long-standing view that personal data derived from Council Tax functions could only be used for those functions, and any other use was unlawful; instead taking the stance that a decision on that point was not for the Commissioner but was for local authorities to make for themselves. In the Guidance the Commissioner has maintained his view of the legal meaning of the term "lawfully" but has reiterated the statements made in his enforcement strategy that he would not take action against a data controller for a technical breach of the law but only where the breach caused a real detriment to the individual.[47]

The area of particular uncertainly appears to centre around the extent that authorities can use either incidental or general powers in order to use personal data obtained for one purpose for a) a linked or similar purpose and b) a wholly different purpose. The Court of Human Rights has considered the point to some extent in the cases of

---

[43] PIU Report, Cabinet Office.
[44] See DCA Guidance and Toolkit on the DCA website.
[45] Serious Crime Bill cl.61 onwards.
[46] Sch.6 proposed amendments to the Audit Commission Act 1998.
[47] Sharing personal information; a new approach ICO December 2006.

Peck[48] and *Copland*.[49] In *Peck* the local authority had a statutory power under the Crime and Disorder Act to run CCTV in public places. It photographed Mr Peck on the CCTV and publicised the images to show that the use of CCTV was a positive contribution to the reduction of problems. The Court held that the action of the authority in publishing the data was lawful because it was incidental to the function for which it had obtained the data. Accordingly the authority had a lawful basis for the processing. However in *Copland* the authority monitored communications data relating to the calls and internet use of the applicant and argued that it had a lawful basis as this was incidental to its general powers to run the institution and its obligations to ensure that public funds were properly used. The Court did not accept that and said it found the argument "unpersuasive". The Court appeared to be influenced by the fact that the use was secret and the legal basis did not therefore meet the standards of being generally known and available law. The tentative conclusion that can be drawn from this is that incidental powers can provide a lawful basis for a use of personal data which would otherwise breach Art.8 as long as the proposed uses are publicly acknowledged or set out in some proper way and the purpose is closely associated with the original purpose for which the data were obtained. The use must be clearly incidental to the main function and forseeable by the person affected. The discussion in the cases on these points are distinctly brief and there has not yet been any academic review but it appears therefore that there are relatively constrained limits on the use of incidental powers. The Court has not considered the general powers such as the local government well-being provisions[50] however it may be suggested that they will not regard these are satisfactory unless the scheme for the use of the data is set out properly in an ascertainable form which citizens have an opportunity to review. In the case of the Consultancy Index, before it was put on a statutory footing, the Court in the UK held that the Index was lawful although based on the general powers of the Secretary of State but appeared to be largely influenced by the fact that the surrounding administrative scheme ensured that those affected were fully informed of their position and rights.

The uncertainty has led to the addition of specfic "gateway" provisions in more recent legislation to make clear that the body has the powers to use or share data, for example in the Serious Organised Crime and Police Act 2005 (SOCA), s.32 allows SOCA to use and disclose information for permitted purposes. However the existence of such provisions creates a degree of uncertainty in those cases where no gateways have been incorportated.

Fairly

5–22   It is submitted that "fairly" must be an objective standard. This was the Registrar's view under the 1984 Act. In the publication *The Guidelines*,[51] the Registrar contended:

> "Standards of fairness and lawfulness must be objectively assessed and applied. To assess the proper standards the Registrar will use the standpoint of the

---

[48] (2003) 36 E.H.R.R. 41.
[49] (2006) 43 E.H.R.R. SE5.
[50] Local Government Act 2000 s.2.
[51] 3rd series, November 1994, at p.59.

'common man'. Thus the Registrar may decide that a data user has contravened the [first] Principle even though the data user did not intend to be unfair and did not consider himself to be acting unfairly."

The point is not dealt with in the Legal Guidance, however, there is no reason to assume that the Commissioner would take a different view.

Fairness under the 1984 Act

5–23   In the Legal Guidance the Commissioner refers to a number of cases decided by the Data Protection Tribunal under the parallel provision (the first Principle) of the 1984 Act. In those cases the Tribunal stated that the purpose of that Act was to protect the rights of the individual about whom data are obtained, stored, processed or supplied, rather than those of the data user.[52] The Tribunal took the view that, in deciding whether processing is fair, the most important single consideration would be the interest of the data subject. The Tribunal weighed the various considerations involved in any particular case but ultimately always gave more weight to the interests of the individual.[53]

It is suggested that the Commissioner goes a little too far in the Legal Guidance in referring to the interests of the data subject being "paramount".[54] Although the Tribunal did use the term in the first credit reference decision, *CCN Systems Limited v The Data Protection Registrar*, it distanced itself from the term in the second decision *Infolink v The Data Protection Registrar*. The cases have been referred to with approval in subsequent cases[55] however in a case decided by the Information Tribunal in an appeal under the Freedom of Information Act 2000 (FOIA) decided in January 2007[56] the Tribunal has indicated that in deciding whether a disclosure of personal data under the FOIA is fair the *CNN* and *Infolink* cases can be distinguished. In that decision the Tribunal made clear that the question of the fairness of the processing has to be considered in all the circumstances of the particular case. In the particular circumstances the processing concerned personal data of public officials which was being processed for the purpose of a public function. In that case the interests of the officials was not first or paramount:

"... we find that when assessing the fair processing requirements under the DPA that the consideration given to the interests of data subjects who are public officials where data are processed for a public function, is no longer first or paramount. Their interests are still important but where data subjects carry out public functions, hold elective office or spend public funds they must have the expectation that their public actions will be subjected to greater scrutiny than would be the case with their private lives."

---

[52] *CCN Systems Ltd v The Data Protection Registrar,* February 1991, para.5.
[53] *Infolink Ltd v The Data Protection Registrar,* June 1991, para.61.
[54] *Legal Guidance,* p. 31.
[55] See *R. (Lord) v Secretary of State for the Home Department* [2003] EWHC 2073.
[56] *The Corporate Officer of the House of Commons v Information Commissioner,* Appeal EA 2006/0015 and 16.

In the same vein the Court of Appeal in *Johnson v Medical Defence Union*[57] agreed that in assessing fairness the position of the data controller must also be considered.

5–24 In other cases the Data Protection Tribunal found that personal information will not be fairly obtained unless the individual has been informed of any non-obvious purpose or purposes intended by the data controller before the information is obtained.[58]

The Tribunal had also found in a direct marketing context, that where data subjects could have been told but were deliberately not told, at the time the data were obtained, of the proposed use of their personal data for marketing purposes, the data user is under an obligation to obtain the positive consent of the data subjects for the subsequent use of their data for this purpose.[59]

Interpretation principles in the 1998 Act

5–25 The interpretation of the first Principle takes up the largest part of the interpretation provisions set out in Pt II of Sch.1 to the 1998 Act. All the interpretation provisions apply to the term "fairly" alone. None relate to the word "lawfully". The Commissioner refers to Sch.1 Pt II paras 1–4, as constituting a "fair processing code".[60] The code addresses the question of notice to the data subject but clearly does not exhaust all the ways in which personal data may be processed fairly or unfairly.

The first provision[61] establishes, that, in determining whether personal data are processed fairly, regard is to be had to the method by which they are obtained, including in particular whether any person from whom they are obtained is deceived or misled as to the purpose or purposes for which they are to be processed. The obtaining of personal data, or the information to be contained in personal data, is an act of processing.

The second part of the paragraph provides that data will be deemed to be obtained fairly if they consist of information obtained from a person who is either authorised by or under any enactment to supply it or obliged to do so either by or under an enactment or an international instrument. This is stated to be subject to para.2 which sets out the information which must be provided to data subjects. The effect of this provision is twofold:

(a) no disclosure of personal data which is required under statute can be restricted on grounds related to the first Principle and the person who obtains personal data for a statutory purpose will not be liable for an act of unfair processing, even if the data subject had not been told of the possible disclosure;

(b) nevertheless the data subject should be provided with the necessary fair processing notice therefore a data controller who has obtained personal data for a statutory purpose in reliance on para.1 will nevertheless be bound to provide the data subject with the "specified information".

---

[57] [2007] EWCA Civ 262.
[58] *Innovations (Mail Order) Ltd v DPR*, September 1993, para.30.
[59] *ibid.* para.31.
[60] *The Data Protection Act 1998—An Introduction*, Office of the Data Protection Registrar, October 1998, at p.11.
[61] Sch.1 Pt II para.1.

To some extent the provision covers the same ground as the exemption in s.35 which exempts disclosures of personal data from the non-disclosure provisions where the exemption is required by or under any enactment.

The "specified information"

5–26 The Act provides that data are not to be treated as being processed fairly unless the data controller ensures so far as practicable that the data subject is provided with certain information at the time that the data are gathered from him or, if the data are obtained by another route, either before the "relevant time" or as soon as practicable thereafter.

"Another route" may include purchase or transfer from another data controller or obtaining the personal data from an associate (wife, parent, etc.) of the data subject.

The "relevant time" is defined in para.2(2) as:

(a) the time when the data controller first processes the data; or

(b) in a case where at that time disclosure to a third party within a reasonable period is envisaged:

  (i) if the data are in fact disclosed to such a person within that period, the time when the data are first disclosed;

  (ii) if within that period the data controller becomes, or ought to become, aware that the data are unlikely to be disclosed to such a person within that period, the time when the data controller does become, or ought to become, so aware; or

  (iii) in any other case, the end of that period.

Subparagraphs (a) and (b)(i) are relatively unproblematic. If a data controller is planning on keeping the personal data to himself, so to speak, then the "relevant time" is when processing first takes place. If the data controller is planning to disclose to a third party then the relevant time is when that disclosure first takes place. Subparagraph (b)(ii) deals with the situation where a data controller originally intends to disclose but then for whatever reason changes his mind—in this case, the relevant time is when the data controller changes his mind. Of subpara.(b)(iii), it can be said that it is otiose since all the possible scenarios appeared to be exhausted by subparas (i) and (ii).

What is the specified information?

5–27 The information to be provided to the data subject is:

(a) the identity of the data controller;

(b) the identity of any nominated representative;

(c) the purpose or purposes for which the data are intended to be processed;

(d) any further information which is necessary, having regard to the specific circumstances in which the data are or are to be processed, to enable processing in respect of the data subject to be fair.

Note: For future reference this will be referred to as the "specified information".

"Nominated representative" is not defined in the 1998 Act, although the phrase also appears in the provisions on notification at s.16(1)(b).

The Commissioner has stated that in deciding whether and, if so, what further information is "necessary" to satisfy the fourth requirement above:

> "Data controllers should consider what processing of personal data they shall be carrying out once the data have been obtained and consider whether or not data subjects are likely to understand the following:
>
> > (a) the purposes for which their personal data are going to be processed;
> > (b) the likely consequences of such processing such that the data subject is able to make a judgment as to the nature and extent of the processing; and
> > (c) whether particular disclosures can reasonably be envisaged,
>
> It would be expected that the more unforeseen the consequences of processing the more likely that it is that the data controller will be expected to provide further information."[62]

The approach recognises that the purpose of the provision of information provides transparency to the data subject, which in itself is regarded as a desirable quality, as well as opening the possibility of empowering the data subject to take a range of steps. The Directive deals with the *purpose* of a fair processing notice in general terms in Recital 38 as follows:

> "Whereas, if the processing of data is to be fair, the data subject must be in a position to learn of the existence of a processing operation and where the data are collected from him, must be given accurate and full information, bearing in mind the circumstances of the collection."

The data subject can be empowered in a number of ways by being made aware of the nature of the processing: he may be put on notice that behaviour is being captured or that information may be shared with others, for example on CCTV or in a credit notice, which may forewarn him to alter behaviour appropriately; he may be made aware that a record is held in respect of which he may wish to exercise his rights of access or, if the data are incorrect, correction; he may be able to assess the notice and decide not to enter into the relationship with the data controller, for example if it is a condition of taking advantage of a special offer that the individual consents to receive direct mail, he may decide not to accept the offer. In its Opinion on the provision of information to passengers in the transfer of PNR data to US authorities[63] the Article 29 Working Party noted that passengers should be made aware of the nature of the processing even if, in practice, the transfer to the US authorities has become a condition of travelling to the US.

The Commissioner acknowledges that complying with the "fair processing code" links and overlaps with the obtaining of the data subject's consent as one of the ways

---

[62] *Legal Guidance*, p.32.
[63] Adopted February 15, 2007.

of legitimising processing. Data subjects must be made fully aware of the ways in which their data may be processed in order that they can give fully informed consent to legitimise processing, in appropriate cases.

In the Directive Art.10—which covers those cases where the data controller collects data directly from the data subject—lists a number of examples of the type of further information which might be relevant to include. These are:

- the recipients or categories of recipients;
- whether the replies to the questions are obligatory or voluntary, as well as the possible consequences of failing to reply;
- the existence of the right of access to and the right to rectify the data concerning him.

Article 11, which covers those cases where the data are not obtained from the data subject suggests:

- the categories of information concerned;
- the recipients or categories of recipients;
- the existence of the right of access to and the right to rectify the data concerning him.

As a matter of good practice it is suggested that data controllers should consider whether to include these in any notice.

Providing the specified information

5–28   The obligation on the data controller is to ensure so far as practicable that the data subject either:

(a) has;

(b) is provided with; or

(c) has made readily available to him

the specified information.

The first term "has" seems to be designed to cover a multi-stage data gathering exercise and to enable the data controller to provide the data subject with the requisite information at just one rather than at every stage. Alternatively, it may cover the situation where data are gathered with the specific intention of passing it to a third party. The original data gatherer may know what the third party's purposes will be and can provide the data subject with the relevant specified information at the time of gathering. The third party would then know that the data subjects already have the specified information.

The last term—"has made readily available to him"—is rather open-ended and ripe for different interpretations. It could be argued that, for example, handing a data subject a notice saying that the requisite information can be obtained by writing to a specified address, would be sufficient. The contrary argument would be that the information was not "readily" available if it was not immediately to hand. In one of the Tribunal cases under the 1984 Act, consideration was given to the stage at which and the manner in which a data subject should be informed of the uses to which it was proposed their data should be put. In *Innovations (Mail Order) v Data Protection Registrar*, the appellants contended that sending a subsequent notice of uses was acceptable. This submission was rejected by the Tribunal. In that case however there would have been no difficulty in providing the information at the point when the personal data were obtained. The data controller wished to use the data for another purpose (the sale of marketing lists to third parties) which was not an necessary adjunct of the main purpose and the data controller deliberately adopted a policy of withholding the relevant notice until the acknowledgement of order was sent and thereby putting the burden of "opting out" of the sale of the names on the data subject. Not surprisingly the Tribunal did not regard this as "fair". However there may well be circumstances in which simply enabling a data subject to access specified information by another means would be sufficient. The development of the internet and the availability of websites with the capacity to include more detailed information on Privacy Statements or their equivalent has led to a significant development in the approach of regulators to the notice provisions with the encouragement of the use of "layered" notices. The Commissioner has issued guidance on this approach and it has been endorsed by the Article 29 Working Party. The concept of making information "readily available" to a data subject did not appear in the provisions for interpreting the 1984 Principles and has not been specifically considered by the Tribunal under the 1998 Act.

The Act is not explicit about when the information has to be placed before the data subject. If the data subject is able to make meaningful decisions based on the information, for example not to enter into the relationship, it will be crucial that the relevant information is provided at that time. To achieve this, the material parts of the information should usually be provided before or at the point at which the data are obtained. However the current guidance on "layered" notices appears to accept that more detailed information or information about matters which will not make a material difference to the individual may be provided at a later date if it would be difficult to provide all the information at the point of obtaining.

5–29   The question of whether a data controller can gain an advantage by deliberately failing to give a fair processing notice arose in the case of *Grow With Us Ltd v Green Thumb (UK) Ltd*[64] in which the court made clear that parties cannot use the Act as a vehicle to avoid commercial obligations freely entered into. Green Thumb had a lawn treatment business in which Grow With Us held a franchise. Grow With Us was obliged under the franchise agreement to supply Green Thumb with a list of its customers' and prospective customers' names and addresses. They had persistently refused to transfer the data to Green Thumb. For that, and other reasons, Green Thumb refused to renew the franchise agreement and Grow With Us took them to court to require them to do. One of the arguments employed by Grow With Us was that the disclosure of the names and addresses would breach the DPA because the

---

[64] [2006] EWCA Civ 1201.

customers had not had proper notice. They also argued that there was no appropriate Sch.2 ground. In relation to the notice point they raised two arguments:

- that the obligation to provide a fair processing notice required them to have regard to the purposes for which the disclosee was to process the personal data and they were not aware in sufficient detail of those purposes to provide an adequate notice; and
- the data protection notice given by Green Thumb on the prospectus which went to customers had not been sufficient to notify customers of the purposes for which Green Thumb intended to process the data.

The judge in the Court of Appeal, Buxton L.J., did not have to decide these points but went on to consider them holding that the data protection notice provided by Green Thumb was perfectly adequate to give a general indication of the nature of the processing which was intended and, on the first point, that it would be for Green Thumb to give the notice about their own processing, not Grow With Us. The wording of the notice which appeared on the prospectus was as follows:

"Green Thumb (UK) Ltd and its franchisees take the issue of protecting your personal information seriously and would be grateful if you would take the time to read the following information about our use of your personal information. We will use your personal information to provide and enhance our services to you; deal with enquiries, administration, security and market research."

As far as the appropriate ground for processing was concerned the Court held that there was no barrier to obtaining customer consent to the disclosure but in any event Ground 6 was probably available to the controller.

5–30   The level of detail to be provided in a notice was also considered in *Johnson v MDU* in which the Court held that a notice which referred to the purpose of risk assessment in general terms was sufficient to enable the MDU to utilise Mr Johnson's data in order to assess the wisdom of continuing to supply him with services.[65] In that case the Court appears to have taken the nature of the recipient into account, commenting that the notice, which was in general terms, should have been sufficient to alert a doctor such as Mr Johnson to the scope of processing likely to be carried out.

5–31   In both these cases and the *House of Commons before the Information Tribunal* case the courts and the Tribunal have been prepared to accept that data protection notices given in reasonably general terms have provided adequate notice to the individuals. In none of the cases have the courts had to deal with the questions which arise where the individual is in a more vulnerable situation or the information is particularly sensitive. In other areas the courts have been assiduous to ensure that in such cases specific notice is provided to the individual in order to protect the interests of that person. In the case of *R. (on the application of B) v Stafford Combined Court*[66] the High Court decided that a 14-year-old girl who had been receiving psychiatric care

---

[65] See para.3–64, above for the notice which was regarded as acceptable by the Court.
[66] [2006] EWHC 1645.

should have been notified of the request for disclosure of her medical records to the defence and given an opportunity to object. In the case the girl had made allegations of abuse against an individual who was being prosecuted in connection with the allegation. The defence had asked for access to her medical records and these had been provided without notice or opportunity to oppose the application for disclosure. The High Court held that her right to privacy meant that the records should not have been handed over with proper notice. The case resulted in a change to the Criminal Procedure Rules

As far as practicable

5–32   There has also been a potential weakening of the notice obligations following consideration of the extent of the obligation imposed by the requirements of para.2(1) of Pt II to Sch.1 in the case of *The Corporate Officer of the House of Commons v Information Commissioner*. The case was an appeal brought under the Freedom of Information Act and the Information Tribunal was considering whether the details of MPs' expense claims should be disclosed. It was argued on behalf of the Commons that the MPs had not been told that the expenses would be disclosed in detail and therefore the Commons would be in breach of the requirements if it made the disclosure. Since the decision to notify the MPs lay within the powers of the Commons the obvious answer would be to disregard the point on the basis that if the Tribunal ordered disclosure it could delay the implementation of the order for 28 days within which the Commons could carry out the notification thereby complying with the requirement. Only if the Commons failed to do so would there be a breach of the DPA and at that stage the Commissioner could take enforcement action if required. However the Tribunal took the more complex option of holding that the obligation had been met sufficiently. The reasoning is not completely clear but it appears that they accepted that because the MPs were aware of the disclosure of some information under the Publication Scheme adopted by the Commons the further disclosure was not regarded as another purpose. They also placed reliance on the fact that the obligation on the data controller to provide the information is not absolute but is only to "ensure so far as practicable" that the information is provided or made available. The Tribunal may therefore be prepared to accept a more generous approach to those cases where a data controller has not managed to provide the necessary information than the Commissioner has generally been prepared to do in the past.

Fairness and contract

5–33   The relationship between the obligations to provide fair processing notices and the terms of a contract were considered in Lady Justice Arden in her dissenting judgment in the case of *Johnson v Medical Defence Union*.[67] In that case the appellant argued that, even though the Medical Defence Union (MDU) had an absolute contractual right to terminate Mr Johnson's membership, if the organisation planned to carry out some processing of which Mr Johnson was wholly unaware in order to assess whether they should continue his membership they should have given him notice. The comments were obiter and also seem to have become mixed up with the question of

---

[67] [2007] EWCA Civ 262.

whether Mr Johnson's consent was required for the processing (which it clearly was not as Ground 6 of Sch.2 could be argued to apply). Nevertheless it does set out the general proposition that a party to a contract cannot use the notice provisions to restrict the processing of information which was foreseeable and was permitted by the contract.[68]

Article 29 Working Party Paper

5–34   Among the papers which have been prepared by the Article 29 Working Party there are a number which deal with the provision of notices. In Opinion 2/2007 on information to passengers about the transfer of Passenger Name Records to US authorities[69] they gave detailed advice on both the content and the delivery of such notices. They dealt with the question of the obligations of intermediaries and took the view that an intermediary who is obtaining personal data for another should ensure that the individual is provided with clear, accurate and comprehensive information which should be provided before the purchase of a ticket. The fact that the data are to be transferred to US authorities and used and stored for long periods for purposes different to the original one must be included in the notice. The information should be provided both before and after purchase of the ticket to cater for those cases where the ticket is purchased by a third party. The model notices consist of a shorter notice to give passengers summary information about the transfers and offer them the possibility to find out more. It is suggested that this notice would be suitable for a booking by telephone. The longer version includes Frequently Asked Questions and more detail and would be suitable where the booking is over the web or at the premises of a travel agent. In terms of delivery the Opinion advises the provision of paper copies where the parties are face-to-face or exchange paper, the short notice being read out over the telephone and the individual directed to a place where the longer notice is available; and the website notice divided into a short form which will be seen automatically and a longer notice which can be linked and accessed. The Opinion therefore applied the best practice guidance given in earlier papers and endorsed by the Commissioner in the UK in respect of the use of appropriately "layered" delivery of the relevant information. In its Opinion on the SWIFT system[70] the Working Party concluded that neither SWIFT itself (which it regarded as a data controller) nor the financial institutions which used its services, had provided notices to comply with Arts 10 and 11 of the Directive. The finding is interesting as it might be assumed that a person transferring money overseas would realise that the service would involve some transfer of personal data overseas, although admittedly not the fact that the data would go to the US where the US authorities would access it for investigative and monitoring purposes.

Exemptions

5–35   The interpretation provisions also allow a fairly substantial exemption to the general obligation to provide the specified information, although only in the situation where information is obtained other than from the data subject. A data controller need

---

[68] paras 143 and 147.
[69] February 15, 2007.
[70] Opinion 10/2006 on the processing of personal data by the Society for Worldwide Interbank Financial Telecommunication.

not, in such a situation, provide the specified information where the "primary conditions"—together with certain additional conditions to be specified by the Secretary of State are met.

The primary conditions are:

"3(2)(a) that the provision of the specified information would involve a disproportionate effort; or
3(2)(b) that the recording or disclosure of the data by the data controller is necessary to comply with a legal obligation other than a contractual obligation."

The additional conditions were specified in The Data Protection (Conditions Under Paragraph 3 of Part II of Schedule 1) Order 2000 (SI 2000/185). These are that the data subject has not made any prior request to be provided with the information for both para.3(2)(a) and (b) and, in the case of para. 3(2)(a) that the controller also records his reason for believing that the effect would be disproportionate.

In those cases where the data controller relies upon the disproportionate effort ground he must keep a record of his reasons for believing that disproportionate effort applies.

"Disproportionate effort" is clearly therefore an important term. It is not defined in the Act. The Commissioner's guidance on the interpretation of "disproportionate effort"[71] states that whether or not something amounts to disproportionate effort will be a question of fact in each case:

"In deciding this the Commissioner will take into account a number of factors, including the nature of the data, the length of time and the cost involved to the data controller in providing the information. The fact that the data controller has had to expend a considerable amount of time and effort and/or cost in providing the information does not necessarily mean that the Commissioner will reach the decision that the data controller can legitimately rely on the disproportionate effort ground. In certain circumstances the Commissioner would consider that a quite considerable effort could reasonably be expected. The above factors will always be balanced against the prejudicial or effectively prejudicial effect on the data subject and in this respect a relevant consideration would be the extent to which the data subject already knows about the processing of their personal data by the data controller."

There are a number of exemptions from the requirements of the Principles, principally from the first Principle, which are covered in the relevant chapters on the exemptions, below.

General identifiers

5–36 Paragraph 4 of the interpretation provisions provides that if personal data include a national identity number or another "general identifier" defined by the Secretary of State, then fair and lawful processing of any such data will additionally

---

[71] *ibid.* p.34.

require compliance with conditions to be specified by the Secretary of State. No order
has been made to date.

Rights to opt-out

5–37   One particular view expounded by the Registrar under the 1984 Act which is
not repeated in the Legal Guidance but which, it is submitted, remains relevant in
assessing fairness relates to the right to opt-out of non-core uses of data. In the previous Guidance it was explained as follows:

> "Although the Act does not expressly require it, there may be circumstances where
> fair obtaining requires a data user to give an individual the opportunity to opt out
> of additional uses and disclosures of the information he or she has provided
> beyond the primary purpose for which it was supplied. This will be the case where
> an individual effectively has no realistic choice other than to use the service of a
> particular data user, for example, where an individual attends an NHS hospital
> for treatment.
>
> In situations where the individual does have a choice, the Registrar considers
> that it is good practice to offer such an opt out."

The suggestion is that even where a data subject is informed about possible uses of
his or her data this may not always be sufficient to establish fairness. The data subject
may additionally have to be given an immediate right to object to certain processing.

Special cases—internet, telephone and fax

5–38   Practitioners should bear in mind that even if the requirements of the first
Principle are satisfied, the collection and processing of personal information may
involve other regulation. Where email addresses and fax numbers are being collected
and used for direct marketing there are specific rules governing the collection and use.
The current rules about email, fax and automated call marketing can be found in the
Privacy and Electronic Communications (EC Directive) Regulations 2003. These
are dealt with in Ch.22, below on electronic communications. There are also special
rules in the Consumer Protection (Contracts Concluded by Means of Distance
Communication) Regulations 2000/42 which set out the information which must be
provided to consumers in distance sales. The Electronic Commerce (EC Directive)
Regulations 2002 contain further provisions regulating transactions conducted electronically. The use of email for sending commercial communications both unsolicited
and solicited is dealt with and in addition to the information specified under the DPA,
businesses affected by these Regulations must make further information "easily,
directly and permanently accessible".

Other requirements of fairness

5–39   Although the interpretation provisions to Principle 1 are detailed they only
deal with one aspect of fairness—that concerned with the way in which data are
obtained. Clearly therefore they do not exhaust the general requirement that the processing of personal data be "fair". The concept of fairness is open-ended and will vary

with the circumstances of the case. It would be impossible to list all the implications given the breadth of the term "processing". The courts have considered whether it is fair to disclose photographs of those accused of criminal activities[72] and the question of the fairness of processing for the purpose of risk management was considered in *Johnson v Medical Defence Union*.[73] In the credit reference cases under the 1984 Act the Tribunal ruled that the processing of personal data by means of a system which would retrieve data about unassociated third parties, which would then be used for the purpose of assessing whether to offer credit to the data subject, amounted to unfair processing. In the *British Gas* case the Tribunal held that the use of personal data which was obtained when British Gas was a statutory monopoly, for the purpose of direct marketing third party products without the consent of data subjects, amounted to unfair processing. Much of the guidance produced by the Commissioner's Office deals with the fairness, or otherwise, of processing for particular purposes, for example whether it is fair to retain markers showing that individuals are considered violent on specific records. Fairness overlaps with proportionality and takes into account the extent to which the individual is aware of the processing, the justification for the processing and the potential harmful impact of the processing on individuals.

Consequences of breach of the first Principle for legal proceedings

5–40   While the most obvious possible consequences may be the risk of action by a data subject or enforcement action by the Commissioner the issue of unfairly obtained information also arises in court proceedings, often in conjunction with concerns over breach of s.55 (covered in Ch.20, below on enforcement). In *St Merryn Meat v Hawkins*[74] breach of the DPA affected the outcome in other legal proceedings. The claimants lost a freezing order on the basis that they had relied upon information obtained in breach of the Data Protection Act 1998 and had failed to make a full and honest disclosure of the fact to the court. The claimants had obtained information about a fraud against them by tapping a telephone. The court had been informed that the telephone was an office, not a home, telephone. On the basis of the evidence they applied for, and were granted, interim freezing and search orders. The defendants applied for its discharge on the basis that it was a private telephone which had been tapped and the claimants had failed to disclose that fact to the court.

The court accepted the defendants' argument and marked its displeasure by discharging the order even though it accepted that the claimants had a strong case and it was judged likely that the defendants would dissipate the assets before judgment. In the case of *Jean Jones v University of Warwick*[75] enquiry agents acting for the University gained access to Ms Jones' home by subterfuge and secretly filmed her using the kettle. The film was then used in evidence to counter her claim for damages against the University arising from an incident in the course of her employment by the University. The claimant sought to have the evidence excluded having been obtained in breach of Art.8 (the DPA was not argued although the same arguments would have applied). The court allowed the evidence and held that the fact that evidence had been

---

[72]   R. *(on the application of Ellis) v the Chief Constable of Essex Police* [2003] EWHC 1321.
[73]   see n.67.
[74]   LTL 2/7/2000 (unreported elsewhere).
[75]   [2003] EWCA Civ 151.

obtained in breach of some other legal obligation did not render it inadmissible but penalised the University in costs.

The High Court has been asked to order disclosure against third parties (Norwich Pharmacal Orders under CPR 31.16) in respect of whom the applicant has well-grounded suspicions that there has been an unlawful obtaining of information, in order to have the necessary information in order to bring proceedings, in several cases. In *Hughes v Carrutu*[76] it came to the attention of the claimant that a third party had obtained information on him when he was contacted by the Office of the Information Commissioner who were investigating a private detective agency. It appeared that the agency had obtained information unlawfully on the claimant but the claimant did not know who the investigator's client was. The court granted him an order so that he was able to pursue a remedy. However the court refused such an order in the case of *Fiona Trust Holding v Yuri Privalov*[77] on the basis that the claimant already had enough material to commence proceedings and the purpose of the Norwich Pharmacal relief was not to allow the victim to "fine tune a pleading".

THE SECOND PRINCIPLE

5–41 This requires that personal data shall be obtained only for one or more specified and lawful purposes and shall not be further processed in any manner incompatible with that purpose or those purposes. There is clearly an overlap with Principle 1. The first Principle requires the data controller (save in certain specified circumstances) to notify a data subject of the purposes for which the data are intended to be processed. The second Principle addresses the circumstances in which notice has not been provided to the data subject. It also admits of the possibility that the purpose specification may be contained elsewhere than the notice to the data subject.

It may be that the second Principle is designed to provide an additional fairness "safety net". This may be relevant where it has not been practicable to provide the notice or where the exemption to the first Principle that has been outlined above applies—i.e. where a data controller who does not gather personal data directly from a data subject decides that providing the specified information would involve a disproportionate effort. Such a controller would still bear a responsibility for specifying the purposes of processing in accordance with Principle 2.

The interpretation provisions allow the purpose or purposes for which personal data are obtained to be specified either in a notice given to the data subject to satisfy the "specified information" requirements of Principle 1 or by notification to the Commissioner.[78] Once the purposes have been specified any further processing must be restricted to a manner not incompatible with the specified purposes.

The use of the word "incompatible" suggests a use that is contradictory to rather than simply different from any originally specified purpose or purposes. Synonyms for "incompatible" are "unsuited", "incongruous", "inconsistent", "unsuitable", "opposite" or "irreconcilable". If this is the correct interpretation then it is open to the data controller to contend that processing which was not specified at the time of the collection of

---

[76] [2006] EWHC 1791.
[77] [2007] EWHC 39.
[78] See Notification in Ch.9, below.

the data but not inconsistent with the original specified lawful purposes does not fall foul of this provision as long as it is subsequently specified by the controller. For example, a data controller who processes data for the purposes of satisfying a mail order from a data subject might contend that the subsequent and unforeseen use of the data for the purposes of further marketing mailshots by third parties was not "incompatible" although it was unspecified when the data were first obtained. The controller would have to specify the new purpose in some appropriate manner and notify the data subject in accordance with the first Principle but would not fall foul of Principle 2.

The interpretation provisions also state that a data controller may in particular specify the purpose or purposes by either of these methods, which carries the implication that specification of purposes may take place by another method. Section 24 of the Act suggests at least one other method by which purpose specification may take place. Section 24 has to be read in light of the requirements specified in s.17.

5–42   Section 17(1) of the Act prohibits processing of personal data unless the data controller has "notified" the Commissioner. Section 17(2) and (3) set out limited exceptions to this basic prohibition. These are, first, where the relevant data are not information which is being processed by means of equipment operating automatically in response to instructions given for the purpose, nor is it information which is recorded with the intention that it should be processed by means of such equipment.[79] In other words the data is information which is recorded as part of a relevant filing system or which forms part of an accessible record as defined by s.68.

Secondly, the prohibition in s.17(1) does not apply where the Secretary of State has exempted particular processing on the basis that it is unlikely to prejudice the rights and freedoms of data subjects.[80] The exemptions from notification are covered in the Notification Regulations.[81]

If either of these exemption applies then a data controller may, nonetheless, give a notification to the Commissioner under s.18. If a data controller chooses not to do so, then any person may still request the "relevant particulars" from the data controller. Under s.24, the data controller is under a duty to supply the particulars in writing within 21 days and free of charge.[82] These particulars are the equivalent of the information which must be notified to the Commissioner. Any data controller who fails to provide the relevant particulars commits an offence.[83] Thus s.24 "relevant particulars" may be a further route by which a data controller may specify purposes.

The interpretation provisions also provide that in determining whether any disclosure of personal data is compatible with the purposes for which those data were obtained, regard is to be had to the purpose or purposes for which the "disclosee" intends to process the data. This provision may put a data controller at risk of enforcement action if he or she discloses to another party who subsequently uses the data for a purpose incompatible with the data controller's original specified purpose. Thus data controllers who disclose to third parties should identify the purpose or purposes for which the relevant data was originally obtained and to impose on the disclosees, by way of contract, obligations to use the data only for compatible purposes. The other

---

[79] 1998 Act s.1(1)(a) and (b).
[80] 1998 Act s.17(3).
[81] The Data Protections (Notification and Notification Fees) Regulations 2000 (SI 2000/188).
[82] 1998 Act s.24(1).
[83] 1998 Act s.24(4).

option would be to revert to the data subject and obtain his or her sanction for any processing for a new and incompatible purpose. It is not clear to what extent the controller has an obligation to enquire into the detail of the purposes of the disclosee. In the *Green Thumb* case referred to earlier the Court appeared to accept that the data controller need only have a general understanding of the purposes of the disclosee. It is submitted that this is the appropriate approach.

Alternatively, data controllers may seek to obtain personal data from data subjects for a very wide range of specified purposes, so as not to inhibit the purposes for which the data may be passed on and used by subsequent recipients. Such blanket notices are increasingly common, however, to date none appear to have been the subject of a challenge by the Commissioner on the basis that their inherent uncertainty or open-ended nature will inevitably lead to unfair processing.

Commissioner's view

5–43   The Commissioner is clearly aware of the potential for data controllers to seize upon what appear to be weaknesses in the second Principle. The Legal Guidance includes the stern warning that:

> "It is to be noted that the Commissioner takes a strict view of the concept of compatibility of processing of personal data."[84]

Unfortunately the basis for the strict view or the implications for data controllers are not further spelt out. On the other hand the Commissioner accepts that consent is not necessary to ensure compatibility in all cases. In the Code of Practice on Employment Records in relation to the use of records for disciplinary purposes it states that:

> "A purpose will not be incompatible if workers have been told in advance that information obtained from them will be used for that purpose."[85]

The Guidance also states, somewhat obscurely, that decisions about the compatibility of uses by third parties ". . . cannot be made retrospectively by data controllers once the data are obtained". The meaning of this is not apparent.

Use for a new purpose: is consent always required?

5–44   There will be circumstances where a data controller wants to use personal data for a purpose not specified to the data subject at the time the data were obtained. It will be a question of fact as to whether it is genuinely a new purpose of which notice could not be given at the point of obtaining. Here we consider a case in which the personal data were obtained fairly and lawfully and in accordance with the first Principle for a particular purpose, giving all the specified information relevant to that purpose. It does not apply where a controller is merely seeking to avoid his responsibilities to inform data subjects and give them proper choices. The controller must consider the impact of the second Principle and decide whether the new use is compatible with that

---

[84] *Legal Guidance*, p.36.
[85] Employment Practices Code, Pt 2: Employment Records, p.53.

for which the data were obtained. If it is compatible he may use the data for the purpose as long as he complies with Principles 1 and 2. Thus he must provide the data subject with the relevant information in accordance with the first Principle. If he cannot do that because it is not practicable, he must specify the new purpose in some other appropriate way, presumably by including it on the register of notifications. The controller must ensure that he has appropriate grounds on which to process the data and if sensitive data are involved those grounds must extend to the sensitive data. He must also ensure the fairness and lawfulness of the processing. These may require that the data subject be asked for positive consent or be given an "opt-out". The requirements of fairness in particular will vary with the circumstances of the case. In practical terms it is likely that the cumulative effect of these requirements means it is prudent to obtain positive consent of the data subject but it is not necessary as a matter of law and there must be cases where consent is not necessary. The Tribunal considered the impact of the second Principle briefly in the *Commons* case described earlier and decided that the disclosure of the travel details to the public in that case was not a use for a new purpose and was not incompatible. It also noted that data controllers comply with this Principle at least in part by means of notification which is done under broad headings.

THE THIRD PRINCIPLE

5–45   This requires that personal data shall be adequate, relevant and not excessive in relation to the purpose or purposes for which they are processed. This substantially repeats the fourth Principle under the 1984 Act. There are no provisions on interpretation for this principle.

Interpretation under the 1984 Act

5–46   Because of the similarity between the third Principle and the fourth Principle under the 1984 Act it may be useful to look at decisions under that Act. It must be emphasised however that the decisions of the Tribunal under the 1984 Act are at best persuasive and not binding. They may, however, give an indication as to the approach which may be adopted.

In the Tribunal case of *Community Charge Registration Officer of Runnymede BC v Data Protection Registrar*,[86] the Tribunal was asked to consider whether the holding by community charge registration officers of information about property types (i.e. whether the property was a flat, bungalow, caravan, etc.) as part of the community charge register was in breach of the Principle. The Tribunal found it was. They found this to be the case even though there was unlikely to be any prejudice to the data subjects. They took the view that public bodies which had the power to oblige people to provide personal information were under a particular onus to ensure that the information demanded was always adequate, relevant and not excessive. The Tribunal also endorsed the approach recommended by the Registrar:

"We were referred in the course of the hearing to the Guideline booklet Number 4 issued by the Data Protection Registrar entitled The Data Protection Principles.

---

[86] CASE DA/90, 24/49/3, October 27, 1990.

Paragraph 4.2 relating to the 4th Principle advises that data users should seek to identify the minimum amount of information about each individual which is required in order properly to fulfil their purpose and that they should try to identify the cases where additional information will be required and seek to ensure that such information is only collected and recorded in those cases. We endorse this general guidance for those wishing to have a test to apply to answer the question whether personal data is adequate, relevant and not excessive for the purposes for which it is held."

This guidance has been repeated in the Legal Guidance on the 1998 Act at p.37.

In *Community Charge Registration Officer of Rhondda BC v Data Protection Registrar*,[87] the Tribunal upheld a similar approach taken with respect to the holding of dates of birth. It was accepted, however, that the holding of dates of birth would be relevant in respect of those persons who would shortly become eligible to vote at the age of 18.

Thus, where a data controller holds an item of information on all individuals which will be used or useful only in relation to some of them, the information is likely to be excessive and irrelevant in relation to those individuals in respect of whom it will not be used or useful and should not be held in those cases. The Commissioner also suggests that it will not be acceptable to hold information on the basis that it might possibly be useful in the future without a view of how it will be used.[88] This, however, should be distinguished from holding information in the case of a particular foreseeable contingency which may never occur, for example, where a data controller holds blood groups of employees engaged in hazardous occupations. It therefore follows that forms used for collecting information about individuals should be reviewed regularly and if necessary restructured so that, when completed, they will provide the right amount and type of information.

The data controller's subjective views as to relevance are not the governing criteria—an objective view will be adopted in all cases. It is likely that where different data users hold data for the same purpose, or where a Code of Practice exists in a particular field of activity, the Commissioner will have regard to the level of information generally found to be necessary to achieve the data user's purpose in considering whether or not the principle has been breached.

5–47   In the *PNR* cases[89] one of the arguments raised against the agreement reached between the EU and the US Government was that the amount of personal data which was to be provided by the airlines to the US Customs Bureau was excessive for the purpose for which it was to be held. A total of 34 data elements were listed which were to be provided for each passenger. The point is dealt with in the Opinion of the Advocate General who held that, given the purpose of the processing of the personal data, the total of the data items was not excessive. In reaching his view he made clear that the term "necessary" in the Directive should carry the same meaning as in the European Convention, that the question be weighted as one of proportionality saying:

---

[87] CASE DA/90, 25/49/2, October 11, 1990.
[88] *Legal Guidance*, p.37.
[89] See Ch.1, above for a full discussion of the cases.

"I am of the opinion that, in adopting the list of 34 personal-data elements as attached to the decision on adequacy, the Commission did not agree to a manifestly inappropriate measure for the purpose of achieving the objective of combating terrorism and other serious crimes. First the importance of intelligence activity in counter-terrorism should be stressed, since obtaining sufficient information may enable a State's security services to prevent a possible terrorist attack. From that point of view, the need to profile potential terrorists may require access to a large number of pieces of data. Second the fact that other instruments relating to the exchange of information within the European Union provide for disclosure of less data is not sufficient to demonstrate that the amount of data required in the specific counter-terrorism instrument constituted by the PNR regime is excessive."[90]

5–48 In the case of *The Chief Constables of West Yorkshire, South Yorkshire and North Wales Police v the Information Commissioner* the Information Tribunal held that conviction information which was retained in accord with the Association of Chief Police Officers Guidelines remained adequate, relevant and not excessive for the purposes of policing and criminal justice but should not be used for employment vetting. The case is considered in more detail in the Case Studies at the end of the chapter. The Tribunal also found that Principle 3 overlaps with Principle 5 and that information which would be in breach of Principle 3 would be likely to be excessive in relation to the purpose. The principle was not argued in the case of *Marper* which held that the retention of fingerprint and DNA data about those who had not been convicted of offences was not a breach of Art.8.

THE FOURTH PRINCIPLE

5–49 This requires that personal data shall be accurate and, where necessary, kept up-to-date. A definition of inaccuracy appears at s.70(2) of the Act:

"For the purposes of this Act data are inaccurate if they are incorrect or misleading as to any matter of fact."

Thus, a mere opinion, which does not purport to be a statement of fact, cannot be challenged on the grounds of inaccuracy.[91]

It is worth noting that the first part of the Principle is unqualified—"personal data shall be accurate". The second part, however, is qualified—data need only be kept up-to-date where "necessary".

The purpose for which the data are used will clearly be relevant in deciding whether updating is necessary. For example, if the data are intended to be used merely as an historical record of a transaction between the data controller and the data subject, then updating would be inappropriate. In other cases updating will be crucial—for example, if the data are used to decide whether to grant credit.

---

[90] *ibid*. para.238.
[91] The issue of accuracy is also discussed in greater depth in Ch.14, below on remedies.

The interpretation provisions allow that there will be no breach of the accuracy requirement where the data are, in fact, inaccurate but where the data controller has accurately recorded the information from a data subject or third party and:

(a) has taken reasonable steps to ensure accuracy (having regard to the purpose or purposes for which the data were obtained and further processed); and

(b) has recorded the data subject's view as to inaccuracy within the relevant data, where such views have been conveyed.

The requirement on the data controller to record accurately information obtained from the data subject or third party presumably means that the data controller cannot claim the benefit of this exemption where the data controller himself is responsible for the inaccuracy but only where the controller accurately records erroneous information where the error originates from the data subject or the third party. The requirements in the exemption to record a data subject's view as to inaccuracy and to "take reasonable steps" mirror the provisions in s.22 of the 1984 Act as to inaccuracy. However, under the 1984 Act, the controller could rebut an allegation of inaccuracy either because he could show he had taken reasonable care or by including the data subject's views. Under the 1998 Act, the controller must leap over both hurdles.

The requirement to take reasonable steps "having regard to the purpose or purposes for which the data were obtained and further processed" is presumably an acknowledgment that inaccuracies in certain types of data (e.g. as to creditworthiness) may have more severe consequences than in others, and that consequently more stringent accuracy checks would be required. What constitutes "reasonable steps" is not defined, but it is submitted that at the very least the controller would have to show a written procedure for checking accuracy.

The Commissioner's powers to take enforcement action for a breach of the fourth Principle are supplemental to the data subject rights to apply for the rectification, blocking, erasure or destruction of inaccurate data.[92]

THE FIFTH PRINCIPLE

5–50   This requires that personal data processed for any purpose or purposes shall not be kept for longer than is necessary for that purpose or those purposes. The Principle is based on Art. 6.1(e) of the Directive which requires that personal data must be "kept in a form which permits identification of data subjects for no longer than is necessary for the purposes for which the data were collected or for which they are further processed".

The UK provision does not reflect the reference to the anonymisation of data and it is not referred to in the Commissioner's Legal Guidance on this Principle however it must be borne in mind that the Principle can be complied with by the removal of all identifiers from the data and not only by deletion.

There are no interpretation provisions for the fifth Principle. The Commissioner advises that data controllers should review their personal data regularly and delete the information which is no longer required for the purposes. The Legal Guidance suggests

---

[92] See s.14 of the 1998 Act and Ch.14, below.

that controllers should adopt a systematic policy of deleting data. This might involve setting a standard life for records of a particular category. At the end of that life the record should be reviewed and deleted unless there is some special reason for keeping it. The length of the review period will depend on the nature of the record. If the data have only a short-term value it may be appropriate to delete them within days or months. Controllers must also be alert to their responsibilities to preserve information.[93] In 2004 Philip Morris was sued for $2.75 million for destroying potential email evidence in a civil racketeering action against the tobacco industry. The firm's policy was to delete all email which was over 60 days old but this was no defence as the court found that the policy should have been suspended once legal proceedings were contemplated. Some statutes set time limits for the retention of data, for example the Companies Act 1985 requires the retention of accounting records for a period of three years from the date on which they are made for a private company and six years for a public company.[94] Codes of Practice may also include relevant provisions. In relation to the public sector the Code of Practice on Records Management issued under s.46 of the Freedom of Information Act is the governing instrument. There are also recommendations in other Codes of Practice, for example the CCTV Code. For the rules on the retention of traffic data under Directive 2006/24 see Ch.23, below. A checklist of the most important stages of a records management policy is included in the practical tools at the end of the chapter. The Code of Practice for Information Security Management ISO 17799 sets out suggested rules on the keeping of documents electronically.

5–51   The Commissioner's Guidance also deals with the case where a relationship has ended as follows:

> "If personal data have been recorded because of a relationship between the data controller and the data subject, the need to keep information should be considered when that relationship ceases to exist. For example, the data subject may be an employee who has left the employment of the data controller. The end of the relationship will not necessarily cause the data controller to delete all the personal data. It may well be necessary to keep some of the information so that the data controller will be able to confirm details of the data subject's employment for say, the provision of references in the future or to enable the employer to provide the relevant information in respect of the data subject's pension arrangements. It may well be necessary in some cases to retain certain information to enable the data controller to defend legal claims which may be made in the future. Unless there is some other reason for keeping them personal data should be deleted when the possibility of such a claim arising no longer exists, i.e. when the relevant statutory time-limit has expired."

In *R v Chief Constable of the Greater Manchester Police Ex p. Christopher John Coombs*[95] the High Court considered whether the Data Protection Act 1984 was breached by the retention of personal data about the defendant. The police were

---

[93] The Institute of Chartered Secretaries and Administrators (ISCA) publishes an excellent book which sets out the recommended retention times for different categories of information held by businesses. It is available from their website. The Chartered Institute of Personnel and Development Professionals (CIPD) publishes a similar set of recommendations in respect of employee data.

[94] Companies Act 1985 s.222.

[95] LTL 24/7/2000 (unreported elsewhere).

entitled to retain records of alleged paedophilia where a conviction was dismissed on appeal because the judge in the original case had misdirected on corroboration.

In the *PNR* cases the question of whether the PNR data would be held for excessive periods was considered in the Opinion of the Advocate General, it having been argued that the periods anticipated were unnecessarily generous. In the Opinion he accepted that the normal period of three years and six months was not manifestly excessive nor was the longer period of eight years for that data which had been accessed in the initial period. Again the Advocate General took account of the nature of the purpose for the processing and determined that the State had a wide margin of appreciation in a case of this nature.

In the case of *The Chief Constables of West Yorkshire, South Yorkshire and North Wales Police v the Information Commissioner* the Information Tribunal held that conviction information which was retained in accord with the Association of Chief Police Officers Guidelines was not excessive for the purposes of policing and criminal justice but should not be used for employment vetting. The case is considered in more detail in the Case Studies at the end of this chapter. The principle was not argued in the case of *Marper* which held that the retention of fingerprint and DNA data about those who had not been convicted of offences was not a breach of Art.8.

In the case of *Rita Pal v General Medical Council*[96] the claimant had brought a claim in defamation and under the Data Protection Act. She claimed that personal data on her was being kept for longer than was necessary. The GMC had applied for summary judgment on the basis that the records complained of could not be destroyed as the GMC was in the process of reconsidering its policy on retention of data and it would be premature to require the deletion of the record complained of. The GMC did not succeed. The court held that it would not be open to the GMC to arrive at a records retention policy that did not comply with the Data Protection Act and there was no justification for striking out the claim on the basis that its policy was not yet settled. Except for the substitution of "processed" for "held", the principle is a duplication of the sixth Principle under the 1984 Act. A short case study of the application of the Principle is set out in the Practical Tools section below.

THE SIXTH PRINCIPLE

5–52   This requires that personal data shall be processed in accordance with the rights of data subjects under the Act. This replaces and extends the seventh Principle under the 1984 Act which required compliance with the data subject's access rights. Subject access rights are, of course, a part of the 1998 Act[97] but data subject rights also include the right to prevent processing likely to cause damage and distress,[98] the right to prevent processing for the purposes of direct marketing[99] and rights in relation to automated decision-taking.[100]

The interpretation provisions rather obviously and rather unhelpfully simply state that any breach of the data subjects rights set out in ss.7 and 10–12 will also

---

[96] [2004] EWHC 1485 (QB).
[97] 1998 Act s.7.
[98] 1998 Act s.10, see Ch.12.
[99] 1998 Act s.11, see Ch.12.
[100] 1998 Act s.12, see Ch.13.

constitute a breach of the sixth Principle. The Commissioner's powers to take enforcement action against a data controller for breaching the sixth Principle are thus supplemental to the right of a data subject to seek specific remedies including compensation, under s.13, for damage or distress suffered as a result of a breach of the data subject rights set out in ss.7–12 of the 1998 Act.

THE SEVENTH PRINCIPLE

5–53   This requires that appropriate technical and organisational measures shall be taken against unauthorised and unlawful processing of personal data and against accidental loss or destruction of, or damage to, personal data. It is supplemented by significant interpretation provisions. This principle replaces the appropriate security measures requirement of the eighth Principle contained in the 1984 Act. Under the 1998 Act the obligations imposed by the seventh Principle are reinforced by the obligation to notify the Commissioner of the security measures in place.[101] The risk of security breach to business is significant. Since 1991 the Department of Trade and Industry (Dti) has sponsored research into information security breaches to help UK businesses understand and deal with the risks that they face. The Information Security Breaches Survey 2004[102] demonstrated the increased dependence of business on electronic information and the systems which process it with the resulting increase in security risks particularly through virus infections and inappropriate use of systems by staff. It reported that two-thirds of business had had a premeditated or malicious incident in the period covered by the survey and concerns about computer security were a significant issue for many businesses.

The Principle reflects Art.17 of the Directive but there are a number of differences between the requirements in the Directive and provisions of the 1998 Act:

(a)   The Directive requires controllers to ensure a level of security appropriate to the risks represented by the processing rather than the harm that might result from a breach and the nature of the data—which is what the Act requires. It is submitted that what is required by the Directive is wider than what is required by the Act.

(b)   The Directive's emphasis on the need for security "in particular where the processing involves the transmission of data over a network" is omitted from the Act.

(c)   The Directive's requirement that "any person acting under the authority of the controller or of the processor who has access to personal data must not process them except on instructions from the controller", is also omitted,[103] although Art.12(a)(ii) imposes a general obligation to ensure that a data processor acts only on instructions from the controller.

(d)   The Directive's requirement that the contract which must be entered into between the data controller and the processor include a requirement that the

---

[101]   1998 Act s.18(2)(b).
[102]   Price Waterhouse Coopers.
[103]   Directive Art.16.

processor shall be bound to comply with the security requirements of the law of the Member State where the processor is established has not been transposed into UK law.

Legal Guidance

5–54   The Commissioner's Legal Guidance on the security requirements runs to three pages.[104] Data Controllers are encouraged to use Privacy Enhancing Technologies[105] as part of their approach to compliance. The Commissioner points out that the level of security must be "appropriate" and therefore a risk-based approach to determining the proper level of security is advised. Areas which should be considered by the data controller are listed although it is pointed out that the list is not comprehensive. The list covers:

- security management;
- controlling access to information;
- ensuring business continuity;
- staff selection and training;
- detecting and dealing with breaches of security.

Those seeking more detailed guidance on security are referred to ISO 27001 or ISO/IEC Standard 17799.

Interpretation under the 1998 Act

5–55   The interpretation provisions (the third longest after those for the first and eighth Principles) commence, again rather tautologously and unhelpfully, by stating that "an adequate level of protection is one which is adequate in all the circumstances of the case".

The interpretation provisions require a controller, in determining "appropriate" security measures, to have regard to:

(a) the state of technological development;

(b) the cost of implementing security measures;

(c) the nature of the data to be protected;

(d) the harm that might result from unauthorised or unlawful processing or from accidental loss destruction and damage of the personal data.

Complying with these requirements can be seen as a balancing act. As the cost of "cutting edge" security measures decreases and their availability increases, then an increasingly heavier onus will lie on the data controller to adopt such measures. Similarly,

---

[104] *Legal Guidance*, pp.40–43.
[105] See the Commissioners website *http://www.informationcommissioner.gov.uk* [Accessed on 2 September 2007] for material on PETs.

more "sensitive" (both in the sense defined in the Act and in its broader meaning) data, the disclosure or other processing of which might cause disproportionate damage and distress, will require more sophisticated and expensive security measures.

With increasing technological developments it is highly likely that a data controller will be expected to consider a range of technical security measures such as firewalls (systems designed to prevent external agencies hacking into a private network) and encryption. Encryption should not, however, be seen as a panacea since its use can in itself lead to security problems. There are risks in allowing employees a free hand in encrypting data and communications. Loss of a private key to encrypted files through either malice or carelessness could expose a company to the risk of serious damage. If such files contain personal data then the loss of an encryption key may be the equivalent of the accidental destruction of the data.

The interpretation provisions also require the data controller to take reasonable steps to ensure the reliability of any employees who have access to the personal data. "Reasonable steps" is, as before, not defined but it is submitted that written recruitment, training and vetting procedures will be a minimum requirement. Although what constitutes "reasonable steps" is not made explicit, it will also depend on the nature and sensitivity of the personal data concerned.

Where the data controller makes use of an external agency to carry out processing (a "data processor") then the controller must choose a data processor providing "sufficient" guarantees with respect to security measures and must take "reasonable steps" to ensure compliance with those measures. The relationship between the controller and the processor must also be governed by a written contract which imposes obligations equivalent to those imposed by the seventh Principle and under which the processor may only act on instructions from the controller. A precedent processor agreement is included at the end of this chapter.

5–56   In 2007 the Commissioner threatened to take enforcement action against a number of banks and other financial institutions unless they improved the security of their processing. There had been repeated media stories that customer records were being left in dustbins outside bank premises, although there were also suspicions that at least some of the material was only being acquired by dint of positive efforts by those wishing to produce a story. Whatever the background the result was that several financial institutions provided the Commissioner with undertakings to abide by and apply proper security procedures in the future. Data Controllers who are subject to the regulation of the Financial Services Authority (FSA) under the Financial Services and Markets Act 2000 are more likely to be concerned at the response of the FSA to a security breach involving personal data than the response of the Information Commissioner following the decision of the FSA in the case of the Nationwide Building Society in February 2007. Principle 3 of the FSA's Principles for Business requires firms to take reasonable care to organise and control their affairs responsibly and effectively with adequate risk management systems. In August 2006 a laptop computer was stolen from the home of one of the Nationwide's employees. The laptop contained customer information which could have been used to further financial crime. The FSA held that the Nationwide had not had an adequate risk management strategy as it had been possible to download large amounts of customer data on to portable devices. The FSA found fault with the way that the information security procedures were structured and made available as well as its training and controls. The FSA fined Nationwide £980,000.00 for the breach.

There is an increased interest in making those businesses which suffer a security breach involving personal information report the breach to the individuals. This security breach notification measure has become more common in the US with the Canadian Policy and Public Interest Clinic reporting that well over half US States have enacted laws requiring customers to be notified when there is a data security breach.[106] In the EU the Commission has suggested the possibility in a consultation paper on the future of the regulation of electronic communications. Increasingly businesses and public bodies are making public statements about disclosures and security breaches so that individuals are able to take action to check their credit card statements or take other measures to deal with the possibility that a breach of security has compromised the position of the individual and left them vulnerable to identity fraud.

There is no specific requirement that the data controller should maintain audit trails but these are important tools to show when the data have been accessed, who has accessed the data and whether and when any alterations have been made.

A suggested security measures checklist appears in the Practical Tools section at the end of this chapter. The checklist proposed by the Commissioner in the Legal Guidance is also extremely helpful.

THE EIGHTH PRINCIPLE

5–57   This requires that personal data shall not be transferred to a country or territory outside the European Economic Area (EEA) unless that country or territory ensures an "adequate" level of protection for the rights and freedoms of data subjects in relation to the processing of personal data. The principle is discussed in detail in regard to overseas transfers in Ch.8, below.

This principle imposes substantial obligations on data controllers to ensure they are not moving personal data from EEA countries to countries with "inadequate" data protection regimes. The interpretation provisions set out a list of factors which must be considered in determining "adequacy", namely:

    (a) the nature of the personal data (presumably an acknowledgment, as with the provisions for accuracy, that certain types of data require better protection than others);

    (b) the country or territory of origin of the information contained in the data;

    (c) the country or territory of final destination of the information;

    (d) the purposes for which and the period during which the data are intended to be processed;

    (e) the law, international obligations, codes of conduct or other rules in force in the country or territory in question. With respect to rules and codes of conduct these may be general or made by arrangement in particular cases;

    (f) the security measures taken in respect of the data in that country or territory.

---

[106] *Approaches to security breach notification*, A White Paper, CIPPIC, January 2007.

Schedule 4 to the 1998 Act sets out a list of circumstances where the eighth Principle does not apply.

The interpretation provisions further provide that in any proceedings under the 1998 Act a Community finding that a particular territory does or does not ensure an "adequate level of protection" is binding. A Community finding is a finding of the European Commission under Art.31(2) of the Data Protection Directive.

RELATION WITH THE PRINCIPLES IN THE 1984 ACT

5–58   A significant attempt was made to echo the Principles from the 1984 Act with which data controllers would already be familiar. Principle 1, which covered "fair and lawful obtaining and processing" in the 1984 Act, became fair and lawful processing in the 1998 Act, but additionally qualified by the requirement that personal data cannot be processed at all unless one of the Sch.2 conditions is fulfilled (and in the case of sensitive personal data, one of the Sch.3 conditions). These conditions are dealt with in their respective chapters.

Principle 2, which was "holding only for one or more specified and lawful purpose" in the 1984 Act, became "obtaining for one or more specified and lawful purpose and not further processing in a manner incompatible with those purposes".

The old Principle 3 (restrictions on disclosures) disappeared. Principles 3–5 (accuracy, relevance, adequacy, etc.) effectively duplicate the old Principles 4–6. The old Principle 7 (data subject access rights) was replaced by Principle 6, which requires personal data to be processed in accordance with the rights of the data subject. Principle 7 (security measures) largely repeats the old Principle 8 while adding significantly to its requirements. Principle 8, which prohibits transfers outside the EEA unless to a country with an "adequate" data protection structure, is entirely new.

While the wording of the Principles mirrors the 1984 Act, the interpretation provisions in Pt II of Sch.1 extend and modify them so as to comply with the requirements of the Directive.

PRACTICAL TOOLS

5–59   In this section we examine a decision of the Information Tribunal and provide some case studies—the case studies illustrate the approach which has been taken to specific principles and are taken from Annual Reports of the Commissioner published since 1999. The comments in italics are the author's comments.

The Chief Constables of West Yorkshire, South Yorkshire and North Wales Police and The Information Commissioner

In the Information Tribunal

Principles three and five

Summary

5–60   The Information Commissioner served enforcement notices on the Chief Constables of the three police forces for breaches of Principles three and five in respect of the retention of personal data on the criminal convictions of three individuals. Principle three requires the data controller to ensure that personal data held for any purpose shall be "adequate, relevant and not excessive in relation to the purpose or purposes for which they are processed". Principle five requires the data controller to ensure that personal data processed for any purpose or purposes, "shall not be kept for longer than is necessary for that purpose or those purposes". The Chief Constables appealed. The appeals were consolidated.

The Tribunal decided that the Chief Constables were not in breach of the Principles by retaining the specific information for the purposes of policing, which it regarded as including the administration of criminal justice, but that the information should not be disclosed for employment vetting. They amended the enforcement notice to require the data controllers to establish a mechanism whereby the conviction information could be withheld from non-police users.

They also directed that the parties could file a written review as to progress regarding the achievability of this aim within four months of the date of the judgment and, in the event that either of the parties considered at a later stage that further persons should have access to policing data, provided that they could make an application on notice to the Tribunal for permission.

The facts

5–61 The data subjects were not identified but were referred to by the initials of the force area, SY, WY and NW.

In 1979, when SY was 15 years old, she was convicted of an offence of occasioning actual bodily harm as a result of which she received a conditional discharge of 12 months. It was not known whether she pleaded guilty or not guilty, whether she was represented at the hearing or any facts surrounding the conviction. The conviction data about her had been placed on the PNC in 1998, apparently because SY had come to the attention of the police at that time, although no one knew how. The judgment quotes a letter from Nottingham (which was clearly prejudicial to SY and which was backed up by no evidence) that the conviction data from 1979 had been put onto the PNC in 1998

> ". . . because of another offence committed in 1998 but subsequently dropped (for reasons not known or researched by myself)" (para 15)

WY had come before the courts twice when he was 18 in 1978: on the first occasion for theft, taking a motor vehicle without consent and driving without insurance and while disqualified; on the second occasion for similar offences including driving without due care and attention, failing to stop after an accident and driving while disqualified.

NW's convictions were 34 years old. He had had 5 arrests for taking and driving away, larceny and receiving during 1967 and 1969.

There was no evidence that the individuals had come before the courts or to the attention of the police since the original convictions apart from the vague material about SY.

Despite the fact that the role of the Tribunal was to determine the relevance of these particular convictions to the policing purpose and despite the statement of the

Tribunal that the question of whether there was a breach of principle would depend on the facts of each case, the Tribunal refused to take evidence from the complainants about the circumstances of the convictions. SY's solicitors had expressed a willingness to provide a statement setting out the relevant facts and a member of WY's family had sent a letter providing background to the circumstances surrounding the incidents which led to the offences. The Tribunal refused to take either of these into account, because of its concerns that the evidence could not be tested under cross-examination. It decided that it could "reach a conclusion upon the substance of the appeals without embarking on the kind of factual inquiry which contested versions of events are bound to lead to" (para 7).

In effect therefore, despite the repeated statement of the Tribunal (para 201) that the judgment was not meant to be a precedent for other cases on conviction data and was being decided on the facts of these cases, the Tribunal treated the conviction information as a class of information in respect of which the retention decisions were to be made.

The arguments of the parties

5–62   The starting point for the case was the existence of guidelines on the retention and removal of conviction data ("weeding") produced by the Association of Chief Police Officers (ACPO). The Commissioner accepted that the weeding guidelines were generally sound and that the types of convictions in question fell within the categories of data which it was acceptable to retain under the guidelines, but he argued that the guidelines were drawn with a very broad brush. His position was that Chief Constables must exercise discretion when applying the guidelines. Where a data subject requests that the data be reviewed the Chief Constable should review the data and consider the purpose for which the conviction data are held and the likelihood of the particular data being useful for each aspect of the purpose. If the data would not be useful for those purposes he should exercise his discretion to remove the data. Applying that approach to these cases it was the Commissioner's view that the data should be removed and that failure to remove the data breached Principles three and five as well as Article 8 of the HRA Convention.

One of the arguments raised against the Commissioner was that such a policy would be unfair to those who **did not** ask for removal of records but the Commissioner rejected the suggestion that there would be unfairness to those data subjects who do not request deletion.

The arguments put forward on behalf of the Chief Constables focussed on the usefulness of conviction data for policing and the difficulty of exercising a discretion in this area. They argued that conviction information is important in operational policing, in particular in investigative work. It is required for employment vetting for certain occupations and there is a statutory obligation under the Police Act 1997 to supply it for those purposes. Consistency in the retention of conviction information is essential and selective erasure would undermine that consistency. The weeding rules do not allow for any discretion, rather they provide a consistent and inflexible rule of practice going far beyond any guidelines. Moreover the imposition of such a discretion would place an unreasonable burden on the police. Finally the removal of conviction data in respect of those who requested it would be unfair to those data subjects who did not make such a request.

Evidence

5–63 The Commissioner relied upon the bare facts of the conviction data, its age and the apparent absence of any further criminal activity by the complainants since the dates of the convictions, to support the argument that the data was excessive and irrelevant to the policing purpose. He did not seek to adduce general evidence on the value of old conviction information and did not call any expert evidence, although he drew attention to some Home Office research which he used to suggest that the existence of a single conviction early in life was not a very good predictor of later criminal activity. However the Tribunal did not accept the research evidence as assisting the Commissioner's case.

5–64 On behalf of the Chief Constables evidence was called that the purpose of policing includes, in addition to operational policing, employment vetting obligations and the obligation to assist in the administration of justice. The deletion of records would lead to inconsistencies in searches of the Criminal Records Bureau. It is desirable, if not absolutely essential, for the CPS to have possession of full conviction information in order to be able to put fully informed and accurate information to a court should evidence of character be required; that a full record of convictions is required for sentencing; that evidence of previous convictions may be relevant to assess the danger to the public from a defendant and that convictions may show how successful previous sentences have been.

The Tribunal heard evidence that conviction history was important information for use in police investigations and that the Probation service depends upon a comprehensive database of convictions to enable them to assess patterns and risk of offending.

In each case the data fell within specific categories for which the Code of Practice set out retention guidelines. The controllers further argued that those guidelines were sound and represented good practice. The retention of the type of conviction data in question was in accord with the guidelines and was relevant to the purpose of policing.

In effect the case presented on behalf of both parties focussed upon the retention of the conviction data as a class and not the retention of the specific records relating to the specific individuals which were at issue in the proceedings.

The legal arguments

5–65 In essence the Commissioner argued that, in considering whether information is excessive or is being held longer than is necessary for the purpose, a balance must be struck between the needs of the purpose and the impact on the individual. The Chief Constables argued that the purpose is paramount and as long as some justification can be shown for the continued retention of data of that type the controller is entitled to retain it.

Findings

5–66 It is not wholly straightforward to discern the findings of the Tribunal however it is suggested that the following list represents a fair summary:

- There is a significant degree of overlap between Principles three and five, so that data which has been kept for longer than is necessary for the purpose is likely also to be excessive in relation to the purpose

- The question of whether data are relevant to the purpose for which they are processed will depend largely on the nature, content and quality of the data

- In order to determine whether it is "necessary" for a data controller to keep particular data for a particular purpose the controller should apply a test of proportionality. If the data are potentially embarrassing or damaging to the data subject he may have to undertake a balancing exercise between the importance of retaining the data for his purposes and the negative impact on the data subject

In relation to policing and conviction information:

- The purpose of policing covers operational policing, assisting the courts in the administration of justice and some employment vetting where such vetting is for the prevention or detection of crime or the apprehension or prosecution of offenders (para 179) even though the standard purpose description in the registerable particulars does not include this (para 134)

- A Chief Constable as data controller can only justify retention of data on the Police National Computer for the purposes of employment vetting insofar as the vetting is for the purpose of the prevention or detection of crime or the apprehension or prosecution of offenders (para 183)

- Conviction information may remain relevant for the element of the policing purpose related to the administration of justice even when it is no longer particularly relevant for operational policing (para 185)

- The way in which the ACPO DP Code of Practice has been interpreted has varied from force to force and in future should be applied on a consistent basis (para 66). In particular the terms "weeding" and "review" in the context of conviction data should be clarified between the Commissioner and ACPO (para 58)

- Better guidance is needed on data protection and informatics by police officers (para 59) and such guidance should be taken into account by all forces (para 69)

- The approach taken in the Bichard Report towards the role of the Information Commissioner in relation to data held by the police for policing purposes is endorsed (para 72). This is that it is for the police to decide whether information is required for operational purposes and the role of the Commissioner is limited to a supervisory role similar to that of a court exercising a judicial review function, "If a reasonable and rational basis exists for a decision 'that should be the end of the story'";

- that although there should be agreement about retaining certain categories of information for specific purposes there could still be a review in individual cases;

- that retention of information involves less interference than using information. (para 72 quoting Bichard 4.45.1)

- The approach taken by Bichard in relation to the disclosure of non-conviction information to employers was endorsed i.e. that the discretion whether or not to disclose non-conviction data on an enhanced disclosure search should be removed from Chief Constables

- The fact that no convictions are recorded against an individual does not raise a presumption that the person is innocent of any crime. While research shows that re-offending rates drop as the age of the offender increases "this is not necessarily an indication that offenders are less likely to commit crime" . . . put simply consistent offenders simply become better at avoiding detection or alternatively they might switch to crimes with lower detection rates etc. The evidence to justify the retention of the conviction data is weak and there is little research into the business benefits to the police of retention (para 54)

- In considering whether there is a breach of the third and fifth principles the critical issue is whether or not the purpose for which the data are processed is no longer justified (para 88) (again applying Bichard)

- Conviction history forms an integral part of the investigative operations of the police force (para 100) (para 207 and 208)

- Conviction data is useful to the courts in considering character (para 208)

- Article 8(5) of Directive 95/46/EC provides that a complete register of convictions will be unlawful unless kept under the control of official authority

- The retention of conviction data by the State engages Article 8(1) (para 173) but is justified within Article 8(2) (para 177)

- The disclosure of spent conviction data by the State for the purposes of a certificate of conviction under section 113 of the Police Act 1997 would breach Article 8(1) and not be justifiable under Article 8(2)

- Section 113 of the Police Act 1997 should be interpreted in accord with the Human Rights Act 1998 so as to restrict the disclosure of information on "spent" convictions to the CRB for the purposes of the standard certificate

- As a matter of evidence the evidence of an "aggrieved data subject" cannot be accepted in relation to convictions without being subject to being tested against police records or court files. Thus where there is no available information from the police the evidence of the data subject must be excluded (para 203);

- The weeding rules do not represent a rigid and unqualified code (para 206)

Commentary

5–67   *One of the most striking aspects of this 95 page judgment is the paucity of reference to the relevant sections of the Act or any legal authorities. The wording of the relevant Principles is set out in para.3 of the judgment. They are then barely mentioned until para.184. Even at that stage there is no examination of the meaning or import of the provisions, no earlier cases are cited and there is no consideration of the Commissioner's formal guidance or how the Principles have been approached by earlier Tribunals.*

This appears to have been the result of a positive decision not to consider how the relevant Principles should be interpreted:

> *"Insofar as the Third and Fifth Data Protection principles are concerned, the Tribunal is not minded to make any concrete determination as to their exact scope and effect if only given the fact that the legislation itself as has been seen stops short of doing so in its explanatory treatment of the principle in Schedule 1 particularly Part 2 to the 1998 Act."*

As can be noted from the list of the finding much of the judgment consists of setting out matters of fact and law dealing with the way that the Police National Computer works, the guidelines in place for dealing with conviction data and the use of conviction data in the criminal justice system.

On the broader issues the Tribunal accepted that a breach of Art.8 would inevitably involve a breach of the Principles, however it appears to have regarded Art.8 and the Principles as co-terminous and failed to explore the argument that the Directive extends and particularises the Art.8 rights in the field of information and a controller may still breach Principles 3- and 5 even if he does not breach Art.8. Disappointingly, although the Tribunal appears to have ruled that the question of retention should be assessed applying a test of proportionality, there was no discussion of proportionality in the specific cases. Oddly enough, although there was a clear statement from the Tribunal that it regarded the information about the convictions as inadequate material on which to found a judgment, there was no finding on adequacy. The Tribunal appears to have been content to judge the information to be inadequate but at the same time relevant and not excessive to the purpose.

In relation to the powers of the Tribunal it considered whether it was able to hear evidence not presented to the Commissioner and decided that it was able to do so.

In making its final order the Tribunal in effect said that the parties might apply to it to review progress in implementation of the order within four months of the judgment. While this may be a practical response it raises the question whether it is within their powers.

Case Study 1: Principle 1

5–68 "The complainant had alleged rent arrears with a housing association. She had vacated the property and provided her employer's address for correspondence purposes. The housing association sent a letter to the employer themselves, [sic] outlining the amount of alleged debt, and seeking the employer's assurance that they would co-operate should an attachment of earnings order be obtained. A letter addressed to the complainant was enclosed in the same envelope. The complainant claimed that she was extremely embarrassed by the disclosure."

Comment. The Association obtained the employer's address details for the purpose of correspondence only. They used the information for another purpose without notice to the employee or offering her an opportunity to opt-out of the use. The processing was therefore in breach of the requirements to provide the specified information.

The processing was unfair in more general terms as it was not justified at the time as no attachment of earnings order had yet been sought. A reasonable person considering the circumstances would have realised that the complainant would be embarrassed by the letter.

The information may also have been disclosed in breach of confidence if the details of the complainant's rent account was regarded as confidential.

Case Study 2: Principle 2

5–69 "A police force disclosed information about a victim of crime to a voluntary organization providing counselling services to victims. The victim complained that this contravened the Act as he did not want his details to be disclosed to a third party unconnected with the investigation of the crime."

Comment. It appeared that the police force had not informed the victim of the transmission of the information or, if it had done so, it had not offered a specific opt-out from the disclosure. If the force had been aware of the intention to pass the information on the victim should have been informed when the data were collected, if this was possible. However if the police force only considered the possible disclosure later they should have reviewed not only the compatibility of the original purpose of collection with the new purpose but also the general fairness of the processing.

Principle 3—see Tribunal case

Case Study 4: Principle 4

5–70 "A complaint was received from a woman who had recently left the employment of a local authority Social Services Department. There were some outstanding administrative issues surrounding her departure. The Council intended to make a note to this effect on one of their systems. Unfortunately, through a clerical error, her name was instead entered onto a list of the Department's clients. This database was accessible by a number of the complainant's ex-colleagues, one of whom brought this to her attention."

Comment. The personal data here became inaccurate and the data controller would be responsible for the inaccuracy.

Principle 5—see Tribunal cases

Case Study 6: Principle 6

5–71 "A local authority failed to provide a copy of a reference within 40 days of a subject access request, after an offer of employment was withdrawn as a result of that reference."

Comment. In this case the breach also caused the individual loss and could have given rise to an application for compensation.

Case Study 7: Principle 7

5–72   "An employee of a further education college complained that other employees, outside the Personnel Department were able to access confidential personal information about her.

The complainant explained that any member of staff on the network neighbourhood system could access documents concerning her, including a memo, which set out a number of concerns she had raised with the line managers. She said that a member of the Personnel Department who had saved them without any password protection and in an open directory had typed these documents. The complainant said that at least seven employees on the network system could have had access to these files, one of which was entitled 'Ms X's claim for extra pay.'

An individual complained that she had received a direct marketing telephone call from a mobile telephone company. It became clear that the company had purchased the individual's personal data from the private company which administered the Driving Theory Test on behalf of the DSA. Without DSA's knowledge or approval, the private company which acted as their data processor for the Driving Theory Test had sold personal data relating to 100,000 candidates to a number of private companies for direct marketing purposes."

Comment.   The case studies show how the security obligations can be breached in very different circumstances. In the first case there appear to have been inadequate internal procedures. In the second the contract with the private sector body did not apparently comply with the requirements of the DPA.

Security measures checklist

5–73   There are a number of useful standards materials which deal with security. ISO 27001 the Information security Management Code gives guidance for technical and operational security measures. The British Standards Institute Code of Practice for Legal Admissibility and Evidential Weight of Information Stored Electronically PD 008 gives guidance to the quality required to ensure that evidence can be used in legal proceedings. BS 4783 Storage Transport and Media Maintenance contains useful guidance on solutions to reduce the chances of damage to data. The obligations imposed by the interpretation provision on the Seventh Principle on security can be distinguished as follows:

1. Ensure a level of security appropriate to:

   (a) the harm that might result from such unauthorised or unlawful processing or accidental loss, destruction or damage as are mentioned in the Seventh Principle, and

   (b) the nature of the data to be protected (Sch.1, para.9):

      (i) A data controller must design and implement a security policy. This will involve:

         • first, defining the security needs of the organisation through a risks audit;

- secondly, producing a policy to tackle the identified risks; and
- thirdly, implementing the policy through instructions and training to relevant staff—the relevant staff should have clearly defined roles, responsibilities and privileges;
- responsibility should be clearly placed with a senior member of staff
- adequate resources should be allocated for the function
- fourthly, having feedback, review and amending mechanisms in place.

(ii) Any security policy will have to guard against unauthorised access to personal data:

- Are security staff needed?
- What arrangements have been made regarding access by third parties to locations where personal data is kept? Do they have to check in and out? Are baggage checks necessary?
- Should personal data be kept in a secure room?
- Is password protection for personal data appropriate? If so are passwords changed regularly?
- How are the media containing personal data stored? Is that storage secure?
- Security policies must address the issue of unauthorised disclosure of personal data and have systems and checks for staff to follow to ensure they are not tricked into disclosing data.
- Consider the positioning of equipment—can computer screens be overlooked?
- Printouts must be treated as securely as information stored on computer.
- Procedures are required to deal with the full and proper disposal of back up tapes, disks and printouts. Redundant equipment must be securely dealt with.

(iii) Any security policy will have to guard against loss of personal data:

- Personal data should be backed up regularly and back ups stored separately from originals.
- Policies must minimise the risk of equipment storing personal data being stolen.
- Are hardware and software reliable?

2. Take reasonable steps to ensure the reliability of any employees who have access to the personal data (Sch.1, para.10):

(i) When is checking appropriate?

- On applying for a job? Remember temporary staff appointments also require vetting.
- On an appraisal?
- On departure from a job?
- Are spot checks appropriate? If so should they be random or notified in advance?

(ii) Is a specific "whistle-blowing" system appropriate for staff to notify breaches committed by colleagues? If so what steps are taken to ensure all relevant staff know how the system operates?

(iii) What types of checks are appropriate?

- References from previous employers—should security breaches be raised as a specific issue for a previous employer to address?
- Are employees' academic and professional qualifications pertinent?

3. Choose a data processor providing sufficient guarantees in respect of the technical and organisational security measures governing the processing to be carried out, and take reasonable steps to ensure compliance with those measures (Sch.1, para.11)

(i) The processor should have a written security policy available for inspection. The policy should offer levels of security depending on the nature of the data and the harm which might result from any breach of security.

(ii) The processor should be able to demonstrate its track record with respect to security measures and produce references from other controllers.

(iii) The processor should permit spot checks to be carried out. The controller should consider whether these should be random or pre-arranged.

A written contract between the data controller and the processor is required (Sch.1, para.12). The contract should incorporate the issues set out in para.3 above and must ensure that the processor may only act on instructions from the data controller.

Records management process

5–74   A good records management system will include processes that broadly correspond to those listed here:

1. Information capture—the process of acquiring or recording/creating information

2. Registration—recording the existence of a record and capturing metadata (data about the data) that can be used to uniquely identify a record and locate it

3. Classification—categorizing information on the basis of business needs which will also inform retention decisions

4. Access and security levels- determining who within an organisation will have access to information and what measures will be taken to ensure the security of the information

5. Life expectancy of the record—determining retention and disposal arrangements whether via archive or destruction

6. Use and tracking of records—the process of using information, retrieving information, tracking location, amendments, version control, distribution of copies

7. Destruction and disposal—the process of destruction and the retention of a record of the nature and time of the destruction or disposal

See also ISO 15489 the international standard for records management

PROCESSOR CONTRACT CLAUSE

5–75   The precedent can be used as the starting point for the production of an appropriate clause whether as part of a larger contract or a stand—alone agreement. Not all of the provisions may be required in a simple agreement. Data controllers must bear in mind that the contract terms are not a substitute for an assessment of the security standards of the processor. Before entering into the contract the data controller must have assessed the level of technical and organisational security measures which are required to protect the personal data which are to be processed and have assured himself that the processor chosen is able to provide that level of security.

In some contracts the level of security required is captured in Schedules and it may be appropriate to refer to those in the clause. In any event if the contract includes such provisions case must be taken to ensure that the clause is consistent with them. Care must also be taken to ensure that the clause is consistent with any confidentiality clause and in particular that the personal data covered by the processor clause is satisfactorily defined. The personal data may be a sub-set of the information which is agreed to be covered by the confidentiality clause.

1 Definitions

All terms used in this clause which appear in the [Data Protection Act 1998] [Data Protection Legislation] have the meaning set out in that [Act][legislation]

Data Protection Legislation means the Data Protection Act 1998, the Privacy and Electronic Communications (EC Directive) Regulations 2003 [*Check that subordinate legislation and amendments are covered in a general clause or add one in*]

Notes—in some precedents the terms are listed individually.

*It is usually straightforward to state who the parties are and which one is the **Data Controller** and which is the **Data Processor**. For the purposes of this precedent it is assumed that the Parties have been defined and we refer to the Parties here as **Client** and **Supplier**.*

*It can be more complex to capture the **Personal Data** which is the subject of the **Controller/Processor** obligations. In some cases the parties will know in advance the categories and types of personal data of personal data which will be processed. In others they will not necessarily know this in advance.*

(a) Where the categories are known then they can be set out by reference to the types of data subject, the types of processing and any other known factors. This approach is taken in the Model Clauses for overseas transfers. The relevant personal data which is the subject of the

contract is described in a separate schedule. The Model Clause formulation includes a description of the data subjects, the types of personal data processed and the nature of the processing.

[Relevant Personal Data][Client Personal Data] means

(a) the Personal Data described in Schedule X

However in other cases there is less clarity about the relevant personal data which will be processed as a result of the contract and another method of defining it must be used.

> *(b) In some cases the contract will have schedules setting out the services to be provided and the data that will be handled by the service provider. In such a case the clause can be drafted by reference to the services provided under the agreement. It will be clear what personal data will be involved, for example if the supplier is providing HR services.*

(b) [the Personal Data processed by the Supplier on behalf of the Client in the delivery of the Services this Agreement]

> *(c) Where the contract is a straightforward outsourcing of an IT function and the **Data Processor** will be receiving the personal data from the **Data Controller** then it can be described in those terms.*

(c) [the Personal Data received by the Data Processor from the Data Controller for the purposes of the Services]

> *(d) In other cases, the personal data with which the parties are concerned will also be generated by the **Data Processor** or may be received from others. In this case contracts sometimes use a formulation which tries to capture the relevant personal data using formulations like **Personal Data processed by the Data Processor in connection with this Agreement** but this may be too wide, for example potentially it captures the personal data about the employees of the **Data Processor** who are employed to work on the contract. This should be considered when deciding which approach to use.*

(d) [the Personal Data processed by the Data Processor in connection with this Agreement]

> *(e) A general formulation which can be used refers to the **Personal Data processed by the Data Processor in connection with this Agreement in respect of which the Client is the Data Controller** however, unless this class of information is described or can be ascertained from some other provisions (for example the description of the services as noted above), the question of whether or not particular data are caught by the provision will be a matter of fact to be ascertained during the lifetime of the contract. The parties will not therefore have the certainty that other methods can provide.*

(e) [Personal Data processed by the Data Processor in connection with this Agreement in respect of which the Client is the Data Controller]

The Parties acknowledge that Client is a Data Controller for the [Relevant Personal Data] [Client Personal Data]

Client appoints the Supplier as a Data Processor to process the [Relevant Personal Data][Client Personal Data] on his behalf

Supplier's obligations

The Supplier shall process the [Relevant Personal Data][Client Personal Data] only in accord with the instructions of the Client [as given from time to time]

The Supplier shall process the [Relevant Personal Data][Client Personal Data] only for the purposes of the Agreement in accord with the instructions of the Client

Notes—these provisions are required by paragraph 12 (a) (ii) of Part II of Schedule 1

The Supplier agrees and warrants that [having regard to the state of technological development and the cost of implementing any measures (a)] and having regard to:

the nature of the [Relevant Personal Data][Client Personal Data] and

the harm that might result from unauthorised or unlawful processing or accidental loss, destruction of or damage to the [relevant Personal Data][Client Personal Data] [in particular where the processing involves the transmission of the [relevant Persona Data][Client personal Data] over a network(b)]

it has in place appropriate technical and organisational measures to protect the [Relevant Personal Data][Client Personal Data] against accidental or unlawful destruction or accidental loss, alteration, unauthorised disclosure or access and all other forms of unlawful processing in accord with the requirements of the Data Protection legislation [law of] [name of Member State in which the Data Processor is established if not the UK (c)] which implements Article 17 of Directive 95/46/EC on the protection of individuals with regard to the processing of personal data and the free movement of such data]

Notes—these provisions are required by paragraph 12 (b). The first set of words in square brackets (a) are not necessary but repeat the provision in principle 7. The second set of words in square brackets (b) which refer to networks are not necessary but reflect the wording of Article 17. Where the processor is established in the UK then the third set of words in square brackets (c) are not necessary however where the processor is outside the UK consideration should be given to including them as Article 17.3 of the Directive requires that the processor shall be required to undertake the security obligations set out in Article 17.1 "as defined by the law of the Member State in which the processor is established".

The Supplier agrees and warrants that it will [take all steps which are necessary to ensure compliance with those measure] [take reasonable steps to ensure compliance with those measures]

The Supplier agrees and warrants that it will take reasonable steps to ensure the reliability of any employees or agents of his who have access to the [relevant Personal Data][Client Personal Data] and in particular will ensure that such persons receive training in data protection, security and the care of personal data.

Notes—the clauses set out above are mandatory for Principle 7. The following clauses set out a number of practical measures to go with them and specific remedies for the data controller. The term Relevant Personal Data is used for the rest of the precedent

The Supplier shall provide the Client with a statement of the technical and organisational measures adopted in order to meet the Supplier's obligations in respect of the Relevant Personal Data together with a statement of the steps taken to ensure the reliability of any employees or agents who will have access to the Relevant Personal Data [before commencement of any processing operations involving the Relevant Personal Data]

The Supplier shall not be entitled to commence processing operations involving the Relevant Personal Data until [the Client has notified the Supplier of its acceptance of the statement] [other trigger event]

If at any time the Supplier becomes aware of a breach of the required standards or is not able to deliver compliance with the required standards he shall promptly inform the Client of the fact and the Client shall be entitled to suspend the processing of the Relevant Personal Data by the Supplier

The Supplier will indemnify the Client against all costs, claims, damages expenses or proceedings which the Supplier may incur arising from a breach of the Supplier's obligations in respect of the Relevant Personal Data

The Client may inspect the Supplier's facilities for the processing of the Relevant Personal Data and may audit the Supplier's procedures to ensure that they meet the standards set out in the accepted statements. The Client shall give reasonable notice of such inspection or audit.

At the termination of this Agreement for whatever cause the Supplier shall immediately stop processing the Relevant Personal Data and shall return the relevant Personal Data to the Client

The Supplier shall comply with any requirement imposed on the Client by any relevant regulator in respect of the Relevant Personal Data and shall comply with any reasonable requirement of the Client in order to ensure compliance with the Data Protection Legislation.

The Supplier will not transfer any of the Relevant Personal Data outside the European Economic Area without the consent of the Client

The Supplier will not disclose any of the Relevant Personal Data to any person other than for the purposes of this Agreement otherwise than in response to a legal requirement.

Notes—These are all biased towards the data controller. They do not include all the possible arrangements that may be made, for example it may be agreed that the data will be destroyed at the end of the contract; the parties may wish to agree who pays for any audit of the processing; the parties may wish to add more detail to the overseas transfer provisions or those dealing with third party disclosures

The following may also be useful to include.

The Supplier may appoint other contractors to process the Relevant Personal Data as further Data Processors on behalf of the Client [with the consent of the Client which shall not be unreasonably withheld] provided that the other contractors are appointed on written term that require equivalent protections for the Relevant Personal Data as are required of the Supplier by this Agreement and provide the Client with equivalent rights against the other contractors

Sometimes contracts permit data processors to sub-contract as long as the terms are equivalent to the main contract and do not require that the sub-contractor enters into a relationship with the data controller. This clause requires the data processor to ensure that the data controller has rights against the sub-contractor. There is an argument that if a data controller allows sub-contracts to which he is not a party or cannot enforce the contract he is in breach of Principle 7. Where a data processor appoints a sub-contractor the sub-contractor is arguably still a data processor for the data controller because as a data processor is "any person (other than an employee of the data controller) who processes the data on behalf of the data controller" (section 1(1)) Principle 7 applies where processing of personal data is carried out by a data processor on behalf of a data controller. The better approach therefore is to ensure that the data controller has the benefit of a written appointment.

The Supplier will, unless prevented by law, promptly inform the Client if it receives any requests in respect of the Relevant Personal Data whether from data subjects or the Information Commissioner or any other persons

The Supplier will promptly provide the Client with any information which the Client requires in order to comply with any subject access request in relation to the processing of the Relevant Personal Data or to respond to any enquiry by any relevant regulator

Notes—the parties may wish to ensure that data subjects are able to benefit from the clauses but if they do not then the rights of third parties under the Third Parties (Rights in Contracts) Act

ADDITIONAL INFORMATION

Derivations

5–76   • Directive 95/46 (see App. B)

    (a) Arts 6 (principles related to data quality), 10 (information in cases of collection from the data subject), 11 (information where data have not been obtained from the data subject), 16 and 17 (confidentiality and security of the processing), 25 (transfer of personal data to third countries).
    (b) Recitals 28, 38, 39, 40, 46, 56, 57.

   • Council of Europe Convention of January 28, 1981 for the Protection of Individuals with regard to automatic processing of Personal Data: Arts 5 (quality of data), 7 (data security).
   • Data Protection Act 1984; s.2 and Sch.1 (the Principles).
   • Organisation for Economic Co-operation and Development Guidelines: Annex, Pt 2 (Basic Principles of National Application 7, 8, 9, 10, 11).

Hansard references

5–77   Vol.586, No.108, col.CWH 21, Lords Grand Committee, February 23, 1998
Principle 1, fair collection, meaning of as soon as practicable

Vol.587, No.127, col.1127, Lords Third Reading, March 24, 1998
Principle 6, para.8, Pt II, Sch.1

Commons Standing Committee, June 4, col.304
Principle 6

ibid., cols 304, 305
Principle 7 arm/risk

Vol.315, No.198, col.611, Commons Third Reading, July 2, 1998
Principle 7 and Year 2000 bug

Case law

5–78   See Data Protection Tribunal cases listed at the end of Ch.3, above.

CHAPTER 6

Legitimate Processing

INTRODUCTION

6–01   This chapter and Ch.7 will consider the conditions for the processing of any personal data and for the processing of sensitive personal data, set out in Schs 2 and 3 to the Act, are considered. The conditions set out in Schs 2 and 3 are continuing conditions; there must be a legitimisation of the processing throughout the processing.

The conditions recognise that the processing of any personal data about another is a trespass into the informational privacy of that person and must therefore either be accepted by the individual or justified on some basis. The threshold to justify processing is not very high but nevertheless must take account of the data subject's rights. This can be seen most clearly in the wording of the "catch-all" ground in Sch.2, which permits processing when:

> "it is necessary for the purposes of legitimate interests pursued by the data controller or by the third party or parties to whom the data are disclosed, except where the processing is unwarranted in any particular case by reason of prejudice to the rights and freedoms or legitimate interests of the data subject."[1]

Data controllers have been inclined to apply a broad interpretation of this ground. In this they have been supported by the Commissioner (see the Legal Guidance referred to later).

There is no explicit duty on the data controller to identify or record the grounds for processing personal data. The registerable particulars submitted for notification do not require him to identify his grounds and he is under no obligation to provide information on this point to the data subject in response to a subject access request. The Commissioner may demand a statement of the grounds for particular processing in an Information Notice under s.43 but only if he has received a demand for assessment or reasonably requires the information to determine whether the controller is complying with the Principles.

A data controller must have proper grounds for the processing of personal data in any particular case. If a data controller does not have proper grounds the Commissioner is able to serve an enforcement notice requiring him to rectify matters, whether by establishing proper grounds or ceasing to process the data temporarily or

---

[1] 1998 Act Sch.2 para.6.

permanently. In proceedings for compensation brought by an individual a court might also order a cessation of particular processing of particular data on the ground that the controller had no proper basis for the processing. However, it is likely that such an order would be limited to the data relating to the individual applicant, not the entire data set, whereas action by the Commissioner could apply to an entire dataset.

SUMMARY OF THE MAIN POINTS

6–02   The first Principle of the Data Protection Principles under the 1998 Act provides that:

> "Personal data shall be processed fairly and lawfully and in particular shall not be processed unless:
>
> (a) at least one of the conditions in Schedule 2 is met, and
> (b) in the case of sensitive personal data at least one of the conditions in Schedule 3 is also met."

In other words, any processing which is permitted must be fair and lawful but no processing is permitted unless at least one of the Sch.2 conditions is satisfied and, additionally, in the case of "sensitive data", at least one of the Sch.3 conditions.

Thus to comply entirely with the first Principle of the 1998 Act, processing must be legitimate (i.e. comply with the Sch. 2 conditions or, in the case of sensitive data, the Sch.3 conditions) and must be fair and lawful. Lawful, it is submitted, encompasses but has a broader meaning than "legitimate" in accordance with Schs 2 and 3. The meaning of "fair and lawful" is discussed in detail in Ch.5, above on the Principles.

LEGITIMATE PROCESSING

6–03   Processing is defined in s.1(1) of the 1998 Act as meaning "obtaining, recording or holding" the data and carrying out various operations with respect to the data including: organising, adapting, altering, retrieving, consulting, using, disclosing, aligning, combining, erasing or blocking the data. In short, almost anything that might be done to or with personal data is covered by "processing". The definition is considered in detail in Ch.3, above. Processing is only permissible if it is carried out where one or more of the Sch.2 conditions apply.

The data subject has given his consent to the processing

6–04   The meaning of consent and its interpretation is discussed in detail in Ch.3, above. This condition contrasts with the parallel provision in Sch.3 (conditions for the processing of sensitive data) which requires the explicit consent of the data subject. By implication, therefore, some form of consent which is not explicit is sufficient to satisfy this Sch.2 condition. There is no requirement that the consent be in writing.

Article 7 of the Directive, which sets out the criteria for making data processing legitimate, refers to the data subject unambiguously giving his consent. The word "unambiguous" is not included in the 1998 Act. Consent may be either express or implied from some relevant action of the data subject. Reference is sometimes made to "opt out" consent. True consent cannot be obtained by merely presenting an "opt out" to the data subject after he has provided information to the data controller, however failure to complete an opt-out box on a coupon or other mechanism which is returned to the data controller can be argued to be an action from which consent may be implied. For example a respondent to a mail order coupon may be presumed to understand that his personal data will be processed for the purposes of dealing with the order. However, if the personal data so gathered are intended to be used for another purpose—in particular direct marketing, either by the original data user or by a third party to whom the data have been sold or transferred—then fairness requires that the data subject must give consent.[2] Such consent might be obtained by sending a communication which has to be returned to the data controller and which includes a description of the proposed new use and an opt-out box prominently situated. Returning the communication with the opt-out box unticked would then be argued to amount to an implied consent.

In practice the specified information requirements of the first Principle and the consent condition of Sch.2 are generally dealt with in tandem by the adoption of written or spoken procedures which both convey information about intended processing to the potential data subject and also obtain his or her consent. This might be achieved, for example, by providing the data subject with a written notice in duplicate detailing the specified information and asking for the return of one copy signed to indicate consent.

6–05   The Directive (Art.2(h)) defines the data subject's consent as meaning any "freely given, specific and informed indication of his wishes by which the data subject signifies his agreement to personal data relating to him being processed". Thus "consent" obtained by trickery or under duress would not suffice, but arguably this adds little to the requirement that personal data is processed fairly in any event. The requirement in the Directive that consent must be informed suggests that there must be some indication that the data subject has understood the nature of the data gathering or other data processing exercise. The Directive uses the term "signifies" rather than "conveys" or "communicates" and, it is submitted, means something potentially less clear than those terms. "Signifies", it is suggested, means "indicates" rather than "tells" or "states".

Under the 1984 Act the Registrar served an Enforcement Notice on British Gas Trading Limited with respect to leaflets sent out informing customers that personal data gathered for the purposes of customer administration would be used for the purpose of marketing products not associated with the supply of gas unless the customers positively signified their dissent. The Registrar's views were upheld by the Tribunal in 1998.[3] The Tribunal considered that where personal data were supplied in order for a data subject to acquire essential services from a company with an effective monopoly then any processing of that data for marketing purposes would be unfair processing unless done with the consent of the data subject.

In considering whether inaction can amount to consent being "signified", common law principles also have to be borne in mind. It is clear from case law that silence cannot

---

[2] *Innovations (Mail Order) Ltd v DPR*, September 1993, para.30. See *Encyclopedia of Data Protection* (Sweet & Maxwell).
[3] *British Gas Trading Ltd v DPR*, 1998. See Encyclopedia of Data Protection (Sweet & Maxwell) or *www.informationtribunal.gov.uk* [Accessed on 2 September 2007].

indicate consent.[4] This issue is discussed in more detail in Ch.3, above. In the case of *Michael Stone v SE Coast Strategis Health Authority*[5] the court appears to have accepted that a data subject could withdraw a consent, although the point was not actually litigated The Health Authority had originally argued that a consent to publication of information, once given, was irrevocable but did not pursue the claim.

Contractual reasons

6–06   Schedule 2 para.2 permits processing where it is necessary:

(a) for the performance of a contract to which the data subject is a party; or

(b) for the taking of steps at the request of the data subject with a view to entering into a contract.

Thus if the data subject replies to a mail order coupon, ordering specific goods, processing for the purposes of obtaining payment for the order and to effect the delivery of the ordered goods would be permissible under this provision (although arguably such activities would also be permitted by way of the data subject's implied consent). Ancillary purposes, such as future mail shots from the data controller regarding additional products, would not be permitted under this provision, since such processing would not be in pursuance of the original contract. Such additional processing might be permissible under the legitimate interest ground or under the consent condition if the data subject's implied or express consent had been obtained to such additional processing at the time that the original contract was entered into—one of the best examples being by way of an "opt-in" or "opt-out" box on the original order form. If the data subject had filled in a mail order coupon to order a catalogue it could be argued that the dispatch of subsequent replacement editions of the same catalogue was justifiable under this head.

The second limb of the "contractual reasons" condition appears to be designed to cover, for example, credit reference checking carried out by the data controller prior to entering into a contract. However, if that is the intention of the limb, then the inclusion of the phrase "at the request of the data subject" seems an odd qualification. A credit reference check is not usually a pre-contractual step "requested" by a data subject. The request for a credit reference check invariably comes from the data controller not the data subject, since its rationale is to protect the lender/controller rather than the borrower/subject. Credit reference checks are procedures which data subjects might consent to, which of course would allow the controller to process in pursuance of the "consent" condition, but they are hardly procedures which a data subject requests. An alternative view would be that a credit reference check is such an essential part of any credit agreement that by requesting a credit agreement a data subject would be deemed to be requesting a credit reference check.

The second limb of the "contractual reasons" condition is clearly wide enough to cover other pre-contractual dealings that require the processing of the data subject's personal data. Given that a "request" from a data subject for processing to take place

---

[4] *Jonathan Cape v AG* (the *Crossman Diaries* case) [1976] Q.B. 752.
[5] [2006] EWHC 1668.

must necessarily involve their consent to such processing, it is difficult to see what situation the second limb is aimed at that would not already be covered by the data controller obtaining the data subject's consent to processing.

6–07   The use of the word "necessary" should also not be overlooked. Presumably "necessary" in the context of the 1998 Act means objectively necessary rather than "considered necessary by the data controller". In the House of Commons on May 21, 1998, the Government spokesman explained that in the Government's view the word embodied the European legal principle of proportionality. Case law since then has made clear that this is the correct approach. In *Michael Stone v SE Coast Strategic Health Authority*[6] Mr Justice Davis commented.

> "It is common ground that the word "necessary", as used in the Schedules to the 1998 Act, carries with it the connotations of the European Convention on Human Rights: those include the proposition that a pressing social need is involved and that the measure employed is proportionate to the legitimate aim being pursued."

It is submitted that, while this correctly states the element of proportionality in relation to the grounds for processing, it is somewhat misleading to refer to a "pressing social need". The social need is set out in the ground—for example that the parties wish to enter into a contract or that the vital interests of the subject require protection and the processing of the personal data must be for that purpose and be proportionate to the purpose.

The Commissioner has not issued any explicit guidance on how the word necessary should be interpreted. The only guidance given by the Commissioner is to require that data controllers "should consider in each case whether the processing is necessary to achieve the purpose".[7] It appears that initially the interpretation favoured by the Commissioner of "necessary" processing was "processing without which the intended purpose will be rendered impossible or impractical", as contrasted with processing which merely facilitates the intended purpose. However this approach was in contradiction to the European approach.

In the case of the first limb of the "contractual reasons" condition, "necessary" does not cause great difficulty. With the placement of an order by mail, processing will be necessary to ensure that the sought goods are correctly delivered to the data subject and to ensure that an account is delivered and paid.

With the second limb, "necessary" arguably adds little. As has already been submitted, any data subject "requesting" such processing will also, arguably, be consenting to such processing and the data controller is not therefore going to be troubled with having to show that such processing is "necessary".

Non-contractual legal obligations

6–08   Schedule 2 para.3 permits processing where it is necessary to comply with any legal obligation to which the data controller is subject, other than an obligation imposed by contract. "Necessary" is used again—see the comments in para.6–07, above. This provision can be seen as complementary to the "contractual reasons"

---

[6] See above.
[7] *ibid.* p.11.

condition, and deals with the situation where a controller is obliged by law to process data rather than with an enforceable agreement with the data subject which necessitates the processing of data. Thus if the law requires the testing of primary school children and the maintenance of individual children's test results the data controller (head teacher/board of governors) can claim to satisfy this condition. The permission of the data subjects (parents/children) does not additionally have to be sought.

The data subject's vital interests

6–09   Schedule 2 para.4 permits processing where it is necessary to protect the vital interests of the data subject. "Necessary" is used again—see the comments, above.

The Commissioner has issued some guidance on the interpretation of "vital interests"; in the Legal Guidance as follows:

> "The Commissioner considers that reliance on this condition may only be claimed where the processing is necessary for matters of life and death, for example, the disclosure of a data subject's medical history to a hospital casualty department treating the data subject after a serious road accident."

This is, however, only an interpretation suggested by the Commissioner—furthermore it is a rather restrictive interpretation open to question. The potential difficulty with the phrase "vital interests" is that the word vital has, effectively, two meanings. Vital may mean "necessary to the continuance of life" or "having or affecting life". Alternatively, it may simply mean "essential" or "very important". The meaning given to "vital" in the context of the 1998 Act will affect how widely or restrictively the phrase is interpreted and whether the Commissioner's restrictive interpretation is upheld. Support for the interpretation being restricted to matters affecting the survival of the data subject comes from the Directive itself.

Recital 31 states that the processing of personal data must be regarded as lawful where it is carried out in order to protect an interest which is essential for the data subject's life. The emphasis here, therefore, is on matters of life. Article 7 of the Directive, upon which Sch.2 to the 1998 Act is closely based, makes use of the term "vital interests" without any further clarification. Reference back to the Recitals in the Directive therefore suggests that "vital interests" should be interpreted restrictively to matters affecting the very survival of the data subject.

Conversely, it can be argued that if the intention of the UK legislature was to confine a data subject's "vital interests" to matters of life and death then an alternative phrase such as "the life and health of the data subject" could have been used in preference to "the vital interests of the data subject". In s.34(8) of the 1984 Act the focus was clearly on health issues—albeit on the health of the data subject and others. It is submitted that if the legislature had wanted to limit a data subject's vital interests to issues of health only then could the wording from the 1984 Act have readily been incorporated into the 1998 Act with little amendment. If the wider interpretation is adopted then "vital interests" may well be held to include issues other than health—in particular, it may be that the phrase includes the financial interests of the data subject.

Public functions

6–10   Schedule 2 para.5 permits processing where it is necessary:

(a) for the administration of justice;

(b) for the exercise of any functions conferred by or under any enactment;

(c) for the exercise of any functions of the Crown, a Minister of the Crown or a government department, or;

(d) for the exercise of any functions of a public nature exercised in the public interest.

(aa) for the exercise of any functions of either House of Parliament.

(Note: "Necessary" is used again—see the comments, above.)

It is submitted that the scope of these provisions applies to processing carried out under a discretionary power rather than a legal obligation. Paragraph (aa) was added by Sch.6, para.6 of the Freedom of Information Act 2000.

Subclause (d) seems to be a rather open-ended "mopping-up" provision that is likely to have its interpretation challenged through the courts by way of judicial review. Indeed, it is submitted that "functions of a public nature" will be those which are capable of judicial review. In *Campbell v MGN* the *Mirror* tried to argue that the publication of material which it described as being in the public interest was the "exercise of a public function". Not unsurprisingly, the court held that the *Mirror* newspaper was not a public body operating in the public interest.

The publication *The Judge over your Shoulder*[8] describes administrative law as:

> "The law governing public administration. It governs the exercise of public functions and thus applies primarily to central and local government and public bodies when exercising statutory or other powers or performing public duties."

Administrative law may therefore extend to and affect some private sector bodies such as self-regulatory organisations or privatised utilities if they are exercising public functions.[9] Judicial review of administrative action is an expanding field of law. The courts appear to be prepared to expand the types of executive action that can be subject to review. For example, in *R. v Ministry of Defence Ex p. Smith*,[10] four servicemen and women sought judicial review of a decision by the Ministry of Defence to discharge them from the RAF and Royal Navy because of their homosexual orientation. This was decided pursuant to a joint policy decision of the three armed services exercising prerogative powers preserved by the Army Act 1955, the Air Force Act 1955 and the Naval Discipline Act 1957. The Ministry argued that the issue was not justiciable. The court did not accept the argument that the exercise of prerogative powers in matters of national defence was not justiciable.

The courts have also extended the range of those who are entitled to bring actions for judicial review. The case of *R. v Secretary of State for Foreign Affairs Ex p. World*

---

[8] 2nd ed., published by the Treasury Solicitors/Cabinet Office.
[9] *R. v Panel on Take-overs and Mergers Ex p. Datafin Plc* [1987] Q.B. 815; *Melton Medes v Security and Investment Board* [1995] 3 All E.R. 880.
[10] [1996] 1 All E.R. 257.

Development Movement Ltd[11] was brought against the Foreign Secretary by the World Development Movement. The court accepted that the organisation had sufficient locus standi to bring the case before the court.

6–11 *The data controller's legitimate interests* Schedule 2 para.6 permits processing where it is necessary:

> "for the purposes of legitimate interests pursued by the data controller or by the third party or parties to whom the data are disclosed, except where the processing is unwarranted in any particular case by reason of prejudice to the rights and freedoms or legitimate interests of the data subject. The Secretary of State may by order specify particular circumstances in which this condition is or is not to be taken to be satisfied."

Note: "Necessary" is used again—see the comments, above.

The term legitimate interests is not in any way further clarified. What is clearly required in determining whether this condition has been satisfied is a balancing act—an assessment of both the legitimate interests of the data subject and of those of the data controller and an appraisal of which should take priority.

The view taken by the Commissioner is that the term is a wide one:

> "The Commissioner takes a wide view of the legitimate interests condition and recommends that two tests be applied to establish whether this condition may be appropriate in any particular case."

The two tests suggested merely repeat the provisions of the condition but do not further explore how the balance is to be struck in any particular case. It is suggested that the "legitimate interests" of the data controller will be all those commercial freedoms which are promoted or indeed guaranteed by the EU Treaties, while the rights and freedoms or legitimate interests of the data subject will be all those rights promoted and guaranteed by the European Convention of Human Rights and UK law.

The pursuit, promotion and marketing of a legitimate business are, it is submitted, all "legitimate interests" of a business-based data controller. What then of the situation where such a data controller decides that he wishes to market a new product by utilising a database of previous customers? Such customers may not have given their consent to such "new" processing and it would not be in pursuance of a contractual or other legal obligation. Can the data controller claim that the marketing, the new processing, is in pursuit of "legitimate interests" and, if so, what are the legitimate interests of a data subject in such a situation, which have to be balanced against those of the data controller? Presumably, the interests of the data subject are not to receive unsolicited marketing material just because they have placed an order for another product. Might it not be argued that this is a minor inconvenience to the data subject? No cost to the data subject is involved and the data subject simply has to read the material and dispose of it if he or she is not interested. Would this minor inconvenience be

---

[11] [1995] 1 All E.R. 611.

held to take priority over the promotion of a business with the possibility of increased profits, tax revenue and employment?

6–12 Such balancing acts are not always easy or straightforward. Even if the condition is broadly interpreted the data controller remains subject to the obligation to process personal data fairly in accordance with the first Principle. Thus even though the legitimate processing hurdle is passed a new use may be in breach of Principle 1. The "specified information" includes the purpose or purposes for which the data are intended to be processed. Although a data controller might be able to claim legitimate processing without the consent of the data subject, by relying on the "legitimate interests" condition, this does not remove the obligation to notify the data subject of the intended use of the data. Third parties (persons to whom personal data are passed by a data gathering data controller) are in an interesting position in that they may be able to claim, where the data has been passed to them without the data subject's consent, that using the data for marketing purposes is in pursuit of a legitimate interest—thus rendering the processing legitimate. They may also be able to claim that they are exempt from providing the specified information to the data subjects because it would involve a "disproportionate effort". However, it is unlikely that they would be able to contend that the processing was still fair.

The provision states that the Secretary of State may make an order as to when this condition is or is not to be taken to be satisfied. The "may" clearly indicates that the Secretary of State has a discretion to issue such clarification, not an obligation. No such order has been made to date.

6–13 In the case of *Proper Officer of the House of Commons* before the Information Tribunal, the Tribunal took the view that the House of Commons as a public body was processing personal data relating to MPs on the basis of Ground 6. It is submitted that this is an erroneous approach and that a public body must base its processing on either Ground 3 (a legal obligation) or Ground 5 (exercise of a discretionary power). Ground 6 is applicable to the private sector only. This approach was supported by the European Court in the joined cases of *Rechnugshof and Österreichischer Rundfunk*[12] where the Court held that the grounds for processing on which public bodies must rely are found in Art.7(2)(c) and (d).

6–14 In Opinion 10/2006 on the SWIFT processing the Article 29 Working Party considered the application of Article 7(f) (the equivalent of Ground 6) to the processing carried out by SWIFT in transferring the personal data of banking customers to the US where the databank would be subject to disclosure to the US authorities under subpoenas. The WP dealt with the balance as follows:

> "It cannot be denied that SWIFT has a legitimate interest in complying with the subpoenas under US law. If SWIFT did not comply with those subpoenas it runs the risk of incurring sanctions under US law. On the other hand it is also crucial that a 'proper balance' is found and respected between the risk of SWIFT being sanctioned by the US for eventual non-compliance with the subpoenas and the rights of individuals.
>
> Article 7(f) of the Directive requires a balance to be struck between the legitimate interest pursued by the processing of personal data and the fundamental rights of

---

[12] C-465/00, C138/01 and C-139/01 [2003] ECR I–4989.

data subjects. The balance of interest test should take into account issues of proportionality, subsidiarity, the seriousness of the alleged offences that can be notified and the consequences for the data subjects. In the context of the balance of interst test adequate safeguards will also have to be put into place. In particular Article 14 of the Directive provides that when data processing is based on Article 7(f) individuals have the right at any time to object on compelling legitimate grounds to the processing of the data relating to them.

SWIFT conducted the processing and mirroring of its data in a 'hidden, systematic, massive and long term' manner without having specified the further incompatible purpose at the time of processing the data and without SWIFT pointing this out to the users of its services. The further processing and mirroring for an incompatible purpose could have far-reaching effects on any individual.

The Working Party therefore considers that the interests for fundamental rights and freedoms of the numerous data subjects over-ride SWIFT's interests not to be sanctioned by the US for eventual non-complicane with the subpoenas."

PRACTICAL TOOLS

6–15   Suggested wording for a notice on a mail order coupon where the data controller wishes to utilise the personal data gathered for the subsequent marketing of the controller's own products:

Name
Shipping Address
Email (not mandatory)
Telephone Number
Item Ordered:
Method of Payment Cheque u Credit card u
Credit Card Number
Expiry Date
Signature (essential if paying by credit card)

The information which you have provided on this form will be used by Bloggs & Co to fulfil the order that you have placed with us. We will not pass your information to any organisation outside this company. However we would also like to use your information to let you know about other products and services offered by this company which we think will be of interest to you. We will do this by mail, telephone or email. If would like to receive this information then please tick the box below. If at any time you wish to stop receiving information from us then please write to Customer Services at the address below. If you do not wish to receive any information you do not need to do anything.

Yes I would like to receive information about Bloggs & Co's other products.

Comments

6–16   The personal data sought does not involve sensitive data and thus only the Sch.2 conditions need to be satisfied for legitimate processing. In respect of the processing to fulfil the original order Bloggs will be able to rely on para.2 (contractual reasons) and probably para.1 (the data subject's implied consent).

In order for the processing to be fair the data controller must comply with the "fair processing code" and in particular must provide the "specified information":

(a) the identity of the data controller;

(b) the identity of any nominated representative;

(c) the purpose or purposes for which the data are intended to be processed;

(d) any further information which is necessary, having regard to the specific circumstances in which the data are or are to be processed, to enable processing in respect of the data subject to be fair.

The wording above informs the data subject of the data controller's identity. Bloggs have not chosen to nominate a representative. The data subject is also told that his or her data will be used to fulfil the order and, if he or she consent, for the marketing of Bloggs' additional products. The data subject is also specifically informed of the use of email and telephone for marketing and will have consented to both methods if he or she ticks the box. If processing for additional products is carried out then it will be legitimate because the data controller has obtained the data subject's explicit consent. Although it might be contended that the data controller will have obtained the data subject's implicit consent if the data subject fails to opt out of receiving further mail shots from Bloggs, it is submitted that requiring the data subject to opt in is both better practice and less contentious in terms of establishing consent. The sentence allowing the data subject to stop mail shots is both an acknowledgment that consent to processing may be withdrawn by the data subject and also an acknowledgment of the data subject's rights to object to processing for direct marketing.

ADDITIONAL INFORMATION

Derivations

6–17   • Directive 95/46 (See App.):

         (a) Art.7 (criteria for making data processing legitimate);
         (b) Recitals 30, 31.

   • Council of Europe Convention of January 28, 1981 for the Protection of Individuals with regard to automatic processing of Personal Data: Art.5 (quality of data).

Hansard references

6–18   Commons Standing Committee D, June 4, 1988, col.307.
Ground 6 of the grounds for legitimate processing:

"The paragraph seeks to reconcile opposing and possibly conflicting interests."

Vol.315, No.198, col.613, Commons Third Reading, July 2, 1998
Political canvassing to be dealt with by orders under para.10.

Previous case law

6–19 None.

CHAPTER 7

Sensitive Data

INTRODUCTION

7–01   Schedule 3 to the 1998 Act sets out nine conditions or grounds, one or more of which must be satisfied in order to legitimise the processing of sensitive personal data. There is also an order-making power to the Secretary of State to specify further circumstances and the conditions have been extended by a number of statutory instruments. "Sensitive personal data" are defined in s.2 of the Act as "personal data consisting of information as to:

(a) the racial or ethnic origin of the data subject;

(b) his political opinions;

(c) his religious beliefs or other beliefs of a similar nature;

(d) whether he is a member of a trade union (within the meaning of the Trade Union and Labour Relations (Consolidation) Act 1992);

(e) his physical or mental health or condition;

(f) his sexual life;

(g) the commission or alleged commission by him of any offence;

(h) any proceedings for any offence committed or alleged to have been committed by him, the disposal of such proceedings or the sentence of any court in such proceedings."

Unlike some other aspects of the 1998 Act which rely on rather ambiguous concepts, the definition of sensitive personal data is relatively clear and specific. That is not to say that the definition is free of all ambiguity. For example, is a record on a personnel file that an employee holds the opinion that his boss "is an oppressive capitalist who will go out of his way to exploit his workers at every opportunity" a record of a political opinion or an awkward employee? It appears to be assumed that biometric data are sensitive personal data. Presumably there is a view that biometric data, particularly genetic data, consists of information as to an individual's "physical or mental health" however the point may be arguable and it might be preferable if the definition of sensitive personal data explicitly covered biometric information. This is particularly the case as biometrics become more common in daily life.[1] It is notable that a Consultation Paper on the "Forensic use of Bioinformation: Ethical Issues", issued by the Nuffield Council on Bioethics, contained no mention of the role of data protection in the debate on the protection of such information.[2]

In the case of *Lord Ashcroft v AG and Department for International Development*[3] the court accepted that data from which an implication of criminal conduct could be drawn could count as sensitive data on a hearing on an application to amend particulars of claim. It was claimed that a reference in a leaked document could constitute sensitive personal data because it could be read as bearing the meaning that Lord Ashcroft had allegedly committed a criminal offence. The judgment reads:

> "The objection is taken that the memorandum does not in terms specify any particular offence and so is not caught by section 2(g). I reject that contention. It is in my view at least arguable that the reference in the memorandum to the laundry arrangements of Lord Ashcroft would be understood to be a reference to the criminal offence of money-laundering."

This was only the hearing on whether the case was arguable and should not be treated as stronger authority than that but at least the judge considered it sufficiently arguable.

7–02   In *Lindqvist*[4] the European Court held that information which Ms Linqvist she had placed on an internet page stating that a named colleague had an injured foot and was working part time was sensitive personal data about the colleague within Art.8(1) of the Directive. On the other hand in the case of *Naomi Campbell v MGN*[5] the court had to consider whether the photographs of Miss Campbell should be treated as sensitive personal data as they revealed her colour. The Court held that the photographs were not sensitive data as that information was not the import or purpose of the photographs.

"Beliefs of a similar nature" may cause uncertainty since it is qualified by but is distinct from religious beliefs. Does it include concepts as uncertain as a "personal moral code" or "principles governing one's lifestyle"? The decision in *Campbell* appears to support the view of the Commissioner that data which would only be sensitive by association or implication should not be treated as caught by the provisions. Nevertheless it is sensible for data controllers to be alert to such issues and ensure that data which might be regarded as sensitive data are not held unless it is genuinely necessary for the purpose involved.

Sensitive data is not a new concept. It occurs in Treaty 108 and also in the 1984 Act. Section 2(3) of the 1984 Act provided:

> "The Secretary of State may by order modify or supplement [the data protection] principles for the purpose of providing additional safeguards in relation to personal data consisting of information as to:

---

[1] In March 2005 the European Commission released a major study on biometrics and how their use will impact on daily lives following the decision to use biometrics in passports, visa applications and residence permits from 2006.

[2] 2006.

[3] [2002] EWHC 1122.

[4] See Ch.3, above for a full discussion.

[5] [2002] EWHC 299.

(a) the racial origin of the data subject;

(b) his political opinions or religious or other beliefs;

(c) his physical or mental health or his sexual life;

(d) his criminal convictions."

No orders were made pursuant to this power.

There is no explicit duty on the data controller to identify or record his grounds for processing personal data. The registerable particulars submitted for notification do not require him to identify his grounds and he is under no obligation to provide information on this point to the data subject in response to a subject access request. The Commissioner may demand a statement of the grounds for particular processing in an Information Notice under s.43 but only if he has received a demand for assessment or reasonably requires the information to determine whether the controller is complying with the principles.

A data controller must have proper grounds for the processing of sensitive personal data in any particular case. If a data controller does not have proper grounds the Commissioner will be able to serve an enforcement notice requiring him to rectify matters, whether by establishing proper grounds or ceasing to process the data temporarily or permanently. In an action for compensation brought by an individual before a court the court might also order a cessation of particular processing of particular data on the basis that the controller had no proper ground for the processing. However, it is possible that such an order would be limited to the data relating to the individual applicant, not the entire data set, whereas action by the Commissioner could apply to an entire data set.

Summary of Main Points

7–03 (a) Schedule 3 sets out the conditions for the legitimate processing of sensitive personal data;

(b) the grounds in Sch.3 have been extended by a number of statutory instruments;

(c) at least one of the conditions must be satisfied in order to legitimise the processing of sensitive personal data as well as at least one of the Sch.2 conditions;

(d) satisfying a Sch.3 condition will not automatically involve the satisfaction of the matching Sch.2 condition;

(e) the conditions in Sch.3 largely follow the grounds set out in Art.8 of Directive 95/46 (the Directive), which requires Member States to prohibit the processing of sensitive data save in particular specified circumstances;

(f) the conditions in Sch.3 which relate to legal advice or proceedings, statutory or Crown purposes or the administration of justice and processing for ethnic monitoring are not to be found in Art.8. However, Art.8 provides that:

> "8.4 Subject to the provision of suitable safeguards, Member States may, for reasons of substantial public interest, lay down exemptions in

addition to those laid down in paragraph 2 either by national law or by decision of the supervisory authority."

(g) the conditions which have been added by statutory instrument also extend the grounds from those set out in the directive in reliance on Art 8.4.

LEGITIMATE PROCESSING OF SENSITIVE DATA

7–04 It is worth recalling the definition of processing. Processing is defined in s.1(1) of the 1998 Act as meaning "obtaining, recording or holding" the data and carrying out various operations with respect to the data including "organising, adapting, altering, retrieving, consulting, using, disclosing, aligning, combining, erasing or blocking the data". The term is discussed in detail in Ch.3, above on definitions.

Processing of sensitive personal data is only permissible if it is carried out in reliance on one or more of the conditions in Sch.3. This increased level of protection for some types of data reflects the case law on Art.8 of the European Convention on Human Rights and Fundamental Freedoms (ECHRFF) in which some categories of information, such as medical records, have been held to be worthy of particular protection from intrusion by the State.[6] The growth in the use of biometrics for identification and developments such as the DNA database meant that increasing amounts of sensitive personal data are held on individuals with an increasing need for safeguards. Schedule 3, however, does not provide any additional safeguards for such data beyond the requirement to be able to assert one or more of the grounds for processing.

The data subject has given his explicit consent to the processing

7–05 (Note: The issue of consent in general is discussed in detail in Ch.3, above.)

This condition contrasts with the parallel provision in Sch. 2 which establishes that processing will be legitimate if the data subject has given his consent. Clearly if explicit consent is established then the parallel provision requiring simple consent in Sch.2 will also be satisfied.

There is no requirement that explicit consent be in writing. Presumably, explicit oral consent will suffice. However, given that "explicit" is likely to be interpreted as meaning "clear and unambiguous", data controllers may prefer to ensure that explicit consent is signified in writing in order to fend off any criticism that the required consent was insufficiently clear and unambiguous. The Commissioner has made it clear that he is looking for informed consent, i.e. a clear understanding on the part of the data subject as to the nature and extent of the relevant processing for which consent is being given. In the case of sensitive data, data controllers may prefer to adopt the protective stance of ensuring that the information relating to the intended processing (including the "specified information") is set out in writing rather than delivered orally and left open to interpretation and misunderstanding. The Commissioner has stated that the use of the word "explicit":

"suggests that the consent of the data subject should be absolutely clear. In appropriate cases it should cover the specific detail of the processing, the particular type

---

[6] See Ch.2, above and the cases of *Z v Finland* (1997) 25 E.H.R.R. 371 and *MS v Sweden* (1997) 28 E.H.R.R. 313.

of data to be processed (or even the specific information), the purposes of the processing and any special aspects of the processing which may affect the individual, for example disclosures which may be made of the data."[7]

The Commissioner has also suggested that in some cases "nothing less than clear written consent will suffice".

Legal Obligations and Rights in the Context of Employment

7–06   Paragraph 2 of Sch.3 permits the processing of sensitive data where the processing is necessary for the purposes of exercising or performing any right or obligation which is conferred or imposed by law on the data controller in connection with employment. The Secretary of State may by Order specify cases where this condition is either excluded altogether or only satisfied upon the satisfaction of further conditions. No such order has been made or proposed at the time of writing.

This condition is not exclusive to employers. It can be claimed by those who oversee compliance by employers as long as the oversight is part of a statutory obligation. The concept of "necessity", which appeared so frequently in the conditions for general processing, reappears here. For a discussion of its interpretation see para.6–07, above. Compliance with many of the conditions under Sch.3 will also entail the satisfaction of the parallel or mirror provision under Sch.2 since the former are in many cases more restrictive restatements of the latter. In the case of this condition, it is submitted that the same facts will be relevant to compliance with Ground 3 in Sch.2:

> "Ground 3 The processing is necessary to comply with any legal obligation to which the data controller is subject, other than an obligation imposed by contract;"

The para.2 provision in Sch.3 covers processing, including disclosures required for statutory purposes, such as disclosures to the Inland Revenue. The Commissioner has accepted that it does not cover some information which an employer may need to hold but to which none of the other conditions apply and for which it may be difficult to obtain the consent of the data subject. An example is the holding of driving or other conviction information about employees where it is necessary for work-related purposes.

7–07   As well as statutory disclosures it will cover employers who wish to monitor the composition or "make up" of their workforce where such monitoring flows from what is necessary for the performance or exercise of any right or obligation conferred or imposed by law.

General statute imposes obligations on employers in relation to discrimination, either direct or indirect, on the grounds of race (Race Relations Act 1976), sex (Sex Discrimination Act 1975), disability (Disability Discrimination Act 1995) age or sexual orientation or perceived sexual orientation. An employer may seek to monitor compliance with non-discrimination obligations imposed by legislation by monitoring the

---

[7] Legal Guidance p.11.

make-up of its workforce and, in particular, the relative proportions of sexes, ethnic groupings and so on. Such monitoring can be seen to facilitate compliance with non-discrimination legislation but may not be a matter of legal compulsion. It will be a question of judgment whether it is "necessary" for such compliance. However, a later condition (para.9 of Sch.3) specifically permits the monitoring of racial or ethnic origin (but not other types of sensitive data) providing certain safeguards are complied with (see para.7–17, below).

An employer may also have other arrangements for monitoring, for example an employer may have an agreement with staff that it will provide health insurance and health checks for staff. The employer would however not be able to rely on this ground to hold the sensitive personal data arising from such an agreement. Even if the agreement was incorporated into contracts of employment this would not create an obligation "imposed by law". Contractual obligations are obligations voluntarily taken on by free parties which, subject to the legal principles governing the law of contract, may be enforced at law. They are not obligations imposed on an individual vis-à-vis the State. It would not, therefore, be open to a data controller to claim the benefit of this condition because of any contractual obligation.

It is worth noting that Sch.2 para.3 uses the term "any legal obligation to which the data controller is subject". This term clearly potentially includes contractual obligations and therefore the paragraph specifically has to exclude them from the ambit of the phrase by adding the qualification "other than an obligation imposed by contract". Schedule 3 para.2(1), however, uses the phrase "any obligation . . . imposed by law". This is materially different from the phrase "any legal obligation to which the data controller is subject" and, it is submitted, clearly excludes contractual obligations.

To protect the vital interests of the data subject or another person where consent cannot be given or is withheld

7–08   This condition allows the processing of sensitive data where it is necessary:

(a)   in order to protect the vital interests of the data subject or another person, in a case where:

   (i)   consent cannot be given by or on behalf of the data subject; or
   (ii)   the data controller cannot reasonably be expected to obtain the consent of the data subject; or

(b)   in order to protect the vital interests of another person, in a case where consent by or on behalf of the data subject has been unreasonably withheld.

Again, "necessity" is a requirement. The parallel Sch.2 condition is clearly the one which allows processing in order to protect the vital interests of the data subject.[8] It is not clear whether "another person" must be another readily ascertainable and distinct person or whether it might include a class or indeed members of the public at large. The distinction may be important, especially in the cases of a data subject who presents a threat to the vital interests of others—for example, through mental health

---

[8] For the discussion on how "vital interests" may be interpreted see para.6–09, above.

problems or an infectious and fatal disease. In such a situation, will it be necessary to show a threat to a specific person or will it be sufficient to show a general threat to the public? It is submitted that the latter interpretation is more effective.

Atypically, the Sch.3 condition appears to be more widely framed than the parallel Sch.2 condition allowing, as it does, the processing of sensitive data when it is necessary to protect the vital interests not just of the data subject but also of "another person".

Thus data controllers need to take care when relying on this Sch.3 condition that they do not assume that the parallel condition under Sch.2 will automatically be satisfied—it may not be. The "vital interests of another person" would appear to allow, for example, the processing of data relating to a data subject's criminal record or mental health where that record discloses offences or behaviour which may put third parties at serious risk. The data subject may have been asked for his or her consent to the relevant processing and may have "unreasonably withheld" that consent. The data controller would thus be able to claim the benefit of this Sch.3 condition but not that of the parallel Sch.2 condition, since the processing is not to protect the vital interests of the data subject but of another. The data controller may well, of course, be able to bring the processing within one of the other conditions—either the Sch.2 condition that allows processing where it is necessary for the exercise of any functions of a public nature exercised in the public interest where a public body is the data controller, or the condition in para.6 of Sch.2 is likely to be applicable where the controller is a private entity. However, the difference between the parallel Schs 2 and 3 conditions remains a curiosity. It is not immediately clear why the Sch.2 "vital interests" condition was not also worded to cover the vital interests of the "data subject or another person".

7–09   The Sch.3 condition deals with three scenarios in which the data subject's consent is not available. If explicit consent is available then of course the data controller need not worry about compliance with this provision at all, since the first Sch.3 condition would then be satisfied.

The three scenarios are:

(a)   Consent cannot be given by or on behalf of the data subject (for example a comatose data subject who requires urgent medical treatment).

(b)   The data controller cannot reasonably be expected to obtain the consent of the data subject (this may apply, for example, where a disclosure of a data subject's mental health or previous convictions is necessary to protect a third party but where seeking the consent of the data subject might seriously aggravate the situation).

(c)   Consent by or on behalf of the data subject has been "unreasonably withheld" (this may apply, for example, where a disclosure of a data subject's mental health or previous convictions is necessary to protect a third party but where sought the data subject's consent is unreasonably withheld).

What is and is not reasonable or unreasonable will have to be evaluated in each individual case. Data controllers may be at risk of enforcement action if they adopt blanket policies for dispensing with data subject consent in a class of cases. To avoid such a scenario, data controllers may have to demonstrate a specific decision-taking process in each case.

This condition introduces the possibility of consent to processing being given by a third party on behalf of, rather than directly by, the data subject himself or herself. The possibility of a third party giving consent is not one that occurs elsewhere in either the Sch.2 or Sch.3 conditions dealing with the consent of the data subject.

This is not to say that the consent of a third party can never satisfy the Schs 2 and 3 conditions requiring the data subject's consent. As is discussed in detail in Chs 10 and 11, below when considering subject rights, the general law does intervene in certain limited circumstances to empower a third party to provide consent on another person's behalf—for example, a parent on behalf of a child or a carer with an Enduring Power of Attorney on behalf of a mental health patient. Thus, even the conditions specifically requiring the data subject's consent may be satisfied by consent being provided by a third party. However, these conditions are silent on this possibility, leaving the general law to intervene when required. Conversely, the Sch.3 condition relating to vital interests specifically raises the possibility of consent being given by a third party. Thus the condition envisages situations of a third party providing consent which are not routinely provided for by the general law.

The condition acknowledges that third parties not covered by the general law may be asked to consent to processing necessary to protect the data subject's vital interests—for example, where a man is brought into a hospital in a coma and his wife is asked to consent to the processing necessary to protect her husband's vital interests. The most common circumstances in which next of kin are asked for consent occur in medical emergencies and the General Medical Council's guidance to doctors covers such eventualities. In such cases the wife is not giving consent "on behalf of" her husband. In the scenario just mentioned, where a wife consents to processing, if she did so "on behalf of" her comatose husband, the hospital would not be able to rely upon the "vital interests" condition as this only applies when consent cannot be given on behalf of the data subject. If the wife can give such consent on behalf of her husband the condition no longer applies.

In the aforementioned scenario, it would also be possible for the hospital to claim the benefit of a later Sch.3 condition (see para.7.21, below) which permits processing which is necessary for medical purposes and is undertaken by:

(a) a health professional; or

(b) a person who in the circumstances owes a duty of confidentiality which is equivalent to that which would arise if that person were a health professional.

7–10 "Medical purposes" includes the purposes of preventative medicine, medical diagnosis, medical research, the provision of care and treatment and the management of healthcare services.

It is worth acknowledging that there is likely to be an overlap between processing necessary for medical purposes and processing necessary to protect the vital interests of the data subject. This will be so especially if, as is the view of the Commissioner, "vital interests" should be confined to matters of life and death (see Ch.6, above).

It is interesting to speculate on which classes of sensitive data might fall to be processed under this condition. Physical or mental health or condition is clearly going to be the most common type of sensitive data that falls to be processed in accordance with this condition. Racial origin may be relevant to the vital interests of the data subject if it discloses a predisposition to certain health conditions or illnesses (e.g. sickle cell anaemia). Sexual life may be pertinent again to determine susceptibility to or causes of certain illnesses. Information relating to offending and sentencing may fall to be disclosed to third parties to protect their vital interests. Religious beliefs may be pertinent to the acceptability of certain types of medical treatment—for example blood transfusions.

It is difficult to see how information relating to political opinions, or trade union membership might fall to be processed legitimately in accordance with this condition.

By certain non-profit making bodies in respect of their members

7–11   This condition permits processing where it:

(a) is carried out in the course of its legitimate activities by any body or association which exists for political, philosophical, religious or trade union purposes and which is not established or conducted for profit;

(b) is carried out with appropriate safeguards for the rights and freedoms of data subjects;

(c) relates only to individuals who are either members of the body or association or who have regular contact with it in connection with its purposes; and

(d) does not involve disclosure of the personal data to a third party without the consent of the data subject.

This is a little like the unincorporated members' club exemption contained in s.33(2)(a) of the 1984 Act which exempted such clubs—which held personal data relating only to members of the club—from the obligation to register and to comply with subject access rights. The exemption could not be claimed unless the members had been asked if they objected and had not done so. The exemption was also lost if there was any incompatible use of the data or disclosure of the data without the data subject's consent. Carrying out the same process of checking whether a member, or person who has regular contact with the association, may be a way of data controllers ensuring that the processing is carried out with "appropriate safeguards for the rights and freedoms of the data subjects" under this 1998 Act condition.

The Commissioner's view is that the ground does not allow data controllers who rely upon it to make subsequent non-consensual disclosures of personal data in reliance upon it.[9]

Where the information has been made public

7–12   Processing of sensitive data is permissible if the information contained in the personal data has been made public as a result of steps deliberately taken by the data subject. At first sight, this seems a straightforward and clear provision. Difficulties arise, however, in determining what constitutes "making public". Clearly, a data

---

[9] Legal Guidance.

subject making a statement about sensitive data relating to him or her on television is making that data public. At the other end of the spectrum, disclosing an issue of sensitive data to one's spouse is not making something public. But what of an announcement to a small gathering of five, 10 or 20 people? And how would the nature of the gathering affect whether a pronouncement constitutes information being "made public"? A disclosure of information at a private dinner party for 20 would be considered by many as a private matter but possibly not an announcement before a public meeting attended by only eight.

It may be helpful to view "making something public" as a disclosure to a random unselected group as opposed to a set or group chosen by or within the control of the publisher.

It is easy to think of this condition as relating only to confidential or hidden information. However, sensitive data may be gleaned from the visibly obvious—for example, information about a person's ethnic origin (or even religion in the case of a Sikh wearing a turban) or disability. A question then arises as to whether the "visibly obvious" constitutes information which has been made public. It is submitted that it has been—can the law really seek to distinguish between someone who is visibly disabled and someone who actually states "I am disabled"? There must, however, be limits to this proposition—for example, if someone is visibly very sick but it is not clear what the precise ailment is, it is submitted that "visible illness" alone would not legitimise the processing of the information that the person was actually suffering from cancer if that had not otherwise been made public but had been gleaned elsewhere.

The requirement of deliberateness also raises some questions. Clearly, this would exclude information gleaned from a private file which is inadvertently dropped in public, but what of the data subject who loses his temper in a public restaurant and shouts something out which he or she otherwise wished to keep private. Is the act of shouting in a public place a "deliberate" disclosure or inadvertent? It is submitted that the approach likely to be taken by the courts is to mirror the approach taken to the cases on private actions in public places described in Ch.2, above, for example the *Von Hannover* case in which photographs of Princess Caroline of Monaco taken while having a private dinner in a restaurant were regarded as covered by the protection of Article 8 of the ECHRFF, albeit the activity took place in a place open to the public. On this basis it would require a clear public statement or overt activity by the data subject to fulfill the condition.

Clearly each case will have to be judged on its own facts.. What must not be overlooked, of course, is that the data controller must still establish one of the Sch.2 conditions for legitimate processing. This particular Sch.3 condition is one of the few that does not have a clear mirror in Sch.2. Any data controllers relying on this condition will not discharge their responsibilities by showing compliance with it alone but must ensure that a relevant Sch.2 condition is also satisfied.

In legal proceedings

7–13   This condition allows the processing of sensitive data where it:

(a) is necessary for the purpose of, or in connection with, any legal proceedings (including prospective legal proceedings);

   (b) is necessary for the purpose of taking legal advice; or

   (c) is otherwise necessary for the purpose of establishing, exercising or defend-
        ing legal rights.

The term "necessary" makes a reappearance. There are no qualifications in these provisions tying them to the data subject. For example, the second subclause does not say
"is necessary for the purpose of the data subject taking legal advice".

Presumably, this condition permits the processing of sensitive personal data relating
to a person not actually seeking the legal advice if the processing of that data was
"necessary" for the purposes of obtaining legal advice. Thus a solicitor may be sanctioned to process sensitive personal data relating to their client's opponent (as well as
their client) if such processing is necessary for the purpose of obtaining legal advice.

There is no clear mirror or parallel condition under Sch.2. The condition that
permits processing where it is necessary for the administration of justice does not
mirror this condition as the administration of justice is an essentially public activity
whereas this condition is concerned with essentially private activities.

Data controllers carrying out the processing of sensitive data which satisfies the
legal proceedings condition in Sch.3 will have to take care to ensure that the processing is also legitimised by a Sch.2 condition. Where the data controller does not have a
direct relationship with a data subject—for example, the scenario outlined above
where a solicitor seeks to process sensitive personal data relating to a client's opponent—the data controller is likely to have to rely on the "legitimate interests" condition. It follows that the controller must ensure that the personal data held about the
opponent or other third parties is proportionate.

The Commissioner voices concerns at the potential breadth of this ground in the
Legal Guidance and states:

> "The Commissioner's view is that (c) is of limited scope and data controllers
> should adopt a narrow interpretation and rely upon another Sch. 3 condition if
> there is any doubt as to whether it applies. In particular it should not be used to
> construct a legal right where none exists."

However the wording of subs.(c) is ambiguous. It refers to "establishing" legal
rights. This could mean proving the existence of legal rights already applicable or the
creation of new legal rights. The Commissioner has advised that the narrow interpretation is the preferred option but gives no basis for this view and a broader approach
is not unarguable.

In the case of *R (on the application of B) v Stafford Combined Court*[10] the Court
held that a witnesses medical records should not have been disclosed to the accused
without a hearing in which she was able to be represented. The case focused on the confidentiality of the records and did not address whether the disclosure could be justified
under Sch.3.

To carry out certain public functions

7–14   The seventh para. of Sch.3 permits processing where it is necessary:

---

[10] [2006] EWHC 1645.

(a) for the administration of justice;

(b) for the exercise of any functions conferred by or under any enactment; or

(c) for the exercise of any functions of the Crown, a Minister of the Crown or a government department.

The Secretary of State may by order specify cases where this condition is either excluded altogether or only satisfied upon the satisfaction of further conditions. This was amended by Sch.6 to the Freedom of Information Act 2000 to add a further Ground 7(b) that the processing is necessary for the exercise of any functions of either House of Parliament.

The ground is an almost exact duplication of the Sch.2 condition which permits processing where it is necessary:

(a) for the administration of justice;

(b) for the exercise of any functions conferred by or under any enactment;

(c) for the exercise of any functions of the Crown, a Minister of the Crown or a government department; or

(d) for the exercise of any functions of a public nature exercised in the public interest, save that the final possibility is omitted.

Compliance with this Sch.3 condition will therefore automatically result in compliance with the parallel but more widely phrased Sch.2 condition.

In *Michael Stone v SE Coast Strategic Health Authority*[11] the Court held that Ground 7 was the basis for the publication of the report of the inquiry under s.2 of the National Health Service Act 1977 and regulations made under it.

For a discussion on the equivalent Sch.2 provisions see Ch.6, above. The parallel Sch.2 condition does not contain the proviso enabling the Secretary of State to restrict the ambit of the condition. No such orders have yet been made.

For medical purposes

7–15 The eighth condition legitimises the processing of sensitive data where the processing is necessary for medical purposes (including the purposes of preventative medicine, medical diagnosis, medical research, the provision of care and treatment and the management of healthcare services) and is undertaken by:

(a) a health professional; or

(b) a person who owes a duty of confidentiality which is equivalent to that which would arise if that person were a health professional.

Section 69 of the 1998 Act sets out the definition of "health professional". Subsection 69(1) provides that in the (Data Protection) Act the phrase means any of the following:

---

[11] [2006] EWHC 1668 (Admin).

(a) a registered medical practitioner;

(b) a registered dentist as defined by s.53(1) of the Dentists Act 1984;

(c) a registered optician as defined by s.36(1) of the Opticians Act 1989;

(d) a registered pharmaceutical chemist as defined by s.24(1) of the Pharmacy Act 1954 or a registered person as defined by Art.2(2) of the Pharmacy (Northern Ireland) Order 1976;

(e) a registered nurse, midwife or health visitor;

(f) a registered osteopath as defined by s.41 of the Osteopaths Act 1993;

(g) a registered chiropractor as defined by s.43 of the Chiropractors Act 1994;

(h) any person who is registered as a member of a profession to which the Professions Supplementary to Medicine Act 1960 for the time being extends;

(i) a clinical psychologist, child psychotherapist or speech therapist;

(j) a music therapist employed by a health service body; and

(k) a scientist employed by such a body as head of a department.

Subsection 69(2) defines "registered medical practitioner" as including any person who is provisionally registered under ss.15 or 21 of the Medical Act 1983 and is engaged in such employment as is mentioned in subs.(3) of s.69.

Subsection (3) of s.69 provides that "health service body" means:

(a) a Health Authority established under s.8 of the National Health Service Act 1977;

(b) a Special Health Authority established under s.11 of that Act;

(c) a Health Board within the meaning of the National Health Service (Scotland) Act 1978;

(d) a Special Health Board within the meaning of that Act;

(e) the managers of a State Hospital provided under s.102 of that Act;

(f) a National Health Service trust first established under s.5 of the National Health Service and Community Care Act 1990 or s.12A of the National Health Service (Scotland) Act 1978;

(g) a Health and Social Services Board established under Art.16 of the Health and Personal Social Services (Northern Ireland) Order 1972;

(h) a special health and social services agency established under the Health and Personal Social Services (Special Agencies) (Northern Ireland) Order 1990; or

(i) a Health and Social Services trust established under Art.10 of the Health and Personal Social Services (Northern Ireland) Order 1991.

The definition of "health professional" is thus extensive but does not cover all the persons who might be responsible for providing medical care and treatment, etc. hence the second limb to the provision covering other persons owing an equivalent duty of confidentiality. Counsellors dealing with health care issues might be one example of persons falling within the second limb.

7–16   There is no single clear parallel provision in Sch.2 which is likely to be automatically satisfied if this Sch.3 condition is relied on. In many cases where medical care is being dispensed direct to the data subject, he or she will also be providing at least implied consent and possibly explicit consent to the processing of sensitive data and will thus satisfy the Sch.2 consent condition. Medical purposes which are more remote from the data subject such as research or management may fall within the public interest, legitimate interests, legal obligations or functions exercised under an enactment conditions. If reliance is placed on the "public interest" condition in Sch.2 then a question may arise as to whether the relevant medical purposes are essentially functions of a public nature.

In the *Stone* case referred to above the court went on to hold that the publication of the report of the inquiry into the care, treatment and supervision of Michael Stone could be sanctioned under para.8 on the basis that the publication was for the "management of healthcare services" and thus within "medical purposes" and the publication would be carried out by persons who owed a duty of confidentiality in respect of the information (albeit that the duty was being overridden in the public interest in this case).

Ethnic monitoring

7–17   The processing of sensitive data is permitted where it:

(a) is of sensitive personal data consisting of information as to racial or ethnic origin;

(b) is necessary for the purpose of identifying or keeping under review the existence or absence of equality of opportunity or treatment between persons of different racial or ethnic origins, with a view to enabling such equality to be promoted or maintained; and

(c) is carried out with appropriate safeguards for the rights and freedoms of data subjects. The Secretary of State may by order specify circumstances in which such processing is, or is not, to be taken to be carried out with appropriate safeguards for the rights and freedoms of data subjects.

This condition relates only to sensitive data relating to racial or ethnic origin and not to any other type of sensitive personal data. Thus if an employer is processing data which records the sexual composition of his workforce or the incidence of disabilities as well as race details then this condition may not be relied on. Other conditions may permit such processing.

This condition is thus narrower than the "employment" condition set out in para.2 of Sch.3. It is also wider in the sense that there is no requirement that the ethnic monitoring be in connection with employment. Thus monitoring in relation to the provision of services (for example, housing) would be covered.

This is a reasonably clear provision although some question may arise as to how the data controller can establish that the data are processed for the purpose of promoting racial equality rather than for another purpose. Presumably, the use to which such data are put should be carefully scrutinised by the data controller.

The concept of "appropriate safeguards for the rights and freedoms of data subjects" reappears. In this condition, however, unlike the fourth condition, the Secretary of State is empowered to direct in which circumstances the "appropriate safeguards" are or are not established. No such orders have been issued. The relevant provisions under Sch.2 which a data controller will most likely seek to rely on if this Sch.3 condition is claimed are the "public interest" or "legitimate interests" conditions.

The final para. of Sch.3 permits the processing of sensitive personal data when "the personal data are processed in circumstances specified in an Order made by the Secretary of State". There is no specific parallel power for the Secretary of State in Sch.2, although the final Sch.2 condition does enable the Secretary of State to specify when the "legitimate interests" condition is (or is not satisfied).

The Data Protection (Processing of Sensitive Personal Data) Order (SI 2000/417)

7–18   The Order sets out additional grounds on which sensitive personal data may be processed without falling foul of the first Principle. As noted above the data controller must also be able to show that a Sch.2 ground applies and must comply with the other Principles in his handling of the data.

Ten grounds are set out in the Order. In most cases the liberty given by the Order only applies where certain protective conditions are met or where the individual does not object. However this is not uniformly the case and para.10 permits the processing of any sensitive data necessary for the exercise of any functions conferred on a constable by any rule of law. This ground has no conditions attached. Each of the 10 grounds is described below.

Substantial public interest

7–19   Under five of the 10 grounds the processing involved must be carried out "in the substantial public interest". This term has been taken directly from Art.8(4) of the Directive and should be approached in accordance with the European legal principle of proportionality. It is therefore difficult to offer a precise guide to how it is likely to be applied other than to comment that a personal or private economic/commercial benefit is unlikely to qualify; the detriment if the processing is not carried out must be more than minimal and it must be in support of an interest generally accepted as being of substantial public significance. The test of whether particular processing is in the substantial subject interest in any case will be a question of fact and law to be determined in accordance with generally accepted social values and standards. It is not a subjective test for each controller.

Necessary (for a particular purpose)

7–20   In eight of the grounds the processing must meet some form of test of necessity. In most cases it must be necessary for one or more specified purposes. Again we are dealing with a term with a European provenance which will apply in this context (see para.6–07, above).

Safeguards

7–21 Article 8(4) permits Member States to extend the grounds for processing personal data "subject to suitable safeguards". The Order does not provide for explicit safeguards in most cases. In the cases of insurance, equality of treatment, political registers and research there are various provisos that the processing must not be used to make individual decisions or cause harm to individuals but these do not appear in all the grounds. It might be argued therefore that, as the United Kingdom has not provided explicit safeguards for all the grounds, the Order is deficient and does not fully comply with Art.8(4). On the other hand, the processing is restricted in all the cases and the Government would no doubt regard the restrictions in themselves as amounting to safeguards.

Paragraph 1

7–22 Sensitive data may be processed where the processing is in the substantial public interest, is necessary for the prevention or detection of any unlawful act and must necessarily be carried out without the explicit consent of the data subject being sought so as not to prejudice those purposes. The term "act" includes a failure to act.

The act or omission need not amount to a breach of the criminal law as the term "unlawful" covers breaches of both civil obligations and criminal prohibitions. The ground can only be relied on where there would be real prejudice to the purpose if the individual were told of the processing and asked to consent. The effect of reliance on this ground is to deprive the individual of the right to exercise a degree of control over sensitive data relating to him or her. As such it is likely to be construed so as to protect the rights of the individual. It will not be available to data controllers who wish to avoid informing data subjects as a matter of convenience or to save them embarrassment.

Paragraph 2

7–23 Sensitive data may be processed where the processing is in the substantial public interest, is necessary for the discharge of functions of a particular type and must necessarily be carried out without the explicit consent of the data subject being sought so as not to prejudice the discharge of the function. The functions are any designed for protecting members of the public against dishonesty, malpractice, or any other seriously improper conduct by, or the unfitness or incompetence of any person, or mismanagement in the administration or of failure in services provided by any body or association. The words, "dishonesty, malpractice, or other seriously improper conduct by, or the unfitness or incompetence of, any person" are exactly the same as those used in the exemption provision in s.31(2)(a) and it would therefore be reasonable to expect them to carry the same meaning. The functions are not otherwise limited in any way. Any function which comes within the description will be covered. The function need not be of a public nature, nor carried out by a public body. There must be some ascertainable role or obligation or duty on a body to offer protection to the public from one or more of the ills described but the relevant processing itself need not be carried out by that body.

Paragraph 3

7–24   This ground relates to the special purposes, that is the journalistic, literary or artistic purposes, and in essence allows the disclosure of wrongdoing to or by the media for the purposes of publication where the publication of the information would be in the public interest. Again the disclosure must be "in the substantial public interest". It must be for one or more of the special purposes and be made "with a view to the publication of those data by any person". Paragraph 3(1)(d) goes on to provide that "the data controller" must reasonably believe that such a publication would be in the public interest.

It should be noted that this ground relates only to the disclosure of information or data and not to other forms of processing. This means that it is a limited ground. It cannot be relied on by a data controller to obtain, record or hold sensitive personal data. Therefore a data controller who legitimately holds relevant sensitive personal data may rely on this provision to disclose information to a journalist but the journalist cannot rely on it to retain the information.

The disclosing data controller must anticipate the publication of the actual data. Therefore it will not cover the disclosure of background information which is not itself intended for publication. The disclosing data controller must also have himself considered and taken a view on the question of whether publication will be in the public interest. This is because the disclosing data controller must reasonably believe that the publication would be in the public interest.

The disclosure must be "in connection with" various types of wrongdoing. The disclosure does not have to be information about actual wrongdoing as long as it is made "in connection with" the issue. For example if an individual has claimed to have been involved overseas in a particular meeting on a particular date and has claimed travel and accommodation expenses, disclosure of information showing that he was in fact in another place at another meeting would be "in connection with" dishonesty or malpractice. The types of wrongdoing are:

(i)   the commission by any person of any unlawful act (whether alleged or established);

(ii)   dishonesty, malpractice, or other seriously improper conduct by, or the unfitness or incompetence of, any person (whether alleged or established); or

(iii) mismanagement in the administration of, or failure in services provided by, any body or association (whether alleged or established).

In each case "act" includes a failure to act.

There need only be an allegation of relevant wrongdoing and there is no explicit limitation as to the credibility of the allegation or the source of it. For example, there is no requirement that the allegation be based on any substantive evidence or reasonable grounds for suspicion. However, the data controller making the disclosure must be able to assert that the disclosure was made in the substantial public interest and that publication of the information would be in the public interest. A data controller who makes a disclosure of sensitive personal data in connection with a wild or irresponsible allegation may have some difficulty in claiming the public interest grounds successfully.

Paragraph 4

7–25   This ground covers the processing of personal data for the provision of counselling or similar services. It is intended to cover for example the counselling of victims of sexual abuse which may involve the processing of sensitive data about the abuser without the abuser's consent. The processing of the sensitive data must be in the substantial public interest, be "necessary for the discharge of any function which is designed for the provision of confidential counselling, advice, support or any other service" and be carried out without the consent of the data subject where consent is absent on one of three grounds. These are that the processing is necessary "in a case where" consent cannot be given by the data subject; that the processing is necessary "in a case where" the data controller cannot reasonably be expected to obtain explicit consent; and that the processing:

> "must necessarily be carried out without the explicit consent of the data subject being sought so as not to prejudice the provision of that counselling, advice, support or other service."

In the first two grounds there is a requirement that the processing be "necessary". This appears to repeat the requirement set out in para.4(b) and it is not clear whether two different elements are being dealt with here or whether the repetition is merely an unfortunate piece of drafting. Under para.4(b) the processing of the sensitive personal data must "be necessary for the discharge of any function etc . . .". Under para.4(c)(i) and (ii) the processing of the sensitive personal data must also be "necessary in a case where consent cannot be given . . ." and be "necessary in a case where the data controller cannot reasonably be expected to obtain the explicit consent of the data subject". A different formulation is then used in para.4(c)(iii), which applies when it would be possible to seek the consent of the data subject, under which the processing "must necessarily be carried out without the explicit consent of the data subject being sought . . .".

Paragraph 5

7–26   This paragraph and the following one deal with processing necessary for carrying on insurance business. Paragraph 6 only applies to data affected by the transitional provisions, but para.5 potentially applies to all data. In essence it allows insurance companies and pension schemes to hold relevant medical information about the family of the insured person or scheme member for use in insurance decisions as long as it is not used for decisions affecting those family members. The processing of the sensitive data must either be necessary for the purpose of carrying on an insurance business or of determining eligibility or benefits payable under occupational pensions schemes under the Pension Schemes Act 1993. "Insurance business" is defined by reference to the Insurance Companies Act 1982 and covers the provision of life and annuity insurance and permanent health insurance including that effected by local authorities on their members under the Local Government Act 1972. The only data which may be processed under this provision are personal data as to the physical or mental health or condition of a person who is, or was, within one of the specified categories of blood relation to the relevant insured person or the relevant member of the pension scheme. It only applies in a case where:

- the data controller cannot reasonably be expected to obtain the explicit consent of the data subject; and

- the data controller is not aware of the data subject withholding his consent.

This paragraph does not expand on what the position will be if the data subject is aware of the processing and objects to it. However, as this is part of the conditions which must be met before the ground is made out it must be that if the data subject registers any objection with the insurance company they will not be able to continue holding the data under this head. The data subject will not have to serve an objection notice under s.10 of the Act.

Paragraph 6

7–27   This deals with the processing of sensitive data which were subject to processing already underway immediately before October 24, 1998. It covers any type of sensitive data, not merely the limited category of health data dealt with under para.5 above. It must be necessary for carrying on life and annuity and permanent health insurance in a case where the data controller cannot reasonably be expected to obtain the explicit consent of the data subject and the data subject has not informed the data controller that he does not consent. This is intended for those cases where the insurance company has obtained sensitive personal data about others as part of the provision of insurance cover in the past but has no way of contacting those persons. It only applies to the historic eligible data. The same comments about subsequent objections by the data subject apply as under para.6 above and in the event of an objection the information must be removed.

Paragraph 7

7–28   This is very similar to para.9 of Sch.3 to the Act which permits the processing of personal data relating to racial or ethnic origin for the purposes of equal opportunities monitoring. It permits the processing of additional categories of personal data relating to religious or other beliefs and mental or physical disabilities for monitoring or promoting equal opportunities. A number of specific safeguards are attached to this ground.

The processing must not support measures or decisions with respect to any particular data subject unless the subject has explicitly consented and must not cause, or be likely to cause, substantial damage or distress to any person. An individual who is the subject of personal data processed by a data controller under this provision may make an objection in writing to such processing. If he does so the data controller must cease processing the data.

Paragraph 8

7–29   This reflects the commitment given during the passage of the Bill through Parliament to permit political parties to process personal data about the political opinions of individuals even if they do not have their consent. The data may only be held by a person registered under the Registration of Political Parties Act 1998. The data controller may only process the data if the processing "does not cause nor is likely to cause, substantial damage or substantial distress to the data subject or any other person". There is a further safeguard provision in para.8(2) under which the data subject may give notice in writing to cease the processing within "such period as is reasonable in the circumstances". The question of what is reasonable will be a matter of judgment depending on the particular circumstances.

Paragraph 9

7–30   This covers the processing of sensitive personal data for research purposes. It adopts the definition in s.33 in which "research purposes" include statistical or historical purposes. As noted in Ch.18, below this is a wide definition, however, the conditions imposed on the processing are restrictive. To some extent they echo those found in s.33 but there are some differences. Moreover they are more restrictive insofar as para.9 requires that the processing of the sensitive personal data must be in the substantial public interest. Sensitive personal data may therefore only be held on this ground where there is some public interest in the research itself. The processing must also be necessary for the research purpose. The other safeguard conditions are that:

- the processing does not support measures or decisions with respect to any particular data subject otherwise than with the explicit consent of the data subject; and

- the processing does not cause, nor is likely to cause, substantial damage or substantial distress to the data subject or any other person.

The wording has been subtly altered from that employed in s.33. In s.33 the processing must not support measures or decisions with respect to "particular individuals" and the processing must not cause damage or distress to "any data subject".

Paragraph 10

7–31   This permits the processing of sensitive personal data where it is necessary for the exercise of any function conferred on a constable by any rule of law. There is no requirement that the processing be in the substantial public interest however it may be being assumed that the exercise of the powers of constables will be carried out in the public rather than any private interest.

Elected representatives

7–32   A further order, the Data Protection (Processing of Sensitive Data) (Elected Representatives) Order 2002 (SI 2002/2905) provides for the disclosure of sensitive data to and processing of sensitive data by elected representatives in certain circumstances.

Elected representatives

7–33   The following are elected representatives for the purposes of the order:

- a member of the House of Commons, National Assembly for Wales, Scottish Parliament or Northern Ireland Assembly;

- a UK member of the European Parliament;

- a mayor or councillor of a local authority or equivalent in the London Assembly, City of London, the Isles of Scilly, Scotland or Northern Ireland.

There are rules as to when terms of office of members end at the dissolution of Parliament or the Assemblies.

Relevant processing

7–34   Paragraph 3 permits the processing of sensitive personal data where it is carried out by an elected representative or a person acting with his authority. The processing must be in connection with the discharge of the functions of the elected representative. The data subject must have asked the representative to take action, either on behalf of the data subject or another individual, and the processing must be necessary for the purposes or in connection with the action reasonably taken by the elected representative. As the processing must be about the data subject and the data subject has asked the politician to help it might be thought that this would be covered by Ground 1. However it may be that in such cases, while the data subject will implicitly have consented to the processing, the consent is thought to be insufficiently explicit to be eligible under the Schedule.

Paragraph 4 permits the processing of sensitive personal data where it is carried out by an elected representative or a person acting with his authority. The processing must be in connection with the discharge of the functions of the elected representative. The paragraph applies where the request is made by an individual other than the data subject to take action either on behalf of the data subject or another. The processing must be carried out without the explicit consent of the data subject because the processing:

- is necessary in a case where explicit consent cannot be given by the data subject;

- is necessary in a case where the elected representative cannot reasonably be expected to obtain the explicit consent of the data subject;

- must necessarily be carried out without the consent of the data subject being sought so as not to prejudice the actions of the elected representative; or

- is necessary in the interests of another individual where the explicit consent of the other individual has been unreasonably withheld.

Disclosures

7–35   Where an elected representative or someone acting with his authority has been in contact with a data controller at the request of a data subject para.5 permits the data controller to make disclosures of sensitive data where it is necessary to respond to the query.

Under para.6 the response can involve personal data about a person other than the data subject if it is necessary to carry out the processing without the explicit consent of the data subject on the same grounds as in para.4 (listed above).

7–36 The Data Protection (Processing of Sensitive Personal Data) Order 2006[12] is the most recent addition to orders made under the Act. It came into effect on July 26, 2006 and allows personal data about some criminal convictions to be held by financial institutions. The intention is to facilitate the revocation of contracts with credit card holders where those credit card holders have used cards to pay for unlawful images over the internet.

The Order provides for the processing of sensitive personal data in circumstances where the processing:

> ". . . about a criminal conviction or caution for an offence listed in paragraph (3) relating to an indecent photograph or pseudo-photograph of a child is necessary for the purpose of administering an account relating to the payment card used in the commission of the offence or for cancelling that payment card."[13]

The relevant offences are listed and cover incitement to commit any of the relevant offences. All the crimes relate to indecent images of children. The main legislation is the Protection of Children Act 1978 (PCA) which makes it an offence to take or distribute indecent photographs or pseudo-photographs of children.[14] The Criminal Justice Act 1988 (CJA) renders mere possession (including on a hard disk) of indecent photographs or pseudo-photographs of a child an offence.[15]

A "pseudo photo" is something that "appears" to be a photo and "appears" to show a child—even if it is not based on a child or indeed a real person. In the Order the term is defined to include an image, whether made by computer graphics or otherwise, which appears to be a photograph. This means that electronically manipulated or created images will be caught.[16] Where payment has been made using a payment card for such images and the offender has been convicted or cautioned the information may be passed to the financial institution by the relevant policing or prosecution authority and the institution is then authorised by the Order to hold the relevant personal data for the purpose of the account. The motivation is to encourage financial institutions to cancel the cards used in such criminal activity. The card issuer will usually have contractual grounds allowing the termination of the contract where the card has been used for criminal activity but the use of the termination power raises many difficult questions. If there is another cardholder on the account the termination will presumably have to be explained and may involve a disclosure of data not already known. The termination may also have the effect of depriving the user of the use of a payment card. While it may be reasonable as a preventative measure to revoke the payment means of persistent offenders to stop them re-offending, termination in other cases looks

---

[12] SI 2006/2068.
[13] art.2.
[14] PCA s.1.
[15] CJA s.160.
[16] PCA s.1(7)–(9).

suspiciously like a punitive action which would arguably breach the individual's human rights. The power does not yet appear to have been exercised; financial institutions have so far shown little appetite for holding lists of internet paedophiles, and it is not clear what effect it will have.

7–37 A further provision has been included in the Serious Crime Bill introduced to the House of Lords in February 2007. Clause 64 would introduce a further ground as follows:

"(1) The processing —

(a) is either

(i) the disclosure of sensitive personal data by a person as a member of an anti-fraud organisation or otherwise in accordance with arrangements made by such an organisation; or

(ii) any other processing by that person or another person of sensitive personal data so disclosed; and

(b) is necessary for the purpose of preventing fraud or a particular kind of fraud.

(2) In this paragraph 'an anti-fraud organisation' means any unincorporated association, body corporate or other person which enables or facilitates any sharing of information to prevent fraud or a particular kind of fraud or which has any of these functions as its purpose or one of its purposes."

This accompanies the provisions which are intended to enable public sector bodies to disclose information to private sector anti-fraud organisations, such as the Credit Industry Fraud Avoidance System (CIFAS). It is not clear what sort of sensitive personal data would be disclosable as one would expect that the bulk of information disclosed would cover benefit claims.

7–38 Although there may appear to be a wealth of Sch.3 grounds the Commissioner has acknowledged that the absence of an equivalent "catch-all" ground to that found in Sch.2 has caused some problems:

"The Commissioner is aware of certain factual circumstances where data controllers processing sensitive personal data experience difficulty in satisfying a Schedule 3 condition. In such circumstances, when considering the exercise of her discretion whether to take enforcement action, the Commissioner would look carefully at the processing, taking into account any damage and distress caused to a data subject as a result of that processing."[17]

7–39 In the Employment Practices Code the Commissioner describes the types of sensitive personal data which will typically be held by an employer as covering physical or mental health, criminal convictions (to assess suitability for some types of employment), disabilities, racial origin and trade union membership.

---

[17] Legal Guidance.

PRACTICAL TOOLS

7–40   Comparison of the Schedule 2 and 3 conditions

Schedule 3 condition	Schedule 2 condition that consequently will be or is likely to be satisfied and to which data controllers should have regard
Paragraph 1—the data subject has given explicit consent.	Paragraph 1—the data subject has his given consent.
Paragraph 2—The processing is necessary re legal obligations and rights in the context of employment.	Paragraph 3—The processing is necessary to comply with any legal obligation to which data controller is subject, other than an obligation imposed by contract. Paragraph 5(b)—The processing is necessary for the exercise of any functions conferred by or under any enactment.
Paragraph 3—The processing is necessary to protect the vital interests of the data subject where consent cannot be of given or is withheld. Paragraph 3—The processing is necessary to protect the vital interests of another person where consent cannot be given or is withheld.	Paragraph 4—The processing is necessary to protect the vital interests in order to protect the vital interests of data subject. Paragraph 5(d)—The processing is necessary for the exercise of any other functions of a public nature exercised in the public interest by any person.
Paragraph 4—By certain non-profit making bodies in respect of their members.	Paragraph 6(1)—The processing is necessary for the purposes of legitimate interests pursued by the data controller or by the third party or parties to whom the data are disclosed, except where the processing is unwarranted in any particular case by reason of prejudice to the rights and freedoms or legitimate interests of the data subject. The Secretary of State may by order specify particular circumstances in which this condition is or is not to be taken to be satisfied. But data controllers should not the "necessity" requirement of this condition.

Schedule 3 condition	Schedule 2 condition that consequently will be or is likely to be satisfied and to which data controllers should have regard
Paragraph 5—Where the information has been made public.	There is no clear parallel condition. Data controllers must take care to ensure that one of the Schedule 2 conditions is satisfied.
Paragraph 6—The processing is necessary in legal proceedings.	There is no clear parallel condition. Data controllers must take care to ensure that one of the Schedule 2 conditions is satisfied.
Paragraph 7—The processing is necessary: a) for the administration of justice; b) for the exercise of any functions conferred by or under any enactment; or c) for the exercise of any functions of the Crown, a Minister of the Crown or a government department.	Paragraph 5—The processing is necessary: a) for the administration of justice; b) for the exercise of any functions conferred by or under any enactment; c) for the exercise of any functions of the Crown, a Minister of the Crown or a government department; or d) for the exercise of any functions of a public nature exercised in the public interest.
Paragraph 8—The processing is necessary for medical purposes.	There is no clear parallel condition. Data controllers must take care to ensure that one of the Schedule 2 conditions is satisfied.
Paragraph 9—The processing is necessary for ethnic monitoring purposes.	Paragraph 5(d)—The processing is necessary for the exercise of any other functions of a public nature exercised in the public interest by any person. Or possibly: Paragraph 6(1)—The processing is necessary for the purposes of legitimate interests pursued by the data controller or by the third party or parties to whom the data are disclosed, except where the processing is unwarranted in any particular case by reason of prejudice to the rights and freedoms or legitimate interests of the data subject.

Schedule 3 condition	Schedule 2 condition that consequently will be or is likely to be satisfied and to which data controllers should have regard
Paragraph 10—By Order of the Secretary of State. ensure	There is no clear parallel condition. Data controllers must take care to that one of the Schedule 2 conditions is satisfied.

ADDITIONAL INFORMATION

Derivations

7–41 • Directive 95/46 (See App.B):

    (a) Art.8 (the processing of special categories of data).
    (b) Recitals 33, 34, 35, 36.

• Council of Europe Convention of January 28, 1981 for the Protection of Individuals with regard to automatic processing of Personal Data: Art.6 (special categories of data).
• Data Protection Act 1984: s.2(3) (sensitive data classes).

Hansard references

7–42 Commons Standing Committee D, May 12, 1998, col.36
Sensitive data, other beliefs of a similar nature

Commons Standing Committee D, June 4, 1998, col.301
Failed attempt to have the canvassing of political opinions exempt and discussion of political opinion information.

ibid., cols 314–316
Criminal conviction information held by various organisations, possible exemptions.

Previous case law

7–43 None.

CHAPTER 8

Overseas or Cross-border Transfers of Personal Data

INTRODUCTION

8–01 The aim of the relevant provisions on cross-border flows of data in the Directive is to ensure that personal data from EU countries are handled in accordance with the Data Protection Principles even when they leave the EEA. The transfer of personal data outside the EEA is prohibited, save for those cases where the exceptions or derogations can be claimed, unless the destination country (which is also taken to include the country of eventual destination if more than one data movement is contemplated) has an adequate level of personal data protection.[1] Although the derogations are reasonably wide they cannot be used in all cases. This has been a source of continued friction since the Directive was passed. The Commission has expressed concern that some Member States have taken too relaxed a view of the prohibition[2]; regulatory authorities in at least one jurisdiction have been challenged before the courts for taking too strict a view of the rules banning transfers[3]; business has been frustrated at the bureaucracy imposed on transfers and lobbied to find more business friendly ways of dealing with the issues[4]: in non-EEA countries the provision has been seen as a way for Brussels to extend the impact of the Directive beyond the borders of the EU and ensure that others adopt a system of regulation similar to the EU model.

8–02 The Commission has the capacity to make findings of adequacy in relation to third countries. The standard it has applied for making such findings in respect of a country is that the country has generally applicable law equivalent to EU regimes. This has enabled the EU to make findings of adequacy in respect of several countries, including Switzerland and Argentina. However in respect of the United States the two adequacy findings (Safe Harbor and the PNR transfer) have not been based on national legislation.

8–03 There is no doubt that US law does not meet the standards which have been required by the EU before making an adequacy finding. US laws on privacy and data protection rights have been and remain undeniably patchwork—often found in regulations applying only to certain sectors of industry or commerce. There has been resistance in the US to the introduction of a federal and legislative-based data protection

---

[1] Dir.95/46 Art.25.1.
[2] First Report on the Implementation of the Directive see Action 3.
[3] Reference case against Spanish data protection supervisory authority.
[4] See the ICC contract clauses and the move to have BCR adopted.

system. This does not mean that the US has no privacy protection. Indeed, while the response to the EU Directive was to regard it as an unnecessary and bureaucratic regulation which would damage free trade and US interests, the last few years have seen the start of a change in the US attitudes to privacy protection.[5]

The "Safe Harbor" agreement with the US reached in July 2000 came into effect in November 2000. This only applies in the US; there is no concept of a Safe Harbor in any other jurisdiction. It enables US companies to adopt a self-regulatory regime which will be taken to satisfy the EU standards of "adequacy". The fact that take-up has been slow has caused commentators to condemn the arrangements as unsatisfactory, and it does have drawbacks. By March 2007 only a comparatively small number of US companies had signed up to the Safe Harbor Agreement.[6] It should be noted however that the number includes a significant number of global businesses. Moreover it should be recognised that a range of options are available to data controllers exporting personal data to the US of which Safe Harbor is only one.

8–04 If the controller cannot bring the transfer into one of the categories of exemption (or derogation), another possible solution to the problems caused by the approach of the Directive to overseas transfers is the adoption of contractual solutions. Contracts have long been considered as potential vehicles to deliver data protection solutions. Work was carried out on contracts by the Council of Europe in the 1980s and has continued, with an increasing degree of sophistication, ever since. The use of approved contracts is sanctioned by the Directive[7] and the Commission has approved three standard form contracts for the export of personal data from the EU to both controllers and processors. The first two were produced by the Commission and provoked criticism from business for their lack of flexibility. As a result the International Chamber of Commerce produced and submitted a third, more "business friendly", contract which was approved by the Commission.

A further possible route to enable transfers to countries without adequate protection is the development of Binding Corporate Rules under which a global company is empowered to establish its own scheme of binding internal contracts which commit the organisation to adhere to an appropriate data protection standard.

8–05 A fundamental difference in attitudes to overseas transfers between the approach of regulators and the pragmatism of business has gradually emerged since 1998. The Directive (and hence the laws of all Member States) allows the export of data where one of the derogations apply. Not unreasonably therefore businesses tend to consider the possibility of using one or more of the derogations as the first option when faced with a transfer to a non-EEA country with no finding of adequacy. Generally, it is only if none of the derogations apply, that businesses look to whether contracts, Safe Harbor or Binding Corporate Rules, or a combination of such measures, offer an acceptable solution. Regulators, on the other hand, are keen to emphasise that derogations should be the last option and only relied upon where no way of providing adequate protection can be found.[8]

---

[5] See research by Ponemon institute and others.
[6] In March 2007 the US Trade Dept website listed 1,135 entries under Safe Harbor, however the exact figure is difficult to ascertain as some entries are no longer current while others represent groups of companies.
[7] Dir 95/46 Art.26(2).
[8] See WP Document 11639/02/EN among others, the most recent being WP114 which represents current thinking.

In its 2003 First Report on the implementation of the Data Protection Directive[9] the Commission drew attention to the continuing unsatisfactory nature of the arrangements for transborder data flows and committed itself to:

> ". . .further discussions with a view to a substantial approximation of existing practices in the Member States and the simplification of the conditions for international transfers."

In pursuance of this aim it committed to making more use of its powers to make findings of adequacy and approve standard form contracts. These aims formed two of its projected workstreams; the other two being to foster the role of Binding Corporate Rules and seek a more uniform interpretation of the derogations.

The Report appears to show a divergence of views between some States, including the UK, and the Commission on both transfer without authorisations and notification of national authorisations granted under Art.26(2) to the Commission. In the relation to the former point the accompanying Analysis document explains that approaches vary in different States:

> "The Member States also take different approaches to the situation pending formal findings of adequacy by either their national authorities or the Commission. In Austria, Greece, Portugal and Spain the law makes clear that in the absence of a Commission finding, only the national authorities can determine that a particular third country provides adequate protection. . . . The law is not that clear in this respect in Italy, in particular because transfers need to be notified to the Authority which may object to the transfer. . . and the situation is unclear in Belgium because of the lack of a Royal Decree that should serve to complete the legislation.
>
> However in other countries it would appear that pending such a formal determination individual controllers can make this assessment for themselves. The different approaches to this question pending formal findings therefore results in substantial divergences between the Member States."[10]

In the body of the Report it is remarked that:

> "The approach adopted by some Member States, where the assessment of the adequacy of protection provided for by the recipient is supposed to be made by the data controller, with very limited control of the data flows by the State or the national supervisory authority, does not seem to meet the requirement placed on Member States by the first paragraph of Article 25(1)."[11]

The Report does not explore this issue further however it also raises concerns that there have been so few notifications to the Commission under Art.26(2).

---

[9] COM (2003) 265 Final.
[10] Para.13.2 Pt 1: Analysis of transposition legislation.
[11] *ibid*. para.4.4.5.

There is no imminent suggestion of infraction proceedings against those Member States which do not impose controls but UK data controllers may wish to be alert to the questions being aired.

SUMMARY OF THE MAIN POINTS

8–06 • The eighth Data Protection Principle[12] provides that:

"Personal data shall not be transferred to a country or territory outside the European Economic Area unless that country or territory ensures an adequate level of protection for the rights and freedoms of data subjects in relation to the processing of personal data."

• The interpretation provisions for the eighth Principle[13] provide an interpretation of the phrase "adequate level of protection":

"There are a number of exemptions[14] to the ban in the Eighth Principle."

• Where a "Community finding" has been made in relation to a particular kind of transfer then any question as to an "adequate level of protection" must be determined in accordance with that finding. A "Community finding" is a finding of the European Commission,[15] that a country or territory outside the European Economic Area does, or does not, ensure an adequate level of protection within the meaning of Art.25(2) of the Directive.

• Transfers to non-EEA countries are included on the data controller's register of notification, but this can be done in very general terms. A transfer is a processing operation in itself and the data controller must also be able to rely on one of the grounds for processing in order to validate any overseas transfer. Transfers may be sanctioned under binding Corporate Rules or approved contracts.

• Failure to comply with the Principle is not an offence but may be subject to enforcement action by the Commissioner.

• As well as complying with the eighth Principle an overseas transfer must comply with the other Principles and issues of fairness, transparency and lawfulness of the transfer must be considered.

WHAT IS A CROSS-BORDER DATA TRANSFER?

8–07 No definition of a transfer was provided in either the 1984 Act or the Directive. Clause 1 of the Data Protection Bill contained a definition of what constitutes a transfer but the proposed definition did not survive into the final Act.

The clause would have provided that:

"A person who:

---

[12] As set out in Sch.1 Pt 1 para.8 of the 1998 Act.
[13] As set out in paras 13–15 of Pt 2 of Sch.1.
[14] Para.14 contains a reference to Sch.4 to the 1998 Act.
[15] Under the procedure provided for in Art.31(2) of the Data Protection Directive.

> a) discloses data to a person in a country or territory; or
> b) otherwise makes the information contained in the data available to a person in a country or territory,
>
> is taken to transfer the data to that country or territory."

This was a broad definition of a "transfer". It would clearly have covered personal data being communicated over the telephone (the "push" transfer) and might have been wide enough to cover the provision of access rights to a third party outside the EEA or placing of material on a website which would potentially be available to persons outside the EEA (the "pull" transfer).

The definition was dropped during consideration of the Bill. In the absence of such a definition it was not clear whether personal data made available for access or posted on an internet site from where it could be accessed would involve a transfer outside the EEA. However the point has now been decided by the European Court in the *PNR* cases and the case of *Bodil Lindqvist*[16] resulting in the decision that the former clearly is a transfer but the latter will not necessarily be and may depend on where the server used is situated.

The Guidance available from the Office of the Information Commissioner[17] distinguishes between transfer and transit as follows:

> "The Act does not define 'transfer' but the ordinary meaning of the word is transmission from one place, person etc. to another. Transfer does not mean the same as mere transit. Therefore the fact that the electronic transfer of personal data may be routed through a third country on its way from the UK to another EEA country does not bring such transfer within the ambit of the Eighth Principle."

The Act provides that the transfer of information in a form in which it would not fall under the UK Act, for example on a paper copy outside the definition of a "relevant filing system", which is intended to be held as data in the overseas jurisdiction, will still be regarded as a transfer.[18]

A data controller may still retain control over the relevant personal data even if it (or a copy) has been transferred overseas. Control may, for example, be retained by way of strict contractual terms between a transferor and transferee.

8–08   In *Lindqvist*[19] Mrs Lindqvist had placed personal data on to a website which was hosted within the EEA. The European Court decided that she had not transferred personal data outside the EEA. There is no transfer to a third country within the meaning of Art.25 of the Directive in such circumstances notwithstanding that it thereby makes the data accessible to anyone who connects to the internet including people in a third country.[20] The Court explained that, if the Directive were interpreted to mean that there was a transfer whenever personal data were loaded on to a website that could be accessed over the internet, then if the Commission found that even one

---

[16] See Ch.3, above for a full explanation of the case.
[17] The eighth Data Protection Principle and international data transfers Version 2.0, June 30, 2006.
[18] DPA s.1(3).
[19] [2004] Q.B. 1014.
[20] See n.19 above para.71.

country did not have adequate protection the Member States would be obliged to prevent any personal data being placed on the internet.

This leaves open the question of who is responsible for the "transfer" when such personal data are accessed from a non-EEA country. The UK Commissioner has considered the intention of the person uploading the data to be a material consideration:

> "In practice data are often loaded onto the internet with the intention that the data be accessed in a third country, and, as this will usually lead to a transfer, the principle in the Lindqvist case will not apply in such circumstances."[21]

While the decision in *Lindqvist* is wholly understandable it leaves a possible lacunae in control. The Commissioner seeks to deal with this by pointing out that, even where there is no intention to transfer, the very fact that the data controller has made the data so widely accessible raises the question of whether the processing is fair.

8–09 The point was further considered by the European Court in the cases concerning the transfer of Passenger Name Record (PNR) data to the US.[22] In this case airlines based in the EU were required by the US authorities to provide them with the information in the PNR about travellers who were to fly to the US. The airlines did not have the systems in place to enable them to extract the data items and transfer them so it was decided to give the US authority, the US Bureau of Customs and Border Protection (CBP), access to the airlines' databases in the EU to enable them to extract the data. When the agreement to allow this was challenged one of the issues raised in defence of the arrangement was that the "pull" system did not constitute a transfer within the terms of the Directive and therefore could not be sanctioned by any finding of adequacy by the Commission. This adventurous proposition did not find favour with the Advocate General or the Court. In the Opinion of the Advocate General:

> "I am of the opinion that, in this case, the access to the PNR data enjoyed by the CBP falls within the concept of a "transfer to a third country". In my view the defining characteristics of such a transfer is the flow of data from a Member State to the third country, in this instance the United States. It does not matter in that regard whether the transfer is carried out by the sender or the recipient. As the EDPS points out, if the scope of article 25 of Directive 95/46 were limited to transfers carried out by the sender it would be easy to evade the conditions laid down by that article."[23]

8–10 There are no restrictions at all on transfers to countries within the European Economic Area (the 25 members of the European Union plus Norway, Iceland and Liechtenstein). Transfers to such countries are governed by the same rules which would cover a disclosure to a different organisation within the United Kingdom. Effectively, therefore, the "border" which has to be crossed for the eighth Data Protection Principle to be relevant is the border running around the EEA rather than that round the United Kingdom.

A data controller based outside the EEA but using equipment in the United Kingdom for the processing of data (otherwise than for the purposes of transit through

---

[21] See n.17 above paras 1, 3, 4.
[22] Joined Cases C-317/04 and C-318/04 [2003] ECR I–4989. See Ch.1, above for a full description of the cases.
[23] *Ibid*. para.91.

the UK) will be subject to UK law.[24] The extent of the "use" required is not defined nor is it clear whether the controller has to make use of the equipment directly or whether a controller who employs another to process personal data is making "use" of the equipment used by the processor. It is suggested that if it had been intended to extend to the circumstances where a third party is involved the construction "uses or causes to be used" would be required and therefore the better view would be that the controller has to use the equipment himself to fall within the provision.

A transfer occurs on each occasion when personal data are dispatched outside the jurisdiction. Therefore prima facie each cross-border transfer should be considered separately. However, in practical terms data controllers make decisions in relation to classes of transfers and the advice from the OIC and the Article 29 Working Party tend to recognise that data controllers will take judgments on classes of data.

Note: For a fuller discussion on the territorial applicability of the 1998 Act, see Ch.3.

Onward transfers

8–11 The Directive does not deal specifically with onward transfers. It simply requires that one of the elements to be taken into consideration when determining adequacy is the "country of final destination", a phrase which is repeated in the UK provision.[25] The question of how far the recipient organisation in a third country is able to make further transfers and to what extent the original exporting data controller should be held responsible for such transfers is an unresolved question. As might be anticipated the Working Party and the Commission have been alert to emphasise to data controllers that, in the view of the Working Party and the Commission onward transfers of personal data to recipients outside the EEA are equally governed by the prohibitions on transfer. The question of onward transfer and how far it should be restricted by the exporting data controller was raised in the *PNR* cases. One of the arguments raised against the agreement to allow the CBP access to the PNR data was that the CBP were not prohibited by the terms of the agreement from further transferring the data to other countries. Therefore they might allow a further transfer to a jurisdiction which had not been assessed as adequate. The point was not considered by the Court and was not directly addressed in the Opinion of the Advocate General. In the Opinion the Advocate treated the issue of the safeguards surrounding the transfer as an Art.8(2) ECHRFF question which was bound up with the question of proportionality and the margin of appreciation which should be available to those dealing with terrorism, crime and security. In relation to the specific point he said.

> ". . .the safeguards surrounding the transfer of PNR data to other government authorities make it possible in my view, to consider that the interference in the private life of airline passengers is proportionate for the purpose of achieving the aim pursued by the PNR regime."

The significance of his approach is that he took a robust and holistic view of the transfer to the CBP, taking into account the purpose of the processing, the nature of

---

[24] DPA s.5(1)(b).
[25] DPA Sch.1 Pt II para.13(c).

the CBP and the data and balanced the privacy impact against the wider justification for the processing.

ADEQUATE PROTECTION

8–12   The core of the provisions relating to cross-border transfers is the assessment as to whether the foreign country offers an adequate level of protection for the rights and freedoms of data subjects in relation to the processing of personal data. The *PNR* cases also gave rise to an interesting expression in the Opinion of the Advocate General in which he distinguished between "adequate protection" and "equivalent protection" as follows:

> "The specific nature of the rules governing the transfer of personal data to third countries can be largely examined by the key role played by the concept of adequate protection. In order to define that concept it must be clearly distinguished from the concept of equivalent protection which would require third countries to recognise and actually apply all the principles contained in Directive 95/46."[26]

Guidance on assessing whether a foreign country offers adequate protection has been produced by the Article 29 Working Group and the UK Commissioner. The UK Commissioner's view is that, as with much of the 1998 Act, the onus is placed upon a data controller to make their own decision as to whether their processing is in accordance with the legislation—and in the specific case of cross-border transfers whether the transferor country ensures an adequate level of protection.[27]

In this chapter the guidance from those sources is considered but, however persuasive such guidance may be, it is not in itself law. Data controllers who wish to rely on their own view that a country provides an adequate standard of protection will have to be able to demonstrate a rational decision-making process to show an assessment of adequacy.

Provisions in the Act

8–13   The Act itself sets out a number of criteria in Sch.1 Pt 2 para.13 to which any data controller must have particular regard in assessing adequacy.

The first of these criteria requires a data controller to have regard to the nature of the data. The clear implication here is that there will be more or less sensitive data (sensitive both in the sense defined by the Act as well as in its more general meaning) which will require correspondingly more or less protection. This is, of course, a parallel of the provision in the interpretation of the seventh Principle on security measures which requires consideration to be given to the nature of the data to be protected in assessing the "appropriateness" (as opposed to "adequacy") of the relevant security system. It is interesting that the two sets of interpretative provisions on two consecutive principles should utilise two different concepts—"appropriateness" and "adequacy". It is submitted that the concept of "adequacy" could easily have been utilised in both sets of provisions and would have provided thereby at least the security of familiarity.

---

[26] Opinion para.88.
[27] The eighth Data Protection Principle and international data transfers, Office of the Information Commissioner, June 2006.

No further guidance is given in the legislation as to how "adequacy" needs to be balanced against the nature of the data, but clearly the minimum requirement is for a data controller to be able to show a rational decision-making process along the lines of "I considered the level of protection, which involves A, B and C, to be offered by country M to be adequate, given that the data we transferred contained details of X, Y and Z".

The second and third criteria to be considered are the country or territory of origin of the information contained in the data and the country and territory of final destination.

8–14 The implication seems to be that if data were gathered in a country with an "inadequate" system of data protection then a transfer to a country with a similarly inadequate system might be acceptable or at least a transfer back to the country of origin. The fourth criterion requires consideration to be given to the purposes for which and the period during which the data are intended to be processed. This is a consideration which goes hand in hand with the requirement that, in assessing adequacy, regard must be had to the nature of the data. A data controller thus must look not only at the nature of the data to be processed but also at the nature of the processing to be carried out in the foreign territory or country and the time when that processing is planned to take place.

Thus the controller will ask:

(a) What is the nature of the data?

(b) What will be done with it?

(c) For how long?

Again no further guidance is given in the legislation as to what types of processing will require more or less protective regimes. But, as with the criteria obliging consideration of the nature of the data, it is submitted that the data controller must be able to demonstrate a rational decision-making which takes into account all these factors.

The fifth to eighth criteria require a data controller to consider the details of the data protection regime or regimes in place in the country of destination and specifically:

(a) the law in force;

(b) the international obligations adhered to;

(c) relevant enforceable codes of conduct or other rules;

(d) security measures taken in respect of the data.

The last provision requires the data controller to consider what security measures are to be taken with respect to the specific data to be transferred, whereas the first three require consideration to be given to the generality of the regimes in place.

The eighth Principle commences by stating that "An adequate level of protection is one which is adequate in all the circumstances of the case, having regard in particular to . . .", before reciting the eight criteria to be considered. Thus the eight criteria are not exhaustive of the matters which a data controller may have to consider in assessing adequacy.

Adequacy assessment

8–15   Help in assessing adequacy has already been provided at both an EU level and at a national level.

EU level

8–16   At the EU level there have been a number of formal decisions as to countries and territories which offer an adequate level of protection. The decisions are "Community findings" under the Directive. The interpretative provisions on the eighth Principle specifically provide for "Community findings" to be taken into account in deciding adequacy.[28] Such findings on particular types of transfer are binding on data controllers and the national data protection enforcement agencies. A "Community finding" is defined as a finding of the European Commission, under the procedure provided for in Art.31(2) of the Data Protection Directive, that a country or territory outside the European Economic Area does, or does not, ensure an adequate level of protection within the meaning of Art.25(2) of the Directive.[29] The decisions have been issued as Commission Decisions which operate as Community legal instruments and are directly applicable without the need for further implementing provisions, however the UK has chosen to have a formal adoption mechanism.

The Commission is also empowered to decide that certain standard contractual clauses offer sufficient safeguards in relation to transfers to countries with data protection regimes providing otherwise inadequate protection.[30] This is discussed more fully below.

Article 29 Paper

8–17   The Article 29 Working Party[31] produced some helpful guidance on the interpretation of Arts 25 and 26 of the EU Directive (the Articles covering cross-border transfers)[32] in July 1998 which has subsequently been relevant in making adequacy assessments and is referred to in later Commission decisions.[33]

The guidance suggests that any meaningful analysis of "adequate protection" must comprise two basic elements: an assessment of the content of the rules applicable and an assessment of the means for ensuring their effective application.

The Working Party also submits that:

"Using Directive 95/46/EC as a starting point, and bearing in mind the provisions of other international data protection texts, it should be possible to arrive at a

---

[28] DPA Sch.1 Pt 2 para.15.
[29] For an explanation of the Art.31 procedure see Ch.25, below.
[30] Art.26 of the Directive paras 2–4.
[31] See para.25–19, below for the constitution and work of the Article 29 Working Party.
[32] "Transfers of personal data to third countries: Applying Articles 25 and 26 of the E.U. data protection directive" DG XV D/5025/98.
[33] See Recital 3 of Council Decision 2001/497.

'core' of data protection 'content' principles and 'procedural/enforcement' requirements compliance with which could be seen as a minimum requirement for protection to be considered adequate."

Those principles and requirements, the Working Party suggests, are as follows:

Content Principles

8–18   The basic principles to be included are the following:

(a) The purpose limitation principle—data should be processed for a specific purpose and subsequently used or further communicated only insofar as this is not incompatible with the purpose of the transfer. The only exemptions to this rule would be those necessary in a democratic society on one of the grounds listed in Art.13 of the Directive.[34]

(b) The data quality and proportionality principle—data should be accurate and, where necessary, kept up-to-date. The data should be adequate, relevant and not excessive in relation to the purposes for which they are transferred or further processed.

(c) The transparency principle—individuals should be provided with information as to the purpose of the processing and the identity of the data controller in the third country, and other information insofar as this is necessary to ensure fairness. The only exemptions permitted should be in line with Arts 11(2), 12 and 13 of the Directive.

(d) The security principle—technical and organisational security measures should be taken by the data controller that are appropriate to the risks presented by the processing. Any person acting under the authority of the data controller, including a processor, must not process data except on instructions from the controller.

(e) The rights of access, rectification and opposition—the data subject should have a right to obtain a copy of all data relating to him/her that are processed, and a right to rectification of those data where they are shown to be inaccurate. In certain situations he/she should also be able to object to the processing of the data relating to him/her. The only exemptions to these rights should be in line with Art.13 of the Directive.

(f) Restrictions on onward transfers—other transfers of the personal data by the recipient of the original data transfer should be permitted only where the second recipient (i.e. the recipient of the onward transfer) is also subject to rules affording an adequate level of protection. The only exceptions permitted should be in line with Art.26(1) of the Directive.

---

[34] Art.13 permits a restriction to the "purpose principle" if such a restriction constitutes a necessary measure to safeguard national security, defence, public security, the prevention, investigation, detection and prosecution of criminal offences or of breaches of ethics for the regulated professions, an important economic or financial interest, or the protection of the data subject or the rights and freedoms of others.

Examples of additional principles to be applied to specific types of processing are:

(a) Sensitive data—where "sensitive" categories of data are involved (those listed in Art.8 of the Directive), additional safeguards should be in place, such as a requirement that the data subject gives his/her explicit consent for the processing.

(b) Direct marketing—where data are transferred for the purposes of direct marketing, the data subject should be able to "opt-out" from having his/her data used for such purposes at any stage.

(c) Automated individual decision—where the purpose of the transfer is the taking of an automated decision in the sense of Art.15 of the Directive, the individual should have the right to know the logic involved in this decision, and other measures should be taken to safeguard the individual's legitimate interest.

Procedural and enforcement mechanisms

8–19 In Europe, there is broad agreement that data protection principles should be embodied in law. There is also broad agreement that a system of "external supervision" in the form of an independent authority is a necessary feature of a data protection compliance system. Elsewhere in the world, however, these features are not always present.

To provide a basis for the assessment of the adequacy of the protection provided, it is necessary to identify the underlying objectives of a data protection procedural system, and on this basis to judge the variety of different judicial and non-judicial procedural mechanisms used in third countries.

The objectives of a data protection system are essentially threefold:

(a) To deliver a good level of compliance with the rules. (No system can guarantee 100 per cent compliance, but some are better than others.) A good system is generally characterised by a high degree of awareness among data controllers of their obligations, and among data subjects of their rights and the means of exercising them. The existence of effective and dissuasive sanctions can play an important part in ensuring respect for rules, as of course can systems of direct verification by authorities, auditors, or independent data protection officials.

(b) To provide support and help to individual data subjects in the exercise of their rights. The individual must be able to enforce his/her rights rapidly and effectively and without prohibitive cost. To do so, there must be some sort of institutional mechanism allowing independent investigation of complaints.

(c) To provide appropriate redress to the injured party where rules are not complied with. This is a key element which must involve a system of independent adjudication or arbitration which allows compensation to be paid and sanctions imposed where appropriate.

Thus to ensure "adequacy" a data controller should consider whether the regimes in the country of transfer provide the elements of protection outlined above.

The Working Party has emphasised that these are minimum requirements. It is clear, therefore, that data controllers may need to consider additional aspects of the data protection regimes in place in the country of transfer depending on the nature of the data to be transferred, and the nature and length of the intended processing.

Adequacy through self-regulation

8–20   Paragraph 13 of the interpretation paragraphs states that an adequate level of protection is one which is adequate "in all the circumstances of the case. . .". Specific reference is made to "any relevant codes of conduct or other rules which are enforceable in that country or territory".

Thus account may be taken of non-legal rules that may be in force in the third country in question, provided that these rules are capable of enforcement. The Working Party emphasises that the mere capacity for the rules to be enforced will not be sufficient—what must be demonstrated is that the rules are complied with.[35] It is in this context that the role of industry self-regulation falls to be considered.

The Working Party suggests that a self-regulatory code (or other instrument) should be taken to mean:

> "any set of data protection rules applying to a plurality of data controllers from the same profession or industry sector, the content of which has been determined primarily by members of the industry or profession concerned."

This would encompass, at one end of the scale, a voluntary data protection code developed by a small industry association with only a few members to, at the other end, the kind of detailed codes of professional ethics applicable to entire professions, such as bankers and doctors, which often have quasi-judicial force.

Evaluation of a self-regulatory code

8–21   The Working Party suggests that evaluation should take the following form:

(a) "Evaluate the content of any code—

   (i)   does it comply with the "content principles"? (para.8–14, above)
   (ii) is it in plain language?
   (iii) does it prevent disclosure to non-members not governed by the code?

(b) Evaluate the prevalence of any code in the relevant industry—the Working Party suggests that industry—or profession wide codes will be preferable to those developed by small groupings of companies within sectors, because:

   (i)   Consumers will find fragmented industries, characterised by rival associations each with its own code, confusing;

---

[35] "Transfers of personal data to third countries: Applying Articles 25 and 26 of the E.U. Data Protection Directive" DG XV d/5025/98, Ch.3.

(ii) It creates uncertainty as to which rules apply if data are passed between different companies within one industry—e.g. direct marketing.

(c) Evaluate the effectiveness of any code—does it achieve:

(i) a good level of compliance?

- How is the code publicised?
- Is it voluntary or compulsory?
- How do members demonstrate compliance?
- What auditing mechanisms apply?
- How are breaches dealt with—are sanctions punitive or merely remedial? (the latter, the Working Party suggests, are likely to be inadequate).

(ii) support and help for data subjects?

- Is there a complaints investigation system and does it have adequate powers?
- How are it and its decisions publicised?
- How are alleged breaches adjudicated—is adjudication independent and impartial? Impartiality might be achieved by using an external adjudicator or by having consumer representatives on any adjudication panel.

(iii) (crucially) appropriate redress including compensation."

Adequacy through contract

8–22 As stated above contractual "solutions" are possible where the level of general legal compliance with data protection norms would otherwise be deemed inadequate. The Working Party paper reviews the role of contracts in achieving or contributing to adequate protection. The Working Party took a reasonably positive view of the possibility of contractual terms ensuring adequate safeguards for the rights and freedoms of data subjects:

"For a contractual provision to fulfil this function, it must satisfactorily compensate for the absence of a general level of adequate protection, by including the essential elements of protection which are missing in any given particular situation."[36]

After acknowledging the difficulties in using contractual terms to provide redress, support and help to data subjects and delivering a good level of compliance the Working Party draws a number of conclusions including:

(a) The contract should set out in detail the purposes, means and conditions under which the transferred data are to be processed, and the way in which the basic Data Protection Principles are to be implemented. Greater legal security is provided by contracts which limit the ability of the recipient of the data to process the data autonomously on his own behalf. The contract

---

[36] "Transfers of personal data to third countries: Applying Articles 25 and 26 of the E.U. Data Protection Directive" DG XV D /5025/98, Ch. 4.

should therefore be used, to the extent possible, as a means by which the entity transferring the data retains decision-making control over the processing carried out in the third country.

(b) Where the recipient has some autonomy regarding the processing of the transferred data, the situation is not straightforward, and a single contract between the parties to the transfer may not always be a sufficient basis for the exercise of rights by individual data subjects. A mechanism may be needed through which the transferring party in the Community remains liable for any damage that may result from the processing carried out in the third country.

(c) Onward transfers to bodies or organisations not bound by the contract should be specifically excluded by the contract, unless it is possible to bind such third parties contractually to respect the same Data Protection Principles.

(d) Confidence that Data Protection Principles are respected after data are transferred would be boosted if data protection compliance by the recipient of the transfer were subject to external verification by, for example, a specialist auditing firm or standards/certification body.

(e) In the event of a problem experienced by a data subject, resulting perhaps from a breach of the data protection provisions guaranteed in the contract, there is a general problem of ensuring that a data subject complaint is properly investigated. EU Member State supervisory authorities will have practical difficulties in carrying out such an investigation.

(f) Contractual solutions are probably best suited to large international networks (credit cards, airline reservations) characterised by large quantities of repetitive data transfers of a similar nature, and by a relatively small number of large operators in industries already subject to significant public scrutiny and regulation. Intra-company data transfers between different branches of the same company group is another area in which there is considerable potential for the use of contracts.

(g) Countries where the powers of State authorities to access information go beyond those permitted by internationally accepted standards of human rights protection will not be safe destinations for transfers based on contractual clauses.

COMMUNITY FINDINGS STATES

8–23 On July 27, 2000 the European Commission issued decisions recognising Switzerland and Hungary as providing adequate protection for personal data on the basis that those countries have generally applicable data protection law which follows the same approach as the Directive. The decisions cover the transfer of all personal data to Switzerland and Hungary.[37] Since the extension of the EU the finding in respect of Hungary has become otiose.

---

[37] Commission Decision of July 26, 2000 [2000] O.J. L215/1-3; Commission Decision July 26, 2000 [2000] O.J. L215/4-6.

On December 20, 2001 the Commission delivered a finding of adequacy in respect of the Canadian regime.[38] This is not a finding for the jurisdiction as the Canadian Act, the Canadian Personal Information Protection and Electronic Documents Act, which came fully into force on January 1, 2004, does not cover personal data held by public bodies or by private organisations and used for non-commercial purposes. Accordingly where the data transfer is to a public body or to a private body for a non-commercial purpose, adequacy will have to be achieved by some other mechanism. Argentina,[39] Guernsey[40] and the Isle of Man[41] have also been added to the list by the Commission.

The Commission may also make a finding that a particular jurisdiction does not offer adequate protection. So far it has not done so overtly, although the refusal to accept some regimes such as the 1986 Isle of Man legislation (subsequently replaced by a regime acceptable to the Commission), as offering adequate protection is tantamount to such a decision. It seems unlikely that formal decisions of inadequacy will ever now be made.

SAFE HARBOR

8–24 As explained in the introduction, the US approach to the protection of personal privacy is different from the EU one. The US has a number of statutory protections but these are piecemeal and specific to sectors or particular problems, for example the Children's Online Privacy Protection Act 1998 (COPPA). Otherwise regulation is based on self-regulatory mechanisms and consumer action. This is very different from the EU approach of universally applicable law. The US Administration was concerned that personal data would stop flowing to the US after implementation of the Directive and accordingly the Safe Harbor Agreement was negotiated. The Safe Harbor Agreement is only one possible mechanism to allow data export to the US; reliance can be placed on any of the derogations, such as consent, or a contractual solution adopted. The Safe Harbor Agreement has not been universally popular. On the European side the Parliament expressed reservations about it as did the Article 29 Working Party. Nevertheless it is a significant initiative.

The details of the Safe Harbor Agreement (the US spelling of the word has become universally accepted in this context) are found in the Commission Decision of July 27, 2000 pursuant to Directive 95/46 of the European Parliament and of the Council on the adequacy of the protection provided by the Safe Harbor Privacy Principles and related Frequently Asked Questions issued by the US Department of Commerce.[42] The papers consist of:

- the Decision itself;

- the Privacy Principles;

- the Frequently Asked Questions;

---

[38] Commission Decision 2002/2/EC of December 20, 2001 [2002] O.J. L2/13-16.
[39] June 30, 2003.
[40] November 21, 2003.
[41] April 28, 2004.
[42] Decision 520/2000.

- a list of the US Statutory Bodies recognised by the EU as being able to deal with complaints and offer redress;

- correspondence from those authorities (the Federal Trade Commission (FTC) and the US Department of Transportation (USDoT)) to the Commission;

- a memorandum outlining the authority of the FTC; and

- a statement of the US law on damages for breach of privacy and explicit authorisations in US law.

The materials can be found on the EU website or the US Department of Commerce website, *http://www.export.gov/safeharbor* [Accessed on 2 September 2007], where a list of those companies which have decided to adopt the Safe Harbor Principles can also be found. The material Recital in the Commission decision is (5) which reads:

"The adequate level of protection for the transfer of data from the Community to the United States recognized by this decision, should be attained if organizations comply with the Safe Harbor Privacy Principles for the protection of personal data transferred from a Member State to the United States (hereinafter 'the Principles') and the Frequently Asked Questions (hereinafter 'the FAQs') providing guidance for the implementation of the Principles issued by the Government of the United States on 21.07.2000. Furthermore the organizations should publicly disclose their privacy policies and be subject to the jurisdiction of the Federal Trade Commission (FTC) under Section 5 of the Federal Trade Commission Act which prohibits unfair or deceptive trade acts or practices in or affecting commerce, or that of another statutory body that will effectively ensure compliance with the Principles implemented in accordance with the FAQs."

This encapsulates the requirements of the Safe Harbor.

Overview

8–25 Participation in Safe Harbor is voluntary. It is only open to organisations which are subject to either s.5 of the Federal Trade Commission Act (FTCA) or the authority of the US Department of Transportation under Title 49, United States Code, s.41712. Section 5 of the FTCA does not apply to banks, savings and loans and credit unions, telecommunications and interstate transportation common carriers, air carriers and packers and stockyard operators. Most of these are therefore excluded from Safe Harbor unless covered by the Department of Transportation. This covers the travel industry and airlines. In order to join the Safe Harbor a US organisation must do one of three things: develop its own self-regulatory privacy policy which complies with the Principles[43]; or participate in an industry self-regulatory programme which meets the Principles, for example the TRUSTe or BBBOnline programmes; or comply with sector-specific regulations that meet the Principles. The organisation must then certify to the Department of Commerce (or its designee) that it is operating in compliance with the Principles. The certification must include specific information

---

[43] In this context "Principles" means the Safe Harbor Privacy Principles.

including a statement that the organisation has a privacy policy, which is available to the public, and which complies with the Principles. The notification lasts 12 months and the organisation must make an annual return to the Department confirming its continued compliance. This is called a verification and may be based upon a self-assessment or a compliance review by an outside body. Participants have to have effective enforcement and dispute resolution mechanisms which can be delivered either by a private sector organisation such as BBBOnline or by committing to co-operate with EU data protection authorities. The co-operation option must be chosen where the data controller in the EU plans to transfer personal data about employees in the EU. Where the co-operation option is chosen the company works with a panel drawn from the supervisory authorities in the EU. Failure to comply with the self-regulatory standards must be actionable under s.5 as an unfair or deceptive act or some other statutory mechanism. The organisation only has to apply the standards to data which it receives by way of transfer from the EEA after the adoption of the Safe Harbor. The standards are not applicable to manual information which falls outside the Directive but can be applied if the organisation chooses. If an organisation wishes to include human resources data in the safe harbor it must indicate that fact specifically in its certification. An organisation can decide to leave Safe Harbor but the personal data which it received from the EU during its membership must continue to be treated in accordance with the Principles.

Safe Harbor—the Privacy Principles

8–26   The seven Privacy Principles are issued by the US Department of Commerce under its statutory duty to foster, promote and develop international commerce. In view of their importance they are set out in full below:

- "Notice
    An organization must inform individuals about the purposes for which it collects and uses information about them, how to contact the organization with any enquiries or complaints, the types of third parties to which it discloses the information, and the choices and means the organization offers individuals for limiting its use and disclosure. This notice must be provided in clear conspicuous language when individuals are first asked to provide personal information to the organization or as soon thereafter as is practicable, but in any event before the organization uses such information for a purpose other than that for which it was originally collected or processed by the transferring organization or discloses it for the first time to a third party.

- Choice
    An organization must offer individuals the opportunity to choose (opt out) whether their personal information is (a) to be disclosed to a third party or (b) to be used for a purpose that is incompatible with the purpose(s) for which it was originally collected or subsequently authorized by the individual. Individuals must be provided with clear, conspicuous, readily available and affordable mechanisms to exercise choice.

    For sensitive information (i.e. personal information specifying medical or health conditions, racial or ethnic origin, political opinions, religious or philosophical beliefs, trade union membership or information specifying the sex life of the individual), they must be given affirmative or explicit (opt in) choice if the information is to be disclosed to a third party or used for a purpose other than those for which it was originally collected or subsequently authorized by the individual through the exercise of an opt in choice. In any case, an organization should treat as sensitive any information received from a third party where the third party treats and identifies it as sensitive.

- Onward transfer

  To disclose information to a third party, organizations must apply the Notice and Choice principles. Where an organization wishes to transfer information to a third party that is acting as an agent, as described in the endnote, it may do so if it first either ascertains that the third party subscribes to the Principles or is subject to the Directive or another adequacy finding or enters into a written agreement with such third party requiring that the third party provide at least the same level of privacy protection as is required by the relevant Principles. If the organization complies with these requirements, it shall not be held responsible (unless the organization agrees otherwise) when a third party to which it transfers such information processes it in a way contrary to any restrictions or representations, unless the organization knew or should have known the third party would process it in such a contrary way and the organization has not taken reasonable steps to prevent or stop such processing.

- Security

  Organisations creating, maintaining, using or disseminating personal information must take reasonable precautions to protect it from loss, misuse and unauthorised access, disclosure, alteration and destruction.

- Data integrity

  Consistent with the Principles, personal information must be relevant for the purposes for which it is to be used. An organisation may not process personal information in a way that is incompatible with the purpose for which it has been collected or subsequently authorized by the individual. To the extent necessary for those purposes, an organization should take reasonable steps to ensure that data is reliable for its intended use, accurate, complete and current.

- Access

  Individuals must have access to personal information about them that an organization holds and be able to correct, amend or delete that information where it is inaccurate, except where the burden or expense of providing access would be disproportionate to the risks to the individual's privacy in the case in question, or where the rights of persons other than the individual would be violated.

- Enforcement

  Effective privacy protection must include mechanisms for assuring compliance with the Principles, recourse for individuals to whom the data relate affected by non-compliance with the Principles, and consequences for the organization when the Principles are not followed. At a minimum such mechanisms must include, (a) readily available and affordable independent recourse mechanisms by which each individual's complaints and disputes are investigated and resolved by reference to the Principles and damages awarded where the applicable law or private sector initiatives so provide; (b) follow up procedures for verifying that the attestations and assertions businesses make about their privacy practices are true and that privacy practices have been implemented as presented; and (c) obligations to remedy problems arising out of failure to comply with the Principles by organizations announcing their adherence to them and consequences for such organizations. Sanctions must be sufficiently rigorous to ensure compliance by organizations."

Comment

8–27   The Privacy Principles do not meet all the requirements of the Directive. In particular the individual rights to object to some kinds of processing and the ban on automated decisions are absent. Moreover there are no specific rules governing telecommunications as there are in Europe under Directive 2002/58. Otherwise the Principles are close to the requirements of the Directive.

The Frequently Asked Questions (FAQs)

8–28   There are 15 FAQs. The FAQs relate to: sensitive data; journalistic exemptions; secondary liability; investment banking and audits; the role of data protection authorities; self-certification under the Safe Harbor; verification of compliance with Safe Harbor; the access principle; personal data used for human resources; processor contracts; dispute resolution and enforcement; timing of opt-outs; travel information; pharmaceutical and medical products; and public record and publicly available information. The FAQs amplify the Principles and deal with the practical points relating to the working of the Safe Harbor.

US regulatory bodies and correspondence from them

8–29   The basis of Safe Harbor is that the organisation "signs up" to a publicly-stated privacy policy that incorporates the standards set out in the Principles and the FAQs. Failure to comply with that privacy policy can be the subject of regulatory action. So the policy becomes enforceable by an independent regulator. The two bodies which exercise relevant regulatory powers are the Federal Trade Commission (FTC) and the US Department of Transportation. Enforcement will take place in the US. The Department of Commerce maintains the public list of subscribers which anyone wishing to export personal data to the US may consult. The list also shows the enforcement body for the subscriber so it can be used by anyone wanting to make a complaint. Enforcement action by the regulator may result in the subscriber being struck off the list and losing Safe Harbor status. If a company loses Safe Harbor status that will be made clear in the list. The FTC has undertaken, in the correspondence with the EU, to give priority to referrals of non-compliance with Safe Harbor received from privacy programmes or EU data protection authorities.

Financial services

8–30 As such services are not subject to s.5 of the Federal Trade Commission Act they are not able to take advantage of the Safe Harbor. Discussions are continuing between the EU and the US over bringing financial services into Safe Harbor but have not yet reached fruition at the time of writing.

Effect of an organisation joining the Safe Harbor

8–31 Organisations in the EU wishing to export personal data to the US may do so to any organisation which appears on the Safe Harbor list and data protection authorities cannot stop such exports except in limited circumstances set out in Art.3 of the Decision. These are broadly where there is a dispute as to whether the subscriber has complied with Safe Harbor or where there are real grounds for concern that the enforcement body is not fulfilling its proper function.

Response to the Safe Harbor

8–32 Companies could sign up for Safe Harbor from November 2000.

Although the requirements of Safe Harbor are lower than those needed to comply with the Directive, US companies have appeared unconvinced that the benefits out-weigh the disadvantages. Those include concerns that adoption will lead to pressures from US citizens to apply the same standards to data emanating from the US, worries about the potential liabilities involved in non-compliance and the cost of changing privacy policies as well as the difficulties of having different privacy policies for data coming from the EU.

The EU Commission reviewed the working of the Safe Harbor in October 2004.[44] The report expressed concerns about whether the organisations which have signed up were adhering to the requirements of Safe Harbor, commenting that a substantial number of organisations had no published privacy policy and of those that did fewer than half of the privacy policies met the standards in the Principles. However, it made clear that there was no question of revoking the finding of adequacy in relation to the Safe Harbor. At the time of writing there are still less than 1,000 active entries on the list of US companies which have joined Safe Harbour.

CONTRACTUAL CLAUSES APPROVED BY THE COMMISSION

8–33 Individual contracts or sets of contractual clauses do not, of course, provide an adequate level of protection for an entire country. Thus contractual clauses are a way of complying with an exemption to the eighth Principle rather than complying with the Principle itself.

The provisions in the Directive have not been translated directly into the 1998 Act. Instead the exemptions set out in Sch.4 provide that the eighth Principle does not apply where:

---

[44] Staff working document, see (2004) 1323 at *http://www.europa.eu/justice_home/fsj/privacy* [Accessed on 2 September 2007].

"The transfer is made on terms which are of the kind approved by the Commissioner as ensuring adequate safeguards for the rights and freedoms of data subjects."[45]

Thus, there is no specific reference to contractual terms or clauses.

There is no barrier to individual data controllers agreeing contracts with third parties for the export of personal data on terms negotiated between the parties. In many EU countries such contracts have to be submitted to the national supervisory authority for approval. The United Kingdom and Ireland are exceptional in that the regulators have not required the submission of contracts. Where contracts have to be submitted the national authority will usually review the terms to ensure that certain standards are met and if it considers the contract to be deficient may require amendments. It can take several months for contracts to be approved. Standard form clauses are intended to shorten the process as the national regulatory authorities have to accept contracts drawn up in accordance with the standard.

Three sets of clauses have been approved by the Commission; two sets of controller to controller clauses and one set of controller to processor clauses. The standard form contracts are very similar even though the legal relationships between the parties are very different. A second set of controller processor clauses is currently under consideration at the time of writing. The contracts have been approved under Art.26(2). They are not mandatory—controllers may still use their own contracts—but where the standard forms are used, in most cases, the national regulators have to accept them as producing adequate protection.

Controller to controller contract

8–34   On June 15, 2001 the Commission approved a standard set of contractual clauses to cover the situation where a data controller in the EU sends personal data to a controller outside the EEA to a jurisdiction which does not offer adequate protection for the personal data.[46] The Decision took effect in September 2001. The UK Information Commissioner authorised transfers made using the model clauses under para.9 of Sch.4 on December 21, 2001. The standard contract has been criticised as it imposes onerous obligations, particularly on the recipient. If a data controller uses the clauses then the contract should be accepted by data protection authorities in all the Member States as providing adequate protection. The contract is intended to take effect under the law of the exporting Member State so the contract has to be altered, at least so as to accommodate any legal requirements to comply with contract law in the Member State.

The standard clauses offer a number of options to reach a standard of adequacy. The contract can incorporate standards equivalent to the data protection law of the sending country; or (if the importer is US based and does not already subscribe to Safe Harbor) the Safe Harbor Principles; or the Principles set out in the standard form contract.[47] The data exporter agrees that the transfer complies with the national law and is liable for compliance with the national law up until the export[48] and remains liable

---

[45] 1998 Act Sch.4 para.8.
[46] Commission Decision 2001/497 of June 15, 2001 on standard contractual clauses for the transfer of personal data to third countries under Dir.95/46.
[47] Commission Decision 2001/497 cl.5b.
[48] Commission Decision 2001/497 cl.4a.

for continued compliance with the Principles jointly with the importer.[49] The individual data subjects are entitled to copies of the contract and to have their queries answered by both parties.[50] They must be told of any sensitive data export[51] and be able to enforce rights under the contract.[52] In the United Kingdom this can now be done under the Contracts (Rights of Third Parties) Act 1999. The importer agrees to abide by rulings of the national supervisory authority in the exporting jurisdiction and to submit to audit by the exporter.[53]

The contract has appendices in which the parties set out the categories of data subjects about whom data are being transferred, the purpose of the transfer, the categories of personal data being exported, the recipients of the data, the storage limit, i.e. the length of time for which the data will be held, and where sensitive data are involved, the types of sensitive data.

The Commission has published a set of FAQs on the standard clauses which is also available on the Commission website and which covers:

- whether the clauses are compulsory;
- whether companies can rely on contracts approved at national level;
- whether Member States can block or suspend transfers where the standard clauses are used;
- whether the clauses can be used as part of a wider contract;
- the relation between the Principles and any derogations to those imposed by the importer's national law;
- the burden of joint and several liability;
- the relation with the "safe harbor";
- whether those who are not members of the "safe harbor" can use the "safe harbor" aspect of the standard.

The adoption of the clauses was preceded by correspondence with the US interests represented by both the US Departments of Treasury and Commerce (April 2001) and an Opinion prepared by the Article 29 Working Party on January 26, 2001. The documents, which are available on the Commission website, show the divergence of positions between the Americans and Europeans over the privacy debate.

Contracts (Rights of Third Parties) Act 1999

8–35   A person who is not a party to a contract may enforce a term of a contract if either, the contract expressly provides that he may, or the term purports to confer a benefit on him, unless it is clear from the contract that this was not

---

[49] Commission Decision 2001/497 cl.6.2.
[50] Commission Decision 2001/497 cll.4c and 5c.
[51] Commission Decision 2001/497 cl.4b.
[52] Commission Decision 2001/497 cl.6.1.
[53] Commission Decision 2001/497 cl.5c and d.

intended by the parties.[54] The third party has to be expressly identified in the contract, either by name or as a member of a class or answering a particular description.[55] This can easily be achieved in overseas transfer contracts by a description of the beneficiaries as employees or some other category. Such a clause will cover future members of the class as well as those in the class at the time the contract is entered into.[56]

The third party's rights apply under the contract so any exclusions or limitations in the contract will apply to him and he will only be able to exercise the remedies that apply under the contract.

Once a third party has become the beneficiary of a contract term his position is protected. The main parties cannot alter the term, or rescind the contract altogether, without the third party's agreement if it would disadvantage the third party because the third party has relied on the term.[57] Otherwise parties could enter into contracts which confer benefits on third parties to allow them to achieve some end, for example make an overseas transfer, and then rescind the contract once the transfer had been made, leaving the third party with no redress. A court however can dispense with the agreement of the third party in some cases.

The implementation of the third party rights has made contractual solutions an option for UK data exporters.

Controller to processor contract

8–36   On December 27, 2001 the Commission approved a set of model clauses to be used where a data controller in the EU sends personal data to a processor outside the EEA in a jurisdiction which does not offer adequate protection for the personal data.[58] The decision took effect on April 3, 2002. The UK Commissioner issued an authorisation in respect of contracts made using this model. The standard contract is designed to give enforceable rights to data subjects. This involves the exporter "agreeing" with the importer that his actions comply with the requirements of the Directive[59] although this seems unnecessarily complicated as the data subject would have a remedy under national law in any event if the exporter had failed in his compliance. The importer agrees to an audit of his processing if required,[60] to only process on the instructions of the processor and to implement the technical security measures which are set out in the Appendix to the contract.[61] The data has to be described in a similar way to the controller to controller contract.[62] Where data subjects suffer damage in the first instance they must seek any remedy against the exporter of the data,[63] however, if the exporter has disappeared or become insolvent the importer agrees that a claim may be made against

---

[54] Contracts (Rights of Third Parties) Act 1999 s.1.
[55] *ibid.* s.1(3).
[56] *ibid.*
[57] Contracts (Rights of Third Parties) Act 1999 s.2.
[58] Commission Decision of December 27, 2001 on standard contractual clauses for the transfer of personal data to processors established in third countries under Dir.95/46.
[59] Decision cl.4.
[60] Decision cl.5f.
[61] Decision cl.5a, b, c.
[62] Decision App.1.
[63] Decision cl.6.1.

him.[64] The contract provides for the return or destruction of the data at the termination of the contract.[65]

Amendment of controller to controller clauses

8–37   The first set of controller to controller Commission approved contracts were not popular with business. The US Department of Commerce and the Department of the Treasury indicated their disagreement with aspects of them, as well as US business organisations. A more business friendly proposed standard contract was prepared by an alliance of business organisations including the International Chamber of Commerce and was accepted by a decision amending the original Commission decision on December 27, 2004.[66] These were authorised by the ICO on May 27, 2004. There are now two sets of model controller to controller clauses, Set I and Set II. Data controllers may chose either set but may not amend the clauses or the sets. Each set is designed to achieve a balance of protection but does so by the use of different mechanisms. In each case the national supervisory authority in the exporting Member State may prohibit the data flows where certain conditions are satisfied. Set II does not include the joint and several liability clauses as between the importer and the exporter, the parties are liable for their own breach. However the exporter has an obligation of due diligence to determine that the data importer is able to satisfy its obligations under the contract and must agree to submit to data audits on reasonable request of the exporter. Where Set II has been adopted the rights of individuals to enforce for breach of the required standards is directed in the first instance to the exporter and only arises against the importer where the exporter has refused to enforce the contract. Set II allows for rather more flexibility over agreements between the parties as to which one should deal with subject access requests. Under Set II rights of termination for breach of the contract are explicitly covered.

BINDING CORPORATE RULES

8–38   Although the Directive does not provide any mechanism for the Commission to approve group-wide codes of conduct as an acceptable mechanism to deliver adequacy, such codes have been increasingly used.[67] They offer global businesses, which may be subject to a large number of different privacy laws, a method of standardising compliance levels in the business. There was some interest in the possibility of developing a standard form code which could be adopted by business and used as a tool to enable the transfer of personal data intra-group.[68] It gradually became clear that one code would not be able to deal with the vast range of data processing activities but the

---

[64] Decision cl.6.2.

[65] Decision cl.11.

[66] Commission Decision of December 27, 2004 amending Decision 2001/497 as regards the introduction of an alternative set of standard clauses for the transfer of personal data to third countries (2004/915).

[67] The code developed by Shell for its global business was the starting point for the ICX draft code which was considered by the IPSE initiative under the work carried out by CEN. See *http://www.cenorm.be* [Accessed on 2 September 2007] for a Report on the IPSE work.

[68] See the work carried out by the Initiative for Privacy Standardisation in Europe at the CEN website *http://www.cen.be* and *www.cenorm.be/issp/DPPP* [Accessed on 2 September 2007].

way forward would be for global companies to develop individual "codes" which meet the necessary standards. These codes are called Binding Corporate Rules and are the latest tool available for use in enabling cross border transfers outside the EEA. In outline a company works with a national supervisory authority to adopt a binding internal code which the supervisory authority then approves under the national implementing provisions of Art.26(2). Article 26(2) allows Member States to authorise transfers to countries which do not ensure an adequate level of protection where the controller:

> ". . .adduces adequate safeguards with respect to the protection of privacy and fundamental rights and freedoms of individuals as regards the exercise of the corresponding rights. . . ."

The scheme put forward for approval must therefore be able to deliver guarantees of compliance and rights of redress for non-compliance. The relevant national supervisory authority is responsible for liaising with the other relevant data protection authorities in other jurisdictions to obtain the agreement of all. On June 3, 2003 the Article 29 Working Party adopted a Working Document on Binding Corporate Rules.[69] The first data controller to obtain a successful authorisation has been the GE Group which pursued its authorisation through the UK Commissioner's office. On December 15, 2005 GE was approved by the UK for the purpose of the worldwide transfer of employee data within the GE group of companies.

Article 29 Working Document on Binding Corporate Rules[70] (BCRs)

8–39   The Working Document makes it clear that BCRs should not be regarded as having superseded contractual solutions; such solutions are being used in increasingly sophisticated ways, for example by having standard clauses with many parties to the contract. It emphasises that BCRs may be used with contractual solutions, for example the initial transfer may be made under BCRs and further onward transfers to other recipients than the data importer under separate contractual arrangements. Such contractual solutions can allow for further transfers where the data subjects have given unambiguous consent (where sensitive data are concerned) or in other cases been given the opportunity to object. The various documents which set out the standards which must be reached to produce BCRs use slightly different terminology and sequence. In this section we examine the topic by reviewing the substantive content required and then the procedure for authorisation. After the adoption of the Working Document the Article 29 Group followed with two further guides: Working Document Setting Forth a Co-operation Procedure for Issuing Common Opinions on Adequate Safeguards resulting from Binding Corporate Rules and Working Document Establishing a Model Checklist Application for Approval of Binding Corporate Rules.[71] These were adopted in April 2005. These follow the same approach as the Checklist produced by the Office of the Information Commissioner

---

[69] Working Document: Transfers of personal data to third countries: Applying Article 26(2) of the EU Data Protection Directive to Binding Corporate Rules for International Data Transfers, 11639/02/EN WP 74.
[70] *ibid.*
[71] 05/EN WP 107 and 05/EN WP 108.

in February 2005.[72] The Working Party has made clear this remains a developing area so any organisation looking to follow the process should ensure that it is aware of any subsequent developments. The most recent addition to the BCR approved document is WP133, an application form adopted in July 2007.

8–40   The application follows a two stage process. Before embarking on the BCR process proper, organisations need to make an initial application to obtain the co-operation of the supervisory authority with which the organisation wishes to work and ascertain that it has the jurisdiction to approve BCRs. As WP 108 makes clear the BCR process is not mandated by the Directive and the participation of supervisory authorities is therefore not required under EU law. WP 108 states that "the participation of data protection authorities in the approval of binding corporate rules is entirely voluntary". While this is accurate in general terms the UK Commissioner has set out the terms and process on which his office will work with organisations in this area. If he failed to honour those public statements without some good reason, an aggrieved applicant might have public law remedies.

Jurisdiction

8–41   A corporate group which wishes to pursue the BCR approach must select the lead data protection supervisory authority using the criteria set out in the guidance. The initial application is made to the selected lead data protection supervisory authority showing the nature and general structure of the processing activities in the EEA/EU with particular attention to:

- the place where decisions are made;
- the location and nature of affiliates in the EU;
- the number of employees or others concerned;
- the means and purpose of the processing;
- all the places from which the transfers to third countries take place; and
- the third countries to which data are transferred.

The recipient authority will forward the information to all of the supervisory authorities which have a supervisory role for the processing described with a statement as to whether it is prepared to be the lead authority. The authorities will agree among themselves within a period of approximately four weeks as to whether the choice of the lead is appropriate. Once the lead authority has been agreed that authority will work with the applicant to agree the substantive provisions and prepare the deliverables for submission.

Data protection lead

8–42   The corporate must identify a member of its corporate structure within the EU which will be the lead for the purposes of data protection compliance. Either this will be the corporate headquarters or the member of the group which has delegated

---

[72] Required Contents of a Submission for Approval of "Binding Corporate Rules" to the Information Commissioner.

data protection responsibilities for the group. This entity works with the supervisory authority for the Member State in which it is situated to achieve the BCR approval. WP108 sets out a set of criteria for choosing the correct entity and jurisdiction if the parent or operational headquarters is situated outside the EU. The chosen corporate entity must be appointed by the parent with data protection responsibilities for the corporate group to ensure that the chosen corporate can impose data protection compliance standards on members of the group outside the EEA, have authority to work with the chosen data protection authority and take responsibility for the payment of compensation for damages resulting from a breach of the BCRs by any liable member of the corporate group.

Description of processing and data flows

8–43 The documents submitted for BCR approval (and there may be a suite of such documents—there is no requirement that applicants submit one compendious document) must identify the nature of the data, for example the rules may only relate to one kind of data such as human resource data, the purposes of the transfer, and the extent of the inter-group transfers. The description of the transfers must cover those within the EEA and those outside the EEA and any onward transfers to third parties from those outside the EEA. The level of detail may mirror a detailed notification.

Data protection safeguards

8–44 The data protection compliance standards adopted in respect of the data must be set out. These must comply with the law of the Member State where the responsible corporate is situated and be consistent with the Directive. These rules are to be applicable to all of the defined personal data transferred through the defined corporate group. It should be noted that there may be different standards of enforceability (see later). The OIC notes that this should be more than a restatement of the DPA and should contain some "added value", for example practical guidance to staff. The Rules must address:

- transparency and fairness to the data subject;
- purpose limitation;
- ensuring data quality;
- security;
- individual rights of access, rectification and objection to processing;
- restrictions on onward transfer out of the multinational company covered by the rules.

Legally binding measures

8–45 The crux of the mechanism is that the rules must be "binding" both within the corporate and for the benefit of individuals. There is a certain inevitable elasticity to the term "binding". Inevitable because to quote WP 74 BCRs are intended to be available to a range of organisations "on the basis of different legal and cultural backgrounds and different business philosophies and practices" . Although the term "binding" appears at first sight to be synonymous with "legally enforceable" a closer reading of the material suggests that BCRs may be acceptable if they are enforced in practice even if the organisation has not been able to offer a mechanism which is entirely legally enforceable:

- Binding within the organisation

  The rules may be made binding by contracts within the group or as corporate codes adopted by a group. WP 74 notes that "under international corporate law affiliates may be able to enforce codes of conduct against each other based on claims of quasi-contractual breach, misrepresentation or negligence". The effect may also be achieved by unilateral undertakings given by the parent company and which are binding on members of the group; by the adoption of codes which are capable of having a regulatory effect within an existing legal framework; or by incorporating the rules into the general business principles of the organisation backed by appropriate policies, audits and sanctions. This last possibility appears in WP 108 but not in the OIC checklist, although such business principles could be taken into account by the UK Commissioner.

- Binding on employees

  Employees must be bound to take account of the rules and this may be achieved by including requirements in contracts together with the provision of appropriate training backed up with sanctions for non-compliance.

- Binding on sub-contractors

  This may be achieved by the incorporation of suitable clauses into contracts.

- Binding for the benefit of individuals

  It is only mandatory that those data subjects whose personal data emanates from the EU have the right to enforce the BCRs, although the extension of the benefit to others will be welcomed by supervisory authorities. This entails both the requirement that individuals are able to pursue a judicial remedy and the requirement that the data protection lead corporate is subject to and accepts the supervision of the data protection supervisory authority. Individuals must be able to lodge their complaints with the member of the group at the origin of the transfer (within the EU) or the group member which is the data protection lead. The lead corporate must demonstrate that it has sufficient financial resource to deal with any claim. The rules must become binding for the benefit of the data subjects by some legal mechanism such as by acquiring third party rights under inter-group contracts. WP 74 notes that in some jurisdictions unilateral declarations by corporates may be sufficient to be the origin of third party rights but in other legal systems this is not the case. The Guidance from the UK Commissioner focuses on the practical steps which must be open to complainants but does not explore the enforceability of the rules by data subjects. WP 74 notes however that all the data subjects will have rights under the data protection laws of the country where personal data relating to them was processed. The remedies available must be equivalent to those mandated by the Directive.

Compliance audit

8–46 The WP attaches significance to the verification of compliance. The rules must provide for audit by either internal or external auditors or a combination. The supervisory authority is entitled to call for the audit programme to be provided to it. The supervisory authorities will be expected to undertake to only have regard to the material relating to the data protection audit and not to other matters of corporate governance.

Mechanism for recording and reporting change

8–47 It is recognised in WP 74 that ". . .corporate groups are mutating entities whose members and practices may change from time to time. . ." and thus the deliverables must include processes to deal with such change. These must ensure that:

- no transfer is made to a new member of the group until the new member is bound by the rules and able to deliver compliance with them;
- an updated list of the group members, the rules and any update to the rules is maintained and made available to the supervisory authority on request; and
- updates and changes are notified to the data protection authorities annually.

Procedures and deliverables

8–48 The lead corporate works with the supervisory authority to ensure that its submission reaches the proper standard. It must submit:

- a background paper setting out how the required substantive elements of the BCR structure have been met;
- the set of materials which comprise the rules which are to be adopted by the group; and
- the contact details of a responsible person in the organisation.

This material, referred to in WP 108 as a "consolidated draft" is distributed among the relevant supervisory authorities for comment. The period allowed for comment is usually one month. The lead authority will transmit the comments to the applicant and, where necessary there will be further work and discussion to deal with any unresolved problems. Once the lead authority considers that the material is satisfactory it will invite the applicant to send a final draft which can be circulated to all the relevant supervisory authorities for confirmation. The formal approval for the BCR will issue from the lead authority but the confirmation from the relevant supervisory authorities acts as authorisation for the transfer arrangements at each national level. National permits must still be obtained and modifications given at national level before transfers can be made from that jurisdiction. Once approval is granted, the Chairman of the Article 29 Working Party will notify all supervisory authorities.

Approval was granted to GE in December 2005, restricted to the export of Employee data. The rules themselves are on the GE website.

National level

8–49 The approval of the GE BCRs which are the first in the EU puts the Office of the Information Commissioner in the UK at the forefront of supervisory authorities in the area and may be seen as a vindication of the approach taken by successive Commissioners which has been pragmatic rather than bureaucratic.

Commissioner's Guidance

8–50 Section 51(6) imposes the following relevant obligation on the Commissioner:

> "The Commissioner shall arrange for the dissemination in such form and manner as he considers appropriate of:
>
> (a) any Community finding as defined by paragraph 15(2) of Part II of Schedule 1;
>
> (b) any decision of the European Commission, under the procedure provided for in Article 31(2) of the Data Protection Directive, which is made for the purposes of Article 26(3) or (4) of the Directive; and
>
> (c) such other information as it may appear to him to be expedient to give to data controllers in relation to any personal data about the protection of the rights and freedoms of data subjects in relation to the processing of personal data in countries and territories outside the European Economic Area."

The "Community findings" referred to in subs.(a) have been discussed in para.8–20, above. Subsection (b) refers to procedures set out in the Directive for approval of standard contractual clauses which have been discussed in paras 8–31 and 8–32, above.

Under the previous Commissioner, Elizabeth France, the approach to cross-border transfers differed from that of some national supervisory authorities. It has been noted earlier that the UK Commissioner has not sought to approve transfers made under the derogations nor individual contracts made between controller and controller. The Guidance issued by the Commissioner also accepted that where a transfer was made from a controller to a processor it was regarded as sufficient to achieve compliance if the parties had entered into a contract which met the requirement of Principle 7. Since the re-issuing of the revised Guidance by Richard Thomas in June 2006, there appears to have been some stepping back from this generous view. The revised Guidance is reviewed in the following paragraphs.

Revised Guidance—the eighth Data Protection Principle and international data transfers: the Information Commissioner's legal analysis and recommended approach to assessing adequacy including consideration of the issue of contractual solutions, binding corporate rules and Safe Harbor[73]

---

[73] Version 2.00, June 30, 2006.

8–51 This has replaced the 1999 document which was issued as a "preliminary view" and re-issued in 2000. The paper consists of an introduction followed by a four step process and a fifth section which deals with outsourcing to controllers located in third countries. In the four step process the final step is a consideration of whether any of the exemptions in Sch.4 apply to the transfer, of which the controller may avail himself. In practical terms, as noted earlier, this is probably an unrealistic approach, as most controllers will look for an exemption rather than go through a complex process of considering whether the overseas regime offers adequate protection.

Introduction

8–52 In the introductory section the Commissioner makes the point that transfers outside the particular jurisdiction fall under the remit of the data protection supervisory authority for that jurisdiction. Thus where a data controller is going to make a transfer of personal data originating from another Member State the advice and guidance of the relevant data protection authority for that Member State should be followed. In respect of transfers out of the UK the Commissioner will expect to see evidence that the controller has followed the precepts set out in his Guidance. As a preliminary step the controller should consider whether his business objectives can be met without the transfer of identifiable personal data as anonymisation will take the data outside of the data protection regime altogether.

Step 1

8–53 Controllers should consider whether there will be a transfer of data to a third country.

Step 2

8–54 Controller's should consider the third country and the circumstances surrounding the transfer and consider the question of whether an adequate level of protection will be given to that data.

In the previous Guidance six types of transfer were examined ranging from transfers to a third party processor who remains under the control of the exporting data controller to transfers which amount to a sale of data to a third party with no continuing relationship with either the data subject or the purchaser. However this classification of types of transfers has been abandoned together with the view that a presumption of adequacy can be made in most, if not all, instances of transfers outside the EEA by exporting controllers to overseas processors.

Step 3

8–55 The Controllers must consider whether the parties have or can put in place adequate safeguards such as Binding Corporate Rules or model clauses.

Step 4

8–56 Controllers consider whether any of the derogations apply to allow the transfer to take place lawfully.

8–57 *Step 1.* The Guidance goes through the nature of a transfer and the questions posed by the decision in *Lindqvist* (see para.8–08, above).

8–58 *Step 2.* In assessing whether an adequate level of protection applies the data controller will be expected to consider whether any Community findings of adequacy apply or the importing organisation has elected to join the Safe Harbor if the option is open to it. In the absence of comfort on either of those grounds the controller should make an adequacy assessment in relation to the particular transfer.

The controller should review the criteria set out in the Act and derived from the Directive, in particular:

- the nature of the personal data;
- the country of origin of the data and the country of final destination;
- the purpose(s) of the proposed transfer;
- the law in force in, any international obligations of, or relevant codes of conduct applicable to the country of final destination;
- the period during which the data are intended to be processed;
- any security measures taken in respect of the data.

In order to do this the controller must have regard to two facets of the adequacy assessment, general adequacy criteria and legal adequacy criteria. It is accepted that if the general adequacy assessment shows that the particular transfer is low risk then there may be less need to investigate the question of legal adequacy as the controller may be satisfied that the transfer may be safely made.

In assessing general adequacy the nature of the transfer, i.e. the data involved, the purpose, and any security measures taken should be reviewed. In assessing legal adequacy the position of the third country, i.e. the country of destination, the legal system in that country, including any relevant codes of conduct in force should be reviewed. The two parts, both of which have to be considered by exporting controllers, provide that an overall balanced assessment of adequacy is made in relation to the particular transfer proposed. The controller should then review the position in the importing country to assess the degree of protection offered to the data. The Commissioner recognises that in most ordinary circumstances such an undertaking would be outwith the resource or expertise of the controller but suggests that an exporting controller might reasonably be expected to be aware of any obvious problems such as political instability and undertake the detailed assessment in some cases such as:

> "where the exporting controller is proposing to set up a permanent operation in a third country and anticipates making regular, large scale transfers to that country."

Exporting controllers may also consider some more general criteria and the following list of questions is suggested:

"(a) Has the third country adopted the OECD Guidelines? And if so what measures has it taken to implement them?

(b) Has the third country ratified Convention 108? And are there appropriate mechanisms in place for compliance with it?

(c) Does the third country have a data protection regime in place which meets the standards set out in the Article 29 Working Party document adopted 24 July 1998 (WP 12)?

(d) Does the third country have any legal framework for the protection of the rights and freedoms of individuals generally?

(e) Does the third country recognise the general rule of law and, in particular, the ability of parties to contract and bind themselves under contracts?

(f) More specifically, are there laws, rules or codes of practice (general or sectoral) which govern the processing of personal data?"

At the conclusion of this exercise the data controller who determines that there is adequate protection may make the transfer, subject to ensuring that any transfer which originates from another Member State meets the criteria required by that State. If adequacy cannot be established the controller should proceed to Step 3.

8–59 *Step 3.* Step 3 is an evaluation of the possibility of putting in place appropriate safeguards such as model contracts or binding corporate rules. The section includes a brief guide to the use of these tools. In respect of the model clauses it explains that any change to the model clauses, even where the change in wording is not material to the meaning, takes the contract outside the protection of the approval granted under para.9 of Sch.4. However the contract may still deliver an adequate level of protection. A contract need not be bilateral and a model contract used to engage several parties will remain within the approval as long as there is no change to the approved clauses.

If neither the model clauses nor binding corporate rules are available the controller should move on to Step 4 and consider the derogations or exemptions set out in Sch.4. The Guidance reviews and comments on the exemptions drawing on the Article 29 approach as set out in WP 114. It concludes that if the transfer falls into one of the derogations the transfer may be made. We have referred to the Commissioner's Guidance on the derogations where appropriate in the section of this chapter which covers the exemptions/derogations.

Section 5—International outsourcing to data processors located in a third country

8–60 This is a new section in the Commissioner's Guidance. It places more focus on satisfying the eighth as well as the seventh Principle than the Guidance Note which it replaces. It rehearses the basic requirements of Principle 7 and emphasises that, where processing of personal data is outsourced to a processor, the data controller remains responsible for compliance with the Principles. This includes the obligation on the controller to ensure that the processor provides appropriate security and is bound by a contract made or evidenced in writing. It suggests that an appropriate way of achieving compliance with both Principles is the use of the model contract for processor or controller to processor transfers, describing this option as possibly "attractive" in international outsourcings. However it recognises that this is not the only way to satisfy Principle 8 and other methods of establishing adequacy as set out under Step 2 of the Guidance may be acceptable. This rather suggests that reliance on the derogations is not considered appropriate. The Guidance only specifically refutes the use of the derogations in relation to one situation which is the argument that a transfer may be made without adequate protection where the transfer is necessary for the performance of a contract between the data controller and a person other than the data subject where such a contract is entered into at the data subject's request or is for the benefit of the data subject.[74] Apparently data controllers (in what appears to be an optimistic defiance of the clear wording and purpose of the derogation) sometimes argue to the Commissioner that this ground would apply where the controller wishes to outsource a function which is necessary for the fulfilment of the controller's obligation to the subject, for example an employer outsourcing its processing of payroll data. As would be expected the Commissioner points out that the outsourcing is to the benefit of the controller and not the employee, who is entitled to be paid wherever the data are processed.

8–61   Interestingly the Commissioner does not wholly close the door on the use of contracts which satisfy Principle 7 although it is clear that the controller who wishes to use such a contract as the basis of the outsourcing transfer must also be able to show that they have made "due diligence checks" in relation to the transfer. As this is an important issue for those outsourcing the relevant paragraph is quoted in full below:

> "5.7 In particular, the model clauses will not be necessary if the data controller establishes that there is adequacy as described in Step 2 of this guidance. In this respect the Commissioner's guidance is that compliance with the Seventh Principle will go some way towards satisfying the adequacy requirements of the Eighth Principle (given the continuing contractual relationship between the parties and the data controller's continued liability for data protection compliance under the Act). However, the Commissioner would still expect the data controller to make due diligence checks in relation to the data processor and conduct some examination of the type of matters usually looked at in relation to adequacy (e.g. the nature of the data, the country in which the data processor is located and the security arrangements in that third country) [*see Step 2.4 and 2.5 for all the adequacy criteria to be taken into account when adducing adequacy*] If such due diligence and analysis did not reveal any particular risks in relation to the transfer, then the controller-processor relationship and security measures implemented further to compliance with the Seventh Principle would be likely to ensure adequacy and, therefore, the transfer would be able to proceed in compliance with the Eighth Principle."

---

[74] DPA para.3 of Sch.4.

Accordingly the Commissioner will no longer be satisfied with the adoption of clauses which satisfy Principle 7[75] but will also require that the controller conducts (and retains evidence of) a risk assessment in relation to the processor and the jurisdiction.

The guidance also considers the position sub-processors, although it stops short of producing precedent clauses. It advises controllers to ensure that the sub-contracting of processing must not be carried out without the consent of the controller; that the sub-processor should be bound to at least the same standards of security as the main processor and any adequacy issues addressed. The Commissioner emphasises that, as the controller remains responsible it should retain control of any sub-processor. This Guidance will therefore strengthen the negotiating position of any controller dealing with a processor who wishes to retain the freedom to appoint sub-processors of its choice. The question of the appointment of processors, sub-processors and the range of contractual options open to the parties is dealt with in Ch.5, above in relation to Principle 7.

Fair processing and overseas transfers

8–62   The provision of information to a data subject about the implications of any cross-border transfer of their personal data is likely to be part of the provision of the "specified information" required by the fair processing code.

The first Principle provides, inter alia, that data are not to be treated as being processed fairly unless the data subject is provided with certain information at the time that the data are gathered from him or, if the data are obtained by another route (presumably purchase or transfer from another data controller), either before the first processing or disclosure or as soon as practicable thereafter.

The information to be provided to the data subject is as follows:

(a) The identity of the data controller;

(b) the identity of any nominated representative;

(c) the purpose or purposes for which the data are intended to be processed;

(d) any further information which is necessary, having regard to the specific circumstances in which the data are or are to be processed, to enable processing in respect of the data subject to be fair.

The "any further information" requirement would appear to encompass providing the data subject with information about any non-obvious country to which his/her personal data may be transferred and the implications of such a transfer.

In practice, therefore, it is likely that the specified information requirements of the first Principle and the consent condition of Sch.4 will be dealt with in tandem so that data controllers develop specific written or spoken procedures which both convey information about any intended overseas transfer to the potential data subject and obtain his or her consent. This might be achieved, for example, by providing the data subject with a written notice in duplicate detailing the specified information and asking for the return of one copy signed to indicate consent.

---

[75] See Ch.5, above for precedent clauses which can be used in contracts between processors and controllers.

ELECTORAL ROLL

8–63 A prohibition on the transfer of personal data was included in the Representation of the People (England and Wales) (Amendment) Regulations 2002 (SI 2002/1871). There was always a cogent argument that this prohibition contravened the Directive and the prohibition has now been repealed by the Representation of the People (England and Wales) (Amendment No. 2) Regulations 2006 which took effect on May 3, 2007.[76] The Regulations were passed to limit the use and disclosure of data taken from the electoral roll, following the judgment in the case of *Robertson v Wakefield*.[77]

Regulation 92(8) provided that a person who obtained a full copy of the register may have it processed for them by a processor but under reg.92(8) the processor had to be one who carries on business in the EEA and the processor could not transmit the data outside the EEA for processing. This provision was therefore a prohibition on the transfer of the register outside the EEA for processing. Curiously the prohibition did not apply to the transfer to a controller outside the EEA. As noted earlier the Directive provides for findings of adequacy by the Commission in respect of third countries and for the sanctioning of exports where the transfer takes place under an approved contract. Moreover the Directive provides in Art.31 that the Commission may adopt measures which shall take effect immediately. It follows that the prohibition in the Regulations contravened EU law and would have been open to attack on that basis.

8–64 Schedule 4 outlines the exemptions to the eighth Principle. The Schedule permits cross-border transfers of personal data without reference to the eighth Principle (and thus potentially to countries or territories with "inadequate" levels of protection) in the following circumstances:

1. The data subject has given his consent to the transfer.

2. The transfer is necessary:

   (a) for the performance of a contract between the data subject and the data controller; or
   (b) for the taking of steps at the request of the data subject with a view to his entering into a contract with the data controller.

3. The transfer is necessary:

   (a) for the conclusion of a contract between the data controller and a person other than the data subject which:

      (i) is entered into at the request of the data subject; or
      (ii) is in the interests of the data subject; or

   (b) for the performance of such a contract.

4. (1) The transfer is necessary for reasons of substantial public interest.

   (2) The Secretary of State may by order specify:

---

[76] SI 2006/2910.
[77] See Ch.2, above for a full discussion of the case. *Brian Robertson v Wakefield City Council* [2001] EWHC Admin 915.

    (a) circumstances in which a transfer is to be taken for the purposes of sub-paragraph (1) to be necessary for reasons of substantial public interest, and

    (b) circumstances in which a transfer which is not required by or under an enactment is not to be taken for the purpose of sub-paragraph (1) to be necessary for reasons of substantial public interest.

5. The transfer:

    (a) is necessary for the purpose of, or in connection with, any legal proceedings (including prospective legal proceedings);

    (b) is necessary for the purpose of obtaining legal advice; or

    (c) is otherwise necessary for the purposes of establishing, exercising or defending legal rights.

6. The transfer is necessary in order to protect the vital interests of the data subject.

7. The transfer is of part of the personal data on a public register and any conditions subject to which the register is open to inspection are complied with by any person to whom the data are or may be disclosed after the transfer.

8. The transfer is made on terms which are of a kind approved by the Commissioner as ensuring adequate safeguards for the rights and freedoms of data subjects.

9. The transfer has been authorised by the Commissioner as being made in such a manner as to ensure adequate safeguards for the rights and freedoms of data subjects.

EXEMPTIONS OR DEROGATIONS

8–65 Schedule 4 to the 1998 Act, following Art.26(1) of the Directive, sets out a limited number of situations in which an exemption from the "adequacy" requirement for third country transfers may apply. The interpretative provisions in Pt 2 of Sch.1 indicate that the eighth Principle simply does not apply to transfers covered by one or more of the criteria set out in Sch.4.

These exemptions, like most of the exemptions to general principles in the 1998 Act, are tightly drawn. Broadly speaking, they cover three situations—first, where the risks to the data subject are relatively small; secondly, where other interests (public interests) override the data subject's rights; and thirdly where the transfer benefits the data subject.

There are many similarities between the exemptions set out in Sch.4 and the conditions for processing set out in Schs. 2 and 3. In some cases, the provisions are identical. The interpretative provisions[78] reserve the right of the Secretary of State to make orders directing that transfers prima facie falling within the list of exemptions may still be governed by the eighth Principle. The first of the exemptions

---

[78] 1998 Act Sch.1 Pt 2 para.14.

in Sch.4 covers cases where the data subject gives his/her consent to the proposed transfer.

Article 26(1)(a) of the Directive refers to the data subject giving his/her unambiguous consent. The word "unambiguous" does not appear in the relevant provision in Sch.4 to the 1998 Act. Article 2(h) of the Directive, which contains the definition of consent, states that it must be freely given, specific and informed. The requirement that consent is informed may be particularly significant as it may mean that the data subject must be properly informed of the particular risk arising from his/her data being transferred to a country lacking adequate protection. Interestingly the Information Commissioner refers only to the definition of consent in the Directive in the relevant section of the Guidance of June 2006.

There are clearly "grey areas" relating to consent and the extent to which it is "freely given", "specific" and "informed". A job applicant, for example, applying for a job with a multinational company and being asked for consent to the transfer of his/her personal data overseas to a country with an "inadequate" data protection regime is not readily going to refuse such consent, and both the Article 29 Working Party and the UK Commissioner in guidance on employment matters have indicated their view that such consent may not be "freely given". The Commissioner quotes the Article 29 comment that "relying on consent may. . .prove to be a 'false good solution', simple at first glance but in reality complex and cumbersome".

The Working Party suggests that the "consent" exemption could be useful in cases where the transferor has direct contact with the data subject and where the necessary information could be easily provided and unambiguous consent obtained.

Contractual requirements

8–66   The second exemption covers transfers necessary for the performance of a contract between the data subject and the controller (or the implementation of pre-contractual measures taken in response to the data subject's request).

Thus a data controller relying upon this condition will only be able to transfer personal data overseas if the contract relied upon is between the data controller and data subject.

The third exemption covers transfers necessary for the conclusion or performance of a contract concluded in the interest of the data subject and entered into at the request of the data subject between the controller and a third party.

The second and third exemptions appear potentially quite wide, but their application in practice is likely to be limited by the "necessity test": all of the data transferred must be necessary for the performance of the contract. Thus if additional non-essential data are transferred or if the purpose of the transfer is not the performance of the contract but rather some other purpose (follow-up marketing, for example) the exemption will be lost. With respect to pre-contractual situations, this would only include situations initiated by the data subject (such as a request for information about a particular service) and not those resulting from marketing approaches made by the data controller.

In spite of these caveats, these second and third exemptions are not without impact. They are applicable, for example, to those transfers necessary to reserve an airline ticket for a passenger or to transfers of personal data necessary for the operation of an international bank or credit card payment. Indeed, Art.26(1)(c) of the Directive provides that the exemption for contracts "in the interest of the data subject" specifically covers the transfer of data about the beneficiaries of bank payments, who, although data subjects, may often not be party to a contract with the transferring controller.

Substantial public interest

8–67   The fourth exemption permits transfers which are necessary for reasons of substantial public interest.

The Working Party suggests that this may cover certain limited transfers between public administrations, although they warn that care must be taken not to interpret this provision too widely. A simple public interest justification for a transfer does not suffice, it must be a question of substantial public interest.

Recital 58, upon which the exemptions are based, actually provides that there should be an exemption:

> "where protection of an important public interest so requires, for example in cases of international transfers of data between tax or customs administrations or between services—competent for social security matters."

This clearly suggests, therefore, that data transfers between tax or customs administrations or between services responsible for social security will generally be covered. Transfers between supervisory bodies in the financial services sector may also benefit from the exemption.

The fourth exemption contains a provision for the Secretary of State to specify by order when relevant transfers are and are not to be taken as necessary for reasons of substantial public interest.

The Immigration and Asylum Act 1998 provides that for the purposes of para.4(1) of Sch.4 the provision of identification data under s.13 is a transfer of personal data which is necessary for reasons of substantial public interest. The section applies where a person is to be removed from the UK to a country of which he is not a national or a citizen, but will not be admitted unless identity data relating to him is provided by the Secretary of State. This appears to be the only time the power has been exercised. The Home Office discussion documents on subordinate legislation did not contain any proposals for such orders.

Legal proceedings

8–68   The fifth exemption covers transfers which are necessary in connection with legal proceedings, for obtaining legal advice, or for establishing, exercising or defending legal rights.

This exemption is identical to the sixth condition for the legitimate processing of sensitive data. Its terms are discussed at Ch.6, above. Clearly again, the satisfaction of this condition for the legitimate processing of sensitive data will also permit the cross-border transfer of such data without consideration of the restrictions in the eighth Principle.

The data subject's vital interests

8–69   The sixth exemption concerns transfers necessary in order to protect the vital interests of the data subject. An obvious example of such a transfer would be the urgent transfer of medical records to a third country where a tourist who had previously received medical treatment in the EU has suffered an accident or has become dangerously ill.

It should be borne in mind, however, that the phrase "vital interests" is not without problems. This exemption is of course identical to the fourth condition for legitimate processing contained in Sch.2. Its terms are discussed in Ch.6, above. Yet again, the satisfaction of this condition for the legitimate processing of sensitive data will also "passport" the cross-border transfer of such data without consideration of the restrictions in the eighth Principle.

In the Guidance, the Commissioner emphasises the view that this exemption may only be relied on where the data transfer is necessary for matters of life and death.

Public registers

8–70   The seventh exemption concerns transfers made from registers intended by law for consultation by the public, provided that in the particular case the conditions for consultation are fulfilled. The Working Party suggest that the intention of this exemption is that where a register in a Member State is available for public consultation or by persons demonstrating a legitimate interest, then the fact that the person who has the right to consult the register is actually situated in a third country, and that the act of consultation in fact involves a data transfer, should not prevent the information being transmitted to him.

Recital 58 of the Directive qualifies the exemption in the following manner:

> "where the transfer is made from a register established by law and intended for consultation by the public or persons having a legitimate interest; whereas in this case such a transfer should not involve the entirety of the data or entire categories of the data contained in the register and, when the register is intended for consultation by persons having a legitimate interest,—the transfer should be made only at the request of those persons or if they are to be the recipients."

Thus the Directive makes it clear that entire registers or entire categories of data from registers should not be permitted to be transferred under this exemption. Given these restrictions, this exemption should not be considered to be a general exemption for the transfer of public register data. For example, it is reasonably clear that mass transfers of public register data for commercial purposes or the trawling of publicly available data for the purpose of profiling specific individuals would not benefit from the exemption.

The authority of the Commissioner

8–71   The eighth and ninth exemptions empower the Commissioner to authorise or approve certain types of cross-border transfers of personal data. The exemptions permit such transfers when:

(a) the transfer is made on terms which are of a kind approved by the Commissioner as ensuring adequate safeguards for the rights and freedoms of data subjects;

(b) the transfer has been authorised by the Commissioner as being made in such a manner as to ensure adequate safeguards for the rights and freedoms of data subjects.

The Commissioner issued formal approval of the EU approved contractual terms under para.8. It is also possible for data controllers to seek such approval of contractual terms or authorisation for particular transfers by application to the Commissioner as well as for the Commissioner to issue such approval or authority on his own initiative after conducting his own investigations.

The Commissioner must consider any applications made by or on behalf of exporting controllers for approval or authorisation under paras 8 or 9, respectively, of Sch.4 to the Act. However, exporting controllers should note that in the past such references have not been encouraged for individual contracts although consent will be given to the adoption of binding corporate rules under this power.

Contract clauses and authorisations

8–72 The current Guidance also states that the controller is entitled to make his own determination on adequacy and a contract can be part of the mechanism used to provide adequacy. If the controller proceeds in this way he does not need to make any submission to the Commissioner. If the controller does wish to make a submission to the Commissioner controllers will have to be able to show that:

(i) they have applied the adequacy test to the particular transfer and reached a negative conclusion;

(ii) they have considered and discounted all other cases where the eighth Principle does not apply as set out in Sch.4 to the Act; and

(iii) they are satisfied that the terms in respect of which they seek the Commissioner's approval or the circumstances for which they seek authorisation ensure adequate safeguards for the rights and freedoms of data subjects.

Any such approvals or authorisations must be referred to the Commission and other Member States for EU-wide approval or rejection in accordance with paras 2–4 of Art.26 of the Directive. Section 54(7) of the 1998 Act provides:

"The Commissioner shall inform the European Commission and the supervisory authorities in other EEA States:

(a) of any approvals granted for the purposes of paragraph 8 of Schedule 4.

(b) of any authorisations granted for the purposes of paragraph 9 of that Schedule."

Accordingly the UK Act does not require that data controllers who make their own assessment of adequacy or establish their own set of contractual protections submit anything to the Commissioner for authorisation. This contrasts with the position in many other Member States. As noted in para.8–05, above the Commission has raised the question of whether the UK is meeting its obligations under the Directive, given the reluctance of the regulator to approve individual contractual arrangements.

The basic prohibition on transfer to third countries which do not provide an adequate means of protection is found in Art.25(1). Art.25(2) sets out the considerations which are relevant to a finding of adequacy. The remainder of the Article provides for determinations of adequacy by the Commission or Member States. It is silent on the question of whether a data controller is entitled to make its own determination on the issue. Article 26 provides for derogations, among them Art.26(2) which provides that:

> "Without prejudice to paragraph 1, a Member State may authorise a transfer or set of transfers of personal data to a third country which does not ensure adequate protection within the meaning of Article 25(2), where the controller adduces adequate safeguards with respect to the protection of the privacy and fundamental rights and freedoms of individuals and as regards the exercise of the corresponding rights; such safeguards may in particular result from appropriate contractual clauses."

Member States must inform the Commission of any such authorisations. Although the Commission has criticised those countries which accept self assessment of adequacy by controllers and lamented the generally low level of authorisations notified to it, it has stopped short of threatening infraction proceedings.

ENFORCEMENT

8–73   Enforcement of the provisions relating to cross-border transfers is by way of the Commissioner serving an enforcement notice in accordance with s.40 of the 1998 Act. For a detailed discussion of the Commissioner's powers of enforcement see Ch.20, below.

PRACTICAL TOOLS

Case studies

Case 1: A transfer of sensitive data in the airline industry

8–74   A Portuguese citizen books a ticket at a Lisbon travel agency for a flight on board an airline based in Country B. The data collected include details of the fact that the citizen is disabled and uses a wheelchair. The data are entered on an international computer reservation system, and from there are downloaded by the airline onto its passenger database located in Country B, where they are retained indefinitely. The airline plans to use the data to provide better service to the passenger if he were to travel with the airline in the future, as well as for internal management planning purposes.

Step one: assessing the adequacy of the protection:

(a) The relevant applicable rules: Although there is an international code of conduct applying to the data held on the computer reservation system, no data protection rules are in place regarding the data held on the airline's own database in Country B.

(b) Evaluation of the content of the applicable rules: None are applicable.

(c) Evaluating the effectiveness of the protection: Not applicable.

Verdict protection levels in Country B are not adequate, particularly given the sensitivity of the data involved.

Step two: searching for a solution. The transfer of data onto the computer reservation system and its use by the airline for the purpose of providing the appropriate service to the disabled passenger for the flight in question is a transfer necessary for the performance of the contract between the passenger and the airline (Art.26(1)(b)). However, the continued retention of the data (including sensitive data about the data subject's health) on the airline's database cannot be justified on these grounds. The transfer of data to the airline must therefore be covered by a different exemption.

Data subject consent would seem to be the best solution. Consent could be obtained by the travel agent in Lisbon on behalf of the airline. The risks of the data being held in Country B should be pointed out to the data subject, as should the fact that the transfer and retention of data in the airline's own database is not necessary for the reasons pertaining to the specific flight being booked.

Case 2: A transfer of marketing list data

8–75 A company in the Netherlands specialises in the creation of mailing lists. Using many disparate sources of public information available in the Netherlands, together with client lists rented from several other Dutch companies, the resulting lists purport to include individuals fitting a particular socio-economic profile. These lists are then sold by the Dutch company to client companies not only in the Netherlands and the EU, but in a multitude of other third countries. The recipient client companies then use the lists (which include postal addresses, telephone numbers, and often email addresses) to contact the individuals on the lists with a view to selling a bewildering array of different products and services. A large number of individuals included in the lists have complained to the Dutch data protection authority about the marketing approaches they have received.

Step one: assessing the adequacy of the protection:

(a) The relevant applicable rules: Some of the client companies who buy in the mailing lists offered by the Dutch company are based in countries which have general data protection legislation in place which includes a right for individuals to opt out of receiving such marketing approaches. Others are in countries without such laws, but are members of self-regulatory associations which have developed data protection codes. Others are subject to no data protection rules at all.

(b) Evaluation of the content of the applicable rules: This single case would require the evaluation of a multitude of different laws and codes. If the Netherlands-based company is to maintain its approach of selling or renting its lists to companies based in any country of the world, then there are necessarily going to be situations where the level of protection is not adequate.

Step two: searching for a solution. In this example, because the data are collected from public sources and without any direct contact with the data subject it would be very problematic for the Netherlands company to seek consent from each and every data subject to his/her inclusion on the mailing lists. In view of this, it is unlikely that any of the exemptions in the Directive are likely to be useful.

The Netherlands company has two possibilities, which could be used as alternatives or together. The first possibility would be for it to limit this trade in mailing lists to companies in jurisdictions which clearly appeared to ensure adequate protection by virtue of laws or effective self-regulatory instruments.

The second possibility would be to require contractual undertakings from all client companies (or at least those in "non-adequate" jurisdictions) regarding the protection of the data transferred. These contractual arrangements seek to create a situation under which the Netherlands company remained liable under Netherlands law for any violation of Data Protection Principles resulting from the actions of the client company to whom the mailing lists had been transferred.

Such a contractual solution, if properly implemented, would help overcome the effective barrier to trade that the lack of adequate data protection in certain third countries creates.

Case study of Multinational Company ABC

8–76   Note: This case study is based upon the systems introduced by a real multinational company to tackle the obligations arising from the Directive in respect of cross-border transfers of personal data.

ABC has its headquarters in the US and operates in over 40 countries. It has 110,000 employees. It has what it describes as a "significant presence" in the EC and has 400 legal entities worldwide. It is a truly global organisation. It is a processor of its customer's personal data and the controller of its own data. It has a need to move data across borders. The company does not regard personal data as generally distinct from other data the company is handling. The company acknowledges that it wishes to transfer data between different legal entities forming part of ABC and also to non-ABC entities which are based in countries with widely differing data protection regimes.

ABC's solution is the "ABC global data protection system" based upon a global data protection Code of Practice. Each individual legal entity within ABC is required to join and adhere to this system. The system is described as EU Directive–compliant. External entities are required to enter into contracts requiring adherence with the global data protection system.

ABC have categorised a number of different types of transfer, namely:

(a) ABC controller to ABC controller;

(b) ABC controller to non-ABC controller;

(c) ABC controller to ABC processor;

(d) ABC controller to non-ABC processor;

(e) ABC processor to ABC processor;

(f) ABC processor to non-ABC processor.

ABC draws a strong distinction between the roles of processor and controller and their respective roles and responsibilities. The different transfers mentioned above are consequently governed by different Principles.

For controller to controller transfers ABC requires that the transferee controller has similar data handling requirements. For controller to processor transfers ABC requires a written agreement which ensures compliance with confidentiality and security requirements.

With respect to cross-border transfers ABC permits only:

1. transfers within the EEA;

2. transfers to another ABC entity;

3. other specifically permitted and regulated transfers.

Compliance with the global data protection system is ensured via:

1. a network of data protection representatives;

2. operational mechanisms;

3. complaint investigation and resolution procedures;

4. compliance auditing.

ADDITIONAL INFORMATION

Derivations

8–77 • Directive 95/46 (See App.B):

    (a) Arts 25 and 26 (transfer of personal data to third countries).
    (b) Recitals 56, 57, 58, 59, 60.

    • Council Decision of Europe Convention of January 28, 1981 for the Protection of Individuals with regard to automatic processing of Personal Data: Art.12 (transborder data flows).

    • Data Protection Act 1984: s.12 (overseas transfers).

    • Organisation for Economic Co-operation and Development Guidelines: Annex Part One 1(c) defines "transborder flows of personal data", Part Three 15, 16, 17, 18 (free flow and legitimate expectation).

Hansard references

8–78   Vol.586, No.108, CWH 25, Lords Grand Committee, February 23, 1998
Adequacy, proposal that contracts should be included as part of programme to achieve adequacy rejected.

Vol.586, No.110, col.124, Lords Grand Committee, February 25, 1998
Derogations.

ibid., cols 129, 130
Data matching codes and preliminary assessment.

Commons Standing Committee D, June 4, 1998, col.317
Transfers for reasons of substantial public interest.

Vol.315, No.198, col.576, Commons Third Reading, July 2, 1998
Partial definition of transfer and a provision setting out the geographical scope of provisions in clause 5 withdrawn.

Case law

8–79   Case C – 101/01 reference to the European Court under Article 234 **Bodil Lindqvist** [2003] ECR I–12971
PNR Judgement ECJ C–317/04, C–318/04 (Opinion of the Advocate General)

CHAPTER 9

Notification

INTRODUCTION

9–01 The function of the public register of notifications is transparency. Transparency, or openness about the uses of personal data, is a key element in data protection. This is emphasised by the importance attached to the rights of subject access and the fair obtaining and processing rules. However, transparency was not the only function of registration under the 1984 Act. Registration under the 1984 Act had a regulatory element to it; applications could be refused where the Registrar believed that the applicant would not comply with the Principles. Under the 1998 Act the Commissioner cannot refuse to place any entry in the register, as long as the application is properly made.

HISTORY OF REGISTRATION/NOTIFICATION

9–02 The concept of a public register of processing operations was a central recommendation of the Lindop Report in 1978 (Report of the Committee on Data Protection—Cmnd.7341). At that time, computing was confined to a few large powerful organisations. It was judged that such powers should not be wielded in secret. The obligation for such organisations to have their processing "vetted", then made public through the system of registration, was seen as a bulwark against the encroachment of Big Brother. This thinking persisted throughout the genesis of the 1984 Act. Accordingly, when the 1984 Act was introduced, the registration provisions were seen as a core element of the regime. Those provisions required each data user to provide descriptions of the purposes of his processing, the data held for those purposes, the sources of the data, disclosures made from the data, and any overseas transfers made. Much of the early work of the Registrar's office was devoted to the development of a comprehensive system of registration in which this information was provided by way of standard descriptions. The aim was to produce a system of registration which was capable of compressing the detail of every conceivable computing usage into a standard format for publication. That aim was to some extent successfully accomplished in the early years of the Registrar's office. But the fact that registration became a legal obligation just as the availability of the personal computer was changing the landscape of computing forever meant that the exercise had a Canute-like quality from the beginning.

By the time the second Registrar, Elizabeth France, was appointed in 1995, the registration system had come to be widely regarded as burdensome, bureaucratic and unnecessarily detailed. The problems of the registration system in terms of content and penetration were widely acknowledged. Estimates of the numbers of those who should have registered but never did so varied, but ranged from 250,000 to over 1 million. The application forms for registration were complex and detailed for data users to complete and difficult for data subjects to follow. In fairness, it must be recognised that no registration system could have kept pace with the rate of change in computing over the relevant period.

9–03   The Registrar's office made efforts to ameliorate the problems with the introduction of a telephone application system based on the use of "templated" applications. In 1996, the Registrar produced detailed proposals for a radical simplification of the registration system but pending the change in the law decided not to implement major changes to the system. The Government was determined to produce a system as simple as possible commensurate with compliance with the Directive. In August 1998, the Home Office issued a Consultation Paper entitled *Subordinate Legislation: Notification Regulations* in which it described its approach to notification thus:

> "The Government considers that the primary purpose of notification under the new data protection scheme should be to promote transparency, that is providing to the public and the Commissioner a clear description in general terms of the processing of personal data. Consistently with proper implementation of the Directive, the Government and the Registrar want the new notification system to be simple, straightforward and readily understandable. It should be useful to members of the public, data controllers and the Commissioner.
>
> Where appropriate, use will be made of the valuable experience gained in operating the registration scheme established under the Data Protection Act 1984. However, the new proposals reflect the fact that notification will be an element of the main regime rather than triggering application of that regime. They also reflect the principles of better regulation—in particular simplifying procedures and making the result more accessible to all."

The opportunity to overhaul the registration system was not missed. After the 1998 Act came into effect a new system was adopted with the old system being gradually phased out. The two systems, the new and the old, ran in parallel until March 2003 when the last register entries under the old system finally disappeared.

The details of the notification scheme do not appear in the primary legislation. The 1998 Act sets out the outline provisions. The detail is to be found in the Data Protection (Notification and Notification Fees) Regulations 2000[1] and administrative arrangements made by the Commissioner. These are set out in the *Notification Handbook: A Complete Guide to Notification*. The Regulations include some crucial aspects of the system, for example exemptions from the obligation to register.

SUMMARY OF MAIN POINTS

9–04   (a)   Notification is not a control mechanism; the Commissioner cannot refuse a notification and exemption from notification confers no exemption from other aspects of the Act.

---

[1] SI 2000/188.

(b) The information to be notified covers the data, the purposes of processing, data subjects, recipients and overseas transfers but does not include sources of the data.

(c) Security information must be notified to the Commissioner but does not appear on the public register.

(d) There is a provision for some processing to be designated "assessable processing". Such processing must be notified to the Commissioner before the commencement of the processing for the Commissioner to assess. No categories of processing have been designated as assessable processing to date.

(e) Manual data does not have to be notified unless it falls into an assessable processing category.

(f) Those who are exempt from making an entry on the public register must still be able to provide an inquirer with information equivalent to that contained in the register, alternatively, voluntary notification is allowed if the data controller wants to make a public statement of processing available.

(g) Only one register entry per data controller is permitted and purpose titles may usually only be used once.

(h) Public authorities must state their status on the register following an amendment introduced by the Freedom of Information Act 2000.

(i) An annual fee is payable for an entry in the register.

(j) Data processors are not required to notify, unlike computer bureau which were required to register under the 1984 Act.

THE DUTY TO NOTIFY

9–05 Section 17(1) provides that personal data must not be processed unless an entry in respect of the data controller is included in the register maintained by the Commissioner. Under s.21(1) the data controller is guilty of an offence if such processing takes place. The details to be included in the register are specified in regulations or administrative arrangements made under them.

Scope of duty

9–06 The duty is imposed on all data controllers unless an exemption can be claimed. Controllers do not have to notify if:

(a) The personal data are exempt from Pt III of the Act. This applies to data held for personal, domestic and recreational purposes under s.36 or if the purposes of national security require that the personal data should not be registered (i.e. should not be put into the public domain[2]). Personal data which are exempt from Pt III are also exempt from prior assessment.

---

[2] s.28.

(b) The sole purpose of the processing is the maintenance of a public register under s.17(4). In theory such processing may still be subject to prior assessment but in fact this would be most unlikely.

(c) The data are manual data covered by the Act. This exemption is provided by s.17(2). Such data may still be subject to prior assessment.

(d) The data fall under one of the exemptions to the duty to notify in the Notification Regulations.

Processing exempt from notification

Exemptions under the Act

9–07   These cover:

(i) Any personal data if the exemption is required for the purpose of national security (s.28(1)).

(ii) Personal data processed by an individual only for the purposes of that individual's personal, family or household affairs (s.36).

(iii) Processing whose sole purpose is the maintenance of a public register (s.17(4)). "Public register" is defined in s.70 as any register which is open to public inspection or open to inspection by any person having a legitimate interest either by or under an enactment or in pursuance of any international agreement.

(iv) Manual data which fall within the definition of a "relevant filing system".

Before the end of the first transitional period in October 2001 there were a number of further transitional exemptions from the obligation to register but these have now been exhausted.

Other exemptions

9–08   Further exemptions may be prescribed by the Secretary of State but only in cases where it appears to him that the processing is unlikely to prejudice the rights and freedoms of data subjects. In order to comply with Art.18(2) of the Directive which sets out the circumstances in which exemptions from notification may be permitted the Secretary of State must specify:

(i) the purposes of the processing;

(ii) the data or categories of data undergoing processing;

(iii) the category or categories of data subject;

(iv) the recipients or categories of recipients to whom the data are to be disclosed;

(v) the length of time the data are to be stored.

The proposals in the consultation paper were for the following exemptions:

   (i) payroll, some personnel and work planning;

  (ii) purchase and sales administration;

 (iii) advertising, marketing and public relations (with the possibility of also exempting promoting the data controller's own business activities but not independent direct marketing);

 (iv) general administration (including any word processing not covered by a more specific exempted purpose);

  (v) unincorporated members' clubs as in the 1984 Act s.33(2)(a) exemption;

 (vi) non-profit seeking bodies with a political, philosophical, religious or trade-union aim (as described in para.4 of Sch.3); and

(vii) small voluntary organisations.

9–09 In the event four exemptions from notification were set out in the Notification Regulations. A data controller must comply with the remainder of the Act even if he is exempt from notification. Moreover, if requested he must be able to produce a description of his processing in accordance with s.24. The exemptions will not apply if the processing is assessable processing[3] although no categories of assessable processing have been declared.

The four categories of exempt processing are:

- processing for staff administration;

- processing for advertising marketing and public relations;

- processing for accounts and record keeping;

- processing of membership information by non-profit making bodies.

In each case the nature of the processing, the data held and the range of acceptable disclosures are described in the Regulations and the data controller must stay within those bounds to be able to claim the exemption. In each case the exemption is not lost where disclosures are made under the non-disclosure exemptions or where they are required by any enactment, rule of law or order of the court.[4]

For each exemption the purpose of the processing, the types of personal data, the types of data subject, the nature of the permitted disclosures and the length of time for which the data are to be held are set out. If the data controller processes outside these parameters he will lose the benefit of the exemption.

9–10 *Staff administration.* This is described as processing for the purpose of:

"appointments or removals, pay, discipline, superannuation, work management or other personnel matters in relation to the staff of the data controller".[5]

---

[3] SI 2000/188 reg.3.

[4] SI 2000/188 reg 3(b).

[5] 1998 Act Sch.1 para 2(a).

The data subjects may be past, present or prospective members of staff. The exemption only applies to data held about the staff of the data controller, however. Staff include employees, office holders, workers under a contract for services and volunteers.[6]

The exemption therefore extends to not-for-profit organisations, such as charity shops, who use volunteers. Information may also be held on other data subjects where it is necessary for the data controller to process personal data about them for the exempt purpose. Thus, for example, data about the nearest relations of employees might be held for contact purposes.

The personal data which may be held about staff under this exemption are limited to name, address, identifiers and information as to qualifications, work experience and pay or "other matters the processing of which is necessary for the exempt purposes".[7] Potentially this covers a wide range of information. Information about health matters, criminal convictions, trade union membership and other sensitive data are often held in relation to personnel and superannuation matters. Data may be disclosed to third parties where it is necessary to make the disclosure in order to carry out the exempt purpose, or where the disclosure is made with the consent of the data subject, or under the non-disclosure exemptions. The non-disclosure exemption means that the data may also be disclosed where the particular conditions are fulfilled in the following cases:

- where there are statutory requirements or court orders;

- for the purposes of national security;

- for the purposes of the prevention or apprehension of offenders, prevention or detection of crime, assessment or collection of any tax or duty;

- for journalistic, literary or artistic purposes;

- for the purpose of or in connection with any legal proceedings or for the purpose of obtaining legal advice or establishing legal rights;

- where the data controller is obliged to make the data public.

To stay within the exemption from notification, the staff data must not be kept beyond the ending of the relationship between the data subject and the controller unless and for so long as is necessary for the purpose of staff administration. However where the data are required for research and fall within the research exemptions it would presumably be possible for the data controller to continue to hold the data for research purposes within the terms of that exemption. In such a case a notification covering the research purpose would be required.

9–11 *Advertising, marketing and public relations.* This is described as processing for the purpose of:

---

[6] 1998 Act Sch.1 para.1: "workers" has the meaning given in the Trade Union and Labour Relations (Consolidation) Act 1992.
[7] SI 2000/188 Sch.1 para.2(c)(iii).

"advertising or marketing the data controller's business, activity, goods or services and promoting public relations in connection with that business or activity, or those goods or services."

The data subjects may be past, existing or prospective customers or suppliers or any other person in respect of whom it is necessary to process personal data for the exempt purpose. This would allow, for example, the processing of personal data about contacts for the purposes of public relations. It is not apparent on the face of it why suppliers have been included as data subjects. Organisations do not usually market to their suppliers as such (unless they hope to convert them to customers) but if the intention is to cover such eventualities they would be covered as prospective customers. The term "prospective" is a wide one, however, it is difficult to see how a narrower term could have been used.

The personal data are limited to name, address and other identifiers or information which it is necessary to process for the exempt purposes. The purpose description is therefore the main restricting factor on the processing which may be carried out under the exemption.

Disclosures are limited to those where the disclosure is necessary for the exempt purposes or is made with the consent of the data subject but includes savings for disclosures made under enactments and the non-disclosure exemptions as for staff administration (see above).

The limitations on retention of data are the same as for staff administration as described above.

9–12 *Accounts and records.*   This is described as processing for the purpose of:

"keeping accounts relating to any business or other activity carried on by the data controller, or deciding whether to accept any person as a customer or supplier, or keeping records of purchases, sales or other transactions for the purpose of ensuring that the requisite payments and deliveries are made or services provided by or to the data controller in respect of those transactions, or for the purpose of making financial or management forecasts to assist him in the conduct of such business or activity."

The data subjects may be past, existing or prospective customers or suppliers or any other person the processing of whose data is necessary for the exempt purposes. As noted above the term "prospective" is a wide term. The data may consist of names, addresses and other identifiers together with information as to financial standing or other data which it is necessary to process for the exempt purposes.

9–13 *Remote credit checks.*   The information relating to financial standing does not include personal data processed by or obtained from a credit reference agency. This provision gives rise to some potential problems. It could mean that a data controller who carries out remote credit checks which involve the automatic processing of personal data by a credit reference agency at the controller's request will not be able to claim the exemption even if he contributes no information and never downloads or otherwise retains the data, in other words does no more than buy the remote service. However, it can be argued that such an interpretation would be incompatible with the basic definitions of a data controller and the nature of the obligation to notify.

A data controller can only be exempt from notifying data which he would have a duty to notify in the first place. A data controller is one who determines the purposes for which and the manner in which data are to be processed. It can be argued that the remote user of a credit reference agency's services who has read-only or equivalent limited access does not determine the purposes and manner of the processing and is therefore not a data controller for the credit reference data within this definition. He will be a recipient of the data and the credit reference agency could be required to notify such customers as recipients of data. Moreover, it is possible that he may obtain information to be contained in personal data from the credit reference agency. Accordingly if he obtains and retains data from the agency he may lose the exemption, however, this cannot extend to the circumstances where he does not retain any data. Applying this line of reasoning it can be argued that he has no obligation to notify his relationship with the credit reference agency and if he has no obligation to notify he cannot be exempt from such an obligation. On this view therefore simply carrying out a remote credit check without retaining any data from it should not lose the exemption.

9–14   However, the guidance issued from the Commissioner's office advises that:

> "Your data classes are restricted to data which are necessary for your accounts and records. This excludes personal data processed by or obtained from a credit reference agency."

Thus the Commissioner supports the view implicit in the Regulations that the person buying the services of the credit reference agency becomes the data controller for the credit data irrespective of whether he retains or controls any data from the search. The Commissioner takes this view on the following basis:

> "that the remote user of a credit reference agency's services who has read-only or equivalent limited access is, in all practical cases, likely to be a data controller.
>   When he enters into an agreement with the credit reference agency and thereafter takes delivery of the equipment required and uses it for the purposes of carrying out credit checks, he decides both the purposes for which and the manner in which the personal data of those persons the subject of such credit checks are, or are to be, processed."

The Commissioner says that because of the wide definition of "processing" in the Act such a person is likely to fall within the definition of data controller even where the processing involved amounts to something less than obtaining or retention. The particular processing activity which may best describe the activity in question is, "consultation", if not "obtaining", "retrieval" or "use".

The Commissioner's view therefore is that even where the person merely buys the results of a search without contributing any data or exercising any control over the agency data the company can be argued to come within the definition of a data controller. This guidance was issued before the decision of the Court of Appeal in *Johnson v Medical Defence Union*,[8] which effectively undermines the approach taken by the Commissioner. In *Johnson* the member of staff employed by the MDU consulted the computer records of references to Mr Johnson, summarised the material on hard copy and then entered it into the computer again. The Court of Appeal held that there was no "processing" involved in that activity. It would seem to follow that if there is no processing of personal data the question of the identity of a data controller does not arise.

The rules relating to disclosures under the accounts exemption are the same as for the other exempt categories, that is disclosures can be made where necessary for the exempt purpose, with the consent of the data subject and under the non-disclosure exemptions. The data must not be retained after the end of the relationship or so long as is necessary for the exempt purpose.

9–15 *Processing by non-profit making organisations.* This is described as processing carried out by a body or association which is not established or conducted for profit and is:

> "for the purposes of establishing or maintaining membership of or support for the body or association or providing or administering activities for individuals who are either members of the body or association or have regular contact with it."

The data subjects may include not only the usual categories of past, existing or prospective members and persons in respect of whom it is necessary to process personal data for the exempt purpose but also any person who has regular contact with the body in connection with the exempt purposes. Accordingly charities are able to keep records of regular beneficiaries without losing the exemption. Interestingly, this appears to mean that the body will lose the benefit of the exemption if it retains records of those contacts who only donate or assist on a "one off" basis.

The personal data may consist of names, addresses and identifiers, information as to eligibility for membership and data necessary for the exempt purposes. As in the other exemptions, disclosures are limited to those made with consent, those necessary for the purpose and those made under the non-disclosure provisions. The data must not be retained beyond the ending of the relationship except so far as is necessary for the exempt purposes.

THE REGISTER

Contents of the register

9–16 Section 16(1) sets out the particulars which the data controller must specify in the public register. The particulars set out in s.16(1) are:

- name and address of data controller;
- identity of a representative (if any);

---

[8] [2007] 1 All E.R. 464.

- description of the personal data being processed and the categories of data subjects;
- description of the purposes of the data processing;
- description of the recipient or recipients of the data;
- names or description of the territories outside the EEA to which the data are to be transferred;
- statement of exempt processing.

Section 71 of the Freeedom of Information Act 2000 added a new provision to the rules concerning the register of notifications which requires public authorities to also include a statement of the fact that they are public authorities for the purpose of the FOIA.

Name and address of data controller

9–17   Under s.16(3) the address given for a registered company must be that of its registered office. The address of any other person carrying on a business must be that of his principal place of business in the United Kingdom The name should be the name by which the person is legally known: in the case of a registered company, its registered name rather than a trading name; in the case of an organisation other than a registered company, its full name as set out in its constitution or other formal document; in the case of an individual the name by which he is usually known.

Name and address of nominated representative

9–18   The previous registration system also included a non-statutory, contact name for use by the Registrar's office. A data user could chose to have correspondence about his entry sent to a nominated contact. This was a useful service for some data users. There is now a provision allowing a controller to include the name and address of a representative where he "has nominated a representative for the purposes of the Act". This is a new provision. It is not amplified in any other part of the Act. There is a requirement in s.5 that a person established overseas without a branch or agent in the jurisdiction who processes personal data in the United Kingdom other than merely for transit must nominate a representative. This appears to contemplate that a data controller may nominate a representative within the jurisdiction to deal with all or some of his data protection matters. Presumably the representative need not be an employee and might be a professional or specialist adviser who deals with data protection matters on behalf of clients. The inclusion of a named representative is not a substitute for the name of the data controller. It cannot be used as a method of avoiding the name appearing on the public register. It is to be included, if at all, as an additional piece of information.

Recipients

9–19   In the 1984 Act both sources and disclosures of personal data had to be registered. Sources no longer figure on the register and disclosures have been replaced by recipients. These are persons to whom data are disclosed other than in pursuance of a legal obligation.

Form of notification

9–20   The Regulations provide that the form of giving notification shall be determined by the Commissioner. Thus the detail of the data subjects, data classes, purposes, recipients, overseas transfers and security measures are determined by the Commissioner. The Commissioner also determines how changes in notification under the Act are to be presented. Information about the notification scheme is available from the Commissioner's office in the *Notification Handbook* or is available from the OIC website. The introduction to the Guidance makes clear that notification is not intended to be a detailed system:

> "It is not however intended nor is it practicable that the register should contain very detailed information about a data controller's processing. The aim is to keep the content at a general level, with sufficient detail to give an overall picture of the processing. More detail is only necessary to satisfy specific statutory requirements or where there is particular sensitivity."

The system remains purpose led, as it was under the 1984 Act. The system is template-based. When notifying online the controller selects the business type which most nearly matches his business from a list and an application template comes up which includes those purposes most commonly used by businesses of that type together with the data classes, subjects and recipients most commonly used in connection with each purpose. The controller can amend the template by adding or removing purposes or adding or removing other categories of information. Telephone applications follow the same pattern. If the application is made on an application form the controller may chose purposes and other categories from the standard lists. There are a number of standard purposes, data subject classes, data classes and recipients. If none of the standard purposes fit the applicant should describe the purpose in his own words.

As will be appreciated from the standardised nature of the system, the descriptions are presented in broad terms. Controllers are prohibited from transferring personal data to states outside the European Economic Area (that is, the European Union, Liechtenstein, Norway and Iceland) unless the rights of the individuals whom the data concerns will be adequately protected. The controller must specify the final destination of personal data if they are to be transferred indirectly through an EU State. The description of overseas transfers is the broadest of all. The applicant has a choice of registering either:

- none outside the EEA;

- worldwide; or

- naming up to 10 individual countries.

Statement of exempt processing

9–21   Where applicable, a notification must contain a statement that the controller also processes or intends to process personal data covered by a notification exemption or personal data which are part of a relevant filing system. This provision in s.16(1)(g) is new to the 1998 Act. There was no similar provision in the old Act. It reflects the fact that not all personal data have to be included on the public register. Section 17(2) exempts from notification manual data which are otherwise covered by the Act, that is data held as part of a relevant filing system or manual data otherwise held as part of an accessible record. Further exemptions are made in the Notification Regulations. A data controller may chose to include any of these categories of exempt data in his register entry on a voluntary basis (see section on voluntary notification below) but if he is registered and decides not to include them his entry must state that he has not done so. If he only holds data exempt from notification this does not apply. The statement of exempt processing on the register is:

> "This data controller also processes personal data which are exempt from notification."

Additional information in the register

9–22 Under s.19(2)(b) of the Act the Regulations may authorise or require the Commissioner to include other information in the register. Regulation 11 provides that the Commissioner may include:

- the registration number;
- the date the entry is treated as starting (which will be the date of receipt of the application);
- the date the entry expires;
- contact information for the data controller.

These are all to be included. In the guidance issued by the Commissioner's office data controllers are asked to provide a company registration number, however this is not a requirement of the Regulations.

SPECIAL CASES

9–23 Under s.18(4) the Act allows special provisions to be made "in any case where two or more persons are the data controllers in respect of any personal data". Such provisions have been made in two cases, for schools and partnerships.

Schools

9–24 The Government was committed to dealing with the situation in which local authorities, governors of schools and head teachers all registered separately under the 1984 Act. This arose because the statutory provisions dealing with education impose separate legal obligations on the local education authority, the governors and the head teacher. Similar incidents of separate legal responsibility imposed on office holders occur in other areas of the public sector; for example, electoral registration officers were required to register separately from the local authority which employs them. It is not a universal pattern and some office holders on whom statutory duties are imposed registered under the name of the employing body. In many cases they were allowed to register under the name of the office, although the office did not have a legal personality of its own. These anomalies arose over the years, particularly as individual responsibilities were increasingly imposed on individual office holders by statute. Most of these have not been affected but special provision has been made for schools. Regulation 6 provides that in those cases where the head teacher and the school are both data controllers for the same data one notification may be given in the name of the school. The process of notification in the name of the school is sparked when one of the existing entries expires. The OIC asks for the number of both entries and replaces the two with one consolidated entry.

Partnerships

9–25 Although it is not expressly stated, the presumption appears to be that generally partners will be data controllers jointly or in common for data used by the partnership. The 1984 Act made no special provision for the registration of partnerships or indeed for any form of joint registration. This caused practical problems for the Registrar's office. In the early years of the office, a pragmatic approach was adopted to allow partnerships to register under the partnership name, subject to providing the names of the current partners. However, the basis for this was not clear given that a partnership, in England and Wales at least, has no legal personality. It could give rise to problems where partnerships split up or where a small partnership was dissolved and one partner wished to carry on the business as a sole trader. In the former case, as long as the partnership name was retained, the Registrar's office allowed the registration to be maintained by the element of the former partnership which had retained the name; in the latter case the individual was required to re-register. Under the 1984 Act, the Registrar made administrative arrangements under which partners registered jointly for the personal data used in the partnership. Those arrangements have now been formalised and reg.5 provides that where persons carry on a business in partnership they may register jointly in the name of the partnership for personal data used for the purposes of the firm. The name and address to be specified is the firm's principal place of business. The names of the partners need not be supplied. This does not of course apply to limited liability partnerships.

Groups of companies

9–26 No special provisions have been made for groups of companies. If companies in the same group are data controllers they must each notify separately. Trading names may be included in the register but not the names of other legal entities.

GENERAL PROVISIONS

Number of entries permitted

9–27 The Commissioner must maintain a public register of those who give him notification of relevant data processing. He can only allow one entry in the register for each data controller, as under s.19(1)(b) he must make an entry following a notification from any person ". . . in respect of whom no entry as a data controller was for the time being included in the register".

Therefore, if a controller already has an entry in the register and purports to make a further application the Commissioner is under no obligation to accept it. Presumably the Commissioner will reject such a purported application as invalid. In the 1996 consultation paper, the Registrar recommended that each data user should only be able to make use of each standard purpose once and this has been put into effect, although the Guidance states that in exceptional circumstances the Commissioner may allow the use of a purpose more than once "where [she] considers that it will aid transparency to the data subjects".

Refusal of a notification of entry

9–28   The Commissioner is given no specific power to refuse an application for notification as long as it is made in the prescribed form. The restriction of applications to the prescribed format should presumably ensure that he is able to treat a purported application for notification which is scurrilous, vexatious or incomprehensible as invalid on the ground that it is not presented in the prescribed form, but does not allow the refusal of any application in the prescribed form however unlikely its contents may be.

Duration of a register entry

9–29   An entry in the register lasts for 12 months or such other period as may be prescribed by the regulations, and different periods may be prescribed for different cases. The entry may be renewed on payment of the relevant annual fee. Fees may be paid by cheque, direct debit or BACS. If an entry is not renewed within the 12-month period it lapses and cannot be renewed. The data controller must make a new application. The practice of the OIC is to send a reminder to data controllers before expiry of the entry, although he has no statutory duty to do so. Where a controller pays by direct debit the entry will be automatically renewed as the fee is taken.

Public access to the register

9–30   The Commissioner must provide facilities for making the contents of the register available for inspection free of charge by members of the public at all reasonable hours. This is a mandatory requirement. The register is kept in electronic, not paper, format. In order to fulfil the requirement physical inspection is available by access to a computer terminal connected to the live register. Such access is only allowed at the Commissioner's Wilmslow office. The Commissioner may also provide such other facilities for making the information contained in the register available free of charge. This is a discretionary power. A copy of the register is available over the internet. Copyright restrictions are placed on the internet copy to ensure that it cannot be used as a mailing list.

Certified copies

9–31   The Commissioner must supply certified copies of the particulars contained in the register to any member of the public who requests one. A fee is payable for such a copy. The fee remains £2. Non-certified copies are available up to a certain number of entries free of charge from the Commissioner's office.

APPLICATIONS FOR REGISTRATION

Method of application

9–32   No particular method of application is prescribed by the Act. Notification regulations may provide for the registrable particulars to be specified in a particular form. This could be in writing but could equally be used to permit applications to be made in electronic form, whether online or by disk. Applications for notification can be made online and over the telephone as well as by completing a form but in each case the applicant has to sign and return a paper form containing a declaration before the transaction is completed.

Security numbers

9–33   The OIC issues each applicant with a "security number" which must be quoted on any application to alter an entry on the register. This replaces the data user number which was issued under the previous system.

Accuracy of applications

9–34   There is no provision dealing with the accuracy of information to be supplied to the Commissioner. In the 1984 Act, it was an offence to knowingly or recklessly provide false information on an application for registration. Separately, the Registrar had a power to refuse an application on the grounds that the information provided by the applicant was insufficient.

The Registrar took the view that inaccurate information could not be regarded as sufficient and was prepared to refuse applications on such grounds. In the absence of either provision, it appears that the Commissioner has no clear power to refuse to place an entry on the public register, even if he knows it to be completely false. By contrast, s.21(2) makes it an offence for a controller to fail to comply with the duty to keep particulars up to date as required under notification regulations.

Fees

9–35   The fees for all notifications are set at £35. No VAT is chargeable on the fee. Changes to entries on the register of notifications is free. Over the last few years there have been a number of "scams" where organisations using similar sounding names to the OIC duped businesses into sending them money to register. A number have now been prevented from trading.

Fees cannot be returned once they have been paid except in exceptional circumstances. Any application for a refund should be made to the OIC setting out the grounds of the application.

Removal of an entry

9–36   The data controller can have an entry in the register removed on application to the OIC as long as he can cite the security number.

Assignment of register entry

9–37   It appears that the benefit of a register entry cannot be assigned or transferred. This is inconvenient where the data controller undergoes a change of legal personality, for example where a sole trader sets up a limited company to carry on the same business the register entry cannot be transferred. The new company must make a fresh application for notification in its own right.

Changes

9–38   In any case where a controller notifies, he must maintain the entry as an accurate record. The extent of the obligation to notify changes, irrespective of whether the notification is voluntary or mandatory, is set out in the Regulations. The purpose is to ensure, so far as is practicable, that at any time the entry contains:

    (a) the controller's current name and address;

    (b) a description of the controller's current processing practices or intentions;

and that a description of the current security measures is lodged with the Commissioner. Failure to keep the entry up-to-date in accordance with the notification regulations is an offence under s.20(2). The offence is one of strict liability although a defence of due diligence is available. Application for changes to the entry must be made in writing and accompanied by the security number. Where the data controller either:

    • alters his processing to the extent that the application or entry no longer accurately or completely reflects his activities; or

    • changes the security arrangements which he has submitted to the Commissioner;

he must notify the Commissioner of the alteration at the latest within 28 days of its taking place, and amend his entry or statement to reflect the current situation.

Obligations of Commissioner

9–39   A data controller is deemed to be notified from the date on which the correctly completed application form together with the fee is received at the Commissioner's office. If the application is made by registered post or recorded delivery the period of notification begins on the date on which the application was posted. The Commissioner must inform applicants for notification when he has included an entry in the register as soon as practicable and at least within 28 days of receipt of the application. A copy of the entry is sent to the controller when it has been added to the register.

Notification of Security provisions

9–40   The 1998 Act includes a requirement which did not appear in the 1984 Act. It was imposed following the Directive and requires a data controller to notify the Commissioner of the security arrangements which the controller has in place to protect the personal data. Under s.18(2)(b) a notification must not only specify the registerable particulars in the form determined by or under the regulations but also include "a general description of the measures to be taken for the purpose of complying with the Seventh Data Protection Principle".

The seventh Data Protection Principle requires that:

> "Appropriate technical and organisational measures shall be taken against unauthorised or unlawful processing of personal data and against accidental loss or destruction of or damage to, personal data."

This security information does not appear on the public register. It is held, and presumably assessed or considered, by the Commissioner.

The seventh Principle is accompanied by interpretation provisions covering the matters to be taken into account in deciding if security measures are appropriate. Broadly these cover the nature of the data, their possible uses, and the practical and financial impact of achieving effective security for the data including:

(a)   standards in handling employees who have access to personal data;

(b)   standards in appointing data processors with access to personal data.

They also require a data controller who is using a processor to process personal data for him to bind the processor by a contract made or evidenced in writing to apply the same standards.

9–41   The security requirements imposed by the seventh Principle are thus specified in some detail. However the actual security technique chosen need not be supplied to the Commissioner in that degree of detail. Under s.18(2) the data controller need only supply "a general description" of the security measures. The Regulations provide that this shall be determined by the Commissioner. These are dealt with by applicants for notification being asked to respond to a list of questions as follows:

- Have you taken any measures to guard against unauthorised or unlawful processing of personal data and against accidental loss, destruction or damage?

- If the answer is "yes" answer the following questions:

- Are the measures based on an assessment of the risks involved in the processing?

- Do they include:

  - adopting an information security policy;
  - taking steps to control physical security;
  - putting in place controls on access to information;
  - establishing a business continuity plan;

- training your staff on security systems and procedures;
- detecting and investigating breaches of security when they occur?

- have you adopted the British Standard on Information Security Management BS 7799 or ISO 17799?

BS 7799

9–42   This security standard which covers the use of personal data was developed by the British Computer Society. It has now been replaced by ISO 17799. It sets out a method of evaluation of risk to data processing and a guide to matching the appropriate level of security to the particular risk assessed. The adoption of a particular standard is optional for any organisation. An organisation could achieve appropriate security by another method. It is questionable whether the Commissioner could seek to make adherence to or adoption of the approach in BS 7799 a requirement, however, the standard has been used as a reference point for the security provisions which may be adopted by controllers. The resulting information is held by the Commissioner but does not appear on the public register. ISO 17799 is the equivalent international standard.

ASSESSABLE PROCESSING

9–43   Section 22 sets out the power of the Secretary of State to determine the categories of assessable processing for the purposes of the Act. No determination has been made so these provisions have not been activated. Section 22 derives from Art.20 of the Directive under which Member States shall:

> "determine the processing operations likely to present specific risks to the rights and freedoms of data subjects and shall check that these processing operations are examined prior to the start thereof."

The Directive does not state how the checks are to be done. In the 1998 Act, the checks are to be carried out following receipt of a notification of assessable processing. It might reasonably be assumed that, following those checks, the supervisory authority would have some appropriate range of responses available to it to deal with cases which did show serious risks to individual rights and freedoms, possibly including the imposition of conditions before the start of processing or even forbidding processing altogether in the most extreme case. While this may appear to be the spirit of the Directive, it does not in terms require that any particular powers are to be available to the supervisory authority if a check shows that the processing would cause serious detriment to the rights and freedoms of any individual. Section 22 follows the letter of the Directive. If a notification reveals to the Commissioner that the assessable processing is unlikely to comply with the Act he must inform the controller of his opinion. The Commissioner has no power to forbid the processing or require it to be amended until the controller actually carries it out. The Commissioner will then be able to take enforcement action under his enforcement powers. However, it is possible that by such time the breach may be irretrievable and the damage done.

The assessable processing provisions therefore cannot be used to initiate the Commissioner's enforcement powers. They could be a catalyst for the exercise of individual rights in an appropriate case if the Commissioner were free to inform individuals who are potentially affected by assessable processing of the imminent risks. This would enable such individuals to take injunctive action or lodge notices of objection to the processing in an appropriate case. This seems an unlikely outcome, however, and as it stands s.22 appears to be little more than a formal nod towards the implementation of Art.20.

Types of processing

9–44 Types of assessable processing may be specified by the Secretary of State by Order. To be specified, processing must appear to him to be particularly likely to:

    (i) cause substantial damage or substantial distress to data subjects; or

    (ii) otherwise significantly to prejudice the rights and freedoms of data subjects.

No further assistance is given as to what amounts to substantial damage or substantial distress. It is not clear whether the test is intended to be subjective or objective.

Three types of processing were canvassed in the consultation in August 1998. They were:

    (i) the processing of genetic data;

    (ii) data matching;

    (iii) processing by inquiry agents.

Each of these had given rise to concern in the past, as reported in the Annual Reports of the Registrar. They continue to be among the most controversial areas of data processing but none have been designated as assessable processing.

Time limits

9–45 Where a controller carries out processing in one of the assessable categories he must not start processing until he has sent a notification to the Commissioner and either the Commissioner has responded or the time limit for the Commissioner's response has elapsed. If he does start processing, he is guilty of an offence under s.22(6).

The time limits for response by the Commissioner are extremely tight. Where the Commissioner receives a notification which shows that assessable processing is being carried out he has 28 days from the date of receipt of the notification to give a notice to the controller stating the extent to which he considers that the processing is likely or unlikely to comply with the provisions of the Act. He may extend that period of 28 days for up to a further 14 days by reason of special circumstances on one occasion only, by giving notice to that effect to the controller. The nature of what might amount to special circumstances is not specified in the Act.

The controller must not start to process until he receives the Commissioner's response or until the end of the 28 days or the extended period if the Commissioner has extended it.

VOLUNTARY NOTIFICATION

9–46   The concept of an openly available opportunity to make a public statement of processing is taken to its logical extreme by s.18(1) which allows, "any data controller who wishes to be included in the register maintained under section 19" to give notice to the Commissioner for inclusion in the register. Applying this, it is possible for controllers who are entitled to claim exemption from the duty to notify to choose to do so voluntarily. If such a controller does notify he is subject to the full rigours of the notification requirements; he must pay fees and becomes subject to the obligation to maintain the entry up-to-date. The possible motive for taking on this obligation is to be found in the s.24 duty to make information generally available as described below.

The option of notifying voluntarily is only open to controllers who are exempt from notification by reason of s.17, or regulations made under s.17. It is not available to those who are exempt under any of the exemptions found in Pt IV.

Thus the option of voluntary notification is not available to those who:

(a) hold personal data only for personal, family or household affairs; or

(b) hold personal data where the national security exemption comes into play.

This is because, by virtue of s.27(1), such data are not to be treated as personal data for the purposes of Pt II (notification).

Those controllers who will be able to notify voluntarily will be those who:

(a) hold manual personal data including accessible records;

(b) are exempt by virtue of regulations;

(c) hold personal data for the purposes of maintaining public registers.

There appears to be no provision allowing a controller who has voluntarily notified to cancel or withdraw a notification, although as notification is renewed annually it will be open to such a controller to chose not to renew the notification at the expiry of the entry.

DUTY TO MAKE INFORMATION AVAILABLE

9–47   Section 24 implements the requirement of Art.21(3) of the Directive that:

"Member States shall provide, in relation to processing operations not subject to notification, that controllers or another body appointed by the Member States make available at least the information referred to in Article 19(1)(a) to (e) in an appropriate form to any person on request."

The information specified in Art.19(1)(a)–(e) is, as may be anticipated, the contents of the register entry. This provision is again based on the belief that all processing should be transparent and information on it freely available. Therefore, even in those cases where a controller does not have to provide a public statement on the register, he must be ready with the equivalent information to provide to any inquirer.

The Art.21 requirement has been enacted as imposing an obligation on those who process manual data and those who are exempt by virtue of notification regulations and who have decided not to notify voluntarily, to respond to requests for information about their processing.

Under s.24(1) the request must be made in writing. This includes sending the notice by legible and preservable electronic means by virtue of s.64(1)(b). On receipt of the request the controller has 21 days in which to make the relevant particulars available in writing to the inquirer. The response must be made free of charge. It does not appear to impose a duty to send a copy to the inquirer and presumably therefore the controller may insist that the inquirer attend his office to view a copy of the written statement of the particulars. The particulars consist of those set out at paras (a)–(f) of s.16(1), that is all the registration details except the security statement. Failure to provide the statement on request is an offence of strict liability although there is a defence of due diligence.

Provision is made in s.24(3) to allow exemptions from this obligation in the notification regulations, however this has not been used.

OFFENCES

9–48 Offences are dealt with in detail elsewhere in the Act. In brief, the offences relating to notification are:

(a) processing without notification (unless exempt)—s.21(1);

(b) failure to notify changes in accordance with regulations—s.21(2);

(c) carrying out assessable processing when no notification has been given to the Commissioner—s.22(6).

DATA PROTECTION SUPERVISORS

9–49 Section 23 contains a novel provision which there appears to be no intention to use. It allows the Secretary of State to establish conditions under which controllers may appoint data protection supervisors who will be responsible for monitoring the controller's compliance with the provisions of the Act. The monitoring must be carried out in an independent manner. Accordingly the data supervisor would have to be independent from his employer or any other influence in relation to his data protection duties. Although the compliance in question is not limited to compliance with notification requirements, the potential exemption applies only to notification. The order may provide that where a supervisor is appointed in accordance with the order and specified conditions are complied with, the provisions of Pt II, that is those dealing with notification, are to have effect "subject to such exemptions or other modifications as may be specified in the order".

Such an order may impose duties on the supervisors in relation to the Commissioner, for example some form of supervisory role might be given to the Commissioner. It may also confer functions on the Commissioner in relation to supervisors.

There were complex transitional arrangements from the old registration system. The final old-style register entries expired on February 28, 2003.

ADDITIONAL INFORMATION

9–50   The Regulations are made under the following sections of the Act:

- s.17(3) (provision of exemptions from notification on the ground that the processing is unlikely to prejudice rights and freedoms);

- s.18(2)(b) (registerable particulars and security measures);

- s.18(4) (joint notifications by partnerships and joint data users);

- s.18(5) (fees provisions);

- s.19(2) (contents of entry including such other material as may be authorised);

- s.19(3) (start date of register entry, i.e. "deemed notification" provision);

- s.19(4) (fees for renewals of entries);

- s.19(5) (time for retention of entries 12 months or otherwise);

- s.20(1) (duty to notify Commissioner of changes to entry);

- s.26(1) (power to vary fees for different cases);

- s.67(2) (general order making powers);

- Sch.14, para.2(7) (power to modify the application of s.20(1), i.e. duty to notify of changes in the case of anyone who has an entry in the register on the basis of a previous register entry under 1984 Act).

Derivations

9–51   • Directive 95/46 (See App.B):

> (a) Arts 18 (obligation to notify the supervisory authority), 19 (contents of notification), 20 (prior checking), 21 (publicising of processing operations).
> (b) Recitals 48, 49, 50, 51, 52, 53, 54.

- Council of Europe Convention of January 28, 1981 for the Protection of Individuals with regard to automatic processing of Personal Data: 8a (additional safeguards for the data subject).

- Data Protection Act 1984: ss.4 (registration of data users and computer bureau); 6 (applications for registration and for amendment of registered particulars); 7 (acceptance and refusal of applications); 8 (duration and renewal of applications); 9 (inspection of registered particulars).

- Organisation for Economic Co-operation and Development Guidelines: Annex, Part Two (Basic principles of national application 12).

Hansard references

9–52 Vol.586, No.108, col.CWH 58, Lords Grand Committee, February 23, 1998
Preliminary assessments, extention of time in special circumstances.

Commons Standing Committee D, May 19, 1998, cols 145–167
Voluntary notification, shared notifications, additional material, schools notification, annual fees, publicly available, preliminary assessments, information made generally available.

ibid., col.175
Notification fees

Vol.315, No.198, Commons Third Reading, July 2, 1998
Preliminary assessment procedure

Previous case law

9–53 None.

CHAPTER 10

Individual Rights—General Points

INTRODUCTION

10–01 This chapter deals with points common to the individual rights: s.7 (subject access), s.10 (objection to processing), s.11 (objection to direct marketing), s.12 (objection to automated decision-making) and ss.13 and 14 (rights to compensation and correction). For example, four of those rights must be exercised by notice in writing. This gives rise to questions as to how the notices must be served. Other common points are whether they can be handled by agents; the exercise of the rights by children; and whether the individual rights can be waived by individuals, for example under a contract.

SUMMARY OF MAIN POINTS

10–02 (a) there are only limited formal requirements for the service of rights notices and requests;

(b) notices and requests can be served by electronic means;

(c) children can exercise the rights on their own behalf if they are of sufficient understanding;

(d) individuals may agree to waive their rights but the rights cannot be excluded otherwise.

FORMALITIES OF NOTICES

10–03 The Directive does not specify how requests to exercise individual rights have to be made, but under the 1998 Act all rights are to be exercised by a notice or request in writing to the data controller.

Address for service

10–04 The Act does not specify any formalities as to service of notices or requests by individuals. The provisions relating to service in s.65 only relate to the service of notices by the Commissioner. A subject access or any other rights request can be made at any valid address for the data controller. Many large organisations have data protection officers and rights requests can be directed to them. When dealing with a large organisation it may be preferable for data subjects to direct requests to the head office of an organisation rather than to a branch office. Many organisations have standard procedures for dealing with rights requests and it may be worth making inquiries as to those procedures before making the formal request.

Notice in writing

10–05   Although notices must be in writing, there are no other formal requirements as to presentation or content. Clearly a request has to be intelligible for the controller to understand it but there is no legal requirement for it to mention the Data Protection Act. Generally, the more relevant information the individual supplies to help the data controller understand and deal with his request the better. In particular, in making a subject access request the provision of information by the data subject will help the controller find the information sought. Where a controller cannot find the information requested without further assistance from the data subject the obligation to respond is deferred until it has been supplied. Data controllers should ensure that staff are trained to be able to recognise Data Protection Act requests and notices. A data controller may find it useful to have standard forms for individuals to complete when requesting subject access or raising objections to particular types of processing to ensure that all the information he needs to deal with the request properly is collected. However, he will not be able to insist that the individual uses the form.

Service by electronic means

10–06   Under s.64 any of the individual notices or requests can be served by electronic means as long as the notice is received in legible form and is capable of being used for subsequent reference.

EXERCISE OF RIGHTS BY MINORS OR ON BEHALF OF OTHERS

Exercise of individual rights by children

10–07   The main right provided by the 1984 Act was the right of subject access. The capacity of children to exercise that right on their own behalf was a difficult area because of the difference between the provisions applying in Scotland and other areas. Under Scots law a child was not able to make an application for subject access on his or her own behalf until the age of 16. Until then the right of subject access had to be exercised by the parent or guardian acting on behalf of the child. In England, Wales and Northern Ireland a parent could make an application on behalf of a child until the child reached an age when he was able to decide for himself whether or not to make the application. The guidance generally followed has been that by the age of 12 a child can be expected to have a sufficient understanding to decide whether or not to make a request. A child may of course achieve that capacity earlier; that will be a question of fact in the particular circumstances. Under the 1998 Act children have all the individual rights and the same guidance should apply to the exercise of all those rights. The position in England, Wales and Northern Ireland remains the same as under the 1984

Act but s.66 has brought the position in Scotland nearer into line with the rest of the UK. Section 66 provides that a child of 12 years or over will be presumed to have sufficient age and maturity to exercise any right conferred by the Act. In other cases a child under that age will still be able to exercise any such right where he has a sufficient general understanding of what it involves.

For children under 12 rights notices or requests will usually be made by parents or guardians acting on the child's behalf. In considering any such request the data controller must give careful thought as to whether he should accept the request. If he has any doubt, for example as to whether the parent making the request is entitled to do so in a case where parents are estranged, it will be prudent to refuse access and leave the issue to be decided by a competent court which can weigh what is in the best interests of the child.

Exercise of rights by agents

10–08   There is no bar on the exercise of the individual rights, for example an application for subject access, being carried out on behalf of another person. An individual can appoint an agent to act in the exercise of his rights for him. However, where someone holds himself out as acting on behalf of another the controller should check that proper authority is held. How the controller does this will depend on the particular circumstances. In some cases it can simply be done by asking the person to confirm in writing that he or she has the appropriate authority. This may be sufficient where the controller is dealing with a solicitor or other professional adviser representing the data subject. In cases where the agent is acting under a formal power the controller may wish to have sight of that power. When the agent is neither a professional adviser nor acting under a formal power the controller should ask for sight of the authorisation provided by the individual, and some proof that it has come from the subject should be obtained. If the controller makes a disclosure to a person without the subject's authority he may be liable for a breach of the Act.

Exercise of rights on behalf of persons with disabilities

10–09   Current legislation governing the protection of those with disabilities is to be changed with the implementation of the Mental Capacity Act 2005. The Act is not in force at the time of writing but will come into force during 2007. It will replace the Enduring Powers of Attorney Act 1985, repeal Pt 7 of the Mental Health Act 1983 and provide for the replacement of the Court of Protection by a new Court with broader powers. Recourse should therefore be had to the new provisions in the future although at the time of writing the old provisions remain in place.

In cases where the person is acting under a power of attorney it will be prudent for the controller to ask to see the power and to check that it is sufficient to provide authority for the action sought. If the request is made under an enduring power of attorney the controller will also need to be provided with evidence that the power has been registered with the Court of Protection.

10–10   Those who are incapable of managing their own affairs may be subject to protective orders of the Court of Protection. The functions of the Court are carried out by the Public Guardianship Office. Under the Mental Health Act 1983 the Court may administer their affairs. Under s.96(1)(k) the power of the Court extends to "the exercise of any power . . . vested in the patient". Under this provision the Court could make a specific order for any of the individual rights to be exercised.

Generally, the Court will order the appointment of a Receiver to manage the affairs of a patient under s.99 and the appointment will authorise the extent of the Receiver's role. If there is doubt as to whether the authority of the Receiver extends to exercising the rights under the Data Protection Act, application for a specific order can be made to the Court under s.96. After the Mental Capacity Act 2005 comes into effect the relevant provisions will be in s.16 of that Act. Under s.16(1) if a person lacks capacity in relation to a matter or matters concerning either the person's welfare or their property and affairs the Court will be able to make an order making a decision on their behalf or appointing a person to make such a decision.

Litigation

10–11   A child or a person incapable of managing his or her own affairs will not be able to bring court proceedings to enforce the individual rights in his or her own name, but must act by a litigation friend in the usual way.

CAN THE RIGHTS BE EXCLUDED?

10–12   The general rule is that a party may contract out of a statutory protection which is intended to be for private benefit, but he may not contract out of a statutory protection which is intended to serve the public interest: *Johnson v Moreton*.[1] In some Acts, there are specific provisions governing this point but neither the Directive nor the Act deals with the possibility of an individual contracting out of the individual rights.

The Data Protection Principles and the individual rights

10–13   Applying the general rule, in the first instance a distinction might be drawn between the Data Protection Principles and the individual rights. On this basis the courts might be prepared to accept that an individual could enter into a contract in which he waived his rights to access or compensation under the Act, but might not countenance a contract under which he purported to waive the application of the Data Protection Principles to the data about him. The reasoning is that the individual rights are for the sole benefit of individuals whereas the Principles set the general standards. However, this application of the general rule does not necessarily stand up on closer examination. The individual rights and the Principles are closely entwined. Principle 4 requires that personal data shall be accurate and, where necessary, kept up-to-date; s.14 provides for individual remedies in respect of inaccurate data. Principle 6 requires that personal data shall be processed in accordance with the rights of data subjects under the Act; s.13 gives a remedy in compensation to a data subject who suffers damage by reason of any contravention of the Act. In addition individuals have the right to ask the Commissioner to assess the lawfulness of processing, thus invoking the supervisory jurisdiction of the regulator.

---

[1] [1980] A.C. 37, see Ch.11, below.

An alternative approach would be to take the view that not all of the Principles set out general standards. On this basis Principle 6 could be distinguished from the others as it simply reinforces the importance of the individual rights, rather than setting a general standard. Equally, not all the matters which give rise to individual remedies would be regarded as being solely for the benefit of the individual. Thus the "right" to request an assessment of processing, which involves the role of the supervisory authority, might be seen as a different sort of right. Following this thinking, a set of individual rights could be distinguished, being the rights found in ss.7 (subject access), 10 (objection to processing), 11 (objection to direct marketing), 12 (rights relating to automated decision-taking), 13 (rights to compensation) and 14 (remedies for inaccuracy). These would be regarded as the individual rights which could be waived by the data subject. However, although an individual could enter into a contract to agree that the rights did not apply to him he could not disapply the powers of the Commissioner to take enforcement action in an appropriate case. Principle 6 may be enforced by the Commissioner.

It might be argued that while the individual could not successfully waive his rights under those sections, he could agree not to assert his remedies in the courts. Thus the rights would continue to apply and the powers of the Commissioner would continue to apply but the individual would agree, by an appropriate contract clause, not to seek to exercise his rights or enforce them in court or make a request to the Commissioner for assessment. It is suggested that this is the better view.

Effect of the Directive and the Human Rights Act 1998

10–14   The relevant requirement of the Directive is found at Art.22, Remedies:

> "without prejudice to any administrative remedy for which provision may be made, inter alia before the supervisory authority referred to in Article 28, prior to referral to the judicial authority, Member States shall provide for the right of every person to a judicial remedy for any breach of the rights guaranteed him by the national law applicable to the processing in question."

It could be argued that it is sufficient for the State to ensure that a remedy is available in the law. There is no requirement that the State restrict individuals from contracting out of the exercise of that remedy.

However, this raises the question whether the national law can allow an individual to contract out of an aspect of those fundamental rights which the State has a duty to maintain.

10–15   The right to respect for private and family life is a Convention right. The Directive is stated to be an exposition of those rights in the context of data processing. Although each separate individual right cannot be traced directly back to Convention roots, overall they can be regarded as manifestations of the right to private life. This raises the question of whether their waiver in a contract would be compatible with the Convention rights.

An individual can consent to acts which would otherwise be a breach of the qualified rights. The consent must be freely given and genuine. In considering whether the consent met those standards a court would be likely to take into consideration the nature and relationship of the contracting parties. It seems unlikely that the courts would find it acceptable for a public authority to require an individual to waive his statutory rights under the Act in order to obtain a State benefit.

Position of private bodies

10–16 Where the other party is a purely private body, exercising a purely private function, an individual should be entitled to contract out of any or all of the rights to take action under the DPA 1998. Leaving aside the question of the terms of the contract and the issues of fairness, which are dealt with below, it could be argued that there is nothing in either the general law, the Human Rights Act or the Convention to forbid such an agreement, and it is therefore within the powers of a private body and a private individual to enter an agreement that the individual would not take court action to enforce certain of his individual rights under the Data Protection Act.

It is suggested that it is lawful for an individual to agree to waive his or her rights to enforce the remedies granted for breach of the individual rights in ss.7, 10, 11, 12, 13 and 14, subject to the requirements that the consent is genuine, freely given and the contract fair and not in breach of the Unfair Terms in Consumer Contracts Regulations 1999. It will not be lawful for anybody to seek to exclude the powers of the Commissioner or the right to complain to the Commissioner.

Contract terms

10–17 The intersection of contract terms and fairness in obtaining and processing information exercised the Registrar considerably under the 1984 Act. In the Act the requirements to achieve fairness in both obtaining and processing are explicitly set out in Sch.1 Pt II paras 2 and 3. A data controller wishing to exclude the individual rights would have to ensure that the clause and its effects are clearly explained to the individual. An exclusion clause would have to be part of a contract agreed with an individual. The data controller cannot unilaterally seek to disapply individual rights. The individual would have to agree and some consideration would have to pass between the parties. The consideration need not be much; it could be as little as an agreement that the data controller send the individual a catalogue. To satisfy Principle 1, the information about the exclusion terms would either have to be imparted or made readily available before the information is provided by the individual or before the first processing or the first disclosure. It would also fall within the scope of para.3(2)(d) of Pt II being:

> "further information which is necessary, having regard to the specific circumstances in which the data are or are to be processed, to enable processing in respect of the data to be fair."

Moreover, to satisfy the requirements of contract law the terms of a contract must be available to the individual before or at the point of entering the contract. If a clause is included in the contract which is an unusually wide exclusion or onerous term or involves giving up a right provided by statute the explicit attention of the individual may have to be drawn to it: *Interfoto Picture Library Ltd v Stiletto Visual Programmes Ltd*.[2] It would not be sufficient therefore to seek to give information about exclusion of rights clauses after the data have been obtained.

---

[2] [1989] Q.B. 433.

The Unfair Terms in Consumer Contracts Regulations 1999 (SI 1999/2083)

10–18   Under the Unfair Terms in Consumer Contracts Regulations 1999 (SI 1999/2083) a contract term may not be binding if, having regard to the relative bargaining position of the parties, it is an unfair term. The Regulations apply to any term in a contract concluded between a seller or supplier and a consumer where the term has not been individually negotiated (reg.3). An "unfair term" is any term which, contrary to the requirement of good faith, causes a significant imbalance in the parties' rights and obligations under the contract to the detriment of the consumer (reg.4(1)). In assessing a term the circumstances of the contract are taken into account (reg.4(2)) and in assessing good faith regard has to be had to a specified list of matters (reg.4(3)). These are: the strength of the bargaining position of the parties; whether the consumer had an inducement to agree to the term; whether the goods or services were to his special order and the extent to which the seller or supplier had dealt fairly or equitably with the consumer (Sch.2). Accordingly the relationship of the parties, the nature of the contract, the relative bargaining position of the parties and the nature of the supply (for example if it is an essential service) will all be relevant in deciding if the exclusion clause is valid. Schedule 3 of the Regulations contains an indicative list of terms which may be regarded as unfair, one of which is a term which has the object or effect of excluding or hindering the consumer's right to take legal action or exercise any other legal remedy (Sch.3 para.1(q)). Thus a contract clause in an agreement covering the use of personal data under which the individual waived his individual rights under the Act would run a significant risk of falling foul of the Regulations.

The Regulations are primarily enforced by the Director General of Fair Trading but the Commissioner may also bring proceedings in respect of unfair terms.

DERIVATIONS

10–19   See Chs 11, 12, 13 and 14, below on individual rights.

CHAPTER 11

Subject Access

INTRODUCTION

11–01 When Sir Norman Lindop reported on data protection in 1978, "the right to know" had proved a controversial topic among those who gave evidence to his committee:

> "This principle of subject access is a prominent feature of much of the legislation abroad, and it was emphasised in all the submissions of those bodies that were primarily concerned with the interests of the data subject . . . For users, however, this objective proved to be highly controversial; many expressed outright disagreement with it (and these included several government departments), and many more expressed grave doubts and reservations."[1]

Despite the reservations of data users, however, the right of access to computerised information passed into law in 1984, albeit with a number of wide exemptions. Its inclusion was in part attributable to the importance accorded to the right in the Convention for the Protection of Individuals with regard to Automatic Processing of Personal Data which had been adopted by the Council of Europe in 1981 and which provided the impetus for the passage of the 1984 Act in the United Kingdom.

Over the 30 years since the Lindop Report, information reflecting every aspect of our lives, has increasingly been captured at an extraordinary rate. As the extent of that information capture has increased, it has become correspondingly even more important for individuals to be able to find out who holds information on them, to learn what that information is and to understand how it may be used by the data controller. Armed with such knowledge the data subject may check its accuracy, challenge its use and even demand its deletion.

11–02 The 1984 Act was one of the first laws to empower individuals to see the information others held about them but it was limited in scope, covering only computerised information. Other specific rights were given by particular statutes. Since 1984, Parliament has extended access rights to other areas, for example the Access to Medical Reports Act 1988. A number of these rights were consolidated in the Data Protection Act 1998 and are now subject to broadly the same regime. The 1998 Act sets out a framework of individual rights in relation to personal information, and subject

---

[1] Lindop, *Report of the Committee on Data Protection*, Cmnd.7341 (1978), paras 5,45–5,46.

access may be regarded as the threshold provision for the exercise of those rights. Unless the individual can learn what information is held about him and what will happen to it, his rights to correct or challenge it may become valueless.

In *Durant v Financial Services Authority*[2] Auld L.J. in the leading judgment commented on the purpose of the subject access provision:

> "In conformity with the 1981 Convention and the Directive, the purpose of section 7, in entitling an individual to have access to information in the form of his 'personal data' is to enable him to check whether the data controller's processing of it unlawfully infringes his privacy and, if so, to take such steps as the Act provides, for example in sections 10 to 14, to protect it. It is not an automatic key to any information, readily accessible or not, of matters in which he may be named or involved. Nor is to assist him, for example, to obtain discovery of documents that may assist him in litigation or complaints against third parties."

This approach, of considering the purpose of the access right and referring it specifically to privacy infringement, is perhaps a more restrictive approach than earlier commentators had tended to take. It mirrored the approach taken by the Court of Appeal to the definitions of "personal data" and "relevant filing system"[3] in the context of a subject access request. These are discussed later in the chapter and in more depth in Ch.3, above on the definitions. The dicta of the Court on the term "personal data" has proved difficult for controllers to apply in practice. At the same time however more general rights of access to information have increased significantly, particularly for information held in the public sector, since the implementation of the Freedom of Information Act 2000 in January 2005.

SUMMARY OF MAIN POINTS

11–03

(a) A wide range of information must be provided to the individual. The definition of personal data is a broad one and the information which must be disclosed will include personal information contained in manual files. Information about the processing must also be provided, not just a copy of the information itself. Third party data must be provided in appropriate circumstances and a set of rules deals with when that will apply.

(b) Access rights which were previously exercised under the Consumer Credit Act 1974, the Access to Health Records Act 1990 and the Access to Personal Files Act 1987 are exercised under the data protection regime.

(c) Where the access request is made to a public authority the right of access extends to all recorded information, with special rules for access to unstructured manual information

---

[2] [2003] EWCA Civ 1746.
[3] See Ch.3, above for a full examination of the decision on the definitions.

(d) A flat rate fee of £10 is payable on most requests, although credit reference searches cost £2, health data previously covered by the Access to Health Records Act 1990 may cost up to £50. The £10 fee must be paid before the controller has to start searching for the data.

(e) Where unstructured manual information is requested the obligation of the public authority is restricted by the imposition of a cost ceiling which limits the amount of information which may be retrieved

(f) There are a number of exemptions from the obligation to provide access

(g) The Commissioner can serve an enforcement notice on any data controller who fails to give subject access and has powers to serve information notices in order to inspect data, to check whether claims for exemptions are justified and to call for further details from the data controller if he is not satisfied with the explanations given.

(h) Individuals can assert their rights in court and seek court orders to provide personal data.

REQUIREMENTS FOR REQUESTING INFORMATION

11–04 The Directive does not specify how requests for information have to be made. Under s.7(2) requests do not give rise to a duty to respond unless they are made in writing. Controllers are therefore under no obligation to respond to oral requests. There is no rule preventing a controller giving information in response to an oral request but it may be a security risk to do so and a controller will need to be sure of the identity of the person making the request before responding.

The advice of the Information Commissioner is that, where an accidental disclosure would not be expected to cause damage or distress, the data controller may rely on the usual signature of the data subject and dispatch the response to the address recorded by the controller as the data subject's address. However, better security precautions should be adopted if the information is such that:

> "its accidental disclosure to an individual impersonating the data subject would be likely to cause damage or distress to the real data subject."[4]

The Commissioner's Legal Guidance suggests that the controller may check identity by:

- Asking the individual to verify identity by providing information which only he or she would know or producing documents which only he or she would have; or

- Asking for the signature on the access request to be witnessed.

---

[4] Office of Information Commissioner (OIC) *Legal Guidance* (October 2001), p.49. It should be noted that this may also involve an offence under s.55 by the person who attempts to procure the information.

Address for service

11–05 The Act does not specify any particular description of address for service therefore a subject access request can be made at any valid address for the data controller. Many large organisations have data protection officers and subject access requests can be directed to them. When dealing with a large organisation it may be advisable to send a request to the head office or administrative centre rather than to a local branch.

Requests in writing

11–06 Once a controller has received a request in writing together with the fee he is under an obligation to respond to it,[5] unless it is not sufficiently clear to enable him to find the information requested[6] or if he has already complied with an identical or very similar request within a reasonable timescale.[7] The Act does not indicate what amounts to a "reasonable interval" between requests but the Guidance from the Commissioner suggests that the following factors should be considered:

- "the nature of the data;
- the purpose for which the data are processed; and
- the frequency with which the data are altered."[8]

Clearly a request has to be intelligible in order for the controller to understand and respond to it and the more information the individual gives to help the controller find the relevant information the better. If the request does not enable the controller to identify the person making the request or locate the information requested he is not obliged to comply with the request as long as he has made reasonable enquiries to the requester and has not received the further information which he requires.[9] An individual who wants to ask for subject access should write to the controller in clear terms, explaining what information he wants. Although he is under no obligation to mention the Data Protection Act it is usually helpful to controllers if he does so.

Data controllers should ensure that staff are trained to recognise and respond to subject access requests. Requests do not have to be provided in a particular form in order to be valid. This means that staff should be trained to understand the nature and existence of the subject access right, not simply to recognise a standard form. A data controller may, however find it useful to have a standard form on which to ask individuals to provide details to help find the information requested. Where a controller has a large organisation and holds large amounts of data a standard form is particularly useful, as it can help to narrow down the areas of data which will have to be searched to deal with the request.

---

[5] 1998 Act s.7(2).
[6] 1998 Act s.7(3).
[7] 1998 Act s.8(3).
[8] OIC, *Legal Guidance* (October 2001), p.48.
[9] 1998 Act s.7(3) as amended by Sch.6 para.1 to the Freedom of Information Act 2000.

Obligations of public authorities under the Freedom of Information Act (FOIA)

11–07   Section 68 of the FOIA amends s.1 of the DPA by the addition of a further category (category (e)) in the definition of data to include recorded information held by a public authority which does not fall within categories (a) to (d). Category (e) data is therefore all recorded information held by a public authority other than that held on computer, recorded with the intention that it should be held on computer, that held on relevant filing systems or that held in accessible records.[10] This category (e) is further broken down into structured and unstructured data.[11] Unstructured personal data is manual data which is part of a set of data relating to individulas where the set is structured by reference to individuals or criteria relating to them but in which specific information is *not* readily accessible. Thus a file with the name of an individual on the cover where the contents are in date order will be covered by this defintion. By contrast unstructured personal data will be information that is held outside any structured filing mechanism, for example references to an individual in diaries or in loose papers.

All of the requirements of s.7 apply to the new category (e) data however where unstructured data are concerned the public authority is not under an obligation to provide the information unless "the request under that section contains a description of the data" (s.9A(2)). There is no further assistance provided on the level of detail at which the description is to be provided. While no one would expect the subject to have to provide an exact location it might be reasonable to ask for an approximate date when the information may have been generated, the subject-matter, the type of information sought, e.g. social service files, or letters to the planning department.

Fees for subject access

11–08   The fee is prescribed in regulations (described in the next section) made by the Secretary of State. Section 7(2) provides that cases may be prescribed in which no fee will be payable but this power has not been used. The fee covers all the categories of information which a subject can request apart from unstructured manual data where the request is made to a public authority. Other than the cases where access rights appeared in predecessor legislation the fee for subject access is now £10.[12] This makes access cheaper than it was under the 1984 Act. Under the 1984 Act the data user could have as many register entries as he wished on the public register. On subject access a fee of £10 was payable per entry. The effect of s.7(2)(b) is that the fee must be paid before the data controller is under any obligation to start looking for the data. This meets the concern that individuals might abuse the access provisions by making extensive access requests and then failing to turn up and collect the information. Section 8(1) allows the Secretary of State to make regulations prescribing that a request for information under one part is to be treated as a request under all parts.

Where the request is made to a public authority which has an obligation to also provide category (e) data any unstructured data will be subject to the appropriate

---

[10] For a detailed analysis of the provisions see Ch.3, above Interpretation and Definitions.
[11] DPA s.9A inserted by s.69 of the Freedom of Information Act 2000.
[12] Data Protection (Subject Access) (Fees and Miscellaneous Provisions) Regulations 2000 (SI 2000/191).

limit prescribed under the Freedom of Information Act. Therefore even where the data subject has been able to provide a proper description of the unstructured information, the authority is not under an obligation to provide it, or to provide any of the information required by s.7(1) "if the authority estimates that the cost of complying with the request so far as relating to those data would exceed the appropriate limit".

This has to be read with the next subs.(4) which provides that subs.(3) does not exempt from the obligation to inform the data subject whether personal data of which the individual is the data subject are being processed by or on behalf of the data controller. In other words to tell the data subject whether the authority has information on him at all. There is no exemption from this part of the subject access obligation unless the estimated cost of complying with that aspect of it alone in relation to the unstructured data would exceed the "appropriate limit". The appropriate limit in these two subsections means the amount prescribed by the Secretary of State and any estimates for the purpose of the section must be made in accordance with regulations under s.12(5) of the FOIA. The cost is assessed on a notional basis of staff time at £25 per hour and the authority is able to take into account the time spent locating and retreiving the informaiton. The limit is currently set at £600 for central government departments and £450 for the rest of the public sector. At the time of writing the basis of the cost calculation is under review.

It should be borne in mind that the access provisions to accessible records continue in force. Accordingly the authority will have to decide when a request is received whether the information sought might fall under any of the accessible records provisions and if so treat those accordingly. Where accessible records are concerned the authority has to provide all the information, both manual and automated irrespective of the method of filing, for the statutory fee.

THE DATA PROTECTION (SUBJECT ACCESS) (FEES AND MISCELLANEOUS PROVISIONS) REGULATIONS (SI 2000/191)

11–09 The subject access provisions in s.7 of the Act are supplemented by these Regulations. They make provision for differential fees and time limits for response in relation to access requests in the special cases of credit reference files and education and health accessible records. They also cover a number of miscellaneous points. Regulation 3 provides that the maximum fee for subject access in all but the special cases referred to above will remain at £10.

Treatment of requests

11–10 Section 8(1) allows the Secretary of State to make regulations prescribing cases in which a request for information under one part of s.7 is to be treated as also being a request for the information under other parts of s.7. Regulation 2 prescribes that a request under any part of s.7(1)(a), (b) or (c) is to be treated as covering all three subsections. However a request will only extend to s.7(1)(d) where it shows an express intention to that effect. The request need not actually mention the subsection but must clearly refer to the requirement to have access to information about the logic of any processing operation. Equally a request made under s.7(1)(d) will not be treated as covering the first three subsections unless it shows an express intention to that effect.

Credit reference agencies

11–11 Section 9(2) of the Act provides that, where access requests are made to credit reference agencies, they are to be treated as being limited to personal data relevant to the financial standing of the requester unless the request shows a contrary intention. Where s.9(2) applies reg.4 makes a number of additional changes to the usual procedure. The maximum fee which the data controller can charge for dealing with the request is set at £2.[13] The data controller must respond within seven working days.[14] Working days do not include weekends, bank holidays in the jurisdiction within which the data controller is situated and Christmas or Good Friday.

Educational records

11–12 Accessible records which are education records within the meaning of Sch.11 are subject to the provisions of reg.5. This applies to the entire record covering the information held as automated data, information recorded in a relevant filing system and information held in the manual files. A data controller cannot charge a fee for giving subject access to such records[15] although he may recover some of the copying charges as allowed under the next subsection. This provides that fees may be charged for providing the information in hard copy form in accordance with the Schedule to the Regulations. The Regulations set a maximum fee of £50 where the information is to be provided other than by a copy in writing. Where the request is to be met by providing copies in writing the Regulations set a sliding scale of charges depending on the number of sheets copied. This runs from £1 for fewer than 20 pages and goes to a maximum of £50 for 500 sheets or more. The time for complying with a request for access to accessible records is set at 15 school days where the data controller is situated in England or Wales.[16]

Health records

11–13 This provision only applies to a limited set of personal data: that which is held on a manual system; that which is a health record within s.68 and was made before October 2001.[17] Where the information is to be supplied in permanent form the maximum fee is set at £50. Unlike the education records provision this does not have to be linked to the number of pages made available. However where the data subject does not want to be supplied with a copy in permanent form, and the data are not automated data but are part of an accessible health record, some of which was recorded within the preceding 40 days before the request, no fee may be charged. This is to enable individuals to view recently made health records at no charge and an individual may specify that his request is so limited.[18]

---

[13] SI 2000/191 reg.4(1)(a).
[14] SI 2000/191 reg.4(1)(b).
[15] SI 2000/191 reg.5(2).
[16] SI 2000/191 reg.5(4).
[17] SI 2000/191 reg.6(1).
[18] SI 2000/191 reg.5(4).

RETRIEVING THE INFORMATION—FINDING WHAT THE DATA SUBJECT WANTS

Authenticity of the request

11–14   A controller who receives a subject access request may not be completely satisfied as to its provenance. Where he is not sure who the request has come from or what information the person wants, the controller is not obliged to provide any information until he is content on these points. Section 7(3) provides that where a controller reasonably requires further information either to satisfy himself as to the identity of the person making the request or to locate the information that the person seeks the controller is not obliged to comply with a request unless he has informed the person making the request of his requirements and unless the person supplies the further information.

This section was inserted into s.7(3) by Sch.6 para.1 to the Freedom of Information Act 2000. There is no absolute obligation on the data controller, nor is there a time limit within which he must make enquiries. This point has caused some concern to the Commissioner who advised:

"... a data controller should act promptly in requesting the fee or any other further information necessary to fulfill the request. A deliberate delay on the part of the controller is not acceptable."

The controller should not however provide access where he has doubts about the authenticity of the request. If a controller does this he risks falling foul of the security and other requirements of the Act because it might lead to an unauthorised disclosure of data. A controller should therefore make further inquiries of the person requesting access where he is unsure on any point, either to satisfy himself that the person making the request is entitled to the data or to find the particular information that the subject has requested. Where he makes such inquiries his obligation to supply the information does not start until he has been provided with the answers by the data subject.

Does all information have to be given?

11–15   In *R. v Chief Constable of B County Constabulary and the Director of the National Identification Service Ex p. R*,[19] Laws J. held that the subject access provisions in s.21(1)(b) of the 1984 Act established "a simple duty to supply the data subject with the whole of the information held upon him by way of personal data when he requests it".

The circumstances of the case were that an individual who had a spent conviction for a minor offence committed 10 years earlier required a subject access certificate to submit to the consulate general of a country in which he sought employment. He wanted the Chief Constable to provide the s.21 search excluding the spent conviction. Laws J. held that the wording of s.21 of the 1984 Act, which read:

---

[19] Unreported, November 1997.

"(1) . . . an individual shall be entitled . . .

> (b) to be supplied by any data user with a copy of the information constituting . . . any such personal data held by him . . ."

did not allow the user to do anything other than supply all the information under the relevant purpose heading.

The rigour of that ruling could have been mitigated by regulations made under s.7(7) that "an individual making a request under this section, may in such cases as may be prescribed, specify that his request is limited to personal data of any prescribed description," but, as the analysis of the relevant regulations (above) shows, this has not been done. In reality however both public sector and private sector data controllers habitually reach agreement with data subjects to limit the information provided on a subject access request. In principle this approach is unobjectionable as long as it is agreed to by both parties and does not involve any connivance in "doctoring" access requests to make them acceptable to third parties, the real mischief involved in the above case.

11–16 In one case, the Act makes statutory provision for a limited search request to be presumed. Where the data controller is a credit reference agency, s.9(2) provides that an individual making a subject access search shall be taken to have limited his request to "personal data relevant to his financial standing" unless the request shows a contrary intention. The limitation is a "carry over" from the provision in s.158 of the Consumer Credit Act 1974 (which no longer applies to individual consumers). Under s.158 consumers had a right of access to the "file" of credit information relating to them held by the credit reference agency, rather than to all the information relating to them which the agency held. The largest credit reference agencies in the United Kingdom handle several million requests for access to credit files every year. For the vast bulk of consumers all the information required is provided on the credit file. The presumption has been that individuals making access requests to credit reference agencies will still want access to their credit files. However, if a consumer wishes to make a wider search he is entitled to do so under s.7 of the 1998 Act. The specific rules for access to credit information are covered below.

What information must be given in response to a request?

11–17 The information that must be given will depend upon the extent of the data regarded as falling within the definition of personal data, information the subject asks for in the particular case, whether any exemptions apply and whether any of the special rules made under regulations made by the Secretary of State (described above) apply. A controller may have to give up to five different types of information to the individual, whereas under the 1984 Act he only had to give two. In summary the controller has an obligation to:

> (a) confirm that processing is taking place, in other words to tell the individual whether the controller is processing information about him;
>
> (b) describe the type of processing by explaining what the purpose of the processing is, what kind of data are being processed and describing the identity of any recipients or categories of recipients of the data;

(c) if available, provide the data sources by providing information either generally or specifically about where the personal data came from;

(d) describe the processing logic involved, that is, provide information about the logic involved in any of the automatic processing (although this only applies in limited circumstances);

(e) provide the data by giving sight of the information constituting the data which the controller holds on the individual.

In *Johnson v MDU* the Court stated that the primary objective of the subject access right is to make it possible for the data subject to learn what information about them is being processed by others. The entitlement to seek information as to the recipients and sources is ancilliary. Accordingly the words "sources of that data" should be construed narrowly.[20] By the same logic therefore the other ancillary rights would fall to be narrowly construed, although this point was not canvassed in the judgment.

Obligation to confirm that processing is taking place

11–18   The first information the person making a request needs to know is whether the controller is processing personal data about him at all. In some cases individuals make subject access requests under the misapprehension that a controller holds information on them. The controller should always respond to a request even if only to tell the inquirer that he holds no data about the person which he is obliged to disclose. Before making any response the controller must ensure that a thorough search of his data is carried out so he can be confident his answer is accurate. A controller is entitled to ask the inquirer for additional information to help him make this search. This may be particularly important, given the extent of the information which is available for subject access.

Obligation to describe the processing

11–19   The subject access rights involve describing the type of processing and providing information about data sources. Under the 1984 Act if an individual wanted to research this information he had to go to the public register for it rather than directly to the data user involved. If the data user was a large organisation with many entries on the public register (and some public bodies could have over 90 separate purposes listed in the entry) it could be difficult for the individual to decide which purposes related to him and, having ascertained those purposes, to work out which of the listed disclosures might relate to him. The information was inevitably set out in general terms on the register and not targeted at each individual data subject, and the categories of information were not related to one another on the public register.

11–20   Under the 1998 Act the controller has to provide some of that information directly to the individual if he asks for it. The information can still be provided in general terms but the controller has to select and supply that which is relevant to the particular data subject. The controller must provide a description of the type of data

---

[20] *Johnson v MDU* [2004] EWHC 347, para.55.

held on the subject, the purposes for which the data are held and the recipients of the data.

A description of the type of data is likely to be acceptable in general terms, although where sensitive data is involved the particular description of the sensitive data should probably be given. It is not clear at what level of detail the purposes for which data is to be held will have to be described. Logically the purpose description might be expected to provide more information than the subject already knows but in practice it seems controllers are providing it at a general level.

11–21   The controller does not have to list the names of the people to whom he may disclose particular data. It is open to him to describe them in general terms instead. Such people are described as "recipients" of personal data.

The term is defined in s.70 of the Act and in relation to personal data it means anyone to whom the data are disclosed, including an employee or agent of the data controller to whom the data are disclosed in the course of the processing. It does not, however, include anyone to whom disclosure is made as a result of or with a view to a particular inquiry made in exercise of any power conferred by law. It therefore includes those who process data under any authority of the controller, but not public authorities which obtain data from controllers because of their statutory functions. A controller therefore must describe those to whom he passes information except where it is disclosed in the course of the statutory inquiry or other inquiry made in exercise of a legal power. For example a data controller would not have to name the Inland Revenue as a disclosure if he only made disclosures to it in response to statutory requests for information. This provision appears in the Directive but the reasoning is not apparent.

Obligation to provide data sources

11–22   Controllers have to provide "any available information" as to the source of their personal data. Curiously, the obligation is not mirrored by an obligation to retain information about data sources. It is therefore up to the data controller to decide how much information he wishes to keep about the sources of his data. If he does keep such information it will have to be given to the data subject when requested. This applies even if the information about the sources is not of itself held as data covered by the Act. The scope of the obligation is undefined. It covers any available information. There is no definition as to what counts as available. In the case of *Johnson v MDU*[21] the Court held that the rights should be narrowly defined and said that:

> "It does not cover every hand through which the data have passed. It does not include the postman or the secretarial and administrative personnel whose job is to do no more than assemble or deliver material."

While presumably it would cover information in the possession of the controller it would not extend to information held by others, even if such information could be ascertained without any particular difficulty.

In reality many data controllers retain records of the sources of their information and will therefore be obliged to disclose them. However, the Act does not specify the

---

[21] [2004] EWHC 347 (Ch), para.55.

level of detail at which such information must be given, and it may be acceptable to provide it in general terms. The obligation is further tempered by the provisions relating to information about third parties. Where the information about recipients or sources reveals the identity of other individuals the rules relating to third party information will apply.

It should be noted that the requirement to provide information about sources on a subject access request is not mirrored by a corresponding provision in the notification scheme. Sources of data do not have to be notified on the public register.

Obligation to describe the processing logic

11–23 The specifically requested data controller must inform the data subject of the "logic involved" in any decision-taking where automatic processing has constituted or is likely to constitute the sole basis for any decision significantly affecting him. This has its origins in Art.15(1) of the Directive and in order to understand the provision it helps to consider Art.15.

One of the fundamental concerns of those framing the Directive was to ensure that individuals should not become subservient to machines—that human values and judgments should always be paramount. One manifestation of this approach is the provision dealing with automated decisions which affect individuals. Individuals have a right to object to important decisions being taken about them by automated means. In support of this right individuals are also entitled to access to information about any such processing as part of the subject access right. The information only has to be given where the processing constitutes, or is likely to constitute, the basis for a decision significantly affecting the data subject. This is not further defined but in the Directive it covers any processing which "produces legal effects concerning the data subject or significantly affects him and which is intended to evaluate certain personal aspects relating to him such as his performance at work, creditworthiness, reliability or conduct".

11–24 It is not clear from s.7(1)(d) how far the individual is intended to be given a detailed explanation of the judgmental basis of the decision-making system. Data controllers hardly wish to provide details of how their decision-making systems work and there is a tendency to provide information only in the most general terms.

Section 8(5) makes it clear that if the information about the logic involved in the decision-making system constitutes a trade secret then it does not have to be provided to the subject. The Act does not define trade secrets, but the Law Commission, in a consultation paper on trade secrets, suggested a provisional definition as covering "information which is not generally known, which derives its value from that fact and as to which its owner has indicated (expressly or implied) his or her wish to preserve its quality of secrecy".[22]

In a Court of Appeal case[23] in the context of employment law, it was held that a trade secret must consist of specific information used in the business which can fairly be regarded as the employer's property and disclosure of which would harm the employer's business.

---

[22] Law Commission, *Legislating the Criminal Code: Misuse of Trade Secrets* (December 1997) para 1.29.
[23] *FSS Travel and Leisure Systems Ltd v Johnson* [1998] I.R.I.R. 382.

Obligation to provide information constituting the data

11–25 This is the core informational right, the prospect of which caused such outrage to some of Lindop's witnesses in 1978. The data controller must open his files and provide the individual with access to the information he holds, and may only withhold information if he can bring himself within one of the exemptions.

The extent of the information which may be involved depends on the view which is taken of the definition of personal data. Personal data means data "which relate to a living individual who can be identified from the data or from that and other information in the possession of, or likely to come into the possession of, the data controller and including any expression of opinion about the individual". It is no longer cut down, as it was under the 1984 Act, by the requirement that the data must be processed by "reference to the data subject" or by the exemption for data used only for text processing. The definition has been considered in the context of subject access request in the cases of *Durant v FSA*,[24] *Johnson v Medical Defence Union*[25] and *Smith v Lloyds TSB*.[26]

In both *Johnson v MDU* and *Smith v Lloyds TSB* the applicants were unsuccessful in trying to persuade the courts to take a wide view of the term "data". In both cases the materials which the applicants wanted were held in manual files which would not be covered by the right of access but information on those files had originally been produced on a word processor or other computing equipment. In both cases the Court rejected the applications and made clear that the information must be held as data at the time of the request. The term "personal data" has also been narrowly construed. In the *Durant* case Auld L.J. applied a narrow meaning to the term. In doing so he took into account the addition to the definition of the words "and includes any expressions of opinion about the individual and any indication of the intentions of the data controller or any other person in respect of the individual" remarking that, if the term "personal data" had the broad construction which the applicant argued for such provision would have been otiose. It is perhaps regrettable that the provenance of this proviso was not drawn to the attention of the court. Commentators have previously suggested that in fact the proviso was otiose, having been inserted as an "avoidance of doubt" provision because the previous definition in the 1984 Act excluded such matters. The Court also took into account the practicalities of the matter, arguing that the facts that the data controller has only 40 days to respond to a request and is only paid a fee of £10, emphasis that the obligation on the data controller is to recover data which are kept in such a way that they can be recovered quickly and cheaply. The court recognised that it can be difficult to decide what information "relates to" an individual and offered two "tests" to apply when the controller is in doubt on the point; whether the information is "biographically significant" and whether the individual is the "focus" of the information. In practice these are difficult to apply. They are open to subjective evaluation that can vary from controller to controller.

11–26 In *Johnson* the Court followed the ruling in *Durant* as far as the evaluation of the term "personal data" was concerned but it also considered the relation between

---

[24] [2003] EWCA Civ 1746.
[25] *Johnson v MDU* [2004] EWHC 347, para.55.
[26] [2005] EWHC 246.

what may be described as individual entries on the one hand and summary documents on the other. This deals helpfully with a point that many data controllers wrestle with when dealing with subject access requests; namely at what level of granularity should the rules on whether the information is personal data be applied? It also demonstrated the difficulty in applying the "tests" suggested in *Durant*.

Mr Johnson was a doctor who had had various dealings with the Medical Defence Union (MDU). One of the sets of documents considered was a summary of the occasions on which Mr Johnson had sought advice or assistance from the MDU. The totality of the document covered about five pages. Individual entries in the document would précis the date and nature of the advice sought on each occasion. The judge considered one particular entry which recorded the name of the patient and the MDU officer who had dealt with the enquiry and took the view that the entry did not contain Mr Johnson's personal data. The focus was the patient, not the surgeon. On the other hand the totality of the document was about Mr Johnson:

> "The difference between this type of summary and the individual entries is significant. If the individual entries are not personal data, then section 7(1) does not apply and the data subject has no entitlement either to the data or the information about the origin and dissemination of them. On the other hand if the complete summary is personal data, as I think it is, then section 7(1) does apply. Mr Johnson is prima facie entitled to be given a description of that personal data and relevant information about the origin and dissemination of that summary."

It would appear from this that the data controller considering materials must have regard to the total document in appropriate cases and if the document, taken as a whole, can be said to be about the data subject must provide that document. Information is not to be artificially divided into small tranches in order to avoid disclosure.

11–27   The data controller must examine all the data held to decide which data are covered by this definition. The obligation is however to provide the "information constituting" the personal data and not the original documentation itself. This was confirmed in *Durant*[27] and the extent of the obligation was considered in *R v Secretary of State for the Home Department Ex p. Lord*.[28] In that case a Category A prisoner sought subject access to the reports prepared by prison staff and other involved professionals which are considered by the service when the classification of prisoners is under consideration. The practice of the service was to summarise the content of the reports— known as the "gist"—and the summary be provided to the prisoner. The reports themselves were not provided to prisoners. A number of issues arose in the case but one of the points made in the judgment was that the summary did not fully reflect the reports. For that, as well as other reasons, the court ordered the disclosure of the originals rather than the summarised "gist". An attempt was made by counsel for the prisoner to argue that the implication of s.7(5) ("and so much of the information sought by the request as can be communicated without disclosing the identity") and s.8(2) ("a copy of the information in permanent for") is that the data controller **must** disclose

---

[27] [2003] EWCA Civ 1746, para.26.
[28] [2003] EWHC 2073 (Admin).

the original documentation and may not provide a summary. This was not however accepted by the Judge.

Subject access to emails

11–28 The obligation to provide all the personal data includes data in email systems, an application which has proved to be a considerable burden for data controllers. There are some specific problems associated with giving access to emails.

Emails have a number of specific features which affect the provision of subject access:

- they may have been deleted from live systems but retained as archived material or back-up;
- they may have been deleted by the sender or recipient but not erased from the system;
- they may be held locally on stand-alone PCs or laptops and not available to the system administrator;
- they are likely to contain third party data, at least in the details of the sender or recipient;
- their tone may be informal or unguarded;
- they may be "private" to the sender or recipient or regarded as personal correspondence.

Data controllers can face problems in locating personal data held in emails, in retrieving such data from their systems and in deciding whether any third party data should be provided on subject access.

The Commissioner's view in advice given in 2001 but which no longer appears on the website was that emails which contain information about identifiable living individuals will be caught on a request for subject access unless they have been printed off, the electronic version wholly deleted and the hard copy version stored in a file which does not fall within the definition of a relevant filing system. His view was that:

> "even though data may have been 'deleted' from the live system, the emails will be caught if they can be recovered by, say, the systems administrator before their final destruction."

The tone of the advice indicated that the Commissioner was aware of the problems that giving access to emails presents for data controllers. It acknowledged that the Commissioner has a discretion as to whether to take enforcement action and considered the exercise of that discretion and the matters that would be taken into account before concluding:

> "to summarise, the Commissioner's approach is that where emails are held on live systems and can be located, she [sic] will seek to enforce subject access if this has been denied. Where data are held elsewhere the Commissioner will weigh the

interests of the data subject against the effort that the controller would have to take to recover the data and in many instances may be likely to decide not to take action."

The advice acknowledges that the data subject may still seek to take action through the courts.

Inevitably there remains a risk associated with access to emails. More importantly for many data controllers there may be a massive cost in tracing and considering emails for access. The importance of robust, clear and consistently enforced email policies as part of a broader policy dealing with communications cannot be stressed strongly enough.

Access to other data

11–29 It must be borne in mind there is no distinction between "official" or "business" data and personal data. Information about sole traders or partners in a partnership or, in some circumstances, directors of a company may all be personal data and liable to be given in response to a subject access request.

In the same way, subject access requests will cover some forms of manual data. The Act covers manual data which is held within a "relevant filing system" (s.1(1)). This means "any set of information relating to individuals to the extent that the set is structured either by reference to the individuals, or criteria relating to individuals, in such a way that particular information relating to a particular individual is readily accessible". The definition was considered in *Durant* in which the Court of Appeal took a narrow approach to the definition which should be applied. A detailed discussion of this provision is found in Ch.2, above; it certainly covers structured forms of information such as card index systems. The Directive provided that manual data already subject to processing underway in October 1998 would remain outside the Act's requirements until 2001 but that has long passed. A further difficult issue for data controllers to resolve in dealing with subject access requests is dealing with data about other individuals.

Data about other living individuals

11–30 Just as our lives are rarely lived in isolation so information about us is rarely held in neat packages. One record will often include facts about a range of people. Medical records will show which health professionals have treated a patient; banking records may show which members of staff handled a transaction; local authority housing records will include details of joint tenants at a property and possibly information about others in their households; police reports will include the identities of the officers who compiled them.

Where an individual asks for access to a record which includes information about others as well as about himself two equally legitimate, but often conflicting, interests come into play: the interest of the subject in having a full and true picture of the information which applies to him and the interest of the other party who features in the record (referred to throughout this section as the third party) in maintaining his privacy. There are special rules for the disclosure of third party data where the information falls under the modification orders dealing with social work, education and health records which are covered in the exemptions in Ch.16, below.

In s.7(4)–(6) the Act attempts to set out a code for data controllers to follow to strike a balance between these two competing interests. Unfortunately some aspects of the code are expressed obliquely. This section explains the background to the provisions, and examines how they apply. A case study on the practical application of the rules is at the end of this chapter.

The United Kingdom used the introduction of the Data Protection Act 1998 to honour its commitment to incorporate the 1988 decision of the ECtHR in *Gaskin v United Kingdom*[29] into UK law. To understand these provisions it is helpful to have an outline of the *Gaskin* case.

11–31   The plaintiff was in the care of Liverpool City Council during his childhood. His childhood was not a settled one. On reaching adulthood he sought to sue the Council for negligence in failing to provide proper care for him as a child. He sought discovery of his personal social work files under the Administration of Justice Act 1970. Initially the Council refused to provide them. The records contained information about third parties such as social workers who had handled his case, doctors, foster parents and others who had been involved in his care. Mr Gaskin took the Council to court and after various proceedings and detailed reconsideration of the issues, Liverpool City Council agreed to provide him with some of the information he sought. However in the interim the Government had issued its own guidance on the disclosure of social services records, and stepped in. The Attorney General obtained an injunction to restrain the Council from providing all the information sought. Eventually it was resolved that records could be provided, but only with the permission of those who generated the records. If any of those people either could not be contacted or refused to give permission, that information would have to be withheld.

Mr Gaskin then took his case to the Court of Human Rights in Strasbourg under Arts 8 and 10 of the Human Rights Convention. He claimed that the failure of the State to provide access to his records was a breach of his right to private life. The Court gave its judgment in 1989 and held that he had a right under Art.8 to access to the records of his childhood as without these he was unable to develop his understanding of himself. However, where information related to others, the public authority should ask such a third party to give permission to the disclosure. If the third party was not available to be asked or unreasonably refused permission there should be some provision to allow the case to be reviewed and a refusal to be overridden in an appropriate case. In short, the Court took the view that there had to be a mechanism for an independent authority to balance the competing rights involved in an individual case.

Is the third party information personal data about the data subject?

11–32   The data controller only has to undertake the balancing exercise where the information relating to the other party forms part of the personal data of the applicant. If it does not do so the question of the balance to be struck never arises.

11–33   *Who is the third party?*   A data controller faced with a subject access request needs to establish whether the records relating to the subject include "third party" data. Although this may sound a simple question it involves quite a complex

---

[29] [1990] 1 F.L.R. 167.

test. A third party is anyone who the person making the request is likely to be able to identify. Section 7(4) refers to this as "information relating to another person who can be identified from that information" but it must be read with s.8(7) which makes clear that for these purposes this means that either the information on its own is sufficient to identify him to a recipient who does not have any special knowledge, or that the controller has reasonable grounds to believe that the information is sufficient to identify the third party to the data subject because of knowledge the subject either has or is likely to get hold of. The controller is therefore faced with considerable uncertainty in those cases where the information about the third party would not on its own be sufficient to identify him. He must consider what the data subject is likely to know or be able to ascertain. Accordingly data controllers have to have regard to what they know about data subjects to decide on this point. It is not easy to see how a controller is to reach any reasonable assessment in the absence of special knowledge of the data subject. If the data are third party data the controller then has to decide whether or not to give them.

11–34 Consent. There is no obligation to seek consent. If the third party consents the data can always be given. The form of consent required is not specified in the Act but the discussion on consent in Ch.3, above is relevant here. Controllers are advised that it would be prudent to obtain clear written consent, particularly before giving information which may prove sensitive if disclosed. There is no clear obligation to consider whether consent should be or can be obtained but it is suggested that controllers should do so.

Third party data can be provided to a data subject without the consent of the third party if "it is reasonable in all circumstances". This is a broad provision but the controller is given some help by s.7(6), which sets out a number of factors to which particular regard should be had in deciding this point. It is clear that the controller is expected to address his mind to the question of reasonableness and not apply a blanket policy of providing or refusing to give third party data. The factors listed are referred to as "particular" factors so are not the only ones to be taken into account, and the data controller must consider whether others are relevant. The provisions were considered in *Durant* in which the Court took the view that the provisions appear to create a presumption or starting point that the information relating to the other, including his identity, should not be disclosed without consent but that the presumption may be rebutted if it is "reasonable in all the circumstances" to disclose the third party data.

The statutory factors to which regard must be given are:

(a) any duty of confidentiality owed to the other individual;

(b) any steps taken by the data controller with a view to seeking the consent of the individual;

(c) whether the other individual is capable of giving consent;

(d) any express refusal of consent by the other individual.

Although the subsection lists the factors to which regard is to be had it does not say how they are to be balanced or what weight is to be given to each factor. The twin issues which have to be balanced here are confidentiality and consent.

11–35 *Confidentiality.* Some relationships are characterised by confidentiality, for example that between doctor and patient. Where there is an obligation of confidence the party to whom information is confided may not divulge it unless he has grounds to do so. The grounds on which an obligation of confidence does not apply or can be breached are:

(i) where the confider consents;

(ii) where there is a legal compulsion to make the disclosure;

(iii) where there is an overriding public interest in the disclosure.

An obligation of confidence can arise in other relationships. In order for an obligation to arise the information must be confidential, in the sense that it is not in the public domain, that it has some substantive content or is more than "mere tittle-tattle",[30] and was imparted, or came into the possession of the party, in circumstances which lead to an expectation of confidentiality.[31]

At first sight the wording of this section might seem to imply that an obligation of confidence could be overridden by a right to subject access, but the point is not free from doubt. Section 27(5) provides that "except as provided by this Part . . . the subject information provisions shall have effect notwithstanding any enactment or rule of law prohibiting or restricting the disclosure, or authorising the withholding of information". This would arguably have the effect that an obligation of confidence was simply overridden. On the other hand the wording of s.7(6)(a) that regard shall be had to "any duty of confidentiality owed to the other individual" might suggest that the obligation was not overridden. The position appears to be that confidentiality will not act as a prohibition as long as the test in s.7(4)(a) is satisfied and it is "reasonable in all the circumstances to comply with the request without the consent of the individual". In these circumstances, however, the individual might still seek to enforce his confidentiality and argue that the disclosure without his consent was not reasonable. To that extent s.27(5) does not necessarily remove the protection of confidentiality from a third party where subject access is involved. A data controller who has to decide whether to give access to confidential data may still risk a breach of confidence action by the third party.

11–36 What does s.7(6)(a) therefore involve? Confidentiality is not an overriding consideration which will stop the disclosure of the data, but equally the controller has no guaranteed protection if he discloses. On the face of it the controller is left between a rock and a hard place. The answer appears to lie in the subsections which deal with consent. Although the section is worded so that there appears to be no obligation to ask for consent, even where it would be practical to do so, in cases where there is an obligation of confidence and it is possible to seek consent the controller would be well advised to do so, particularly those data controllers in the public sector who will be subject to public law remedies.

If the controller obtains consent he can give the data, assuming that he has decided that it is not against his own interest to do so. It seems reasonable to assume that a

---

[30] *Coco v Clark (Engineers)* [1969] R.P.C. 41.
[31] See Ch.2, above for a discussion of the law of confidence.

private sector data controller is entitled to take his own interests into account in determining whether to provide third party information, although the section does not explicitly say so and the contrary might be argued. If consent is refused the controller has a legitimate basis on which to withhold the data. Clearly there may be cases where it is impossible or impractical to obtain consent. In such cases the controller must still consider whether it is reasonable in all the circumstances to provide third party data.

The data controller can of course only weigh those circumstances known to him and inevitably his knowledge may be deficient or partial. The sort of considerations a data controller will bear in mind are:

(i) the nature of the data about the third party, in particular whether it might be damaging or cause harm or bad feeling between the parties;

(ii) the nature of the third party's role—there will be less justification for withholding information about someone who acted in a formal and official capacity for example a nurse or a lawyer than someone who acted in a private and personal capacity;

(iii) whether it is likely that the data are already known to the data subject or are readily ascertainable to him;

(iv) whether the information might be of particular importance to the data subject for example in pursuing some legitimate claim or interest which can be weighed against the interest of the third party.

11–37 In *Durant* the Court confirmed that much of the balancing test will depend on the nature of the information and its legitimate value to the data subject. The point was considered in detail in *Re Lord*[32] where one of the justifications for the preparation of the "gist" rather than the provision of the reports themselves was to protect the identities of the authors of the reports and the opinions which they express. In the case the authors of the reports had not consented to the disclosure of the reports to the prisoner. The argument was made on behalf of the Secretary of State that, in the case of such reports, the mere redaction of the names of the authors would not be sufficient to protect their identities as it would be apparent to the applicant which reports emanated from a psychologist or a probation officer, for example, and that there was a potential risk to the report writers in disclosure to dangerous prisoners, although it was accepted that in the particular case there was no specific threat. Moreover the writers of the reports had an expectation of confidentiality as the reports had not previously been disclosed. Giving judgment Mr Justice Munby did not accept that the balance could be struck by applying a blanket policy. He accepted that the authors of the reports were themselves data subjects and had important privacy interests in the material which they had written which had to be brought into balance. He also accepted that they had historically been some expectation of confidentiality, albeit that there was a recognition that confidentiality would not be absolute. However he held that the balance between the legitimate interests of

---

[32] [2003] EWHC 2073 (Admin).

the prisoner and the officials had to be struck on case-by-case basis and the blanket policy of non-disclosure of third party data by the use of the "gist" system could not be justified.

11–38 Following this analysis we can see there appear to be three broad categories of third party information:

(i) Information where there is no obligation of confidence and no concern or sensitivity attached to disclosure. In those cases it is reasonable to give the information without asking for prior consent, although it would be advisable to notify the third party of the disclosure.

(ii) Information subject to a clear duty of confidence. Consent should be sought to give the information. If consent is given the information should be provided. If consent is not given or cannot be asked for the controller must undertake a balancing test, but would need strong reasons to give it and override an obligation of confidence.

(iii) Information where there is no clear duty of confidence but disclosure may be sensitive and it would be prudent to seek consent before giving it. If consent is obtained the information can be given; if consent is not obtained the controller must weigh the benefit of providing the information to the data subject and the possible harm to others that might be caused if he did so.

11–39 In *Durant* the Court also considered how far an appellate court should be expected to scrutinise the application of the third party rules by the data controller. In *Durant* the Court decided not to inspect the material in dispute and took the view that the role of the court is a reviewing one rather than one which assumes the role of primary decision-maker on the merits of the case.

Cases where the data controller is not obliged to provide access

11–40 Leaving aside the substantive exemptions, which are dealt with below, data controllers do not have to comply with a request where they have already complied with an "identical or similar request" by the data subject unless a "reasonable interval" has elapsed between the two.[33] Section 8(4) provides that in deciding whether the interval is reasonable the controller should consider:

- the nature of the data;
- the purpose of the processing; and
- the frequency with which the data are altered.

TIME FOR RESPONSE

11–41 Having received the request for subject access, obtained the appropriate fee, satisfied himself that he is dealing with a valid request and has sufficient information

---

[33] 1998 Act s.8(3).

to find the relevant data required, the data controller then has a period of 40 days within which to supply the information to the data subject.[34] Where any of the data are third party data for which consent is being sought for disclosure a separate 40-day clock ticks for that data only.[35]

The 40-day period is allowed as a "long stop" period. The controller's duty under s.7(8) is to comply with a request "promptly". The 40-day period is a prescribed period which may be varied by the Secretary of State by order made under s.7(11), and different periods may be prescribed for different classes of request.

CHANGES IN THE DATA

11–42 Many data controllers must continue routine processing irrespective of receipt of a subject access request, and the Act allows for this to continue. Under s.8(6) the information given must be based on the data held at the time the request is received. It should be noted this appears to refer to the time of the initial request and not the receipt of the fee if that comes later, or the provision of further information from the subject if that is needed to find the data. However, where the controller would have made amendments or deletions irrespective of receipt of the request, these can still be made and the information can still be given based on the data as they are at the time of satisfying the request. This provision only allows for routine processing which would have taken place in any event and does not permit the controller to make other changes to the data.

Offence of altering personal data

11–43 The Freedom of Information Act 2000 creates a new offence, which will apply to public sector data controllers only, of altering records after receipt of an access request under either the Data Protection Act 1998 or the Freedom of Information Act 2000. See Ch.4, above for a discussion of this provision.

HOW CAN THE INFORMATION BE GIVEN?

11–44 Under the 1984 Act the controller was under a straightforward duty to supply a copy of the information constituting the data. For some types of data this proved cumbersome, for example if the data user had a massive tranche of records it could involve an enormous amount of work to print out the data. The 1998 Act broadened the scope of how information may be supplied. While the usual method of dealing with a subject access request remains the supply of a copy of the information in permanent form, this is not necessary if:

    (i) the individual agrees to accept subject access in another form; or

    (ii) the supply of a copy is not possible; or

    (iii) the supply of a copy would involve disproportionate effort.

---

[34] 1998 Act s.7(8) and SI 2000/191 reg.3.
[35] 1998 Act s.7(4) and (8).

There has never been a prohibition on supplying information in alternative form to hard copy where the individual consents. For example, for some medical body scans or X-rays which could only be seen on special equipment, subject access can only be given by providing a patient with an opportunity to see the information displayed. This provision affords the controller a statutory basis for restricting the method by which he provides access to data which cannot be adequately rendered in hard copy. It is more difficult to see the basis for the other provision which allows for information to be given in an intelligible form other than hard copy where the provision of hard copy would "involved disproportionate effort".

The provision does not release the data controller from the obligation to provide access to the data in an intelligible form, so it applies to data which it is possible to supply in hard copy, unlike the medical scans, but which involve a disproportionate effort to print out. It may be of assistance where a large amount of information would be difficult to print but could be transferred easily to a disk, and this may be what it is intended to cover. The provision to allow a response other than in hard copy only applies to the actual data and not to information about the processing or the logic involved in decision-making. The issue of what constitutes disproportionate effort was one of the points considered in *R v Lord* in which the Secretary of State had argued that the work involved in checking an entire file to redact material which should be removed as being third party data or because it is exempt from the obligation to disclose amounted to a disproportionate effort. The argument was not accepted by the Court:

> "Section 8(2)(a) cannot justify withholding from the claimant information in the form in which he would otherwise be entitled to receive it. The administrative burden –light as it is here- has in any event to be assessed in the context of the significance of the information that is otherwise required to be disclosed. Section 8(2)(a) exonerates a data controller from "disproportionate effort", but in determining what is proportionate one necessarily, as it seems to me, has to have regard to the intrinsic significance of the information whose disclosure is being sought and its importance to the data subject."[36]

The advice of the OIC[37] is that it will be a question of fact as to whether the supply amounts to a disproportionate effort in each case. When making an assessment the Commissioner will take into account:

> "the cost of provision of the information, the length of time it may take to provide the information, how difficult or otherwise it may be for the data controller to provide the information and also the size of the organization of which the request has been made. Such matters will always be balanced against the effect on the data subject."

---

[36] *R v Lord* [2003] EWHC 2073, para.155.
[37] OIC, *Legal Guidance* (October 2001), p.46.

EXEMPTIONS

11–45   These are fully covered in Chs 15 to 16, below. For convenience, this section includes an outline of the subject access exemptions. Information may be able to claim exemption if it falls within the following categories, but in each case there are conditions attached or limitations to the exemption.

Subject access is one part of the "subject information provisions" under s.27. The other part of the subject information provisions consists of the rules about providing information to individuals contained in para.2 of Pt II of Sch.1.

Any exemption applies to all aspects of the subject access rights not just the provision of the data.

National security

11–46   Any data or processing can be exempt from controls in the Act, including subject access, under s.28 if the exemption, "is required for the purpose of safeguarding national security". The judge of whether that applies is a Minister of the Crown who can provide a certificate of exemption. An individual who is refused subject access on the basis of such a certificate and is therefore directly affected by it can challenge the certificate on the grounds on which judicial review could be sought. Any such challenge will be heard by a specially constituted Information Tribunal. The Commissioner cannot challenge a national security certificate, although he may apply to be heard in any proceedings brought by an individual.[38]

Crime and taxation

11–47   Personal data processed for the purposes of the prevention or detection of crime, the apprehension or prosecution of offenders or the collection of any tax or duty or imposition of a similar nature are exempt where it would prejudice those purposes in a particular case to give subject access. This exemption extends to anyone to whom the data are transferred for a statutory purpose. The exemption in s.29 largely reproduces the exemption in its predecessor, s.28 of the 1984 Act, although extended by a provision covering risk assessment information for these purposes. The impact of the exemption and the approach to be taken to it in the context of subject access was considered in *R. v Lord* in which the court confirmed that information must be approached on a case-by-case basis and the degree of risk assessed in a realistic manner.

Health, social work and education

11–48   Section 30(1) of the Data Protection Act 1998 provides that the Secretary of State may by order exempt personal data from the subject information provisions, or modify those provisions, in relation to personal data consisting of information as to the physical or mental health or condition of the data subject. The relevant order is the Data Protection (Subject Access Modification) (Health) Order 2000 (SI 2000/413). The terms of the order are discussed in full in Ch.16, below. The presumption where

---

[38] The Commissioner made such an application in the appeal by Tom Baker MP.

information falls under this Order is against disclosure save with medical authorisation. The OIC Guidance states:

> ". . . the information should not be provided unless the appropriate health professional (also defined) has been consulted. The exception to the rule is where the data controller already has a written opinion from the appropriate health professional obtained within the previous six months that an exemption to the right of subject access exists because the disclosure is likely to cause serious harm to the physical or mental health of the data subject or any other person."[39]

Section 30(3) provides for the modification of access rights in the case of social work information and s.30(2) for education information. The relevant orders are the Data Protection (Subject Access Modification) (Social Work) Order 2000 (SI 2000/415) and The Data Protection (Subject Access Modification) (Education) Order 2000 (SI 2000/414) respectively. All three orders include special provisions dealing with third party data.

Regulatory activity

11–49 This exemption applies on a case-by-case basis where access to information would prejudice any of the wide list of regulatory activities which fall within s.31. In most circumstances only data controllers who have a regulatory function can rely on these exemptions.

Journalism, art and literature

11–50 Subject access is included among the widespread exemptions from control where processing is undertaken for any of these purposes with a view to publication and where the controller reasonably believes that the publication is in the public interest and the provision of subject access would be incompatible with these purposes.

Research, historical and statistical information

11–51 Personal data are exempt where they are processed for the research purposes and are not used to make individual decisions for as long as the processing does not cause damage or distress to the individual and the research itself does not identify any data subject.

Other categories

11–52 (i) information which is publicly available[40];

(ii) Crown employment or ministerial appointments where they fall under SI 2000/416;

---

[39] OIC, *Legal Guidance* (October 2001).
[40] 1998 Act s.34

  (iii)　information used only for domestic purposes[41];

  (iv)　confidential references in some cases[42];

  (v)　information relating to the Armed Forces in some cases[43];

  (vi)　information relating to judicial appointments and honours[44];

  (vii)　information used for management forecasts or planning in some cases[45];

  (viii)　information relevant to negotiations in some cases[46];

  (ix)　information processed in relation to corporate finance under SI 2000/184;

  (x)　examination marks for a period of time[47];

  (xi)　examination scripts[48];

  (xii)　information relating to human embryos, adoption or related matters where they fall under SI 2000/1865;

  (xiii)　legal professional privilege[49];

  (xiv)　information which would breach the privilege against self-incrimination[50];

  (xv)　personnel information about public sector employees held in unstructured manual form.[51]

RELATIONSHIP WITH OTHER LEGAL CONSTRAINTS

11–53　A large number of statutes restrict the disclosure of information about individuals. A convenient example can be found at s.59 of the Act itself. Under this section it becomes an offence to disclose any information relating to an identified or identifiable individual or business which has been provided to the Commissioner for the purpose of the Act except under specified circumstances. In the case of s.59 those circumstances include a provision to allow disclosure with the consent of the individual, but this is not always possible. Compliance with a subject access request will often entail the disclosure of information which would otherwise be restricted. The Act negates the possibility of conflict between such prohibitions and the right of subject access in s.27(5) which provides that, except as provided by Pt IV of that Act, the subject access provisions shall prevail over any rule of law or legislation forbidding access. This means that a data controller must give precedence to the right of subject access where there is a potential conflict. In *R. v Lord* the Secretary of State sought to

---

[41]　1998 Act s.36
[42]　1998 Act Sch.7 para.1.
[43]　1998 Act Sch.7 para.2.
[44]　1998 Act Sch.7 para.3.
[45]　1998 Act Sch.7 para.5.
[46]　1998 Act Sch.7 para.7.
[47]　1998 Act Sch.7 para.8.
[48]　1998 Act Sch.7 para.9.
[49]　1998 Act Sch.7 para.10.
[50]　1998 Act Sch.7 para.11.
[51]　Inserted by Freedom of Information Act 2000.

argue that the fact that prisoners could have access to some material under other arrangements in effect displaced the right of access under the DPA. A practice of providing prisoners with information about reports had been instituted following the decisions of the court culminating in *R v Secretary of State for the Home Department Ex p. McAvoy*.[52] The court did not accept that submission and agreed that the prisoner had a statutory right to apply for subject access which was not displaced by the existing administrative arrangements. By the same token the courts have held that the mere fact that a data subject was unsuccessful in obtaining subject access to data under the provisions of the DPA does not debar him from exercising his rights to access information under other regimes. In *Johnson v MDU*[53] Mr Johnson sought pre-action disclosure under the Civil Procedure Rules having been unsuccessful in his attempt to gain access to information held by the MDU under the subject access provisions. The MDU resisted the application on the basis that the court had already heard and determined Mr Johnson's application for access to information. The attempted defence was rejected by the court which held that there were two completely separate causes of action and Mr Johnson remained able to exercise his rights under the CPR despite the failure of his subject access application.

REMEDIES FOR FAILURE TO GIVE SUBJECT ACCESS

11–54 The data controller faces the possibility of action by either the Commissioner or the individual data subject if he fails to provide proper subject access.

Data subject remedies

11–55 A data subject can apply to a court under s.7(9) for a specific order to make the controller provide the information which he has failed to give. This right exists independently from the general right of a data subject to seek compensation if a contravention of any of the requirements of the Act has caused him loss or damage.[54] The general compensation right is covered in Ch.14, below but it should be borne in mind that if an application is made to court on behalf of the data subject under s.7(9), consideration as to whether any additional loss has been incurred should be taken into account and the possibility of making a s.13 application should be considered at the same time. Before making an order under s.7(9) the court has to be satisfied that a valid request has been made and that the controller has not provided the information as and when he should have done. The jurisdiction is exercisable by the county court or the High Court in England and Wales or a Sheriff Court in Scotland.[55] In *R v Lord* the court held that there is no obligation on the data subject to make an application to the Commissioner before being entitled to make an application to the court. The extent of the discretion available to the court has been considered in a number of cases. In *P v Wozencroft (expert evidence: Data Protection)*[56] the Court held that there was a discretion as to whether to order the disclosure of documents. The applicant had

---

[52] [1998] 1 W.L.R. 790.
[53] [2004] EWHC 2509 (Ch).
[54] 1998 Act s.13.
[55] 1998 Act s.15.
[56] [2002] 2 F.L.R. 1118.

argued that as s.7(1) provides that an individual is "entitled" to his right to access and as the Directive requires that Member States shall "guarantee" every data subject the right to obtain data from the controller, then the court which finds that an individual has not been given personal data to which he was entitled under the section **must** order disclosure even though s.7(9) provides that a court which is satisfied that there has been a failure to comply with the obligation by a data controller **may** order him to comply with the request. The discretion of the court was confirmed by the Court of Appeal in *Durant* which went on to consider by what principles a court should be guided in exercising its discretion under s.7(9). In the lower court the judge had set out three reasons why, even had he held that the FSA was in possession of personal data about Mr Durant, he would not have ordered disclosure. These comments were obiter. When the case reached the Court of Appeal it agreed that there was no relevant personal data which should be disclosed and therefore did not need to decide the discretion point however Auld L.J. commented that he would agree with the views expressed by Munby J. in *R v Lord* in which he had held that the discretion was general and untrammelled.[57]

In order to decide whether the applicant should have access to the information he seeks, a court can require the controller to produce the data for inspection. This will include any data for which the controller is claiming an exemption. Curiously, the court does not appear to be able to require sight of all the other information now covered by subject access, that is information as to the sources of data and the nature of the processing, although s.15(2) provides that the court may require information as to the logic involved in any decision-taking be available for inspection. This absence of a statutory power may not prove a difficulty where the action is brought in the High Court (or the Court of Session), where the court may require production of the information under its inherent powers. However, it means that county courts will be limited in their capacity to deal with applications which involve other parts of the information as well as simply the data. When data are made available for inspection to the court they must not be revealed to the applicant unless and until the case is resolved in his favour.[58]

Where the data concern health care an application to the court can be made by a third party to prevent the disclosure of information to the data subject in limited circumstances. See Ch.16, below on the effect of the modification order covering data consisting of information as to the physical or mental health of the data subject.

The Commissioner

11–56 Subject access is one of the individual information rights now covered by Principle 6 found in Pt 1 of Sch.1, which requires that:

> "personal data shall be processed in accordance with the rights of data subjects under this Act."

There is an interpretation provision to this Principle in Sch.1 Pt II para.8 which states that failure to supply information which has been duly requested under s.7 will be a contravention of Principle 6. In such a case the subject can apply to the Commissioner

---

[57] para.74.
[58] 1998 Act s.15(2).

for an "assessment" of his case under s.42. The nature of assessments and the enforcement provisions are dealt with in detail at Chs 20 and 23, below. Where the Commissioner makes an assessment he may or may not take action. An assessment may involve the service of an information notice or the issue of a warrant or lead directly to an enforcement notice in an appropriate case.

11–57 An information notice under s.43 may require the controller to supply the Commissioner with all of the information which might be provided under a subject access search. An information notice is therefore wider than the power of the court: however the powers of the court may be exercised with more expedition. There is a right of appeal to the Information Tribunal against an information notice.[59] Where an appeal is lodged it may be some time before the issues raised by the notice are resolved. Although in theory a warrant could be used to obtain sight of information requested under subject access search, in practice warrants have never been used for this purpose. This may be because of the difficulties of finding particular data on any large and complex system.

Where the Commissioner is satisfied that subject access should have been given, he may serve an enforcement notice on the controller requiring him to give subject access to the data. The procedures for service of an enforcement notice are set out at Ch.20, below. Failure to comply with an enforcement notice is an offence under s.47 of the Act. It is also an offence for a person knowingly or recklessly to make a false statement in response to an information notice.

CONSUMER CREDIT ACT INFORMATION

11–58 It has been noted above that requests by individuals for access to files held by credit reference agencies about them now fall under the Data Protection Act. Credit reference agencies hold data on individual consumers covering, among other things, electoral role information, county court judgments, debts and credit card payments. It is important to individuals that such information is accurate as it may affect their ability to obtain credit. Credit reference agencies are regulated by the Consumer Credit Act 1974 (CCA) which deals with licensing and other regulatory matters. The CCA is enforced by the Director General of Fair Trading. Under the CCA consumers, partnerships and companies had rights to access information held on their credit files by credit reference agencies under s.157 of the CCA. Agencies were obliged to provide consumers with a copy of the file relating to them on payment of a fee of £2. A "file" is defined in s.157(5) to mean all the information kept on an individual by a credit reference agency regardless of how it is stored. Accordingly, under these provisions, consumers had access to more information than that covered by the DPA.

Section 62 of the DPA 1998 amended the access provisions under s.158 of the CCA with the effect that those provisions only apply to "partnership or other unincorporated body of persons not consisting entirely of bodies corporate". Accordingly all access requests made by individual consumers now come under the DPA 1998 but subject to a number of special provisions. These are contained partly in the Act itself and partly in Regulations made under it. In effect this creates a specific regime dealing with access to and rectification of credit information.

---

[59] 1998 Act s.48.

The Consumer Credit (Credit Reference Agency) Regulations (SI 2000/290)

11–59 The Regulations came into force on March 1, 2000 with the Act. They deal with the provision of information to consumers by credit reference agencies and are made under s.9(3) of the DPA and ss.157(1), 158(1) and 159(5) of the CCA.

Under s.9(2) of the DPA 1998 an individual who makes a subject access request to a credit reference agency shall be taken to have limited his request to data relating to his financial standing, i.e. his credit information, unless the request specifies otherwise. Where a data controller which is a credit reference agency receives a subject access request, in addition to the usual subject access response, the controller must give the individual a statement of his rights under s.159 of the CCA, in the form prescribed in the Regulations. This sets out the individual's rights to make objections on grounds of inaccuracy and to request the insertion of notices of correction if he considers that the information is incorrect and he is likely to be prejudiced if it is not corrected.[60] A credit agency must respond to a request for a credit file within seven working days.[61]

11–60 Regulation 5 sets out the procedure to be followed where there is a dispute about the accuracy of a record and a notice of correction has not been agreed between the parties.[62] If the agency receives an objection but does not consider that the information should be altered the individual may have a notice of correction filed with the information held.[63] If the credit reference agency does not accept the notice of correction then there is a dispute resolution procedure for which the Commissioner is the adjudicator. The Regulations prescribe the equivalent forms to be given under the CCA where searches are made by partnerships and other unincorporated bodies.[64]

The CCA also contained provisions[65] setting out procedures to be followed where individuals disagreed with the contents of a credit file. They could insist on notices of correction being filed with the credit data. If the agency and the consumer could not agree on the contents of a notice of correction the Director General of Fair Trading was the adjudicator. This has now altered and, where the information concerns individuals, the adjudicator has become the Commissioner.

11–61 An application for adjudication on a dispute as to accuracy may be made by an agency or one who is the subject of credit data. In each case the one who objects must supply the name and address of the agency and the other party and indicate when the disputed notice of correction was served.[66] Where an agency makes an application it must send:

- a copy of the file supplied;

- a copy of the notice of correction;

- a copy of any related correspondence.

---

[60] CCA s.159(1).
[61] SI 2000/290 reg.3.
[62] CCA s.159(5).
[63] CCA s.195(3).
[64] SI 2000/290 Schs 2 and 3.
[65] CCA s.159.
[66] SI 2000/290 reg.5(2).

It must also state the ground on which it considers that it would be improper for it to publish a notice of correction.[67]

An application by a data subject must give particulars of the entry in the file or the information received from the agency. He must explain why he considers the information to be incorrect and why he considers he is likely to be prejudiced if the information is not corrected.[68]

11–62 A fee is payable on making the application. The Commissioner may make such an order as he thinks fit. Under s.159(6) of the CCA it is an offence for any person to fail to comply with such an order in the time.

Individuals have rights under the DPA in respect of inaccurate data. However the CCA covers all records, both manual and computerised. The s.159 rights to removal or amendment of information continue to apply to all information both manual and automated.

The DPA rights apply to:

(i) automated data;

(ii) manual data falling within relevant filing systems.

This was subject to the special transitional provisions in Sch.8 Pt II para.4.

Data about other persons may appear on consumer credit files. The extent of such information has in the past been a source of disagreement between the credit industry and the Commissioner. There is now an industry-wide agreement on the extent of third party data which is provided on a credit search.

ACCESSIBLE RECORDS

11–63 Access rights to health records were given under the Access to Health Records Act 1990, and to personal information held for social work purposes and to personal information held for public sector tenancies under the Access to Personal Files Act 1987. In each case the access rights given by the particular legislation only applied to information held in manual form; access to automated data came under the 1984 DPA. This meant that someone wanting access to his or her entire set of records would have to make two applications, one under the DPA 1984 for the computerised record and one under the particular legislation for the manual information. The rules for applying for information were slightly different and remedies for non-compliance were different. The DPA 1998 brought all the access rights together by bringing all manual health records into the data protection regime, including those which do not fall within the definition of a manual filing system. This was achieved by classifying "accessible records" as data.

"Accessible records" are defined at s.68 as either:

"(a) a health record as defined by subsection (2); or
(b) an accessible public record as defined by Schedule 11."

---

[67] SI 2000/290 reg.5(4).
[68] SI 2000/290 reg.5(3).

11–64   A health record in its turn is further defined as:

". . . any record which—
(a) consists of information relating to the physical or mental health or condition of an individual; and
(b) has been made by or on behalf of a health professional in connection with the care of that individual."

Apart from in one instance it is irrelevant whether the health professional was in the public or private sector. Moreover the record falls under the Act whenever it was made. This is different from the Access to Medical Records Act 1988, which only applied to records compiled after November 1, 1991 (except insofar as access to the earlier record was required to make intelligible the records to which access was permitted).

Section 69(2) contains a list of 15 categories of medical practitioners who are "health professionals" for the purposes of this section. The categories cover health professionals such as doctors or dentists employed in the public or private sector, however a "music therapist" will only be covered by these provisions if employed by a "health service body" as defined in s.69(3). The record must have been made by the health professional "in connection with the care of that individual". In the Access to Health Records Act 1990 s.11, care is defined as indicating "examination, investigation, diagnosis and treatment".

This definition has not been imported into the 1998 Act but in a case of ambiguity a court might find it of persuasive assistance. The 1990 Access to Medical Records Act remains in force to govern access by personal representatives of deceased patients to a deceased's medical records, but does not otherwise apply.

11–65   The second limb of s.68(1) refers to Sch.11 which contains the provisions which originated in the Access to Personal Files Act 1987, now repealed. The two sets of records covered are housing tenancy information and social work records. Tenancy information is defined as information:

"held for any purpose of the relationship of landlord and tenant of a dwelling [house] which subsists, has subsisted or may subsist between [the authority] [or as the case may be Scottish homes] [the Executive] and any individual who is, has been or, as the case may be, has applied to be a tenant of [the authority] [theirs] [the Executive]."

Note: The words in square brackets apply respectively to the positions in England, Wales, Scotland and Northern Ireland because different bodies are responsible for public sector housing in each area but the rights given by the provision and the information covered are the same. It covers information held for "any purpose" of the tenancy or putative tenancy relationship and would cover among other records allocation of tenancy, conduct of a tenancy, rent payments and arrears, repairs, and termination proceedings. In England and Wales it is specified that housing action trusts established under Pt III of the Housing Act 1988 are covered. However, it will not extend to housing associations as they are not local authorities for the purposes of s.4(e) of the Housing Act 1985. Given that housing associations are publicly funded this may not seem an obvious distinction. It should be noted also that where housing estates have been transferred to the private sector the access rights will not have been transferred.

11–66 The social work records to which individuals are entitled are those held by a local social services authority in England and Wales, a social work authority in Scotland and a health and social services board in Northern Ireland. In each case the records cover information "held for the purpose of any past, current or proposed exercise" of a social services function of one of the defined authorities. The records held by such authorities may cover child care, fostering, adoption, nurseries, special needs, disabilities, or care of the elderly. Again, only information held by public sector bodies is covered.

All of these records, now covered by the term "accessible records", have been brought under the DPA 1998 for the purpose of providing subject access and providing rights of correction. While the aim of consolidating the access provisions is welcome the method of doing so is ungainly. The guiding principles in the consolidation appear to have been:

   (i) all the records should be covered by the same regime;

  (ii) none of the existing rights should be diminished;

 (iii) no additional rights should be given unless it was inescapable to do so.

These aims are not easy to reconcile. The final resolution will be reached in October 2007 when all accessible records will come under the same regime as other automated and manual records. The subject access position is straightforward. Individuals are entitled to access to all manual records held for these purposes, unless a specific exemption can be claimed. All the s.7 access rights apply.

11–67 The provisions in relation to remedies are slightly varied. While the Commissioner's powers to take enforcement action or serve information notices in respect of any breach of Principle 6 still apply, the rights of individuals to apply to the courts for specific remedies were reduced until October 2001. The reduced rights are found in s.12A.[69] They also apply between 2001 and 2007 to a subset of manual data, that is the manual data held immediately before October 24, 1998 which cannot claim the exemption for historical research.

Although the policy was to seek to maintain the existing rules as far as possible, inevitably, the transition of the access rights to the Data Protection Act has resulted in a number of changes. In particular the exemptions which were set out on the face of the earlier Acts have now been transferred to orders made under s.30. These are dealt with at Ch.16, below.

EDUCATION RECORDS

11–68 The rights of access to education records, which were embodied in the Education (Schools Records) Regulations 1989 made under ss.218 and 232 of the Education Reform Act 1988 and corresponding enactments in Scotland and Northern Ireland have also been transferred to the Data Protection Act as "accessible records". In

---

[69] 1998 Act Sch.13.

broad terms the Regulations provided for a right of access to pupil records held by schools, although they excluded those kept by teachers purely for their personal use. Section 68(1) now covers such records as well as health and personal social work records.

The relevant records are defined in Sch.11. Paragraphs 2, 3 and 4 cover the position in England and Wales; paras 5 and 6 cover the position in Scotland; and paras 7 and 8 cover the position in Northern Ireland. In each case information processed by a teacher solely for the teacher's own use is excluded from the right.

In the case of England, Wales and Northern Ireland the information must:

    (i) relate to a person who is or has been a pupil at the school;

    (ii) be processed on behalf of a teacher or a governing body at specified types of schools;

    (iii) have been supplied from specified sources;

before access to it can be claimed.

11–69 Not all schools are subject to this provision. Ordinary private schools are excluded. The access right covers schools funded by education authorities, that is, grant maintained and maintained schools. It also applies to any special school as defined in the Education Act 1996 s.6(2).

The sources of the information are:

    (i) teachers and other school-related local authority employees;

    (ii) the pupil to whom the record relates;

    (iii) the parents of that pupil.

Information obtained from other sources, such as local police liaison officers, will not be covered. In the case of Scotland, the right covers any record processed by an education authority (as defined) for the purpose of providing education or further education to a pupil within the meaning of the Education (Scotland) Act 1980.

SECTION 12A PENALTIES

11–70 Section 12A is found in Sch.13 to the Act. It entitles a data subject to give notice to a controller where the subject believes that the controller is holding personal data which are inaccurate or incomplete, or which are being held in a manner incompatible with the legitimate purposes of the controller.

The notice must be given in writing and state the reasons for the subject's belief that the contravention has occurred. Where the subject alleges that the data are incomplete or inaccurate he can require the controller to rectify, block, erase or destroy the data. Where the subject alleges that the data are being held in a way incompatible with the controller's legitimate purposes he may require the controller to cease holding the data in such a way.

If a court is satisfied that a subject has given such a notice which is justified, or justified to any extent and that the controller has failed to comply with it, the court may order the controller to do so. Data are incomplete for these purposes if they would be inadequate or are out of date (s.12A(5)).

PRACTICAL TOOLS

Precedent

11–71

Request for Subject Access

Comments	Letter
Give your full address and postcode and a phone number if possible	Mrs J. J. 101 High Street Anytown Countyshire AN2 3AB Tel: 0123 533333 (daytime)
Address to head office	To: Import Finance Ltd 123 Commerce Street Bigtown Metropol B12 2CD
Date and keep a copy of the letter.	22nd February 2003
	Dear Sirs
Make it clear this is a formal request.	**Data Protection Act 1998** **Subject Access Request**
Help the organisation deal with your request.	I wish to exercise my rights under data protection to obtain access to data you have about me. If you do not deal with this for your [company] [organisation] please pass this letter to the person who does.
Provide relevant information to help the controller identify you and find the information you want.	I am a customer of your company and have done business with you since 1989. My customer account number is 123XYZ.

Comments	Letter
	Are you or anyone acting on your behalf processing any personal data about me?
	If so, provide me with the following information about any processing covered by the 1998 Data Protection Act.
Section 7(1)(b)(i), 1998 Act	1. What type of data do you have about me?
Section 7(1)(b)(ii), 1998 Act	2. What purposes is it being processed or likely to be processed for?
Section 7(1)(b)(ii), 1998 Act	3. Who is the data being disclosed to or likely to be disclosed to?
Section 7(1)(c)(ii), 1998 Act	4. If you have any information about where the data comes from or who gave it to you please supply that information.
There is no statutory obligation on the controller to answer this query.	5. Have you taken, or to your knowledge has anyone else taken, any significant decision about me on the basis of data automatically processed by you or on your behalf?
Section 7(1)(d), 1998 Act	6. If the answer to question 5 is yes, describe the logic involved in that decision.
Section 7(1)(c)(i), 1998 Act	Please provide me with a copy of the information constituting the data which you hold about me.
Under the Act this must be supplied before the data are provided	I enclose a fee of £10.00.
Section 7(9), 1998 Act	You have 40 days in which to deal with my request. The 40 days will end on ....
	I look forward to hearing from you. Yours sincerely,

Note: Remember to enclose the fee and appropriate authority if you are acting for another person.

Case Study

Third Party Data Subject Access Case Study

11–72   The Chief Police Officer of Anytown, Chief Constable Copa, is responsible for the records held by his force. He is the registered data controller for them. His records include a report of an alleged incident of criminal damage at a local fish and chip shop which led to the arrest of a youth named Albert Bracegirdle (AB).

The record includes the date of the alleged incident; the name and address of AB; a record of the fact that AB was arrested but never charged; the name and address of the owner of the fish and chip shop, a Mr Christopher Dent (CD); the collar number and station of the two officers who attended the scene (numbers 123 and 456, Blue Hill); the names and addresses of two passers-by (EF and GH) who gave statements about what they saw of the incident.

There is also information contained in the text about another individual (X) who is not named. This person was seen by both EF and GH, who provided clear descriptions of him. The substance of the report is that the officers were called to the fish and chip shop by CD at the close of business. CD had been in the back of the shop closing up for the day when he heard the crash of the shop window breaking. He ran into the front part of the shop and saw AB running out of the door. He grabbed AB and held on to him. He then called the police who arrested AB. When questioned AB denied that he had caused any damage or indeed any trouble. He explained that he had entered the shop and was trying to attract CD's attention, hoping for a late night chip supper, when he heard the crash and saw the window had been smashed inward. When CD came running out obviously in a rage AB panicked and made a run for it. He had seen no one else. He had not been looking at the window when the damage occurred.

11–73 In response to local enquiries EF and GH made statements later. They had been walking home and had seen a youth running away at around the same time just after they had heard the crash. They described the youth as a white male of medium height, with a bald head, wearing a green leather jacket and appearing to have a scar on one side of his face. Their statements supported AB's contention. The damage also supported AB's statement in that it was clear that the damage had been caused by a blow to the outside of the window as the glass was on the floor inside. The youth with the leather jacket was never found. AB was released without charge. The youth is referred to in the record as X.

AB applies for subject access. How much of the third party information on this record does he have to be given and what information can be withheld?

The first point to make is that the Chief Constable must provide AB with as much of the information as he can without disclosing the identity of other persons. The fact that third parties feature in a record or are identified in it is not a reason for withholding access to the record itself. The data controller must start from the basis that he has an obligation to give the information and can only withhold third party information on specific grounds applicable to each third party.

11–74 The Chief Constable will have to decide whether there is information on the record which relates to third parties who can be identified from that information. In the case study CD, EF and GH can clearly be identified from the information on the records. Their names and addresses are provided. The police officers can also be identified by AB who saw them, was arrested by them and would be able to identify them by a combination of the knowledge in his possession and the information on the record which contains their collar numbers and the station from which they work. The identity of X, however, is problematic.

On the information available from the record no-one without special knowledge would be able to identify X. The controller has to consider whether it is possible that a person having special knowledge could do so. In this case it is suggested identification would be possible because this is such a clear and specific description. There cannot have been many bald, scarred young men in green leather jackets running around the vicinity of the fish and chip shop at the time of the incident. It is possible therefore that X could be identified by a combination of the information available on the record and the special knowledge of anyone who already knows the person answering his description or who might be placed to establish it by making local inquiries. In this case the controller may reasonably assume further inquiries would be as fruitless as they were for the police officers but it is still possible that AB already has the special knowledge that would allow him to identify X.

The controller must decide whether it is likely AB has such special knowledge. In making this assessment the controller will have to have regard as to what is already known about AB. It is not open to him to make inquiries of AB as to the extent of his knowledge because that might be tantamount to disclosing the third party data.

11–75 It is suggested that in the absence of positive evidence that AB has sufficient information to identify X, the data controller cannot form a reasonable belief that such knowledge is or is likely to become available to him and accordingly he should treat the information about X as not being third party data. Once it is established that data is not third party data it must be given to the subject. AB is therefore entitled to the information about X.

The next information considered is that relating to the police officers. In this case it would be reasonable for the Chief Constable to provide the data. There is nothing confidential about it. It is not within the sensitive data categories within the Act. It is already at least partly known to the data subject who was interviewed by the officers and may recall their names. The officers were acting in their formal working capacity.

The shopkeeper (CD). In this case it might depend upon the extent of the data involved and what AB already knows. AB already clearly knows his identity and the shop address. He probably will also know that CD has given a statement but the record also includes CD's home address and this might not be known to AB and might cause some sensitivity. It would be reasonable to seek CD's consent, therefore, before imparting that information.

The passers-by (EF and GH). There is no reason to suppose that this information is already known to AB. These people may have no idea their information might be made available to him. Unless they had been warned of a potential disclosure it would be appropriate to seek their consent before disclosing information about them.

11–76 In the case study, therefore AB will be given the identifying data about the officers. CD will be asked for consent to disclose his home address. EF and GH will be asked to consent to the disclosure of information to AB. if CD, EF or GH refuse, the Chief Officer will have to consider whether to give the information despite their refusal. He might decide that there is no reason why AB's request should outweigh the privacy of the witnesses and decide not to give it. AB will also be given the data on X because X was not classed as a third party.

The Chief Constable has 40 days from the receipt of AB's initial request to provide all the data except the third party data for which he decides to seek consent. If in this case he asked CD's consent to disclose his home address 20 days after receiving AB's request, if CD takes a further month to answer his letter, the Chief Constable would have to provide the bulk of the data at the expiry of 40 days from the receipt of AB's request, but as far as the information on CD was concerned he would have another 40 days from receipt of CD's consent.

Checklist for data controller: subject access

How to use this checklist

11–77 The average data controller may not need to use all of the points on this checklist. It is suggested he should select those appropriate to his particular circumstances. He may also find it necessary to add further details under some of the headings. The checklist should therefore be used as a starting point in producing a subject access procedure.

- Is the request written or sent electronically or is it oral?
- If the request is oral is it appropriate to respond to it or to insist on a written request or one sent by electronic means?
- At which office or branch was the request received?
- On what date was the request received?
- Is the request accompanied by the correct fee?
- Has the person making the request given an intelligible name and address or other contact to which the controller can respond?
- Has the person making the request provided sufficient information on which the controller can be satisfied as to his or her identity?
- Is this a request for which the 40-day period is the maximum response time?
- If the 40-day period does not apply, what is the maximum response time?
- On what date does the maximum response time expire?
- Has an acknowledgement of receipt of the request been sent to the individual?
- Has the person making the request made any previous subject access requests?
- If this is the case, what period of time has elapsed since the last request?
- If this is the case, is it reasonable for another request to be made and responded to now?
- Is a copy of any previous response to a subject access request available?
- Is this request made by the individual to whom it relates or by another acting on his or her behalf?
- If it is made by another, in what capacity is that person acting?
- Is proof of authority to apply on behalf of the other required or has it been supplied by the applicant?
- Is the request made by a child?
- Is the request made by a child in Scotland?
- If the request is made on behalf of a child, does the person making it have locus standi to do so in respect of the child?

- What is the child's age?

- Has the person making the request provided sufficient information to locate the data and information sought?

- Has the person making the request specified that the request is limited to any particular type of personal data?

- Does the request relate to any form of accessible record, that is a health record, social work record, housing record in the public sector, education record?

- Does the controller hold unstructured manual data [in the case of a public authority]?

- Does the request relate to a credit file?

- Are any sources of the data available?

- Have any disclosures been made from the data or are any planned to be made from this data?

- Who are the recipients of such disclosures? Can they be described specifically or generally?

- Have all internal available information sources been searched for information in relation to this inquiry including manual sources and word processing sources?

- Is any of the data which is held sensitive data?

- For what purposes is this date held or used?

- Is any data relating to the person making the request being processed by or on behalf of the controller by any other parties?

- Is any of the data processed by automatic means so as to form the basis of any decision affecting the data subject?

- Is the effect of such a decision likely to be significant to the data subject?

- Is the processing the sole basis for such a decision?

- Is the logic involved in that decision-making available to be supplied to the individual?

- Does any of the logic constitute a trade secret?

- Does the data contain any information relating to other living individuals?

- Can any of those individuals be identified from that information?

- Is it likely that any of those individuals could be identified by the data subject from his or her own knowledge or knowledge which he or she is likely to acquire?

- Have the third parties been contacted and asked for their consent to disclose the data relating to them?

- Have they been asked to consent within a specific time scale?

- Have the third parties consented or refused to consent to the disclosure of data relating to them?

- Is any obligation of confidentiality owed to any of the third parties?

- Does any of the data relating to the third parties arise from their professional roles?

- Is it reasonable to disclose data relating to any of the third parties without their consent?

- Is it appropriate to claim any of the exemptions from subject access in respect of any of the data?

- Is it possible to supply a copy of the data in permanent form or must other arrangements for supply be made?

- Is the data in an intelligible form or should explanations be supplied with it?

ADDITIONAL INFORMATION

Derivations

11–78 • Directive 95/46 (See App.B)
    (a) Art.12 (right of access).
    (b) Recital 41.

- European Convention for the Protection of Human Rights and Fundamental Freedoms 1950: Art.8 (right to respect for private and family life).

- Council of Europe Convention of January 28, 1981 for the Protection of Individuals with regard to automatic processing of Personal Data: Art.8b (additional safeguards for the data subject).

- Data Protection Act 1984: s.21 (subject access).

- Organisation for Economic Co-operation and Development Guidelines: Annex Part Two (basic principles of national application) 13.

Hansard references

11–79 Vol.586, No.108, CWH 44, Lords Grand Committee, February 23, 1998
Trade secrets and whether the term should be widened to cover all intellectual property.

Vol.586, No.110, col.107, Lords Grand Committee, February 25, 1998
Disclosure of references.

Vol.587, No.127, col.1094, Lords Third Reading, March 24, 1998
Subject access general.

Commons Standing Committee D, May 12, 1998, col.20, 23
Accessible records.

Commons Standing Committee D, May 14, 1998, col.69, 70
Consumer credit information requests made to credit reference agencies.

ibid., col.79, 80, 90
Sources of data, the logic of decision making, access to third party data.

ibid., col.108
Reasonable interval.

ibid., col.112
Trade secret.

ibid., col.115
Data to be provided as at the time of the request.

Commons Standing Committee D, June 4, 1998, col.296
Accessible records amendments made.

Vol.315, No.198, col.577, Commons Third Reading, July 2, 1998
Access to decision making logic.

ibid.
Trade credit references.

Vol.591, No.184, col.1477, 1478, Lords consideration of Commons amendments, July 10, 1998
Intention behind provisions dealing with accessible records.

ibid., col.1482
Credit reference searches.

ibid., col.1484
"Trade secret" wide enough to cover credit scoring algorithms.

Previous case law

11–80   *R. v Chief Constable of B County Constabulary and the Director of the National Identification Service Ex p. R* reported in Annual Report of the Data Protection Registrar 1997. In this case the High Court held that under the 1984 Act a Chief Constable did not have discretion to give only part of a record in response to a subject access request.

CHAPTER 12

Rights to Prevent Processing

INTRODUCTION

12–01   The Act contains two distinct rights to prevent processing. Section 11 provides individuals with a specific right to prevent processing for the purposes of marketing. Section 10 affords a more general right of objection, but the circumstances in which it can apply are limited. Both sections are covered in this chapter. The s.11 right is an absolute right; s.10 is subject to a balancing test.

Section 10 sets out the right to "prevent processing" however the grounds on which processing may be prevented have been restrictively transposed from the Directive. It is not clear that the national provisions adopted are sufficient to comply with the Directive. The issue is dealt with at the end of this chapter. In this chapter an interpretation which seeks to accord with the terms in the Directive has been suggested where possible. Even as curtailed, however, s.10 is a significant step towards establishing control over one's information. While individuals cannot stop the tax man calculating what he is owed or the police keeping records of speeding convictions they can, in some circumstances, stop particular disclosures or have records to which they object removed.

SUMMARY OF MAIN POINTS

12–02

(a) A specific right is provided in the case of direct marketing. This is not subject to conditions.

(b) A data controller who is aware that a transferee of the data intends to use the personal data for direct marketing must take account of any objections to the transfer for that use.

(c) The right of objection applies to all direct marketing, whatever the medium used, but there are further restrictions on marketing by telephone, fax and email.[1]

(d) The right to insist that marketing material is stopped applies to a company's own marketing to its customers, as well as marketing by third parties.

---

[1] See Ch.22, below on Privacy and Electronic Communications for these provisions.

(e) There is no right to prevent processing (other than for marketing) where the controller relies on one or more of the primary grounds, that is the first four grounds of Sch.2, to legitimise his processing.

(f) The individual must show that the grounds of his objection are made out before the controller is obliged to comply with the objection (other than for marketing).

(g) In deciding whether to accept an objection (other than for marketing) the controller has to balance his reasons for processing against the grounds of objection.

(h) There are no special provisions in relation to sensitive data however:

(i) it is unlikely that sensitive data will be available to use for direct marketing as explicit consent would be required;

(ii) the processing of sensitive data would be more likely to give rise to damage or distress than non-sensitive data so it is more likely that a s.10 notice of objection would succeed where such data are concerned.

(i) The s.10 right can be exercised by an individual who objects to the disclosure of personal data by a public authority under the Freedom of Information Act 2000.

RIGHT TO PREVENT PROCESSING FOR DIRECT MARKETING

12–03   This gives individuals an absolute right to require the controller to stop such processing. It was the only provision in the Bill which was given whole-hearted endorsement by both Lord Williams for the Government and Lord Astor for the Opposition on the First Reading of the Bill in the House of Lords on February 3, 1998.

Direct marketing is defined in s.11(3) as meaning:

"the communication (by whatever means) of any advertising or marketing material which is directed to particular individuals."

It covers processing directly aimed at producing personal mail, fax, telephone calls or any other form of communication. It would also be sufficient to cover host mailings, that is, inserts with other mail, or "stuffers" as they are known. Although the point has not yet been tested, it probably extends beyond preventing the receipt of marketing approaches. It may enable an individual to require a controller to cease profiling, screening or data-mining activities even where they do not result in the direct arrival of marketing materials to the individuals. This is because the right in s.11(1) is to require the data controller "to cease, or not to begin, processing for the purposes of direct marketing personal data in respect of which he is the data subject". Data may be processed for the purposes of direct marketing even though the processing does not result in the arrival of marketing material to the individual.

12–04   In the Commissioner's Legal Guidance[2] it is stated:

---

[2] OIC, *Legal Guidance*, p.55.

"The Commissioner regards the term 'direct marketing' as covering a wide range of activities which will apply not just to the offer for sale of goods or services, but also the promotion of an organisations' aims and ideals. This would include a charity or political party making an appeal for funds or support and, for example an organization whose campaign is designed to encourage individuals to write to their MP on a particular matter or attend a public meeting or rally."

The broad meaning of this term was endorsed by the Information Tribunal in *Scottish National Party v Information Commissioner*. In that case the Commissioner took action under the Privacy and Electronic Communications (EC Directive) Regulations 2003 (PECR) against the Scottish Nationalist Party (SNP). The SNP had made unsolicited automated calls playing a recorded message exhorting listeners to support the Party. They refused to stop despite complaint because they claimed that the message was not a marketing message and therefore did not fall under the rules in the PECR. The Tribunal did not agreed and upheld the broad meaning of the term. The right applies in circumstances where the data controller "anticipates" that the personal data will be used for marketing. The effect of this term was considered in the case of *R. (Robertson) v City of Wakefield and Home Office*[3] described earlier.[4] Mr Robertson objected to the sale of the electoral roll to third parties who would use it for, among other commercial purposes, direct marketing. The electoral registration officer who sold the roll did not himself use the data for direct marketing. The question for the court was whether the electoral registration officer could be prevented by a notice under s.11 from passing on the data to the third parties. The judge considered Art.14(b) of the Directive on which s.11 is based and which provides that the data subject must have the right:

"to object, on request and free of charge, to the processing of personal data relating to him which the controller anticipates being processed for the purposes of direct marketing, or to be informed before personal data are disclosed for the first time to third parties or used on their behalf for the purposes of direct marketing, and to be expressly offered the right to object free of charge to such disclosures or uses."

12–05 It was common ground that the United Kingdom had implemented the first limb of the Article in s.11. The claimant submitted that domestic law did not meet the requirement in Art.14 as the electoral registration officer had a statutory duty to sell copies of the electoral register and there was no provision in the relevant Regulations for individuals to register their rights of objection to the subsequent use of the data for direct marketing.

The judge found as a matter of fact that the register was sold for marketing:

". . . for many years, the data contained in the Register have been purchased by commercial interests and it has been obvious to EROs and to others that the data so purchased have been used for, among other things, direct marketing purposes."

---

[3] [2001] EWHC Admin 915.
[4] See Ch.2, above for fuller discussion.

The judge held that s.11 will apply where the data controller "anticipates" that personal data will be processed for direct marketing, even if that processing is carried out by another. He considered that such a reading of s.11 was compliant with the Directive. The judge made clear that he was seeking to establish an interpretation which would accord with the purpose of the provision. He also referred to the construction as being supported by the recital to the Directive, when read as a whole. On the facts he held that the electoral registration officer should have accepted the claimant's objection. Despite the fact that the finding on s.11 in *Robertson* was potentially wide it does not appear to have impacted on any other public registers.

12–06　The prohibitory notice may cover the marketing of the company's own goods or services, not just the goods or services of others. Thus it will be wider in scope than the addition of a name to the Mailing Preference Service (MPS) suppression file. This is an industry initiative, run by the Direct Marketing Association, under which individuals who object to the receipt of direct mail may have their names added to a database which is then made available as a tool against which mailing lists are "cleaned".[5]

The recommended database management technique to deal with objection is to add suppression markers next to names and addresses where the individuals have objected to the receipt of marketing materials, rather than to erase those names and addresses. This ensures that the names and addresses cannot be added on again from other sources. However, where this technique is adopted, the data continue to be held and processed. If an individual continues to object in cases where a data controller wishes to use suppression markers, the controller may have to argue that processing the data so marked is not processing for the purposes of direct marketing.

12–07　The right is equivalent to a strict liability provision. The formalities for service of the notice are limited. Notice must be given in writing but it need not mention the section. A controller has no obligation to reply to a notice but it would usually be reasonable to expect him to do so. Failure to comply may result in court action by the individual or a complaint to the Commissioner.

The individual must specify the time in which he requires the notice of objection to take effect, which is to be "such period as is reasonable in all the circumstances". This must be a question of fact. It may be appropriate to allow longer to cease existing mailing than it would to not begin new mailing because of the length of time over which mailings may run.

If a controller fails to comply with a notice the individual may apply to court and the court may order a controller to take steps to comply with the requirement as the court sees fit. Failure to comply with an individual's objection may also lead to enforcement by the Data Protection Commissioner under Principle 6. In the Directive an obligation is imposed on the Member States to take necessary measures to ensure that data subjects are aware of the existence of this right.

Opt-out boxes and s.11

12–08　Opt-out boxes are the little boxes on forms or websites, etc. that can be ticked or checked to signify that the individual does not want to receive marketing material. They accompany notices which usually explain the various kinds of

---

[5] To register with the MPS visit *www.mpsonline.org.uk* or telephone MPS Registration line 0845 703 4599.

marketing which the data controller intends to carry out. They appear on reply coupons and order forms, any mechanism which the individual has to return to the controller. A common form wording is:

"We may pass your details to third parties so they may offer goods and services which may be of interest to you. Tick here if you would prefer not to receive such offers."

Sometimes the notice and options offered are more detailed. The customer may be offered options about receiving material from the data controller itself or telephone or email or SMS contact as well as third party marketing, sometimes an easy opt-out from third party marketing, such as a tick box, but a more difficult mechanism to opt-out of the data controller's own marketing is offered. The precise content and extent of the collection notice required will depend on the circumstances in which the data are obtained and what the data controller intends to do with the information. A discussion of the requirements for collection notices can be found in Ch.5, above in relation to Principle 1. In this section the relationship with s.11 is considered. Section 11 does not make "opt-out" boxes mandatory, although trade association codes of practice may do so. The controller must comply with Principle 1 and must honour any objections lodged in accordance with s.11. However the most commonly accepted way of providing both notice and choice is to combine notice with an easy option on any collection form or mechanism which a data subject must return to a data controller. The opt-out may cover both the data controller's marketing and the use of the data for third party marketing.

In some forms of trading, particularly mail order trading, it is not realistic to offer an opt-out from the data controller's own marketing and the opt-out box may be confined to use for third party marketing or only third party marketing.

Right to Prevent Other Processing

12–09 As is explained in Ch.6, above no one can process personal data unless he can justify the processing as being within at least one of the grounds listed in Sch.2. These are divided into the four primary grounds set out in paras 1–4 and the remaining secondary grounds in paras 4–6. In practice it is likely that controllers will seek to rely on more than one of the grounds for any processing. Although technically an individual only has the right to object where the processing is based on one of the secondary grounds, in reality he will usually also be able to object where one of the primary grounds is relied upon, that is the consent ground, because in most cases consent can be revoked. In this context, therefore, consent is dealt with separately from the other three primary grounds for processing.

No right to object

12–10 An individual cannot object under s.10 where the processing is carried out with consent or on one of the following Sch.2 grounds:

"(2) The processing is necessary:

    (a) for the performance of a contract to which the data subject is a party; or

    (b) for the taking of steps at the request of the data subject with a view to entering into a contract;

(3) The processing is necessary for compliance with any legal obligation to which the data controller is subject, other than an obligation imposed by contract; or

(4) The processing is necessary in order to protect the vital interests of the data subject."

The Secretary of State has the power to prescribe additional cases in which individuals will have no right of objection to particular processing.[6]

If they wish to escape the possibility of s.10 objections, data controllers will wish to rely on one of the primary grounds for processing. Controllers should consider whether they can bring their processing within one of those grounds. There may also be cases where classes of controllers will wish to lobby the Secretary of State to make s.10(2)(b) orders in order to overcome the possible problems caused by the right to object, particularly where they are otherwise dependent upon consent.

Processing on the basis of consent

12–11 Under Sch.2 para.1 the fact that "the data subject has given his consent to the processing" is a legitimising ground for processing.[7] The consent must apply to the relevant processing. The existence of consent validates processing. A consent once given can be presumed to continue for so long as the particular relevant processing to which it relates continues; however, reliance on consent entails a risk to the controller that the consent may be withdrawn. Data controllers who rely on consent may seek to couple it with an interest or make it irrevocable or only capable of withdrawal upon express notice, in order to lessen this risk. Nevertheless, revocation must remain a possibility. In *Johnson v MDU*[8] there was a brief consideration of the relationship between the terms of a contract and the question of consent to processing. The point is not wholly clear but the view of the judge appeared to be that the data subject could not withdraw consent for the processing of personal data which was necessary for performance of a contractual relationship. The better view might be that the data subject can withdraw consent but the data controller can then rely on another ground.

If a data subject who has previously consented to a form of processing notifies the controller of an objection to the processing, that objection may operate as a withdrawal of the consent. In determining whether consent has been withdrawn regard will have to be had to the terms of the consent which was originally obtained and any provisions for withdrawal. Once consent to processing has been withdrawn the controller must rely on another ground. A private sector data controller may then be forced to rely upon para.6 of Sch.2(1) that the:

"processing is necessary for the purposes of legitimate interest pursued by the controller or by the third party or parties to whom the data are disclosed, except

---

[6] 1998 Act s.10(2)(b)—no orders have been made or proposed up to the data of writing.

[7] For a more detailed discussion of the meaning of consent see Ch.3, above.

[8] [2007] 1 All E.R. 467.

where the processing is unwarranted in any particular case by reason of prejudice to the rights and freedoms or legitimate interest of the data subject."

A public sector data controller would (assuming he was not processing as a result of a mandatory duty, in which case consent would be irrelevant) be forced to rely upon para.5 of Sch.2(1) that the processing is necessary for one of the purposes or functions set out in the ground.

Where these grounds are relied upon, a s.10 objection can be raised to the processing. An individual who wishes to exercise a s.10 right should therefore ensure that any existing consent has been revoked, although it should be recognized that a court may in any event be prepared to treat a s.10 request as a revocation in itself, if it is sufficiently explicit. On the other hand, controllers will wish to bind individuals to maintain their consent and may look for ways to make consent difficult to revoke even if irrevocability cannot be achieved.

Grounds to which objections may be made

12–12   If the controller bases his processing on Grounds 5 or 6 of Sch.2 then the data subject will have the right to object to the processing. Ground 5 reads:

"5. The processing is necessary:

(a) for the administration of justice,
(b) for the exercise of any functions conferred on any person by or under any enactment,
(c) for the exercise of any functions of the Crown, a Minister of the Crown, or a government department, or
(d) for the exercise of any other functions of a public nature exercised in the public interest by any person."

In order to establish which activities will be covered by these grounds it helps to look back to para.3 of Sch.2 which covers those cases where processing is "necessary for compliance with a legal obligation to which the controller is subject".

Grounds 3 and 5 must be intended to apply to different circumstances. Any organisation, whether in the public or private sector, which is processing in order to fulfill a legal duty will be able to rely on the para.3 ground. The Inland Revenue is under an obligation to assess the tax liability of citizens. The police have an obligation to keep records of reportable offences; these will process in reliance on Ground 3. It follows therefore that, where data controllers in the public sector are concerned, such controllers will rely on para.5 where the controller is relying on a discretionary power. Applying this approach the individual will be unable to object to processing carried out by a public body where the controller is fulfilling a legal duty but he will be able to do so where the controller is exercising a discretionary power. The right to object to processing in the public sector therefore appears to apply where the controller is carrying out a function on the basis of a power rather than a duty. As a matter of principle this seems to be a reasonable interpretation and one which would accord with the Directive.

In the private sector, Ground 6 may be widely relied upon for marketing and uses of data which are ancillary to the primary relationship. As noted above, it involves balancing the competing interests of the individual and the data controller.

WHICH PROCESSING CAN BE PREVENTED?

12–13 Having ascertained whether the right applies to the processing in question, the controller must consider the extent of that right and the grounds on which it may be exercised. The right can perhaps best be regarded as a right to restrict the extent of processing. Section 10 offers the individual a flexible range of requirements which he can seek to impose upon the controller. The individual cannot restrict the processing of data about anyone else, only about himself, although the grounds for restricting it include damage or distress to another. The individual may require the controller to stop processing already under way or to refrain from starting prospective processing. He can seek to restrict the processing by reference to:

(a) the purpose of the processing;

(b) any particular type of processing;

(c) any data held in respect of him.

Processing is defined in s.1 of the Act and covers a wide range of information activities including dissemination of data, alteration of data or their recording. The individual can therefore require that a record should be erased not simply marked; that the controller stop making disclosure of data to others for their purposes; that the controller cease to hold any data about him; cease to disseminate data to particular people; cease to process data for particular purposes; erase particular data fields or make other detailed amendments to his processing. In the notice to the controller the individual must set out the precise processing to which he objects and which he requires to be changed. Despite the right being potentially a wide one there have been very few cases in which it has been raised. It has not been used in the majority of the cases on privacy described in Ch.2, above or if cited has not been the main ground relied upon. In several cases the court have taken the view that a claim under the DPA adds nothing to the rights of the individual under Art.8 of the European Convention on Human Rights and Fundamental Freedoms (ECHRFF). In both the *Campbell* and the *Douglas* cases the s.10 right was initially raised but never became part of the final case.

GROUNDS OF OBJECTION: WHAT DOES THE INDIVIDUAL HAVE TO SHOW?

12–14 The individual must:

(a) describe the data involved and the processing to which he objects stating:

    (i) that the processing in question is causing or is likely to cause substantial damage or substantial distress to himself or another; and

    (ii) that that damage or distress would be unwarranted.

(b) give the reasons why he asserts the processing would cause such distress and would be unwarranted.

Section 10 was amended by the Government during its passage through Parliament. Originally the individual had to show that the processing was unwarranted and was likely to cause substantial damage or substantial distress to him or another. The amendment has reversed the order of the two grounds, and appears to have applied the test of being "unwarranted" to the damage or distress involved. This anticipates that processing could be carried out on one of the secondary grounds, could cause substantial damage or distress to the individual but that damage or distress could be justified by the controller as being "warranted". Each of the elements the individual must cover is dealt with below.

Describe the data and the processing

12–15   A description of the data will be sufficient if it sets out the categories of information involved, for example personnel data, education records, records of insurance contracts; or it may be more specific and relate to particular detailed information, for example the age of the individual.

The individual must describe the processing to which he objects. He can describe it in general terms or he can describe it by reference to a purpose or to a particular activity. Where a description is to be given by reference to a purpose it may be appropriate to consider how purpose is specified in other parts of the Act. Principle 2 deals with the specification of purpose, requiring that:

"personal data shall be obtained only for one or more specified and lawful purposes . . ."

Paragraph 5 of Pt II of Sch.1, which gives definitions, states that the purpose or purposes for which personal data are obtained may in particular be specified:

"(i) in a notice given for the purpose of paragraph 2 by the controller to the subject; or

(ii) in a notification given to the Commissioner under Part III of this Act."

It is suggested that it will be sufficient for the individual to adopt any of these methods of describing the purpose of the processing as long as the description is sufficient to enable the data controller to pinpoint the particular data involved and to understand which purpose he has in mind. The individual may alternatively describe the processing by referring to the processing activity being undertaken, for example he may refer specifically to disclosure of the data by transmission, dissemination or otherwise making it available or to recording or holding the data. Once he has described the data and the relevant processing the individual must go on to specify how the processing is causing or is likely to cause substantial damage or distress to himself or another and why that would be unwarranted.

Show substantial damage or distress is likely

12–16 The damage or distress has to be related to the processing and not to the nature of the data, although as processing includes the holding of data this may be a meaningless distinction. A likelihood of damage or distress is also required. This appears to be intended to be a stronger test than a mere risk of damage or distress. It is not clear what would constitute substantial damage or substantial distress. The test of substantiality raises problems of construction. Prima facie the test of substantiality must be the same in relation to both damage and distress. The term "substantial" is one of those words, like significant or reasonable, that import the concept of proportionality and thus depend greatly on context. In the Shorter Oxford English Dictionary "substantial" affords a wide range of shades of meaning as:

"(a) is or exists as a substance, having a real existence;

  (b) (law) belonging to or involving essential right, or the merits of a matter;

  (c) (of food) ample;

  (d) (of structures) solid and workmanlike;

  (e) of ample or considerable amount, quantity or dimensions."

For the purposes of the Contempt of Court Act 1981, under which penalties may be imposed for activities which create a "substantial risk" of prejudice to a fair trial, it has been held that a substantial risk means a real risk, more than a remote risk.[9] It is suggested that in the context of the Act the test of substantiality should be no more onerous. The Directive refers only to the individual having "compelling legitimate grounds" for his objection. It does not require damage or distress to be involved. It is suggested that it is sufficient that there be a real likelihood of damage or distress arising as a result of the processing.

A further question arises as to how substantial distress is to be ascertained. This could be determined on either a subjective or an objective basis. If a data subject is particularly sensitive to what others think of him he may be prone to extreme distress by knowing that something detrimental is recorded about him. It appears there would be some difficulty in adopting a subjective test. If the test were subjective an individual's rights might vary with the depth of his sensibilities. It is suggested that the test should be objective. If the individual can show that the processing would be likely to cause distress to a person of ordinary sensibility in the shoes of the data subject the ground should be made out. This must be distinguished from the evidential difficulty. Clearly if an individual asserts that particular processing is likely to cause real distress the controller is not likely to be in a position to disprove this. Damage will mean actual damage. (For a discussion of what constitutes damage see Ch.14, below.)

Unwarranted damage and distress

12–17 This appears to entail a balancing test between the reasons of the data controller for the processing and the effect on the individual. The reasons for the subject's

---

[9] *Attorney-General v Independent Television News Ltd* [1995] 2 All E.R. 370.

objection need to be set out sufficiently to allow the controller to consider them and decide whether he accepts them. The subject must explain why he considers the processing would cause unwarranted damage or distress. The damage or distress point is a matter for the individual to assert. Then he must show why it is unwarranted. The most likely reasons which may be given as unwarranted are that the processing will amount to a breach of the private or family life of the individual, for example that the data user is holding sensitive data which is not justified by the particular circumstances and which may be intrusive, or that the processing amounts to a breach of the Data Protection Principles, for example that the data is being held for longer than is necessary by the data controller.

It is unlikely that inaccuracy of the data would be sufficient to rely upon as there is a specific remedy where data is inaccurate, but a breach of one of the other Principles could well give grounds for making an application for objection. The data may be irrelevant to the purpose; they may be excessive or inadequate, may have been held for longer than is necessary for the purpose or may have been obtained by trickery or deception or used in a way which is incompatible with the purpose for which they were obtained.

Formalities of the objection

12–18 A s.10 notice must be given in writing. It does not have to be served at a specific address but it would be advisable to send it to the data controller's head office or administrative centre and it may be helpful to address it to a data protection officer. The request does not have to refer to s.10 or be in any particular form although it will probably be helpful to controllers if it does so.

The notice has to specify a time within which the controller is required to comply. A reasonable time for compliance will depend upon the particular processing involved unless it is essential to comply in a shorter time scale, e.g. to restrain a proposed disclosure is unlikely to be less than 28 days, which is the equivalent minimum time within which a controller would be expected to comply with an enforcement notice.

How should a data controller respond?

12–19 A data controller must tell the subject, by written notice, whether he agrees to take the action or objects to it within 21 days of receiving the objection notice. In his response under s.20(3) he must state that he has complied or intends to comply with the notice or state his reasons for regarding the data subject's notice as unjustified and the extent (if any) to which he has complied or intends to comply with it. The controller may therefore agree to a request in whole or in part. Alternatively a controller may choose to respond by requesting further information from the data subject to enable the controller to find the particular data or to isolate the processing. Although such exchanges are not required by statute, in any subsequent court hearing a court is likely to consider how the data controller has dealt with the request. Equally, a data controller may wish to enter into negotiations to find an alternative method of dealing with the individual's concerns. The cost of complying with a requisition is not dealt with in the section and it is not clear how far a controller is entitled to take this into account. Cost alone will probably not be a sufficient reason to justify refusal to comply with a requisition, unless the cost is thoroughly disproportionate; it may however be a relevant factor for a court to consider in deciding how an application which it decides is justified should be complied with. The section gives no assistance on this point or on what a controller should do if he cannot comply with the requisition without making major changes to the processing or if he cannot comply with the requisition because the data also relate to a third party. The Act is silent on these points.

Once a controller receives a request not to process in a specific way, for example by making a disclosure which he plans to make, he is under no obligation to stop the processing involved immediately. Receipt of a requisition does not impose a ban upon processing. However, it is possible that an individual could seek an injunction to restrain the controller from continuing to process, for example by making a specified disclosure. If a disclosure were made without justification after receipt of a s.10 objection which the court later upheld, the individual might subsequently be able to claim damages under s.13 of the Act. Under the Freedom of Information Act 2000 the fact that an individual has lodged a valid s.10 objection which has been accepted by the data controller may be a ground upon which the personal data relating to the data subject may be exempt from the obligation to disclose in response to a request. The provision is dealt with in Ch.4, above.

Objection to processing after the death of the data subject

12–20   The DPA only applies to the living individuals and gives no privacy protection to the dead. This can be a cause of great distress to families. It is not clear whether an objection lodged during the lifetime of the individual can endure after death or if the data controller ceases to be bound by the objection once the individual has died. If the objection can endure for the benefit of the estate it would enable individuals to protect the privacy of their personal information after death. This would be of particular interest now that the Freedom of Information Act 2000 is fully in force. If individuals could serve s.10 notices on public bodies, such as their GP or the HM Revenue and Customs, who held personal information about them which would endure after death, they would be able to preserve at least some of their privacy into the grave.

Relation to the Principles

12–21   Failure to comply with a notice under s.10 may be a breach of the sixth Data Protection Principle by virtue of para.3 of Pt II of Sch.1. Principle 6 requires that "personal data shall be processed in accordance with the rights of data subjects under this Act".

Under para.3 of the interpretation section to this principle, a person is to be regarded as contravening the sixth Principle if, and only if:

"(b) he contravenes section 10 or 11 by failing to comply with a notice duly given under that section."

The wording here suggests that the extent of the obligation under ss.10 and 11 are equivalent but in fact they differ considerably. Where a notice is duly given under s.11 the controller must comply with it and this will be enforced by a court. A s.10 notice, however, requires a balancing exercise to be performed as described above. Where a justified requisition has not been complied with then the Commissioner may serve an enforcement notice under s.40 of the Act in an appropriate case.

Powers of the court

12–22   As well as asking the Commissioner to assess the processing involved an individual may make an application to court for an order that the controller comply with the requisition. The court must be satisfied:

    (a) that the notice has been duly given;

    (b) that the controller has failed to comply with the notice; and

    (c) that the requisition is justified whether in whole or in part.

The court will be required to balance the competing interests of the data controller and the subject. It will have to take into account the grounds on which the controller processes and the respective interests of the parties. This will be similar to the considerations which apply where the processing is based on the Sch.2 para.6 provision— that is:

> "that the processing is necessary for the purposes of the legitimate interests pursued by the controller or by the third party or parties to whom the data are disclosed except where the processing is unwarranted in any particular case by reason of prejudice to the rights and freedoms or legitimate interests of the data subject."

Among the rights and freedoms to be taken into account will be those set out in the Human Rights Convention.

A court may order the controller to take specific steps to comply with the notice and has a wide discretion as to what it may require.

How can an individual use this right?

12–23   The right is likely to be most useful where the individual is dealing with specific data or specific relationships which are not contractual, for example, data recorded and processed during pre-contractual negotiations. In theory an individual could use his or her rights under the DPA to conduct a privacy audit by carrying out subject access searches and then raising objections to any processing which he or she considers objectionable. It might, however, take a particularly motivated individual to go to such lengths. To date the author is only aware of its being used to seek erasure of data.

PRACTICAL TOOLS

Case Studies

Case Study 1: The Credit Agency

12–24   Mr Bean borrows money to buy a car. Mr Bean agrees to the lender's terms and conditions which permit the lender to disclose data reflecting how he deals with the loan to a credit reference agency. Unfortunately Mr Bean defaults on the loan without completing all his payments. The lender terminates the agreement by serving a default notice. Mr Bean subsequently pulls himself together and manages to pay off the outstanding sum so he is never taken to court. The credit reference agency continues to hold the details of the default after the contract is terminated.

Mr Bean does not want the credit agency to hold information about the loan. Even if it continues to hold it for credit purposes he objects to it being used for anything else, for example, pre-screening for mailing lists or being used as part of profiling information. Can Mr Bean require the credit reference agency to remove the record or can he restrict the uses and the disclosures that can be made of the data in their hands?

Case Study 2: The Housing Authority

12–25 Miss Brown is 19 years old. She has been living in a Housing Association property with her mother who has remarried. It is also the home of her mother's new husband's son by a former marriage. The tenancy is in the husband's name. The Housing Association has a record of all the occupants of the property. When residents move the Association's records show the previous addresses at which they resided, which will be linked to the current address on the records. The son develops a fixation with the girl. He has previous convictions for violence and it causes her a great deal of distress. She moves to another part of the town, to accommodation provided by the same Association but she wishes to ensure that her new address can never be connected with the address from which she has moved. This is to stop either the young man or any of her family contacting her. Can Miss Brown use her s.10 rights to achieve this end?

Case Study 3: The Model Agency

12–26 Miss Jones is a particularly pretty girl. She is 19 years old and has just taken her A-levels. She is waiting for the results although she fears she has not done very well. As an alternative career option she considers doing some modelling work. She visits a model agency (agency A) and they are very impressed with her looks. They arrange to have photographs taken and they compile a record on her appearance. They explain that they need the information to be able to assess what sort of work would suit her and have a record of her clothes size and colouring for possible assignments.

She gets her A-level results and finds she has done a great deal better than she expected. After discussions with her family she decides she would do better to finish her studies and consider modelling at a later date. She contacts the agency and tells them she is no longer interested. She never enters into any contract with the agency.

Several months later she is surprised to be contacted by another agency (agency B) who offer her some photographic work. They say they are specifically looking for petite redheads with green eyes. She is surprised at the contact and asks them where they obtained her details and how they know what she looks like. She is told that they hold a record of her appearance which they have acquired from agency A.

Miss Brown does not want to have the records on her retained, nor does she wish to receive any further offers of modelling contracts. Is she able to use her s.10 rights against either agency A or agency B?

Case Study 4: The Estate Agent

12–27 Just after Mrs Jones put her house on the market at £190,000 a national organisation announced that it was opening a major administrative centre nearby. At the same time house prices generally started to move. Mrs Jones decided to take her property off the market with a view to offering it at a higher price some months later. In doing so she fell out with her estate agent who had a prospective purchaser nearly ready to make an offer. Mrs Jones does not want anyone to be able to find out the price at which she had offered it on the market. She wants the estate agent to remove the record of the offer price.

Is Mrs Jones able to use her s.10 rights in order to achieve this end? The estate agent does not want to remove the price record, he considers it an important part of his database of local price movements. Can the estate agent resist Mrs Jones' request?

Analysis of Case Studies

12–28 Having considered the provisions relating to s.10 we can look at the various case studies as follows:

Case Study Comments 1: The Credit Agency

12–29 The processing carried out by the credit reference agency was probably originally based on a consent given as part of Mr Bean's contractual arrangements with the lender. The contract however is at an end and the continued holding of the data by the credit reference agency is not necessary for the performance of a contract to which he is a party. The functions exercised are not functions of a public nature. The credit agency will therefore be depending upon para.6(1) of Sch.2 for its ground for processing unless the contract included a consent clause stating that the consent to the holding of data by the agency would endure after termination of the contract.

Mr Bean knows which processing of which data he wishes to have stopped. He may state that the processing is unfair to him if data is disclosed for purposes other than credit searches because it was only collected for credit purposes in the first instance. However, he may have difficulty in showing any ground of substantial damage or distress although possibly he could claim that he would suffer distress if the data were disclosed.

Case Study Comments 2: The Housing Association

12–30 The Housing Association is processing data under either para.5(d) or para.6(1). The individual can therefore make a s.10 requisition. She is able to show that the processing may cause a risk to her safety if it allows the young man to trace her, and she is able to show that it may cause substantial damage or substantial distress. The controller must consider her application. In this case the Association must weigh its reasons for holding data in this way—administrative convenience—against the possibility of its causing damage to the individual. In this case it appears that if she were to be traced by the young man there could be serious consequences for her so it is suggested her application should be successful.

Case Study Comments 3: The Model Agency

12–31   Miss Jones is probably able to stop both agencies disclosing data relating to her. She may be able to stop agency B holding information about her and she may be able to stop agency A holding information.

Agency A originally held the data on the basis of consent. It could be argued that this was a limited consent and only endured for the purpose of the negotiations and that the retention of the data afterwards is in breach of Principle 5, being kept for longer than is necessary for the purpose of the negotiations. Equally, agency A might argue that it has a reasonable basis for retaining information about possible models in case they return. Certainly the disclosure which was made was in breach of Principle 2 because it was processed in a manner contrary to that which she had been led to believe. If there is a consent to agency A it can be revoked by Miss Jones stating that she no longer consents to the retention of data following the termination of her discussions with the agency. She could require agency A to either erase all the data about her or to refrain from disclosing them on the grounds that it is a breach of Principle 2 and therefore unwarranted and likely to cause her substantial damage or distress because she is upset at being contacted by third parties.

She can require agency B to cease to hold the data relating to her as it must be relying on para.6(1), and she can state that it was unfairly obtained by agency B under Principle 1 and that its use without her consent is causing her substantial damage or distress.

The weakness in her case is in asserting that any problems it caused her give rise to substantial damage or distress.

Case Study Comments 4: The Estate Agent

12–32   The estate agent is probably relying on para.1 consent or the para.2 ground that the processing was necessary for the performance of a contract or taking steps with a view to entering a contract. Mrs Jones can revoke her consent and after the termination of the contract Ground 2 no longer applies. The estate agent is therefore relying upon para.6(1) that it is for the purposes of the legitimate interests he is pursuing and not unwarranted in a particular case by any prejudice to her rights or freedoms or legitimate interests. He could consider anonymising the data by removing her name but as she can be identified easily from her address this would probably not be a sufficient action to anonymise it. Mrs Jones is in difficulty in finding grounds for the removal of the data, although she might be able to argue that its retention may cause her a financial detriment if someone finds out the original asking price. It is unlikely Mrs Jones can successfully object to the processing.

Precedents

Objection Notice: direct marketing under s.11(1)

12–33

Comments	Letter
Give full name address and postcode	Mrs J. J. 101 High street Anytown Countyshire AN2 3AB Tel: 012 53333 (day time)

Address to head office	To: Import Finance Ltd
	    123 Commerce Street
	    Bigtown
	    Metropol
	    B12 2CD

Date and keep copy of letter	22 February 2003
Refer to the relevant section	Dear Sirs **Data Protection Act 1998** **Direct Marketing: Notice of Objection** **s.11**
Provide information to help the organisation find its record on you	[I am a customer of your shop in Bigtown] [My account number is XY2123] [My mailing reference is ABC 987]
Set a reasonable period of time for the data controller to comply in	I require that after 5 April 2003 (that is, six weeks from the date of this letter) you stop processing personal data about me for direct marketing.
	Any breach of this prohibition may result in court proceedings. Yours sincerely

Precedent Objection Notice: general under s.10(1)

12–34

Comments	Letter
Give full name address and postcode	Mrs J. J. 101 High Street Anytown Countyshire AN2 3AB Tel: 012 53333 (day time)

Address to head office	To: Import Finance Ltd
	      123 Commerce Street
	      Bigtown
	      Metropol
	      B12 2CD

Date and keep copy of letter	22 February 2003
Refer to the relevant section	Dear Sirs **Data Protection Act 1998** **Objection to processing personal data** **Section 10**
Provide information to Help the organisation find its record on you	[I am a tenant of the above property] [customer of your subsidiary company xyz]
Specify the data and the processing to which you object	You process or intend to process data about me by [disclosing my name, address and credit records to enquiries]
Explain why it will cause damage or distress and why that is not justified in the circumstances	This processing is likely to cause substantial damage or substantial distress to [me] [name of other] which is not warranted because [my former wife is seeking to prevent me having access to my children and is looking to discredit me to everyone. I know she plans to enquire about my credit history to help her do this. It has nothing to do with her but she will gossip about it to everyone and use it against me. It is unfair to me for her to be able to find out about my credit rating]
	I look forward to receiving your reply within the next 21 days. Yours sincerely

Precedent: Response/Counter Notice by data controller under s.10(3)

12–35

Comments	Letter
Controller's name and address or that of agent	Import Finance Ltd 123 Commerce St Bigtown Metropol B12 2CD Tel: 987—654321
Controller must respond within 21 days of receipt of notice	Mr J. J. 101 High Street Anytown Countyshire AN2 3AB
Date and keep copy of letter	28 February 2003
	Dear Mr J. J. **Data Protection Act 1998** **Notice of Objection received 1st Oct 1999**
Refer to the relevant section	I acknowledge receipt of your notice dated 24 February 2003 requiring the company not to process credit information relating to you, in order to disclose to enquiries.
If the grounds for refusing to comply are that the processing is carried out on one of the primary grounds controllers are advised to set that out	The company will not comply with your notice to the extent you have required. Credit enquiries should only be made by subscribers to the agency services where the customer has requested credit. Therefore the processing of credit enquiry information is carried out on the basis of consent, and is also necessary for the taking of steps at the data subject's request with a view to entering a contract. Accordingly you have no right to object to the processing in question.
	Subscribers are bound by contract to only make enquiries in such circumstances.
State to what extent, if any, the controller is prepared to comply	I note, however, you are concerned that a subscriber facility might be abused to obtain information for other purposes. I have therefore arranged for a "special care" flag to be attached to your records so

Comments	Letter
	no enquiry will be answered without further contact with you to ensure the enquiry is genuine. I trust this meets your concerns.
	Yours sincerely,
Sent by or on behalf of the controller	Mrs P. S. On behalf of Import Finance

Checklist for data controllers

How to use this checklist

12–36   The average data controller may not need to use all the points on this check-list. It is suggested he should select those appropriate to his particular circumstances. He may also find it necessary to add further details under some of the headings. The checklist should therefore be used as a starting point in producing a procedure to deal with objection notices.

- Does the objection relate to marketing or another form of processing?
- Does it relate to direct marketing within the definition in the section?
- Is it in writing or sent electronically or oral?
- If it is not in writing or electronic is it appropriate to deal with it as sent or should the individual be required to put it in writing or send it by electronic means?
- At which branch or office was it received?
- On what date was the request received?
- Has the individual making the request given an intelligible name and address to which the controller can respond?
- When does the 21 days for response expire on a s.10 notice?
- What time scale has the individual specified to stop marketing processing on a s.11 notice?
- What marketing processing is affected?
- Is more time needed to comply with the requirement?
- How is the marketing data held? Is it manual or automated or some of both?
- Does the s.10 objection apply to manual or automated data?
- Has the individual described the data?

- Has the individual described the processing?

- Has the individual explained why unwarranted damage and distress would be caused?

- On what grounds are the data being processed?

- Can one of the primary grounds be claimed?

- Does the notice amount to a revocation of an existing consent?

- Is it possible to comply with the objection?

- Is processing about others affected?

- Would compliance mean system changes?

ADDITIONAL INFORMATION

Compliance with the Directive

12–37   The data subject's general right to object is found at Art.14 which states:

"Member States shall grant the data subject the right, at least in the cases referred to in Article 7(e) and (f) to object at any time on compelling legitimate grounds relating to his particular situation to the processing of personal data relating to him, save where otherwise provided by national legislation. Where there is a justified objection, the processing instigated by the controller may no longer involve those data."

It is dealt with in the recitals by Recital 45:

"Whereas in cases where data might lawfully be processed on grounds of public interest, official authority or the legitimate interests of a natural or legal person, any data subject should nevertheless be entitled, on legitimate and compelling grounds relating to his particular situation, to object to the processing of any data relating to himself; whereas Member States may nevertheless lay down national provisions to the contrary."

The Article and the recital are in almost identical terms. Under Art.14 an objection can be made on "compelling and legitimate grounds" which relate to the individual's particular situation. Under s.10, however, the individual must show that the processing is likely to cause or is causing "substantial damage or substantial distress" which would be "unwarranted".

This appears to impose a different, and narrower, test than is imposed by the Directive. For example, it might be argued that a breach of Principle by a data controller which affected an individual would give rise to a legitimate ground of objection by that individual. If the effect on the individual was detrimental and not outweighed by any countervailing public interest in the processing being undertaken, it might reasonably be regarded as a compelling objection. However, the individual might struggle to show that he suffered "substantial damage or distress" within the terms of s.10.

As was explained in Ch.3, above it is the duty of the Member States to implement a Directive. One of the tools adopted in order to achieve this end is for the courts to construe statutes in accordance with the Directive. It is possible therefore that the courts may be minded to interpret the s.10 rights generously to ensure that they correspond to the rights as set out in Art.14. Such an approach has been taken in the case studies and examples given in this chapter.

Considerable concern was expressed in Parliamentary debate that the section failed to transpose the Art.14 rights adequately. These are reflected in the Hansard references cited below.

Derivations

12–38 • Directive 95/46 (See App.B):
        (a) Art.14 (the data subject's right to object).
        (b) Recitals 25, 30, 45.

Hansard references

12–39   Vol.586, No.108, col.CWH 47, Lords Grand Committee, February 23, 1998
Whether the term "substantial damage and distress" properly reflects the requirements of the Directive.

ibid., CWH 50
Direct marketing covers not-for-profit mailings.

Vol.587, No.122, col.496, Lords Report, March 16, 1998
Notices of objection to processing, general objection clause revised.

ibid., cols 500, 501
Compelling legitimate grounds and substantial damage and distress.

Vol.587, No.127, col.1129, Lords Third Reading, March 24, 1998
Consent in section 10.

Commons Standing Committee D, May 14, cols 117–121
Rights to prevent processing, substantial damage and distress.

ibid., col.123
Right to prevent processing to direct marketers, notice to consumers.

ibid., col. 125
Emails are covered by the right to object to processing.

Vol.591, No.184, col.1486, Lords consideration of Commons amendments, July 10, 1998

Right to prevent processing for direct marketing, tick boxes as objections.

Previous case law

12–40 *R v Brian Reid Robertson and City of Wakefield Metropolitan Council and Secretary of State for the Home Department* [2001] EWHC Admin 915.

CHAPTER 13

Rights Relating to Automated Decisions

INTRODUCTION

13–01 Section 12 allows individuals to insist that some decisions should not be taken by automated means. It also provides that individuals must be specifically informed about some decisions taken on an automated basis and allows them to raise subsequent objections and require those decisions to be reconsidered. It originates from a provision in the French data protection law. It appears to have been little used The section was significantly changed by Government amendment during the passage of the Bill. In its original form it would have imposed a ban on relevant automated decision-making. As enacted, however, the individual must activate the ban.

SUMMARY OF MAIN POINTS

13–02

(a) The right does not affect any use of manual data but only automated processing.

(b) An individual is able either to ban the taking of automated decisions by a data controller or to make a data controller undertake a non-automated review of a relevant decision.

(c) The right does not necessarily allow the individual to have the decision over-turned although that may be the effect of a reconsideration.

(d) A significant number of ordinary commercial decisions are exempt from this right, as are those taken under statutory powers. Where data controllers make use of any systems (either their own systems or those provided by others) which are affected by this provision they must take steps to ensure that:

   (i) individuals who have objected are not subject to decisions made by such systems;

   (ii) appropriate notices can be given to individuals where decisions are made by such systems; and

   (iii) they have procedures to take account of any objections raised and to allow decisions to be reconsidered with human intervention.

PROCESSING AFFECTED

13–03   The s.12 rights apply to any:

"decision taken by or on behalf of the data controller which significantly affects that individual [and which] is based solely on the processing by automatic means of personal data of which that individual is the data subject for the purpose of evaluating matters relating to him such as, for example, his performance at work, his creditworthiness, his reliability or his conduct [except where those decisions are exempt decisions]."

The s.12 rights derive from Art.15 of the Directive, which provides that:

"Member States shall grant the right to every person not to be subject to a decision which produces legal effects concerning or significantly affects him and which is based solely on automated processing of data intended to evaluate certain personal aspects relating to him, such as his performance at work, credit worthiness, reliability, etc."

NATURE OF THE DECISION

13–04   The right of objection applies only where processing is carried out in order to make assessments of, or pass judgments on, individuals. The right applies to the taking of any decisions based on such an assessment without some form of human intervention. The decision may be about anything; however, four specific examples are given, three of them taken from the Directive. The four specific examples are performance at work, creditworthiness, reliability or conduct. It is clear these are not exclusive but they indicate the kind of evaluations which are contemplated by this provision. While the general words are wide enough to encompass a broad range of activities, the examples given are taken from a relatively narrow range.

Significant effects

13–05   In all cases the assessment or evaluation must be capable of resulting in a decision which significantly affects the individual. The term "significantly affects" is not defined. A decision may affect a data subject by causing emotional distress. It does not necessarily have to result in physical damage or financial loss. Nor indeed does the section require that the effect on the individual should be detrimental. On the other hand it would seem unlikely that a data subject will object to receipt of an unsolicited benefit even if it has occurred because of automated processing. The effect need not be a legal effect. For example, an individual may be significantly affected by being stopped or searched or questioned even where he is not subsequently arrested or charged.

The provision is silent as to whether the test of whether an individual is significantly affected by a decision is to be assessed objectively or subjectively. The examples given are ones which would be generally regarded by reasonable persons as significantly affecting someone. On the other hand, an individual may be significantly affected by matters which would not be of concern to others because he or she may have particular sensitivities. On this basis the test could be subjective. The point does not appear to have been litigated to date. It will be for the courts to resolve this issue. It is perhaps unlikely that a court will require a decision to be retaken unless objectively it is seen to have a detrimental effect on an individual.

Nature of the Processing

13–06 The prohibition can be applied only where a decision is based solely on automated processing. This suggests that any human intervention, however slight, will be sufficient to overcome this prohibition.

The decision must be taken "by or on behalf of the data controller". The person who takes the decision is described as the "responsible person" in s.12(9). The responsible person therefore need not be the data controller or the one who carries out the actual processing but must be the one who makes a decision. This opens possible questions about liability for breach where the data controller and responsible person are different persons, although it seems unlikely that such a split would occur in most cases.

The prohibition cannot be applied in a number of cases, described as exempt decisions, which are considered below. There is a possible ambiguity in the drafting of s.12 because the prohibition can only be applied to decisions about a data subject based solely on "the processing by automatic means of personal data in respect of which he is the data subject".

Article 15 of the Directive is not limited to data in respect of which the individual is the sole data subject but simply refers to automated processing of data. The wording adopted in s.12 leaves it open to argument that if the processing is based on personal data about both the data subject and another or others it would fall outside the prohibited category. This would seem to be an absurd result and presumably was not intended. If correct it would significantly undermine the rights given by the section, as many forms of automated decision-making will involve data about others. For example, in a job evaluation scheme a decision may be based on the processing of data about a group of individuals, not just one data subject. In view of the wording of the Directive the better view therefore will be that such processing is covered and that the term "solely" relates only to the automated processing in question and not the data subject.

Exempt Decisions

13–07 Section 12(4) provides that a prohibition notice will not be effective in respect of an "exempt decision". An "exempt decision" is one which meets the criteria in s.12(6) and (7), or which is made in other circumstances prescribed by the Secretary of State.

No orders prescribing additional circumstances have been made or proposed at the time of writing so the only current exemptions are to be found in s.12(6) and (7). Section 12(6) sets out, (rather wordily) four circumstances in which decisions may be made, and s.12(7) sets out two conditions which can apply to them. This combination gives eight separate circumstances in which decisions will be exempt. They are listed below using the wording taken from the section (which explains the constructions employed).

Categories of exempt decisions

13–08

(a) The decision is made in the course of steps taken for the purpose of considering whether to enter into a contract with the data subject and the effect of the decision is to grant the request of the data subject;

(b) The decision is made in the course of steps taken for the purpose of considering whether to enter into a contract with the data subject and steps have been taken to safeguard the legitimate interests of the data subject (for example by allowing him to make representations);

(c) The decision is made in the course of steps taken with a view to entering into a contract with the data subject and the effect of the decision is to grant a request of the data subject;

(d) The decision is made in the course of steps taken with a view to entering into a contract with the data subject and steps have been taken to safeguard the legitimate interests of the data subject (for example by allowing him to make representations);

(e) The decision is made in the course of steps taken in performing a contract with the data subject and the effect of the decision is to grant a request of the data subject;

(f) The decision is made in the course of performing a contract with the data subject and steps have been taken to safeguard the legitimate interests of the data subject (for example by allowing him to make representations);

(g) The decision is authorised or required by or under any enactment and the effect of the decision is to grant the request of the data subject;

(h) The decision is authorised or required by or under any enactment and steps have been taken to safeguard the legitimate interests of the data subject (by allowing him to make representations).

It will have been noted that three of the conditions in s.12(6) deal with contractual situations and the remaining one applies where processing has a statutory basis. The conditions in s.12(7) are intended to ensure that the interests of the individual are safeguarded. Therefore either the effect of the decision must be to grant a request of the individual or his interests must have been protected in some way.

The data subject need not know about the automated processing before it takes place or at all in the case of exempt decisions. However, where the request condition applies there must have been some form of request which can be relied upon and which the data controller is dealing with. On the face of it, the request need not be proximate in time to the automated processing. It is not clear what degree of particularity the request must have. For example it might be argued that a data subject who has ticked an "opt in" box relating to the marketing of financial products could be described as having "requested" that he be considered for the purpose of considering whether to enter into a contract with the data subject and therefore targeted for the receipt of marketing material on an automated basis. However this is perhaps a bold construction, and the better view is probably that a request must be a specific request to a specific data controller resulting in a specific case of automated decision-making.

Contractual situations

13–09   Where one of the contractual grounds is to be relied upon the contract must be with the data subject about whom the data are processed and not with any other person. The decision need not necessarily be proximate to the pre-contractual considerations. The connection need only be sufficient to fall within the broad parameters of "in the course of steps taken for the purpose of considering". The processing may take place at a different time or the decision be taken by a different controller to the one who enters into the contract. Example (a) and example (c) in the above list are extremely similar. Possibly the former applies where an application is considered and rejected, and the latter applies when the application is considered and accepted in principle but the automated decision relates to the terms of the offer. The latter appears to be intended to be more proximate to the contract and could possibly cover circumstances where the customer has made an application for credit. Where the decision is taken in the course of performing a contract such automated decisions are therefore permitted. That permission will cease once a contract has been concluded or negotiations have been terminated.

Statutory authorisation

13–10   For a decision to be authorised or required under any enactment the controller must be able to point to a specific statutory provision. The few remaining government departments which operate under the prerogative powers, such as the Passport Agency, will therefore be unable to rely on this. Although the decision must have a statutory basis the specific authorisation for automated processing need not be found in statute. For example, if the Benefits Agency is empowered to make a statutory determination as to the amount of benefit payable it does not need specific authority to use a computerised system to make the automated decision.

SAFEGUARDS

13–11   Where the effect of processing which falls within one of the exempt processing categories is to grant a request of the data subject, no further action by the data controller is required. It is assumed that the data subject has no cause for complaint. Where the request of the data subject is not granted then the data controller must take steps to ensure that the subject's interests are safeguarded, for example he may provide an opportunity to make representations. This would entail informing the individual of the result of the decision, of his right to make representations and giving a fair hearing to those representations. It is not clear how far the subject has to be informed of the nature of the processing or indeed that the decision is as the result of automated processing.

The right to make representations is only one method of safeguarding the legitimate interests of the data subjects. Other methods may be used. Possibly these would include a right of appeal to an ombudsman or an internal review in which the individual is not involved.

The steps taken must safeguard "the legitimate interests of the data subject". Those legitimate interests are not specified. In this context, however, it is suggested that they cover at least the right to respect for private life and family accorded under the European Convention on Human Rights, and the economic interests of the individual as a consumer and an employee.

When the courts consider whether steps have been taken to safeguard the legitimate interests of the data subjects, they may also take into account whether proper procedures have been followed which ensure that the relevant considerations are weighed in making the decision.

Prohibition notices served by individuals

13–12 Under s.12(1) an individual is entitled to prohibit a data controller by notice from taking any such automated decision at any time in relation to him. The notice must be in writing although the Act does not specify how or where it should be served. The formalities of service set out in s.65 of the Act only apply to service of notices by the Commissioner. A prohibition notice could be served on a data controller at a local office or branch office of a big organisation, although it would perhaps be prudent for anyone serving such a notice to do so at the head office or registered office in the case of a limited company.

A prohibition notice requires the controller to ensure that no decision which falls within the section is taken by or on behalf of the controller. A notice is not time limited; once served it will continue to apply until revoked by the individual. It will only apply to that individual, so for example a prohibition by an employee on the application of an automated assessment system will only apply to that individual and not to the post which he or she holds.

There is no prohibition on the service of a notice on behalf of another, so a solicitor could serve on behalf of a client or a parent on behalf of a child. The same considerations in relation to service of a notice on behalf of another will apply here as in the case of subject access. These are discussed in full at Ch.10, above. The notice need not mention s.12(1) but it would be prudent to do so to assist controllers to recognise such a notice.

Obligations of data controllers

13–13 If a s.12(1) notice is not in effect and a controller takes an automated decision which falls within the section, then the controller must, "as soon as is reasonably practicable" notify the individual that the decision was taken on an automated basis and that he is entitled to request that it be reviewed or reconsidered. It is not clear how far there is a difference between a requirement to reconsider a decision or take a new decision otherwise on an automated basis. Possibly the latter is a requirement to take the decision de novo without reference to the earlier one.

Notification by data controller

13–14 The notification need not be in writing (unlike other s.12 notices) although it would be prudent for a controller to commit himself to writing. Nor does the notification have to be given within a specified period (again unlike the other s.12 notices).

It must be given "as soon as reasonably practicable" after the relevant decision is taken. It appears that the notice need not be given before the decision is implemented, although controllers would be well-advised to delay implementation of any decision which has a significant impact if it is possible for them to do so. This allows for the possibility of a successful objection by the individual. The alternative might be a difficult process of unpacking the effects of a decision which has been implemented. Moreover, it could be argued that the possibility of making an objection only after such a decision has been implemented is not sufficient to comply with the Art.15 requirement that every person "shall have the right not to be subject to such a decision".

While equally it could be argued that the existence of the initial right of objection contained in s.12(1) implements the prior objection provision of Art.15 and the s.12(2) right is additional to that, the point cannot be free from doubt and it is suggested that the better course for controllers would be to notify the individual of a decision and then withhold implementation until any objection can be considered.

Section 12(2)(a) does not specify the level of detail at which the notification must be given. As the decision involved is one which will significantly affect the individual in any event it might be anticipated that the controller will be communicating with the data subject in the circumstances. It is suggested that the controller should inform the individual:

(a) of the actual decision taken;

(b) of any effect that the decision will have on the individual;

(c) of the fact that it was based solely on automated processing;

(d) of the individual's entitlement to require the controller to reconsider or take a new decision.

It has to be said that it is not completely clear from the wording that the controller is under an obligation to notify the individual of his right to object, but a public authority would be under an obligation to do so as a matter of good faith and proper conduct. It is suggested that failure to do so would be maladministration by a public authority and it would be prudent for any data controller to do so.

Data subject response

13–15   Section 12(2)(b) entitles the individual who has received notice of an automated decision from the data controller to serve a counter notice within 21 days of receipt. The counter notice must be given in writing and requires the controller to reconsider the decision or take a new decision "otherwise than on" an automated basis. The data subject is not entitled to set any other parameters or conditions, for example he cannot insist on the decision being taken in a particular way or by a particular person. He may, however, be entitled to distinguish between requiring a decision to be reconsidered or taken afresh. It might be expected that a data subject would require decisions to be taken afresh to overcome any possible bias towards the initial decision made by the machine and even to insist that the person taking the decision on a non-automated basis should not be made aware of the automated decision. Once a controller receives a valid notice of objection the individual has clearly activated his Art.15 right and the controller should not implement the disputed decision even though this causes him inconvenience.

Counter-notice by data controller

13–16   The controller who receives a s.12(2)(b) notice of objection must respond in writing to the individual within 21 days of receipt. In his response he must "specify the steps that he intends to take to comply with the data subject notice". The section does not deal with the level of detail at which the steps are to be specified but as a minimum it might be expected to:

(a) explain that the controller is going to reconsider the decision or have it taken on a new basis;

(b) state when this will be done;

(c) explain any effects this will have on the individual.

It would also be reasonable for the controller to subsequently inform the individual of the results of the reconsideration or retaking of the decision although again it is not a statutory requirement to do so. However for a public body it might be maladministration to fail to do so.

BREACH OF S.12

Failure to observe a s.12(1) or 12(2)(b) notice

13–17   Section 12(8) gives the court power to make a specific order to have the decision reconsidered or retaken in cases in which a prohibition notice has been ignored. The data subject must apply to the court for such an order. The section provides that the order be made against "the responsible person", that is "a person taking a [relevant] decision in respect of [a data subject]". This formula may have been used to cover those cases where the decision is taken by another on behalf of the data controller. However, since the data controller is the person ultimately responsible for the processing and notices of objection are to be served on the data controller, to which the controller is responsible for responding, it seems unlikely that the responsible person will be anyone other than the controller in the vast majority of cases. An order under s.12(8) that a decision be reconsidered or retaken shall not affect the rights of any person other than the data subject or the responsible person. This is the effect of s.12(9). Thus if a decision has been implemented so as to affect the rights of another those rights will not be affected even if the decision is reconsidered or overturned. The position of a controller or third party might be affected, but any right to redress, for example in contract, against the responsible person will stand. Otherwise it might be argued that the contract was avoided due to the successful statutory objection. The provision appears to be aimed at ensuring that the responsible person carries the risk of implementing a challengeable automated decision and not any other affected person. This appears to be an equitable position where the affected person is a third party. A person who risks being an affected third party in such a situation should ensure he is covered by an appropriate clause in his contract with the data controller. However the point is less clear where the person affected is himself the data controller.

Compensation

13–18   Failure to comply with the s.12 rights will give rise to compensation rights under s.13 if it causes damage. The compensation rights are dealt with in Ch.14, below.

Powers of the Commissioner

13–19   Failure to comply with the requirements of s.12 may give rise to enforcement action by the Commissioner for breach of Data Protection Principle 6. The powers of the Commissioner are dealt with in Chs 20 and 23, below.

Failure to serve a s.12(2)(a) notice

13–20   Unfortunately, no specific remedy is provided for the individual in circumstances where a controller takes a relevant automated decision but neglects to inform the individual of his rights. The controller could be subject to enforcement action by the Commissioner and the individual will be able to claim compensation if damage is caused to him. However, a lower court may not be able to order the controller to give the appropriate notice or to reconsider the decision, although the High Court could do so under its inherent powers.

Practical Tools

Examples of automated decision-making

13–21

(a) A solicitors' firm using an automated debt collection system to despatch final demands, followed by the issue of court summonses without human intervention.

(b) A financial services company using an automated system to target, select and, more importantly, reject customers for particularly good credit offers.

(c) Investigative agencies using a computer programme which profiles information about travellers in order to pinpoint particular travellers who fall within the profile of typical drug smugglers, to stop and search their luggage.

(d) A lottery company selecting name and address by random programme from electoral information and sending one individual a cheque for having won the lottery.

(e) The police issuing a court summons to a person recorded as a vehicle keeper with DVLA on the basis of a police camera record of the vehicle speeding without further investigation or intervention.

Precedents

Individual prohibition on automated decision-taking

13–22

Comments	Letter
Give full name and address and postcode	Mrs J. J. 101 High Street Anytown Countyshire AN2 3AB Tel: 0123 53333 (daytime)
Address to head office	To: Import Finance Ltd 123 Commerce Street Bigtown Metropol B12 2CD
Date and keep a copy of letter	22 February 2003
Refer to the relevant section	Dear Sirs **Data Protection Act 1998** **Automated Decision Prohibition Notice** **Section 12(1)**
Provide relevant information to help the organisation identify you	[I am an employee of your company. I am employed as the baking assistant in the Glasgow bakery.] [I am a customer of your company]. [My mail order account number is XY2 999.]
Specify the particular processing if you have a specific concern	I give notice that from the date of receipt of this letter you must ensure that: No decision which significantly affects me [in particular no decision affecting the grant of credit to me]: Is taken by or on [your] behalf [of your organisation], based solely on the processing by automatic means of personal data in respect of which I am the data subject the purpose of evaluating matters relating to me, unless it is an "exempt decision". Any breach of this prohibition may result in court proceedings.
If you think the organisation will wish for further proof the notice is valid, have it countersigned.	Yours sincerely Countersigned .... Mr JP/MD Local Practice

Notification of an automated decision by a data controller

13–23

Comments	Letter
Controller's name and address or that of agent	Import Finance Ltd 123 Commerce Street Bigtown Metropol B12 2CD
There is no obligation to give a telephone number. Controllers may prefer not to do so although individuals will find it helpful.	Ring: 9871-65432 & ask for Mrs P. S.
	To: Mrs J. J. 101 High Street Anytown Countyshire AN2 3AB
Must be sent as soon as reasonably practicable after the decision but no specific timescale is imposed.	20 February 2003
Refer to the relevant section	Dear Mrs J. J. **Data Protection Act 1998** **Notice of an automated decision—** **Section 12(2)**
The section does not in terms require the controller to notify individuals of the right to object or the timescale. Public sector controllers should do so.	This is a notice I am required to send you by law. You do not have to respond to it but if you wish to do so you must write to the address above within 21 days of receiving this notice marked for the attention of Mrs P. S.
	I regret to inform you that [your application for the post of master baker has been rejected].
There is no bar on seeking to minimise request for reconsideration	This decision was taken by an automated evaluation system which evaluated your qualities and experience compared to those of other applicants. I can assure you that the system has been extensively tested and is fair and unbiased. However should you wish to request that the decision be reconsidered or re-taken otherwise than by the automated system you are entitled to do so.
Sent by or on behalf of Controller	Yours sincerely Mrs P. S. On behalf of Import Finance

Individual response to a notice of automated processing

13–24

Comment	Letter
	Mrs J. J. 101 High Street Anytown Countyshire AN2 3AB Tel: 012 53333 (days only)
	To: Import Finance Ltd. 123 Commerce Street Bigtown Metropol B12 2CD
The response to be within 21 days of receiving the notice from the Controller	28 February 2003
	Dear Mrs P. S., Thank you for your letter dated 24th October which I received on 5th November.
Specify whether the decision is to be reconsidered or re-taken	I require Import Finance Ltd. to [reconsider the decisions.] [take a new decision about my application for the post as Master Baker] not on an automated basis.
	Yours sincerely

Controller's response to a s.12(2)(b) notice

13–25

Comment	Letter
	Import Finance Ltd 123 Commerce Street Bigtown Metropol B12 2CD

Comment	Letter
	To: Mrs J. J. 101 High Street Anytown Countyshire AN2 3AB Ring 9871-65432 and ask for Mrs P. S.
Response by the Controller must be within 21 days of the request	14 March 2003
	Mrs J. J., **Data Protection Act 1998** **Notice under section 12(2)(3)**
This specifies the steps which will be taken as required. It does not give the *outcome* of the reconsideration	I received your letter of 28 February on 4 March. As a result of your request the papers relating to your application will be considered by the Personnel Department in comparison with those applicants selected for interview by the automated system. The Personnel Department will decide on the basis of those papers whether you should be called to interview.
	Yours sincerely Mrs P. S. On behalf of the Data Controller

Checklist for data controllers: automated decisions

How to use this checklist

13–26   The average data controller may not need to use all the points on this checklist. It is suggested he should select those appropriate to his particular circumstances. He may also find it necessary to add further details under some of the headings. The checklist should therefore be used as a starting point in producing a procedure to deal with objection notices.

     Objections under s.12(1)

- Is the objection made in writing or electronically or oral?

- If it is not in writing or in electronic form is it appropriate to accept it or should the individual be asked to put it into written or electronic form?

- At which branch or office was it received?

- On what date was it received?

- Has the individual lodging the objection given an intelligible name and address?

- Is the individual lodging the objection an existing data subject?

- Is the objection lodged by the individual to whom it relates or by another acting on his or her behalf?

- If it is made by another, in what capacity is that person acting?

- Is proof of authority to object on behalf of another required or has it been supplied?

- Is the objection lodged by a child?

- Is it lodged by a child in Scotland?

- What is the child's age?

- If it is lodged on behalf of a child does the person lodging it have locus standi to do so in respect of the child?

- Is a proper record kept of all valid objections lodged under s.12(1)?

- Can all automated decision-making within s.12(1) be recognised by the organisation?

- Is all such processing checked to see if one or more of the exemptions apply to it?

- Is the personal data to be subject to non-exempt automated decision making checked against the s.12(1) record of objections before the process is run?

Procedures to be followed under 12(2)

13–27 • Is a record kept of each incident of non-exempt automated decision-making processing?

- Is there a proper system for notifying individuals significantly affected by such decisions?

- Has the date of the non-exempt processing been recorded?

- When was the data subject notified of the non-exempt processing?

- Has the decision been implemented or suspended pending a response from the data subject?

- Has a response been received from the data subject within the time allowed?

- What does the data subject notice require?

- How is the response to be handled?

- Has the data subject been notified of the final decision?

Additional Information

Derivations

13–28   • Directive 95/46 (See App.B):

    (a) Art.15 (automated individual decisions).
    (b) Recital 41.

Hansard references

13–29   Commons Standing Committee D, May 19, 1998, cols 137–143
Exercise of objection rights.

Previous case law

13–30   None.

CHAPTER 14

Compensation and Other Individual Remedies (including the Assessment of Claims by the Commissioner)

INTRODUCTION

14–01 Since October 2001, when the Act came fully into effect for all automated and most manual data, data controllers have faced an increased likelihood of civil action for breach of its provisions. While there have been relatively few cases under the Act to date, the courts have acknowledged that this is a growing and developing area of law.[1] Individuals may not only take action to enforce their individual rights, but take action for compensation for other contraventions of the Act.

In this chapter, the remedies available through the courts in such actions are categorised under four headings:

(a) rights orders;

(b) compensation orders;

(c) accuracy orders;

(d) other orders.

The term "rights order" is not found in the Act but breaches of the individual rights described in Chs 10 to 13, above, that is the right of subject access and the rights to object to the taking of automated decisions, to processing for direct marketing and to other specified forms of processing, are mirrored by specific remedies which can be granted by the courts. These are referred to here as "rights orders". The award of compensation is not limited to cases where there has been a breach of the individual rights. Compensation can be sought for any contravention of the Act which has caused damage to the individual. One of the most important provisions in this context is the requirement that personal data shall be accurate. That requirement is dealt with in this chapter. Where compensation can be claimed the courts can make associated orders, such as orders to rectify the data in question.

---

[1] See *Sofola v Lloyds TSB* [2005] EWHC 1335, QB; and *Pal v GMC* [2004] EWHC 1485.

"Accuracy orders" is another term not found in the Act. It is used here as a generic term to describe the wide range of actions which a court may take to deal with cases where data are or have been deemed to be inaccurate.

Although the remedies are presented here sequentially, in any particular case it may be appropriate to pursue more than one remedy; for example it would be usual to bring an action both for damages and for rectification where inaccurate data have caused loss and are being maintained on an individual's file. Moreover, it is increasingly likely that the action will include a claim for breach of the Human Rights Act 1998, although not every breach of the individual rights in the DPA will also be a breach of the Convention rights.[2]

Note: A case study is included in Section II.

SUMMARY OF MAIN POINTS

14–02 The 1998 Act did not weaken or remove any of the remedies which were available under the 1984 Act (although special procedural provisions are introduced in respect of the special purposes[3]). It significantly increased the range of remedies available through the courts.

In summary:

(a) The individual rights are accompanied by a specific remedy for breach of each right.

(b) Compensation may be claimed for any contravention of the Act which causes damage and associated distress, or, in some circumstances, which causes distress alone.

(c) Where data are inaccurate the powers available to the court are both flexible and extensive. In particular the court can order that further inquiries be made, can provide for data to be "blocked" and can require alterations in data to be notified to third parties who had previously received inaccurate information.

(d) Accuracy rights as well as remedies are significantly strengthened. A data controller must consider the accuracy of data received from a third party. Under the 1984 Act it was sufficient to mark the data as "received data" in order to be protected from a compensation claim in respect of inaccuracy.

RIGHTS ORDERS MADE BY THE COURTS

Subject access orders

14–03 Under s.7(9) a court may order a data controller to comply with a valid subject access request which has been made to him. In such a case the claimant must satisfy the court that a request has been made under the provisions of s.7 which complied with the requirements of that provision and that the controller has failed to comply with that request.

---

[2] See Ch.2, above for a discussion of the HRA and the overlap with the DPA.
[3] See Ch.17, below for a full treatment of these special provisions.

The court has a discretion as to whether to order the controller to comply. The extent of this discretion has been the subject of consideration by the Court of Appeal in the case of *Durant v FSA*.[4] The existence of a discretion is clear from the use of the word "may" in s.7(9). However, on the face of it there are limits to the court's discretion. In the 1984 Act the factors which the court was to take into account in deciding whether to make a subject access order were described at s.21(8), which provided that:

> "A court shall not make an order under this sub-section if it considers that it would, in all the circumstances, be unreasonable to do so, whether because of the frequency with which the applicant has made requests to the data user under these provisions or for any other reason."

Therefore, under the 1984 Act, it was clear that the court had a wide-ranging power to consider all the relevant circumstances in deciding whether or not to make the order, and could decline to do so if it considered it unreasonable. The considerations were narrowed in the 1998 Act to those which appear in s.8. These are:

(a) a discretion as to how the information must be supplied;

(b) an ability to withhold data in view of the frequency of requests;

(c) an ability to withhold data if the data constitute a trade secret;

(d) an ability to withhold data if the data relate to third parties.

Thus it is clear that a court may still take into account whether the individual has made unreasonably frequent requests. This may provide the data controller with a defence against an application to a court for an order for access. Under s.8(3) a controller who has previously complied with a subject access request does not have to comply with an identical or very similar request until a reasonable interval has elapsed between the two. Under s.8(4) a reasonable interval must be determined taking account of the nature of the data, the purpose of the processing and the frequency with which the data are altered.

14–04 The data controller who has determined not to respond to a second or subsequent request on this ground and who is faced with an action against him would be able to apply to strike out the action under the Civil Procedure Rules (CPR) r.3.4 or contest an application for a court order on the ground that he had satisfied the same or a sufficiently similar subject access request reasonably recently. An application to strike out would be made on the basis that the statement of case discloses no reasonable grounds for bringing a claim.[5]

Subject access may also be refused, at least in part, if the logic involved in the relevant decision-making involved constitutes a trade secret. This is found in s.8(5).

14–05 Under s.7(9) the court is not, in terms, empowered to order a subject access request to be complied with only in part or refuse because it appears to be vexatious or for any other reason, even if it might seem to be a reasonable and just response. Thus the discretion does not appear to be as extensive as the powers of the court under the 1984 Act. It also contrasts with the power a court enjoys in making an order dealing with

---

[4] [2003] EWCA Civ 1746.
[5] CPR r.3.4(2)(a).

an objection to processing under s.10 of the Act, where an order can be made that the individual's request should be complied with "to any extent". However in *Lord*[6] Mumby J. held that the discretion conferred by s.7(9) is general and untrammeled,[7] a view later supported by the Court of Appeal in *Durant*[8] where the Court held that it has a general discretion as to the manner of dealing with such cases and the orders which it makes. The question which the Court of Appeal considered in *Durant* was as follows:

> "By what principles should a court be guided in exercising its discretion under section 7(9) of the Act to order a data controller who has wrongly refused a request for information under section 7(1) to comply with the request?"[9]

In the particular case it was not necessary to answer the question as the Court found that the data controller did not hold any personal data relating to the requester. In the High Court the judge had added that, even if the applicant had been entitled to the data, he would not have ordered its disclosure for three reasons; that he (the judge) could not see that the information would be of any practical value to the applicant; that the purpose of the legislation was to ensure that accurate records are held and allow the individual to challenge any inaccuracy and in this case the applicant wanted the information in order to take proceedings against Barclay's Bank; and finally that the FSA had acted throughout with good faith. On appeal the applicant had argued that these were not legitimate reasons to refuse to provide access; the subject access right was not limited to checking the accuracy of information and the reason that Mr Durant wanted the data was not relevant to the exercise of discretion under s.7(9). It was further argued that Art.12 of the Directive, which requires Member States to "guarantee" every data subject the right to obtain access to their personal data, meant that the Court enforcing s.7 rights was obliged to order disclosure if it was shown that the request under s.7 was otherwise justified. In granting leave for the appeal Ward L.J. had paid particular attention to the discretion arguments as a ground for appeal. However, the argument that the court's discretion was curtailed in any way did not find favour with Auld L.J. in the Court of Appeal.

14–06 This overcomes the potential problems which could arise if the court had no such discretion. For example, if the court had to decide a case in which a subject access request had been made for both archive and live data, which the court considered would require an unreasonably extensive trawl of the archive data held by the controller, if the court could not order compliance in part the only option open to the judge would be to require the request to be complied with in full. In *R. v Chief Constable of B County Constabulary*,[10] the High Court held that a data controller could not be required to make a selective response to a subject access request. In that case the data subject wished the controller to omit "spent" convictions from a subject access response. The subject had been required to obtain the subject access information by an overseas government for submission in support of an application for a permit to teach in that country. Applying the case it could be argued that a data subject cannot chose to make a partial

---

[6] [2003] EWHC 2073 (Admin).

[7] *ibid.*, para.160.

[8] [2003] EWCA Civ 1746.

[9] *Durant*, above para.20.

[10] Unreported, November 1997.

access request, nor a controller to grant one. An alternative view of the case is that the parties cannot use subject access to present a falsely partial picture by omitting relevant material from a particular record, but that there would be no difficulty in confining the request and the answer to defined records or data sets.

14–07 Under s.15(2) a court considering an application under s.7(9) is entitled to inspect any relevant data or information as to the logic involved in any decision-making in order to determine whether it should be made available to the claimant. However, it must not permit disclosure of such information to the claimant prior to determination of the case.

Prevention of processing order

14–08 Under s.10(4) a court may order a data controller to desist from the processing of personal data to the same extent as an individual could so require under s.10; that is, to cease within a reasonable time, or not to begin, processing or processing for a specified purpose or in a specified manner any personal data. The power is exercisable where a court:

". . . is satisfied, on the application of any person who has given a notice under subsection(1) which appears to the court to be justified . . . that the data controller in question has failed to comply with the notice . . ."

The claimant must therefore show that:

(a) he has given notice under s.10(1);

(b) the notice was wholly or partly justified in that the processing has caused or is likely to cause substantial damage or substantial distress to him or another;

(c) that the damage or distress is unwarranted; and

(d) that his notice to desist has not been complied with.

However his claim will be completely defeated if the processing by the data controller was based on one of the primary grounds for processing set out in Sch.2.[11] It appears that the evidential burden of showing that none of those grounds apply lies with the claimant as the right to serve a notice does not apply where the relevant conditions in the Schedule are met.

If the court is satisfied under these heads, and the respondent does not succeed in dislodging the application, whether by showing that he processed on a primary ground, or disputing the facts, the court may order the controller to take such steps to comply with the notice as it thinks fit.

The order may therefore require partial compliance with the notice. Rights orders will be similar to mandatory injunctions and in all cases orders should be drawn with care to ensure that they are specific and leave the controller in no doubt of what actions are required to comply with the order. Where mandatory injunctions are granted they must be in such a form that the recipient knows what he must do in order to comply:

---

[11] By this is meant the first four grounds in the Schedule. See Ch.6, above for Sch.2.

Redland Bricks Ltd v Morris[12]; *Video Arts Ltd v Paget Industries Ltd*[13]; *Harris v Harris*.[14] This is particularly the case with orders to prevent processing. The order will need to specify the processing in question, the purposes of the processing, the duration and any other relevant matters.

The direct marketing order

14–09 Under s.11(2) a court may order a data controller to desist from processing for direct marketing to the same extent that an individual might do so, that is to cease within a reasonable time, or not to begin, processing particular personal data for the purpose of direct marketing. The claimant must show that he has given notice under s.11(1) and that the controller has failed to comply with the notice. There is no defence to the application, although the court retains a general discretion as to whether or not to grant the order. It should be noted that the court can order any processing for the purpose of direct marketing to be stopped, not just that which results in the receipt of direct mail. The provision was considered in *Robertson v Electoral Registration Officer for Wakefield*[15] in which the judge held that such a notice could be served on a data controller who does not himself carry out direct marketing but supplies data to another in the knowledge that the data will be used for the purpose.

Automated decisions orders

14–10 These derive from the individual rights in s.12. There are two separate rights but only one type of order to remedy a breach of those rights. Under s.12(8) a court may order a person who has taken a decision based solely on automated processing to reconsider the decision or take a new one on a non-automated basis. Under s.12(1) an individual may serve notice on a controller requiring him to ensure that no decision within the terms of the subsection is taken in respect of him. If the controller breaches this requirement and takes such a decision the data subject may apply to the court. If he satisfies the court that:

(a) he has served such a notice; and

(b) the controller has made a prohibited decision which is not an exempt decision;

the court may order the data controller to reconsider the decision or take a new one not based on such processing. However, it is not apparent how the individual will know that such a decision has been taken, as the controller's obligation in s.12(2) to notify an individual that such a decision has been taken only applies where no notice under s.12(1) has been served. It may have been assumed that, if the processing significantly affects the individual, then he or she will inevitably learn of it, but this cannot be a foregone conclusion. The decision may be one which has no immediate impact, as for example an evaluation of work performance which is noted on a record but only to be used when a question of promotion or redundancy is raised. Moreover, the individual

---

will not necessarily know that a decision has been taken on the basis of automated processing even if he is aware of the result of the decision. It is suggested that the provision is unsatisfactory in this regard.

14–11 The court may also make an order where the controller has not complied with a notice served under s.12(2)(b). Under s.12(2) a controller must inform an individual of the taking of a decision within s.12(1) which is not an exempt decision (unless as noted above a s.12(1) notice has been served). In such a case the individual is entitled to serve a counter-notice under s.12(2)(b) requiring the controller to reconsider or retake the decision.

If the controller breaches this requirement and fails or refuses to reconsider or retake the decision the data subject may apply to the court and must satisfy the court that:

(a) there has been an automated decision within s.12(1) of which he received written notice;

(b) within the relevant time of receiving notice (21 days) he gave notice in writing to the controller requiring him to reconsider or retake the decision; and

(c) the controller has failed to comply with the requirement.

If he can show that this is the case the court may order the data controller to reconsider the decision or take a new one not based on such processing. However, it is not clear what routes are open to the individual if the controller fails in his duty to notify the individual but the individual becomes aware of the processing. It is suggested that in such a case the individual should serve the s.12(2)(b) notice, if possible within 21 days of learning of the relevant processing. The data controller should not be able to rely on his own failure to comply with the law to remove the individual's right to object.

It has to be remarked that the procedure set out by the section is unwieldy and unclear. In the Bill as originally drafted it appeared as a relatively straightforward prohibition. It was substantially amended at Report Stage in Parliament. The difficulties described above are largely attributable to the complexity of the amendment.

ACCURACY

Accuracy of data

14–12 Under s.70(2) data are inaccurate if they are "incorrect or misleading as to any matter of fact". There appear to be three possible types of inaccuracy:

(a) a record of an opinion may be inaccurate if it fails to reflect the opinion truly held;

(b) an opinion itself may be inaccurate, particularly if it is based on an inaccurate assessment of the facts; or

(c) the purported record of fact may not accurately reflect the reality.

Under s.14(1) an individual will have a remedy against both the holding of inaccurate data and against the record of any opinion which appears to a court to be based on the data held. If an opinion is inaccurate but not related to inaccurate data held there will be no remedy. This can be demonstrated by an example. A data controller may have a record of a worker showing that he or she never turns in for work on a Friday. That record is accurate. The controller may be of the opinion that the worker does not like working on Fridays because he or she is lazy. If the controller adds a note to the record to the effect that in his opinion the worker is not committed because he never attends work on a Friday (which is the firm's busiest day) that opinion will not give rise to any action for inaccuracy. This is the case even if the opinion is misguided because in fact the worker has to go for hospital treatment on a Friday. There will be no remedy, however, because the inaccurate opinion is based on an accurate data record.

Data may be misleading if a material aspect of the information is omitted. On the other hand there is no requirement that data needs to be exhaustive. This point again may be illustrated by a simple example. A man may be called Jacque Marie Ivan Johnson-Court. His name may be recorded in various ways:

(a) J Marie I. Johnson-Court;

(b) J M I Johnson-Court;

(c) J M I Court.

In the first example, the record is arguably misleading as to a matter of fact (his gender). In the second example, his name has been abbreviated but is not misleading because it gives accurate information about him. In the third example, the data are inaccurate because they omit a material part of his surname. Jacque Marie could have the data in the first and third examples corrected as being misleading and incorrect respectively but could not insist in the second example that all his names were set out in full.

14–13   Where data are received from a third party, Sch.1 Pt II para.7 provides that the fourth principle is not regarded as being contravened where the data "accurately record information obtained by the data controller from the data subject or a third party" and where two conditions are satisfied. Those conditions are (a) that the data controller has taken reasonable steps to ensure the accuracy of the data having regard to the purposes for which the data were obtained and further processed; and (b) if the data subject has notified the controller that he considers the data inaccurate, that the data are marked to indicate that fact. Where these conditions have been complied with the Commissioner cannot enforce Principle 4. However, even where the data accurately record information obtained from a third party and the conditions have been complied with the individual may still have a remedy against inaccuracy on an application to the court.

These provisions are different from the s.22 provisions in the 1984 Act, under which the obligation of the data user was simply to indicate that data had been received from the third party and ensure any such indication was extracted when the data themselves were extracted. In the 1998 Act the controller is under no statutory obligation to mark the data. His obligation is to ensure that they are accurate. The data subject may apply for a remedy for inaccuracy in respect of "personal data of which the applicant is the subject". It does not allow the data subject to apply for the amendment of data which relate to others. The position becomes more difficult where the same data relate to more than one person but only one party claims that the data are inaccurate. In such circumstances it is suggested that the most appropriate remedy may be a supplementary statement rather than any amendment to the data.

Accuracy Orders

14–14 Faced with a charge of inaccuracy a court has a wide and flexible range of powers. On an application made under s.14(1) a court may order the data controller to:

(a) rectify the data;

(b) block the data;

(c) erase the data; or

(d) destroy the data.

In each of those cases the order may also cover any other personal data which contain an expression of opinion which appears to the court to be based on the inaccurate data. The court may also order:

(a) verification inquiries;

(b) supplementary statements; or

(c) communication orders.

None of the terms used in s.14 for the remedies granted, that is rectification, erasure, blocking or destruction, are defined in the Act. Their meanings must therefore be ascertained by reference to their ordinary meaning in the English language, and any relevant interpretative instruments. They are important terms and their meanings will determine the extent of individual rights under the Act. Each of the terms is considered below.

Rectification orders

14–15 This appeared in the 1984 Act at s.24(1) in a similar context to its current one. Under s.24(1) a court could "order the rectification or erasure of any data". There is no case law on the terms rectification or erasure in this context. They never appear to have been litigated. The term rectification appears in the OECD Guidelines at para.13(d) in relation to individual rights and in Treaty 108 at Art.8.d, again in relation to individual rights. In both cases, however, it appears without further gloss.

In the Directive it only appears in Art.32 in relation to the transitional provisions relating to manual data. This Article provides that Member States may allow a transitional period of up to three years for controllers to comply with the requirements for "processing under way" as at October 24, 1998. For manual filing systems the Member States may allow a further period for controllers to comply with Arts 6 (data quality); 7 (lawfulness); and 8 (sensitive data). Article 32 then continues:

"Member States shall however grant the data subject the right to obtain, at his request . . . the rectification, erasure or blocking of data which are incomplete, inaccurate or stored in a way incompatible with the legitimate purpose of the controller."

This provision is, unfortunately, not of much assistance in understanding what the term rectification is meant to entail. It is clear that under the Directive rectification need only be available in these limited circumstances. Leases or other contracts which fail to reflect the common intentions of the parties may be rectified by the courts to give effect to the common intentions.[16]

14–16 The Shorter Oxford English Dictionary (OED) meaning of rectification includes:

(a) to put or set right, to remedy, to correct, amend, make good;

(b) to restore to a sound and healthy condition;

(c) to correct by removal of errors or mistakes.

Setting a record right would usually entail removing or altering an old version and replacing it with a new one. This may be acceptable on a register, however, in terms of handling personal information, this can be a difficult issue as this may destroy the continuity of the record—unless, that is, the record itself shows when it was altered and why. In many cases the preservation of an audit trail is important to show that the security requirements of the Act are being complied with.

It is suggested that, where data are shown to be inaccurate and rectification is chosen as the appropriate route, the data should be "rectified" by a change being made in such a manner that it clearly shows when and why the change was made in order to ensure that an audit trail is kept. It is suggested that rectification is a preferred option to erasure for remedying inaccuracy. If removal of the data is chosen, by whatever method, it may be appropriate to keep a record as to why the data were removed for the purposes of audit.

This may give rise to difficult decisions. For example, if a patient has been wrongly diagnosed as having an illness or condition which is socially sensitive, whether it be a sexually transmitted disease or headlice, he may want the record completely removed. However, the medical record may show that he has been sent for particular tests or given particular treatment. Those parts of the record are not inaccurate but will be difficult to understand or may be open to misinterpretation without the information about the inaccurate diagnosis.

Blocking orders

14–17 This term appears in s.1(1) of the Act in the definition of "processing", without further explanation. It is a relative newcomer to data protection legal instruments as it makes no appearance in the 1984 Act or in either the OECD Guidelines or Treaty 108. It appears in the Directive in Art.28(3) as an example of the powers of intervention with which a supervisory authority should be endowed and again in

---

[16] *Toronto-Dominion Bank v Oberoi* [2002] EWHC 3216.

Art.32 (set out above). No assistance as to its meaning can be drawn from either of those provisions.

The OED entry for "block" is lengthy. Its meanings include:

(a) to obstruct or close with obstacles;

(b) to shut up or in by obstructing ingress or egress;

(c) to obstruct the course of (something).

If one applies these meanings in the context of data it appears that a blocking order may require a controller to ensure that particular data, while remaining on the record, are made inaccessible either in general or to particular recipients. The term "recipients", it will be recalled, includes servants or agents of the controller. There is no guidance as to how a controller is to deal with data which have been made subject to a blocking order if the data are subsequently requested under a statutory provision. It is submitted that the best course would be for the controller to make an application to the court to lift the blocking order and allow for disclosure.

In the absence of any definition it is also unclear whether blocking can only restrict disclosure of data or whether the use of the data, either by the controller or by others, can also be blocked. In view of these uncertainties it is recommended that anyone applying for a blocking order should specify precisely how the order requested is intended to operate and what it is intended to cover.

A blocking order may be a useful tool to ensure compliance with Principle 2 under which personal data are restricted from being processed in a manner incompatible with the purposes for which they were obtained.

Erasure and destruction

14–18 These terms are dealt with together to cover the point that, in the context of information, they should have the same effect, although they appear to envisage different activities. If actions to erase or destroy information are successful then the information content should no longer exist. The difference between them would appear to relate to the context in which particular data occur. If only the inaccurate data are held on a single medium that medium may be physically destroyed. A disk can be crushed; paper can be shredded; marked cards can be burnt. The data can be destroyed with the medium. On the other hand, if the target data are held in a medium with other data some of which are not inaccurate, for example on a disk with other information or as part of paper records which relate to others, then the medium cannot be destroyed. In such cases, however, the offending data will need to be removed by erasure, leaving the remainder of the record intact.

14–19 Erasure. This appeared in the 1984 Act in s.24 under which a court could order the erasure of data. The term was not defined in the 1984 Act. There is no case law on it. It appears in the OECD Guidelines at para.13.d in relation to individual rights and Treaty 108 as Art.8.d. In both cases it appears without further gloss. In the Directive it occurs in Art.28 together with blocking and destruction but no further assistance as to its meaning is to be gained from that provision.

The OED entry for "erase" includes:

(a) to scrape or rub out, to efface, expunge;

(b) to obliterate from the mind or memory;

(c) to destroy utterly.

A consideration of erasure in relation to data raises a technical point on how data can be erased. On a normal computer hard disk the "delete" command does not actually delete the digitised information. It simply removes the index reference to the file so the file can no longer be retrieved using the computerised index. This frees that part of the disk or other medium for re-use. However the data held in that file have not been erased and will not be removed until they have been overwritten. That may never occur. Accordingly routine deletion will not erase data and specialist assistance may be necessary to comply with an erasure order. Moreover it may be prudent for the order itself to specify that simple deletion from an index will not be sufficient to ensure compliance with such an order.

14–20   Destruction.   This term appeared in the 1984 Act in s.23 as one of the occurrences which could give rise to an action against a data user, not as a potential remedy. It was not defined and there is no case law on it. It does not appear in Treaty 108 or the OECD Guidelines.

It appears in the Directive in Art.28(3) together with blocking and erasure but not in Art.32. Again these Articles give no assistance and neither the recitals nor the rest of the Directive help us.

The OED definition of "destroy" includes:

(a) to pull down or undo;

(b) to lay waste;

(c) to undo, break up, reduce into a useless form.

Although in the paragraph above a distinction was drawn between erasure and destruction it has to be said it is not obvious that the requirement to destroy data must entail a requirement to also destroy the medium. On the face of it destruction means no more than erasure. However, there may be cases where erasure of information would not be practicable, for example where the information appears on sheets of typed paper and destruction is the only practicable option.

Bearing these points in mind it is suggested that an order for erasure or destruction should be framed to cover both possibilities to ensure that any offending data are effectively dealt with.

Verification inquiries

14–21   This term has been used to describe the provision which is found in s.14(2)(b). Such inquires can be ordered:

(a) where the controller has obtained personal data from a third party or the data subject on trust as to their accuracy and;

(b) has taken no further independent steps to verify their accuracy or indeed to include the data subject's view if the data subject disputes their accuracy.

In such a case, where the data subject disputes the accuracy of the record and takes the matter to court, under s.14(2)(b) the court can order the controller to follow the verification requirements which apply to received data and which are set out in Sch.1 Pt II para.7, that is to take:

"(a) . . . reasonable steps to ensure the accuracy of the data; and

(b) if the data subject has notified the data controller of the data subject's view that the data are inaccurate, the data indicates that fact."

Presumably, the court can direct that inquiries be made both of the data subject and of any third party. As the data subject has brought the action inquiries can be made in the course of the proceedings and his views taken on board. One would anticipate, however, that the very fact that the data subject has brought proceedings must mean the data subject disputes the accuracy of the data. Inquiries of third parties may be difficult to make the subject of court orders as, on the face of it, the third parties have no obligation to respond to the data controller. However, this difficulty could be dealt with by calling any third party who supplied the data or who can speak to its accuracy, as a witness, if necessary by issue of a witness summons. An alternative is to seek discovery against the third party under the *Norwich Pharmacal* rules.[17] This enables an application for discovery to be made against one who is not a party to litigation where that party is known to be in possession of relevant information or material. Such applications are governed by CPR r.31.17. The court can then evaluate the evidence of accuracy.

Presumably, having directed inquiries and heard evidence, the court can order that the data subject's views should be added to the data record as they could have been by the controller under s.7(b). This is on the basis that the court may "make such order as it thinks fit for securing compliance with those requirements". Although it appears that this would be within the powers of the court it seems more likely that the court would find on the accuracy of the data and order a supplemental statement of the true facts to be added. It may do so under both s.14(2)(a) and (b).

Supplemental statement

14–22 The court may order a supplemental statement both where verification inquiries have been ordered and where the data controller has already complied with the Sch.1 Pt II para.7 requirement. A supplemental statement as to the "true facts relating to the matters dealt with by the data" can only be ordered where the disputed data are "received data". The court can also make rectification, blocking, erasure or destruction orders in respect of such data.

Communication orders

14–23 Where inaccurate data have been ordered to be rectified, erased, blocked or destroyed the court can make a communication order under s.14(3). The order will

---

[17] *Norwich Pharmacal v Commissioners for Customs and Excise* [1974] A.C. 133.

require the controller to notify third parties to whom the data have previously been disclosed of the action taken. The court can only make such an order if it is reasonably practicable for the data controller to comply with it. In deciding whether it is reasonably practicable s.14(6) requires the court to have regard, in particular, to the number of persons who would have to be notified. Clearly this is only one consideration and it will also be relevant to take into account how difficult such communication would be. A controller may have an existing effective method of regular communication even if he has a large number of disclosees, and in those circumstances he should not be relieved from his responsibilities by the weight of numbers. The court will also need to weigh:

(a) the nature of the inaccurate data;

(b) the damage it may cause to the data subject; and

(c) the risk of further damage caused by disclosures if dissemination is not stopped.

The High Court considered the application of s.14 in *P v Wozencroft*[18] and held that an application under s.14 for rectification of an expert report delivered to the court in family proceedings was an abuse of process and should be struck out. P was a litigant in person who was seeking access to a child. Dr Wozencroft was a consultant child psychiatrist who was charged with producing a report for the court in the proceedings. He duly produced a report, of which P was deeply critical. In the family proceedings the judge made an order which followed the recommendation of the expert. P appealed the order unsuccessfully. Several months later P made a subject access request seeking a copy of the report and subsequently challenged the accuracy of the report in an action under s.14. The subject access request was resolved however the rectification application was considered by the court. P asked the court that various statements in the report which related to him be "rectified". It was accepted that the report was personal data within the Act. The question of whether the data controller was CAFCASS, which had commissioned the report, or Dr Wozencroft, who had written it, was not decided. The judge did not rule on the accuracy of the data in the report. He ruled that it would be wholly inappropriate for a court to exercise the discretion to retrospectively amend a report given to a court and therefore it was not necessary to consider the accuracy of the contents:

> "In my judgment it is clear that the claimant could never persuade the court to exercise its discretion to make an order for rectification under section 14 of the Act. This forum, is quite simply, wholly inappropriate for articulation of the issues which the claimant raises in relation to the defendant's reports."

He pointed out that a claimant had an opportunity to challenge the report in cross-examination and to appeal the decision and challenges to the accuracy of the contents of the report should have be disposed of in that forum:

---

[18] [2002] EWHC 1724, Fam.

"It is entirely inapt that over a year later there should be free-standing proceedings in this court in which the claimant seeks to do what he should have done at the hearing."

The case was dismissed as an abuse of process. It would have been an interesting case had it gone to hearing. It seems highly unlikely that any claimant would succeed in showing that opinions delivered by an expert were inaccurate in that they were not honestly the true opinion of the expert. It is suggested that had the case gone to hearing, and had the judge been satisfied that any data relating to P were inaccurate, it would not be appropriate to alter a report which had been put before the court. The appropriate remedy would be to order a supplemental statement to be held with the original report. However, these can only be ordered where the data are "received" data. Such an order would therefore have to be made on the basis that CAFCASS are the data controller and have "received" the data from the expert.

COMPENSATION AND ASSOCIATED COURT ORDERS

Who can sue?

14–24 An individual who suffers damage by reason of any contravention of the Act is able to sue for compensation. The individual need not be the data subject affected by the processing for these purposes. It is sufficient that a contravention of the Act has caused that person damage. The usual rules as to capacity of parties to take action will apply. For example a child will be unable to bring proceedings in his or her own name even though she or he was competent to make a subject access request or exercise any of the other rights, but must sue by a litigation friend unless the court makes an order permitting the child to conduct proceedings without one under CPR r.21.2.

Who can be sued?

14–25 The controller whose contravention of the requirement of the Act has caused the damage or the distress will be liable. It is possible that controllers may be jointly liable particularly where they share or otherwise pool data. In such a case one would expect the court to apportion liability in accordance with the degree of responsibility. The usual rules as to vicarious liability will apply, with an employer being liable for actions carried out within the scope of his employment.[19]

What must be proved?

14–26 The claimant must show that the contravention has caused him to suffer damage. The term "damage" is not defined. In general it would cover pecuniary loss such as loss of profits or earnings, and non-pecuniary loss such as pain or suffering and loss of amenity.[20] Damages for pain and suffering depend on the individual's awareness of the pain.[21] Damages for loss of amenity are assessed on an objective basis

---

[19] *Lister v Hesley Hall Ltd* [2001] 2 All E.R. 76a.
[20] *Hassell v Abnoof* (2002) QBD CO/101.
[21] *Lim v Camden Health Authority* [1979] 2 All E.R. 910.

to calculate for the actual loss.[22] Damage may also consist of damage to reputation.[23] However in the case of *Johnson v Medical Defence Union*[24] Buxton L.J. rejected the possibility of such a head of claim in a data protection case where the appellant relied upon assumptions that his reputation had been damaged and a financial value could be put on that:

"I am certainly not prepared to import those assumptions, peculiar to, and in the view of some an unedifying feature of, the English law of defamation into this wholly different chapter of law."[25]

In the case of *Sofola v Lloyds TSB*[26] Mr Justice Tugendhat was prepared to contemplate that a claim to have been refused banking facilities on the basis of inaccurate data could be argued as damage under s.14 although the point was not determined. In the case of *Dr Rita Pal v General Medical Council*[27] the court accepted that the retention of data in breach of the Act which has an impact on the individual could found an action. In general damages for distress are not recoverable save in those circumstances in which extreme distress which results in damage may count as actual damage, for example in cases of psychiatric injury:

"The courts have developed sufficient confidence in medical expertise to be willing to award damages for mental disturbances which manifest themselves in bodily symptoms (such as miscarriage) or in a recognised psychiatric illness. The latter is distinguished from shock, fear, anxiety or grief are regarded as a normal consequence of a distressing event and for which damages are not awarded."[28]

However, a number of statutes specifically provide for damages to be payable for distress.

Compensation is intended to place the individual in the position which he would have been in apart from the wrong which has been done. It is not intended to be punitive. There may however be aggravated damages which can be awarded where the behaviour of the respondent aggravates the original injury. In the High Court aggravated damages were awarded against the Mirror newspaper in the case brought by Naomi Campbell[29] although the decision was later overturned on appeal. It is possible that exemplary damages might be awarded in a sufficiently serious case[30].

14–27 Section 13(2) provides that an individual who suffers distress as well as damage because of the contravention may claim for that distress. Where processing is for the special purposes, that is journalistic, artistic or literary purposes, distress on its own will be sufficient as a basis of a claim.[31]

---

[22] *Denis Damien O'Brien v Constance Harris* (2001) QBD CO/102.
[23] *Victoria Mandeville Gillick v Brook Advisory Centres* (No. 1) [2001] EWCA 1263.
[24] [2007] EWCA Civ 262.
[25] *ibid.*, para.78.
[26] See *Sofola v Lloyds TSB* [2005] EWHC 1335, QB.
[27] [2004] EWHC 1485 (QB).
[28] *White v Chief Constables of Yorkshire* [1999] 1 All E.R. 1, per Lord Hoffman at 40b.
[29] See Ch.2, above.
[30] *Rookes v Barnard* [1074] A.C. 1129; *Kuddus v Chief Constable of Leicestershire Constabulary* [2001] UKHL 29.
[31] Section 13(3).

The claimant need only show that any of the requirements of the Act have been breached. This is a very broad provision and would cover breach of the notification requirements, failure to honour the individual rights or breaches of the following requirements of the Principles:

(a) personal data shall be processed fairly and lawfully;

(b) personal data shall be kept up to date where necessary;

(c) personal data shall be adequate;

(d) personal data shall be relevant to the purpose or purposes for which it is collected and processed;

(e) personal data shall not be excessive (in relation to the purposes of the processing);

(f) personal data shall not be kept for any longer than is necessary for the purpose.

Breach of any of these requirements in a way which causes damage to an individual may give rise to an action by the individual. The security obligation under the Directive is treated rather differently to the other obligations and perhaps it is not correct to characterise it as a data subject right. However, it may also give rise to an action for compensation. It should however be noted that in the *Campbell* case the Court of Appeal suggested that the exemption for the processing of personal data for the special purposes would usually apply so as to defeat a claim for damages, at least as far as the daily media are concerned. In *Lord Ashcroft v AG*[32] Lord Ashcroft brought a claim against the Government in respect of the leaking of two documents which he claimed were unlawfully disclosed and the disclosure of which caused him to lose standing and interfered with his private life. Several months after the proceedings had been started he sought to amend his claim to include claims for breach of the Data Protection Act 1984 and 1998. The judge had to decide whether to allow the amendments, the test being whether they showed an arguable case. In respect of the claim under the 1984 Act, Lord Ashcroft argued that he had a right to take action for breach of the Principles. The respondent argued that the rights under the 1984 Act were limited to those specifically given in ss.21 to 23. The judge held that any breach of the Principles under the 1984 Act was a matter for the Registrar only and could not give rise to a private action in damages however the claimant would be able to claim under s.23 of the 1984 Act for damage caused by an unauthorised disclosure. The judge also accepted that the position under the 1998 Act is different as far as individual rights of action are concerned and that Lord Ashcroft could claim for any breach of the 1998 Act which caused damage. He rejected a further (and particularly adventurous) contention that the DPA obliged the Government to carry out adequate inquiries into any allegation of breach of private life, a point contended by the claimant as part of his complaint in respect of the alleged inadequacy of the leak inquiry. He considered the further contention that, while the disclosure complained of pre-dated the 1998 Act and thus could not found an action for breach of Principle under that Act, the documents

---

[32] [2002] EWHC 1122, QB.

in issue continued to be held by the Government after the 1998 Act came into force and, as the 1998 Act requires personal data to be relevant and accurate, the continued holding of the data amounted to unfair processing in breach of Principle 1 under the 1998 Act. The judge agreed that an arguable case could be mounted along those lines and allowed this part of the pleadings to stand. In the case of *Sofola v Lloyds TSB*[33] Mr Sofola took action against the bank for damage caused to him by unlawful processing of personal data and inaccurate data. The bank succeeded in having the claim struck out, apparently, in part at least, under the mistaken belief that the bank had deleted the offending record. It transpired that in fact the record had not been deleted and Mr Justice Tugendhat took the unusual step of allowed the appeal to be reinstated on the data protection issues.

Level of payments for distress

14–28   There is no guidance as to the level of payment that may be appropriate when a claimant has suffered distress. There may be a wide spectrum depending on the particular facts of the case, ranging from a limited amount for injury to feeling caused by a minor inaccuracy, to substantial damages for intense and justified distress. There are no obviously analogous areas. A wide range of levels can apply to cases for injury to feelings arising as a result of discrimination on grounds of sex or race. In *Armitage v Johnson*[34] £20,000 was awarded for injury to feelings in a particularly bad case for 18 months of suffering. In *Noone v North West Thames Health Authority (No. 1)*[35] the applicant was awarded £3,000 for injury to feelings. See also *ICTS (UK) Ltd v Tchoula*[36] as cited in *Doshoki v Draeger Ltd.*[37] In *Crofton v Yeoboah*[38] the claimant was awarded £25,000 (a reduction of the original £45,000 awarded) for injury to feelings. In *Vento v Chief Constable of West Yorkshire*[39] three bands of compensation were set for injury to feelings. The top band is between £15,000 and £25,000. Only in exceptional cases should damages exceed £25,000.

In any action for compensation it is a defence to a claim for the controller to prove that he has taken: "such care as in all the circumstances was reasonably required to comply with the requirement concerned". This is found in s.13(3). The obligation on data controllers is to comply with the Data Protection Act. This does not involve any issue of foreseeability of loss to the individual or the person affected. However, the foreseeable risk will be relevant in assessing whether the controller has taken such care as was reasonably required "in all the circumstances". Those circumstances would presumably include matters such as the risk of possible damage to individuals, and the extent of such damage.

Associated orders

14–29   The court has an additional power to order rectification, erasure, destruction or blocking of the data under s.14(4) where:

---

[33] [2005] EWHC 1335, QB.
[34] [2002] I.R.L.R. 341.
[35] [1998] I.C.R. 813.
[36] [2001] I.R.L.R. 643.
[37] [2002] I.R.L.R. 3410.
[38] EAT April 2003.
[39] [2002] EWCA Civ 1871.

(a) an individual has suffered damage;

(b) in circumstances in which he would be entitled to compensation under s.13; and

(c) there is a substantial risk of further failure by the controller to comply with the Act in respect of that data in the same circumstances.

The claimant does not have to bring an action for compensation under s.13 in order to invoke this provision. However, as the conditions for a s.13 action must be met it is difficult to envisage circumstances in which a claimant would not make such an application at the same time. In effect, this provision enables the court faced with a s.13 application to make a related order dealing with the data in order to prevent further damage occurring.

Other orders of the court—powers of the court

14–30   The remedies sought will determine the court in which the proceedings are to be brought. Under s.15(1) the jurisdiction conferred by ss.7 to 14 is exercisable by the High Court or a county court, or in Scotland by the Court of Session or the Sheriff's Court.

Under the CPR which took effect from April 26, 1999 claims are allocated to three tracks:

- small claims—for claims up to £5,000;

- fast track—£5,000 to £15,000;

- multi-track—£15,000 plus.

Proceedings under the Act have not been classified as "specialist proceedings" under CPR Pt 49.

It might be expected that claims for compensation will fall under the small claims or fast track procedures.

High Court

14–31   The High Court is not the most obvious venue for a data protection action. The level of damages usually claimed and the nature of the orders sought might seem unlikely to justify the expense for an individual claimant. However, it may be considered appropriate in some circumstances, particularly if the claimant also seeks other orders such as injunctions under the High Court's inherent powers. Applications for injunctions may be made on an interim (interlocutory) or final basis to the Court for an order that a particular action, in these cases processing of a particular nature, cease. As an injunction is an equitable remedy it is never available as a matter of right and the Court always has a discretion whether or not to grant it. The main consideration in whether to grant an interim injunction (i.e. until trial or further order) is whether the claimant can be adequately recompensed by money for the wrong done. An injunction may be refused where the wrong done is minor and there is no danger that it will be repeated. If he is to succeed in an application for an interim injunction the claimant must show that he has an arguable case, that there is a serious issue to be tried and that he cannot be adequately remedied for any injury done pending trial by money damages. In the case of *Microsoft Corporation v Paul Martin McDonald (also known as Garry A Webb) (trading as BIZADS and BIZADS UK[40])* the High Court granted an injunction as relief for an action brought by Microsoft under reg.30 of the Privacy and Electronic Communications (EC Directive) Regulations 2003. Regulation 30 provides that a "person who suffers damage by reason of any contravention of any requirement of these Regulation by any other person shall be entitled to bring proceedings for compensation from that other person for that damage". The respondent sold lists of email addresses for use for unsolicited commercial email. The court agreed that Microsoft, whose services were detrimentally affected by the sending of such emails, fell within the scope of the provision and was entitled to claim damages and granted an injunction under the provisions of the Supreme Court Act 1981.

A permanent injunction can be obtained without interim relief being applied for. An order for a speedy trial can be sought in appropriate case.

County Court

14–32   This is the more likely venue for individual claims. Claims for damages below £5,000 will fall within the small claims limit. County courts are creatures of statute and do not have the inherent powers of the High Court. In relation to actions for compensation under s.13 they will be able to issue associated orders under s.14(4). However, their powers will be limited to providing remedies in accordance with the Act. A court order for a money sum will operate as a money judgment to be enforced in the usual way. Where an order to take specific action or refrain from taking specific action has been made by a court and not complied with an action for contempt can be brought and eventually the contemptor condemned to prison until the contempt has been purged.

FINANCIAL SUPPORT FOR LITIGATION

14–33   Claimants bringing claims under the 1998 Act are not eligible for legal aid. Such claims would be eligible for conditional fee arrangements. Section 58 of the Courts and Legal Services Act 1990 as amended by s.27 of the Access to Justice Act 1999 makes such agreements lawful (provided that they satisfy certain requirements) both when they do not include a success fee and when they do. Such conditional fee agreements are now widely used, however, they only allow for the recovery of costs where costs are awarded. It is therefore unlikely that solicitors will enter into them in small claims where the normal rule is that no costs are awarded.

COMMISSIONER'S POWERS

Request for assessment

14–34   Under s.42 a person may ask the Commissioner for an assessment of any processing by which he believes himself to be directly affected. An assessment in this

---

[40] [2006] EWHC 3410.

context means an assessment as to whether it is likely or unlikely that any processing of personal data has been or is being carried out in compliance with the Act. The request can be made by the person directly or by another on his behalf and the person must be, or believe himself to be, directly affected by the processing in question. The power to request an assessment cannot be used as a general check by someone who is not affected by particular processing. The request does not have to specify whether the person has any grounds for suspicion that the processing is being carried out in contravention of the Act.

The Commissioner has a duty to make an assessment when requested. This is subject to the Commissioner's being satisfied as to the identity of the person making the request and being able to ascertain the relevant processing which is complained of. However, the Commissioner has a degree of discretion in the manner in which he fulfils his duty to make an assessment. Under s.42(2) he may "make an assessment in such manner as appears to him to be appropriate". This would cover a range of possible options, from a consideration limited to evaluating only the information given in a letter of complaint, to a full-scale investigation by officers of the Commissioner. The former course might be followed for example where a letter of complaint raised a matter already adjudicated by the courts or tribunal and where the judgment could be applied directly to the case; alternatively, a full investigation including interviews and inquiries of the controller, might be the preferred approach in a case alleging breach of s.55 (unlawful procuring of data).

In deciding how to make his assessment the Commissioner may have regard to the consideration set out in s.42(3)(a)–(c), that is:

> "(a) the extent to which the request appears to him to raise a matter of substance;
>
> (b) any undue delay in making the request; and
>
> (c) whether the person making the request is entitled to make an application under s.7 [subject access] in respect of the personal data in question."

14–35   As the right in s.42 applies to "persons" rather than individuals, it follows that requests for assessment may be made by limited companies and other bodies, not just individual data subjects. However, the rights to subject access in s.7 only apply to individuals. Accordingly, it appears that the Commissioner can take into account under s.42(3)(c) whether the complainant is an individual. The list in s.42(3) is clearly not exclusive and other factors may also be relevant to the particular case.

The Commissioner only has a limited obligation to disclose the results of his consideration of an assessment. Under s.42(4) he need only notify the person who made the request whether an assessment has been made and of any view the Commissioner has formed or action taken as a result of the request. He does not have to provide information about the nature of the assessment, whether any further inquiries were undertaken or provide any finding of fact or evidence.

The Commissioner has powers to require the production of information and evidence from data controllers by the use of an Information Notice, or the issue of a warrant, but again an individual will have no right to access any information obtained by such means. The Commissioner may serve an enforcement notice on a data controller for breach of the Act but an individual has no right to be consulted on the form or effect of such a notice, even where it was provoked by his initial complaint.

Accordingly, although an individual may make a formal complaint to the Commissioner in the form of a request for assessment, once he has made that request the matter is out of his hands and out of his control. The Commissioner does not have the same powers as a court. Moreover, the Commissioner has a regulatory role and while he may actively investigate an alleged breach, which a court cannot do, he will not act on behalf of the complainant in a matter. In addition he has no power to award compensation and his enforcement powers are more limited than the order-making powers of a court. If the complainant is unhappy with the way the Commissioner handles the case his only recourse might be to complain to the ombudsman or seek judicial review of the Commissioner's actions or decisions if he believed the Commissioner had either failed to carry out his obligations or carried them out improperly.

The prosecution and enforcement powers of the Commissioner are treated in full at Ch.20, below.

Assistance in cases involving special purposes

14–36 The special purposes are treated in detail in Ch.17, below. However, the assistance provisions are mentioned here as a special case where the Commissioner may act on behalf of or in concert with a complainant.

The powers only apply where the case concerns data processed for the special purposes. Those are defined in s.3 of the Act as meaning any one or more of the following:

> "(a) the purposes of journalism;
>
> (b) artistic purposes;
>
> (c) literary purposes."

These terms are not further defined within the Act. A full treatment of the terms will be found in Ch.17, below. There are exemptions in s.32 for data held and used for the special purposes. Under s.53 an individual who brings any proceedings for:

(a) failure to provide subject access;

(b) failure to comply with an objection to processing;

(c) inaccuracy of data;

(d) failure to comply with a notice in respect of automated decision-taking; or

(e) action for compensation,

which relate to personal data processed for the special purposes may apply to the Commissioner for assistance in relation to those proceedings.

This provision is supplemented by Sch.10 to the Act, under which the assistance provided may include the making of arrangements for the Commissioner to bear the cost of legal advice and assistance and legal representation of the applicant in preliminary proceedings or in negotiations. It should be noted that no special provision is included to cover the disclosure of investigative material obtained by the Commissioner during any investigation into a complaint or a request for assessment covering the special purposes, but there would be no bar to the Commissioner making appropriate disclosures in a case where assistance is provided, as long as the disclosures are necessary for the discharge of the Commissioner's functions.

The Commissioner is only empowered to provide assistance if in his opinion the case involves a matter of substantial public importance. To the extent provided for by s.53 and Sch.10, therefore, the Commissioner may directly assist an individual in bringing his or her case but those provisions are relatively narrow.

Access to Commissioner's papers

14–37   Complainants and their representatives sometimes seek to deal with a breach of the Act both by making a complaint to the Commissioner and, in appropriate cases, by taking private action before a court. In order to pursue the private proceedings complainants may seek access to reports or statements arising from any investigation carried out by the Commissioner. However, practitioners should be aware that they cannot rely on evidence from the Commissioner's investigations being made available to them. The Commissioner's powers are regulatory and the Commissioner's papers are rarely made available on a voluntary basis to assist with private actions. The case law on information generated during a criminal inquiry is clear on this point. In the case of *Bunn v BBC*[41] the court held that statements made to the police by an accused person under caution enjoyed confidentiality. This was because it was clearly implicit in the relationship between the police and the accused that the information was only to be used for the purposes for which it was to be provided, although on the particular facts of that case the information in the statements was in the public domain because they had been read in open court. However the same reasoning would apply to statements made under caution to another investigating agency such as the Commissioner. In *Taylor v Serious Fraud Office*[42] the House of Lords held that there was an implied undertaking for material disclosed by the prosecution in criminal proceedings that they should not be used for a collateral purpose. If the circumstances so required the court could release the undertaking. In other cases the courts have ruled on how far information acquired by a public authority in the course of its functions may be used or disclosed for other purposes.[43] In broad terms a public body will usually only be able to disclose confidential information with the consent of the person who provided it, unless the disclosure is in the public interest.[44] This ruling applies to material gathered during an investigation. It follows that papers generated during an inquiry by the Commissioner, even if not dealing with a

---

[41] [1998] 3 All E.R. 552.
[42] [1998] 4 All E.R. 801.
[43] *Bunn v BBC* [1998] 3 All E.R. 552; *Woolgar v Chief Constable of Sussex* [1999] 3 All E.R. 604; *R. v A Police Authority in the Midlands Ex p. LM* (2000) UK.H.R.R.143.
[44] *Hellewell v Chief Constable of Derbyshire* [1005] 4 All E.R. 473.

possible criminal offence, are unlikely to be available to assist an individual in taking a private action.

Freedom of information

14–38 The Information Commissioner is a public authority covered by the Freedom of Information Act 2000 (FOIA) but this does not provide for extended access to case papers. The FOIA includes exemptions for information which is subject to an enforceable obligation of confidence and which is subject to a statutory barrier on disclosure. Moreover, there are exemptions for information relating to the investigation and prosecution functions of bodies carrying out law enforcement and regulatory activities, such as the enforcement work of the Commissioner.[45]

PRACTICAL TOOLS

Case Study—Compensation

14–39 Mrs Jones had a nervous illness some 10 years ago. It was caused by particularly stressful family circumstances at the time and has never recurred. She now works for the university as a lecturer. She has not disclosed her previous illness. She was not asked to do so on her application form which only asked for information about illness in the last five years. There is a record of the illness on her medical records held by her GP. Unfortunately one of the dates on the medical record is wrong and records the illness as having occurred in 1998 instead of 1989.

The GP, Dr Smith, has a notification on the public register maintained by the Information Commissioner which shows that the practice holds data for medical purposes.

Dr Smith is approached by a researcher from the same university to provide him with data for research purposes. Dr Smith agrees to provide the data, believing it is a worthwhile project and has the blessing of the ethical committee, but fails to amend his registration to notify the disclosure. This is contrary to ss.15(1)(e) and 16(1) of the Act.

The data which are disclosed to the researcher include the personal data about Mrs Jones and show the date of the illness as 1998. The GP does not inform Mrs Jones of his intention to disclose the data. He did not intend to disclose them at the date they were first recorded but he does not now make a further contact with her under Sch.1 Pt 2(1)(a).

When the researcher, Mrs Black, starts to go through the information with which she has been provided she realises that this record must refer to Mrs Jones. She is concerned about the record and speaks to Mrs Jones' senior at the university. He looks at the information the researcher has been provided with and, because of the inaccuracy of the data, assumes that Mrs Jones lied in applying for the lecturing post she currently holds. Mrs Jones is dismissed on the basis that she provided inaccurate information on her application.

Does Mrs Jones have a remedy under the Data Protection Act against either Dr Smith, the researcher Mrs Black, or her senior officer?

---

[45] FOIA ss.30 and 31.

Approach

14–40 In approaching any case analysis it is advisable to:

- consider whether the information falls under the Act in the hands of each person who deals with it;
- Consider whether it is held as data within the Act or on a relevant filing system, and whether it is personal data;
- assess who the data controller is in each incident, for example whether it is a limited company or an unincorporated organisation or an individual, in doing so distinguish between employees and employers;
- consider the nature of the data and in particular whether it is sensitive data, and assess the grounds for the processing;
- check the notification requirements have been complied with;
- check through the Principles assessing whether there has been compliance with all of them in the circumstances;
- check through the individual rights assessing whether those have been complied with;
- assess whether any exemption could be claimed.

Dr Smith and Mrs Jones

14–41 Dr Smith was a data controller for the personal data about Mrs Jones as the data were held in automated form and he controlled the purposes and manner of the processing. The data are sensitive data. We can take it that Dr Smith had appropriate grounds for holding those data for medical purposes. Either consent or the legitimate interest ground would allow him a legitimate ground for processing under Sch.2 and he was entitled to hold the sensitive data on the basis that it was necessary for medical purposes under Sch.3.

Dr Smith was properly notified to hold the data for medical purposes but when he made the disclosure to the researcher he was not properly registered to make it and contravened ss.15(1)(e) and 16(1).

There is a question mark over whether Dr Smith had grounds under Schs 2 and 3 for disclosing the data. The act of disclosing for another's purpose may be regarded as processing for that purpose (although the point is not completely clear in the Act). If it is so regarded Dr Smith would have to rely on the legitimate interest ground in Sch.2 and the ground relating to medical uses in Sch.3. However the Sch.3 ground, (Ground 8), only applies where the processing is:

"Necessary for medical purposes and is undertaken by

(a) a health professional, or
(b) a person who in the circumstances owes a duty of confidentiality which is equivalent to that which would arise if that person were a health professional."

Medical purposes includes the purpose of medical research.

Dr Smith owed Mrs Jones an obligation of confidence as the information is obviously confidential.[46] Applying that legal position to these circumstances the University and the researcher were bound by the equivalent obligation of confidence as Dr Smith. Accordingly Dr Smith could argue that he had an appropriate ground under Sch.3 for making the disclosure.

Unfortunately Dr Smith failed to comply with the Principles in several ways. He did not give notice to Mrs Jones of the disclosure as he should have done under Sch.1 Pt II para.2(1)(a) so he processed the data unfairly. Moreover the data themselves are inaccurate.

There is nothing to suggest that Mrs Jones has served any notices on Dr Smith which would have prevented him making the disclosure.

Dr Smith has therefore contravened the Act by holding inaccurate data. Moreover he has disclosed that data unfairly and without notification to the Commissioner. Mrs Jones clearly has a remedy in respect of the inaccuracy and may go to court to have the data rectified under s.14(1). Mrs Jones has also suffered damage by the loss of her job, however, Dr Smith may defend any action against him for compensation on the basis that he was not responsible for that damage; the University was. We therefore turn to the position of the University.

The University

14–42   It appears that the University employed both the researcher and Mr White and there is nothing to suggest that they were acting outside the course of their employment in this matter so the University can be regarded as the relevant person with legal responsibility for the data. The data were not anonymised so they were still personal information relating to Mrs Jones in the hands of the University. It is not clear from the case outline whether they were held as data or in a manual filing system within the terms of the Act or are outside the Act so we should consider the position in each case.

On the basis that the data fall within the Act the University could rely on the legitimate interest ground to legitimise holding the data in the first instance and would have to rely on ground 8 as the basis for holding the sensitive data. Ground 8 could be claimed on the basis set out above, that a person who comes into possession of information which is clearly confidential is himself in turn bound by that obligation. On this basis the University and its staff who dealt with the data will have owed Mrs Jones on obligation of confidence in respect of the data and were bound to use them only for the purposes for which they were disclosed. However, the University has breached that obligation by using the data for another purpose, the purpose of dealing with employment matters. As the University had breached its obligation by using the data for another purpose it has forfeited its ground for holding the sensitive data; it has processed it unlawfully and has also become liable for a breach of confidence action by Mrs Jones.

No information is given about the University's notification so we will assume it covers the situation.

The University was not responsible for the original inaccuracy of the data. However they made no further inquiries to establish its accuracy. The interpretation provision

---

[46] *A v B*; see Ch.2, above.

for Principle 4 provides that it is not to be regarded as contravened where the data accurately record date obtained from a third party in a case where:

"(a) having regard to the purpose or purposes for which data were obtained and further processed, the data controller has taken reasonable steps to ensure the accuracy of the data, and

(b) if the data subject has notified the data controller of the data subject's view that the data are inaccurate, the data indicate that fact."

It is submitted that in this case the University has not taken reasonable steps to ensure the accuracy of the data before processing them for the purposes of employment. They should have made further inquiries. Accordingly the University has breached Principle 4.

Mrs Jones therefore has a claim under s.13 of the Act against the University on the basis that she has suffered damage by reason of contraventions of the requirement of the Act and she is entitled to compensation for both the damage and her associated distress. Although she may launch her action against both Dr Smith and the University it is suggested that the primary liability rests with the University.

However, if the University is not a data controller for the data and the information as held by the University falls outside the Act she can still make her claim against Dr Smith. The University may be liable for breach of confidence and wrongful dismissal in any event.

ADDITIONAL INFORMATION

Derivations

14–43 • Directive 95/46 (See App.B):

(a) Arts 12(b) and (c) (right of access and rectification), 22 (remedies), 23 (liability), 28 (supervisory authority), 32 (final provisions);
(b) Recital 55.

• Council of Europe Convention of January 28, 1981 for the Protection of Individuals with regard to automatic processing of Personal Data: Art.8c, 8d (additional safeguards for the data subject).

• Data Protection Act 1984: ss.22 (compensation for inaccuracy), 23 (compensation for loss or unauthorised disclosure), 24 (rectification and erasure), 25 (jurisdiction and procedure).

• Organisation for Economic Co-operation and Development Guidelines: Annex, Part Two (basic principles of national application 13(d)).

Hansard references

14–44 Vol.586, No.108, col.CWH 52, Lords Grand Committee, February 23, 1998 Power of court to require controller to tell of rectification when correction otherwise than by order of court

Vol.585, No.95, col.523, Lords Report, March 16, 1998
Information commissioner must give to individuals following making of assessments

Vol.587, No.127, col.1095, Lords Third Reading
Compensation rights

Commons Standing Committee D, May 14, 1998, col.101
Scope of requests for assessment to Commissioner

ibid., cols 126–129
Damages include compensation for pure financial loss, levels of compensation for distress under special purposes, notices to third parties of orders made

Vol.315, No.198, col.580, Commons Third Reading, July 2, 1998
Powers of court to order rectification.

Previous case law

14–45   *R. v Chief Constable of B County Constabulary*, unreported, November 1997
Pascal v Barclays Bank Plc, unreported
Mayor and City of London Court, May 11, 1999, case under s.22 of the DPA 1984
Campbell v Mirror Group Newspapers [2002] EWCA Civ 1373
A v B [2002] 3 W.L.R. 542
Gaskin v UK (1989) 12 E.H.R.R. 36
P v Wozencroft [2002] EWHC 1724, Fam

CHAPTER 15

Exemptions for Regulation, National Security, Crime Control and Taxation

INTRODUCTION

15–01 The first three aspects of the title of this chapter may appear to form a logical set whereas the last one looks slightly out of place. The exemption for processing for the purpose of the collection of taxes has been included with these provisions because s.29 applies the same exemptions to processing for the purpose of taxation as to crime prevention and the apprehension and prosecution of offenders.

It could be argued that the usual rule, that the Directive is the primary source of interpretation, should not apply to the exemptions for national security and crime control in the same way as to other parts of the Act. Where the function falls outside Community competence it could be argued that the relevant provision does not rely for its interpretation upon the provisions of the Directive. However, insofar as the same exemptions will cover data which are used for some purposes within and some purposes outside Community competence and insofar as the Act was passed to give effect to the Directive this may be a purely academic distinction. It should be expected that the courts will have regard to the terms of the Directive in construing the application of any exemption in the 1998 Act. The point arose indirectly in the case of *R. (on the application of SSHD) v The Information Tribunal & the Commissioner (interested party)*.[1] The case is considered in more detail below but it was argued on behalf of the Secretary of State that the impact of Art.3 of the Directive, which provides that it does not apply in the course of activities falling outside the scope of Community law, meant that any issues concerned with national security are wholly outside the remit of the Information Commissioner who is not even able to question whether the exemption has been properly applied. This was rejected by the court which held that, while Art.3 sets out the general principle, the combination of Arts 13 and 28(4) which deal with the application of specific exemptions and restrictions in national implementing provisions and the powers of national supervisory authorities to check whether these exemptions and restrictions are being properly applied respectively, means that the role of the national supervisory authority cannot simply be ousted where exemption on the grounds are

---

[1] [2006] EWHC Admin 2958.

claimed. However once the exemption is made out it appeared to be accepted that the Directive could have no further impact on interpretation or approach.

All the exemptions in this chapter, except the national security exemption, are to be applied on a case-by-case basis. The text follows the same pattern for each exemption, describing who can claim the exemption, what the exemption covers and when it can be claimed, followed by specific points relating to the particular sections.

Summary of Main Points

15–02   (a) The exemption for processing for regulatory purposes is in the body of the Act. Under the 1984 Act the functions were specified by statutory instrument. This made them difficult to research and not easily accessible, as the detail was in the secondary legislation. On the other hand it provided certainty as to which functions were covered. The exemption is widely drawn.

(b) The national security exemption is a class exemption and certificates can have "prospective" effect. There are two limited forms of appeal to the Data Protection Tribunal on specific grounds. There are additional special procedures dealing with such appeals.

(c) The crime and taxation exemptions include those who receive information in pursuance of statutory functions and include an additional exemption for risk classification systems.

(d) There is a specific exemption for the armed forces.

National Security

Who can claim the exemption?

15–03   Any data controller may be able to claim the benefit of the exemption because it applies to any personal data where the exemption is necessary for the purpose of securing national security. There is an evidential provision that a certificate by a Minister of the Crown shall be conclusive evidence of that point but the exemption does not depend on that certificate. It is a matter of fact as to whether the exemption is required for the purpose of safeguarding national security.

What does the exemption cover?

15–04   The exemption covers Pts II, III and V of the Act, the Principles and s.55, that is the individual rights, notification, the Commissioner's powers of enforcement, compliance with the Principles, and restrictions on the unlawful procuring of information. This is the broadest exemption in the Act. The exemption does not however apply to ss. 51 to 54 which includes the general powers of the Commissioner in s.51 to ". . . so perform his functions under this Act as to promote the observance of the requirements of this Act by data controllers". If it is necessary for the purpose of safeguarding national security any data may be released from the mechanisms of control under the Act. The ground covered by the exemption is the same as in the 1984 Act although the mechanism for achieving it is different. In the 1984 Act personal data were exempt from Pt II of the Act, which covered registration, and from ss.21–24 which dealt with individual rights. Because the enforcement powers of the Registrar and the provisions of the Act depended upon registration, exemption from registration had the effect of exempting the data from any other control. In the 1998 Act notification and the other regulatory provisions are divorced and accordingly in s.28(1) the Act lists the exemptions from the Principles and the other relevant provisions specifically.

When can the exemption be claimed?

15–05 There is no definition in the Act as to what amounts to "safeguarding national security". The decision to claim the exemption rests, in the first instance with the data controller, which will usually be a Government Department.

Certificates and evidence

15–06 Section 28(2) provides that a certificate signed by a Minister of the Crown certifying that the exemption is, or at any time was, required for the purpose shall be conclusive evidence of that fact. The certificate may identify the personal data by means of a general description and may be expressed to have prospective effect. This is contained in s.28(3). A general description presumably means exactly what it says and would be satisfied by a broad phrase, for example "personal data held by the Home Office for the purpose of immigration", although there must be a question about how general the description may lawfully be. It is not clear, however, what is meant by the provision that the certificate "may be expressed to have prospective effect". This co-exists with the requirement that the exemption is at any time or was required for the purpose. While the term "prospective" suggests that a certificate may have future effect, the limitation to the exemption being currently required or having previously been required suggests it should not be able to have future effect.

The certificate must be provided by a Minister. There is a further provision dealing with evidence which allows a certified copy of a certificate to be received in evidence. This is contained in s.28(9). Section 28(8) provides that a document purporting to be a Minister's certificate shall be received in evidence and deemed to be such a certificate unless the contrary is proved. The relationship between these provisions is not immediately apparent. The copy is not conclusive evidence. It appears that where the actual certificate is produced that will be conclusive evidence unless the contrary is proved but where a certified copy of the certificate, which by its very nature cannot be a "document purporting to be a Minister's certificate", is produced then it must be accompanied by evidence to produce it and can be dislodged by contrary evidence.

Nature of appeals

15–07 There is a separate National Security appeals panel of the Information Tribunal, members of which are designated and appointed to hear appeals under s.28 of the Data Protection Act 1998.

These appeals are against a certificate issued by a Minister of the Crown, providing conclusive evidence that the exemptions from the sections of the Data Protection Act

1998 identified in s.28(1) of the Act are required for the purposes of national security. Anyone directly affected by the issue of a certificate may appeal against it. The Tribunal applies the principles of judicial review to the certificate, as to whether the Minister had reasonable grounds for issuing the certificate. In the case of *SSHD* the Tribunal accepted that the Commissioner may be a person directly affected by a certificate as such a certificate is able to oust his supervisory powers.

When personal data are identified by a data controller, and a certificate is issued, an appeal may be made under s.28(6) of the Data Protection Act 1998, on the ground that the certificate does not apply to the data in question.

15–08 There are thus two separate appeals provided for by s.28 of the Data Protection Act 1998. A person "directly affected by the issuing of a certificate" can appeal under s.28(4) to the Data Protection Tribunal "against the issue of the certificate". A business or commercial or voluntary body could be directly affected and as the term "person" covers legal persons[2] the appellant might not be an individual. The appeal will be determined upon judicial review grounds. Section 28(5) provides that where the Tribunal finds that, applying the principles applied by the court on an application for judicial review, the Minister did not have reasonable grounds for issuing the certificate, the Tribunal may allow the appeal and quash the certificate. The Tribunal's powers appear to be limited to quashing the certificate in whole and not in part. The only ground is that the Minister did not have reasonable grounds for issuing the certification, that is that the decision to grant the certificate was Wednesbury unreasonable, that is it was so unreasonable that no reasonable Minister properly directed could have made that decision.[3] The decision would have to be so unreasonable that no reasonable Minister properly directed could have issued the certificate.

The other provision for appeal is in s.28(6). This applies where proceedings have been brought under or by virtue of the Data Protection Act 1998, in other words where there are actions for individual rights under Pt II of the Act, actions by the Commissioner under the enforcement provisions or prosecutions brought by the Commissioner or the DPP's office. In any of these proceedings a data controller may claim that a certificate under s.28(2) which identifies the personal data by means of general description in accordance with s.28(3), applies to any personal data. The other party to the proceedings may then appeal to the Tribunal under s.28(6) on the basis that the certificate does not apply to the personal data in question. In any of these proceedings, therefore, the controller may lay claim to the exemption. The other party, irrespective of whether he could appeal under s.28(4) in respect of the certificate, can, if the certificate is worded in general terms, appeal to the Tribunal on the grounds that the certificate does not cover the particular data.

On the face of the provisions, although the controller will be a party to the appeal and of course the party who objects to the breadth of the certificate will be the appellant, it is possible that the Minister of the Crown who issued the certificate would not be a party. On the other hand it is difficult to see how the Tribunal could reach a determination as to what data are covered by a certificate in the absence of evidence from or on behalf of the relevant Minister who provided the certificate. The Tribunal rules

---

[2] Interpretation Act 1978 Sch.1.
[3] *Associated Provincial Picture Houses v Wednesbury Corporation* [1948] 1 K.B. 223, CA.

of procedure have dealt with this. The Rules are the Information Tribunal (National Security Appeals) Rules 2005 and are covered in Ch.26, below.

On the hearing of an appeal the Tribunal may determine under s.28(7) that the certificate does not apply to the particular personal data which are the subject of the appeal.

Procedure on appeals

15–09 Schedule 6 includes special provisions for s.28 appeals. The Lord Chancellor designates particular members of the Tribunal from among the Chair and Deputy Chairs. Subject to subsequent rules the Tribunal members who are able to hear s.28 appeals will hear appeals as to certificates granted under s.28 ex parte. It is not explicitly spelt out but this presumably means that the appellant will present his/her case separately from the data controller. The Tribunal is dealt with in Ch.26, below.

National Security Appeals Panel Decisions

15–10 As at the end of 2006 the National Security Appeals Panel of the Tribunal had issued decisions in three appeals.

In the matter of *Norman Baker MP v The Secretary of State for the Home Department* the appellant, a Member of Parliament, believed that the Security Service, a data controller under the Act, held personal data about him, and he made a subject access application to establish whether or not his belief was correct and to require the Security Services to disclose the data to him. The respondent to the appeal was the Secretary of State for the Home Department. He signed a certificate dated July 22, 2000 which purported to exempt the Security Service from complying with the provisions of inter alia Pt II of the Data Protection Act 1998, which includes s.7. The Service responded to the appellant's request in ambiguous terms which neither confirmed nor denied that any data were held. It also relied upon the certificate as conclusive evidence that any data which it held were exempt from the requirements of s.7 of the Act. In doing so the Secretary of State was adopting a "neither confirm nor deny" (NCND) policy which was considered to be the standard response to such requests. Effectively what was being sought by the Home Secretary was a blanket exemption for the Security Service in relation to any subject access request.

Mr Baker appealed to the panel under s.28(4) as a person "directly affected" by the issue of the certificate. He believed that the Security Service held information about his involvement with ecological and environmental pressure groups in the 1980s and that although the file on him had been closed it still existed.

The Secretary of State contended to the panel that there were reasonable grounds for authorising the Service to give a non-committal reply to this and other requests, because this was considered necessary to safeguard national security. Much of the evidence was directed towards justifying the NCND policy in relation to the operations of the Service. This evidence was not challenged. The appellant, supported by the Data Protection Commissioner (as the Information Commissioner was then known), who intervened in the proceedings, accepted that the NCND policy is justified in relation to s.7(1)(a) requests for information made to the Service, in all cases where the Service lawfully determines that a positive response would be harmful to national security.

15–11 The validity of the certificate in question was disputed, however, on the ground that its terms were wide enough to relieve the Service from any obligation to decide whether or not national security would be harmed by a positive response to the particular request. The appellant and the Information Commissioner contended that the Minister did not have reasonable grounds for issuing the certificate in such wide terms, which could permit the Service to give the NCND reply even in cases where a positive response would not be harmful to national security.

The Panel addressed only the narrow issue as to whether the Minister did have reasonable grounds for issuing the certificate in terms which exempted the Service from the obligation to respond positively to any request made to it under s.7(1)(a) of the Act, regardless of whether or not national security would be harmed by a positive response in the particular case. The panel concluded, applying the principles of judicial review as they are applied by the courts, that the Minister did not have reasonable grounds for issuing the certificate which had this "unnecessarily wide effect". The panel quashed the Home Secretary's Certificate dated July 22, 2000 but acknowledged that this did not prevent the Home Secretary from issuing a fresh certificate aimed at circumventing the panel's criticisms. The panel refrained from attempting to draft the terms in which a valid certificate might be issued.

The decision of the panel was delivered on October 1, 2001 and is available in full at *http://www.informationtribunal.gov.uk* [Accessed on 2 September 2007].

15–12 In the matter of *Mohamed Al Fayed v The Secretary Of State For The Home Department* the panel considered similar issues to those considered in the Baker case. In the Al Fayed case the appellant had made subject access applications to the Security Service (commonly known as MI5) and the Secret Intelligence Service (commonly known as MI6).

Certificates, similar in terms to those issued in the *Baker* case, were issued by the respective Secretaries of State. The panel's decision in *Baker* however had the effect of quashing the certificate issued by the Home Secretary and the Foreign Secretary conceded, in light of the *Baker* decision, that his two certificates should be withdrawn. At the hearing before the panel on December 11, 2001 the only contentious issue was that of the appellant's costs. The respondents contended that as the respective certificates had been either withdrawn or quashed prior to the hearing the panel had no power to award the appellant his costs. The panel rejected this argument and awarded the appellant costs.

The decision was delivered by the panel on February 28, 2002 and is available in full at *http://www.informationtribunal.gov.uk*.

15–13 In the case of *SSHD*[4] the case was appealed to the High Court which supported the view which had been taken by the Tribunal. The original applicant had sought subject access from the Immigration and Nationality Department (IND) and received a Neither Confirm Nor Deny (NCND) in the following terms:

> "We have processed your request and enclose copies of all the information which IND is required to supply under the Data Protection Act."

SSHD applied to the Information Commissioner for an assessment and the Commissioner wished to check that the s.28 exemption had been properly claimed.

---

[4] See n.1, above.

The Commissioner served an Information Notice asking for sight of information which the Department claimed was covered by the exemption in order to check that the exemption was being properly applied. The Department responded by obtaining a Ministerial Certificate. The form of the Certificate is not set out in the High Court judgment but the Tribunal explained that the certificate was signed on the premise that the Commissioner had no statutory role within the context of the s.28 exemption. The Commissioner then appealed against the Certificate as a person "directly affected". The Tribunal agreed that he was a person directly affected and had the locus to mount an appeal and the Certificate was liable to be quashed as it had been issued on the basis that the Commissioner had no proper role:

> "As the certificate was signed on the premise that the Commissioner had no statutory role within the context of section 28 exemptions it must follow that the Secretary of State fundamentally misdirected himself as to the law and accordingly did not have reasonable grounds for issuing the certificate. This means that the certificate is liable to be quashed."

The Secretary of State appealed to the High Court which dismissed the appeal and agreed with the Tribunal. The interesting aspect of the case is that, on a reading of the Act, it would appear that the effect of s.28 was intended to exclude the Commissioner from the process. All the regulatory powers of the Commissioner are excluded by s.28. However the High Court followed the Tribunal in finding that the Commissioner's general remit as set out in s.51 was a sufficient basis to allow him to at least make efforts to check the assertions of Government Departments. In doing so they applied an interpretation which accords with Arts 13 and 28(4) of the Directive.

CRIME AND TAXATION

Who can claim the exemption?

15–14 Section 29 was amended during its passage through Parliament as a result of intense debate. It covers two distinct elements of exemption. The first element, contained in s.29(1)–(3), largely reproduces exemptions which appeared in the 1984 Act. The second element, contained in s.29(4)–(5), deals with systems of risk assessment, and was new in the 1998 Act. The risk assessment exemption is dealt with at the end of this section.

As with national security, and indeed most of the exemptions, the first exemptions in s.29(1)–(3) are not determined by the identity of the person who claims them. Anyone who can fulfill the exemption conditions may lay claim to the exemptions. The exemptions apply to anyone who processes for 1 of 10 purposes and who fulfils the necessary conditions. The purposes are set out in s.29(1)(a), (b) and (c). Broken down, they cover the following:

(a) the prevention of crime;

(b) the detection of crime;

(c) the apprehension of offenders;

    (d) the prosecution of offenders;

    (e) the assessment of any tax;

    (f) the collection of any tax;

    (g) the assessment of any duty;

    (h) the collection of any duty;

    (i) the assessment of any imposition of a similar nature to a tax or duty;

    (j) the collection of any imposition of a similar nature to a tax or duty.

The processing must have been carried out for one of these purposes. It is clear that the provision will apply to those bodies for which the investigation of crime or the prosecution of offenders is their primary purpose. It is less clear where the boundaries lie for those who might be described as carrying out such processing for "secondary purposes", that is otherwise than for the core purposes of the organisation. There may be actions by a private body or a public body where a crime is not central to the reason for the processing action or decision. For example, the investigation of dishonesty in an employee may be investigated primarily to be treated as a disciplinary matter by an employer. The employer may choose not to report it to the police. Nevertheless the actions of the employee were criminal. It is not clear whether the controller could claim the exemption for the apprehension of crime for any processing involved. The heading "prevention of crime" could cover a very wide area. It is suggested that the proper approach is to construe these narrowly as they are exemptions. Prosecution is limited to criminal proceedings and does not cover civil proceedings.

What does the exemption cover?

15–15 The exemption covers the First Data Protection Principle (except to the extent to which it requires compliance with Schs 2 and 3) and s.7 but only in any case to the extent to which the application of those provisions to the data would prejudice the particular purpose. It should be noted that it does not cover Schs 2 and 3 hence the provisions that data processing shall be carried out on legitimate grounds and the requirement for specific additional grounds for holding sensitive data remain. It does cover the requirement that personal data shall be processed fairly and lawfully together with the detailed requirements in paras 1 and 2 of Pt II of Sch.I. The requirements to inform individuals of the identity of the controller and the purposes of the processing, the fair obtaining and processing code, therefore only apply to the extent that they would not prejudice the relevant purpose. The data will also be exempt from the right of subject access to the same extent.

    The subject access and the fair obtaining and processing code exemptions can also be "transferred" from the person who had information for 1 of the 10 purposes which are covered by s.29(1) and which has been passed on to someone who processes for the purpose of discharging statutory functions. Under s.29(2) such data are exempt to the same extent as they were in the hands of the original controller.

    The further element of the exemption is the non-disclosure exemption. In s.29(3) personal data are exempt from the non-disclosure provisions where the disclosure is for 1 of the 10 purposes and the exemption provisions apply, that is, that compliance with the provision of the Act would prejudice any of those 10 purposes. It should be noted, however, that the non-disclosure provisions cannot be transferred to third parties. The non-disclosure provisions mean the Data Protection Principles, apart from Principle 7 dealing with security, to the extent which they are inconsistent with the disclosure in question.

For example, the Principles include a restriction on disclosures which are incompatible with the purpose of processing and on a prohibition on transfer. If the exemption applies a controller may make any disclosure, even if it would otherwise be unfair or incompatible, if it is for one of the crime or taxation purposes and the application of the Principle would prejudice any of those matters in relation to that particular disclosure.

When can the exemption be claimed?

15–16   The exemption can only be claimed on a case by case basis. It is not a blanket exemption. In *R v Secretary of State for the Home Department Ex p. Lord*[5] the Secretary of State sought to argue that review reports on Category A prisoners should never be disclosable in response to a subject access request because the reports were held for the purpose of preventing and detecting crime and disclosure would prejudice those purposes. It was argued that the disclosure would lead to less frank assessments being made because of the concerns of prison officers for their safety. Further it was submitted that some reports might contain information the disclosure of which would prejudice prison security for example by providing information on prisoners' associates or revealing intelligence information. In effect this was an argument for a class exemption to be applied to the reports. In deciding the point the judge referred to the decision of the Tribunal in relation to the equivalent provision of the 1984 Act in the case of *Equifax Europe Limited v The Data Protection Registrar*[6] in which the Tribunal had accepted that the term "in any case" meant "in any particular case" and that the test had to be applied on a case-by-case basis. The judge agreed that the data controller must show that one or more of the statutory purposes would be prejudiced or be likely to be prejudiced by the disclosure of the particular information in the particular case. He did however accept that the data controller remains able to take into account the potential consequential effect that disclosure in one case may have in others.[7] This applies equally to data in the hands of the original controller or in the hands of the person discharging the statutory functions to whom they have been passed, and applies to the non-disclosure exemptions as well as to the subject information provisions. Data will only be exempt in a particular case to the extent to which the application of the relevant provisions to the data would be likely to prejudice any of the functions listed in this section.

15–17   Whether there is a likelihood of prejudice in a particular case will be a question of fact and judgment. In order for there to be prejudice there must be a positively detrimental effect and likelihood will be judged on the basis of whether it is more likely than not. In *R v Lord*[8] the court considered the meaning of the term "likely", pointing

---

[5]   [2003] EWHC 2073.
[6]   *Encyclopaedia of Data Protection*, reference DA 90 25/49/7.
[7]   *Lord* para.122.
[8]   n.5, above.

out that the term has "neither a single nor even a prima facie meaning". He quoted Chadwick L.J. in *Three Rivers District Council v Governor and Company of the Bank of England (No. 1)*[9] in which he said that:

> " 'likely' does not carry any necessary connotation of 'more probable than not'. It is a word which takes its meaning from context. And where the context is a jurisdictional threshold to the exercise of a discretionary power, there may be good reason to suppose that the legislature—or the rule-making body, as the case may be—intended a modest threshold of probability."

He explained that in *Re H*[10] the House of Lords treated the word "likely" in s.31(2) of the Children Act 1989 as meaning that there has to be a real, a substantial rather than merely speculative, possibility. Whereas in the *Three Rivers* case the word imported simply a test that the outcome was "more than fanciful". He summed up the correct approach as follows:

> "I accept that 'likely' in section 29(1) does not mean more probable than not. But on the other hand it must connote a significantly greater degree of probability than merely 'more than fanciful'. A 'real risk' is not enough. I cannot accept that the important rights intended to be conferred by section 7 are intended to be set at nought by something which measures up only to the minimal requirement of being real, tangible or identifiable rather than merely fanciful. Something much more significant and weighty than that is required. After all the Directive, to which I must have regard in interpreting section 29(1) permits restrictions on the data subject's right of access to information about himself only (to quote the language of recital (43)) 'in so far as they are *necessary* to safeguard' or (to quote the language of Article 13(1)) 'constitute a *necessary* measure to safeguard' the prevention and detection of crime (emphasis added). The test of necessity is a strict one. The interference with the rights conferred on the data subject must be proportionate to the reality as well as to the potential gravity of the public interests involved. It is for those who seek to assert the exemption in section 29(1) to bring themselves within it and moreover to do so convincingly, not by mere assertion but by evidence that establishes the necessity contemplated by the Directive.
>
> In my judgment 'likely' in section 29(1) connotes a degree of probability where there is a very significant and weighty chance of prejudice to the identified public interests. The degree of risk must be such that there 'may very well' be prejudice to those interests, even if the risk falls short of being more probable than not."[11]

15–18   In relation to the equivalent provision under the 1984 Act the view of the Registrar was that the assessment of likelihood of prejudice should be an objective assessment. The question would not be whether the controller believed there to be a likelihood of prejudice but whether in fact there would be prejudice.

---

[9] [2003] 1 W.L.R. 210.
[10] [1996] A.C. 563.
[11] *Lord* paras 99, 100.

There have been a range of cases which have considered the disclosure of personal data but most of them have been dealt with as raising questions under Art.8 of the Convention rights rather than Data Protection Act issues.[12] It was mentioned briefly in *Re R (A Child) (2004)*[13] but only for the Court to comment that the Act neither prevented nor required the disclosure of particular information.

Risk assessment classifications systems

15–19   Section 29(4) provides for an exemption from the rights of subject access contained in s.7 for personal data which consist of some risk assessment information.

The data controller for the personal data must be either a government department, or a local authority or another authority administering housing benefit or council tax benefit. It applies where the authority operates a system of risk assessment in connection with its functions which it applies to data subjects to evaluate the risk (broadly) of non-payment, non-compliance or fraud. If the authority had to provide the risk markers attached to particular records in response to subject access requests it might undermine the operation of the system. The risk assessment system has to be operated for one of the following purposes:

(a) the assessment or collection of any tax or duty or any imposition of a similar nature; or

(b) the prevention or detection of crime, or apprehension or prosecution of offenders, where the offence concerned involves any unlawful claim for any payment out of, or any unlawful application of public funds; and

(c) the personal data involved must be processed for one of these purposes.

By virtue of s.29(5) "public funds" includes funds provided by any Community institution. The subject access exemption is available "to the extent to which the exemptions [are] required in the interests of the operation of the system". This provision had a stormy passage through Parliament. The original version of s.29(4) was the subject of the only defeat for the Government. It provided for a sweeping exemption which was subsequently significantly narrowed down to its current limits. The passage of the Bill through Parliament is dealt with in Ch.1, above.

Responding to requests by law enforcement agencies for personal data

15–20   A data controller who is the subject of a request from the police or other law enforcement agency for the disclosure of personal data may find that they have to engage in a difficult balancing act between satisfying the requirements of the police and protecting the interests of their clients or customers. On the one hand the data controller will have to consider the data subject's rights as established by the Data Protection Act 1998, albeit subject to the exemptions contained in s.29, plus their rights under the Human Rights Act 1998 and, in particular, the qualified right to privacy effectively established by Art.8 of the ECHR; and on the otherhand the question of

---

[12] See the discussion of case law in Ch.2, above.
[13] [2004] EWHC 2085 (Fam).

any duty or obligation to provide information to the authorities. Section 29 itself does not provide any obligation to disclose information so the obligation, if it exists, must be found elsewhere.

15–21   Part 3 of the Anti-Terrorism Crime and Security 2001 (ATCSA) extended the grounds for large scale data holders to disclose personal and/or confidential information to law enforcement agencies. In general terms, the extended purposes are those of any criminal investigation or proceedings, whether in the United Kingdom or elsewhere. Part 3 of ATCSA also removes statutory restrictions on the disclosure of information including personal or confidential information contained in no less than 66 Acts. These Acts include the Data Protection Act 1998. ATCSA does not however compel the holders of personal data to disclose such information to the law enforcement agencies.

15–22   The case of R *(on the application of NTL Group Ltd) v Crown Court at Ipswich*[14] provides some clarification for a data controller seeking to balance apparently conflicting statutory obligations relating to the disclosure of personal data to law enforcement agencies.

The claimant, NTL, was a telecommunications company which had a computer system which automatically stored emails from the relevant internet provider. Those emails were destroyed one hour after being read by the recipient. Unread emails were kept for a further limited period. The police had good reason to believe that a number of persons were involved in a widespread conspiracy to defraud members of the public. A detective constable served on the claimant a notice of application for the production of special procedure material under s.9 of and Sch.1 to the Police and Criminal Evidence Act 1984 (PACE). Paragraph 11 of Sch.1 provided that where a notice of application for an order had been served on a person, he should not conceal, destroy, alter or dispose of the material to which the application related except with the leave of the judge or written permission of a constable until the application was dismissed or abandoned or he had complied with an order made on the application.

The claimant was of the opinion that the only way to comply with the notice was to intercept the emails by transferring them to a different email address to that intended for the recipient which would involve it in committing an offence under s.1 of the Regulation of Investigatory Powers Act 2000 (RIPA), namely intentionally and without lawful authority intercepting any communication in the course of its transmission. It accordingly wrote to the police constable requesting permission to destroy or dispose of the material to which the application related. That request was turned down and it therefore applied to the Crown Court. The judge ruled that the claimant would not be committing a criminal offence once they had received the notice of application.

The claimant applied for judicial review of that decision contending that by preserving the emails it would be necessary to modify or interfere with its telecommunications system or its operation and monitor transmissions made by means of the telecommunication system, the purpose of which would be to make some or all of the contents of the communication available, while being transmitted, to a person other than the sender or intended recipient of the communication and thus would fall within meaning of interception contained in s.2(2), (7) and (8) of RIPA.

15–23   The Divisional Court dismissed the application. Reading s.2(2) in conjunction with s.2(7) and s.2(8) of the 2000 Act, it was clear that where an email was pre-

---

[14] [2002] EWHC Admin 1585.

served by transmitting it to a different address to that of the recipient an offence would be committed. However, it was implicit in the terms of para.11 of Sch.1 to PACE that the body, subject to an notice of application for special procedure material under s.9 of PACE, had the necessary power to take the action which it had to take in order to conserve communications by email within its system until such time as the court decided whether or not to make an order. No harm would be caused to any third party because unless a judge was prepared to make the order and therefore remove the protection which would otherwise exist for third parties the police would have no right to be informed of the contents of the material retained by the claimant. It followed that the judge had come to the correct conclusion.

15–24 The case of *Totalise Plc v Motley Fool Ltd*[15] is also relevant in this area. In this case the defendants were companies who operated websites, which incorporated discussion forums for various companies including the claimant, Totalise Plc. An anonymous contributor known as Z made numerous entries on each forum, which made wide-ranging defamatory allegations about Totalise. After complaints by Totalise, both defendants eventually banned Z from their websites and removed all of the items he had posted. They refused however Totalise's request for Z's details. Totalise brought an application for disclosure of Z's identity. Both defendants resisted the application on the basis that their internal policies were not to reveal the identity of their users. They relied upon s.10 of the Contempt of Court Act 1981, which provided that:

> "No court may require a person to disclose, nor is any person guilty of contempt of court for refusing to disclose the source of information contained in a publication for which he is responsible, unless it be established to the satisfaction of the court that disclosure is necessary in the interest of justice or national security or for the prevention of disorder or crime."

The defendants further relied upon the Data Protection Act 1998. They submitted that s.35 of the 1998 Act, which provided that personal data was exempt from the non-disclosure provisions where the disclosure was required by law in connection with legal proceedings, should be given a restrictive interpretation so that the identity of Z in the instant case should be protected by the general principles of the 1998 Act, which prevented disclosure without the consent of the data subject. Totalise submitted that, as operators of a bulletin board, the defendants were not "responsible" for contents placed there by others outside their control, except in the circumstances provided by s.1 of the Defamation Act 1996, upon which no reliance had been placed. Totalise also submitted that there was no justification for a restricted interpretation of s.35 of the 1998 Act and that the established principles in relation to the court's jurisdiction to require a person "mixed up in the tortious acts of others" were preserved and not restricted by the 1988 Act.

The High Court ruled:

(1) Section 10 of the 1981 Act was concerned with protecting journalists' sources and balancing the right of a free press with the legal rights of others. In the instant case, the defendants had no responsibility for and exercised no legal

---

[15] [2003] 2 All E.R. 872.

or editorial control over the items on the websites; they merely provided a facility for discussion. They were accordingly not "responsible" for publication for the purposes of s.10.

(2) There was no justification for a restrictive interpretation of s.35 of the 1998 Act: that section clearly preserved and did not restrict the right of the claimant to obtain disclosure of a tortfeasor's identity in accordance with the pre-existing law. In the instant case, it was clear on the facts that Z had defamed Totalise in a very serious manner and as part of a concerted campaign. Z was hiding behind anonymity and Totalise had no other practical means of establishing his identity. The balance weighed clearly in favour of granting the relief sought. If it were otherwise, it would be possible for individuals to defame with impunity on websites such as those of the defendants.

Costs were ordered against the two defendants. The second defendant appealed this order to the Court of Appeal which considered the matter in December 2001. The Court of Appeal ruled that the costs order was wrong in a case where the party had refused to disclose due to a genuine doubt that the person requesting disclosure was entitled to it, or was under an appropriate legal obligation not to disclose, or could be subject to proceedings if disclosure was voluntary, or the disclosure would or might infringe another's legitimate interest.

The inference from this decision is that where there is doubt over the legitimacy of a disclosure a party being asked to disclose is not at fault for asking the party seeking disclosure to obtain a court order for disclosure.

In summary the subject of an approach by a law enforcement agency for disclosure of personal data who is uncertain about the applicability or ambit of the exemptions in the Data Protection Act 1998 and the legitimacy of the disclosure would not be wrong to require that the agency obtain an order or warrant under appropriate enabling legislation. At the very least it would not be unreasonable to seek written confirmation from the police stating that personal data are required for a criminal investigation and that seeking the data subject's consent would undermine the investigation. The problem with making such demands may be that the police will seek a warrant of exceptionally wide ambit enabling them, for example, to uplift servers or other equipment vital to their business. A preferable approach may therefore be to ensure that the initial agreement with data subjects makes it clear that personal data will be disclosed to a law enforcement agency where the data controller has reasonable grounds for believing that an unlawful act has been committed.

REGULATORY ACTIVITY

Who can claim the exemption?

15–25   A range of bodies can claim exemption under s.31. Like the crime and taxation exemption and the national security exemption it applies to personal data processed for particular functions rather than to specific bodies or organisations. However, in this case it is difficult to find a general term which covers the different categories of functions.

Section 31(2) applies to "relevant functions" which broadly cover regulatory activities of a public nature. The regulatory activity must be carried out by or under any enactment, or by the Crown or a Minister of the Crown or government department or be exercised in the public interest and be of a public nature. Although the last category does not limit the nature of the legal persons who can carry it out, it limits the function, in that broadly speaking it must be one which would be judicially reviewable.

The exemption can be claimed where personal data are processed for the purpose of discharging any of the functions specified in s.31(2) as long as those functions are carried out by one of the types of bodies specified in s.31(3).

The relevant functions cover those designed for protecting members of the public from financial loss caused by dishonesty or malpractice of various kinds. They would, for example, cover the functions of the Law Society regulating the conduct of solicitors insofar as they are relevant to providing protection against malpractice, dishonesty or other seriously improper conduct or in relation to the unfitness or incompetence of persons authorised to carry on professional activity. It only applies, however, where the relevant function relates to persons "authorised" to carry on any professional activity. Therefore it would not apply if there was no need for authorisation to conduct the activity. So for example the functions of the Advertising Standards Authority which is a self-regulatory organisation would not be covered because practitioners are not authorised to practise by that body.

The charity functions relate to those for protecting charities against misconduct or mismanagement in their administration, protecting the property of charities from unlawful misapplication or for the recovery of the property of charities. The provision allowing exemption where recovery of property is involved is wider than any other and extends into an area which is not covered by any other exemption.

There are then further provisions where functions are designed for securing the health, safety and welfare of persons at work or for protecting persons other than persons at work against risk to health or safety arising out of or in connection with the actions of persons at work.

Section 31(4) applies to a further set of personal data, that is personal data processed for the purpose of discharging the functions of ombudsmen designed for protecting members of the public against maladministration by public bodies or failures in public services. Insofar as it covers maladministration it is only maladministration by public bodies. Therefore it does not cover the functions of the private ombudsmen who regulate by contractual agreements, as for example the banking ombudsman or the insurance or pensions ombudsmen.

15–26 Section 31(5) covers personal data processed for the purpose of discharging any function which is conferred on the Director General of Fair Trading and is designed for one of three particular functions. Those functions are, broadly, those of:

(a) protecting members of the public against sharp or improper business behaviour;

(b) regulating anti-competitive agreements;

(c) preventing abuse of dominant position in the market.

Section 233 of the Financial Services and Markets Act 2000 (FSMA) inserts a new s.31(4A) as follows:

"(4A) Personal data processed for the purpose of discharging any function which is conferred by or under Part XVI of the Financial Services and Markets Act 2000 on the body established by the Financial Services Authority for the purposes of that Part are exempt from the subject information provisions in any case to the extent to which the application of those provisions to the data would be likely to prejudice the proper discharge of the function."

Part XVI of the FSMA establishes an ombudsman scheme—described as a scheme whereby certain disputes may be resolved quickly and with minimum formality by an independent person. The disputes potentially covered relate to complaints of misbehaviour within the ambit of activities regulated by the Financial Services Authority.

15–27   Regulation 29 of the Enterprise Act 2002 (Amendment) Regulations 2006 inserts a new s.31(5A) as follows:

"(5A) Personal data processed by a CPC enforcer for the purpose of discharging any function conferred on such a body by or under the CPC Regulation are exempt from the subject information provisions in any case to the extent to which the application of those provisions to the data would be likely to prejudice the proper discharge of that function."

What does the exemption cover?

15–28   A CPC enforcer for the purposes of this provision means the same as in s.213(5A) of the Enterprise Act 2002, excluding the Office of Fair Trading. The Regulations provide enforcement powers for bodies which are responsible for enforcing consumer rights to deal with cross border infringements of specified legislation.

The content of the exemption is relatively narrow. It applies to the subject information provisions, namely the first Data Protection Principle insofar as it requires compliance with the fair obtaining and processing code and s.7, that is the right of subject access.

When can the exemption be claimed?

15–29   It can be claimed in any case to the extent to which the application of the fair obtaining and processing code or the subject access provisions would be likely to prejudice the proper discharge of the particular function. The test of prejudice and likelihood and the provision for a case-by-case basis are the same as in relation to crime and taxation as above.

The exemption only applies to the extent required for the particular function and the particular exemption. For example, if a function would only be affected by the fair obtaining provisions the data controller dealing with it may only lay claim to that exemption and not also to the subject access provisions. If he wishes to claim the subject access exemption that must be justified separately.

ARMED FORCES

Who can claim the exemption?

15–30 This exemption is contained in para.2 of Sch.7. It exempts personal data from the subject information provisions. The exemption can be claimed by any data controller as long as the controller can establish that to comply with the subject information provisions would prejudice the combat effectiveness of the armed forces.

What is covered?

15–31 The exemption covers the subject information provisions, namely, the fair obtaining and processing code in para.2 of Pt II of Sch.I and the subject access provisions in s.7.

When can it be claimed?

15–32 It can be claimed in any case to the extent to which the application of those provisions would be likely to prejudice the combat effectiveness of any of the armed forces of the Crown. This will be a question of fact. Presumably the view of a senior officer of the Crown will be decisive in establishing whether there is a likelihood of prejudice. The comments in relation to the extent of prejudice and the nature of likelihood in the section on crime and taxation are equally applicable to this provision.

ADDITIONAL INFORMATION

Derivations

15–33 • Directive 95/46 (See App.B):

> (a) Arts 3 (scope), 13 (exemptions and restrictions)
> (b) Recitals 13, 43, 44.

• Council of Europe Convention of January 28, 1981 for the Protection of Individuals with regard to automatic processing of Personal Data: Art.9 (exceptions and restrictions).

• Data Protection Act 1984: ss.27 (national security), 28 (crime and taxation), 30 (regulation of financial services etc.).

• Organisation for Economic Co-operation and Development Guidelines: Annex, Part One (scope of guidelines).

Hansard references

15–34 Vol.586, No.108, col.CWH 60, Lords Grand Committee, February 23, 1998 Exemptions for national security

Vol.586, No.110, col.67, Lords Grand Committee, February 23, 1998 "In any case"

ibid., cols 70, 71
Effect on exchanges of information under the Crime and Disorder Bill 1998.

ibid., cols 73, 74
Exemption from First Principle

Vol.587, No.127, col.1097, Lords Third Reading, March 24, 1998
Regulatory bodies

Commons Standing Committee D, May 19, col.177, 1998
Extent of the non-disclosure exemption in cl.28

ibid., col.180
National security certificates

Commons Standing Committee D, May 21, cols 184–190, 1998
Extent of section 28 exemptions and relation to data sharing

ibid., cols 192–195
Insertion of Government amended cl.28(4)

ibid., cols 201, 203, 204
Addition of Ombudsmen to regulatory list

Vol.315, No.198, cols 586–591, Commons Third Reading, July 25, 1998
Crime and taxation

Vol.591, No.184, col.1494, Lords consideration of Commons amendments, July 10, 1998
  Consideration of section 28(4) as amended

Previous case law

15–35 *Equifax (Europe) Ltd v Data Protection Registrar* (1991) Data Protection Tribunal. In this case the Tribunal held the exemption in s.28 of the 1984 Act applied on a case-by-case basis.

CHAPTER 16

Exemptions for the Protection of the Individual: Family, Employers, Health, Social Work and Schools Information

INTRODUCTION

16–01 This chapter covers those exemptions which are intended to protect individuals rather than business or professional interests. The health, social work, education and embryology exemptions are contained in orders made by the Secretary of State.

Where the conditions are fulfilled the exemptions cover any type of data held for the relevant purpose, whether manual or automated and whether part of an accessible record or not. If data are covered by an exemption the data controller may not have to tell the individual that the exemption is being claimed. Thus if information is withheld when a subject access request has been made the controller may not be required to tell the individual of that. As is the case of all exemptions a court will construe them strictly against the party seeking to rely on them. Where the subject access exemption applies to data which are otherwise covered by the Act the courts will have no powers to enforce the subject access rights or to deal with any associated claims for failure to give subject access. The Commissioner will have no power to take enforcement actions. However the other individual rights will continue to apply in respect of the personal data. An individual could, in theory, serve a s.10 notice of objection or a s.12 prohibition in respect of automated decision-making in respect of data to which the controller did not have to give access. It is not clear how the individual could describe the data or how the controller could respond in such a case. In practice, the other individual rights lose much of their force where the subject access right is removed.

SUMMARY OF MAIN POINTS

16–02 (a) The health and social work exemptions cover the right of subject access and, in some limited cases, the fair obtaining and processing code found in Sch.1 Pt II para.2.

(b) Even where the exemption covers the fair obtaining and processing code (as described above) it does not exempt the controller from the general duty to comply with the first Principle and therefore to process data fairly and lawfully.

(c) An exemption is included for pupil records held in schools, and in Scotland in further education establishments. This reproduces provisions originally found in the Education (Schools Records) Regulations 1989. The exemption mirrors the transfer of the access rights to records previously provided for under these Regulations.

(d) The health and social work exemptions apply on a case-by-case basis.

(e) The Freedom of Information Act 2000 introduced a new subject access exemption which applies only to manual data held by public authority and covers personnel records.

PERSONAL AND FAMILY INFORMATION

16–03 Section 36 provides that personal data processed by an individual only for the purpose of that individual's personal, family or household affairs (including recreational purposes) are exempt from the Data Protection Principles and the provisions of Pt II and Pt III. This exemption derives from Art.3.2 of the Directive, which provides that the Directive shall not apply to the processing of personal data "by a natural person in the course of a purely personal or household activity". It is very similar in wording to s.33(1) of the 1984 Act which provided exemption for:

"Personal data held only by an individual and concerned only with the management of his personal, family or household affairs, or held by him only for recreational purposes . . ."

In the 1998 Act, Pt II covers the rights of data subjects but Pt III only covers notification. The exemption covers the individual rights of data subjects but does not disapply the supervisory regime. Thus the Commissioner is able to serve information notices in respect of such data. This was probably not necessary to comply with the Directive but brings the exemption into line with other exemptions under the Act. Section 55 of the Act also applies to the data, so it may be an offence to obtain, disclose or procure the disclosure of such information to another without the authority of the controller.

There was no case law on the equivalent provision in the 1984 Act and there has been no UK case law. In the past it has given rise to queries about circumstances where the individual uses his or her own computer to assist a local voluntary organisation and the regulator has made clear that the exemption does not apply where personal data are processed for an organisation, but is confined to purely personal use.

16–04 The originating provision in the Directive was considered in *Linqvist*.[1] Mrs Lindqvist had posted information about members of her congregation on a website

---

[1] See Ch.3, above for a full discussion of the case.

and been prosecuted under the Swedish legislation for doing so without having notified the processing to the regulator. Article 3.2 includes two exceptions from the scope of the Directive, the second of which covers the processing of personal data:

"by a natural person in the course of a purely personal or household activity"

The European Court held that that exception,

". . . must therefore be interpreted as relating only to activies which are carried out in the course of private or family life of individuals which is clearly not the case with the processing of personal data consisting in publication on the internet so that those data are made accessible to an indefinited number of persons."

This decision in effect answers the concerns expressed by the Commissioner in submissions to the Home Office, made as part of the post-implementation appraisal of the Act (see Ch.1, above):

"An exemption for domestic purposes is clearly justified but potentially has very wide effect. For example an individual who installs a CCTV camera on his/her house for security purposes can direct it through a neighbour's bedroom window deliberately yet still be exempt from the Act. It is in relation to the Internet that many problems arise. One individual can publish a great deal of offensive and damaging material about others on the world wide web. This involves the processing of personal data but falls outside the scope of the Act if it is only for the individual's personal, family or household affairs (including recreational purposes)."

It is clear from *Lindqvist* that a very narrow interpretation should be placed on the exception and it would not apply where information is posted on the internet.

HEALTH INFORMATION

16–05 Section 30(1) contains an order-making power for the Secretary of State to exempt or modify the subject information provisions in relation to personal data consisting of information as to the physical or mental health or condition of the data subject. The Data Protection (Subject Access Modification) (Health) Order 2000 (SI 2000/413) was made under this section and came into force on March 1, 2000 with the Act.

The Data Protection (Subject Access Modification) (Health) Order 2000 (SI 2000/413)

Introduction

16–06 The 1984 Act contained a similar provision which applied only to the subject access provisions. In the 1998 Act some data may also be exempt from the obligation to provide information at the point of collection from the data subject. The Order applies to personal data consisting of information as to the physical or mental health or condition of the data subject. It does not apply to data which could also fall under the s.38 Order (the social work Order).

Court proceedings

16–07   Certain personal data falling under the Order which are processed by a court are exempt from both the fair obtaining and processing codes in para.2 Pt II Sch.I and the subject access provisions in s.7.[2] In essence this provision preserves the confidentiality of certain reports provided to the court in proceedings concerned with the care of children. In order to qualify for the exemption the information must be related to the physical or mental health of the individual and be supplied in a report or evidence given to the court in the course of specified proceedings relating to the care of children in which the rules of court provide for the contents of the report or evidence to be withheld. The report may be made by a local authority, Health & Social Services Board or Trust, probation officer or other person making a report in the course of the specified proceedings. As with the social work and educational records orders it is not clear whether the exemption only applies when the data are in the hands of the court or when they are in the hands of the supplying person. This part of the exemption is not subject to any test of prejudice nor is it applied on a case by case basis.

Serious harm to physical or mental health

16–08   By para.5 other personal data may be exempt from the s.7 subject access rights in any case to the extent that the application of the subject access rights would be likely to cause serious harm to the physical or mental health or condition of the data subject or any other person. Thus the data subject might not be told that the controller holds data on him or her if to say even so much would be likely to cause serious harm. Regulation 7 provides for data controllers to obtain written confirmation from a health professional that information on an individual should be withheld but controllers must not rely on such a statement if it is over six months old or it is unreasonable to do so. The written confirmation may cover all the personal data held. However, more commonly, data controllers will only consider the possibility of the exemption when actually faced with a request for access and data will only be withheld in part.

A data controller cannot withhold data which he knows has already been seen by the subject or is already within his knowledge no matter how much harm repetition or confirmation of the data might cause.[3] A data controller who is not himself a health professional as defined in the Order must consult the appropriate health professional before withholding data under the provision.[4] The appropriate health professional is defined in para.2. The data controller should refer to the health professional who is currently or most recently responsible for providing care in relation to the matters covered by the request or if there is more than one such professional the one most suitable to advise on the issue. In the event that there is no appropriate health professional to turn to, or in those cases where the data relating to physical or mental health have been processed in relation to benefit claims under Child Support or pensions provisions, then advice should be sought from any health professional with the necessary experience and qualifications.[5]

---

[2] SI 2000/413 reg.4(2).
[3] SI 2000/413 reg.6(2).
[4] SI 2000/413 reg.5(2).
[5] SI 2000/413 reg.2.

Access by those acting on behalf of the data subject

16–09   As was noted in Ch.10, above subject access requests may be made by a third party on behalf of the data subject. The Order deals with the possibility that the data subject may not want the person acting for him to have access to some information. Where the data subject is a child for whom the person with parental responsibility has exercised the subject access right or it has been exercised for the data controller by a person appointed by a court to manage his or her affairs, personal data which fall under the Order will not be disclosed if:

- the information was provided by the data subject with the expectation that it would not be disclosed to the person making the request;

- the information was obtained as a result of an examination or investigation to which the data subject agreed in the expectation that it would not be disclosed to the person making the request; or

- the data subject has expressly indicated that the information should not be so disclosed.

It is expressly provided that the data subject can alter his own mind and allow access to data which he or she had previously vetoed.[6]

Information about health professionals

16–10   Regulation 8 modifies s.7(4) of the Act which deals with access to third party data. The effect of the modification is that information on those who have contributed to the health record as professionals, usually those who have provided health care to the data subject, cannot be withheld on the basis that it relates to another individual who can be identified from that information.

The court is given power to decide how far a data controller should give or not give subject access to such data which it may either exercise at the request of the data subject or on the application of:

> "any other person to whom serious harm to whose physical or mental health or condition would be likely to be caused by compliance with any such request in contravention of those provisions."

This is designed to protect those about whom information would otherwise be given, for example, because they have provided health care.

SOCIAL WORK INFORMATION

16–11   Unlike the health provisions the order-making power in s.30(3) is subject to a prejudice test. There is no apparent reason for this difference. It was not the subject of any Parliamentary debate and appears to have been carried forward from the 1984 Act which made the same distinction. The Secretary of State may only make

---

[6] SI 2000/413 reg.5.

exemption or modification orders to the extent that he considers the relevant requirements of the Data Protection Act would "be likely to prejudice" the carrying out of social work.

Social work is not defined in the section. The relevant order is the Data Protection (Subject Access Modification) (Social Work) Order 2000[7] which came into effect on March 1, 2000 with the main Act. The 2000 Order has been modified by the Data Protection (Subject Access Modification) (Social Work) (Amendment) Order 2005[8] which added the Children and Family Court Advisory and Support Service (CAFCASS) to the list of bodies which are covered by the provisions.

The Data Protection (Subject Access Modification) (Social Work) Order 2000 (SI 2000/415) 2000

16–12   The social work Order will not apply where any of the health, education or miscellaneous subject access exemption orders apply.

Court proceedings

16–13   Under para.4 certain personal data which are processed by a court are exempt from both the fair obtaining and processing codes in para.2 Pt II Sch.I and the subject access provisions in s.7. The data must be "processed by a court" but it is not clear whether the exemption only applies to the personal data while they are in the hands of the court or to the same data in the hands of the person supplying it. The data will almost inevitably also be held by another because the data must consist of information supplied in a report or other evidence by a person in the course of legal proceedings dealing with the welfare of children. The proceedings are ones in which the court has the power under the applicable Rules to withhold information from the data subject.[9] The data in the hands of the person supplying it may well be eligible for the more general social work exemption from subject access described below but the exemption from the fair obtaining and processing codes would not apply. This part of the exemption is not applied on a case-by-case basis and involves no test of prejudice.

Social work

16–14   By para.5 other personal data may be exempt from the s.7 rights, apart from the requirement in s.7(1)(a) that the subject be informed whether the data user holds information on him, but only:

> "In any case to the extent to which the application of those provisions would be likely to prejudice the carrying out of social work by reason of the fact that serious harm to the physical or mental health or condition of the data subject or any other person would be likely to be caused."

Serious harm is not defined. The order lists activities which are regarded as "carrying out of social work" in para.1 of the Schedule. As the explanatory note states:

---

[7] SI 2000/413.
[8] SI 2005/467.
[9] 1998 Act Sch.1 para.2.

"The Order principally applies to data processed by local authorities, in relation to their social services and education welfare functions, and health authorities to whom such data are passed and by probation committees and the National Society for the Prevention of Cruelty to Children. The Order also applies to data processed for similar purposes by the corresponding bodies in Northern Ireland. Data processed by government departments for certain purposes connected with social work and by officers such as guardians ad litem and (in Scotland) the Principal Reporter of the Scottish Children's Reporter Administration are also within the scope of the Order. Provision is made enabling other voluntary organisations or other bodies to be added to the list of bodies whose data are subject to the provisions of the Order where the data are processed for purposes similar to the social services functions (or in Scotland social work functions) of local authorities.

In the case of social work authorities in Scotland who receive certain data from the Principal Reporter, the Order requires such data controllers to obtain the Principle Reporter's approval before complying with any section 7 request."

16–15 Section 7(4) of the Act, which deals with access to third party data, is modified so that information on those who provide social work functions in a professional capacity cannot be withheld on a subject access search.[10]

The court is given power to restrain a data controller from giving subject access in breach of the provisions of the Order in respect of such data on the application of "any person to whom serious harm to whose physical or mental health or condition would be likely to be caused by compliance with any such request in contravention of those provisions". The provision is designed to protect those about whom information would otherwise be given because they have provided social work functions. It is not clear how this provision could apply in any other situation. It is not likely that any other person would know that a subject access request which might affect him or her had been made, or be aware that he might be seriously affected by the information to be given on a subject access request.[11]

Access by those acting on behalf of the data subject

16–16 As was noted in Ch.10, above subject access requests may be made on behalf of data subjects. The Order recognises that, even in such cases, there are situations where a data subject may not want anyone else to have access to certain information about him or her. Where the data subject is a child for whom the person with parental responsibility has exercised the subject access right or it has been exercised for the data subject by a person appointed by a court to manage his or her affairs, personal data which fall under the Order will not be disclosed if:

- the information was provided by the data subject with the expectation that it would not be disclosed to the person making the request;

---

[10] 1998 Act s.7(1)(a) and (2).
[11] 1998 Act s.7(1)(b).

- the information was obtained from an investigation or examination to which the data subject had consented in the expectation that it would not be so disclosed;

- the data subject has expressly indicated that the information should not be disclosed.

It is expressly provided that the data subject can alter his or her mind and allow access which had previously been vetoed.

EDUCATION INFORMATION

16–17   The order-making power in s.30(2) mirrors the health data power in s.30(1). It contains no test of prejudice. It extends to the subject information provisions so it covers both subject access and the fair obtaining and processing code in para.2 Pt II of Sch.I. It allows the Secretary of State to exempt data from the subject information provisions or modify them in the case of personal data about pupils. The provisions are slightly different for Scotland, although in relation to primary and secondary schools the effect is the same. The exemption covers personal data which fulfils two conditions:

(a) the data controller must either be the proprietor of, or a teacher at, a school, or an education authority in Scotland; and

(b) the data must relate to persons who are or have been pupils at the school or are receiving or have received further education provided by the education authority.

"Proprietor" is defined in s.30(5)(a) at some length. In brief it has the same meaning as in the Education Act 1996 in England and Wales, that is broadly covering the governing bodies of state schools and the equivalent controlling bodies, whether Boards or owners, of the various types of independent schools. The term has the same import in Scotland and in Northern Ireland although the particular arrangements and therefore the detailed list are different.

The Data Protection (Subject Access Modification) (Education) Order 2000 (SI 2000/414)

16–18   The Data Protection (Subject Access Modification) (Education) Order (the education Order) will not apply where the health or miscellaneous orders apply. The exemption order came into force on March 1, 2000 with the main Act. The order applies to personal data in educational records as defined in Sch.11 to the Act.

Court proceedings

16–19   Under para.4 certain personal data which are processed by a court are exempt from the fair obtaining and processing codes in para.2 Pt II Sch.1 and the subject access provisions in s.7. The data must be "processed by a court" but it is not clear whether the exemption only applies to the personal data while they are in the hands of the court or to the same data in the hands of the person supplying it. The data will almost inevitably also be held by another because the data must consist of information supplied in a report or other evidence by a person in the course of legal proceedings dealing with education matters relating to children. The proceedings are ones in which the court has the power under the applicable rules to withhold information from the data subject.[12] The data in the hands of the person supplying it may well be eligible for the more general exemption for educational records from subject access described below but the exemption from the fair processing and fair obtaining codes would not apply. This part of the exemption is not subject to prejudice and is not applied on a case by case basis.

Educational records

16–20 By para.5 other personal data may be exempt from the s.7 rights in any case to the extent to which the application of the subject access right would "be likely to cause serious harm to the physical or mental health or condition of the data subject or any other person". Serious harm is not defined.

Personal data may also be exempt even where there is no likelihood of harm if, in certain circumstances, it would be in the best interests of the data subject that access should be withheld. This does not apply in Scotland but otherwise applies where a request is made by another person acting for the data subject being either a parent or a person appointed by the court to manage another's affairs. In such a case, personal data "consisting of information as to whether the data subject is or has been the subject of or may be at risk of child abuse" are exempt to the extent to which it would not be in the best interests of the data subject to give the information. "Child abuse" includes physical injury as well as physical and emotional neglect, ill-treatment and sexual abuse of a child.

16–21 Section 7(4) of the Act, which deals with access to third party data, is modified so that information on those who are employed in providing education services in a professional capacity cannot be withheld on a subject access search. However, such individuals are not left without protection where it is appropriate. The court is given power to restrain a data controller from giving subject access in contravention of the provisions of the Order in respect of such data on the application of:

> "any person to whom serious harm to whose physical or mental health or condition would be likely to be caused by compliance with any such request in contravention of those provisions."

It is not clear how this provision could apply in any other circumstance as it is not likely that any other person would know a subject access request had been made or would know that he or she might be seriously affected by it.

Education authorities in Scotland who receive and detain data from the Principal Reporter in Scotland are required to obtain his opinion on whether the disclosure of the information might cause serious harm to anyone before disclosing it in response to a subject access request.

---

[12] 1998 Act s.4(2).

HUMAN EMBRYOS

16–22 These are dealt with under the Data Protection (Miscellaneous Subject Access Exemptions) Order 2000[13] (amended by the Data Protection (Miscellaneous Subject Access Exemptions) (Amendment) Order 2000.[14]

The Data Protection (Miscellaneous Subject Access Exemptions) Order 2000 (SI 2000/419)

16–23 This Order was made under s.38(1) and came into effect on March 1, 2000 with the main Act. It sets out a number of legal provisions which prohibit or restrict the disclosure of information and provides that where they apply the prohibition takes precedence over the subject access rights in s.7. The list comes in three parts: the Human Fertilisation and Embryology Act 1990 which applies throughout the United Kingdom; provisions relating to adoption records and papers which apply in England and Wales; the equivalent provisions in Scotland. The exemption has no test of prejudice. It is limited to subject access and does not exempt any of the information from the fair obtaining and processing codes.

Background

16–24 An additional subject access exemption was inserted into the 1984 Act by s.33(8) of the Human Fertilisation and Embryology Act 1990 as s.35A. The 1990 Act established the Human Fertilisation and Embryology Authority. It contains detailed provisions under which individuals born as a result of fertility treatment are able to research their genetic heritage. The Authority maintains a register which includes information about individuals who have been born or might be born as a result of fertility treatment.

The exemption from subject access under the Data Protection Act was inserted to ensure that access to such data would be gained under the aegis of the Authority, rather than via a data protection route. The Human Fertilisation and Embryology Act contains safeguards surrounding such access. These deal with the form in which a request for access to the register maintained by the Authority is to be made and sets out the information which may be disclosed. The exemption applied except so far as the disclosure of the data was in accord with s.31 of the 1990 Act.

In an early draft of the Data Protection Bill a form of exemption was included which also acted as an exemption from the subject information provisions. However, this was left out of the Bill in its final stages. The exemption in the 1984 Act has been replaced by an order made under s.38(1).

16–25 An order under s.38(1) reverses the general rule that subject access rights take precedence over other legal prohibitions on disclosure of information. This is set out in s.27(5) which provides that:

> ". . . the subject information provisions shall have effect notwithstanding any enactment or rule of law prohibiting or restricting the disclosure, or authorising the withholding, of information."

---

[13] SI 2000/419.
[14] SI 2000/1865.

Section 38(1) empowers the Secretary of State to override this. In effect an order under this section re-imposes the prohibition which is otherwise lifted by s.27(5). The powers prevail so far as is necessary to safeguard the interests of the data subject or the rights or freedoms of any other individual.

The equivalent order-making power was used under the 1984 Act to provide for a raft of miscellaneous subject access exemptions which have been re-enacted under the 1998 Act. The order applied to information held in pursuance of various statutory functions largely concerned with the care of children, for example adoption records and reports.

PERSONNEL RECORDS

New exemption for personnel records

16–26   A new subject access exemption was added by the Freedom of Information Act 2000 (FOIA) for the purposes of category (e) data only; that is structured or unstructured manual data which is not held on a relevant filing system. The FOIA extended the right of subject access to cover such data where it is held by public bodies covered by it. The exemption covers category (e) data which is also data held for personnel matters. The policy behind the new exemption appears to be to maintain parity between employees in the public and private sectors. If the exemption had not been added a public sector employee would enjoy a far wider right of access to his employment records than an employee in the private sector via subject access. It also has the effect of preserving such information from third party inquirers because the existence of a subject access exemption means that the public authority must apply the exemption when dealing with a request for data by a third party.

16–27   The additional subject access exemption is found in s.70(1) of the FOIA which inserts a new s.33A into the DPA. Section 33A(2) exempts this class of data from all the data protection principles, from the individual rights, from notification and from s.55 (unlawful obtaining of personal data). It is not exempted from the powers of the Commissioner which means that the power of the Commissioner to serve an information notice under s.43 to ascertain whether the DPA applies will still bite.

The new exemption applies to:

"(2) Personal data which fall within paragraph (e) of the definition of 'data' in section 1(1) and relate to appointments or removals, pay, discipline, superannuation or other personnel matters, in relation to—

(a) service in any of the armed forces of the Crown
(b) service in any office or employment under the crown or under any public authority, or
(c) service in any office or employment, or under any contract for services, in respect of which power to take action, or to determine or approve the action taken, in such matter is vested in Her Majesty, any Minister of the Crown, the National Assembly for Wales, any Northern Ireland Minister (within the meaning of the Freedom of Information Act 2000) or any public authority."

It should be noted that the existence of an exemption places the authority under no obligation to rely on it and many authorities follow an open records practice for personnel records.

Data covered by the exemption for personnel records

16–28 The line between personnel matters and administrative/management matters may be a grey one. It is possible that the exemption could be used to remove more information than anticipated from the public domain. A similar question arises to that raised in respect of the media. When does data fall into one category or the other?

The position of contractors in relation to the personnel exemption

16–29 Under s.5(1) of the FOIA the Secretary of State may designate as a public authority for the purposes of the Act any person who is neither listed in Sch.1 nor capable of being added but who appears to the Secretary of State to exercise functions of a public nature or is providing under a contract made with a public authority any service whose provision is a function of that authority. The order may designate a specific person or office. The order must specify the services provided under the contract to which the designation applies. Only information held in relation to those services will be covered by the designation. The interaction of a designation and the extended right of subject access and new exemption is problematic. For example a contractor may provide facilities management or processing services under a Private Finance Initiative (PFI) contract. The contractor will have a responsibility for the provision of the services under the contract. As long as he meets the agreed service levels set out in the contract he will fulfil his contractual obligations. The power of the public authority over the detail of how he fulfils those obligations may be limited. The employees who carry out the service will be employed by the contractor, not the public authority. Where the Secretary of State designates a contractor as being one who is providing a service whose provision is a function of the authority and designates the services being carried out under the contract it is not clear whether the contractor will be counted as a public authority for all purposes.

16–30 If the result of a designation is to give employees of the contractor the benefit of the extension to subject access it is arguable that the contractor does not recieve the benefit of the exemption. The employees of the contractor do not appear to fall clearly within any of the classes in s.33A(2) (a) to (c). It could be argued that the employment is "service in any office or employment under the Crown or under any public authority" or that it is service "in any office or employment or under any contract for services in respect of which power to take action or determine or approve the action taken is vested in [one of the specified list]" but either interpretation seems to stretch the wording of the section. If the wording cannot be stretched then the employees of the designated contractor would obtain extended subject access without the employer having the benefit of the exemption. The prudent course might be for those entering into contracts to include a clause making clear, for the avoidance of any doubt that the particular contract, is, for the purposes of the DPA a contract falling in (b) or (c).

ADDITIONAL INFORMATION

Derivations

16–31 • Directive 95/46 (See App.B):

  (a) Arts 3.2 (scope); 13.1g (exemptions and restrictions).
  (b) Recitals 12, 22.

• Council of Europe Convention of January 28, 1981 for the Protection of Individuals with regard to automatic processing of Personal Data: Art.9 (exceptions and restrictions).

• Data Protection Act 1984: ss.29 (health and social work) (3391) (domestic or other limited purposes); 34A (human embryos).

• Data Protection (Subject Access Modification) (Health) Order 1987 No. 1903.

• Data Protection (Subject Access Modification) (Social Work Order) Order 1987 No. 1904.

• Data Protection (Miscellaneous Subject Access Exemptions) Order 1997 No. 1906.

• Organisation for Economic Co-operation and Development Guidelines: Annex Part One (scope of guidelines).

Hansard references

16–32 On May 10, Mr George Howarth announced that the drafts of six of the statutory instruments, which include the exemption orders for education, social work and embryology, were to be published on the internet. The Home Office had previously consulted on the form of the orders.

1998—the Home Office issued a consultation paper on proposals for orders to be made under the Act.

Commons Standing Committee D, May 21, 1998, cols 199–200
Excluded data.

Vol.315, No.198, col.593, Commons Third Reading, July 2, 1998
Education information exemption.

Previous case law

16–33 None.

CHAPTER 17

Exemptions for the Special Purposes: Journalistic, Literary and Artistic

INTRODUCTION

17–01 Provisions dealing with the special purposes and the exemptions which apply to those purposes are set out in ss.3, 32, 44, 45, 53 and Sch.10. The reason for this spread throughout the Act is that the exemptions are complex.

They:

- allow for non-compliance with some of the standards set out in the Act;

- restrict the powers of the court prior to publication of material;

- restrict the power of the Commissioner to take enforcement action both prior to and after publication;

- provide for the Commissioner to fund proceedings where the special purposes are in question.

All of these elements are dealt with in this chapter. The provisions of the Human Rights Act, the regulation of the press and the relationship between privacy and freedom of expression are covered in more detail in Ch.2, above.

The provisions have given a generous interpretation to Art.9 of the Directive as far as journalistic, artistic and literary works are concerned. They go beyond what might have been required to provide for an Art.9 exemption. From another point of view, however, they are a narrow application of the exemption provided in the Directive for freedom of expression. Freedom of expression has been equated with three particular areas of activity: journalism, artistic and literary work. No other activities have the benefit of the "freedom of expression" exemption. If one partner in a firm of solicitors writes a letter to another setting out his suspicions about a member of his staff and the basis for them, the partnership would be unable to refuse subject access to that information on the basis of the special purposes exemption. If the partnership intends to publish it, however, it may lay claim to the exemption, at least before publication.

Background

17–02   After adoption of the Directive and before the Data Protection Bill was published there was negative reporting of it in the written press. One or two pieces suggested that the Directive would spell the end of a free press as it is known. The Bill was much delayed in publication. It was to be published in November 1997, then it was delayed until December 1997 and finally saw the light of day in January 1998. It appears from the positive response the Bill evoked from the press when it did appear, including the comments from Lord Wakeman of the Press Complaints Commission speaking in the House of Lords in the opening debate, that the time was spent by the Government resolving the differences with the press interests. The resulting provisions are complex. They have not however protected the media from the gradual restriction of intrusive journalism since the implementation of the Human Rights Act (HRA).

The data subject who wishes to restrict publication in reliance under the Data Protection Act faces a labyrinth of provisions. It is not simply that the provisions are complex, but that the shifts in responsibility and in the burden of proof at crucial points in the proceedings, together with the multiple possible adjudications and appeals before final disposal, make the case difficult to conclude. As predicted individuals have not sought to use the DPA to restrict publication of material. However to date this has not proved to be a barrier to the issue of injunctions or "gagging" orders in appropriate cases. The High Court has been prepared to contemplate such orders to protect individuals' rights to confidentiality and has increasingly aligned the concepts of privacy and confidentiality in cases brought under the HRA.

The development of this case law has been explored in Ch.2, above and is not repeated here, although some of the cases on Art.10 are included. Any consideration of the exemption for journalistic, literary and artistic material must take into account the developments under the HRA and it is suggested that this chapter should be read together with Ch.2, above.

Section 32 was considered in the case of *Naomi Campbell v Mirror Group Newspapers*[1] which is discussed later in the chapter.

SUMMARY OF MAIN POINTS

17–03   (a) The s.32 exemption works on a case by case basis; it is not a blanket exemption.

   (b) The exemption includes a balancing test, taking into account an assessment of public interest; it is not an absolute exemption.

   (c) Protection against court action by individuals is given to journalistic, literary or artistic work prior to publication; once material is no longer being processed with a view to publication that procedural element of the exemption no longer applies.

   (d) After the material has been published individuals can take court action but the publisher may have a defence as the substantive element of the exemption continues to apply.

---

[1] See Ch.2, above; [2002] EWCA Civ 1373.

(e) When the substantive exemption comes into play it is extremely powerful. It can provide both a sword and a shield. It can be used to mount a defence against actions taken against publishers under the Act. The individual rights and the principles, apart from the security principle, give way. Even the rules requiring legitimacy of processing and restricting the use of sensitive data may be overridden.

(f) The powers of the Commissioner to take enforcement action are also restricted in relation to the special purposes.

(g) Private actions involving the special purposes can be funded by the Commissioner where issues of significant public interest arise.

PROPOSALS FOR PRESS REGULATION

Background information

17–04   Before the introduction of the Data Protection Act there was extensive discussion of the possibility of privacy legislation particularly aimed at curbing the worst behaviour of the written media. Following pressure from Members of Parliament for privacy legislation, the Government in 1989 set up a committee under the chairmanship of David Calcutt Q.C. to consider what measures might be needed to protect "individual privacy from the activities of the press". This Committee on Privacy and Related Matters reported in June 1990.[2] Largely as a result of the pressure resulting from its report, the Press Complaints Commission (PCC) was strengthened and the press given "one final chance" to show that legislation was not needed and that voluntary self-regulation could be made to work.

Two years later Sir David Calcutt Q.C. (as he had then become) was asked to conduct a review of press self-regulation which was presented to Parliament in January 1993.[3] The review recommended that the Government should give further consideration to the introduction of a tort of infringement of privacy and on January 14, 1993 the Government announced that it would consider this proposal.

The issues arising from media intrusion and related privacy matters were also considered by the National Heritage Select Committee which recommended the enactment of a Protection of Privacy Bill.[4]

In July 1993 the Lord Chancellor's Department and the Scottish Office issued a consultation paper entitled *Infringement of Privacy*, seeking responses on the proposal that a civil tort of infringement of privacy should be created. The consultation exercise took some time. In a response published in July 1995[5] the Government responded to both the consultation paper and the National Heritage Select Committee Report at the same time. The Government concluded that no persuasive case had been made out for statutory regulation of the press and announced that it had no plans to introduce a statutory right to privacy.

---

[2] *Report of the Committee on Privacy*, Cmnd.1102.
[3] Cmnd.2135.
[4] *Fourth report of the Committee*, March 1993.
[5] Privacy and Media Intrusion, Cmnd.2918.

Although these initiatives came to nothing they demonstrate both the depth of concern caused by media intrusion and the strength of the opposition to any government control over its behaviour. They provide the background to the strong opposition mounted to the Data Protection Directive and later the Bill by the media which, having fought off the various moves to impose statutory regulation, viewed the new law as an attempt to achieve similar ends by the "back door".

The 1998 Act imposed a stronger regime than was in force under the 1984 Act with increased individual rights. It has had the effect of bringing into the open the tension between the right to respect for private life in the information context and the right to freedom of expression. That tension was present throughout the development of the Directive. It was one of the first issues to occupy the Article 29 Working Party of representatives of supervisory authorities set up under the Directive. In February 1997, the Working Party adopted Recommendation 1/97 Data Protection Law and the Media. In the Recommendation the Working Party acknowledged the tension but took the view it had a positive side:

"However, the two fundamental rights must not be seen as inherently conflicting. In the absence of adequate safeguards for privacy individuals may be reluctant to freely express their ideas. Similarly identification and profiling of readers and users of information services is likely to reduce the willingness of individuals to receive and impart information."

Parliamentary interest in the regulation of the media has continued since the implementation of the 1998 Act. In 2002–2003 the Culture Media and Sport Committee of the House of Commons produced its report on *Privacy and Media Intrusion*. It recognised the start (as it was at the time) of the judge-made law on Art.8 and the route towards a privacy law that it was likely to take. It recommended that, rather than leaving the development to the courts, the Government should bring forward legislative proposals and deliver a privacy law to protect individuals from unwarranted press intrusion. This has not been acted upon and, as we have seen in Ch.2, above the law has been developed as foretold. The other recommendations argued for the strengthening of the Press Complaints Commission (PCC), improving its independence and the sanctions available as well as some changes to strengthen the Code itself.

WHAT ARE THE SPECIAL PURPOSES?

17–05 The special purposes are set out in s.3 of the Act being:

"(a) the purposes of journalism;

(b) artistic purposes; or

(c) literary purposes."

No further assistance is offered in respect of these definitions. Accordingly the terms must be given their ordinary and natural meaning. As in any provision based on the Directive the courts will take a purposive approach to interpretation, seeking to give effect to the intent of the Directive. This exemption is derived from Art.9. Article 9 is headed "Processing of personal data and freedom of expression". It provides that Member States shall provide for exemptions or derogations ". . . for the processing of personal data carried out solely for journalistic purposes or the purposes of artistic or literary expression . . .". The Directive gives no further assistance in describing what these purposes are. The terms themselves are extremely broad. Journalistic, artistic and literary endeavours are clearly meant to be different matters.

A number of questions are evoked by the term "journalistic" purposes. It is not immediately apparent whether this covers any work for any publication in any medium whether or not the author is paid. The Shorter Oxford English Dictionary (OED) describes a "journalist" as "one who earns his living by editing or writing for a public journal or journals. One who keeps a journal".

The first part of the definition suggests that payment of some sort is necessary, however this appears to be an unnecessary restriction. In the Recommendation of the Article 29 Working Party the point is made that it is not the journalist but the freedom to express views which is protected by the exemption:

> "Article 9 of the Directive respects the right of individuals to freedom. Derogations and exemptions under Article 9 cannot be granted to the media or to journalists as such, but only to anybody processing data for journalistic purposes."

It appears, therefore, that a piece written without payment for a parish magazine could count as journalism. Journalism does not appear to be limited to the reporting of fact but may include associated comments on reporting of fact. Presumably it is wide enough to include comment irrespective of whether any factual reporting is involved. The work does not have to be done by a journalist as the relevant processing may be undertaken by "any person".[6]

17–06 The terms "artistic" and "literary" purposes are equally imprecise. Literary works must presumably involve the use of words. In the first edition we suggested that "therefore artistic work, by exclusion, will not do so". However, this is probably too narrow a view. There seems no reason why an artistic work could not include words as well as other material. How a literary or artistic work is to be judged is not clear. If a hopeful would-be author or artist works on a piece which is never finished, or which indeed turns out to have no literary or artistic merit, is he within the definitions? Is it possible to judge whether a piece is a literary or artistic work until the vision which inspired it is crystallised in the finished creation? In relation to copyright protection under the Copyright, Design and Patents Act 1988 a literary work is any original written material. There is no test of literary merit attached. It is suggested that this is also the correct approach to the concept of literary work in the context of the DPA. This approach is based on the same reasoning as is applied above in relation to journalism, that the purpose of the exemption is to protect freedom of expression.

One may presumably have a work which is both literary and artistic, as in a multimedia presentation. Can a database be a literary work? Is a piece of software a literary work? If an interactive business game is based on real people will that be a literary work containing personal data?

---

[6] 1998 Act s.32(1)(a).

Unfortunately, the Act provides no answers to these questions. One can say that as one is dealing with exemptions from the rigour of the Act the general rule of statutory interpretation is that they will be interpreted strictly against the party seeking to rely on them. On the other hand as the purpose of the exemption is to protect the right to freedom of expression a purposive approach tends towards a generous interpretation of the terms. In any event it is difficult to see how such broad and general terms can be strictly interpreted. It is more likely that the courts will take a liberal approach to those activities which may give rise to a claim to the exemption but apply a strict construction to the terms of the exemption itself. This accords with the general principle that exemptions are to be construed strictly.

WHAT ARE THE GROUNDS OF THE EXEMPTION?

17–07   The exemption can be claimed where personal data are processed only for the special purposes and where three separate conditions are fulfilled. Before considering these three conditions it should be emphasised that the personal data involved must be processed only for the special purposes.[7] It is not clear how proximate the processing must be to the special purposes in order to fulfil this test. One might argue that fulfilling the personnel function or dealing with the accounts of a media business involves processing personal data for the purposes of journalism, but it is suggested that a tighter line should be drawn in this area and that the exemption should be restricted to the processing of matter which is itself intended for publication. This is the approach taken by the Article 29 Working Party in its Recommendation:

> "Derogations and exemptions may cover only data processing for journalistic (editorial) purposes including electronic publishing. Any other form of data processing by journalists or the media is subject to the ordinary rules of the Directive. This distinction is particularly relevant in electronic publishing. Processing of subscriber data for billing purposes or processing for direct marketing purposes (including processing of data on media use for profiling purposes) fall under the ordinary data protection regime."

The question of whether information is held "otherwise than for the purposes of journalism" has been litigated in the Information Tribunal under the Freedom of Information Act 2000. That Act covers the public service broadcasters but only for information held otherwise than for their journalistic purposes. In the Tribunal a narrow view of the term was taken however the case is currently under appeal to the High Court.

There must exist a definable act of processing carried out for the special purposes, not simply an intention to process for those purposes, or processing to which those purposes are incidental. Presumably any processing which fulfils any part of the definition of processing may qualify for the exemption.

---

[7] 1998 Act s.32(1).

With a view to publication

17–08   The first test is that the processing is undertaken with a view to the publication by any person of any journalistic, literary or artistic material.[8] Publication is not defined but the term "publish" is defined in s.32(6) as meaning, for the purposes of this Act, as "making material available to the public or any section of the public".

Clearly something will be made available to the public if it is published in a newspaper, or on a website, on the internet, or in a book on public sale, or displayed at a public art gallery so that any person may look at it. It is less clear what is envisaged by the term "a section of the public". The same wording is used in the Contempt of Court Act 1981,[9] the Race Relations Act 1968 and in law relating to charities. It appears to cover groups as opposed to individuals but where there is no selection of the membership of such groups. The essential difference seems to be between controlled and public access.

The processing must have taken place "with a view" to publication. It is not clear how specific this view must be. Must the material be due to be published within the foreseeable future? It is presumably a question of fact as to whether or not there is a genuine view to publication. As a matter of law it should not be necessary to point to a particular publication date but there must be a genuine aim to publish. This would suggest that data kept on file as background to a potential story would not necessarily be eligible for exemption on this ground.

Publication in the public interest

17–09   The second condition is that the data controller must reasonably believe that, having regard to the special importance of the public interest in freedom of expression, publication would be in the public interest.[10]

Public interest is a notoriously elusive concept. To compound the possible ambiguity the term appears twice in the same subsection. Regard must be had to the specific interest in freedom of expression as part of a broader concept of public interest. Public interest tests arising in other contexts may be of only limited assistance. In the context of publication by the press it has been held that public interest is not the same as what is interesting to the public. In *Lion Laboratories Ltd v Evans*[11] the Court considered a case in which a newspaper had obtained confidential documents from an ex-employee which disclosed doubts about the reliability of the Lion Intoximeter 3000. The question for the court was whether disclosure of the information in the documents was in the public interest. It was held that it was in the public interest to disclose it, even if the information had been obtained in breach of confidence and there was no wrongdoing on the part of the company. The court held that in deciding whether publication was in the public interest there was no requirement there should be misconduct on the part of the person to be "exposed" but it had to take into account (a) the difference between what is interesting to the public and what is in the public interest; (b) the fact that the media have an interest in publishing things which will increase circulation; and (c) the fact that the public interest might be best served

---

[8] DPA s.32(1)(a).
[9] Contempt of Court Act 1981 s.2(1).
[10] DPA s.32(1)(b).
[11] [1984] 2 All E.R. 417.

by someone going to the police not the press. It then had to weigh the nature of the material, the competing interests in confidentiality and whether the publication went to matters of real public concern.

The question of public interest in publication was re-visited by Lord Woolf in *A v B*.[12] The approach taken by Lord Woolf suggests a more generous view of the public interest and in particular acknowledges that there is a broad public interest in the existence of a free and vigorous press. For a full discussion of *A v B* see Ch.2, above. The generous view does not appear to have been universally applied in subsequent cases. In this section the controller is given additional assistance by s.32(3) which states that, in considering for the purposes of subs.1(1)(b) whether a belief that publication is in the public interest was a reasonable one, regard may be had to compliance with any code of practice which is relevant to the publication in question and is designated by the Secretary of State by order for the purpose of this subsection.

Since the Human Rights Act 1998 came into effect the courts have had to weight competing interests in freedom of expression and other areas of public interest in a large number of cases. A selection of the most significant involving personal privacy are dealt with in Ch.2, above. Others have concerned the publication of material which may lead to threats to those involved or matters affecting taste and decency.

17–10 In *R. (on the application of ProLife Alliance) v British Broadcasting Corporation*[13] the House of Lords held that the question of whether the BBC as a regulator had imposed an improper restriction on the broadcasting of a political programme had to be considered by reference to the principles of judicial review and the court should not substitute its views for those of the regulator unless it could be shown that the regulator had applied an inappropriate standard. Prolife campaigns against abortion. In the 2001 General Election they fielded sufficient candidates to be entitled to air time for a party political broadcast. The BBC and other broadcasters refused to screen the material prepared by Prolife on the grounds that it did not comply with the BBC producer's guidelines on taste and decency. The film included footage which dealt with late stage abortion and was described as "graphic and disturbing" but it was accepted by the broadcasters that it was not sensationalised and imparted an accurate depiction. The Court of Appeal held that Art.10 was engaged and had been breached without justification. However the House of Lords reversed the decision pointing out that the BBC was acting in its quasi-regulatory or regulatory role. Both parties accepted that the BBC had such a role and its decision was made pursuant to the role.

In *H (a healthcare worker) v Associated Newspapers Limited*[14] the Court of Appeal lifted a ban which had been imposed in the High Court to stop journalists from soliciting information which might lead to the discovery of a healthcare worker who had been diagnosed as HIV positive. The court held that this was too wide a restriction to place on the press and was an unacceptable fetter on the right to freedom of expression. In a similar vein the High Court held that an injunction restraining the publication by the BBC of the identity of social workers who had been involved with a celebrated case

---

[12] [2002] 3 W.L.R. 542.
[13] [2003] UKHL 23.
[14] [2002] EWCA Civ 195.

would be a disproportionate interference with the Art.10 rights of the BBC and two children who wished to disclose their own story.[15] Similar decisions were made in *Re Webster (A Child) sub nom Norfolk CC v Nichola Webster*[16] in which an interim order restricting access by the media to an interim hearing was held to be too wide and interfered with the Art.10 rights of the parents. In that case however the interests of the parents were not the only factor in favour of openness; there were other strong interests, in particular the need to command full confidence in the judicial process. In *Leeds City Council v Channel Four Television Group*[17] the court held that Channel 4 was entitled to screen a documentary including film shot covertly in a local secondary school which showed the disruptive and defiant behaviour of children and the demoralised response of staff. While it was accepted that the disclosures involved an intrusion into the Art.8 rights of the children the balance came down in favour of publication in view of the serious issues of public interest raised and the fact that the surreptitious filming appeared to be the only way of exposing the problems. In *R. v Shayler*[18] the House of Lords held that the Official Secrets Act 1989, which prohibited the disclosure, without lawful authority, of any documents or information which came into the individual's possession as a member of the security services was not incompatible with Art.10. The sections created an offence of disclosure of prohibited information for which the defendant had been prosecuted. He had sought to raise a defence of public interest. The court held that although Art.10 was engaged and his rights to freedom of speech had been restricted it had been done in furtherance of one of the objectives specified in Art.10(2), and the restriction was proportionate as there was a proper mechanism by which he could seek to challenge the ban on publication. The court held that as part of his employment he had given a binding undertaking of confidentiality and if he sought to be relieved of that he must seek official authorisation. If authorisation was refused he could challenge it by judicial review but if his challenge failed he had to abide by the ruling of the court. In *Venables and Thompson v News Group Newspapers Ltd*[19] the court had to weight the Art.10 rights against the right to life and security. The case arose as Venables and Thompson reached 18 years of age. There had been injunctions in place banning anyone from disclosing information about them. As they approached 18 applications were made for the injunctions to be maintained against all the world so as to ensure that their whereabouts and current identities were not published. The court held that their rights to security and safety outweighed the rights protected by Art.10. Lifetime protection was also accorded to the woman formerly known as Mary Bell and her daughter in similar circumstances. Mary Bell (as she had been) had been convicted of the manslaughter of two young children when she was herself 11 years old. The court held that in the exceptional circumstances the balance favoured the protection of the privacy of the individual and granted an order *contra mundum*.[20]

As noted in Ch.2, above neither the European Court of Human Rights nor the UK courts have stretched the impact of the Art.10 rights to include a right to obtain access to information held in the public sector. Nevertheless the Freedom of Information Act

---

[15] *BBC v Rochdale Metropolitan Borough Council* [2005] EWHC 2862 (Fam).
[16] [2006] EWHC 2733.
[17] [2005] EWHC 3522.
[18] [2002] UKHL 11.
[19] [2001] 1 All E.R. 908.
[20] *X (formerly known as Mary Bell) v SO* [2003] EWHC 1101 (QB).

2000, which came fully into force on January 1, 2005, has given rise to some decisions of the Information Tribunal which suggest that the public interest in access to official information is supported by, or possibly is a part of, the Art.10 right. It has to be noted however that these are first instance decisions of a statutory tribunal. Moreover the reasoning is not wholly clear, accordingly they should perhaps be treated with some caution.[21]

Codes of practice

17–11 The code of practice referred to in s.32(3) need not necessarily be one made under the Data Protection Act. The designated codes[22] are the Press Complaints Commission Code of Practice, the Broadcasting Standards Commission Code on Fairness and Privacy under s.107 of the Broadcasting Act 1996, the Independent Television Commission Programme Code under s.7 of the Broadcasting Act 1990, the British Broadcasting Corporation Producers' Guidelines and the Radio Authority Code under s.91 of the Broadcasting Act 1990. The Broadcasting Standards Code is now a legacy code superseded by the Ofcom Broadcasting Code.

Under the PCC Code, public interest is not exhaustively defined but "includes":

"1.   i) detecting or exposing crime or serious impropriety;
   ii) protecting public health and safety;
   iii) preventing the public being misled by some statement or action of an individual or organisation"
2. There is a public interest in freedom of expression itself
3. Whenever the public interest is invoked the PCC will require editors to demonstrate fully how the public interest was served
4. the PCC will consider the extent to which material is already in the public domain, or will become so.
5. In cases involving children under 16, editors must demonstrate an exceptional public interest to over-ride the normally paramount interest of the child."

The belief that publication is in the public interest must be held by the data controller for the personal data involved. If the data controller is a corporate entity it would follow that the reasonable belief should be attributable to a responsible individual who acts for the company in this regard and has addressed his mind to the case in question. In *Tesco Supermarkets Ltd v Nattrass*[23] the House of Lords considered the attribution of mental capacity to a corporation in relation to an offence under the Trade Descriptions Act 1968. They held that the mental element required for the offence had to be attributable to a senior official or manager who could be regarded as part of the management of the organisation. This followed the judgment of Denning L.J. in *HL Bolton (Engineering) Co Ltd v T J Graham & Sons Ltd*[24] in which he likened a company to a human body in which some workers act as the hands and arms of the company but others represent the "directing mind". It would appear that the same

---

[21] *Information Commissioner v Derry Council*, unreported. See *www.informationtribunal.gov.uk*.
[22] Data Protection (Designated Codes of Practice) (No.2) Order 2000 (SI 2000/1864).
[23] [1971] 2 All E.R. 127.
[24] [1956] 3 All E.R. 624.

person should also have directed his mind to the third condition, that is the test set out in the following subsection.

Incompatibility with the special purposes

17–12 The third test which must be fulfilled before the controller can claim the exemption is that he reasonably believes that, in all the circumstances, compliance with the relevant provision of the Act is incompatible with the special purposes.[25] It is a question of fact as to whether the controller did reasonably believe that the matters would be incompatible. The term incompatible is used on a number of occasions in the Act and is never defined. It must therefore be given its ordinary meaning. The OED defines incompatible as:

> "1. Of benefices, etc., incapable of being held together;
> 2. Mutually intolerant; incapable of existing together in the same subject; discordant, incongruous, inconsistent;
> 3. Unable to 'get on' together; at variance;
> 4. Irreconcilable."

This sets quite a high standard and suggests that the controller must reasonably believe that he will be unable to publish either in total or a substantial part of the work if he complies with the relevant requirement of the Act. It does not apply only to the action of publication but may apply to any of the processing which leads up to publication and is necessary to achieve it, for example the collection of information from an individual without the provision of a collection notice.

WHAT DOES THE EXEMPTION COVER?

17–13 If the test in s.32(1) is met, that is, putting it broadly, that the controller reasonably believes that if he complies with the relevant data protection provision either he will be unable to publish material which it would be in the public interest to publish, or he will be unable to do so effectively or fully, then he is not bound by the particular data protection provision in that case. The relevant data protection provisions from which he may be exempt are found in the Principles (except the Security Principle) and a number of the individual rights.

The Principles

17–14 The controller may claim exemption from any of the Data Protection Principles, apart from Principle 7 which covers the security of data processing. The linked provisions in Schs 2, 3 and 4 are also covered by this exemption. This allows the controller to disregard the prohibition on sensitive data holding, the requirement for legitimacy of processing and the prohibition on overseas transfer where he reasonably believes that the s.32(1) tests are made out. The balancing test involved in assessing whether the publication is in the public interest and whether the relevant data protection provision would be incompatible with publication is likely to be particularly

---

[25] DPA s.32(1)(c).

difficult where the data controller seeks to avoid compliance with these fundamental provisions. The courts have to balance these issues when claims for compensation come before them to be met by media claims for exemption. As is seen in the discussion on s.32(4) below this moment is likely to be postponed until after publication of the material.

The exemptions from the Principles will come into play pro-actively in that the controller will have to make a positive decision not to comply with the relevant Principle(s) in a particular case. The controller will also have to be prepared to defend this position if challenged. It is suggested that those involved in journalistic, literary and artistic areas who are likely to wish to claim the exemption should establish procedures to ensure that clear decisions are made on appropriate grounds where the exemptions are claimed and that a record of the use of the exemptions is retained in case of future challenge.

Individual rights

17–15 These are:

(a) The right of subject access—s.7. Where subject access is refused the attendant information rights, for example to a statement of the logic involved in any processing decision, may also be refused.

(b) The right to prevent processing likely to cause damage or distress—s.10.

(c) The right to object to automated decision taking—s.12.

(d) The rectification blocking and erasure provisions dealing with inaccurate data—s.14(1)–(3).

These exemptions will be claimed reactively when an individual seeks to exercise the relevant right. It is suggested that those data users who may wish to take advantage of these exemptions adopt an appropriate system for authorising the exemption claim to ensure that any claim complies with the s.32(1) provisions. The exemptions may either be claimed when the individual request is first made to the data controller and the response refused, or may be claimed in proceedings brought by the individual to enforce his or her rights. Where the exemption is claimed in legal proceedings brought by an individual before publication the issues cannot be adjudicated by the court unless the Commissioner has made a finding that the processing was not taking place only for the special purposes following the procedure which is described later in the chapter.

How Long Do the Exemptions Last?

17–16 The policy behind these exemptions is to protect freedom of expression. A major consideration in formulating the provisions appears to have been to ensure that there can be no prior restraint of publication and that data protection restraints will not be used to stifle freedom of the press when that freedom is exercised in the public interest. The protection afforded against prior restraint accords with the balance between the right to freedom of expression and individual liberties accepted in previous UK case law.

In *Schering Chemicals Ltd v Falkman Ltd*[26] Lord Denning M.R. dealt with the question of the freedom of the press to publish thus:

> "The freedom of the press is extolled as one of the great bulwarks of liberty. It is entrenched in the constitutions of the world. But it is often misunderstood. I will first say what it does not mean. It does not mean that the press is free to ruin a reputation or break a confidence, or to pollute the course of justice or to do anything which is unlawful. I will next say what it does mean. It means that there should be no censorship. No restraint should be placed on the press as to what they should publish. Not by a licensing system. Not by executive direction. Not by court injunction."

The accepted restriction on prior restraint accounts for the provision in s.32(4) which is designed to provide for a stay of proceedings where such proceedings are brought prior to publication, and will apply even though there has been one publication in the previous 24 hours. This extension to a previous 24-hour application period is intended to ensure that the daily media cannot be restrained between the issue of editions.

The procedural exemption continues to apply to any processing which is undertaken "with a view to publication". It endures for as long as there is an intention to publish. The exemption may be claimed afresh for each publication but will only apply to that particular publication.

Application after publication

17–17   Once the material has been published it is clear that the prohibitions on court proceedings brought by data subjects no longer applies. This point was considered by the High Court and subsequently the Court of Appeal in the case of *Naomi Campbell v Mirror Group Newspapers*. In the High Court the *Mirror* argued that the court was wholly prohibited from hearing any case in relation to the special purposes until s.32(5) was satisfied, that is until the Commissioner had made a determination under s.45. The judge ruled against the *Mirror* on this point and held that he could consider the case. He ruled that the restriction on bringing proceedings in s.34(4) only applied prior to publication and once the material has been published the court could consider the case under the DPA. Thus once s.32(4) is no longer satisfied a court has no grounds on which to stay proceedings. In relation to the substantive aspect of the exemption the judgment was less clear. (The Court of Appeal subsequently decided that he had held that the substantive element of the exemption also ceased to apply.) In any event he held that on the facts the *Mirror* would not be able to claim the benefit of the exemption. In the Court of Appeal it was held that the data controller who published material can claim the benefit of the substantive exemption after publication and on the facts of the case the *Mirror* was entitled to it.

This is clearly the logical approach to the application of the exemption in cases where the possibility of compliance with the relevant provision from which the data controller claimed exemption, for example the requirement to provide a collection

---

[26] [1982] 1 Q.B. 1.

notice, has been exhausted. However, where the data controller only required the benefit of the exemption in order to be able to publish, and could comply with the requirement after publication without any detrimental effect to the special purposes, it seems right that he should have to do so. An example would be a subject access request. A data controller may receive a subject access request prior to the publication of material and be of the honest and well founded view that he does not have to provide the data as the exemption applies. He then publishes the material, or significant parts of it. Following publication there would be no difficulty in providing access to the material. Despite this the data controller appears to be under no obligation to give the material unless the data subject serves another request. (This is not confined however to this provision; the same may occur when an exemption from subject access is claimed on other grounds. It is a specific example of the more general question as to the effect of a change in the circumstances affecting a data controller after receipt of a subject access request.)

Facts

17–18 The claimant was a well-known fashion model who had denied in public that she had drug problems. She was photographed leaving a clinic where she had been having treatment for addiction. The photograph was published by the *Mirror* newspaper in February 2001 which also published the fact that she was being treated by having therapy. After she complained about the disclosures of the information and the publication of the photograph the newspaper published further material criticising her complaint and claim for breach of privacy. She took action against the newspaper claiming damages for breach of confidentiality and compensation under s.13 of the DPA in respect of the articles and photographs published. The claimant accepted that the paper was entitled to publish the basic fact that she was addicted to drugs and was having treatment, but argued that it was not entitled to use photographs of her or give detail of the treatment, i.e. the therapy or the therapist. The paper refuted any claim for breach of confidence or breach of the DPA. It argued that, even if the information was confidential, there was a public interest in publishing it as she had misled the public about her drug use. Her claim eventually succeeded in the House of Lords. The DPA issues were canvassed in the High Court and the Court of Appeal.

Judge Morland in the High Court reviewed the evidence relating to Ms Campbell's statements about addiction and ruled that, as she was a role model and had made public statements that she was not addicted, the *Mirror* was entitled to disclose that she had lied and did have drug addiction problems. She had been prepared to make statements about drug use in the fashion business and had put the issue into the public domain. There was a public interest in revealing that she had lied. However the newspaper was not entitled to go beyond that into material which she had not put into the public domain. The details which were revealed about her treatment amounted to an invasion of her privacy which was not justified by any public interest.

He considered both the claim under the DPA and the application of the exemption for journalistic material. He referred to the background of the DPA in the Directive and to the treatment of the right to freedom of expression under Art.10 of the Covention rights and the derogation in Art.9 of the Directive. He also considered the Article 29 Working Party Recommendation 1/97 on Data Protection and the Media. The *Mirror* submitted that the exemption in s.32 applied to the publication and argued that not only did the substantive exemption apply but the procedural exemption in s.32(5) continued to apply post-publication and thus the Court was precluded from hearing the case until the Commissioner had made a determination under s.45. The Court rejected the contention that the procedural provision applied post-publication (citing among other authorities the first edition of this text) and went on to consider the application of the substantive exemption.

17–19 The Court held that the information about the applicant's drug use and treatment related to her physical or mental health or condition and thus was sensitive data. It held that the photographs of the applicant leaving the clinic were unfairly obtained as they were taken by a photographer concealed in a car at a distance. Ms Campbell had no opportunity to evade the shot or refuse consent. Moreover the fact that the photographs and information were obtained in breach of confidence meant that they were obtained unlawfully. The judge then considered which of the Sch.2 grounds legitimised the processing by the *Mirror*.[27] He rejected the argument put forward by the newspaper that it could rely on Ground 5, which relates to processing for the exercise of a public function. He accepted that Ground 6 was available to the newspaper, however, he said that some of the material failed the balancing test in Ground 6 as the publication of the details of the treatment and the photograph went beyond the legitimate interests of the paper. He then considered the Sch.3 Grounds[28] and SI 2000/417, Ground 3(1) which permits the disclosure of wrongdoing to the media where publication would be in the public interest.[29] He held that the conditions in Ground 3(1) were cumulative. The newspaper had submitted otherwise. He also held that the publication of the nature of Ms Campbell's treatment was not in the substantial public interest. Moreover her actions were not in connection with the commission of offences but with efforts not to commit offences. He concluded that none of the three requirements of the first Principle, fair processing, lawful processing, or grounds under Schs 2 and 3, were made out. Accordingly there had been a breach of the DPA. There was no defence that the newspaper had taken reasonable care to avoid such breach, on the contrary it was a deliberate and knowing action. He then considered the effect of s.13 and agreed that where the special purposes were concerned the applicant did not have to show actual damage but was entitled to compensation for distress. The judge assessed the amount of the damages for distress and injury to feelings as £2,500. The claimant had claimed aggravated damages for the behaviour of the *Mirror* after the publication. These however could be compensatory only and not punitive. On the aggravated damages issue the judge held that the paper was entitled to assert that the claim against it should not have been made and say so in print. However in this case, in doing so it had belittled the claimant in relation to her claim. He therefore held that she was entitled to aggravated damages as the article "trashed her as a person". The claimant was awarded a further £1,000 in aggravated damages bringing the total damages to £3,500.

Although the Court of Appeal overturned the judgment holding that there was no breach of confidence in relation to the photograph as it was a photograph of the

---

[27] See Ch.6, above for an analysis of the grounds for processing.
[28] See Ch.7, above for an analysis of the grounds for processing sensitive data.
[29] See para.7–24, above.

claimant taken in a public place Miss Campbell finally succeeded in the House of Lords. The data protection point was not considered in the Lords but in the Court of Appeal the Court agreed that the publication of the material was processing within the terms of the DPA and did not appear to depart from the reasoning and approach of Judge Morland to the application of the DPA. However the Court held that the *Mirror* was entitled to the benefit of the substantive exemption in s.32 as publication was in the public interest and the written material about the treatment and the photograph were not severable from the publication of the fact that the claimant was an addict, in respect of which it was accepted that publication was in the public interest. The Court accepted that the grounds of the exemption applied in particular that the *Mirror*, through its editor, held a reasonable belief that compliance with the requirements of the DPA would be incompatible with the purpose of journalism.

RESTRICTIONS ON INDIVIDUAL ACTIONS

17–20   A data controller who processes for one of the special purposes and against whom court proceedings are brought by an individual to enforce his rights under ss.7, 10, 12 or 14 (1)–(3) before publication of the material in question can insist that the proceedings are halted until the Information Commissioner has made a declaration that the processing is no longer carried out for the special purposes or is not carried out only for the special purposes. In effect this allows the data controller to have proceedings stayed until after publication of the relevant material. This procedure, under which specified issues are transferred from the courts to the jurisdiction of the Commissioner, appears to have no counterpart in other statutes. It applies in addition to the substantive exemption and is a procedural aspect of the exemption. Section 32(4) and (5) provide:

> "(4) Where at any time ('the relevant time') in any proceedings against a data controller under sections 7(9), 10(4), 12(8) or 14, or by virtue of section 13 the data controller claims, or it appears to the court, that any personal data to which the proceedings relate are being processed:
>
> > (a) only for the special purposes; and
> > (b) with a view to the publication by any person of any journalistic, literary or artistic material which, at the time twenty four hours immediately before the relevant time, had not previously been published by the data controller,
>
> the court shall stay the proceedings until either of the conditions in sub-section (5) is met.
>
> > (5) Those conditions are:
>
> > (a) that a determination of the Commissioner under section 45 with respect to the data in question takes effect, or
> > (b) in a case where the proceedings were stayed on the making of a claim, that the claim is withdrawn."

Under this provision, if the data controller is able to claim that the processing in question is carried out with a view to publication for the first time by that controller, the power of the court to deal with the case is stayed until an external determination is made on whether the exemption applies. A Commissioner's determination under s.45 may only be made to the effect that personal data are not being processed only for the special purposes, or are not being processed with a view to publication by any person of any journalistic, literary or artistic material which has not previously been published by the data controller. The Commissioner may therefore lift the stay on the court proceedings where he is able to make a determination to that effect but otherwise the stay will continue to apply. The matter however does not end there. Where the Commissioner has made such a determination the data controller may appeal to the Information Tribunal against the determination. This gives those who process for the special purposes a potent weapon to resist any interference with publication on data protection grounds.

17–21 It is not apparent why Parliament decided that the determination has to be made by the Commissioner. It would be far simpler for the courts to make appropriate determinations as to whether the processing was being carried out for the special purposes. The court seized of the matter would be able to hear witnesses on the claim and cross-examination on the issue. The Commissioner is not in a position to do this.

It could be suggested that, as the Commissioner has the power to serve a "special information notice" under s.44 of the Act in relation to the special purposes, in which he may require the data controller to furnish him with information for the purpose of ascertaining whether the personal data are being processed only for the special purposes, or whether they are being processed with a view to the publication by any person of any journalistic, literary or artistic material which has not previously been published by the data controller, he has an advantage over the courts in making such a decision. However, a special information notice is limited under s.44. The Commissioner may only serve one where he has received a request by a data subject to consider any particular processing or where he has reasonable grounds for suspecting, in a case in which the data controller has made a claim under s.32 in any proceedings, that the personal data to which the proceedings relate are not being processed only for the special purposes or are not being processed with a view to the publication by any person of any journalistic, literary or artistic material which has not previously been published by the data controller.

The effect of this is to place the Commissioner in a difficult position. He may only serve a s.44 notice to enable him to make a determination under s.45 where he has reasonable grounds for suspecting that the claim made by the data controller is not made out, however the data controller may make the claim giving no evidence of grounds. The Commissioner therefore faces an evidential burden before he can even seek information from the data controller whereas the data controller may assert the exemption before a court without showing any grounds. The effect appears to be to allow the case to be prolonged and to make it particularly difficult for an individual to bring any proceedings.

However, eventually publication must take place. The Commissioner will then be able to make the s.45 determination and a court will be able to consider the substantive claim. At that stage the court will have to assess whether the grounds in s.32(1)(b) and (c) were made out at the time the processing took place.

POWERS OF THE COMMISSIONER

17–22 These have been referred to above. There are special provisions affecting the Commissioner's powers to deal with personal data processed for the special purposes.

Special information notices

17–23 A special information notice is served under s.44. It can only be served where one of two conditions applies: either the Commissioner has received a request for an assessment under s.42 or, as explained above, a stay has been claimed under s.32 in court proceedings brought against a data controller. In the case of a s.32 claim the Commissioner can only serve the notice where he has reasonable grounds for suspecting that either the data are not being processed for the special purposes or they are not being processed with a view to publication of material which has not been published previously. He must state his grounds for his suspicions in the notice. The notice is limited to ascertaining whether the grounds for a s.32 claim are made out, that is whether the data are being processed only for the special purposes with a view to first publication. The recipient of such a notice may appeal to the Tribunal. The usual provisions as to cases of urgency apply.

Information notices

17–24 Section 46(3) provides that the Commissioner cannot serve a standard information notice under s.43 with respect to the special purposes unless he has first made a s.45 determination which has taken effect. This means that before the Commissioner can even require any information from a controller about data processed for the special purposes, other than the specific information dealt with by a special information notice, he has to go through a formal process of determining that the exemption could not be claimed and allow for an appeal against that determination.

In the case of either a special information notice or ordinary information notice, if the controller appeals the information need not be furnished pending the determination or withdrawal of the appeal.

Enforcement notices

17–25 Section 46 provides that the Commissioner may not serve an enforcement notice on a data controller with respect to the processing of personal data for the special purposes unless he has made a s.45(1) determination and the court has granted leave for the notice to be served. This restriction applies even after publication of the material in question.

The relevant court will be the county court or High Court in England and Wales or a Sheriff Court in Scotland. Where the Commissioner makes an application for leave to serve a notice the court shall not grant leave unless it is satisfied that the Commissioner has reason to suspect a contravention of the Principles which is of substantial public importance and, except where the case is one of urgency, that the data controller had been given notice in accordance with the rules of court of the application for leave.

17–26 It is not clear, and no assistance is given in the text, as to what constitutes substantial public importance in relation to the contravention of the Data Protection

Principles, nor is it clear whether it differs from public interest or if so how. The Commissioner must have grounds to suspect the contravention of the Principles and that contravention must be of substantial public importance. The Commissioner must then satisfy the court that he has reasons for this view. It is not clear whether the Commissioner has to satisfy the court that the matters actually are of substantial public importance or simply that the Commissioner reasonably believes that they are.

It could be suggested that examples of issues of particular public importance would be where sensitive data are alleged to have been misused or where processing has been unlawful or where particularly damaging allegations or inaccurate statements have been made about a data subject.

Particular weight may be attached to a breach of the right to private and family life. It could be argued that there is a particular public importance that the Convention rights, as fundamental or higher order rights, be upheld by the courts. On this basis almost any breach of the right to private life could be the basis for enforcement action. The contrary argument would be that the right to freedom of speech is also a fundamental right which must be upheld by the courts. The task for the court is to balance the competing rights in any particular case. When the Commissioner serves an enforcement notice that notice may also be appealed to the Information Tribunal.

The relevant time

17–27   It is not clear from s.32(4) how the relevant time is crystallised. It appears that the controller must assert his claim in court proceedings, asserting also the date and time of the relevant processing in order to allow the 24-hour countdown. The application presumably will be to the court for a stay, supported by an affidavit.

ASSISTANCE OF THE COMMISSIONER

17–28   Section 53 provides that an individual who brings proceedings for individual rights which relate to personal data processed for the special purposes may seek assistance from the Information Commissioner. When the Commissioner receives an application for assistance he must consider it and decide whether and to what extent to grant it but he can only grant the application for assistance if in his opinion the case involves a matter of substantial public importance. It will be noted that this is the same test which is applied in s.46(2)(a) in respect of an application for leave to the court to take proceedings by enforcement action. Proceedings need not actually be in train, but may include prospective proceedings. If the Commissioner decides to provide assistance he must notify the applicant. If he decides not to provide assistance he must also notify the applicant of that decision and he may provide reasons for his decisions but is under no obligation to do so.

A matter of substantial public importance would appear to denote some degree of public interest or benefit to the public at large or of societal values whether of justice, fairness, privacy or otherwise. The comments above in respect of the relevance of Convention rights will be applicable here also. These provisions are supplemented by Sch.10, which provides that the Commissioner must ensure that the person against whom proceedings are commenced is informed that assistance will be provided in those proceedings. Schedule 10 also provides that assistance may include making arrangements for the Commissioner to bear the cost of legal advice or assistance or representation or assistance in the proceedings or steps preliminary or incidental to the proceedings.

The reasoning behind the inclusion of this provision may be to ensure that the individual faced by the procedural claims under s.32(4) can obtain a fair hearing in compliance with Art.6 of the Human Rights Convention. Legal aid is not available for cases under the Data Protection Act. In the absence of some form of support for litigants it might be argued that the complexity of the provisions means there is an "inequality of arms" between the respondent (which will most commonly be a media organisation) and the individual who seeks to assert his individual rights.

Where assistance is provided it shall include an agreement to indemnify the applicant for costs arising by virtue of any order, subject to any exceptions specified in the notification to the individual.

PRACTICAL TOOLS

Example of the application of the special procedures applicable before publication—journalistic purposes

17–29   Note: This case study differs from others in the book as it does not analyse the legal issues. It is included to illustrate how the special provisions could apply in a practical situation.

A young woman, Anna Brown (AB), was the subject of an article in the *Weekly Wonder Magazine* (WWM) last year. The article dealt with her relationship with her father, who is now deceased. It alleged she had behaved extremely badly to him in his dying years and had extorted money from him in his final illness. AB is suing the WWM for defamation in respect of the article about her.

She learns from friends that a reporter with the WWM, one David Edwards (DE), has been making inquiries about her relationship with her elderly mother-in-law. AB suspects that DE is making the inquiries for the purposes of defending the defamation proceedings against the WWM although the reason he has given for the inquiries is that he is researching for another story about AB.

AB makes a subject access request to WWM under s.7 of the Act. WWM refuses to respond to her request so AB asks the Commissioner to make an assessment under s.42 as to whether WWM is complying with Principle 6 (personal data shall be processed in accordance with the rights of data subjects under this Act). At the same time she makes an application to the county court for an order under s.7(9) that the WWM provide subject access to any personal data held about her.

The Commissioner makes further inquiries of both AB and of WWM. He is informed by WWM that the inquiries about AB were made, and the resulting data are held, with a view to the publication of material not previously published about AB. AB on the other hand informs the Commissioner of her suspicions that the inquiries are not being made in connection with a further article but in connection with the defamation proceedings. The Commissioner considers whether it would be appropriate to serve a special information notice under s.44. However, before a decision on that is made the proceedings under s.7(9) are listed for trial. At that stage in the proceedings the WWM serves an affidavit from the editor which states that all the personal data held about AB are being processed for the purpose of journalism with a view to the publication of material which has not previously been published by it.

17–30   AB believes that most of the data WWM holds are data that were obtained and used in the publication of the previous article. As a result of some comments made by the reporter DE during his conversations with her friends she suspects WWM does not want to publish the material or at least that is not its primary purpose and in fact it wishes to use the information in the defamation proceedings.

The court has no option but to stay the proceedings and AB presses the Commissioner to make a determination relating to the data held by the WWM. After considering the information available the Commissioner decides that it throws reasonable doubt on the assertions of the WWM. He serves a special information notice on the WWM under s.44(1) stating his grounds for suspecting that the data are not being processed only for the journalistic purposes with a view to first publication. In the notice he asks a series of detailed questions about the data held, the purposes for which they may be used and the publication plans of the WWM.

On receipt of the special information notice the WWM appeals against it to the Information Tribunal and the case goes to a contested hearing. It is several months before the hearing but finally, after a two-day hearing before the Tribunal, it rules that the WWM must respond to the special information notice and allows it 28 days to do so. The WWM decides not to appeal the Tribunal decision but to respond to the notice.

The Commissioner considers the response to be equivocal. In the response the WWM states that the data held on AB are being used to prepare for its defence in the defamation proceedings and that much of the data was previously published but that the information is also being held for the purpose of the publication of a second piece to come out after the conclusion of the defamation proceedings. This planned article will contain additional material which has not previously been published.

The Commissioner decides that in those circumstances the WWM cannot claim the s.32 stay, certainly not for all the data held, and makes a determination under s.45 that the personal data are not being processed only for the purposes of journalism. He serves notice of the determination on the WWM which appeals the determination to the Information Tribunal. It takes some months for the matters to come to hearing; however after a three-day hearing before the Tribunal the Tribunal agrees with the Commissioner's view and upholds the determination.

The Commissioner then considers whether enforcement action is appropriate and decides that he should serve an enforcement notice to require the WWM to give AB access to the data. Before he can do so he must seek permission of the court under s.46. He serves notice on the WWM under s.46(2)(b) that he intends to apply to the court for leave to serve an enforcement notice and makes his court application under s.46(1)(b). The Commissioner argues that the failure to give subject access on the grounds cited by WWM raises an issue of substantial public importance which justifies the court giving leave for service of the notice. The application is contested by WWM and after some months it comes to hearing. After a contested hearing lasting two days the court decides to give leave and the Commissioner serves his enforcement notice under s.40 for failure to give subject access to AB. WWM appeals the enforcement notice to the Information Tribunal on the substantive grounds in s.32(1) that even though the processing is not taking place only for the special purposes eventual publication is still one of the purposes of the processing; it is in the public interest that the article be published and if subject access is given to AB publication will become impossible. It takes some months for the matter to come to a hearing and the contested proceedings last four days. The Tribunal upholds the enforcement notice and orders subject access be given to AB.

Clearly there could be further appeals to higher courts at any stage but even assuming there are no such further appeals it will have taken four contested hearings and probably several years of litigation to secure AB's subject access rights. AB discontinues her action in the court.

ADDITIONAL INFORMATION

Derivations

17–31 • Directive 95/46 (See App.B):

    (a) Art.9
    (b) Recitals 17, 37.

• Council of Europe Convention of January 28, 1981 for the Protection of Individuals with regard to automatic processing of Personal Data: Art.9 (exceptions and restrictions).

• Organisation for Economic Co-operation and Development Guidelines: Annex, Part One (scope of guidelines).

• European Convention for the protection of Human Rights and Fundamental Freedoms: Art.10 (freedom of expression).

Hansard references

17–32 Vol.586, No.110, col.90, Lords Grand Committee, February 25, 1998
Meaning of publishing sufficient to include any media

ibid., cols 95–97
Effect of the exemption

ibid., col.99
Codes to be designated

ibid., col.103
Accuracy exemption

Vol.587, No.127, cols 1115–1117, Lords Third Reading, March 24, 1998
Extent of exemption and relation with ECHR

Commons Standing Committee D, May 12, 1998, cols 53–55
Definition of the special purposes

Commons Standing Committee D, May 21, cols 211–229
Effect of exemption

Commons Standing Committee D, June 2, 1998, col.249
Special information notices

Commons Standing Committee D, June 4, 1998, cols 323, 324
Effect of information notice on issue of warrants.

CHAPTER 18

Research

INTRODUCTION

18–01   Research which entails the use of personal data must comply with the Act. Some of the standards required by the Act and set out in the Data Protection Principles present difficulties in the context of research. For example the requirements that individuals should be told of the potential uses of personal data at the time of collection, that data should only be used for the purposes for which they were collected, or compatible purposes, and only retained for so long as is necessary to fulfill those purposes may be difficult to meet. The Act includes only limited exemptions for research so researchers need to understand and be able to apply the Principles.

Practical problems arise in applying the Principles to the use of personal data for research because:

(a) researchers may wish to use personal data which were originally collected or generated for other purposes when no one was aware of the potential use for research; for example medical researchers may wish to refer to records of childhood illnesses or use samples taken for clinical rather than research purposes;

(b) researchers may wish to re-use material or information originally collected for a limited or different research purpose, for example research into a specific illness;

(c) the information which may be useful for research may not be needed for the primary purpose of collection, for example the investigation of a road traffic accident may not require the age of the driver to be available but it may be useful information for researchers investigating patterns of road accidents;

(d) researchers may wish to retain and use data long after the primary use for which the data were collected has ceased, for example a researcher into housing needs and provision may wish to access tenancy records long after the tenants have moved away or a house been sold;

(e) it may be difficult for researchers to provide subject access to personal data.

Personal data are increasingly important in carrying out research and researchers need to be sure that they are complying with all aspects of the law, relevant ethical standards and professional guidance. The law is not just found in the data protection standards.

When dealing with personal information researchers must also consider the Human Rights Act 1998 and the law of confidence.

Human Rights Act 1998

18–02   In Ch.2, above the impact of the right to respect for private and family life, home and correspondence under the Human Rights Act is explained. This right may also impact upon research.

The law of confidence

18–03   Principle 1 requires that all personal data be processed "lawfully". Thus, in considering Principle 1, other legal standards have to be considered. In the context of much research the law of confidence is relevant. In Ch.2, above the law of confidence as it impacts on personal information is examined and in Ch.5, above the interface with Principle 1 is explained.

Ethical and professional standards

18–04   Because Principle 1 also requires that personal data be processed "fairly" relevant standards of fairness have to be considered when it is applied. Ethical and profession standards will therefore be regarded as part of the obligations in Principle 1.

Where personal data are used for research the researcher should look at all these matters.

Dealing with this range of legal and ethical standards is not always easy. In addition to uncertainties about data protection, researchers, and those charged with making decisions on the use of personal data in the research area, such as members of ethics committees, have, in the past, faced uncertainty over the impact of the Human Rights Act 1998 and the law of confidence. The difficulties faced by the research community were emphasised in a 2006 report from the Academy of Medical Sciences; *Personal data for Public Good: using health information in medical research* which recommended, among other proposals, that consent should cease to be regarded as the basis for the use of personal data in research.

The use of records relating to individuals—general issues

18–05   Research may be records-based. The nature and extent of the records available for possible research have increased dramatically over the last 50 years but society is still working towards a satisfactory way of resolving the tensions between research needs and individual autonomy in respect of such records. Many records are held by the state as a result of the provision of care at the public expense or the exercise of policing functions. The most striking examples are patient records held by the NHS, records held in the national DNA database (NDNAD) and fingerprint databases held by the police. The use of NHS records has given rise to controversy in the past. The government has acted to resolve some of the problems by legislation (dealt with later in this chapter) but the issues remain controversial. There is a move among the research and academic communities to find ways to free databases for use by researchers.[1]

---

[1] See the report *Personal Data for Public Good: using health information in medical research* by the Academy of Medical Sciences, January 2006.

Genetic material

18–06   Genetic material gives rise to particular concern. The UK now has the largest forensic DNA database in the world.[2] Samples are taken from those who are arrested and from volunteers. The samples from those who are arrested are retained even if no legal action is taken against them or they are acquitted.[3] Without clear restrictions on the use of such material the ever-increasing databanks will inevitably be attractive to researchers.

In 2002 the Human Genetics Commission published a major report into the storage and use of personal genetic information, "Inside Information—Balancing Interests in the Use of Personal Genetic Data". This contained a number of recommendations which would impose clear limits on the uses of genetic information without real consent including restrictions on use by employers, ring-fencing of research databases so they could not be accessed for other purposes, independent oversight of genetic databases and the creation of a criminal offence for testing or access without consent for non-medical purposes. Not all of the recommendations have been taken forward at the time of writing and the difficult issues raised by bio-information continue to give rise to concerns.[4] It has however become an offence to take a DNA sample without consent save for statutory medical or criminal investigative purposes under the Human Tissue Act 2004 which came into effect in September 2006.

Historical records

18–07   Difficult questions are also raised by the fact that the Data Protection Act is only concerned with the living and there is no provision to protect the privacy of the dead. Once, when most ordinary people died, the record of their lives died with them. For some there was an inscription on a tombstone or a life event recorded in a parish register; sometimes records of individual lives survived but these were unusual and fragmented. This is no longer the case. The most insignificant of us will leave behind a personal historical record more complete than those left by the emperors of the past. The histories of our jobs, pensions, children, health, DNA, finances will outlive us in one way and another. They may also live on to have an effect on our descendants.

The DPA only applies to personal data about living individuals but should it, or can it already, be used to give us a say in what happens to those records after death? Should individuals be entitled to chose obscurity in death?[5] While a doctor may be bound by an ethical obligation to keep patient information confidential after the patient dies the more general rights to privacy protected by the Data Protection Act will no longer apply. At least one step has been taken in the direction of providing such protection; in the Freedom of Information (Scotland) Act 2002 the exemption for personal privacy extends to the medical records of a deceased person. In a case decided by the Information Commissioner under the Freedom of Information Act 2000 the Commissioner ruled that

---

[2] Home Office *DNA Expansion programme 2000–2005; Reporting Achievement* (2005).
[3] *R. v Chief Constable of South Yorkshire Police Ex p. LS R v Chief Constable of South Yorkshire Police Ex p. Marper* [2004] UKHL 39.
[4] See *Forensic Use of bioinformation: ethical issues*, Consultation Paper, Nuffield Council on Bioethics, January 2007.
[5] In Ch.12, above the question of whether the individual right to object to processing could be used to require post-humorous privacy is considered briefly.

the medical records of a deceased individual did not have to be disclosed and could still be regarded as subject to an obligation of confidence which remained binding on the public authority.[6]

Records-based research

18–08 Where research is records-based the researcher will usually not meet the individual whose record he or she peruses. Some of those who are the subject of records may be dead (in which case the Act will no longer be applicable) but, unless the researcher is dealing with records which are at least over a century old, there can be no certainty that all of the individuals on a database are dead. Research may involve samples or tissue. This may be linked to records identifying individuals or may in itself be sufficient to identify unique individuals.

While in some cases material can be anonymised, in other cases this is not possible, for example, where the research seeks to check correlations between life incidents which are removed in time from one another the identity of the individual may be necessary to ensure that the correct records are matched. Such data will be personal data under the Act.

The 1998 Act has introduced stricter controls over the use of personal data than those previously in force. The transitional reliefs have now expired.[7] This chapter describes the exemptions in the Act which deal with research in the context of the broader issues.

SUMMARY OF MAIN POINTS

18–09   (a) Research is broadly defined in the Act and includes statistical and historical studies.

(b) The use of personal data for research is subject to the Principles which involve:

    (i) the detailed rules governing, fairness, lawfulness and the provision of notice to individuals;

    (ii) the need to show a legal justification for any processing and the more stringent rules for sensitive data;

    (iii) the restriction on the uses that may be made of personal data to those for which they were collected or those compatible with the purposes of collection;

    (iv) the quality standards and limitations on retention;

    (v) the rights of individuals;

    (vi) the security requirements;

    (vii) the ban on overseas transfers.

(c) There are two "safeguard conditions" which researchers can apply. These are that:

    (i) the research must not be used to make decisions about the individuals to whom the data relate; and

---

[6] Decision of the Information Commissioner re: *Epsom and St Helier University NHS Trust.*
[7] See Ch.1, above for a brief analysis of the remaining transitional exemptions.

(ii) the processing must not cause substantial damage or distress to the individuals whose data are utilised in the research.

(d) If the safeguard conditions are met personal data may be used for research even if they were not originally collected for a research purpose.

(e) If the safeguard conditions are met personal data may be retained indefinitely for the purposes of research.

(f) If the results of the research are anonymised and the safeguard conditions are met the individual data subject may be refused access to the data.

(g) These exemptions can apply to any research, whether carried out in the public or private sector, whether commercial or academic, as long as the safeguard conditions are met.

(h) The use of data held prior to October 1998 can continue for research without having to comply with the Act in full, subject to fulfilling the safeguard conditions.

It follows that researchers can use personal data for research purposes even if the individual has not been told of that use and retain the data indefinitely even if to do so breaches the Principles as long as the research fulfills all the necessary safeguard conditions for these exemptions. However, there are no exemptions from the requirement that data controllers have a legitimate basis for processing personal data or from the fair obtaining and processing codes.[8] It should be noted that there are only limited grounds for the processing of sensitive personal data for the purposes of medical and other research. Sensitive personal data are defined in s.2 of the Act as data concerned with:

- racial or ethnic origin;
- political opinions;
- religious or similar beliefs;
- trade union membership;
- physical or mental health or condition;
- sexual life;
- the commission or alleged commission of any offence or any criminal proceedings.

BACKGROUND

Recommendations R(83)10 and R(97)18

18–10 The tension between the needs of the research community for information and moves by international bodies to protect personal data led to an early focus on this

---

[8] See Chs 5–7, above for the principles.

area among data protectors. Treaty 108 specifically refers to the use of data for research, and in 1983 the Council of Europe gave further guidance to signatory states on the use of personal data for research in Recommendation R(83)10. This has been replaced by the later Recommendation R(97)18 but the description of the issues remains applicable today.

In the Explanatory Memorandum to R (83)10 the problems are clearly explained in the following terms:

"Personal data frequently play an important, if not vital, role in research. Sociological studies, with their questionnaires and interviews, are probably the best-known example of interest in personal data, but there are many others. Special studies into cancer incidence or multiple births also demonstrate how greatly epidemiology, for instance, depends on access to named data which can be used for research based on the case histories of individuals. The same is true of psychology and educational research. Thus disciplines may vary but broad areas of research still require information about identifiable persons.

For a long time no particular justification for the use of personal data was necessary. The mere fact that data were needed for research was sufficient, and the few rare criticisms were met by reference to codes of professional ethics. Since the beginning of the 1970s, however, the situation has begun to change as a result of developments in data protection legislation in several member countries. The need for rules stipulating the conditions under which personal data may be collected, stored, transmitted or used in any form is coming to be recognised openly in legislation.

Research is bound by the same fundamental rules as any other activity involving the use of personal data. The laws on data protection do not recognise privilege. They may well adapt their requirements to the particular structure and specific objects of the information process, but they do not allow any exception to the duty to observe the restrictive principles which they lay down.

Thus data protection legislation may be clear in its attitude. The consequences are no less so. With or without data protection longitudinal studies on child development demand knowledge of a minimum of personal data. The aetiology of heart diseases and the efficiency of certain forms of treatment cannot be understood without access to information on the behaviour of patients. Any critical analysis of social policy rests largely on the availability of micro-data. No one can seriously claim that research in any of these cases should be abandoned on grounds of data protection."

The Recommendation R(83)(10) sets out a general approach to the use of personal data for research based on the principle of "functional separation". Broadly, exemptions from the standards required by data protection are acceptable as long as the data are not used to make decisions about, or take actions which may affect, the individual. A separate Recommendation dealt specifically with the uses of medical data banks.[9]

On September 30, 1997 the Committee of Ministers adopted a further Recommendation R(97)18 concerning the protection of personal data collected and processed for

---

[9] Recommendation R(81)1 replaced by R(97)5.

statistical purposes. The revised Recommendation was considered necessary in the light of the progress which has been made in statistical methods and information technology since 1983.

The revised Recommendation closely reflects the provisions of the Directive.[10] These are also of course reflected in the Data Protection Act 1998. It contains detailed rules governing the fair collection of data and covers questions of transborder data flows and lawfulness of processing which are set out in the Principles, as described in para.18–09, above. It also strengthens the exhortations to anonymise personal data as soon as it is no longer necessary to retain them in an identifiable form.

Directive 95/46

18–11 The Directive deals with the tension between the needs of research and the requirements of data protection in similar ways to Recommendation R(83)10, although in considerably less detail. Article 6 contains derogations for the processing of personal data for historical, statistical or scientific purposes which provide that such uses shall not be regarded as incompatible with the original purpose of collection of the data, and that data may be kept for longer periods than required for the purposes for which they were collected, provided that Member States provide sufficient safeguards. There are further provisions to allow for exemption from providing information where personal data are passed on for the purposes of research and from the right of subject access.

Despite these provisions for derogations and exemptions compliance with the following elements of the Directive gives rise to some difficulties for researchers:

(a) the right of individuals to know of the use of personal data for research purposes;

(b) the right of individuals to consent or object to the use of personal data for research purposes;

(c) the right of individuals to prevent the use of personal data for research purposes in an appropriate case;

(d) the right to have records which are used for research restricted in the extent of disclosures made from them and to have adequate security provided to them.

CURRENT ISSUES

18–12 Despite the efforts to provide protection for the privacy of individuals in the face of data-hungry research, significant problems still arise from this area. Perhaps the best known is the controversy over the Icelandic databank. Iceland has a small population which has been largely untouched by immigration. Icelanders have a passion for genealogy and the records available allow family ties to be traced back through recorded history. Health care has been provided by the State since early last century. The combination of this material means that Iceland

---

[10] Dir.95/46.

presents a wealth of material which can be mined for genetic research. In 1998 the Icelandic Parliament passed the Health Sector Database Act. The Act allowed the Ministry of Health to grant a licence to create an electronic database. The Act passed the Icelandic Parliament on December 17, 1998 by a slim margin.[11] It did not require consent from individual data subjects for the research to be carried out on genetic data relating to them. The Act is based on the presumed "consent" of individual Icelanders. In 2000 the Ministry then granted the licence to a private company called deCODE. The licence permitted deCODE to cross-reference the data on medical records with genetic data collected on individual Icelanders and genealogical data. The grant provoked fierce controversy. The pressure group Mannvernd— (which means "human protection") successfully campaigned for Icelanders to have the right to opt-out of inclusion in the database.[12] However the opt-out was only applicable to living data subjects . A case was then brought by one of the Mannvernd supporters, Ragnhildur Gudmundsdottir, on behalf of her deceased father objecting to the inclusion of data relating to him in the database. She was successful in her claim and in November 2003 the Icelandic Supreme Court ruled that she had the right to object as information about her could be inferred from the information about the parent.

MEDICAL RESEARCH

UK developments in the use of personal data in the NHS

18–13   In the United Kingdom there has been a significant development in the attitude of the Government to the use of personal data for medical purposes, including research. This is attributable, in part at least, to the Alder Hey Inquiry which followed the disclosure of information about the widespread removal and retention of organs, ostensibly for future research, without the full knowledge or consent of the next of kin[13] and the similar problems experienced in Bristol which resulted in the passage of the Human Tissues Act.2004. The Office of the Information Commissioner had been critical of the approach taken to the use of patient information in the NHS for research and other non-treatment purposes for some years. In 2000 the General Medical Council (GMC) revised its 1995 guidance on confidentiality[14] and in doing so advised a more restrictive view on the use of data for research by clinicians.[15] The current Guidance to doctors was issued in 2006.[16] It advises that express consent is usually needed before the disclosure of identifiable information for purposes such as research and epidemiology. If the patient withholds consent, or consent cannot be obtained then disclosures may only be made where they are required by law or can be justified in the public interest or are covered by a regulation made under s.60 of the Health and Social Care Act 2001.

---

[11] Reported in the *Sunday Times*.
[12] See article at *http://www.CIO.com*, *"Privacy v Progress"* by Stephanie Overby.
[13] Report of the *Royal Liverpool Hospital Inquiry* (January 30, 2001).
[14] GMC, *Duties of a Doctor: Confidentiality* (1995).
[15] GMC, *Confidentiality: Protecting and Providing Information* (September 2000).
[16] GMC, *Confidentiality: Protecting and Providing Information* (September 2000).

Human Rights Act 1998

18–14 The collection, storage, use and disclosure of medical information by the NHS, and probably private sector health providers as well, clearly engages Art.8 of the Convention. Where the information is used in connection with the provision of care the use will be justified by the consent which has been given to treatment, however for all other uses and disclosures of information the NHS should be able to point to either a full and informed consent given by the patient or a justification which fulfills the three requirements of Art.8(2). They are a legal basis, justification in one of the specified list of interests and a proportional response. One of the problems which may arise where research is carried out in reliance on consent is the difficulty of obtaining the consent of those without capacity or who lose of mental capacity part way through the research project. This has been addressed in the Mental Capacity Act 2005 ss.30–34 and Mental Capacity Act 2005 (Loss of Capacity during Research Project) (England) Regulations 2007.[16a]

Guidance

18–15 In November 2003 the Department of Health issued its NHS Code of Practice on Confidentiality which followed a wide consultation and was endorsed by the Information Commissioner, the General Medical Council (GMC) and the British Medical Association (BMA).

The Code of Practice was the end product of a project to address health information in the wider context of the "Connecting for Health" programme. In December 2001 the Department of Health issued a policy document: "Building the Information Core—Protecting and Using Confidential Patient Information: A strategy for the NHS". The document quoted the Minister for Health speaking to the Commons Committee:

> "Informed consent is crucial to the Government's view of how a modern NHS should work. We simply cannot move to a patient centred service if patients are not informed and consenting participants in the services they receive.
>
> But we all know too well that this is not the way the NHS operates at the moment. Much of what is done in the NHS relies upon implied consent. In some cases this is appropriate, for example sharing information within a hospital to ensure a patient receives appropriate care, but in other cases the definition of implied consent is pushed too far."

The Code provides guidance to NHS bodies and related bodies on confidentiality issues. It states that medical research is not part of the provision of healthcare, although closely related, and that the informed consent of the patient should generally be the basis of the use of personal data in research. There is therefore a consensus among those advising researchers in the area of medical research on the issue of informed consent. The emphasis on the need for consent has however caused significant problems for researchers in accessing data for epidemiological research and led in its turn to pressure from parts of the academic and research community for there to be less emphasis on consent and more on the public interest benefits of research.[17]

[16a] SI 2007/679.
[17] See the report referenced at n.1, above.

Although the Government may have intended the provisions in the Health and Social Care Act 2001 to provide a way of dealing with the tension between privacy and research, until consents become the norm the view of many researchers is that it has not done so.

HEALTH AND SOCIAL CARE ACT 2001 s.60

18–16   Under s.60 the Secretary of State may make regulations to:

"... make such provision for and in connection with requiring or regulating the processing of prescribed patient information for medical purposes as he considers necessary or expedient—

(a) in the interests of improving patient care, or
(b) in the public interest."

The regulations may not regulate the processing of personal data for the provision of care, and cannot override the DPA. Section 61 provides for the establishment of a Patient Information Advisory Group to advise on the content of the regulations and other matters concerned with patient information. The regulations may contain provisions dealing with both confidential and non-confidential patient material and may authorise disclosures to prescribed persons subject to safeguards and conditions. Where disclosures are made in accordance with such authorisations they are taken to be lawful. Thus the regulations provide a basis in law for disclosures without the consent of the patient, including disclosures for research purposes.

The Health Service (Control of Patient Information) Regulations 2002[18]

18–17   The Regulations came into effect on June 1, 2002. The Regulations permit the processing of confidential medical information in certain circumstances subject to the condition that the processing is carried out by a health professional or person who owes an equivalent obligation of confidence and is limited to that necessary to achieve the purpose and in particular that:

- personally identifying particulars are removed as far as possible;

- access to the information is restricted to properly trained employees on a need-to-know basis;

- the information is held securely; and

- there is an annual review of the necessity of holding the information.

The responsible body must also make available information about compliance with the standards on request.[19]

18–18   The Regulations apply to all medical information, not merely those categories of information that are subject to the DPA 1998, but the provisions clearly reflect

---

[18] S1 2002/1438.
[19] S1 2002/1438 reg.7.

the requirements of the DPA. The definitions of health professional and processing are the same as in the DPA. The Regulations do not replace the requirement to have a ground for processing sensitive data and are worded so as to ensure conformity with the grounds. However they will, in effect, provide for exemption from the remainder of Principle 1 of Sch.1 to the DPA. The processing will not involve a breach of confidence, because reg.4 provides that there will be no breach of confidence where patient information is processed in accordance with the Regulations. It will also have a basis in law which will go part way to satisfying the requirements of Art.8. If the Secretary of State exercises his powers under Art.4 of reg.2(4) the fair processing, or collection notice, otherwise required under para.2(1)(b) of Sch.1, will not have to be provided as it will be exempt by virtue of reg.3(2) of The Data Protection (Conditions under Paragraph 3 of Part II of Schedule 1) Order 2000. However the removal of this safeguard might lead to arguments about proportionality under the HRA and therefore risk an argument that the process still does not satisfy Art.8. This may prove a difficult point to resolve.

18–19 The Regulations permit the processing of confidential patient information about patients referred for the diagnosis or treatment of neoplasia ("the cancer registries") for medical purposes which includes research approved by research ethics committees, by approved and authorised persons where the Secretary of State considers it necessary in the public interest.[20] In respect of patients with other conditions, confidential patient information may be processed with the approval of the Secretary of State:

- to anonymise or pseudonymise identifiable information;

- to identify geographical locations which may be relevant for research purposes;

- to identify and contact patients to approach them for consent;

- to link or validate data from more than one source; or

- for quality audit of the provision of healthcare.

Where the processing is for medical research the research must also be approved by an ethics committee.[21]

The Patient Information Advisory Group (PIAG) advises the Secretary of State on the grant of approvals and considers applications from organisations:

"for support to obtain patient identifiable data without consent of the patients concerned to carry out research and other activities under section 60 of the Health and Social Care Act."

The approvals are meant to be an interim measure until consent is available and have to be reviewed annually. The PIAG publishes annual reports on its work and a list of

---

[20] *ibid.* reg.2.
[21] *ibid.* reg.5 and Sch.1.

databases for which approval is required, among these are the United Kingdom Association of Cancer Registries (UKACR). Cancer registries are responsible for the compilation of national registers of cancer sufferers. These are databases on which clinicians register information about patients diagnosed as suffering from particular cancers. The databases are non-statutory. They are maintained by the cancer charities. The functions of the cancer registries include monitoring trends, evaluating prevention and treatment and investigating causes. Analysis of the registers, which have been kept since 1971, can show survival rates for different cancers in different parts of the country and allow comparison with treatment results in other countries.

In the absence of authorisation under the regulations, the disclosure of the information on to the register without individual consent could constitute a breach of the obligation of confidence owed to the patient. In the past it appears that clinicians have often not informed patients that their details will be registered on the databases, let alone obtained consent. In making the submission for authorisation the UKACR expressed concerns that patients may object and refuse to be registered, with resulting degradation in the quality of the data or, if they discover that they have been registered without consent, may seek to be removed from the registers.

After considering the UKACR submission the PIAG expressed reservations regarding the poor communication with patients about the work of the registries and the failures to disclose information to patients; the disclosure of information from the registers to third parties and the absence of appropriate retention and disposal policies for the data, all of which issues it said should be addressed by the registries. Subject to those caveats however it recommended that disclosure of patient data to the registries be authorised.

RESEARCH PURPOSES

Data controller

18–20   The definition of a data controller is covered in Ch.3, above. In any research context it is important to ascertain the identity of the data controller. In most cases it will be the academic institution but it may be the funding organisation or the head of the research team. In all cases responsibility for compliance with the DPA will rest with the data controller.

Definitions

18–21   The exemptions apply to personal data used for "research purposes". Section 33 states that "'Research purposes' include statistical or historical purposes". None of these terms is further defined. In the OED research is defined as:

> "The act of searching (closely and carefully); an investigation directed to the discovery of some fact by careful study of a subject; a course of critical or scientific inquiry."

Statistical purposes are presumably aimed at the study of or the production of statistics. Historical purposes could reasonably be regarded as covering historical studies. However, these are only specific elements covered by the definition and research purposes may be substantially wider than these two. As the exemption does not depend solely on fulfilling the definition of research but is only triggered where a further set of conditions apply, it does not appear to be particularly material that the definition of research is a broad one. Research may thus be purely academic or "blue sky" research or targeted commercial research or anything in between. In the area of medical research it will cover epidemiological studies and clinical studies. However, research will only qualify for one or more of the exemptions if it fulfils the relevant safeguard conditions. These vary with the particular exemption involved.

Permitted disclosures

18–22 Section 33(5) sets out a list of disclosures that may be made from personal data without risking the loss of any of the research exemptions. These cover:

(a) disclosure to any other person for research purposes only;

(b) disclosure to the data subject or to a person acting on his behalf;

(c) disclosure at the request of a data subject or someone acting on his behalf or with his consent;

(d) disclosure where the person making the disclosure has reasonable grounds for believing it falls within one of the above.

EFFECT OF THE ACT ON RESEARCH

18–23 Three provisions of the 1998 Act appear to have most impact on the use of data for research.

Grounds for legitimate processing

18–24 The use of data for research is not of itself a legitimising ground for processing. The two grounds which might be expected to be relied upon by researchers are Ground 1—that the data subject has consented to the processing, and Ground 6—that the processing is necessary for the purposes of legitimate interests pursued by the data controller or by the third party or third parties to whom the data are disclosed, except where the processing is unwarranted in any particular case by reason of prejudice to the rights and freedoms or legitimate interests of the data subject. In the case of research required by law, for example for pharmaco-vigilance Ground 3 may be relevant—that the processing is necessary for compliance with any legal obligation to which the data controller is subject, other than an obligation imposed by a contract.

Grounds for holding sensitive personal data

18–25 Schedule 3 contains a limited provision in Ground 8 for sensitive personal data to be processed for medical research purposes. Sensitive data may be processed for medical research under Ground 8 where:

"(1) The processing is necessary for medical purposes and is undertaken by:

> (a) a health professional, or
>
> (b) a person who in the circumstances owes a duty of confidentiality which is equivalent, to that which would arise if that person were a health professional.

(2) In this paragraph 'medical purposes' includes the purposes of preventative medicine, medical diagnosis, medical research, the provision of care and treatment and the management of health care services."

Health professional is defined in s.69. Where the research is undertaken by a health professional it appears to be immaterial that no obligation of confidence subsists between the data subject and the professional, although in fact there will be such an obligation in most cases and sub-para.(b) assumes that there will always be one. Where the research is carried out by another, that person must owe a duty of confidentiality to the subject. Where information is obtained by the third party from a person who is under an obligation of confidentiality to the subject and is obtained with knowledge of that obligation the third party will be equally bound by it.[22] Thus if information is obtained subject to an obligation of confidentiality it can be transferred subject to the same obligation. Ground 8 may therefore offer considerable scope for medical researchers but will not necessarily cover all medical research. The alternatives are Ground 1—the individual has given his explicit consent to the processing of the personal data or the further ground inserted by the Data Protection (Processing of Sensitive Personal Data) Order 2000 in relation to research. This provides that sensitive personal data may be processed if necessary for research purposes as long as the processing is "in the substantial public interest" and the two safeguard conditions in s.33 are met.[23] It is also possible that research involving ethnic or racial data may be carried out on the limited basis and to the limited extent specified in Ground 9 of Sch.3.

The application of the fair obtaining and processing codes

18–26 These require that an individual is told at the time of collection of the data of the proposed uses and disclosures or, if that does not occur, is told before data are processed for the relevant purpose. The application of this principle would require that, where an individual has not been told at the time the data were collected that the information would be used for research purposes he should be so informed when they are to be so used and given the identity of the controller, if that person is different from the one who first collected the data, or at least should have this information made readily available to him. As far as is practicable this should be done before the processing for the research starts or, if disclosures are involved, the disclosures are made. The rigour of these provisions may be mitigated in two circumstance, either if the provision of such notice "would involve disproportionate effort" under Sch.1, Pt II to the DPA or if the processing is carried out to fulfill a legal obligation, other than one imposed by a contract, and in each case the data controller complies with the further conditions prescribed in the Data Protection (Conditions under

---

[22] *Spycatcher (No.2)*. See Ch.2, above for a discussion of the developing law of confidence.

[23] See para.18–28, below for the safeguard conditions.

Paragraph 3 of Part II of Schedule 1) Order 2000. Different conditions are prescribed for each of the two circumstances.[24]

Researchers must also comply with the data quality requirements of Principles 3 and 4; the individual rights, apart from in those cases where the limited exemption from subject access may be claimed; the security requirements of Principle 7 and the prohibition on overseas transfers to jurisdictions without an adequate system of data protection in Principle 8.

Applicable Exemptions

18–27   These can only be claimed if the safeguard conditions in s.33(1) are met.

Safeguard conditions

18–28   These are twofold. The data must not be processed to "support measures or decisions with respect to particular individuals nor processed in such a way that substantial damage or substantial distress is, or is likely to be, caused to any data subject". The first condition carries forward the concept of "functional separation" referred to in R(83)10, para.18–10 above. The prohibition appears to be aimed at the use of particular personal data, not the use of the results of the research. So research leading to statistical findings, for example that a particular drug has positive effects on a particular type of patient, which are then used as a basis to make decisions in individual cases, is within the exemption; but research based on personal data, for example on the genetic make-up of members of the same family which are used to take a decision on treatment for a child of the family, is not within it. Thus translational research, that is where the result might impact on the treatment of the patient, will not be able to claim the exemption. The second element of the exemption, that there must be no damage caused to the data subject, fits in with the approach taken throughout the Directive, and in turn in the implementing legislation, of allowing exemptions only in cases where the risk to the rights and freedoms of individuals is low.

Where the safeguard conditions apply the researcher is exempt from three of the requirements of the Act:

- Principle 2;
- Principle 5;
- Subject access.

There is a further exemption which applies to "historical research" which is explained below. However, this only applies to some limited data. It is also complicated to apply so it may only be of limited use.

Exemption from Principle 2

18–29   Principle 2 requires that personal data shall be obtained only for one or more specified and lawful purposes, and shall not be further processed in any manner

---

[24] See Ch.7, above for a full explanation of the conditions.

incompatible with that purpose or those purposes. The exemption in s.33(2) only applies to the second limb of the Principle. The use only for research purposes will not be regarded as incompatible with the purposes for which the data were obtained as long as the safeguard conditions (see above) are complied with. The data must still be obtained for specified and lawful purposes. If it is known that data are to be used for research or it is likely this will occur at some later stage the data controller should notify the individual at the point of collection or otherwise in accordance with the requirements of Principle 1.

Exemption from Principle 5

18–30 Principle 5 requires that personal data processed for any purpose or purposes shall not be kept for longer than is necessary for that purpose or those purposes. Under s.33(3) personal data which are processed only for research purposes subject to the safeguard conditions (see above) may be kept indefinitely despite the strictures of Principle 5.

Exemption from the Right of Subject access

18–31 Section 7 provides for individuals to have access to personal data held about them (see Ch.11, above). Section 33(4) provides that personal data processed only for research purposes are exempt from the s.7 rights, subject to the safeguard conditions, and a further condition which relates only to subject access, namely that the results of any research or the resulting statistics are not made available in a form which identifies the data subjects or any of them.

Exemption for historical research

18–32 This exemption in Sch.8, Pt IV started in 2001. As with the other exemptions the researcher must comply with the safeguard conditions. The exemption is twofold.

The two provisions both apply to personal data processed only for the purposes of "historical research". This term is not defined. The term may have been intended to cover research carried out using pre-October 24, 1998 data. The effect would be that research which involved the use of personal data and which was started before October 1998 but not concluded by October 2001 would not be jeopardised. It is suggested a broad meaning is justified for the term by the same reasoning justifying a broad meaning for the term "research" set out in para.18–20, above. There are two sets of exemptions. One applies to eligible manual data and to eligible automated data which are not processed by reference to the data subject. The other applies to eligible automated data which are processed by reference to the data subject. Therefore in order to determine which of the exemptions applies in dealing with any particular data set, the researcher will have to consider whether the processing which is to be carried out for the research purpose proposed is to be done by reference to the data subject.

Example

18–33 Research programme A is looking at the nature of car accidents which occur at a particular junction. Among the data are personal data about named drivers. The data are searched by reference to the make of car, never by reference to the driver. The identity of the driver is immaterial to the research. These data are not processed by reference to the data subject.

Research programme B is seeking to ascertain which treatment is most successful in treating drug addicts. Most addicts have several attempts at treatment and the research tracks addicts to look at which treatments they received. It requires the personal data to be searched and extracted by reference to the individual addict. These data are processed by reference to the data subject.

The exemption for automated data not processed by reference to the data subject may not prove to be of much practical assistance as it is difficult to envisage a reason for processing data incorporating personal identifiers if it is not processed by reference to the data subject.

Eligible manual data and eligible automated data not processed by reference to the data subject

18–34 The definitions of eligible manual and automated data are dealt with in Ch.1, above on transition. Eligible manual data processed only for historical research purposes subject to the safeguard conditions are exempt from:

(a) Principle 1—the requirement that personal data shall be processed fairly and lawfully and in particular subject to the conditions for legitimacy of processing and the processing of sensitive personal data, except for the fair obtaining and processing code contained in para.2 of Pt II of Sch.1;

(b) Principle 2—that personal data shall be obtained for specified and lawful purposes and not further processed in any manner compatible with those purposes;

(c) Principle 3—that personal data shall be adequate, relevant and not excessive for the purpose for which they are being processed;

(d) Principle 4—that personal data shall be accurate and where necessary kept up-to-date;

(e) Principle 5—that personal data shall not be kept for longer than is necessary for the purposes for which it was processed;

(f) the right to accuracy orders granted by the courts under s.14(1)–(3).

Eligible automated data processed by reference to the data subject

18–35 Data falling into this category are exempt from Principle 1 to the extent that it requires compliance with:

(a) Schedule 2—the requirement that personal data be processed subject to one of the legitimacy conditions;

(b) Schedule 3—the requirement that sensitive personal data be processed subject to one of the sensitive data conditions.

ANONYMISATION

18–36 Anonymisation and pseudonymisation are increasingly popular terms in the data protection area. The paper issued for the Public Consultation Exercise leading

up to the issue of the Commissioner's Guidance on the Use and Disclosure of Health
Data (May 2002) contained the following description of the process:

> "By anonymisation is meant the effectively permanent removal of personal iden-
> tifiers from personal data. Typically this occurs when data are aggregated with a
> view to the production of statistics (for instance the proportion of the population
> which has contracted a particular disease). Anonymisation only occurs if there is
> no reasonable possibility that data from which the personal identifiers have been
> removed will not in the future be linked once again with the data subject to whom
> the data related.[25]
>
> Pseudonymisation occurs when a true identity (e.g. name, address, National
> Health number etc.) is replaced by a pseudonym, that is an identifier by which a
> patient is known within the system but which does not readily identify him or her
> as a person in the real world. Pseudonymisation is typically reversible in that
> information linking the pseudonym to a real identity is held in a secure part of a
> computer system (or away from the system as a whole)."

Where research uses genuinely anonymised data the DPA will not apply. In the recitals
to the Directive it is accepted that the use of anonymised data falls outside its remit:

> "*Recital 26*
>
> . . . whereas the principles of protection shall not apply to data rendered anony-
> mous in such a way that the data subject is no longer identifiable . . ."

However, there is no definition of what amounts to anonymisation in the Directive
and the definition of personal data in Art.2(a) is so wide that it is questionable whether
data can be successfully anonymised and still relate to a specific living individual.[26]
Nevertheless the techniques of anonymisation and pseudonnymisation, described as
Privacy Enhancing Technologies, are regarded by privacy regulators as the preferred
approach to system design, particularly where sensitive data like medical data are concerned.

Cases on anonymisation and disclosure

18–37   While anonymised data falls outside the DPA the processing required to
achieve it must entail the use of personal data. It also leaves open the question of
whether the use or disclosure of anonymised data breach Art.8 or an obligation of confidentiality. There have been two cases in which the use or disclosure of anonymised
data have been considered.

A Health Authority v X[27]

18–38   In this case a Health Authority had sought to obtain disclosure of patient
records in order to consider the compliance of a medical practice with the terms of
service of the practitioners. Two patients had not given consent to the disclosure and

---

[25] *Draft Guidance* (May 2001) para.29.
[26] See Ch.3, above on the definitions.
[27] May 10, 2001, High Court; affirmed by Court of Appeal, December 2001.

therefore the GPs involved, not wishing to risk a breach of confidence by disclosing the information, applied to the court for a ruling as to whether they were entitled to make the disclosure. The court considered the ECtHR decisions in *Z v Finland* and *MS v Sweden* on medical data under Art.8.[28] It ordered the disclosure of the records but on safeguard conditions that the confidentiality of the personal information should be maintained and the patients' anonymity preserved as far as possible. While prima facie the disclosure of medical records without consent would be a breach of Art.8 in this case the disclosure was justified but in any event the privacy of the patients could be safeguarded. The safeguards would include anonymisation of the material.

The Court also stipulated that the data could not be disclosed more widely than was necessary to deal with the problem.

R. v Department of Health Ex p. Source Informatics Limited[29]

18–39   Source Informatics Limited (Source) wished to obtain information about the prescribing habits of GPs, which information they intended to sell to pharmaceutical companies for marketing purposes. Source proposed to obtain this information from pharmacists, who would gather it, with the consent of GPs, from prescription records. The data would be stripped of patient identifying data and passed on to Source. Both GPs and pharmacists were to receive some small consideration. In 1997 the Department of Health (DoH), which was concerned that the outcome would be to increase the NHS drugs bill, issued guidance to pharmacists that patient confidentiality would be breached by the disclosure of the prescription data even though the identifying particulars of the patients were removed. Source sought judicial review of the DoH advice.

The DoH argued that the use of the patient identifiable data to anonymise it and then to sell the data, albeit anonymised, was a use for a purpose other than that for which the data had been disclosed, that it amounted to a misuse of the information and thus a breach of confidence. Source argued that neither the processing to anonymise nor the disclosure of the anonymous information would constitute a breach of confidence.

The Court of Appeal held that, as long as the patients' privacy was not put at risk, there could be no breach of confidence involved in either the processing required to anonymise the data or the disclosure of the anonymised information.

Although the case pre-dates the implementation of the DPA, reference was made to the Directive, with both sides seeking to rely on it. It was argued by one side that the processing for the purpose of anonymisation was processing which fell within the Directive and therefore would require the consent of the patient or other grounds in Schs 2 and 3, and by the other that such processing should be regarded as outwith the Directive as it is intended to produce data which are not personal data. The judge did not have to decide the point but favoured the later view saying:

> "Although this is clearly not the appropriate occasion to attempt a definitive ruling on the scope of the Directive—and still less of the impending legislation—I have to say that common sense and justice alike would appear to favour the [latter] contention."

---

[28] See Ch.2, above on privacy for a discussion of these cases.
[29] [2000] 1 All E.R. 786.

Various arguments on the extent and nature of implied consent were raised with the judge which he did not find necessary to determine. However, he did not find acceptable the contention that consent could be implied to a range of uses of which individual patients might not be aware. He thought that the preferable approach was to accept that some of the more innocuous uses of personal information, such as use for stocktaking, did not breach any obligation of confidence as the equitable duty of confidence "ought not to be drawn too widely in the first place".

FUTURE DEVELOPMENTS

18–40   The area of medical research using personal data is one in which the law is still developing. The NHS has taken a robust stance that consent is the proper basis but that stance is not universally accepted by those working in the research area. It is possible that the courts may be sympathetic towards the view of researchers that such research is carried out in the public interest and that interest should be capable of overriding personal confidentiality, except in unusual cases.. On the other hand there is a strong argument in favour of the traditional approach to confidentiality, as exemplified by the GMC guidance, which stresses that in the a culture of confidentiality patients will be more open with those who treat them.

PRACTICAL TOOLS

18–41   The Government published a Research Governance Framework for Health and Social Care, revised April 2005, which must be followed by anyone doing research in those areas.

Data protection checklist for researchers

18–42   This checklist is intended to help those carrying out research to check compliance with the Act and assess whether the exemptions apply to the particular research project being carried out. The list should be adapted or modified for the particular circumstances as necessary. It will also be necessary to consider Ethics Committee or other guidance/requirements. If the two conditions are not satisfied, the remaining points are not relevant.

- Does the research involve personal data within the meaning of s.1 of the DPA, that is data which relate to a living individual who can be identified from that data or other information in the possession of or likely to come into the possession of the controller?

- Does the research have to involve personal data or could the data be anonymised?

- Is there a description of the research project?

- Does the project come within the research definitions in s.33(1), that is it being carried out for a research, historical or statistical purpose?

- Who is to be the data controller for the personal data, that is the person who controls the purposes and manner of the processing?

- Has a notification been made to the Commissioner if necessary?

- Has the controller checked the grounds in Sch.2 and decided upon which grounds he can rely?

- Are any of the data sensitive data?

- If so has the controller checked the grounds in Sch.3 and the Order and decided upon which grounds he can rely in respect of the sensitive data?

- Does the research project involve any overseas transfers? For example is it a joint project with an overseas body?

- If this is the case will personal data be transferred overseas as part of the research project?

- If so has the controller checked that the receiving country has adequate protection or that one of the grounds in Sch.4 applies to the transfer?

- Was the data obtained by the data controller? If it was obtained by another person does the controller know who obtained the data and in what circumstances? Were individuals told that the data would be used or disclosed for research?

- Has the controller checked that the individuals were told of the proposed use for research either at the time the data were obtained or subsequently? If they have not been told the controller must either arrange to have them informed of the proposed use or ensure that the provisions relating to disproportionate effort in Sch.1 Pt II, para.3 apply.

- Are the data confidential? If so consent will usually be required and not mere notice.

- Are the results of the research going to be used to make decisions about any of the research subjects; for example does the research concern patients with a particular illness and could the results may determine subsequent treatment for one member of the group of patients? If this applies no research exemptions can be claimed and the provisions of the Principles and the individual rights apply to the personal data used for the research.

- Could the data processing being carried out result in any damage or distress to the individual data subjects? If this is the case no research exemptions can be claimed and the provisions of the Principles and the individual rights apply to the personal data used for the research.

If all the above points on the checklist have been satisfied then the research project can claim the benefit of the first aspect of the exemption, that is:

(a) the personal data may be used for the research project even if the use for research would otherwise be incompatible with the purpose for which the data were obtained; and

(b) the personal data may be kept indefinitely.

- How are the results of the research to be made public? Will they be made public in an anonymised form only?

If this point can also be satisfied subject access to the data may be withheld to the personal data used in the research.

- Can any Privacy Enhancing Technologies (PETs) be applied to the research?

ADDITIONAL INFORMATION

Derivations

18–43 • Directive 95/46 (See App.B).

    (a) Art.13 (exemptions and restrictions).
    (b) Recitals 23, 29, 34, 40.

- Council of Europe Convention of January 28, 1981 for the Protection of Individuals with regard to automatic processing of Personal Data: Art.9 (exceptions and restrictions).

- Data Protection Act 1984: Sch.1 Pt II para.7.

- Organisation for Economic Co-operation and Development Guidelines: Annex, Part One (scope of guidelines).

Hansard references

18–44   Vol.587, No.95, col.122, Lords Report, March 16, 1998
Use of research to trace beneficiaries

Commons Standing Committee D, May 21, 1998, col.230
Meaning of research

Previous case law

18–45   *R. v Department of Health Ex p. Source Informatics* [2000] 1 All E.R. 786
A Health Authority v X, May 10, 2001, HC affirmed by Court of Appeal in December 2001

Commissioner's Guidance

18–46   Use and Disclosure of Health Data (May 2002).

CHAPTER 19
Miscellaneous Exemptions

INTRODUCTION

19–01   A review of the remaining areas of exemption can give the impression that the Act consists more of exemptions than of anything else. The impression would be unfair but there are a considerable number of individual exemptions which are difficult to categorise conveniently. Although the fact that an exemption applies does not place the data controller under any obligation to take advantage of it.

SUMMARY OF MAIN POINTS

19–02   (a)   There is a wide exemption for legal rights which covers almost any disclosure of information where there is any possibility of legal proceedings at any stage.

(b)   There are exemptions for the purposes of business management planning, corporate finance and examination scripts.

(c)   In many cases where there is an exemption from subject access there is also an exemption from the fair obtaining and processing code.

(d)   The Act includes an order-making power for further exemptions.

BUSINESS EXEMPTIONS

Confidential references

19–03   Schedule 7 para.1 exempts personal data from the subject access provisions in s.7 if they consist of a reference. The reference must be given or to be given in confidence[1] by the data controller for one of three purposes. The purposes are:

(a)   education, training or employment, or prospective education, training or employment of the data subject;

(b)   the appointment or prospective appointment of the data subject to any office; or

(c)   the provision or prospective provision by the data subject of any service.

---

[1] For an explanation of the law of confidence see Ch.2, above.

The exemption applies both before and after the reference is given but it only applies to "the data controller". Hence it appears that the only data controller who can claim the benefit of the exemption is the data controller who provides the reference and not the party who obtains the reference. This seems somewhat illogical but would appear to be the result of a strict reading of the paragraph, although the alternative view is not unarguable. The Directive is of no interpretative assistance as this provision does not derive from the Directive. The Commissioner in the Legal Guidance has supported the view that the exemption only applies to the provider of the reference.

The reference must be given in confidence. Controllers who wish to claim the exemption should therefore specify that they intend references they provide to be confidential.

The exemption only applies where the reference is for one or more of the purposes listed above, of education or employment or the provision of services. Therefore it does not apply to those entering into business partnerships and does not appear to apply to bankers' references or credit references or financial assessment. The exemption from subject access is absolute. It is not subject to any test of prejudice. It therefore covers all the aspects of s.7.

Management forecasts

19–04   Under Sch.7 para.5 personal data processed for the purpose of management forecasting or management planning to assist the data controller in the conduct of any business or other activity are exempt from the subject information provisions in any case, to the extent that the application of those provisions would be likely to prejudice the conduct of that business or other activity.

This exemption applies to all the subject information provisions and therefore covers both subject access and the fair obtaining and processing code. It only applies in an individual case to the extent that giving subject access or giving notification of subsequent uses or disclosures under the code would be likely to prejudice the particular business or activity.

The personal data can be processed for one of two purposes, either the purpose of management forecasting or the purpose of management planning. These must be intended to assist the data controller in the conduct of any business or other activity. The exemption is therefore not limited to businesses and may apply to some other form of venture or activity such as a charity or an educational establishment.

The terms management forecasting and management planning are not defined and therefore should be given their ordinary meaning. There must be some business or venture in the course of operation because the only application of the exemption is "in the conduct" of any business or other activity. The exemption may allow businesses to plan for staff progression; however, in order to claim the exemption the data controller must be able to show that providing subject access or complying with the fair information and processing code would be likely to cause prejudice to the conduct of that business or the activity carried out.

Negotiations

19–05   Schedule 7 para.7 provides that personal data which consist of records of the intentions of the data controller in relation to any negotiations with the data subject are exempt from the subject information provisions in any case to the extent to which the application of those provisions would be likely to prejudice those negotiations.

As with management forecasts, this exemption applies to both subject access and the fair obtaining and processing code. It must be applied on a case-by-case basis and only applies to the extent to which the provision of those individual rights would be likely to prejudice the negotiations. The exemption was a new addition to the 1998 Act. The explanation for the exemption may lie in problems which had previously been experienced in the insurance industry with individuals seeking subject access to reserve figures held by insurance companies in relation to claims. It is not clear whether the exemption achieves the aim of exempting these figures from subject access, as reserve figures could be argued to be held in connection with financial forecasting rather than negotiation.

It should be noted that the prejudice test applies to prejudicing the particular negotiations. It is not a general prejudice to the position of one party or to the position of the controller. The risk to negotiations is probably that there is a risk of the failure of negotiations. Alternatively it could be argued that the risk may be that the bargaining position of one of the parties would be substantially weaker. The exemption is particularly useful in personnel matters, for example, in industrial tribunal proceedings.

CORPORATE FINANCE

19–06   Under Sch.7 para.6 there are two exemptions from the subject information provisions. They are primarily intended to ensure that the individual rights given by the Act cannot be employed to affect price-sensitive information in financial markets. They are dependent on detailed conditions being fulfilled and it is not easy to explain them in simple terms.

Financial instruments

19–07   Under Art.(1)(a) the first exemption applies in any case in which:

(a) the personal data are processed for the purposes of, or in connection with, a corporate finance service;

(b) the service is provided by a "relevant person";

(c) there is a financial "instrument" either already in existence or to be created; and

(d) giving access to the personal data or complying with the fair obtaining and processing code could affect the price of the instrument or the data controller reasonably believes it could do so.

The effect need not be prejudicial, but the presumption would appear to be that any artificially induced price movement would be prejudicial to the functioning of the financial market.

Important interest of the United Kingdom

19–08   Under Art.(1)(b) the second exemption applies in any case in which:

(a) the data are processed for the purpose of, or in connection with, a corporate finance service;

(b) the service is provided by a "relevant person";

(c) giving subject access to the data or complying with the fair obtaining and processing code could affect an important economic or financial interest of the United Kingdom; and

(d) that interest requires to be safeguarded against such an effect.

The question of whether a particular interest is an important economic or financial one for the United Kingdom which requires safeguarding appears to be a matter for the data controller to determine in the particular case. However, it is not left to the discretion of the data controller. The Secretary of State is empowered to make an order specifying matters to be taken into account in determining whether the exemption is required. He may also specify circumstances in which the exemption is not to be taken to be required. The relevant order is the Data Protection (Corporate Finance Exemption Order) 2000 (SI 2000/184).

The circumstances specified in the Order are where:

- the data controller reasonably believes that giving subject access to particular personal data could affect a decision whether to deal in or subscribe to or issue a financial instrument or cause any person to act in a way that might affect business activity; and

- giving subject access to such data (whether regularly or occasionally) will result in a prejudicial effect on the orderly functioning of financial markets or the efficient allocation of capital within the economy.

The reference to an effect on business activity includes, in particular, a reference to an effect on the industrial strategy of any person, or on the capital structure of an undertaking or on the legal or beneficial ownership of a business or asset.

Corporate finance services

19–09   These exemptions will only apply to a limited range of services. These "corporate finance services" are defined in Art.3.(3)(a) to (c) to cover underwriting in respect of issues, or the placing of issues, of any instruments and advice and services relating to such underwriting. An instrument is defined in technical terms as:

"any instrument listed in section C of Annex 1 to Directive 2004/39/EC of the European Parliament and of the Council of April 21, 2004 on markets in financial instruments"

The reference to Sch.1 to the Investment Services Regulations 1995 which previously appeared in the definition has been replaced by the Financial Services and Markets Act (Markets in Financial Instruments) Regulations 2007.[2] The most common instruments

---

[2] SI 2007/126.

to which this applies would appear to be stocks and shares. As well as share issues a corporate finance service covers advice to undertakings on capital structure, industrial strategy and related matters, and advice and services relating to mergers and the purchase of undertakings.

An example of how this applies might be an adviser (who must fall within the definition of a relevant person for these purposes) who is working for a company which is considering a bid for another undertaking and who carries out inquiries into the directors of the target undertaking. If those inquiries were to become known, via response to a subject access request, it could trigger price movements in the shares in the target company. For the purpose of this provision price includes value, thus covering movements in the market value of instruments even when they are not sold.

Relevant person

19–10   As noted above, the corporate finance service must be provided by a "relevant person" and four categories of persons are listed as follows:

"(a) any person who, by reason of any permission he has under Part IV of the Financial Services and Markets Act 2000, is able to carry on a corporate finance service without contravening the general prohibition, within the meaning of section 19 of that Act;

(b) an EEA firm of the kind mentioned in paragraph 5(a) or (b) of Schedule 3 to that Act which has qualified for authorization under paragraph 12 of that Schedule and may lawfully carry on a corporate finance service;

(c) any person who is exempt from the general prohibition in respect of any corporate finance service:

 (i) as a result of an exemption order made under section 38(1) of that Act, or

 (ii) by reason of section 39(1) of that Act (appointed representatives);

(cc) any person, not falling within paragraph (a), (b) or (c) who may lawfully carry on a corporate finance service without contravening the general prohibition".[3]

LEGAL EXEMPTIONS

Legal professional privilege

19–11   Schedule 7 para.10 re-enacts the professional privilege exemption in s.31(2) of the 1984 Act. However, in the 1984 Act the exemption was limited to subject access whereas in the 1998 provision the personal data are exempt from the subject information provisions. The exemption applies if the data consist of information in respect of which a claim to legal professional privilege, or in Scotland confidentiality as between client and professional legal adviser, could be maintained in legal proceedings. Legal

---

[3] Substituted by the Financial Services and Markets Act 2000 (Consequential Amendments) Order 2002 (SI 2002/1555).

privilege is the privilege of the clients. It has been held by the ECtHR to be part of the right to privacy guaranteed by Art.8.[4] It is also a right recognised by the European Court of Justice as part of European law.[5] Once information can claim privilege it may last forever.[6] Accordingly where subject access is sought to information which was originally subject to legal professional privilege but where the litigation has been concluded, access to that data can be blocked forever.[7] As the privilege is the client's it is up to the client whether to claim the exemption or give subject access. There is no test of prejudice attached to this exemption.

It is difficult to see how the exemption from the fair collection element of the subject information provisions can apply in practice. It might be argued that it allows a solicitor acting on behalf of a client in legal proceedings to obtain information for use in those proceedings without complying with the fair obtaining and processing code. This seems an unlikely scenario and might not accord with rules of professional conduct.

Self-incrimination

19–12   Paragraph 11 of s.7 re-enacts s.34(9) of the 1984 Act providing that a person need not comply with a subject access request if to do so would reveal evidence of the commission of an offence other than an offence under this Act. It further provides that information disclosed by any person in compliance with a subject access request, or order made following a request, will not be admissible in proceedings for an offence under the Data Protection Act. The effect is that a person need not give subject access if to do so would reveal evidence of a non-data protection offence which would expose him to proceedings for that offence. It should be noted that it will only apply where he would be exposed to proceedings. Given that subject access overrides other prohibitions contained in statute (see s.26) the usual statutory provisions forbidding the disclosure of information would not expose an individual to proceedings for any of the prohibitory offences. This exemption applies where the actual content of the subject access reply would provide evidence of another offence. Where information shows a data protection offence it is not admissible in proceedings against an individual for such offence.

Disclosures required by law or made in connection with legal proceedings, etc.

19–13   The etcetera in this heading is fraught with understatement. This is a very wide exemption. The exemption has no test of prejudice nor are its terms limited to a case-by-case basis. It is divided into three separate provisions. The first covers mandatory disclosures.

Mandatory disclosures

19–14   Section 34(1) exempts personal data from the non-disclosure provisions where the disclosure is required by or under any enactment, by any rule of law or by order of the court. An enactment means an Act of Parliament or a statutory instrument.

---

[4] See *Campbell v United Kingdom* (1992) 15 E.H.R.R. 137.
[5] See Case 155/79 *AM&S Europe Ltd Commission of the European Communities* [1983] Q.B. 878.
[6] See *Calcraft v Guest* [1898] Q.B. 759.
[7] The has changed for the public sector since the Freedom of Information Act came into effect and the exemption is subject to a public interest test.

A rule of law will usually be a common law rule and an order of the court will be an order of any court or tribunal having the status of a court. The range of information which is available in the public domain has been widened since the passage of the Freedom of Information Act 2000 and the Environmental Information Regulations 2004. These, and the relation with s.34, are explored in detail in Ch.4, above. However it should be noted that, when applying the exemptions to protection personal privacy under the access legislation, the application of s.34 is disregarded. There has also been a widening of the rights to see court papers with changes to the Civil Procedure Rules which now allow non-parties to litigation to obtain a range of documents such as particulars and statements of claim without the need for the court's permission.[8] A court may restrict the access to materials but will only do so on the application of the party. It follows that a party which wishes to protect personal information from disclosure by these means must make a specific application to the court under the relevant provisions.

Elective disclosures

19–15 These are dealt with in in s.35(2). This was considered by the Court of Appeal in the case of *Totalise Plc v The Motley Fool Ltd*.[9]

19–16 *Totalise Plc v The Motley Fool.* The two defendants, the Motley Fool and Interactive Investor Limited, operated websites which included "discussion" or bulletin boards for business information. Users could post material in these areas relating to businesses, both opinions and information. A user going under the name Zeddust posted material about Totalise Plc. Totalise Plc contacted both website operators and complained that the statements by Zeddust were defamatory and asked that the postings be removed, that Zeddust's rights to post material be withdrawn and that the identity of Zeddust be revealed to them.

Interactive responded that the combination of their privacy policy and the effect of the Data Protection Act meant that they could not disclose the information requested. Totalise applied to the court for a *Norwich Pharmacal* order. This is named after the case *Norwich Pharmacal Co v Commissioners for Customs and Excise*.[10] It allows disclosure to be ordered by the court against a third party who has become "mixed up" in tortuous activity through no fault of his own.

The court at first instance made the order against both defendants and ordered the defendants to pay the costs of the application. The judge said:

"... it was perfectly plain from the outset that the postings on both websites were highly defamatory and the claimants were the victims of a sustained campaign amounting to an actionable tort. There was no other way in which the claimants could have proceeded, save by requiring identification of Zeddust from both defendants."

19–17 He held that the defendants should have supplied the information requested without waiting for a court order. They would be entitled to make the disclosure

---

[8] The Civil Procedure (Amendment) Rules 2006.
[9] [2002] 1 W.L.R 1233, Case No. A2/2001/0558.
[10] [1974] A.C. 133.

applying the exemption under s.35 of the DPA which exempts disclosures necessary for the purposes of establishing, exercising or defending legal rights and thus should bear the costs of the court order.

19–18 On behalf of the second defendant it was argued that it would have been wrong for Interactive to make the disclosure without a court order as they were under an obligation of confidence to their customer, Zeddust, and the data involved was covered by the Data Protection Act 1998.

On appeal against the costs order the Court of Appeal accepted that s.35(2) applied to the disclosure but said that the provision could not be looked at in isolation. The disclosure amounted to a processing operation and thus required the data controller to be able to justify the disclosure on one of the grounds in Sch.2. The Court referred to Ground 5(a) which allows disclosure for the purposes of the administration of justice but went on to consider Ground 6 and whether the disclosure was out weighted by any prejudice to the rights and freedoms of the data subject. It considered that:

> "it is legitimate for a party [such as the defendant] who reasonably agrees to keep information confidential and private to refuse to voluntarily hand over such information."

19–19 The Court held that Interactive should not be liable to pay the costs of the application by Totalise Plc as they were justified in waiting for a court order before disclosing the information.

The Court implicitly recognised that the mere existence of a non-disclosure exemption does not impose an obligation on the data controller to make the requested disclosure and the data controller must consider all the circumstances of the case, in particular the privacy rights of the data subject and any undertakings given to him, before making a disclosure.

19–20 The approach taken by the court in Totalise has much in common with a number of cases concerned with the disclosure of personal information for the purpose of other types of legal proceedings. In *Bennet v Compass Group UK & Ireland*[11] the Court of Appeal decided that defendants in personal injury cases should not be given authority to have direct access to claimants' medical records. Whereas it was formerly the practice for the court to order claimants to sign authorisations allowing direct access to claimants' records, in *Bennet* the Court of Appeal decided that such orders could infringe the Art.8 rights of claimants. In future such access should be via the claimants' solicitors. The orders for disclosure should be clear as to the documents to be disclosed. In *Asda Stores v Thompson*[12] the Employment Appeal Tribunal made an order aimed at preserving the privacy of "whistleblowers" who made statements in the course of investigations into a claim of gross misconduct and who were offered confidentiality. The EAT overruled an order for blanket discovery by the Tribunal and said that the applicants did not need to know the identity of those making statements which led to the investigation.

Section 34(2) provides for exemptions from the non-disclosure provisions where the disclosure is necessary for:

---

[11] (2002) L.T.L. April 18.
[12] (2002) I.R.L.R. 245.

(a) the purpose of or in connection with legal proceedings (including prospective legal proceedings); or

(b) for the purpose of obtaining legal advice.

In the case of *Matthew Mensah v Robert Jones*[13] the High Court considered the application of s.35 where a doctor disclosed medical records relating to a patient in order to obtain his own legal advice on a claim that the patient was threatening to bring against him. The patient then claimed that the doctor was in breach of the DPA in making the disclosure as the complaint was in respect of an alleged assault and the disclosure of the medical records was not "necessary" for the purpose of taking legal advice. Mr Justice Lightman dismissed the claim stating that it was indeed necessary for the defendant to disclose all the circumstances surrounding the case to his solicitors.

This is a widening of the provision which appeared in the 1984 Act. In the previous provision the disclosure in connection with legal proceedings had to be made where the person involved was a party or a witness to the proceedings. This was found to be unnecessarily narrow in practice. It made it difficult for a prospective witness to make appropriate disclosures or for an affidavit to be filed on the basis of which proceedings were to be started, because the exemption only applied where legal proceedings were in existence. The matter could have been dealt with by removing the words "to which the person making the disclosure is a party or a witness", or by adding the words "including prospective legal proceedings". The draftsman has chosen to adopt both of these solutions to the present problem and the effect is to widen the non-disclosure provision considerably. Prospective legal proceedings may be of any nature. It is not clear how prospective they must be or whether a settled intention to take action is required.

Although the disclosure must be necessary for these purposes it is not necessary to show that the proceedings or the advice will be prejudiced if there is a failure to make the disclosure. Despite the widening of the provision the courts have not treated it as a "get out of jail free" provision.

Legal rights disclosures

19–21 The section includes a further provision which allows the personal data to be exempt from the non-disclosure provisions where the disclosure is "otherwise necessary for the purposes of establishing exercising or defending legal rights".

Clearly in these cases there do not need to be current or even prospective legal proceedings, and it must be wider than obtaining legal advice because that is dealt with in s.34(2)(b). Although on a strict grammatical reading it appears to suggest that the disclosure is necessary to establish the legal right, it may be that the intention was that the disclosure was necessary for the purpose of establishing the existence of a legal right, not the legal right itself.

This could allow organisations to carry out wide matching, trawling or tracing activities free from the non-disclosure provisions if they can show that the disclosures are necessary for the purpose of establishing exercising or defending legal rights. For example, the Child Support Agency has a legal right to collect maintenance from absconding or absenting fathers. This provision might enable it to process personal

---

[13] [2004] EWHC 2699.

data exempt from the non-disclosure provisions, on the grounds that the disclosure of data to it is necessary for establishing that it has a right to obtain payment from particular parents. It might also apply to insurance fraud databases or other investigative agencies.

The provision exempts personal data from the non-disclosure provisions, namely the Data Protection Principles, insofar as those are incompatible with the disclosure, and from other rights, so an individual may be deprived of his right to prevent processing or to require the blocking of inaccurate data. However, both the Principles and any possibility of compensation derived from breach of those Principles as far as they affect disclosure, are taken out of the picture. Although the term disclosure in the singular is used, the Interpretation Act 1978 provides that the singular includes the plural unless the contrary is clear from the context. In this case, therefore, widespread unregulated disclosures might be possible under the exemption.

This possibility has obviously been of concern to the Commissioner's Office and in the Legal Guidance it is emphasised that the disclosure must be "necessary" for the purposes. However, it appears this may be less stringent than it appears at first sight as the term "necessary" has to be interpreted as importing a test of proportionality.[14]

GOVERNMENT USES

Judicial appointments and honours

19–22   Paragraph 3 of Sch.7 provides an exemption from the subject information provision where personal data are processed for the purposes of assessing any person's suitability for judicial office or the office of Queen's Counsel or the conferring by the Crown of any honour. There is no test of prejudice available attached. The exemption does not attach itself to any particular data controller; as long as the controller processes personal data for those purposes exemption may be claimed. The exemption is absolute and does not have to be considered on a case-by-case basis nor does it only apply to the extent of any incompatibility. This is an absolute extension. It could presumably apply to an employer who provides a reference, or recommendation of a voluntary group that provides a recommendation for the provision of an honour or someone who provides "soundings" for judicial office. The exemption applies not only to the subject access provision but also to the fair obtaining and processing code.

Parliamentary privilege

19–23   Schedule 6, paras 2 to 5 inclusive to the Freedom of Information Act 2000 insert provisions extending the coverage of the Act to the processing of personal data by or on behalf of either of the Houses of Parliament[15] and providing for matching exemptions to preserve parliamentary privilege. In the absence of such provisions legislation does not extend to the Houses of Parliament.

The data controllers are to be the Corporate Officers of the two Houses where personal data are processed by or on behalf of the Houses. The Corporate Officers may

---

[14] See *Hansard* quoted in Ch.3, above and discussion of the terms in para.6–07, above.
[15] FOIA 2000 para.3 inserting new s.63A after s.63 of the DPA.

not be prosecuted but s.55 (unlawful obtaining of data) and para.12 of Sch.9 (obligation to assist with the execution of a warrant) will apply.

Schedules 2 and 3 of the DPA are amended by the insertion of grounds for processing which cover the exercise of any function of either House of Parliament. The exemption provision extends to:

- the first Principle (except as far as it relates to Schs 2 and 3);

- the second, third, fourth and fifth Principles;

- the right of subject access in s.7;

- the rights of objection, rectification, compensation in ss.10 to 14(1) to (3);

if the exemption is required for the purpose of avoiding an infringement of the privileges of either House of Parliament.[16]

EDUCATIONAL EXEMPTIONS

Examination marks

19–24 Paragraph 7 of Sch.7 re-enacts the provisions of s.35 of the 1984 Act almost word for word. It amends the subject access provisions in relation to examination marks. The data to which it applies are personal data consisting of marks or other information processed by a controller for the purpose of determining the results of professional, academic or other examinations. Any form of examination, assessment, report or work will be covered as long as it falls within this definition. The definition is contained in sub-para.7(5) under which "examination" includes any process for determining the knowledge, intelligence, skill or ability of a candidate by reference to his performance in any test, work or other activity. Clearly there must be a candidate who performs in some way which must be subject to a valuation process producing a result, but it can be any type of valuation process or indeed any type of examination. Playing the piano at a local music festival, a Grade I ballet examination, the completion of a Brownie badge or the primary school SATs tests rank with university finals and everything in between in falling within this omnibus definition.

The exemption appears to apply to the data consisting of actual marks and marking schemes and to data processed as a consequence of the determination of results. This would appear to cover the pass-mark, the rankings, and any re-marking. Where the exemption applies the controller may delay responding to a subject access request until the time when he would have given the examination results. The provision is designed to stop students jumping the queue to obtain the results of examinations earlier than they would do in the normal scheme of things.

Where the controller receives a subject access request and the appropriate fee before the results are due to be announced then the subject access response time (40 days) either does not start to run until after the exam result is announced or, if that date would be more than five months away, the controller must give the data within the five

---

[16] FOIA 2000 para.2, *ibid.*

month period. If the period before giving the response is going to be longer than the usual 40-day period the controller must provide a fuller set of data than usual, being all the changes to the data until the time they are finally provided. This may act as a disincentive to controllers trying to take advantage of the five-month maximum. The five-month maximum has presumably been arrived at on the basis of assessments from the start of an academic session onward. Results are treated as given when the candidates are told of them or they are published.

Examination scripts

19–25   This was a new exemption to the 1998 Act inserted by para.8 of Sch.7. It provides that personal data consisting of information recorded by candidates during an academic, professional or other examination are exempt from s.7. "Examination" is given the same extended meaning as in the previous provision relating to examination marks.

There is no test of prejudice and it appears to be an absolute exemption to subject access. It is difficult to ascertain how this can be justified under the Directive or indeed in commonsense terms, given that the personal data would have been provided by the subject directly in the examination. The Commissioner in the Legal Guidance suggests that the exemption does not extend to "comments recorded by the examiner in the margins of the script" which it advises should be given "even though they may not appear to the data controller to be of much value without the script itself".[17] This assumes that the scripts are covered by the Act, however, if they fall outside the definition of a "relevant filing system" they may not be covered.

OTHER EXEMPTIONS

Publicly available information

19–26   Section 34 provides a wide exemption for data which consist of information which the data controller is obliged by or under any enactment to make available to the public, whether by publishing it, by making it available for inspection or otherwise, whether gratuitously or by payment of a fee. This has the same effect as s.34 of the 1984 Act. The exemption applies to the subject information provisions, the fourth Data Protection Principle (accuracy), s.14(1) to (3) and the non-disclosure provisions.

The subject information provisions cover both subject access and the fair obtaining and processing code. The fourth Principle deals with accuracy and s.14 deals with the rights of individuals to take action for the correction of inaccurate data. The non-disclosure provisions mean any provisions incompatible with the disclosure required. Schedules 2 and 3, which deal with legitimacy of processing and sensitive data, still apply as does Principle 3 which requires that data should be adequate, relevant and not excessive in relation to the purpose or purposes for which they are processed.

The exemption only applies when the data are in the hands of the particular data controller who is under an obligation to make it public. It would not apply, for example, to the electoral roll when it is sold and passes into the hands of another party. In the case of the electoral roll there are now special provisions enabling individuals to

---

lodge a notice of objection to use by third parties. The objection is lodged with the Electoral Registration Officer. The name of the objector will be removed from what is called the edited register which is sold to the private sector without any restriction on the use of the list. However the objector cannot thereby opt-out of all use of the roll by the private sector. It can still be used for money laundering and credit checking purposes.[18] The exemption only applies to the information that the data controller is obliged to publish not to supporting information in the hands of the controller.

Relation with the Freedom of Information Act 2000 (FOIA)

19–27 As s.34 applies to information which the data controller is obliged to make public there was a concern that the publication or provision of access to information under the FOIA would deprive individuals of the rights they would otherwise have. Thus prima facie, where an authority was willing to give access to personal information to the public under a request for access, the data subject would thereby be deprived both of his individual rights of access and his remedies for wrongful disclosure and inaccuracy. While the former would be of less moment, save where there were disputes about the data covered, as the individual would be able to find the information anyway as a member of the public, the later would mean that the individual was deprived of one of his rights guaranteed by the Directive. Section 72 of the FOIA deals with this by inserting the words "other than an enactment contained in the Freedom of Information Act" into s.34. Accordingly where the information is disclosed under some other legal provision, e.g. an obligation to publish planning applications, the exemption will still apply but not otherwise.

This appears to apply to s.21 as well as specific disclosures. Section 21 of the FOIA exempts information from FOIA requests if the information is reasonably accessible to the applicant other than under s.1, i.e. other than in response to a specific request. It applies where the public authority is obliged to communicate the information by or under any enactment to members of the public on request or under a publication scheme. Thus it can only apply to personal data that would be freely available to the public. So where personal data are contained in a publication scheme they will be exempt from the individual right of access under FOIA by virtue of s.21.

They would also be covered by the exemption under s.34 of the DPA 1998 but that now excludes the class of information available under FOIA but not under other legislation. So there are:

- Personal data which are exempt from access under the FOIA under s.21 because such data are generally publicly available to anyone, e.g. planning application data. The data are then exempt from subject access, accuracy and the non disclosure bars under DPA 1998 under s.34.

- Personal data, not falling within the above, which are made available under the FOIA or under the Environmental Information Access Regulations, thus available under an enactment contained in the FOIA, but the amendment to s.34 means that the data are not exempt from subject access or the accuracy rights as far as the position of individuals are concerned.

---

[18] See Ch.2, above for an explanation of the relevant regulations.

FURTHER ORDERS

Orders under s.38

19–28   There are two order-making provisions under s.38. Section 38(1) re-enacts the provision found in s.34(9) of the 1984 Act which allows the Secretary of State to exempt personal data from the subject access provisions if they consist of information the disclosure of which would be prohibited or restricted by or under any enactment. In this case the Secretary of State may order an exemption from the subject information provisions but only if and to the extent he considers it necessary for safeguarding the interests of the data subjects or the rights and freedoms of any other individual, or considers that the prohibition or restriction in the original Act ought to prevail over the subject information provisions. The relevant order is SI 2000/419 and is dealt with at the end of Ch.11, above. The second sub-section of s.38 provides that the Secretary of State may by order exempt from the non-disclosure provision disclosures made in circumstances specified in the order. He may only do this if he considers the exemption necessary for safeguarding the interest of the data subject or the rights and freedoms of any other individual. No such orders have been made.

Crown Employment

19–29   Paragraph 4 provides for the Secretary of State to make an order exempting personal data from the subject information provisions where that data are processed for the purpose of assessing suitability for particular public appointments. Those are either employment by or under the Crown or an office through which appointments are made by Her Majesty, a Minister of the Crown or by the Northern Ireland Department. The relevant order is the Data Protection (Crown Appointments) Order 2000 (SI 2000/416). The appointments listed in the order include senior clerical appointments in the Church of England, the Poet Laureate, the Astronomer Royal and the Provost of Eton.

FURTHER POWERS

19–30   In addition to the exemptions set out in these chapters, there are some specific "exemption possibilities" in other parts of the Act. For example Sch.1 para.1 has a provision allowing for additional exemptions from the fair obtaining and processing code, and Sch.3 para.9 provides for further exemptions to be made from the sensitive data provisions. Orders under Sch.3 are dealt with in Ch.7, above.

ADDITIONAL INFORMATION

Derivations

19–31 • Directive 95/46 (See App.B).

   (a) Art.13 (exemptions and reservations)
   (b) Recitals 42, 43, 44, 45.

- Council of Europe Convention of January 28, 1981 for the Protection of Individuals with regard to automatic processing of Personal Data: Art.9 (exceptions and restrictions).

- Data Protection Act 1984: ss.31 (judicial appointments and legal professional privilege), 34 (other exemptions), 35 (examination marks).

- Organisation for Economic Co-operation and Development Guidelines: Annex, Part One (scope of guidelines).

Hansard references

19–32 Commons Standing Committee D, May 21, 1998, col.232
Prospective legal proceedings is not intended to cover purely speculative or fishing expeditions

Commons Standing Committee D, June 4, 1998, col.320
Exemption for negotiations should cover intentions in the event of future negotiations (such as insurance budget allocations)

Commons Standing Committee D, June 10, 1998, col.340
Exemption for corporate financial activities

Vol.315, No.198, col.595, Commons Third Reading, July 2, 1998
Publicly available registers

Statutory instruments

19–33 SI 2000/184: The Data Protection (Corporate Finance Exemption) Order
SI 2000/416: The Data Protection (Crown Appointments) Order
SI 2000/419: The Data Protection (Miscellaneous Subject Access Exemptions) Order

Case law

19–34 *Totalise Plc v The Motley Fool Limited* [2001] EWCA Civ 1897.

CHAPTER 20

Enforcement and Prosecutions

INTRODUCTION

20–01   The Act imposes a considerable number of obligations on data controllers and provides data subjects with a number of rights. In order to ensure that those obligations are heeded and the rights are capable of being exercised the Act has to support both with an enforcement framework. That framework has two elements—first, the Commissioner is empowered to take enforcement action against data controllers who are not processing personal data in accordance with the Act and to commence prosecutions in the criminal courts if a data controller or third party commits any one of a number of criminal offences created by the Act; second, individuals have the right to take action in the courts to enforce their rights. This chapter covers the enforcement and prosecution powers of the Commissioner. The provisions dealing with the enforcement of individual rights will be found in Chs 10–14, above.

20–02   The role of the Commissioner as regulator expanded significantly under the 1998 Act. Under the 1984 Act the Registrar could only enforce the Principles against registered data users. Individuals could only make a subject access application to registered data users. It therefore followed that the focus of actions under the 1984 Act was to ensure that data users were registered. Those restrictions were removed within the 1998 Act under which a failure to notify with the Commissioner, although still an offence in itself, does not protect the data controller from other regulatory action.

SUMMARY OF MAIN POINTS

20–03   (a) The enforcement powers of the Commissioner also apply to breaches of the Privacy and Electronic Communications (EC Directive) Regulations 2003, with some amendments and the Commissioner has similar enforcements powers in relation to breaches of the Freedom of Information Act 2000.

(b) The Commissioner has an obligation to make an assessment of processing if a data subject seeks one.

(c) The Commissioner has powers to require data controllers to provide him with information by means of the service of an information notice.

(d) The Commissioner may seek a warrant of entry to premises where evidence of a contravention of the Act may be found.

(e) The Commissioner may serve enforcement notices on data controllers who have contravened or are contravening the Principles.

(f) Data controllers served with notices under the Act may appeal to the Information Tribunal.

(g) The Act imposes a range of criminal sanctions including sanctions for breach of notices, for unlawfully procuring information, for some breaches of the notification requirements and for breach of the confidentiality obligations imposed on the Commissioner and his staff.

(h) The offence of procuring information has become a matter of increasing concern and the penalties for this offence are likely to include imprisonment in the near future.

(i) Prosecutions may be brought by the CPS under other provisions in relation to information protected by the Data Protection Act such as misfeasance in public office.

Enforcement powers, policy and strategy

20–04   The questions of policy and strategy on enforcement and prosecution have been difficult ones for the Commissioner and his predecessors. Over the two decades since the first Data Protection Act came into force the policy and approach on enforcement has gradually tightened and focused on specific areas which are seen to be of concern. Nevertheless there remains a sense that the enforcement powers of the Commissioner's office are not as tough or as well-used as they might be. One of the problems is that the Commissioner has no power to impose penalties, a contrast to the data protection regulators in other jurisdictions who may impose direct fines for breaches. In March 2007 it was reported, for example, that the Spanish Commissioner had fined a hospital in Barcelona 60,100 Euros (about £40,000) for inappropriate disclosure of medical records of patients. It also contracts with other regulators in the UK, for example the Financial Services Authority which in February 2007 imposed a financial penalty of £980,000 on the Nationwide Building Society in respect of a failure of compliance matters including security. The Commissioner has made various representations seeking increased powers to deal with particular problems, such as unsolicited faxes or the unlawful procuring of personal data. In recent months there has been a more sympathetic approach in Government to increasing the powers of the Commissioner and the s.55 offence of unlawful procuring of data will become punishable by imprisonment when the Criminal Justice and Immigration Bill comes into force. If and when it does it will mark a watershed in the treatment of personal data—an acceptance that the abuse of data may amount to a real mischief and not merely an administrative oversight.

Assessment procedure

20–05   The Act includes an assessment procedure by which any person who is, or believes himself to be, directly affected by any processing of personal data may ask the Commissioner for an assessment of whether it is likely or unlikely that data processing has been carried out by a data controller in compliance with the provisions of the

Act.[1] The belief on the part of an individual that they are affected by processing is almost certainly a subjective belief rather than an objectively reasonable belief. The latter could have been established by inserting the word "reasonably" before "believes". On receiving such a request the Commissioner is placed under an obligation to carry out an assessment although he is given a discretion as to how the assessment is carried out.[2]

The obligation on the Commissioner is tempered by the qualification that the Commissioner need not carry out such assessments where the complainant (or another person) fails to provide information to satisfy the Commissioner of the identity of thecomplainant or to enable the Commissioner to identify the processing in question. Such information may be "reasonably required" by the Commissioner for the purpose.[3]

The qualification is however very limited. If a Mr Smith were to write to the Commissioner stating that he held the [objectively wholly unreasonable belief] that Bloggs supermarket were holding details about him and his family including details of their sex lives and political opinions then, providing Mr Smith identified himself and his concerns accurately, the Commissioner has an obligation to assess the matter.

20–06 The Act, whilst denying the Commissioner any discretion over whether to conduct an assessment, does provide a considerable discretion as to the form of the assessment. Section 40(3) allows the Commissioner, in determining the appropriate form of the assessment, to take in to account:

- the extent to which the request appears to him to raise a matter of substance;

- any undue delay in making the request; and

- whether or not the person making the request is entitled to make an application under s.7 (which establishes the right of access to personal data—see Ch.11, above on Subject Access) in respect of the personal data in question.[4]

20–07 The basic obligation—to carry out some form of assessment as to whether it is likely or unlikely that the processing has been or is being carried out in compliance with the Act—is not removed, however, just tempered. It would appear that even the most trivial or out-of-date complaints must trigger some form of inquiry by the Commissioner. Thus it is presumably not permissible for the Commissioner to respond "your complaint is now too old to be considered" but it is permissible to respond "due to the age of your complaint the Commissioner does not propose to contact the data controller. However, on the basis of the information provided he considers it likely/unlikely that the processing was carried out in compliance with the Act". This is still however an onerous burden placed on the Commissioner.

20–08 Section 42(4) provides that the Commissioner must notify the applicant:

(a) whether he has made an assessment as a result of the request; and

---

[1] 1998 Act s.42(1).
[2] 1998 Act s.42(2).
[3] 1998 Act s.42(2).
[4] 1998 Act s.42(3).

(b) to the extent that he considers appropriate, having regard in particular to any exemption from s.7 applying in relation to the personal data concerned, of any view formed or action taken as a result of the request.

Subsection (a) thus implies a discretion as to whether an assessment is carried out at all although presumably, given the wording of the rest of the section, this will only be a permissible response where the Commissioner lacks information about the identity of the applicant or the relevant processing.

Subsection (b) allows for the possibility that the Commissioner may, as a result of the assessment, become party to information that the data controller would not be obliged to disclose to the applicant because a subject access exemption applies. In such a case the Commissioner may only provide limited information to the applicant about the results of his assessment. The Act does not provide any guidance on the form of a request for an assessment. In practice it appears that the Commissioner's office interprets any written reference or complaints as a request for assessments.

Enforcement under the Privacy and Electronic Communications (EC Directive) Regulations 2003

20–09 Under the Privacy and Electronic Communications (EC Directive) Regulations 2003 (PECR), Pt V of the DPA 1998 is applied with the appropriate modifications set out in Sch.1 to the Regulations. The complaint and assessment provisions are worded differently from s.42. Whereas under s.42 an individual who is or believes himself to be affected by processing may make a request to the Commissioner for an assessment of the processing in question, this does not apply under the PECR. Instead, under reg.32 either OFCOM or a person aggrieved by an alleged contravention of the Regulations may request the Commissioner to exercise his enforcement functions in respect of a contravention. The Regulations do not in terms impose a duty to consider such a request or make a determination following it but applying the principles of public law the Commissioner will be under an obligation to consider any request properly made to him under the legislation. In order to decide whether to exercise his enforcement functions the Commissioner will have to make a decision on whether or not the processing involved complies with the Regulations. The Commissioner may exercise his enforcement powers where he is satisfied that a person has contravened or is contravening the requirements of the Regulations. The Commissioner's powers are therefore not limited to breaches committed by data controllers as under the Act. In deciding whether to exercise his powers the Commissioner is not required to consider whether distress has been caused to any person, but merely damage. The Commissioner may also service information notices on any person for the purpose of determining whether that person has complied or is complying with the relevant requirements. The provisions in relation to special purposes (including special information notices and determinations in relation to the special purposes) are omitted as are other provisions which are not relevant to the PECR.

Assessments in practice

20–10 The Information Commissioner's Annual Reports over the years show a steady growth in the number of requests for assessment. In the year 2000–2001 the

Commissioner's office received 8,875 requests for assessment; the following year that figure had risen to 12,479. In 2005–2006 the Annual Report provided a figure of 22,059 new cases received. However over half of these were resolved by providing advice and guidance, which would suggest that the basis for counting a "case" is not necessarily that it raises a substantive issue requiring investigation.

With a view to streamlining the assessment request procedure the Information Commissioner issued a document entitled Policy on Handling Assessments which is available on the Commissioner's website at *http://www.ico.gov.uk/dpr/dpdoc.nsf* [Accessed on September 2, 2007]. Version 2 of the document is dated April 11, 2002. It appears to be still the main guiding policy although there have been specific campaigns in respect of particular areas, such as s.55 offences, over the last few years. The Policy sets out the following principles for the handling of assessment requests by the Commissioner's office:

"2. Guiding Principles

2.1 In handling any requests for assessment that [she] receives the Commissioner will use the limited resources available to her to best effect in meeting her more general duty of promoting observance of the requirements of the Act by data controllers. It is in this light that she has adopted the following as guiding principles on which to base her strategy for handling individual requests and to provide general direction for her staff involved in this work.

2.2 All requests should receive initial consideration.

2.3 Consistent criteria should be followed in deciding how to handle individual requests and the resources to be applied to them.

2.4 Regard should always be paid to the extent to which a request raises significant and widespread concerns about observance of the requirements of the Act by data controllers.

2.5 Persons making a request should be treated in a courteous, sympathetic and businesslike manner and should be given assistance if they have difficulty in communicating with us.

2.6 Individuals should be encouraged to help themselves as far as possible and be provided with information and assistance to enable them to do so.

2.7 Individuals who are primarily seeking to resolve complaints should be directed to use other complaints resolution mechanisms and should be provided with information to enable them to do so. Such information may include an assessment made by the Commissioner.

2.8 Approaches to data controllers should be courteous, constructive and aimed at securing compliance with the Act. Where a data controller does not co-operate in an investigation, the use of the Commissioner's formal powers to obtain information should be considered.

2.9 The Commissioner's duty is to make an independent assessment of whether the provisions of the Act have been contravened and what if any action is appropriate. In doing so she has to act impartially, rather than as the representative of the person making the request or the person on whose behalf the request is made.

2.10 Where the Commissioner considers that action by a data controller is required this should normally be sought through discussion and negotiation. Where such an approach fails, the data controller is clearly in breach of basic requirements of the Act, or the circumstances of the assessment make this approach inappropriate, the use of formal enforcement powers should be considered.

2.11 There should be a seamless process from assessment through to enforcement in those cases where the Commissioner considers that formal enforcement is appropriate.

2.12 Persons requesting an assessment who are dissatisfied with the way their requests have been handled should have an opportunity to have their cases reviewed."

20–11 Paragraph 2.1 with its reference to "limited resources" appears to be an acknowledgment that it is impractical for the Commissioner's office to fulfil the statutory duty to the letter and to deal with every assessment request in detail. Paragraph 2.4 suggests that the Commissioner is likely to take effective action in those cases where a large number of complaints are received about a particular data controller or about a particular type of breach. Paragraph 2.6 suggests that a data subject will be expected to contact the data controller first with their complaint prior to referring the matter to the Commissioner's office and para.2.7 indicates that an aggrieved data subject may be expected to use the data controller's formal complaints procedure before raising the issue with the Information Commissioner.

Section 3 of the Policy also contains the requirement that a person requesting an assessment must provide "reasonable prima facie evidence of a breach" of the Data Protection Principles. This is not a statutory requirement but a hurdle introduced by the Commissioner. In practice the Commissioner's office will reject requests for assessments where the complainant has not, at least, first written to the data controller and received a written response from the data controller. Furthermore the written response from the data controller must fail to deal or promise to deal with the issues raised.

Investigation in the absence of a request for assessment

20–12 In considering matters of non-compliance or setting in train investigations the Commissioner is not limited to those cases where he has received an request for an assessment but may use his own discretion to investigate matters of concern. This is explicit in the provisions dealing with information notices and other powers which may be exercised either when he has received a request for assessment or if he reasonably requires any information for the purpose of determining whether the controller has complied or is complying with the principles. In a number of cases the Commissioner has set in train projects to investigate particular problems, such as the unlawful procuring of information, without being requested to do so by data subjects.

Information notices

20–13 The power to serve information notices was new in the 1998 Act. In practice it has been little used although use is increasing. The Commissioner may, upon receiving a request for an assessment, or on his own initiative, serve an information notice on the data controller requiring the provision of information to enable the Commissioner to determine whether the data controller has complied or is complying with the Data Protection Principles.[5] The notice must state whether the information is sought in response to an assessment request or because the Commissioner is conducting his own inquiry into a possible breach of the Principles. In the latter case the Commissioner must also state the reasons for regarding the information sought as relevant.[6] An information notice must set out the rights of appeal.[7]

The Commissioner has discretion over:

- the timescale for compliance with the notice—subject to appeal time limits; and

- the form in which the required information is to be provided.[8]

There is a procedure for urgent information notices.[9]

Timescale for compliance

20–14 Subject to the provisions on appeals and urgent notices it is for the Commissioner to determine the appropriate timescale. The Commissioner, save in urgent cases, may not require compliance with the information notice before the end of the appeal period. Furthermore, if there is an appeal by the data controller then the need for compliance is suspended until the determination or withdrawal of the appeal.[10]

In urgent cases the Commissioner may require compliance after a minimum period of seven days from the service of the notice. It is for the Commissioner to determine whether the situation is urgent. The Act merely indicates that such a decision may be reached by "reason of special circumstances". Clearly urgent information notices will be relevant when the Commissioner has concerns that something is about to happen vis-à-vis the relevant personal data—for example there is about to be a (another) transfer overseas in breach of the principles or there is about to be a (another) disclosure in breach of the Act. In such circumstances he may require the information to be supplied immediately to enable him to take emergency enforcement action. The word "another" is used in parentheses since the Act only allows an information notice to be served with respect to current breaches—which would appear to exclude anticipated future breaches.

20–15 There are exemptions to the general obligation on a data controller to respond to an Information Notice in respect of:

- material covered by legal professional privilege in so far as it relates to advice given in relation to the 1998 Act;

- material which would incriminate the recipient of the information notice insofar as it discloses offences other than offences under the 1998 Act.[11]

---

[5] 1998 Act s.43.
[6] 1998 Act s.43(2).
[7] 1998 Act s.43(3).
[8] 1998 Act s.43(1).
[9] 1998 Act s.43(5).
[10] 1998 Act s.40(7).
[11] 1998 Act s.43(6)–(8).

The Commissioner is empowered to cancel but not (unlike enforcement notices) to vary the terms of information notices.[12]

20–16 The Commissioner may also serve a special information notice in order to investigate suspected breaches or abuses of the "special purposes" exemptions specified in s.32 of the Act either in response to an assessment request or in certain other limited circumstances. If the Commissioner decides that the exemption has been wrongly claimed then he may issue a determination to this effect.

The ability of the Commissioner to investigate a suspected abuse of the "special purposes" exemption without a request for an assessment is limited to situations where a court has stayed proceedings brought under the Act in response to a claim by a data controller, that the special purposes exemption applies. Any such stay will be for the specific purpose of the Commissioner making a determination as to whether the "special purposes" exemption has been wrongly claimed. The procedure is governed by s.32(4)–(5) of the 1998 Act.[13]

The provisions relating to the mandatory contents of special information notices (SINs), rights of appeal, urgent SINs, cancelling SINs and exemptions for legal professional privilege and self-incrimination are identical to those for ordinary information notices. The Commissioner may not serve an "ordinary" (as opposed to "special") information notice on a data controller who claims to be processing personal data only for the "special purposes" without first issuing a determination to the effect that the "special purposes" exemption has been wrongly claimed.[14] Any such determination, like other notices, must set out the rights of appeal and cannot take effect until the appeal time limit has passed or, if there is an appeal, until that has been determined or withdrawn.[15] Unlike other notices there is no procedure for urgent determinations.

ENFORCEMENT

Enforcement notices

When may they be served?

20–17 The Commissioner is empowered to serve an enforcement notice on any data controller that the Commissioner is satisfied is breaching one or more of the Data Protection Principles[16] or on any person if satisfied that the person is breaching any provision of the Privacy and Electronic Communications (EC Directive) Regulations 2003 (see Ch.22, below for the detailed provision of the PECR). The Commissioner must be satisfied that there has been a breach of the relevant provisions. Generally therefore there will be some form of investigation procedure before enforcement action is taken. When deciding whether to serve an enforcement notice, the Commissioner must take into account whether any person has or is likely to be caused damage or distress by the suspected breach.[17]

---

[12] 1998 Act s.43(9).
[13] See Ch.17, above.
[14] 1998 Act s.46(3) and s.43(10).
[15] 1998 Act s.45.
[16] 1998 Act s.40.
[17] 1998 Act s.40(2).

What can notices require?

20–18 The purpose of the enforcement notice issued by the Commissioner is to ensure compliance with the breached Principles or other relevant provisions. The notice will set out the steps to be taken (or to be avoided) to rectify the breach and a timescale for rectification.[18]

The enforcement notice may also specify that the data controller must cease processing:

- any type of personal data;

- any specified class of personal data;

- any personal data or specified class of personal data for a specified purpose or purposes or in a specified manner.[19]

20–19 When dealing with a breach of the fourth Principle (the requirement that data be accurate and up-to-date) the Commissioner may, in an enforcement notice, require the data controller:

- to rectify, block, erase or destroy inaccurate data;

- to rectify, block, erase or destroy other data held by the data controller containing an expression of opinion which appears to the Commissioner to be based on inaccurate data;

- with respect to personal data accurately recording information from a data subject or third party to take "reasonable steps" to ensure the accuracy of the data;

- with respect to personal data accurately recording information from a data subject or third party to incorporate an approved statement of the true facts.[20]

The latter two possibilities obviously envisage a situation where the data controller has accurately recorded inaccurate information from a third party or data subject and the data subject has objected. In addition to the general powers to require rectification, etc. the Commissioner may also require the data controller to take reasonable steps to check the accuracy of the information and/or may require the addition of an approved statement of the true facts. It is the Commissioner rather than any other party who "approves" the statement. These provisions stem directly from the interpretative provisions for the fourth Principle set out in para.7 of Pt II of Sch.1.[21]

Any enforcement notice requiring rectification, blocking, erasure or destruction of personal data (i.e. not just an enforcement notice dealing with the Fourth Principle) may require a data controller, if "reasonably practicable", to notify third parties to whom the data have been disclosed of the rectification, etc. The Commissioner may

---

[18] 1998 Act s.40(1)(a).
[19] 1998 Act s.40(1)(b).
[20] 1998 Act s.40(3) and (4).
[21] See Ch.5, above on The Principles.

also require this step to be taken if he is satisfied that data which have been rectified, etc. had been processed in breach of any of the principles.[22]

The Act provides that in determining what is "reasonably practicable" regard must be had, in particular, to the number of third parties to be notified.[23] The insertion of the words "in particular" clearly mean that the number of third parties to be notified is not the only matter to be considered when deciding on practicability but it is a major factor. It will be the responsibility of the Commissioner in the first instance to determine what is and is not reasonably practicable. The data controller may challenge the Commissioner's interpretation by an appeal to the Tribunal.

Timescale for compliance

20–20 Subject to the provisions on appeals and urgent notices it is for the Commissioner to determine the appropriate timescale. The Commissioner, save in urgent cases, may not require compliance with an enforcement notice before the end of the appeal period. Furthermore, if there is an appeal by the data controller then the need for compliance is suspended until the determination or withdrawal of the appeal.[24]

In urgent cases the Commissioner may require compliance after a minimum period of seven days from the service of the notice. It is for the Commissioner to determine whether the situation is urgent. The Act merely indicates that such a decision may be reached by "reason of special circumstances".

What must a notice contain?

20–21 The enforcement notice must contain:

- a statement of the Data Protection Principle or Principles which the Commissioner is satisfied have been or are being contravened and his reasons for reaching that conclusion;

- details of the data controller's rights of appeal against the enforcement notice[25]; and

- with urgent enforcement notices, a statement that compliance is required as a matter of urgency and a statement of the Commissioner's reasons for reaching that conclusion.[26]

Cancellation and variation

20–22 The Commissioner is empowered to vary or cancel any enforcement notice.[27] Conversely the subject of any enforcement notice may apply for cancellation or variation but only after the expiry of the appeal time limit. Under the 1984 Act the Registrar alone was empowered to cancel (rather than cancel or vary) enforcement

---

[22] 1998 Act s.40(5).
[23] 1998 Act s.40(5).
[24] 1998 Act s.40(7).
[25] 1998 Act s.40(6).
[26] 1998 Act s.40(8).
[27] 1998 Act s.41.

notices.[28] The power of variation was therefore new in the 1998 Act although it made little practical difference as under the 1984 Act the Registrar could cancel an enforcement notice and then issue a new one containing varied terms.

Enforcement notices served

20–23   In May 2000 the Information Commissioner issued two enforcement notices against Second Telecom Limited and Top 20 Ltd under the Telecommunications (Data Protection and Privacy) Regulations 1999 in relation to the sending of unsolicited "junk" faxes to individuals.

Regulation 24 prohibited the use of publicly available telecommunications services for communication of material for direct marketing purposes, by means of facsimile transmission, where the called line was that of a subscriber who was an individual who has not previously notified the caller that he consents for the time being to such communications being sent by, or at the instigation of the caller on that line.

Both companies appealed to the Tribunal. During the appeal process discussions between the companies and the Commissioner took place which led to an agreement between the Commissioner and the companies over what action needed to be taken to ensure compliance with the 1999 Regulations. This agreement was endorsed by the Tribunal, under s.49 of the 1998 Act, on November 20, 2000 and led to new enforcement notices being issued by the Commissioner. See Ch.22, below for a full discussion of the rules on unsolicited faxes.

In July 2004 the Commissioner issued enforcement notices against the Chief Constables of West Yorkshire, South Yorkshire and North Wales Police in relation to the retention of information on criminal convictions. The Commissioner sought the erasure or destruction of old conviction information. On appeal the Information Tribunal allowed the appeal as far as the retention of the information for policing purposes but not in respect of vetting (see Ch.5, above for a detailed analysis of the case).

The Commissioner has accepted undertakings from a number of financial organisations such as banks and building societies in respect of concerns about the security of hard copies of personal data about customers. The undertakings were published on the Commissioner's website in February 2007. The existence of the undertakings may however owe more to the finance industry's unwillingness to upset the regulator than any real breach of their legal obligations and for that reason they are not examined here.

Service of notices

20–24   Section 64 provides that individuals may serve any of the notices under the Act by electronic means as long as the resulting notice is received in legible form and capable of being used for subsequent reference. This provision does not apply to notices serviced by the Commissoner in the exercise of his regulatory functions. Service of notices by the Commissoner is covered under s.65 which sets out how notices may be served on individuals, bodies corporate or incorporate and partnerships in Scotland. The provisions are without prejudice to other lawful methods of service or giving notice. A notice may be served on an individual by delivering it to him, sending

---

[28] 1984 Act s.10(8).

it by post to his usual or last known place of residence or business, or leaving it for him at that place. A notice may be served on a body corporate or incorporate by sending it by post to or leaving it at its principal office addressed to the proper officer. A notice may be served on a partnership in Scotland by addressing it to the partnership and either posting it to or leaving it at the principal office of the partnership.

Rights of appeal against notices and determinations

20–25   A person upon whom an enforcement, information or special information notice or a determination has been served is given various rights of appeal by s.48 of the 1998 Act. All appeals are to the Information Tribunal (see Ch.).
The rights are:

- the right to appeal against any notice[29];
- the right to appeal against the refusal of an application by the recipient to cancel or vary an enforcement notice[30];
- the right to appeal against the decision by the Commissioner to include a statement that the notice is urgent and the right to appeal against any timescale consequently imposed[31];
- the right to appeal against a determination made under s.45.

Section 48 needs to be read in conjunction with Sch.6 to the 1998 Act which provides more detail on appeal procedures. The composition and powers of the Tribunal are covered in Ch.26.

ENFORCEMENT OF DATA SUBJECT'S RIGHTS

20–26   The Commissioner may also enforce data subjects' rights as breaches of the Principles. These are the rights to subject access[32]; to prevent processing likely to cause damage or distress[33]; to prevent direct marketing[34]; or to object to automated decision-making.[35] This is in addition to the rights of the data subjects to apply for court orders. These rights and their enforcement by the data subjects are discussed more fully in the chapters on data subject's rights (Chs 10–13, above).

ENTRY AND INSPECTION

20–27   The 1998 Act contains powers, virtually identical to those in the 1984 Act, for the Commissioner to obtain a warrant for his officers to enter and search premises and to seize evidence where a breach of the legislation is suspected. The powers of entry and inspection are contained in Sch.9.

---

[29] 1998 Act s.48(1).
[30] 1998 Act s.48(2). The ability to make such an application is set out in s.41(2).
[31] 1998 Act s.40(3). The procedures for urgent notices are set out in ss.40(8), 43(5) and 44(6).
[32] 1998 Act s.41.
[33] 1984 Act s.10(8).
[34] 1998 Act s.42(1).
[35] 1998 Act s.42(2).

For the grant of a warrant a circuit judge (sheriff in Scotland, county court judge in N. Ireland) must be satisfied of several matters. He must be satisfied by information on oath, supplied by the Commissioner, that there are reasons for suspecting that a data controller has contravened or is contravening any of the Data Protection Principles or that an offence under the Act has been or is being committed.[36] The power to grant a warrant therefore only applies in respect of past and current breaches of the Act. It does not apply when it is expected that an offence will be committed in the future. He must also be satisfied that there is information that evidence of the contravention or offence is at the specified premises.[37] "Premises" include any vessel, vehicle, aircraft or hovercraft.[38] Save in exceptional circumstances the warrant will not be issued unless the judge is satisfied that the Commissioner has given seven days' notice in writing to the occupier demanding access[39] and:

- access was demanded at a reasonable hour and unreasonably refused; or

- although entry to the premises was granted, the occupier unreasonably refused to comply with a request to permit the Commissioner's staff to exercise any of the rights covered by the warrant;[40] and

- the occupier has been notified of the warrant application has had an opportunity to make representations to the judge.[41]

Even when satisfied of all these matters, a judge still has a discretion to decline to grant a warrant.[42]

20–28 The exceptional circumstances permitting the grant of a warrant without notice to an occupier are if the judge is satisfied that the case is one of urgency or that compliance with the notice provisions would defeat the object of the entry.[43] "Urgency" is not more precisely defined but in practice the Commissioner will have to show some evidence or suspicion of an imminent act which could thwart the investigation. Given that, as already stated, warrants may not be granted with respect to future possible misconduct this exception should be quite limited.

No warrant may be issued in relation to data processed for the "special purposes" unless a s.45 determination (see para. 20–16, above) by the Commissioner has already been made.[44]

A warrant must be executed within seven days. The warrant authorises the Commissioner or any of his officers or staff to enter the premises, to search them, to inspect, examine, operate and test any equipment found there which is used or intended to be used for processing personal data and to inspect and seize any documents or other material found there which may be evidence of a breach of the principle or a commission of an offence under the Act.

---

[36] 1998 Act Sch.9 para.1(1).
[37] 1998 Act Sch.9 para.1(1).
[38] 1998 Act Sch.9 para.13.
[39] 1998 Act Sch.9 para.2(1)(a).
[40] 1998 Act Sch.9 para.2(1)(b).
[41] 1998 Act Sch.9 para.2(1)(c).
[42] 1998 Act Sch.9 para.1.
[43] 1998 Act Sch.9 para.2(2).
[44] 1998 Act Sch.9 para.1(2).

Search warrants under the Act are not limited to premises occupied by data controllers. Other premises may be searched providing the warrant criteria set out above are satisfied.

Reasonable force may be used in the execution of the warrant.[45] The warrant should be executed at a "reasonable hour" unless it is reasonably suspected that the relevant evidence would not be found at such a time.[46] "Reasonable hour" is not more precisely defined. For business premises it is likely to mean ordinary working hours. For domestic premises the term most likely excludes ordinary sleeping hours (23.00–08.00 approximately).

The warrant should be shown, and a copy provided, to the occupier of the premises or, if the occupier is not there, then a copy of a warrant should be left in a prominent place on the premises.[47]

20–29 If property is seized under the warrant then a receipt must be given if it is requested.[48] The legislation is not specific on when this must be done. The Codes of Practice made pursuant to the Police and Criminal Evidence Act 1984 state that with respect to the seizure of property by the police a list or description of the seized property must be provided within a reasonable time.[49] The absence of any time limit in the 1998 Act suggests that the receipt must be given on demand.

The "seizer" of property is empowered to hold it "as long as is necessary" in all the circumstances.[50] In practice this will mean that once property has been eliminated from an investigation then it must be returned forthwith. Property which is the subject of a prosecution or enforcement action may be retained until the end of that action and, if its destruction is not ordered, will have to be returned at the conclusion. In practice there is likely to be a considerable delay with respect to data retained on computer or disk (or other removable storage media) before such property is returned. This is because such property has to be examined with care—in particular to ensure that the examination does not result in an alteration of the data. Typically such forensic examinations are carried out by experts and within the criminal justice system there is a very high demand for their services. Even computers and disks which turn out not to contain "offending" material can thus be out of the owner's possession for a considerable period of time whilst awaiting forensic examination.

20–30 The PACE Codes of Practice, which are not binding on data protection investigators but to which they seek to adhere, contain the following provision:

> "Where an officer considers that a computer may contain information which could be used in evidence, he may require the information to be produced in a form which can be taken away and in which it is visible and legible."[51]

Under the 1998 Act the occupier must also be provided with copies of anything seized if they so request and if the person executing the warrant considers that it can

---

[45] 1998 Act Sch.9 para.4.
[46] 1998 Act Sch.9 para.5.
[47] 1998 Act Sch.9 para.6.
[48] 1998 Act Sch.9 para.7(1).
[49] PACE 1984 Code By para.6.8.
[50] 1998 Acts ch.9 para.7(2).
[51] PACE Code B para.6.5.

be done without undue delay.[52] This obligation contrasts with the parallel obligation under the PACE Codes. There the obligation is that copies should be provided within a reasonable time of any request unless providing copies would prejudice the investigation.[53] In police investigations the police would rarely allow copying to take place during any search—the fear would be that the occupier might tamper with the evidence during the copying process. The police would thus rely on the "prejudice to the investigation" exception. Furthermore, the police would use the "within a reasonable time" qualification to decline to provide copies during any search.

There are no parallel exceptions in the 1998 Act and it would appear therefore that if the occupier, for example, requests copies of any data disks and if copying facilities are readily available then such copying must be allowed unless undue delay would result. This is a valuable right which should be exercised by all data controllers subject to seizure of their property not least because it will enable them to continue operating pending any investigation.

20–31   There are no powers of inspection and seizure in relation personal data which are exempt to protect national security under s.28 of the Act. The exemptions are considered in detail in Ch.15, above. Furthermore, the powers of inspection and seizure do not apply to:

- communications between a professional legal adviser and his client with respect to legal advice given about the 1998 Act;

- communications between a professional legal adviser and his client, or between such an adviser or his client and any other person, made in connection with or in contemplation of proceedings under the 1998 Act.[54]

Anything held by a person other than the professional legal adviser or his client and anything held with the intention of furthering a criminal purpose is excluded from this exemption.[55] "Client" does however include any person representing such a client.[56]

In practice, those professional legal advisers engaged in dispensing advice on the 1998 Act would be well advised to implement the practice of marking correspondence as privileged so that any such documents can be readily identified during any search. Otherwise the person executing the warrant may not have the time, patience or inclination to listen to detailed representations regarding unmarked correspondence.

20–32   In the case of *R. v Chesterfield Justices Ex p. Bramley*[57] the High Court considered the responsibilities of the police in relation to material that was claimed to be the subject of legal professional privilege. The facts were as follows:

During the course of a criminal investigation concerning B, the police applied for warrants to search two premises for documents. Under the criteria, a magistrate could issue a search warrant only if he had reasonable grounds for believing, inter alia, that the material on the premises did not consist of or include items subject to legal privilege. However, no reference was made to the possibility that there was material subject to legal

[52] 1998 Act Sch.9 para.7(2).
[53] PACE Code B para.6.9.
[54] 1998 Act Sch.9 para.9(1).
[55] 1998 Act Sch.9 para.9(2).
[56] 1998 Act Sch.9 para.9(4).
[57] [2000] 1 All E.R. 411.

professional privilege at the two premises. The magistrates granted the warrants, and the police duly carried out the searches. No one was present at the first site where certain privileged documents were inspected only to the extent necessary to establish their nature. At the other site, a claim by B to privilege in respect of certain documents was rejected and those documents removed from the site, but the police returned them without inspection following representations from B's solicitors. B subsequently applied for judicial review of the magistrates' decision to grant the warrants, and of the police's decision to seize privileged documents. In particular, the court was asked to determine whether the police were entitled to remove documents from premises for later sifting, whether they were entitled to remove documents from the premises for sifting elsewhere and whether the police could sift on site documents which were said to be privileged.

The court held (Jowitt J. dissenting):

"(1) If the officer who made the application did not volunteer information on the specific issue of privilege, the magistrate should ask whether the material sought consisted of or included items subject to such privilege and if there were reasonable grounds for believing that the material sought included items subject to privilege, the targeted material would have to be redefined in such a way as to enable the magistrate to be satisfied that there were no longer reasonable grounds for such a belief, otherwise he could not issue the warrant.

(3) In order to decide how much of the available material fell within the scope of the warrant, the searchers would have to look at the documents, but if there was a lot of material and it was not possible to sort the relevant material reasonably quickly and easily, the statute did not enable the officer to remove all or a large part of the material to sort it out properly elsewhere.

(4) Whether or not an officer had reasonable grounds for believing an item was not subject to privilege was a question of fact, to be decided in the context of any given case. It was preferable for an agreement to be reached at the time of the search as to what was and what was not subject to privilege, but if that was not possible, the officer conducting the search should package separately for later examination items which were relevant but which he believed might be subject to privilege.

(5) If there was a difference of opinion which could not be resolved during the search as to whether an item seized was within the warrant or was subject to privilege the issue should be determined preferably by means of an action for trespass to goods, although it would be possible to proceed by way of judicial review."

20–33 The decision was distinguished in *R. (on the application of H) v Inland Revenue Commissioners*[58] in which the Revenue seized two computers from the applicant's home having entered his premises under a warrant granted under the Taxes Management Act 1970. The officers could not copy the hard drives in situ so they removed the computers and then copied the hard drives. The court held that a hard drive should be regarded as a single "thing" that could be required as evidence for the purposes of the Taxes Management Act.

---

[58] [2002] EWHC 2164.

20–34   There is, moreover , a significant and potentially material difference between the provisions in the Police and Criminal Evidence Act 1984 (PACE) and those in the Data Protection Act 1998.

Section 19(6) of PACE provides that:

> "No power of seizure conferred on a constable under any enactment (including an enactment contained in an Act passed after this Act) is to be taken to author-ise the seizure of an item which the constable exercising the power has reasonable grounds for believing to be subject to legal privilege."

The *Chesterfield Justices* cases establishes that whether an officer has reasonable grounds for believing that material is subject to legal privilege is a question of fact to be decided on a case-by-case basis but if such reasonable grounds for believing are established then any seizure will be illegal.

In the Data Protection Act 1998 Sch.9 para.9(1) simply states that the powers of inspection and seizure conferred by a warrant issued under Sch.9 are not exercisable in respect of material which is the subject of legal privilege.

This, on the face of it, seems to put the Commissioner's investigators in an impossi-ble position since if material is in fact the subject of legal privilege then any inspection and seizure will be automatically unlawful. There is no "reasonable grounds for believ-ing" qualification in the Data Protection Act 1998. Thus if the occupier of premises being searched by the Commissioner's investigators claims legal privilege but an inves-tigator proceeds to check the assertion by an on-site inspection and the material does turn out to be privileged it would appear that the inspection will have been unlawful, Similarly if the disputed material is removed for an off-site inspection and it turns out that the material is in fact privileged then both the seizure and inspection will be unlaw-ful. It appears that it would not be open to an investigator to claim that at the time of inspection of seizure they held a reasonable belief that the material was privileged.

20–35   If an occupier objects to the inspection or seizure of any material on the grounds that it consists partly of privileged material then he must, if the person exe-cuting the warrant so requests, still provide copies of the non-privileged parts.[59] Warrants must be endorsed and returned to the issuing court after being executed or, if not executed, within seven days. The endorsement must state what powers have been exercised under the warrant.[60]

Offences and Prosecutions

20–36   Prosecutions for actions such as disclosure of information without authori-sation may also be brought under other provisions. The 1998 Act creates several criminal offences. Section 63(5) of the 1998 Act provides that neither a government department nor the person who is the data controller for the Royal Household (the Keeper of the Privy Purse), the Duchy of Lancaster and the Duchy of Cornwall shall be liable to prosecution under the Act. However the provisions in s.55 (unlawful obtaining and disclosing of personal data—and the provisions relating to obstructing

---

[59] 1998 Act Sch.9 para.10.
[60] 1998 Act Sch.9 para.11.

the execution of a warrant) do apply to a person in the service of the Crown as they apply to any other person.

In England, Wales and Northern Ireland the Commissioner and the Director of Public Prosecutions are the only people able to bring proceedings for an offence under the Act.[61] Almost all the offences under the Act are either way offences carrying the statutory maximum financial penalties (£5,000 in the magistrates' court and an unlimited fine in the Crown Court). Community Service Orders may also be imposed. In addition to imposing a penalty on conviction the court may also, for most offences, order that any document or other material used in connection with the processing of personal data and appearing to the court to be connected with the commission of the offence be forfeited, destroyed or erased.[62] A court may not make such an order where a person other than the offender claims an interest in the relevant material unless the person is given an opportunity to be heard.[63]

20–37   Prosecutions have been brought against police officers who disclosed information from the Police National Computer under the common law offence of misfeasance in public office. Offences under this provision are imprisonable, whereas offences under the Data Protection Act are not. In the case of *AG's reference (No. 1 of 2007) sub nom R. v James Andrew Hardy*[64] the Attorney General referred a sentence of imprisonment which had been suspended and a requirement to undertake 300 hours' unpaid work to the Court of Appeal as being unduly lenient. The Court held that on the facts the officer's misconduct had required a sentence of immediate imprisonment and the minimum sentence for the offence should have been 18 months.

Failure to comply with a notice

20–38   Section 47 of the 1998 Act creates two criminal offences relating to enforcement and other notices. First, a person who fails to comply with a notice under the legislation commits an offence.[65] It is a defence to show that all due diligence was exercised to comply with the notice.[66] The concept of "due diligence" is one that appeared in the 1984 Act as a defence to a charge of failing to comply with an enforcement notice or a transfer prohibition notice.[67]

There have been very few prosecutions for failing to comply with an enforcement notice and none which have involved an appeal to the higher courts. Therefore despite the concept of "due diligence" having been in existence in the context of data protection for nearly 20 years there are no useful authorities on its interpretation. The concept of "due diligence", especially as a defence, does appear in many other criminal statutes. Section 96(4) of the Banking Act 1987 provides:

> "In any proceedings for an offence under this Act it shall be a defence for the person charged to prove that he took all reasonable precautions and exercised all due diligence to avoid the commission of such an offence by himself or any person under his control."

---

[61] 1984 Act s.6(5).
[62] 1998 Act s.60(4).
[63] 1998 Act s.60(5).
[64] [2007] EWCA Crim 760.
[65] 1998 Act s.47(1).
[66] 1998 Act s.47(3).
[67] 1984 Act ss.10(9) and 12(10).

There are, however, no helpful authorities on the interpretation of due diligence within the context of the Banking Act 1987 either.

20–39   Section 47 of the 1998 Act creates a second offence of knowingly or recklessly providing information which is false in a material respect in response to any information/special information notice. The requirement that the information is false in a material respect will exclude trivial or inconsequential falsehoods.

The offence under s.47 may be committed "knowingly or recklessly". Both terms are well established concepts in criminal legislation. Where the word knowingly is included in the definition of an offence it makes it plain that the doctrine of *mens rea* applies to that offence. When the term is used the prosecution must prove knowledge on the part of the offender of all the material circumstances of the offence. For example, on a charge of "knowingly having in his possession an explosive substance", the prosecution must prove that the accused knew both that he had it in his possession and that it was an explosive substance.[68] Applying this principle to the offence under s.47 would mean that the prosecution must prove that the provider of the information knew that the information was false in a material respect.

Archbold[69] suggests that there is some authority for the view that in the criminal law "knowledge" includes "wilfully shutting one's eyes to the truth": (see, e.g. per Lord Reid in *Warner v Metropolitan Police Commissioner*[70] or *Atwal v Massey*[71]) but counsels that such a proposition must be treated with great caution. The view of the courts at present is that this is a matter of evidence, and that nothing short of actual knowledge will suffice. See the dictum of Lord Bridge in *Westminster City Council v Croyalgrange Ltd*.[72]

The exclusion of "wilfully shutting one's eyes to the truth" from the ambit of "knowingly" arguably has little impact on the offence under s.47 of the 1998 Act since the offence can be committed "knowingly or recklessly" and it is likely that "wilful eye closure" will be covered by the latter concept.

20–40   In the case of *R v G*[73] the House of Lords considered the requirement for *mens rea* in the case of an offence under the Criminal Damage Act 1971. The House departed from the decision in the case of *Caldwell* in which it had held that the defendant would be reckless if a reasonable person would have recognised the risk. The House held that this was capable of leading to obvious unfairness and the need to correct it was compelling. Accordingly a person would be taken to act recklessly within the meaning of s.1 with respect to circumstances when he was aware of a risk that existed or would exist and, being aware of the risk it was unreasonable to take it. The meaning of recklessness has been subject to some modification in the context of sexual offences. The offence of rape for example may be committed if the defendant knows that his victim is not consenting or is reckless as to whether he or she does consent.

In *R. v Taylor (Robert)*[74] Lord Lane C.J. said that in rape, the defendant is reckless if he does not believe the woman is consenting and could not care less whether she is consenting or not but presses on regardless.

---

[68] *R. v Hallam* [1957] 1 Q.B. 569; (1957) 41 Cr.App.R. 111, CCA.
[69] 1998 ed. at para.17–49.
[70] [1969] 2 A.C. 256 at 279, HL.
[71] (1972) 56 Cr.App.R. 6, DC.
[72] (1986) 83 Cr.App.R. 155 at 164, HL.
[73] [2003] UKHL 50.
[74] (1985) 80 Cr.App.R. 327, CA.

20–41 The courts had an opportunity to consider the term "recklessly" within the context of the 1984 Act in *Data Protection Registrar v Amnesty International*.[75] The brief facts were that the defendant was a charity which was registered under the 1984 Act. It entered into an agreement with another charity which involved it disclosing its database of supporters to a mailing house so that the mailing house could carry out a mailing on behalf of the second charity. The Registrar alleged that as a consequence Amnesty International had operated outside the terms of their registration entry and had committed offences under s.5(2)(b) and 5(2)(d) of the 1984 Act. The particular offences were the use of personal data for an unregistered purpose—namely trading in personal information and the disclosure of personal data to a person (the mailing house) not described in the registration entry. One of the consequences of Amnesty's action was that their supporters received a mailing seeking contributions to the second charity. One of the recipients complained to the Registrar. The Registrar put the case on the basis that Amnesty International had operated outside the terms of its register entry and had committed the s.5(2) offences recklessly rather than knowingly. It was contended that it had altered the use of the personal data they held without giving any consideration to whether this had implications for their data protection registration.

20–42 The stipendiary magistrate dismissed the informations at the conclusion of the trial. One of the reasons given was that Amnesty's actions had not caused any "serious harmful consequences" as apparently required by the *Lawrence/Caldwell* definition of "recklessness". The stipendiary magistrate took the consequences of Amnesty's action to be the receipt of unwanted "begging" letters by Amnesty's supporters and took the view that this could only sensibly be described as irritating rather than "serious" or "harmful".

The Registrar appealed to the Divisional Court on the basis that the phrase in the *Lawrence/Caldwell* definition "the kind of serious harmful consequences that the section that created the offence was intended to prevent" had to be read in the context of the particular piece of legislation. In the context of the 1984 Act it meant no more than the kind of consequences (i.e. a data user operating outside the terms of their register entry) that s.5(2) of the 1984 Act was intended to prevent. The words "serious" and "harmful" really only had meaning within the context of the offences that *Lawrence* and *Caldwell* were considering—causing death by reckless driving and criminal damage respectively.

The Divisional Court held that this was the correct interpretation. Amnesty's acquittals however stood as the Registrar did not seek to have the matter remitted to the magistrates' court.

For a consideration of recklessness on the part of a corporation in the context of the Data Protection Acts 1984 and 1998 see the discussion of *Information Commissioner v Islington LBC*[76] below.

The two offences under s.47 are either way offences. Both are punishable by a fine—maximum £5,000 in the magistrates' court, unlimited in the Crown Court.

Notification offences

20–43 Under the 1998 Act the system of registration by data users was replaced by one of notification by data controllers. Unfortunately, the supporting criminal offences

---

[75] [1995] Crim. L.R. 633.
[76] [2002] EWHC Admin 1036; [2002] All E.R. (D) 381.

which buttress the requirement of notification are no longer neatly contained in one comprehensible section of the legislation (as with s.5 of the 1984 Act).

The requirement to notify the Commissioner is set out in ss.16–20 of the Act. These provisions require data controllers to notify the Commissioner of:

- their name and address;
- a description of the personal data;
- the purpose(s) for which they are held;
- the recipients of disclosures;
- non-EEA countries to which the data may be transferred;
- security measures to comply with Principle 7.

For a more detailed consideration of Notification see Ch.9, above.

Section 21 makes it an offence to fail to notify the Commissioner of the processing of personal data and also to keep the Commissioner notified of relevant changes (for example as to the address of the controller, or to the intentions of the controller with respect to the processing of personal data, or to the security measures to comply with Principle 7). The failure to "notify" and the failure to notify changes are either way offences punishable with a maximum £5,000 fine in the magistrates' court or an unlimited fine in the Crown Court.

Failure to provide relevant particulars (s.24)

20–44   Section 17(1) of the Act prohibits processing of personal data unless the data controller has "notified" the Commissioner. Section 17(2) and (3) set out limited exceptions to this basic prohibition. These are, first, where the relevant data is not information which is being processed by the means of equipment operating automatically in response to instructions given for purpose nor is it information which is recorded with the intention that it should be processed by means of such equipment.[77] In other words the data is information which is recorded as part of a relevant filing system or which forms part of an accessible record as defined by s.68. These have come to be known as "manual records".

Secondly, the prohibition in s.17(1) does not apply where the Secretary of State has exempted particular processing of the basis that it is unlikely to prejudice the rights and freedoms of data subjects.[78] This power has been used to exempt some forms of common processing from the requirement to notify. The categories of processing which have been determined as falling within this class are set out in the Notification Regulations and are described in the chapter on notification, above.

If either of these exceptions apply then a data controller may, nonetheless, give a notification to the Commissioner under s.18. If a data controller chooses not do so then any person may still request the "relevant particulars" from the data controller. The data controller is under a duty to supply the particulars in writing within 21 days

---

[77] 1998 Act s.1(1)(a) and (b).
[78] 1998 Act s.17(3).

and free of charge.[79] These particulars are the equivalent of the information which must be notified to be Commissioner.

Any data controller who fails to provide the relevant particulars commits an offence.[80] It is a defence for the data controller to show that he exercised due diligence to comply with the duty to supply the relevant particulars. For a discussion of the concept of "due diligence" see above. Again the offence is an either way offence and punishable with the statutory maximum financial penalty.

Unlawful obtaining and disclosing of personal data

20–45 Section 55 of the 1998 Act radically reworked aspects of the equivalent offences in the 1984 Act. In 2007 it was the subject of a major consultation by the Commissioner's office and has become one of the most important criminal provisions in the Act. However it did not appear in the original 1984 Act and does not derive from the Directive. The section addresses the growing and troublesome problem of third parties obtaining information by deception, sometimes referred to as "blagging" and sometimes (more mysteriously given the usual meaning of the phrase) as "social engineering". In this text it is referred to as the practice of obtaining information by deception.

The problem came to prominence with a news story about the then new head of British Intelligence, Stella Rimington. In 1994 Ms Rimington was the first named head of British Intelligence and the press decided to celebrate this limited openness by seeing what other information could be unearthed about her. "Investigative" journalists therefore set about finding out details about her affairs. This did not result in any major disclosures; the most startling appeared to be that she routinely shopped at Marks and Spencer on a Thursday evening, but it did raise the question of how material about her could be accessed so readily. It transpired that the information had been obtained by deceptive telephone calls to her financial services providers. When a complaint was made to the Office of the Data Protection Registrar (ODPR) it was decided that no prosecution could be brought since the duped data users had not committed any knowing or reckless breach of their register entry.

Clearly this incident alone did not spark the alterations to the 1984 Act—rather it was symptomatic of a general concern about the ease with which private detectives and journalists were apparently able to obtain purportedly confidential personal information. Some private investigators even boasted in advertisements that they could obtain "full financial profiles" of any named individual. The issue was addressed in 1994 by amendments to the 1984 Act introduced by the Criminal Justice and Public Order Act 1994.

20–46 The amendments introduced three new offences:

S.5(6)—a person who procures the disclosure to him of personal data the disclosure of which to him is in contravention of subs.5(2) or 5(3), knowing or having reason to believe that the disclosure constitutes such a contravention shall be guilty of an offence.

S.5(7)—A person who sells personal data shall be guilty of an offence if (in contravention of subs.6) he has procured the disclosure of the data to him.

---

[79] 1998 Act s.24(1).
[80] 1998 Act s.24(4).

S.5(8)—A person who offers to sell personal data shall be guilty of an offence if (in contravention of subs.(6) he has procured or subsequently procures the disclosure of the data to him.

The amendments were fraught with potential difficulties, particularly because the offences were linked to registration, that being the fundamental concept under the 1984 Act. There were a number of successful prosecutions but they were difficult to bring home and the wording of the provision was revised in the 1998 Act.

20–47   Under the 1998 Act it is an offence knowingly or recklessly:

- to obtain or disclose personal data or the information contained in personal data; or

- to procure the disclosure to another person of the information contained in personal data,

without the consent of the data controller.

For a discussion of "knowingly or recklessly" see para.20–41, above.

The obtaining/disclosing/procuring without the consent of the data controller will not be an offence if the perpetrator can prove on the balance of probabilities that:

- it was necessary for the prevention or detection or crime;

- it was required or authorised by statute, rule of law, or court order;

- the "obtainer or procurer", etc. acted in the reasonable belief that he had a right in law to act as he did or that he would have had the consent of the controller if they had known of the particular circumstances; or

- it was, in the particular circumstances, justifiable as being in the public interest.

In any criminal proceedings the onus will initially be on the relevant person to raise one or more of these issues as a defence. If that initial onus is satisfactorily discharged then the onus will shift to the Commissioner to prove beyond reasonable doubt that the defence claimed does not apply.

The requirement that the "obtainer", etc. held a reasonable belief imposes an objective standard. In other words it will not be sufficient for the "obtainer" to hold an honest belief about particular circumstances if that belief was objectively unreasonable. The defence based on the reasonable belief that the obtainer, etc. had in law the right to obtain, etc. obviously undermines the basic proposition that ignorance of law is generally no defence. Such defences are not, however, unknown in the criminal law. For example, under s.2(1) of the Theft Act 1968 a person is not to be regarded as dishonest "if he appropriates the property in the belief that he has in law the right to deprive the other of it".

20–48   While the drafting clearly addresses some of the problems encountered with the earlier provision s.55 is not without problems—"without the consent of the data controller" may require some careful examination. In many prosecutions under s.5(6) of the 1984 Act the fundamental allegation was that the data user had been duped into disclosing personal data. It could be contended that although the data user was deceived the disclosure was not without their consent.

However, the law on consent in the context of sexual offences addresses this issue and case law has held that a mistake as to the identity of the person carrying out an action will vitiate apparent consent as will a fraud as to the nature of the act *R. v Linekar*.[81] As to frauds as to the nature of the act, see for example *R. v Flattery*,[82] where the consent was induced by the pretence that the act of intercourse was a form of medical treatment, and *R. v Williams*,[83] where a choirmaster pretended to be testing a girl's breathing powers with an instrument. As to fraud as to the identity of the perpetrator of the act, s.1(3) of the Sexual Offences Act 1956 makes express provision for the case of a man inducing a married woman to have sexual intercourse with him by impersonating her husband. This provision was first introduced by the Criminal Law Amendment Act 1885 for the purpose of reversing the decision in *R. v Barrow*.[84] As to other instances of impersonation, it is possible that the principle in *Barrow* will still prevail; but it was dissented from in *R. v Dee*,[85] and doubt about the correctness of the decision was expressed in *Flattery*. What was said in *Linekar* as to fraud as to identity vitiating consent was obiter, the case not concerning mistake as to identity at all, but the editors of Archbold submit that the view of the Court of Appeal represents the modern and better view.[86]

20–49 The most common type of deception employed on a data controller by those seeking to obtain personal data unlawfully is a deception as to their identity. Typically they pretend to be the data subject or someone authorised to act on their behalf. Applying the principle that "fraud as to identity vitiates consent" derived from sexual offences cases to the context of personal data ought to mean the most common type of deception vitiates the "consent" of the data controller. The requirement in the Directive that the data subject's consent must be "freely given, specific and informed"[87] may also be pertinent. The Commissioner may argue that the data controller's consent must be similarly informed, which would exclude consent obtained by deception.

20–50 It is also an offence to sell or to offer to sell personal data that has been unlawfully obtained/procured/disclosed. An offer to sell includes an advertisement indicating that personal data are or may be for sale. The offences do not apply to personal data where an exemption is necessary for the purposes of national security (see s.55(8)). Thus such deceptive means of obtaining information may continue to be used by those concerned with national security where it is necessary for the purpose. Nor does s.55 apply to the new category of recorded information added by the amendments in the Freedom of Information Act 2000. These offences again are either way offences and again attract the statutory maximum financial penalties.

20–51 In November 2002 one of the first prosecutions under s.55 came to trial before the Kingston Crown Court. In *R. v Codrington* (unreported) C was an employee of the Benefits Agency who had abused his access to the Agency's computer equipment to look up personal data relating to friends and family. He was prosecuted by the

---

[81] (1995) 2 Cr.App.R. 49, CA.
[82] (1877) 2 Q.B.D. 410.
[83] [1923] 1 K.B. 340; (1924) 17 Cr.App.R. 56, CCA.
[84] (1868) L.R. 1 C.C.R. 156.
[85] (1884) 15 Cox C.C. 579.
[86] 1998 ed., para.20–29.
[87] Directive Art.2(h).

Commissioner under both s.5(6) of the Data Protection Act 1984 and s.55 of the Data Protection Act 1998 since the alleged behaviour occurred both before and after March 1, 2000. The matter was contested but C was convicted of all matters.

In the course of the trial the trial judge was asked to direct the jury on the meaning and ambit of the term "knowingly or recklessly" in the context of s.55. The trial judge agreed with prosecution counsel's submission that the term applied both to the lack of consent of the data controller and to the "obtaining", "disclosing" or "procuring".

Section 55(1) reads:

> "A person must not knowingly or recklessly, without the consent of the data controller:
>
> (a) obtain or disclose personal data or the information contained in personal data; or
>
> (b) procure the disclosure to another person of the information contained in personal data."

The trial judge in *Codrington* considered that "knowingly or recklessly" had to apply to the lack of consent of the data controller as otherwise the phrase would have appeared after "without the consent of the data controller".

Thus the prosecution in *Codrington* had to demonstrate knowledge or recklessness on the part of the defendant in respect of the lack of the consent of the Benefits Agency and the obtaining of the personal data. Of course most "obtaining" of personal data is going to be with knowledge but it is clearly possible to envisage a reckless "disclosure" of personal data.

20–52 In the case of *R v Rooney*[88] the defendant was charged with having knowingly or recklessly obtained and disclosed personal data relating to her sister's estranged partner. The defendant was an employee of Staffordshire police in the HR department. She accessed the computer records of the address of her sister's ex-partner on several occasions and following the last occasion she disclosed to her sister that the officer had moved to "an address in Tunstall". She was convicted of having disclosed personal data and appealed on the grounds that the information disclosed did not fall within the definition of personal data as no one could be identified from it. The appeal was dismissed on the grounds that it was sufficient that she had disclosed information contained in personal data and it was not an essential component of the offence that the identity of the individual be disclosed.

20–53 The mischief addressed by the section has grown as more and more parties seek to access information about others, often for journalistic purposes but occasionally for other reasons such as the collection of debts. The Information Commissioner has been active in pursuing such offences. In May 2006 he presented a report to Parliament under his powers in s.52(2) of the Act[89] in which he set out the problems arising from the illicit trade in personal data and made an argument for significantly increasing the penalties available for the offences. The core recommendation of the report was that the Government should raise the penalty for conviction on indictment for s.55 offences to a maximum two years imprisonment or a fine or both, and for

---

[88] [2006] EWCA Crim 1841.

[89] *What price privacy? The unlawful trade in confidential personal information*, May 10, 2006, HC 1056.

summary conviction to a maximum of six months imprisonment or a fine or both. The report included a number of other recommendations as follows:

- businesses buying information should only buy information which they are confident has been properly obtained;

- the Security Industry Authority should include a caution or conviction for a s.55 offence among the grounds for refusing or revoking a licence for a private investigator;

- the Association of British Investigators should include explicit reference to the offences in its training standards;

- the Press Complaint Commission should take a stronger line to address the use of such tactics by the press;

- the Office of Fair Trading should amend its debt collection guidance to condemn s.55 offences.

The Commissioner also signalled that he would continue discussions with all the relevant parties, seek further evidence from the public and publish a follow-up report in six months time.

20–54 The follow-up report was duly published in December 2006[90] and Richard Thomas was able to report on six months of effective progress. In particular he welcomed the decision of the Department of Constitutional Affairs to launch a public consultation on the possibility of increasing the penalties for deliberate and wilful misuse of personal data.[91] The consultation document proposed an increase in the criminal sanctions in line with the recommendation from the Office of the Information Commissioner. The consultation had closed in October 2006. The recommendations in the report which has received a very broadly positive response. On February 7, 2007 the Government announced its intention to increase the penalties as sought by the Commissioner when a suitable legislative opportunity presented itself.

Offences committed in relation to warrants

20–55 It is an offence under para.12 of Sch.9 to intentionally obstruct the execution of a warrant or to fail, without reasonable excuse, to give reasonably required assistance for the execution. Examples of the latter type of obstruction might be the refusal to give a password to access a computer system or the refusal to unlock a filing cabinet.

The most common form of obstruction in the criminal justice system is the obstruction of a police constable in the execution of his duty.[92] A defendant obstructs a police constable if he makes it more difficult for him to carry out his duty.[93] No physical act

---

[90] *What price privacy now? The first six months progress in halting the unlawful trade in confidential personal information*, December 13, 2006, HC 36.
[91] July 24, 2006.
[92] Police Act 1996 s.89.
[93] *Hinchcliffe v Sheldon* [1955] 1 W.L.R. 1207.

is necessary to constitute obstruction. Simple refusal to answer questions does not constitute an obstruction.[94] Answering questions incorrectly may, however, amount to obstruction.[95] A person may obstruct by omission but only if they are under an initial duty to act.[96] There is also a common law offence of refusing to aid a constable who is attempting to prevent or to quell a breach of the peace and who calls for assistance.[97]

Thus it can be seen that the obligation to assist a person executing a warrant under the 1998 Act is an extension to the usual concept of "obstruction" and a potentially onerous obligation. There maybe situations where the obligation clashes or appears to clash with a suspect's right against self-incrimination as stated in the European Convention on Human Rights.[98] For example, if an occupier is asked to provide a password to a computer system which the occupier knows contains incriminating information does the obligation to assist imposed by Sch.9 breach the right again self-incrimination? Unlike other offences under the 1998 Act this obstruction offence may only be dealt within the magistrates' court and is punishable with a maximum fine of £5,000.

Enforced subject access

20–56 This subject is more fully discussed in Ch.21, below. However it is worthwhile in this section highlighting the offence created by s.56(5), although the offence remains not yet in force. This makes it an offence for a person in connection with:

- the recruitment of another person as an employee;
- the continued employment of another person; or
- any contract for the provision of services to him by another person,

to require that other person or a third party to supply him with a "relevant record".

Similarly, it is an offence for a person concerned with the provision of goods, facilities or services to public or a section of public to require, as a condition of providing such goods, etc. to another person, that other person or a third party to supply him with a "relevant record". "Relevant record" is given a lengthy and specific definition in s.56(6) and this is discussed in detail in Ch.21, below.

Liability of directors

20–57 Section 61 provides that where an offence has been committed by a body corporate and is proved to have been committed with the consent or connivance of or to be attributable to any neglect on the part of any director, manager, secretary or similar officer or any one acting in such capacity that person shall be guilty of the offence as well as the body corporate and be liable to be proceeded against and punished in the same way. Offences by bodies corporate which require *mens rea* can only be successfully prosecuted where a senior officer of the body corporate or a "directing

---

[94] *Rice v Connolly* [1966] 2 Q.B. 414.
[95] *Green v DPP* (1991) 155 J.P. 816.
[96] *Lunt v DPP* [1993] Crim. L.R. 534.
[97] *Waugh, The Times*, October 1, 1986.
[98] European Convention on Human Rights, Art.6.

OFFENCES AND PROSECUTIONS

mind" can be shown to have the necessary mental element. This is an additional provision that enables the prosecutor to seek a penalty against the individual in his or her own right arising from that person's engagement in the offence. It is a pre-condition that the prosecution prove the offence against the body corporate. Section 61 is essentially parasitic. The standard required to be shown in respect of the senior officer is relatively low; the offence need only be with their consent, connivance or even attributable to neglect. Where a body corporate is managed by its members, then the section applies equally to members who hold management positions and in a Scottish partnership (which is an entity with separate legal personality from its partners) to partners in the same position.

Additional penalties

20–58   In addition to the penalties by way of fine and costs the prosecution may, in the case of some offences, apply to the court dealing with the prosecution for an order that any document or other material used in connection with the processing of personal data connected with the offence be forfeited, destroyed or erased.

The relevant offences are failure to notify, failure to keep a notification up-to-date, the unlawful procuring of data, enforced subject access and breach of an enforcement notice. Where a person (not the offender) claims to be the owner of or otherwise a person interested in the material in question the court must give them an opportunity to be heard and explain why such an order should not be made.

Unlawful disclosure by the Commissioner's staff

20–59   Section 59(3) makes it a criminal offence for the Commissioner, his staff and agents to disclose information obtained in connection with the Act unless disclosure is made with lawful authority. The information must relate to an identified or identifiable individual or business and must not already be in the public domain.[99]

A disclosure will only be with lawful authority if:

- it is made with consent;

- the information was provided for the purpose of being made public in accordance with the Act;

- the disclosure is required by the Act or any Community obligation;

- disclosure is for the purpose of any civil or criminal proceedings;

- disclosure is in the public interest having regard to the rights and freedoms or legitimate interests of any person.[100]

Assessable processing

20–60   "Assessable processing" is defined in s.22(1) as processing specified in an order made by the Secretary of State as appearing particularly likely to cause substantial damage or distress to data subjects or otherwise significantly to prejudice the rights

---

[99]   1998 Act s.59(1)(a).
[100]   1998 Act s.59(2).

and freedoms of data subjects. The Commissioner is placed under an obligation by s.22(2) on receiving notification to consider whether any of the relevant processing is assessable processing and, if so, whether it is likely to comply with the provisions of the 1998 Act.

If the Commissioner decides that assessable processing is involved then within 28 days of receiving notification (the period may exceptionally be extended by up to 14 days) the Commissioner must give notice to data controller of the decision and the opinion as to whether the processing is likely or unlikely to comply with the Act. This provision does not give the Commissioner the power to prohibit processing—only to give an opinion. If the Commissioner wishes to prohibit processing then she must use the enforcement notice procedure.

No assessable processing, in respect of which a notification has been given to the Commissioner, may be carried on unless:

- the 28-day period (or exceptionally extended period) has expired; or

- before the end of that period the data controller has received the notice of the Commissioner's opinion.

If a data controller breaches this requirement then an offence is committed.[101] There is no statutory defence of being able to show due diligence. In either it is a way offence punishable with the maximum financial penalties. However, no orders have been made and no processing is currently classed as assessable processing, nor do there appear to be any proposals to change this.

Procedural issues and delay

20–61 Investigations conducted by the Information Commissioner's office are often quite prolonged—for a variety of reasons including staffing levels. There have quite often been substantial delays between the receipt of a complaint of an alleged offence and the commencement of a prosecution. However the current position under UK law would appear to be that the courts are rarely concerned, in relation to Art.6 rights, with the delay between the start of an investigation and the commencement of a prosecution unless the defendant can show "material prejudice" prior to being summonsed. It is difficult to envisage "material prejudice" occurring during an investigation conducted by the Information Commissioner since the Commissioner's investigators have no power of arrest and detention and cannot even insist on an interview taking place. It is just about possible to imagine "material prejudice" occurring if the alleged offender is in a business where the secure processing of personal data is crucial and details of the investigation become widely known.

Rather the courts' concern in relation to delay is what happens post charge or summons. There are rarely significant delays attributable to the Information Commissioner in DPA prosecutions post summons. Thus although abuse of the process arguments based on Art.6 rights and delay have been threatened and indeed presented in DPA prosecutions, to date none have been successful.

---

[101] 1998 Act s.22(6).

ENFORCEMENT UNDER THE 1984 ACT

20–62   There were a number of problems with the offence provisions of the 1984 Act which are now of no more than historical interest. There was also a period of some uncertainty after the implementation of the 1998 Act in March 2000 in relation to offences committed before implementation. These are covered briefly in this section, although it is unlikely that they will have any ongoing relevance. For a full discussion see earlier editions of this text.

Procuring information

20–63   As explained earlier, this section had been added by an amendment and the wording caused some problems. In particular it appeared that an offence was only committed if the procurer obtained a disclosure to himself. This was an apparent loophole which appeared ripe for exploitation. For example, a private detective agency procuring the disclosure of confidential financial information could arrange for the data to be disclosed direct to their client rather than to the original procurer of the information.

A further problem was related to registration. It was a requirement of a s.5(6) offence that the procurement resulted in a breach of s.5(2) or 5(3) of the 1984 Act— the provisions which obliged a data user to operate within the terms of the user's data protection register entry.

Finally, problems arose with trying to establish the mental element in s.5(6) offences. The section required that the procurer "knows or has reason to believe" that a breach of s.5(2) has resulted from their actions. In practice, knowledge was extremely difficult to establish since it suggested a detailed knowledge on the part of the defendant of the duped data user's data protection register entry. "Reason to believe" sounded like a familiar legal concept but in reality was a phrase that did not appear anywhere else in the criminal law. In practice the Registrar invited the courts to infer "reason to believe" whenever a deception was practised by the procurer—on the basis that no deception would have been used if the procurer believed that they were acting within the terms of the data user's register entry. All of those problems have been addressed in the current provisions.

CRIMINAL ENFORCEMENT FOR MATTERS BEFORE MARCH 1, 2000

20–64   Since the 1998 Act repealed the 1984 Act, including all the provisions creating criminal offences, and since the transitional provisions of the 1998 Act did not specifically preserve the 1984 Act criminal offences, question arose as to how offences under the 1984 Act could be prosecuted and warrants obtained post March 1, 2000 in respect of earlier transgressions.

Article 7 of the ECHR provides:

> "(1) No one shall be held guilty of any criminal offence on account of any act or omission which did not constitute a criminal offence under national or international law at the time when it was committed. Nor shall a heavier penalty be imposed than the one that was applicable at the time the criminal offence was committed.

(2) This Article shall not prejudice the trial and punishment of any person for any act or omission which, at the time it was committed, was criminal according to the general principles of law recognised by civilised nations."

The first limb of Art.7(1) prohibits the retroactive application of criminal offences so as to penalise conduct which was not criminal at the time when the relevant act or omission occurred.

The view was taken by the Commissioner's office that s.16 of the Interpretation Act 1978 applied:

"General savings
(1) Without prejudice to section 15, where an Act repeals an enactment, the repeal does not, unless the contrary intention appears—
revive anything not in force or existing at the time at which the repeal takes effect;
affect the previous operation of the enactment repealed or anything duly done or suffered under that enactment;
affect any right, privilege, obligation or liability acquired, accrued or incurred under that enactment;
affect any penalty, forfeiture or punishment incurred in respect of any offence committed against that enactment;
affect any investigation, legal proceeding or remedy in respect of any such right, privilege, obligation, liability, penalty, forfeiture or punishment;
and any such investigation, legal proceeding or remedy may be instituted, continued or enforced, and any such penalty, forfeiture or punishment may be imposed, as if the repealing Act had not been passed."

Thus post March 1, 2000 it would appear that offences under the 1984 Act could still be investigated and prosecuted. This assertion was not however without controversy.

The relevant provision in the Interpretation Act is s.16(1)(e) which in effect provides that the legal proceedings for offences under the 1984 Act may be instituted as if the 1984 Act had not been repealed. This clearly enabled the offence to be prosecuted however there was some uncertainty as to whether the Information Commissioner could bring the prosecutions.

The Data Protection Registrar was a creature of statute and only had the powers to do those things which he was empowered to do by the Data Protection Act 1984. The Information Commissioner is equally a creature of statute. Neither had or has a general power to prosecute. They could not and cannot bring prosecutions other than for offences under the data protection legislation. This is in contrast with the Director of Public Prosecutions or a Procurator Fiscal in the Scottish system both of which are prosecutors with general powers.

20–65   The argument that s.16(1)(e) was effective to protect prosecution cases brought in respect of breaches of the 1984 Act by the Information Commissioner post March 2000 depended on arguing that the provision preserves both the effect of the section which made the act an offence and invests the Commissioner with the power to bring the prosecution. This might have been open to dispute. It is not a necessary implication of the section. The Corporation Sole, that is the legal personality, which was the Data Protection Registrar continued in existence as the Information Commissioner when the 1998 Act repealed and replaced the 1984 Act but the powers of the Registrar disappeared wholly. However the point was not argued in any of the cases brought in the relevant period and is now of merely academic and historical interest.

20–66   The position was even less clear in relation to warrants. None of the provisions of the Interpretation Act, quoted above, would seem to extend to the ability to apply for a warrant under the 1984 Act. The transitional provisions set out in Sch.14 to the 1998 Act were of no assistance either. Although there is a section relating to warrants issued under the 1984 Act it merely relates to and preserves the validity of warrants that had already been issued under the 1984 Act before March 1, 2000. The fact that the transitional provisions were silent on the ability to apply for a 1984 Act warrant post March 1, 2000 appeared to be confirmation that no such power persisted.

20–57   It could not be argued that warrants under the 1998 Act were available in relation to investigations into 1984 Act offences since one of the pre-requirements for obtaining a 1998 Act warrant was that a judge had to be satisfied that there were reasons for suspecting that a data controller had contravened or was contravening any of the data protection principles or that an offence under "this Act" had been or was being committed. In short, 1998 Act warrants are only available to investigate 1998 Act offences or the breach of 1998 Act Data Protection Principles. Since the relevant parts of the 1998 Act did not come into force until March 1, 2000 it follows that 1998 Act warrants were only available in relation to post March 1, 2000 behaviour.

There was thus a lacuna in the powers of the Commissioner to investigate 1984 Act offences post March 1, 2000 in that it was not possible for the Commissioner to obtain a search warrant to assist in such investigations. The validity of this analysis was been acknowledged by the Commissioner's Office which did not apply for any warrants for 1984 Act offence investigations after March 1, 2000.

Applicability of Tribunal and court decisions on enforcement action under the 1984 Act

20–67   It must be emphasised that decisions of the Tribunal are persuasive rather than binding. This was the case even with respect to decisions made entirely under the 1984 Act. Arguably, the persuasiveness of Tribunal decisions under the 1984 Act will be weaker with respect to appeals against notices or determinations under the 1998 Act. However, where the Commissioner takes enforcement action under the 1998 Act with respect to a principle which largely or wholly replicates a principle under the 1984 Act then relevant Tribunal decisions under the earlier legislation will still be persuasive. The Courts and the Tribunal have had regard to earlier decisions in a number of cases and these are referred to in the text under the relevant provision. There were six cases where the courts have considered the interpretation of the 1984 Act. These are:

R. v Brown [1996] 1 All E.R. 545.

R. v Chief Constable of B County Constabulary (unreported) November 1997.

Rowley v Liverpool Corporation, The Times, October 26, 1987, CA.

Amnesty International (British Section) v Data Protection Registrar [1995] Crim. L.R. 633.

Griffin v Data Protection Registrar [1994] E.C.C. 369.
Information Commissioner v Islington LBC [2002] EWHC 1036; [2002] All E.R. (D) 381.

Of these the unreported case of *R. v Chief Constable of B County Constabulary* relates to the issue of data subject access and is not, therefore, directly pertinent to issues of enforcement and prosecution. It is discussed in the Ch.11, above on Subject Access.

Similarly, the *Rowley* case relates to a potential loss of the accounts and payroll exemptions under the 1984 Act. *Griffin* also relates to the ambit of the accounts exemption. The accounts and payroll exemptions do not exist in the 1998 Act and the decisions will not therefore be pertinent to enforcement and prosecution under the new legislation. *Amnesty International* is a case on the meaning of recklessness within the Data Protection Act 1984. It is discussed earlier in this chapter at para.20–41. It is submitted that the decision may still be pertinent to the concept of recklessness under the 1998 Act.

R v Brown

20–68   The case of *Brown* is interesting in that it is the only case on the interpretation of the 1984 Act to reach the House of Lords. The facts of *Brown* were simple. A police officer called PC Brown had had searches carried out on the Police National Computer. The results of the searches were duly reported to him. The searches were on the registration numbers of vehicles. The first search did not reveal any personal data as it showed that the vehicle was owned by a limited company. The second search did show personal data. In due course it was discovered that the searches were not carried out in connection with PC Brown's policing duties but had been carried out for his own purposes. It was shown that he had a connection with a debt collection business and it appeared that he had gained access to information for some purpose in connection with that business and not one for which he was authorised to have access. The prosecution could not, however, prove that anything had been done with the information. They could not prove that he had passed it on to any other person or employed it in any particular way. All that could be shown was that he had browsed the information.

In *Brown* the House of Lords was asked to consider if the 1984 Act made such an activity a criminal offence. The charge against Brown was that he used personal data for a purpose other than one described in the register entry of the Chief Constable contrary to s.5(2)(b) of the 1984 Act. The issue was whether the mere accessing or browsing of data amounted to a "use" of data.

By a 3:2 majority the court held that mere "browsing" did not constitute a use of the data and did not therefore amount to a criminal offence under the 1984 Act. "Use" was given its ordinary and natural meaning. It was held that any application of the information extracted from the data would, however, amount to a "use".

The concept of "using" data is, effectively, abandoned by the 1998 Act. Instead the Act is concerned with "processing". Processing is defined in s.1(1) of the 1998 Act as meaning "obtaining, recording or holding" the data and carrying out various operations with respect to the data including: organising, adapting, altering, retrieving, consulting, using, disclosing, aligning, combining, erasing or blocking the data. In short almost anything that might be done to or with personal data (apart, possibly, from just letting it sit there) is covered by "processing". It is submitted that the definition of processing clearly covers "browsing" (it would be included in "consulting" for example) and thus that the decision in *Brown* no longer has any validity under the 1998 Act.

The *Islington LBC* case is a decision of the Divisional Court relating to a prosecution under the 1984 Act but handed down in May 2002, more than two years after the coming into force of most of the 1998 Act. It concerned registration under the 1984 Act and is therefore of little relevance today in relation to registration but it did deal with the question of knowledge by a corporate body.

Hence, it is submitted that the principle in *Islington LBC* is of general application and would still be relevant to prosecutions brought under the 1998 Act against corporations, public authorities and such like. Archbold helpfully restates the general principle from Islington LBC in the following terms:

> "In the case of an offence involving proof of mens rea, it may be possible to combine proof of the actus reus on the part of an employee of the corporation who would not form part of the controlling mind with proof of mens rea on the part of a person who does form part of the controlling mind. Thus, in *Information Commissioner v. Islington L.B.C.* it was held that on a prosecution of a local authority for an offence, contrary to section 5(5) of the Data Protection Act 1984 (rep.), of recklessly using data for a purpose other than the purpose or purposes described in the entry in the data protection register relating to the authority (the registration for that purpose having lapsed), the act of one of its employees in using data for an unauthorised purpose could be combined with the recklessness of the controlling minds of the authority as to the lack of registration, where there was evidence of such an act (but no evidence that the actor knew or was reckless as to the lapse of the registration) and of such recklessness (but no evidence that the controlling minds had any individual knowledge of the particular act)."[102]

ADDITIONAL INFORMATION

Derivations

20–69 • Directive 95/46:

- • Recital 63—Whereas such authorities must have the necessary means to perform their duties, including powers of investigation and intervention, particularly in cases of complaints from individuals, and powers to engage in legal proceedings; whereas such authorities must help to ensure transparency of processing in the Member States within whose jurisdiction they fall;

- • Recital 55—Whereas, if the controller fails to respect the rights of data subjects, national legislation must provide for a judicial remedy; whereas any damage which a person may suffer as a result of unlawful processing must

---

[102] para.17–32a, 2003 ed.

be compensated for by the controller, who may be exempted from liability if he proves that he is not responsible for the damage, in particular in cases where he establishes fault on the part of the data subject or in case of force majeure; whereas sanctions must be imposed on any person, whether governed by private of public law, who fails to comply with the national measures taken under this Directive;

- Art.22—Remedies

- Art.23—Liability

- Art.24—Sanctions.

CHAPTER 21

Access to Criminal Records and Enforced Subject Access

INTRODUCTION

21–01   Over the last 20 years there has been a significant change in attitudes to access to criminal records. Gradually the number of instances where prospective employers and others are expected or required to check the antecedents of employees or volunteers has risen and opposition to the disclosure of records has diminished. The Criminal Records Bureau (CRB) was established in March 2002 under Pt V of the Police Act 1997. It became an Executive Agency of the Home Office in 2003 and is run under a public–private partnership with Capita. The CRB currently obtains records from the Police National Computer (PNC) of the 43 local forces, Scottish police forces via a cross-border police intelligence system and the Departments of Health and Education and Skills in respect of the lists of those registered as unsuitable to work with vulnerable people and children. Under the Serious Organised Crime and Police Act 2005 it was given powers to obtain information from a range of other sources including other policing bodies in the UK, such as the British Transport Police and police forces in the Channel Island and the Isle of Man. One of its primary functions is to disclose information drawn from these records to Registered Bodies acting for employers and others for vetting purposes. The disclosures are made under specific provisions in the Police Act 1997, taking account of the Rehabilitation of Offenders Act 1974 (ROA). Although the introduction of the system has greatly reduced the number of enforced subject access requests the system of Basic Disclosures has not yet been introduced in England and Wales and therefore s.56 of the DPA has not been implemented. In this chapter we cover the nature of criminal records, the background to the protection and disclosure of criminal records, the relevant provisions of the ROA and the Police Act 1997, the reasons for and the effect of s.56.

SUMMARY OF MAIN POINTS

21–02   (a) Criminal records are retained both nationally and within the 43 individual police forces in England and Wales.

(b) The Report of the Bichard Enquiry which was held after the murder of two children by Ian Huntley made a number of recommendations for improvements in records and extension of access for vetting. There has also been an extension of the registers of those regarded as unsuitable to work with the vulnerable.

(c) As a result of the Bichard Enquiry there has been a review of criminal records and arrangements for their maintenance and access.

(d) Access to criminal records is currently provided in England, Wales and Northern Ireland under Pt V of the Police Act 1997 at two levels: Standard and Enhanced Disclosure. It is planned that Basic Disclosure will also be introduced.

(e) Scotland has its own system. In Scotland Basic Disclosure is also available.

(f) Enforced subject access is made an offence of strict liability in s.56 of the DPA. It is anticipated that the section will be brought into force after arrangements for the issue of Basic Certificates in England, Wales and Northern Ireland.

(g) The prohibition on enforced subject access only extends to information associated with criminal convictions and National Insurance records, although there is a power to extend the provision to other records.[1]

The Nature of Criminal Records

21–03 Criminal records include both intelligence and conviction records. Conviction information is very powerful personal data. The existence of a conviction can make it more difficult to find employment, accommodation or services. There is a strong public interest in conviction information being available to those with a need to know and an equally strong public interest in encouraging those who have had convictions in the past to rehabilitate themselves in society. Since convictions are declared in open court they are not generally treated as confidential information, certainly while they can still be researched from public domain information, nevertheless there are restrictions on their use and dissemination. In *R. v Chief Constable of North Wales Police*[2] a police officer had shown the owner of a caravan site cuttings from a newspaper covering the criminal convictions of two persons who were resident on the site. The Court of Appeal held that there was no breach of confidence as the material was from a publication but endorsed the fact that the force was required to treat disclosure seriously and only make disclosures in appropriate circumstances. Criminal records are sensitive data under the Data Protection Act and a disclosure will be a breach of an individual's right to respect for private life, accordingly it must be lawful, justifiable under one of the exemptions in Art.8 (2), and be proportionate to the aim served by the breach.[3] In the case of *R (Ellis) v The Chief Constable of Essex Police*[4] the Court

---

[1] In her response to the post-implementation appraisal of the DPA in December 2000 the Information Commissioner noted that enforced subject access might also be sought to health records and gave notice that she would seek an extension to cover such records if the practice spread.

[2] Home Office Circular No.45/1986, dated July 17, 1986, para.2.

[3] See Ch.2, above, for a full treatment of the effect of Art.8.

[4] [2003] F.L.R. 566 The Chief Constable of Essex introduced an offender-naming scheme with a view to reducing burglary and car crime. The claimant was selected to be the first offender used in the scheme.

held that the disclosure of the identifying of an individual convicted of offences by displaying posters showing photographs of the offender and details of his offence risked breaching the HRA. The Court held that the scheme could not be assessed in principle but a judgment would have to be made on the facts of the case. In the particular case the claimant was withdrawn from the scheme. The Court expressed concerns as to whether the intrusion into Art.8 rights was proportionate to the benefits claimed. A person who obtains access to conviction information under a Standard or Enhanced Disclosure will be guilty of an offence under s.124 of the Police Act 1997 if he makes an unauthorised disclosure of that information.

21–04 Before the Police Act 1997 came into force criminal records were disclosed on non-statutory grounds under administrative arrangements set out in Home Office Circulars. Although in a case concerned with the retention and disclosure of information from records held by the Department of Health relating to fitness to work with children the Court of Appeal held that such administrative arrangements could amount to a lawful basis for the purposes of Art.8, the statutory basis for disclosure in the Police Act 1997 clearly provides a firmer footing for disclosure.

21–05 The primary source of records available are those held on the Police National Computer (PNC). Records of reportable offences and sometimes of cautions are held on the PNC. The PNC is run as a common policing service involving chief police officers and the Home Office. In effect the PNC acts as a vast pool of data. All police forces have access to it, all add information to it and there are rules allocating responsibility for the inclusion of inaccurate data. The PNC is to be replaced by a new police system called IMPACT. The IMPACT programme aims to vastly improve the extent and quality of the data available to be shared between police forces by providing access to all (or nearly all) policing databases.

21–06 The more recent the record the more likely that it will be held on the PNC. The first criminal records database, Phoenix, became operational in 1995 and some older records which had previously been held on microfiche were transferred to it when it started. However, even if the record was generated since 1995, if the punishment was of a minor nature it might not have been recorded centrally, although such matters should now be recorded. All recordable offences are centrally recorded. Recordable offences are those designated by the Secretary of State under regulations made under s.27(4) of the Police and Criminal Evidence Act 1984. In addition to the PNC records every force will hold its own databases of information and intelligence covering for example stolen property, intelligence and protection of children. In June 2004 Sir Michard Bichard delivered his Report into the circumstances surrounding the deaths of Holly Wells and Jessica Chapman. The Bichard Enquiry recommended (among other things) that there should be a procedure to allow for cross-force searching of records, systems to exchange information with Scottish forces and a Code of Practice on Information Management under the Police Reform Act 2002. In 2006 the CRB set up the police border intelligence service to cover exchange with Scottish records. It has also implemented the Police Rocal Cross Referencing System (I-PLX) and the IMPACT Nominal Index which provides an index to the main databases held in forces, but does not act as a gateway to the actual information. It is planned that the IMPACT programme will provide the functionality for automated access to all the databases held by all the police forces.

21–07 IMPACT will therefore be an enormous and ambitious IT project. It is already facing difficulties because of problems in assuring data compatibility and quality across forces. There has been repeated criticisms of the quality of police records, both on the PNC and locally. Since 1995 there have been no fewer than five reports on the problems associated with the criminal records system. For example, in December 2001 the Chief Inspector of Constabulary delivered a Report on the Data Quality and Timeliness of Police National Computer Criminal Records. In the Report he noted that previous reports had highlighted concerns with the quality and timeliness of the criminal records but there were still outstanding problems. He singled out particular problems with substantial delays in the initial input of arrest/summons details and the final entry of impending case results. The Report made 10 recommendations for actions which were needed to bring about improvements. Despite the fact that, following the Bichard Enquiry which criticised the arrangements for retrieval of and disclosure of intelligence information between forces and the commitment to improvement in late 2006, it was revealled that the records of thousands of British residents who had been convicted of crimes abroad had never been added to the PNC. As a result the Home Secretary proposed a review of the way that such information is shared between countries and used by them. There has been a clear commitment by Government to improve the criminal record and intelligence system. Since the Bichard Report targets have been introduced for the timeliness of entry of information about arrests and summons to the PNC. However, a progress report on Bichard in May 2006 showed that there were still problems in about one third of forces and the focus on improved timeliness meant that there had not been the resources to improve the quality of data on force records. In April 2007 it was announced that the proposed Cross Region Information Sharing Project (CRISP), which was to be an interim data-sharing arrrangement before the next generation of the PNC under IMPACT, had been shelved largely because of the poor qulaity of existing data and the lack of compatibility between different forces' systems.

21–08 The data protection compliance issues associated with the retention of police records of convictions were raised in the case of the *Chief Constable of West Yorkshire, South Yorkshire and North Wales v the Information Commissioner*.[5] The case is examined in Ch.[], above but includes a detailed and largely irrelevant discussion of criminal records. The Information Commissioner had served enforcement notices requiring the erasure or removal of old records of spent convictions on the basis that the records were excessive and being retained for longer than was necessary for the purpose. The Tribunal held that the records could be retained for policing purposes and the administration of justice but should not be used or disclosed for any other purposes such as vetting.

21–09 The questioning of whether the retention of fingerprints and DNA samples constituted an interference with an individual's right to a private life under Art.8 was considered by the House of Lords in *R (Marper) v Chief Constable South Yorkshire*.[6] The House held that mere retention did not constitute an interference, but even if that were not the case any interference would be modest and justifiable under Art.8(2). In the *South Yorkshire* case the Tribunal distinguished this and held that the Tribunal distinguished this and that the retention of conviction information would engage Art.8(1).

---

[5] In the Information Tribunal 2006.
[6] [2004] 1 W.L.R. 2196.

BACKGROUND TO THE PROTECTION AND DISCLOSURE OF CRIMINAL RECORDS

Conflicting pressures

21–10   Originally criminal records were kept for use by the police in investigating crime and for the purposes of the criminal justice system, for example use by the courts in sentencing offenders. Apart from these uses the approach was that police information (including criminal records) should not be disclosed "unless there are important considerations of public interest to justify departure from the general rule of confidentiality".[7]

The three areas of exception where disclosure was traditionally regarded as being in the public interest were:

- for the purposes of national security;
- to ensure probity in the administration of law;
- for the protection of vulnerable members of society.

Those who were considered to fall within the exceptions were listed in Home Office circulars. The circulars also listed the persons authorised to make such searches. However, they only provided for access to a limited number of persons and in a limited number of circumstances. In 1993, the Home Office issued a consultation paper on the Disclosure of Criminal Records for Employment Vetting Purposes.[8] The paper considered the then current arrangements in England and Wales, outlined the pressures on the system and explored the options for making new arrangements. The consultation paper described a situation in which access to criminal records for vetting varied across different police areas and was haphazard in effect. It also listed the Home Office circulars which dealt with disclosure of criminal records. It described the existing arrangements as "obviously muddled". One of the options it considered as part of the remedy for the situation was the establishment of a central unit to deal with handling access to criminal records. In responding to the consultation paper the then Data Protection Registrar, Eric Howe, commented:

> "It is undoubtedly true that, over the last few years, pressure has increased to make available details of an individual's criminal records in a wide variety of circumstances. From my position as Data Protection Registrar I see particularly the escalating use of enforced subject access whereby individuals are obliged to use their right of access under the Data Protection Act 1984 to obtain a copy of their criminal record from the police and pass it on to the prospective employer. I have argued frequently that this is an abuse of individual's rights and should be prevented by criminal sanctions.
>
> The growth of the use of enforced subject access highlights the need to review the current arrangements for disclosure. It is important to note that it is not only the criminal record which is a target for enforced subject access. National Insurance records too are being used increasingly as a source of information

---

[7] Home Office Circular No. 45/1986, dated July 17, 1986, para.2.
[8] Cmnd.2319.

which can reveal a period spent in prison. Potentially, Court registers could become a target as they become computerised.

If wider access is to be permitted it is important that a proper framework is established within which such access can take place and that access outside that framework is effectively restricted."[9]

In May 1997 the Government issued a consultation letter discussing a number of possible ways of dealing with the problem. After considering the responses it determined that criminalisation of enforced subject access together with a proper and more generous framework for legitimate access was the only effective solution. In order to achieve this it created the offence of enforced subject access in s.56 coupled with the provisions for criminal certificates in the Police Act 1997. It has always been intended that the two legal provisions would be implemented in tandem, with s.56 delayed until ss.112, 113 and 115 of the Police Act are working. Section 56 has not yet been brought into force but most of the relevant provisions of the Police Act 1997 were brought into force on March 1, 2002.[10]

It should be noted that the offence provisions in s.56 in the DPA 1998 have not been extended to cover enforced subject access to all data: only those highlighted as being particular problems, that is criminal records and National Insurance records. However, the formula adopted allows the Secretary of State to add further categories of records if problems should arise in other areas.

The provisions of Pt V of the Police Act are intended to strike a balance between rights to legitimate access and the protection of those who are rehabilitated.

REHABILITATION OF OFFENDERS ACT 1974 (ROA)

21–11   The ROA is predicated on the basis that an individual who has paid the penalty for a crime committed should be able to rehabilitate himself and build a new life. The Act allows for certain convictions to be "spent" and s.4(1) provides that, in respect of spent convictions, the offender "shall be treated for all purposes in law as a person who has not committed or been charged with or prosecuted for or convicted of or sentenced for the offence or offences which were the subject of that conviction".

Convictions for serious crimes which result in lengthy periods of imprisonment are excluded from the Act and will never be spent. Broadly speaking convictions are spent at between six months and ten years after conviction, depending on the gravity of the offence as reflected in the sentence passed. The Secretary of State has power to exclude the application of s.4(1) by Order.

Exemptions

21–12   The Rehabilitation of Offenders Act 1974 (Exceptions) Order 1975 as amended[11] sets out a wide range of circumstances in which convictions will not be treated as spent. They cover appointments in the criminal justice system, appointment to posts concerned with the provision of care to children and young persons, and

---

[9] *Annual Report of the Data Protection Registrar* (June 1994).
[10] The Police Act 1997 (Commencement No. 9) Order 2002 (SI 2002/413).
[11] SI 1975/1023.

appointments in social or medical services where the carer is concerned with looking after vulnerable persons. The Order also contains a list of excepted professions where members of the profession must disclose any convictions where appropriate and a list of licences and permits, applications for which also require the disclosure of convictions which would otherwise be spent. Further amends have been made to the Exceptions Order by recent statutory instruments which (inter alia):

- provide for exceptions where the suitability of persons with permission under the Financial Services and Markets Act 2000 are involved[12];

- add justices' chief executive to the excepted offices and employment and extend the definition of "working with children"[13];

- add a range of further professions and offices and employment such as the Crown Prosecution Service and receivers for the Court of Protection.[14]

Access to criminal records

21–13 The CRB was established in 2001 in order to deal with requests for access to criminal records under the Police Act 1997. It went live in March 2002. Initially it had problems in handling the task allotted to it and there were serious backlogs in dealing with requests.[15] In broad terms, individuals will be able to access their own records for the purposes of supplying information to a third party, but will only obtain limited information. There is no limitation on the use that an individual can make of these records. Wider, and direct, legitimate access to criminal records is available to employers of those concerned with the care of children and the vulnerable, those who work in the criminal justice system, and those concerned with granting various applications for licences and permits. Access is also available for national security vetting.

Provisions for certificates under the Police Act 1997

21–14 Part V of the Police Act 1997 provides for three types of certificates of criminal records to be provided. Requests for England, Wales and Northern Ireland are made to the CRB which issues certificates on behalf of the Secretary of State. The Scottish equivalent is called "Disclosure Scotland". It is an autonomous organisation although its functions are very similar to the CRB.

The certificates are:

(a) Criminal Convictions Certificates (Basic Disclosures);

(b) Criminal Records Certificates (Standard Disclosures); and

(c) Enhanced Criminal Records Certificates (Enhanced Disclosures).

As the names suggest there is a gradation in the range and depth of information available under each one.

---

[12] Rehabilitation of Offenders (Exceptions) (Amendment) (No.2) Order 2001 (SI 2001/3816).
[13] Rehabilitation of Offenders (Exceptions) (Amendment) Order 2001 (SI 2001/192).
[14] Rehabilitation of Offenders (Exceptions) (Amendment) Order 2002 (SI 2001/441).
[15] Reported in *The Times*, July 3, 2002.

Arrangements for Standard and Enhanced Disclosure have been made. The rules governing these are set out in the Police Act (Criminal Records) Regulations 2002 (SI 2002/233).[16] The Regulations make detailed provisions for the matters which are to appear on the certificates. As well as criminal records these include information about those prohibited from working with children or disqualified from working with children or vulnerable adults. The criminal records included on the certificates include cautions, and reprimands or warnings given to children or young persons under s.65 of the Crime and Disorder Act 1998. The Information Tribunal considered the implications of its ruling in the South Yorkshire case that some of the old convictions should not be used or disclosed for vetting purposes (see para.21–08, above). The Regulations define what is covered by the term "recorded in central records" in s.113(3) of the Police Act 1997. Compliance with the restrictions imposed by the Tribunal would mean that some of the old records which on the face of it are "recorded in central records" and fall within the scope of the Regulations would have to be withheld on a CRB search. The Tribunal dealt with this by holding that the term could be construed so as to comply with Directive 95/46 and Art.8 of the Human Rights Convention.[17] The ruling has not been appealed. Accordingly a CRB search will not necessarily show all convictions, cautions or warnings recorded in central records as some older ones (of 25 years or more) may be withheld on the obligation to issue criminal record certificates.

Criminal Convictions Certificates or Basic Disclosures

21–15 The CRB has not yet made arrangements for the issue of the Basic Disclosure.[18] The launch of this part of the scheme has been postponed. They will be available to any individual and will show the records relating to that individual. They must be applied for in the prescribed form and a fee may be prescribed. The individual will obtain a certificate which will show any conviction recorded against him in central records or state that there is no such conviction. It will show offences kept on central records, which means such records held for the use of police forces as may be prescribed.[19] It will not show spent offences. This will be the basic form of certificate available to allow individuals to prove their bona fides in certain circumstances.

There is no limitation on the uses to which the certificates may be put. It is possible therefore that in the future insurance companies, hire car companies and a range of other service providers may require sight of the certificates before being prepared to enter into contracts.

Criminal Records Certificates or Standard Disclosures[20]

21–16 These certificates are available where the applicant produces:

 (a) an application countersigned by a registered person; and

---

[16] As amended by the Police Act 1997 (Criminal Records) (Amendment) Regulations 2007 from April 1, 2007.

[17] *Ghaidan v Godin-Mendoza* [2004] UK HL 30; [2004] A.C. 557.

[18] Police Act 1997 s.112.

[19] *ibid.* s.112(3).

[20] *ibid.* s.113.

(b) a statement that the certificate is required in connection with "an exempted question", that is a question excluded from the effect of the ROA under an order made by the Secretary of State.

Such a certificate will show convictions recorded in the central records including spent convictions and any cautions, reprimands or warnings held in central records.[21] The certificate will also show whether the individual appears on any of the lists maintained by the Department for Education or the Department of Health. A caution is not a conviction but is a record of an admitted offence in respect of which a prosecution could have been brought. Cautions, reprimands and final warnings are brought within the scope of central records by reg.9. A fee is payable for the certificate. Such a certificate will still not be a full record of all data held in the criminal justice system.

Enhanced Criminal Records Certificates or Enhanced Disclosures[22]

21–17   These are available where the applicant produces:

(a) an application countersigned by a registered person; and

(b) a statement by the registered person that the certificate:

   (i) is required in connection with an "exempted question" that is a question excluded from the effect of ROA by an order of the Secretary of State made under s.4(4) of the Rehabilitation of Offenders Act 1974; and
   (ii) is in relation to one of the specified range of activities (being broadly those concerned with betting and gaming or the care of children) listed in s.115(6).

The provision of an enhanced criminal record certificate will produce the fullest search of the three possibilities. This will show all convictions including spent convictions, cautions, reprimands and warnings, whether the individual appears on lists maintained by the Department for Education and Skills or the Department of Health plus information from local police force records of which the CRB is aware as a result of records shown on the I-PLX. The extent of such information is left to the discretion of the local force which determines what information might be relevant for the purposes of the particular certificate and ought to be included. However where additional information is held locally which it would not be appropriate to put into the certificate itself, because it is not in the interest of the prevention or detection of crime that the individual should see such information, this may still be sent directly to the countersignatory to the request. The guidance issued to forces both by the Association of Chief Police Officers (ACPO) and the Home Office is that only in very exceptional circumstances should information be provided to the Registered Body instead of being shown on the face of the CRB disclosure itself.[23]

---

[21] *ibid.* s.113(5).
[22] *ibid.* s.115.
[23] Home Office Circular No. 5/2005 "Criminal Records Bureau: Local checks for the purpose of enhanced disclosures".

The registered persons who act as countersignatories for both Standard Disclosure and Enhanced Disclosure have to abide by a Code of Practice drawn up by the Secretary of State. The Code and Explanatory Guide for Registered Persons are intended to ensure that the information released will be used fairly and that the information is handled and stored appropriately and kept for only as long as is necessary. The Code does not apply to Basic Disclosures.

The Act sets out those who may be approved to countersign applications and contains provisions to deal with disputes about the identity of applicants and the accuracy of records. It is an offence, under s.124 of the Police Act 1997, to pass Disclosure information to those who do not need to have access to it in the course of their duties. There is provision for umbrella bodies to act as registered persons for smaller organisations and thus provide a conduit for the disclosure of information, particularly for the voluntary sector.

As will be appreciated from this brief outline, the Police Act 1997 sets out a complex regime. While these provisions may appear to provide fully for any reasonable need to access conviction information, it must be recognised that they will not provide the same range and detail as a subject access response. It is therefore possible that the abuse of subject access might continue despite the availability of certificates under the Police Act. Accordingly the Government has also acted to make enforced subject access an offence.

ENFORCED SUBJECT ACCESS

21–18 Section 56 deals with the problem of enforced subject access. It does not derive from the Directive or from earlier legislation. It was inserted in response to a problem which developed in the United Kingdom under the 1984 Act. Enforced subject access occurs where a person, often a prospective employer, makes the offer of a benefit, such as employment or the provision of services, conditional on sight of the material given in response to a subject access request made by the individual to a third party. The requests are usually made for criminal records. The use of enforced subject access provides the prospective employer with information about the individual, usually the contents of any criminal record.

Section 56 makes enforced subject access a criminal offence. The section has not been brought into force at the time of publication. It is anticipated that the Order bringing it into force will be brought forward once the arrangements for Basic Disclosure are in place.

The pressure to use the subject access right to obtain details about prospective employees' previous convictions was foreseen during the passage of the 1984 Act. The response of Ministers was to reassure Parliament that if there proved to be a problem it would be dealt with by the police by "administrative measures". In due course the problem occurred as had been foreseen but, despite the best attempts of police forces, no administrative remedy for it could be found. Gradually the practice of requiring individuals to provide subject access searches in order to vet for previous criminal records became widespread among employers. It has also been used by overseas governments as a method of vetting prospective immigrants' criminal records. In a debate on the Data Protection Bill in June 1998 Mr George Howarth outlined the problem which the clause was intended to tackle in the following terms:

"That term covers the circumstances when one person forces another to hand over his data protection subject access record as a condition of being considered for, or obtaining, some form of benefit, such as a job.

This happens mainly with criminal records. Some employers tell job applicants to hand over a data protection subject access printout obtained from the police if they want to be considered for a job. Sometimes they ask for Department of Social Security contributions records, believing that gaps in contributions show a period in custody. The police and the DSS believe that of the approximately 100,000 subject access applications they receive each year, the vast majority are enforced. Often the letters come in standard form, for example, as prescribed by employees."

Types of record covered by s.56

21–19 In general terms s.56 makes it an offence for a prospective employer to require an individual to produce a subject access search as a condition of employment. The offence is however rather technical and only applies to "relevant records". These are defined in s.56(6), being those containing the particular information specified in respect of particular data controllers as set out in an accompanying table. This apparently obscure method of describing the information means that further categories can be added if and when necessary.

Convictions and cautions

21–20 The information specified includes information relating to convictions and cautions obtained by a data subject from a chief officer of police in England, Wales, Scotland or Northern Ireland; or the National Criminal Intelligence Service or the Director General of the National Crime Squad.[24] Information "relating to" convictions or cautions may be wider than simply a record of a conviction or a caution and would be wide enough to embrace a record of a decision not to give a caution or a record of a conviction which had been overturned on appeal. It would not cover criminal intelligence, although it seems unlikely such information would be forthcoming on a subject access request in any event, as it would be more than likely to be withheld under the exemption for crime prevention.

"Relevant Record" is described as one which "has been or is to be obtained by a data subject from [one of the specified data controllers]". It follows that the data do not have to be retained or processed by the data controller to whom the request is made or who supplies the data in response to the request. This reflects the somewhat diffuse nature of control over records of convictions and cautions as described above. Cautions and convictions are defined in s.56(7). In England and Wales a caution may be given instead of a prosecution where there is evidence of guilt sufficient to give a reasonable prospect of conviction and there is an unequivocal admission. Cautions are non-statutory responses to criminal incidents. Cautions are dealt with under Home Office circulars.

Under s.56(7) a caution means a caution given in England or Wales in respect of an admitted offence. The concept of a caution does not exist in Scotland. In Scotland the Procurator Fiscal may issue an admonition which is of a similar nature and which may

---

[24] Now the Serious Organised Crime Agency.

be recorded on the Scottish Criminal Records Office System. Conviction has the same meaning as in the ROA. The Secretary of State may amend these definitions and may therefore add to or alter the categories of caution and conviction. In the ROA conviction is defined in s.1. A further four sets of information controlled by the Secretary of State are in the prohibited list.

Records relating to young persons

21–21   Records relating to the functions of the Secretary of State under the Powers of the Criminal Courts Act 1973, s.90 and 91, replacing s.53 of the Children and Young Persons Act 1933 and the equivalent provisions for Scotland and Northern Ireland in respect of any young person sentenced to detention are covered. The Act makes provision for the detention of those under 18 at ss.90 and 91. Under s.90 children and young persons between the ages of 10 and 18 may be sentenced to detention in legal custody or imprisonment for offences the sentence for which is fixed by law as life imprisonment, such as manslaughter or murder during Her Majesty's pleasure. It should be noted that such records will largely duplicate information held in the register of criminal convictions and cautions.

Prison information

21–22   A further category of prohibited information is that relating to the functions of the Secretary of State under the Prison Act 1952 and its equivalents in Scotland and Northern Ireland. Thus any record containing information as to any function of the Secretary of State under the 1952 Act is prohibited. The 1952 Act was a consolidating statute bringing together provisions governing, inter alia, the central administration of prisons, the consignment and treatment of prisoners and various offence provisions connected to the prison service.

National Insurance records

21–23   National Insurance records held pursuant to the Social Security Benefits Act 1992 may be a target for employers because a certain category of National Insurance record contributions indicate that a person has spent time in custody. The data also show gaps in continuity of employment to check against an applicant's declared job history. The functions of the Secretary of State under the Social Security Benefits Act 1992 and other benefits legislation have therefore been included.

Police Act 1997

21–24   Functions under Pt IV of the Police Act 1997, which deals with the provision of criminal records (dealt with above), have also been included in the list of prohibited records.

Prohibited circumstances

21–25   A person is prohibited on pain of criminal penalties from requiring another to exercise his subject access right in respect of any of the prohibited data categories in three circumstances. These are:

(a) employment;

(b) a contract for services;

(c) the provision of goods, facilities and services.

Employment

21–26   By s.5(10) the term "employee" is given an extended definition. It not only covers those who would be regarded as employees for most legal and employment purposes but also any individual who works under a contract of employment as designated by s.230(2) of the Employment Rights Act 1996. This is the definition applied in employment law in relation to employment rights but this definition excludes those who hold office under other arrangements, for example, police officers or those who provide services as independent contractors. However, for the purposes of s.56 office holders are included as employees by s.56(10)(b).

In the case of either employees, or those treated as employees by virtue of this provision, it is immaterial whether the individual is entitled to any remuneration. The term remuneration is a wide term sufficient to cover payment in kind or honoraria. Thus a scout leader or a church choir master who holds office would be covered even though these are voluntary organisations and the individuals would not normally be regarded as employees and do not receive any payment. The employment prohibition applies in connection with both the recruitment of any person or the continued employment of any person (s.56(1)(a) and (b)).

Contract for services

21–27   A contract for services is distinguished from an employment relationship as the parties are not master and servant. There are a number of tests to ascertain whether a relationship is one of employee/employer or independent contractor, such as the degree of control exercised[25] and whether the individual has a choice when and how to carry out the work.[26] Such distinctions are immaterial in the case of enforced subject access. The offence extends to any contract for the provision of services. Thus, any service from providing window-cleaning to an engineering consultancy would be within its scope.

A person must not, in connection with either employment or any contract for the provision of services, require another person or a third party to supply him with a relevant record. The requirement need not be a condition of the employment offer or the contract to fall foul of the prohibition; it needs simply to be made "in connection with" it.

The provision of goods or services

21–28   In respect of the provision of goods or services it is prohibited to make the provision conditional on the supply of a relevant record, under s.56(2):

---

[25] *Yewens v Noakes* (1880) 6 Q.B.D. 530.
[26] *Ready Mixed Concrete (South East) Ltd v Minster of Pensions and National Insurance* [1968] 1 All E.R. 433.

"A person concerned with the provision (for payment or not) of goods, facilities or services to the public or a section of the public must not, as a condition of providing or offering to provide any goods facilities or services to another person, require that other person or a third party to supply him with a relevant record or to produce a relevant record to him."

The prohibition applies to voluntary groups, clubs, churches and other non-profit making bodies as well as to commercial relationships such as those of landlord and tenant. "Goods, facilities or services" is a broad phrase and capable of covering anything from the sale of consumer goods on credit terms through to financial services, property transactions and legal services. The person must, however, be concerned with the provision of such services to the public or a section of the public. The public means any person who may be interested; a section of the public will be relevant where a service is offered to a number of persons of a particular class but there is no selection to enter that class. An employer who offers discounted goods to his employees would possibly not be covered by the prohibition, therefore, and could make it a condition of their claiming a staff discount that individuals should supply a subject access search.

Crime reports

21–29 Although it might be thought that the new regime offers ample opportunity to those with a "need to know" to obtain and verify information from the police the pressure on police records continues to grow. It is now common that insurance companies and loss reporters have begun to require those claiming under insurance policies to provide access to crime reports compiled by the police, on occasions by the use of enforced subject access. The report is then compared to the insurance claim submitted by the individual.[27]

Empty records

21–30 A record which shows no data will still be caught by the prohibition as s.56(9) provides that for the purposes of this section an "empty" record is to be taken as a record containing information relating to that matter.

Mens Rea

21–31 The requirement to produce a relevant record in the prohibited circumstances is the *actus reus* of the offence. It is an offence of strict liability.[28] Section 56(5) states that "a person who contravenes sub-section (1) or (2) is guilty of an offence". It is immaterial that the person requiring the search neither knew it was wrong nor intended to break the law. However, there are two defences to the offence.

Defences

21–32 The prohibitions in s.56(1) and (2) will not bite in two sets of circumstances. In each case, the person who requires the data subject to obtain his records will carry

---

[27] In fact this happened to the author when claiming under a travel insurance policy for a mobile telephone which had been stolen.

[28] In other words the prosecution do not have to show that the accused knew that the act was wrong.

the burden of proof and must show that those circumstances apply. In any proceedings for an offence in which one of the defences is raised, the burden of proof on the defence will be to prove it to the civil standard.[29]

Compulsion of law

21-33   An enforced subject access requirement will not be prohibited if the person who demanded it shows that it was required or authorised under any enactment by any rule of law or by the order of a court. To the best of the writer's knowledge, there exists no enactment or rule of law which requires an individual to require another to obtain subject access. It is moreover not easy to conceive of one under which it could be authorised. Possibly a person under a duty of care or due diligence who required an employee or contractor to obtain subject access might seek to argue that the imposition was "required" so they could comply with their legal obligations of care. However, as certificates of criminal conviction are available lawfully it may be anticipated that any requirement or authorisation to obtain a criminal record information will be interpreted as a requirement or authority which applies to those records which may be lawfully obtained, as opposed to those which may not. The circumstances under which a court might make such an order are left at large but it is difficult to envisage a court ordering an individual to commit what would otherwise be a criminal offence.

Public interest

21-34   Public interest makes a further appearance in the Act in this context. Enforced subject access will not be prohibited if the person requiring it can show that "in the particular circumstances" the imposition of the requirement "was justified as being in the public interest". In this case, public interest is partially defined by exclusion. Section 54(4) states that:

> "having regard to the provisions of Part V of the Police Act 1997 (certificates of criminal records etc), the imposition of the requirement referred to in sub-section (1) or (2) is not to be regarded as being justified as being in the public interest on the grounds that it would assist in the prevention or detection of crime."

Although this removes one, and probably the most often asserted, public interest justification, it leaves other aspects at large. The requirement that regard must be had to the provisions of Pt V implies that where Pt V of the Police Act 1997 deals with the provision of criminal record information which is relevant to assessing the suitability of applicants for particular positions that would preclude the use of the defence in s.56(3)(b).

PROSECUTIONS

Prosecutors

21-35   As with all offences under the Act, there can be no private prosecutions. Any proceedings must be brought either by the Commissioner or by or with the consent of

---

[29] *R. v Carr-Briant* [1943] K.B. 607.

the Director of Public Prosecutions, or in Northern Ireland the Director of the Public Prosecution for Northern Ireland (s.60(1)).

Courts

21–36   The offence is triable either way and accordingly a prosecution may be brought in any magistrates' court, although usually proceedings will be brought in the court for the area in which the offence was committed.

Proceedings

21–37   The power to charge any director or other person treated as a directing mind of a body in appropriate circumstances where the offence is committed other than by an individual applies to the enforced subject access offence.[30] The court's power to order the forfeiture or destruction of any data connected with the commission of the offence also applies.[31] For a full discussion of the criminal regimes, see Ch.20, above.

Immunity from prosecution

21–38   Diplomatic immunity is available to the staff of foreign embassies and consulates under international conventions. Enforced subject access has been used in the past by overseas governments via the embassy or consulate in the United Kingdom in connection with the grant of visa and work or entry permits. It is possible that the offence provisions will not prevent this aspect of the abuse.

Health records

21–39   Section 57 contains a provision aimed at dealing with the problem of enforced subject access to health records. This provision makes void any contractual requirement that an individual shall seek subject access to a health record. It does not provide for any criminal sanction. The reason for the two different approaches appears to be historical. Section 57 derives from the Access to Health Records Act 1988. It repeats a provision of the earlier Act. There does not appear to be a problem of enforced subject access to health records and at this stage there are no plans to extend the provisions of s.56 to such records.

21–40   Section 56 was amended by the Freedom of Information Act 2000 to make it explicit that the prohibition on enforced subject access does not extend to the new category of data falling within s.1(e). The reasoning behind this is very difficult to follow. The effect is that enforced subject access to recorded information not falling within the original definition in the DPA will not be an offence when s.56 comes into effect. The abuse of subject access can therefore continue in respect of such information. It may not prove to be a practical problem as the provisions in respect of the need for the applicant to describe unstructured data will possibly cut down that which will be potentially available under this anyway, but as a matter of principle one might have expected the protection to be afforded to all the personal information.

---

[30] DPA s.61.
[31] DPA s.60(4).

Extent of the problem

21–41   Giving evidence to the Information Tribunal in the *South Yorkshire* case Mr Smith, Deputy Information Commissioner, estimated that the overwhelming majority of the 200,000 requests received per year are as a result of enforced subject access.

ADDITIONAL INFORMATION

Derivations

21–42 • Fourteenth Report of the Data Protection Registar—June 1998, p.22 (report on *R. v Director of "B" County Constabulary and the Director of National Identification Services Ex p.* R, November 25, 1997), p.46

Website: *http://www.crb.gov.uk* [Accessed on September 2, 2007]

Directive

21–43   Although it is accurate to say that the provision does not derive from the Directive it has been suggested that the ban on enforced subject access is required by Art.12 which requires "Member States shall guarantee every data subject to the right of subject access 'without constraint' ".

Hansard references

21–44   Commons Standing Committee D, June 2, 1998, cols 270–272
Enforced subject access

Vol.591, No.184, col.1502, Lords consideration of Commons amendments, July 10, 1998
Enforced subject access

Previous case law

21–45   *R. v Chief Constable of B County Constabulary; Director of the National Identification Services Ex p.* R, unreported, November 1997:—see Ch.11, above, Subject Access for an analysis of this case.

CHAPTER 22

Electronic Communications and the Privacy and Electronic Communications (EC Directive) Regulations 2003

INTRODUCTION

22–01 Developments in the telecommunications industry over the past two decades have been dynamic and extensive. The digitalisation of networks and availability of broadband have extended the modes in which information can be transmitted; services and service providers have multiplied and converged. The developments in technology, and the expansion in the number of operators, have led to particular pressures on personal privacy: location data is available from mobile telephones; directory services are no longer the province of the dominant operator and can be offered in a range of ways; "cookies"[1] can track web usage; caller line identification has enabled those called to see the number from which they are being called. The passage of a specific sectoral Directive in 1997 (Dir. 97/66) relating to data protection and telecommunications, reflected the significance of these developments. This Directive was repealed and replaced within a mere five years. In the replacement Directive the term "telecommunications" was replaced by "electronic communications" throughout, evidence of the importance to the Commission of achieving a "technology neutral" regime. Directive 97/66 required revision, not only because of further developments in the telecommunications industry, for example the continuing development of digital mobile networks, but also because some important provisions in it had been interpreted in different ways in different Member States. As an example the position of the UK government had been that email was excluded from the ambit of the marketing rules in the implementing regulations. There was also pressure to alter the strict rules on the retention and use of

---

[1] Cookies is the term used for small files used in the delivery of internet communications. A webserver can automatically send these bits of code to a user's computer when a user visits a website. They are used, for example, to enable the website to recognise the visitor on a subsequent occasion. They can be used for tracking and web usage. For more information about how cookies work and are used visit *http://computer.howstuffworks.com/cookie1.htm* [Accessed on September 2, 2007].

traffic data both from a security perspective and to enable the telecommunications industry to develop new services based on location data.[2]

22–02   Directive 97/66 was replaced by Directive 2002/58 of the European Parliament and the Council of July 12, 2002 concerning the processing of personal data and the protection of privacy in the electronic communications sector (the Privacy and Electronic Communications Directive or Directive 2002/58). Agreement was reached on the revised Directive in July 2002.[3]

Many of the provisions of Directive 2002/58 were unchanged from Directive 97/55. The main areas of change being:

- the reference to telecommunications has been altered throughout to electronic communications;

- the definitions have become both tighter and more extensive;

- the coverage of traffic data has been extended;

- the restriction on service providers using personal data about users to market only their own services has been lifted;

- notice of the use of "cookies" is now required with users having the option to decide not to accept cookies, except where the cookie is essential to deliver contracted services;

- a set of rules governing the uses of location data has been included;

- emergency services must be able to have access to location data;

- the rules relating to directory information have been changed to deal with developments in the use and availability of directories;

- it has been made explicit that email (which includes SMS) marketing requires consent save in certain cases where the marketer has an existing trading relationship with the subscriber.

SUMMARY OF MAIN POINTS

22–03   (a) The Regulations apply in addition to the Data Protection Act 1998.

(b) They apply to those who use and provide electronic communications services; it follows that those subject to the Regulations may not be data controllers for the purposes of the Data Protection Act 1998.

(c) The use of electronic communications services (including email) for direct marketing is regulated.

(d) The sending of unsolicited faxes for direct marketing to individual subscribers is banned; such faxes can only be sent with consent.

---

[2] The retention of communications data and the rules governing the interception of telecommunications are dealt with in Ch.23, below.

[3] *http://www.berr.gov.uk* [Accessed on September 2, 2007].

(e) The sending of unsolicited faxes for direct marketing to corporate subscribers is permitted but the sender must stop sending them if the subscriber objects either directly or by electing to be included on the fax preference list.

(f) Unsolicited marketing "calls" to individual subscribers are still allowed but there is a "stop list" of numbers of subscribers who do not want such calls. Calls must not be made to those numbers on the list or the numbers of those who have objected directly to the caller.

(g) The use of automated calling systems for direct marketing without consent is banned whether the marketing is to individuals or other subscribers.

(h) Direct marketing is widely defined and includes advertising even if nothing is being offered for sale.

(i) The use of cookies or equivalent tools without the consent of the subscriber or user is restricted.

(j) Limits are placed on the retention of traffic data and the purposes for which they can be used.

(k) Limits are placed on the processing of location data.

(l) Callers must be able to block the presentation of their calling line identification; equally those receiving calls where the CLI has been blocked must be entitled to refuse to accept such calls.

(m) Individuals are given the right to limit the information about them which is published in directories or available from directory enquiry services and may go ex-directory free of charge.

(n) Security standards are required for networks.

(o) Subscribers may opt to receive non-itemised bills.

IMPLEMENTATION OF DIRECTIVES 97/66 AND 2002/58

Implementation of Directive 97/66

22–04   The implementation of Directive 97/66 had been a torturous process. The DTI issued draft regulations in July 1998. The draft regulations covered all the areas of the Directive except Art.5, which deals with security of communication and interception rules and did not have to be implemented until 2000. That Article was implemented under the Regulation of Investigatory Powers Act 2000, a provision which has not subsequently altered (see Ch.23, below). It then became clear that there would be some delay in bringing all the provisions of the new Regulations into force but that unsolicited calls and faxes were matters of immediate concern. Political pressure developed for an early implementation of provisions to deal with these. Accordingly this area was hived off into a separate instrument, the Telecommunications (Data Protection and Privacy) (Direct Marketing) Regulations 1998 (the TDPPDM Regulations). These came into force on May 1, 1999. The enforcement provisions of the Data Protection Act 1984 applied to breaches of the Regulations and the Registrar was the supervisory authority for them. The staggered implementation also allowed work to be started on the telephone suppression service which would otherwise have been held up until implementation of the DPA 1998.

The TDPPDM Regulations were replaced by the Telecommunications (Data Protection and Privacy) Regulations 1999 (SI 1999/2093) (TDPP Regulations) which came into force with the Data Protection Act 1998 on March 1, 2000. The provisions dealing with direct marketing were almost identical to those in the TDPPDM Regulations. There were a few minor drafting alterations, but nothing of any substance. The TDPP Regulations were amended by the Telecommunications (Data Protection and Privacy) (Amendment) Regulations 2000.

Implementation of Directive 2002/58

22–05   Implementing legislation was required by October 31, 2003. In the UK the timetable lagged slightly. In March 2003 the DTI issued a Consultation Document, *Implementation of the Directive on Privacy and Electronic Communications*, which reviewed the options for implementing those changes required by the Directive. It also reviewed the way that the regulations which had implemented Directive 97/66, the Telecommunications (Data Protection and Privacy) Regulations 1999 (SI 199/2093), had worked so far and whether any additional amendments were required to those Regulations. Following the consultation the Privacy and Electronic Communications (EC Directive) Regulations 2003[4] (PECR) came into force on December 11, 2003. These replaced the Telecommunications (Data Protection and Privacy) Regulations 1999 (TDPP Regulations). The Regulation of Investigatory Powers Act 2000 was unaffected, and the Telecommunications (Lawful Business Practice) Regulations 2000 were subject to minor amendment only. A further development occurred in June 2004 when the PECR were amended by the Privacy and Electronic Communications (EC Directive)(Amendment)Regulations 2004 to allow businesses to register with the Telephone Preference service.

Subsequent developments have focused on the rules governing the retention and use of communications data. These are covered in Ch.23, below.

BACKGROUND

Council of Europe Recommendation R(95)

22–06   The EU is not the only body to be concerned about the impact of developments in telecommunications on the individual's right to private life. The Council of Europe's Committee of Experts on data protection were working on an equivalent Recommendation to Member States during the 1990s (for a discussion of the role and significance of Recommendations under Treaty 108 see Ch.3, above). In February 1995, the Committee of Ministers of the Council of Europe adopted Recommendation R(95)4 on the protection of personal data in the area of telecommunication services,

---

[4] SI 2003/2426 amended by the Privacy and Electronic Communications (EC Directive)(Amendment) Regulations 2004 (SI 2004/1039).

with particular reference to telephone services. It is accompanied by detailed explanatory memoranda. The Recommendation lists the then new features of the digitised telecommunications world which may pose particular threats to personal privacy as calling-line identification, call forwarding and mobile telephone use, as well as call-tracing devices, automatic dialling devices and itemised phone bills. On most of those topics the points covered by the Recommendation shadow those in Directives 97/66 and 2002/58. The explanatory memoranda helpfully sets out much of the background thinking on the approaches taken to these issues across Europe. Although the Recommendation is now somewhat dated it still provides helpful material on those areas.

Article 29 Working Party

22–07   The Article 29 Working Party has a continued interest in telecommunications and associated matters and has issued a range of Opinions on these issues. In February 2004 it adopted an Opinion on unsolicited communications for marketing purposes under Art.13 of Directive 2002/58. In the Opinion the Working Party states that, despite the fact that Directive 2002/58 has introduced a harmonised regime for marketing using electronic communications, some of the concepts used in the Directive "appear to be subject to differences of interpretation". In particular they emphasise that the term electronic mail covers a wide range of services, including newsletters sent by email; that the level of consent required for the sending of electronic marketing must meet the standards required by Directive 95/46; and that the derogation for the marketing of similar products and services must be narrowly interpreted. While the Guidance issued by the UK regulator confirms the first point, his approach to the second and third issues is perhaps more generous than that taken by the Working Party.

Method of regulation of telecommunications in the United Kingdom

22–08   Prior to the Communications Act 2003, there were five different regulatory regimes covering media, telecommunications and radio communication. This meant that there were five different regulators namely:

- Independent Television Commissioner;
- Broadcasting Standards Commission;
- Radio Authority;
- Office of Telecommunications (Oftel); and
- Radio Communications Agency.

The telecommunications sector was regulated by the Telecommunications Act 1984 and the Wireless Telegraphy Acts. In each case, providers of telecommunications services were required to obtain a licence. The Telecommunications Act 1984 licensed the telecommunications system used rather than the provision of the actual telecommunications services. The licences were either licences specific to the operator or class licences and covered voice telecommunications, data telecommunications and reseller arrangements. The licence granted under the Wireless Telegraphy Act 1949 licensed the use of parts of the radio spectrum. In each case the licence specified the scope of the activities permitted under it and the terms applicable to that licence.

The existing regime was struggling to keep pace with the developments in the telecommunications sector. The telecommunications market has in a relatively short time moved from being a State monopoly to the current open market with numerous telecommunication service providers all vying for a share of the market.

The EU Commission is keen to ensure that consumers of telecommunication services are protected and that they enjoy the benefits of open competition. In this respect, the use of a tight regulatory regime is considered to be undesirable. The main concern is that technology and the use of technology changes rapidly and tight regulation is not able to keep pace. Licences are seen as too rigid and a light touch regulatory approach is preferred when combined with the use of open market and economic-based competition law principles. Such an approach is seen to be more flexible, able to provide the protections sought by the EU Commission and able to promote competition. The aim is to produce a vibrant market and eventually one which is self regulating.

In virtually all European countries, there was an incumbent telecommunications supplier which was either owned by the State or had originally been so. The concern was that with no incentive to change, these incumbents could create a bottleneck thereby stifling competition. In order to deal with this, the EU Commission decided that it would be necessary for there to be a degree of ex ante regulation which would be designed to modify the behaviour of the incumbents and to promote competition. The continued convergence between broadcasters and communication companies, between those supplying content and those delivering it, means that it is sensible to appoint one regulator in each Member State with responsibility for the whole of the communications sector within that Member State.

Communications Act 2003

22–09   The objectives of the EU Commission are to:

- promote competition within the telecommunications market, in part by ensuring that access to telecommunication services and the services themselves are interoperable thus providing a greater choice for consumers;

- develop the internal market and in particular the harmonisation of EU regulations relating to the provision of telecommunication services;

- promote the interests of EU citizens.

The aim is for all legislation flowing from the Directives to be technology neutral.

The Communications Act 2003 implemented a number of EU Directives that underpinned the above objectives. In particular:

- Directive 2002/19 on access to and interconnection of electronic communications networks and associated facilities (Access Directive)[5];

---

[5] [2002] O.J. L108/7.

- Directive 2002/20 on the authorisation of electronic communications networks and services (Authorisation Directive)[6];

- Directive 2002/21 on a common regulatory framework for electronic communications networks and services (Framework Directive)[7];

- Directive 2002/22 on universal service and users' rights relating to electronic communications networks and services (Universal Service Directive)[8]; and

- Directive 2002/58 concerning the processing of the personal data and the protection of privacy in the electronic communications sector (Privacy Directive).[9]

The Communications Act 2003 also implemented the Radio Spectrum Decision.[10]

Even though the Communications Act 2003 has over 400 sections and nearly 20 Schedules, it provides the United Kingdom with a light touch regulatory regime. Under the current regime, there is one unified regulator, which is the Office of Communications ("Ofcom"). Ofcom is the national regulatory authority for the United Kingdom and represents the United Kingdom in Europe. It is the single regulator for the entire communications sector and has taken over the roles of the five previous regulators. The provisions of the Wireless Telegraphy Acts and the licences granted thereunder are still in force but now are regulated by Ofcom.

22–10   As part of its function, Ofcom is required to undertake market reviews of the various communications markets. Following these reviews it determines whether any organisation has a significant market power and is required to establish conditions which may be imposed ex ante to ensure that the service providers within that market segment provide a competitive offering. Such conditions and the market itself are monitored by Ofcom. Any conditions imposed by Ofcom are subject to periodic review in light of changes in the market. Ofcom is also the enforcement agency in relation to the regulation of the communications sector and acts as a dispute resolver for both communication service providers and their customers.

The original licensing regime has been replaced with a general authorisation regime. This means that provided a service provider complies with the obligations imposed by a set of general conditions and with any specific conditions imposed on it by Ofcom, there is a general permission to provide electronic communication services or to operate electronic communication networks (see definitions below). However, certain areas such as broadcasting and the provision of mobile telecommunication services are still subject to licensing regimes set out in the Broadcasting Act 1990 and the Wireless Telegraphy Act 1949 respectively.

22–11   Ofcom has published a number of conditions which relate to the provision of electronic communications services and the operation of electronic communications networks. These conditions, which are set out below, do not apply to the content of the communications. The conditions are:

---

[6] [2002] O.J. L108/21.
[7] [2002] O.J. L108/33.
[8] [2002] O.J. L108/51.
[9] [2002] O.J. L201/37.
[10] Decision 2002/676 on a regulatory framework for radio inspection policy in the European community [2002] O.J. L229/15.

- general conditions of entitlement;

- significant market power conditions and market reviews;

- universal service conditions;

- privileged supply conditions; and

- access related conditions.

The provision of premium rate services (such as television votelines, competitions, mobile ringtones, interactive TV games, adult entertainment, information (weather, traffic, etc.) and directory enquiry services) continue to be regulated by the Independent Committee for the Supervision of Standards of the Telephone Information Services ("ICSTIS"). Ofcom appointed ICSTIS as an approved enforcement authority for the premium rate sector and ultimately enforces any sanctions that ICSTIS may impose.

Directive 2002/58

22–12　Directive 2002/58 was agreed under the Art.189b co-decision procedure introduced after Maastricht as part of the move to strengthen the powers of the European Parliament in making new European law.

Scope of the Directive

22–13　Directive 2002/58 applies in addition to the general Directive 95/46. It applies irrespective of whether personal data are being processed. Where personal data are involved the data controller must comply with the rules in the Data Protection Act 1998 and the Regulations implementing Directive 2002/58. The Guidance issued by the Information Commissioner (see below) confirms that information which identifies living individuals, such as mailing lists of individuals names, will be regarded as personal data for the purposes of the Regulations.[11]

Technical features and standardisation

22–14　One of the reasons for a specific Directive on personal data and telecommunications is a concern that different data protection rules arising from different national applications of the general rules on public telecommunications could undermine technical and legal harmonisation in this area. The development of a European market in telecommunications is an aim of the Community. This is reflected in Art.14 which requires that, in implementing Directive 2002/58 Member States must not impose any mandatory technical requirements which could impede the free market in telecommunications equipment.

Where provisions of the Directive can only be implemented by requiring that telecommunications equipment has specific technical features, Member States have to

---

[11] The question of whether such information is caught arises because of the case of *Durant v FSA*. The Guidance makes clear that the Commissioner regards names as covered by the Regulations in the Introduction to the Guidance.

inform the Commission (Art.14(2)) and the Commission will consider the reference in the light of its powers to impose common standards.

Services (digital and analogue exchanges)

22–15   Article 3 states that the Directive shall apply to the processing of personal data in all publicly available electronic communications services in public communications networks in the Community. However, whereas Arts 8, 10 and 11 apply to subscriber lines connected to digital exchanges they only apply to such lines connected to analogue exchanges where it is technically possible to apply them and where it does not involve a disproportionate economic effort to implement those standards. Member States should inform the Commission of those cases in which it is not possible to implement the provisions of these Articles for those reasons. Articles 8 and 10 cover Calling and Connecting Line Identification and Art.11 covers automatic call-forwarding. The PECR include provisions to reflect this by imposing the requirements on prevention of calling line identification only where the facility is available.

Method of implementation of the Directive

22–16   Directive 2002/58 was implemented by regulations made under s.2(2) of the European Communities Act 1972. This means that the Regulations do not apply to matters outside Community competence. This was used as the basis for the retention of communications data for an extended period of time for the purposes of crime prevention. In all other ways, however, the interpretation of the Regulations should be approached as the main Act. A full description of the approach is set out at Ch.3, above. In particular a purposive approach must be taken to interpretation bearing in mind the aims of the Directives.

GUIDANCE FROM THE INFORMATION COMMISSIONER

22–17   The Information Commissioner has issued detailed guidance on the PEC Regulations. Version 3 was issued in May 2004.[12] The Guidance is divided into two sections: Pt 1 covers Marketing by Electronic Means and Pt 2 covers Security, Confidentiality, Traffic and Location data, Itemised Billing, CLI and Directories. Part 1 includes a set of Marketers FAQs which provide practical guidance on common problems.

DEFINITIONS AND OTHER GENERAL PROVISION

22–18   The definitions from the Data Protection Act 1998 apply for the purposes of the Regulations and, subject to the specific definitions in the Regulations and the 1998 Act, expressions taken from Directive 2002/58 have the same meaning as in that Directive. Directive 2002/58 does not import the complex technical definitions of the predecessor provisions dealing with the telecommunications network, or telecommunications services.

22–19   The PECR directly imports core definitions from the following sources:

---

[12] Guidance to the Privacy and Electronic Communications (EC Directive) Regulations 2003.

— the Communications Act 2003;

— the Broad Broadcasting Act 1990; and

— the Electronic Commerce (EC Directive) Regulations 2002.

The definitions imported are:

"public electronic communications network";
"public electronic communications service";
"communications provider";
"electronic communications service";
"electronic communications network";
"programme service"; and
"information society services".

All the definitions are deliberately generic to protect the legislation from obsolescence as the technologies that underpin communications and media evolve.

The series of definitions in the Communications Act 2003 distinguishes those services that provide the public with the ability to communicate, in essence the communications networks, from the content and information services that are transmitted over them. The defined terms are to be found in ss.32, 151 and 405 (note the terms underlined are also defined terms but are not set out in this section) as follows:

" 'public electronic communications network' (s.151) means an electronic communications network provided wholly or mainly for the purpose of making electronic communications services available to members of the public;

'public electronic communications service' (s.151) means any electronic communications service that is provided so as to be available for use by members of the public.

'communications provider' (s.405) means a person who (within the meaning of section 32(4)) provides an electronic communications network or an electronic communications service;

'electronic communications service' (s.32) means a service consisting in, or having as its principal feature, the conveyance by means of an electronic communications network of signals, except in so far as it is a content service.

'electronic communications network' (s.32) means:

(a) a transmission system for the conveyance, by the use of electrical, magnetic or electro-magnetic energy, of signals of any description; and

(b) such of the following as are used, by the person providing the system and in association with it, for the conveyance of the signals—
  (i) apparatus comprised in the system;
  (ii) apparatus used for the switching or routing of the signals; and
  (iii) software and stored data.

'content service' means so much of any service as consists in one or both of the following—

    (a) the provision of material with a view to its being comprised in signals conveyed by means of an electronic communications network;

    (b) the exercise of editorial control over the contents of signals conveyed by means of a such a network."

Section 201 of the Broadcasting Act 1990 defines a programme service as:

" 'programme service' means any of the following services (whether or not it is, or it requires to be, licenses), namely:

    (a) any service which is a programme service within the meaning of the Communications Act 2003;

    (b) any other service which consists in the sending, by means of an electronic communications network (within the meaning of the Communications Act 2003), of sounds or visual images or both either:

        (i) for reception at two or more places in the United Kingdom (whether they are so sent for simultaneous reception or at different times in response to requests made by different users of the service); or

        (ii) for reception at a place in the United Kingdom for the purpose of being presented there to members of the public or to any group of persons."

The Communications Act 2003 definition of programme service referred to above is defined in s.405 of that Act as:

"(a) a television programme service;

 (b) the public teletext service;

 (c) an additional television service;

 (d) a digital additional television service;

 (e) a radio programme service; or

 (f) a sound service provided by the BBC."

22–20 The definition of "information society services" is summarised in the Electronic Commerce (EC Directive) Regulations 2002 by reference to the original EC Directive as follows:

" 'information society services' (which is summarised in recital 17 of the Directive as covering 'any service normally provided for remuneration, at a distance, by means of electronic equipment for the processing (including digital compression) and storage of data, and at the individual request of a recipient of a service') has the meaning set out in Article 2(a) of the Directive, (which refers to Article 1(2) of Directive 98/34/EC of the European Parliament and of the Council of 22 June 1998 laying down a procedure for the provision of information in the field of technical standards and regulations, as amended by Directive 98/48/EC of 20 July 1998)."[13]

---

[13] The full definition is set out in a subsequent amendment (Directive 98/48 of July 20, 1998).

The use of remuneration captures both subscription services and those sites that derive revenue from other sources, for instance advertising. The requirement that the services are provided for remuneration is very broad and includes sites which are established solely to promote a business and from which there is no direct revenue. The DTI's guidance notes indicate that the definition catches all e-commerce sites including those of businesses providing free information on a website as well as all online ads, email, etc. This means that virtually all business websites are caught. Best practice is to assume that any form of commercial website is caught by the definition of information society services.

SUBSCRIBERS

22–21   The Regulations distinguish between individual subscribers and others; the extent of the protection given depending on the category into which the subscriber falls, whether as an individual or a corporate subscriber.

Subscriber

22–22   A subscriber is defined in reg.2(1) as a person who is party to a contract with a provider of public electronic communications services for the supply of such services. The subscriber is the legal being who enters into the contract to pay for the services. In an ordinary household the subscriber will be the person whose name is on the bill and who signed the original agreement. In a company it will be the name of the corporate entity which enters into the legal agreement. Some rights given by the Regulations have to be exercised by or in the name of the subscriber. The subscriber is usually the person whose name appears in the directory.

Corporate subscriber

22–23   This means a subscriber who is an incorporated company, a partnership in Scotland, a corporation sole and any other body corporate or entity which is a legal person distinct from its members.

Unincorporated bodies are not defined but will be treated in the same way as individual subscribers. The definition of an individual in reg.2(1) specifically includes an unincorporated body of such individuals. Accordingly organisations such as local groups and societies will have the wider protection given to individuals. This may be particularly useful where the secretarial functions for such groups are exercised, as is often the case, by an individual member from his or her home address. An individual subscriber is a living individual.

Definitions of "bill" and "user" are also included. " 'Bill' includes an invoice, account, statement or other instrument of similar character and 'billing' shall be construed accordingly", and " 'user' means any individual using a public electronic communications service".

Also defined are:

> *Call*—a call is specifically a connection established by means of a telephone service available to the public allowing two-way communication in real time.
>
> *Communication*—means any information exchanged between a finite number of parties by means of a public electronic communications service

but is distinguished from a broadcast. Thus a distinction is drawn between SMS, email and other methods of asyncratic electronic communication and telephone communication. Electronic mail is a form of communication which has a separate definition.

Electronic mail—means any text, voice, sound or image message sent over a public electronic communications network which can be stored in the network or in the recipient's terminal equipment until it is collected by the recipient and includes messages sent using a short message service.

Location data—means any data processed in an electronic communications network which shows the geographical position of the user of terminal equipment, who is using a public telecommunications service. Location data in fact includes not only immediate location but also the direction of travel and the time the location was recorded.

Traffic data—means any data processed for the purpose of the conveyance of a communication on a network or for the purpose of billing for the communication and includes data relating to the routing, duration or time of communication.

Value added service—means any service which requires the processing of traffic or location data beyond that necessary for the transmission of the communication or the billing in respect of the communication.

Guidance issued by the Office of the Information Commissioner[14] ("the PECR Guidance") includes "caller" in the section on definitions stating:

" *'Caller'*—this means the instigator of a call. This is usually a legal person. The call would not be made or the fax/email/text/picture message would not be sent unless the caller paid for it to be made or sent."

However there is no legal definition of the term "caller" and in the Regulations a distinction appears to be drawn between the caller and the instigator of a call.

22–24 Regulation 27 provides that any provision of a contract between a subscriber and service provider or a service provider and a network provider which would be inconsistent with the Regulations shall be void. Accordingly it is clear that subscribers cannot contract out of the protection of the Regulations. While the position in the main Act is not completely clear (see detailed discussion at Ch.10, above the position in the Regulations is therefore made explicit in reg.27.

DIRECT MARKETING

Who is covered?

22–25 In most cases the rules are of general application and apply to any person. "Person" includes any legal entity, a corporate entity or individual and includes any

---

[14] Guidance to the Privacy and Electronic Communications (EC Directive) Regulations 2003 Pt 1, Marketing by Electronic Means, version 3, May 2004.

body of persons (Interpretation Act 1978). Some provisions apply only apply to sub-scribers and the provisions in reg.24 which deal with the provision of information apply to persons "using" the service or "instigating the use of the service".

It appears that the "instigator" may be a different person to the caller, nor need the caller necessarily be employed by the "instigator". Clearly the term would cover the sit-uation where an employee is acting in the course of his employment, therefore if a mar-keting business employs staff to make telephone sales calls the employing organisation will be responsible for complying with the Regulations and open to penalties for non-compliance. The term "instigate", however, is wider than "require" or even "cause". It would appear to be sufficient to cover an organisation which encourages individuals who are ostensibly self-employed and acting on a commission sales basis to make direct marketing approaches using the telecommunications network. It is probably wide enough to apply to charitable organisations which encourage volunteers to use their home telephones to make calls recruiting helpers to sell raffle tickets or conduct house-to-house collections for the charity. There is no requirement that the "instigator" should have a financial relationship with the caller.

A person need not be a data controller or a data processor to be caught by this aspect of the Regulations. He or she does not need to have a computer or to process personal data. All the caller has to do is use the telephone for direct marketing and the relevant provisions will apply.

Public electronic communications network and services

22–26 The definition of "public electronic communications network" refers to a network which is made available to the members of the public. Equally, the definition of "public electronic communications services" talks about services available for use by members of the public. In neither case is there any further explanation as to what is meant by making the network or use of the services available to the public. Accordingly, the words must be given their ordinary meaning. It follows that Directive 97/66 does not cover private branch exchange systems (PBX systems), for example those used internally by hotels or by large companies for their workplaces. These are covered by the provisions of the DPA 1998 but not by PECR.

Direct marketing

22–27 This is not defined in either Directive 2002/58 or Directive 95/46. The defi-nition in the Regulations is the same as that in s.11 of the DPA 1998. Under reg.21(2) any reference to direct marketing is a reference to the communication of any advertis-ing or marketing material on a particular line. It should be noted that any reference to line shall be construed as a reference to anything that performs the functions of a line and the term "connected" in relation to a line is to be construed in the same way.[15]

There is no definition of marketing or direct marketing in Directive 2002/58. In the draft regulations a form of definition was proposed as "any reference to direct mar-keting in these Regulations is a reference to the communication of any advertising or marketing on a particular line" (Art.(2(5)). However this did not appear in the final version.

---

[15] PECR reg.2(4).

Direct marketing has been given a broad definition under the Data Protection Act 1998 by the Information Tribunal. In the case of *Scottish National Party v Information Commissioner*[16] the SNP argued that the playing of pre-recorded telephone messages from Mr Alex Salmond and Sir Sean Connery supporting the SNP were not undertaken as direct marketing. The Commissioner held that the activity constituted direct marketing and not-for-profit organisations such as political parties were not excluded from the ambit of the Regulations. The Tribunal supported the broad view which has been adopted by the Commissioner. The advertising need not be of a commercial product, nor need anything be offered for sale. This fits with the commonly used sense of the term. In Recommendation R(85)20 of the Council of Europe on the Protection of Personal Data used for the purposes of Direct Marketing, for the purposes of the Recommendation "direct marketing":

> "comprises all activities which make it possible to offer goods or services or to transmit other messages to a segment of the population by post, telephone or other direct means aimed at informing or soliciting a response from the data subject as well as any service ancillary thereto."

In the Direct Marketing (UK) Code of Practice, prepared under the aegis of the Director General of Fair Trading and the Data Protection Registrar and issued in September 1997, various marketing-related terms have been adopted from the Distance Selling Directive (97/7). Direct marketing is not specifically defined but advertising is. The term advertising, "is to be taken to include all forms of direct marketing communication, including any sales promotion or fund raising, whether or not it contains an offer or an invitation to treat".

22–28 In Recommendation R(95)4 it is made clear that direct marketing includes not only commercial marketing, but also political marketing and approaches made by trade unions, charitable organisations and others.[17]

The Federation of European Direct Marketing, which represents the direct marketing sector at European level, issued its view of the meaning of direct marketing in its response to the Council of Europe Privacy Guidelines on the internet in July 1998 thus:

> "Direct marketing is a series of marketing strategies, using various delivery techniques designed to provide the receiver (consumers and companies) with information at a distance. Direct marketing is principally but not exclusively database, one-to-one relationship marketing.
>
> Direct marketing is not a homogenous marketing discipline but rather a series of different strategies using different means of approach (e.g. broadcasting, printed press, mail, telephone, on-line services). It is used to sell products, to deliver information, public announcements, and for after sales services, customer care services, charity and political appeals."

The Article 29 Working Party confirmed that, in its view Art.13 covers:

---

[16] Appeal EA/2005/0021, Information Tribunal.
[17] Explanatory Memorandum para.85.

". . . any form of sales promotion, including direct marketing by charities and political organisations (e.g. fund raising etc..)."[18]

The ICO Guidance refers to the definition in s.11 of the Act and explains that the Commissioner takes the view that the term covers a wide range of activities including the promotion of an organisation's aims and ideals. While these are not legal definitions for this purpose they show that the term has been given a wide meaning and this has been followed by the Tribunal.

Automated calling systems

22–29   Regulation 19 bans the use of automated calling systems for direct marketing without the prior consent of the subscriber. This provision affords equal protection to individuals and corporate subscribers. The subscriber must have previously notified the caller or the instigator of the call that he consents to receiving calls via an automated call system for the time being. The term "automated calling system" is defined as a system which is capable of automatically initiating a sequence of calls to more than one destination in accordance with instructions stored in that system and transmitting sounds which are not live speech for reception by persons at some or all of the destinations called. This is a restricted meaning of the term "call" and excludes any form of communication other than voice. The systems were described in Recommendation R(95)4 at para.95 as:

"robotic dialling devices [which] allow for the random dialling of pre-recorded marketing messages. They feed on lists of numbers which are dialled over and over again until the subscriber replies."

The essence of such a system is not only that the calls are dialled automatically but that the same message is given automatically to all recipients. Thus pre-set dialling devices which allow human operators to have numbers dialled for them and then be ready to pick them up when someone answers the telephone are not caught The PECR Guidance points out that, in the Commissioner's view, marketing by text/picture/video message, fax or emails are not caught by this prohibition. The Guidance also states that automated calls are caught even if one of the recorded options is to press a digit and speak to a live operator and warns that the Commissioner will be taking a firm line on the use of automated calling systems. In addition the person "using or instigating the use of the system" must ensure that the name of that person and either an address or telephone number at which he can be reached is provided with the communication. This means that the automated call must include this information.

Automated diallers and silent calls

22–30   The use of automated diallers has given rise to the problem of subscribers receiving silent calls. The problem does not arise from automated calling systems but from ones where the marketer uses staff to speak to targets. It arises because the

---

[18] Para.3.3 Opinion 5/2004 on unsolicited communications for marketing purposes of the Article 29 Working Party 11601/EN WP 90.

marketing organisation wishes to maximise the number of contacts that staff can make. Therefore they use a programme which dials numbers automatically before there is an operative ready to pick them up. If no member of staff is ready to take another call the recipient picks up the telephone to find no one on the other end. These silent calls can be extremely worrying for recipients and, in the past, telecommunications service providers have been reluctant to tell the recipient the identity of the caller organisation, allegedly for data protection reasons (although the cynical might suspect it has more to do with preserving a lucrative line of business). The Guidance firmly lays to rest the argument that service providers cannot divulge the identity of the calling organisation, pointing out that reg.15 explicitly provides that information on nuisance or malicious calls can be made available to a person with a legitimate interest in knowing the identity of the calling subscriber even where the subscribers has withheld the calling line identity (as is usually the case with this type of call).

More surprisingly the ICO has taken the view that such calls do not fall under the PECR:

> "As disturbing as silent calls can be, no marketing material is being transmitted and therefore the marketing rules in these Regulations do not apply."[19]

While it is clear that a nuisance call cannot be caught by the Regulations the provisions of reg.21 apply to the "use" of a public electronic communications service for the purpose of unsolicited calls and reg.24 applies to the instigation of the use of public electronic communications service for direct marketing purpose. It is suggested that a more robust view could have been taken by the Commissioner on this point. However the subscriber who is troubled by such calls is not left with a remedy because OFCOM has been active in taking action to restrict the impact of these systems in relation to silent calls under its powers to take action against network use which causes avoidable nuisance, annoyance or anxiety. In October 2006 it was reported that OFCOM had acted against marketing organisations which had failed to restrict the number of marketing calls which resulted in silent calls to subscribers

Unsolicited commercial email or "spam"

22–31   The term "spam" or "spamming" is popularly used to describe unsolicited commercial emails sent over the internet. This may be on an individual basis or take the form of unsolicited bulk email. In some cases email addresses are "harvested", that is gleaned by automated programmes which pull addresses out of newsgroups and web pages. Some users deluge the networks with spam using automated sending facilities. Increasingly service providers strive to filter out spamming and once a service provider is alerted to the practice it will usually terminate the user's account, but by that time the damage may have been done. Spam may also be sent by SMS messages to mobile telephones. It was not clear whether email and SMS were covered by the TDPP Regulations however under PECR the position is clear.

A recent case[20] under the Computer Misuse Act 1990 ("CMA") considered the situation where a former employee deluged his former employer's systems with email using

---

[19] PECR Guidance p.10.
[20] *Director of Public Prosecutions v David Lennon* [2006] EWHC 1201 (Admin).

a mail bomb program. In fact, Mr Lennon used software to send in the region of 5 million emails to a server belonging to Domestic and General Group Plc (his former employer). In the first instance, the judge in the Youth Court held that there was no case to answer on the basis that the employer's email system had been set up to receive email and so there was an implied consent to send email to it. Even if such implied consent did not extend to sending multiple emails to the email address, it was not possible to determine at what point such implied consent came to an end and so no offence could have been committed. The case turned on the wording of s.3 of the CMA and whether there had been a modification to the employer's systems. Not surprisingly the prosecution appealed the decision and the matter was considered by the High Court.

In the High Court Jack J. held that a denial of service (DOS) attack amounted to a breach of the CMA. Typically, DOS attacks are performed using software that automatically sends emails to nominated email servers. The volume of emails overwhelms the server, in essence preventing it from sending or receiving email. Jack J. found that the receipt of emails by the email server was an "unauthorised modification" for the purposes of the CMA on the basis that the implied consent could not be considered to extend to the sending of malicious emails, purportedly from another user, with the express intent of overwhelming the email system. Other forms of DOS attack exist, however the aim, in all cases, is to deny genuine users access to specific computing resources.

It was not clear whether email and SMS were covered by the TDPP Regulations however under PECR the position is clear: the Commissioner can take enforcement action to restrain the culprit, if he or she can be found, culminating if necessary in prosecutions. Clearly this depends on being able to trace those responsible and the efficacy of the remedy will also depend on where the actions are deemed to be carried on. As much spam originates outside the United Kingdom, for example in Korea or China, the relevant territorial provisions will be important. It is now also possible for a person who suffers damage because of the effect of unsolicited direct marketing to bring an action for compensation under reg.30 (see below for an examination of this provision). While the damage to an individual from the receipt of unsolicited email would be negligible the damage to a service provider affected by a deluge of spam could be significant. Realistically however those who perpetrate such attacks are either likely to be outside the jurisdiction or disgruntled "men of straw" who would not be worth suing.

Use of electronic mail for direct marketing purposes

22–32 The question of whether email was covered under the predecessor Regulations was a point of some doubt. The Office of the Information Commissioner (OIC) advised that email was covered, while the Government took the view that it was not. The OIC also took the position that SMS messages were "calls" within the meaning of the TDPP Regulations and therefore subject to the Regulations. Neither of these points were considered by a court and they remained undecided. The point was unequivocally dealt with in Directive 2002/58 as email is explicitly covered and defined to include SMS messaging.

Relevant provisions in Directive 2002/58

22–33 Under Art.13(1) the use of electronic mail for the purposes of direct marketing without the consent of the recipient is not permitted. Electronic mail is widely defined and the definition is sufficient to cover messages left as voicemail calls on telephone systems as well as text messages to mobile telephones.

Individual and corporate subscribers

22–34 Regulation 22 of the PECR implements the new provisions covering unsolicited commercial email in Art.13. The opt-in rule is incorporated in reg.22(2) which applies to the transmission of unsolicited communications by means of electronic mail to recipients. Where the subscriber to a line is an individual subscriber the rights apply to those who receive electronic communications using that line. Such persons are referred to as recipients. The term recipient is not defined in the PECR. It is defined in the Act in relation to personal data only however the provisions of reg.22 apply irrespective of whether the messages contain personal data. The better view therefore is that the technical definition in the Act will not apply but may be of persuasive value. This leaves open the question of whether a recipient can be a legal person as well as a natural person. It could be argued that, as the term recipient in the Act would cover legal as well as natural persons, where the subscriber is an individual who allows a legal entity to use the relevant line the legal entity itself could be regarded as a recipient. However reg.22(1) restricts the provisions to the transmission of unsolicited communications to individual subscribers so the better view is probably that the term recipient in the Regulations should not be regarded as covering corporate bodies. It also follows that where an individual subscriber allows several other individuals to use a facility such as a PC each individual will be a recipient and be able to make his or her own choices about the receipt of e mail marketing. This leads to an interesting issue where the subscriber is a large partnership which would more usually be regarded as the equivalent of a corporate entity. The ICO Guidance in its FAQs accepts however that in such a case the wishes of the subscriber should override the choices of the employees, using the example of an employer who wants an employee to keep in regular contact with conference organisers, an obligation which means the employee has to accept the receipt of marketing materials.

The provision does not apply where the subscriber is a corporate body and therefore does not cover spam aimed at individuals at their corporate email addresses or mobile telephones, although where personal data are involved, such marketing will be covered by the provisions of the Act.[21]

Under reg.22(2):

> ". . . a person shall neither transmit, nor instigate the transmission of , unsolicited communications for the purposes of direct marketing by means of electronic mail unless the recipient of the electronic mail has previously notified the sender that he consents for the time being to such communications being sent by or at the instigation of the sender."

There are a number of potential ambiguities in this regulation; the meaning of the term "unsolicited"; the distinction between that and "consent"; and the duration of "the time being".

---

[21] The ICO Guidance notes that the Committee of Advertising Practice Code restricts the sending of individual marketing emails to corporate addresses.

The obligation to comply falls on the subscriber whose line is used for the transmission of the marketing material. It follows that where such a person acts as an agent for others, or provides marketing services or allows others to use his lines for email marketing the subscriber must ensure that the rules are being followed.

The restriction to consent is subject to the proviso in Art.13(2) that, where email addresses have been obtained from customers in the context of the provision of goods or services with full notice, they can be used for the marketing of similar products or services subject to the subject being given the opportunity to object free of charge and in an easy manner to such use when the data are collected and to there being a consistent opt-out message on every subsequent communications. The context of the provision of goods and services is defined as being where the sender or instigator of the mailing:

"(a) . . . has obtained the contact details of the recipient of that electronic mail in the course of the sale or negotiation for the sale of a product or service to that recipient;

(b) the direct marketing is in respect of that person's similar products and services only: and

(c) the recipient has been given a simple means of refusing (free of charge except for the costs of the transmission of the refusal) the use of his contact details for the purposes of such direct marketing, at the time when the details were initially collected, and, where he did not initially refuse the use of the details, at the time of each subsequent communication."

The particular issues to be considered are: what amounts to the course of negotiations for the sale of a product and how similar products and services should be interpreted. The Consultation Paper proposed that a customer relationship should include cases where someone has registered an interest in a product and does not require an actual purchase. The PECR Guidance accepts that where a person has actively expressed an interest in purchasing a company's products and services and not opted out of further marketing of that product or service or similar products or services when their details were collected then the marketer can continue to use their details for his own marketing. In relation to similar products the Consultation Paper suggested that these should cover products that the addressee would reasonably have expected the marketer to market at the time that the contact details were provided but not those of a new business or a new product range. The PECR Guidance is not quite as explicit and refers to promotional material that the individual would reasonably expect. As noted earlier the Article 29 Working Party paper takes a less generous line that the ICO.

When is a call "unsolicited"?

22–35 Regulation 22 covers "unsolicited" direct marketing communications but does not define the term "unsolicited". The ICO Guidance described an unsolicited marketing communication as one:

"..that you have not specifically invited but you have positively indicated that you do not mind receiving it."

This gnomic advice is followed by a rather more helpful example of the contrast between asking someone to buy you a drink and being offered a drink and accepting the offer. The essence of the definition is that the individual must have done something from which the marketer is able to infer consent to the marketing. In relation to the meaning of the term "consent" the Guidance points out that where personal data are concerned the definition in the main directive, Directive 95/46, continues to apply. The consent must therefore be freely given, informed and signified to the recipient.[22] Where consent if being obtained online it need not be restricted to a tick-box but may be some other mechanism such as clicking on an icon or sending an email. It is crucial however that some clear action is taken by the subscriber. One of the repeated questions from marketers is whether notice coupled with a failure to register an objection, i.e. an "opt-out" mechanism, is sufficient to be regarded as a consent. The ICO makes clear that such a mechanism alone will not be sufficient but may be combined with other mechanisms to achieve a sufficient consent:

> "However, in context, a failure to indicate objection may be **part of** the mechanism whereby a person indicates consent. For example, if you receive a clear and prominent message along the following lines, the fact that a suitably prominent opt-out box has not been ticked may help establish that consent has been given: e.g. 'By submitting this registration form, you will be indicating your consent to receiving email marketing messages from us **unless** you have indicated and objection to receiving such messages by ticking the above box'."

For a consent to be informed the collector of the email address must have given a proper notice of the intended use. The consent is specific to the "sender" of the email marketing but there is no restriction on the beneficiary of the marketing. In other words the sender may obtain consent to market goods being sold by third parties but may not pass on the names and email addresses for others to carry out the marketing themselves unless he has obtained a consent which applies directly to the third party. For example a company may seek an individual's consent on behalf of itself and all its affiliated companies. The question of whether such a consent is valid and effective will depend on the facts of the case and particularly the level of detailed information provided to the recipient. The ICO Guidance takes a relatively generous view of how consent may be obtained and suggests that a positive response to a question phrased in general terms will be sufficient, for example:

> "We would like to pass your details on to specially selected third parties so that they can send you more information about holidays in America. Do you agree to this?"

would be sufficient to obtain a consent for the third parties as long as it evoked a positive response.

For the time being

22–36   The phrase is used in regs 20, 21, 22, 25 and 26. Subscribers may notify the holders of the preference service lists or marketers that they do not "for the time being"

---

[22] For a full discussion of the meaning of the term see Ch.3, above.

wish to receive unsolicited communications or may notify the senders of marketing materials by facsimile or email that they "consent for the time being" to receiving such communications, or, in reg.20(5) "do not object for the time being" to unsolicited facsimiles. The term is not derived from the Directive. It must therefore be given its usual meaning subject to the obligation to apply a purposive approach to achieve the aims of the Directive. Under the Directive the provisions on unsolicited communications are dealt with in Art.13. The material section is Art.13(3) which provides that Member States:

> "shall take appropriate measures to ensure that, free of charge, unsolicited communications for the purposes of direct marketing, in cases other than those referred to in paragraphs 1 and 2 [**Comment: these deal with consent and the exception for similar goods and services in the case of e mail marketing**] are not allowed either without the consent of the subscribers concerned or in respect of subscribers who do not wish to receive these communications, the choice between these options to be determined by national legislation."

It is extremely difficult to work out what, if anything, the phrase "for the time being" adds. Perhaps the simplest approach is that it makes explicit that contributors are always able to change their minds and therefore neither a consent nor an objection is an eternal choice. It appears to add nothing else save possibly an additional layer of unnecessary confusion. The Directive makes clear that some forms of marketing require consent and for others marketers may be made subject to an opt-out regime. Consent must be given its normal meaning and the question of whether a consent continues to apply should be determined on the basis of the evidence available. Where there is a choice in the Directive the UK has provided for an opt-out regime. Its obligation is to ensure that unsolicited communications are not allowed to **subscribers who do not wish to receive these communications**. This is not the same as subscribers who have registered on a preference service. It is suggested therefore that the term adds nothing of value to the concept of consent and a narrow meaning should be attributed to it in the context of objections to marketing.

It appears from the ICO Guidance that it has been suggested that the addition of the term to the requirement for consent suggests that consent must inevitably lapse after a certain period. As noted above we would suggest that whether consent exists or not must be a question of fact. The Guidance takes what appears to be the same view and suggests that an initial consent will remain valid:

> ". . . . Where there are good grounds for believing that the recipient remains happy to receive the marketing communications in question, for example where the recipient has responded **positively** (i.e. other than to object) to previous recent marketing e mails."

Means of refusing

22–37 Regulation 22(37)(c) requires that the recipient must have been provided with a simple means of refusing the use at the point of initial collection of his contact details and at the time of each subsequent communication. While this is relatively straightforward on websites and emails, being achieved by the use of the "unsubscribe" option, it can present practical problems where the marketing is being sent by SMS. The ICO comments that the practical limitations of standard mobile screens do not mean that marketers can ignore the rules about giving proper initial notice and advocates the provision of information via advertisements or websites where individuals sign up for services. The ICO is more sympathetic to the difficulties caused in providing the subsequent notice. In the Guidance it is explained that the Commissioner had originally considered that opt-out notices should provide a postal or email address but after further consultation with the industry has agreed that a short code can be used as long as the sender has been clearly identified, the short code message is not a premium rate charge and the short code is valid.

ICO Guidance

22–38   In addition to the issues canvassed above the ICO Guidance covers viral marketing and the implementation of pan-European marketing campaigns by email. On viral marketing it points out that a marketer which encourages recipients to pass on material will be an "instigator" of electronic mail for direct marketing purposes and remain responsible under the Regulations. This is particularly the case where the marketer offers a reward of some form for sending on the material. Where a marketer encourages recipients to pass the names and contact details of friends they must not use the details unless satisfied that the individuals know and have consented. In relation to pan-European campaigns it simply notes that some jurisdictions have taken a more stringent line than the UK and, although there is an argument that the law of the jurisdiction in which the marketer is based is the applicable one, the question may be arguable if the marketer is using information collected in another State.[23] In addition the ICO provides some practical guidance on giving notices and marketing options for those who employ several means of delivery.

Transitional provisions

22–39   The PECR Regulations came into effect on December 11, 2003. The transitional provisions in Sch.2 contain no savings for lists of email addresses collected for marketing use without consent or without falling into the excepted category. The ICO indicated in the Guidance issued at the time of implementation that, at least initially, marketing lists of email addresses compiled in accordance with privacy legislation in force at the time, and which had been used recently without the recipients indicating any objection, could continue to be used as long as an opt-out was provided with every mailing. The Guidance went on to indicate that the ICO would continue to take a generous view of the use of mailing lists compiled and used only for the sender's own marketing as long as the lists are updated and weeded regularly. Clearly any data collected after December 2003 must comply with the consent requirements. This indefinite period of grace does not however apply to lists which are rented out to third parties. There is no legal right in the Regulations to continue to use such lists but the Commissioner has indicated publicly that this is his policy and marketers may therefore rely on the statements in the Guidance. Unlike the telephone and fax services there is no statutory email preference service.

---

[23] See para.22–99 and Ch.3 for a discussion on territorial application.

Concealment of the identity of the sender of direct marketing by email

Rights of subscriber

22–40 Regulation 2 covers unsolicited calls for direct marketing purposes.

Regulation 23 prohibits "any person" from transmitting or instigating the transmission of a communication for the purposes of direct marketing by means of electronic mail where the identity of the person on whose behalf the communication has been sent has been disguised or concealed or where a valid address to which the recipient of the communication may send a request that such communication cease has not been provided. A "valid address" must be provided. The ICO accepts that in the online environment this could be an email address and in text messages a short code could amount to a valid address. As good practice however it recommends a website address or PO Box number should be included. This imposes an obligation on the person "on whose behalf" the marketing is sent to ensure that there is no deception.

There is no positive requirement in relation to electronic mail in the PECR that the sender must include the identity of the organisation responsible for the marketing. This contrasts with the obligations imposed by reg.24 on those who make telephone calls, use automated calling systems or market by fax.

However, reg.7 of the Electronic Commerce (EC Directive) Regulations 2002 requires the originating party to be identified where any "commercial communications" (see definition below) are made on its behalf. In addition any such communication should clearly identify:

- that it is commercial communication;
- any promotional offers;
- any promotional competitions; and
- in an accessible, clear and unambiguous way the terms and conditions surrounding any promotional offer or competition.

Regulation 2(1) defines "commercial communications" as:

"a communication, in any form, designed to promote, directly or indirectly, the goods, services or image of any person pursuing a commercial, industrial or craft activity or exercising a regulated profession, other than a communication—

(a) consisting only of information allowing direct access to the activity of that person including a geographic address, a domain name or an electronic mail address; or

(b) relating to the goods, services or image of that person provided that the communication has been prepared independently of the person making it (and for this purpose, a communication prepared without financial consideration is to be taken to have been prepared independently unless the contrary is shown)."

In addition, reg.8 requires service providers to clearly identify unsolicited commercial communications sent by electronic mail so that it is clear to the recipient, upon receipt, that the communication is unsolicited.

Regulation 21 covers unsolicited calls for direct marketing purposes. A person must not use, or instigate the use of, or permit his line to be used where an objection has been lodged by the subscriber for the line in question. An objection can be lodged either by the subscriber notifying the caller that unsolicited calls should not "for the time being" be made on the line or by the subscriber listing the line number on the stop list kept by Ofcom. The provisions protect both individual and corporate subscribers and since June 2004 corporate subscribers have also been able to register with the Telephone Preference Service (TPS). The protection applies to subscribers and not to recipients of calls (contrast the provisions relating to email marketing covered above) and therefore if the subscriber for a line has registered an objection either directly or on the TPS unsolicited calls cannot be made on that line. However solicited calls are not affected and therefore if a user of the line who is not the subscriber has agreed to receive marketing calls this is still permissible.

Unsolicited

22–41   As in reg.22(2) this is not defined. This does not mean, as a matter of law, that any call should be treated as unsolicited unless the subscriber has explicitly agreed to accept direct marketing from or at the instigation of that particular caller. It is possible that a call could be treated as not unsolicited in other circumstances but in most cases a call will be unsolicited if the subscriber has not clearly agreed to the caller, or someone acting at his behest, contacting him via the telephone (see para.x, above for a discussion of the term as used in reg.22(2)). In general terms the Commissioner takes the view that it has its ordinary natural meaning of "uninvited".

22–42   Regulation 21(4) provides that the fact that the subscriber registers with the TPS will not automatically override a notification of non-objection to the receipt of calls. Such calls may be made by the caller on the line even though the number is registered with the TPS. It is not completely clear from the wording whether this is meant to apply to prior or subsequent notification however the Information Commissioner takes the view in the Guidance that where the subscriber has previously agreed to receive calls from a specific organisation a general registration on the TPS does not override that consent. Clearly the question of whether a consent remains valid will be a question of fact and it may not be wise for an organisation to rely on an old consent which has not been used regularly as the basis for making marketing calls as against a subscriber who has registered on the TPS in the intervening period. In practice, in most cases therefore, where a subscriber has notified a caller that he does not object to receiving direct marketing calls, the caller may rely on this until it is specifically revoked, usually by the caller being directly advised otherwise.

Subscribers who register on the TPS should therefore specifically notify organisations which they have previously agreed could call them, if they wish to stop future calls. A notification does not have to be made in writing but it may be prudent for evidential purposes to give a written notice and retain a copy. Subscribers should allow 28 days for the TPS registration to take effect. A call within the first 28 days of registration will not breach the Regulation.[24]

---

[24] PECR reg.21(4).

Marketing sent by fax

Rights of individual subscribers

22–43 Regulation 20 deals with unsolicited direct marketing faxes. Such faxes are prohibited without consent "for the time being". The prohibition covers a person transmitting or instigating the transmission of such faxes or a subscriber permitting his line to be used for their transmission. In the case of a subscriber who permits others to use a line for which he is the named subscriber the regulation is not specific as to the extent of knowledge required before he is held responsible for permitting the use. In *Sweet v Parsley*[25] it was held that the term "permit" connotes actual knowledge or grounds for suspicion that the prohibited act is going on and an unwillingness to act to prevent it. This was a case under the Dangerous Drugs Act 1965 in which the occupier of premises was charged with permitting premises to be used for drug taking. This was confirmed in *R. v Souter*.[26] The knowledge or suspicion must go to the relevant aspects of the prohibited activity. If actual knowledge is required the subscriber would have to be aware that the user of the line was undertaking the prohibited acts before he could be held to have "permitted" them. Alternatively it may be argued that, as in *Sweet v Parsley*, suspicion coupled with turning a blind eye may be sufficient.

Consent

22–44 An individual subscriber must have "previously notified the caller that he consents for the time being to such communications being sent by or at the instigation of the caller." The consent must be provided to the caller before the fax is sent. Applying general principles, consent may be implied from a relevant action but cannot be implied from inertia or silence (see discussion of consent in Ch.3, above). The consent must be explicit as to the particular kind of marketing ("such communications"), so a general consent to the receipt of marketing materials will not be sufficient to cover fax marketing. It must also be specific to the caller in question ("notified the caller"), so a general consent to receive fax marketing will not suffice. The consent must emanate from the subscriber for the line, not merely from one of the household. It is not explicit in the Regulations how a user is to distinguish individual subscribers in all cases. Clearly a number may be allocated to a named individual and shown so in the directory. Equally the directory entry may show the name of a limited company. It will be apparent from those that the subscriber is an individual or a corporate subscriber respectively. However in some cases a trading name may be used and it may not be clear whether the subscriber is an individual or a corporate entity. In the case of a corporate entity the caller does not need prior consent but only to respond to an objection if notified (see below). The fact that there may be some possible confusion in some cases should not, in the long term, be a detriment to the individual subscriber as he may also make use of the fax stop provisions designed for corporate subscribers. If an individual subscriber's line continues to be used for marketing faxes, possibly because it appears from directory information to belong to a corporate entity, then the individual can also exercise the rights described below. It does however have the effect of reducing the effective level of protection to

[25] [1969] 1 All E.R. 347.
[26] [1971] 1 W.L.R. 1187.

opt-out in such cases. This is borne out by the agreement reached by the regulator in a case brought in 2000.

22–45   In January 2001 the Information Commissioner settled cases brought against two companies, Second Telecom Ltd and Top 20 Ltd, for sending unsolicited faxes by an agreed enforcement notice which imposed obligations on both companies to routinely screen their existing databases against list of residential subscribers so as to exclude those who appeared on such databases from their marketing lists. The agreed notice was accompanied by an order of the Tribunal, again agreed by both sides, which imposed obligations on both companies not to send faxes to anyone who had opted-out of receiving faxes either by notifying the Commissioner or the companies themselves or who appears on the Fax Preference service stop list.

Because of the definitions used for corporate subscribers and individual subscribers it appears that partnerships, whatever their size, will fall to be treated as individual subscribers unless they are limited liability partnerships. Partners are persons who carry on business together with a view to profit (Partnership Act 1890). A partnership is not a corporate entity with a legal personality of its own and therefore does not fall into the definition of corporate subscriber in reg.2(1). While it may seem strange that some of the very large accountancy or legal partnerships are entitled to be treated as individual subscribers it appears that is the case.

A caller may rely on a previous consent until he is notified that it no longer applies. Where a subscriber who has consented to the despatch of marketing faxes is no longer the subscriber for that line, it will be helpful to his successor to the line if he either tells those to whom he has given the consents of the change, or leaves his successor a list of those to whom he has given consent. However this is perhaps asking a lot and it may not be a common occurrence.

A subscriber who has given consent may withdraw consent at any time.[27]

Rights of corporate subscribers

22–46   Although this section is headed the rights of corporate subscribers, in fact, as explained above, individual subscribers are also able to take advantage of the stop list. Under reg.20(1)(a) transmitting, instigating the transmission of or permitting the use of a line to make unsolicited direct marketing faxes is not allowed where either:

(a)   the called line is that of a corporate subscriber who has previously notified the caller that such unsolicited communications should not be sent on that line; or

(b)   the number allocated to the subscriber is on the stop list run by Ofcom.

In the first case, the notification must have been made to the caller, not the person whose line is being used. The notice need not be in writing. The notice must have told the caller that unsolicited faxes for marketing should not be sent on that line.

The 28-day period of grace also applies to the fax preference service stop list. Under reg.20(5) where a subscriber who has registered on the stop list "has notified a caller that he does not for the time being object to such communication being sent by that

---

[27] PECR reg.20(6).

caller on that line" such communications may continue to be sent notwithstanding the appearance on the stop list.

Information to be notified on marketing materials

22–47   On all direct marketing sent using public electronic communication services certain information must be provided by virtue of reg.24. The name of the person using or instigating the service must be given for all calls whether fax, telephone or an automated call. In relation to fax and automated calls the address of the person or a telephone number at which he can be reached free of charge must be provided. In the case of other direct marketing that information must be communicated if the recipient of the call so requests. It should be noted that the request may be made by the recipient of the call. It need not be the subscriber. The information must therefore be available when the call is made. It will not be sufficient for a caller to say it will be sent by post or is available in some other place.

Arrangements for the stop lists

22–48   Regulations 20 and 21 refer to the stop lists for both fax and telephone lines. A telephone preference service and a fax preference service were previously run by the direct marketing industry. These were replaced by the statutory arrangements. In essence these set up "stop" lists of those who have stated that they do not want to be subject to fax or telephone marketing. Both allow for individuals and business to register. The responsibility for the lists rests with Ofcom under regs 25 and 26. The arrangements for each list are similar.

Fax Preference Service (FPS) and Telephone Preference Service (TPS)

Any subscriber, whether a corporate subscriber or an individual, can notify Ofcom that he or she does not wish for the time being to receive unsolicited direct marketing faxes on a particular line.[28]

Any subscriber may notify Ofcom that they do not want for the time being to receive unsolicited direct marketing calls.[29] Until June 25, 2004 the right to register with the TPS was restricted to individual subscribers however this was altered by the Privacy and Electronic Communications (EC Directive)(Amendment) Regulations 2004[30] which permitted corporate subscribers to register. Corporate subscribers can register numbers allocated to particular lines by notice in writing to Ofcom. Ofcom must send all registered corporate subscribers a reminder of their registration every 12 months. This does not apply to individual subscribers.

The notices do not have to be in writing, apart from the notices provided by corporate users of the TPS, although clearly it will be helpful if subscribers put their objections in writing. Ofcom must maintain and keep up-to-date a list of all the fax numbers notified to them in this way and a list of the telephone numbers notified to them. If Ofcom has reason to believe that the subscriber who notified the objection is no longer the holder of that particular line number they must remove the number from the stop list.

---

[28] *ibid.* reg.25.
[29] *ibid.* reg.26.
[30] SI 2004/1039.

Ofcom has corresponding duties under regs 25(3) and 26(3) to make information from the stop lists available to any person who wants to send unsolicited direct marketing faxes or make calls for unsolicited direct marketing. Thus the marketer will be able to check that none of the numbers which he intends to contact belong to those who have objected. Ofcom must also make information from the records available to subscribers who want to check whether their number is on the list and have it removed. Ofcom can charge fees for making the information available and may charge different fees for providing different information, subject to an overriding duty to ensure that the systems break even and pay for themselves

The Regulations do not set out how the stop lists are to be run. Ofcom may keep the records in electronic or in printed form. Ofcom is permitted to make arrangements with another or others to provide the stop list mechanisms, but not the power to set the fees for use.

28-day time delay

22–49   A 28-day time delay is built in to allow for the appearance of the number on the stop list. It may take time for a number to appear on the list. If a subscriber objects just after the marketer has received his copy of the list the marketer may (quite innocently) telephone or fax that subscriber despite the fact that he has objected to the Director. Regulations 20(4) and 21(3) deal with this situation by providing that the caller will not be held to have contravened if the number was not on the list within the preceding 28 days before the call. In effect callers will not be able to rely on copies of the stop lists any older than 28 days.

CONFIDENTIALITY OF COMMUNICATIONS

22–50   Regulation 6 covers the use of any device used to store information or gain access to information stored on a user's terminal equipment. These are sometimes referred to as "spyware". The best known examples are probably "Cookies". Cookies are one of the types of software code that can be inserted into the memory of one computer by another, however the provisions of reg.6 are not technology specific. The essence of such programs is that they are sent to a user's computer when he visits a website and lodged in the memory. This may allow the website to recognise the computer in the future; spyware can also be used to trace the computer activities of the user or garner information from the host computer. The programs may do more than. Such programs can be useful, allowing the user to shop online more efficiently for example, but may also be very privacy intrusive. Under the regulation, unless the sole purpose of the device is to carry out or facilitate the communication itself or is strictly necessary for the provision of an information society service which the subscriber or user has requested the consent of the subscriber or user is required for such devices. An information society service is given the meaning that it has in the Electronic Commerce (EC Directive) Regulations 2002. This is:

> "any service normally provided for remuneration, at a distance, by means of electronic equipment for the processing (including digital compression) and storage of data, and at the individual request of a recipient of a service."

The provision of broadband is an information society service whereas shopping online for groceries is not.

The terms of the two exceptions from the requirement to give a notice and opt-out are very tight. In the case of facilitating the communication itself the device must be used for that sole purpose. In the case of the provision of an information society service the device must be "strictly necessary". As the term "necessary" is a term implying a balance the test here is specific and strict.

The restrictions apply irrespective of whether the information to which access is being gained is personal data. This means for example that the use of gifs or web beacons in email marketing campaigns as tracking devices to assess how many people opened the marketing email are not acceptable without the prior specific consent of the target. Apart from the exclusions described above the user or subscriber must be given clear and comprehensive information about the purposes of the storage or access involved and offered an opportunity to refuse the device. The notice and opportunity to opt-out need only be given once. The Regulation does not say who has to provide the notice. It might be thought that it is implicit in the provision that the person responsible for inserting the device should give the notice, however the Guidance from the Information Commissioner suggests that a third party might have the responsibility in some cases:

> "We recognise that it is possible for organisations to use cookie type devices on websites seemingly within the control of another organisation, for example through a third party advertisement on a website. In such cases the organisation to whom the site primarily refers will be obliged to alert users to the fact that a third party advertiser operates cookies. It will not be sufficient for that user to provide a statement to the effect that they cannot be held responsible for any use of such devices employed by other persons they allow to place content on their websites. In addition the third party would also have a responsibility to provide the user with the relevant information." (para.2.3 Version 2 November 2003)

The Guidance also stresses that the notice must be "sufficiently full and intelligible to enable individuals to gain a clear appreciation of the potential consequences of allowing storage and access to the information collected by the device should they wish to do so".

As the information must only "be provided" it is possible that it could be provided using a third party. The Interactive Advertising Bureau (IAB) is an industry body which has a website which explains the functions of cookies at *http://www.allaboutcookies. org* [Accessed on September 2, 2007] and website owners can link their sites to the information provided.

The regulation is not specific as to how the user or subscriber should be provided with the opportunity to refuse. The Commissioner's view, not surprisingly, is that the opportunity should be clear and the mechanism for refusal "prominent, intelligible and readily available to all, not just the most computer literate or technically aware". He goes on to advise that where the refusal mechanism is part of the privacy policy this should be signposted and easily accessible within the policy.

The regulation does not distinguish between the subscriber and the user. These may be different people. It is left to the individuals or organisations concerned to decide whose wishes would take precedence if there is a difference of views.

Traffic and Billing Data

22–51   The use of telecommunications generates vast amounts of personal data about the users. Directive 97/66 started from the basis that those users have rights to privacy in respect of that data; rights which do not amount to ownership of the information but restrict the uses that service and network providers could make of the data generated in providing telecommunications services. The same approach is seen in Recommendation R(95)4 at para.2.1 of the appendix to the Recommendation which states:

> "Telecommunications services, and in particular telephone services which are being developed, should be offered with due respect for the privacy of users, the secrecy of correspondence and the freedom of communication."

This recognises that the rights of individuals can be seen as an aspect of the right to freedom of expression. So, an internet service provider will not have the right to sell lists of subscribers who have visited particular sites or otherwise exploit the data about subscribers arising from his control of the service provision. The uses of such data are restricted. In this respect the rights of corporate subscribers are protected as well as those of individuals. This part of the Regulations deals with the uses which can be made of the data generated in the running of the services either with or without the consent of the subscriber. In broad terms the uses are restricted to those which are necessary to run the services. The subscriber may be asked to consent to some wider uses but even those are restricted in scope. The restrictions specify and make explicit the purpose specification restrictions imposed by the main Act.

Meaning of the terms traffic data, location data, and value added service

22–52   "Traffic" data are the data arising from the running of the network. "Traffic" data are defined in reg. 2(1) as:

> "any data processed for the purpose of the conveyance of a communication on an electronic communications network or for the billing in respect of that communication and includes data relating to the routing, duration or time of a communication."

Traffic data are distinguished from "location data". There are specific rules for the two sets of data, although the end result is very similar. "Value-added services" are not defined and the term is capable of covering a whole range of new services from interactive advertisements to navigation and breakdown services based on location.

Traffic data do not have to be personal data to be covered by the definition, although the restrictions imposed only apply to traffic data relating to subscribers or users which are processed and stored by a public communications provider. It follows that anonymised traffic data which can no longer be said to "relate" to a subscriber or user, or traffic data which do so relate but are processed and stored by any other person, are outside the specific restrictions imposed by reg.7. There is no separate definition of billing data (although the term "bill" is defined). If the data fall within reg.7 the basic rule is that they should be erased or, where the identifying data relates to an identifiable individual or corporate entity, anonymised when no longer required for the purpose of the transmission of a communication. The rules on erasure have however been modified by Directive 2005/0182 on the retention of data generated or processed in connection with the provision of publicly available electronic communications services or of public communications networks which has amended Directive 2002/58 in relation to retention. Directive 2005/0182 has not yet been implemented in the UK. The impact of the new Directive is dealt with in Ch.23, below. The provision requires that personal data should be modified so that it is no longer personal data and, in relation to corporate subscribers "modified so that they cease to be data that would be personal data if that subscriber was an individual". This, rather horrid, definition in respect of corporate subscribers absorbs the elements of the definition of personal data so presumably data will be relevant data for these purposes about a corporate subscriber if they relate to that corporate subscriber, and the corporate subscriber can be identified from that information or that and other information in the possession of the telecommunications service provider. Presumably a corporate subscriber will be identified by its legal name and address or identifying number such as a company registration number, but it is possible that a trading name would be regarded as sufficient. However, of necessity, providers are entitled to use the data to send bills to customers and a number of other legitimate uses of the data are permitted.

Applying the definition of "bill" in the general definitions in which bill includes an invoice, account, statement or other document of similar character, billing data will be any information relating to invoices, accounts, statement or other instruments of the like character.

Permitted uses of traffic data

Billing

22–53   Predictably enough traffic data held for the purposes of assessing and levying charges by a subscriber or in respect of interconnection payments may be processed and stored until the payment has been completed. Interconnection payments are the amounts one provider charges to another for the use of connections. The data can continue to be processed until the debt in respect of which they are processed becomes time-barred or until any proceedings, including appeals, arising from non-payment are concluded (reg.7(5)–(6)). It appears that they should then be erased. The OIC advises in the Guidance on the Regulations that such data should not be routinely retained for the maximum six-year period but should only be retained as long as they are actually needed. The subscriber or user must be told what types of traffic data are to be processed for this purpose and how long the processing will last, although prior consent is not required (reg.8(1))(para.3.1 guidance checked).

Authorised activities

22–54   Under reg.8(2) the only processing of traffic data which may be carried out is restricted to that which is required for one or more of a restricted list of purposes and even then subject to a range of conditions. The purposes are:

- the management of billing and traffic;
- customer enquiries;

- the prevention or detection of fraud;
- the marketing of electronic communications services; or
- the provision of value added services.

In all cases the activity may only be carried out by the provider or those acting under his authority. Accordingly a provider cannot sell or disclose the traffic data to third parties for their purposes (reg.8(2)).

Marketing and value-added services

22–55   Under reg.7(3) traffic data relating to a subscriber or user may be used for marketing telecommunications services or the provision of value-added services to that subscriber or user with the informed consent of the subscriber or user. The services marketed or the value-added services may be supplied by a third party. The subscriber or user must have been provided with information about the types of traffic data which are to be processed and the duration of the processing before the provider seeks consent. It is not explicit how the consent of a corporate subscriber is to be given. Presumably the service provider can rely on the consent of anyone who holds himself out as being able to give consent on behalf of the company. As in all other cases where consent is required it must be real consent, and although it may be implied it must be implied by a relevant action; lack of response cannot be treated as consent (for a full discussion of consent see Ch.3, above). The marketing need not be conducted by the telephone but may involve any form of marketing initiative. Under reg.7(4) subscribers must be able to withdraw their consent at ay time.

Dispute resolution

22–56   Regulation 8(4) states that nothing in the Regulations shall prevent the disclosure of traffic data to a competent authority for the purposes of the settlement of disputes by any statutory mechanism. This is parallel to the non-disclosure exemption for legal proceedings in the DPA 1998.

Customer inquiries

22–57   No further definition is included of what customer inquiries covers. It could be that the inquiries must be put by customers but equally it could be argued that they need only be about customers. If they are restricted to inquiries by customers it is not clear whether they must be about the customer's own particular account or whether the provider can give information in response to one customer's inquiry about another's account. The OIC view was previously that the inquiries are limited to those made by customers about their own accounts however the point is not covered in the November 2003 Guidance.

Prevention or detection of fraud

22–58   This only covers fraud. It does not cover the detection of other criminal activity such as offences against the person or drugs offences. Although on the words the fraud does not appear to have to be directed against the service operator or the provider this appears to be the reason for the specific provision. It is not clear whether it applies where the fraud is perpetrated against another customer, for example by making dishonest use of his line. Where other criminal activities are concerned there are exemptions in reg.29 from restrictions on processing where it is carried out for the prevention or detection of crime. Fraud has now been defined in the Fraud Act 2006, which came into effect in January 2007. An offence of fraud may cover a wide range of activities.

Management of billing or traffic

22–59 Again no definition is included so the term "management" has to be given its ordinary meaning. The management purposes must be the purposes of the provider, not the purpose of others.

Restrictions on the processing of location data

22–60 Regulation 14 specifically covers location data. It does not apply to traffic data. Location data are defined and mean any data processed in an electronic communications network indicating the geographical position of the terminal equipment of the user of a public electronic communications service including data relating to the latitude, longitude or altitude of the terminal equipment, the direction of travel of the user, or the time the location information was recorded.

Location data allow for a range of new services but also allow for significant surveillance and intrusion. The Regulations provides that location data relating to a user or subscriber of a public electronic communications network or service cannot be processed for anything other than the provision of value added services and even then with consent. The prohibition does not apply if the data have been successfully anonymised so that the user or subscriber cannot be identified (reg.14(2)).

The consent must be fully informed, in that the provider must have told the user or subscriber the types of location data that will be processed, the purposes and duration of the processing and whether the data will be passed to a third party for the service to be provided (reg.14(3)). The user or subscriber has a right to withdraw consent and there must be a continuing right of opt-out on a transaction basis. In other words, at every point of connection or each transmission to be given the right to opt-out "using a simple means and free of charge".

The processing must be restricted to that necessary for the purpose of providing the value-added service. There are also restrictions on the persons who may carry out such processing. These are restricted to the provider in question or someone acting for him and under his authority, or the third party provider of the services or those acting for him and under his authority (reg.14(5)).

However there is no restriction on the processing of location data by the users of the Emergency numbers, 999 and 112.[31] This means that emergency services can always trace the location of callers to these numbers.

Itemised billing

22–61 Regulation 9 deals with itemised billing. Regulation 9 provides that any subscriber, not simply an individual, shall be entitled to require the communications

---

[31] PECR reg.16(1)(c).

service provider to submit to him bills which are not itemised. The intent of this is to preserve the privacy of members of a household. In Recommendation R(95)4 the potential privacy problems in itemised billing were described thus:

> "Nevertheless urgent data protection problems are raised by the provision of itemised bills to subscribers, as well as by the retention by the network operator of the service data on which the bill is based . . . the provision of an itemised bill to a subscriber enables him or her to examine the telephone use of other people living in the household. In particular it allows the principal subscriber to identify the co-respondents of the co-users."[32]

Regulation 9(2) imposes a general duty on Ofcom to have regard to the needs to reconcile the rights of subscribers to receive itemised bills and the privacy rights of callers and recipients when exercising various powers under the Communications Act 2003. It draws attention to the possibility of using privacy-enhancing methods of communication or payment. The sort of facilities considered may be pre-paid telephone cards.

Call forwarding

22–62   Call forwarding is the term used for diverting calls. For a description it is helpful to turn again to Recommendation R(95)4:

> "Call forwarding allows a user to re-route his incoming calls to the terminal of a third party. This service is not dependent on the digitalisation of the network since it has always been available in the analogue system."[33]

Regulation 17 requires a service provider to remove a divert at the request of the subscriber to whose line calls are being diverted where the divert is "as a result of action taken by a third party". Presumably if the divert has been requested by the subscriber himself then the right of removal does not apply (although it seems unlikely that a service provider would insist on retaining a divert the subscriber did not want). The divert has to be removed without any charge and must be removed without any avoidable delay. The subscriber's service provider may have to ask other network or service providers to assist in achieving this and they in turn are subject to duties to comply with any reasonable request made by the subscriber's service provider for the purpose of achieving this end.

Calling or connected line identification

22–63   Calling line identification (CLI) was seen as a highly privacy-invasive feature when introduced and there was concern that callers should be able to protect anonymity of calls by blocking incoming CLI. Recommendation R(95)4 set out the potential problems with CLI in terms that seem almost quaint:

> "The digitalisation of networks has made possible this new service feature in voice telephony. With the aid of a display unit on a subscriber's terminal, it is now

---

[32] Explanatory Memoranda para.99.
[33] Explanatory Memoranda para.114.

possible to identify the source of incoming calls, that is the identity of the calling party . . .

This new service feature brings with it many advantages for subscribers. First, it allows them to be in control when the telephone rings. With the incoming number displayed even before the communication takes place, the subscriber is in a position to decide whether or not to speak to the calling party. Secondly, the new service feature is a useful tool to combat abusive or malicious calls since those responsible for them will no longer be able to conceal their identity (provided of course that they are telephoning from a terminal connected to the ISDN network). Thirdly, the display of the incoming number on the called party's terminal presents obvious advantages for emergency services such as police, ambulance and fire brigade . . .

The perceived advantages indicated in the preceding paragraph need to be evaluated in the light of a number of possible privacy problems which have been identified by the data protection community. First, the service feature may possibly undermine the anonymity which is guaranteed by ex-directory facilities. Secondly, calling line identification constitutes an obstacle to the freedom of communication of individuals contacting help line services, such as Alcoholics Anonymous, advice centres or the Samaritans . . . Thirdly the release of a telephone number to a commercial or marketing agency as a result of a telephone enquiry regarding a particular product or service may give rise to unwanted calls of a commercial or marketing nature."[34]

CALLING LINE IDENTIFICATION (CLI)

22–64 The Regulations now cover calling or connected line identification in relation to both incoming and outgoing calls. The rules on the use of CLI are set out in regs 10–13. Information about the identity of the calling line may be available to the subscriber or end user in two ways; either from a display on the telephone equipment in use or from a call return service. The identity of the calling line is always known to the service provider. In the United Kingdom CLI has been available through a call return service by dialling 1471 since 1994. It is also governed by Ofcom's General Conditions of Entitlement and the Guidelines for the provision of Calling Line Identification Facilities and other related services over Electronic Communications Networks Version 2.[35]

Publicity

22–65 CLI is perceived as a service to consumers which may be of benefit to them and which they should be entitled to use. Accordingly, where CLI services are available any public electronic communications service provider who offers those facilities must provide information to the public about the service and the options open to users and subscribers.[36] However, CLI is not always to be available and may be overridden in some particular circumstances.

---

[34] Explanatory memoranda para 107–110.
[35] Both available from *http://www.ofcom.org.uk* [Accesssed on September 2, 2007].
[36] PECR reg.12.

Malicious and nuisance calls

22–66   The provisions allowing callers to withhold numbers cannot be used as a cloak by nuisance callers. Under reg.15(1) a communications provider can override anything which is done to prevent the presentation of CLI where it is necessary or expedient to trace the source of malicious or nuisance calls on a subscriber's line. The subscriber has to apply to the service provider to trace the source of such calls. This right will override any contract term to the contrary. Moreover the provider may let any person with a legitimate interest know the identity of the subscriber for the line from which the nuisance calls have been made. Clearly a person with a legitimate interest would cover the police or another enforcement agency, but it also appears wide enough to cover the subscriber who is receiving the nuisance calls. It will not necessarily identify the actual caller, particularly where it is a line to which a number of people have access, but will pinpoint the physical location of the calls.

Emergency number calls

22–67   The other circumstance in which CLI will not be available is on calls to emergency services. CLI cannot be blocked for calls made to either 999 or 112 (the European emergency number). As noted earlier location data may also be processed in relation to calls to the emergency numbers.

Apart from these special cases subscribers are to be able to exercise several choices over the presentation of identity and acceptance of calls from others without identifying information. Where a subscriber has more than one line the rights apply separately to each line so a subscriber might have a different policy on accepting calls on different lines.[37]

Preventing outgoing presentation of CLI

22–68   Regulation 10 sets out two choices for blocking presentation of identity; per call blocking by users and per line blocking by subscribers. Anyone using a telephone line which offers the technical facility for blocking must be able to prevent the presentation of the identity of the line he is using on a call-by-call basis (per call blocking). Any subscriber, that is the one who has a contract with the service provider, must be able to block any CLI presentation for all calls on the line (per line blocking). These facilities must be provided by a simple mechanism and must be free of charge by the service provider.

Third country calls

22–69   In Art.8(5) the Directive requires that the blocking of CLI must apply to calls originating in the Community and made to third countries. The only way this can be achieved, other than by agreements between service providers in Europe and third countries, is by the service provider marking such calls as CLI unavailable. No specific provision in the Regulations deal with this requirement; no such duty is imposed on service providers.

---

[37] PECR reg.10(3).

Presenting incoming presentation of CLI

22–70   At first sight it is not easy to see why a subscriber would want to disable CLI presentation but it can occur where a help line wishes to guarantee anonymity of calls made to it or to preserve individual privacy in a shared household. To deal with such cases reg.11(2) provides that where CLI is available the subscriber whose line is being called can prevent the CLI of the caller being made available to him. This is a self-denying ordinance. It applies to the line and not to individual calls.

Preventing outgoing presentation of CLI

22–71   Regulation 11(4) is intended to allow a subscriber to prevent the presentation of the "real" number being called from being made available to a caller where the call comes through a connected line. This will apply where a caller is ringing a number and the call is being forwarded on to another number. For example a GP may have his calls routed through the surgery number but actually be taking them at home. He may not want his home number presented to calling patients. This provision allows him to block the presentation of the number of the connected line, that is the home number.

Refusing calls without CLI

22–72   If CLI is available to the person being called before the call is taken and the caller has blocked the CLI of the call, then the person being called will be able to see that is the case before he takes the call. Regulation 12(3) provides that where a person being called is aware that CLI has been blocked on a call he must have a simple means to reject the call or all such calls. It need not be a free service. The right to refuse to take a call on which the number has been blocked is contained in Art.8(3) of the Directive.

22–73   The appropriate way to deal with this has been a matter of some debate. The problem is that, while fixed networks can offer a service called Anonymous Call Rejection (ACR) there is no direct equivalent on mobile networks. Where ACR is available calls without CLI are not delivered to the subscriber, and the subscriber gets a message explaining why the call has been rejected and how to overcome the rejection, by releasing the CLI.

On mobile networks however this facility is not available so the only way of rejecting a call is for the user to press "busy". This does not tell the caller that the call is being rejected or why the call is being rejected and how to overcome the problem.

In the consultation paper in July 2002 the DTI canvassed the method of complying with this requirement and, at that time it seemed that the regulator, Oftel, considered that the industry should come up with a satisfactory technical fix. However the current Guidance from the Commissioner's Office seems to accept that the position has been abandoned. The Guidance states that:

> "It is the Commissioner's current understanding, on the basis of advice received from Oftel, that as the relevant regulation applies to the automatic rejection of voice calls only, this can be implemented relatively simply using a recorded message."

In other words mobile users should record a voicemail message explaining to callers that their calls may have been rejected because of the absence of CLI, then press the busy button when presented with a call without CLI that they do not want to accept and divert to voicemail. This is hardly a consumer friendly approach, particularly as the customer has to pay for voicemail messages.

There is a separate problem with international calls which does not appear to have any solution. The OIC paper sets out the problem as follows:

"The current technical standards do not distinguish between a situation where CLI has been deliberately withheld and where CLI is unavailable, for example, in relation to incoming international calls. Therefore, a subscriber who chooses not to receive calls with CLI withheld will also not receive international calls."

Co-operation by providers

22–74   Regulation 13 requires all communication service providers to comply with reasonable requests made by others to give effect to the CLI rights of subscribers and users.

DIRECTORIES

22–75   In the United Kingdom both directories and directory inquiries in relation to telephone subscribers have been opened to competition. All providers enter subscriber data into one central database which is operated by BT but is available to all providers. There is no equivalent for fax, mobile telephones or email addresses. Regulation 18 covers any directory of subscribers. The term "subscriber" is defined as meaning a person who is a party to a contract with a provider of public electronic communications services for the supply of such services. The directory may be in printed or electronic form but must be made available to members of the public or a section of the public including by means of a directory enquiry service. It follows that directories may cover fax numbers, email numbers, or mobile telephone numbers and this is how the Information Commissioner has interpreted the provision.[38] They are not limited to directories of telephone numbers. It does not matter who compiles them or offers the directory service, nor does the form of the directory matter, whether on CD-ROM or paper or given over the telephone in response to a request. The provisions do not apply to any editions of directories published before December 11, 2003 when the Regulations came into force.

22–76   Subscribers have rights to have details relating to them to be omitted from further editions of directories; they cannot require existing or previous editions to be amended. Whenever a revised version of a directory is issued it is deemed to be a new edition.[39]

22–77   Obligations are laid upon both those who "collect" personal data and those who "produce" directories. Neither of these terms are defined and therefore must be given their natural meaning. The rights to be notified of the inclusion in the directory and to withdraw rest with the subscriber rather than the user. The Regulations appears to be based on the assumption that the subscriber will be the user of the telephone. It is not clear how it applies in other cases, for example where parents subscribe to mobile telephones for use by children.

---

[38] Guidance to PECR para.7 Pt 1.
[39] PECR reg.18(7).

Individual subscriber entries

22–78   Before details relating to an individual subscriber are included in a directory he must be told by the person who collects the personal data that it is intended for inclusion. He must be given the opportunity to have particular information omitted from a directory but cannot insist that specific information is included. There is no specific requirement that the subscriber provides prior consent to inclusion, an opt-out appears to be sufficient. In his guidance the Commissioner refers to these provisions as reflecting the transparency requirements of the first data protection principle and emphasises that the nature of the directory product and potential use should be considered. In particular the more information is to be included in a directory and the more sophisticated the product, the more information should be provided to the subscriber:

> ". . . those collecting information. . . . will need to ensure subscribers appreciate that their information will be made available via a variety of directory products and services what will enable those who know their name and address to obtain their phone number. Where there are a range of ex-directory options these should be drawn to subscribers' attention."

An individual subscriber can also "verify, correct or withdraw" his entry without charge at any time.

Corporate subscriber entries

22–79   Corporate subscribers have the right to be omitted from a directory where the corporate subscriber has notified the producer of the directory that it does not want "its" data to be included. This would presumably allow a corporate subscriber to require that all its direct dial numbers should be omitted from a directory.[40]

Directory inquiries

22–80   The rules about directories appear to apply equally to directory inquiry services although the point is not made explicit.

Reverse searching

22–81   The Regulations include provisions which deal with directories which offer reverse searching, that is the provision of the name and address from the telephone number. This was not covered under the previous Regulations but the OIC took action against providers who offered this service without the consent of the subscriber as being unfair processing. Subscribers must be expressly informed and give express consent before their details can be included in a directory which allows reverse searching of facsimile or telephone numbers.[41]

22–82   It should be noted that directory services are treated as a mandatory service to subscribers under other telecoms provisions. For example the Telecommunications (Open Network Provision)(Voice Telephony) Regulations 1998

---

[40] PECR reg.18(4).
[41] PECR reg.18(3).

require all providers of publicly available telephone services who have a contract with a subscriber in respect of which a number has been allocated to offer the subscriber an entry in a publicly available directory and a directory enquiry service. This obligation is repeated in the new regulatory framework under which Member States are required to ensure at least one comprehensive subscriber directory. This obligation is imposed on British Telecommunications plc and Kingston Communications plc (in respect of Hull) by the Universal Service Obligations specifically imposed on each of those companies.

22–83   Under the Regulations all licensees and "system less service providers", that is providers who do not have fixed networks, like mobile phone operators, have to offer subscribers a place in a directory enquiry service and in a publicly available directory of subscribers. They also have to make "copies" of their subscribers' details available to those who request them and in doing so have to follow a non-discriminatory policy. Thus the information about subscriber numbers is available to anyone who wants it to make a directory. In order to ensure that this does not undermine data protection safeguards for individuals in the use of their information, the provider who passes on that information must ensure that the person who obtains it from him will comply with data protection standards.

The Regulations insert standard clauses into the licences of those who are licensed operators under s.7 of the Telecommunications Act 1984 requiring them to comply with the Data Protection Act in the handling of directory information and particularising the standards as being those set out in the Code of Practice. They are bound to comply with the Code, therefore, as part of their licence conditions. Breach of the Code will be a breach of licence conditions and enforceable by the Director. However this mechanism does not work for all directory producers, as they will not necessarily be licence holders. They are bound to honour the terms of the Code by threat of having the supply of information to them cut off if they fail to do so. Service providers who supply directory information to non-licensed persons must make it a condition of supply that the person agrees to comply with the Code and may withhold supply if they do not do so.

Telecommunications Directory Information—A Fair Processing Code

22–84   A Code was brought in under the Data Protection Act 1984 but re-issued under the 1998 Act in due course. It deals with the fair processing of personal data for directories. It applies to any personal data processed to provide a directory service or product (except for private directories, such as those produced internally by large organisations).

The Code states that in order to be fair the processing for directories must only be carried out in order to make available information "in line with the wishes and expectations of data subjects". In effect therefore directory services will be expected to stay as they are unless the individual consents to the change. Therefore unless the individual has consented directory services will be restricted to:

(a) searches on name and address only;

(b) alphabetical ordering;

(c) restrictions on address only search;

(d) a ban on reverse searching;

(e) choice of title and form of address to be determined by the subscriber.

It recognises that directory compilers will have to pass data on to third parties and encourages them to make it more difficult for third parties to process the data outside these confines by imposing technical barriers such as making bulk copying difficult.

SECURITY OF ELECTRONIC COMMUNICATIONS

22–85 Regulation 5 is based on Art.4 of the Directive and requires adequate security for public electronic communications services. The security concerns are to some extent fuelled by a recognition of the inherent insecurity of mobile telephone networks. The provisions require providers to take appropriate security measures and also to alert users to particular security risks. The primary obligation to take appropriate technical and organisational measures to ensure the security of the service falls on the service provider, but the network provider also has an obligation to respond to any reasonable request made by the service provider for security purposes. It is not clear whether the network provider can be liable to enforcement action if he fails to comply with the reasonable request of the service provider, but it appears that he has a mandatory duty to take security measures in conjunction with the service provider and accordingly could be liable if he fails in that duty.

Where there is still a significant risk to the security of the service despite the efforts of the service and network providers, then the service provider is under an obligation to provide a number of relevant pieces of information to the subscriber. No explanation of what constitutes a "significant" risk is provided. The Directive uses the term "particular" risk. A risk might be regarded as significant if it affects a large number of users, to the extent that even though the effects of the breach of security might be minor the risk of it happening to any subscriber is high. To take a fanciful example, there might be a risk that snatches of conversations could be heard on other mobile telephones occasionally. However they would never be more than a few words and not in a way that would show the identity of the speakers. Alternatively a risk might be relatively unlikely but if it did occur could involve a major loss of privacy. To give an even more fanciful example, there might be a risk that someone using a mobile telephone in the vicinity of a public address system point could find the entire conversation picked up and broadcast over the public address system. The risk might be relatively remote but if it did occur it could mean a major breach of privacy. Both could be regarded as significant risks. It is suggested that, given the use of the word "particular" in the Directive it would be more prudent to take a broad view of the word "significant" and regard both as falling within the category.

22–86 The obligation of the service provider is to inform the subscriber of:

(a) the nature of the risk;

(b) any appropriate measures that the subscriber may take to safeguard against the risk; and

(c) the likely costs involved in taking such measures.

The factors which determine whether measures are appropriate are the cost of implementing the solution and the state of the technology. These have to be measured against the risks against which he is being guarded. The service provider is not under an obligation to proffer advice on untested expensive new solutions for problems, but to give mainstream advice on reasonably costed remedies. The information must be provided free of charge.

EXEMPTIONS

22–87   As noted above, specific exemptions are included in relation to the use of traffic data. There are also more general exemptions in regs 28 and 29 relating to national security and law enforcement.

These exemptions apply to the specific requirements of the PECR Regulations.

Relationship between the exemptions in the Regulations and the DPA 1998

22–88   The DPA 1998 sets out a regulatory regime for personal data and allows some disclosures to be made outside that regime or some of the rights to be abrogated where there is a strong countervailing interest such as the prevention of crime. The exemptions in the main Act apply to the requirements of the main Act. The exemptions in the PECR apply to the requirements of the Regulations only, not to the requirements of the DPA 1998. The two are without prejudice to one another so the same facts would be able to give rise to an exemption claim under s.28 of the DPA 1998 and one under reg.29 of the PECR but each would apply separately to the processing involved.

National security

22–89   This is dealt with by way of a general exemption from the Regulations in reg.28 if such an exemption is required in order to safeguard national security. This is followed by detailed provisions under which conclusive evidence of the requirement for the exemption is to be provided by a certificate signed by a Minister of the Crown and for appeal to the Tribunal on limited grounds. The provisions relating to the certificates, the rights of appeal and the constitution of the Tribunal are the same as those in the main Act, which are dealt with fully at Ch.15, above and are not repeated here.

Legal proceedings and law enforcement

22–90   Under reg.29 none of the provisions of the Regulations shall require a communications provider to do anything or stop him doing anything:

(i) inconsistent with any requirement imposed by or under an enactment, or order of a court; or

(ii) likely to prejudice the prevention or detection of crime or apprehension or prosecution of offenders.

The communications provider will also be exempt from any requirement of the Regulations if exemption is:

(iii) required for the purpose of legal proceedings including prospective legal proceedings;

(iv) necessary for the purpose of obtaining legal advice; or is

(v) otherwise necessary for the purpose of establishing or exercising legal rights.

This is similar to the legal proceedings exemption in the DPA 1998. There is no exemption for the collection of tax or duty.

In the Directive exemptions were dealt with in Art.15. It includes a requirement that any exemptions must meet the standards of proportionality required for any breach of Art. 8 of the ECHRFF. It also includes a specific provision for communications data:

". . . Member States may inter alia adopt legislative measures providing for the retention of data for a limited period justified in grounds laid down in this paragraph. All the measures referred to in this paragraph shall be in accordance with the general principles of Community law, . . ."

The topic of retention of communications data is covered in Ch.23.

ENFORCEMENT AND INDIVIDUAL RIGHTS

Compensation

22–91 Regulation 30 provides that a person who suffers damage by reason of any contravention of any of the requirements of the Regulations by any other person shall be entitled to bring proceedings for compensation for the damage. There is no compensation for associated distress in these cases, unlike the provisions in respect of the main Act. Damage means actual damage (see discussion of what constitutes damage in Ch.14, above). It is difficult to envisage what actual damage is likely to be caused by unsolicited telephone calls, although in the case of fax messages and spam email there is a cost to the subscriber associated with the receipt of the messages. The cost is extremely small and it might be thought that it would hardly be worth seeking monetary compensation but it would enable an individual to bring an action before the courts. The court would then be able to use any other powers at its disposal to deal with the case. It appears however that an enterprising data subject has succeeded in an action in the Edinburgh Sheriff Court against Transcom for the damages associated with receipt of an unsolicited email. It is reported on a website[42] that he was awarded damages of £750 plus costs of £617 (the court having lifted the usual cap on costs in a small claims action) against Transcom for sending an unsolicited email to his personal email address.

In *Microsoft v McDonald*[43] Microsoft took action under reg.30 against a spammer who had used their network services. Regulation 30 allows "any person" who has suffered damages as a result of breach of the regulations to seek compensation. The Court held that Microsoft was within the class of persons entitled to claim under reg.30. In the case Microsoft sought an injunction to restrain the spammer from repeating his

---

[42] *http://www.scotchspam.org.uk* [Accessed on September 2, 2007].
[43] [2006] EWHC 3410.

actions. The High Court granted the injunction under its powers under the Supreme Court Act 1981.

If proceedings for compensation are brought under this regulation it is a defence for the defendant to prove that he had taken such care as in all the circumstances was reasonably required to comply with the requirement. It is suggested that, as far as the marketing aspects are involved, this would cover giving proper training and instructions to staff; making sure proper stop lists are maintained of those who notify objections to direct marketing by these methods; ensuring regular use of the current stop lists; ensuring the relevant information is given and available when requested; ensuring notifications given are passed on expeditiously to Ofcom or the persons running the stop lists on his behalf.

Enforcement

22–92   The enforcement provisions are drafted by reference to the DPA 1998. Part V of the DPA 1998 is applied with appropriate modifications set out in Sch.1. These powers are covered in Ch.x. The complaint and assessment provisions are worded differently from the DPA 1998. Under s.42 of the DPA 1998 an individual who is or believes himself to be affected by processing may make a request to the Commissioner for an assessment of the processing in question. The Commissioner then has obligations to make the assessment and respond to the individual. Under reg.32 either Ofcom or a person aggrieved by an alleged contravention of the Regulations may request the Commissioner to exercise his enforcement functions in respect of that contravention The Regulations do not in terms impose a duty to consider such a request or make a determination following it but applying the principles of public law the Commissioner will be under an obligation to consider any request properly made to him under the legislation. In order to decide whether to exercise his enforcement functions the Commissioner will have to make a decision on whether or not the processing involved complies with the Regulations.

Assistance of Ofcom

22–93   Under reg.33 Ofcom has a duty to provide technical advice to the Commissioner on matters relating to electronic communication if requested. The request of the Commissioner must be a reasonable one.

Enforcement notices

22–94   The Commissioner may serve an enforcement notice on any person who contravenes the requirements of the Regulations. In considering whether to serve a notice the Commissioner must have regard to whether the contravention has caused any individual damage but not distress. The provisions of s.41 of the DPA 1998 under which those subject to enforcement notices may apply to the Commissioner to have the notice cancelled or varied by reason of a change of circumstances also apply. Notices may apply as a matter of urgency.

Information notices

22–95   The power to serve information notices applies to breaches of the Regulations. A notice may be served where the Commissioner reasonably requires any information for the purpose of determining whether a person has complied or is complying with the relevant requirements of the Regulations. The notice may require him to furnish such information relating to compliance as is specified in the notice. The notice must contain a statement that the Commissioner regards the specified information as relevant for the purpose of determining whether the person has complied or is complying and his reason for regarding it as relevant.

Prosecutions and warrants

22–96   Failure to comply with an enforcement or information notice is an offence. The Commissioner's powers to apply for warrants will apply to breaches of the Regulations.

Appeals

22–97   There are appeals to the Tribunal against both notices and any urgency provisions which are included with them.

Adequacy of enforcement powers

22–98   The Commissioner has made public his view that he does not consider that his information gathering and enforcement powers are sufficient to deal with serious abuses. In his response to the Consultation Paper issued before implementation the Commissioner made this point. The paper posed a number of questions about the efficacy of the remedies available under the TDPP Regulations and whether they were adequate to deal with all the mischiefs. It covered the reluctance of service providers to pass information to the regulator (or to complainants) where the complaint concerned repeated "nuisance" calls which emanate from marketing firms, that is calls where no one speaks and where the number had been withheld. It posed the possibility that network and service providers should be under a requirement to disclose the source of a call which is suspected of breaching the marketing rules. The paper also considered whether there should be a strengthened regime against those who flouted the rules on unsolicited marketing communications and even suggested consideration of the use of administrative fines or "Stop Now" orders backed by criminal sanctions. The Commissioner's Office was therefore disappointed that none of these stronger powers were included in the Regulations but remains optimistic that the DTI will eventually recognise the problems and provide a stronger enforcement mechanism.

TERRITORIAL APPLICATION

22–99   Directive 2002/58 and the Regulations are silent on the issue of territorial application. The provisions of the DPA 1998 are not applied to the Regulations and accordingly the general law will apply. In general terms therefore the Regulations will apply where actions are carried out in the jurisdiction of the UK courts. In relation to control of traffic and billing data this is likely to be where the data are held. If a service or network provider is established in the United Kingdom then there is unlikely to be any problem. The issues becomes more cloudy in relation to obligations placed on those who use telephone services. This applies to the marketing uses. If a person outside the United Kingdom uses a telephone network within the United Kingdom to send marketing material it is not clear whether the "use" takes place within the United Kingdom or outside it and whether a call is made where it is started or where it is received.

If a person uses the telephone network to transfer personal data overseas the usual rules in the DPA 1998 will apply. There are no special rules for overseas transfers and the use of telecom systems. The Articles 29 and 31 Groups have a locus standi to consider and report on Directive 2002/58 as on the main Directive.

TRANSITION

22–100   The transitional arrangements are dealt with in Sch.2. The complex transitional provisions of the DPA 1998 are not relevant.

Directories

22–101   Regulation 18, which provided additional rights in relation to entries in directories does not apply to previously published editions of a directory. Exclusion rights do not apply to editions published before implementation.

Notifications

22–102   Broadly speaking, all consents or objections registered under the predecessor Regulations continue to have effect under the new provisions.

CHAPTER 23

Monitoring of Communications and Data Retention

INTRODUCTION

23–01 Respect for the confidentiality of communication is a fundamental aspect of the right to privacy as set out in Art.8 of the European Convention on Human Rights and Fundamental Freedoms ("the Human Rights Convention"). Article 8 requires the State to respect "private and family life, home and correspondence". Article 5 of Directive 2002/58 applies this right to the provision of electronic communications by public service providers. Crucially Art.5 restricts eavesdropping on electronic conversations or monitoring the use of communications systems in public electronic communications systems. In an era in which government is increasingly reliant on surveillance of communications the scope of the restrictions imposed by Art.5 and its predecessor in Directive 97/66 has been a matter of considerable controversy. The importance of surveillance and monitoring of communications for the purposes of tackling crime and terrorism has thrown the impact of these restrictions into sharp relief.

In this chapter we cover the European legal background to the rules governing the monitoring of communications, the scope of the European legal instruments, the regulation of interception in the UK under the Regulation of Investigatory Powers Act ("RIPA") and the Telecommunications (Lawful Practice) (Interception of Communications) Regulations 2000 ("LBP Regulations") and the retention of data generated by the use of public electronic communications systems. The broader context of European co-operation in relation to security is covered in Ch.24, below.

RIPA covers the entire spectrum of interception, covert surveillance, use of intelligence sources and related matters. Only Pt 1 of Ch.I—Interception of Communications and Ch.II—Acquisition and Disclosure of Communications Data are covered in this chapter.

The scope of the European legal instruments is important in this context as it affects how much freedom the UK has to decide on its own rules in some of these areas. The relationship with the European legal instruments is therefore considered.

Interception of Communications

Introduction

23–02   The rules which govern this area are derived from supra-national legal instruments: the Human Rights Convention, Directive 2002/58 and its predecessor Directive 1997/66. Retention of communications data is regulated by Directive 2006/24.

There are different rules for interception of communications and for access to communications data. Interception has a legal definition in RIPA but broadly covers any access to the **content** of communications. Interception may take place either by **monitoring**, that is listening into the conversation or viewing an email exchange while is is taking place, or **recording** that is accessing the communication and taking a copy to listen to or read later. Access to communications data means having access to the traffic data **about** the communication. Communications data is the information generated as a result of electronic communications (such as the number called or the length of the call) rather than the content of the communication. There are special rules which allow businesses (which includes the public sector for these purposes) to intercept the contents of communications on their own systems subject to safeguards. These are found in the LBP Regulations made under RIPA. There are no provisions which allow businesses (including the public sector) to access or use the communications data on their systems.

Summary of Main Points

23–03   (a) Interception of communications and access to communications data involve breaches of Art.8 of the Convention rights.

(b) Interception, access to communications data and retention of communications data are covered by a number of intersecting provisions.

(c) Organisations (whether public or private) carrying out interception of content on private electronic communications systems which they control (e.g. internal government department systems) are subject to Art.8 of the Convention and have a lawful basis for their interference with those rights as long as they apply the LBP Regulations.

(d) Organisations (whether public or private) carrying out surveillance or accessing communications data on private electronic communications systems which they control (e.g. internal government department systems) are subject to Art.8 of the Convention but have no lawful basis for the interference as they are not able to rely on Ch.II of RIPA and the LBP Regulations do not cover communications data.

(e) Public bodies carrying out interception or access to communications data on public telecommunications systems are subject to Art.8 of the Convention and Art.5 of Directive 2002/58 and have a lawful basis for their interference with those rights as long as they have proper authority under RIPA.

(f) The retention of communications data by providers of public electronic communications service providers is covered by Directive 2006/24 but this has not yet been implemented in the UK.

BACKGROUND

Article 8 of the Convention rights

23–04   The interception or surveillance of a communication is clearly an interference with the Art.8 right of an individual.[1] Article 8 provides:

"(1) Everyone has the right to respect for his private and family life, his home and his correspondence.
(2) There shall be no interference by a public authority with the exercise of this right except such as is in accordance with law and is necessary in a democratic society in the interests of national security, public safety or he democratic well-being of the country, for the prevention of disorder or crime, for the protection of health or morals, or for the protection of the rights and freedoms of others."

This is now part of UK law by virtue of the Human Rights Act 1998. In the past the UK was found wanting before the European Court of Human Rights because of its failure to regulate comprehensively the interception of communications. The first statute to regulate the interception of communications was the Interception of Communications Act 1985 ("IOCA") which was passed following an adverse finding against the UK in the case of *Malone v UK*.[2] UK practice had been for telephone taps to be carried out under administrative practices with no comprehensive statutory code governing surveillance activities. Thus the practice did not comply with the standards necessary to meet Art.8(2) as it was not set out in a legal scheme sufficiently clear or transparent to enable the citizen to understand in what circumstances and in what conditions public authorities were empowered to carry out such activities.[3]

The IOCA made it an offence to intentionally intercept a communication in the course of transmission by a public telecommunications system, unless either it was done with the authority of a warrant issued by the Secretary of State or the interceptor had reasonable grounds for believing that either the sender or the recipient had consented to the interception. However the limited remit of the IOCA meant that the UK continued to face adverse findings by the Court at Strasbourg in relation to interception. In the case of *Alison Halford v UK*[4] the Court found that the tapping of a telephone which was part of a private network was not covered by the IOCA and was thus without a proper legal basis. In a variety of cases the Court also found that the failure by the UK to regulate surveillance by electronic eavesdropping in other ways breached Art.8.[5] In the UK courts

---

[1] See Ch.2, above for a full description of the impact of the HRA and the case law on Art.8 since October 2000. Concerns about the impact of interception on private life were expressed by the Article 29 Working Party in its Recommendations in the Respect of Privacy in the Context of Interceptions of Telecommunications of May 3, 1999.
[2] (1985) & E.H.R.R. 14.
[3] For a more detailed analysis see *Keir Starmer European Human Rights Law*.
[4] (1997) 24 E.H.R.R. 523.
[5] *Khan v UK* (2001) 31 E.H.R.R. 45; *PG JH v UK* [2002] Crim. L.R. 308.

in *R. v Effick*[6] it was held that calls from a cordless telephone which were intercepted between the base unit and the telephone were not covered by the IOCA.

Most recently the Court has found against the UK in the case of *Copland v UK*.[7] The case is dealt with below.

When the Convention rights were implemented in the United Kingdom by the HRA it was imperative that the entire area of surveillance was reviewed and put on to a proper statutory footing. The Government decided that the appropriate approach was to deal with both Art.5 of Directive 97/66 and Art.8(2) of the Convention rights in the same legislation and did so in RIPA and the LBP Regulations.

Article 5 of Directive 97/66 and 2002/58

23–05   Article 5(1) of Directive 2002/58 requires Member States to ensure the confidentiality of:

> ". . . communications and the related traffic data by means of a public communications network and publicly available electronic communications services, through national legislation. In particular they shall prohibit listening, tapping, storage or other kinds of interception or surveillance of communications and the related traffic data by persons other than users, except with the consent of the users concerned, except when legally authorised to do so in accordance with Article 15(1)."

This largely restates Art.5 of Directive 1997/66; the difference is in the addition of the reference to "and related traffic data" which is dealt with below. However in respect of the interception of the content of communications the provision is identical. It requires Member States to prohibit the interception of communications and access to communication data on public networks except **either** where users of the communication system have consented **or** the interception is legally authorised.

The scope of areas where legal authority may permit an interference is not in fact limited to the derogations provided for by Art.15(1) as Art.5(2) further provides that:

> "(2) Paragraph 1 shall not affect any legally authorised recording of communications and the related traffic data when carried out in the course of lawful business practice for the purposes of providing evidence of a commercial transaction or of any other business communication."

Recital 23 provides some further explanation of the scope of this derogation as follows:

> "Confidentiality of communications should also be ensured in the course of lawful business practice. Where necessary and legally authorised, communications can be recorded for the purpose of providing evidence of a commercial transaction. Directive 95/46/EC applies to such processing. Parties to the communications should be informed prior to the recording about the recording, its

---

[6] [1994] 3 All E.R. 458.
[7] (2006) E.H.R.R. 43 SE5.

purposes and the duration of its storage. The recorded communication should be erased as soon as possible and in any case at the latest by the end of the period during which the transaction can be lawfully challenged."

23–06 The derogations provided for by Art.15(1) permit Member States to adopt legislative measures to restrict the scope of the rights and obligations where the restriction constitutes a necessary, appropriate and proportionate measure within a democratic society to safeguard:

". . . national security (i.e. State security), defence, public security, and the prevention, investigation, detection and prosecution of criminal offences or of unauthorised use of the electronic communication system."

The Article makes it explicit that Member States may adopt laws to provide for the interception of communications where the reasons fall outside community competence but the measures must be limited to those allowed by the Article. Any abrogation of the confidentiality of communications must also be in accord with Community law including the Principles in Art.6(1) and (2) of the Treaty. The Principles in Art.6(1) and (2) enshrine the fact that the Union is founded on the principles of liberty, democracy, respect for human rights and fundamental freedoms.[8]

The Directive does not apply to areas outside the scope of EU law and thus interception may take place for matters outside scope. Recital 11 of Directive 2002/58 makes this point explicit but also makes it explicit that the Convention rights continue to apply to such interception. RIPA is primary legislation and its provisions apply to all interception which is within its scope.

Confidentiality of communications data

23–07 As noted above Directive 97/66 did not impose any restriction on the access to communications data. It did impose restrictions on how such data can be used by those who provide public electronic services which have now been repeated in Directive 2002/58 and are implemented in the UK by the Privacy and Electronic Communications (EC Directive) Regulation 2003 (PECR) (see Ch.22, above). RIPA covers the acquisition and disclosure of communications data by designated public authorities from public service providers but does not cover the access to communications data or the use of such data by operators of private systems, such as employers. As far as private networks are concerned the LBP Regulations did not deal with communications data. The current situation therefore is that operators of private networks (usually employers) access and use communications data without any general supervisory regime other than the Data Protection Principles; specifically there is no legal basis for accessing such data. It can be assumed that the view of the UK Government has been that operators of private systems, whether the system controller is in the public or the private sector, need no additional powers to access or use communications data. The case of *Copland*[9] however suggests that this is not the view of the EctHR and will need to be addressed. Directive 2002/58 placed communications data arising from public electronic communications

---

[8] Treaty Art.15(1).
[9] See n.1, above.

services on the same footing and subject to the same restrictions as interception. There has however been no subsequent change of the relevant statutory provisions in RIPA which suggests that the view of the UK Government is that the combination of the restrictions in PECR and the RIPA regime is sufficient to meet Art.5.

Copland v UK

23–08 Mrs Copland was employed by a Further Education College. During the course of her employment her telephone and internet usage were monitored by her employer. There was some dispute over whether interception of contents took place but the Court took the view that it did not have to decide that as the monitoring of the communications data amounted to a breach of Art.8 in any event. Mrs Copland had not been told that her communications would be monitored. The UK Government had argued that the monitoring of the communications data did not amount to an interference in private life but the Court held that it did. The Government also argued that, if there was an interference it was on lawful grounds, being incidental to the powers of the college, and was proportionate. The Court held that there was no lawful basis as there was no express power and therefore the question of proportionality did not arise. It found against the UK on Art.8 and also Art.13 in that Mrs Copland did not have an effective remedy for the breach of her Art.8 rights. This leaves the UK in a difficult position in relation to the monitoring of communications data on private networks operated by public sector bodies. The impact on the private sector is less clear but as Art.8 has been held to have horizontal effect there is a cogent argument that they are also affected.

Coverage of Directives

23–09 Areas which are outside Community competence are outside the remit of Community law. Article 3(2) of Directive 95/46 specifically sets out those limits by providing that the Directive does not apply to the processing of personal data carried out in the course of activities which fall outside the scope of Community law and explicitly not to processing operations:

> "concerning public security, defence, State security (including the economic well-being of the State when the processing operation relates to State security matters) and the activities of the State in the areas of criminal law."

A directive itself may also be limited in scope because of the basis on which it was made. Directives are secondary legislation of the Community. A legal basis for the making of a directive must be found in the Treaties.[10] Directive 95/46 was made as an internal market measure on the basis of Art.95. Any purported action under the Directive must fall within the scope of Art.95.

23–10 The limitations of the legal basis were emphasised by the ruling of the European Court of Justice in the cases heard on the transmission of Passenger Name records (PNR) to the United States.[11] Following the terrorist attacks of November 9,

---

[10] For a fuller discussion of the scope of Community law see paras 1–16 onwards, above.
[11] Joined Cases C-317/04 and C-318/04 of the European Court of Justice, May 30, 2006.

2001 the United States had required airlines to disclose detailed passenger information relating to those who travelled to the country. In order to provide a lawful basis for the required disclosures the European Commission had adopted two decisions, the first holding that the US Bureau of Customs and Border Protection (CBP) provided a sufficient level of protection for the personal data being transferred and the other embodying an agreement with the US authorising the transfers.[12] The European Parliament applied for the decisions to be annulled on the basis that the decisions were outwith the competence of the Council and the Commission.

Community competence

23–11 The institutions of the Community do not have competence to rule on matters that are not within the Treaties of the Union. Security is outside the scope of Community competence. The agreement with the US on PNR was for the purposes of security and thus the Commission and the Council were not able to made binding instruments in relation to it. The European Court agreed with the Parliament and the Decisions were annulled with effect from September 30, 2006.[13]

A Member State is not required by EU law to apply a provision of a Community instrument, such as a directive, to an activity outside an area of Community competence, although the Member State may chose to apply the standards required by a directive to all areas of relevant behaviour by national law. When implementing the data protection Directives the UK had a choice as to how it would implement. It could have implemented by secondary legislation and made regulations under the European Communities Act 1972. Regulations can be made under this Act only in relation to areas falling within Community competence. Alternatively it could have passed primary legislation. The Community could not make the United Kingdom apply Directive 95/46 to personal data processed for purposes outside Community competence such as policing. The United Kingdom has chosen to do so by passing primary legislation and making the Data Protection Act 1998 generally applicable national law, including those areas which are not covered by Community competence. Directives 1997/66 and 2002/58 however were implemented by regulations made under the European Communities Act 1972 and are therefore only applicable within the UK to areas covered by Community competence.

Directive 2002/58 applies, and will be relevant as an aid to interpretation, where the surveillance or interception falls within areas of Community competence, as with the monitoring of business calls, but does not apply, and is only persuasive, at best, when the surveillance or interception is carried out for purposes outside Community competence such as policing or national security. It should be noted however that Art.5 (see para.23–06, above) of the predecessor Directive was implemented by primary legislation, RIPA. The LBP Regulations are made under that primary legislation. RIPA will

---

[12] Commission Decision 2004/535 of May 14, 2004 on the adequate protection of personal data contained in Passenger Name Record of air passengers transferred to the United States Bureau of Customs and Border Protection ([2004] O.J. L235/11/) and Council Decision 2004/496 of May 17, 2004 on the conclusion of an Agreement between the European Community and the United States of America on the processing and transfer of PNR data by Air Carriers to the United States of America on the transfer and processing of PNR data by Air Carriers to the United States Department of Homeland security, Bureau of Customs and Border Protection ([2004] O.J. L183/83/).

[13] For a more detailed review see paras 1–16 onwards, above.

therefore apply irrespective of the rules relating to Community competence. The tortuous relationship between the two is recognised in reg.3(3) of the LBP Regulations which provides that interception or monitoring falling within certain grounds (those in para.1(i)(a), that is those which relate to ordinary business use) are only authorised to the extent permitted by Art.5. Implicitly therefore monitoring for other purposes, which cover areas such as national security which are outside Community competence, may exceed the remit of Art.5 as Directive 2002/58 is irrelevant to those areas. Nevertheless such activities will still be covered by RIPA 2000 and the DPA 1998 which are both primary legislation of general application in the UK.

This is relevant to the issues raised by the debate on the retention of traffic data as well as to the surveillance debate. Where Article 8 of the Convention rights applies however interception, and now it appears following *Copland*, access to and use of communications data, must comply with Article 8(2) of the Convention rights as an interference with communication.

SCOPE OF CONVENTION RIGHTS

23–12 The Human Rights Convention and the HRA are only directly binding on public authorities. In some circumstances the ECtHR has held that the State has an obligation to ensure the protection of rights against the actions of another private person. The Court has said that this applies to Art.8. Although the exact extent of the obligation is unclear the courts in the UK have applied Art.8 to private bodies such as the media in respect of the publication of information since the HRA came into effect in 2000.[14] It seems likely therefore that the Art.8 right will be applied as against private bodies as well as public ones in other spheres of action.

As far as public bodies are concerned they are bound by Art.8 of the Convention rights and the same is probably the case for private bodies but they have no mechanism for obtaining prior approval of interception or surveillance outside the LBP Regulations and, as the LBP Regulations do not cover monitoring of communications data, no mechanism for obtaining authorisation for the monitoring of such data. Public bodies are only able to apply for authorisation for interception or access to communications data under the relevant provisions of RIPA for the purpose of their public functions. This point was made clear in the case of *C v The Police and Secretary of State for the Home Department*.[15]

C v The Police and Secretary of State for the Home Department[16]

23–13 The Investigatory Powers Tribunal has exclusive jurisdiction to hear complaints about the misuse of powers relating to surveillance authorised or carried out under RIPA. A retired police officer complained to the Tribunal that he had been subject to covert surveillance by private investigators acting for the police force. The complainant had taken early retirement on medical grounds. He had been awarded compensation and an "enhanced injury" award after tripping over a carpet in a police station. The force wished to check the extent of the injuries he had suffered. The

---

[14] See Chap.2 for the cases on privacy and the media decided since October 2000.
[15] In the Investigatory Powers Tribunal No.IPT/03/32/H November 14, 2006.
[16] *ibid.*

complainant asserted that the surveillance should have been authorised under the provisions of s.26 of RIPA. This provides for the authorisation of planned covert surveillance which is not intrusive; is carried out "for the purpose of a specific investigation or specific operation"; and will result in the obtaining of private information about a person.

23–14   The case hinged on whether the surveillance by a public authority for a private law purpose such as employment-related matters was covered by s.26. The Tribunal held that it was not and that only surveillance for the purposes of the investigatory functions of public bodies can be authorised and carried out under RIPA. Accordingly the claimant had to bring his claim within the general law, applying Art.8 and data protection and privacy rights, rather than having any remedy before the specialist tribunal.

23–15   As part of its judgment the Tribunal made some general comments on the nature of surveillance which reinforce the approach which has been taken by the courts to the taking of photographs and the obtaining of information more generally:

> "Surveillance by public authorities (or indeed anyone else) is not in itself unlawful at common law, nor does it necessarily engage Article 8 of the Convention. For example, general observation of members of the public by the police in the course of carrying out their routine public duties to detect crime and to enforce the law is lawful. It does not interfere with the privacy of the individual citizen in a way that requires specific justification; see, for example, *Friedl v Austria* (1995 21 EHRR)."

REGULATION OF INVESTIGATORY POWERS ACT 2000 (RIPA)

Communications data

23–16   Communications data under RIPA covers traffic data under Directive 2002/58 but is a wider definition. Chapter II makes provision for authorised persons to obtain communications data from telecommunication operators subject to service of appropriate notices and places operators under obligations to make disclosures. However it imposes no obligation on operators to retain data for any specific length of time, a point which caused problems for both operators and authorities as the prohibition in Directives 97/66 and 2002/58 on the retention of traffic data was opposed to the wishes of the investigation and intelligence communities to have widespread access to such data accumulated over significant periods.

Definition of Communications Data

23–17   This is defined as:

"(a) any traffic data comprised in or attached to a communication (whether by the sender or otherwise) for the purposes of any postal service or telecommunications system by means of which it is being or may be transmitted;

(b) any information which includes none of the contents of a communication (apart from any information falling within paragraph (a)) and is about the use made by any person—of any postal service or telecommunications service; or in connection with the provision to or use by any person of any telecommunications service, of any part of a telecommunications system;

(c) any information not falling within paragraph (a) or (b) that is held or obtained, in relation to persons to whom he provides the service, by a person providing a postal service or telecommunications service."[17]

The contents of any communication are not included in the definition. Traffic data is defined in relation to any communication as:

"(a) any data identifying, or purporting to identify, any person, apparatus or location to or from which the communication is or may be transmitted,

(b) any data identifying or selecting, or purporting to identify or select, apparatus through which, or by means of which, the communication is or may be transmitted,

(c) any data comprising signals for the actuation of apparatus used for the purposes of a telecommunication system for effecting (in whole or in part) the transmission of any communication, and

(d) any data identifying the data or other data as data comprised in or attached to a particular communication, but that expression includes data identifying a computer file or computer programme access to which is obtained, or which is run, by means of the communication to the extent only that the file or program is identified by reference to the apparatus in which it is stored."[18]

It appears from the breadth of the definition that cookies would be capable of being communications data. If that is the case then, under Directive 2002/58, an employer who reviews the cookies on the system to see which websites have been visited by employees would be accessing communications data.

23–18 It is further provided that traffic data includes any references to the actual apparatus through which it is transmitted.[19] Chapter II applies to conduct in relation to a postal service or telecommunications service for obtaining communications data other than conduct consisting in the interception of communications in the course of their transmission by means of such a service or system and the disclosure to any person of communications data. It provides that conduct to which the Chapter applies shall be lawful where it is conducted by an authorised person in accordance with the authorisation.[20] As noted earlier however it makes no provision for establishing the lawfulness of access to and use of communications data other than under Ch.II.

It provides for designated persons to serve notice on postal or telecommunications service operators requiring the operator to disclose specified communications data[21] and places a duty on the service providers to comply with the requirements of the notice[22] as far as is reasonably practicable.[23] If the operator does not already have

---

[17] RIPA s.21(4).
[18] RIPA s.21(5).
[19] RIPA s.21(7).
[20] RIPA s.21(1).
[21] RIPA s.22(4).
[22] RIPA s.22(6).
[23] RIPA s.22(7).

the data in his possession the notice may require him to obtain it, if the operator is capable of doing so. The obligation on the operator may be enforced by civil proceedings for an injunction by the Secretary of State "or other appropriate relief".[24]

The designated person must believe that it is necessary to obtain the communications data in one of the specified interests or purposes and that it is proportionate to the objective to be achieved that the data be obtained.

Specified interests or purposes

23–19   These are partially set out in reg.22(2) but the list is not exhaustive as it includes a provision for the Secretary of State to specify further purposes by order. There has been one order under this provision.[25] The purposes provided for in the subsection are:

— the interests of national security;

— the purpose of preventing or detecting crime or of preventing disorder;

— the interests of the economic well-being of the United Kingdom;

— the purpose of protecting public health;

— the purpose of assessing or collecting any tax, duty, levy or other imposition, contribution or charge payable to a government department;

— the purpose, in an emergency, of preventing death or injury or any damage to a person's physical or mental health, or of mitigating any injury or damage to a person's physical or mental health.

The categories of designated persons are to be officials or office holders for public authorities as listed or as prescribed by the Secretary of State.[26] Such persons are then entitled to authorise others of the same level or rank to exercise the powers. All authorisations and notices must be given in writing and contain prescribed particulars.[27] A notice may have effect for a month but may be renewed. Notices may also be cancelled. The Secretary of State may make arrangements for contributing to the cost of complying with notices under these provisions.

These provisions potentially allow officials of public authorities widespread powers to serve notices requiring communications data. The Home Secretary brought out a draft order under s.25(2) in June 2002 which listed a wide range of public authorities including government departments, local authorities, fire authorities and others as prescribed authorities. The draft met with stiff opposition and was withdrawn by the Government.[28] It was replaced by a narrower list under which access to all categories of

---

[24] RIPA s.22(8).
[25] The Regulation of Investigatory Powers (Communications Data)(Additional Functions and Amendment) Order 2006 (SI 2006/1878).
[26] RIPA s.25(2).
[27] RIPA s.23(1) and (2).
[28] See the website for the Foundation for Information Policy research *http://www.fipr.org* [Accessed on September 2, 2007] for relevant press releases.

communications data was restricted to broadly policing and associated organisations while other public bodies have access to only a sub-set of the possible categories of communications data.[29]

23–20   The term operator simply means a person who provides a telecommunications service. It would therefore appear that notices can be served on those who provide services other than as a public telecommunications service, such as providers of private systems. It may also be wide enough to cover those who run systems for their own businesses.

Codes of Practice

23–21   The provisions relating to codes are found in ss.71 and 72. Section 71 provides that the Secretary of State must issue one or more codes of practice relating to the exercise and performance of the powers and duties under Pts I to III of RIPA (inter alia). Before issuing a code the Secretary of State has to prepare and publish a draft and consider any representations made about the draft. The codes have to be laid before Parliament.

Under s.72 a person exercising or performing a power or duty in relation to which provision is made in a code shall in doing so have regard to every relevant code of practice. Failure to comply with a code results in no civil or criminal penalty but the code is admissible and may be taken into account by, inter alia, any court or tribunal conducting any civil or criminal proceedings (s.72(4)). Four codes came into force in July 2002; three impose obligations on public authorities in relation to the authorisation, disclosure and copying of information. One code imposes obligations on service providers to maintain an intercept capacity.[30]

There was a widespread negative response to the original proposals on access to communications data. The Foundation for Information Policy Research (FIPR) campaigned against the extent of the powers and the lack of effective oversight. In particular FIPR comments that the only supervision of this Part of the Act is via the Interception Commissioner but he cannot possibly oversee all the communications notices—no central records have to be kept of notices requesting communications data.

23–22   A distinction must be made between the **retention** of communications data and the right to access such data. As has been discussed in this section RIPA covers **access** to such data however since RIPA came into effect there has been continuing uncertainty over the obligations on service providers to **retain** such data in the first place so that the rights of access can be exercised. The area is now covered by Directive 2006/24. This must be implemented in respect of data generated by use of telephony by September 2007. A consultation paper on implementation was issued in March 2007. The consultation will close in June 2007. The consultation paper includes a draft of the proposed regulations, the Electronic Communications Data Retention (EC Directive) Regulations 2007. In this section we review the draft regulations.

---

[29] The Regulation of Investigatory Powers (Communications Data) Order 2003 (SI 2003/3172) amended by the Regulation of Investigatory Powers (Communications Data)(Additional Functions and Amendment) Order 2006 (SI 2006/1878).

[30] The Regulation of Investigatory Powers (Interception of Communications: Code of Practice) Order 2002 (SI 2002/1693).

RETENTION OF COMMUNICATIONS DATA

23–23   As noted above under Directives 97/66 and 2002/58 service providers are under an obligation to erase traffic data when they no longer have a need for it for the specified purposes. To some extent the length of time for which service providers retain such information is therefore a matter of judgment for them and will vary depending on their business needs. Information which is used for the purposes of national security and policing will be outside the scope of the Directives and therefore could be retained without worrying about the restrictions in Directives 1997/66 and 2002/58. This was acknowledged in both Directives. Moreover in Art.15(1) of Directive 2002/58 the rights of Member States to adopt measure to restrict the obligations to erase (in effect to require retention) are recognised where:

> "such restriction constitutes a necessary, appropriate and proportionate measure within a democratic society to safeguard national security (i.e. State security) defence, public security, and the prevention, investigation, detection and prosecution of criminal offences or of unauthorised use of the electronic communication system as referred to in Article 13(1) of Directive 95/46/EC. To this end Member States may *inter alia* adopt legislative measures providing for the retention of data for a limited period justified on the grounds laid down by this paragraph."

However service providers cannot tell whether communications data will be required for those purposes at the point when they are generated. The only way that communications data can be preserved so that relevant data can be made available is for all data to be retained. It is therefore extremely difficult to be sure that the retention of data which is within the scope fulfils the criteria required by Art.15(1). Member States had very different responses to the question of requiring the retention of communications data.

In the UK the Government evinced a clear wish to ensure the preservation of all such data for the purpose of subsequent access if required for law enforcement. However it was reluctant to pass legislation requiring service providers to retain all the communications data and instead sought to agree an industry standard for retention by setting up a procedure for the establishment of voluntary codes of practice under the Anti Terrorism, Crime and Security Act 2001 (ATCSA).

23–24   The ATCSA includes provisions dealing with retention in Pt II. The notes to the Act explain that:

> "This Part contains provisions to allow communications service providers to retain data about their customers' communications for national security purposes. Retained data can then be accessed by the security, intelligence and law enforcement agencies under the terms of a code of practice, which is being drawn up in consultation with industry and the Information Commissioner."

The notes go on to state that it provides for a:

> "voluntary code of practice defined in statute to ensure that service providers have a clear remit for retaining data which complements the powers given to public authorities under RIPA[to obtain **access** to such data] It also contains a reserve

power to review these arrangements and issue directions under secondary legislation if necessary. The need to maintain a reserve power must be reviewed every two years and may be renewed by affirmative order. Once the power has been exercised, there is no need for further review."

And that:

"RIPA sets out clear limits on the purposes for which the security intelligence and law enforcement agencies may request access to data relating to specific communications, i.e. relating to a particular customer or telephone line. Fishing expeditions are not permitted."

The reserve power in s.104 (the sunset clause) has been reviewed twice to date and the current consultation paper proposes a further extension. Ostensibly this is to deal with the possible implementation of Directive 2006/24 in relation to internet traffic data although the explanation in the consultation paper in not wholly clear on the point.

The UK Government has not exercised the powers to issue directions but has proceeded by way of a voluntary code of practice. In March 2003 it conducted a consultation following which it published the Code of Practice on Voluntary Retention of Communications Data. However, as the Government acknowledges in the regulatory Impact Statement in the current consultation, some providers have indicated that they would not comply with the voluntary code, while others have indicated that, while they are prepared to do so in the short term, they would prefer to be placed under a statutory requirement to retain. The reluctance of providers can be explained by a concern that they could be held to be in breach of reg.7 of the PECR which requires that traffic data should be erased or anonymised when no longer required for the purposes of the transmission.[31] The Information Commissioner however appears to have taken a wholly permissive view of the current programme of retention.

Developments in Europe

23–25   The UK was not alone in facing problems in achieving the retention of communications data. Even though law enforcement agencies throughout Europe were lobbying for more retention, by 2005 the European Commission reported that about 15 of the Member States did not have mandatory data retention, in about half of those with mandatory retention laws in place the retention was not operational as the legislation had not been implemented, and in those which had retention legislation in place the periods of retention and the scope of the obligations varied substantially.[32]

23–26   The pressure for harmonised retention periods became more intense after the terrorist bombings in Madrid in March 2004. In April 2004 four countries (France, Ireland, Sweden and the UK) put forward a proposal for a third pillar

---

[31] See Ch.22 for a full discussion of this provision.
[32] Commission Staff Working Document—Extended Impact Assessment. Annext to the proposal on the retention of data processed in connection with the provision of public electronic services and amending Directive 2002/58 (COM) (2005) 438 final SEC (2005) 1131.

Framework Decision for the retention of communications data. If taken forward this would have led to a decision of the Council.[33] There was however considerable unease in the European Parliament and the Commission about the proposed use of a third pillar mechanism to legislate for matters of data protection and electronic communications which fall within the first pillar. One of the legal concerns expressed was that a Framework Decision could not legitimately alter or amend a directive.[34] Politically the privacy or data protection governance of matters covered by third pillar instruments have tended not to be as transparent or responsive as first pillar matters.[35] There were serious concerns at the impact on privacy which mandatory retention would entail.[36] The debate illustrates not only the political difficulty of the issue but the fact that the particular topic, the retention of data generated for communication so it can be accessed when required for purposes of crime and security, straddles the areas of Community and national competence.[37] The Parliament rejected the proposal for the framework decision and at the same time, in September 2005, the Commission proposed a new Directive which would require retention and amend Directive 2002/58. The proposal was put forward as a harmonisation measure because retention requirements have an economic impact on service providers but also to meet the need for access for the purposes of policing and security. The justification for Directive 2006/24 falling within Art.95 is not wholly satisfactory but it appears to have been accepted by the Parliament and the Commission, possibly because of a concern that the Council would press ahead with a Framework Decision if the Directive was not accepted (see Ch.1 para.1–23, above for a fuller discussion). The legal basis of the Directive has now been challenged by Ireland and Slovakia in the European Court. The consultation paper on implementation describes this as a "legal technicality" and comments that, even if the challenge succeeds the proposed regulations will be "unaffected".[38] However, while the Regulations would remain on the UK statute book, it is difficult to accept that they would be "unaffected". They would be open to challenge for being incompatible with Directive 2002/58 because, as discussed below, Directive 2006/24 amends the mandatory destruction provisions in Directive 2002/58.

23–27 Directive 2006/24 of March 15, 2006 on the retention of data generated or processed in connection with the provision of publicly available electronic communications services or of public communications networks and amending Directive 2002/58 (the data retention Directive) came into effect on May 3, 2006. The Directive not only deals with retention of communications data but also the grounds and procedures required for access to such data. Directive 2006/24 is dealt with in full below. The implementing regulations are then reviewed. It should be noted however that the regulations do not include any changes to the access regime under RIPA.

---

[33] For an explanation of the difference between first and third pillar areas see Ch.24 para.x onwards, below.
[34] Art.47 Title VIII Final provisions (ex Art.M).
[35] See Ch.24, below for a discussion of the data protection supervisory regimes for third pillar matters.
[36] See for instance Art.29 Data Protection Working Party Opinion of October 21, 2005 1868/05/EN WP 113 on the proposed directive.
[37] On July, 30 2004 DG INFSO-DG JAI consultation document on traffic data retention was issued to seek "input from a broad range of stakeholders on a number of questions raised by the issue of traffic data retention".
[38] Consultation paper para.6.5.

Scope of Data Retention (EC Directive) Regulations

23–28   The regulations only cover retention of communications data derived from fixed line or mobile telecommunications, not internet use. The Directive allows Member States to postpone implementation in relation to internet traffic data until March 2009. The UK has elected to take advantage of that provision. In the consultation paper it was noted that the retention of traffic data from internet use "is a more complex issue involving much larger volumes of data and a considerably broader set of stakeholders within the industry" (para.2.10). However such data is already retained by some service providers under the current voluntary code of practice and the Government will continue with those arrangements. One effect of the deferral is that, as noted earlier, the Government proposes to extend the sunset clause in s.106 of the ATCSA.

DIRECTIVE 2006/24

Retention

23–29   Directive 2006/24 amends Art.15 of Directive 2002/58 by the insertion of the following paragraph:

> "1a. Paragraph 1 shall not apply to data specifically required by Directive 2006/24/EC of the European Parliament and of the Council of 15 March 2006 on the retention of data generated or processed in connection with the provision of publicly available electronic communications or of public communications networks to be retained fro the purposes of Article 1(1) of that Directive."[39]

Thus, as long as the retention complies with Directive 2006/24 Member States are not at risk of transgressing any of the prohibitions in Directive 2002/58. Directive 2006/24 requires Member States to retain data described in six categories[40] "generated or processed by providers of publicly available electronic communications services or of a public communications service within their jurisdiction in the process of supplying the communication services concerned".[41] The categories are:

- data necessary to trace and identify the source of a communication;

- data necessary to identify the destination of a communication;

- data necessary to identify the date, time and duration of a communication;

- data necessary to identify the type of communication;

- data necessary to identify users' communication equipment or what purports to be their equipment; and

- data necessary to identify the location of mobile communication equipment.

---

[39] Directive 2006/24 Art.11.
[40] Directive 2006/24 Art.5.
[41] Directive 2006/24 Art.3(1).

For each category Art.5 specifies what the category comprises for telephones (both fixed and mobile) and for internet use (including internet telephony, email and internet access). The data to be retained are therefore specified in detail. As an example, under data necessary to identify the type of communication for mobile telephony six types of data must be retained, not only the calling and called numbers, the IMSI[42] of the calling and called party, the IMEI[43] of the calling and called party but also:

> "in the case of pre-paid anonymous services, the date and time of he initial activation of the service and the location label (Cell ID) from which the service was activated."

23–30   The Directive applies to data in the specified categories on both legal entities and natural persons and includes the related data necessary to identify the subscriber or user. It therefore covers some data which would not be covered by the data protection directives. Content is expressly excluded, including the content of material accessed during the use of the internet. The retention obligation extends to "unsuccessful call attempts", that is calls that are connected but are not answered, but only to the extent that the service providers retains records of such calls. Not all providers keep such records. This was an issue of some dispute during the passage of the Directive. Some States were keen to have this information retained[44] however an obligation to retain such data would have had significant cost implications for service providers. Data about unconnected calls does not have to be retained. The term "unconnected calls" is not among the defined terms. There is no provision in the Directive to require Member States to compensate service providers for the costs involved in meeting the requirements.[45] The UK already funds the cost of providing additional facilities to allow for interception and proposes to continue with the practice.

23–31   The Directive covers:

- the obligation to retain data;
- procedures to provide access to data;
- the period of retention;
- data security and storage requirements;
- supervision, remedies, liabilities and penalties;
- evaluation, statistics and future measures; and
- implementation in national laws.

Definitions

23–32   Where terms defined in either of the data protection Directives (1995/46 or 2002/58) or the telecommunications Directive (2001/21) are used the terms have the

---

[42] International Mobile Subscriber Identity.
[43] International Mobile Equipment Identity.
[44] Data of this nature had been helpful in discovering those responsible for the bombings which killed 191 people and injured approximately 1800 on March 11, 2004.
[45] Such a provision was included by the Commission in the proposal but was removed by the Parliament. It will be a matter for Member States.

same meaning. Accordingly there are very few defined terms. The term "communications data" is not used and the Directive simply refers to "data" which means traffic data, location data (both defined in Directive 2002/58, see Ch.22, above) and the related data necessary to identify the subscriber or user. A "user" is anyone who makes use of a "publicly available electronic communications service, whether for public or private use, and does not have to be a subscriber". "Telephone service" is widely defined and is distinct from other electronic communications services. A "user ID" is the unique identifier allocated to person who register with an internet service and a "cell ID" is the cell from which a call on a mobile was made or was received.

The obligation to retain data

23–33　　The obligation to retain the data is set out in Art.3 (see above for the scope of the obligation and the nature of the data to be retained). Member States must ensure that the data are retained for a minimum period of six months after the communication up to a maximum of two years at which point they must be erased.[46] The only data which may be held after the maximum period are those records which have been accessed for the authorised purposes and in respect of which there is therefore a reason to retain them further.

Procedures to provide access to data

23–34　　Article 4 deals with access to the stored data and provides that Member States must adopt measures to ensure that the retained data are provided only to "the competent national authorities" in specific cases and in accordance with national law. The scope of this is not clear. It must presumably be read with Art.1 which states that the purpose of the retention is to make the data available for the purposes of the investigation, detection and prosecution of "serious crime as defined by each Member State in its national law". While Member States clearly have some leeway as to what is defined as "serious crime" the restriction to serious crime is intended to place a limitation on the types of illegal activity in respect of which communications data can be made available to investigators. In the current UK regime under RIPA the specified interests and purposes are far wider than the area of serious crime. Under RIPA crime is not limited to serious crime and the purposes also include the prevention of disorder and the protection of public health. It must be assumed that the UK will be forced to narrow the list of purposes and the list of public bodies which are currently authorised to access communications data or face claims that it is in breach of the data protection Directives. Article 4 further restates the requirement that access procedures and conditions must be necessary and proportionate in accord with EU and Convention law. Moreover individuals must be provided with remedies for breach of the Directive which are equivalent to the rights they have in respect of breaches of the Data Protection Act.[47] Currently individuals do not have a right to challenge access orders under RIPA in the normal courts but are restricted to the specialist Tribunal; once Directive 2006/24 is implemented it is arguable that such rights will be required, at least for access to traffic data.

---

[46] Directive 2006/24 Arts 6 and 7(d).
[47] Directive 2006/24 Art.13(1).

Data storage and security requirements

23–35   Service providers will not only be required to retain the communications data but to store it in such a way that it is accessible and can be provided to the competent authorities without undue delay.[48] They will have to ensure that the retained data do not degrade during storage. The stored data must be of the same quality as the data on the network. In addition the data must be held securely to ensure that only authorised personnel can access them.[49] This is without prejudice to the existing obligations which apply to personal data. Article 13(2) requires Member States to impose penalties in respect of intentional and illegitimate access to the stored data.

Supervision, remedies, liabilities and penalties

23–36   Each Member State must designate a supervisory authority for the purpose of oversight of the **storage** obligation only. The authority will be charged with monitoring the security of storage and the compliance with the rules. It could be the data protection authority but there is no requirement that this be the case and in the UK it may be the Security Commissioner under RIPA. The question of individual remedies has been dealt with above.

Implementation

23–37   The Directive must be implemented by September 2007 but States can postpone the implementation in respect of internet access, telephony and email until March 2009. The UK declared that it would take advantage of this period of postponement as did 15 other Member States for varying lengths of time.[50]

Evaluation, statistics and future measures

23–38   Member States must provide the Commission with annual figures showing how many cases of access to communications data took place each year, the age of the data for each case and any cases where data could not be retrieved. Within five years of the passage of the Directive, that is by September 2010, the Commission has a duty to evaluate the working of the Directive and report to Parliament and the Council on its economic impact. In doing so it shall consider the types of data retained, the length of retention and the statistics which it has garnered from Member States.[51]

THE DATA RETENTION (EC DIRECTIVE) REGULATIONS 2007

Retention period and scope of data

23–39   The Regulations will come into effect on October 1, 2007. The retention period under the Regulations[51a] is 12 months.[52] This is the period which was

---

[48]   Directive 2006/24 Art.8.
[49]   Directive 2006/24 Art.7.
[50]   Directive 2006/24 Art.15.
[51]   Directive 2006/24 Art.14.
[51a] SI 2007/2199.
[52]   Regulations reg.4(2).

determined to be appropriate after the consultation on the voluntary code. In the consultation the Government set out the justification for the 12-month retention period. It stated that, while most requests for communications data are for data less than six month sold, research carried out by the Association of Chief Police Officers (ACPO) in 2005 showed that there were a significant number of requests for older data and that these were in connection with more serious crimes. In the Regulatory Impact Assessment paper it explains that the period of 12 months was regarded as "the optimal trade-off" between law enforcement requirements and the intrusion into personal privacy. It explained that in order to determine the appropriate length of time the factors to be weighted were:

- the degree of intrusion in to personal life;
- the public policy need for the data; and
- the adequacy of the safeguards to prevent abuse.

23–40   The data to be retained are set out in reg.5 as follows:

- the telephone number from which the call was made;
- the name and address of the subscriber to that telephone and registered user of that service;
- the telephone number dialled and, in cases involving supplementary services such as call forwarding or call transfer, the telephone number to which the call is forwarded or transferred;
- the name and address of the subscriber of any such telephone number called;
- the date and time of the start and end of the call; and
- the telephone service used.

A telephone service is defined in reg.2 as calls, including voice, voicemail and conference and data calls; supplementary services including call forwarding and call transfer; plus messaging and multi-media services including short message services, enhanced media services and multi-media services. It is made explicit in reg.4(5) that data derived from internet access, internet email or internet telephony are not covered by these regulations.

23–41   In relation to mobile telephony the following must also be retained:

- the IMSI and the IMEI of the telephone which is used for the call[53];
- the IMSI and the IMEI of the telephone called;
- in the case of pre-paid services anonymous services the data and time of the initial activation of the service and the cell ID from which the service was activated;

---

[53] IMSI—international mobile subscriber identity IMEI;—international mobile equipment identity.

- the cell ID at the start of the communication; and

- data identifiying the geographic location of cells by refernce to their cell ID.[54]

The cell ID is the location of a call on a mobile line. All areas of the UK have a cell ID. The anonymous service provisions are included to allow for at least some information to be available to deal with those users of pay as you go telephones who have never registered the identity of the user.

These requirements cover those listed in Article 5 of the Directive. The obligation applies to the data generated or processed by public communications providers in the process of supplying the communication services.[55] Data derived from unsuccessful call attempts where such data exists. Unsuccesful call attempts are defined as communications where a telephone call has been successfully connected but not answered or there has been network management intervention.[56] However data relating to unconnected calls does not have to be retained.[57]

Application

23–42   The obligation to retain the data is placed upon all public communications providers. This covers those who provide networks and those who provide services[58] and the definitions are as set out in the Communications Act 2003 s.151.[59] However where one public communications service provider retains the same data as another provider the data will only be retained by one of them. The Regulatory Impact Assessment paper explains that this approach has been discussed with the European Commission and achieves several ends: it ensures that the same data are only retained once, in accord with Recital 13 of the Directive; it reduces the burden on the private sector; moreover minimising the number of public communications service providers who are involved will reduce the number of those who the public sector deals with and encourage a "smaller pool of more experienced industry partners".[60] The mechanism can be utilised because of the structure of the industry, in which a significant number of providers actually provide services across networks owned by other service providers. It follows that the vast bulk of the burden will fall on to a few larger providers such as BT. The legal provisions are set out in reg.3. Regulation 3 provides that the regulations shall not apply to a service provider where the data are retained by another public service provider. If only part of one service providers' data are retained by another then the first provider must still retain the other parts independently. The Secretary of State will decide which service providers will be responsible for the primary retention. He is empowered to give a written notice to the providers in question. It is clear from reg.3(4) that he may specify a class of providers. The notice must be given or published in an appropriate manner so it comes to the attention of the providers. The notice mechanism will also be used to specify the extent to which and the date from which the Regulations apply.

---

[54] Draft Regulations reg.5.
[55] Draft Regulations reg.4(1).
[56] Draft Regulations reg.2.
[57] Draft Regulations reg.4(4).
[58] Draft Regulations reg.2 interpretation.
[59] See Ch.22, above for the relevant definitions.
[60] Regulatory impact assessment para.4.12.1.

Security and storage

23–43   Regulations 6 and 7 deals with data security and access. They implement Arts 7 and 8 of the Directive. The data have to be retained in such a way that they can be transmitted without undue delay in response to requests. In the Regulatory Impact Assessment, in the discussion of costs and reimbursement, the point is made that effective retention and effective retrieval mechanisms are part of the same solution. While the data aere held the security requirements are as follows:

- the retained data must be the same quality and subject to the same security as the data in the live service;

- the data must be subject to appropriate technical and organisational security to ensure that they can only be access by authorised personnel and protected against unlawful access, loss, destruction or disclosure;

- the data must be destroyed at the end of the period of retention.

The Information Commissioner (IC) becomes the relevant Supervisory Authority for the security of the data.[61] The terminology used in reg.6 in relation to the security obligation echoes closely the security obligation in Principle 7. The obligation of the IC is to "monitor" the application of the regulations with respect to security. The term is used in Art.9 of the Directive, to which reg.8 refers. The IC is given no enforcement powers in respect of the stored data. Clearly where the data involve personal data then, if there is a security breach which would also be a breach of the Data Protection Act, he will be able to use his enforcement powers under that Act. Moreover the provisions of s.55 which create the offence of unlawful procuring of personal data will apply, and of course it is likely that the s.55 offences will carry prison sentences by the time the Regulations are implemented. The Recitals to the Directive refer to the sanctions required by the Data Protection Directive (95/46) and to the rights of those who have suffered damage as a result of unlawful processing to redress and compensation. The UK is not proposing any other specific provisions, presumably on the basis that the existing Data Protection Act and Computer Misuse Act provisions are adequate to provide appropriate sanctions if the stored data are violated.

Statistics

23–44   Every 12 months providers will be required to supply the Secretary of State with statistics showing the number of occasions when data have been disclosed in response to a request and the number of occasions data have been refused.

Payments

23–45   There was no commitment in the Directive to make any payments to service providers to assist with the cost of retention and retrieval system. However the UK had already made that commitment in the ATCSA. Regulation 10 provides a power for the Secretary of State to reimburse any expenses incurred by a service provider in complying with the Regulations. The Secretary of State has a power and

---

[61] Draft Regulations reg.8.

not a duty so he is free to determine how it is to be exercised. Where a service provider claims for reimbursement there is a concomitant power for the Secretary of State to require that the organisation complies with any audit that he may reasonably require in respect of the payments made. In the accompanying papers it is explained that experience to date has shown that efficient retrieval systems are essential to realise the benefits of the data. The reimbursment of costs will be restricted to the cost of additional capacity provided for the purposes of RIPA access. If this were not reimbursed those providers which receive a high volume of disclosure requests would be put at a competitive disadvantage. It is explained that consideration was given to separating the costs associated with retention from those associated with retrieval and only reimbursing costs associated with retrieval but the view has been taken that this would give an unfair advantage to those which receive the highest volume of requests. It is therefore proposed that the current arrangements in the UK should remain in force.

Public and private systems

23–46   The rules and provisions for interception and access to communications data vary depending on whether the system is part of the public system or a private one. A private telecommunications system is defined in the LBP Regulations as a system which is not a public system but which is attached directly or indirectly to a public service and includes apparatus in the system located in the United Kingdom for making the connection to the public system. A public system is one by which a public telecommunications service is provided. Many private systems are run by the organisation which uses them but others may be run by third party service providers.

Are providers of private telecommunications systems and services data processors?

23–47   Although this may be regarded as a fundamental questions about the way that electronic services work it is only obliquely addressed directly in the legislative scheme. The Article 29 Working Party in Opinion 2/2006 refers to Recital 47 in the general Directive 95/46 which states:

> "whereas a message containing personal data is transmitted by means of a telecommunications or electronic mail service, the sole purpose of which is the transmission of such messages, the controller in respect of the personal data contained in the message will normally be considered to be the person from whom the message originates, rather than the person offering the transmission service; whereas nevertheless, those offering such services will normally be considered controllers in respect of the processing of the additional personal data necessary for the operation of the service."

Where the service provider is a public telecommunications service provider and is therefore subject to the requirements of Directive 2002/58, which imposes limits and restrictions on the use of the traffic and billing data, this is an effective approach. However where the service is provided on a private system to an organisation we would submit that the better view is that the organisation itself remains the data controller and the provider should be treated as a mere processor and required to enter into a processor agreement which restricts the rights of the processor as to the data generated as a result of the service and requires the provision of appropriate security controls.

Impact of the retention requirements on private service providers

23–48 It is not clear whether retention obligations will be imposed on those who supply private electronic communications systems. In a French case on a provision of the 1986 Liberty of Communications Act (*Loi relative a la liberte de communication*) as amended, in 2000 the Paris Court of Appeal found that there was no difference in the obligations in respect of data retention imposed on those who offer public services and those who run private networks where the private network provider allows staff access to the internet.[62] While this is a French case on a French law and not directly applicable it indicates the view that might be taken in principle.

MONITORING OF COMMUNICATIONS

23–49 Interception of communications on the public telecommunication system is treated more seriously than interception of communications on private systems. It is a criminal offence for any person "intentionally and without lawful authority to intercept at any place in the United Kingdom, any communication in the course of its transmission" if the transmission was by a public postal service or public telecommunication system.[63](In this chapter we are only concerned with the interception of telecommunications and not postal services.) The Court considered what amounted to the "right to control the operation or use" of a system in *R. v Clifford Stanford*.[64] In that case the court held that the right to control the operation and use meant more then mere rights to access and included a right to control how the system was used and operated by others. In the case an ousted director had persuaded an ex-colleague to divert emails to him. He had argued that, as the ex-colleague had legitimate access to the email system, the ex-colleague was entitled to control its operation and there was therefore no offence of unauthorised interception. His contentions were not accepted by the Court.

23–50 The question of whether an interception has taken place on a public telecommunications system has been litigated several times in criminal cases. This may be because s.17 of RIPA precludes any material being adduced in evidence which discloses or suggests that interception under a warrant has taken place. Hence the tendency of accused who have been unfortunate enough to have incriminating calls recorded to claim that the evidence has been obtained by interception (and thus the incriminating material should be excluded). The courts have been correspondingly keen to find that there is no interception. In *R. v Hardy* (October 2002) the Court of Appeal held that the tape recording of a telephone conversation by an undercover officer with the suspect did not amount to the interception of a communication in the course of its transmission by a telecommunications system within the meaning of s.2(2) of RIPA. In *R. v E*[65] the police obtained the necessary permission to place a

---

[62] *BNP Paribas v World Press online*, February 4, 2005.
[63] RIPA s.1(1).
[64] [2006] EWCA Crim 258.
[65] [2004] EWCA Crim 1243.

surveillance device in E's car under provisions in the Police Act 1997 and RIPA. They recorded E speaking into a mobile telephone. E claimed that the recording was obtained as a result of an interception which was unlawful. The Court of Appeal considered the definition of "interception" in s.2(2) of RIPA under which an interception must take place "in the course of transmission". They held that the natural meaning was that this involved some interference with the signal in the course of transmission whereas the voices recorded in the car were recorded independently of the transmission system. This was consistent with *R v Effik and Morgans v DPP*.[66] In *AG reference (No.5 of 2002) sub nom R v W (2003)* the court held that a judge was entitled to hear evidence to decide whether a system was public or private in order to decide whether interceptions were of a public or private communication system.

23–51 There are only limited circumstances in which an interception will be protected by "lawful authority". On private systems it is an offence, intentionally and without lawful authority, to intercept a communication in the course of transmission unless the interceptor is a person with the right to control the operation of the system or he has the express or implied consent of such a person.[67] However if the interceptor is the person with the right to control the system or has been given consent by such a person the only penalties involved are civil penalties. The sender or recipient, or intended recipient, has a private right of action in tort unless the communication takes place with lawful authority.[68]

The limits of the public/private telecommunications system and the meaning of the terms "interception" and "in the course of transmission" are therefore significant.

"In the course of transmission"

23–52 The relevant provisions of s.2 reads:

> "(7) For the purposes of this section the times while a communication is being transmitted by means of a telecommunications system shall be taken to include any time when the system by means of which the communication is being, or has been, transmitted is used for storing it in a manner that enables the intended recipient to collect it or otherwise to have access to it.
>
> (8) For the purposes of this section the cases in which any contents of a communication are to be taken as made available to a person while being transmitted shall include any case in which any of the contents of the communication, while being transmitted, are diverted or recorded so as to be available to a person subsequently." This is an important definition in the context of email as email is not usually instantaneously received nor is it instantaneously erased on being read. It sits on servers waiting to be read and is stored by recipients in mailboxes after being read. On a straightforward reading of the definition in s.2(7) any reading of email by another would be interception irrespective of whether it had already been opened by the recipient as long as the storage was in a manner that enabled the recipient to continue to access it."

---

[66] [2001] 1 A.C. 315.
[67] RIPA s.1(6).
[68] RIPA s.1(3).

However the Information Commissioner in the code on monitoring employees in the workplace and the Home Office have both expressed the view that once an email has been "collected" (and presumably read) by the recipient then s.2(7) no longer applies even though it is still stored in a manner that allows the recipient to have further access to it. This is on the basis that an "interception" must occur before the receipt of the material, and subsequent reading is not an "interception". It is suggested that this interpretation is wrong on both a straightforward reading of the words of the provision and as a matter of interpretation. If the provision is read in the light of the requirement in the HRA to interpret statutes so as to give effect to the Convention rights it is clear that the only interpretation that gives effect to the Art.8 obligations of respect for private life and correspondence is to treat stored and opened emails as covered. As a matter of principle it is inconsistent to suggest that the right to respect disappears once the material has been opened by the intended recipient. Regrettably the point was not considered by the Court of Appeal in *R. v Ipswich Crown Court Ex p. NTL Ltd.*[69] The case was not on this particular point but in passing the Court commented that the effect of s.2(7) was to extend the time within which an interception could be made until the intended recipient had collected it. They did not address whether there would still be an interception if the recipient left the read message on the server and it was subsequently read by another.

Interception

23–53   A person intercepts a communication in the course of transmission if he does any of the following acts:

"(a) so modifies or interferes with the system or its operation
 (b) so monitors transmissions made by means of the system, or
 (c) so monitors transmissions made by wireless telegraphy to or from some apparatus comprised in the system,

as to make some or all of the contents of the communication available, while being transmitted, to a person other than the sender or intended recipient of the communication."

A communication broadcast for general reception cannot be intercepted and there is no interception involved in the operator ascertaining information to allow the communication to be sent, for example in cases where the postal service has to open a returned communication to find where it should be returned to. The contents of communication are distinguished from traffic data associated with a communication. The monitoring of communications data is not interception.

Public telecommunications service and system

23–54   There are interlocking definitions of "telecommunications service" and "telecommunications system". A system is:

"any system (including the apparatus included in it) which exists (whether wholly or partly in the United Kingdom or elsewhere) for the purpose of facilitating the

---

[69] [2002] EWHC 1585 (Admin).

transmission of communications by any means involving the use of electrical or electro-magnetic energy."

A service is:

"any service that consists in the provision of access to, and of facilities for making use of, any telecommunications system (whether or not one provided by the person providing the service)."

A public service is one offered or provided to the public or a substantial part of the public in the United Kingdom and a public system is one by which a public telecommunications service is provided. A private service is not defined but a private system is a system which is not a public system but which is attached directly or indirectly to a public service and includes apparatus in the system located in the United Kingdom for making the connection to the public system.

It follows from this that a telecommunications system which is entirely internal and has no connection with a public external network is entirely outside the province of these provisions.

Lawful authority

23–55 As interception with lawful authority will not attract civil or criminal penalties this is an important concept. What amounts to lawful authority varies depending on whether the communication is intercepted on a public or private system. It will also depend on whether the communication is a "stored communication".

Any communication may be intercepted with the authority of a warrant.[70] A stored communication may be intercepted by exercise of a statutory power to require the supply of information or the provision of any document or property.[71] There is no explanation of what amounts to a "stored communication". It would seem to cover any message in the possession of the person who controls the system. It appears that this conduct amounts to an interception and this gives added weight to the argument set out above that access to a read message is interception just as much as access to a message not yet read.

Interception may otherwise have lawful authority under ss.3 or 4 or regulations made under s.4(2).

Interceptions—overseas authorities

23–56 In the area of international co-operation in criminal and other matters of justice and security there are agreements for mutual assistance which may involve authorities in the United Kingdom making requests for assistance overseas and the Secretary of State must ensure than no such requests are made by officials in the United Kingdom without lawful authority.[72] Interception will also be authorised where it is in relation to a person outside the United Kingdom, and carried out at the behest of an

---

[70] RIPA s.1(5)(b).
[71] RIPA s.1(5)(c).
[72] RIPA s.1(4).

overseas authority which is subject to legal obligations to carry out the interception under the laws of the overseas territory. Such situations are subject to further conditions to be prescribed by the Secretary of State.[73]

Consent

23–57   An interception is lawful if it is an interception of a communication to which both parties to the communication have consented or the interceptor has reasonable grounds for so believing.[74] Recipient and sender are not defined in this Pt. The assumption which has been made by commentators appears to be that the sender and recipient are the specific living individuals who compose and read the material respectively however there might be circumstances in which it could be argued that the sender and/or recipient in an particular case was the legal person who received or sent the materials and the individual who acted as the "hands" was the mere instrument. If this could be argued then a legal entity could consent to have all its material intercepted by a third party, thus obviating the need for individual employee consent. The consent could only apply to material produced by the employees in the course of the business but the third party interceptor would be able to argue that he had reasonable grounds for believing in that consent and thus was protected from suit by an unhappy employee.

In this connection it is not clear who the employee would regard as the appropriate defendant. It could be the controller of the system who permitted the interception but it could be the third party interceptor themselves if different. It is suggested that any third party who monitors for an employer should obtain a warranty and indemnity from the employer or other controller of the system at whose behest he intercepts.

Interception and covert surveillance

23–58   Where the interception is part of a surveillance which has been authorised under Pt II of the RIPA and one party has consented the interception will be lawful.[75]

Service providers and wireless telegraphy

A service provider who intercepts in connection with the provision of the service or enforcement of legal requirements in connection with the service is authorised as is interception with the authority of a designated person under the Wireless Telegraphy Act 1949 for purposes under that Act.[76]

Prisons and other institutions

23–59   Interceptions in prisons or secure hospital units may be carried out under the specific rules governing such institutions.[77]

---

[73] RIPA s.4(1).
[74] RIPA s.3(1).
[75] RIPA s.2(2).
[76] RIPA s.4(4)–(6).
[77] RIPA s.4(4)–(6).

Relation with orders under the Police and Criminal Evidence Act 1984 (PACE)

23–60 In *R. v Ipswich Crown Court Ex p. NTL Ltd*[78] the court considered the relationship between the prohibition in s.1 of RIPA and the service of notices to preserve material under PACE. NTL were asked by the police to retain emails passing between suspects on their system pending an application by the police for a warrant under PACE to give them access to the emails. NTL queried whether they were entitled to do this before they received the order as the only method they had of retaining the material was to intercept and copy it. The Court decided that the notice of intent served by the police under PACE was sufficient lawful authority under RIPA to enable the service provider to preserve the material. The judge commented that in any event NTL would not be able to disclose the material until it was served with the court order.

MONITORING OF BUSINESS COMMUNICATIONS

23–61 Directive 97/66 covered the use of public telecommunications networks, not wholly private ones. This is equally the case with Directive 2002/58. Article 5(2) provides a "carve out" for the:

> "legally authorised recording of communications and the related traffic data when carried out in the course of lawful business practice for the purpose of providing evidence of a commercial transaction or any other business communication"

made using such a network. It should be noted that the provision allows for the "recording" of calls in such circumstances. It should further be noted that the phrase "related traffic data" was not included in Directive 97/66 and traffic data are therefore not covered in the LBP. Article 15 provides for derogation from the ban on interception for any of the purposes set out in that article.

Section 4(2) of RIPA enables the Secretary of State to make regulations authorising such conduct:

> "as appears to him to constitute a legitimate practice reasonably required for the purpose, in connection with the carrying on of any business, of monitoring or keeping a record of—
>> communications by means of which transactions are entered into in the course of that business; or
>> other communications related to that business or taking place in the course of its being carried out."

Although s.4(2) and the Regulations made under it primarily reflect Art.5(2), it also implement aspects of Art.15. Thus they permit interception for a wider range of purposes than would be permissible under Art.5(2) alone (even taking a generous view of Art.5(2)).

---

[78] See n.63, above.

Lawful Business Practice Regulations 2000 (LBP)

23–62 The LBP Regulations are difficult to follow. To some extent this is caused by the use of the Regulations to deal, not only with the exemption in Art.5(2), but with aspects of the derogation in Art.15. The drafting adopted has conflated the two aspects. It therefore assists to "unpick" the two aspects to make sense of the Regulations. Article 5(2) only covers recording communications data in the course of business for providing evidence of commercial transactions, however the Regulations are not confined to this. They also cover the monitoring of electronic communications systems by public bodies for national security and crime prevention purposes. Section 4(7) provides that business includes references to activities of government departments, public authorities and those who hold office under statute; and the purposes for which monitoring may be conducted includes crime-related matters and national security. The use of the Regulations for this purpose has given rise to some stresses and ambiguities which only the courts will be able to resolve if the Regulations come before them. Oddly enough, even though it allows public bodies to monitor communications of those using their systems without oversight or the restrictions otherwise imposed by RIPA, this aspect of the Regulations does not appear to have attracted particular criticism on civil libertarian grounds, although it might have been expected to do so, particularly as it could be suggested that s.4(2) of RIPA does not authorise the use of the regulations for this purpose.

Recording and monitoring

23–63 The terms are not defined but monitoring appears to mean the consistent monitoring, as in having a person actually listening to the conversations in real time, whereas recording would appear to allow a copy of the communication to be taken to listen to or read at another time.

23–64 The Regulations can only authorise interception of communications on the system used for the purposes of a business by, or on behalf of, the person carrying on the business.[79] In the Regulations any interception must take place by or with the consent of the system controller.[80] The system controller is the one who, in relation to the particular telecommunications system, has the right to control the operation of the system,[81] see *R v Clifford Stanford*[82] referred to earlier. The system controller would usually be the data controller for any personal data held on the system.

The Regulations only cover interceptions and not the monitoring of communications data. As has been noted earlier the case of *Copland* suggests that access to communications data also engages Art.8 and requires a lawful basis.

Conditions relevant to all interception under the LBP Regulations

23–65 Under reg.3(3) any interception:

- must be limited to the purpose of monitoring or keeping a record of communications relevant to the system controller's business;

---

[79] RIPA s.4(3).
[80] LBP reg.3(1).
[81] LBP reg.2(d).
[82] [2006] EWCA Crim 258.

- only take place on a telecommunication system provided for use wholly or partly in connection with that business; and

- the system controller must have made "all reasonable efforts" to inform everyone who may use the system that communications on it may be intercepted.

The first condition causes difficulty when dealing with the vexed issue of personal communications and is dealt with below. The last condition can give rise to practical difficulties in informing those who are sending incoming communications for the first time and in respect of whom there is no obvious way of providing the information in every case. However, as the requirement is for the system controller to have made all reasonable efforts it appears that the practical difficulties have been appreciated.

Monitoring and keeping records of communications

23–66 Regulation 3(1)(a) sets out the purposes for which communications may be both monitored and recorded. It lists five purposes as follows:

- monitoring for standards purposes;

- national security;

- the prevention or detection of crime;

- investigation or detection of unauthorised use of a telecommunications system;

- ensuring the effective use of the system.

There are then two purposes for which the system controller may monitor but not record communications, which are:

- deciding whether the communication is related to the system controller's business; or

- monitoring the use of confidential telephone lines.

Monitoring for standards purposes

23–67 This is a messy provision. The relation between (aa) and the rest of the subsection is not as clear as it might be and it could be read as allowing the system controller to monitor or record in order to establish any set of facts for any purpose. This appears to be the view taken by the Commissioner's office however it is suggested that this would be wrong and the establishment of facts must be linked to ascertaining compliance with regulatory or self-regulatory practices. This is borne out by reg.3(3) which provides that conduct falling within this paragraph is only allowed to the extent permitted by Art.5.

Regulatory or self-regulatory practices or procedures

23–68 Monitoring is allowed in connection with regulatory or self-regulatory practices or procedures which are applicable to the system controller in the carrying on of his business or applicable to another person in the carrying on of his business where that person is supervised by the system controller in respect of those practices or procedures.[83]

Regulatory or self-regulatory practices or procedures are defined as:

- any practices or procedures recommended or required by the law of any State within the EEA, or standards or codes of practice which meet certain criteria; or

- any practices or procedures applied for the purpose of reaching compliance with those laws or standards or codes of practice.

The standards or codes must meet certain criteria. Those are that the standard or code:

- published by or on behalf of a body which is established in a State in the EEA; and

- includes amongst its objectives the publication of standards or codes of practice for the conduct of business.

So under this heading a code or standard set by the Press Complaints Commission (PCC) or the Advertising Standards Authority (ASA) would qualify as would an in-house practice or procedure adopted in order to meet the requirements of the PCC or ASA code.

The system controller can monitor to:

- establish the existence of facts;

- ascertain compliance with the standards or codes; or

- ascertain or demonstrate standards applicable to users of the system for these purposes.

Effective use of the system

23–69 This permits monitoring and recording by the system controller to secure, or as an inherent part of, the effective operation of the system. It includes monitoring or recording by those who provide telecommunications services of their own services in relation to provision or enforcement under any enactment.

Prevention and detection of crime

23–70 There is no definition of these terms. There is no test of reasonableness or proportionality in the Regulations. The Principles under the DPA will continue to apply, assuming that personal data are being processed as part of the interception. The OIC advises that in order for the processing to be fair the interception should be objectively justifiable and no more intrusive than necessary for the purpose. If the system controller is a public authority directly subject to the HRA then the intrusion would

---

[83] LBP reg.3(1)(a)(i)(bb).

have to be justifiable in terms of Art.8(2) of the Convention rights. It will be a matter of fact as to whether the particular interception was justified and proportionate for these purposes.

National security

23–71   There is no definition of national security imported into the Regulations. In relation to oversight of the interception of communications the position is as described above in relation to the prevention or detection of crime. In circumstances where a system controller intercepts in the interests of national security it seems likely that the exemption under the DPA would also be claimed. This exemption involves no test of proportionality and a certificate under the DPA is conclusive proof of the application of the exemption.

Oversight of interception under the LBPR

23–72   There is no provision for oversight of such interceptions. If a system controller intercepts outside the protection given by the Regulations the individual whose communications have been intercepted could take private action in tort under s.1(3) of RIPA.

INTERCEPTION OR MONITORING OF "PERSONAL" COMMUNICATIONS

23–73   The question which has produced more comment than any other in relation to interception has been whether "personal" communications, usually telephone calls and emails, sent by employees can be intercepted by employers and if so in what circumstances. It has to be borne in mind that the ECtHR has held that telephone calls from business premises are covered by Art.8 as are emails.[84] The interception and monitoring of such calls must be justified within the LBP. The question here is where the calls and emails are about personal matters rather than about work matters.

Do the Regulations apply to "personal" communications sent using an employer's electronic communications system?

23–74   By personal communications are meant any communications sent or received by an employee in a personal capacity, the contents of which are not related to work. There are different kinds of personal communications: they may be passed between employees or work contacts on non-work related matters or exchanged with those wholly unconnected with the employer. It could be suggested that Art.5 does not allow the monitoring or recording of such communications, unless they fall within the exceptions in Art.14, as they are not a "business communication", on the other hand it can be argued that if they are sent in business hours using the business network system then they can validly be regarded as "business communications".

The exemptions in Art.14 allow for circumstances where the interception is for the "prevention, investigation, detection or prosecution . . . of unauthorised use of the

---

[84] See discussion of *Copland* above.

telecommunications system". If the employer has a rule that the employees must only use the communications systems for business or sets limits on the authorisation given to employees in the use of the system for private purposes, then it appears to follow that the employer may monitor in order to detect unauthorised use. Personal communications sent in business time using the business system could be regarded as being sent and received "in the course" of the business being carried on but the term is ambiguous. The Regulations use the phrase in reg.2(b)(ii), "a communication which otherwise takes place in the course of the carrying on of that business".

It is submitted that the phrase is sufficient to cover personal calls made in works time where employees are authorised to make some calls within limits. Regulation 3(1)(a)(iv) and (v) allow for monitoring for the purpose of investigating or detecting unauthorised use of the system (or any other telecommunications system) where the activity is undertaken in order to secure, or as an inherent part of, the effective operation of the system. Regulation 3(1)(b) allows for monitoring (but not recording) of incoming communications for the purpose of determining whether they are communications relevant to the system controller's business which he is entitled to review for the purposes of facts, self-regulatory standards or business standards within reg.3(a)(i).

If the argument set out above is correct it would follow that an employer who sets a clear policy on what use may be made of the system would be entitled to monitor to ensure that the system is being used in accordance with the authorisation given as long as the monitoring was within the limits notified to the employees and was proportionate. It might be regarded as proportionate to carry out an initial review of communications data only in those cases where there is some ground for concern and only to intercept messages marked as personal where there was good cause. In effect this is the approach adopted in the Employment Code of Practice. The position would be more difficult where the employer puts no limits at all on the private uses of the system and employees can make any calls they wish from the employer's telecommunications system. In those circumstances, although reg.3(1)(b) would still provide for the monitoring of incoming calls to check that they fall within reg.3(1)(a)(i), there would arguably be no basis for the monitoring of outgoing personal calls by employees.

Right to private calls

23–75   Employees have no legal right to enjoy the benefit of using an employer's business facilities to send and receive personal communications during the course of employment. (If they do send or receive such communications the question of whether they have the right to keep them private from the employer is a separate issue.) There do not appear to be any cases establishing a right to personal correspondence at work although the Article 29 Working Party in Opinion 2/2006 quotes an academic comment to the effect that "impeding" someone's right to initiate correspondence must be a breach. Cases before the ECtHR which deal with rights to correspondence and privacy of correspondence have been mainly in circumstances where the individual has had no opportunity, other than via the mechanism which has been intercepted, to communicate freely with others, for example in the case of mail from prisoners. Although the Home Office issued a recommendation to employers in the public sector that they should offer employees the use of a pay phone which could be available for private use there is no legal requirement for this. In the absence of such a positive right for employees the question hinges on what is in the contract between the parties. While it might be arguable that an employer could make it a term of the employment contract that the employee would not use any of the employer's facilities for personal communication it would possibly be seen as unreasonable and unfair in today's environment. In practice it will depend on what is in the company policy and what has become practice or is accepted by the employer. In one case in France where an employee had used the employer's facilities with either agreement or acquiescence a court held that the employee was entitled to a degree of privacy in the communication.[85] It seems that once the employer allows some degree of personal use of work facilities the corollary is that, for reasons of fairness and respect for personal privacy and privacy of correspondence, he will also be expected to afford the individual a degree of privacy of that use.

Practical considerations in relation to private communications

23–76   If an employer is monitoring to check for other compliance matters there are practical problems in respecting employee privacy of correspondence. Unless the system has some method of allowing employees to mark private communications as such it is difficult to see how the employer can ensure that he never intercepts any such calls. The OIC advises that the employer should have regard to the "header" of messages to see whether they are likely to be personal in content and not intercept or monitor ones which appear to be unless it is necessary to do so to ensure that the system is not being used in an unauthorised manner. Even where messages are marked as private the employer may need to view them if there are grounds to suspect misuse of the system.

Stored messages

23–77   As noted above the Home Office and the OIC have taken the view that stored messages once read by the recipient are not covered by the ban on interception. However it is clear that they are outside the definition of communications data. If the Home Office and OIC view is correct there is no privacy protection for stored messages once read other than that afforded by the DPA and the HRA. For the reasons set out it is suggested that the better view is that they are covered by the ban on interception and any access to them should be in accordance with the LBP Regulations.

Interception under Warrants Issued under RIPA

23–78   Warrants for the interception of communications on public telephone systems are dealt with under ss.5–20 of RIPA. Only a brief description of the arrangements is given here as such interceptions are not affected by the terms of Directive 2002/548. The interception will either relate to a matter which falls outside Community competence or will be covered by one of the exemptions in Art.14.

Interception warrants may be issued by the Secretary of State, or in urgent or overseas cases by a senior official,[86] on the application of a limited number of public officials

---

[85] See Ch.3, above for a note of the case *Nikon v M.Frederic*, para.3–07.
[86] RIPA s.7(1).

whose roles are connected with policing or security.[87] The Secretary of State may only issue a warrant if he is satisfied that it is necessary:

- in the interests of national security;

- to prevent or detect serious crime;

- to safeguard the economic well-being of the United Kingdom;

- to give mutual assistance to an overseas authority in equivalent matters.

The Secretary must believe that the conduct authorised by the warrant is proportionate to the aim to be achieved.[88]

Warrants must identify either the person whose communications are to be intercepted or the premises in respect of which the interception is required.[89] They may be revoked, renewed or modified.

The Secretary of State may impose obligations on providers of telecommunications and postal services to ensure the intercept capability of systems and may contribute to the costs of establishing or maintaining such capability.[90] There are restrictions on the disclosure of intercepted material[91] and restrictions on the disclosure of the existence of interceptions backed up by offence provisions for tipping off offences.[92]

Interception for the purposes of email screening

23–79   The difficulties associated with the development of electronic communications, the way that a balance can be struck between the privacy rights of the individual, the legitimate business needs of employers and others and the needs of the State continue to be a source of debate and review. Most recently the Article 29 Working Party has commented on the interception of emails for the purpose of detecting viruses, filtering spam and other mail related services in Opinion 2/2006.[93] It has advised that the filtering of emails for the purpose of detecting viruses and for removing spam can be justified under the obligations of the security requirements of Directive 2002/58, subject to notice to the users. However it raised concerns at the screening of email content for other reasons, for example to remove pre-determined content without the consent of the users of the system, and took the view that such activity amounts to an unlawful interception. The last area which it considered were other email-related services which involve an assessment by the service provider of the way that the recipient has handled the communication, for example by letting the sender know whether the email has been opened. It expressed "the strongest opposition" to this processing being carried out secretly and advised that these services should require the consent of the recipient.

---

[87] RIPA s.6.
[88] RIPA s.5.
[89] RIPA s.8(1).
[90] RIPA s.12.
[91] RIPA s.15.
[92] RIPA s.19.
[93] 00451/06/EN.

The Courts have sent out a strong signal about the respect due to the privacy of telephone calls when they imposed a custodial sentence in early 2007 on the journalist who tapped telephone calls of the Royal family on the public network.

ADDITIONAL INFORMATION

Extract Employment Practices Code Policy for the Use of Electronic Communications

23–80 Employers should consider integrating the following data protection features into a policy for the use of electronic communications:

- Set out clearly to workers the circumstances in which they may or may not use the employer's telephone systems (including mobile phones), the email system and the internet for private communications.

- Make clear the extent and type of private use that is allowed, for example restrictions on overseas phone calls or limits on the size and/or type of email attachments that they can send or receive.

- In the case of internet access specify clearly any restrictions on material that can be viewed or copied. A simple ban on "offensive material" is unlikely to be sufficiently clear for people to know what is and is not allowed. Employers may wish to consider giving examples of the sort of material that is considered offensive, for example material containing racist terminology or nudity.

- Advise workers about the general need to exercise care, about any relevant rules, and about what personal information they are allowed to include in particular types of communication.

- Make clear what alternatives can be used, e.g. the confidentiality of communications with the company doctor can only be ensured if they are sent by internal post, rather than by email, and are suitably marked.

- Lay down clear rules for private use of the employer's communication equipment when used from home or away from the workplace, e.g. the use of facilities that enable external dialling into company networks.

- Explain the purposes for which any monitoring is conducted, the extent of the monitoring and the means used.

- Outline how the policy is enforced and penalties which exist for a breach.

Case Study

23–81 Mr and Mrs Block have been married for over 20 years and have together built up a successful retail business. They started out with a shop in the nearby town of Amchestan and now have several shops as well as having franchised their business concept, "Blocks 4 Rocks Limited" to franchisees throughout the UK. Mrs Block still spends time in the Amchestan shop but Mr Block runs the wider business from the head office attached to their home. They tend to also work at home quite a bit. As a result they have a sophisticated telephone system which connects the shops with the head office and the house.

They have no children but their nephew works with them in the business and expects to take it over in due course. The nephew runs one of the shops in Bradcester (not franchised).

Sadly Mrs Block has become suspicious over her husband's behaviour. She has found him putting down the telephone quickly when she enters the room. Her nephew's wife runs an advertising and PR agency which provides services to Blocks 4 Rocks and Mrs Block is beginning to wonder whether he may be having an affair with her. The wife, who is called Christina, occasionally works from the office in the Blocks 4 Rocks Bradcester shop. When she works there she uses one of the Block's mobile telephones.

Mrs Block decides to have a look at the business call records. She finds that a unusually large number of calls have been made between the Bradcester shop and one of the franchisees and another large number of calls between the mobile telephone used by the Bradcester shop and the head office. She is hesitating by the telephone at home deciding whether to confront her husband when she notices a small lead coming from the telephone. She is outraged to realise that her own telephone appears to have been "bugged". When Mr Block returns she confronts him with all the evidence and demands an explanation.

Mr Block breaks down and confesses all. He had a brief fling with Christina over 12 months ago but, after only a couple of weeks realised what a fool he had been and stopped. Since then Christina has kept telephoning him and threatening to tell Mrs Block unless he increases the fees for her services. He planned to record the calls and then tell her that he would take them to the police and accuse her of blackmail if she did not stop. He also explains that he suspects Christina is having an affair with the franchisee and he has asked a private enquiry agent to try to listen in to the calls she makes from the mobile.

Case Study—Analysis

23–82   It appears that the limited company Blocks 4 Rocks is the system controller for the telephone system in use. The system covers the house, the head office and the shops. If Mrs Block is a director or senior manager in the business she will be entitled to intercept or authorise interception under the LBP Regulations however she simply looks at the call records. This may amount to communications data. If it does and the company has not notified its employees that such data may be monitored Christina could argue that her Art.8 rights have been breached (as Mrs Copland did). On the other hand Blocks 4 Rocks is a private body and a court may not be prepared to extend protection to Christina in respect of the actions of a private body.

Mr Block does carry out an interception. If he is a Director or senior manager in the business he will be entitled to authorise this but must comply with the LBP. One of those requirements is that users of the system should be informed of any monitoring or recording and he has not done this. The purpose of the interception must also be in accord with the Regulations. He could argue that it is for the prevention or detection of crime, if he can claim that Christina's pressure on him amounts to criminal conduct. Mr Black's main problem however will be in arguing that the monitoring is for the purpose of the system controller's business. It can be argued that he is monitoring for personal rather than business purposes. The instructions to the enquiry agent are clearly unlawful. If the agent intercepts calls on the public system he will be committing a criminal offence under the RIPA.

CHAPTER 24

Data Protection Supervision of EU Co-operation in Immigration, Asylum, Customs, Policing and Judicial Matters, Role of the European Supervisor and the Information Commissioner

INTRODUCTION

24–01   It is necessary to look outside the Data Protection Act 1998 and the Directives for the data protection measures relating to significant European instruments in the areas of asylum, immigration, home affairs and security, justice and customs.

Several European legal instruments involve the creation of at least one major database of personal data shared between the participating states:

- The Schengen Convention, which established arrangements to facilitate the removal of border controls between contracting States on mainland Europe, governs the Schengen Information System (to be replaced by Schengen II) and includes data protection provisions. As the United Kingdom has decided to take part in the Schengen arrangements (although not as a full member) the UK Commissioner has a role in relation to those provisions.

- The Convention on the establishment of a European Police Force (the Europol Convention)[1] establishes information sharing arrangements for policing purposes and has its own supervisory mechanism including data protection rules.

- The Convention on the use of Information Technology for Customs Purposes involves information sharing and data protection provisions.

- The Council decision setting up Eurojust[2] establishes Eurojust as a body of the European Union aimed at improving judicial co-operation and includes provisions on data-sharing and supervisory arrangements.

---

[1] [1995] O.J. C316/2.
[2] 2002/187/JHA O.J. L 63, March 6, 2002, p.1.

There are other information-sharing arrangements, which are now part of the first pillar, but in which there are specific rules applicable to data sharing and data protection:

- EURODAC, an information system which holds information about requests for asylum made in different Member States and on illegal immigrants. Supervision of the EURODAC system now falls directly under the EU as asylum and immigration have become first pillar matters, although the database was originally established under the Convention determining the State responsible for examining Applicants for Asylum lodged in one of the Member States of the European Communities (the Dublin Convention).

- The Visa Information System (VIS), a central information system on visa applications with an interface in each Member State set up under a Council Decision of June 2004.[3]

Information sharing arrangements, and concomitant data protection provisions, are also necessary for the success of other initiatives such as the Convention on Mutual Assistance in Criminal Matters[4] May 2000; the exchanging of information extracted from Criminal Records[5] and the European Arrest Warrant[6] however these do not give rise to the existence of shared databases.

24–02 The fragmentation of data protection supervision in this area is a result of the history of, and the current arrangements for, co-operation between Member States of the European Community in matters relating to immigration, border control, justice, customs and home affairs. These arrangements are complex and continue to evolve at a rapid pace. The complexity arises partly from the mismatch between the fast pace of policy and practical initiatives for co-operation in these areas and the slow pace of developments in the EU legal regime. This has resulted in a patchwork of different initiatives and arrangements for co-operation which have evolved over a period of time.

Since the first edition of this book in 1999 there has been a radical increase in the extent and depth of co-operation between Member States in border control, law enforcement and related matters. The policy of the EU is now to achieve an area of freedom, security and justice (AFSJ). The website of the European Parliament describes the AFSJ in the following terms:

"an area of freedom, where citizens can move without restriction. Its establishment involves the abolition of controls at internal borders and the adoption of measures for third country nationals;

an area of security aimed at preventing and combating the threats that hang over the Union and its citizens. The Union is working to combat all types of

---

[3] 2004/512.

[4] This covers procedures for mutual assistance including interception of communications and includes restrictions on the use of personal data obtained from another State under the Convention O.J. E.U. (197 of July 12, 2000) p.3.

[5] Council Decision 2005/876/JHA of November 21, 2005.

[6] The warrant entered into force on January 1, 2004 between eight of the EU Member States including the UK and Ireland.

serious crimes, such as organised crime, terrorism, drug trafficking, trafficking in human beings, fraud against the European Community's financial interests, cybercrime and money laundering;

an area of justice, which comprises two areas: First judicial co-operation in civil matters. The idea is to ensure that national legal systems do not pose obstacles to citizens in their professional activity or in their family life. . . . Second judicial co-operation in criminal matters. The aim here is to keep a criminal investigation from coming up against a dead end at national borders. The Union is working to ensure that criminals find no refuge in Union territory."

Europe already felt its prosperous and (generally) law abiding democracies to be under threat before September 11, 2001. The growth of organised crime without respect for national frontiers and the pressures from would-be economic migrants had contributed to an agenda of increased data surveillance and co-operation even before September 11, 2001. The events of that day provided a further impetus and, perhaps more importantly, produced a level of popular support, for measures which might otherwise have been met with resistance as undermining individual liberties. The terrorist attacks in Madrid and London in March 2004 and July 2005 produced a further political impetus with the focus moving from economic crime and uncontrolled immigration to the threat of terrorist activity. The European Council adopted the Hague Programme: strengthening freedom, security and justice in the European Union[7] in March 2005 to address the need to take a more co-ordinated approach.

It would be a task well beyond this book to attempt to analyse the development of co-operation in these areas in any detail. This chapter aims to provide a general introduction to the development of the shared information systems and the corresponding data protection supervisory arrangements. The chapter does not attempt any detailed analysis. It presents a broad outline in order to put the data protection safeguards and instruments into context. It does not contain practical tools or derivations. In the first part of the chapter a general introduction to the European background is given (without which the arrangements are unfathomable), then the legal basis and general nature of the main arrangements for sharing information are described. In the second part the data protection supervisory arrangements are described. It should be recognised however that this chapter only describes one aspect of a broad policy of co-operation across the EU and these arrangements apply in that broad context. As an example, the introduction of technical specifications for the introduction of biometric identities into passports and other travel documents throughout the EU will increase the effectiveness of identification and hence eventually the quality of the data of the shared databases.[8]

SUMMARY OF MAIN POINTS

24–03   (a) There are currently six main European data sharing arrangements: the Schengen Information System (SIS), the Europol databases, the Customs Information System (CIS), the Visa Information System (VIS)

---

[7] 52005XG0000303(01) [2005] O.J. C053, March 3, 2005, p.001–0014.
[8] Council Regulation 2252/2004.

and EURODAC. There are proposals for others. There are also separate arrangements for the exchange of information in specific areas such as arrests/warrants.

(b) Each database was established for a specific purpose with, usually, provisions for limited access by third parties or use for other purposes, but there have been pressures to extend both access and use and increasingly the EU is looking to maximise access to all the available data for law enforcement purposes.

(c) Each database and its use is subject to a set of data protection rules. Each governing legal instrument incorporates or references provisions relating to the use, disclosure and supervision of personal data. Although the standards for data protection are broadly the same the particular arrangements for data handling and supervision are currently different in each case.

(d) Insofar as the data protection rules are based on a common instrument it is not universally the general Directive (95/46) but Council of Europe Treaty 108 and the Recommendation on Policing.

(e) The processing of personal data in the SIS, Europol, Eurojust, and the CIS are subject to regulatory oversight by joint supervisory bodies, that is in each case a regulatory body whose membership is drawn from the Member States, usually the national data protection regulators.

(f) EURODAC is supervised by the EU Data Protection Supervisor (EDPS) but pending his appointment an interim joint supervisory body was convened. VIS is supervised by the EDPS.

(g) Eurojust is subject to specific Rules of Procedure on the processing and protection of personal data at Eurojust adopted by the college of Eurojust and approved by the Council.[9]

(h) The relation with the European Union varies depending on the area involved:

— immigration and asylum, the issue of visas and judicial co-operation in civil matters are now matters within EU competence so they are subject to Community supervision and part of the institutions of the Community;

— despite the greatly increased co-operation over policing and criminal justice, these remain "third pillar" areas in which Member States of the European Union co-operate under Title VI of the Treaty on European Union.

(i) There is a separate international agreement for co-operation in the exchange and availability of information including personal data, DNA, fingerprints and vehicle registration information which also includes specific data protection provisions. This agreement was initially adopted

---

[9] Council approval February 24, 2005, O.J. C068, March 19, 2005, p.001–0010.

outside the legal framework of the EU (the Prum Agreement) but it has now been incorporated into the EU framework.

(j) Although legal instruments under Title VI are entered into under the aegis of the Community their status varies. Conventions entered into under Title VI are not legal instruments of the Community so they are of inter-pretative value only in cases of ambiguity in UK law.

(k) As the Title VI instruments are not a source of legal powers for the Commissioner, the Commissioner's powers to fulfil obligations under them have to be found within the terms of the 1998 Act or orders made under it.

There is considerable concern at the patchwork of legal measures in this area and the problems that this causes for data subjects who are affected by these initiatives. Many commentators are deeply critical of the lack of consistent standards or supervision.[10]

History of European Co-operation over Justice, Home Affairs and Immigration

Overview

24–04   The European Community was founded under the Treaty of Rome in 1958 with the objective of establishing a common market without barriers to promote trade between Member States. At its inception its remit only covered economic matters, so foreign and security matters, justice and home affairs, including immigration control, were outside the scope of Community competence. Since its foundation the Community has matured towards economic and social integration. In 1987 the Single European Act came into force. Its aim was to remove the internal barriers within the Community to the free movement of people, goods, services and capital, creating a single internal market. As noted in Ch.1, above, Directives 95/46, 97/66 and 2002/58 have been introduced as internal market measures. After the Single European Act the next stage in the movement towards European unity was the Treaty on European Union negotiated at Maastricht in December 1991. The Treaty had to be ratified by all the Member States before it could come into force. This process was completed by November 1993.

The effect of the Treaty of Maastricht

24–05   The Maastricht Treaty extended the role of the Community in three ways:

(a) The areas of Community competence were extended, for example, two of the new areas of competence were public health and consumer protection. The new areas were absorbed into the existing framework of Community institu-tions which are referred to as "first pillar" matters.

---

[10] As an example the European Data Protection Supervisor expressed his concern at the Prum Agreement in the course of giving his Opinion on the Proposal for a Framework Decision on the protection of personal data in the framework of police and judicial cooperation in criminal matter (COM (2005) 475 final).

(b) Agreement was reached on moving to intergovernmental co-operation in foreign and security matters. This co-operation between governments does not involve the institutional framework of the Community. These subjects are referred to as "second pillar" matters.

(c) The Treaty laid the foundations of a "third pillar" of the Community, co-operation in justice and home affairs. This co-operation was also intergovernmental and did not involve the institutions of the Community. It required unanimous agreement between all the governments of the Member States to institute relevant measures. Areas included in the third pillar were asylum, immigration from third countries, co-operation in combating drug addiction, fraud and terrorism.

The Treaty of Amsterdam

24-06 The spirit of co-operation in third pillar areas was taken further by the Amsterdam Treaty signed on October 2, 1997 which entered into force on May 1, 1999 having completed the processes of ratification in Member States. Title IV of the Treaty covers visa, asylum, immigration and other policies related to the free movement of persons. These provided that within the five years following the entry into force of the Treaty measures in relation to external border controls, asylum and immigration were be adopted by the Council and therefore within the first pillar. Over the five-year transitional period the Council had to act unanimously to introduce measures in any of these areas. This Title is subject to a Protocol on the position of the United Kingdom and Ireland. By this Protocol none of the provisions of Title IV or measures adopted pursuant to it shall be binding on or applicable to the United Kingdom or Ireland. However, they may chose to participate in any such measures and there are provisions dealing with the procedures to be adopted should they chose to do so. The issues of visas, asylum, immigration and judicial co-operation in civil matters are now therefore part of the first pillar.

24-07 Title VI of the Treaty sets out steps for co-operation in police and judicial co-operation in criminal matters. Article 29 recites that one of the "objects of the Union" is to provide for its citizens "a high level of safety within an area of freedom, security and justice by developing common action among Member States in the fields of police, judicial co-operation in criminal matters and by preventing and combating racism and xenophobia". Fighting crime encompasses fighting drugs, terrorism and organised crime. Policing and judicial co-operation in criminal matter remain areas of inter-governmental activity.

Mechanisms for inter-governmental co-operation

24-08 Article 34 sets out the mechanisms which are available to the Council to take action in these areas. These are the adoption of common positions, framework decision, decisions, or conventions.

Common positions define the approach of the EU to a particular matter. Framework decisions are formal instruments which are intended to achieve harmonisation of the laws of Member States. They do not have direct effect but Member States must ensure that the results required by the decision are achieved in national law. Decisions are instruments which apply to the EU itself but do not impact on the laws of Member States. Conventions are separate legal instruments which are recommended to Member States and to which Member States may adhere. The Court of Justice can rule on the validity and interpretation of decisions, framework decisions and the interpretation of convention.

The complexity of the third pillar arrangements has given rise to problems and challenges, as with the challenge to the Council decision on PNR data.

24–09 The Treaty of Amsterdam did not alter the legal structure of conventions already in force, therefore the Europol and Customs Conventions remained unaffected by the changes wrought by Amsterdam.

The Treaty of Nice amended Title VI to include an obligation on the Council to encourage co-operation in the investigation and prosecution of criminal matters through Eurojust. Eurojust was established following a Council decision in February 2002.

24–10 Since the Treaty of Amsterdam was finalised co-operation in the areas of policing has continued to expand. A further Convention under the third pillar was agreed in May 2000; the Convention on Mutual Assistance in Criminal Matters which replaces earlier arrangements made under the aegis of the Council of Europe.

24–11 The next stage in European integration was anticipated to be the adoption of the European Constitution. This would, among other measures, have abolished the third pillar and brought the arrangements for police and judicial co-operation in criminal matters under the first pillar. The terms of the Constitution were agreed after much negotiation and the Constitution was signed in October 2004. However it was subject to referenda in several Member States. Once France and Holland voted against adoption the process of adoption ground to a halt, despite the fact that a number of the governments in other Member States had agreed to the terms. Since then the growth of the EU by accession has meant that any re-negotiation of the terms of the Constitution would be even more difficult. The current Presidency of Angela Merkel of Germany is keen to restart the process of adoption of the Constitution but some Member States do not share her enthusiasm. The pressure to increase co-operation in policing matters and home affairs however has not abated and initiatives under the third pillar have continued to develop.

The development of co-operative arrangements was given renewed urgency by the Madrid bombing in March 2004 and the London bombing in July 2005. As noted earlier, in November 2005 the European Council adopted the Hague Programme which has brought together the initiatives being taken forward to create the area of freedom justice and security to:

> "improve the common capability of the Union and its Member States to guarantee fundamental rights, minimum procedural safeguards and access to justice, to provide protection in accordance with the Geneva Convention on Refugees and other international treaties to persons in need, to regulate migration flows and to control the external borders of the Union, to fight organised cross-border crime and repress the threat of terrorism, to realise the potential of Europol and Eurojust, to carry further the mutual recognition of judicial decisions and certificates both in civil and criminal matters, and to eliminate legal and judicial obstacles in litigation in civil and family matters with cross-border implications."

The ambitious reach of the Programme is matched by its aims in relation to the sharing of data. One of its key aims is improving the exchange of information, to which end it introduces the concept of the "principle of availability". It should be noted that this is not a legal principle adopted by the EU but a statement of policy aspiration which has, to date, not resulted in any completed legal instruments. The Commission's first report on the implementation of the Hague Programme, delivered in June 2006, accepts that progress in implementing this aim has been slower than was hoped.

COMMENT

24–12 The ambitious programme for increased co-operation is therefore being implemented under a set of legal instruments, those covered by Title VI, which are not best suited for the task. The obscurity of the provisions and the lack of democratic accountability remain major problems. This has been a constant refrain, particularly focused on the perceived deficit in the protection of personal data. In resolutions of March 27, 2003 and March 9, 2004 the European Parliament called for the creation of uniform data protection rules across the third pillar to provide equivalent standards to those in Directive 95/46. The European Data Protection Authorities in their spring conference in 2005 called for the adoption of a legal framework for data protection applicable in third pillar activities and more recently the European Parliament has called for a more radical solution, the abolition of the third pillar and the transfer of all functions to the first pillar to enhance democratic accountability[11] even if the Constitution itself is not adopted. As Peter Hustix, the European Data Protection Supervisor (EDPS) puts it, the Opinion on the framework proposal on personal data:

".... the present general framework for data protection in this area is insufficient. In the first place Directive 95/46/EC does not apply to the processing of personal data in the course of activities which fall outside Community law, such as those provided for by Title VI. Although in most Member States the scope of the implementing legislation is wider than the directive itself requires and does not exclude data processing for the purpose of law enforcement, significant difference in national law exist. In the second place the Council of Europe Convention No 108 by which all the Member States are bound, does not provide for the necessary preciseness in the protection as has been recognised already at the time of the adoption of Directive 95/46/EC. In the third place neither of these two legal instruments takes into account the specific characteristics of the exchange of data by police and judicial authorities."[12]

SUPERVISION OF COMMUNITY INSITUTIONS

24–13 At least in one area there was an improvement in supervisory mechanisms for personal data post-Amsterdam as those activities which are carried out under the first pillar became subject to the requirements of Directive 95/46. Article 286 of the

---

[11] CAVADA Resolution June 8, 2005.
[12] [2006] O.J. C47/12 para.4.

Treaty of Amsterdam dealt with data protection in the Community. It was incorporated to remedy the much-criticised failure of the Community to apply data protection standards and supervision to its own processing or that of organisations under its control. Article 286 states that Community Acts (i.e. data protection directives) on the protection of individuals with regard to the processing of personal data and the free movement of such data shall apply to the institutions and bodies set up by or on the basis of the Treaty. It also requires the Council to establish an independent supervisory body responsible for monitoring the application of the Acts to Community institutions and bodies. Accordingly post-Amsterdam the Directive has been applied to Community processing and compliance with it is now supervised by the European Data Protection Supervisor.

24–14 The proposal for the post of EDPS was adopted in November 2000 and established by Regulation of the Council in December 2000.[13] This was confirmed and supplemented by a Decision of September 13, 2004. The supervisory role covers all Community institutions and bodies and applies to the processing of personal data carried out in the exercise of their activities all or part of which fall within the scope of Community law. The processing is subject to the standards set out in Directive 95/46. The post is established in Brussels. The post-holder is appointed by the European Parliament and the Council for a period of five years. He has a position and independence equivalent to that of a judge of the Court of Justice of the European Communities. The EDPS, Peter Hustinx and his assistant supervisor, Joaquin Bayo Delgado, were appointed on January 17, 2004. The Supervisor can receive complaints, conduct enquiries and is entitled to access rights to enable him to do so. He can order the rectification, blocking, erasure or destruction of all data processed in breach of the standards; impose a temporary or permanent ban on processing and warn or admonish the data controller. Each Community institution or body must also have a data protection officer who is responsible for ensuring that the body complies with data protection standards. EURODAC is subject to the supervision of the EDPS.

Since his appointment Peter Hustinx has issued a number of opinions on developing policies and issues which have been influential in the development of policy in this area and are referred to in this chapter.

The Nature of Third Pillar Instruments

24–15 Third pillar instruments, even ratified conventions, have an anomalous position in terms of European Community law. There is no recourse to the European Court as a matter of Community law, other than on interpretation or the validity of implementing measures, although one may be provided for under the particular instrument. There will be no direct effect stemming from a decision, framework decision or convention as it is not part of Community law. Neither framework decisions nor conventions are directly applicable in UK law. The UK Government has an obligation to implement them via appropriate national legislation. In the case of any ambiguity the UK courts will strive to interpret the law in accordance with the UK's international obligations (see Ch.3, above for a discussion of this point). There is no case law on how they will be treated by the UK courts, although one would expect

---

[13] Reg.45/2001 of December 18, 2000.

them to be influential. The Europol Convention was the first of the third pillar conventions to enter into force.

As noted above the third pillar agreements have given rise to concerned debate over the perceived democratic deficit of such arrangements.

The subject-matter of third pillar instruments

24–16 One of the pressures leading to agreement over third pillar arrangements was the need to co-operate to combat criminal activity. Although the remit of the Community excluded justice and criminal areas, in practice it has not always been easy to ascertain where the boundaries of such activities lie. Moreover there has been a need for increased co-operation between Member States in these areas. Those who deal in drugs, people or weapons or pursue other types of criminal activity do so without regard for national frontiers. At first such co-operative arrangements ran in parallel with the development of the Community. Thus in 1967 Member States signed a Convention on Mutual Assistance between Customs Administrations. In 1975 the "Trevi" group of Ministers for Home Affairs developed with the aim of combating terrorism. The growth of these separate initiatives outside the structure of the Community led to a complex set of co-operative arrangements. Arrangements under the third pillar were intended to simplify and streamline co-operation in these areas, although it is not immediately apparent that they have done so.

Given the subject-matter of the third pillar areas it is inevitable that they involve the use of personal data. An early proposal by the Commission that there should be a framework data protection convention applying to all third pillar conventions to ensure that the same data protection rules applied to each did not come to fruition. As it stands the instruments in force have rather different data protection arrangements to one another although a Joint Secretariat deals with the supervisory arrangements for some of the initiatives.

INTERNAL BORDERS AND SCHENGEN

24–17 Customs control is sometimes used as a synonym for border control, that is the exercise by a State of powers over the entry of goods and people into its territory. Border controls can cover a range of areas such as immigration, control over the movement of drugs, drug precursors, firearms or other undesirable imports, health checks on food imports and restrictions on livestock movements as well as anti-smuggling checks and the imposition of taxes on goods. In different European States such controls have traditionally been exercised in different ways. In the United Kingdom HMRC are responsible for supervising the movement of goods while the Immigration Service deals with the movement of people. Given the many, and important, issues for States in border control the challenge of eliminating internal barriers in the European Community has been a considerable one.

The dismantling of barriers

24–18 The focus of the Single European Act was to remove the three main barriers to the movement of goods between States:

(a) physical barriers of frontier controls;

(b) technical barriers of different technical requirements for goods;

(c) fiscal barriers of tax and customs duty.

Single European Act measures, such as the abolition of customs documentation for intra-EU trade, were successful in largely eliminating these barriers, although there remain areas of control exercised at the borders between the Member States, for example the import of pets into the United Kingdom is still controlled. There remain controls over individuals who come from outside the Community including controls on immigration, asylum seekers and third country nationals. These significant controls are exercised at the external borders of the Community. One of the consequences of the gradual elimination of internal controls has meant that Member States are heavily dependent on those States with external frontiers to stop the entry of undesirable goods or persons into Europe in the first place. Responsibility for the control or surveillance of external borders falls to national authorities but there is a recognition that the burden falls unequally among EU countries. A European Agency for External Border Management became operational in May 2005 which can provide analysis and intelligence support. The Schengen Agreement or Accord was important in establishing the framework in which the free movement of people between the continental States could be achieved and now largely removes the internal barriers to the movement of people around much of Europe.

The Schengen Accord

24–19 The "Schengen Accord" was adopted in 1990 between those Community countries which agreed to abolish border controls between themselves (starting with the Benelux countries). The removal of border controls required consistency between the participating countries in the exclusion of those regarded as undesirable, the treatment of aliens and asylum seekers, documentation for those who entered the area and policing of borders. If an individual had been expelled from one State or was regarded as an undesirable entrant the individual should not be able to enter via the territory of another participating state. The Schengen Accord covered these areas.

The Schengen Information System (SIS)

24–20 A core element in making the agreement workable was the agreement to share information and institute an "alert" system which would pick up any attempted entry by anyone in the categories regarded as a threat or undesirable or the movement of objects described as either stolen or lost. This was achieved by the pooling of information between the participating countries via the Schengen Information System (SIS). The Schengen system has also been developed to allow for the issue of short term visas and residence permits. Over the years the Schengen area was extended as Member States joined the Accord. Italy signed in 1990, Spain and Portugal in 1991, Greece in 1992, Austria in 1995 and Denmark, Sweden and Finland in 1996. There are parallel agreements with Iceland, Norway and Switzerland.

Under Schengen the participating countries agreed to share data on a range of matters. Unlike Europol there is no central unit which holds data or analyses intelligence. A copy of the entire Schengen database is held in each participating country and, while, there are also rules governing which data might be held, retention periods and the like, essentially each copy is subject to the laws of the holding country. The SIS became operational in March 1995. The Schengen acquis became partially applicable in Ireland in 2002 and the United Kingdom on December 22, 2004. The UK and Ireland only take part in respect of some aspects of Schengen, namely police and judicial co-operation in criminal matters and the fight against drugs, but will take part in SIS II when it comes on stream.

Iceland and Norway, which are non-EU States, are full members and Switzerland joined in 2005. The current SIS is not open to the accession States as its technical capacity is limited to 18 states. Thus the accession States are not currently part of the area without internal frontiers. Although they had to accept the Schengen acquis at accession not all the provisions of the acquis apply to them.

24-21 The SIS database holds records put in by each of the members which are then accessible to others. The SIS database is supported by separate SIRENE (supplementary information requests at the national entity) Bureaux in each State which provide, on request, more detailed information or intelligence. Under the Amsterdam Treaty immigration and visas became first pillar matters and the Schengen acquis (agreement plus a conglomeration of associated extensions and additional arrangements) was incorporated into the EU's institutional framework, with the Schengen Secretariat integrated into the General Secretariat of the Council. However as part of the function of the SIS is to maintain public security, amendments to the governing regime (the Schengen acquis), have to be achieved by parallel instruments based on the different pillars. The functions of the SIS were extended to assist with the fight against terrorism by a Council Regulation 871/2004 of April 29, 2004 and a Council Decision 2005/211 of February 24, 2005 both concerning the introduction of some new functions for the Schengen Information System, in particular in the fight against terrorism. These instruments amend the Schengen Convention to:

- give access to the SIS to Europol and the national members of Eurojust;
- extend the list of missing objects for which alerts can be registered to include boats, aircraft, containers, residence permits, registration certificates and means of payment;
- give access to the SIS to national authorities responsible for the investigation and prosecution of crime;
- require Member States to record all transmissions of personal data and extent the period for which records are kept to three years; and
- set out a common legal basis for the SIRENE network.

A second generation, more sophisticated, version of the Schengen Information System is being developed (SIS II) which will cover the new accession States, have additional capacity to provide crime-pattern analysis and profiling of offenders, deal with visa information and interface with the VIS and other systems. The legal basis for SIS II has been considered in a Commission proposal of June 3, 2005 on legal instruments which recognises its mixed functions which will cover police and judicial co-operation in criminal matters as well as its original role of the control of persons at external borders or national territories and the issue of short term visas. On December 20, 2006 the arrangements for the management, supervisory and data protection arrangements for SIS II were set out in Regulation 1987/2006. These are referred to in more detail later.

The development of SIS II shows how far the Schengen Information System has moved from the original purpose of external border control and the increased willingness of Member States to provide data for security and broadly related purposes since September 11.

Access and interoperability

24–22 On November 24, 2005 the Commission adopted a communication relating to the interoperability between SIS II, VIS and EURODAC. This looked forward in the longer term towards bringing together the various systems and considering how they could more effectively work in harmony to deal with crime and terrorism and facilitate the free movement of persons and the prevention of illegal immigration. The communication considers steps towards the adoption of a harmonised approach to biometric identifiers and data in the EU for all travellers.

EUROPOL

Police co-operation in Europe before Europol

24–23 As the Treaty of Rome did not cover policing, co-operation in policing matters evolved separately from mainstream Community development. "Interpol", which is an organisation based on co-operation between operational police forces, had been in existence for many years but is international rather than European. In addition it could not satisfy the growing pressures for information sharing and exchange. As noted above, the "Trevi Group" was established in 1975 consisting of the EC Ministers for Justice and Home Affairs with the aim of developing counter-terrorist measures. Over the years following its establishment its remit was gradually extended to cover police training and technology, serious crime, public order and disaster prevention.

As might be anticipated, pressures grew for a more sophisticated mutual policing arrangement and in 1991 the establishment of a European Police Office was proposed by Germany. Those proposals were taken forward by the Community in Maastricht.

Adoption of the Europol Convention

24–24 The German proposal for a European police unit was agreed in the Maastricht Treaty at Art.K.1 as one of the action areas of common interest thus:

> "police co-operation for the purposes of preventing and combating terrorism, unlawful drug trafficking and other serious forms of international crime, including if necessary certain aspects of customs co-operation, in connection with the organisation of a Union-wide system for exchanging information within a European Police Office (Europol)."

This has now been replaced by Art.29 which was noted above.

According to the Report of the Select Committee of the House of Lords on the European Communities (April 1995), these forms of crime were included in the Treaty not because they are the most serious of crimes, but because they display particular trans-border elements.

The headquarters of Europol are at The Hague in the Netherlands. As a precursor of Europol the Europol Drugs Unit (EDU) was established under Ministerial agreement and became operational in January 1994. The Ministerial agreement prohibited the storage of personal data in a central collection prior to the full Convention being agreed and coming into force. Thus the EDU common database was limited to holding only non-personal data. The initial role of the EDU was to exchange information about organised drug trafficking, but illicit trafficking in radioactive substances, clandestine immigration networks and illicit vehicle trafficking were added by a Justice and Home Affairs Council "Joint Action" in March 1995, followed by trafficking in human beings (which includes the sexual exploitation of children) in December 1996.

The terms of the Europol Convention were agreed between Member States in 1995. The recital to the Convention sums up the relationship between the Europol agreement and the Community thus:

> "Whereas the activities of Europol under this Convention are without prejudice to the powers of the European Communities; whereas Europol and the Communities have a mutual interest, in the framework of the European Union, in establishing types of co-operation enabling each of them to perform their respective tasks as efficiently as possible."

The Europol Convention was ratified by the United Kingdom in 1997, with the UK being the first Member State to ratify, and entered into force on October 1, 1998 at which date the EDU became Europol. However Art.45(4) of the Convention did not allow it to take up its activities until various rules and procedures under the Convention enter into force. These included the rules of procedure of the joint supervisory body (JSB) under Art.24(7). These were delayed because of a dispute between Member States over the status of the JSB but Europol commenced its full activities on July 1, 1999.

Role and nature of Europol

24–25 Europol is a supra-national organisation with legal personality. Its principal tasks are described in Art.3 of the Convention as being:

> "(1) to facilitate the exchange of information between Member States;
> (2) to obtain, collate and analyse information and intelligence;
> (3) to notify the competent authorities of Member States without delay via the national units referred to in Article 4 of information concerning them and of any connections identified between criminal offences;
> (4) to aid investigations in the Member States by forwarding all relevant information to the national units;
> (5) to maintain a computerised system of collected information containing data in accordance with Articles 8, 10 and 11."

It has an additional role to improve co-operation between Member States and assist through advice and research. However the manipulation of information, usually about living individuals, is its primary function. This restriction to the exchange of information sits uneasily with the political aim, described elsewhere in this chapter, to strengthen co-operation in the area of policing. Under the Hague programme the European Council urged Member States to give Europol the backing to play a central role in the fight against serious and organised crime and increase co-operation in operational policing. Under the European Constitution policing would fall under EU competence. While the Constitution languishes unresolved the best that the Council can do is exhort Member States to develop cross-border police co-operation in investigative techniques, forensic investigations, training and specific operations.

24–26   The criminal activities which fall under the Europol remit are set out in Art.2(2) as being unlawful drug trafficking, trafficking in nuclear and radioactive substances, illegal immigrant smuggling, trade in human beings and motor vehicle crime. It also deals with forgery of money and other means of payment and terrorist activities. Its competence extends to related crimes such as secondary offences. Since November 2000 it has dealt with money laundering regardless of the type of offence from which the money originates. Its role is involved where an organised criminal structure is in place and two or more Member States are involved.

24–27   Although Europol is not an operational force its role in operational matters in co-operation with national forces has developed. The European Council in June 1997 adopted recommendations which would give it "operative" powers. These would enable it to support operational activities by Member States and to ask Member States to conduct investigations in specific cases. In September 2000 the Council requested Member States to deal with requests from Europol to initiate or conduct investigations in specific cases and inform Europol of the results. The following month, November 2000, the Council asked Member States to utilise Europol support for joint investigative teams by supporting teams with analysis, advice and intelligence.

In December 2002, a draft protocol amending the Europol Convention was agreed by the Council. This would extend the remit of Europol to:

> "improve the effectiveness and co-operation of the competent authorities in the Member States in combating serious international crime where there are factual indications or reasonable grounds for believing that an organized criminal structure is involved and two or more Member States are affected in such a way as to require a common approach by the Member States owing to the scale, significance and consequences of the offences concerned."

A Supplemental Agreement has been reached between the United States and Europol on the exchange of personal data and related information.[14] Discussions are currently underway in One Council to replace the Europol Convention with a Council Decision.

The nature of the Europol Information System

24–28   The information system and the allocation of responsibilities for processing between Europol, the liaison officers and Member States are described in

---

[14] Reported at the meeting of the Justice and Home Affairs Council, December 2002.

this section. The computerised system maintained by Europol is covered explicitly in the Convention. It falls into three parts: the information system described in Arts 7 and 8, the work files described in Art.10 and the index system described in Art.11.

The various elements of the system were graphically described in the House of Lords Report as an outer and inner ring:

> "In the outer ring is information which can be directly extracted by Europol and by national units of Member States. Article 7 [now 8] describes the data which may be stored on the outer system. Only the unit which entered the data may amend, correct or delete it. Articles 10 10a and 11 describe the inner ring of sensitive data resulting from analysis by Europol."

Contents of the information system (Arts 7 and 8)

24–29 This holds identification, criminal intelligence and conviction information on the crimes within Europol's remit and related crime, that is related secondary offences such as procuring. The primary set of personal data held is prescribed and limited to names, date and place of birth, nationality, sex and identification information. Additional information may be held on the offences or suspected offences, modus operandi and suspected membership of criminal organisations.

Work files (Art.10)

24–30 As well as the identification intelligence record described in Arts 7 and 8 there is a system of analysis files which can hold a range of data on a wider number of associated persons such as contacts of the suspect, possible witnesses and victims of offences. The work files are to assist in particular criminal investigations. The investigation may be specific to a particular case or strategic, for example looking at the courier routes for drug-smuggling into Europe or analysing patterns of intelligence. The opening of a work file is governed by Art.12. The purpose and content of each work file must be specified and the approval of the Management Board of Europol gained before it can be opened.

Index system (Art.11)

24–31 The index system operates as a flag or marker on the outer ring to indicate there is further information in the inner ring but without giving away what it might be.

Allocation of information responsibilities between Europol and Member States

24–32 Each Member State must have a designated national unit which works with Europol (Arts 1(2) and (4)). In the United Kingdom this national unit is the Serious Organized Crime Agency. The national unit is subject to UK law. Information is supplied to the Europol system by the Member States' national unit. Each national unit must second at least one liaison officer to Europol. The liaison officers are instructed by the national units and their task is to assist in the exchange of information between the national unit and Europol by facilitating the necessary exchanges of information between the two. The liaison officers are subject to the national law of the seconding Member State (Art.5). The liaison officers work at Europol Headquarters in The Hague.

Only national units, liaison officers and appropriate Europol officials can input and retrieve data directly from the information system. Only the unit which entered the data can modify, correct or delete it. There are rules as to rectification of inaccuracies noted by another unit (Art.9). Europol can also obtain information from third parties, subject to safeguards, and can disclose to third parties, again subject to safeguards (Arts 10(4) and 18).

The provisions of the Convention for securing data protection compliance are analysed in the second part of this chapter.

Customs Information System

Background to the Convention

Aims of the Convention

24–33 The development of Customs co-operation has to be seen within the movement to harmonise the treatment of border issues described in the sections on Maastricht and Amsterdam above. The preamble to the Convention sets out the context of the Convention thus:

> "CONSIDERING that customs administrations are responsible, together with other competent authorities, at the external frontiers of the Community and within the territorial limits thereof, for the prevention, investigation and suppression of offences against not only Community rules, but also against national laws [. . .]
>
> CONSIDERING that a serious threat to public health, morality and security is constituted by the developing trend towards illicit trafficking of all kinds [. . .]
>
> Bearing in mind that the customs administrations in their day to day work have to implement both Community and non-Community provisions, and that there is consequently an obvious need to ensure that the provisions of mutual assistance and administrative co-operation in both sectors evolve as far as possible in parallel."

It will be noted from this that an important driver for the development of these arrangements is the need to co-operate to combat drug trafficking.

There has been co-operation between Customs authorities since the 1960s, however the Customs Information System (CIS) was not established until 1992. The Convention on the use of information technology for customs purposes was agreed in July 1995 under Art.K3(2)(c) of the Maastricht Treaty, that is as part of Title VI covering co-operation in justice and home affairs. It entered into force three months after a majority of Member States had ratified it. By December 1998 five states had ratified and it came into force in the first half of 1999. The UK Government designated the Data Protection Registrar the national supervisory authority on January 14, 1997 in an answer to a Parliamentary question.

Other use of the information system infrastructure

24–34   The infrastructure of the CIS system is also used for the exchange of information at Community level about "frauds and irregularities in the customs and agricultural domains" (Regulation 515/97). The provision for common usage is made by Commission Regulation 696/98 of March 27, 1998 implementing Council Regulation 515/97 on mutual assistance between the administrative authorities of the Member States. The use of a common infrastructure may be eminently practical but is legally fraught, as this element of the system falls within Community competence and is therefore a first pillar matter. This complicates the data protection supervisory arrangements as post-Amsterdam these become the responsibility of the new European Data Protection Supervisor.

Nature of the Convention

24–35   Unlike Europol the Customs Convention does not involve the establishment of a separate legal organisation. To that extent the arrangements are much simpler than those for Europol. The database is set up and supervised by the Commission (Art.3(2)). The Commission is responsible for the technical management of the facility. It reports to a Committee of representatives of the Member States' Customs' Administrations set up under Art.16. The Management Committee must ensure that the terms of the Convention are carried out and that the system functions properly, technically and operationally. Thus it is responsible for maintaining the standards for information and security set out in Arts 12 and 19 respectively. The Committee reports to the Council of Ministers of the Community.

The aims of the CIS are set out in Art.2(2) as being:

> ". . . in accordance with the provisions of this Convention, . . . to assist in preventing, investigating and prosecuting serious contravention of the national laws by increasing, through the rapid dissemination of information, the effectiveness of the co-operation and control procedures of the customs administrations of Member States."

The Information System

24–36   The CIS consists of a computerised network with a dedicated database of information which allows customs enforcement organisations throughout the Community to exchange information. There are terminals at ports and entry points to the Community. The central database is accessible via terminals in every Member State. The data included can cover personal data but restrictions are placed upon the nature of the personal data which can be held and the purposes for which they can be used. The purposes are limited to:

    (a) sighting and reporting;

    (b) carrying out discreet surveillance; or

    (c) specific checks, for the purposes of investigating customs matters concerning:

        (i) commodities;

    (ii) means of transport;
    (iii) businesses;
    (iv) persons,

where there are real indications to suggest that the person has committed, is in the act of committing or will commit, serious contraventions of national laws (Arts 3 and 5). The relevant national laws are those dealing with the movement of prohibited or restricted goods within the Treaty (very broadly, dangerous goods) and anything related to drug trafficking (Art.1). The personal data which can be held are set out in Art.4. They must not include data in the sensitive categories set out in Art.6 of Treaty 108 and in any event must not cover more than name, date and place of birth, nationality, sex, physical description, warning codes for dangerous persons, reason for inclusion of the data and suggested actions.

Joint Secretariat

24–37 A Council Decision of October 17, 2000 established a secretariat for the joint supervisory data protection bodies set up by the Europol Convention, the CIS Convention and the Schengen Convention. The secretary is appointed for three years and is responsible to the joint supervisory bodies. The decision has applied from September 2001.

VIS—Visa Information System

24–38 The development of co-operation over policing and judicial matters was given an additional impetus by the events of September 11, 2001. One of the most significant issues to be addressed has been the pressure on the external borders of the EU which is a source of grave concern to Member States. The issue of visas at borders is now to be supported by the VIS.

Note: the Channel Islands and the Isle of Man are not covered by the conventions but may choose to subscribe to them.

The introduction of a uniform EU short-term visa valid throughout the territory of the participating Member States was an important element of the Schengen Convention. Visa control became part of the first pillar after the Treaty of Amsterdam and since then the EU has taken forward the uniform visa policy including establishing lists of countries whose nationals require visas, uniform procedures and EU-wide agreements with other States. Despite the efforts towards harmonisation there remain significant problems with visas resulting in the proposal for a uniform system to reduce visa fraud. The VIS was established by Council Decision 2004/512 of June 2004[15] to support the common visa policy of the Union. The Regulation sets out the legal basis for the development of the system and its inclusion in the EU budget but does not deal with operational issues, supervision or safeguards: The aim of the system is the reduction of document fraud in visas (counterfeiting and falsification of visas) and the practice of "visa shopping", that is simultaneously submitting applications in different Member States.[16] The VIS will be

---

[15] [2004] O.J. L213 of June 15, 2004, p.0005–0007.
[16] See *http://www.europarl.europa.eu* [Accessed on September 2, 2007] for debates of Parliament on this topic.

one of the largest cross-border systems. It will contain the details of all those who apply for a Schengen visa (a short term visa) as well as long term visa, amounting to around some 20 million new entries every year. The United Kingdom and Ireland do not participate in the common visa policy and the VIS Regulation do not apply to them. However they will have access to the data for limited purposes.

The Decision is to be implemented by a Regulation of the Parliament and the Council (the VIS Regulation) as a first pillar measure. In December 2004 the Commission adopted a proposal for the Regulation accompanied by an Extended Impact Assessment (EIA). This proposal set out the proposed operational arrangements in respect of the system and the accompanying data protection safeguards. The proposal was submitted to the EDPS who provided an Opinion on the proposal in July 2005.[17] No further documents are yet publicly available so the final arrangements and data protection safeguards are not known however it is perhaps unlikely that there will be much variation between the proposal and the final arrangements.

The central information system will store data on all visas including those applied for, issued, rejected and cancelled. There will be a national system in each Member State that will facilitate checks at external borders and within Member States.

24–39   Data will be collected on applicants for visas and stored on the central system. The data will include

- identifying information about the applicant;

- nationality and place and country of birth;

- information on the visa and travel documents;

- destination and purpose of travel.

Fingerprints and photographs will be part of the data to be stored. There will be a central information system and an interface in each Member State. The interface will provide the connection to the relevant central national authority in the Member State and the connection to the central information system.

Proposed data protection arrangements

24–40   The processing carried out in the central system will be subject to Regulation 45/2001 and the processing carried out in each Member State subject to the national legislation which implents Directive 95/46. The relationship between these two was one of the points which the EDPS recommended should be clarified.

Under the proposal the categories of data to be retained will be specified as will the different processing operations which will be possible (entering data, consulting it, amending and so on) together with the authorities which will have access to the data for the purposes of the system. The retention period would be five years and strict security and access controls would be in place. Subject access would be through the Member State as would the exercise of any other individual rights.

In his Opinion the EDPS stresses the importance of the purpose limitation in the system, distinguishing between the purpose of the system and the other, incidental

---

[17] [2005] O.J.C181/6.

benefits, but emphasising that access and use must be related to the core purpose. The EDPS states that he favours the introduction of biometric identifiers provided there are adequate safegurds provided and judged that the VIS proposal complies with data protection standards subject to the acceptance of a list of recommendations to clarify and tighten the supervisory regime. Given that the system will hold biometric identifiers the impetus for law enforcement authorities to have routine access will be strong.

At the time of writing the revised proposal has not been published.

Access to the VIS for law enforcement

24–41 In line with the developing policy to maximise access to all relevant information for law enforecment purposes, in November 2005 the Commission presented a proposal for a Council Decision giving access to the VIS to national authorities responsible for internal security and Europol for the purposes of the prevention, detection and investigation of terrorist offences and the types of crimes and offences in respect of which Europol is competent to act.[18] The UK and Ireland would be allowed to access the data despite the fact that they do not take part in the common visa policy. This proposal was made under Title VI and therefore outside Regulation 45/2001. As a result the proposal includes detailed data protection provisions. The EDPS was invited to deliver an Opinion and issued a further Opinion on this proposal in January 2006[19] in which he drew attention to the problems involved with granting access to first pillar databases to law enforcement agencies, saying:

> "One must bear in mind that the VIS is an information system developed in view of the European visa policy and not as a law enforcement tool. Routine access would indeed represent a serious violation of the principle of purpose limitation."

Under the proposal:

- authorities responsible for internal security and Europol would have access to the VIS;

- access would only be allowed for the purpose of prevention, detection and investigation of terrorist offences and other serious criminal offences;

- each Member State would have to designate a single national unit with responsibility for consultation with the VIS, as would Europol;

- access must be justifiable in each case and would only be avaialable on a case-by-case basis;

- the further transfer or disclosure of data from the VIS is restricted;

- full records of the access, reasons for the access and authority for access must be kept.

There are also monitoring and evaluation provisions.

---

[18] COM (2005) 600 Final.
[19] Opinion of the European Data Protection Supervisor on COM (2005) 600 final.

Data Protection safeguards proposed for access provisions

24–42 It is proposed that the access by Europol should be subject to the data protection standards in the Europol Convention, access by the European Commission or other institutions should be subject to Regulation 45/2001 and other access should be subject to the Proposal for a Council Framework Decision on the protection of personal data processed in the framework of police and judicial co-operation in criminal matters.[20] Article 13 of the draft would make the entry into force of the Framework Decision a condition precedent to the introduction of the Decision on access.

The Framework Decision on the protection of personal data was put forward as the conmomitant instrument to accompany the Proposal for a Council Framework Decision on the exchange of information under the principle of availability.[21] The twin proposals have been adopted by the Commission[22] but have since progressed only slowly and there is no guarantee that the Framework Decision on the protection of personal data will be adopted. If it is not adopted then some other data protection standards instrument would have to be referenced in the access provisions.

The access regime itself is restricted as set out above. In addition a sub-committee of the Article 31 Working Party (not the Article 29 Working Party) would have a reviewing role and the relevant data protection supervisory authorities in the Member States would be under an obligation to investigate and report on the lawfulness of the processing of personal data under the regime at least once annually.

This is yet another of the proposals for increased access to personal data originally gathered for other purposes. It is not clear at the time of writing whether it will be carried forward or how.

The EDPS in his Opinion suggests that the access proposal to the VIS is a precursor for access rights to other systems and should therefore be taken seriously as it may be a precedent. In suggesting improvements he particularly recommends that:

- the conditions for access to the data should require that the access would contribute "substantially" to dealing with a specific case;

- the purpose of travel and the photograph of the visa holder or applicant should only be avialable as supplementary information;

- self-auditing requiremetns for data protection comliance should be introduced.

UK BORDERS

24–43 Although the UK does not share the common visa policy it has a separate project to control access and to record the details of every traveller to and from the UK. The system, referred to as eBorders, will record all movements. It is assumed that it would be subject to the UK Data Protection Act 1998 and no other special form of regulation. We have not been able to trace any public statements on the data protection supervisory provisions, or rules on access to the eBorders data.

---

[20] COM (2005) 475.
[21] COM (2005) 490.
[22] October 4, 2005.

European passports

24–44 On December 13, 2004 the Council adopted a Regulation creating an obligation on Member States to include biometrics in passports. Member States will have to issue passports that include:

- a digital photograph within 18 months of entry into force of the provision; and

- digital fingerprints 36 months after entry into force.

Eurojust

24–45 Eurojust is the mechanism by which the EU seeks to facilitate judicial co-operation over investigation and prosecution in criminal matters. In many States there is judicial oversight of the investigation process. There is clearly the possibility of some overlap between Europol and Eurojust and a need for the two organisations to work together. Eurojust was recognised in the EU Treaty of Nice in December 2000[23] and subsequently established up by Council Decision of February 28, 2002[24] as a body of the EU with legal personality. Eurojust has its headquaters at the Hague. The role of Eurojust is to improve the way that requests for legal assistance between States are handled, extradition requests are implemented, requests for assistance and information are dealt with and generally make cross-border work on investigations and prosecutions more efficient.

Eurojust can deal with the range of crimes covered by Europol plus computer crime, fraud and corruption, money laundering, environmental crime, organised crime and any associated offences. There must be a cross-border aspect to the investigation.

It consists of a College made up of members drawn from the judiciary of the Member States. The College is responsible for working with the national members. The College may carry out various tasks such as setting up joint investigations or passing on information. It appears that Eurojust as an organisation has no power over national judicial or policing organisations but is limited to asking national authorities for co-operation, for example over joint investigations.

Its powers to deal with information however are rather more extensive. It must establish an index of the investigations in which it is concerned and associated work files including personal data of suspects and witnesses and victims. It has powers to disclose information including the power to disclose information to international bodies or organisations or non-EU States for the purposes of its functions. Disclosure must be approved by the national member from the country which contributed the data and will be subject to requirements of adequate protection in the receiving jurisdiction, although there are exceptions where required in emergencies to "counter imminent serious danger threatening a peerson or public security". The handling of personal data is subject to a specific data protection regime in the Decision and more detailed rules which may be adopted by the College.

---

[23] Amendment of Art.31 of the EU Treaty.
[24] 2002/187/JHA [2002] O.J. L63, March 6, 2002, p.1.

Data Protection Supervisory arrangements

24–46 Eurojust has its own individual supervisory scheme for data protection. It is not subject to Regulation 2001/45 or the supervision of the EDPS. The Decision sets out the role of the Data Protection Officer and the application of the data protection principles to Eurojust. Articles 14–22 of the Decision set out the data protection standards which Eurojust must achieve; Art.23 provides for the establishment of an independent joint supervisory body with an obligation to monitor the level of compliance achieved by Eurojust with these standards; Art.24 provides that Eurojust may be liable for damage to individulas caused by unauthorised or incorrect processing of personal data in accor with the national law of the state in which it is situated. The range of personal data that may be processed for its purposes is specified[25] but may be extended in exceptional circumstances. If either sensitive personal data or an extended range of data are held the Data Protection Officer must be notified. This official must be appointed by Eurojust and be granted a degree of independence of operation.[26] He must ensure that the rules are followed, that records of disclosures are maintained and deal with requests for subject acccess. In the event of non-compliance he may refer the matter to the joint supervisory body if the College does not deal with it to his satisfaction. The Decision deals with:

- rights of subject access, procedure and exemptions from the right of access[27];

- correction and deletion of personal data;

- time limits for the storage of personal data; and

- data security standards.

In addition the College may adopt rules of procedure on the processing and protection of personal data which must be approved by the Council. The College exercised this power in October 2004 and Council approval followed in February 2005.[28]

EURODAC

24–47 The Dublin Convention on asylum of June 15, 1990 contained provisions to deal with determining which Member State was responsible for asylum seekers in the Community. As it pre-dated the Treaty of Maastricht it was not a third pillar instrument, although it covers third pillar areas and was made between Member States. It set out a framework within which applications for asylum could be considered by one Member State. It sought to ensure that applicants for asylum were not shuffled from one county to another and that applicants were not able to make multiple applications within the Community. Article 15 provided for the communication and sharing of information on applicants among the States but was not specific as to the information to be shared. If Member States wished to computerise all or part of the information

---

[25] Decision Arts 15 and 16.
[26] Decision Art.17.
[27] Decision Art.19.
[28] [2005] O.J. C68, March 19, 2003, p.0001–0010.

held for the purposes of determining applications and implementing the Convention they would have to have in place laws equivalent to Treaty 108 and an independent supervisory authority. The Dublin Convention was due to come into effect in September 1995 but was never fully implemented because of changes in both the institutional position of its subject-matter and political decisions on how to deal with asylum and associated areas.

A Declaration on asylum was included in 1 of the 33 declarations at the end of the Maastricht Treaty. These declarations did not have legal force but were significant policy statements. In this they highlighted the determination to work to a harmonised asylum policy throughout the Community. Following on from Maastricht further work was carried out on the proposed co-operation and information-sharing with a new draft third pillar Convention published in 1996 (8665/5/96). The draft related to the proposed establishment of EURODAC:

> "for the collection, storage, exchange and comparison of fingerprints of applicants for asylum in connection with Article 15 of the . . . Dublin Convention."

The proposal was similar in form to the Customs Information System, a common database with restrictions upon the data which may be put into it, restrictions on its use by participating States, rules about accuracy, access and individual rights and provisions for national and joint supervisory bodies. Subsequently the proposal was extended by the addition of a protocol which dealt with illegal immigrants in the Community. Under this protocol the fingerprints of both asylum seekers and persons "apprehended for an irregular border crossing" were to be taken and passed to EURODAC if the person was at least 14 years old and the data were to be retained for comparison with any subsequent asylum application. The UK and Ireland opted into EURODAC.

Work on EURODAC stalled over a number of issues, such concerns as the extension of fingerprinting to an unknown number of illegal immigrants and the minimum age for fingerprinting. As asylum is one of the areas which moved to the first pillar following the arrangements adopted after ratification of the Amsterdam Treaty the proposals were held in abeyance until after the legal basis and procedures for handling instruments in the area changed. EURODAC now takes effect as a first pillar measure under Council Regulation of December 11, 2000. It has been implemented by a further Council Regulation in February 2002, referred to as the Dublin II Regulation.

The Regulation establishes a series of criteria for allocating responsibility for examining an asylum application to the Member State that permitted the applicant to enter or reside. That Member State is responsible for examining the asylum application and has to take back its applicants who are in other Member States without permission.

How the system works

24–48　The following description is taken from SCADPlus and it should be noted that the database does not contain the name and address of asylum seekers, relying on an Automated Fingerprint Identification System (AFIS):

> "Eurodac consists of a Central Unit within the Commission equipped with a computerized central database for comparing the fingerprints of asylum applicants

and a system for electronic data transmission between Member States and the database.

In addition to fingerprints, data sent by Member States will include in particular the Member State of origin, the place and date of the asylum application if applicable, sex and reference number. Data are collected for anyone over 14 years of age and are encoded directly into the database by the Central Unit or the Member State of origin.

In the case of asylum seekers, data are kept for 10 years unless the individual obtains the citizenship of one of the Member States, when their particulars are immediately erased. Data relating to foreign nationals apprehended when attempting to cross an external border irregularly are kept for two years from the date on which the fingerprints were taken. Data are immediately erased before the end of the two years if the foreign national receives a residence permit, or has left the territory of the Member State

In the case of foreign nationals found illegally present within a Member State, Eurodac makes it possible to check their fingerprints against those in the central database to determine whether the individual has previously lodged an asylum application in another Member State. After the fingerprints have been transmitted for comparison purposes they are not stored by Eurodac."

The data protection supervisory role falls to the EDPS as described above and the applicable standards are those set out in the Directive.

DATA PROTECTION SUPERVISION OF THE SHARED DATABASES

Introduction

24–49   There are valid criticisms to be made of the data protection supervisory arrangements for these various supra-national information-sharing initiatives. They are complex and relatively obscure. It is difficult for those on whom data are held to understand or exercise their data protection rights under these various instruments. The development of co-operative arrangement has been criticised for being undertaken without putting human rights safeguards in place.

Schengen Information System—Data Protection Supervisory Arrangements

24–50   The Schengen Information System (SIS) is an alert system. It allows participating countries to access the SIS to check for alerts on:

"persons and property for the purposes of border checks and other police and customs checks carried out within the country in accordance with national law and, in the case of the specific category of alerts referred to in Article 96, for the purposes of issuing visas, residence permits and the administration of legislation on aliens in the context of the application of the provisions of this Convention relating to the movement of persons."[29]

---

[29] Convention of June 19, 1990 implementing the Schengen Agreement of June 14, 1985, Art.92. Convention as last amended O.J. L191, June 22, 2005, p.18.

The purpose of the SIS is to:

> "maintain public policy and public security, including national security, in the territories of the Contracting Parties and to apply the provisions of this Convention relating to the movement of persons in those territories, using information communicated via this system."[30]

Each country can issue an alert and the central processing support facility immediately copies this to every other SIS database. Alerts fall into different categories. Article 102 restricts the use of alerts to the purposes for which they were registered. Every tenth transmission of personal data is checked to audit whether the search is for an admissible purpose under Schengen.[31]

The UK is not a full member of the Schengen accord but takes part in relation to several aspects including judicial co-operation, drugs co-operation, Arts 26 and 27 and police co-operation.[32] The data protection arrangements described below are binding on the UK and the UK takes part in the supervisory arrangements.

The copy of the SIS in each country and the use of alerts are governed by the national data protection law in force in that country unless the Schengen Convention itself lays down more stringent measures. The party issuing the alert is responsible for the accuracy of the data[33] and only that party can modify, add to or delete the data which it has entered. There are provisions for resolving differences over the accuracy of data entered by different parties and if resolution is not possible the matter will be referred to the joint supervisory body for resolution.[34]

The Convention requires participating States to have in place national law which meets the standards of the Council of Europe Convention for the Protection of Individuals with regard to Automatic Processing of Personal Data of January 28, 1981 and Recommendation R(87)15 of September 17, 1987 of the Committee of Ministers of the Council of Europe regulating the use of personal data in the police sector. No data could be transferred until such legislation was in place.[35]

24–51   Individual rights of access are exercisable in accordance with the national law.[36] Access can be refused either because such refusal is "indispensable for the performance of a lawful task in connection with the alert or for the protection of rights and freedoms of third parties". Individuals can seek correction of inaccurate data and bring action before the national courts for rectification of data held on the SIS or seek compensation in accordance with the national law.

There are restrictions on the time for which data in the various categories may be retained on the database, usually three years, but the period is longer for some material and may be extended if the circumstances warrant such extension.[37]

---

[30] *ibid.*, Art.93.
[31] *ibid.*, Art.103.
[32] Council Decision 2000/365 of May 29, 2000 and Council Decision 2004/926 of December 22, 2004.
[33] *ibid.* (n.29), Art.105.
[34] *ibid.*, Art.106.
[35] *ibid.*, Art.117.
[36] *ibid.*, Art.109.
[37] *ibid.*, Art.114.

Each participating State must designate a supervisory authority responsible for carrying out independent supervision of the data file of the national section of the SIS in accordance with national law and for checking that the processing and use of data entered in the SIS does not violate the rights of the data subject. For this purpose, the supervisory authority must have access to the data file of the national section of the SIS.

Individuals have the right to ask the supervisory authorities to check data which relate to them entered in the SIS and the use made of such data. That right is governed by the national law of the participating State to which the request is made. If the data have been entered by another State the check must be carried out in close co-ordination with that Contracting Party's supervisory authority.[38]

The joint supervisory authority which is responsible for supervising the technical support function of the SIS consists of two representatives from each national supervisory authority. Each Contracting Party has one vote. The standards for supervision are those set out in the Schengen Convention itself, those set out in the Council of Europe Convention of January 28, 1981 for the Protection of Individuals with regard to the Automatic Processing of Personal Data, taking into account Recommendation R(87)15 of September 17, 1987 of the Committee of Ministers of the Council of Europe regulating the use of personal data in the police sector, and those set out in the national law of the Contracting Party responsible for the technical support function. The national law is the French law as the database is supported from Strasbourg.

The joint supervisory authority is responsible for checking that the provisions of the Convention are properly implemented in respect of the technical support function. In order to achieve this task the members have access to the technical support function.

24–52   The joint supervisory authority is also responsible for examining any difficulties of application or interpretation that may arise during the operation of the SIS, for studying any problems that occur with the exercise of independent supervision by the national supervisory authorities or in the exercise of the right of access to the system, and for drawing up harmonised proposals for joint solutions to existing problems. Reports drawn up by the joint supervisory authority are submitted to the authorities to which the national supervisory authorities submit their reports.[39]

Each State is responsible, in accordance with its national law, for any injury caused to a person through the use of the national data file of the SIS. If an individual suffers injury because of the issue of an alert, because another State party entered inaccurate data or stored data unlawfully the national authority is still liable but is entitled to reimbursement of any sums paid out as compensation.[40]

Under Art.118 a participating State undertakes, in relation to its national section of the SIS, to adopt the necessary measures in order to:

(a)   deny unauthorised persons access to data-processing equipment used for processing personal data (equipment access control);

(b)   prevent the unauthorised reading, copying, modification or removal of data media (data media control);

---

[38] *ibid.*, Art.114.
[39] *ibid.*, Art.115.
[40] *ibid.*, Art.116.

(c) prevent the unauthorised input of data and the unauthorised inspection, modification or deletion of stored personal data (storage control);

(d) prevent the use of automated data-processing systems by unauthorised persons using data communication equipment (user control);

(e) ensure that persons authorised to use an automated data-processing system only have access to the data covered by their access authorisation (data access control);

(f) ensure that it is possible to verify and establish to which bodies personal data may be transmitted using data communication equipment (communication control);

(g) ensure that it is subsequently possible to verify and establish which personal data have been input into automated data-processing systems and when and by whom the data were input (input control);

(h) prevent the unauthorised reading, copying, modification or deletion of personal data during transfers of personal data or during transportation of data media (transport control).

Special measures must be taken to ensure the security of data while they are being communicated to services located outside the territories of the Contracting Parties. Such measures must be notified to the joint supervisory authority. Staff who process data in the national section of the SIS must have undergone appropriate security checks and be properly trained.

The Information Commissioner is the United Kingdom's designated national supervisory authority for the SIS and attends the Joint Supervisory Authority as an observer.[41]

Doubts were cast on the quality of the data entered onto the SIS in a study conducted in 2005. The Joint Supervisory Authority of Schengen decided to review the processes adopted for the reporting of unwanted aliens to SIS. They asked relevant national authorities to evaluate whether reporting complied with the Schengen Convention. According to the report submitted by the Danish Data Protection Agency out of the 443 cases referred 22 had been wrongly reported, a further 17 had had data wrongly keyed in, and a further 7 had later been the subject of updated information which had not been passed on. There were also problems with compliance with procedures and the quality of data. The Danish National Commissioner was reported to have taken steps to correct the problems.

SIS II

24–53   The decision to develop the next generation of the Schengen system has been described earlier. There were three proposals for the legal basis of SIS II which would provide the legal framework for the single information-sharing system. The detailed arrangements for SIS II have now been set out in Regulation 1987/2006 on the establishment, operation and use of the second generation SIS. As the UK is a participant in

---

[41] *Annual report of the Information Commissioner.*

the SIS II (although not a full participant) the data entry and supervisory arrangements will apply to the UK. The regulation sets out the categories of data that can be entered on to the system, the purposes of use, the criteria for entry, authorised access and the rules on data protection.

SIS II will have a central management body responsible for the system. It will have a central system, national applications and interfaces between the two. It will hold alerts for those to whom entry to the EU will be refused. These alerts should generally be automatically be removed after three years although they may be retained longer on a case-by-case basis. Biometrics may be part of the data to ensure correct identification.

The central system will be based in Strasbourg and will be subject to Regulation 45/2001 while the national applications will be subject to the standards in Directive 95/46 in the Member States. Supervision will be exercised in a similar way with the national application subject to the national data protection supervisory authority and the central system subject to the EDPS. Access is limited to the purposes of border control, including police and customs control, but access for other purposes, including criminal proceedings may be given subject to judicial authority.[42] However data processed on SIS II must not be transferred or made available to third countries or international organisations.[43]

Responsibility for the accuracy of data rests with the national authority which enters it on to the system and there are procedures to exchange information and reconcile difference between different entries.[44]

Individuals will have rights of subject access plus rights of rectification and compensation in relation to inaccurate data. Subject access is the responsibility of the Member States but if the application is made to a State other than the one which issued the alert the issuing State must be consulted. Exemptions from subject access are available to protect the rights and freedoms of others.[45]

The supervisory authorities must ensure that the national arrangements are audited every four years. There is, as yet, no indication of how the UK will deal with these supervisory obligations.

EUROPOL—DATA PROTECTION SUPERVISORY ARRANGEMENTS

Development of data protection standards in the area of policing

24–54 Just as European co-operation in policing and justice matured so did European work on maintaining the rights of individuals in a data-rich policing environment. Following on from the adoption of Treaty 108 by the Council of Europe in 1981 (see Ch.1, above), its Committee of Experts continued to work on formulating recommendations for signatory States to follow in specific areas of concern. Policing was one of those areas and in 1987 the Council of Europe agreed Recommendation R(87)15 of the Committee of Ministers to Member States regulating the use of personal data in the police sector. This has proved to be both enduring and ubiquitous. The Recommendation itself, or reference to it, appears in several instruments. Together

---

[42] Art.27.
[43] Art.39.
[44] Arts 34 and 35.
[45] Arts 41, 42, 43.

with Treaty 108 it set the standard required for participating countries in the Schengen arrangements. It is a part of the standard setting mechanism for Europol. It is referred to explicitly in both documents. Consideration has been given to up-dating the Recommendation however no changes have been deemed necessary. Despite the popularity of reference to R(87)15 it is not clear how much influence it has on day-to-day policing, for example it does not appear in the United Kingdom's Association of Chief Police Officers Data Protection Code of Practice.

In view of its ubiquity it is examined at the end of the chapter in some detail. It is based on Treaty 108 and sets out specific recommendations in applying the standards of Treaty 108 to data held for policing. The Recommendation covers the core safeguards provided by data protection; purpose limitation; individual rights of access and independent supervision. However it is expressed in general terms. The provisions in the Europol Convention are particularised.

Data protection standards—outline

24–55   The data protection arrangements for Europol are rather complicated. To put it broadly the data processing responsibilities are split three ways, between Europol itself, the national liaison officers and the national units. Different data protection compliance standards and supervisory mechanisms apply to each one. The provisions can be broken down as follows:

(a) rules in the Convention which apply to the processing of personal data by Europol itself;

(b) rules in the Convention which apply to the processing of personal data used for Europol purposes by Member States;

(c) rules in the Convention which apply to the processing of personal data by liaison officers of Member States;

(d) a requirement that Europol itself takes account of Treaty 108 and Recommendation R(87)15 in handling personal data;

(e) a requirement that all Member States have national law equivalent to Treaty 108;

(f) a requirement that all Member States take account of Recommendation R(87)15 in their national laws;

(g) a requirement that Member States contribute members to the joint supervisory body which "oversees" data protection compliance within Europol;

(h) a requirement that each Member State designates a supervisory body for its national participants in Europol to supervise their compliance with national data protection standards.

Data protection standards

24–56   Responsibility for observing data protection rules for data stored at Europol, in particular as regards the legality of the collection, the transmission to Europol and the input of data as well as their accuracy, their up-to-date nature and verification of their storage time limits lies with the Member State which input or communicated the data insofar as the data came from a Member State but for other data which might have been collected by Europol for third parties or result from their analyses it rests with Europol (Art.15(1)).

Europol is responsible for the data that it holds and processes in accordance with the rules set out in the Convention itself. Europol must store the data it receives in such a way that it is clear which Member State has contributed it (Art.15(2) and (3)).

In addition, every Member State has to designate a national supervisory body which must independently monitor the permissibility of the input, retrieval and communication of the Member State to Europol in accordance with its national law and ensure that the liaison unit is acting in accordance with the national law in doing so (Art.23).

The standard for Europol

24–57　If the Convention set a particular standard for data protection compliance for Europol itself then it should comply with that. (The mechanism to require compliance may be imperfect but the standard is clear enough.) If the Convention sets no standard then the residual standard of data protection is incorporated by Art.14 as Treaty 108 and Recommendation R(87)15. Europol is to "take account" of these.

There has been criticism of this uneven requirement. However, on the other hand, the Convention itself sets out data protection safeguards and this is the primary instrument of control.

Data protection standards in the body of the Europol Convention

24–58　Management Board approval is required before a data file can be opened[46] and the use of Europol data by Member States is restricted[47] as is the ability to link the Europol computer with other computers.[48]

The only liaison with Member States is to be through the liaison unit and liaison officers are limited in their rights to consult Europol work files.[49]

The content of the information system is defined and limited and restrictions are imposed on the purposes for which data may be collected and used by Europol.[50] There are restrictions on data input and rules as to modification, correction, deletion of data[51] as well as rules on the correction of data by Europol.[52] Any liability for damage caused by inaccuracy lies with the Member State in whose jurisdiction the damage occurred.[53]

The time limit for storage of data files is three years with provision for review after that period. Report data must be deleted after six months.[54]

---

[46] Art.12.
[47] Art.17.
[48] Art.6(2).
[49] Art.4(2).
[50] Art.5.
[51] Arts 2, 3 and 10.
[52] Art.9(2).
[53] Art.20.
[54] Art.38.

Requests for subject access must be made to Member States and passed on to Europol. The Convention includes rules to deal with such requests and provisions for appeals.[55]

Access to the information system is restricted and there are requirements for security measures for Europol to protect data[56] as well as requirements of confidentiality and discretion.[57]

As is clear from the above the standards in the Convention mirror, and to large extent meet, the standards in Directive 95/46. Concerns that the standards of data protection compliance for Europol are insufficient therefore may be overstated. However, concerns that the supervisory mechanisms for ensuring that Europol itself complies with those standards are insufficient are better founded. The supervisory mechanisms are dealt with below.

The standard for Member States

24–59   Each Member State must have in its national law a standard of data protection which corresponds to Treaty 108 and also must take account of Recommendation R(87)15. The references to Treaty 108 and the Recommendation are however somewhat misleading when applied to the UK situation. The basic rule is that the national units must comply with the national law. A UK court would therefore have to apply the UK national law rather than Treaty 108 or any other instrument. In the unlikely event of a conflict between the national law and the Convention, the UK courts would be bound to apply the national law.

Personal data cannot be passed to a Member State until it has ratified the Convention having passed national law which complies with the Recommendation and Treaty 108.

Independent supervision of data protection standards

24–60   The Convention not only sets out the required standards for data protection but also requires a supervisory mechanism for those standards. Article 16 contains a self-audit mechanism under which Europol has to check 1 in 10 retrievals from the information system for data protection compliance.

Role of the Joint supervisory body

24–61   An independent joint supervisory body oversees the activities of Europol to ensure that the rights of individuals are not violated by the data processing carried out by Europol and to monitor the transmission of data by Europol to third parties. The joint supervisory body is made up of two representatives of each national supervisory body. Europol must assist the joint supervisory body with its work and respond to requests for information. The joint supervisory body also appears to have jurisdiction to advise the national supervisory bodies and individuals may complain direct to the joint supervisory body (JSB) (Art.24(4)). The JSB has no hard enforcement powers. It exercises its oversight through a system of reports and recommendations. It acts as a form of appellate body in respect of refused subject access requests which have been

---

[55] Art.21.
[56] Art.16.
[57] Art.10.

made for Europol data and requests to correct or delete data which have been refused (Arts 19(7) and 20(4)). It has considered several complaints and delivered appeal judgments on it. If the JSB notes a violation of the convention in relation to data protection matters it may refer the issue to the Director General of Europol and request a reply from him. It must report regularly to the Council and may chose to publish its reports. The JSB has met and formulated rules to govern its own procedures. The Commissioner is the UK representative.

Supervision by the national supervisory authority

24–62 As noted above, the national units and the liaison officers are under an obligation to comply with the national law. Article 23 requires that:

> "1. Each Member State shall designate a national supervisory body, the task of which shall be to monitor independently, in accordance with its respective national law, the permissibility of the input, the retrieval and any communication to Europol of personal data by the Member State concerned and to examine whether this violates the rights of the data subject. For this purpose the supervisory body shall have access at the national unit or at the liaison officer's premises to the data entered by the Member State in the information system and in the index system in accordance with the relevant national procedures. For their supervisory purposes, national supervisory bodies shall have access to the offices and documents of their respective liaison officers at Europol. In addition, in accordance with the relevant national procedures, the national supervisory bodies shall supervise the activities of national units under Article 4(4) and the activities of liaison officers under Article 5(3), points 1 and 3, and Article 5(4) and (5), in so far as such activities are of relevance to the protection of personal data.
>
> 2. Each individual shall have the right to request the national supervisory body to ensure that the entry or communication of data concerning him to Europol in any form and the consultation of the data by the Member State concerned are lawful. This right shall be exercised in accordance with the national law of the Member State to the national supervisory body of which the request is made."

The obligations on the national supervisory authority can be regarded as threefold:

(a) to oversee the standards of data entered by the Member State;

(b) to oversee the activities of the liaison officers and the national units in handling the personal data involved;

(c) to check on behalf of individuals whether personal data is processed to the correct standards.

In each case, the compliance standard is to the national law. In the United Kingdom the national unit is the Serious Organised Crime Agency established under the Serious Organised Crime and Police Act 2005. The Commissioner is the national supervisory authority.

Beneath the Convention there are a number of sets of rules governing specific areas. These are:

- rules applicable to Europol analysis files;
- rules and obligations of liaison officers;
- rules on the confidentiality of Europol information;
- financial regulations;
- rules concerning the receipt of information by Europol from third parties;
- rules governing the transmission of personal data by Europol to third States and third parties;
- rules governing Europol's external relations with European Union related bodies;
- rules governing Europol's external relations with third States and non-European Union related bodies;
- public access to Europol documents.

UK concerns about Europol

24–63 Europol involves the collection of vast pools of personal data. Inevitably it has been of concern to data protection authorities and those concerned with civil liberties since its inception. In 1994 the House of Lords Select Committee on the European Communities reported to Parliament on the then draft Convention. The Report examined widespread concern not only with the contents of the Convention but with the way the EDU had expanded its activities without any formal legal basis.

The UK Registrar prepared a Memoranda for the Committee in which she commented thus:

> "The adequacy of protection for personal data is a matter of concern. Police activity whilst directed at entirely proper social objectives, necessarily poses a threat to individuals. If that police activity is misdirected the consequences for the individual can be most damaging. Consequently proposals to collect, exchange and analyse personal information for policing purposes raise greater data protection concerns than are raised by more benign activities."

The Report broadly supported the aims of Europol but expressed concerns on a number of issues. Its data protection comments are found in paras 117 to 120. In those it:

- welcomed the requirements that all participating States should comply with Treaty 108 and Recommendation R(87)15;
- expressed concern about limitations on data subjects rights of access to data;
- supported the provisions for data exchange with third parties;
- supported the appointment of national and joint supervisory bodies.

One of the areas of concern expressed by those giving evidence related to the perceived democratic deficit of the arrangements. The Report of the House of Lords Committee on the European Communities on Europol[58] reflected expressions of concern made in evidence to it by Liberty and Justice and IPPR (Institute for Public Policy Research), that the Convention had not been available in draft for public comments and no proper debate or democratic process was involved in its adoption. One of the conclusions reached by the Committee related to the perceived democratic deficit:

"National parliaments if they are to be responsible for democratic supervision of measures under the Justice and Home Affairs pillar must be able to consider drafts when they can make a constructive input rather than when they can only endorse or reject the measure."

From other quarters, such as Justice, concern has also been expressed over the "legal deficit"of the Convention, that is the absence of enforcement mechanisms against Europol itself and appropriate judicial mechanisms for resolving possible disputes over the application of the Convention either between Member States or between Europol and Member States. Although the joint supervisory body is set up to monitor Europol's adherence to the Convention standards and its decisions are final, it has no enforcement powers and is limited to making recommendations to the Director of Europol. There are no mandatory mechanisms within the Convention for resolving disputes between all States. A partial solution has been reached in that all the signatories except the United Kingdom have committed themselves to a declaration that in the event of disputes they will submit the dispute to the rulings of the Court of Justice of the Communities. However this regime for resolution does not apply to all signatories.

Data protection standards in the Customs Information System

24–64 Under Art.13 each Member State must have national legislation equivalent to Treaty 108. It must have a designated supervisory authority to oversee data protection compliance and in addition:

"In order to ensure the proper application of the data protection provisions in this Convention the Customs Information System shall be regarded in every Member State as a national data file subject to the national provisions [for data protection] and any more stringent provisions contained in this Convention."

The Convention therefore imposes two requirements:

(a) that the information system is treated as a "national data file" falling under UK data protection law; and

(b) that the UK data protection law delivers compliance with the standards set out in the Convention for data protection.

This is a different approach to that of the Europol Convention.

---

[58] Art.10.

National data file

24–65 The entire information system appears to have to be regarded as a national data file, not simply the data entered on to the system by the United Kingdom. The data are not stored in the United Kingdom, although the authorities in the United Kingdom have access to them and they are extracted and used in the United Kingdom.

Standards in the Convention

24–66 The limitations on the data to be held and the purposes for which they may be held have been described earlier in the chapter. In addition the Member State must ensure that it is unlawful for information from the system to be used for other purposes.[59] Direct access to the system is reserved to the national authorities designated by the Member State, although if there is unanimous agreement between them access may be provided to international or regional organisations.[60] The information obtained from the system must only be used for the purposes set out in the Convention.[61]

The accuracy of data is the responsibility of the State which supplied it. Only the supplying State has the right to alter or delete data it has included. There are rules to deal with cases where the accuracy of data supplied by one state is called into question by another.[62]

The time for which data are to be retained is limited and must be reviewed annually.[63] Data must not be copied from the system to other data files.[64] Subject access, accuracy and other individual rights are to be handled in accordance with the national provisions.[65] Individuals must also have the right to ask for checks to be made on the data held about them.[66] The national authorities are subject to security requirements in respect of the data and the national terminals.[67]

Disputes under the Convention are dealt with at Art.27. Initially disputes are to be examined by the Council under the procedures set out in Title VI of the Maastricht Treaty and if not resolved by that may be referred to the European Court of Justice by one of the parties. Disputes between the Commission and a Member State also may be submitted to the Court. However submission to the Court is not mandatory.

Data protection supervision

24–67 Article 17 requires each Member State to designate a national supervisory authority to supervise personal data included in the Customs Information System. As with Europol the supervisory authority is to carry out independent supervision and checks to ensure that the processing of data in the system does not violate the rights of individuals. Individuals may also ask the national supervisory authority to carry out

[59] Session 1994–5, 10th Report, April 1995.
[60] Art.14.
[61] Art.7.
[62] Art.11.
[63] Art.12.
[64] Art.15.
[65] Art.15.
[66] Art.17(2).
[67] Art.19.

checks on the processing of data relating to them. The Commissioner has been designated as the national supervisory authority under the 1998 Act.

Article 18 requires a joint supervisory authority to be set up composed of two representatives from each separate independent authority to carry out its task applying the standards in the Convention itself, Treaty 108 and taking account of Recommendation R(87)15. The JSB has a generally supervisory role but no specific powers under Art.18. If it discovers problems they are to be reported to the national supervisory authorities.

Data protection supervision of the EURODAC arrangements

24–68 The following description of the requirements relating to data protection are taken from the SCAD plus information on EURODAC:

"Member States of origin must ensure that finger prints are taken lawfully as well as all operations involving the use, transmission, conservation or erasure of the data themselves. The Commission must see to the proper application of the Regulation within the Central Unit, and take the necessary measures to ensure the safety of the Central Unit. It also informs the European Parliament and the Council of the measures it takes. Any person or Member State that has suffered damage as a result of an unlawful processing operation or an act incompatible with the Regulation is entitled to receive compensation. That State may however be exempted from its liability, in whole or in part, if it can prove that it is not responsible for the event giving rise to the damage."

Until the EDPS was established supervision was carried out by an interim joint supervisory body drawn from the regulatory authorities of the Member States.

DATA PROTECTION SUPERVISION OF EUROJUST

24–69 Eurojust has a specific scheme for internal data protection set out in rules of Procedure adopted by the College and approved by the Council.

In the rules the definitions from Directive 95/46 are adopted and the rules are applied to all information collected and further processed by Eurojust but not to information handled by National Members exclusively in the context of their national judicial powers. Eurojust data is divided into case-related and non-case-related data. Case-related is that data linked to the operational tasks of Eurojust. The rules set out a detailed data protection policy for Eurojust covering (inter alia) the grounds to establish lawfulness of processing, quality and security, information to be provided on the collection of information and specific rules dealing with the internal telecommunications network. The standards reflect those in Directives 95/46 and 2002/58 rather than Treaty 108. While the standards reflect those in Directive 95/46 in some areas they are more specific and even go beyond those in Directive 95/46, for example Art.5.2 imposes a responsibility to anonymise data where possible; Art.6.1 includes an obligation to erase or rectify inaccurate data; and there is a specific protection for whistleblowing reports of non-complaince in Art.12.3 as well as an obligation of co-operation.

The rules include clear data-purpose limitations to case-related data although there the restriction is not as tight in relation to non-case-related data.[68] Where individuals

---

[68] Arts 15 and 31 respectively.

wish to exercise access rights these must be done either through the authority appointed for that purpose in the relevant member state or by sending the access request to Eurojust. There are detailed provisions setting out the rules for the automated case management system and access to each work file. Broadly access is restricted to the National Member responsible for the work file and those others to whom he or she accords access. No-one except the National Member can modify the information on a work file. Although the standards have more in common with Directive 95/46 the adequacy of third party recipients is to be assessed by reference to Treaty 108.[69]

DATA PROTECTION SUPERVISION OF VIS

24–70   The outline of the supervisory scheme proposed is described at para.24–40 earlier. No detailed rules of procedure have yet been made.

RELATION BETWEEN THE CONVENTIONS AND UK LAW

24–71   Conventions and other third pillar instruments are not self-executing in UK law. Therefore the instruments are not directly effective in UK law nor a source of power for the Commissioner. There are provisions under the 1998 Act to allow the Secretary of State to make orders to deal with international commitments. Under s.54(3) he may make provisions to deal with co-operation with other data protection authorities. Other international obligations are dealt with by order making powers under s.54(4), under which the Commissioner shall carry out:

> "Any data protection functions which the Secretary of State by order may direct him to carry out for the purpose of enabling Her Majesty's Government in the United Kingdom to give effect to any international obligations of the United Kingdom."

This enables the Secretary of State to direct the Commissioner to be the supervisory authority for the purpose of third pillar instruments. However it is not completely clear how this interrelates either with the powers of the Commissioner or the territorial scope of his powers. It is arguable that if the powers of the Commissioner vested in him by the Act are not sufficient to carry out the functions which he is appointed to do under such a direction they cannot be widened by an order made under this section.

In order to carry out the function of supervisory authority as required by Art.23 of the Europol Convention the national authority must have a right of access to the national unit and the offices and documents of the liaison officers. The 1998 Act does not give the Commissioner a right of access to premises or papers in the absence of a warrant. However s.81 of the Crime (International Co-operation) Act 2003 provides the commissioner with inspection powers for Schengen, Europol and the CIS. On the territorial point it is arguable that under the territorial provisions in s.5 of the 1998 Act the liaison officers based in The Hague are outside the Commissioner's jurisdiction.

The contrary argument is that s.54(4) is wide enough to enable the Secretary of State to endow the Commissioner with specific powers of entry as of right for the purposes

---

[69] Art.28.

of the Europol Convention. In respect of the liaison officers the view would be taken that they are processing within the context of an establishment for which the data controller is established in the United Kingdom, being the SOCA, and therefore fall under the 1998 Act by virtue of s.5(1)(a).

As noted earlier a court faced with any ambiguity in legislation will presume that the United Kingdom intended to comply with its international obligations and as far as is possible will resolve the ambiguity so as to give effect to those obligations. As the Europol Convention requires the United Kingdom to appoint a supervisory body with the required powers of access as of right perhaps the better view of s.54(4) is that it does give the Secretary of State the power to give the Commissioner additional powers to carry out his duties. On the issue of territorial application, in order to fulfil the obligations on the United Kingdom for supervision by the national supervisory authority the view can be taken that the liaison officers in The Hague process in the context of the establishment of the national unit based in the United Kingdom under s.5(1)(a).

24–72   The same reasoning and approach is suggested to the CIS Convention. The more difficult question in the customs context is whether the UK Act can be argued to apply to the entire CIS file as required by the Convention as s.5 limits the application of the Act to data processed in the context of an establishment of a data controller in the United Kingdom. In s.1 a data controller is defined as one who, alone or jointly or in common with others, controls the purposes for which and the manner in which personal data are processed. The relevant UK customs authority is the Commissioners of Customs and Excise. While the Commissioners of Customs and Excise are clearly to be regarded as established in the United Kingdom it is rather strained to say that all the data held jointly by the different Member States on the CIS are processed "in the context of" their establishment but that is the approach which must be applied to argue that all the data are within a national data file. Again the safer position may be to argue that, as the United Kingdom has an obligation to comply with the Convention and as s.5 deals with the processing of personal data carried out in the context of an establishment in the United Kingdom and as the Commissioners have obligations and powers in respect of the CIS, then that system should be regarded for the purposes of s.5 as processed within in the context of the Commissioners' role and accordingly as a data file within the jurisdiction of the United Kingdom. This requires a rather more elastic view of s.5 than the equivalent argument in respect of the liaison officers for Europol. It also leads to the uneasy conclusion that the United Kingdom might assert that the entire system could be subject to the enforcement powers of the United Kingdom Commissioner and not just the data for which the United Kingdom is primarily responsible. On the other hand, it would be possible to regard the control of the database as being exercised in common with other customs authorities and to limit any supervisory action to data contributed by the United Kingdom.

In relation to the CIS Convention it appears that the provisions of the 1998 Act together with the general law should be sufficient to satisfy the requirements of the Convention, although that might be open to question in the area of the mandatory purpose limitations. It would have to be argued that such a limitation could be found in the law as it applies to the Commissioners of Customs and Excise either generally or in the particular statutory provisions which govern their activities, as none appears in the 1998 Act.

UK LEGISLATION

24–73   The UK has had to legislate in order to ensure that it can meet its obligations in respect of the various European instruments. The UK legislation is not examined here but it should be noted that a range of UK legal instruments include provisions dealing with disclosure of information. These include the Serious Organised Crime and Police Act 2001 and the Crime (International Co-operation) Act 2003.

Anti-terrorism, Crime and Security Act 2001

24–74   This included an enabling power to implement by secondary legislation terrorism-related EU agreements on Justice and Home Affairs as well as increased powers for disclosure of information by government bodies.

Part 4 s.36 repeals a provision in the Immigration and Asylum Act 1999 which required the destruction of fingerprints taken and, in effect, provides for the retention of fingerprints taken in asylum and certain immigration cases:

> "This is to help prevent applicants who have had cases resolved from re-applying and creating multiple identities which can be used in the perpetration of terrorism or other serious crimes. It is necessary because finger prints are the only sure way of establishing a person's identity beyond doubt."

Part 13 allows for rapid implementation of measures agreed by EU leaders under third pillar arrangements by SI on:

- joint investigative teams;
- measures to simplify seizure of terrorist assets across Europe;
- measures to speed up extradition between Member States.

IMPACT AND FUTURE PLANS

Impact of the development of co-operative arrangements

24–75   There has been enormous development of European co-operation in the areas of immigration, asylum, policing and justice in the last five years. The political will to increase the information held on citizens and others, to bring the information held together and to share it with others cannot be doubted. The Hague Programme sets the position on Biometrics and Information Systems without hesitation:

> "The management of migration flows, including the fight against illegal immigration should be strengthened by establishing a continuum of security measures that effectively links visa application procedures and entry and exit procedures at external border crossings. Such measures are also of importance for the prevention and control of crime, in particular terrorism. In order to achieve this, a coherent approach and harmonised solutions in the EU on biometric identifiers and data are necessary . . .

The European Council invites the Council, the Commission and Member States to continue their efforts to integrate biometric identifiers in travel documents, visa, residence permits, EU citizens passports and information standards without delay and to prepare for the development of minimum standards for national identity cards, taking into account ICAO standards."

Proposal for a Council Framework Decision on the exchange of information under the principle of availability[70]

24–76 One of the most ambitious proposals, which has so far not advanced further than a proposal, has been the proposal for the "principle of availability" of law enforcement relevant information between the Member States. This was one of the Hague Programme proposals and is essentially a proposal that information needed for the fight against crime should be available across the internal borders of the EU without any obstacles, the availability to be facilitated by the use of an index system.[71] The initiative appears to have stalled, although a number of States have entered their own arrangements (see above on the Prum Convention) however the proposal did bring the need to deal with the data protection arrangements for the increase in information exchange into the political arena.

It was accepted that one of the key conditions for the acceptance of such a principle would have to be a uniform agreement on data protection. In October 2005 the Commission put forward a proposal for a Council Framework Decision on the protection of personal data processed in the framework of police and judicial co-operation in criminal matters "the Framework Proposal".[72] This would set out a uniform standard for the protection of personal data processed under third pillar arrangements and would do away with the need for the separate data protection provisions set out in the SIS, CIS, Europol and other instruments that we have examined in this chapter. The Commission carried out a programme of consultation and review over the initiative and found the proposal widely supported by the supervisory authorities in the Member States, the Parliament and the EDPS, although the appetite among governments appear to have been more variable. The Framework is largely reflective of the standards in Directive 95/46 with the addition of specific safeguards in relation to disclosures to other authorities, accuracy of data, security arrangements, further transmission and processing and international transfers. However the EU Multidisciplinary Group on Organised Crime (MDG) which was tasked with taking the proposal forward was unable to agree the measure and in early 2007 the incoming German Presidency proposed that the Commission be asked to produce a "revised" version.[73] At the moment however progress appears to be extremely slow.

We are therefore left with a continuation of the current unsatisfactory arrangements in which the complexity and relative obscurity of these arrangements make for a number of difficulties for all concerned. It is unlikely that those on whom data are held can understand or exercise their data protection rights under these various instruments. It is difficult for data controllers to keep abreast of the developments in these areas which

---

[70] COM (2005) 490 final.
[71] See COM (2004) 429 final—Towards enhancing access to information by law enforcement agencies.
[72] 2005/0202 (CNS) COM (2005) 475 final.
[73] Statewatch Vol.16 No. 5/6 December 2006 reports that one of the main stumbling blocks lay in Art.15 of the original draft which would have required any non-EU State to which data was to be passed to have adequate data protection standards.

may affect them and be sure they are complying as they ought. It even makes for difficulties for the supervisory authority as the resource demands of the co-operative arrangements on the national supervisory authority are considerable. The increasing number of international commitments under the Conventions together with the working groups under the Directive, and the continuing work of the Council of Europe place considerable burdens placed on the Information Commissioner's Office. From a broader social perspective the development of international systems to register the movement of people, the increased exchange of data between States and the integration of security and policing are seen as part of the move to a "global surveillance infrastructure". In April 2005 a group of civil liberties and non-governmental organisations lauded ICAMS (International Campaign Against Mass Surveillance) calling on governments to seek other ways of dealing with security and terrorist threats. While it may be regarded as overly dramatic to describe the growth of co-operative arrangements as "global surveillance" there can be no doubt that the lack of transparency and hence real accountability for the vast and intrusive databases being developed should be a matter of proper concern to anyone involved in the regulation of privacy and personal data.

Channel Tunnel

24–77   These were set out in Channel Tunnel (International Arrangements) Order 1993,[74] made under the Channel Tunnel Act 1987. Personal data held by the French police for policing functions in the control zones are treated as subject to French data protection law and the same applies to data held by the UK police in the control zones. Similar arrangements apply under the Nationality, Immigration and Asylum Act 2002 (Juxtaposed Controls) Order 2003.[75]

ADDITIONAL INFORMATION

Outline of Recommendation R(87)15 and the Second Evaluation Report of the Recommendation

24–78   The principles in the Recommendation apply to the collection, storage, use and communication of personal data for police purposes which are subject to automatic processing.

Police purposes are defined as covering all the tasks which police authorities must perform for the prevention and suppression of criminal offences and the maintenance of public order. The Recommendation sets out eight principles under each of which there are more detailed provisions. The eight principles, although covering broadly the same areas as those in Treaty 108, are not exactly the same or presented in the same sequence as in Treaty 108. They are not in the same order as the Principles under the 1984 or 1998 Acts.

Principle 1—Control and notification

24–79   Supervision of personal data in police systems by an independent supervisory authority is recommended, as is notification to the supervisory authority of the data held for policing.

---

[74] SI 1993/1813 (as amended).
[75] SI 2003/2818.

Principle 2—Collection of data

24–80 It is recommended that the collection of data for policing purposes be limited to that "necessary for the prevention of a real danger or the suppression of a specific criminal offence. Any exception to this provision should be the subject of national legislation". This is a particularly tight provision and could prevent the collection of intelligence information if narrowly construed.

It provides for notice to an individual of the collection of data about him, where this would not prejudice policing purposes; restriction on the collection of data by technical surveillance and restriction on the collection of sensitive data on discrete groups without special authorisation. The restriction on technical surveillance could have a distinctly chilling effect on the spread of CCTV if rigorously applied.

Note: The United Kingdom entered reservations to those provisions which cover notification to individuals that data on them are being stored and special controls on collection of sensitive data.

Principle 3—Storage of data

24–81 This deals with the accuracy of stored data, providing that storage should be limited to accurate data necessary for the performance of the police functions. Different categories of data should be stored separately and enhanced by accuracy markers. Facts should be distinguished from opinions.

Principle 4—Use

24–82 Subject to the rules on communication in Principle 5, police data should be used exclusively for police purposes.

Principle 5—Communication of data

24–83 This is a long and detailed provision divided into sub-paragraphs setting out rules which specify the limitations on the disclosure of police data, broadly being the restriction of disclosures to those made in accordance with the law and in the public interest.

Principle 6—Publicity, right of access to police files, right of rectification and right of appeal

24–84 This sets out provisions on access to data and correction of inaccurate data.

Principle 7—Length of storage and updating of data

24–85 This includes criteria for retention and recommends that there should be rules setting out different retention times for different categories of data.

Principle 8—Data security

24–86 This recommends that adequate security measures should be taken bearing in mind the nature of the particular files.

CHAPTER 25

The Commissioner

INTRODUCTION

25–01   On March 1, 2001 the Data Protection Registrar became the Data Protection Commissioner and then on January 30, 2002 the Information Commissioner.[1] The Commissioner has a broad remit to educate and inform the public about data protection as well as specific regulatory powers. This chapter covers his general role and those of his powers under the Data Protection Act 1998 (DPA)(the Act) and the Privacy and Electronic Communications (EC Directive) Regulations 2003 which are dealt with in other chapters. The Commissioner's powers and role are set out in Pt VI of the Act. The Commissioner's powers under the Freedom of Information Act 2000 (FOIA) are dealt in Ch.4, above insofar as they affect his role as data protection regulator. This book does not cover the Commissioner's general role under the FOIA although it should be recognised that many of the roles overlap. For example the Commissioner's obligation to promote good practice in data protection is mirrored by an equivalent obligation under s.47(1) of the FOIA.

SUMMARY OF MAIN POINTS

25–02   (a)   The Commissioner has a regulatory role and can serve enforcement and information notices and bring prosecutions.

(b)   The Commissioner has a role in European co-operation and oversight of associated Treaty obligations.

(c)   The Commissioner may assist individuals in special cases under the provisions dealing with journalistic, artistic or literary purposes.

(d)   The Commissioner's staff and the Commissioner are subject to criminal penalties if improper disclosures of information given to them are made.

(e)   The Commissioner has an explicit role in encouraging good practice and codes of practice. A formal procedure is introduced for settling codes of practice. He also has a power to carry out audits with consent.

(f)   Codes of practice may be made at EU level by the Article 29 Working Party.

---

[1]   Freedom of Information Act 2000 s.18(1) and 87(2)(a).

NATIONAL ROLES

National Offices

25–03 The Commissioner operates from four offices. Although originally the Commissioner's office was based in the North West and the Wilmslow office remains the commissioner's Headquarters, since the expansion of his role it has been necessary to establish offices in Northern Ireland, Scotland and Wales. The addresses and contact details are given on the website at *http://www.ico.gov.uk* [Accessed on September 2, 2007].

Promotional work

Good Practice

25–04 Under the 1984 Act the Registrar had an obligation to fulfil his statutory roles so as to "promote the Data Protection Principles". A similar provision occurs in s.51(1) but applies beyond the Principles to cover not only all aspects of the new Act but also the promotion of good practice. This emphasises that the Commissioner's job in carrying out promotional work goes beyond promoting the legally enforceable standards in the Act. This is explicit in the definition of good practice in s.51(9), where it is defined as meaning:

> "such practice in the processing of personal data as appears to the Commissioner to be desirable having regard to the interests of data subjects and others, and includes (but is not limited to) compliance with the requirements of this Act."

"Good practice" may cover a range of activities including practices aimed at achieving compliance and practices which support standards beyond legal compliance. For example, under this heading the Commissioner may promote the adoption of Privacy Enhancing Technologies although he might not be able to require data controllers to adopt them.

Information and advice

25–05 The Commissioner has an obligation to disseminate information to the public about both good practice and other matters under the Act. He is not restricted as to the means used to fulfil his statutory duty or as to the extent of the information he provides. The obligation is simply to disseminate "in such form and manner as he considers appropriate" such information "as it may appear to him expedient to give to the public". The Commissioner also has a power to provide advice to any person on matters under the Act.

The Commissioner's office is active in the provision of advice on all aspects of the previous legislation including via training videos and student packages. The Office has also initiated online seminars, an online newsletter and produced a CD-ROM for schools. Since 2004 the Commissioner has focused on producing practical guidance and the website lists a range of Good Practice Notes on a range of issues in the index of data protection guidance materials. While the commitment of the Commissioner to provide guidance, and indeed the range of guidance available, is welcome, it can sometimes be difficult to keep track of where guidance has altered or developed or how authoritative it is meant to be as there are different types of guidance (introductory, practical application, and detailed specialist guides) and the date is not always given on the document. It should also be noted that extensive guidance is produced by European bodies on specific issues as noted below.

Charges

25–06 Under s.51(8) the Commissioner may charge for services provided under these provisions, that is broadly the education, advisory or audit functions. Charges must have the consent of the Secretary of State. This provision has been included to allow the Commissioner to provide wider information and educational services. The Registrar had no power to impose any charge under the previous Act, even to recover the costs of materials. The power has yet to be exercised.

International information

25–07 The Commissioner is not limited to the dissemination of information about national issues. The information provided must include material about data protection in other countries outside the European Economic Area and any findings made under the provisions of the Act of adequacy or inadequacy of protection in third countries.

Codes of Practice

Background and general comments

25–08 Codes are generally intended to include practical guidance on the application of the legislation. They may be either sectoral, for example covering policing or direct marketing, or functional, covering for example employment. There can also be general codes. Some large multinational corporations have their own company codes. There is no definition of what counts as a code and they vary widely. The concept of codes of practice has been an enduring one in data protection terms and has surfaced in the Directive.

The Directive includes provision for both national and European codes. The Younger Report recommended the adoption of codes of conduct in 1972. Under s.36(4) of the 1984 Act codes of practice could be adopted and one of the tasks of the Registrar was to promote the adoption of such codes. There was a flurry of code-related data protection activity in the years immediately after the passage of the 1984 Act and various codes came into being at that time. However, codes were not being widely used in the United Kingdom between 1986 and 2000. In the 1998 Act s.51(3)–(5) sets out a procedure for the formulation and determination of codes.

Current codes

25–09 There is a code on the use of CCTV cameras, and an Employment Practices Code. The Secretary of State has issued a code of practice to accompany data matching exercises undertaken under the Social Security Administration (Fraud) Act 1997 but that is no longer available on the Department of Work and Pensions (DWP) website. The Association of Chief Police Officers have a data protection code of practice. The Commissioner's office has produced guidance on how to produce codes.[2]

---

[2] This does not appear to be available from the website but should be available from the ICO.

Codes vary in usefulness and relevance. They may simply repeat the standards set out in the legislation, adding no particular value, or they may provide detailed and helpful guidance. Codes may provide something of a subsequent embarrassment where the regulator's thinking moves on if he has agreed to a generous provision in a particular code. For that reason regulators' endorsements of codes of practice are often hedged about with cautious provisos. Codes may have a legal effect, that is they may be taken into account by a court or tribunal, or may have persuasive force only, that is they can be referred to but the court does not have to follow them. Even if they are of persuasive value only they are likely to be considered by a court or tribunal when assessing matters of judgment such as fairness. Codes under the DPA 1998 do not have statutory force as, for example, the Highway Code does.

Secretary of State sponsored codes

25–10 The Secretary of State has a potential role in code development and may direct the Commissioner to create a code of practice. This is done by an order of the Secretary of State. Such an order must describe the personal data or the processing to which the code is to relate and may also describe the persons or classes of persons to whom it is to relate. Those classes need not be types of data controllers but might be classes of data subject. For example, the Secretary of State could require the Commissioner to prepare a code relating to the processing of personal data about children by internet users.

Where the Secretary of State has ordered the production of a code under s.52(3) the Commissioner must lay the completed code before Parliament either alone or as part of an annual or special report. The provision dealing with Secretary of State sponsored codes was inserted during the Committee Stage in the House of Lords, following amendments proposed by Baroness Nicholson of Winterbourne. The amendments followed concerns about the absence of control of data matching exercises being carried out by central government agencies and local authorities. The provision has not yet been used but potentially it allows the Secretary of State a considerable power to direct the use of the Commissioner's resources.

Other codes

25–11 The Commissioner may prepare codes where he considers it appropriate to do so. In any case where a code is to be prepared the procedure to be followed is the same. The Commissioner must engage in a consultation with trade associations, data subjects or persons representing data subjects "as appear to him to be appropriate". Trade associations are defined in s.51(9) as including anybody representing data controllers. They may therefore cover representative bodies from public sector organisations which would not normally be described as trade associations, for example, the Association of Chief Police Officers. The aim of the codes is to provide "guidance as to good practice". Codes may also be produced by trade associations themselves. The Commissioner may encourage such associations to prepare codes of practice and has specific responsibilities if presented with a code prepared by such an association. If such a code is submitted to him he must consider it and notify the association whether, in his opinion, the code promotes the following of good practice. Before reaching his conclusion the Commissioner must carry out appropriate consultations with data subjects, or persons representing them, as he considers appropriate.

Commissioner's code on employment practices

25–12   There is a procedure for dealing with and generating codes of practice under the 1998 Act. The main thrust of the Commissioner's code related work has been on the employment code, The Employment Practices Data Protection Code. This was completed in 2004. It proved a difficult task because the issues covered involved quite complex relationships and overlapped with other areas of law. Yet, in order to provide real added value the code has had to give advice in such areas. The completion of the Code and its general acceptance marks a significant achievement for the Commissioner's office and owes much to the work of the Assistant Commisisoner responsible, David Smith.

Preparatory work started in 1999 when a report on data protection and privacy issues in the workplace was commissioned by the Data Protection Registrar. The resulting report was published in 1999. As soon as the 1998 Act came into force, in March 2000, the Commissioner's office was ready to start work on the draft code. The first draft was issued in October 2000 with a consultation period which was intended to run to January 2001. The draft covered managing data protection, recruitment, employment records, access and disclosure, contract and agency staff, employee monitoring, medical testing, discipline and dismissal and retention of records. The timing of the draft was unfortunate. It appeared at the same time as the Regulations covering the monitoring of communications under the Telecommunications (Lawful Business Practice) (Interception of Communications) Regulations 2000.[3] There was no time to insert a section on the Regulations in the draft code and there was some uncertainty as to whether the two were fully compatible. The draft code dealt with some very contentious areas. One of the most difficult was monitoring employees' use of telephone, email and the internet. The draft code took a privacy protective stance and the responses to the consultation from industry groups were almost universally negative. The consultation period was extended until June 2001, with a consultation conference being held in Manchester in June 2001. The Commissioner then decided to issue the code in sections covering recruitment and selection; records management; monitoring at work; and medical information. The first section was released in March 2002 on one of the less contentious aspects, recruitment practices and data protection. This was followed by the release of a further draft of the section dealing with monitoring. The section was again greeted by hostility and negative comment. In August 2002 the section on records management was issued. The section on monitoring was issued finally in 2004. The Code takes the form of the main document with the addition of detailed supplementary guidance for those who need to delve deeper into the issues. There is also a simpler guide to the Code for those smaller employers who require more general advice.

Audit powers

25–13   Section 51(7) provides for a power to audit with consent however it stops well short of the provision the regulator had sought. Section 51(7) provides that the

---

[3] SI 2000/2699.

Commissioner may "with the consent of the data controller, assess any processing of personal data for the observance of good practice". The Commissioner has prepared an Audit Manual which his staff will follow when carrying out an audit. This is available on the Commissioner's website and available for others to use.

There is clearly a risk to the controller in inviting the regulator to carry out an audit inspection. Such an inspection might lead to the discovery of breaches of the Act which would leave the controller at the risk of supervisory action. It would hardly be possible for the Commissioner to agree to ignore such breaches in view of his statutory obligations. The power has been used however and it appears that it has been used by public sector bodies rather than by private sector bodies.

Reports to Parliament

25–14 Section 52 re-enacts the report provisions in very similar form to those found in the 1984 Act. The Commissioner is required to lay an annual report before Parliament. The report must deal with the exercise of his functions under the Act. The Commissioner's annual report has traditionally been laid in mid-July. Annual reports contain useful case studies and position papers on current issues. The Commissioner may also lay other reports on functions as he thinks fit. The Commissioner used this power to raise the problems associated with the unlawful trade in personal data in the report "What Price Privacy?" delivered to Parliament in early 2006.

Funding for assistance in special cases

25–15 The Commissioner's powers to fund individual action in some cases are dealt with at Ch.17, above. In summary, the Commissioner is given a role under s.53 and Sch.10 to provide financial assistance to an individual who brings proceedings in the civil courts for enforcement of his individual rights in a case where the special purposes (that is journalistic, artistic or literary purposes) are involved. The assistance may only be granted where the Commissioner considers that the case involves a matter of substantial public importance. Supplementary provisions cover the Commissioner's duty to notify the parties affected and the procedure which must be followed in such cases.

Disclosure of information to the Commissioner

25–16 Section 58 allows any person to disclose information to the Commissioner or Tribunal where it is necessary for the discharge of their functions under the DPA or the FOIA, together referred to as "the information Acts". Such a disclosure may be made irrespective of any enactment or rule of law prohibiting or restricting it. This allows for example a solicitor who is bound by client confidentiality to disclose information to the Commissioner in pursuance of the Commissioner's inquiries. Section 58 does not require the disclosure of information and cannot be used to demand information, although the Commissioner may demand information by service of an information notice in an appropriate case under both sets of legislation. Section 58 simply ensures that the person who discloses information in appropriate circumstances has a defence against a prosecution for unauthorised disclosure or an action for breach of confidence or any other legal action based on the disclosure. The equivalent section under the 1984 Act was never litigated and the precise effect of this provision is not clear. It could be viewed as a complete bar to any proceedings for breach of the prohibitory rule or as a defence to any such proceedings.

Controllers who wish to rely on s.58 are advised to obtain a written record from a duly authorised official employed by the Commissioner stating that the information in question is necessary for the discharge of the Commissioner's functions. It may even be prudent to ask the Commissioner to specify which functions are involved. In cases where data controllers are asked by police forces to release data under the s.29 exemption the regulator has suggested that users request information about the reason for the disclosure to be provided to them as an additional safeguard to ensure the non-disclosure exemptions are not abused. It might therefore be prudent for controllers to apply the same approach as representing best practice in these circumstances.

If a controller has adopted best practice by making appropriate inquiries and obtaining full authority from the Commissioner's office he should be in a strong position to defend himself from any proceedings brought as a result of a disclosure.

Section 76 of and Sch.7 to the FOIA provide for the disclosure of information by and to the OIC by a number of other bodies which would otherwise be precluded from making disclosures. Section 76 provides for the disclosure of information "obtained by or furnished to" the Commissioner for the purposes of the FOIA or the DPA to a list of Ombudsmen. Schedule 7 provides for disclosure to the Commissioner by the Parliamentary Commissioner for Administration, the Local Commissioner for Administration, the Health Service Commissioner, the Welsh Administration Ombudsman, the Northern Ireland Commissioner for Complaints and the Assembly Ombudsman for Northern Ireland.

INTERNATIONAL ROLE

General

25–17   Directive 95/46 has a life beyond implementation. In particular it provides for:

(a) the continued involvement of the European Commission in the regulation of personal data in Europe;

(b) continued co-operation between Member States in this area;

(c) continued co-operation between the supervisory authorities of Member States.

In addition, the United Kingdom has entered into a number of third pillar agreements which involve data protection co-ordination. These are dealt with in Ch.24, above. The Commissioner has a role in all of these areas.

Community Codes of Conduct

25–18   Article 27(1) of the Directive provides that both Member States and the Commission shall encourage the:

"drawing up of codes of conduct intended to contribute to the proper implementation of the national provisions adopted by the Member States pursuant to this Directive, taking account of the specific features of the various sectors."

The provisions dealing with national codes of practice have been implemented in s.51 (described above) but there is no provision in the 1998 Act for the adoption of Community-wide codes. Article 27(3) appears to envisage such Community codes as specific instruments applicable throughout the Community and as such one would have expected some mechanism for national adoption. Such a mechanism appears to be absent. Article 27(3) provides that draft Community codes and amendments or extensions to existing Community codes may be submitted to the Article 29 Working Party. The Working Party must consider whether the codes are in accordance with the national provisions adopted pursuant to the Directive. Presumably this means all 15 sets of national provisions. It further provides that "the authority" may seek the views of data subjects or their representatives on such draft codes. It is not clear which authority is meant here but it seems reasonable to assume it covers either a relevant national authority or the Commission itself. Once codes are approved by the Working Party the Commission may ensure appropriate publicity for them.

The codes must be sectoral and formulated by an industry or other representative group. Production of a code and Working Party approval is time consuming. The Working Party published a procedure for the submission and approval of codes in September 1998. The procedure is for:

- submission of the code and agreement by the Working Party to accept it for consideration;
- preparation of a written opinion of the Working Party;
- publication of the opinion and communication to those concerned.

Draft codes must have been prepared "by an organization representative of the sector concerned and established or active in a significant number of Member States". Preferably data subjects should have been involved in the preparation. It must clearly define the sector or organisation to which it is intended to apply. Draft codes must be sent in a Community language accompanied by a translation in English and French. Premature drafts or drafts which do not meet these criteria will not be considered. The draft will usually be considered by a sub-group or task force of the Working Party which will prepare a Report. They will consider whether or not the draft:

"is in accordance with the Data Protection Directives and, where relevant, the national provisions adopted pursuant to those Directives and is of sufficient quality and internal consistency and provides sufficient added value to the Directives and other applicable data protection legislation, specifically whether the draft code is sufficiently focused on the specific data protection questions and problems in the organization or sector to which it is intended to apply and offers sufficiently clear solutions for these questions and problems."

Codes have been put forward by the Federation of European Direct Marketing Associations (FEDMA) and the International Travel Agents Association (IATA). The dialogue with FEDMA resulted in the approval of the Code. However, the IATA proposal was submitted to the Article 29 Working Party in 1997 but it did not meet the requirements of the sub-group set up to consider it and it did not prove possible for the parties to resolve their differences. In October 2000 the IATA passenger service conference adopted the proposal as a Recommended Practice but it has not become a Community Code.

The Working Party itself cannot issue codes. This means it does not have an obvious vehicle on which to issue policy statements similar to the Recommendations formulated by the Council of Europe on specific topics which set out ways of handling issues like the development of genetic databases. It has overcome this by issuing Opinions and Working Papers (for which see below).

Article 29 Working Party

Constitution

25–19 The Directive provides for two separate representative groups to be set up: a group of representatives of the Member States, attended on behalf of the United Kingdom by an official from the sponsor department previously the Home Office and now the Lord Chancellor's Department; and a group of representatives of the supervisory authorities of the Member States, attended on behalf of the United Kingdom by the Commissioner. These are the Article 31 Committee and the Article 29 Working Party respectively.

Under s.54(1)(b) of the Act the Commissioner is the designated supervisory authority in the United Kingdom for the purposes of the Directive. This entails his attendance at the Article 29 Working Party. Under Art.29(1) the Working Party is to have advisory status and must act independently. Its advice will be aimed primarily at the Commission but may go to Member States, to the Article 31 Committee and presumably also to data controllers and subjects where appropriate. Although it acts independently its members under Art.29(2) consist of representatives of the supervisory authorities, a representative of the "authority or authorities established for the Community institutions and bodies" and a representative of the Commission. The representative of the authority established for the Community institutions reflects the commitment of the Commission to implement one of the core recommendations of the original data protection motion proposed in 1990 that the Commission itself should apply data protection norms and standards to its own functions and institutions. The Commission is in the process of appointing an official to carry out this undertaking and to supervise data protection standards throughout the Community institutions. One of his tasks is to sit on the Art.29 group. The other member is a representative of the Commission itself. The remainder of Art.29 outlines the constitution of the Working Party which is then left to settle its own rules of procedure. Article 29 provides that decisions are to be taken by a simple majority of the representatives of the supervisory authorities, so the Commission and the supervisory authority for the Commission do not have votes. The Secretariat is provided by the Commission. The relevant Directorate of the Commission for data protection matters is Directorate General XV which is responsible for the internal market and financial services. The Working Party elects a chairman who holds office for two years. The agenda is formulated from items listed by the chairman either at the request of the supervisory authority or the Commission or at the chairman's own behest.

Role

25–20 The role of the Working Party is to consider the implementation of the Directive in the Member States and to provide information and advice and recommendations to the Commission on matters arising from their considerations. They are charged with four specific areas:

(a) considering questions of harmonisation within the Union;

(b) advising on levels of protection within the Union and in third countries;

(c) advising the Commission on any proposed changes to the Directive or related or additional Community measures affecting data protection;

(d) giving opinions on Community-wide codes.

The Working Party has various functions and obligations arising from these considerations. It must draw up an annual report on data protection in the Community and in third countries which must be made public. The Working Party was set up after adoption of the Directive in 1995 and has met regularly since then. The first annual report was issued in June 1997 and consisted of a summary of developments in the Union, the Council of Europe, third countries and in other international fora such as the International Labour Organisation. As well as its representative members the working party accepts observers from Iceland and Norway.

Papers and opinions produced by the Article 29 Working Party

25–21 The Working Party has a general role to make recommendations on "all matters relating to the protection of persons with regard to the processing of personal data in the Community". It has produced approximately 135 papers up to the time of writing in April 2007. A number are routine or administrative, that is annual reports, implementation reviews, procedural documents for codes of practice and opinions on other instruments. The work on substantive topics has focused on:

- overseas transfers and adequate protection in other jurisdictions;
- internet and telecommunications issues;
- employment;
- the tension between privacy and security.

There are also Opinions or other papers on a range of other issues such as data protection and the media, whistleblowing, public sector information and marketing. The work on some areas is ongoing. For example the paper on employment matters, Opinion 8/2001 on the processing of personal data in the employment sector, was adopted in autumn 2001. In effect the Opinion is similar to a code and covers many of the same areas. A list of the papers produced by the Article 29 Working Party is included on the website at *http://www.europa.eu/justice_home/fsj/Privacy* [Accessed on September 2, 2007].

The Working Party has a duty to inform the Commission if it discovers divergences in data protection between Member States which are likely to affect the achievement of equivalent protection throughout the Union. The Working Party's opinions and rec-ommendations must be forwarded to both the Commission and the Article 31 Committee. This triggers an equivalent obligation on the Commission (but not the Article 31 Committee) to produce a report informing the Working Party of the actions the Commission has taken in response to their opinions and recommendations. Such a report must also go to the European Parliament and the Council. Although the Working Party's advice and recommendations do not have to be made public the Committee's report does.

Article 31 Committee

25–22   The Article 31 Committee is composed of representatives of Member States and chaired by a representative of the Commission. Its role is to assist the Commission in drafting Community implementing measures for data protection. The measures in question will be those allowed for under the Directive to supplement or extend the existing provisions. The Commission is not given a free-standing remit to propose major changes to the Directive. The relevant provisions appear in Arts 3, 25 and 27. Article 33 requires the Commission to report on the implementation of the Directive to the Council and the European Parliament at regular intervals starting in the year 2001, that is three years after implementation throughout the Community. In particu-lar the Commission must report on the data processing of sound and image data and shall submit "any appropriate proposals which prove to be necessary, taking account of developments in information technology and in the light of the state of progress in the information society". The report is currently underway.

Article 27 has been covered above and deals with Community codes of conduct and the introduction of such codes. Article 29 covers the assessment of adequacy and find-ings of adequacy of protection in third countries in connection with data transfers. The Commission has the power to make formal findings that particular third countries either do or do not ensure an adequate standard of equivalent protection. Such findings must then be acted on by Member States. The findings of the Commission can only be made following the procedure set out in Art.31 involving the Article 31 Committee.

The Art.31 procedure is for the Commission's representative to submit a draft of a proposed measure to the Committee which must then give its opinion on the proposal within a timescale which is to be set down by the chairman of the Committee, taking into account the urgency of the matter. The voting on the proposed measure is by qual-ified majority measure in accordance with Art.148(2) of the Treaty of European Union. The chairman does not have a vote in this process.

In the event of a dispute between the Commission and the Committee the proposed measure must not be adopted for three months and in that time it must be submitted to the Council of Ministers for a decision. This procedure will allow any particularly thorny questions of third country adequacy to be resolved at the highest political level. If a pro-posal is approved by the Committee it can be adopted immediately by the Commission.

The decisions taken by the Commission on adequacy under Art.25 are binding on the UK Commissioner by virtue of s.54(6), which provides that where the Commission makes a decision on adequacy or otherwise of a third country under the Art.31(2) procedure the Commissioner "shall comply with that decision in exercising his functions" in deter-mining questions of adequacy relating to transfers from the United Kingdom.

Convention co-operation

25–23 The Commissioner has obligations to co-operate with other supervisory bodies under two international instruments. The Convention for the protection of individuals with regard to automatic processing of personal data (Treaty 108) to which the United Kingdom remains a signatory and the Directive.

Section 54(1) replaces s.37 of the 1984 Act. Under s.54(1) the Commissioner continues to be the designated authority for the purposes of Art.13 of Treaty 108. Article 13 deals with mutual assistance between contracting States. Signatories to Treaty 108 agree to designate a national authority which will be obliged to co-operate with other designated national authorities to provide general information on law and administrative practice in the field of data protection in their jurisdiction and particular information in specific instances. Section 54(2) allows the Secretary of State to make provision for the functions to be discharged by the Commissioner. Provision was made by the Data Protection (Functions of Designated Authority) Order 2000.[4] It specifies the actions required of the Commissioner as designated authority. In particular, the Commissioner must provide information to foreign authorities if requested. He must also proffer assistance to individuals in the United Kingdom to exercise their rights in other convention countries and assist individuals in other convention countries to exercise their rights in the United Kingdom.

Directive co-operation

25–24 Article 28(6) requires supervisory authorities in different Member States to co-operate with one another to the extent necessary for the performance of their duties, in particular, by the exchange of useful information. This is implemented in the United Kingdom by s.53(3). Under this the Secretary of State may make provision by order as to co-operation by the Commissioner with the European Commission or other supervisory authorities. Such co-operation in particular can extend to the exchange of information and the exercise of the Commissioner's powers in respect of processors whose processing is carried out in the United Kingdom but who are subject to the law of another Member State. This can occur under the application of the territoriality provisions found in s.5 of the 1998 Act.

Informal co-operation

25–25 The Commissioner's role in working with other supervisory authorities overseas is not limited to fulfilling his statutory obligations. The Commissioner undertakes a considerable amount of additional co-operative work. His staff attend meetings of some OECD working parties and the Council of Europe Committee of Experts. Since 1984 Commissioners from privacy and data protection supervisory authorities throughout the world have met for an annual international conference to discuss issues of mutual concern. Most recently conferences have been in Warsaw (2004), Montreaux (2005) and London (2006). In addition, there are ongoing and informal contacts between supervisory authorities in which the European Commission has no role.

---

[4] SI 2000/186.

Colonies

25–26 Section 54(5) provides for the Secretary of State to direct the Commissioner to assist with the exercise of data protection functions in any UK colony. The terms as to such assistance may include terms as to payment. This provision has been inserted in the Act to allow dependencies, and in particular Gibraltar, to rely on expertise and services provided by the Commissioner's office rather than having to set up a separate administrative system for data protection in Gibraltar. As far as can be ascertained at the date of writing (April 2007) no arrangements have been made in respect of Gibraltar.

European Supervisory Bodies

25–27 There is a brief provision in s.54(4) behind which lurks a major area of work carried out by the Commissioner. Section 54(4) simply provides that:

> "the Commissioner shall also carry out any data protection function which the Secretary of State may by order direct him to carry out for the purpose of enabling Her Majesty's Government in the United Kingdom to give effect to any international obligation of the U.K."

The United Kingdom has entered into a number of international treaties which include obligations to co-operate in data protection areas. A full description is to be found in Ch.24, above.

Adequacy

25–28 As well as implementing Community findings under Art.25, s.54(7) requires that the Commissioner must inform the Commission where he approves contractual terms under para.8 of Sch.4 and where he authorises transfers under para.9 of the same Schedule. This has been done in the case of the Commission—approved contract clauses for the export of personal data to countries which do not offer adequate protection.

OFFICE OF THE COMMISSIONER

Appointment and tenure

25–29 The formal provisions dealing with the Commissioner's appointment and tenure are set out in s.6 and Sch.5. Under s.6 the office of the Data Protection Registrar was to continue but under the new name of Data Protection Commissioner. It became the Information Commissioner under Sch.2 of the FOIA in January 2002. The Commissioner is appointed by Letters Patent. The Commissioner is not a Crown servant. He is an independent official answerable directly to Parliament and not answerable to a Minister. He exercises legal powers which are vested directly in him and are not delegated by a Minister. He has legal personality as a corporation sole. This is a little used form of corporate personality employed where powers and responsibilities are vested in an individual office-holder. The usual example of a corporation sole is of a bishop. The Commissioner holds office for a five-year term and may be appointed for up to three consecutive terms. The usual appointment would be a maximum of two terms but a third term may be permitted if there are "special circumstances" which make the reappointment desirable in the public interest. The Commissioner must in any event retire after reaching 65. The Commissioner can seek to be removed from office at his own choice but can only be forced to go by the Queen in pursuance of an address from both Houses of Parliament. This is a procedure equivalent to impeachment. The Commissioner's salary and pension are to be determined by Parliament. In practice the Commissioner's post is treated as equivalent to that of a senior member of the civil service.

Staff

25–30   The Commissioner may employ such staff as he considers appropriate and must determine their salary and terms of service. In practice his staffing levels, the terms of appointment and pension arrangements are equivalent to those of civil servants. He must appoint two statutory deputies who fulfil the functions of the Commissioner during any vacancy in that office or if the Commissioner is unable to act for any reason. Apart from the statutory delegation to the deputy the Commissioner has a general power to authorise officers and staff to perform any of his functions on his behalf.

Staff confidentiality

25–31   The DPA contains, at s.59, a provision that did not appear in the 1984 Act which creates a criminal penalty for the Commissioner and his staff of knowingly or recklessly disclosing information without lawful authority. The prohibition covers information obtained under both the DPA and the FOIA, current and past Commissioners, members of the Commissioner's staff and agents of the Commissioner. They are precluded from disclosing information which is not already in the public domain, which relates to an identified or identifiable individual or business and which has been provided to the Commissioner for the purposes of the Act. This prohibition applies in everything other than six prescribed circumstances. Those circumstances are:

(a) the disclosure is made with the consent of the individual or business;

(b) the information was provided for the purpose of being made public;

(c) the disclosure is necessary for the exercise of the Commissioner's functions under the Act;

(d) the disclosure is necessary for complying with Community obligations;

(e) the disclosure is made for the purpose of any proceedings;

(f) the disclosure is necessary for reasons of substantial public interest having regard to the rights and freedoms or legitimate interests of any person.

This provision has been included to implement the Art.28(7) requirement that Member States shall provide that members and staff of the National Supervisory Authority are to be subject to a duty of professional secrecy with regard to confidential information to which they have access.

The Directive's requirement only applies to confidential information whereas the s.59 prohibition applies to any information about an individual or business which comes into the possession of the Commissioner. It is not clear why the Art.28(7) prohibition has been so transposed or why a criminal penalty has been attached. There are also a number of ambiguities with this provision. The term "business" is indeterminate and it is not clear therefore whether the prohibition applies to information relating to or held in the public sector or if so, how much of such information would be covered. It is clear, however, that some information would be confidential in the ordinary use of the term.

Formalities and seal

25–32 The Commissioner has a seal which is authenticated by his signature or that of another person duly authorised for that purpose (para.6 of Sch.5). There is a presumption of authenticity for documents purporting to be issued under the Commissioner's seal and signed by or on behalf of the Commissioner and they are to be received in evidence and deemed to be authentic unless the contrary is shown (para.7 of Sch.5).

Financial provisions and accounts

25–33 The Commissioner receives income from a variety of sources. His income mainly derives from registration fees but small sums come from legal costs and miscellaneous items such as payment for certified copies of entries in the public register. All such receipts must be paid to the Secretary of State, except insofar as the Secretary of State with the consent of the Treasury so directs. This provision allows for the introduction of a financial regime under which the Commissioner may retain some moneys derived from the exercise of his functions however no action has been taken to implement this provision. Where the Secretary of State receives monies from the Commissioner he must pay those into the Consolidated Fund.

The Commissioner receives grant in aid, that is moneys voted in Parliament and paid to the Commissioner via the Secretary of State. The Commissioner is under an obligation to keep proper accounts which must be provided annually to the Comptroller and Auditor General and laid each year before Parliament.

ADDITIONAL INFORMATION

Derivations

25–34• Directive 95/46 (See App.B):

  (a) Arts 27 (codes of conduct), 28 (supervisory authority), 29 and 30 (working party).
  (b) Recitals 61, 62, 63, 64, 65.

• Council of Europe Convention of January 28, 1981 for the Protection of individuals with regard to automatic processing of personal data: Art.10 (sanctions and remedies).

- Data Protection Act 1984: s.3 and Sch.2 (the Registrar), s.36 (general duties of Registrar), s.37 (co-operation between parties to the Convention).

- Organisation for Economic Co-operation and Development Guidelines: Annex, Part Five (International co-operation).

Hansard references

25–35   Vol.586, No.110, col.89, Lords Grand Committee, February 25, 1998
Audit powers of Commissioner.

ibid., col.120, 121
Good practice, compliance duties, codes of practice.

ibid., col.123
Power to assist in special cases.

Vol.587, No.122, cols 509, 510, Lords Report, March 16, 1998
Information and audits.

ibid., col.524
Assistance to Gibraltar.

ibid., col.531
Duty to consult on codes of practice.

Commons Standing Committee D, June 2, 1998, col.252
Encouraging codes of practice.

ibid., col.258
Assistance in special cases.

ibid., col.256
Reports to Parliament and international co-operation.

ibid., col.268
Confidentiality requirement.

Vol.315, No.198, cols 602, 603, Commons Third Reading, July 2, 1998
Confidentiality requirement for Commissioner's staff.

Previous case law

25–36   None.

Article 29 Working Party Papers

25–37   There are now too many to list so reference should be made to the website.

CHAPTER 26

Information Tribunal

INTRODUCTION

26–01 The Act maintains the specialist Tribunal set up under the 1984 Act but now called the Information Tribunal. The Tribunal hears appeals against notices served under the Data Protection Act 1998, the Freedom of Information Act 2000 and the Privacy and Electronic Communications (EC Directive) Regulations 2003 (PECR). The Freedom of Information Act 2000 changed the name of the Tribunal to the Information Tribunal[1] and made a number of consequential amendments.[2] The rules of procedure are dealt with in statutory instruments.[3] The rules made under the Data Protection Act 1998 were amended in 2000 and 2002 to make the technical changes necessary to enable the Tribunal to deal with appeals under the Freedom of Information Act 2000 (FOIA) but in 2005 the entire set of Rules were replaced. There are separate rules of procedure for those hearings involving national security certificates. The Tribunal dealt with only 10 appeals between 1984 and 1999, sitting only nine times, one appeal being dealt with by written submissions; since the 1998 Act came into effect it has dealt with only three appeals under the Data Protection Act, one of which concerned national security certificates.[4] It has heard many more appeals under the FOIA. The Tribunal Secretariat is based in Leicester but the Tribunal itself has no permanent accommodation and sits whereever it is required.

This chapter explains the membership, jurisdiction, powers and rules of the Information Tribunal. In considering its role and powers practitioners must bear in mind that this is a statutory Tribunal and therefore its powers must be found in the governing statute or the statutory instrument setting out its rules of procedure. The Tribunal has no inherent powers.

SUMMARY OF MAIN POINTS

26–02   (a) The Tribunal hears appeals against the service of enforcement and information notices under both the DPA, the PECR and the FOIA and on the

---

[1] Freedom of Information Act 2000 s.18(2).
[2] FOIA s.18(3) and Sch.4.
[3] The Information tribunal (Enforcement Appeals) Rules 2005 (SI 2005/14).
The Information Tribunal (Enforcment Appeals) (Amendment) Rules 2005 (SI 2005/450).
The Information Tribunal (National Security Appeals) Rules 2005 (SI 2005/13).
[4] *Baker v Secretary of State for the Home Office* at *www.informationtribunal.gov.uk* [Accessed on September 2, 2007].

application of the national security exemptions under the legislation There are special provisions for the appointment of members to hear national security appeals.

(b) Its workload has increased significantly since January 2005 with addition of appellate functions in relation to decision notices under the FOIA.

TRIBUNAL MEMBERSHIP

26–03 Section 6(3) of the DPA provides for the continued existence of the Data Protection Tribunal. The Tribunal consists of a legally qualified chairman and one or more deputies. They must have been qualified as solicitors in England or Wales, Scotland or Northern Ireland for at least seven years to be eligible for such appointment. The legal appointments are made by the Lord Chancellor after consultation with the Lord Advocate. The Lord Chancellor must specifically designate a number of persons among the chair and deputies appointed who are to hear appeals lodged under s.28 of the DPA or s.60 of the FOIA concerning national security matters. Such designation may be revoked at any time.

An unspecified number of lay members are also appointed to membership of the Tribunal. They represent:

- the interests of data subjects;

- the interests of data controllers;

- the interests of those who make requests under the FOIA; or

- the interests of public authorities under the FOIA.[5]

This follows the pattern set in the Employment Tribunal appointments where lay members represent employer and employee interests respectively. The membership of the Tribunal therefore consists of a panel of members who may be called upon to sit. Appointments are dealt with in detail in Sch.5 Pt II.

There is no fixed term of appointment for members. All members hold office "in accordance with the terms of their appointment". In practice appointments last for five years. Members can resign during that term by notice to the Lord Chancellor. Members are eligible for reappointment on the expiry of their membership. There is no specified retirement age except that the legally qualified members have to retire when they reach the age of 70 years. This, however, is subject to the provision in the Judicial Pensions and Retirement Act 1993 which empowers the Lord Chancellor to authorise the continued holding of judicial office up to the age of 75. The chair and deputies could therefore serve until the age of 75. Members of the Tribunal are paid a daily allowance for each day they sit.[6]

---

[5] DPA s.6(6) as amended by para.16 of Sch.2, Pt II FOIA.
[6] DPA Sch.5 para.13.

SECRETARIAT

26–04 The Tribunal has a secretariat which deals with administrative arrangements. Notices of appeal and other correspondence for the Tribunal should go to the Secretary to the Information Tribunal.

SITTINGS

26–05 The Tribunal has premises in Nottingham but it can sit anywhere. It may choose to hold several hearings at the same time as it may decide to sit in two or more divisions. However, the number of hearings would be limited by the number of deputy chairmen available, as each sitting Tribunal must include either the chair or one of the deputies. In the past the Tribunal held its hearings in London but no longer does so. Two deputies have been appointed to the Tribunal. It has never had more than one hearing at a time. The provisions in s.6 of and Sch.6 to the DPA would allow for an expansion in the Tribunal's workload to be dealt with within the existing framework.

The rules of procedure for the Tribunal allow for the chair or deputy to sit alone in particular circumstances. In particular, preliminary or incidental matters can be dealt with by the chair or deputy sitting alone and appeals against information notices can be dealt with in the same way. Subject to those special cases however, a Tribunal shall consist of a chair or deputy who presides over the proceedings and an equal number of the lay members who are appointed to represent the relevant interests on each side. The membership of each individual tribunal is nominated by the chairman. In making nominations the chairman has to take account of the desirability of having lay members with specialist knowledge of a particular subject but must also ensure that such members will not approach the case with a preconceived or settled view.

The constitution of the Tribunal is rather different when national security appeals are to be heard. The Secretary of State may make special rules regulating the procedure for such appeals. In doing so, he must have regard, in particular, to the need to ensure that information is not disclosed contrary to the public interest.[7] Subject to any special rules national security appeals are to be heard by a Tribunal which does not contain any lay members and is made up only of the legally qualified members specifically designated by the Lord Chancellor to hear such appeals. Any Tribunal decision is to be made in accordance with the opinion of the majority.

JURISDICTION

National Security Certificates—Data Protection Act

26–06 Appeals may be brought under s.28(4) and (6). These are explained in Ch.15, above on regulation, crime and taxation. To recap briefly here, s.28 exempts personal data from data protection control if the exemption is required in order to safeguard national security. "Conclusive evidence" of the fact that the exemption is required for that purpose is to be provided by a certificate signed by a Minister of the

---

[7] DPA Sch.6 para.7(3).

Crown. The certificate must identify the personal data to which it applies. Where such a certificate has been issued there are two possibilities of appeal:

(i) Under s.28(4) a person directly affected by a certificate may appeal to the Tribunal on the ground that the Minister who issued it did not have reasonable grounds for doing so. The test to be applied will be that employed in judicial review cases. The decision may only be overruled if it was "Wednesbury" unreasonable, that is following the principle in *Associated Provincial Picture Houses v Wednesbury Corporation*[8] that it was so unreasonable that no reasonable authority could have reached it taking account of proper considerations. On hearing such a case the Tribunal can either allow the appeal or quash the certificate or dismiss the appeal. The Tribunal does not appear to have any power to vary the certificate, unlike the powers in respect of enforcement notices. The applicant in the case of *Baker v Secretary of State* appealed successfully on this ground and the certificate was revoked.

(ii) Under s.28(6) the possibility of appeal is only open to someone who is a party to other proceedings under the Data Protection Act. If such a litigant is confronted by a national security certificate which describes personal data by a general description and which the defendant data controller claims covers personal data which are the subject of those proceedings then the litigant can refer the question of whether or not it properly does so to the Tribunal by way of an appeal. Presumably, under general principles, the other proceedings will have to be stayed pending the determination of the Tribunal on the matter of the certificate. The Tribunal's powers in such a case are limited to determining that the certificate does or does not apply to the personal data in question.

National Security Certificates—Freedom of Information Act

26–07 Appeals may be brought by the Commissioner or an applicant whose request for information has been affected under s.60 where a certificate under ss.23(2) or 24(3) has been issued.

Section 23 allows for a Minister of the Crown to issue a certificate that the information applied for under the FOIA is exempt because it relates to or was supplied by one of the listed national security bodies. Such a certificate is conclusive evidence of such a fact. Nevertheless an appeal may be made to the Tribunal on the grounds that the information is not entitled to the exemption and if the Tribunal makes a finding that it was not so entitled the Tribunal may allow the appeal and quash the certificate.

Section 24 allows a Minister of the Crown to issue a certificate that the information applied for under the FOIA is exempt because the exemption is necessary for the purpose of safeguarding national security. Such a certificate is conclusive evidence of such a fact. Nevertheless, an appeal may be made to the Tribunal on the ground that the Minister who issued it did not have reasonable grounds for doing so. The test to be applied will be that applied in judicial review cases (see para.26–06, above).

---

[8] [1948] 1 K.B. 223.

Section 60(4) also allows appeals on the ground that a certificate issued under s.24(3) which identifies information in general terms does not in fact cover the information which is being withheld. The Tribunal may determine whether the certificate covers the information.

26–08 In the case of *R (on the application of SSHD) v The Information Tribunal and the Information Commissioner*[9] the High Court held that the Information Tribunal was correct to allow the Information Commissioner to appeal where there was a question as to whether a s.28 certificate had been properly applied. The facts of the case were that the data subject made a subject access request to the Immigration and Nationality Directorate of the Home Office (IND). The subject was not satisfied with the response he received and made an application to the Commissioner for an assessment. The ICO contacted the IND and was informed that the IND considered that s.28, the national security exemption, was applicable. The ICO asked the IND to allow the Commissioner to have sight of the data in question, to supply a s.28 certificate and queried whether the subject had been informed of the IND's reliance on s.28. The IND responded that it did not intend to inform the data subject and would not allow the Commissioner to see the data in question. The Commissioner then served an Information Notice under s.43 seeking access to the information which had been withheld and the IND served a certificate under s.28 stating, not that the personal data was exempt from the subject access right for the purpose of safeguarding national security, but that the personal data was exempt from the power of the Information Commissioner to service the Information Notice under s.43. In fact s.28(11) states that the Commissioner cannot exercise any of his regulatory functions in relation to any personal data to which a s.28 certificate applies in any event.

26–09 Section 28(4) states that any person directly affected by the issuing of a certificate may appeal to the Tribunal against the certificate. The Information Commissioner appealed to the Tribunal as a person "directly affected". The IND also appealed against the service of the Information Notice but that was deferred pending the hearing of the Commissioner's application. Where the Tribunal finds, applying the principles applied by a court on an application for judicial review, that the Minister did not have reasonable grounds for issuing the certificate, it may quash the certificate. The Tribunal considered the IND's arguments and took the view that the IND could not purport to remove the Commissioner's right to appeal the certificate and quashed the certificate. The IND appealed to the High Court which upheld the decision of the Tribunal.

Other appeals under the Data Protection Act

26–10 Section 48 sets out the other matters which may be appealed to the Tribunal under the DPA. They are:

   (i) appeals against enforcement notices (s.48(1));

   (ii) appeals against refusals of the Commissioner to cancel or vary existing enforcement notices (s.48(2));

---

[9] [2002] EWHC 2958 Admin.

(iii) appeals against the inclusion of urgency provisions in any notices (s.48(3));

(iv) appeals against information notices or special information notice (s.48(1));

(v) appeals against a determination by the Commissioner under s.45 (s.48(4)).

Only data controllers may appeal. Individuals have no route by which to appeal to the Tribunal apart from under the national security certificate provisions. There may also be appeals against notices served under the PECR. In every notice served, the Commissioner must inform the controller of the extent of any rights of appeal available and the time within which such appeals must be brought. Appeals can be brought on various grounds primarily on matters of fact and law although in cases where the discretion of the Commissioner is involved an appeal may also be brought against the exercise of the discretion. In most cases appeals must be lodged within 28 days, although the Tribunal will have the power to accept late notices of the appeal.

Other appeals under the Freedom of Information Act

26–11 Section 57 of the FOIA sets out the other matters which may be appealed. They are:

(i) appeals by public authorities against enforcement notices;

(ii) appeals by public authorities against information notices;

(iii) appeals public authorities against decision notices by; or

(iv) appeals by individuals against decision notices.

The Commissioner must inform those on whom notices are served of the rights of appeal.

POWERS OF THE TRIBUNAL

Evidence and information

26–12 The provision that no enactment or rule of law prohibiting or restricting the disclosure of information shall preclude a person from furnishing information necessary for the discharge of functions applies to the Tribunal as it does to the Commissioner.[10] The Tribunal rules may provide for the summoning of witnesses and administration of oaths; securing the production of documents and material used for the processing of personal data; and for the inspection, examination, operating and testing of equipment or material used in connection with the processing of personal data. The 1985 Rules provided for the Tribunal to take expert evidence of its volition although this power was never used and has not been repeated in the current Rules. The Tribunal determines the evidence it will receive. It has accepted evidence *de bene esse* in the past (that is, evidence which it is prepared to hear but on which it will make a separate determination as to the weight to be attributed to it).

---

[10] DPA s.58 as amended by Sch.2 para.18 to the FOIA.

Decisions of the Tribunal

26–13   The Tribunal has different powers to deal with different types of appeal before it. These are set out fully in ss.49 of the DPA and 58 of the FOIA. The powers vary with the pieces of legislation.

Enforcement and information notices under both DPA and FOIA

26–14   The Tribunal has wide powers in respect of enforcement and information notices. It may decide that the notice served by the Commissioner was not "in accordance with the law". This could cover a substantial range of defects, including:

(a) that the formalities of the notice have not been complied with, for example it had not been properly addressed or served;

(b) that the Commissioner failed to consider a relevant issue which would have altered his judgment;

(c) that the Commissioner was mistaken in his understanding of the facts on which the decision was based; or

(d) that the Commissioner was wrong in his view of the meaning or effect of the relevant law.

The Tribunal may review any determination of fact on which a notice is based. This means that the Tribunal will proceed by rehearing in any case where the facts are in dispute. For this reason most cases before the Tribunal proceed by way of oral hearings because issues of fact are in dispute between the parties. Even if the Tribunal decides that the disputed decision was correct in law it may overturn or vary the Commissioner's decision if that decision involved the exercise of a discretion and it is the Tribunal's view that the discretion should have been exercised differently. In decisions under the 1984 Data Protection Act the Tribunal tended to use its ability to look again at the exercise of discretion to try to find a compromise solution between the position of the parties on appeal.

The Tribunal may allow an appeal in full and quash the notice or order involved or may substitute such other order or determination as could have been made by the Commissioner. It may not make a determination broader than that which could have been made by the Commissioner when considering the original matter.

Application for cancellation or change of an enforcement notice under the DPA

26–15   Under s.49(3) of the DPA the Tribunal has a narrower power when hearing these cases. It may vary or cancel an existing enforcement notice only where there has been a change of circumstances. The Tribunal must consider that there is something in that change of circumstances which means that the notice ought to be altered or revoked. Any alterations to the notice must be in response to the change. The Tribunal cannot make changes to the notice unconnected to the change in circumstances.

Appeal against inclusion of an urgency provisions under the DPA

26–16 Supervisory notices generally do not take effect for 28 days after service and if an appeal is lodged the effect of the notice is suspended until the appeal is decided. However, any notice may include an urgency provision stating that, because of special circumstances, the notice should be complied with as a matter of urgency and giving the reasons why the Commissioner has reached that conclusion. In such a case a notice can take effect within seven days. This applies to enforcement notices (s.40(7)), information notices (s.43(6)) and special information notices (s.44(7)).

A controller can appeal against the inclusion of an urgency provision even if he does not appeal against the rest of the notice. On such an appeal the Tribunal can either strike out the urgency provision in whole, so the entire notice no longer takes effect in the seven days, or it can strike it out in part so that some of the notice provisions might come in as a matter of urgency and others not. The Tribunal might also make associated modifications to give effect to its decision on the urgency provisions. The most usual modification would be to replace the seven-day period for the notice taking effect with a 28-day or longer period.

Special purpose determination under the DPA

26–17 A s.45 determination is made by the Commissioner where he decides that personal data are not being processed only for the special purposes or are not being processed with a view to publication of materials which has not previously been published by the data controller for the special purposes. Such a determination will be a matter of both fact and law. The appeal against such a determination may be on either fact or law. Where an appeal against such a determination is brought the Tribunal may either dismiss the appeal or cancel the determination. The Tribunal has a narrower power to deal with such appeals than with other matters of appeal. It has no power to vary or modify the determination even if it finds as a matter of fact that part of the data are being processed for the special processes.

Obstruction and contempt

26–18 The Tribunal may deal with a matter being any act or omission in relation to proceedings before it that would amount to contempt in a court by certifying the offence to the High Court or the Court of Session in Scotland. Where the Tribunal certifies an offence of contempt the court to which it is referred may hear the case and deal with it as if a contempt of the superior court had been committed.

HEARINGS

Ex parte hearings

26–19 Subject to the rules of procedure, Tribunal hearings on national security appeals and appeals against the inclusion of urgency provisions in notice are to be heard in the absence of the respondent to the appeal. One would expect the appeals against the Commissioner's notice to be heard *inter partes* and the national security appeal to allow the Minister to be heard *ex parte*.

Other hearings

26–20 Apart from these provisions hearings are *inter partes* and are also held in public. There is provision in the Rules for hearings to be conducted wholly or partly in private in appropriate cases. The Rules allow for appeals to be determined without a hearing. In most cases both parties are legally represented but there is no requirement for legal representation and a party may represent himself. Legal aid is not available for Information Tribunal hearings.

PROCEDURE

26–21 The Tribunal's procedure is determined by the Tribunal Rules which are made under Sch.6 to the DPA as amended by Sch.4 to the FOIA. Paragraph 7(2) of Sch.6 to the DPA sets out a list of matters for which particular provision may be made. A number of these have been referred to already in this chapter. In addition they deal with the publication of reports of the Tribunal's decisions. The Tribunal has a website on which all its decisions are published.

The Information Tribunal (Enforcement Appeals) Rules 2005 as amended

26–22 These Rules[10a] came into force on February 1, 2005. They apply to appeals brought under s.48 of the DPA by data controllers in respect of:

- enforcement notices;
- special information notices;
- information notices;
- the inclusion or effect of urgency provisions in any such notice;
- determinations that data are not being processed only for the special purposes or with a view to the publication by any person of journalistic, literary or artistic material which has not previously been published by the data controller;
- refusals by the Commissioner to vary existing notices, the rules do not apply to appeals against the issue of national security certificates under s.28 of the DPA. A separate set of rules covers these cases.

They also apply to appeals brought under s.57 of the FOIA by public authorities in respect of:

- decision notices;
- information notices;
- enforcement notices

and to appeals brought under s.57 in respect of environmental information under the Environmental Information Regulations 2004.

[10a] SI 2005/14.

Burden of Proof

26–23 It is for the Commissioner to satisfy the Tribunal that the decision which is the subject of the appeal should be upheld except where the appeal is brought under s.48(3) of the DPA against the inclusion of a provision that the notice must take effect as a matter of urgency.[11] In such cases the Commissioner will not necessarily be notified of the appeal or be present at any hearing. The rules are silent as to where the burden of proof falls in such cases.

Hearings to be in public

26–24 Any member of the Council on Tribunals or the Scottish Committee of the Council on Tribunals acting in his capacity as such may attend any hearing, whether it is in public or in private, and remain present at the deliberations of the Tribunal but not take part in them. The general rule is that all hearings, including preliminary hearings, are to be held in public unless the Tribunal directs that the hearing or any part of the hearing is to be held in private. The Tribunal may direct that hearings are to be held in private for the purpose of safeguarding the privacy of data subjects, or commercially sensitive information or any matter in respect of which an exemption under the FOIA is claimed.[12] However, even where a hearing is private the chair or any deputy of the Tribunal may attend, notwithstanding they are not involved in the particular case, and any other person with the leave of the Tribunal and the consent of the parties.

Costs

26–25 Costs are not usually awarded in Tribunal cases but there are provisions allowing for their award in special cases. The Tribunal may make a costs order against the appellant where it considers that the appeal was manifestly unreasonable; against the Commissioner where it considers that the disputed decision was manifestly unreasonable; against either party where it considers that party to have been responsible for frivolous, vexatious, improper or unreasonable action; or for any failure to comply with a direction or a delay which could have been avoided with due diligence. Where the Tribunal is considering awarding costs against a party it must give that party an opportunity to make representations on the point. Where costs are awarded they may be by way of a fixed sum or as taxed if not agreed. Taxation is to be carried out in the county court according to such of the scales set out in the county court rules as is directed by the costs order.[13] The Tribunal awarded costs against Nottingham County Council in a case brought under the FOIA by the Information Commissioner where the Council had repeatedly failed to comply with its obligations.

Appeals to be in writing

26–26 All appeals have to be started by a written notice of appeal. Rule 31 provides that service of any notice or other document for the purpose of the Rules may be effected by sending the notice or document to the proper address by post in a registered

---

[11] Information Tribunal Rules reg.26.
[12] Information Tribunal Rules reg.22.
[13] Information Tribunal Rules reg.29.

letter or by the recorded delivery service. In the case of the Tribunal the proper address is that of the proper officer (the Secretary); in the case of the Commissioner his office; in the case of an appellant the address he gives for service as part of his notice of appeal; in the case of an occupier the address of the relevant premises. The written notice of appeal should be lodged with the Secretary to the Tribunal within 28 days of service of the disputed decision on the appellant.[14] However, the Tribunal may accept appeals served out of time if it is of the opinion that, by reason of special circumstances, it is just and right to do so. The notice of appeal may include a request for an early hearing and if so should also include the appellant's reasons for making such a request. The notice must:

- state the name and address of the appellant;

- identify the disputed decision;

- provide the date of service of the notice of the disputed decision;

- set out the grounds of the appeal;

- state whether the appellant wishes a hearing to be held;

- give an address for service of notices and other documents;

- where an appeal is made out of time, state the special circumstances on which the appellant relies.[15]

As the Rules provide for appeals against information notices to be heard by the chairman sitting alone an appellant who wishes such an appeal to be heard by a full Tribunal must include in his notice of appeal representations as to why it is necessary in the interests of justice for it to be decided by a full Tribunal. The chairman may decide that an appeal against an information notice may be heard by a full Tribunal if it is necessary in the interests of justice.

If a notice of appeal is sent by post it is treated as having been served when received for despatch by the Post Office.[16]

Procedure before hearing

26–27 On receipt of the notice of appeal it will be acknowledged. The acknowledgment must include a statement of the Tribunal's power to award costs. Where an appeal is made against the inclusion of an urgency provision there is no obligation to send a copy to the Commissioner unless the Tribunal is of the opinion that the interests of justice require the Commissioner to assist by giving evidence or being heard and in such cases the Tribunal cannot decide on the inclusion of the urgency provision ex parte. In any other case a copy of the appeal must be sent to the Commissioner by the Secretary to the Tribunal. The Commissioner must respond by sending the Tribunal a written acknowledgment stating whether he intends to oppose the appeal and giving his grounds for doing so. The grounds are likely to amount to a restatement

---

[14] Information Tribunal Rules reg.5.
[15] Information Tribunal Rules reg.4.
[16] Information Tribunal Rules reg.5(3).

of the decision notice. If the appellant has indicated that he will not wish a hearing to be held the Commissioner's response must state whether he agrees with that choice. The Commissioner may also make representations on whether an appeal brought in respect of an information notice should be heard by the chairman sitting alone. The response may also include a request for an early hearing.[17] If, in any case other than an appeal on urgency provisions alone, the Commissioner considers that there are no grounds for the appeal or there is some fundamental flaw in the appeal then he can apply for the appeal to be struck out. Such an application can be heard as a preliminary issue in the appeal.[18] The time limits allowed for response by the Commissioner are 21 days after receipt of the notice of appeal in most cases but such period as the Tribunal allows in other cases.

Appeals may be amended, supplemented, withdrawn or consolidated. Amendments and additions require the leave of the Tribunal and where such changes are allowed the amended grounds must be served on the Commissioner and responses lodged as for the substantive appeal. The Commissioner may also amend his reply to the appeal with the leave of the Tribunal.[19] Withdrawal of an appeal must be done by written notice. Once an appeal is withdrawn a fresh appeal on the same decision cannot be brought without leave of the Tribunal.[20] The Tribunal may order appeals to be consolidated or heard together where it appears to them that some common question of fact or law arises in both or all or that for some other reason it is desirable to proceed with them together. The parties must be afforded an opportunity to comment before such an order is made.[21]

Directions may be made by the Tribunal in the absence of the parties to enable the parties to prepare for the hearing or assist the Tribunal to deal with the issues.[22] The Tribunal has a wide power to issue directions. Wherever it does so notice of the directions must be served on the parties. The Tribunal may also vary or set aside directions on the application of either party. The directions may provide for issues to be dealt with as preliminary issues. Its powers to deal with pre-hearing matters include provisions relating to discovery and inspection; exchange of statements and evidence and the provision of skeleton arguments, chronologies or other documents. The Tribunal may also direct the conduct of the hearing for example by limiting the length of oral submissions or the number of expert witnesses to be called by each side. Its powers to require the production of documents or other material is restricted to those things which a party could be compelled to produce to a court of law in the part of the United Kingdom where the appeal is to be determined. The rules include a specific restriction on the use of any information or material provided. Any recipient of such information must only use it for the purposes of the appeal. The term recipient is potentially a wide one and therefore one who is not a party to the appeal would be bound by it.

The chairman may act for the Tribunal in dealing with any preliminary or incidental matters in relation to accepting appeals out of time, accepting applications by the Commissioner for an extension of time within which to lodge his response to an

---

[17] Information Tribunal Rules reg.8(6).
[18] Information Tribunal Rules reg.9.
[19] Information Tribunal Rules reg.11.
[20] Information Tribunal Rules reg.12.
[21] Information Tribunal Rules reg.13.
[22] Information Tribunal Rules reg.14.

appeal, amendments to grounds, consolidation of appeals, withdrawals, directions, orders of entry to premises, and hearing dates.[23]

Entry to premises

26–28 The rules provide for the possibility that the Tribunal itself may wish to enter premises to inspect, examine, operate or test equipment or other material connected with the processing of personal data in order to determine an appeal and they empower the Tribunal to enter such premises. This power applies even if the occupier of the premises is one of the parties to the appeal. The Tribunal exercises this power by making an order requiring the occupier of any premises to permit entry by the Tribunal together with the parties and such officers and staff as the Tribunal considers necessary. The order must specify the time of entry and at least seven days must elapse between service of the order and the date set for the entry. A copy of the order must be served on both the occupier and the parties. If the occupier applies the Tribunal may set the order aside. It may also vary the time for entry on the application of either the occupier or the parties. If it does vary the time it must notify those affected but does not have to serve another seven day notice. The usual rules as to documents or other material which cannot be compelled to produce apply.[24]

Determination without hearing

26–29 The circumstances in which an appeal may be decided without a hearing are limited. It can be done where the parties agree in writing. Otherwise a previous appeal by the same appellant must have been decided by the Tribunal and the facts of the current appeal must not materially differ from those in the previous appeal. If the Tribunal considers in such a case that that the issues raised on the appeal have already been determined in the previous appeal it may decide either the entire appeal or particular issues without a hearing. However before doing so it must allow the parties an opportunity to make representations. If it decides to proceed without a hearing the Tribunal may direct any party to provide any further written information relevant to the appeal and set a time within which such information must be provided.

Hearings

26–30 At any hearing a party may conduct his own case or be represented by another.[25] The time and date of the hearing is set by the Tribunal which must have due regard to the convenience of the parties. At least 14 days' notice of the date must be given to the parties unless the appeal relates to the inclusion of an urgency provision in the notice. The parties are notified of the hearing date by the Secretary who must also inform them of the consequences of non-appearance at the hearing under reg.17. This provides that if a party who has been duly informed of a hearing date fails to appear without giving sufficient reason for his absence the Tribunal may dismiss the appeal if he is the appellant or otherwise hear and determine the case and

---

[23] Information Tribunal Rules reg.26.
[24] Information Tribunal Rules reg.15.
[25] Information Tribunal Rules reg.19.

make any order as to costs which it thinks fit. The Tribunal has powers to postpone or adjourn the hearing or alter the place of the hearing and if it does so must notify the parties.

Witnesses and evidence

26–31   The Tribunal has a wide power to consider material presented to it. It may receive any document or information in evidence notwithstanding that such document or information would be inadmissible in a court of law. It may require oral evidence to be given on oath or affirmation and the chairman or officer has the power to take such oaths or affirmations.[26] The Tribunal may issue witness summonses to any person in the United Kingdom to attend as a witness, answer questions and produce documents under his custody or control as relate to any matter in question in the appeal. It must give the witness at least seven days' notice of the time and date of the hearing unless the witness agrees otherwise and informs the Tribunal of his agreement. A witness cannot be compelled to give evidence or produce any document which he could not be compelled to produce in a court of law. A person who attends as a witness in response to a summons is entitled to a sum in respect of travelling expenses and attendance as is set by the Tribunal.[27]

Conduct at hearing

26–32   Except as provided by the Rules the Tribunal shall conduct the proceedings as it considers appropriate and shall seek to avoid formality in its proceedings. At the hearing it shall give each party an opportunity to address the Tribunal and amplify the written statements previously served, call witnesses, give evidence, cross examine the witnesses for the other side and on completion of the evidence make representations on the evidence and subject-matter of the appeal generally.[28]

Joinder of other persons to appeals

26–33   Where appeals are heard under the Freedom of Information Act (or the linked provisions of the Environmental Information Regulations) the Tribunal may order a party to be joined as a party to the appeal. It may do this by serving a "joinder notice" to the person. A person may also apply of their own choice to be joined to an appeal.[29]

Exclusion of parties from hearings

26–34   A Minister of the Crown may apply ex parte for a party or parties to be excluded from proceedings and the Tribunal may order this where it considers that it is necessary for reasons of substantial public interest. It must also, as far as possible, inform the parties of the reason for the exclusion.[30]

---

[26] Information Tribunal Rules reg.27.
[27] Information Tribunal Rules reg.27(2).
[28] Information Tribunal Rules reg.24.
[29] Information Tribunal Rules reg.7.
[30] Information Tribunal Rules reg.23.

Decisions

26–35   As soon as practicable after the Tribunal has decided the appeal the chairman shall certify the decision in writing and sign and date the certificate. The certificate shall include any material finding of fact and the reasons for the decision. The Secretary shall send a copy to the parties. The Tribunal must make arrangements for publishing its decisions but in doing so must have regard to the privacy of data subjects and any commercially sensitive information as well as preserving the information which is exempt under the FOIA and may make amendments to the text of the certificate in order to protect those.[31]

Irregularities

26–36   Rule 30 provides that failure to comply with any of the provisions of the Rules before the Tribunal has reached its decision shall not render the proceedings void but the Tribunal may, and shall if any person has been prejudiced by the irregularity, give directions to take steps to cure any irregularity. Clerical errors can be corrected by the chairman by certificate.

National Security Appeals Procedure

26–37   The procedure is, as far as possible, the same as that followed for normal hearings. In this section only the aspects which differ are covered. There is a specific obligation on the Tribunal to ensure that information is not disclosed contrary to the interests of national security.[32] The notice of appeal is not sent to the Commissioner, other than where he is the appellant, but to the relevant Minister, and in the case of an appeal under s.28(6) to the relevant data controller.[33] The Minister then has 42 days in which to respond. He must send the Tribunal a copy of the certificate to which the appeal relates, and a statement stating whether he intends to oppose the appeal. If he does contest it he must send a summary of the grounds relating to the issue of the certificate and the reasons for issuing it, and statements of the grounds on which he relies for opposing the appeal and the evidence upon which he relies. Unless the Minister objects the Tribunal then sends a copy of the material to the appellant, and the Commissioner.[34] The Minister may object to the disclosure on the grounds that the disclosure of information would be contrary to the interests of national security. If he does so he must state his reasons for doing so and prepare a form of notice which can be disclosed.[35]

Where an appeal is brought under s.28(6), that is one in which the certificate itself is not challenged, but the appellant disputes that the certificate covers the data in issue, the respondent also has a period of 42 days within which to state whether he opposes the appeal and, if so, his grounds. A Minister given notice of such an appeal must state whether he supports the appeal. The Minister's response will be served on the relevant data controller and the data controller's response on the Minister.

---

[31] Information Tribunal Rules reg.28.
[32] Information Tribunal Rules reg.4(1).
[33] Information Tribunal Rules reg.7.
[34] Information Tribunal Rules reg.8.
[35] Information Tribunal Rules reg.13.

The usual rules as to directions apply however the Tribunal is obliged to give the Minister prior notice of proposed direction, witness summons or publication of a determination. The Minister may then make an application to the Tribunal to reconsider the proposal in whole or in part.[36] The hearing of such an objection is ex parte save for the attendance of the Minister and he has the right to make oral representations. If the Tribunal decides to overrule the Minister and insist upon the disclosure of material the Minister has the option of choosing not to rely on it in opposing the appeal. If the Minister so chooses the Tribunal must not disclose, nor can it insist on the Minister's disclosing, the material in question.[37] The Tribunal has power to dispose of the appeal on a summary basis although it must give the appellant notice of intention to do so and allow him to make representations in writing or orally, if it so permits, against the proposal to summarily dismiss. All hearings are to be in private except so far as the Tribunal with the consent of the Minister and the parties directs. Persons, other than the Minister, may be excluded from the hearing by the Tribunal but, as far as is compatible with the interests of national security, must be told why.

FURTHER APPEALS

26–38   Under s.49(6) there is an appeal from a decision of the Tribunal on a point of law only to the High Court for England and Wales, the Court of Session in Scotland or the High Court in Northern Ireland. The appropriate court will be determined by the address of the registered office of the person who was the appellant before the Tribunal. Any appeal must be brought within 28 days. The relevant rules are to be found in CPR.

ADDITIONAL INFORMATION

Derivations

26–39 • Data Protection Act 1984: s.3 and Sch.2 (Tribunal and appeal proceedings), s.13 (rights of appeal), s.14 (determination of appeals)

  • The Data Protection Tribunal Rules 1985 (SI 1985/1568)

Hansard references

26–40   Vol.587, No.122, col.526, Lords Report, March 16, 1998
Tribunal appointments for national security appeals.

Commons Standing Committee D, May 12, 1998, col.64
Tribunal appointments.

Previous case law

26–41   None.

---

[36] Information Tribunal Rules reg.17.
[37] Information Tribunal Rules reg.18(6).

CHAPTER 27

Data Protection Law in Jersey, Guernsey and the Isle of Man

INTRODUCTION

27–01 Many organisations work closely with associated or other entities based in the Channel Islands and the Isle of Man. Each of these is a separate jurisdiction. The UK Data Protection Act does not apply in any of these jurisdictions and therefore each of the jurisdictions has had to pass its own legislation. Neither the Channel Islands nor the Isle of Man belong to the European Economic Area (EEA). If dealing with a specific problem in one of the islands the practitioner should check the specific legislation for that jurisdiction. Although the wording and import of most of the provisions are in most instances identical to the UK Act there are differences. Each Act is arranged slightly differently and therefore the section numbers may differ, even where the content is the same. Some of the differences are significant, for example in the Isle of Man, on the application of an aggrieved data subject, the High Court can order a data controller who has not dealt with a subject access request properly to pay a penalty of up to £5,000. In addition each jurisdiction has a separate independent regulator whose approach may not be the same as the one taken by the Information Commissioner in the UK.

SUMMARY OF MAIN POINTS

27–02 (a) In order to apply to the European Commission for a finding that each jurisdiction affords adequate protection the legislature of each of the islands has had to pass data protection law which meets the requirements of the Directive.

(b) In Jersey the law is the Data Protection (Jersey) Law 2005 which came in to effect on December 1, 2005 and replaced the Data Protection (Jersey) Law 1987.

(c) In Guernsey this is the Data Protection (Bailiwick of Guernsey) Law 2001 which came into effect on August 1, 2002 and replaced the Data Protection (Bailiwick of Guernsey) Law 1986.

(d) In the Isle of Man the law is the Data Protection Act 2002 which came into effect on April 1, 2003 and replaced the Data Protection Act 1986.

(e) The EU made findings of adequacy in respect of Guernsey and the Isle of Man on November 21, 2003 and April 28, 2004 respectively (see Ch.4, above for a full discussion of the implications of a finding of adequacy).

(f) The States of Jersey asked Department of Constitutional Affairs to make an application to the EU on February 20, 2006. The EU is currently considering the position of Jersey and an adequacy finding is anticipated in the very near future.

(g) Each of the regimes follows closely the UK Act but there are some areas of difference.

RELATION WITH THE DIRECTIVE

27–03 As the islands are not part of the EU the Data Protection Directive does not apply, nor are the courts under any obligation to take account of the Directive as a matter of general law. This is dealt with by the inclusion of specific interpretative provisions in the Isle of Man Act but not in the other two laws. In the Isle of Man law s.62(3) provides that:

"in construing any provision of this Act any court or tribunal shall have regard to any provision of the Convention or of the Data Protection directive which appears to the court or tribunal to be relevant."

SUPERVISORY AUTHORITIES

27–04 As each jurisdiction has its own legislation which implements the Directive it follows that each Act sets up an independent supervisory body. In the Isle of Man this is the role of the Isle of Man Data Protection Supervisor, in the States of Jersey the Data Protection Commissioner and in the Bailiwick of Guernsey the Data Protection Commissioner. The Bailiwick of Guernsey also covers Alderney and Sark, although there are slightly different provisions for the courts on Alderney and Sark.

Each of the supervisory authorities is the relevant designated authority for the purposes of Art.13 of the Convention for the Protection of Individuals with regard to the Automatic Processing of Personal Data (Treaty 108). The Islands do not directly ratify treaties, instead treaties are extended to the Islands by the UK which formally notifies the Council of the ratification. Treaty 108 was confirmed in the territorial extensions to the ratification of the UK in 1993 covering the Isle of Man and Guernsey. Jersey has been unable to apply until recently, when the new law came into force and is currently reviewing the position.

INTER-ISLANDS CO-OPERATION

27–05 The regulatory authorities of the UK, the islands and Ireland hold regular meetings to discuss matters of common interest. In many cases the guidance issued by the regulators follows the same lines, this is however not universally the case and reference should be made to the websites for specific guidance (see *http://www.gov.im/odps*, *http://www.dataprotection.gov.je* and *http://www.gov.gg/dataprotection* [Accessed on September 2, 2007]).

OVERVIEW OF DIFFERENCES

27–06   There are inevitable differences arising simply from the difference in jurisdictions. The UK DPA amends the Consumer Credit Act 1974 (s.62) and deals with the exercise of rights by children in Scotland (s.66) while none of the other pieces of legislation make similar amends. There are provisions in the UK Act which deal with educational records and accessible records but which are not are not covered by the Jersey or Guernsey acts, although the Isle of Man does cover accessible records.

Section numbers

Jersey law

27–07   In the UK Act and the Jersey law the section numbers and topics are the same up to s.60 of the Jersey law. The Jersey law adds a specific provision which deals with the provision of false information as s.60. It also has a specific provision excluding civil liability by the Commissioner or Tribunal in s.66. The UK's s.62 is omitted and thereafter the sections differ slightly as the Jersey provisions for definitions are contained in the initial definition section rather than separated as in the UK Act. The schedule numbers are the same up until Schs 11 and 12 which in the UK deal with educational records and accessible records which have no counterpart in the Jersey law.

Isle of Man

27–08   In the UK Act and the Isle of Man law the section numbers diverge at s.3 as the Isle of Man deals with sensitive personal data and special purposes in the first section containing the interpretative provisions. There are further differences and the section numbers never converge. The schedule numbers are the same until Sch.9 as the Isle of Man Act includes specific provisions dealing with the register of electors, notification of concerns about specific registrations to the Tribunal and there is no provision for assistance in cases where the special purposes are relevant.

Guernsey

27–09   The section references in the Guernsey Law are the same up to s.62 where the UK provision which covers the amendments to the Consumer Credit Act does not apply. However in Guernsey Statutory Instrument 2002 No.12 includes an analogous statement of rights. The Schedule numbers are the same up to Sch.6 which in the Guernsey Act covers miscellaneous exemptions.

Freedom of Information Act 2000 (FOIA)

27–10   The amendments to the UK DPA made by the FOIA are not applicable in any of the islands as none of the islands have yet passed such legislation, although there is draft legislation under consideration in Jersey and the Isle of Man. The extension of subject access to unstructured manual files in the public sector is therefore not currently applicable to the islands.

OTHER AMENDMENTS TO THE LAWS

27–11 The Jersey law was amended by the Data Protection (Amendment) Jersey Law 2005 in April 2005 to clarify the powers of the States to provide for exemptions which would apply where enactments or rules of law outside the jurisdiction prohibited or restricted the disclosure of information or authorised a person to withhold it. The States of Guernsey has approved a proposal to alter the law in Guernsey to increase the annual fee for notification from £35 (which is the level charged in the UK) to £50 which is the same as Jersey and to exempt charities from payment of the fee. The fee in the Isle of Man is £40. The Commissioner has also recommended that his office be provided with further powers to obtain information when he is conducting investigations, and to clarify the application of the law to the Crown and to public sector organisations to make clear that he may serve regulatory notices on the Chief executive or Head of such a body.

COMPARATIVE ANALYSIS

Definition

27–12 Inevitably there are some technical differences in definitions, for example the courts are different through the jurisdictions. The definitions are also dealt with rather differently. In the Jersey law all the interpretation provisions are included in s.1 whereas in the other laws the main definitions are in s.1 but with further lists of defined terms at the end of the law. There are no significant alterations in the definitions between the legislation however the user should check whether specific terms are defined terms as not all the same defined terms are covered in each law.

Individual rights

Subject access

27–13 The subject access provisions in ss.7, 8, and 9 of the UK Act are mirrored by almost identical provisions in the other three sets of provisions. There are some minor drafting differences but only one major difference which is found in the Isle of Man provisions. In drafting terms the Jersey law makes it explicit that the data controller responding to a subject access request is only required to describe the purposes for which that data controller processes the data, and not the purposes of others and the same is true in respect of the descriptions of recipients. The Jersey law also includes the 40-day time scale as a default provision in the section itself rather than in secondary legislation. The provisions which deal with making a request of the data subject for further identifying information are now the same following the amendment to the UK Act brought about by the Freedom of Information Act. The Isle of Man and the Guernsey laws include the powers of the court to view information in the procedural provisions for subject access rather than under the powers of the court but the effect of the provisions is the same. In Guernsey the statutory period for responding to a subject access request is 60 days.

27–14 The substantive difference lies in the Isle of Man law which provides that where an individual succeeds on an application to the High Court in obtaining an order that a data controller has failed to comply with a subject access request served in accord with the relevant provisions then:

> "(9)(b) if the court is satisfied that the failure was unjustified and that the data controller knew or ought to have known that it was unjustified, [the court may] impose on him a penalty of such amount (not exceeding £5000) as the court thinks fit."

The penalty is treated as a fine imposed by the criminal court. It does not appear that this provision has been used by the courts but it affords a strong incentive to data controllers in the Isle of Man to comply with their subject access obligations.

Rights to object to processing

27–15   The rights to object to processing and to processing for the purposes of direct marketing are identical in all four laws.

Rights of rectification and correction

27–16   Here the Guernsey law follows the UK Act in full but both the Isle of Man and Jersey provide stronger rights to compensation. In the UK and Guernsey an individual may only claim compensation for distress where the distress is either caused by the same contravention for which the individual has been able to recover damage or there has been a contravention of the Act in connection with processing for the special purposes. However the Jersey law provides that an individual who suffers distress by reason of any contravention by a data controller of any requirement imposed by or under the law may recover compensation for that distress. The Isle of Man is not so generous but does allow for recovery for distress caused by a failure to deal properly with a subject access request where the High Court has imposed a penalty.

Rectification and other remedies

27–17   The provisions are identical as are the provisions which provide that a court may view personal data which is the subject of a disputed access application but must not disclose the data to the individual of its own volition. The Guernsey Act sets out which cases are to go to which courts in the islands as between Guernsey, Alderney and Sark.

Notification

27–18   The provisions for notification in all the laws follow the UK model. There are some slight differences in wording in the Jersey law but there are only one or two substantive differences throughout the sections of the laws that deal with notification. The substantive difference of significance is the provision in the Isle of Man law which enables the Supervisor to refer an application for notification to the Tribunal. This breaks the mould of notification as merely an administrative function and is another of the features that marks the Isle of Man Act as more seriously committed to the protection of the individual than others.

Section 20 of the Isle of Man Act provides that if it appears to the Supervisor that a notification of processing made shows that the processing would contravene any of the principles he may refer the notification to the Tribunal. He must, at the same time, specify the principle or principles that he considers would be contravened and why he is making the reference. The Supervisor is not expected to refer merely technical breaches. The section provides that, in deciding whether to make the reference he must consider whether the processing in question has caused or would cause any person damage or distress.

Where the Tribunal are satisfied that the processing would cause such a breach it may direct the Supervisor to either cancel the entry in the register or vary it to such an extent as the Tribunal directs. Schedule 6 sets out the procedures to be followed and there is an appeal to the High Court for a party who is affected by the reference to the Tribunal.

The effect of the provision is to make the process of notification capable of being used as a supervisory regime. To date there have been no references to the Tribunal however the power has been helpful to the Supervisor who has been able to query notifications and ensure that amendments are made. To date no data controller has refused to make amendments that the Supervisor has considered necessary.

27–19   All of the regimes provide for the State authorities to determine particular types of processing as assessable processing but none has done so; nor has the power to provide for data protection officers as independent overseers been used.

27–20   In relation to overseas transfers all the islands provide that the notification must be of transfers outside the particular jurisdiction, rather than outside the EEA as the UK Act requires.

27–21   Only Jersey follows s.16(1)(g) in requiring that the controller include a statement on the register of notifications that the data controller also holds personal data which are exempt from the obligation to notify.

Exemptions

27–22   The basic definition of the nature of exemptions, that is non-disclosure exemptions or subject information exemptions, are common to all the laws. The exemption for public or national security works the same way although the bodies which issue the certificates and hear appeals are distinct for each jurisdiction. The appeals provisions in Jersey and Guernsey which cover those appeals which may be made by a person directly affected by a certificate against the issue thereof do not refer to the application of the principles of judicial review but merely to the question of whether the issue of the certificate was reasonable.

27–23   In relation to the exemption for crime and security the substantive provisions are the same for all the laws, apart from the references to the administrative units which are relevant public authorities for the purposes of the risk classification aspect of the exemption. However the Guernsey and Jersey laws both make it explicit that the investigations may take place in other places and may cover offences that may have been committed either in or outside the jurisdiction. The Jersey law refers to the investigation "anywhere of crime" and the Guernsey law to crime "within or outside the Bailiwick".

27–24   In relation to health, education and social work each law includes enabling provisions which allows exemptions from the right of subject access to be made by order and is the same (apart from a slight difference in wording in the last paragraph of the Jersey law) in each provision. We have not examined the substantive orders and if a data controller wishes to rely on any of those orders the specific wording of the order should be consulted.

27–25   In relation to regulatory activity the main provisions are the same for all the laws however this is an exemption which has been differently drafted in the detail of the materials covered. In the UK provision s.31(4) lists a number of regulatory authorities and provides for a subject information exemption in respect of the functions which they carry out for a list of purposes which are for the protection of the public. This is not repeated in the Guernsey or Isle of Man laws. In the Jersey law there is provision for the relevant authorities or be designated by order and the protective functions listed are more widely drawn to cover cases where the protective function relates to various business activities. In the Guernsey law the designated functions include those designed to protect the reputation and standing of the Bailiwick.

27–26   In relation to the special purposes of journalism, art and literature the exemption is identical in each case apart from some slight drafting alterations (for example using one paragraph instead of two) and the administrative provisions for the designation of relevant codes of practice.

27–27   In relation to research, history and statistics the terms of this exemption are identical in all the laws.

27–28   In relation to information available to the public the exemptions are the same apart from a provision in Art.34(2)(b) of the Guernsey law. In the Guernsey law "public information" is defined not only as that which a data controller is obliged by or under an enactment to make public but as including also:

"(b) information or any type or class of information held by any person or body designated by the Committee for the purposes of this section."

27–29   In relation to legal proceedings, domestic purposes and the power to make further exemptions by order the provisions are the same in each law.

27–30   The Isle of Man has an exemption for the privileges of Tynwald. If it is required for the purpose of avoiding an infringement of the privileges of Tynwald (the Isle of Man parliament) the Council (the Isle of Man Cabinet) or the Keys (the Isle of Man Upper house) then there is a very wide exemption. This allows for exemption from:

- the first Principle except for Schs 2 and 3;

- the second, third, fourth and fifth Principles, s.5 (that is the right of subject access) and ss.8 and 12(1) to (3) (that is rights of rectification).

Miscellaneous exemptions

27–31   The miscellaneous exemptions from subject access or the subject information provisions are the same as the UK in all the laws, apart from some technical and necessary differences in dealing with corporate finance. Anyone seeking to rely on that exemption would need to consider the specific definitions in the individual law. In the Guernsey law there is an additional exemption from subject access in para.12 of Sch.6. Paragraph 12 covers personal data which consist of records of criminal convictions or cautions of data subjects who are not ordinarily resident in the Bailiwick. Where such persons are able to obtain access to such records "under and subject to the law of a jurisdiction other than the Bailiwick" then the records are exempt from the subject information provisions under the Guernsey law. The intention of this provision was to prevent "back-door" enforced subject access to criminal records from the UK via Guernsey. It is notable that the data are not merely exempt from the subject access provisions but from the subject information provisions. The effect of this is that a data controller subject to the Guernsey law may not have to provided notice of processing of such data to the data subjects. The exemption however only applies where the subject would be able to obtain access under the law of another jurisdiction. The access presumably need not be obtained under a data protection law but could be any legal basis. It is not clear whether the individual must simply have the right to apply for access (and implicitly may fail in an access request if an exemption applies) or the data controller must be satisfied that the individual would actually succeed in obtaining access to the information.

ENFORCEMENT

27–32 The enforcement provisions, including provisions in relation to the special purposes and appeals follow exactly the same approach. The only difference in substance between all four jurisdictions is that in Jersey information notices and special information notices may be served on data processors and processors are obliged to respond. If notices are served on such processors a copy must, at the same time, be served on the data controller and both parties are entitled to appeal against the service of the notices.

MISCELLANEOUS AND GENERAL PROVISIONS

27–33 The provisions are again largely the same although, unexpectedly given that the law is in other ways more supportive of individual rights than the others, the Isle of Man does not provide for the Supervisor to assist individuals in cases involving the special purposes. There is no equivalent of s.53 in the UK Act in the Isle of Man. Jersey includes a specific offence provision covering the provision of false information which, in effect, not only criminalises the act of lying to the Commissioner, but appears to also criminalise the provision of false information in response to a subject access request. The drafting of s.60 is not easy to follow. It provides that any person who, knowingly or recklessly, provides the Commissioner *or any other person entitled to information under this Law or under Regulations made under this Law*, with information that is false or misleading in a material particular shall be guilty of an offence. The provision applies where the information is provided either directly in meeting the legal requirement to provide information or indirectly where information is provided:

". . . in circumstances in which the person providing the information intends, or could reasonably have been expected to know, that the information would be used by the Commissioner for the purpose of carrying out the Commissioner's functions under this Law."

It would appear therefore that a person who makes a false report of non-compliance with the Law could fall foul of this provision. The section goes on to provide that a person who knowingly or recklessly provides the Commissioner or any other person entitled to information under the Law with information in connection with an application under the Law that is false or misleading in a material particular shall be guilty of an offence. The offence carries a term of imprisonment of up to five years.

27–34 The general duties of the regulatory authorities are the same in all the jurisdictions save that, in the Isle of Man, the Supervisor has no obligation to promulgate Community Findings or Commission decisions on adequacy. In Guernsey the obligation to lay an annual report before the legislature is found in Sch.5 and, like the other, simply requires a report every 12 months, whereas in Jersey the obligation is not only imposed but is specific as to the timescale within which such a report must be laid.

The provisions in relation to international co-operation vary slightly between the laws. None of the islands have the equivalent of s.54(5) of the UK Act which provides that the Commissioner shall assist with data protection in any specified colony.

27–35 The criminal offences of procuring and selling personal data without the consent of the data controller appear in all the laws even thought they would not be required for the purpose of achieving a finding of adequacy from the Commission. The only difference, again apart from some minor drafting changes, is that in the Jersey law the prohibition applies even where the obtaining was in relation to national security. The UK and the other laws preserve the right of those dealing with national security to use surreptitious methods where it is necessary for the purposes of national security but this is not the case with the Jersey regime.

The remaining provisions which deal with enforced subject access, access to health records, disclosure of information by the supervisory authority, obligations of confidentiality and prosecutions are identical in effect. There remain the administrative and technical provisions including definitions but again the only differences are either minor drafting ones or ones that reflect the different composition of the government in the particular jurisdiction.

Schedules 1–4

27–36 In view of their significance we have considered Schs 1–4 and Sch.7 (exemptions) in detail, however we have not carried out the equivalent detailed assessment of all of the others. In this section therefore we provide only an overview. There are no significant differences in the schedules, although they are not numbered the same in each case. The Guernsey law does not include a schedule dealing with appeals however as appeals are made the courts this is because the relevant provisions are found in procedural rules of the courts. Rules of court have been drafted which are similar to the UK rules which apply to the Information Tribunal.

The Principles and the interpretative provisions

27–37 All of these are identical apart from a small drafting addition in the Jersey law and the fact that the additional safeguards which are applied where the disproportionate effort provision is relied upon where personal data are obtained from a third party appear on the face of the Act in the Isle of Man provisions rather then in secondary legislation.

Schedule 2

27–38　Apart from one omission from the Jersey law and the most minor drafting differences (the movement of "for" into the first part of a phrase in Principle 2 in the Jersey law) the provisions are identical throughout. In the Jersey law "prospective legal proceedings" are omitted. It is difficult to assess whether this could make a material difference but clearly it could be used to base an argument that the provision in Jersey is narrower than in the other jurisdictions.

Schedule 3

27–39　The provisions of Sch.3 are identical, again apart from the most minor drafting differences, until one comes to Grounds 10 onward of the Isle of Man Act. The Isle of Man has included in the Schedule the grounds set out in the UK in SI 2000/417, the Data Protection (Processing of Sensitive Personal data) Order 2000. The only omission is Ground 8 in SI 2000/417 which relates to information held by political parties for the purposes of legitimate political activities.

Schedule 4

27–40　The provisions of Sch.4 are identical apart from some slightly different wording in the Jersey law and again the omission of the reference to "prospective" legal proceedings.

REGISTER OF ELECTORS—ISLE OF MAN

27–41　The Isle of Man used the opportunity of the passage of its Data Protection Act to insert primary legislation authorising the passage of regulations to deal with the use of the electoral roll for marketing and the rights of electors to opt-out of the full register for that purpose. Schedule 9 to the Act amends the Jury Act 1980 to allow the Council of Ministers to make the appropriate regulations.

SECONDARY LEGISLATION

27–42　The secondary legislation for all of the islands follows the pattern of the UK with amendments to reflect the local situation or differences in the primary legislation highlighted in this chapter. Guernsey Statutory Instrument 2002/19 provides a specific exemption from the subject information provisions in the following terms. The disclosure to a relevant body of personal data, consisting of information relating to any person, is exempt from the non-disclosure provisions where the disclosure is necessary for the purpose of protecting that person or any other person from suffering serious harm.

TRANSITIONAL ARRANGEMENTS

27–43　The provisions are the same as the UK and all end on October 23, 2007 with the ending of the second transitional period with the exception of Jersey which ends the first transitional period in December 2008 and the second in December 2011.

ADDITIONAL INFORMATION

27–44   Data Protection Supervisor Isle of Man Supervisor
Iain McDonald
PO Box 69
Douglas
Isle of Man IM99 1EQ

Tel: +44 (0) 1624 693260
Web: *http://www.gov.im/odps* [Accessed on September 2, 2007]
Email: *enquiries@odps.gov.im*

The Isle of Man has Regulations which cover email and telephone marketing—the
Unsolicited Communications Regulations 2005.

Data Protection Commissioner Jersey
Emma Martins

Tel: +44 (0) 1534 441064
Fax: +44 (0) 1534 441065
Web: *http://www.dataprotection.gov.je* [Accessed on September 2, 2007]

Data Protection Commissioner Guernsey
Dr Peter Harris
Data Protection Office
PO Box 642
Frances House
Sir William Place
St Peter Port
Guernsey GY1 3JE

Tel: +44 (0) 1481 742074
Web: *http://www.gov.gg*

Appendix A

Data Protection Act 1998

(1998, c.29)

Part I

Preliminary

1. *Basic interpretative provisions*

(1) In this Act, unless the context otherwise requires—

"data" means information which—

- (a) is being processed by means of equipment operating automatically in response to instructions given for that purpose,
- (b) is recorded with the intention that it should be processed by means of such equipment,
- (c) is recorded as part of a relevant filing system or with the intention that it should form part of a relevant filing system,
- (d) does not fall within paragraph (a), (b) or (c) but forms part of an accessible record as defined by section 68; or
- (e) is recorded information held by a public authority and does not fall within any of paragraphs (a) to (d);

"data controller" means, subject to subsection (4), a person who (either alone or jointly or in common with other persons) determines the purposes for which and the manner in which any personal data are, or are to be, processed;

"data processor", in relation to personal data, means any person (other than an employee of the data controller) who processes the data on behalf of the data controller;

"data subject" means an individual who is the subject of personal data;

"personal data" means data which relate to a living individual who can be identified—

- (a) from those data, or
- (b) from those data and other information which is in the possession of, or is likely to come into the possession of, the data controller,

and includes any expression of opinion about the individual and any indication of the intentions of the data controller or any other person in respect of the individual;

"processing", in relation to information or data, means obtaining, recording or holding the information or data or carrying out any operation or set of operations on the information or data, including—

    (a) organisation, adaptation or alteration of the information or data,

    (b) retrieval, consultation or use of the information or data,

    (c) disclosure of the information or data by transmission, dissemination or otherwise making available, or

    (d) alignment, combination, blocking, erasure or destruction of the information or data;

"public authority" means a public authority as defined by the Freedom of Information Act 2000 or a Scottish public authority as defined by the Freedom of Information (Scotland) Act 2002;

"relevant filing system" means any set of information relating to individuals to the extent that, although the information is not processed by means of equipment operating automatically in response to instructions given for that purpose, the set is structured, either by reference to individuals or by reference to criteria relating to individuals, in such a way that specific information relating to a particular individual is readily accessible.

(2) In this Act, unless the context otherwise requires—

    (a) "obtaining" or "recording", in relation to personal data, includes obtaining or recording the information to be contained in the data, and

    (b) "using" or "disclosing", in relation to personal data, includes using or disclosing the information contained in the data.

(3) In determining for the purposes of this Act whether any information is recorded with the intention—

    (a) that it should be processed by means of equipment operating automatically in response to instructions given for that purpose, or

    (b) that it should form part of a relevant filing system,

it is immaterial that it is intended to be so processed or to form part of such a system only after being transferred to a country or territory outside the European Economic Area.

(4) Where personal data are processed only for purposes for which they are required by or under any enactment to be processed, the person on whom the obligation to process the data is imposed by or under that enactment is for the purposes of this Act the data controller.

(5) In paragraph (e) of the definition of "data" in subsection (1); the reference to information "held" by a public authority shall be construed in accordance with section 3(2) of the Freedom of Information Act 2000 or section 3(2), (4) and (5) of the Freedom of Information (Scotland) Act 2002.

(6) Where

    (a) section 7 of the Freedom of Information Act 2000 prevents Parts I to V of that Act or

    (b) section 7(1) of the Freedom of Information (Scotland) Act 2002 prevents that Act

from applying to certain information held by a public authority, that information is not to be treated for the purposes of paragraph (e) of the definition of "data" in subsection (1) as held by a public authority.[1]

2. Sensitive personal data

In this Act "sensitive personal data" means personal data consisting of information as to—

    (a) the racial or ethnic origin of the data subject,

---

[1] existing text renumbered as s.1(6)(a) and s.1(6)(b) inserted by Freedom of Information (Scotland) Act 2002 (Consequential Modifications) Order 2004/3089 art. 2(2)(c)

(b) his political opinions,

(c) his religious beliefs or other beliefs of a similar nature,

(d) whether he is a member of a trade union (within the meaning of the Trade Union and Labour Relations (Consolidation) Act 1992),

(e) his physical or mental health or condition,

(f) his sexual life,

(g) the commission or alleged commission by him of any offence, or

(h) any proceedings for any offence committed or alleged to have been committed by him, the disposal of such proceedings or the sentence of any court in such proceedings.

3. *The special purposes*

In this Act "the special purposes" means any one or more of the following—

(a) the purposes of journalism,

(b) artistic purposes, and

(c) literary purposes.

4. *The data protection principles*

(1) References in this Act to the data protection principles are to the principles set out in Part I of Schedule 1.

(2) Those principles are to be interpreted in accordance with Part II of Schedule 1.

(3) Schedule 2 (which applies to all personal data) and Schedule 3 (which applies only to sensitive personal data) set out conditions applying for the purposes of the first principle; and Schedule 4 sets out cases in which the eighth principle does not apply.

(4) Subject to section 27(1), it shall be the duty of a data controller to comply with the data protection principles in relation to all personal data with respect to which he is the data controller.

5. *Application of Act*

(1) Except as otherwise provided by or under section 54, this Act applies to a data controller in respect of any data only if—

(a) the data controller is established in the United Kingdom and the data are processed in the context of that establishment, or

(b) the data controller is established neither in the United Kingdom nor in any other EEA State but uses equipment in the United Kingdom for processing the data otherwise than for the purposes of transit through the United Kingdom.

(2) A data controller falling within subsection (1)(b) must nominate for the purposes of this Act a representative established in the United Kingdom.

(3) For the purposes of subsections (1) and (2), each of the following is to be treated as established in the United Kingdom—

   (a) an individual who is ordinarily resident in the United Kingdom,

   (b) a body incorporated under the law of, or of any part of, the United Kingdom,

   (c) a partnership or other unincorporated association formed under the law of any part of the United Kingdom, and

   (d) any person who does not fall within paragraph (a), (b) or (c) but maintains in the United Kingdom—

      (i) an office, branch or agency through which he carries on any activity, or
      (ii) a regular practice;

and the reference to establishment in any other EEA State has a corresponding meaning.

6. *The Commissioner and the Tribunal*

(1) For the purposes of this Act and of the Freedom of Information Act 2000 there shall be an officer known as the Information Commissioner (in this Act referred to as "the Commissioner").

(2) The Commissioner shall be appointed by Her Majesty by Letters Patent.

(3) For the purposes of this Act and of the Freedom of Information Act 2000 there shall be a tribunal known as the Information Tribunal (in this Act referred to as "the Tribunal").

(4) The Tribunal shall consist of—

   (a) a chairman appointed by the Lord Chancellor after consultation with the Lord Advocate,

   (b) such number of deputy chairmen so appointed as the Lord Chancellor may determine, and

   (c) such number of other members appointed by the [Secretary of State][2] as he may determine.

(5) The members of the Tribunal appointed under subsection (4)(a) and (b) shall be—

   (a) persons who have a 7 year general qualification, within the meaning of section 71 of the Courts and Legal Services Act 1990,

   (b) advocates or solicitors in Scotland of at least 7 years' standing, or

   (c) members of the bar of Northern Ireland or solicitors of the Supreme Court of Northern Ireland of at least 7 years' standing.

(6) The members of the Tribunal appointed under subsection (4)(c) shall be—

   (a) persons to represent the interests of data subjects,

  (aa) persons to represent the interests of those who make requests for information under the Freedom of Information Act 2000,

   (b) persons to represent the interests of data controllers. and

  (bb) persons to represent the interests of public authorities.

(7) Schedule 5 has effect in relation to the Commissioner and the Tribunal.

---

[2] words substituted by Secretary of State for Constitutional Affairs Order 2003/1887 Sch.2 para.9(1)(a)

7. *Right of access to personal data*

(1) Subject to the following provisions of this section and to sections 8, 9 and 9A, an individual is entitled—

(a) to be informed by any data controller whether personal data of which that individual is the data subject are being processed by or on behalf of that data controller,

(b) if that is the case, to be given by the data controller a description of—

(i) the personal data of which that individual is the data subject,
(ii) the purposes for which they are being or are to be processed, and
(iii) the recipients or classes of recipients to whom they are or may be disclosed,

(c) to have communicated to him in an intelligible form—

(i) the information constituting any personal data of which that individual is the data subject, and
(ii) any information available to the data controller as to the source of those data, and

(d) where the processing by automatic means of personal data of which that individual is the data subject for the purpose of evaluating matters relating to him such as, for example, his performance at work, his credit worthiness, his reliability or his conduct, has constituted or is likely to constitute the sole basis for any decision significantly affecting him, to be informed by the data controller of the logic involved in that decision-taking.

(2) A data controller is not obliged to supply any information under subsection (1) unless he has received—

(a) a request in writing, and

(b) except in prescribed cases, such fee (not exceeding the prescribed maximum) as he may require.

(3) Where a data controller—

(a) reasonably requires further information in order to satisfy himself as to the identity of the person making a request under this section and to locate the information which that person seeks, and

(b) has informed him of that requirement, the data controller is not obliged to comply with the request unless he is supplied with that further information.

(4) Where a data controller cannot comply with the request without disclosing information relating to another individual who can be identified from that information, he is not obliged to comply with the request unless—

(a) the other individual has consented to the disclosure of the information to the person making the request, or

(b) it is reasonable in all the circumstances to comply with the request without the consent of the other individual.

(5) In subsection (4) the reference to information relating to another individual includes a reference to information identifying that individual as the source of the information sought by the request; and that subsection is not to be construed as excusing a data controller from communicating so much of the information sought by the request as can be communicated without disclosing the identity of the other individual concerned, whether by the omission of names or other identifying particulars or otherwise.

(6) In determining for the purposes of subsection (4)(b) whether it is reasonable in all the circumstances to comply with the request without the consent of the other individual concerned, regard shall be had, in particular, to—

(a) any duty of confidentiality owed to the other individual,

(b) any steps taken by the data controller with a view to seeking the consent of the other individual,

(c) whether the other individual is capable of giving consent, and

(d) any express refusal of consent by the other individual.

(7) An individual making a request under this section may, in such cases as may be prescribed, specify that his request is limited to personal data of any prescribed description.

(8) Subject to subsection (4), a data controller shall comply with a request under this section promptly and in any event before the end of the prescribed period beginning with the relevant day.

(9) If a court is satisfied on the application of any person who has made a request under the foregoing provisions of this section that the data controller in question has failed to comply with the request in contravention of those provisions, the court may order him to comply with the request.

(10) In this section—

"prescribed" means prescribed by the [Secretary of State][3] by regulations:

"the prescribed maximum" means such amount as may be prescribed:

"the prescribed period" means forty days or such other period as may be prescribed:

"the relevant day", in relation to a request under this section, means the day on which the data controller receives the request or, if later, the first day on which the data controller has both the required fee and the information referred to in subsection (3). (11) Different amounts or periods may be prescribed under this section in relation to different cases.

8. *Provisions supplementary to section 7*

(1) The [Secretary of State][4] may by regulations provide that, in such cases as may be prescribed, a request for information under any provision of subsection (1) of section 7 is to be treated as extending also to information under other provisions of that subsection.

(2) The obligation imposed by section 7(1)(c)(i) must be complied with by supplying the data subject with a copy of the information in permanent form unless—

(a) the supply of such a copy is not possible or would involve disproportionate effort, or

(b) the data subject agrees otherwise;

and where any of the information referred to in section 7(1)(c)(i) is expressed in terms which are not intelligible without explanation the copy must be accompanied by an explanation of those terms.

(3) Where a data controller has previously complied with a request made under section 7 by an individual, the data controller is not obliged to comply with a subsequent identical or similar request under that section by that individual unless a reasonable interval has elapsed between compliance with the previous request and the making of the current request.

(4) In determining for the purposes of subsection (3) whether requests under section 7 are made at reasonable intervals, regard shall be had to the nature of the data, the purposes for which the data are processed and the frequency with which the data are altered.

---

[3] words substituted by Secretary of State for Constitutional Affairs Order 2003/1887 Sch.2 para.9(1)(a)
[4] words substituted by Secretary of State for Constitutional Affairs Order 2003/1887 Sch.2 para.9(1)(a)

(5) Section 7(1)(d) is not to be regarded as requiring the provision of information as to the logic involved in any decision-taking if, and to the extent that, the information constitutes a trade secret.

(6) The information to be supplied pursuant to a request under section 7 must be supplied by reference to the data in question at the time when the request is received, except that it may take account of any amendment or deletion made between that time and the time when the information is supplied, being an amendment or deletion that would have been made regardless of the receipt of the request.

(7) For the purposes of section 7(4) and (5) another individual can be identified from the information being disclosed if he can be identified from that information, or from that and any other information which, in the reasonable belief of the data controller, is likely to be in, or to come into, the possession of the data subject making the request.

9. *Application of section 7 where data controller is credit reference agency*

(1) Where the data controller is a credit reference agency, section 7 has effect subject to the provisions of this section.

(2) An individual making a request under section 7 may limit his request to personal data relevant to his financial standing, and shall be taken to have so limited his request unless the request shows a contrary intention.

(3) Where the data controller receives a request under section 7 in a case where personal data of which the individual making the request is the data subject are being processed by or on behalf of the data controller, the obligation to supply information under that section includes an obligation to give the individual making the request a statement, in such form as may be prescribed by the [Secretary of State][5] by regulations, of the individual's rights—

(a) under section 159 of the Consumer Credit Act 1974, and

(b) to the extent required by the prescribed form, under this Act.

9A. *Unstructured personal data held by public authorities*

(1) In this section "unstructured personal data" means any personal data falling within paragraph (e) of the definition of "data" in section 1(1), other than information which is recorded as part of, or with the intention that it should form part of, any set of information relating to individuals to the extent that the set is structured by reference to individuals or by reference to criteria relating to individuals.

(2) A public authority is not obliged to comply with subsection (1) of section 7 in relation to any unstructured personal data unless the request under that section contains a description of the data.

(3) Even if the data are described by the data subject in his request, a public authority is not obliged to comply with subsection (1) of section 7 in relation to unstructured personal data if the authority estimates that the cost of complying with the request so far as relating to those data would exceed the appropriate limit.

(4) Subsection (3) does not exempt the public authority from its obligation to comply with paragraph (a) of section 7(1) in relation to the unstructured personal data unless the estimated cost of complying with that paragraph alone in relation to those data would exceed the appropriate limit.

---

[5] words substituted by Secretary of State for Constitutional Affairs Order 2003/1887 Sch.2 para.9(1)(a)

(5) In subsections (3) and (4) "the appropriate limit" means such amount as may be prescribed by the [Secretary of State]⁶ by regulations, and different amounts may be prescribed in relation to different cases.

(6) Any estimate for the purposes of this section must be made in accordance with regulations under section 12(5) of the Freedom of Information Act 2000.

10. *Right to prevent processing likely to cause damage or distress*

(1) Subject to subsection (2), an individual is entitled at any time by notice in writing to a data controller to require the data controller at the end of such period as is reasonable in the circumstances to cease, or not to begin, processing, or processing for a specified purpose or in a specified manner, any personal data in respect of which he is the data subject, on the ground that, for specified reasons—

    (a) the processing of those data or their processing for that purpose or in that manner is causing or is likely to cause substantial damage or substantial distress to him or to another, and

    (b) that damage or distress is or would be unwarranted.

(2) Subsection (1) does not apply—

    (a) in a case where any of the conditions in paragraphs 1 to 4 of Schedule 2 is met, or

    (b) in such other cases as may be prescribed by the [Secretary of State]⁷ by order.

(3) The data controller must within twenty-one days of receiving a notice under subsection (1) ("the data subject notice") give the individual who gave it a written notice—

    (a) stating that he has complied or intends to comply with the data subject notice, or

    (b) stating his reasons for regarding the data subject notice as to any extent unjustified and the extent (if any) to which he has complied or intends to comply with it.

(4) If a court is satisfied, on the application of any person who has given a notice under subsection (1) which appears to the court to be justified (or to be justified to any extent), that the data controller in question has failed to comply with the notice, the court may order him to take such steps for complying with the notice (or for complying with it to that extent) as the court thinks fit.

(5) The failure by a data subject to exercise the right conferred by subsection (1) or section 11(1) does not affect any other right conferred on him by this Part.

11. *Right to prevent processing for purposes of direct marketing*

(1) An individual is entitled at any time by notice in writing to a data controller to require the data controller at the end of such period as is reasonable in the circumstances to cease, or not to begin, processing for the purposes of direct marketing personal data in respect of which he is the data subject.

(2) If the court is satisfied, on the application of any person who has given a notice under subsection (1), that the data controller has failed to comply with the notice, the court may order him to take such steps for complying with the notice as the court thinks fit.

---

⁶ words substituted by Freedom of Information Act 2000 *c*. 36 Pt VII s.69
⁷ words substituted by Secretary of State for Constitutional Affairs Order 2003/1887 Sch.2 para.9(1)(a)

(2A) This section shall not apply in relation to the processing of such data as are mentioned in paragraph (1) of regulation 8 of the Telecommunications (Data Protection and Privacy) Regulations 1999 (processing of telecommunications billing data for certain marketing purposes) for the purposes mentioned in paragraph (2) of that regulation.[8]

(3) In this section "direct marketing" means the communication (by whatever means) of any advertising or marketing material which is directed to particular individuals.

12. *Rights in relation to automated decision-taking*

(1) An individual is entitled at any time, by notice in writing to any data controller, to require the data controller to ensure that no decision taken by or on behalf of the data controller which significantly affects that individual is based solely on the processing by automatic means of personal data in respect of which that individual is the data subject for the purpose of evaluating matters relating to him such as, for example, his performance at work, his credit worthiness, his reliability or his conduct.

(2) Where, in a case where no notice under subsection (1) has effect, a decision which significantly affects an individual is based solely on such processing as is mentioned in subsection (1)—

    (a) the data controller must as soon as reasonably practicable notify the individual that the decision was taken on that basis, and

    (b) the individual is entitled, within twenty-one days of receiving that notification from the data controller, by notice in writing to require the data controller to reconsider the decision or to take a new decision otherwise than on that basis.

(3) The data controller must, within twenty-one days of receiving a notice under subsection (2)(b) ("the data subject notice") give the individual a written notice specifying the steps that he intends to take to comply with the data subject notice.

(4) A notice under subsection (1) does not have effect in relation to an exempt decision; and nothing in subsection (2) applies to an exempt decision.

(5) In subsection (4) "exempt decision" means any decision—

    (a) in respect of which the condition in subsection (6) and the condition in subsection (7) are met, or

    (b) which is made in such other circumstances as may be prescribed by the [Secretary of State][9] by order.

(6) The condition in this subsection is that the decision—

    (a) is taken in the course of steps taken—

        (i) for the purpose of considering whether to enter into a contract with the data subject,

        (ii) with a view to entering into such a contract, or

        (iii) in the course of performing such a contract, or

    (b) is authorised or required by or under any enactment.

(7) The condition in this subsection is that either—

    (a) the effect of the decision is to grant a request of the data subject, or

    (b) steps have been taken to safeguard the legitimate interests of the data subject (for example, by allowing him to make representations).

---

[8] added by Telecommunications (Data Protection and Privacy) Regulations 1999/2093 Sch.1(II) para.3
[9] words substituted by Secretary of State for Constitutional Affairs Order 2003/1887 Sch.2 para.9(1)(a)

(8) If a court is satisfied on the application of a data subject that a person taking a decision in respect of him ("the responsible person") has failed to comply with subsection (1) or (2)(b), the court may order the responsible person to reconsider the decision, or to take a new decision which is not based solely on such processing as is mentioned in subsection (1).

(9) An order under subsection (8) shall not affect the rights of any person other than the data subject and the responsible person.

12A. *Rights of data subjects in relation to exempt manual data*

(1) A data subject is entitled at any time by notice in writing—

    (a) to require the data controller to rectify, block, erase or destroy exempt manual data which are inaccurate or incomplete, or

    (b) to require the data controller to cease holding exempt manual data in a way incompatible with the legitimate purposes pursued by the data controller.

(2) A notice under subsection (1)(a) or (b) must state the data subject's reasons for believing that the data are inaccurate or incomplete or, as the case may be, his reasons for believing that they are held in a way incompatible with the legitimate purposes pursued by the data controller.

(3) If the court is satisfied, on the application of any person who has given a notice under subsection (1) which appears to the court to be justified (or to be justified to any extent) that the data controller in question has failed to comply with the notice, the court may order him to take such steps for complying with the notice (or for complying with it to that extent) as the court thinks fit.

(4) In this section "exempt manual data" means—

    (a) in relation to the first transitional period, as defined by paragraph 1(2) of Schedule 8, data to which paragraph 3 or 4 of that Schedule applies, and

    (b) in relation to the second transitional period, as so defined, data to which [paragraph 14 or 14A][10] of that Schedule applies.

(5) For the purposes of this section personal data are incomplete if, and only if, the data, although not inaccurate, are such that their incompleteness would constitute a contravention of the third or fourth data protection principles, if those principles applied to the data.

13. *Compensation for failure to comply with certain requirements*

(1) An individual who suffers damage by reason of any contravention by a data controller of any of the requirements of this Act is entitled to compensation from the data controller for that damage.

(2) An individual who suffers distress by reason of any contravention by a data controller of any of the requirements of this Act is entitled to compensation from the data controller for that distress if—

    (a) the individual also suffers damage by reason of the contravention, or

    (b) the contravention relates to the processing of personal data for the special purposes.

(3) In proceedings brought against a person by virtue of this section it is a defence to prove that he had taken such care as in all the circumstances was reasonably required to comply with the requirement concerned.

---

[10] words inserted by Data Protection Act 1998 c. 29 Sch.13 para.1

14. *Rectification, blocking, erasure and destruction*

(1) If a court is satisfied on the application of a data subject that personal data of which the applicant is the subject are inaccurate, the court may order the data controller to rectify, block, erase or destroy those data and any other personal data in respect of which he is the data controller and which contain an expression of opinion which appears to the court to be based on the inaccurate data.

(2) Subsection (1) applies whether or not the data accurately record information received or obtained by the data controller from the data subject or a third party but where the data accurately record such information, then—

    (a) if the requirements mentioned in paragraph 7 of Part II of Schedule 1 have been complied with, the court may, instead of making an order under subsection (1), make an order requiring the data to be supplemented by such statement of the true facts relating to the matters dealt with by the data as the court may approve, and

    (b) if all or any of those requirements have not been complied with, the court may, instead of making an order under that subsection, make such order as it thinks fit for securing compliance with those requirements with or without a further order requiring the data to be supplemented by such a statement as is mentioned in paragraph (a).

(3) Where the court—

    (a) makes an order under subsection (1), or

    (b) is satisfied on the application of a data subject that personal data of which he was the data subject and which have been rectified, blocked, erased or destroyed were inaccurate,

it may, where it considers it reasonably practicable, order the data controller to notify third parties to whom the data have been disclosed of the rectification, blocking, erasure or destruction.

(4) If a court is satisfied on the application of a data subject—

    (a) that he has suffered damage by reason of any contravention by a data controller of any of the requirements of this Act in respect of any personal data, in circumstances entitling him to compensation under section 13, and

    (b) that there is a substantial risk of further contravention in respect of those data in such circumstances,

the court may order the rectification, blocking, erasure or destruction of any of those data.

(5) Where the court makes an order under subsection (4) it may, where it considers it reasonably practicable, order the data controller to notify third parties to whom the data have been disclosed of the rectification, blocking, erasure or destruction. (6) In determining whether it is reasonably practicable to require such notification as is mentioned in subsection (3) or (5) the court shall have regard, in particular, to the number of persons who would have to be notified.

15. *Jurisdiction and procedure*

(1) The jurisdiction conferred by sections 7 to 14 is exercisable by the High Court or a county court or, in Scotland, by the Court of Session or the sheriff.

(2) For the purpose of determining any question whether an applicant under subsection (9) of section 7 is entitled to the information which he seeks (including any question whether any relevant data are exempt from that section by virtue of Part IV) a court may require the information constituting any data processed by or on behalf of the data controller and any information as to the logic involved in any decision-taking as mentioned in section 7(1)(d) to be made available for its own inspection but shall not, pending the determination of that question in the

applicant's favour, require the information sought by the applicant to be disclosed to him or his representatives whether by discovery (or, in Scotland, recovery) or otherwise.

16. *Preliminary*

(1) In this Part "the registrable particulars", in relation to a data controller, means—

(a) his name and address,

(b) if he has nominated a representative for the purposes of this Act, the name and address of the representative,

(c) a description of the personal data being or to be processed by or on behalf of the data controller and of the category or categories of data subject to which they relate,

(d) a description of the purpose or purposes for which the data are being or are to be processed,

(e) a description of any recipient or recipients to whom the data controller intends or may wish to disclose the data,

(f) the names, or a description of, any countries or territories outside the European Economic Area to which the data controller directly or indirectly transfers, or intends or may wish directly or indirectly to transfer, the data, and

[(ff) where the data controller is a public authority, a statement of that fact,][11]

(g) in any case where—

(i) personal data are being, or are intended to be, processed in circumstances in which the prohibition in subsection (1) of section 17 is excluded by subsection (2) or (3) of that section, and

(ii) the notification does not extend to those data,

a statement of that fact.

(2) In this Part—

"fees regulations" means regulations made by the Secretary of State under section 18(5) or 19(4) or (7);

"notification regulations" means regulations made by the Secretary of State under the other provisions of this Part;

"prescribed", except where used in relation to fees regulations, means prescribed by notification regulations.

(3) For the purposes of this Part, so far as it relates to the addresses of data controllers—

(a) the address of a registered company is that of its registered office, and

(b) the address of a person (other than a registered company) carrying on a business is that of his principal place of business in the United Kingdom.

17. *Prohibition on processing without registration*

(1) Subject to the following provisions of this section, personal data must not be processed unless an entry in respect of the data controller is included in the register maintained by the

---

[11] added by Freedom of Information Act 2000 c. 36 Pt VII s.71

Commissioner under section 19 (or is treated by notification regulations made by virtue of section 19(3) as being so included).

(2) Except where the processing is assessable processing for the purposes of section 22, subsection (1) does not apply in relation to personal data consisting of information which falls neither within paragraph (a) of the definition of "data" in section 1(1) nor within paragraph (b) of that definition.

(3) If it appears to the [Secretary of State][12] that processing of a particular description is unlikely to prejudice the rights and freedoms of data subjects, notification regulations may provide that, in such cases as may be prescribed, subsection (1) is not to apply in relation to processing of that description.

(4) Subsection (1) does not apply in relation to any processing whose sole purpose is the maintenance of a public register.

18. *Notification by data controllers*

(1) Any data controller who wishes to be included in the register maintained under section 19 shall give a notification to the Commissioner under this section.

(2) A notification under this section must specify in accordance with notification regulations—

    (a) the registrable particulars, and

    (b) a general description of measures to be taken for the purpose of complying with the seventh data protection principle.

(3) Notification regulations made by virtue of subsection (2) may provide for the determination by the Commissioner, in accordance with any requirements of the regulations, of the form in which the registrable particulars and the description mentioned in subsection (2)(b) are to be specified, including in particular the detail required for the purposes of section 16(1)(c), (d), (e) and (f) and subsection (2)(b).

(4) Notification regulations may make provisions as to the giving of notification—

    (a) by partnerships, or

    (b) in other cases where two or more persons are the data controllers in respect of any personal data.

(5) The notification must be accompanied by such fee as may be prescribed by fees regulations.

(6) Notification regulations may provide for any fee paid under subsection (5) or section 19(4) to be refunded in prescribed circumstances.

19. *Register of notifications*

(1) The Commissioner shall—

    (a) maintain a register of persons who have given notification under section 18, and

    (b) make an entry in the register in pursuance of each notification received by him under that section from a person in respect of whom no entry as data controller was for the time being included in the register.

---

[12] words substituted by Secretary of State for Constitutional Affairs Order 2003/1887 Sch.2 para.9(1)(a)

(2) Each entry in the register shall consist of—

    (a) the registrable particulars notified under section 18 or, as the case requires, those particulars as amended in pursuance of section 20(4), and

    (b) such other information as the Commissioner may be authorised or required by notification regulations to include in the register.

(3) Notification regulations may make provision as to the time as from which any entry in respect of a data controller is to be treated for the purposes of section 17 as having been made in the register.

(4) No entry shall be retained in the register for more than the relevant time except on payment of such fee as may be prescribed by fees regulations.

(5) In subsection (4) "the relevant time" means twelve months or such other period as may be prescribed by notification regulations; and different periods may be prescribed in relation to different cases.[. . .][13]

(6) The Commissioner—

    (a) shall provide facilities for making the information contained in the entries in the register available for inspection (in visible and legible form) by members of the public at all reasonable hours and free of charge, and

    (b) may provide such other facilities for making the information contained in those entries available to the public free of charge as he considers appropriate.

(7) The Commissioner shall, on payment of such fee, if any, as may be prescribed by fees regulations, supply any member of the public with a duly certified copy in writing of the particulars contained in any entry made in the register.[[14]][15]

20. *Duty to notify changes*

(1) For the purpose specified in subsection (2), notification regulations shall include provision imposing on every person in respect of whom an entry as a data controller is for the time being included in the register maintained under section 19 a duty to notify to the Commissioner, in such circumstances and at such time or times and in such form as may be prescribed, such matters relating to the registrable particulars and measures taken as mentioned in section 18(2)(b) as may be prescribed.

(2) The purpose referred to in subsection (1) is that of ensuring, so far as practicable, that at any time—

    (a) the entries in the register maintained under section 19 contain current names and addresses and describe the current practice or intentions of the data controller with respect to the processing of personal data, and

    (b) the Commissioner is provided with a general description of measures currently being taken as mentioned in section 18(2)(b).

(3) Subsection (3) of section 18 has effect in relation to notification regulations made by virtue of subsection (1) as it has effect in relation to notification regulations made by virtue of subsection (2) of that section.

---

[13] renumbering existing subsection (4)(c) as (b) and subsection (b) repealed by Data Protection (Notification and Notification Fees) Regulations 2000/188 Reg.15

[14] in relation to any entry in respect of a person which is for the time being included in the register under paragraph 2(6) of Schedule 14 to the Data Protection Act 1998 as set out in regulation 15 to the Data Protection (Notification and Notification Fees) Regulations 2000

[15] renumbering existing subsection (4)(c) as (b) and subsection (b) repealed by Data Protection (Notification and Notification Fees) Regulations 2000/188 Reg.15

(4) On receiving any notification under notification regulations made by virtue of subsection (1), the Commissioner shall make such amendments of the relevant entry in the register maintained under section 19 as are necessary to take account of the notification.

21. *Offences*

(1) If section 17(1) is contravened, the data controller is guilty of an offence.

(2) Any person who fails to comply with the duty imposed by notification regulations made by virtue of section 20(1) is guilty of an offence.

(3) It shall be a defence for a person charged with an offence under subsection (2) to show that he exercised all due diligence to comply with the duty.

22. *Preliminary assessment by Commissioner*

(1) In this section "assessable processing" means processing which is of a description specified in an order made by the [Secretary of State][16] as appearing to him to be particularly likely—

(a) to cause substantial damage or substantial distress to data subjects, or

(b) otherwise significantly to prejudice the rights and freedoms of data subjects.

(2) On receiving notification from any data controller under section 18 or under notification regulations made by virtue of section 20 the Commissioner shall consider—

(a) whether any of the processing to which the notification relates is assessable processing, and

(b) if so, whether the assessable processing is likely to comply with the provisions of this Act.

(3) Subject to subsection (4), the Commissioner shall, within the period of twenty-eight days beginning with the day on which he receives a notification which relates to assessable processing, give a notice to the data controller stating the extent to which the Commissioner is of the opinion that the processing is likely or unlikely to comply with the provisions of this Act.

(4) Before the end of the period referred to in subsection (3) the Commissioner may, by reason of special circumstances, extend that period on one occasion only by notice to the data controller by such further period not exceeding fourteen days as the Commissioner may specify in the notice.

(5) No assessable processing in respect of which a notification has been given to the Commissioner as mentioned in subsection (2) shall be carried on unless either—

(a) the period of twenty-eight days beginning with the day on which the notification is received by the Commissioner (or, in a case falling within subsection (4), that period as extended under that subsection) has elapsed, or

(b) before the end of that period (or that period as so extended) the data controller has received a notice from the Commissioner under subsection (3) in respect of the processing.

(6) Where subsection (5) is contravened, the data controller is guilty of an offence.

(7) The [Secretary of State][17] may by order amend subsections (3), (4) and (5) by substituting for the number of days for the time being specified there a different number specified in the order.

---

[16] words substituted by Secretary of State for Constitutional Affairs Order 2003/1887 Sch.2 para.9(1)(a)
[17] words substituted by Secretary of State for Constitutional Affairs Order 2003/1887 Sch.2 para.9(1)(a)

23. *Power to make provision for appointment of data protection supervisors*

(1) The [Secretary of State][18] may by order—

   (a) make provision under which a data controller may appoint a person to act as a data protection supervisor responsible in particular for monitoring in an independent manner the data controller's compliance with the provisions of this Act, and

   (b) provide that, in relation to any data controller who has appointed a data protection supervisor in accordance with the provisions of the order and who complies with such conditions as may be specified in the order, the provisions of this Part are to have effect subject to such exemptions or other modifications as may be specified in the order.

(2) An order under this section may—

   (a) impose duties on data protection supervisors in relation to the Commissioner, and

   (b) confer functions on the Commissioner in relation to data protection supervisors.

24. *Duty of certain data controllers to make certain information available*

(1) Subject to subsection (3), where personal data are processed in a case where—

   (a) by virtue of subsection (2) or (3) of section 17, subsection (1) of that section does not apply to the processing, and

   (b) the data controller has not notified the relevant particulars in respect of that processing under section 18,

the data controller must, within twenty-one days of receiving a written request from any person, make the relevant particulars available to that person in writing free of charge.

(2) In this section "the relevant particulars" means the particulars referred to in paragraphs (a) to (f) of section 16(1).

(3) This section has effect subject to any exemption conferred for the purposes of this section by notification regulations.

(4) Any data controller who fails to comply with the duty imposed by subsection (1) is guilty of an offence.

(5) It shall be a defence for a person charged with an offence under subsection (4) to show that he exercised all due diligence to comply with the duty.

25. *Functions of Commissioner in relation to making of notification regulations*

(1) As soon as practicable after the passing of this Act, the Commissioner shall submit to the Secretary of State proposals as to the provisions to be included in the first notification regulations.

(2) The Commissioner shall keep under review the working of notification regulations and may from time to time submit to the [Secretary of State][19] proposals as to amendments to be made to the regulations.

---

[18] words substituted by Secretary of State for Constitutional Affairs Order 2003/1887 Sch.2 para.9(1)(a)
[19] words substituted by Secretary of State for Constitutional Affairs Order 2003/1887 Sch.2 para.9(1)(a)

(3) The [Secretary of State]²⁰ may from time to time require the Commissioner to consider any matter relating to notification regulations and to submit to him proposals as to amendments to be made to the regulations in connection with that matter.

(4) Before making any notification regulations, the [Secretary of State]²¹ shall—

(a) consider any proposals made to him by the Commissioner under subsection (2) or (3), and

(b) consult the Commissioner.

26. Fees regulations

(1) Fees regulations prescribing fees for the purposes of any provision of this Part may provide for different fees to be payable in different cases.

(2) In making any fees regulations, the [Secretary of State]²² shall have regard to the desirability of securing that the fees payable to the Commissioner are sufficient to offset—

(a) the expenses incurred by the Commissioner and the Tribunal in discharging their functions under this Act and any expenses of the [Secretary of State]²³ in respect of the Commissioner or the Tribunal so far as attributable to their functions under this Act, and

(b) to the extent that the [Secretary of State]²⁴ considers appropriate—

(i) any deficit previously incurred (whether before or after the passing of this Act) in respect of the expenses mentioned in paragraph (a), and

(ii) expenses incurred or to be incurred by the [Secretary of State]²⁵ in respect of the inclusion of any officers or staff of the Commissioner in any scheme under section 1 of the Superannuation Act 1972.

27. Preliminary

(1) References in any of the data protection principles or any provision of Parts II and III to personal data or to the processing of personal data do not include references to data or processing which by virtue of this Part are exempt from that principle or other provision.

(2) In this Part "the subject information provisions" means—

(a) the first data protection principle to the extent to which it requires compliance with paragraph 2 of Part II of Schedule 1, and

(b) section 7.

(3) In this Part "the non-disclosure provisions" means the provisions specified in subsection (4) to the extent to which they are inconsistent with the disclosure in question.

(4) The provisions referred to in subsection (3) are—

(a) the first data protection principle, except to the extent to which it requires compliance with the conditions in Schedules 2 and 3,

---

²⁰ words substituted by Secretary of State for Constitutional Affairs Order 2003/1887 Sch.2 para.9(1)(a)
²¹ words substituted by Secretary of State for Constitutional Affairs Order 2003/1887 Sch.2 para.9(1)(a)
²² words substituted by Secretary of State for Constitutional Affairs Order 2003/1887 Sch.2 para.9(1)(a)
²³ words substituted by Secretary of State for Constitutional Affairs Order 2003/1887 Sch.2 para.9(1)(a)
²⁴ words substituted by Secretary of State for Constitutional Affairs Order 2003/1887 Sch.2 para.9(1)(a)
²⁵ words substituted by Secretary of State for Constitutional Affairs Order 2003/1887 Sch.2 para.9(1)(a)

(b) the second, third, fourth and fifth data protection principles, and

(c) sections 10 and 14(1) to (3).

(5) Except as provided by this Part, the subject information provisions shall have effect notwithstanding any enactment or rule of law prohibiting or restricting the disclosure, or authorising the withholding, of information.

28. *National security*

(1) Personal data are exempt from any of the provisions of—

(a) the data protection principles,

(b) Parts II, III and V, and

(c) [sections 54A and 55][26]

if the exemption from that provision is required for the purpose of safeguarding national security.

(2) Subject to subsection (4), a certificate signed by a Minister of the Crown certifying that exemption from all or any of the provisions mentioned in subsection (1) is or at any time was required for the purpose there mentioned in respect of any personal data shall be conclusive evidence of that fact.

(3) A certificate under subsection (2) may identify the personal data to which it applies by means of a general description and may be expressed to have prospective effect.

(4) Any person directly affected by the issuing of a certificate under subsection (2) may appeal to the Tribunal against the certificate.

(5) If on an appeal under subsection (4), the Tribunal finds that, applying the principles applied by the court on an application for judicial review, the Minister did not have reasonable grounds for issuing the certificate, the Tribunal may allow the appeal and quash the certificate.

(6) Where in any proceedings under or by virtue of this Act it is claimed by a data controller that a certificate under subsection (2) which identifies the personal data to which it applies by means of a general description applies to any personal data, any other party to the proceedings may appeal to the Tribunal on the ground that the certificate does not apply to the personal data in question and, subject to any determination under subsection (7), the certificate shall be conclusively presumed so to apply.

(7) On any appeal under subsection (6), the Tribunal may determine that the certificate does not so apply.

(8) A document purporting to be a certificate under subsection (2) shall be received in evidence and deemed to be such a certificate unless the contrary is proved.

(9) A document which purports to be certified by or on behalf of a Minister of the Crown as a true copy of a certificate issued by that Minister under subsection (2) shall in any legal proceedings be evidence (or, in Scotland, sufficient evidence) of that certificate.

(10) The power conferred by subsection (2) on a Minister of the Crown shall not be exercisable except by a Minister who is a member of the Cabinet or by the Attorney General or the Lord Advocate.

(11) No power conferred by any provision of Part V may be exercised in relation to personal data which by virtue of this section are exempt from that provision.

(12) Schedule 6 shall have effect in relation to appeals under subsection (4) or (6) and the proceedings of the Tribunal in respect of any such appeal.

---

[26] word substituted by Crime (International Co-operation) Act 2003 c. 32 Sch.5 para.69

29. *Crime and taxation*

(1) Personal data processed for any of the following purposes—

(a) the prevention or detection of crime,

(b) the apprehension or prosecution of offenders, or

(c) the assessment or collection of any tax or duty or of any imposition of a similar nature,

are exempt from the first data protection principle (except to the extent to which it requires compliance with the conditions in Schedules 2 and 3) and section 7 in any case to the extent to which the application of those provisions to the data would be likely to prejudice any of the matters mentioned in this subsection.

(2) Personal data which—

(a) are processed for the purpose of discharging statutory functions, and

(b) consist of information obtained for such a purpose from a person who had it in his possession for any of the purposes mentioned in subsection (1),

are exempt from the subject information provisions to the same extent as personal data processed for any of the purposes mentioned in that subsection.

(3) Personal data are exempt from the non-disclosure provisions in any case in which—

(a) the disclosure is for any of the purposes mentioned in subsection (1), and

(b) the application of those provisions in relation to the disclosure would be likely to prejudice any of the matters mentioned in that subsection.

(4) Personal data in respect of which the data controller is a relevant authority and which—

(a) consist of a classification applied to the data subject as part of a system of risk assessment which is operated by that authority for either of the following purposes—

(i) the assessment or collection of any tax or duty or any imposition of a similar nature, or

(ii) the prevention or detection of crime, or apprehension or prosecution of offenders, where the offence concerned involves any unlawful claim for any payment out of, or any unlawful application of, public funds, and

(b) are processed for either of those purposes, are exempt from section 7 to the extent to which the exemption is required in the interests of the operation of the system.

(5) In subsection (4)—

"public funds" includes funds provided by any Community institution;

"relevant authority" means—

(a) a government department,

(b) a local authority, or

(c) any other authority administering housing benefit or council tax benefit.

30. *Health, education and social work*

(1) The Secretary of State may by order exempt from the subject information provisions, or modify those provisions in relation to, personal data consisting of information as to the physical or mental health or condition of the data subject.

(2) The Secretary of State may by order exempt from the subject information provisions, or modify those provisions in relation to—

(a) personal data in respect of which the data controller is the proprietor of, or a teacher at, a school, and which consist of information relating to persons who are or have been pupils at the school, or

(b) personal data in respect of which the data controller is an education authority in Scotland, and which consist of information relating to persons who are receiving, or have received, further education provided by the authority.

(3) The Secretary of State may by order exempt from the subject information provisions, or modify those provisions in relation to, personal data of such other descriptions as may be specified in the order, being information—

(a) processed by government departments or local authorities or by voluntary organisations or other bodies designated by or under the order, and

(b) appearing to him to be processed in the course of, or for the purposes of, carrying out social work in relation to the data subject or other individuals;

but the Secretary of State shall not under this subsection confer any exemption or make any modification except so far as he considers that the application to the data of those provisions (or of those provisions without modification) would be likely to prejudice the carrying out of social work.

(4) An order under this section may make different provision in relation to data consisting of information of different descriptions.

(5) In this section—

"education authority" and "further education" have the same meaning as in the Education (Scotland) Act 1980 ("the 1980 Act"), and

"proprietor"—

(a) in relation to a school in England or Wales, has the same meaning as in the Education Act 1996,

(b) in relation to a school in Scotland, means—

    (i) [. . .][27]

    (ii) in the case of an independent school, the proprietor within the meaning of the 1980 Act,

    (iii) in the case of a grant-aided school, the managers within the meaning of the 1980 Act, and

    (iv) in the case of a public school, the education authority within the meaning of the 1980 Act, and

(c) in relation to a school in Northern Ireland, has the same meaning as in the Education and Libraries (Northern Ireland) Order 1986 and includes, in the case of a controlled school, the Board of Governors of the school.

31. *Regulatory activity*

(1) Personal data processed for the purposes of discharging functions to which this subsection applies are exempt from the subject information provisions in any case to the extent to which the application of those provisions to the data would be likely to prejudice the proper discharge of those functions.

(2) Subsection (1) applies to any relevant function which is designed—

(a) for protecting members of the public against—

---

[27] repealed by Standards in Scotland's Schools etc. Act 2000 asp 6 (Scottish Act) Sch.3 para.1

    (i) financial loss due to dishonesty, malpractice or other seriously improper conduct by, or the unfitness or incompetence of, persons concerned in the provision of banking, insurance, investment or other financial services or in the management of bodies corporate,

    (ii) financial loss due to the conduct of discharged or undischarged bankrupts, or

    (iii) dishonesty, malpractice or other seriously improper conduct by, or the unfitness or incompetence of, persons authorised to carry on any profession or other activity,

(b) for protecting charities or community interest companies against misconduct or mismanagement (whether by trustees, directors or other persons) in their administration,

(c) for protecting the property of charities or community interest companies from loss or misapplication,

(d) for the recovery of the property of charities or community interest companies,

(e) for securing the health, safety and welfare of persons at work, or

(f) for protecting persons other than persons at work against risk to health or safety arising out of or in connection with the actions of persons at work.

(3) In subsection (2) "relevant function" means—

(a) any function conferred on any person by or under any enactment,

(b) any function of the Crown, a Minister of the Crown or a government department, or

(c) any other function which is of a public nature and is exercised in the public interest.

(4) Personal data processed for the purpose of discharging any function which—

(a) is conferred by or under any enactment on—

    (i) the Parliamentary Commissioner for Administration,

    (ii) the Commission for Local Administration in England,

    (iii) the Health Service Commissioner for England,

    (iv) the Public Services Ombudsman for Wales,

    (v) the Assembly Ombudsman for Northern Ireland,

    (vi) the Northern Ireland Commissioner for Complaints, or

    (vii) the Scottish Public Services Ombudsman, and

(b) is designed for protecting members of the public against—

    (i) maladministration by public bodies,

    (ii) failures in services provided by public bodies, or

    (iii) a failure of a public body to provide a service which it was a function of the body to provide,

are exempt from the subject information provisions in any case to the extent to which the application of those provisions to the data would be likely to prejudice the proper discharge of that function.

(4A) Personal data processed for the purpose of discharging any function which is conferred by or under Part XVI of the Financial Services and Markets Act 2000 on the body established by the Financial Services Authority for the purposes of that Part are exempt from the subject information provisions in any case to the extent to which the application of those provisions to the data would be likely to prejudice the proper discharge of the function.

(5) Personal data processed for the purpose of discharging any function which—

(a) is conferred by or under any enactment on the the Office of Fair Trading, and

(b) is designed—

    (i) for protecting members of the public against conduct which may adversely affect their interests by persons carrying on a business,

(ii) for regulating agreements or conduct which have as their object or effect the prevention, restriction or distortion of competition in connection with any commercial activity, or

(iii) for regulating conduct on the part of one or more undertakings which amounts to the abuse of a dominant position in a market,

are exempt from the subject information provisions in any case to the extent to which the application of those provisions to the data would be likely to prejudice the proper discharge of that function.

(5A) Personal data processed by a CPC enforcer for the purpose of discharging any function conferred on such a body by or under the CPC Regulation are exempt from the subject information provisions in any case to the extent to which the application of those provisions to the data would be likely to prejudice the proper discharge of that function.

(5B) In subsection (5A)—

(a) "CPC enforcer" has the meaning given to it in section 213(5A) of the Enterprise Act 2002 but does not include the Office of Fair Trading;

(b) "CPC Regulation" has the meaning given to it in section 235A of that Act.

(6) Personal data processed for the purpose of the function of considering a complaint under section 113(1) or (2) or 114(1) or (3) of the Health and Social Care (Community Health and Standards) Act 2003, or [section 24D, 26 or 26ZB of the Children Act 1989][28], are exempt from the subject information provisions in any case to the extent to which the application of those provisions to the data would be likely to prejudice the proper discharge of that function.

32. *Journalism, literature and art*

(1) Personal data which are processed only for the special purposes are exempt from any provision to which this subsection relates if—

(a) the processing is undertaken with a view to the publication by any person of any journalistic, literary or artistic material,

(b) the data controller reasonably believes that, having regard in particular to the special importance of the public interest in freedom of expression, publication would be in the public interest, and

(c) the data controller reasonably believes that, in all the circumstances, compliance with that provision is incompatible with the special purposes.

(2) Subsection (1) relates to the provisions of—

(a) the data protection principles except the seventh data protection principle,

(b) section 7,

(c) section 10,

(d) section 12, and

(dd) section 12A,

(e) section 14(1) to (3).

(3) In considering for the purposes of subsection (1)(b) whether the belief of a data controller that publication would be in the public interest was or is a reasonable one, regard may be had to his compliance with any code of practice which—

---

[28] word repealed by Education and Inspections Act 2006 c. 40 Sch.18(5) para.1

(a) is relevant to the publication in question, and

(b) is designated by the [Secretary of State][29] by order for the purposes of this subsection.

(4) Where at any time ("the relevant time") in any proceedings against a data controller under section 7(9), 10(4), 12(8), 12A(3) or 14 or by virtue of section 13 the data controller claims, or it appears to the court, that any personal data to which the proceedings relate are being processed—

(a) only for the special purposes, and

(b) with a view to the publication by any person of any journalistic, literary or artistic material which, at the time twenty-four hours immediately before the relevant time, had not previously been published by the data controller,

the court shall stay the proceedings until either of the conditions in subsection (5) is met.

(5) Those conditions are—

(a) that a determination of the Commissioner under section 45 with respect to the data in question takes effect, or

(b) in a case where the proceedings were stayed on the making of a claim, that the claim is withdrawn.

(6) For the purposes of this Act "publish", in relation to journalistic, literary or artistic material, means make available to the public or any section of the public.

33. *Research, history and statistics*

(1) In this section—

"research purposes" includes statistical or historical purposes;

"the relevant conditions", in relation to any processing of personal data, means the conditions—

(a) that the data are not processed to support measures or decisions with respect to particular individuals, and

(b) that the data are not processed in such a way that substantial damage or substantial distress is, or is likely to be, caused to any data subject.

(2) For the purposes of the second data protection principle, the further processing of personal data only for research purposes in compliance with the relevant conditions is not to be regarded as incompatible with the purposes for which they were obtained.

(3) Personal data which are processed only for research purposes in compliance with the relevant conditions may, notwithstanding the fifth data protection principle, be kept indefinitely.

(4) Personal data which are processed only for research purposes are exempt from section 7 if—

(a) they are processed in compliance with the relevant conditions, and

(b) the results of the research or any resulting statistics are not made available in a form which identifies data subjects or any of them.

(5) For the purposes of subsections (2) to (4) personal data are not to be treated as processed otherwise than for research purposes merely because the data are disclosed—

(a) to any person, for research purposes only;

(b) to the data subject or a person acting on his behalf,

---

[29] words substituted by Secretary of State for Constitutional Affairs Order 2003/1887 Sch.2 para.9(1)(a)

(c) at the request, or with the consent, of the data subject or a person acting on his behalf, or

(d) in circumstances in which the person making the disclosure has reasonable grounds for believing that the disclosure falls within paragraph (a), (b) or (c).

33A. *Manual data held by public authorities*

(1) Personal data falling within paragraph (e) of the definition of "data" in section 1(1) are exempt from—

(a) the first, second, third, fifth, seventh and eighth data protection principles,

(b) the sixth data protection principle except so far as it relates to the rights conferred on data subjects by sections 7 and 14,

(c) sections 10 to 12,

(d) section 13, except so far as it relates to damage caused by a contravention of section 7 or of the fourth data protection principle and to any distress which is also suffered by reason of that contravention,

(e) Part III, and

(f) section 55.

(2) Personal data which fall within paragraph (e) of the definition of "data" in section 1(1) and relate to appointments or removals, pay, discipline, superannuation or other personnel matters, in relation to—

(a) service in any of the armed forces of the Crown,

(b) service in any office or employment under the Crown or under any public authority, or

(c) service in any office or employment, or under any contract for services, in respect of which power to take action, or to determine or approve the action taken, in such matters is vested in Her Majesty, any Minister of the Crown, the National Assembly for Wales, any Northern Ireland Minister (within the meaning of the Freedom of Information Act 2000) or any public authority,

are also exempt from the remaining data protection principles and the remaining provisions of Part II. [30]

34. *Information available to the public by or under enactment*

Personal data are exempt from—

(a) the subject information provisions,

(b) the fourth data protection principle and sections 12A and 14(1) to (3), and

(c) the non-disclosure provisions,

if the data consist of information which the data controller is obliged by or under any enactment [other than an enactment contained in the Freedom of Information Act 2000][31] to make available to the public, whether by publishing it, by making it available for inspection, or otherwise and whether gratuitously or on payment of a fee.

---

[30] added by Freedom of Information Act 2000 c. 36 Pt VII s.70(1)
[31] words inserted by Freedom of Information Act 2000 c. 36 Pt VII s.72

35. *Disclosures required by law or made in connection with legal proceedings etc*

(1) Personal data are exempt from the non-disclosure provisions where the disclosure is required by or under any enactment, by any rule of law or by the order of a court.

(2) Personal data are exempt from the non-disclosure provisions where the disclosure is necessary—

(a) for the purpose of, or in connection with, any legal proceedings (including prospective legal proceedings), or

(b) for the purpose of obtaining legal advice,

or is otherwise necessary for the purposes of establishing, exercising or defending legal rights.

35A. *Parliamentary privilege*

Personal data are exempt from—

(a) the first data protection principle, except to the extent to which it requires compliance with the conditions in Schedules 2 and 3,

(b) the second, third, fourth and fifth data protection principles,

(c) section 7, and

(d) sections 10 and 14(1) to (3),

if the exemption is required for the purpose of avoiding an infringement of the privileges of either House of Parliament.[32]

36. *Domestic purposes*

Personal data processed by an individual only for the purposes of that individual's personal, family or household affairs (including recreational purposes) are exempt from the data protection principles and the provisions of Parts II and III.

37. *Miscellaneous exemptions*

Schedule 7 (which confers further miscellaneous exemptions) has effect.

38. *Powers to make further exemptions by order*

(1) The [Secretary of State][33] may by order exempt from the subject information provisions personal data consisting of information the disclosure of which is prohibited or restricted by or under any enactment if and to the extent that he considers it necessary for the safeguarding of the interests of the data subject or the rights and freedoms of any other individual that the prohibition or restriction ought to prevail over those provisions.

---

[32] added by Freedom of Information Act 2000 c. 36 Sch.6 para.2
[33] words substituted by Secretary of State for Constitutional Affairs Order 2003/1887 Sch.2 para.9(1)(a)

(2) The [Secretary of State][34] may by order exempt from the non-disclosure provisions any disclosures of personal data made in circumstances specified in the order, if he considers the exemption is necessary for the safeguarding of the interests of the data subject or the rights and freedoms of any other individual.

39. *Transitional relief*

Schedule 8 (which confers transitional exemptions) has effect.

40. *Enforcement notices*

(1) If the Commissioner is satisfied that a data controller has contravened or is contravening any of the data protection principles, the Commissioners may serve him with a notice (in this Act referred to as "an enforcement notice") requiring him, for complying with the principle or principles in question, to do either or both of the following—

(a) to take within such time as may be specified in the notice, or to refrain from taking after such time as may be so specified, such steps as are so specified, or

(b) to refrain from processing any personal data, or any personal data of a description specified in the notice, or to refrain from processing them for a purpose so specified or in a manner so specified, after such time as may be so specified.

(2) In deciding whether to serve an enforcement notice, the Commissioner shall consider whether the contravention has caused or is likely to cause any person damage or distress.

(3) An enforcement notice in respect of a contravention of the fourth data protection principle which requires the data controller to rectify, block, erase or destroy any inaccurate data may also require the data controller to rectify, block, erase or destroy any other data held by him and containing an expression of opinion which appears to the Commissioner to be based on the inaccurate data.

(4) An enforcement notice in respect of a contravention of the fourth data protection principle, in the case of data which accurately record information received or obtained by the data controller from the data subject or a third party, may require the data controller either—

(a) to rectify, block, erase or destroy any inaccurate data and any other data held by him and containing an expression of opinion as mentioned in subsection (3), or

(b) to take such steps as are specified in the notice for securing compliance with the requirements specified in paragraph 7 of Part II of Schedule 1 and, if the Commissioner thinks fit, for supplementing the data with such statement of the true facts relating to the matters dealt with by the data as the Commissioner may approve.

(5) Where—

(a) an enforcement notice requires the data controller to rectify, block, erase or destroy any personal data, or

(b) the Commissioner is satisfied that personal data which have been rectified, blocked, erased or destroyed had been processed in contravention of any of the data protection principles,

an enforcement notice may, if reasonably practicable, require the data controller to notify third parties to whom the data have been disclosed of the rectification, blocking, erasure or destruction;

---

[34] words substituted by Secretary of State for Constitutional Affairs Order 2003/1887 Sch.2 para.9(1)(a)

and in determining whether it is reasonably practicable to require such notification regard shall be had, in particular, to the number of persons who would have to be notified.

(6) An enforcement notice must contain—

(a) a statement of the data protection principle or principles which the Commissioner is satisfied have been or are being contravened and his reasons for reaching that conclusion, and

(b) particulars of the rights of appeal conferred by section 48.

(7) Subject to subsection (8), an enforcement notice must not require any of the provisions of the notice to be complied with before the end of the period within which an appeal can be brought against the notice and, if such an appeal is brought, the notice need not be complied with pending the determination or withdrawal of the appeal.

(8) If by reason of special circumstances the Commissioner considers that an enforcement notice should be complied with as a matter of urgency he may include in the notice a statement to that effect and a statement of his reasons for reaching that conclusion; and in that event subsection (7) shall not apply but the notice must not require the provisions of the notice to be complied with before the end of the period of seven days beginning with the day on which the notice is served.

(9) Notification regulations (as defined by section 16(2)) may make provision as to the effect of the service of an enforcement notice on any entry in the register maintained under section 19 which relates to the person on whom the notice is served.

(10) This section has effect subject to section 46(1).

41. *Cancellation of enforcement notice*

(1) If the Commissioner considers that all or any of the provisions of an enforcement notice need not be complied with in order to ensure compliance with the data protection principle or principles to which it relates, he may cancel or vary the notice by written notice to the person on whom it was served.

(2) A person on whom an enforcement notice has been served may, at any time after the expiry of the period during which an appeal can be brought against that notice, apply in writing to the Commissioner for the cancellation or variation of that notice on the ground that, by reason of a change of circumstances, all or any of the provisions of that notice need not be complied with in order to ensure compliance with the data protection principle or principles to which that notice relates.

42. *Request for assessment*

(1) A request may be made to the Commissioner by or on behalf of any person who is, or believes himself to be, directly affected by any processing of personal data for an assessment as to whether it is likely or unlikely that the processing has been or is being carried out in compliance with the provisions of this Act.

(2) On receiving a request under this section, the Commissioner shall make an assessment in such manner as appears to him to be appropriate, unless he has not been supplied with such information as he may reasonably require in order to—

(a) satisfy himself as to the identity of the person making the request, and

(b) enable him to identify the processing in question.

(3) The matters to which the Commissioner may have regard in determining in what manner it is appropriate to make an assessment include—

    (a) the extent to which the request appears to him to raise a matter of substance,

    (b) any undue delay in making the request, and

    (c) whether or not the person making the request is entitled to make an application under section 7 in respect of the personal data in question.

(4) Where the Commissioner has received a request under this section he shall notify the person who made the request—

    (a) whether he has made an assessment as a result of the request, and

    (b) to the extent that he considers appropriate, having regard in particular to any exemption from section 7 applying in relation to the personal data concerned, of any view formed or action taken as a result of the request.

43. *Information notices*

(1) If the Commissioner—

    (a) has received a request under section 42 in respect of any processing of personal data, or

    (b) reasonably requires any information for the purpose of determining whether the data controller has complied or is complying with the data protection principles,

he may serve the data controller with a notice (in this Act referred to as "an information notice") requiring the data controller, within such time as is specified in the notice, to furnish the Commissioner, in such form as may be so specified, with such information relating to the request or to compliance with the principles as is so specified.

(2) An information notice must contain—

    (a) in a case falling within subsection (1)(a), a statement that the Commissioner has received a request under section 42 in relation to the specified processing, or

    (b) in a case falling within subsection (1)(b), a statement that the Commissioner regards the specified information as relevant for the purpose of determining whether the data controller has complied, or is complying, with the data protection principles and his reasons for regarding it as relevant for that purpose.

(3) An information notice must also contain particulars of the rights of appeal conferred by section 48.

(4) Subject to subsection (5), the time specified in an information notice shall not expire before the end of the period within which an appeal can be brought against the notice and, if such an appeal is brought, the information need not be furnished pending the determination or withdrawal of the appeal.

(5) If by reason of special circumstances the Commissioner considers that the information is required as a matter of urgency, he may include in the notice a statement to that effect and a statement of his reasons for reaching that conclusion; and in that event subsection (4) shall not apply, but the notice shall not require the information to be furnished before the end of the period of seven days beginning with the day on which the notice is served.

(6) A person shall not be required by virtue of this section to furnish the Commissioner with any information in respect of—

    (a) any communication between a professional legal adviser and his client in connection with the giving of legal advice to the client with respect to his obligations, liabilities or rights under this Act, or

(b) any communication between a professional legal adviser and his client, or between such an adviser or his client and any other person, made in connection with or in contemplation of proceedings under or arising out of this Act (including proceedings before the Tribunal) and for the purposes of such proceedings.

(7) In subsection (6) references to the client of a professional legal adviser include references to any person representing such a client.

(8) A person shall not be required by virtue of this section to furnish the Commissioner with any information if the furnishing of that information would, by revealing evidence of the commission of any offence other than an offence under this Act, expose him to proceedings for that offence.

(9) The Commissioner may cancel an information notice by written notice to the person on whom it was served.

(10) This section has effect subject to section 46(3).

44. *Special information notices*

(1) If the Commissioner—

(a) has received a request under section 42 in respect of any processing of personal data, or

(b) has reasonable grounds for suspecting that, in a case in which proceedings have been stayed under section 32, the personal data to which the proceedings relate—

   (i) are not being processed only for the special purposes, or
   (ii) are not being processed with a view to the publication by any person of any journalistic, literary or artistic material which has not previously been published by the data controller,

he may serve the data controller with a notice (in this Act referred to as a "special information notice") requiring the data controller, within such time as is specified in the notice, to furnish the Commissioner, in such form as may be so specified, with such information as is so specified for the purpose specified in subsection (2).

(2) That purpose is the purpose of ascertaining—

(a) whether the personal data are being processed only for the special purposes, or

(b) whether they are being processed with a view to the publication by any person of any journalistic, literary or artistic material which has not previously been published by the data controller.

(3) A special information notice must contain—

(a) in a case falling within paragraph (a) of subsection (1), a statement that the Commissioner has received a request under section 42 in relation to the specified processing, or

(b) in a case falling within paragraph (b) of that subsection, a statement of the Commissioner's grounds for suspecting that the personal data are not being processed as mentioned in that paragraph.

(4) A special information notice must also contain particulars of the rights of appeal conferred by section 48.

(5) Subject to subsection (6), the time specified in a special information notice shall not expire before the end of the period within which an appeal can be brought against the notice and, if such an appeal is brought, the information need not be furnished pending the determination or withdrawal of the appeal.

(6) If by reason of special circumstances the Commissioner considers that the information is required as a matter of urgency, he may include in the notice a statement to that effect and a statement of his reasons for reaching that conclusion; and in that event subsection (5) shall not apply, but the notice shall not require the information to be furnished before the end of the period of seven days beginning with the day on which the notice is served.

(7) A person shall not be required by virtue of this section to furnish the Commissioner with any information in respect of—

(a) any communication between a professional legal adviser and his client in connection with the giving of legal advice to the client with respect to his obligations, liabilities or rights under this Act, or

(b) any communication between a professional legal adviser and his client, or between such an adviser or his client and any other person, made in connection with or in contemplation of proceedings under or arising out of this Act (including proceedings before the Tribunal) and for the purposes of such proceedings.

(8) In subsection (7) references to the client of a professional legal adviser include references to any person representing such a client.

(9) A person shall not be required by virtue of this section to furnish the Commissioner with any information if the furnishing of that information would, by revealing evidence of the commission of any offence other than an offence under this Act, expose him to proceedings for that offence.

(10) The Commissioner may cancel a special information notice by written notice to the person on whom it was served.

45. *Determination by Commissioner as to the special purposes*

(1) Where at any time it appears to the Commissioner (whether as a result of the service of a special information notice or otherwise) that any personal data—

(a) are not being processed only for the special purposes, or

(b) are not being processed with a view to the publication by any person of any journalistic, literary or artistic material which has not previously been published by the data controller,

he may make a determination in writing to that effect.

(2) Notice of the determination shall be given to the data controller; and the notice must contain particulars of the right of appeal conferred by section 48.

(3) A determination under subsection (1) shall not take effect until the end of the period within which an appeal can be brought and, where an appeal is brought, shall not take effect pending the determination or withdrawal of the appeal.

46. *Restriction on enforcement in case of processing for the special purposes*

(1) The Commissioner may not at any time serve an enforcement notice on a data controller with respect to the processing of personal data for the special purposes unless—

(a) a determination under section 45(1) with respect to those data has taken effect, and

(b) the court has granted leave for the notice to be served.

(2) The court shall not grant leave for the purposes of subsection (1)(b) unless it is satisfied—

(a) that the Commissioner has reason to suspect a contravention of the data protection principles which is of substantial public importance, and

(b) except where the case is one of urgency, that the data controller has been given notice, in accordance with rules of court, of the application for leave.

(3) The Commissioner may not serve an information notice on a data controller with respect to the processing of personal data for the special purposes unless a determination under section 45(1) with respect to those data has taken effect.

47. *Failure to comply with notice*

(1) A person who fails to comply with an enforcement notice, an information notice or a special information notice is guilty of an offence.

(2) A person who, in purported compliance with an information notice or a special information notice—

(a) makes a statement which he knows to be false in a material respect, or

(b) recklessly makes a statement which is false in a material respect, is guilty of an offence.

(3) It is a defence for a person charged with an offence under subsection (1) to prove that he exercised all due diligence to comply with the notice in question.

48. *Rights of appeal*

(1) A person on whom an enforcement notice, an information notice or a special information notice has been served may appeal to the Tribunal against the notice.

(2) A person on whom an enforcement notice has been served may appeal to the Tribunal against the refusal of an application under section 41(2) for cancellation or variation of the notice.

(3) Where an enforcement notice, an information notice or a special information notice contains a statement by the Commissioner in accordance with section 40(8), 43(5) or 44(6) then, whether or not the person appeals against the notice, he may appeal against—

(a) the Commissioner's decision to include the statement in the notice, or

(b) the effect of the inclusion of the statement as respects any part of the notice.

(4) A data controller in respect of whom a determination has been made under section 45 may appeal to the Tribunal against the determination.

(5) Schedule 6 has effect in relation to appeals under this section and the proceedings of the Tribunal in respect of any such appeal.

49. *Determination of appeals*

(1) If on an appeal under section 48(1) the Tribunal considers—

(a) that the notice against which the appeal is brought is not in accordance with the law, or

(b) to the extent that the notice involved an exercise of discretion by the Commissioner, that he ought to have exercised his discretion differently, the Tribunal shall allow the appeal or substitute such other notice or decision as could have been served or made by the Commissioner; and in any other case the Tribunal shall dismiss the appeal.

(2) On such an appeal, the Tribunal may review any determination of fact on which the notice in question was based.

(3) If on an appeal under section 48(2) the Tribunal considers that the enforcement notice ought to be cancelled or varied by reason of a change in circumstances, the Tribunal shall cancel or vary the notice.

(4) On an appeal under subsection (3) of section 48 the Tribunal may direct—

    (a) that the notice in question shall have effect as if it did not contain any such statement as is mentioned in that subsection, or

    (b) that the inclusion of the statement shall not have effect in relation to any part of the notice,

and may make such modifications in the notice as may be required for giving effect to the direction.

(5) On an appeal under section 48(4), the Tribunal may cancel the determination of the Commissioner.

(6) Any party to an appeal to the Tribunal under section 48 may appeal from the decision of the Tribunal on a point of law to the appropriate court; and that court shall be—

    (a) the High Court of Justice in England if the address of the person who was the appellant before the Tribunal is in England or Wales,

    (b) the Court of Session if that address is in Scotland, and

    (c) the High Court of Justice in Northern Ireland if that address is in Northern Ireland.

(7) For the purposes of subsection (6)—

    (a) the address of a registered company is that of its registered office, and

    (b) the address of a person (other than a registered company) carrying on a business is that of his principal place of business in the United Kingdom.

50. *Powers of entry and inspection*

Schedule 9 (powers of entry and inspection) has effect.

51. *General duties of Commissioner.*

(1) It shall be the duty of the Commissioner to promote the following of good practice by data controllers and, in particular, so to perform his functions under this Act as to promote the observance of the requirements of this Act by data controllers.

(2) The Commissioner shall arrange for the dissemination in such form and manner as he considers appropriate of such information as it may appear to him expedient to give to the public about the operation of this Act, about good practice, and about other matters within the scope of his functions under this Act, and may give advice to any person as to any of those matters.

(3) Where—

    (a) the [Secretary of State][35] so directs by order, or

    (b) the Commissioner considers it appropriate to do so,

---

[35] words substituted by Secretary of State for Constitutional Affairs Order 2003/1887 Sch.2 para.9(1)(a)

the Commissioner shall, after such consultation with trade associations, data subjects or persons representing data subjects as appears to him to be appropriate, prepare and disseminate to such persons as he considers appropriate codes of practice for guidance as to good practice.

(4) The Commissioner shall also—

(a) Where he considers it appropriate to do so, encourage trade associations to prepare, and to disseminate to their members, such codes of practice, and

(b) where any trade association submits a code of practice to him for his consideration, consider the code and, after such consultation with data subjects or persons representing data subjects as appears to him to be appropriate, notify the trade association whether in his opinion the code promotes the following of good practice.

(5) An order under subsection (3) shall describe the personal data or processing to which the code of practice is to relate, and may also describe the persons or classes of persons to whom it is to relate.

(6) The Commissioner shall arrange for the dissemination in such form and manner as he considers appropriate of—

(a) any Community finding as defined by paragraph 15(2) of Part II of Schedule 1,

(b) any decision of the European Commission, under the procedure provided for in Article 31(2) of the Data Protection Directive, which is made for the purposes of Article 26(3) or (4) of the Directive, and (c) such other information as it may appear to him to be expedient to give to data controllers in relation to any personal data about the protection of the rights and freedoms of data subjects in relation to the processing of personal data in countries and territories outside the European Economic Area.

(7) The Commissioner may, with the consent of the data controller, assess any processing of personal data for the following of good practice and shall inform the data controller of the results of the assessment.

(8) The Commissioner may charge such sums as he may with the consent of the [Secretary of State][36] determine for any services provided by the Commissioner by virtue of this Part.

(9) In this section—

"good practice" means such practice in the processing of personal data as appears to the Commissioner to be desirable having regard to the interests of data subjects and others, and includes (but is not limited to) compliance with the requirements of this Act;

"trade association" includes any body representing data controllers.

52. Reports and codes of practice to be laid before Parliament

(1) The Commissioner shall lay annually before each House of Parliament a general report on the exercise of his functions under this Act.

(2) The Commissioner may from time to time lay before each House of Parliament such other reports with respect to those functions as he thinks fit.

(3) The Commissioner shall lay before each House of Parliament any code of practice prepared under section 51(3) for complying with a direction of the [Secretary of State][37], unless the code is included in any report laid under subsection (1) or (2).

---

[36] words substituted by Secretary of State for Constitutional Affairs Order 2003/1887 Sch.2 para.9(1)(a)
[37] words substituted by Secretary of State for Constitutional Affairs Order 2003/1887 Sch.2 para.9(1)(a)

53. *Assistance by Commissioner in cases involving processing for the special purposes*

(1) An individual who is an actual or prospective party to any proceedings under section 7(9), 10(4), 12(8)[, 12A(3)][38] or 14 or by virtue of section 13 which relate to personal data processed for the special purposes may apply to the Commissioner for assistance in relation to those proceedings.

(2) The Commissioner shall, as soon as reasonably practicable after receiving an application under subsection (1), consider it and decide whether and to what extent to grant it, but he shall not grant the application unless, in his opinion, the case involves a matter of substantial public importance.

(3) If the Commissioner decides to provide assistance, he shall, as soon as reasonably practicable after making the decision, notify the applicant, stating the extent of the assistance to be provided.

(4) If the Commissioner decides not to provide assistance, he shall, as soon as reasonably practicable after making the decision, notify the applicant of his decision and, if he thinks fit, the reasons for it.

(5) In this section—

(a) references to "proceedings" include references to prospective proceedings, and

(b) "applicant", in relation to assistance under this section, means an individual who applies for assistance.

(6) Schedule 10 has effect for supplementing this section.

54. *International co-operation*

(1) The Commissioner—

(a) shall continue to be the designated authority in the United Kingdom for the purposes of Article 13 of the Convention, and

(b) shall be the supervisory authority in the United Kingdom for the purposes of the Data Protection Directive.

(2) The Secretary of State[39] may by order make provision as to the functions to be discharged by the Commissioner as the designated authority in the United Kingdom for the purposes of Article 13 of the Convention.

(3) The Secretary of State[40] may by order make provision as to co-operation by the Commissioner with the European Commission and with supervisory authorities in other EEA States in connection with the performance of their respective duties and, in particular, as to—

(a) the exchange of information with supervisory authorities in other EEA States or with the European Commission, and

(b) the exercise within the United Kingdom at the request of a supervisory authority in another EEA State, in cases excluded by section 5 from the application of the other provisions of this Act, of functions of the Commissioner specified in the order.

---

[38] words inserted by Data Protection Act 1998 c. 29 Sch.13 para.4
[39] words substituted by Secretary of State for Constitutional Affairs Order 2003/1887 Sch.2 para.9(1)(a)
[40] words substituted by Secretary of State for Constitutional Affairs Order 2003/1887 Sch.2 para.9(1)(a)

(4) The Commissioner shall also carry out any data protection functions which the [Secretary of State][41] may by order direct him to carry out for the purpose of enabling Her Majesty's Government in the United Kingdom to give effect to any international obligations of the United Kingdom.

(5) The Commissioner shall, if so directed by the [Secretary of State][42], provide any authority exercising data protection functions under the law of a colony specified in the direction with such assistance in connection with the discharge of those functions as the [Secretary of State][43] may direct or approve, on such terms (including terms as to payment) as the [Secretary of State][44] may direct or approve.

(6) Where the European Commission makes a decision for the purposes of Article 26(3) or (4) of the Data Protection Directive under the procedure provided for in Article 31(2) of the Directive, the Commissioner shall comply with that decision in exercising his functions under paragraph 9 of Schedule 4 or, as the case may be, paragraph 8 of that Schedule.

(7) The Commissioner shall inform the European Commission and the supervisory authorities in other EEA States—

(a) of any approvals granted for the purposes of paragraph 8 of Schedule 4, and

(b) of any authorisations granted for the purposes of paragraph 9 of that Schedule.

(8) In this section—

"the Convention" means the Convention for the Protection of Individuals with regard to Automatic Processing of Personal Data which was opened for signature on 28th January 1981;

"data protection functions" means functions relating to the protection of individuals with respect to the processing of personal information.

54A. *Inspection of overseas information systems*

(1) The Commissioner may inspect any personal data recorded in—

(a) the Schengen information system,

(b) the Europol information system,

(c) the Customs information system.

(2) The power conferred by subsection (1) is exercisable only for the purpose of assessing whether or not any processing of the data has been or is being carried out in compliance with this Act.

(3) The power includes power to inspect, operate and test equipment which is used for the processing of personal data.

(4) Before exercising the power, the Commissioner must give notice in writing of his intention to do so to the data controller.

(5) But subsection (4) does not apply if the Commissioner considers that the case is one of urgency.

(6) Any person who—

(a) intentionally obstructs a person exercising the power conferred by subsection (1), or

---

[41] words substituted by Secretary of State for Constitutional Affairs Order 2003/1887 Sch.2 para.9(1)(a)
[42] words substituted by Secretary of State for Constitutional Affairs Order 2003/1887 Sch.2 para.9(1)(a)
[43] words substituted by Secretary of State for Constitutional Affairs Order 2003/1887 Sch.2 para.9(1)(a)
[44] words substituted by Secretary of State for Constitutional Affairs Order 2003/1887 Sch.2 para.9(1)(a)

(b) fails without reasonable excuse to give any person exercising the power any assistance he may reasonably require,

is guilty of an offence.

(7) In this section—

"the Customs information system" means the information system established under Chapter II of the Convention on the Use of Information Technology for Customs Purposes,

"the Europol information system" means the information system established under Title II of the Convention on the Establishment of a European Police Office,

"the Schengen information system" means the information system established under Title IV of the Convention implementing the Schengen Agreement of 14th June 1985, or any system established in its place in pursuance of any Community obligation.[45]

55. *Unlawful obtaining etc. of personal data*

(1) A person must not knowingly or recklessly, without the consent of the data controller—

(a) obtain or disclose personal data or the information contained in personal data, or

(b) procure the disclosure to another person of the information contained in personal data.

(2) Subsection (1) does not apply to a person who shows—

(a) that the obtaining, disclosing or procuring—

  (i) was necessary for the purpose of preventing or detecting crime, or
  (ii) was required or authorised by or under any enactment, by any rule of law or by the order of a court,

(b) that he acted in the reasonable belief that he had in law the right to obtain or disclose the data or information or, as the case may be, to procure the disclosure of the information to the other person,

(c) that he acted in the reasonable belief that he would have had the consent of the data controller if the data controller had known of the obtaining, disclosing or procuring and the circumstances of it, or

(d) that in the particular circumstances the obtaining, disclosing or procuring was justified as being in the public interest.

(3) A person who contravenes subsection (1) is guilty of an offence.

(4) A person who sells personal data is guilty of an offence if he has obtained the data in contravention of subsection (1).

(5) A person who offers to sell personal data is guilty of an offence if—

(a) he has obtained the data in contravention of subsection (1), or

(b) he subsequently obtains the data in contravention of that subsection.

(6) For the purposes of subsection (5), an advertisement indicating that personal data are or may be for sale is an offer to sell the data.

(7) Section 1(2) does not apply for the purposes of this section; and for the purposes of subsections (4) to (6), "personal data" includes information extracted from personal data.

---

[45] added by Crime (International Co-operation) Act 2003 c. 32 Pt 4 s.81

(8) References in this section to personal data do not include references to personal data which by virtue of [section 28 or 33A][46] are exempt from this section.

56. *Prohibition of requirement as to production of certain records*

(1) A person must not, in connection with—

    (a) the recruitment of another person as an employee,

    (b) the continued employment of another person, or

    (c) any contract for the provision of services to him by another person,

require that other person or a third party to supply him with a relevant record or to produce a relevant record to him.

(2) A person concerned with the provision (for payment or not) of goods, facilities or services to the public or a section of the public must not, as a condition of providing or offering to provide any goods, facilities or services to another person, require that other person or a third party to supply him with a relevant record or to produce a relevant record to him.

(3) Subsections (1) and (2) do not apply to a person who shows—

    (a) that the imposition of the requirement was required or authorised by or under any enactment, by any rule of law or by the order of a court, or

    (b) that in the particular circumstances the imposition of the requirement was justified as being in the public interest.

(4) Having regard to the provisions of Part V of the Police Act 1997 (certificates of criminal records etc.), the imposition of the requirement referred to in subsection (1) or (2) is not to be regarded as being justified as being in the public interest on the ground that it would assist in the prevention or detection of crime.

(5) A person who contravenes subsection (1) or (2) is guilty of an offence.

(6) In this section "a relevant record" means any record which—

    (a) has been or is to be obtained by a data subject from any data controller specified in the first column of the Table below in the exercise of the right conferred by section 7, and

    (b) contains information relating to any matter specified in relation to that data controller in the second column,

and includes a copy of such a record or a part of such a record.

TABLE

Data controller	Subject-matter

1. Any of the following persons—
 	
   (a) a chief officer of police of a police force in England and Wales.
   (b) a chief constable of a police force in Scotland.
   (c) the Chief Constable of the Royal Ulster Constabulary.
	(a) Convictions.
	 (b) Cautions.

[46] words added by Freedom of Information Act 2000 c. 36 Pt VII s.70(2)

TABLE—contd

Data controller	Subject-matter
(d) the Director General of the Serious Organised Crime Agency.[47]	
2. The Secretary of State.	(a) Convictions.
	(b) Cautions.
	(c) His functions under section 92 of the Powers of Criminal Courts (Sentencing) Act 2000, section 205(2) or 208 of the Criminal Procedure (Scotland) Act 1995 or section 73 of the Children and Young Persons Act (Northern Ireland) 1968 in relation to any person sentenced to detention.
	(d) His functions under the Prison Act 1952, the Prisons (Scotland) Act 1989 or the Prison Act (Northern Ireland) 1953 in relation to any person imprisoned or detained.
	(e) His functions under the Social Security Contributions and Benefits Act 1992, the Social Security Administration Act 1992 or the Jobseekers Act 1995.
	(f) His functions under Part V of the Police Act 1997.
3. The Department of Health and Social Services for Northern Ireland.	Its functions under the Social Security Contributions and Benefits (Northern Ireland) Act 1992, the Social Security Administration (Northern Ireland) Act 1992 or the Jobseekers (Northern Ireland) Order 1995.

(6A) A record is not a relevant record to the extent that it relates, or is to relate, only to personal data falling within paragraph (e) of the definition of "data" in section 1(1).

(7) In the Table in subsection (6)—

"caution" means a caution given to any person in England and Wales or Northern Ireland in respect of an offence which, at the time when the caution is given, is admitted;
"conviction" has the same meaning as in the Rehabilitation of Offenders Act 1974 or the Rehabilitation of Offenders (Northern Ireland) Order 1978.

(8) The Secretary of State may by order amend—

(a) the Table in subsection (6), and

(b) subsection (7).

(9) For the purposes of this section a record which states that a data controller is not processing any personal data relating to a particular matter shall be taken to be a record containing information relating to that matter.

---

[47] words substituted by Serious Organised Crime and Police Act 2005 c. 15 Sch.4 para.112

(10) In this section "employee" means an individual who—

(a) works under a contract of employment, as defined by section 230(2) of the Employment Rights Act 1996, or

(b) holds any office,

whether or not he is entitled to remuneration; and "employment" shall be construed accordingly.

57. *Avoidance of certain contractual terms relating to health records*

(1) Any term or condition of a contract is void in so far as it purports to require an individual—

(a) to supply any other person with a record to which this section applies, or with a copy of such a record or a part of such a record, or

(b) to produce to any other person such a record, copy or part.

(2) This section applies to any record which—

(a) has been or is to be obtained by a data subject in the exercise of the right conferred by section 7, and

(b) consists of the information contained in any health record as defined by section 68(2).

58. *Disclosure of information*

No enactment or rule of law prohibiting or restricting the disclosure of information shall preclude a person from furnishing the Commissioner or the Tribunal with any information necessary for the discharge of their functions under this Act [or the Freedom of Information Act 2000][48].

59. *Confidentiality of information*

(1) No person who is or has been the Commissioner, a member of the Commissioner's staff or an agent of the Commissioner shall disclose any information which—

(a) has been obtained by, or furnished to, the Commissioner under or for the purposes of the information Acts.

(b) relates to an identified or identifiable individual or business, and

(c) is not at the time of the disclosure, and has not previously been, available to the public from other sources,

unless the disclosure is made with lawful authority.

(2) For the purposes of subsection (1) a disclosure of information is made with lawful authority only if, and to the extent that—

(a) the disclosure is made with the consent of the individual or of the person for the time being carrying on the business,

(b) the information was provided for the purpose of its being made available to the public (in whatever manner) under any provision of the information Acts,

---

[48] words added by Freedom of Information Act 2000 c. 36 Sch.2(II) para.18

(c) the disclosure is made for the purposes of, and is necessary for, the discharge of—

    (i) any functions under the information Acts, or

    (ii) any Community obligation,

(d) the disclosure is made for the purposes of any proceedings, whether criminal or civil and whether arising under, or by virtue of, the information Acts or otherwise, or

(e) having regard to the rights and freedoms or legitimate interests of any person, the disclosure is necessary in the public interest.

(3) Any person who knowingly or recklessly discloses information in contravention of subsection (1) is guilty of an offence.

(4) In this section "the information Acts" means this Act and the Freedom of Information Act 2000.[49]

60. *Prosecutions and penalties*

(1) No proceedings for an offence under this Act shall be instituted—

(a) in England or Wales, except by the Commissioner or by or with the consent of the Director of Public Prosecutions;

(b) in Northern Ireland, except by the Commissioner or by or with the consent of the Director of Public Prosecutions for Northern Ireland.

(2) A person guilty of an offence under any provision of this Act other than [section 54A and paragraph 12 of Schedule 9][50] is liable—

(a) on summary conviction, to a fine not exceeding the statutory maximum, or

(b) on conviction on indictment, to a fine.

(3) A person guilty of an offence under paragraph 12 of Schedule 9 is liable on summary conviction to a fine not exceeding level 5 on the standard scale.

(4) Subject to subsection (5), the court by or before which a person is convicted of—

(a) an offence under section 21(1), 22(6), 55 or 56,

(b) an offence under section 21(2) relating to processing which is assessable processing for the purposes of section 22, or

(c) an offence under section 47(1) relating to an enforcement notice,

may order any document or other material used in connection with the processing of personal data and appearing to the court to be connected with the commission of the offence to be forfeited, destroyed or erased.

(5) The court shall not make an order under subsection (4) in relation to any material where a person (other than the offender) claiming to be the owner of or otherwise interested in the material applies to be heard by the court, unless an opportunity is given to him to show cause why the order should not be made.

61. *Liability of directors etc*

(1) Where an offence under this Act has been committed by a body corporate and is proved to have been committed with the consent or connivance of or to be attributable to any

---

[49] added by Freedom of Information Act 2000 c. 36 Sch.2(II) para.19(3)

[50] words inserted by Crime (International Co-operation) Act 2003 c. 32 Sch.5 para.70

neglect on the part of any director, manager, secretary or similar officer of the body corporate or any person who was purporting to act in any such capacity, he as well as the body corporate shall be guilty of that offence and be liable to be proceeded against and punished accordingly.

(2) Where the affairs of a body corporate are managed by its members subsection (1) shall apply in relation to the acts and defaults of a member in connection with his functions of management as if he were a director of the body corporate.

(3) Where an offence under this Act has been committed by a Scottish partnership and the contravention in question is proved to have occurred with the consent or connivance of, or to be attributable to any neglect on the part of, a partner, he as well as the partnership shall be guilty of that offence and shall be liable to be proceeded against and punished accordingly.

62. *Amendments of Consumer Credit Act 1974*

(1) In section 158 of the Consumer Credit Act 1974 (duty of agency to disclose filed information)—

    (a) in subsection (1)—

        (i) in paragraph (a) for "individual" there is substituted "partnership or other unincorporated body of persons not consisting entirely of bodies corporate", and
        (ii) for "him" there is substituted "it",

    (b) in subsection (2), for "his" there is substituted "the consumer's", and

    (c) in subsection (3), for "him" there is substituted "the consumer".

(2) In section 159 of that Act (correction of wrong information) for subsection (1) there is substituted—

"(1) Any individual (the "objector") given—

    (a) information under section 7 of the Data Protection Act 1998 by a credit reference agency, or
    (b) information under section 158,

who considers that an entry in his file is incorrect, and that if it is not corrected he is likely to be prejudiced, may give notice to the agency requiring it either to remove the entry from the file or amend it."

(3) In subsections (2) to (6) of that section—

    (a) for "consumer", wherever occurring, there is substituted "objector", and

    (b) for "Director", wherever occurring, there is substituted "the relevant authority".

(4) After subsection (6) of that section there is inserted—

"(7) The Data Protection Commissioner may vary or revoke any order made by him under this section.

(8) In this section "the relevant authority" means—

    (a) where the objector is a partnership or other unincorporated body of persons, the Director, and
    (b) in any other case, the Data Protection Commissioner."

(5) In section 160 of that Act (alternative procedure for business consumers)—

    (a) in subsection (4)—

        (i) for "him" there is substituted "to the consumer", and

     (ii) in paragraphs (a) and (b) for "he" there is substituted "the consumer", and for "his" there is substituted "the consumer's", and

  (b) after subsection (6) there is inserted—

  "(7) In this section "consumer" has the same meaning as in section 158."

63. *Application to Crown*

(1) This Act binds the Crown.

(2) For the purposes of this Act each government department shall be treated as a person separate from any other government department.

(3) Where the purposes for which and the manner in which any personal data are, or are to be, processed are determined by any person acting on behalf of the Royal Household, the Duchy of Lancaster or the Duchy of Cornwall, the data controller in respect of those data for the purposes of this Act shall be—

  (a) in relation to the Royal Household, the Keeper of the Privy Purse,

  (b) in relation to the Duchy of Lancaster, such person as the Chancellor of the Duchy appoints, and

  (c) in relation to the Duchy of Cornwall, such person as the Duke of Cornwall, or the possessor for the time being of the Duchy of Cornwall, appoints.

(4) Different persons may be appointed under subsection (3)(b) or (c) for different purposes.

(5) Neither a government department nor a person who is a data controller by virtue of subsection (3) shall be liable to prosecution under this Act, but [sections 54A and 55 and paragraph 12 of Schedule 9][51] shall apply to a person in the service of the Crown as they apply to any other person.

63A. *Application to Parliament*

(1) Subject to the following provisions of this section and to section 35A, this Act applies to the processing of personal data by or on behalf of either House of Parliament as it applies to the processing of personal data by other persons.

(2) Where the purposes for which and the manner in which any personal data are, or are to be, processed are determined by or on behalf of the House of Commons, the data controller in respect of those data for the purposes of this Act shall be the Corporate Officer of that House.

(3) Where the purposes for which and the manner in which any personal data are, or are to be, processed are determined by or on behalf of the House of Lords, the data controller in respect of those data for the purposes of this Act shall be the Corporate Officer of that House.

(4) Nothing in subsection (2) or (3) is to be taken to render the Corporate Officer of the House of Commons or the Corporate Officer of the House of Lords liable to prosecution under this Act, but section 55 and paragraph 12 of Schedule 9 shall apply to a person acting on behalf of either House as they apply to any other person.[52]

---

[51] word substituted by Crime (International Co-operation) Act 2003 c. 32 Sch.5 para.71
[52] added by Freedom of Information Act 2000 c. 36 Sch.6 para.3

64. *Transmission of notices etc. by electronic or other means*

(1) This section applies to—

(a) a notice or request under any provision of Part II,

(b) a notice under subsection (1) of section 24 or particulars made available under that subsection, or

(c) an application under section 41(2),

but does not apply to anything which is required to be served in accordance with rules of court.

(2) The requirement that any notice, request, particulars or application to which this section applies should be in writing is satisfied where the text of the notice, request, particulars or application—

(a) is transmitted by electronic means,

(b) is received in legible form, and

(c) is capable of being used for subsequent reference.

(3) The [Secretary of State][53] may by regulations provide that any requirement that any notice, request, particulars or application to which this section applies should be in writing is not to apply in such circumstances as may be prescribed by the regulations.

65. *Service of notices by Commissioner*

(1) Any notice authorised or required by this Act to be served on or given to any person by the Commissioner may—

(a) if that person is an individual, be served on him—

  (i) by delivering it to him, or

  (ii) by sending it to him by post addressed to him at his usual or last-known place of residence or business, or

  (iii) by leaving it for him at that place;

(b) if that person is a body corporate or unincorporate, be served on that body—

  (i) by sending it by post to the proper officer of the body at its principal office, or

  (ii) by addressing it to the proper officer of the body and leaving it at that office;

(c) if that person is a partnership in Scotland, be served on that partnership—

  (i) by sending it by post to the principal office of the partnership, or

  (ii) by addressing it to that partnership and leaving it at that office.

(2) In subsection (1)(b) "principal office", in relation to a registered company, means its registered office and "proper officer", in relation to any body, means the secretary or other executive officer charged with the conduct of its general affairs.

(3) This section is without prejudice to any other lawful method of serving or giving a notice.

66. *Exercise of rights in Scotland by children*

(1) Where a question falls to be determined in Scotland as to the legal capacity of a person under the age of sixteen years to exercise any right conferred by any provision of this Act, that

---

[53] words substituted by Secretary of State for Constitutional Affairs Order 2003/1887 Sch.2 para.9(1)(a)

person shall be taken to have that capacity where he has a general understanding of what it means to exercise that right.

(2) Without prejudice to the generality of subsection (1), a person of twelve years of age or more shall be presumed to be of sufficient age and maturity to have such understanding as is mentioned in that subsection.

67. *Orders, regulations and rules*

(1) Any power conferred by this Act on the [Secretary of State][54] to make an order, regulations or rules shall be exercisable by statutory instrument.

(2) Any order, regulations or rules made by the [Secretary of State][55] under this Act may—

(a) make different provision for different cases, and

(b) make such supplemental, incidental, consequential or transitional provision or savings as the [Secretary of State][56] considers appropriate;

and nothing in section 7(11), 19(5), 26(1) or 30(4) limits the generality of paragraph (a).

(3) Before making—

(a) an order under any provision of this Act other than section 75(3),

(b) any regulations under this Act other than notification regulations (as defined by section 16(2)),

the [Secretary of State][57] shall consult the Commissioner.

(4) A statutory instrument containing (whether alone or with other provision) an order under—

> section 10(2)(b),
>
> section 12(5)(b),
>
> section 22(1),
>
> section 30,
>
> section 32(3),
>
> section 38,
>
> section 56(8),
>
> paragraph 10 of Schedule 3, or
>
> paragraph 4 of Schedule 7,

shall not be made unless a draft of the instrument has been laid before and approved by a resolution of each House of Parliament.

(5) A statutory instrument which contains (whether alone or with other provisions)—

(a) an order under—section 22(7),

> section 23,
>
> section 51(3),

---

[54] words substituted by Secretary of State for Constitutional Affairs Order 2003/1887 Sch.2 para.9(1)(a)
[55] words substituted by Secretary of State for Constitutional Affairs Order 2003/1887 Sch.2 para.9(1)(a)
[56] words substituted by Secretary of State for Constitutional Affairs Order 2003/1887 Sch.2 para.9(1)(a)
[57] words substituted by Secretary of State for Constitutional Affairs Order 2003/1887 Sch.2 para.9(1)(a)

section 54(2), (3) or (4),

paragraph 3, 4 or 14 of Part II of Schedule 1,

paragraph 6 of Schedule 2,

paragraph 2, 7 or 9 of Schedule 3,

paragraph 4 of Schedule 4,

paragraph 6 of Schedule 7,

(b) regulations under section 7 which—

   (i) prescribe cases for the purposes of subsection (2)(b),
   (ii) are made by virtue of subsection (7), or
   (iii) relate to the definition of "the prescribed period",

(c) regulations under section 8(1), 9(3) or 9A(5),

(d) regulations under section 64,

(e) notification regulations (as defined by section 16(2)), or

(f) rules under paragraph 7 of Schedule 6,

and which is not subject to the requirement in subsection (4) that a draft of the instrument be laid before and approved by a resolution of each House of Parliament, shall be subject to annulment in pursuance of a resolution of either House of Parliament.

(6) A statutory instrument which contains only—

(a) regulations prescribing fees for the purposes of any provision of this Act, or

(b) regulations under section 7 prescribing fees for the purposes of any other enactment,

shall be laid before Parliament after being made.

68. Meaning of "accessible record"

(1) In this Act "accessible record" means—

(a) a health record as defined by subsection (2),

(b) an educational record as defined by Schedule 11, or

(c) an accessible public record as defined by Schedule 12.

(2) In subsection (1)(a) "health record" means any record which—

(a) consists of information relating to the physical or mental health or condition of an individual, and

(b) has been made by or on behalf of a health professional in connection with the care of that individual.

69. Meaning of "health professional"

(1) In this Act "health professional" means any of the following—

(a) a registered medical practitioner,

(b) a registered dentist as defined by section 53(1) of the Dentists Act 1984,

(c) a registered dispensing optician or a registered optometrist within the meaning of the Opticians Act 1989,

(d) [a registered pharmacist or registered pharmacy technician within the meaning of the Pharmacists and Pharmacy Technicians Order 2007][58] or a registered person as defined by Article 2(2) of the Pharmacy (Northern Ireland) Order 1976,

(e) a registered nurse or midwife,

(f) a registered osteopath as defined by section 41 of the Osteopaths Act 1993,

(g) a registered chiropractor as defined by section 43 of the Chiropractors Act 1994,

(h) any person who is registered as a member of a profession to which the Health Professions Order 2001 for the time being extends,

(i) a clinical psychologist or child psychotherapist, and

(j) [. . .]

(k) a scientist employed by such a body as head of a department.

(2) In subsection (1)(a) "registered medical practitioner" includes any person who is provisionally registered under section 15 or 21 of the Medical Act 1983 and is engaged in such employment as is mentioned in subsection (3) of that section.

(3) In subsection (1) "health service body" means—

(a) a Strategic Health Authority established under section 13 of the National Health Service Act 2006,

(b) a Special Health Authority established under section 28 of that Act, or section 22 of the National Health Service (Wales) Act 2006,

(bb) a Primary Care Trust established under section 18 of the National Health Service Act 2006,

(c) a Health Board within the meaning of the National Health Service (Scotland) Act 1978,

(d) a Special Health Board within the meaning of that Act,

(e) the managers of a State Hospital provided under section 102 of that Act,

(f) a National Health Service trust first established under section 5 of the National Health Service and Community Care Act 1990, section 25 of the National Health Service Act 2006, section 18 of the National Health Service (Wales) Act 2006 or section 12A of the National Health Service (Scotland) Act 1978,

(fa) an NHS foundation trust,

(g) a Health and Social Services Board established under Article 16 of the Health and Personal Social Services (Northern Ireland) Order 1972,

(h) a special health and social services agency established under the Health and Personal Social Services (Special Agencies) (Northern Ireland) Order 1990, or

(i) a Health and Social Services trust established under Article 10 of the Health and Personal Social Services (Northern Ireland) Order 1991.[59,60]

70. *Supplementary definitions*

(1) In this Act, unless the context otherwise requires—

---

[58] words substituted by Pharmacists and Pharmacy Technicians Order 2007/289 Sch.1(1) para.7
[59] In relation to England: s.69 is modified
[60] In relation to Wales: s.69 is modified

"business" includes any trade or profession;

"the Commissioner" means the Information Commissioner;

"credit reference agency" has the same meaning as in the Consumer Credit Act 1974;

"the Data Protection Directive" means Directive 95/46/EC on the protection of individuals with regard to the processing of personal data and on the free movement of such data;

"EEA State" means a State which is a contracting party to the Agreement on the European Economic Area signed at Oporto on 2nd May 1992 as adjusted by the Protocol signed at Brussels on 17th March 1993;

"enactment" includes an enactment passed after this Act and any enactment comprised in, or in any instrument made under, an Act of the Scottish Parliament;

"government department" includes a Northern Ireland department and any body or authority exercising statutory functions on behalf of the Crown;

"Minister of the Crown" has the same meaning as in the Ministers of the Crown Act 1975;

"public register" means any register which pursuant to a requirement imposed—

    (a) by or under any enactment, or
    (b) in pursuance of any international agreement,

is open to public inspection or open to inspection by any person having a legitimate interest;

"pupil"—

    (a) in relation to a school in England and Wales, means a registered pupil within the meaning of the Education Act 1996,
    (b) in relation to a school in Scotland, means a pupil within the meaning of the Education (Scotland) Act 1980, and
    (c) in relation to a school in Northern Ireland, means a registered pupil within the meaning of the Education and Libraries (Northern Ireland) Order 1986;

"recipient", in relation to any personal data, means any person to whom the data are disclosed, including any person (such as an employee or agent of the data controller, a data processor or an employee or agent of a data processor) to whom they are disclosed in the course of processing the data for the data controller, but does not include any person to whom disclosure is or may be made as a result of, or with a view to, a particular inquiry by or on behalf of that person made in the exercise of any power conferred by law;

"registered company" means a company registered under the enactments relating to companies for the time being in force in the United Kingdom;

"school"—

    (a) in relation to England and Wales, has the same meaning as in the Education Act 1996,
    (b) in relation to Scotland, has the same meaning as in the Education (Scotland) Act 1980, and
    (c) in relation to Northern Ireland, has the same meaning as in the Education and Libraries (Northern Ireland) Order 1986;

"teacher" includes—

    (a) in Great Britain, head teacher, and
    (b) in Northern Ireland, the principal of a school;

"third party", in relation to personal data, means any person other than—

(a) the data subject,

(b) the data controller, or

(c) any data processor or other person authorised to process data for the data controller or processor;

"the Tribunal" means [the Information Tribunal][61].

(2) For the purposes of this Act data are inaccurate if they are incorrect or misleading as to any matter of fact.

71. *Index of defined expressions*

The following Table shows provisions defining or otherwise explaining expressions used in this Act (other than provisions defining or explaining an expression only used in the same section or Schedule)—

accessible record	section 68
address (in Part III)	section 16(3)
business	section 70(1)
the Commissioner	section 70(1)
credit reference agency	section 70(1)
data	section 1(1)
data controller	sections 1(1) and (4) and 63(3)
data processor	section 1(1)
the Data Protection Directive	section 70(1)
data protection principles	section 4 and Schedule 1
data subject	section 1(1)
disclosing (of personal data)	section 1(2)(b)
EEA State	section 70(1)
enactment	section 70(1)
enforcement notice	ection 40(1)
fees regulations (in Part III)	section 16(2)
government department	section 70(1)
health professional	section 69
inaccurate (in relation to data)	section 70(2)
information notice	section 43(1)
Minister of the Crown	section 70(1)
the non-disclosure provisions	section 27(3)
(in Part IV)	
notification regulations (in Part III)	section 16(2)
obtaining (of personal data)	section 1(2)(a)
personal data	section 1(1)
prescribed (in Part III)	section 16(2)
processing (of information or data)	section 1(1) and paragraph 5 of Schedule 8
public authority	section 1(1).[62]
public register	section 70(1)
publish (in relation to journalistic, literary	section 32(6)
or artistic material)	
pupil (in relation to a school)	section 70(1)
recipient (in relation to personal data)	section 70(1)
recording (of personal data)	section 1(2)(a)
registered company	section 70(1)

---

[61] words substituted by Freedom of Information Act 2000 c. 36 Sch.2(I) para.14(b)

[62] entry added to table by Freedom of Information Act 2000 c. 36 Pt VII s.68(5)

72. *Modifications of Act*

During the period beginning with the commencement of this section and ending with 23rd October 2007, the provisions of this Act shall have effect subject to the modifications set out in Schedule 13.

73. *Transitional provisions and savings*

Schedule 14 (which contains transitional provisions and savings) has effect.

74. *Minor and consequential amendments and repeals and revocations*

(1) Schedule 15 (which contains minor and consequential amendments) has effect.

(2) The enactments and instruments specified in Schedule 16 are repealed or revoked to the extent specified.

75. *Short title, commencement and extent*

(1) This Act may be cited as the Data Protection Act 1998.

(2) The following provisions of this Act—

    (a) sections 1 to 3,

    (b) section 25(1) and (4),

    (c) section 26,

    (d) sections 67 to 71,

    (e) this section,

    (f) paragraph 17 of Schedule 5,

    (g) Schedule 11,

    (h) Schedule 12, and

(i) so much of any other provision of this Act as confers any power to make subordinate legislation,

shall come into force on the day on which this Act is passed.

(3) The remaining provisions of this Act shall come into force on such day as the [Secretary of State][63] may by order appoint; and different days may be appointed for different purposes.

(4) The day appointed under subsection (3) for the coming into force of section 56 must not be earlier than the first day on which sections 112, 113 and 115 of the Police Act 1997 (which provide for the issue by the Secretary of State of criminal conviction certificates, criminal record certificates and enhanced criminal record certificates) are all in force.

(5) Subject to subsection (6), this Act extends to Northern Ireland.

(6) Any amendment, repeal or revocation made by Schedule 15 or 16 has the same extent as that of the enactment or instrument to which it relates.

SCHEDULE 1—THE DATA PROTECTION PRINCIPLES

PART I

THE PRINCIPLES

1. Personal data shall be processed fairly and lawfully and, in particular, shall not be processed unless—

(a) at least one of the conditions in Schedule 2 is met, and

(b) in the case of sensitive personal data, at least one of the conditions in Schedule 3 is also met.

2. Personal data shall be obtained only for one or more specified and lawful purposes, and shall not be further processed in any manner incompatible with that purpose or those purposes.

3. Personal data shall be adequate, relevant and not excessive in relation to the purpose or purposes for which they are processed.

4. Personal data shall be accurate and, where necessary, kept up to date.

5. Personal data processed for any purpose or purposes shall not be kept for longer than is necessary for that purpose or those purposes.

6. Personal data shall be processed in accordance with the rights of data subjects under this Act.

7. Appropriate technical and organisational measures shall be taken against unauthorised or unlawful processing of personal data and against accidental loss or destruction of, or damage to, personal data.

8. Personal data shall not be transferred to a country or territory outside the European Economic Area unless that country or territory ensures an adequate level of protection for the rights and freedoms of data subjects in relation to the processing of personal data.

---

[63] words substituted by Secretary of State for Constitutional Affairs Order 2003/1887 Sch.2 para.9(1)(a)

PART II

INTERPRETATION OF THE PRINCIPLES IN PART I

The first principle

1.—(1) In determining for the purposes of the first principle whether personal data are processed fairly, regard is to be had to the method by which they are obtained, including in particular whether any person from whom they are obtained is deceived or misled as to the purpose or purposes for which they are to be processed.

(2) Subject to paragraph 2, for the purposes of the first principle data are to be treated as obtained fairly if they consist of information obtained from a person who—

(a) is authorised by or under any enactment to supply it, or

(b) is required to supply it by or under any enactment or by any convention or other instrument imposing an international obligation on the United Kingdom.

2.—(1) Subject to paragraph 3, for the purposes of the first principle personal data are not to be treated as processed fairly unless—

(a) in the case of data obtained from the data subject, the data controller ensures so far as practicable that the data subject has, is provided with, or has made readily available to him, the information specified in sub-paragraph (3), and

(b) in any other case, the data controller ensures so far as practicable that, before the relevant time or as soon as practicable after that time, the data subject has, is provided with, or has made readily available to him, the information specified in sub-paragraph (3).

(2) In sub-paragraph (1)(b) "the relevant time" means—

(a) the time when the data controller first processes the data, or

(b) in a case where at that time disclosure to a third party within a reasonable period is envisaged—

    (i) if the data are in fact disclosed to such a person within that period, the time when the data are first disclosed,

    (ii) if within that period the data controller becomes, or ought to become, aware that the data are unlikely to be disclosed to such a person within that period, the time when the data controller does become, or ought to become, so aware, or

    (iii) in any other case, the end of that period.

(3) The information referred to in sub-paragraph (1) is as follows, namely—

(a) the identity of the data controller,

(b) if he has nominated a representative for the purposes of this Act, the identity of that representative,

(c) the purpose or purposes for which the data are intended to be processed, and

(d) any further information which is necessary, having regard to the specific circumstances in which the data are or are to be processed, to enable processing in respect of the data subject to be fair.

3.—(1) Paragraph 2(1)(b) does not apply where either of the primary conditions in sub-paragraph (2), together with such further conditions as may be prescribed by the [Secretary of State][64] by order, are met.

(2) The primary conditions referred to in sub-paragraph (1) are—

    (a) that the provision of that information would involve a disproportionate effort, or

    (b) that the recording of the information to be contained in the data by, or the disclosure of the data by, the data controller is necessary for compliance with any legal obligation to which the data controller is subject, other than an obligation imposed by contract.

4.—(1) Personal data which contain a general identifier falling within a description prescribed by the [Secretary of State][65] by order are not to be treated as processed fairly and lawfully unless they are processed in compliance with any conditions so prescribed in relation to general identifiers of that description.

(2) In sub-paragraph (1) "a general identifier" means any identifier (such as, for example, a number or code used for identification purposes) which—

    (a) relates to an individual, and

    (b) forms part of a set of similar identifiers which is of general application.

The second principle

5. The purpose or purposes for which personal data are obtained may in particular be specified—

    (a) in a notice given for the purposes of paragraph 2 by the data controller to the data subject, or

    (b) in a notification given to the Commissioner under Part III of this Act.

6. In determining whether any disclosure of personal data is compatible with the purpose or purposes for which the data were obtained, regard is to be had to the purpose or purposes for which the personal data are intended to be processed by any person to whom they are disclosed.

The fourth principle

7. The fourth principle is not to be regarded as being contravened by reason of any inaccuracy in personal data which accurately record information obtained by the data controller from the data subject or a third party in a case where—

    (a) having regard to the purpose or purposes for which the data were obtained and further processed, the data controller has taken reasonable steps to ensure the accuracy of the data, and

    (b) if the data subject has notified the data controller of the data subject's view that the data are inaccurate, the data indicate that fact.

The sixth principle

8. A person is to be regarded as contravening the sixth principle if, but only if—

---

[64] words substituted by Secretary of State for Constitutional Affairs Order 2003/1887 Sch.2 para.9(1)(b)
[65] words substituted by Secretary of State for Constitutional Affairs Order 2003/1887 Sch.2 para.9(1)(b)

(a) he contravenes section 7 by failing to supply information in accordance with that section,

(b) he contravenes section 10 by failing to comply with a notice given under subsection (1) of that section to the extent that the notice is justified or by failing to give a notice under subsection (3) of that section,

(c) he contravenes section 11 by failing to comply with a notice given under subsection (1) of that section,

(d) he contravenes section 12 by failing to comply with a notice given under subsection (1) or (2)(b) of that section or by failing to give a notification under subsection (2)(a) of that section or a notice under subsection (3) of that section.

[or

(e) he contravenes section 12A by failing to comply with a notice given under subsection (1) of that section to the extent that the notice is justified.][66]

The seventh principle

9. Having regard to the state of technological development and the cost of implementing any measures, the measures must ensure a level of security appropriate to—

(a) the harm that might result from such unauthorised or unlawful processing or accidental loss, destruction or damage as are mentioned in the seventh principle, and

(b) the nature of the data to be protected.

10. The data controller must take reasonable steps to ensure the reliability of any employees of his who have access to the personal data.

11. Where processing of personal data is carried out by a data processor on behalf of a data controller, the data controller must in order to comply with the seventh principle—

(a) choose a data processor providing sufficient guarantees in respect of the technical and organisational security measures governing the processing to be carried out, and

(b) take reasonable steps to ensure compliance with those measures.

12. Where processing of personal data is carried out by a data processor on behalf of a data controller; the data controller is not to be regarded as complying with the seventh principle unless—

(a) the processing is carried out under a contract—

(i) which is made or evidenced in writing, and
(ii) under which the data processor is to act only on instructions from the data controller, and

(b) the contract requires the data processor to comply with obligations equivalent to those imposed on a data controller by the seventh principle.

The eighth principle

13. An adequate level of protection is one which is adequate in all the circumstances of the case, having regard in particular to—

---

[66] added by Data Protection Act 1998 c. 29 Sch.13 para.5

(a) the nature of the personal data,

(b) the country or territory of origin of the information contained in the data,

(c) the country or territory of final destination of that information,

(d) the purposes for which and period during which the data are intended to be processed,

(e) the law in force in the country or territory in question,

(f) the international obligations of that country or territory,

(g) any relevant codes of conduct or other rules which are enforceable in that country or territory (whether generally or by arrangement in particular cases), and

(h) any security measures taken in respect of the data in that country or territory.

14. The eighth principle does not apply to a transfer falling within any paragraph of Schedule 4, except in such circumstances and to such extent as the [Secretary of State][67] may by order provide.

15.—(1) Where—

(a) in any proceedings under this Act any question arises as to whether the requirement of the eighth principle as to an adequate level of protection is met in relation to the transfer of any personal data to a country or territory outside the European Economic Area, and

(b) a Community finding has been made in relation to transfers of the kind in question,

that question is to be determined in accordance with that finding.

(2) In sub-paragraph (1) "Community finding" means a finding of the European Commission, under the procedure provided for in Article 31(2) of the Data Protection Directive, that a country or territory outside the European Economic Area does, or does not, ensure an adequate level of protection within the meaning of Article 25(2) of the Directive.

SCHEDULE 2—CONDITIONS RELEVANT FOR PURPOSES OF THE FIRST PRINCIPLE: PROCESSING OF ANY PERSONAL DATA

1. The data subject has given his consent to the processing.

2. The processing is necessary—

(a) for the performance of a contract to which the data subject is a party, or

(b) for the taking of steps at the request of the data subject with a view to entering into a contract.

3. The processing is necessary for compliance with any legal obligation to which the data controller is subject, other than an obligation imposed by contract.

4. The processing is necessary in order to protect the vital interests of the data subject.

5. The processing is necessary—

(a) for the administration of justice,

---

[67] words substituted by Secretary of State for Constitutional Affairs Order 2003/1887 Sch.2 para.9(1)(b)

[(aa) for the exercise of any functions of either House of Parliament,][68]

(b) for the exercise of any functions conferred on any person by or under any enactment,

(c) for the exercise of any functions of the Crown, a Minister of the Crown or a government department, or

(d) for the exercise of any other functions of a public nature exercised in the public interest by any person.

6.—(1) The processing is necessary for the purposes of legitimate interests pursued by the data controller or by the third party or parties to whom the data are disclosed, except where the processing is unwarranted in any particular case by reason of prejudice to the rights and freedoms or legitimate interests of the data subject.

(2) The [Secretary of State][69] may by order specify particular circumstances in which this condition is, or is not, to be taken to be satisfied.

SCHEDULE 3—CONDITIONS RELEVANT FOR PURPOSES OF THE FIRST PRINCIPLE: PROCESSING OF SENSITIVE PERSONAL DATA

1. The data subject has given his explicit consent to the processing of the personal data.

2.—(1) The processing is necessary for the purposes of exercising or performing any right or obligation which is conferred or imposed by law on the data controller in connection with employment.

(2) The [Secretary of State][70] may by order—

(a) exclude the application of sub-paragraph (1) in such cases as may be specified, or

(b) provide that, in such cases as may be specified, the condition in sub-paragraph (1) is not to be regarded as satisfied unless such further conditions as may be specified in the order are also satisfied.

3. The processing is necessary—

(a) in order to protect the vital interests of the data subject or another person, in a case where—

  (i) consent cannot be given by or on behalf of the data subject, or
  (ii) the data controller cannot reasonably be expected to obtain the consent of the data subject, or

(b) in order to protect the vital interests of another person, in a case where consent by or on behalf of the data subject has been unreasonably withheld.

4. The processing—

(a) is carried out in the course of its legitimate activities by any body or association which—

  (i) is not established or conducted for profit, and
  (ii) exists for political, philosophical, religious or trade-union purposes,

(b) is carried out with appropriate safeguards for the rights and freedoms of data subjects,

---

[68] added by Freedom of Information Act 2000 c. 36 Sch.6 para.4
[69] words substituted by Secretary of State for Constitutional Affairs Order 2003/1887 Sch.2 para.9(1)(b)
[70] words substituted by Secretary of State for Constitutional Affairs Order 2003/1887 Sch.2 para.9(1)(b)

(c) relates only to individuals who either are members of the body or association or have regular contact with it in connection with its purposes, and

(d) does not involve disclosure of the personal data to a third party without the consent of the data subject.

5. The information contained in the personal data has been made public as a result of steps deliberately taken by the data subject.

6. The processing—

(a) is necessary for the purpose of, or in connection with, any legal proceedings (including prospective legal proceedings),

(b) is necessary for the purpose of obtaining legal advice, or

(c) is otherwise necessary for the purposes of establishing, exercising or defending legal rights.

7.—(1) The processing is necessary—

(a) for the administration of justice,

[(aa) for the exercise of any functions of either House of Parliament,][71]

(b) for the exercise of any functions conferred on any person by or under an enactment, or

(c) for the exercise of any functions of the Crown, a Minister of the Crown or a government department.

(2) The Secretary of State may by order—

(a) exclude the application of sub-paragraph (1) in such cases as may be specified, or

(b) provide that, in such cases as may be specified, the condition in sub-paragraph (1) is not to be regarded as satisfied unless such further conditions as may be specified in the order are also satisfied.

8.—(1) The processing is necessary for medical purposes and is undertaken by—

(a) a health professional, or

(b) a person who in the circumstances owes a duty of confidentiality which is equivalent to that which would arise if that person were a health professional.

(2) In this paragraph "medical purposes" includes the purposes of preventative medicine, medical diagnosis, medical research, the provision of care and treatment and the management of health care services.

9.—(1) The processing—

(a) is of sensitive personal data consisting of information as to racial or ethnic origin,

(b) is necessary for the purpose of identifying or keeping under review the existence or absence of equality of opportunity or treatment between persons of different racial or ethnic origins, with a view to enabling such equality to be promoted or maintained, and

(c) is carried out with appropriate safeguards for the rights and freedoms of data subjects.

(2) The [Secretary of State][72] may by order specify circumstances in which processing falling within sub-paragraph (1)(a) and (b) is, or is not, to be taken for the purposes of sub-paragraph (1)(c) to be carried out with appropriate safeguards for the rights and freedoms of data subjects.

---

[71] added by Freedom of Information Act 2000 c. 36 Sch.6 para.5
[72] words substituted by Secretary of State for Constitutional Affairs Order 2003/1887 Sch.2 para.9(1)(b)

10. The personal data are processed in circumstances specified in an order made by the [Secretary of State][73] for the purposes of this paragraph.

SCHEDULE 4—CASES WHERE THE EIGHTH PRINCIPLE DOES NOT APPLY

1. The data subject has given his consent to the transfer.

2. The transfer is necessary—

   (a) for the performance of a contract between the data subject and the data controller, or

   (b) for the taking of steps at the request of the data subject with a view to his entering into a contract with the data controller.

3. The transfer is necessary—

   (a) for the conclusion of a contract between the data controller and a person other than the data subject which—

     (i) is entered into at the request of the data subject, or
     (ii) is in the interests of the data subject, or

   (b) for the performance of such a contract.

4.—(1) The transfer is necessary for reasons of substantial public interest.

(2) The [Secretary of State][74] may by order specify—

   (a) circumstances in which a transfer is to be taken for the purposes of sub-paragraph (1) to be necessary for reasons of substantial public interest, and

   (b) circumstances in which a transfer which is not required by or under an enactment is not to be taken for the purpose of sub-paragraph (1) to be necessary for reasons of substantial public interest.

5. The transfer—

   (a) is necessary for the purpose of, or in connection with, any legal proceedings (including prospective legal proceedings),

   (b) is necessary for the purpose of obtaining legal advice, or

   (c) is otherwise necessary for the purposes of establishing, exercising or defending legal rights.

6. The transfer is necessary in order to protect the vital interests of the data subject.

7. The transfer is of part of the personal data on a public register and any conditions subject to which the register is open to inspection are complied with by any person to whom the data are or may be disclosed after the transfer.

8. The transfer is made on terms which are of a kind approved by the Commissioner as ensuring adequate safeguards for the rights and freedoms of data subjects.

9. The transfer has been authorised by the Commissioner as being made in such a manner as to ensure adequate safeguards for the rights and freedoms of data subjects.

---

[73] words substituted by Secretary of State for Constitutional Affairs Order 2003/1887 Sch.2 para.9(1)(b)
[74] words substituted by Secretary of State for Constitutional Affairs Order 2003/1887 Sch.2 para.9(1)(b)

SCHEDULE 5—THE DATA PROTECTION COMMISSIONER AND THE DATA PROTECTION TRIBUNAL

PART I

THE COMMISSIONER

Status and capacity

1.—(1) The corporation sole by the name of the Data Protection Registrar established by the Data Protection Act 1984 shall continue in existence by the name of the [Information Commissioner][75].

(2) The Commissioner and his officers and staff are not to be regarded as servants or agents of the Crown.

2.—(1) Subject to the provisions of this paragraph, the Commissioner shall hold office for such term not exceeding five years as may be determined at the time of his appointment.

(2) The Commissioner may be relieved of his office by Her Majesty at his own request.

(3) The Commissioner may be removed from office by Her Majesty in pursuance of an Address from both Houses of Parliament.

(4) The Commissioner shall in any case vacate his office—

    (a) on completing the year of service in which he attains the age of sixty-five years, or

    (b) if earlier, on completing his fifteenth year of service.

(5) Subject to sub-paragraph (4), a person who ceases to be Commissioner on the expiration of his term of office shall be eligible for re-appointment, but a person may not be re-appointed for a third or subsequent term as Commissioner unless, by reason of special circumstances, the person's re-appointment for such a term is desirable in the public interest.

3.—(1) There shall be paid—

    (a) to the Commissioner such salary, and

    (b) to or in respect of the Commissioner such pension,

as may be specified by a resolution of the House of Commons.

(2) A resolution for the purposes of this paragraph may—

    (a) specify the salary or pension,

    (b) provide that the salary or pension is to be the same as, or calculated on the same basis as, that payable to, or to or in respect of, a person employed in a specified office under, or in a specified capacity in the service of, the Crown, or

    (c) specify the salary or pension and provide for it to be increased by reference to such variables as may be specified in the resolution.

(3) A resolution for the purposes of this paragraph may take effect from the date on which it is passed or from any earlier or later date specified in the resolution.

---

[75] words substituted by Freedom of Information Act 2000 c. 36 Sch.2(I) para.15(2)

(4) A resolution for the purposes of this paragraph may make different provision in relation to the pension payable to or in respect of different holders of the office of Commissioner.

(5) Any salary or pension payable under this paragraph shall be charged on and issued out of the Consolidated Fund.

(6) In this paragraph "pension" includes an allowance or gratuity and any reference to the payment of a pension includes a reference to the making of payments towards the provision of a pension.

4.—(1) The Commissioner—

(a) shall appoint a deputy commissioner or two deputy commissioners, and

(b) may appoint such number of other officers and staff as he may determine.

(1A) The Commissioner shall, when appointing any second deputy commissioner, specify which of the Commissioner's functions are to be performed, in the circumstances referred to in paragraph 5(1), by each of the deputy commissioners.

(2) The remuneration and other conditions of service of the persons appointed under this paragraph shall be determined by the Commissioner.

(3) The Commissioner may pay such pensions, allowances or gratuities to or in respect of the persons appointed under this paragraph, or make such payments towards the provision of such pensions, allowances or gratuities, as he may determine.

(4) The references in sub-paragraph (3) to pensions, allowances or gratuities to or in respect of the persons appointed under this paragraph include references to pensions, allowances or gratuities by way of compensation to or in respect of any of those persons who suffer loss of office or employment.

(5) Any determination under sub-paragraph (1)(b), (2) or (3) shall require the approval of the [Secretary of State][76].

(6) The Employers' Liability (Compulsory Insurance) Act 1969 shall not require insurance to be effected by the Commissioner.

5.—(1) The deputy commissioner or deputy commissioners shall perform the functions conferred by this Act or the Freedom of Information Act 2000 on the Commissioner during any vacancy in that office or at any time when the Commissioner is for any reason unable to act.

(2) Without prejudice to sub-paragraph (1), any functions of the Commissioner under this Act [or the Freedom of Information Act 2000][77] may, to the extent authorised by him, be performed by any of his officers or staff.

Authentication of seal of the Commissioner

6. The application of the seal of the Commissioner shall be authenticated by his signature or by the signature of some other person authorised for the purpose.

Presumption of authenticity of documents issued by the Commissioner

7. Any document purporting to be an instrument issued by the Commissioner and to be duly executed under the Commissioner's seal or to be signed by or on behalf of the Commissioner

---

[76] words substituted by Secretary of State for Constitutional Affairs Order 2003/1887 Sch.2 para.9(1)(c)
[77] words added by Freedom of Information Act 2000 c. 36 Sch.2(II) para.21(3)

shall be received in evidence and shall be deemed to be such an instrument unless the contrary is shown.

SCHEDULE 5—THE DATA PROTECTION COMMISSIONER AND THE DATA PROTECTION TRIBUNAL

PART I

THE COMMISSIONER

Money

8. The [Secretary of State][78] may make payments to the Commissioner out of money provided by Parliament.

9.—(1) All fees and other sums received by the Commissioner in the exercise of his functions under this Act, under section 159 of the Consumer Credit Act 1974 or under the Freedom of Information Act 2000 shall be paid by him to the [Secretary of State][79].

(2) Sub-paragraph (1) shall not apply where the [Secretary of State][80], with the consent of the Treasury, otherwise directs.

(3) Any sums received by the [Secretary of State][81] under sub-paragraph (1) shall be paid into the Consolidated Fund.

Accounts

10.—(1) It shall be the duty of the Commissioner—

(a) to keep proper accounts and other records in relation to the accounts,

(b) to prepare in respect of each financial year a statement of account in such form as the [Secretary of State][82] may direct, and

(c) to send copies of that statement to the Comptroller and Auditor General on or before 31st August next following the end of the year to which the statement relates or on or before such earlier date after the end of that year as the Treasury may direct.

(2) The Comptroller and Auditor General shall examine and certify any statement sent to him under this paragraph and lay copies of it together with his report thereon before each House of Parliament.

(3) In this paragraph "financial year" means a period of twelve months beginning with 1st April.

---

[78] words substituted by Secretary of State for Constitutional Affairs Order 2003/1887 Sch.2 para.9(1)(c)
[79] words substituted by Secretary of State for Constitutional Affairs Order 2003/1887 Sch.2 para.9(1)(c)
[80] words substituted by Secretary of State for Constitutional Affairs Order 2003/1887 Sch.2 para.9(1)(c)
[81] words substituted by Secretary of State for Constitutional Affairs Order 2003/1887 Sch.2 para.9(1)(c)
[82] words substituted by Secretary of State for Constitutional Affairs Order 2003/1887 Sch.2 para.9(1)(c)

Application of Part I in Scotland

11. Paragraphs 1(1), 6 and 7 do not extend to Scotland.

PART II

THE TRIBUNAL

Tenure of office

12.—(1) Subject to the following provisions of this paragraph, a member of the Tribunal shall hold and vacate his office in accordance with the terms of his appointment and shall, on ceasing to hold office, be eligible for re-appointment.

(2) Any member of the Tribunal may at any time resign his office by notice in writing to the Lord Chancellor [(in the case of the chairman or a deputy chairman) or to the Secretary of State (in the case of any other member)][83].

(3) A person who is the chairman or deputy chairman of the Tribunal shall vacate his office on the day on which he attains the age of seventy years; but this sub-paragraph is subject to section 26(4) to (6) of the Judicial Pensions and Retirement Act 1993 (power to authorise continuance in office up to the age of seventy-five years).

Salary etc.

13. The [Secretary of State][84] shall pay to the members of the Tribunal out of money provided by Parliament such remuneration and allowances as he may determine.

Officers and staff

14. The [Secretary of State][85] may provide the Tribunal with such officers and staff as he thinks necessary for the proper discharge of its functions.

Expenses

15. Such expenses of the Tribunal as the [Secretary of State][86] may determine shall be defrayed by the [Secretary of State][87] out of money provided by Parliament.

16. [. . .][88]

17. [. . .][89]

---

[83] words inserted by Secretary of State for Constitutional Affairs Order 2003/1887 Sch.2 para.9(2)
[84] words substituted by Secretary of State for Constitutional Affairs Order 2003/1887 Sch.2 para.9(1)(c)
[85] words substituted by Secretary of State for Constitutional Affairs Order 2003/1887 Sch.2 para.9(1)(c)
[86] words substituted by Secretary of State for Constitutional Affairs Order 2003/1887 Sch.2 para.9(1)(c)
[87] words substituted by Secretary of State for Constitutional Affairs Order 2003/1887 Sch.2 para.9(1)(c)
[88] repealed by Freedom of Information Act 2000 c. 36 Sch.8(II) para.1
[89] repealed by Freedom of Information Act 2000 c. 36 Sch.8(II) para.1

SCHEDULE 6—APPEAL PROCEEDINGS

Hearing of appeals

1. For the purpose of hearing and determining appeals or any matter preliminary or incidental to an appeal the Tribunal shall sit at such times and in such places as the chairman or a deputy chairman may direct and may sit in two or more divisions.

Constitution of Tribunal in national security cases

2.—(1) The Lord Chancellor shall from time to time designate, from among the chairman and deputy chairman appointed by him under section 6(4)(a) and (b), those persons who are to be capable of hearing appeals under section 28(4) or (6) or under section 60(1) or (4) of the Freedom of Information Act 2000.

(2) A designation under sub-paragraph (1) may at any time be revoked by the Lord Chancellor.

[(3) The Lord Chancellor may make, or revoke, a designation under this paragraph only with the concurrence of all of the following—

(a) the Lord Chief Justice;

(b) the Lord President of the Court of Session;

(c) the Lord Chief Justice of Northern Ireland.

(4) The Lord Chief Justice of England and Wales may nominate a judicial office holder (as defined in section 109(4) of the Constitutional Reform Act 2005) to exercise his functions under sub-paragraph (3) so far as they relate to a designation under this paragraph.

(5) The Lord President of the Court of Session may nominate a judge of the Court of Session who is a member of the First or Second Division of the Inner House of that Court to exercise his functions under sub-paragraph (3) so far as they relate to a designation under this paragraph.

(6) The Lord Chief Justice of Northern Ireland may nominate any of the following to exercise his functions under sub-paragraph (3) so far as they relate to a designation under this paragraph—

(a) the holder of one of the offices listed in Schedule 1 to the Justice (Northern Ireland) Act 2002;

(b) a Lord Justice of Appeal (as defined in section 88 of that Act).][90]

Constitution of Tribunal in national security cases

[3. (1) The Tribunal shall be duly constituted—

(a) for an appeal under section 28(4) or (6) in any case where the application of paragraph 6(1) is excluded by rules under paragraph 7, or

(b) for an appeal under section 60(1) or (4) of the Freedom of Information Act 2000,

if it consists of three of the persons designated under paragraph 2(1), of whom one shall be designated by the Lord Chancellor to preside.

---

[90] added by Constitutional Reform Act 2005 c. 4 Sch.4(1) para.275(2)

(2) The Lord Chancellor may designate a person to preside under this paragraph only with the concurrence of all of the following—

(a) the Lord Chief Justice of England and Wales;

(b) the Lord President of the Court of Session;

(c) the Lord Chief Justice of Northern Ireland.

(3) The Lord Chief Justice of England and Wales may nominate a judicial office holder (as defined in section 109(4) of the Constitutional Reform Act 2005) to exercise his functions under this paragraph.

(4) The Lord President of the Court of Session may nominate a judge of the Court of Session who is a member of the First or Second Division of the Inner House of that Court to exercise his functions under this paragraph.

(5) The Lord Chief Justice of Northern Ireland may nominate any of the following to exercise his functions under this paragraph—

(a) the holder of one of the offices listed in Schedule 1 to the Justice (Northern Ireland) Act 2002;

(b) a Lord Justice of Appeal (as defined in section 88 of that Act).][91]

Constitution of Tribunal in other cases

4.—(1) Subject to any rules made under paragraph 7, the Tribunal shall be duly constituted for an appeal under section 48(1), (2) or (4) if it consists of—

(a) the chairman or a deputy chairman (who shall preside), and

(b) an equal number of the members appointed respectively in accordance with paragraphs (a) and (b) of section 6(6).

(1A) Subject to any rules made under paragraph 7, the Tribunal shall be duly constituted for an appeal under section 57(1) or (2) of the Freedom of Information Act 2000 if it consists of—

(a) the chairman or a deputy chairman (who shall preside), and

(b) an equal number of the members appointed respectively in accordance with paragraphs (aa) and (bb) of section 6(6).

(2) The members who are to constitute the Tribunal in accordance with sub-paragraph (1) [or (1A)][92] shall be nominated by the chairman or, if he is for any reason unable to act, by a deputy chairman.

Determination of questions by full Tribunal

5. The determination of any question before the Tribunal when constituted in accordance with paragraph 3 or 4 shall be according to the opinion of the majority of the members hearing the appeal.

---

[91] existing Sch.6 para.3 renumbered as Sch.6 para.3(1) and Sch.6 para.3(2)–(5) inserted by Constitutional Reform Act 2005 c. 4 Sch.4(1) para.275(3)

[92] words inserted by Freedom of Information Act 2000 c. 36 Sch.4 para.3(3)

Ex parte proceedings

6.—(1) Subject to any rules made under paragraph 7, the jurisdiction of the Tribunal in respect of an appeal under section 28(4) or (6) shall be exercised ex parte by one or more persons designated under paragraph 2(1).

(2) Subject to any rules made under paragraph 7, the jurisdiction of the Tribunal in respect of an appeal under section 48(3) shall be exercised ex parte by the chairman or a deputy chairman sitting alone.

Rules of procedure

7.—(1) The [Secretary of State][93] may make rules for regulating—

  (a) the exercise of the rights of appeal conferred—

      (i) by sections 28(4) and (6) and 48, and
     (ii) by sections 57(1) and (2) and section 60(1) and (4) of the Freedom of Information Act 2000, and

  (b) the practice and procedure of the Tribunal.

(2) Rules under this paragraph may in particular make provision—

  (a) with respect to the period within which an appeal can be brought and the burden of proof on an appeal,

  (aa) for the joinder of any other person as a party to any proceedings on an appeal under the Freedom of Information Act 2000,

  (ab) for the hearing of an appeal under this Act with an appeal under the Freedom of Information Act 2000,

  (b) for the summoning (or, in Scotland, citation) of witnesses and the administration of oaths,

  (c) for securing the production of documents and material used for the processing of personal data,

  (d) for the inspection, examination, operation and testing of any equipment or material used in connection with the processing of personal data,

  (e) for the hearing of an appeal wholly or partly in camera,

  (f) for hearing an appeal in the absence of the appellant or for determining an appeal without a hearing,

  (g) for enabling an appeal under section 48(1) against an information notice to be determined by the chairman or a deputy chairman,

  (h) for enabling any matter preliminary or incidental to an appeal to be dealt with by the chairman or a deputy chairman, (i) for the awarding of costs or, in Scotland, expenses,

  (j) for the publication of reports of the Tribunal's decisions, and

  (k) for conferring on the Tribunal such ancillary powers as the [Secretary of State][94] thinks necessary for the proper discharge of its functions.

(3) In making rules under this paragraph which relate to appeals under section 28(4) or (6) the [Secretary of State][95] shall have regard, in particular, to the need to secure that information is not disclosed contrary to the public interest.

---

[93] words substituted by Secretary of State for Constitutional Affairs Order 2003/1887 Sch.2 para.9(1)(d)
[94] words substituted by Secretary of State for Constitutional Affairs Order 2003/1887 Sch.2 para.9(1)(d)
[95] words substituted by Secretary of State for Constitutional Affairs Order 2003/1887 Sch.2 para.9(1)(d)

Obstruction etc.

8.—(1) If any person is guilty of any act or omission in relation to proceedings before the Tribunal which, if those proceedings were proceedings before a court having power to commit for contempt, would constitute contempt of court, the Tribunal may certify the offence to the High Court or, in Scotland, the Court of Session.

(2) Where an offence is so certified, the court may inquire into the matter and, after hearing any witness who may be produced against or on behalf of the person charged with the offence, and after hearing any statement that may be offered in defence, deal with him in any manner in which it could deal with him if he had committed the like offence in relation to the court.

SCHEDULE 7—MISCELLANEOUS EXEMPTIONS

Confidential references given by the data controller

1. Personal data are exempt from section 7 if they consist of a reference given or to be given in confidence by the data controller for the purposes of—

   (a) the education, training or employment, or prospective education, training or employment, of the data subject,

   (b) the appointment, or prospective appointment, of the data subject to any office, or

   (c) the provision, or prospective provision, by the data subject of any service.

Armed forces

2. Personal data are exempt from the subject information provisions in any case to the extent to which the application of those provisions would be likely to prejudice the combat effectiveness of any of the armed forces of the Crown.

Judicial appointments and honours

3. Personal data processed for the purposes of—

   (a) assessing any person's suitability for judicial office or the office of Queen's Counsel, or

   (b) the conferring by the Crown of any honour [or dignity],[96]

are exempt from the subject information provisions.

Crown employment and Crown or Ministerial appointments

4. (1) The [Secretary of State][97] may by order exempt from the subject information provisions personal data processed for the purposes of assessing any person's suitability for—

---

[96] words added by Freedom of Information Act 2000 c. 36 Sch.6 para.6
[97] words substituted by Secretary of State for Constitutional Affairs Order 2003/1887 Sch.2 para.9(1)(e)

(a) employment by or under the Crown, or

(b) any office to which appointments are made by Her Majesty, by a Minister of the Crown or by a Northern Ireland authority.

(2) In this paragraph "Northern Ireland authority" means the First Minister, the deputy First Minister, a Northern Ireland Minister or a Northern Ireland department.

Management forecasts etc.

5. Personal data processed for the purposes of management forecasting or management planning to assist the data controller in the conduct of any business or other activity are exempt from the subject information provisions in any case to the extent to which the application of those provisions would be likely to prejudice the conduct of that business or other activity.

Corporate finance

6.—(1) Where personal data are processed for the purposes of, or in connection with, a corporate finance service provided by a relevant person—

(a) the data are exempt from the subject information provisions in any case to the extent to which either—

(i) the application of those provisions to the data could affect the price of any instrument which is already in existence or is to be or may be created, or

(ii) the data controller reasonably believes that the application of those provisions to the data could affect the price of any such instrument, and

(b) to the extent that the data are not exempt from the subject information provisions by virtue of paragraph (a), they are exempt from those provisions if the exemption is required for the purpose of safeguarding an important economic or financial interest of the United Kingdom.

(2) For the purposes of sub-paragraph (1)(b) the Secretary of State may by order specify—

(a) matters to be taken into account in determining whether exemption from the subject information provisions is required for the purpose of safeguarding an important economic or financial interest of the United Kingdom, or

(b) circumstances in which exemption from those provisions is, or is not, to be taken to be required for that purpose.

(3) In this paragraph—

"corporate finance service" means a service consisting in—

(a) underwriting in respect of issues of, or the placing of issues of, any instrument,
(b) advice to undertakings on capital structure, industrial strategy and related matters and advice and service relating to mergers and the purchase of undertakings, or
(c) services relating to such underwriting as is mentioned in paragraph (a);

"instrument" means any instrument listed in [section C of Annex I to Directive 2004/39/EC of the European Parliament and of the Council of 21 April 2004 on markets in financial instruments][98];

---

[98] words substituted by Financial Services and Markets Act 2000 (Markets in Financial Instruments) Regulations 2007/126 Sch.6(1) para.12

"price" includes value;

"relevant person" means—

    (a) any person who, by reason of any permission he has under Part IV of the Financial Services and Markets Act 2000, is able to carry on a corporate finance service without contravening the general prohibition, within the meaning of section 19 of that Act;

    (b) an EEA firm of the kind mentioned in paragraph 5(a) or (b) of Schedule 3 to that Act which has qualified for authorisation under paragraph 12 of that Schedule, and may lawfully carry on a corporate finance service;

    (c) any person who is exempt from the general prohibition in respect of any corporate finance service—

        (i) as a result of an exemption order made under section 38(1) of that Act, or

        (ii) by reason of section 39(1) of that Act (appointed representatives);

    (cc) any person, not falling within paragraph (a), (b) or (c) who may lawfully carry on a corporate finance service without contravening the general prohibition;

    (d) any person who, in the course of his employment, provides to his employer a service falling within paragraph (b) or (c) of the definition of "corporate finance service", or

    (e) any partner who provides to other partners in the partnership a service falling within either of those paragraphs.

Negotiations

7. Personal data which consist of records of the intentions of the data controller in relation to any negotiations with the data subject are exempt from the subject information provisions in any case to the extent to which the application of those provisions would be likely to prejudice those negotiations.

Examination marks

8.—(1) Section 7 shall have effect subject to the provisions of sub-paragraphs (2) to (4) in the case of personal data consisting of marks or other information processed by a data controller—

    (a) for the purpose of determining the results of an academic, professional or other examination or of enabling the results of any such examination to be determined, or

    (b) in consequence of the determination of any such results.

(2) Where the relevant day falls before the day on which the results of the examination are announced, the period mentioned in section 7(8) shall be extended until—

    (a) the end of five months beginning with the relevant day, or

    (b) the end of forty days beginning with the date of the announcement, whichever is the earlier.

(3) Where by virtue of sub-paragraph (2) a period longer than the prescribed period elapses after the relevant day before the request is complied with, the information to be supplied pursuant to the request shall be supplied both by reference to the data in question at the time when the request is received and (if different) by reference to the data as from time to time held in the period beginning when the request is received and ending when it is complied with.

(4) For the purposes of this paragraph the results of an examination shall be treated as announced when they are first published or (if not published) when they are first made available or communicated to the candidate in question.

(5) In this paragraph—

"examination" includes any process for determining the knowledge, intelligence, skill or ability of a candidate by reference to his performance in any test, work or other activity;

"the prescribed period" means forty days or such other period as is for the time being prescribed under section 7 in relation to the personal data in question;

"relevant day" has the same meaning as in section 7.

Examination scripts etc.

9.—(1) Personal data consisting of information recorded by candidates during an academic, professional or other examination are exempt from section 7.

(2) In this paragraph "examination" has the same meaning as in paragraph 8.

Legal professional privilege

10. Personal data are exempt from the subject information provisions if the data consist of information in respect of which a claim to legal professional privilege [or, in Scotland, to confidentiality of communications][99] could be maintained in legal proceedings.

Self-incrimination

11.—(1) A person need not comply with any request or order under section 7 to the extent that compliance would, by revealing evidence of the commission of any offence other than an offence under this Act, expose him to proceedings for that offence.

(2) Information disclosed by any person in compliance with any request or order under section 7 shall not be admissible against him in proceedings for an offence under this Act.

SCHEDULE 8—TRANSITIONAL RELIEF

Part I

Interpretation of Schedule

1.—(1) For the purposes of this Schedule, personal data are "eligible data" at any time if, and to the extent that, they are at that time subject to processing which was already under way immediately before 24th October 1998.

(2) In this Schedule—

"eligible automated data" means eligible data which fall within paragraph (a) or (b) of the definition of "data" in section 1(1);

---

[99] words substituted by Freedom of Information Act 2000 c. 36 Sch.6 para.7

"eligible manual data" means eligible data which are not eligible automated data;

"the first transitional period" means the period beginning with the commencement of this Schedule and ending with 23rd October 2001;

"the second transitional period" means the period beginning with 24th October 2001 and ending with 23rd October 2007.

Part II

Exemptions available before 24th October 2001

Manual data

2.—(1) Eligible manual data, other than data forming part of an accessible record, are exempt from the data protection principles and Parts II and III of this Act during the first transitional period.

(2) This paragraph does not apply to eligible manual data to which paragraph 4 applies.

3.—(1) This paragraph applies to—

(a) eligible manual data forming part of an accessible record, and

(b) personal data which fall within paragraph (d) of the definition of "data" in section 1(1) but which, because they are not subject to processing which was already under way immediately before 24th October 1998, are not eligible data for the purposes of this Schedule.

(2) During the first transitional period, data to which this paragraph applies are exempt from—

(a) the data protection principles, except the sixth principle so far as relating to sections 7 and 12A,

(b) Part II of this Act, except—

(i) section 7 (as it has effect subject to section 8) and section 12A, and
(ii) section 15 so far as relating to those sections, and

(c) Part III of this Act.

4.—(1) This paragraph applies to eligible manual data which consist of information relevant to the financial standing of the data subject and in respect of which the data controller is a credit reference agency.

(2) During the first transitional period, data to which this paragraph applies are exempt from—

(a) the data protection principles, except the sixth principle so far as relating to sections 7 and 12A,

(b) Part II of this Act, except—

(i) section 7 (as it has effect subject to sections 8 and 9) and section 12A, and
(ii) section 15 so far as relating to those sections, and

(c) Part III of this Act.

Processing otherwise than by reference to the data subject

5. During the first transitional period, for the purposes of this Act (apart from paragraph 1), eligible automated data are not to be regarded as being "processed" unless the processing is by reference to the data subject.

Payrolls and accounts

6.—(1) Subject to sub-paragraph (2), eligible automated data processed by a data controller for one or more of the following purposes—

(a) calculating amounts payable by way of remuneration or pensions in respect of service in any employment or office or making payments of, or of sums deducted from, such remuneration or pensions, or

(b) keeping accounts relating to any business or other activity carried on by the data controller or keeping records of purchases, sales or other transactions for the purpose of ensuring that the requisite payments are made by or to him in respect of those transactions or for the purpose of making financial or management forecasts to assist him in the conduct of any such business or activity,

are exempt from the data protection principles and Parts II and III of this Act during the first transitional period.

(2) It shall be a condition of the exemption of any eligible automated data under this paragraph that the data are not processed for any other purpose, but the exemption is not lost by any processing of the eligible data for any other purpose if the data controller shows that he had taken such care to prevent it as in all the circumstances was reasonably required.

(3) Data processed only for one or more of the purposes mentioned in sub-paragraph (1)(a) may be disclosed—

(a) to any person, other than the data controller, by whom the remuneration or pensions in question are payable;

(b) for the purpose of obtaining actuarial advice,

(c) for the purpose of giving information as to the persons in any employment or office for use in medical research into the health of, or injuries suffered by, persons engaged in particular occupations or working in particular places or areas,

(d) if the data subject (or a person acting on his behalf) has requested or consented to the disclosure of the data either generally or in the circumstances in which the disclosure in question is made, or

(e) if the person making the disclosure has reasonable grounds for believing that the disclosure falls within paragraph (d).

(4) Data processed for any of the purposes mentioned in sub-paragraph (1) may be disclosed—

(a) for the purpose of audit or where the disclosure is for the purpose only of giving information about the data controller's financial affairs, or

(b) in any case in which disclosure would be permitted by any other provision of this Part of this Act if sub-paragraph (2) were included among the non-disclosure provisions.

(5) In this paragraph "remuneration" includes remuneration in kind and "pensions" includes gratuities or similar benefits.

Unincorporated members' clubs and mailing lists

7. Eligible automated data processed by an unincorporated members' club and relating only to the members of the club are exempt from the data protection principles and Parts II and III of this Act during the first transitional period.

8. Eligible automated data processed by a data controller only for the purposes of distributing, or recording the distribution of, articles or information to the data subjects and consisting only of their names, addresses or other particulars necessary for effecting the distribution, are exempt from the data protection principles and Parts II and III of this Act during the first transitional period.

9. Neither paragraph 7 nor paragraph 8 applies to personal data relating to any data subject unless he has been asked by the club or data controller whether he objects to the data relating to him being processed as mentioned in that paragraph and has not objected.

10. It shall be a condition of the exemption of any data under paragraph 7 that the data are not disclosed except as permitted by paragraph 11 and of the exemption under paragraph 8 that the data are not processed for any purpose other than that mentioned in that paragraph or as permitted by paragraph 11, but—

(a) the exemption under paragraph 7 shall not be lost by any disclosure in breach of that condition, and

(b) the exemption under paragraph 8 shall not be lost by any processing in breach of that condition,

if the data controller shows that he had taken such care to prevent it as in all the circumstances was reasonably required.

11. Data to which paragraph 10 applies may be disclosed—

(a) if the data subject (or a person acting on his behalf) has requested or consented to the disclosure of the data either generally or in the circumstances in which the disclosure in question is made,

(b) if the person making the disclosure has reasonable grounds for believing that the disclosure falls within paragraph (a), or

(c) in any case in which disclosure would be permitted by any other provision of this Part of this Act if paragraph 8 were included among the non-disclosure provisions.

Back-up data

12. Eligible automated data which are processed only for the purpose of replacing other data in the event of the latter being lost, destroyed or impaired are exempt from section 7 during the first transitional period.

Exemption of all eligible automated data from certain requirements

13.—(1) During the first transitional period, eligible automated data are exempt from the following provisions—

(a) the first data protection principle to the extent to which it requires compliance with—

    (i)   paragraph 2 of Part II of Schedule 1,

    (ii)   the conditions in Schedule 2, and

    (iii)   the conditions in Schedule 3,

(b)   the seventh data protection principle to the extent to which it requires compliance with paragraph 12 of Part II of Schedule 1;

(c)   the eighth data protection principle,

(d)   in section 7(1), paragraphs (b), (c)(ii) and (d),

(e)   sections 10 and 11,

(f)   section 12, and

(g)   section 13, except so far as relating to—

    (i)   any contravention of the fourth data protection principle,

    (ii)   any disclosure without the consent of the data controller,

    (iii)   loss or destruction of data without the consent of the data controller, or

    (iv)   processing for the special purposes.

(2) The specific exemptions conferred by sub-paragraph (1)(a), (c) and (e) do not limit the data controller's general duty under the first data protection principle to ensure that processing is fair.

PART III

EXEMPTIONS AVAILABLE AFTER 23RD OCTOBER 2001 BUT BEFORE 24TH OCTOBER 2007

14.—(1) This paragraph applies to—

(a)   eligible manual data which were held immediately before 24th October 1998, and

(b)   personal data which fall within paragraph (d) of the definition of "data" in section 1(1) but do not fall within paragraph (a) of this sub-paragraph.

but does not apply to eligible manual data to which the exemption in paragraph 16 applies.

(2) During the second transitional period, data to which this paragraph applies are exempt from the following provisions—

(a)   the first data protection principle except to the extent to which it requires compliance with paragraph 2 of Part II of Schedule 1,

(b)   the second, third, fourth and fifth data protection principles, and

(c)   section 14(1) to (3).

[**14A.**—(1) This paragraph applies to personal data which fall within paragraph (e) of the definition of "data" in section 1(1) and do not fall within paragraph 14(1)(a), but does not apply to eligible manual data to which the exemption in paragraph 16 applies.

(2) During the second transitional period, data to which this paragraph applies are exempt from—

(a)   the fourth data protection principle, and

(b)   section 14(1) to (3).][100]

---

[100]   added by Freedom of Information Act 2000 c. 36 Pt VII s.70(3)

Part IV

Exemptions after 23rd October 2001 for historical research

15. In this Part of this Schedule "the relevant conditions" has the same meaning as in section 33.

16.— (1) Eligible manual data which are processed only for the purpose of historical research in compliance with the relevant conditions are exempt from the provisions specified in sub-paragraph (2) after 23rd October 2001.

(2) The provisions referred to in sub-paragraph (1) are—

  (a) the first data protection principle except in so far as it requires compliance with para-graph 2 of Part II of Schedule 1,

  (b) the second, third, fourth and fifth data protection principles, and

  (c) section 14(1) to (3).

17.—(1) After 23rd October 2001 eligible automated data which are processed only for the purpose of historical research in compliance with the relevant conditions are exempt from the first data protection principle to the extent to which it requires compliance with the conditions in Schedules 2 and 3.

(2) Eligible automated data which are processed—

  (a) only for the purpose of historical research,

  (b) in compliance with the relevant conditions, and

  (c) otherwise than by reference to the data subject,

are also exempt from the provisions referred to in sub-paragraph (3) after 23rd October 2001.

(3) The provisions referred to in sub-paragraph (2) are—

  (a) the first data protection principle except in so far as it requires compliance with para-graph 2 of Part II of Schedule 1,

  (b) the second, third, fourth and fifth data protection principles, and

  (c) section 14(1) to (3).

18. For the purposes of this Part of this Schedule personal data are not to be treated as processed otherwise than for the purpose of historical research merely because the data are disclosed—

  (a) to any person, for the purpose of historical research only,

  (b) to the data subject or a person acting on his behalf,

  (c) at the request, or with the consent, of the data subject or a person acting on his behalf, or

  (d) in circumstances in which the person making the disclosure has reasonable grounds for believing that the disclosure falls within paragraph (a), (b) or (c).

Part V

Exemption from section 22

19. Processing which was already under way immediately before 24th October 1998 is not assessable processing for the purposes of section 22.

SCHEDULE 9—POWERS OF ENTRY AND INSPECTION

Issue of warrants

1.—(1) If a circuit judge is satisfied by information on oath supplied by the Commissioner that there are reasonable grounds for suspecting—

    (a) that a data controller has contravened or is contravening any of the data protection principles, or

    (b) that an offence under this Act has been or is being committed,

and that evidence of the contravention or of the commission of the offence is to be found on any premises specified in the information, he may, subject to sub-paragraph (2) and paragraph 2, grant a warrant to the Commissioner.

(2) A judge shall not issue a warrant under this Schedule in respect of any personal data processed for the special purposes unless a determination by the Commissioner under section 45 with respect to those data has taken effect.

(3) A warrant issued under sub-paragraph (1) shall authorise the Commissioner or any of his officers or staff at any time within seven days of the date of the warrant to enter the premises, to search them, to inspect, examine, operate and test any equipment found there which is used or intended to be used for the processing of personal data and to inspect and seize any documents or other material found there which may be such evidence as is mentioned in that sub-paragraph.

2.—(1) A judge shall not issue a warrant under this Schedule unless he is satisfied—

    (a) that the Commissioner has given seven days' notice in writing to the occupier of the premises in question demanding access to the premises, and

    (b) that either—

        (i) access was demanded at a reasonable hour and was unreasonably refused, or
        (ii) although entry to the premises was granted, the occupier unreasonably refused to comply with a request by the Commissioner or any of the Commissioner's officers or staff to permit the Commissioner or the officer or member of staff to do any of the things referred to in paragraph 1(3), and

    (c) that the occupier, has, after the refusal, been notified by the Commissioner of the application for the warrant and has had an opportunity of being heard by the judge on the question whether or not it should be issued.

(2) Sub-paragraph (1) shall not apply if the judge is satisfied that the case is one of urgency or that compliance with those provisions would defeat the object of the entry.

3. A judge who issues a warrant under this Schedule shall also issue two copies of it and certify them clearly as copies.

Execution of warrants

4. A person executing a warrant issued under this Schedule may use such reasonable force as may be necessary.

5. A warrant issued under this Schedule shall be executed at a reasonable hour unless it appears to the person executing it that there are grounds for suspecting that the evidence in question would not be found if it were so executed.

6. If the person who occupies the premises in respect of which a warrant is issued under this Schedule is present when the warrant is executed, he shall be shown the warrant and supplied with a copy of it; and if that person is not present a copy of the warrant shall be left in a prominent place on the premises.

7.—(1) A person seizing anything in pursuance of a warrant under this Schedule shall give a receipt for it if asked to do so.

(2) Anything so seized may be retained for so long as is necessary in all the circumstances but the person in occupation of the premises in question shall be given a copy of anything that is seized if he so requests and the person executing the warrant considers that it can be done without undue delay.

Matters exempt from inspection and seizure

8. The powers of inspection and seizure conferred by a warrant issued under this Schedule shall not be exercisable in respect of personal data which by virtue of section 28 are exempt from any of the provisions of this Act.

9.—(1) Subject to the provisions of this paragraph, the powers of inspection and seizure conferred by a warrant issued under this Schedule shall not be exercisable in respect of—

(a) any communication between a professional legal adviser and his client in connection with the giving of legal advice to the client with respect to his obligations, liabilities or rights under this Act, or

(b) any communication between a professional legal adviser and his client, or between such an adviser or his client and any other person, made in connection with or in contemplation of proceedings under or arising out of this Act (including proceedings before the Tribunal) and for the purposes of such proceedings.

(2) Sub-paragraph (1) applies also to—

(a) any copy or other record of any such communication as is there mentioned, and

(b) any document or article enclosed with or referred to in any such communication if made in connection with the giving of any advice or, as the case may be, in connection with or in contemplation of and for the purposes of such proceedings as are there mentioned.

(3) This paragraph does not apply to anything in the possession of any person other than the professional legal adviser or his client or to anything held with the intention of furthering a criminal purpose.

(4) In this paragraph references to the client of a professional legal adviser include references to any person representing such a client.

10. If the person in occupation of any premises in respect of which a warrant is issued under this Schedule objects to the inspection or seizure under the warrant of any material on the grounds that it consists partly of matters in respect of which those powers are not exercisable, he shall, if the person executing the warrant so requests, furnish that person with a copy of so much of the material as is not exempt from those powers.

Return of warrants

11. A warrant issued under this Schedule shall be returned to the court from which it was issued—

(a) after being executed, or

(b) if not executed within the time authorised for its execution;

and the person by whom any such warrant is executed shall make an endorsement on it stating what powers have been exercised by him under the warrant.

Offences

12. Any person who—

(a) intentionally obstructs a person in the execution of a warrant issued under this Schedule, or

(b) fails without reasonable excuse to give any person executing such a warrant such assistance as he may reasonably require for the execution of the warrant,

is guilty of an offence.

Vessels, vehicles etc.

13. In this Schedule "premises" includes any vessel, vehicle, aircraft or hovercraft, and references to the occupier of any premises include references to the person in charge of any vessel, vehicle, aircraft or hovercraft.

Scotland and Northern Ireland

14. In the application of this Schedule to Scotland—

(a) for any reference to a circuit judge there is substituted a reference to the sheriff,

(b) for any reference to information on oath there is substituted a reference to evidence on oath, and

(c) for the reference to the court from which the warrant was issued there is substituted a reference to the sheriff clerk.

15. In the application of this Schedule to Northern Ireland—

(a) for any reference to a circuit judge there is substituted a reference to a county court judge, and

(b) for any reference to information on oath there is substituted a reference to a complaint on oath.

SCHEDULE 10—FURTHER PROVISIONS RELATING TO ASSISTANCE UNDER SECTION 53

1. In this Schedule "applicant" and "proceedings" have the same meaning as in section 53.

2. The assistance provided under section 53 may include the making of arrangements for, or for the Commissioner to bear the costs of—

(a) the giving of advice or assistance by a solicitor or counsel, and

(b) the representation of the applicant, or the provision to him of such assistance as is usually given by a solicitor or counsel—

  (i) in steps preliminary or incidental to the proceedings, or
  (ii) in arriving at or giving effect to a compromise to avoid or bring an end to the proceedings.

3. Where assistance is provided with respect to the conduct of proceedings—

(a) it shall include an agreement by the Commissioner to indemnify the applicant (subject only to any exceptions specified in the notification) in respect of any liability to pay costs or expenses arising by virtue of any judgment or order of the court in the proceedings,

(b) it may include an agreement by the Commissioner to indemnify the applicant in respect of any liability to pay costs or expenses arising by virtue of any compromise or settlement arrived at in order to avoid the proceedings or bring the proceedings to an end, and

(c) it may include an agreement by the Commissioner to indemnify the applicant in respect of any liability to pay damages pursuant to an undertaking given on the grant of interlocutory relief (in Scotland, an interim order) to the applicant.

4. Where the Commissioner provides assistance in relation to any proceedings, he shall do so on such terms, or make such other arrangements, as will secure that a person against whom the proceedings have been or are commenced is informed that assistance has been or is being provided by the Commissioner in relation to them.

5. In England and Wales or Northern Ireland, the recovery of expenses incurred by the Commissioner in providing an applicant with assistance (as taxed or assessed in such manner as may be prescribed by rules of court) shall constitute a first charge for the benefit of the Commissioner—

(a) on any costs which, by virtue of any judgment or order of the court, are payable to the applicant by any other person in respect of the matter in connection with which the assistance is provided, and

(b) on any sum payable to the applicant under a compromise or settlement arrived at in connection with that matter to avoid or bring to an end any proceedings.

6. In Scotland, the recovery of such expenses (as taxed or assessed in such manner as may be prescribed by rules of court) shall be paid to the Commissioner, in priority to other debts—

(a) out of any expenses which, by virtue of any judgment or order of the court, are payable to the applicant by any other person in respect of the matter in connection with which the assistance is provided, and

(b) out of any sum payable to the applicant under a compromise or settlement arrived at in connection with that matter to avoid or bring to an end any proceedings.

SCHEDULE 11—EDUCATIONAL RECORDS

Meaning of "educational record"

1. For the purposes of section 68 "educational record" means any record to which paragraph 2, 5 or 7 applies.

England and Wales

2. This paragraph applies to any record of information which—

   (a) is processed by or on behalf of the governing body of, or a teacher at, any school in England and Wales specified in paragraph 3,

   (b) relates to any person who is or has been a pupil at the school, and

   (c) originated from or was supplied by or on behalf of any of the persons specified in paragraph 4,

other than information which is processed by a teacher solely for the teacher's own use.

3. The schools referred to in paragraph 2(a) are—

   (a) a school maintained by a local education authority, and

   (b) a special school, as defined by section 6(2) of the Education Act 1996, which is not so maintained.

4. The persons referred to in paragraph 2(c) are—

   (a) an employee of the local education authority which maintains the school,

   (b) in the case of—

   (i) a voluntary aided, foundation or foundation special school (within the meaning of the School Standards and Framework Act 1998), or
   (ii) a special school which is not maintained by a local education authority,

   a teacher or other employee at the school (including an educational psychologist engaged by the governing body under a contract for services),

   (c) the pupil to whom the record relates, and

   (d) a parent, as defined by section 576(1) of the Education Act 1996, of that pupil.

Scotland

5. This paragraph applies to any record of information which is processed—

   (a) by an education authority in Scotland, and

   (b) for the purpose of the relevant function of the authority,

other than information which is processed by a teacher solely for the teacher's own use.

6. For the purposes of paragraph 5—

   (a) "education authority" means an education authority within the meaning of the Education (Scotland) Act 1980 ("the 1980 Act") [. . .][101],

   (b) "the relevant function" means, in relation to each of those authorities, their function under section 1 of the 1980 Act and section 7(1) of the 1989 Act, and

   (c) information processed by an education authority is processed for the purpose of the relevant function of the authority if the processing relates to the discharge of that function in respect of a person—

---

[101] words repealed by Standards in Scotland's Schools etc. Act 2000 asp 6 (Scottish Act) Sch.3 para.1

(i) who is or has been a pupil in a school provided by the authority, or

(ii) who receives, or has received, further education (within the meaning of the 1980 Act) so provided.

Northern Ireland

7.—(1) This paragraph applies to any record of information which—

(a) is processed by or on behalf of the Board of Governors of, or a teacher at, any grant-aided school in Northern Ireland,

(b) relates to any person who is or has been a pupil at the school, and

(c) originated from or was supplied by or on behalf of any of the persons specified in paragraph 8,

other than information which is processed by a teacher solely for the teacher's own use.

(2) In sub-paragraph (1) "grant-aided school" has the same meaning as in the Education and Libraries (Northern Ireland) Order 1986.

8. The persons referred to in paragraph 7(1) are—

(a) a teacher at the school,

(b) an employee of an education and library board, other than such a teacher,

(c) the pupil to whom the record relates, and

(d) a parent (as defined by Article 2(2) of the Education and Libraries (Northern Ireland) Order 1986) of that pupil.

England and Wales: transitory provisions

9.—(1) Until the appointed day within the meaning of section 20 of the School Standards and Framework Act 1998, this Schedule shall have effect subject to the following modifications.

(2) Paragraph 3 shall have effect as if for paragraph (b) and the "and" immediately preceding it there were substituted—
"(aa) a grant-maintained school, as defined by section 183(1) of the Education Act 1996,
(ab) a grant-maintained special school, as defined by section 337(4) of that Act, and
(b) a special school, as defined by section 6(2) of that Act, which is neither a maintained special school, as defined by section 337(3) of that Act, nor a grant-maintained special school."

(3) Paragraph 4(b)(i) shall have effect as if for the words from "foundation", in the first place where it occurs, to "1998)" there were substituted "or grant-maintained school".

SCHEDULE 12—ACCESSIBLE PUBLIC RECORDS

Meaning of "accessible public record"

1. For the purposes of section 68 "accessible public record" means any record which is kept by an authority specified—

(a) as respects England and Wales, in the Table in paragraph 2,

(b) as respects Scotland, in the Table in paragraph 4, or

(c) as respects Northern Ireland, in the Table in paragraph 6,

and is a record of information of a description specified in that Table in relation to that authority.

Housing and social services records: England and Wales:

2. The following is the Table referred to in paragraph 1(a).

TABLE OF AUTHORITIES AND INFORMATION

The authorities	*The accessible information*
Housing Act local authority.	Information held for the purpose of any of the authority's tenancies.
Local social services authority.	Information held for any purpose of the authority's social services functions.

3.—(1) The following provisions apply for the interpretation of the Table in paragraph 2.

(2) Any authority which, by virtue of section 4(e) of the Housing Act 1985, is a local authority for the purpose of any provision of that Act is a "Housing Act local authority" for the purposes of this Schedule, and so is any housing action trust established under Part III of the Housing Act 1988.

(3) Information contained in records kept by a Housing Act local authority is "held for the purpose of any of the authority's tenancies" if it is held for any purpose of the relationship of landlord and tenant of a dwelling which subsists, has substituted or may subsist between the authority and any individual who is, has been or, as the case may be, has applied to be, a tenant of the authority.

(4) Any authority which, by virtue of section 1 or 12 of the Local Authority Social Services Act 1970, is or is treated as a local authority for the purposes of that Act is a "local social services authority" for the purposes of this Schedule; and information contained in records kept by such an authority is "held for any purpose of the authority's social services functions" if it is held for the purpose of any past, current or proposed exercise of such a function in any case.

(5) Any expression used in paragraph 2 or this paragraph and in Part II of the Housing Act 1985 or the Local Authority Social Services Act 1970 has the same meaning as in that Act.

Housing and social services records: Scotland

4. The following is the Table referred to in paragraph 1(b).

TABLE OF AUTHORITIES AND INFORMATION

The authorities	*The accessible information*
Local authority. Scottish Homes.	Information held for the purpose of any of the body's tenancies.
Social work authority.	Information held for any purpose of the authority's functions under the Social Work (Scotland) Act 1968 and the enactments referred to in section 5(1B) of that Act.

5.—(1) The following provisions apply for the interpretation of the Table in paragraph 4.

(2) "Local authority" means—

    (a) a council constituted under section 2 of the Local Government etc. (Scotland) Act 1994,

    (b) a joint board or joint committee of two or more of those councils, or

    (c) any trust under the control of such a council.

(3) Information contained in records kept by a local authority or Scottish Homes is held for the purpose of any of their tenancies if it is held for any purpose of the relationship of landlord and tenant of a dwelling-house which subsists, has subsisted or may subsist between the authority or, as the case may be, Scottish Homes and any individual who is, has been or, as the case may be, has applied to be a tenant of theirs.

(4) "Social work authority" means a local authority for the purposes of the Social Work (Scotland) Act 1968; and information contained in records kept by such an authority is held for any purpose of their functions if it is held for the purpose of any past, current or proposed exercise of such a function in any case.

Housing and social services records: Northern Ireland

6. The following is the Table referred to in paragraph 1(c).

TABLE OF AUTHORITIES AND INFORMATION

The authorities	*The accessible information*
The Northern Ireland Housing Executive.	Information held for the purpose of any of the Executive's tenancies.
A Health and Social Services Board.	Information held for the purpose of any past, current or proposed exercise by the Board of any function exercisable, by virtue of directions under Article 17(1) of the Health and Personal Social Services (Northern Ireland) Order 1972, by the Board on behalf of the Department of Health and Social Services with respect to the administration of personal social services under— (a) the Children and Young Persons Act (Northern Ireland) 1968;

The authorities	The accessible information
	(b) the Health and Personal Social Services (Northern Ireland) Order 1972; (c) Article 47 of the Matrimonial Causes (Northern Ireland) Order 1978; (d) Article 11 of the Domestic Proceedings (Northern Ireland) Order 1980; (e) the Adoption (Northern Ireland) Order 1987; or (f) the Children (Northern Ireland) Order 1995.
An HSS trust	Information held for the purpose of any past, current or proposed exercise by the trust of any function exercisable, by virtue of an authorisation under Article 3(1) of the Health and Personal Social Services (Northern Ireland) Order 1994, by the trust on behalf of a Health and Social Services Board with respect to the administration of personal social services under any statutory provision mentioned in the last preceding entry.

7.—(1) This paragraph applies for the interpretation of the Table in paragraph 6.

(2) Information contained in records kept by the Northern Ireland Housing Executive is "held for the purpose of any of the Executive's tenancies" if it is held for any purpose of the relationship of landlord and tenant of a dwelling which subsists, has subsisted or may subsist between the Executive and any individual who is, has been or, as the case may be, has applied to be, a tenant of the Executive.

SCHEDULE 13—MODIFICATIONS OF ACT HAVING EFFECT BEFORE 24TH OCTOBER 2007

1. After section 12 there is inserted—

"12A.—Rights of data subjects in relation to exempt manual data.

(1) A data subject is entitled at any time by notice in writing—

(a) to require the data controller to rectify, block, erase or destroy exempt manual data which are inaccurate or incomplete, or

(b) to require the data controller to cease holding exempt manual data in a way incompatible with the legitimate purposes pursued by the data controller.

(2) A notice under subsection (1)(a) or (b) must state the data subject's reasons for believing that the data are inaccurate "or incomplete or, as the case may be, his reasons for believing that they are held in a way incompatible with the legitimate purposes pursued by the data controller.

(3) If the court is satisfied, on the application of any person who has given a notice under subsection (1) which appears to the court to be justified (or to be justified to any extent) that the data controller in question has failed to comply with the notice, the court may order him to take such steps for complying with the notice (or for complying with it to that extent) as the court thinks fit.

(4) In this section 'exempt manual data' means—

(a) in relation to the first transitional period, as defined by paragraph 1(2) of Schedule 8, data to which paragraph 3 or 4 of that Schedule applies, and

(b) in relation to the second transitional period, as so defined, data to which [paragraph 14 or 14A][102] of that Schedule applies.

(5) For the purposes of this section personal data are incomplete if, and only if, the data, although not inaccurate, are such that their incompleteness would constitute a contravention of the third or fourth data protection principles, if those principles applied to the data."

2. In section 32—

(a) in subsection (2) after "section 12" there is inserted—

"(dd) section 12A," and

(b) in subsection (4) after "12(8)" there is inserted, "12A(3)".

3. In section 34 for "section 14(1) to (3)" there is substituted "sections 12A and 14(1) to (3)."

4. In section 53(1) after "12(8)" there is inserted, "12A(3)".

5. In paragraph 8 of Part II of Schedule 1, the word "or" at the end of paragraph (c) is omitted and after paragraph (d) there is inserted "or

(e) he contravenes section 12A by failing to comply with a notice given under subsection (1) of that section to the extent that the notice is justified."

SCHEDULE 14—TRANSITIONAL PROVISIONS AND SAVINGS

Interpretation

1. In this Schedule—

"the 1984 Act" means the Data Protection Act 1984;

"the old principles" means the data protection principles within the meaning of the 1984 Act;

"the new principles" means the data protection principles within the meaning of this Act.

Effect of registration under Part II of 1984 Act

2.—(1) Subject to sub-paragraphs (4) and (5) any person who, immediately before the commencement of Part III of this Act—

---

[102] words added by Freedom of Information Act 2000 c. 36 Pt VII s.70(4)

(a) is registered as a data user under Part II of the 1984 Act, or

(b) is treated by virtue of section 7(6) of the 1984 Act as so registered,

is exempt from section 17(1) of this Act until the end of the registration period[. . .][103].

(2) In sub-paragraph (1) "the registration period", in relation to a person, means—

(a) where there is a single entry in respect of that person as a data user, the period at the end of which, if section 8 of the 1984 Act had remained in force, that entry would have fallen to be removed unless renewed, and

(b) where there are two or more entries in respect of that person as a data user, the period at the end of which, if that section had remained in force, the last of those entries to expire would have fallen to be removed unless renewed.

(3) Any application for registration as a data user under Part II of the 1984 Act which is received by the Commissioner before the commencement of Part III of this Act (including any appeal against a refusal of registration) shall be determined in accordance with the old principles and the provisions of the 1984 Act.

(4) If a person falling within paragraph (b) of sub-paragraph (1) receives a notification under section 7(1) of the 1984 Act of the refusal of his application, sub-paragraph (1) shall cease to apply to him—

(a) if no appeal is brought, at the end of the period within which an appeal can be brought against the refusal, or

(b) on the withdrawal or dismissal of the appeal.

(5) If a data controller gives a notification under section 18(1) at a time when he is exempt from section 17(1) by virtue of sub-paragraph (1), he shall cease to be so exempt.

(6) The Commissioner shall include in the register maintained under section 19 an entry in respect of each person who is exempt from section 17(1) by virtue of sub-paragraph (1); and each entry shall consist of the particulars which, immediately before the commencement of Part III of this Act, were included (or treated as included) in respect of that person in the register maintained under section 4 of the 1984 Act.

(7) Notification regulations under Part III of this Act may make provision modifying the duty referred to in section 20(1) in its application to any person in respect of whom an entry in the register maintained under section 19 has been made under sub-paragraph (6).

(8) Notification regulations under Part III of this Act may make further transitional provision in connection with the substitution of Part III of this Act for Part II of the 1984 Act (registration), including provision modifying the application of provisions of Part III in transitional cases.

Rights of data subjects

3.—(1) The repeal of section 21 of the 1984 Act (right of access to personal data) does not affect the application of that section in any case in which the request (together with the information referred to in paragraph (a) of subsection (4) of that section and, in a case where it is required, the consent referred to in paragraph (b) of that subsection) was received before the day on which the repeal comes into force.

(2) Sub-paragraph (1) does not apply where the request is made by reference to this Act.

---

[103] words repealed by Freedom of Information Act 2000 c. 36 Sch.8(I) para.1

(3) Any fee paid for the purposes of section 21 of the 1984 Act before the commencement of section 7 in a case not falling within sub-paragraph (1) shall be taken to have been paid for the purposes of section 7.

4. The repeal of section 22 of the 1984 Act (compensation for inaccuracy) and the repeal of section 23 of that Act (compensation for loss or unauthorised disclosure) do not affect the application of those sections in relation to damage or distress suffered at any time by reason of anything done or omitted to be done before the commencement of the repeals.

5. The repeal of section 24 of the 1984 Act (rectification and erasure) does not affect any case in which the application to the court was made before the day on which the repeal comes into force.

6. Subsection (3)(b) of section 14 does not apply where the rectification, blocking, erasure or destruction occurred before the commencement of that section.

Enforcement and transfer prohibition notices served under Part V of 1984 Act

7.—(1) If, immediately before the commencement of section 40—

    (a) an enforcement notice under section 10 of the 1984 Act has effect, and

    (b) either the time for appealing against the notice has expired or any appeal has been determined,

then, after that commencement, to the extent mentioned in sub-paragraph (3), the notice shall have effect for the purposes of sections 41 and 47 as if it were an enforcement notice under section 40.

(2) Where an enforcement notice has been served under section 10 of the 1984 Act before the commencement of section 40 and immediately before that commencement either—

    (a) the time for appealing against the notice has not expired, or

    (b) an appeal has not been determined,

the appeal shall be determined in accordance with the provisions of the 1984 Act and the old principles and, unless the notice is quashed on appeal, to the extent mentioned in sub-paragraph

(3) the notice shall have effect for the purposes of sections 41 and 47 as if it were an enforcement notice under section 40.

(3) An enforcement notice under section 10 of the 1984 Act has the effect described in sub-paragraph (1) or (2) only to the extent that the steps specified in the notice for complying with the old principles or principles in question are steps which the data controller could be required by an enforcement notice under section 40 to take for complying with the new principles or any of them.

8.—(1) If, immediately before the commencement of section 40—

    (a) a transfer prohibition notice under section 12 of the 1984 Act has effect, and

    (b) either the time for appealing against the notice has expired or any appeal has been determined,

then, on and after that commencement, to the extent specified in sub-paragraph (3), the notice shall have effect for the purposes of sections 41 and 47 as if it were an enforcement notice under section 40.

(2) Where a transfer prohibition notice has been served under section 12 of the 1984 Act and immediately before the commencement of section 40 either—

(a) the time for appealing against the notice has not expired, or

(b) an appeal has not been determined,

the appeal shall be determined in accordance with the provisions of the 1984 Act and the old principles and, unless the notice is quashed on appeal, to the extent mentioned in sub-paragraph (3) the notice shall have effect for the purposes of sections 41 and 47 as if it were an enforcement notice under section 40.

(3) A transfer prohibition notice under section 12 of the 1984 Act has the effect described in sub-paragraph (1) or (2) only to the extent that the prohibition imposed by the notice is one which could be imposed by an enforcement notice under section 40 for complying with the new principles or any of them.

Notices under new law relating to matters in relation to which 1984 Act had effect

9. The Commissioner may serve an enforcement notice under section 40 on or after the day on which that section comes into force if he is satisfied that, before that day, the data controller contravened the old principles by reason of any act or omission which would also have constituted a contravention of the new principles if they had applied before that day.

10. Subsection (5)(b) of section 40 does not apply where the rectification, blocking, erasure or destruction occurred before the commencement of that section.

11. The Commissioner may serve an information notice under section 43 on or after the day on which that section comes into force if he has reasonable grounds for suspecting that, before that day, the data controller contravened the old principles by reason of any act or omission which would also have constituted a contravention of the new principles if they had applied before that day.

12. Where by virtue of paragraph 11 an information notice is served on the basis of anything done or omitted to be done before the day on which section 43 comes into force, subsection (2)(b) of that section shall have effect as if the reference to the data controller having complied, or complying, with the new principles were a reference to the data controller having contravened the old principles by reason of any such act or omission as is mentioned in paragraph 11.

Self-incrimination, etc.

13.—(1) In section 43(8), section 44(9) and paragraph 11 of Schedule 7, any reference to an offence under this Act includes a reference to an offence under the 1984 Act.

(2) In section 34(9) of the 1984 Act, any reference to an offence under that Act includes a reference to an offence under this Act.

Warrants issued under 1984 Act

14. The repeal of Schedule 4 to the 1984 Act does not affect the application of that Schedule in any case where a warrant was issued under that Schedule before the commencement of the repeal.

Complaints under section 36(2) of 1984 Act and requests for assessment under section 42

15. The repeal of section 36(2) of the 1984 Act does not affect the application of that provision in any case where the complaint was received by the Commissioner before the commencement of the repeal.

16. In dealing with a complaint under section 36(2) of the 1984 Act or a request for an assessment under section 42 of this Act, the Commissioner shall have regard to the provisions from time to time applicable to the processing, and accordingly—

    (a) in section 36(2) of the 1984 Act, the reference to the old principles and the provisions of that Act includes, in relation to any time when the new principles and the provisions of this Act have effect, those principles and provisions, and

    (b) in section 42 of this Act, the reference to the provisions of this Act includes, in relation to any time when the old principles and the provisions of the 1984 Act had effect, those principles and provisions.

Applications under Access to Health Records Act 1990 or corresponding
Northern Ireland legislation

17.—(1) The repeal of any provision of the Access to Health Records Act 1990 does not affect—

    (a) the application of section 3 or 6 of that Act in any case in which the application under that section was received before the day on which the repeal comes into force, or

    (b) the application of section 8 of that Act in any case in which the application to the court was made before the day on which the repeal comes into force.

(2) Sub-paragraph (1)(a) does not apply in relation to an application for access to information which was made by reference to this Act.

18.—(1) The revocation of any provision of the Access to Health Records (Northern Ireland) Order 1993 does not affect—

    (a) the application of Article 5 or 8 of that Order in any case in which the application under that Article was received before the day on which the repeal comes into force, or

    (b) the application of Article 10 of that Order in any case in which the application to the court was made before the day on which the repeal comes into force.

(2) Sub-paragraph (1)(a) does not apply in relation to an application for access to information which was made by reference to this Act.

SCHEDULE 14—TRANSITIONAL PROVISIONS AND SAVINGS

Applications under regulations under Access to Personal Files Act 1987
or corresponding Northern Ireland legislation

19.—(1) The repeal of the personal files enactments does not affect the application of regulations under those enactments in relation to—

    (a) any request for information,

    (b) any application for rectification or erasure, or

(c) any application for review of a decision,

which was made before the day on which the repeal comes into force.

(2) Sub-paragraph (1)(a) does not apply in relation to a request for information which was made by reference to this Act.

(3) In sub-paragraph (1) "the personal files enactments" means—

(a) in relation to Great Britain, the Access to Personal Files Act 1987, and

(b) in relation to Northern Ireland, Part II of the Access to Personal Files and Medical Reports (Northern Ireland) Order 1991.

Applications under section 158 of Consumer Credit Act 1974

20. Section 62 does not affect the application of section 158 of the Consumer Credit Act 1974 in any case where the request was received before the commencement of section 62, unless the request is made by reference to this Act.

SCHEDULE 15—MINOR AND CONSEQUENTIAL AMENDMENTS

[. . .]

Representation of the People Act 1983 (c. 2)

7. In Schedule 2 of the Representation of the People Act 1983 (provisions which may be included in regulations as to registration etc), in paragraph 11A(2)—

(a) for "data user" there is substituted "data controller", and

(b) for "the Data Protection Act 1984" there is substituted "the Data Protection Act 1998".

Access to Medical Reports Act 1988 (c. 28)

8. In section 2(1) of the Access to Medical Reports Act 1988 (interpretation), in the definition of "health professional", for "the Data Protection (Subject Access Modification) Order 1987" there is substituted "the Data Protection Act 1998".

9. [. . .][104]

Education (Student Loans) Act 1990 (c. 6)

10. Schedule 2 to the Education (Student Loans) Act 1990 (loans for students) so far as that Schedule continues in force shall have effect as if the reference in paragraph 4(2) to the Data Protection Act 1984 were a reference to this Act.

---

[104] repealed by Violent Crime Reduction Act 2006 c. 38 Sch.5 para.1

Access to Health Records Act 1990 (c. 23)

11. For section 2 of the Access to Health Records Act 1990 there is substituted—

"2. Health professionals.
In this Act 'health professional' has the same meaning as in the Data Protection Act 1998."

12. In section 3(4) of that Act (cases where fee may be required) in paragraph (a), for "the maximum prescribed under section 21 of the Data Protection Act 1984" there is substituted "such maximum as may be prescribed for the purposes of this section by regulations under section 7 of the Data Protection Act 1998".

13. In section 5(3) of that Act (cases where right of access may be partially excluded) for the words from the beginning to "record" in the first place where it occurs there is substituted "Access shall not be given under section 3(2) to any part of a health record".

Access to Personal Files and Medical Reports (Northern Ireland)
Order 1991 (1991/1707 (N.I. 14))

14. In Article 4 of the Access to Personal Files and Medical Reports (Northern Ireland) Order 1991 (obligation to give access), in paragraph (2) (exclusion of information to which individual entitled under section 21 of the Data Protection Act 1984) for "section 21 of the Data Protection Act 1984" there is substituted "section 7 of the Data Protection Act 1998".

15. In Article 6(1) of that Order (interpretation), in the definition of "health professional", for "the Data Protection (Subject Access Modification) (Health) Order 1987" there is substituted "the Data Protection Act 1998".

Tribunals and Inquiries Act 1992 (c. 53)

16. In Part 1 of Schedule 1 to the Tribunals and Inquiries Act 1992 (tribunals under direct supervision of Council on Tribunals), for paragraph 14 there is substituted—

"Data protection

(a) The Data Protection Commissioner appointed under section 6 of the Data Protection Act 1998;

(b) the Data Protection Tribunal constituted under that section, in respect of its jurisdiction under section 48 of that Act."

17. For paragraphs (1) and (2) of Article 4 of the Access to Health Records (Northern Ireland) Order 1993 there is substituted—

"(1) In this Order 'health professional' has the same meaning as in the Data Protection Act 1998."

18. In Article 5(4) of that Order (cases where fee may be required) in sub-paragraph (a), for "the maximum prescribed under section 21 of the Data Protection Act 1984" there is substituted "such maximum as may be prescribed for the purposes of this Article by regulations under section 7 of the Data Protection Act 1998".

19. In Article 7 of that Order (cases where right of access may be partially excluded) for the words from the beginning to "record" in the first place where it occurs there is substituted "Access shall not be given under Article 5(2) to any part of a health record".

SCHEDULE 16—REPEALS AND REVOCATIONS

PART I

REPEALS

Chapter	Short title	Extent of repeal
1984 c. 35.	The Data Protection Act 1984.	The whole Act.
1986 c. 60.	The Financial Services Act 1986.	Section 190.
1987 c. 37.	The Access to Personal Files Act 1987.	The whole Act.
1988 c. 40.	The Education Reform Act 1988.	Section 223.
1988 c. 50.	The Housing Act 1988.	In Schedule 17, paragraph 80.
1990 c. 23.	The Access to Health Records Act 1990.	In section 1(1), the words from "but does not" to the end. In section 3, subsection (1)(a) to (e) and, in subsection (6)(a), the words "in the case of an application made otherwise than by the patient". Section 4(1) and (2). In section 5(1)(a)(i), the words "of the patient or" and the words "other". In section 10, in subsection (2) the words "or orders" and in subsection (3) the words "or an order under section 2(3) above". In section 11, the definitions of "child" and "parental responsibility".
1990 c. 37.	The Human Fertilisation and Embryology Act 1990.	Section 33(8).
1990 c. 41.	The Courts and Legal Services Act 1990.	In Schedule 10, paragraph 58.
1992 c. 13.	The Further and Higher Education Act 1992.	Section 86.
1992 c. 37.	The Further and Higher Education (Scotland) Act 1992.	Section 59.
1993 c. 8.	The Judicial Pensions and Retirement Act 1993.	In Schedule 6, paragraph 50.

Chapter	Short title	Extent of repeal
1993 c. 10.	The Charities Act 1993.	Section 12.
1993 c. 21.	The Osteopaths Act 1993.	Section 38.
1994 c. 17.	The Chiropractors Act 1994.	Section 38.
1994 c. 19.	The Local Government (Wales) Act 1994.	In Schedule 13, paragraph 30.
1994 c. 33.	The Criminal Justice and Public Order Act 1994.	Section 161.
1994 c. 39.	The Local Government etc. (Scotland) Act 1994.	In Schedule 13, paragraph 154.

PART II

REVOCATIONS

Number	Title	Extent of revocation
S.I. 1991/1142.	The Data Protection Registration Fee Order 1991.	The whole Order.
S.I. 1991/1707 (N.I. 14).	The Access to Personal Files and Medical Reports (Northern Ireland) Order 1991.	Part II. The Schedule.
S.I. 1992/3218.	The Banking Co-ordination (Second Council Directive) Regulations 1992.	In Schedule 10, paragraphs 15 and 40.
S.I. 1993/1250 (N.I. 4).	The Access to Health Records (Northern Ireland) Order 1993.	In Article 2(2), the definitions of "child" and "parental responsibility". In Article 3(1), the words from "but does not include" to the end. In Article 5, paragraph (1)(a) to(d) and, in paragraph (6)(a), the words "in the case of an application made otherwise than by the patient". Article 6(1) and (2). In Article 7(1)(a)(i), the words "of the patient or" and the word "other".
S.I. 1994/429 (N.I. 2).	The Health and Personal Social Services (Northern Ireland) Order 1994.	In Schedule 1, the entries relating to the Access to Personal Files and Medical Reports (Northern Ireland) Order 1991.
S.I. 1994/1696.	The Insurance Companies (Third Insurance Directives) Regulations 1994.	In Schedule 8, paragraph 8.

Number	Title	Extent of revocation
S.I. 1995/755 (N.I. 2).	The Children (Northern Ireland) Order 1995.	In Schedule 9, paragraphs 177 and 191.
S.I. 1995/3275.	The Investment Services Regulations 1995.	In Schedule 10, paragraphs 3 and 15.
S.I. 1996/2827.	The Open-Ended Investment Companies (Investment Companies with Variable Capital) Regulations 1996.	In Schedule 8, paragraphs 3 and 26.

Freedom of Information Act 2000

(2000, c.36)

Part VII

Amendments of Data Protection Act 1998

Amendments relating to personal information held by public authorities

68. Extension of meaning of "data"

(1) Section 1 of the Data Protection Act 1998 (basic interpretative provisions) is amended in accordance with subsections (2) and (3).

(2) In subsection (1)—

(a) in the definition of "data", the word "or" at the end of paragraph (c) is omitted and after paragraph (d) there is inserted "or

(e) is recorded information held by a public authority and does not fall within any of paragraphs (a) to (d);" and

(b) after the definition of "processing" there is inserted—

" 'public authority' has the same meaning as in the Freedom of Information Act 2000;".

(3) After subsection (4) there is inserted—

"(5) In paragraph (e) of the definition of 'data' in subsection (1); the reference to information "held" by a public authority shall be construed in accordance with section 3(2) of the Freedom of Information Act 2000.

(6) Where section 7 of the Freedom of Information Act 2000 prevents Parts I to V of that Act from applying to certain information held by a public authority, that information is not to be treated for the purposes of paragraph (e) of the definition of 'data' in subsection (1) as held by a public authority."

(4) In section 56 of that Act (prohibition of requirement as to production of certain records), after subsection (6) there is inserted—

"(6A) A record is not a relevant record to the extent that it relates, or is to relate, only to personal data falling within paragraph (e) of the definition of "data" in section 1(1)."

(5) In the Table in section 71 of that Act (index of defined expressions) after the entry relating to processing there is inserted—

"public authority. section 1(1)".

69. *Right of access to unstructured personal data held by public authorities*

(1) In section 7(1) of the Data Protection Act 1998 (right of access to personal data), for "sections 8 and 9" there is substituted "sections 8, 9 and 9A".

(2) After section 9 of that Act there is inserted—

"9A.—Unstructured personal data held by public authorities

(1) In this section 'unstructured personal data' means any personal data falling within paragraph (e) of the definition of "data" in section 1(1), other than information which is recorded as part of, or with the intention that it should form part of, any set of information relating to individuals to the extent that the set is structured by reference to individuals or by reference to criteria relating to individuals.

(2) A public authority is not obliged to comply with subsection (1) of section 7 in relation to any unstructured personal data unless the request under that section contains a description of the data.

(3) Even if the data are described by the data subject in his request, a public authority is not obliged to comply with subsection (1) of section 7 in relation to unstructured personal data if the authority estimates that the cost of complying with the request so far as relating to those data would exceed the appropriate limit.

(4) Subsection (3) does not exempt the public authority from its obligation to comply with paragraph (a) of section 7(1) in relation to the unstructured personal data unless the estimated cost of complying with that paragraph alone in relation to those data would exceed the appropriate limit.

(5) In subsections (3) and (4) 'the appropriate limit' means such amount as may be prescribed by the [Secretary of State][1] by regulations, and different amounts may be prescribed in relation to different cases.

(6) Any estimate for the purposes of this section must be made in accordance with regulations under section 12(5) of the Freedom of Information Act 2000."

(3) In section 67(5) of that Act (statutory instruments subject to negative resolution procedure), in paragraph (c), for "or 9(3)" there is substituted ", 9(3) or 9A(5)".

70. *Exemptions applicable to certain manual data held by public authorities*

(1) After section 33 of the Data Protection Act 1998 there is inserted—

"33A.—Manual data held by public authorities

(1) Personal data falling within paragraph (e) of the definition of 'data' in section 1(1) are exempt from—

    (a) the first, second, third, fifth, seventh and eighth data protection principles,

    (b) the sixth data protection principle except so far as it relates to the rights conferred on data subjects by sections 7 and 14,

    (c) sections 10 to 12,

    (d) section 13, except so far as it relates to damage caused by a contravention of section 7 or of the fourth data protection principle and to any distress which is also suffered by reason of that contravention,

---

[1] words substituted by secretary of State for Constitutional Affairs Order 2003/1887 Sch 2 para 12 (1)(b)

(e) Part III, and

(f) section 55.

(2) Personal data which fall within paragraph (e) of the definition of 'data' in section 1(1) and relate to appointments or removals, pay, discipline, superannuation or other personnel matters, in relation to—

(a) service in any of the armed forces of the Crown,

(b) service in any office or employment under the Crown or under any public authority, or

(c) service in any office or employment, or under any contract for services, in respect of which power to take action, or to determine or approve the action taken, in such matters is vested in Her Majesty, any Minister of the Crown, the National Assembly for Wales, any Northern Ireland Minister (within the meaning of the Freedom of Information Act 2000) or any public authority, are also exempt from the remaining data protection principles and the remaining provisions of Part II."

(2) In section 55 of that Act (unlawful obtaining etc. of personal data) in subsection (8) after "section 28" there is inserted "or 33A" .

(3) In Part III of Schedule 8 to that Act (exemptions available after 23rd October 2001 but before 24th October 2007) after paragraph 14 there is inserted—

"**14A.**—(1) This paragraph applies to personal data which fall within paragraph (e) of the definition of 'data' in section 1(1) and do not fall within paragraph 14(1)(a), but does not apply to eligible manual data to which the exemption in paragraph 16 applies.

(2) During the second transitional period, data to which this paragraph applies are exempt from—

(a) the fourth data protection principle, and

(b) section 14(1) to (3)."

(4) In Schedule 13 to that Act (modifications of Act having effect before 24th October 2007) in subsection (4)(b) of section 12A to that Act as set out in paragraph 1, after "paragraph 14" there is inserted "or 14A".

71. *Particulars registrable under Part III of Data Protection Act 1998*

In section 16(1) of the Data Protection Act 1998 (the registrable particulars), before the word "and" at the end of paragraph (f) there is inserted—

"(ff) where the data controller is a public authority, a statement of that fact,".

72. *Availability under Act disregarded for purpose of exemption*

In section 34 of the Data Protection Act 1998 (information available to the public by or under enactment), after the word "enactment" there is inserted "other than an enactment contained in the Freedom of Information Act 2000".

73. *Further amendments of Data Protection Act 1998*

Schedule 6 (which contains further amendments of the Data Protection Act 1998) has effect.

PART VIII

MISCELLANEOUS AND SUPPLEMENTAL

74. *Power to make provision relating to environmental information*

(1) In this section "the Aarhus Convention" means the Convention on Access to Information, Public Participation in Decision-making and Access to Justice in Environmental Matters signed at Aarhus on 25th June 1998.

(2) For the purposes of this section "the information provisions" of the Aarhus Convention are Article 4, together with Articles 3 and 9 so far as relating to that Article.

(3) The Secretary of State may by regulations make such provision as he considers appropriate—

 (a) for the purpose of implementing the information provisions of the Aarhus Convention or any amendment of those provisions made in accordance with Article 14 of the Convention, and

 (b) for the purpose of dealing with matters arising out of or related to the implementation of those provisions or of any such amendment.

(4) Regulations under subsection (3) may in particular—

 (a) enable charges to be made for making information available in accordance with the regulations,

 (b) provide that any obligation imposed by the regulations in relation to the disclosure of information is to have effect notwithstanding any enactment or rule of law,

 (c) make provision for the issue by the Secretary of State of a code of practice,

 (d) provide for sections 47 and 48 to apply in relation to such a code with such modifications as may be specified,

 (e) provide for any of the provisions of Parts IV and V to apply, with such modifications as may be specified in the regulations, in relation to compliance with any requirement of the regulations, and

 (f) contain such transitional or consequential provision (including provision modifying any enactment) as the Secretary of State considers appropriate.

(5) This section has effect subject to section 80.

[. . .]

SCHEDULE 2—THE COMMISSIONER AND THE TRIBUNAL

[. . .]

PART II

AMENDMENTS RELATING TO EXTENSION OF FUNCTIONS OF COMMISSIONER AND TRIBUNAL

Interests represented by lay members of Tribunal

16. In section 6(6) of the Data Protection Act 1998 (lay members of Tribunal)—

    (a) for the word "and" at the end of paragraph (a) there is substituted—

        "(aa) persons to represent the interests of those who make requests for information under the Freedom of Information Act 2000," and

    (b) after paragraph (b) there is inserted "and

    (bb) persons to represent the interests of public authorities."

17. In section 26(2) of that Act (fees regulations), in paragraph (a)—

    (a) after "functions" there is inserted "under this Act", and

    (b) after "Tribunal" there is inserted "so far as attributable to their functions under this Act" .

18. In section 58 of that Act (disclosure of information to Commissioner or Tribunal), after "this Act" there is inserted "or the Freedom of Information Act 2000".

19.—(1) Section 59 of that Act (confidentiality of information) is amended as follows.

(2) In subsections (1) and (2), for "this Act", wherever occurring, there is substituted "the information Acts".

(3) After subsection (3) there is inserted—

    "(4) In this section "the information Acts" means this Act and the Freedom of Information Act 2000."

20.—(1) Paragraph 4 of Schedule 5 to that Act (officers and staff) is amended as follows.

(2) In sub-paragraph (1)(a), after "a deputy commissioner" there is inserted "or two deputy commissioners".

(3) After sub-paragraph (1) there is inserted—

    "(1A) The Commissioner shall, when appointing any second deputy commissioner, specify which of the Commissioner's functions are to be performed, in the circumstances referred to in paragraph 5(1), by each of the deputy commissioners."

21.—(1) Paragraph 5 of Schedule 5 to that Act (exercise of functions of Commissioner during vacancy etc.) is amended as follows.

(2) In sub-paragraph (1)—

    (a) after "deputy commissioner" there is inserted "or deputy commissioners", and

(b) after "this Act" there is inserted "or the Freedom of Information Act 2000".

(3) In sub-paragraph (2) after "this Act" there is inserted "or the Freedom of Information Act 2000".

22. In paragraph 9(1) of Schedule 5 to that Act (money) for "or section 159 of the Consumer Credit Act 1974" there is substituted ", under section 159 of the Consumer Credit Act 1974 or under the Freedom of Information Act 2000".

[...]

SCHEDULE 4—APPEAL PROCEEDINGS: AMENDMENTS OF SCHEDULE 6 TO DATA PROTECTION ACT 1998

Constitution of Tribunal in national security cases

1. In paragraph 2(1) of Schedule 6 to the Data Protection Act 1998 (constitution of Tribunal in national security cases), at the end there is inserted "or under section 60(1) or (4) of the Freedom of Information Act 2000".

2. For paragraph 3 of that Schedule there is substituted—

"**3.** The Tribunal shall be duly constituted—

(a) for an appeal under section 28(4) or (6) in any case where the application of paragraph 6(1) is excluded by rules under paragraph 7, or

(b) for an appeal under section 60(1) or (4) of the Freedom of Information Act 2000,

if it consists of three of the persons designated under paragraph 2(1), of whom one shall be designated by the Lord Chancellor to preside."

3.—(1) Paragraph 4 of that Schedule (constitution of Tribunal in other cases) is amended as follows.

(2) After sub-paragraph (1) there is inserted—

"(1A) Subject to any rules made under paragraph 7, the Tribunal shall be duly constituted for an appeal under section 57(1) or (2) of the Freedom of Information Act 2000 if it consists of—

(a) the chairman or a deputy chairman (who shall preside), and

(b) an equal number of the members appointed respectively in accordance with paragraphs (aa) and (bb) of section 6(6)."

(3) In sub-paragraph (2), after "(1)" there is inserted "or (1A)".

4.—(1) Paragraph 7 of that Schedule (rules of procedure) is amended as follows.

(2) In sub-paragraph (1), for the words from "regulating" onwards there is substituted "regulating—

(a) the exercise of the rights of appeal conferred—

(i) by sections 28(4) and (6) and 48, and

(ii) by sections 57(1) and (2) and section 60(1) and (4) of the Freedom of Information Act 2000, and

(b) the practice and procedure of the Tribunal."

(3) In sub-paragraph (2), after paragraph (a) there is inserted—

"(aa) for the joinder of any other person as a party to any proceedings on an appeal under the Freedom of Information Act 2000,

(ab) for the hearing of an appeal under this Act with an appeal under the Freedom of Information Act 2000,"

Appendix C

Directive 95/46/EC of the European Parliament and of the Council of 24 October 1995 on the protection of individuals with regard to the processing of personal data and on the free movement of such data

DIRECTIVE 95/46/EC OF THE EUROPEAN PARLIAMENT AND OF THE COUNCIL
of 24 October 1995

on the protection of individuals with regard to the processing of personal data and on the free movement of such data

THE EUROPEAN PARLIAMENT AND THE COUNCIL OF THE EUROPEAN UNION,

Having regard to the Treaty establishing the European Community, and in particular Article 100a thereof,

Having regard to the proposal from the Commission,[1]

Having regard to the opinion of the Economic and Social Committee,[2]

Acting in accordance with the procedure referred to in Article 189b of the Treaty,[3]

(1) Whereas the objectives of the Community, as laid down in the Treaty, as amended by the Treaty on European Union, include creating an ever closer union among the peoples of Europe, fostering closer relations between the States belonging to the Community, ensuring economic and social progress by common action to eliminate the barriers which divide Europe, encouraging the constant improvement of the living conditions of its peoples, preserving and strengthening peace and liberty and promoting democracy on the basis of the fundamental rights recognized in the constitution and laws of the Member States and in the European Convention for the Protection of Human Rights and Fundamental Freedoms;

---

[1] OJ No C 277, 5.11.1990, p. 3 and OJ No C 311, 27.11.1992, p. 30.

[2] OJ No C 159, 17.6.1991, p. 38. (3) Opinion of the European Parliament of 11 March 1992 (OJ No C 94, 13.4.1992, p. 198), confirmed on 2 December 1993 (OJ No C 342, 20.12.1993, p. 30); Council common position of 20 February 1995 (OJ No C 93, 13.4.1995, p. 1) and Decision of the European Parliament of 15 June 1995 (OJ No C 166, 3. 7.1995).

[3] OJ No L 197, 18.7.1987, p. 33.

(2) Whereas data-processing systems are designed to serve man whereas they must, whatever the nationality or residence of natural persons, respect their fundamental rights and freedoms, notably the right to privacy, and contribute to economic and social progress, trade expansion and the well-being of individuals;

(3) Whereas the establishment and functioning of an internal market in which, in accordance with Article 7a of the Treaty, the free movement of goods, persons, services and capital is ensured require not only that personal data should be able to flow freely from one Member State to another, but also that the fundamental rights of individuals should be safeguarded;

(4) Whereas increasingly frequent recourse is being had in the Community to the processing of personal data in the various spheres of economic and social activity whereas the progress made in information technology is making the processing and exchange of such data considerably easier;

(5) Whereas the economic and social integration resulting from the establishment and functioning of the internal market within the meaning of Article 7a of the Treaty will necessarily lead to a substantial increase in cross-border flows of personal data between all those involved in a private or public capacity in economic and social activity in the Member States whereas the exchange of personal data between undertakings in different Member States is set to increase whereas the national authorities in the various Member States are being called upon by virtue of Community law to collaborate and exchange personal data so as to be able to perform their duties or carry out tasks on behalf of an authority in another Member State within the context of the area without internal frontiers as constituted by the internal market;

(6) Whereas, furthermore, the increase in scientific and technical cooperation and the coordinated introduction of new telecommunications networks in the Community necessitate and facilitate cross-border flows of personal data;

(7) Whereas the difference in levels of protection of the rights and freedoms of individuals, notably the right to privacy, with regard to the processing of personal data afforded in the Member States may prevent the transmission of such data from the territory of one Member State to that of another Member State whereas this difference may therefore constitute an obstacle to the pursuit of a number of economic activities at Community level, distort competition and impede authorities in the discharge of their responsibilities under Community law whereas this difference in levels of protection is due to the existence of a wide variety of national laws, regulations and administrative provisions;

(8) Whereas, in order to remove the obstacles to flows of personal data, the level of protection of the rights and freedoms of individuals with regard to the processing of such data must be equivalent in all Member States whereas this objective is vital to the internal market but cannot be achieved by the Member States alone, especially in view of the scale of the divergences which currently exist between the relevant laws in the Member States and the need to coordinate the laws of the Member States so as to ensure that the cross-border flow of personal data is regulated in a consistent manner that is in keeping with the objective of the internal market as provided for in Article 7a of the Treaty whereas Community action to approximate those laws is therefore needed;

(9) Whereas, given the equivalent protection resulting from the approximation of national laws, the Member States will no longer be able to inhibit the free movement between them of personal data on grounds relating to protection of the rights and freedoms of individuals, and in particular the right to privacy whereas Member States will be left a margin for manoeuvre, which may, in the context of implementation of the Directive, also be exercised by the business and social partners whereas Member States will therefore be able to specify in their national law the general conditions governing the lawfulness of data processing whereas in doing so the

Member States shall strive to improve the protection currently provided by their legislation whereas, within the limits of this margin for manoeuvre and in accordance with Community law, disparities could arise in the implementation of the Directive, and this could have an effect on the movement of data within a Member State as well as within the Community;

(10) Whereas the object of the national laws on the processing of personal data is to protect fundamental rights and freedoms, notably the right to privacy, which is recognized both in Article 8 of the European Convention for the Protection of Human Rights and Fundamental Freedoms and in the general principles of Community law whereas, for that reason, the approximation of those laws must not result in any lessening of the protection they afford but must, on the contrary, seek to ensure a high level of protection in the Community;

(11) Whereas the principles of the protection of the rights and freedoms of individuals, notably the right to privacy, which are contained in this Directive, give substance to and amplify those contained in the Council of Europe Convention of 28 January 1981 for the Protection of Individuals with regard to Automatic Processing of Personal Data;

(12) Whereas the protection principles must apply to all processing of personal data by any person whose activities are governed by Community law whereas there should be excluded the processing of data carried out by a natural person in the exercise of activities which are exclusively personal or domestic, such as correspondence and the holding of records of addresses;

(13) Whereas the acitivities referred to in Titles V and VI of the Treaty on European Union regarding public safety, defence, State security or the acitivities of the State in the area of criminal laws fall outside the scope of Community law, without prejudice to the obligations incumbent upon Member States under Article 56 (2), Article 57 or Article 100a of the Treaty establishing the European Community whereas the processing of personal data that is necessary to safeguard the economic well-being of the State does not fall within the scope of this Directive where such processing relates to State security matters;

(14) Whereas, given the importance of the developments under way, in the framework of the information society, of the techniques used to capture, transmit, manipulate, record, store or communicate sound and image data relating to natural persons, this Directive should be applicable to processing involving such data;

(15) Whereas the processing of such data is covered by this Directive only if it is automated or if the data processed are contained or are intended to be contained in a filing system structured according to specific criteria relating to individuals, so as to permit easy access to the personal data in question;

(16) Whereas the processing of sound and image data, such as in cases of video surveillance, does not come within the scope of this Directive if it is carried out for the purposes of public security, defence, national security or in the course of State activities relating to the area of criminal law or of other activities which do not come within the scope of Community law;

(17) Whereas, as far as the processing of sound and image data carried out for purposes of journalism or the purposes of literary or artistic expression is concerned, in particular in the audiovisual field, the principles of the Directive are to apply in a restricted manner according to the provisions laid down in Article 9;

(18) Whereas, in order to ensure that individuals are not deprived of the protection to which they are entitled under this Directive, any processing of personal data in the Community must be carried out in accordance with the law of one of the Member States whereas, in this connection, processing carried out under the responsibility of a controller who is established in a Member State should be governed by the law of that State;

(19) Whereas establishment on the territory of a Member State implies the effective and real exercise of activity through stable arrangements whereas the legal form of such an establishment, whether simply branch or a subsidiary with a legal personality, is not the determining factor in this respect whereas, when a single controller is established on the territory of several Member States, particularly by means of subsidiaries, he must ensure, in order to avoid any circumvention of national rules, that each of the establishments fulfils the obligations imposed by the national law applicable to its activities;

(20) Whereas the fact that the processing of data is carried out by a person established in a third country must not stand in the way of the protection of individuals provided for in this Directive whereas in these cases, the processing should be governed by the law of the Member State in which the means used are located, and there should be guarantees to ensure that the rights and obligations provided for in this Directive are respected in practice;

(21) Whereas this Directive is without prejudice to the rules of territoriality applicable in criminal matters;

(22) Whereas Member States shall more precisely define in the laws they enact or when bringing into force the measures taken under this Directive the general circumstances in which processing is lawful whereas in particular Article 5, in conjunction with Articles 7 and 8, allows Member States, independently of general rules, to provide for special processing conditions for specific sectors and for the various categories of data covered by Article 8;

(23) Whereas Member States are empowered to ensure the implementation of the protection of individuals both by means of a general law on the protection of individuals as regards the processing of personal data and by sectorial laws such as those relating, for example, to statistical institutes;

(24) Whereas the legislation concerning the protection of legal persons with regard to the processing data which concerns them is not affected by this Directive;

(25) Whereas the principles of protection must be reflected, on the one hand, in the obligations imposed on persons, public authorities, enterprises, agencies or other bodies responsible for processing, in particular regarding data quality, technical security, notification to the supervisory authority, and the circumstances under which processing can be carried out, and, on the other hand, in the right conferred on individuals, the data on whom are the subject of processing, to be informed that processing is taking place, to consult the data, to request corrections and even to object to processing in certain circumstances;

(26) Whereas the principles of protection must apply to any information concerning an identified or identifiable person whereas, to determine whether a person is identifiable, account should be taken of all the means likely reasonably to be used either by the controller or by any other person to identify the said person whereas the principles of protection shall not apply to data rendered anonymous in such a way that the data subject is no longer identifiable whereas codes of conduct within the meaning of Article 27 may be a useful instrument for providing guidance as to the ways in which data may be rendered anonymous and retained in a form in which identification of the data subject is no longer possible;

(27) Whereas the protection of individuals must apply as much to automatic processing of data as to manual processing whereas the scope of this protection must not in effect depend on the techniques used, otherwise this would create a serious risk of circumvention whereas, nonetheless, as regards manual processing, this Directive covers only filing systems, not unstructured files whereas, in particular, the content of a filing system must be structured according to specific criteria relating to individuals allowing easy access to the personal data whereas, in line with the definition in Article 2(c), the different criteria for determining the constituents of a structured set of personal data, and the different criteria governing access to such a set, may be

laid down by each Member State whereas files or sets of files as well as their cover pages, which are not structured according to specific criteria, shall under no circumstances fall within the scope of this Directive;

(28) Whereas any processing of personal data must be lawful and fair to the individuals concerned whereas, in particular, the data must be adequate, relevant and not excessive in relation to the purposes for which they are processed whereas such purposes must be explicit and legitimate and must be determined at the time of collection of the data whereas the purposes of processing further to collection shall not be incompatible with the purposes as they were originally specified;

(29) Whereas the further processing of personal data for historical, statistical or scientific purposes is not generally to be considered incompatible with the purposes for which the data have previously been collected provided that Member States furnish suitable safeguards whereas these safeguards must in particular rule out the use of the data in support of measures or decisions regarding any particular individual;

(30) Whereas, in order to be lawful, the processing of personal data must in addition be carried out with the consent of the data subject or be necessary for the conclusion or performance of a contract binding on the data subject, or as a legal requirement, or for the performance of a task carried out in the public interest or in the exercise of official authority, or in the legitimate interests of a natural or legal person, provided that the interests or the rights and freedoms of the data subject are not overriding whereas, in particular, in order to maintain a balance between the interests involved while guaranteeing effective competition, Member States may determine the circumstances in which personal data may be used or disclosed to a third party in the context of the legitimate ordinary business activities of companies and other bodies whereas Member States may similarly specify the conditions under which personal data may be disclosed to a third party for the purposes of marketing whether carried out commercially or by a charitable organization or by any other association or foundation, of a political nature for example, subject to the provisions allowing a data subject to object to the processing of data regarding him, at no cost and without having to state his reasons;

(31) Whereas the processing of personal data must equally be regarded as lawful where it is carried out in order to protect an interest which is essential for the data subject's life;

(32) Whereas it is for national legislation to determine whether the controller performing a task carried out in the public interest or in the exercise of official authority should be a public administration or another natural or legal person governed by public law, or by private law such as a professional association;

(33) Whereas data which are capable by their nature of infringing fundamental freedoms or privacy should not be processed unless the data subject gives his explicit consent whereas, however, derogations from this prohibition must be explicitly provided for in respect of specific needs, in particular where the processing of these data is carried out for certain health-related purposes by persons subject to a legal obligation of professional secrecy or in the course of legitimate activities by certain associations or foundations the purpose of which is to permit the exercise of fundamental freedoms;

(34) Whereas Member States must also be authorized, when justified by grounds of important public interest, to derogate from the prohibition on processing sensitive categories of data where important reasons of public interest so justify in areas such as public health and social protection — especially in order to ensure the quality and cost-effectiveness of the procedures used for settling claims for benefits and services in the health insurance system— scientific research and government statistics whereas it is incumbent on them, however, to provide specific and suitable safeguards so as to protect the fundamental rights and the privacy of individuals;

(35) Whereas, moreover, the processing of personal data by official authorities for achieving aims, laid down in constitutional law or international public law, of officially recognized religious associations is carried out on important grounds of public interest;

(36) Whereas where, in the course of electoral activities, the operation of the democratic system requires in certain Member States that political parties compile data on people's political opinion, the processing of such data may be permitted for reasons of important public interest, provided that appropriate safeguards are established;

(37) Whereas the processing of personal data for purposes of journalism or for purposes of literary of artistic expression, in particular in the audiovisual field, should qualify for exemption from the requirements of certain provisions of this Directive in so far as this is necessary to reconcile the fundamental rights of individuals with freedom of information and notably the right to receive and impart information, as guaranteed in particular in Article 10 of the European Convention for the Protection of Human Rights and Fundamental Freedoms whereas Member States should therefore lay down exemptions and derogations necessary for the purpose of balance between fundamental rights as regards general measures on the legitimacy of data processing, measures on the transfer of data to third countries and the power of the supervisory authority whereas this should not, however, lead Member States to lay down exemptions from the measures to ensure security of processing whereas at least the supervisory authority responsible for this sector should also be provided with certain ex-post powers, e.g. to publish a regular report or to refer matters to the judicial authorities;

(38) Whereas, if the processing of data is to be fair, the data subject must be in a position to learn of the existence of a processing operation and, where data are collected from him, must be given accurate and full information, bearing in mind the circumstances of the collection;

(39) Whereas certain processing operations involve data which the controller has not collected directly from the data subject whereas, furthermore, data can be legitimately disclosed to a third party, even if the disclosure was not anticipated at the time the data were collected from the data subject whereas, in all these cases, the data subject should be informed when the data are recorded or at the latest when the data are first disclosed to a third party;

(40) Whereas, however, it is not necessary to impose this obligation of the data subject already has the information whereas, moreover, there will be no such obligation if the recording or disclosure are expressly provided for by law or if the provision of information to the data subject proves impossible or would involve disproportionate efforts, which could be the case where processing is for historical, statistical or scientific purposes whereas, in this regard, the number of data subjects, the age of the data, and any compensatory measures adopted may be taken into consideration;

(41) Whereas any person must be able to exercise the right of access to data relating to him which are being processed, in order to verify in particular the accuracy of the data and the lawfulness of the processing whereas, for the same reasons, every data subject must also have the right to know the logic involved in the automatic processing of data concerning him, at least in the case of the automated decisions referred to in Article 15(1); whereas this right must not adversely affect trade secrets or intellectual property and in particular the copyright protecting the software whereas these considerations must not, however, result in the data subject being refused all information;

(42) Whereas Member States may, in the interest of the data subject or so as to protect the rights and freedoms of others, restrict rights of access and information whereas they may, for example, specify that access to medical data may be obtained only through a health professional;

(43) Whereas restrictions on the rights of access and information and on certain obligations of the controller may similarly be imposed by Member States in so far as they are necessary

to safeguard, for example, national security, defence, public safety, or important economic or financial interests of a Member State or the Union, as well as criminal investigations and prosecutions and action in respect of breaches of ethics in the regulated professions whereas the list of exceptions and limitations should include the tasks of monitoring, inspection or regulation necessary in the three last-mentioned areas concerning public security, economic or financial interests and crime prevention whereas the listing of tasks in these three areas does not affect the legitimacy of exceptions or restrictions for reasons of State security or defence;

(44) Whereas Member States may also be led, by virtue of the provisions of Community law, to derogate from the provisions of this Directive concerning the right of access, the obligation to inform individuals, and the quality of data, in order to secure certain of the purposes referred to above;

(45) Whereas, in cases where data might lawfully be processed on grounds of public interest, official authority or the legitimate interests of a natural or legal person, any data subject should nevertheless be entitled, on legitimate and compelling grounds relating to his particular situation, to object to the processing of any data relating to himself whereas Member States may nevertheless lay down national provisions to the contrary;

(46) Whereas the protection of the rights and freedoms of data subjects with regard to the processing of personal data requires that appropriate technical and organizational measures be taken, both at the time of the design of the processing system and at the time of the processing itself, particularly in order to maintain security and thereby to prevent any unauthorized processing whereas it is incumbent on the Member States to ensure that controllers comply with these measures whereas these measures must ensure an appropriate level of security, taking into account the state of the art and the costs of their implementation in relation to the risks inherent in the processing and the nature of the data to be protected;

(47) Whereas where a message containing personal data is transmitted by means of a telecommunications or electronic mail service, the sole purpose of which is the transmission of such messages, the controller in respect of the personal data contained in the message will normally be considered to be the person from whom the message originates, rather than the person offering the transmission services whereas, nevertheless, those offering such services will normally be considered controllers in respect of the processing of the additional personal data necessary for the operation of the service;

(48) Whereas the procedures for notifying the supervisory authority are designed to ensure disclosure of the purposes and main features of any processing operation for the purpose of verification that the operation is in accordance with the national measures taken under this Directive;

(49) Whereas, in order to avoid unsuitable administrative formalities, exemptions from the obligation to notify and simplification of the notification required may be provided for by Member States in cases where processing is unlikely adversely to affect the rights and freedoms of data subjects, provided that it is in accordance with a measure taken by a Member State specifying its limits whereas exemption or simplification may similarly be provided for by Member States where a person appointed by the controller ensures that the processing carried out is not likely adversely to affect the rights and freedoms of data subjects whereas such a data protection official, whether or not an employee of the controller, must be in a position to exercise his functions in complete independence;

(50) Whereas exemption or simplification could be provided for in cases of processing operations whose sole purpose is the keeping of a register intended, according to national law, to provide information to the public and open to consultation by the public or by any person demonstrating a legitimate interest;

(51) Whereas, nevertheless, simplification or exemption from the obligation to notify shall not release the controller from any of the other obligations resulting from this Directive;

(52) Whereas, in this context, ex post facto verification by the competent authorities must in general be considered a sufficient measure;

(53) Whereas, however, certain processing operation are likely to pose specific risks to the rights and freedoms of data subjects by virtue of their nature, their scope or their purposes, such as that of excluding individuals from a right, benefit or a contract, or by virtue of the specific use of new technologies whereas it is for Member States, if they so wish, to specify such risks in their legislation;

(54) Whereas with regard to all the processing undertaken in society, the amount posing such specific risks should be very limited whereas Member States must provide that the supervisory authority, or the data protection official in cooperation with the authority, check such processing prior to it being carried out whereas following this prior check, the supervisory authority may, according to its national law, give an opinion or an authorization regarding the processing whereas such checking may equally take place in the course of the preparation either of a measure of the national parliament or of a measure based on such a legislative measure, which defines the nature of the processing and lays down appropriate safeguards;

(55) Whereas, if the controller fails to respect the rights of data subjects, national legislation must provide for a judicial remedy whereas any damage which a person may suffer as a result of unlawful processing must be compensated for by the controller, who may be exempted from liability if he proves that he is not responsible for the damage, in particular in cases where he establishes fault on the part of the data subject or in case of force majeure whereas sanctions must be imposed on any person, whether governed by private of public law, who fails to comply with the national measures taken under this Directive;

(56) Whereas cross-border flows of personal data are necessary to the expansion of international trade whereas the protection of individuals guaranteed in the Community by this Directive does not stand in the way of transfers of personal data to third countries which ensure an adequate level of protection whereas the adequacy of the level of protection afforded by a third country must be assessed in the light of all the circumstances surrounding the transfer operation or set of transfer operations;

(57) Whereas, on the other hand, the transfer of personal data to a third country which does not ensure an adequate level of protection must be prohibited;

(58) Whereas provisions should be made for exemptions from this prohibition in certain circumstances where the data subject has given his consent, where the transfer is necessary in relation to a contract or a legal claim, where protection of an important public interest so requires, for example in cases of international transfers of data between tax or customs administrations or between services competent for social security matters, or where the transfer is made from a register established by law and intended for consultation by the public or persons having a legitimate interest whereas in this case such a transfer should not involve the entirety of the data or entire categories of the data contained in the register and, when the register is intended for consultation by persons having a legitimate interest, the transfer should be made only at the request of those persons or if they are to be the recipients;

(59) Whereas particular measures may be taken to compensate for the lack of protection in a third country in cases where the controller offers appropriate safeguards whereas, moreover, provision must be made for procedures for negotiations between the Community and such third countries;

(60) Whereas, in any event, transfers to third countries may be effected only in full compliance with the provisions adopted by the Member States pursuant to this Directive, and in particular Article 8 thereof;

(61) Whereas Member States and the Commission, in their respective spheres of competence, must encourage the trade associations and other representative organizations concerned to draw up codes of conduct so as to facilitate the application of this Directive, taking account of the specific characteristics of the processing carried out in certain sectors, and respecting the national provisions adopted for its implementation;

(62) Whereas the establishment in Member States of supervisory authorities, exercising their functions with complete independence, is an essential component of the protection of individuals with regard to the processing of personal data;

(63) Whereas such authorities must have the necessary means to perform their duties, including powers of investigation and intervention, particularly in cases of complaints from individuals, and powers to engage in legal proceedings whereas such authorities must help to ensure transparency of processing in the Member States within whose jurisdiction they fall;

(64) Whereas the authorities in the different Member States will need to assist one another in performing their duties so as to ensure that the rules of protection are properly respected throughout the European Union;

(65) Whereas, at Community level, a Working Party on the Protection of Individuals with regard to the Processing of Personal Data must be set up and be completely independent in the performance of its functions whereas, having regard to its specific nature, it must advise the Commission and, in particular, contribute to the uniform application of the national rules adopted pursuant to this Directive;

(66) Whereas, with regard to the transfer of data to third countries, the application of this Directive calls for the conferment of powers of implementation on the Commission and the establishment of a procedure as laid down in Council Decision 87/373/EEC (1);

(67) Whereas an agreement on a modus vivendi between the European Parliament, the Council and the Commission concerning the implementing measures for acts adopted in accordance with the procedure laid down in Article 189b of the EC Treaty was reached on 20 December 1994;

(68) Whereas the principles set out in this Directive regarding the protection of the rights and freedoms of individuals, notably their right to privacy, with regard to the processing of personal data may be supplemented or clarified, in particular as far as certain sectors are concerned, by specific rules based on those principles;

(69) Whereas Member States should be allowed a period of not more than three years from the entry into force of the national measures transposing this Directive in which to apply such new national rules progressively to all processing operations already under way whereas, in order to facilitate their cost-effective implementation, a further period expiring 12 years after the date on which this Directive is adopted will be allowed to Member States to ensure the conformity of existing manual filing systems with certain of the Directive's provisions whereas, where data contained in such filing systems are manually processed during this extended transition period, those systems must be brought into conformity with these provisions at the time of such processing;

(70) Whereas it is not necessary for the data subject to give his consent again so as to allow the controller to continue to process, after the national provisions taken pursuant to

this Directive enter into force, any sensitive data necessary for the performance of a contract concluded on the basis of free and informed consent before the entry into force of these provisions;

(71) Whereas this Directive does not stand in the way of a Member State's regulating marketing activities aimed at consumers residing in territory in so far as such regulation does not concern the protection of individuals with regard to the processing of personal data;

(72) Whereas this Directive allows the principle of public access to official documents to be taken into account when implementing the principles set out in this Directive,

HAVE ADOPTED THIS DIRECTIVE:

CHAPTER I

GENERAL PROVISIONS

Article 1

Object of the Directive

1. In accordance with this Directive, Member States shall protect the fundamental rights and freedoms of natural persons, and in particular their right to privacy with respect to the processing of personal data.

2. Member States shall neither restrict nor prohibit the free flow of personal data between Member States for reasons connected with the protection afforded under paragraph 1.

Article 2

Definitions

For the purposes of this Directive:

(a) "personal data" shall mean any information relating to an identified or identifiable natural person ("data subject"); an identifiable person is one who can be identified, directly or indirectly, in particular by reference to an identification number or to one or more factors specific to his physical, physiological, mental, economic, cultural or social identity;

(b) "processing of personal data" ("processing") shall mean any operation or set of operations which is performed upon personal data, whether or not by automatic means, such as collection, recording, organization, storage, adaptation or alteration, retrieval, consultation, use, disclosure by transmission, dissemination or otherwise making available, alignment or combination, blocking, erasure or destruction;

(c) "personal data filing system" ("filing system") shall mean any structured set of personal data which are accessible according to specific criteria, whether centralized, decentralized or dispersed on a functional or geographical basis;

(d) "controller" shall mean the natural or legal person, public authority, agency or any other body which alone or jointly with others determines the purposes and means of the processing of personal data where the purposes and means of processing are determined by national or Community laws or regulations, the controller or the specific criteria for his nomination may be designated by national or Community law;

(e) "processor" shall mean a natural or legal person, public authority, agency or any other body which processes personal data on behalf of the controller;

(f) "third party" shall mean any natural or legal person, public authority, agency or any other body other than the data subject, the controller, the processor and the persons who, under the direct authority of the controller or the processor, are authorized to process the data;

(g) "recipient" shall mean a natural or legal person, public authority, agency or any other body to whom data are disclosed, whether a third party or not however, authorities which may receive data in the framework of a particular inquiry shall not be regarded as recipients;

(h) "the data subject's consent" shall mean any freely given specific and informed indication of his wishes by which the data subject signifies his agreement to personal data relating to him being processed.

Article 3

Scope

1. This Directive shall apply to the processing of personal data wholly or partly by automatic means, and to the processing otherwise than by automatic means of personal data which form part of a filing system or are intended to form part of a filing system.

2. This Directive shall not apply to the processing of personal data:

— in the course of an activity which falls outside the scope of Community law, such as those provided for by Titles V and VI of the Treaty on European Union and in any case to processing operations concerning public security, defence, State security (including the economic well-being of the State when the processing operation relates to State security matters) and the activities of the State in areas of criminal law,

— by a natural person in the course of a purely personal or household activity.

Article 4

National law applicable

1. Each Member State shall apply the national provisions it adopts pursuant to this Directive to the processing of personal data where:

(a) the processing is carried out in the context of the activities of an establishment of the controller on the territory of the Member State when the same controller is established on the territory of several Member States, he must take the necessary measures to ensure that each of these establishments complies with the obligations laid down by the national law applicable;

(b) the controller is not established on the Member State's territory, but in a place where its national law applies by virtue of international public law;

(c) the controller is not established on Community territory and, for purposes of processing personal data makes use of equipment, automated or otherwise, situated on the territory of the said Member State, unless such equipment is used only for purposes of transit through the territory of the Community.

2. In the circumstances referred to in paragraph 1 (c), the controller must designate a representative established in the territory of that Member State, without prejudice to legal actions which could be initiated against the controller himself.

CHAPTER II

GENERAL RULES ON THE LAWFULNESS OF THE PROCESSING OF PERSONAL DATA

Article 5

Member States shall, within the limits of the provisions of this Chapter, determine more precisely the conditions under which the processing of personal data is lawful.

SECTION I

PRINCIPLES RELATING TO DATA QUALITY

Article 6

1. Member States shall provide that personal data must be:

(a) processed fairly and lawfully;

(b) collected for specified, explicit and legitimate purposes and not further processed in a way incompatible with those purposes. Further processing of data for historical, statistical or scientific purposes shall not be considered as incompatible provided that Member States provide appropriate safeguards;

(c) adequate, relevant and not excessive in relation to the purposes for which they are collected and/or further processed;

(d) accurate and, where necessary, kept up to date every reasonable step must be taken to ensure that data which are inaccurate or incomplete, having regard to the purposes for which they were collected or for which they are further processed, are erased or rectified;

(e) kept in a form which permits identification of data subjects for no longer than is necessary for the purposes for which the data were collected or for which they are further processed. Member States shall lay down appropriate safeguards for personal data stored for longer periods for historical, statistical or scientific use.

2. It shall be for the controller to ensure that paragraph 1 is complied with.

Criteria for making data processing legitimate

Article 7

Member States shall provide that personal data may be processed only if:

 (a) the data subject has unambiguously given his consent; or

 (b) processing is necessary for the performance of a contract to which the data subject is party or in order to take steps at the request of the data subject prior to entering into a contract; or

 (c) processing is necessary for compliance with a legal obligation to which the controller is subject; or

 (d) processing is necessary in order to protect the vital interests of the data subject; or

 (e) processing is necessary for the performance of a task carried out in the public interest or in the exercise of official authority vested in the controller or in a third party to whom the data are disclosed; or

 (f) processing is necessary for the purposes of the legitimate interests pursued by the controller or by the third party or parties to whom the data are disclosed, except where such interests are overridden by the interests for fundamental rights and freedoms of the data subject which require protection under Article 1(1).

Section III

Special categories of processing

Article 8

The processing of special categories of data

1. Member States shall prohibit the processing of personal data revealing racial or ethnic origin, political opinions, religious or philosophical beliefs, trade-union membership, and the processing of data concerning health or sex life.

2. Paragraph 1 shall not apply where:

 (a) the data subject has given his explicit consent to the processing of those data, except where the laws of the Member State provide that the prohibition referred to in paragraph 1 may not be lifted by the data subject's giving his consent; or

 (b) processing is necessary for the purposes of carrying out the obligations and specific rights of the controller in the field of employment law in so far as it is authorized by national law providing for adequate safeguards; or

 (c) processing is necessary to protect the vital interests of the data subject or of another person where the data subject is physically or legally incapable of giving his consent; or

 (d) processing is carried out in the course of its legitimate activities with appropriate guarantees by a foundation, association or any other non-profit-seeking body with a political, philosophical, religious or trade-union aim and on condition that the processing relates solely to the members of the body or to persons who have regular contact with it in connection with its purposes and that the data are not disclosed to a third party without the consent of the data subjects; or

(e) the processing relates to data which are manifestly made public by the data subject or is necessary for the establishment, exercise or defence of legal claims.

3. Paragraph 1 shall not apply where processing of the data is required for the purposes of preventive medicine, medical diagnosis, the provision of care or treatment or the management of health-care services, and where those data are processed by a health professional subject under national law or rules established by national competent bodies to the obligation of professional secrecy or by another person also subject to an equivalent obligation of secrecy.

4. Subject to the provision of suitable safeguards, Member States may, for reasons of substantial public interest, lay down exemptions in addition to those laid down in paragraph 2 either by national law or by decision of the supervisory authority.

5. Processing of data relating to offences, criminal convictions or security measures may be carried out only under the control of official authority, or if suitable specific safeguards are provided under national law, subject to derogations which may be granted by the Member State under national provisions providing suitable specific safeguards. However, a complete register of criminal convictions may be kept only under the control of official authority.
Member States may provide that data relating to administrative sanctions or judgements in civil cases shall also be processed under the control of official authority.

6. Derogations from paragraph 1 provided for in paragraphs 4 and 5 shall be notified to the Commission.

7. Member States shall determine the conditions under which a national identification number or any other identifier of general application may be processed.

Article 9

Processing of personal data and freedom of expression

Member States shall provide for exemptions or derogations from the provisions of this Chapter, Chapter IV and Chapter VI for the processing of personal data carried out solely for journalistic purposes or the purpose of artistic or literary expression only if they are necessary to reconcile the right to privacy with the rules governing freedom of expression.

SECTION IV

INFORMATION TO BE GIVEN TO THE DATA SUBJECT

Article 10

Information in cases of collection of data from the data subject

Member States shall provide that the controller or his representative must provide a data subject from whom data relating to himself are collected with at least the following information, except where he already has it:

(a) the identity of the controller and of his representative, if any;

(b) the purposes of the processing for which the data are intended;

(c) any further information such as

— the recipients or categories of recipients of the data,

— whether replies to the questions are obligatory or voluntary, as well as the possible consequences of failure to reply,

— the existence of the right of access to and the right to rectify the data concerning him in so far as such further information is necessary, having regard to the specific circumstances in which the data are collected, to guarantee fair processing in respect of the data subject.

Article 11

Information where the data have not been obtained from the data subject

1. Where the data have not been obtained from the data subject, Member States shall provide that the controller or his representative must at the time of undertaking the recording of personal data or if a disclosure to a third party is envisaged, no later than the time when the data are first disclosed provide the data subject with at least the following information, except where he already has it:

(a) the identity of the controller and of his representative, if any;

(b) the purposes of the processing;

(c) any further information such as

— the categories of data concerned,

— the recipients or categories of recipients,

— the existence of the right of access to and the right to rectify the data concerning him in so far as such further information is necessary, having regard to the specific circumstances in which the data are processed, to guarantee fair processing in respect of the data subject.

2. Paragraph 1 shall not apply where, in particular for processing for statistical purposes or for the purposes of historical or scientific research, the provision of such information proves impossible or would involve a disproportionate effort or if recording or disclosure is expressly laid down by law. In these cases Member States shall provide appropriate safeguards.

Section V

The data subject's right of access to data

Article 12

Right of access

Member States shall guarantee every data subject the right to obtain from the controller:

(a) without constraint at reasonable intervals and without excessive delay or expense:

— confirmation as to whether or not data relating to him are being processed and information at least as to the purposes of the processing, the categories of data concerned, and the recipients or categories of recipients to whom the data are disclosed,

— communication to him in an intelligible form of the data undergoing processing and of any available information as to their source,

— knowledge of the logic involved in any automatic processing of data concerning him at least in the case of the automated decisions referred to in Article 15(1);

(b) as appropriate the rectification, erasure or blocking of data the processing of which does not comply with the provisions of this Directive, in particular because of the incomplete or inaccurate nature of the data;

(c) notification to third parties to whom the data have been disclosed of any rectification, erasure or blocking carried out in compliance with (b), unless this proves impossible or involves a disproportionate effort.

SECTION VI

EXEMPTIONS AND RESTRICTIONS

Article 13

Exemptions and restrictions

1. Member States may adopt legislative measures to restrict the scope of the obligations and rights provided for in Articles 6(1), 10, 11(1), 12 and 21 when such a restriction constitutes a necessary measures to safeguard:

(a) national security;

(b) defence;

(c) public security;

(d) the prevention, investigation, detection and prosecution of criminal offences, or of breaches of ethics for regulated professions;

(e) an important economic or financial interest of a Member State or of the European Union, including monetary, budgetary and taxation matters;

(f) a monitoring, inspection or regulatory function connected, even occasionally, with the exercise of official authority in cases referred to in (c), (d) and (e);

(g) the protection of the data subject or of the rights and freedoms of others.

2. Subject to adequate legal safeguards, in particular that the data are not used for taking measures or decisions regarding any particular individual, Member States may, where there is clearly no risk of breaching the privacy of the data subject, restrict by a legislative measure the rights provided for in Article 12 when data are processed solely for purposes of scientific research or are kept in personal form for a period which does not exceed the period necessary for the sole purpose of creating statistics.

Article 14

The data subject's right to object

Member States shall grant the data subject the right:

(a) at least in the cases referred to in Article 7(e) and (f), to object at any time on compelling legitimate grounds relating to his particular situation to the processing of data relating to him, save where otherwise provided by national legislation. Where there is a justified objection, the processing instigated by the controller may no longer involve those data;

(b) to object, on request and free of charge, to the processing of personal data relating to him which the controller anticipates being processed for the purposes of direct marketing, or to be informed before personal data are disclosed for the first time to third parties or used on their behalf for the purposes of direct marketing, and to be expressly offered the right to object free of charge to such disclosures or uses.

Member States shall take the necessary measures to ensure that data subjects are aware of the existence of the right referred to in the first subparagraph of (b).

Article 15

Automated individual decisions

1. Member States shall grant the right to every person not to be subject to a decision which produces legal effects concerning him or significantly affects him and which is based solely on automated processing of data intended to evaluate certain personal aspects relating to him, such as his performance at work, creditworthiness, reliability, conduct, etc.

2. Subject to the other Articles of this Directive, Member States shall provide that a person may be subjected to a decision of the kind referred to in paragraph 1 if that decision:

(a) is taken in the course of the entering into or performance of a contract, provided the request for the entering into or the performance of the contract, lodged by the data subject, has been satisfied or that there are suitable measures to safeguard his legitimate interests, such as arrangements allowing him to put his point of view; or

(b) is authorized by a law which also lays down measures to safeguard the data subject's legitimate interests.

Section VIII

Confidentiality and security of processing

Article 16

Confidentiality of processing

Any person acting under the authority of the controller or of the processor, including the processor himself, who has access to personal data must not process them except on instructions from the controller, unless he is required to do so by law.

Article 17

Security of processing

1. Member States shall provide that the controller must implement appropriate technical and organizational measures to protect personal data against accidental or unlawful destruction or accidental loss, alteration, unauthorized disclosure or access, in particular where the processing involves the transmission of data over a network, and against all other unlawful forms of processing.

Having regard to the state of the art and the cost of their implementation, such measures shall ensure a level of security appropriate to the risks represented by the processing and the nature of the data to be protected.

2. The Member States shall provide that the controller must, where processing is carried out on his behalf, choose a processor providing sufficient guarantees in respect of the technical security measures and organizational measures governing the processing to be carried out, and must ensure compliance with those measures.

3. The carrying out of processing by way of a processor must be governed by a contract or legal act binding the processor to the controller and stipulating in particular that:

— the processor shall act only on instructions from the controller,

— the obligations set out in paragraph 1, as defined by the law of the Member State in which the processor is established, shall also be incumbent on the processor.

4. For the purposes of keeping proof, the parts of the contract or the legal act relating to data protection and the requirements relating to the measures referred to in paragraph 1 shall be in writing or in another equivalent form.

SECTION IX

NOTIFICATION

Article 18

Obligation to notify the supervisory authority

1. Member States shall provide that the controller or his representative, if any, must notify the supervisory authority referred to in Article 28 before carrying out any wholly or partly automatic processing operation or set of such operations intended to serve a single purpose or several related purposes.

2. Member States may provide for the simplification of or exemption from notification only in the following cases and under the following conditions:

— where, for categories of processing operations which are unlikely, taking account of the data to be processed, to affect adversely the rights and freedoms of data subjects, they specify the purposes of the processing, the data or categories of data undergoing processing, the category or categories of data subject, the recipients or categories of recipient to whom the data are to be disclosed and the length of time the data are to be stored, and/or

— where the controller, in compliance with the national law which governs him, appoints a personal data protection official, responsible in particular:

> — for ensuring in an independent manner the internal application of the national provisions taken pursuant to this Directive
> — for keeping the register of processing operations carried out by the controller, containing the items of information referred to in Article 21(2),

thereby ensuring that the rights and freedoms of the data subjects are unlikely to be adversely affected by the processing operations.

3. Member States may provide that paragraph 1 does not apply to processing whose sole purpose is the keeping of a register which according to laws or regulations is intended to provide information to the public and which is open to consultation either by the public in general or by any person demonstrating a legitimate interest.

4. Member States may provide for an exemption from the obligation to notify or a simplification of the notification in the case of processing operations referred to in Article 8(2)(d).

5. Member States may stipulate that certain or all non-automatic processing operations involving personal data shall be notified, or provide for these processing operations to be subject to simplified notification.

Article 19

Contents of notification

1. Member States shall specify the information to be given in the notification. It shall include at least:

(a) the name and address of the controller and of his representative, if any;

(b) the purpose or purposes of the processing;

(c) a description of the category or categories of data subject and of the data or categories of data relating to them;

(d) the recipients or categories of recipient to whom the data might be disclosed;

(e) proposed transfers of data to third countries;

(f) a general description allowing a preliminary assessment to be made of the appropriateness of the measures taken pursuant to Article 17 to ensure security of processing.

2. Member States shall specify the procedures under which any change affecting the information referred to in paragraph 1 must be notified to the supervisory authority.

Article 20

Prior checking

1. Member States shall determine the processing operations likely to present specific risks to the rights and freedoms of data subjects and shall check that these processing operations are examined prior to the start thereof.

2. Such prior checks shall be carried out by the supervisory authority following receipt of a notification from the controller or by the data protection official, who, in cases of doubt, must consult the supervisory authority.

3. Member States may also carry out such checks in the context of preparation either of a measure of the national parliament or of a measure based on such a legislative measure, which define the nature of the processing and lay down appropriate safeguards.

Article 21

Publicizing of processing operations

1. Member States shall take measures to ensure that processing operations are publicized.

2. Member States shall provide that a register of processing operations notified in accordance with Article 18 shall be kept by the supervisory authority.

The register shall contain at least the information listed in Article 19(1)(a) to (e).
The register may be inspected by any person.

3. Member States shall provide, in relation to processing operations not subject to notification, that controllers or another body appointed by the Member States make available at least the information referred to in Article 19(1)(a) to (e) in an appropriate form to any person on request.

Member States may provide that this provision does not apply to processing whose sole purpose is the keeping of a register which according to laws or regulations is intended to provide information to the public and which is open to consultation either by the public in general or by any person who can provide proof of a legitimate interest.

CHAPTER III

JUDICIAL REMEDIES, LIABILITY AND SANCTIONS

Article 22

Remedies

Without prejudice to any administrative remedy for which provision may be made, inter alia before the supervisory authority referred to in Article 28, prior to referral to the judicial authority, Member States shall provide for the right of every person to a judicial remedy for any breach of the rights guaranteed him by the national law applicable to the processing in question.

Article 23

Liability

1. Member States shall provide that any person who has suffered damage as a result of an unlawful processing operation or of any act incompatible with the national provisions adopted

pursuant to this Directive is entitled to receive compensation from the controller for the damage suffered.

2. The controller may be exempted from this liability, in whole or in part, if he proves that he is not responsible for the event giving rise to the damage.

Article 24

Sanctions

The Member States shall adopt suitable measures to ensure the full implementation of the provisions of this Directive and shall in particular lay down the sanctions to be imposed in case of infringement of the provisions adopted pursuant to this Directive.

CHAPTER IV

TRANSFER OF PERSONAL DATA TO THIRD COUNTRIES

Article 25

Principles

1. The Member States shall provide that the transfer to a third country of personal data which are undergoing processing or are intended for processing after transfer may take place only if, without prejudice to compliance with the national provisions adopted pursuant to the other provisions of this Directive, the third country in question ensures an adequate level of protection.

2. The adequacy of the level of protection afforded by a third country shall be assessed in the light of all the circumstances surrounding a data transfer operation or set of data transfer operations particular consideration shall be given to the nature of the data, the purpose and duration of the proposed processing operation or operations, the country of origin and country of final destination, the rules of law, both general and sectoral, in force in the third country in question and the professional rules and security measures which are complied with in that country.

3. The Member States and the Commission shall inform each other of cases where they consider that a third country does not ensure an adequate level of protection within the meaning of paragraph 2.

4. Where the Commission finds, under the procedure provided for in Article 31(2), that a third country does not ensure an adequate level of protection within the meaning of paragraph 2 of this Article, Member States shall take the measures necessary to prevent any transfer of data of the same type to the third country in question.

5. At the appropriate time, the Commission shall enter into negotiations with a view to remedying the situation resulting from the finding made pursuant to paragraph 4.

6. The Commission may find, in accordance with the procedure referred to in Article 31(2), that a third country ensures an adequate level of protection within the meaning of paragraph 2 of this Article, by reason of its domestic law or of the international commitments it has entered into, particularly upon conclusion of the negotiations referred to in paragraph 5, for the protection of the private lives and basic freedoms and rights of individuals.

Member States shall take the measures necessary to comply with the Commission's decision.

Article 26

Derogations

1. By way of derogation from Article 25 and save where otherwise provided by domestic law governing particular cases, Member States shall provide that a transfer or a set of transfers of personal data to a third country which does not ensure an adequate level of protection within the meaning of Article 25(2) may take place on condition that:

(a) the data subject has given his consent unambiguously to the proposed transfer; or

(b) the transfer is necessary for the performance of a contract between the data subject and the controller or the implementation of precontractual measures taken in response to the data subject's request; or

(c) the transfer is necessary for the conclusion or performance of a contract concluded in the interest of the data subject between the controller and a third party; or

(d) the transfer is necessary or legally required on important public interest grounds, or for the establishment, exercise or defence of legal claims; or

(e) the transfer is necessary in order to protect the vital interests of the data subject or (f) the transfer is made from a register which according to laws or regulations is intended to provide information to the public and which is open to consultation either by the public in general or by any person who can demonstrate legitimate interest, to the extent that the conditions laid down in law for consultation are fulfilled in the particular case.

2. Without prejudice to paragraph 1, a Member State may authorize a transfer or a set of transfers of personal data to a third country which does not ensure an adequate level of protection within the meaning of Article 25(2), where the controller adduces adequate safeguards with respect to the protection of the privacy and fundamental rights and freedoms of individuals and as regards the exercise of the corresponding rights such safeguards may in particular result from appropriate contractual clauses.

3. The Member State shall inform the Commission and the other Member States of the authorizations it grants pursuant to paragraph 2.

If a Member State or the Commission objects on justified grounds involving the protection of the privacy and fundamental rights and freedoms of individuals, the Commission shall take appropriate measures in accordance with the procedure laid down in Article 31(2).

Member States shall take the necessary measures to comply with the Commission's decision.

4. Where the Commission decides, in accordance with the procedure referred to in Article 31(2), that certain standard contractual clauses offer sufficient safeguards as required by paragraph 2, Member States shall take the necessary measures to comply with the Commission's decision.

CHAPTER V

CODES OF CONDUCT

Article 27

1. The Member States and the Commission shall encourage the drawing up of codes of conduct intended to contribute to the proper implementation of the national provisions adopted by the Member States pursuant to this Directive, taking account of the specific features of the various sectors.

2. Member States shall make provision for trade associations and other bodies representing other categories of controllers which have drawn up draft national codes or which have the intention of amending or extending existing national codes to be able to submit them to the opinion of the national authority.

Member States shall make provision for this authority to ascertain, among other things, whether the drafts submitted to it are in accordance with the national provisions adopted pursuant to this Directive. If it sees fit, the authority shall seek the views of data subjects or their representatives.

3. Draft Community codes, and amendments or extensions to existing Community codes, may be submitted to the Working Party referred to in Article 29. This Working Party shall determine, among other things, whether the drafts submitted to it are in accordance with the national provisions adopted pursuant to this Directive. If it sees fit, the authority shall seek the views of data subjects or their representatives. The Commission may ensure appropriate publicity for the codes which have been approved by the Working Party.

CHAPTER VI

SUPERVISORY AUTHORITY AND WORKING PARTY ON THE PROTECTION OF INDIVIDUALS WITH REGARD TO THE PROCESSING OF PERSONAL DATA

Article 28

Supervisory authority

1. Each Member State shall provide that one or more public authorities are responsible for monitoring the application within its territory of the provisions adopted by the Member States pursuant to this Directive.

These authorities shall act with complete independence in exercising the functions entrusted to them.

2. Each Member State shall provide that the supervisory authorities are consulted when drawing up administrative measures or regulations relating to the protection of individuals' rights and freedoms with regard to the processing of personal data.

3. Each authority shall in particular be endowed with:

— investigative powers, such as powers of access to data forming the subject-matter of processing operations and powers to collect all the information necessary for the performance of its supervisory duties,

— effective powers of intervention, such as, for example, that of delivering opinions before processing operations are carried out, in accordance with Article 20, and ensuring appropriate publication of such opinions, of ordering the blocking, erasure or destruction of data, of imposing a temporary or definitive ban on processing, of warning or admonishing the controller, or that of referring the matter to national parliaments or other political institutions,

— the power to engage in legal proceedings where the national provisions adopted pursuant to this Directive have been violated or to bring these violations to the attention of the judicial authorities.

Decisions by the supervisory authority which give rise to complaints may be appealed against through the courts.

4. Each supervisory authority shall hear claims lodged by any person, or by an association representing that person, concerning the protection of his rights and freedoms in regard to the processing of personal data. The person concerned shall be informed of the outcome of the claim.

Each supervisory authority shall, in particular, hear claims for checks on the lawfulness of data processing lodged by any person when the national provisions adopted pursuant to Article 13 of this Directive apply. The person shall at any rate be informed that a check has taken place.

5. Each supervisory authority shall draw up a report on its activities at regular intervals. The report shall be made public.

6. Each supervisory authority is competent, whatever the national law applicable to the processing in question, to exercise, on the territory of its own Member State, the powers conferred on it in accordance with paragraph 3. Each authority may be requested to exercise its powers by an authority of another Member State.

The supervisory authorities shall cooperate with one another to the extent necessary for the performance of their duties, in particular by exchanging all useful information.

7. Member States shall provide that the members and staff of the supervisory authority, even after their employment has ended, are to be subject to a duty of professional secrecy with regard to confidential information to which they have access.

Article 29

Working Party on the Protection of Individuals with regard to the Processing of Personal Data

1. A Working Party on the Protection of Individuals with regard to the Processing of Personal Data, hereinafter referred to as "the Working Party", is hereby set up.

It shall have advisory status and act independently.

2. The Working Party shall be composed of a representative of the supervisory authority or authorities designated by each Member State and of a representative of the authority or authorities established for the Community institutions and bodies, and of a representative of the Commission.

Each member of the Working Party shall be designated by the institution, authority or authorities which he represents. Where a Member State has designated more than one supervisory authority, they shall nominate a joint representative. The same shall apply to the authorities established for Community institutions and bodies.

3. The Working Party shall take decisions by a simple majority of the representatives of the supervisory authorities.

4. The Working Party shall elect its chairman. The chairman's term of office shall be two years. His appointment shall be renewable.

5. The Working Party's secretariat shall be provided by the Commission.

6. The Working Party shall adopt its own rules of procedure.

7. The Working Party shall consider items placed on its agenda by its chairman, either on his own initiative or at the request of a representative of the supervisory authorities or at the Commission's request.

Article 30

1. The Working Party shall:

  (a) examine any question covering the application of the national measures adopted under this Directive in order to contribute to the uniform application of such measures;

  (b) give the Commission an opinion on the level of protection in the Community and in third countries;

  (c) advise the Commission on any proposed amendment of this Directive, on any additional or specific measures to safeguard the rights and freedoms of natural persons with regard to the processing of personal data and on any other proposed Community measures affecting such rights and freedoms;

  (d) give an opinion on codes of conduct drawn up at Community level.

2. If the Working Party finds that divergences likely to affect the equivalence of protection for persons with regard to the processing of personal data in the Community are arising between the laws or practices of Member States, it shall inform the Commission accordingly.

3. The Working Party may, on its own initiative, make recommendations on all matters relating to the protection of persons with regard to the processing of personal data in the Community.

4. The Working Party's opinions and recommendations shall be forwarded to the Commission and to the committee referred to in Article 31.

5. The Commission shall inform the Working Party of the action it has taken in response to its opinions and recommendations. It shall do so in a report which shall also be forwarded to the European Parliament and the Council. The report shall be made public.

6. The Working Party shall draw up an annual report on the situation regarding the protection of natural persons with regard to the processing of personal data in the Community and in third countries, which it shall transmit to the Commission, the European Parliament and the Council. The report shall be made public.

CHAPTER VII

COMMUNITY IMPLEMENTING MEASURES

Article 31

The Committee

1. The Commission shall be assisted by a committee composed of the representatives of the Member States and chaired by the representative of the Commission.

2. The representative of the Commission shall submit to the committee a draft of the measures to be taken. The committee shall deliver its opinion on the draft within a time limit which the chairman may lay down according to the urgency of the matter.

The opinion shall be delivered by the majority laid down in Article 148(2) of the Treaty. The votes of the representatives of the Member States within the committee shall be weighted in the manner set out in that Article. The chairman shall not vote.

The Commission shall adopt measures which shall apply immediately. However, if these measures are not in accordance with the opinion of the committee, they shall be communicated by the Commission to the Council forthwith. It that event:

— the Commission shall defer application of the measures which it has decided for a period of three months from the date of communication,

— the Council, acting by a qualified majority, may take a different decision within the time limit referred to in the first indent.

FINAL PROVISIONS

Article 32

1. Member States shall bring into force the laws, regulations and administrative provisions necessary to comply with this Directive at the latest at the end of a period of three years from the date of its adoption.

When Member States adopt these measures, they shall contain a reference to this Directive or be accompanied by such reference on the occasion of their official publication. The methods of making such reference shall be laid down by the Member States.

2. Member States shall ensure that processing already under way on the date the national provisions adopted pursuant to this Directive enter into force, is brought into conformity with these provisions within three years of this date.

By way of derogation from the preceding subparagraph, Member States may provide that the processing of data already held in manual filing systems on the date of entry into force of the national provisions adopted in implementation of this Directive shall be brought into conformity with Articles 6, 7 and 8 of this Directive within 12 years of the date on which it is adopted. Member States shall, however, grant the data subject the right to obtain, at his request and in particular at the time of exercising his right of access, the rectification, erasure or blocking of data which are incomplete, inaccurate or stored in a way incompatible with the legitimate purposes pursued by the controller.

3. By way of derogation from paragraph 2, Member States may provide, subject to suitable safeguards, that data kept for the sole purpose of historical research need not be brought into conformity with Articles 6, 7 and 8 of this Directive.

4. Member States shall communicate to the Commission the text of the provisions of domestic law which they adopt in the field covered by this Directive.

Article 33

The Commission shall report to the Council and the European Parliament at regular intervals, starting not later than three years after the date referred to in Article 32(1), on the implementation of this Directive, attaching to its report, if necessary, suitable proposals for amendments. The report shall be made public.

The Commission shall examine, in particular, the application of this Directive to the data processing of sound and image data relating to natural persons and shall submit any appropriate proposals which prove to be necessary, taking account of developments in information technology and in the light of the state of progress in the information society.

Article 34

This Directive is addressed to the Member States.

Done at Luxembourg, 24 October 1995.
For the European Parliament
The President
K. HAENSCH

For the Council
The President
L. ATIENZA SERNA

APPENDIX D

Privacy and Electronic Communications (EC Directive) Regulations

(2003/2426)

Made: 18 September 2003

Laid before Parliament: 18 September 2003

Coming into force: 11 December 2003

The Secretary of State, being a Minister designated[1] for the purposes of section 2(2) of the European Communities Act 1972 in respect of matters relating to electronic communications, in exercise of the powers conferred upon her by that section, hereby makes the following Regulations:

1. *Citation and commencement*

These Regulations may be cited as the Privacy and Electronic Communications (EC Directive) Regulations 2003 and shall come into force on 11th December 2003.

2. *Interpretation*

(1) In these Regulations—

"bill" includes an invoice, account, statement or other document of similar character and "billing" shall be construed accordingly;

"call" means a connection established by means of a telephone service available to the public allowing two-way communication in real time;

"communication" means any information exchanged or conveyed between a finite number of parties by means of a public electronic communications service, but does not include information conveyed as part of a programme service, except to the extent that such information can be related to the identifiable subscriber or user receiving the information;

"communications provider" has the meaning given by section 405 of the Communications Act 2003[2];

"corporate subscriber" means a subscriber who is—

---

[1] S.I. 2001/3495.

[2] For the commencement of section 405, see section 411(2) and (3) of the same Act.

(a) a company within the meaning of section 735(1) of the Companies Act 1985;

(b) a company incorporated in pursuance of a royal charter or letters patent;

(c) a partnership in Scotland;

(d) a corporation sole; or

(e) any other body corporate or entity which is a legal person distinct from its members;

"the Directive" means Directive 2002/58/EC of the European Parliament and of the Council of 12 July 2002 concerning the processing of personal data and the protection of privacy in the electronic communications sector (Directive on privacy and electronic communications);

"electronic communications network" has the meaning given by section 32 of the Communications Act 2003[3];

"electronic communications service" has the meaning given by section 32 of the Communications Act 2003;

"electronic mail" means any text, voice, sound or image message sent over a public electronic communications network which can be stored in the network or in the recipient's terminal equipment until it is collected by the recipient and includes messages sent using a short message service;

"enactment" includes an enactment comprised in, or in an instrument made under, an Act of the Scottish Parliament;

"individual" means a living individual and includes an unincorporated body of such individuals;

"the Information Commissioner" and "the Commissioner" both mean the Commissioner appointed under section 6 of the Data Protection Act 1998[4];

"information society service" has the meaning given in regulation 2(1) of the Electronic Commerce (EC Directive) Regulations 2002;

"location data" means any data processed in an electronic communications network indicating the geographical position of the terminal equipment of a user of a public electronic communications service, including data relating to—

(f) the latitude, longitude or altitude of the terminal equipment;

(g) the direction of travel of the user; or

(h) the time the location information was recorded;

"OFCOM" means the Office of Communications as established by section 1 of the Office of Communications Act 2002;

"programme service" has the meaning given in section 201 of the Broadcasting Act 1990[5];

"public communications provider" means a provider of a public electronic communications network or a public electronic communications service;

"public electronic communications network" has the meaning given in section 151 of the Communications Act 2003[6];

"public electronic communications service" has the meaning given in section 151 of the Communications Act 2003;

---

[3] For the commencement of section 32, see article 2(1) of S.I. 2003/1900 (C. 77).

[4] Section 6 was amended by section 18(4) of and paragraph 13(1) and (2) of Part 1 of Schedule 2 to the Freedom of Information Act 2000 (c. 36).

[5] Section 201 was amended by section 148(1) of and paragraph 11 of Schedule 10 to the Broadcasting Act 1996 (c. 55).

[6] For the commencement of section 151, see article 2(1) of S.I. 2003/1900 (C. 77).

"subscriber" means a person who is a party to a contract with a provider of public electronic communications services for the supply of such services;

"traffic data" means any data processed for the purpose of the conveyance of a communication on an electronic communications network or for the billing in respect of that communication and includes data relating to the routing, duration or time of a communication;

"user" means any individual using a public electronic communications service; and

"value added service" means any service which requires the processing of traffic data or location data beyond that which is necessary for the transmission of a communication or the billing in respect of that communication.

(2) Expressions used in these Regulations that are not defined in paragraph (1) and are defined in the Data Protection Act 1998 shall have the same meaning as in that Act.

(3) Expressions used in these Regulations that are not defined in paragraph (1) or the Data Protection Act 1998 and are defined in the Directive shall have the same meaning as in the Directive.

(4) Any reference in these Regulations to a line shall, without prejudice to paragraph (3), be construed as including a reference to anything that performs the function of a line, and "connected", in relation to a line, is to be construed accordingly.

3. *Revocation of the Telecommunications (Data Protection and Privacy) Regulations 1999*

The Telecommunications (Data Protection and Privacy) Regulations 1999 and the Telecommunications (Data Protection and Privacy) (Amendment) Regulations 2000 are hereby revoked.

4. *Relationship between these Regulations and the Data Protection Act 1998*

Nothing in these Regulations shall relieve a person of his obligations under the Data Protection Act 1998 in relation to the processing of personal data.

5. *Security of public electronic communications services*

(1) Subject to paragraph (2), a provider of a public electronic communications service ("the service provider") shall take appropriate technical and organisational measures to safeguard the security of that service.

(2) If necessary, the measures required by paragraph (1) may be taken by the service provider in conjunction with the provider of the electronic communications network by means of which the service is provided, and that network provider shall comply with any reasonable requests made by the service provider for these purposes.

(3) Where, notwithstanding the taking of measures as required by paragraph (1), there remains a significant risk to the security of the public electronic communications service, the service provider shall inform the subscribers concerned of—

(a) the nature of that risk;

(b) any appropriate measures that the subscriber may take to safeguard against that risk; and

(c) the likely costs to the subscriber involved in the taking of such measures.

(4) For the purposes of paragraph (1), a measure shall only be taken to be appropriate if, having regard to—

(a) the state of technological developments, and

(b) the cost of implementing it,

it is proportionate to the risks against which it would safeguard.

(5) Information provided for the purposes of paragraph (3) shall be provided to the subscriber free of any charge other than the cost to the subscriber of receiving or collecting the information.

6. *Confidentiality of communications*

(1) Subject to paragraph (4), a person shall not use an electronic communications network to store information, or to gain access to information stored, in the terminal equipment of a subscriber or user unless the requirements of paragraph (2) are met.

(2) The requirements are that the subscriber or user of that terminal equipment—

(a) is provided with clear and comprehensive information about the purposes of the storage of, or access to, that information; and

(b) is given the opportunity to refuse the storage of or access to that information.

(3) Where an electronic communications network is used by the same person to store or access information in the terminal equipment of a subscriber or user on more than one occasion, it is sufficient for the purposes of this regulation that the requirements of paragraph (2) are met in respect of the initial use.

(4) Paragraph (1) shall not apply to the technical storage of, or access to, information—

(a) for the sole purpose of carrying out or facilitating the transmission of a communication over an electronic communications network; or

(b) where such storage or access is strictly necessary for the provision of an information society service requested by the subscriber or user.

7. *Restrictions on the processing of certain traffic data*

(1) Subject to paragraphs (2) and (3), traffic data relating to subscribers or users which are processed and stored by a public communications provider shall, when no longer required for the purpose of the transmission of a communication, be—

(a) erased;

(b) in the case of an individual, modified so that they cease to constitute personal data of that subscriber or user; or

(c) in the case of a corporate subscriber, modified so that they cease to be data that would be personal data if that subscriber was an individual.

(2) Traffic data held by a public communications provider for purposes connected with the payment of charges by a subscriber or in respect of interconnection payments may be processed and stored by that provider until the time specified in paragraph (5).

(3) Traffic data relating to a subscriber or user may be processed and stored by a provider of a public electronic communications service if—

(a) such processing and storage are for the purpose of marketing electronic communications services, or for the provision of value added services to that subscriber or user; and

(b) the subscriber or user to whom the traffic data relate has given his consent to such processing or storage; and

(c) such processing and storage are undertaken only for the duration necessary for the purposes specified in subparagraph (a).

(4) Where a user or subscriber has given his consent in accordance with paragraph (3), he shall be able to withdraw it at any time.

(5) The time referred to in paragraph (2) is the end of the period during which legal proceedings may be brought in respect of payments due or alleged to be due or, where such proceedings are brought within that period, the time when those proceedings are finally determined.

(6) Legal proceedings shall not be taken to be finally determined—

(a) until the conclusion of the ordinary period during which an appeal may be brought by either party (excluding any possibility of an extension of that period, whether by order of a court or otherwise), if no appeal is brought within that period; or

(b) if an appeal is brought, until the conclusion of that appeal.

(7) References in paragraph (6) to an appeal include references to an application for permission to appeal.

8. *Further provisions relating to the processing of traffic data under regulation 7*

(1) Processing of traffic data in accordance with regulation 7(2) or (3) shall not be undertaken by a public communications provider unless the subscriber or user to whom the data relate has been provided with information regarding the types of traffic data which are to be processed and the duration of such processing and, in the case of processing in accordance with regulation 7(3), he has been provided with that information before his consent has been obtained.

(2) Processing of traffic data in accordance with regulation 7 shall be restricted to what is required for the purposes of one or more of the activities listed in paragraph (3) and shall be carried out only by the public communications provider or by a person acting under his authority.

(3) The activities referred to in paragraph (2) are activities relating to—

(a) the management of billing or traffic;

(b) customer enquiries;

(c) the prevention or detection of fraud;

(d) the marketing of electronic communications services; or

(e) the provision of a value added service.

(4) Nothing in these Regulations shall prevent the furnishing of traffic data to a person who is a competent authority for the purposes of any provision relating to the settling of disputes (by way of legal proceedings or otherwise) which is contained in, or made by virtue of, any enactment.

9. *Itemised billing and privacy*

(1) At the request of a subscriber, a provider of a public electronic communications service shall provide that subscriber with bills that are not itemised.

(2) OFCOM shall have a duty, when exercising their functions under Chapter 1 of Part 2 of the Communications Act 2003, to have regard to the need to reconcile the rights of subscribers

receiving itemised bills with the rights to privacy of calling users and called subscribers, including the need for sufficient alternative privacy-enhancing methods of communications or payments to be available to such users and subscribers.

10. *Prevention of calling line identification—outgoing calls*

(1) This regulation applies, subject to regulations 15 and 16, to outgoing calls where a facility enabling the presentation of calling line identification is available.

(2) The provider of a public electronic communications service shall provide users originating a call by means of that service with a simple means to prevent presentation of the identity of the calling line on the connected line as respects that call.

(3) The provider of a public electronic communications service shall provide subscribers to the service, as respects their line and all calls originating from that line, with a simple means of preventing presentation of the identity of that subscriber's line on any connected line.

(4) The measures to be provided under paragraphs (2) and (3) shall be provided free of charge.

11. *Prevention of calling or connected line identification—incoming calls*

(1) This regulation applies to incoming calls.

(2) Where a facility enabling the presentation of calling line identification is available, the provider of a public electronic communications service shall provide the called subscriber with a simple means to prevent, free of charge for reasonable use of the facility, presentation of the identity of the calling line on the connected line.

(3) Where a facility enabling the presentation of calling line identification prior to the call being established is available, the provider of a public electronic communications service shall provide the called subscriber with a simple means of rejecting incoming calls where the presentation of the calling line identification has been prevented by the calling user or subscriber.

(4) Where a facility enabling the presentation of connected line identification is available, the provider of a public electronic communications service shall provide the called subscriber with a simple means to prevent, without charge, presentation of the identity of the connected line on any calling line.

(5) In this regulation "called subscriber" means the subscriber receiving a call by means of the service in question whose line is the called line (whether or not it is also the connected line).

12. *Publication of information for the purposes of regulations 10 and 11*

Where a provider of a public electronic communications service provides facilities for calling or connected line identification, he shall provide information to the public regarding the availability of such facilities, including information regarding the options to be made available for the purposes of regulations 10 and 11.

13. *Co-operation of communications providers for the purposes of regulations 10 and 11*

For the purposes of regulations 10 and 11, a communications provider shall comply with any reasonable requests made by the provider of the public electronic communications service by means of which facilities for calling or connected line identification are provided.

14. *Restrictions on the processing of location data*

(1) This regulation shall not apply to the processing of traffic data.

(2) Location data relating to a user or subscriber of a public electronic communications network or a public electronic communications service may only be processed—

    (a) where that user or subscriber cannot be identified from such data; or

    (b) where necessary for the provision of a value added service, with the consent of that user or subscriber.

(3) Prior to obtaining the consent of the user or subscriber under paragraph (2)(b), the public communications provider in question must provide the following information to the user or subscriber to whom the data relate—

    (a) the types of location data that will be processed;

    (b) the purposes and duration of the processing of those data; and

    (c) whether the data will be transmitted to a third party for the purpose of providing the value added service.

(4) A user or subscriber who has given his consent to the processing of data under paragraph (2)(b) shall—

    (a) be able to withdraw such consent at any time, and

    (b) in respect of each connection to the public electronic communications network in question or each transmission of a communication, be given the opportunity to withdraw such consent, using a simple means and free of charge.

(5) Processing of location data in accordance with this regulation shall—

    (a) only be carried out by—

        (i) the public communications provider in question;
        (ii) the third party providing the value added service in question; or
        (iii) a person acting under the authority of a person falling within (i) or (ii); and

    (b) where the processing is carried out for the purposes of the provision of a value added service, be restricted to what is necessary for those purposes.

15. *Tracing of malicious or nuisance calls*

(1) A communications provider may override anything done to prevent the presentation of the identity of a calling line where—

    (a) a subscriber has requested the tracing of malicious or nuisance calls received on his line; and

    (b) the provider is satisfied that such action is necessary and expedient for the purposes of tracing such calls.

(2) Any term of a contract for the provision of public electronic communications services which relates to such prevention shall have effect subject to the provisions of paragraph (1).

(3) Nothing in these Regulations shall prevent a communications provider, for the purposes of any action relating to the tracing of malicious or nuisance calls, from storing and making available to a person with a legitimate interest data containing the identity of a calling subscriber which were obtained while paragraph (1) applied.

16. *Emergency calls*

(1) For the purposes of this regulation, "emergency calls" means calls to either the national emergency call number 999 or the single European emergency call number 112.

(2) In order to facilitate responses to emergency calls—

    (a) all such calls shall be excluded from the requirements of regulation 10;

    (b) no person shall be entitled to prevent the presentation on the connected line of the identity of the calling line; and

    (c) the restriction on the processing of location data under regulation 14(2) shall be disregarded.

17. *Termination of automatic call forwarding*

(1) Where—

    (a) calls originally directed to another line are being automatically forwarded to a subscriber's line as a result of action taken by a third party, and

    (b) the subscriber requests his provider of electronic communications services ("the subscriber's provider") to stop the forwarding of those calls,

the subscriber's provider shall ensure, free of charge, that the forwarding is stopped without any avoidable delay.

(2) For the purposes of paragraph (1), every other communications provider shall comply with any reasonable requests made by the subscriber's provider to assist in the prevention of that forwarding.

18. *Directories of subscribers*

(1) This regulation applies in relation to a directory of subscribers, whether in printed or electronic form, which is made available to members of the public or a section of the public, including by means of a directory enquiry service.

(2) The personal data of an individual subscriber shall not be included in a directory unless that subscriber has, free of charge, been—

    (a) informed by the collector of the personal data of the purposes of the directory in which his personal data are to be included, and

    (b) given the opportunity to determine whether such of his personal data as are considered relevant by the producer of the directory should be included in the directory.

(3) Where personal data of an individual subscriber are to be included in a directory with facilities which enable users of that directory to obtain access to that data solely on the basis of a telephone number—

    (a) the information to be provided under paragraph (2)(a) shall include information about those facilities; and

    (b) for the purposes of paragraph (2)(b), the express consent of the subscriber to the inclusion of his data in a directory with such facilities must be obtained.

(4) Data relating to a corporate subscriber shall not be included in a directory where that subscriber has advised the producer of the directory that it does not want its data to be included in that directory.

(5) Where the data of an individual subscriber have been included in a directory, that subscriber shall, without charge, be able to verify, correct or withdraw those data at any time.

(6) Where a request has been made under paragraph (5) for data to be withdrawn from or corrected in a directory, that request shall be treated as having no application in relation to an edition of a directory that was produced before the producer of the directory received the request.

(7) For the purposes of paragraph (6), an edition of a directory which is revised after it was first produced shall be treated as a new edition.

(8) In this regulation, "telephone number" has the same meaning as in section 56(5) of the Communications Act 2003[7] but does not include any number which is used as an internet domain name, an internet address or an address or identifier incorporating either an internet domain name or an internet address, including an electronic mail address.

19. *Use of automated calling systems*

(1) A person shall neither transmit, nor instigate the transmission of, communications comprising recorded matter for direct marketing purposes by means of an automated calling system except in the circumstances referred to in paragraph (2).

(2) Those circumstances are where the called line is that of a subscriber who has previously notified the caller that for the time being he consents to such communications being sent by, or at the instigation of, the caller on that line.

(3) A subscriber shall not permit his line to be used in contravention of paragraph (1).

(4) For the purposes of this regulation, an automated calling system is a system which is capable of—

(a) automatically initiating a sequence of calls to more than one destination in accordance with instructions stored in that system; and

(b) transmitting sounds which are not live speech for reception by persons at some or all of the destinations so called.

20. *Use of facsimile machines for direct marketing purposes*

(1) A person shall neither transmit, nor instigate the transmission of, unsolicited communications for direct marketing purposes by means of a facsimile machine where the called line is that of—

(a) an individual subscriber, except in the circumstances referred to in paragraph (2);

(b) a corporate subscriber who has previously notified the caller that such communications should not be sent on that line; or

(c) a subscriber and the number allocated to that line is listed in the register kept under regulation 25.

(2) The circumstances referred to in paragraph (1)(a) are that the individual subscriber has previously notified the caller that he consents for the time being to such communications being sent by, or at the instigation of, the caller.

(3) A subscriber shall not permit his line to be used in contravention of paragraph (1).

---

[7] For the commencement of section 56(5), see article 2(1) of S.I. 2003/1900 (C. 77).

(4) A person shall not be held to have contravened paragraph (1)(c) where the number allocated to the called line has been listed on the register for less than 28 days preceding that on which the communication is made.

(5) Where a subscriber who has caused a number allocated to a line of his to be listed in the register kept under regulation 25 has notified a caller that he does not, for the time being, object to such communications being sent on that line by that caller, such communications may be sent by that caller on that line, notwithstanding that the number allocated to that line is listed in the said register.

(6) Where a subscriber has given a caller notification pursuant to paragraph (5) in relation to a line of his—

    (a) the subscriber shall be free to withdraw that notification at any time, and

    (b) where such notification is withdrawn, the caller shall not send such communications on that line.

(7) The provisions of this regulation are without prejudice to the provisions of regulation 19.

21. Unsolicited calls for direct marketing purposes

(1) A person shall neither use, nor instigate the use of, a public electronic communications service for the purposes of making unsolicited calls for direct marketing purposes where—

    (a) the called line is that of a subscriber who has previously notified the caller that such calls should not for the time being be made on that line; or

    (b) the number allocated to a subscriber in respect of the called line is one listed in the register kept under regulation 26.

(2) A subscriber shall not permit his line to be used in contravention of paragraph (1).

(3) A person shall not be held to have contravened paragraph (1)(b) where the number allocated to the called line has been listed on the register for less than 28 days preceding that on which the call is made.

(4) Where a subscriber who has caused a number allocated to a line of his to be listed in the register kept under regulation 26 has notified a caller that he does not, for the time being, object to such calls being made on that line by that caller, such calls may be made by that caller on that line, notwithstanding that the number allocated to that line is listed in the said register.

(5) Where a subscriber has given a caller notification pursuant to paragraph (4) in relation to a line of his—

    (a) the subscriber shall be free to withdraw that notification at any time, and

    (b) where such notification is withdrawn, the caller shall not make such calls on that line.

22. Use of electronic mail for direct marketing purposes

(1) This regulation applies to the transmission of unsolicited communications by means of electronic mail to individual subscribers.

(2) Except in the circumstances referred to in paragraph (3), a person shall neither transmit, nor instigate the transmission of, unsolicited communications for the purposes of direct marketing by means of electronic mail unless the recipient of the electronic mail has previously notified the sender that he consents for the time being to such communications being sent by, or at the instigation of, the sender.

(3) A person may send or instigate the sending of electronic mail for the purposes of direct marketing where—

    (a) that person has obtained the contact details of the recipient of that electronic mail in the course of the sale or negotiations for the sale of a product or service to that recipient;

    (b) the direct marketing is in respect of that person's similar products and services only; and

    (c) the recipient has been given a simple means of refusing (free of charge except for the costs of the transmission of the refusal) the use of his contact details for the purposes of such direct marketing, at the time that the details were initially collected, and, where he did not initially refuse the use of the details, at the time of each subsequent communication.

(4) A subscriber shall not permit his line to be used in contravention of paragraph (2).

23. *Use of electronic mail for direct marketing purposes where the identity or address of the sender is concealed*

A person shall neither transmit, nor instigate the transmission of, a communication for the purposes of direct marketing by means of electronic mail—

    (a) where the identity of the person on whose behalf the communication has been sent has been disguised or concealed; or

    (b) where a valid address to which the recipient of the communication may send a request that such communications cease has not been provided.

24. *Information to be provided for the purposes of regulations 19, 20 and 21*

(1) Where a public electronic communications service is used for the transmission of a communication for direct marketing purposes the person using, or instigating the use of, the service shall ensure that the following information is provided with that communication—

    (a) in relation to a communication to which regulations 19 (automated calling systems) and 20 (facsimile machines) apply, the particulars mentioned in paragraph (2)(a) and (b);

    (b) in relation to a communication to which regulation 21 (telephone calls) applies, the particulars mentioned in paragraph (2)(a) and, if the recipient of the call so requests, those mentioned in paragraph (2)(b).

(2) The particulars referred to in paragraph (1) are—

    (a) the name of the person;

    (b) either the address of the person or a telephone number on which he can be reached free of charge.

25. *Register to be kept for the purposes of regulation 20*

(1) For the purposes of *regulation 20* OFCOM shall maintain and keep up-to-date, in printed or electronic form, a register of the numbers allocated to subscribers, in respect of particular lines, who have notified them (notwithstanding, in the case of individual subscribers, that they enjoy the benefit of regulation 20(1)(a) and (2)) that they do not for the time being wish to receive

unsolicited communications for direct marketing purposes by means of facsimile machine on the lines in question.

(2) OFCOM shall remove a number from the register maintained under paragraph (1) where they have reason to believe that it has ceased to be allocated to the subscriber by whom they were notified pursuant to paragraph (1).

(3) On the request of—

(a) a person wishing to send, or instigate the sending of, such communications as are mentioned in paragraph (1), or

(b) a subscriber wishing to permit the use of his line for the sending of such communications,

for information derived from the register kept under paragraph (1), OFCOM shall, unless it is not reasonably practicable so to do, on the payment to them of such fee as is, subject to paragraph (4), required by them, make the information requested available to that person or that subscriber.

(4) For the purposes of paragraph (3) OFCOM may require different fees—

(a) for making available information derived from the register in different forms or manners, or

(b) for making available information derived from the whole or from different parts of the register,

but the fees required by them shall be ones in relation to which the Secretary of State has notified OFCOM that he is satisfied that they are designed to secure, as nearly as may be and taking one year with another, that the aggregate fees received, or reasonably expected to be received, equal the costs incurred, or reasonably expected to be incurred, by OFCOM in discharging their duties under paragraphs (1), (2) and (3).

(5) The functions of OFCOM under paragraphs (1), (2) and (3), other than the function of determining the fees to be required for the purposes of paragraph (3), may be discharged on their behalf by some other person in pursuance of arrangements made by OFCOM with that other person.

26. *Register to be kept for the purposes of regulation 21*

(1) For the purposes of regulation 21 OFCOM shall maintain and keep up-to-date, in printed or electronic form, a register of the numbers allocated to subscribers, in respect of particular lines, who have notified them that they do not for the time being wish to receive unsolicited calls for direct marketing purposes on the lines in question.

(1A) Notifications to OFCOM made for the purposes of paragraph (1) by corporate subscribers shall be in writing.

(2) OFCOM shall remove a number from the register maintained under paragraph (1) where they have reason to believe that it has ceased to be allocated to the subscriber by whom they were notified pursuant to paragraph (1).

(2A) Where a number allocated to a corporate subscriber is listed in the register maintained under paragraph (1), OFCOM shall, within the period of 28 days following each anniversary of the date of that number being first listed in the register, send to the subscriber a written reminder that the number is listed in the register.

(3) On the request of—

(a) a person wishing to make, or instigate the making of, such calls as are mentioned in paragraph (1), or

(b) a subscriber wishing to permit the use of his line for the making of such calls, for information derived from the register kept under paragraph (1), OFCOM shall, unless it is not reasonably practicable so to do, on the payment to them of such fee as is, subject to paragraph (4), required by them, make the information requested available to that person or that subscriber.

(4) For the purposes of paragraph (3) OFCOM may require different fees—

(a) for making available information derived from the register in different forms or manners, or

(b) for making available information derived from the whole or from different parts of the register,

but the fees required by them shall be ones in relation to which the Secretary of State has notified OFCOM that he is satisfied that they are designed to secure, as nearly as may be and taking one year with another, that the aggregate fees received, or reasonably expected to be received, equal the costs incurred, or reasonably expected to be incurred, by OFCOM in discharging their duties under paragraphs (1), (2) and (3).

(5) The functions of OFCOM under paragraphs (1), (2)[, (2A)][8] and (3), other than the function of determining the fees to be required for the purposes of paragraph (3), may be discharged on their behalf by some other person in pursuance of arrangements made by OFCOM with that other person.

27. Modification of contracts

To the extent that any term in a contract between a subscriber to and the provider of a public electronic communications service or such a provider and the provider of an electronic communications network would be inconsistent with a requirement of these Regulations, that term shall be void.

28. National security

(1) Nothing in these Regulations shall require a communications provider to do, or refrain from doing, anything (including the processing of data) if exemption from the requirement in question is required for the purpose of safeguarding national security.

(2) Subject to paragraph (4), a certificate signed by a Minister of the Crown certifying that exemption from any requirement of these Regulations is or at any time was required for the purpose of safeguarding national security shall be conclusive evidence of that fact.

(3) A certificate under paragraph (2) may identify the circumstances in which it applies by means of a general description and may be expressed to have prospective effect.

(4) Any person directly affected by the issuing of a certificate under paragraph (2) may appeal to the Tribunal against the issuing of the certificate.

(5) If, on an appeal under paragraph (4), the Tribunal finds that, applying the principles applied by a court on an application for judicial review, the Minister did not have reasonable grounds for issuing the certificate, the Tribunal may allow the appeal and quash the certificate.

(6) Where, in any proceedings under or by virtue of these Regulations, it is claimed by a communications provider that a certificate under paragraph (2) which identifies the circumstances

---

[8] word inserted by Privacy and Electronic Communications (EC Directive) (Amendment) Regulations 2004/1039 Reg. 2(5).

in which it applies by means of a general description applies in the circumstances in question, any other party to the proceedings may appeal to the Tribunal on the ground that the certificate does not apply in those circumstances and, subject to any determination under paragraph (7), the certificate shall be conclusively presumed so to apply.

(7) On any appeal under paragraph (6), the Tribunal may determine that the certificate does not so apply.

(8) In this regulation—

(a) "the Tribunal" means the Information Tribunal referred to in section 6 of the Data Protection Act 1998;

(b) Subsections (8), (9), (10) and (12) of section 28 of and Schedule 6 to that Act apply for the purposes of this regulation as they apply for the purposes of section 28;

(c) section 58 of that Act shall apply for the purposes of this regulation as if the reference in that section to the functions of the Tribunal under that Act included a reference to the functions of the Tribunal under paragraphs (4) to (7) of this regulation; and

(d) subsections (1), (2) and (5)(f) of section 67 of that Act shall apply in respect of the making of rules relating to the functions of the Tribunal under this regulation.

29. *Legal requirements, law enforcement etc.*

(1) Nothing in these Regulations shall require a communications provider to do, or refrain from doing, anything (including the processing of data)—

(a) if compliance with the requirement in question—

(i) would be inconsistent with any requirement imposed by or under an enactment or by a court order; or

(ii) would be likely to prejudice the prevention or detection of crime or the apprehension or prosecution of offenders; or

(b) if exemption from the requirement in question—

(i) is required for the purposes of, or in connection with, any legal proceedings (including prospective legal proceedings);

(ii) is necessary for the purposes of obtaining legal advice; or

(iii) is otherwise necessary for the purposes of establishing, exercising or defending legal rights.

30. *Proceedings for compensation for failure to comply with requirements of the Regulations*

(1) A person who suffers damage by reason of any contravention of any of the requirements of these Regulations by any other person shall be entitled to bring proceedings for compensation from that other person for that damage.

(2) In proceedings brought against a person by virtue of this regulation it shall be a defence to prove that he had taken such care as in all the circumstances was reasonably required to comply with the relevant requirement.

(3) The provisions of this regulation are without prejudice to those of regulation 31.

31. *Enforcement—extension of Part V of the Data Protection Act 1998*

(1) The provisions of Part V of the Data Protection Act 1998 and of Schedules 6 and 9 to that Act are extended for the purposes of these Regulations and, for those purposes, shall have effect subject to the modifications set out in Schedule 1.

(2) In regulations 32 and 33, "enforcement functions" means the functions of the Information Commissioner under the provisions referred to in paragraph (1) as extended by that paragraph.

(3) The provisions of this regulation are without prejudice to those of regulation 30.

32. *Request that the Commissioner exercise his enforcement functions*

Where it is alleged that there has been a contravention of any of the requirements of these Regulations either OFCOM or a person aggrieved by the alleged contravention may request the Commissioner to exercise his enforcement functions in respect of that contravention, but those functions shall be exercisable by the Commissioner whether or not he has been so requested.

33. *Technical advice to the Commissioner*

OFCOM shall comply with any reasonable request made by the Commissioner, in connection with his enforcement functions, for advice on technical and similar matters relating to electronic communications.

34. *Amendment to the Telecommunications (Lawful Business Practice) (Interception of Communications) Regulations 2000*

In regulation 3 of the Telecommunications (Lawful Business Practice) (Interception of Communications) Regulations 2000, for paragraph (3), there shall be substituted—

"(3) Conduct falling within paragraph (1)(a)(i) above is authorised only to the extent that Article 5 of Directive 2002/58/EC of the European Parliament and of the Council of 12 July 2002 concerning the processing of personal data and the protection of privacy in the electronic communications sector so permits."

35. *Amendment to the Electronic Communications (Universal Service) Order 2003*

(1) In paragraphs 2(2) and 3(2) of the Schedule to the Electronic Communications (Universal Service) Order 2003, for the words "Telecommunications (Data Protection and Privacy) Regulations 1999" there shall be substituted "Privacy and Electronic Communications (EC Directive) Regulations 2003".

(2) Paragraph (1) shall have effect notwithstanding the provisions of section 65 of the Communications Act 2003[9] (which provides for the modification of the Universal Service Order made under that section).

---

[9] For the commencement of section 65, see article 2(1) of S.I. 2003/1900 (C. 77).

36. *Transitional provisions*

The provisions in Schedule 2 shall have effect.

SCHEDULE 1—MODIFICATIONS FOR THE PURPOSES OF THESE REGULATIONS TO PART V OF THE DATA PROTECTION ACT 1998 AND SCHEDULES 6 AND 9 TO THAT ACT AS EXTENDED BY REGULATION 31

1. In section 40—

(a) in subsection (1), for the words "data controller" there shall be substituted the word "person", for the words "data protection principles" there shall be substituted the words "requirements of the Privacy and Electronic Communications (EC Directive) Regulations 2003 (in this Part referred to as "the relevant requirements") and for the words "principle or principles" there shall be substituted the words "requirement or requirements";

(b) in subsection (2), the words "or distress" shall be omitted;

(c) subsections (3), (4), (5), (9) and (10) shall be omitted; and

(d) in subsection (6)(a), for the words "data protection principle or principles" there shall be substituted the words "relevant requirement or requirements."

2. In section 41(1) and (2), for the words "data protection principle or principles", in both places where they occur, there shall be substituted the words "relevant requirement or requirements".

3. Section 42 shall be omitted.

4. In section 43—

(a) for subsections (1) and (2) there shall be substituted the following provisions—

"(1) If the Commissioner reasonably requires any information for the purpose of determining whether a person has complied or is complying with the relevant requirements, he may serve that person with a notice (in this Act referred to as "an information notice") requiring him, within such time as is specified in the notice, to furnish the Commissioner, in such form as may be so specified, with such information relating to compliance with the relevant requirements as is so specified.

(2) An information notice must contain a statement that the Commissioner regards the specified information as relevant for the purpose of determining whether the person has complied or is complying with the relevant requirements and his reason for regarding it as relevant for that purpose."

(b) in subsection (6)(a), after the word "under" there shall be inserted the words "the Privacy and Electronic Communications (EC Directive) Regulations 2003 or";

(c) in subsection (6)(b), after the words "arising out of" there shall be inserted the words "the said Regulations or"; and

(d) subsection (10) shall be omitted.

5. Sections 44, 45 and 46 shall be omitted.

6. In section 47—

(a) in subsection (1), for the words "an information notice or special information notice" there shall be substituted the words "or an information notice"; and

(b) in subsection (2) the words "or a special information notice" shall be omitted.

7. In section 48—

(a) in subsections (1) and (3), for the words "an information notice or a special information notice", in both places where they occur, there shall be substituted the words "or an information notice";

(b) in subsection (3) for the words "43(5) or 44(6)" there shall be substituted the words "or 43(5)"; and

(c) subsection (4) shall be omitted.

8. In section 49 subsection (5) shall be omitted.

9. In paragraph 4(1) of Schedule (6), for the words "(2) or (4)" there shall be substituted the words "or (2)".

10. In paragraph 1 of Schedule 9—

(a) for subparagraph (1)(a) there shall be substituted the following provision—

"(a) that a person has contravened or is contravening any of the requirements of the Privacy and Electronic Communications (EC Directive) Regulations 2003 (in this Schedule referred to as "the 2003 Regulations") or";

and

(b) subparagraph (2) shall be omitted.

11. In paragraph 9 of Schedule 9—

(a) in subparagraph (1)(a) after the words "rights under" there shall be inserted the words "the 2003 Regulations or"; and

(b) in subparagraph (1)(b) after the words "arising out of" there shall be inserted the words "the 2003 Regulations or".

SCHEDULE 2—TRANSITIONAL PROVISIONS

Interpretation

1. In this Schedule "the 1999 Regulations" means the Telecommunications (Data Protection and Privacy) Regulations 1999 and "caller" has the same meaning as in regulation 21 of the 1999 Regulations.

2.—(1) Regulation 18 of these Regulations shall not apply in relation to editions of directories first published before 11th December 2003.

(2) Where the personal data of a subscriber have been included in a directory in accordance with Part IV of the 1999 Regulations, the personal data of that subscriber may remain included in that directory provided that the subscriber—

(a) has been provided with information in accordance with regulation 18 of these Regulations; and
(b) has not requested that his data be withdrawn from that directory.

(3) Where a request has been made under subparagraph (2) for data to be withdrawn from a directory, that request shall be treated as having no application in relation to an edition of a directory that was produced before the producer of the directory received the request.

(4) For the purposes of subparagraph (3), an edition of a directory, which is revised after it was first produced, shall be treated as a new edition.

3.—(1) A notification of consent given to a caller by a subscriber for the purposes of regulation 22(2) of the 1999 Regulations is to have effect on and after 11th December 2003 as a notification given by that subscriber for the purposes of *regulation 19(2)* of these Regulations.

(2) A notification given to a caller by a corporate subscriber for the purposes of regulation 23(2)(a) of the 1999 Regulations is to have effect on and after 11th December 2003 as a notification given by that subscriber for the purposes of regulation 20(1)(b) of these Regulations.

(3) A notification of consent given to a caller by an individual subscriber for the purposes of regulation 24(2) of the 1999 Regulations is to have effect on and after 11th December 2003 as a notification given by that subscriber for the purposes of regulation 20(2) of these Regulations.

(4) A notification given to a caller by an individual subscriber for the purposes of regulation 25(2)(a) of the 1999 Regulations is to have effect on and after the 11th December 2003 as a notification given by that subscriber for the purposes of regulation 21(1) of these Regulations.

4.—(1) A notification given by a subscriber pursuant to regulation 23(4)(a) of the 1999 Regulations to the Director General of Telecommunications (or to such other person as is discharging his functions under regulation 23(4) of the 1999 Regulations on his behalf by virtue of an arrangement made under *regulation 23(6)* of those Regulations) is to have effect on or after 11th December 2003 as a notification given pursuant to regulation 25(1) of these Regulations.

(2) A notification given by a subscriber who is an individual pursuant to regulation 25(4)(a) of the 1999 Regulations to the Director General of Telecommunications (or to such other person as is discharging his functions under regulation 25(4) of the 1999 Regulations on his behalf by virtue of an arrangement made under regulation 25(6) of those Regulations) is to have effect on or after 11th December 2003 as a notification given pursuant to regulation 26(1) of these Regulations.

5. In relation to times before an order made under section 411[10] of the Communications Act 2003 brings any of the provisions of Part 2 of Chapter 1 of that Act into force for the purpose of conferring on OFCOM the functions contained in those provisions, references to OFCOM in these Regulations are to be treated as references to the Director General of Telecommunications.

Explanatory Note

These Regulations implement Articles 2, 4, 5(3), 6 to 13, 15 and 16 of Directive 2002/58/EC of the European Parliament and of the Council of 12 July 2002 concerning the processing of personal data and the protection of privacy in the electronic communications sector (Directive on privacy and electronic communications) ("the Directive").

The Directive repeals and replaces Directive 97/66/EC of the European Parliament and of the Council of 15 December 1997 concerning the processing of personal data and the protection of privacy in the telecommunications sector which was implemented in the UK by the Telecommunications (Data Protection and Privacy) Regulations 1999. Those Regulations are revoked by regulation 3 of these Regulations.

Regulation 2 sets out the definitions which apply for the purposes of the Regulations.

Regulation 4 provides that nothing in these Regulations relieves a person of any of his obligations under the Data Protection Act 1998.

Regulation 5 imposes a duty on a provider of a public electronic communications service to take measures, if necessary in conjunction with the provider of the electronic communications network by means of which the service is provided, to safeguard the security of the service, and requires the provider of the electronic communications network to comply with the service

---

[10] For the commencement of section 411, see section 411(2) and (3) of the Communications Act 2003 (c. 21).

provider's reasonable requests made for the purposes of taking the measures ("public electronic communications service" has the meaning given by section 151 of the Communications Act 2003 and "electronic communications network" has the meaning given by section 32 of that Act). Regulation 5 further requires the service provider, where there remains a significant risk to the security of the service, to provide subscribers to that service with certain information ("subscriber" is defined as "a person who is a party to a contract with a provider of public electronic communications services for the supply of such services").

Regulation 6 provides that an electronic communications network may not be used to store or gain access to information in the terminal equipment of a subscriber or user ("user" is defined as "any individual using a public electronic communications service") unless the subscriber or user is provided with certain information and is given the opportunity to refuse the storage of or access to the information in his terminal equipment.

Regulations 7 and 8 set out certain restrictions on the processing of traffic data relating to a subscriber or user by a public communications provider. "Traffic data" is defined as "any data processed for the purpose of the conveyance of a communication on an electronic communications network or for the billing in respect of that communication". "Public communications provider" is defined as "a provider of a public electronic communications network or a public electronic communications service".

Regulation 9 requires providers of public electronic communications services to provide subscribers with non-itemised bills on request and requires OFCOM to have regard to certain matters when exercising their functions under Chapter 1 of Part 2 of the Communications Act 2003.

Regulation 10 requires a provider of a public electronic communications service to provide users of the service with a means of preventing the presentation of calling line identification on a call-by-call basis, and to provide subscribers to the service with a means of preventing the presentation of such identification on a per-line basis. This regulation is subject to regulations 15 and 16. Regulation 11 requires the provider of a public electronic communications service to provide subscribers to that service with certain facilities where facilities enabling the presentation of connected line identification or calling line identification are available.

Regulation 12 requires a public electronic communications service provider to provide certain information to the public for the purposes of regulations 10 and 11, and regulation 13 requires communications providers (the term "communications provider" has the meaning given by section 405 of the Communications Act 2003) to co-operate with reasonable requests made by providers of public electronic communications services for the purposes of those regulations.

Regulation 14 imposes certain restrictions on the processing of location data, which is defined as "any data processed in an electronic communications network indicating the geographical position of the terminal equipment of a user of a public electronic communications service, including data relating to the latitude, longitude or altitude of the terminal equipment; the direction of travel of the user; or the time the location information was recorded."

Regulation 15 makes provision in relation to the tracing of malicious or nuisance calls and *regulation 16* makes provision in relation to emergency calls, which are defined in regulation 16(1) as calls to the national emergency number 999 or the European emergency call number 112.

Regulation 17 requires the provider of an electronic communications service to a subscriber to stop, on request, the automatic forwarding of calls to that subscriber's line and also requires other communications providers to comply with reasonable requests made by the subscriber's provider to assist in the prevention of that forwarding.

Regulation 18 applies to directories of subscribers, and sets out requirements that must be satisfied where data relating to subscribers is included in such directories. It also gives subscribers the right to verify, correct or withdraw their data in directories.

Regulation 19 provides that a person may not transmit communications comprising recorded matter for direct marketing purposes by an automated calling system unless the line called is that of a subscriber who has notified the caller that he consents to such communications being made.

Regulations 20, 21 and 22 set out the circumstances in which persons may transmit, or instigate the transmission of, unsolicited communications for the purposes of direct marketing by means of facsimile machine, make unsolicited calls for those purposes, or transmit unsolicited communications by means of electronic mail for those purposes. Regulation 22 (electronic mail) applies only to transmissions to individual subscribers (the term "individual" means "a living individual" and includes "an unincorporated body of such individuals").

Regulation 23 prohibits the sending of communications by means of electronic mail for the purposes of direct marketing where the identity of the person on whose behalf the communication is made has been disguised or concealed or an address to which requests for such communications to cease may be sent has not been provided.

Regulation 24 sets out certain information that must be provided for the purposes of *regulations 19, 20 and 21.*

Regulation 25 imposes a duty on OFCOM, for the purposes of regulation 20, to maintain and keep up-to-date a register of numbers allocated to subscribers who do not wish to receive unsolicited communications by means of facsimile machine for the purposes of direct marketing. Regulation 26 imposes a similar obligation for the purposes of regulation 21 in respect of individual subscribers who do not wish to receive calls for the purposes of direct marketing.

Regulation 27 provides that terms in certain contracts which are inconsistent with these Regulations shall be void.

Regulation 28 exempts communications providers from the requirements of these Regulations where exemption is required for the purpose of safeguarding national security and further provides that a certificate signed by a Minister of the Crown to the effect that exemption from a requirement is necessary for the purpose of safeguarding national security shall be conclusive evidence of that fact. It also provides for certain questions relating to such certificates to be determined by the Information Tribunal referred to in section 6 of the Data Protection Act 1998.

Regulation 29 provides that a communications provider shall not be required by these Regulations to do, or refrain from doing, anything if complying with the requirement in question would be inconsistent with a requirement imposed by or under an enactment or by a court order, or if exemption from the requirement is necessary in connection with legal proceedings, for the purposes of obtaining legal advice or is otherwise necessary to establish, exercise or defend legal rights.

Regulation 30 allows a claim for damages to be brought in respect of contraventions of the Regulations. Regulations 31 and 32 make provision in connection with the enforcement of the Regulations by the Information Commissioner (who is the Commissioner appointed under *section* 6 of the Data Protection Act 1998).

Regulation 33 imposes a duty on OFCOM to comply with any reasonable request made by the Commissioner for advice on technical matters relating to electronic communications.

Regulation 34 amends the Telecommunications (Lawful Business Practice) (Interception of Communications) Regulations 2000 and regulation 35 amends the Electronic Communications (Universal Service) Order 2003.

Regulation 36 provides for the transitional provisions in Schedule 2 to have effect.

A transposition note setting out how the main elements of the Directive are transposed into law and a regulatory impact assessment have been placed in the libraries of both Houses of Parliament. Copies are also available from the Department of Trade and Industry, Bay 202, 151 Buckingham Palace Road, London SW1W 9SS and can also be found on *www.dti.gov.uk.*

APPENDIX E

Telecommunications (Lawful Business Practice) (Interception of Communications) Regulations

2000/2699

1. *Citation and commencement*

These Regulations may be cited as the Telecommunications (Lawful Business Practice) (Interception of Communications) Regulations 2000 and shall come into force on 24th October 2000.

2. *Interpretation*

In these Regulations—

(a) references to a business include references to activities of a government department, of any public authority or of any person or office holder on whom functions are conferred by or under any enactment;

(b) a reference to a communication as relevant to a business is a reference to—

  (i) a communication—

    (aa) by means of which a transaction is entered into in the course of that business, or

    (bb) which otherwise relates to that business, or

  (ii) a communication which otherwise takes place in the course of the carrying on of that business;

(c) "regulatory or self-regulatory practices or procedures" means practices or procedures—

  (i) compliance with which is required or recommended by, under or by virtue of—

    (aa) any provision of the law of a member state or other state within the European Economic Area, or

    (bb) any standard or code of practice published by or on behalf of a body established in a member state or other state within the European Economic Area which includes amongst its objectives the publication of standards or codes of practice for the conduct of business, or

(ii) which are otherwise applied for the purpose of ensuring compliance with anything so required or recommended;

(d) "system controller" means, in relation to a particular telecommunication system, a person with a right to control its operation or use.

3. *Lawful interception of a communication*

(1) For the purpose of section 1(5)(a) of the Act, conduct is authorised, subject to paragraphs (2) and (3) below, if it consists of interception of a communication, in the course of its transmission by means of a telecommunication system, which is effected by or with the express or implied consent of the system controller for the purpose of—

(a) monitoring or keeping a record of communications—

    (i) in order to—

        (aa) establish the existence of facts, or
        (bb) ascertain compliance with regulatory or self-regulatory practices or procedures which are—

        applicable to the system controller in the carrying on of his business or

        applicable to another person in the carrying on of his business where that person is supervised by the system controller in respect of those practices or procedures, or

        (cc) ascertain or demonstrate the standards which are achieved or ought to be achieved by persons using the system in the course of their duties, or

    (ii) in the interests of national security, or
    (iii) for the purpose of preventing or detecting crime, or
    (iv) for the purpose of investigating or detecting the unauthorised use of that or any other telecommunication system, or
    (v) where that is undertaken—

        (aa) in order to secure, or
        (bb) as an inherent part of,

the effective operation of the system (including any monitoring or keeping of a record which would be authorised by section 3(3) of the Act if the conditions in paragraphs (a) and (b) thereof were satisfied); or

(b) monitoring communications for the purpose of determining whether they are communications relevant to the system controller's business which fall within regulation 2(b)(i) above; or

(c) monitoring communications made to a confidential voice-telephony counselling or support service which is free of charge (other than the cost, if any, of making a telephone call) and operated in such a way that users may remain anonymous if they so choose.

(2) Conduct is authorised by paragraph (1) of this regulation only if—(a) the interception in question is effected solely for the purpose of monitoring or (where appropriate) keeping a record of communications relevant to the system controller's business;

(b) the telecommunication system in question is provided for use wholly or partly in connection with that business;

(c) the system controller has made all reasonable efforts to inform every person who may use the telecommunication system in question that communications transmitted by means thereof may be intercepted; and

    (d) in a case falling within—

        (i) paragraph (1)(a)(ii) above, the person by or on whose behalf the interception is effected is a person specified in section 6(2)(a) to (i) of the Act;

       (ii) paragraph (1)(b) above, the communication is one which is intended to be received (whether or not it has been actually received) by a person using the telecommunication system in question.

(3) Conduct falling within paragraph (1)(a)(i) above is authorised only to the extent that Article 5 of Directive 2002/58/EC of the European Parliament and of the Council of 12 July 2002 concerning the processing of personal data and the protection of privacy in the electronic communications sector so permits.[1]

---

[1] substituted by Privacy and Electronic Communications (EC Directive) Regulations 2003/2426 reg. 34

APPENDIX F

Regulation of Investigatory Powers Act 2000

(2000 C.23)

PART I

COMMUNICATIONS

CHAPTER I

INTERCEPTION

Unlawful and authorised interception

1. *Unlawful interception*

(1) It shall be an offence for a person intentionally and without lawful authority to intercept, at any place in the United Kingdom, any communication in the course of its transmission by means of—

(a) a public postal service; or

(b) a public telecommunication system.

(2) It shall be an offence for a person—

(a) intentionally and without lawful authority, and

(b) otherwise than in circumstances in which his conduct is excluded by subsection (6) from criminal liability under this subsection,

to intercept, at any place in the United Kingdom, any communication in the course of its transmission by means of a private telecommunication system.

(3) Any interception of a communication which is carried out at any place in the United Kingdom by, or with the express or implied consent of, a person having the right to control the operation or the use of a private telecommunication system shall be actionable at the suit or instance of the sender or recipient, or intended recipient, of the communication if it is without lawful authority and is either—

(a) an interception of that communication in the course of its transmission by means of that private system; or

(b) an interception of that communication in the course of its transmission, by means of a public telecommunication system, to or from apparatus comprised in that private telecommunication system.

(4) Where the United Kingdom is a party to an international agreement which—

(a) relates to the provision of mutual assistance in connection with, or in the form of, the interception of communications,

(b) requires the issue of a warrant, order or equivalent instrument in cases in which assistance is given, and

(c) is designated for the purposes of this subsection by an order made by the Secretary of State,

it shall be the duty of the Secretary of State to secure that no request for assistance in accordance with the agreement is made on behalf of a person in the United Kingdom to the competent authorities of a country or territory outside the United Kingdom except with lawful authority.

(5) Conduct has lawful authority for the purposes of this section if, and only if—

(a) it is authorised by or under section 3 or 4;

(b) it takes place in accordance with a warrant under section 5 ("an interception warrant"); or

(c) it is in exercise, in relation to any stored communication, of any statutory power that is exercised (apart from this section) for the purpose of obtaining information or of taking possession of any document or other property;

and conduct (whether or not prohibited by this section) which has lawful authority for the purposes of this section by virtue of paragraph (a) or (b) shall also be taken to be lawful for all other purposes.

(6) The circumstances in which a person makes an interception of a communication in the course of its transmission by means of a private telecommunication system are such that his conduct is excluded from criminal liability under subsection (2) if—

(a) he is a person with a right to control the operation or the use of the system; or

(b) he has the express or implied consent of such a person to make the interception.

(7) A person who is guilty of an offence under subsection (1) or (2) shall be liable—

(a) on conviction on indictment, to imprisonment for a term not exceeding two years or to a fine, or to both;

(b) on summary conviction, to a fine not exceeding the statutory maximum.

(8) No proceedings for any offence which is an offence by virtue of this section shall be instituted—

(a) in England and Wales, except by or with the consent of the Director of Public Prosecutions;

(b) in Northern Ireland, except by or with the consent of the Director of Public Prosecutions for Northern Ireland.

2. Meaning and location of "interception" etc

(1) In this Act—

"postal service" means any service which—

(a) consists in the following, or in any one or more of them, namely, the collection, sorting, conveyance, distribution and delivery (whether in the United Kingdom or elsewhere) of postal items; and

(b) is offered or provided as a service the main purpose of which, or one of the main purposes of which, is to make available, or to facilitate, a means of transmission from place to place of postal items containing communications;

"private telecommunication system" means any telecommunication system which, without itself being a public telecommunication system, is a system in relation to which the following conditions are satisfied—

(a) it is attached, directly or indirectly and whether or not for the purposes of the communication in question, to a public telecommunication system; and

(b) there is apparatus comprised in the system which is both located in the United Kingdom and used (with or without other apparatus) for making the attachment to the public telecommunication system;

"public postal service" means any postal service which is offered or provided to, or to a substantial section of, the public in any one or more parts of the United Kingdom;

"public telecommunications service" means any telecommunications service which is offered or provided to, or to a substantial section of, the public in any one or more parts of the United Kingdom;

"public telecommunication system" means any such parts of a telecommunication system by means of which any public telecommunications service is provided as are located in the United Kingdom;

"telecommunications service" means any service that consists in the provision of access to, and of facilities for making use of, any telecommunication system (whether or not one provided by the person providing the service); and

"telecommunication system" means any system (including the apparatus comprised in it) which exists (whether wholly or partly in the United Kingdom or elsewhere) for the purpose of facilitating the transmission of communications by any means involving the use of electrical or electro-magnetic energy.

(2) For the purposes of this Act, but subject to the following provisions of this section, a person intercepts a communication in the course of its transmission by means of a telecommunication system if, and only if, he—

(a) so modifies or interferes with the system, or its operation,

(b) so monitors transmissions made by means of the system, or

(c) so monitors transmissions made by wireless telegraphy to or from apparatus comprised in the system,

as to make some or all of the contents of the communication available, while being transmitted, to a person other than the sender or intended recipient of the communication.

(3) References in this Act to the interception of a communication do not include references to the interception of any communication broadcast for general reception.

(4) For the purposes of this Act the interception of a communication takes place in the United Kingdom if, and only if, the modification, interference or monitoring or, in the case of a postal item, the interception is effected by conduct within the United Kingdom and the communication is either—

(a) intercepted in the course of its transmission by means of a public postal service or public telecommunication system; or

(b) intercepted in the course of its transmission by means of a private telecommunication system in a case in which the sender or intended recipient of the communication is in the United Kingdom.

(5) References in this Act to the interception of a communication in the course of its transmission by means of a postal service or telecommunication system do not include references to—

(a) any conduct that takes place in relation only to so much of the communication as consists in any traffic data comprised in or attached to a communication (whether by the sender or otherwise) for the purposes of any postal service or telecommunication system by means of which it is being or may be transmitted; or

(b) any such conduct, in connection with conduct falling within paragraph (a), as gives a person who is neither the sender nor the intended recipient only so much access to a communication as is necessary for the purpose of identifying traffic data so comprised or attached.

(6) For the purposes of this section references to the modification of a telecommunication system include references to the attachment of any apparatus to, or other modification of or interference with—

(a) any part of the system; or

(b) any wireless telegraphy apparatus used for making transmissions to or from apparatus comprised in the system.

(7) For the purposes of this section the times while a communication is being transmitted by means of a telecommunication system shall be taken to include any time when the system by means of which the communication is being, or has been, transmitted is used for storing it in a manner that enables the intended recipient to collect it or otherwise to have access to it.

(8) For the purposes of this section the cases in which any contents of a communication are to be taken to be made available to a person while being transmitted shall include any case in which any of the contents of the communication, while being transmitted, are diverted or recorded so as to be available to a person subsequently.

(9) In this section "traffic data", in relation to any communication, means—

(a) any data identifying, or purporting to identify, any person, apparatus or location to or from which the communication is or may be transmitted,

(b) any data identifying or selecting, or purporting to identify or select, apparatus through which, or by means of which, the communication is or may be transmitted,

(c) any data comprising signals for the actuation of apparatus used for the purposes of a telecommunication system for effecting (in whole or in part) the transmission of any communication, and

(d) any data identifying the data or other data as data comprised in or attached to a particular communication, but that expression includes data identifying a computer file or computer program access to which is obtained, or which is run, by means of the communication to the extent only that the file or program is identified by reference to the apparatus in which it is stored.

(10) In this section—

(a) references, in relation to traffic data comprising signals for the actuation of apparatus, to a telecommunication system by means of which a communication is being or may be transmitted include references to any telecommunication system in which that apparatus is comprised; and

(b) references to traffic data being attached to a communication include references to the data and the communication being logically associated with each other;

and in this section "data", in relation to a postal item, means anything written on the outside of the item.

(11) In this section "postal item" means any letter, postcard or other such thing in writing as may be used by the sender for imparting information to the recipient, or any packet or parcel.

3. *Lawful interception without an interception warrant*

(1) Conduct by any person consisting in the interception of a communication is authorised by this section if the communication is one which, or which that person has reasonable grounds for believing, is both—

    (a) a communication sent by a person who has consented to the interception; and

    (b) a communication the intended recipient of which has so consented.

(2) Conduct by any person consisting in the interception of a communication is authorised by this section if—

    (a) the communication is one sent by, or intended for, a person who has consented to the interception; and

    (b) surveillance by means of that interception has been authorised under Part II.

(3) Conduct consisting in the interception of a communication is authorised by this section if—

    (a) it is conduct by or on behalf of a person who provides a postal service or a telecommunications service; and

    (b) it takes place for purposes connected with the provision or operation of that service or with the enforcement, in relation to that service, of any enactment relating to the use of postal services or telecommunications services.

(4) Conduct by any person consisting in the interception of a communication in the course of its transmission by means of wireless telegraphy is authorised by this section if it takes place—

    (a) with the authority of a designated person under section 48 of the Wireless Telegraphy Act 2006 (interception and disclosure of wireless telegraphy messages); and

    (b) for purposes connected with anything falling within subsection (5).

(5) Each of the following falls within this subsection—

    (a) the grant of wireless telegraphy licences under the Wireless Telegraphy Act 2006;

    (b) the prevention or detection of anything which constitutes interference with wireless telegraphy; and

    [(c) the enforcement of—

        (i) any provision of Part 2 (other than Chapter 2 and sections 27 to 31) or Part 3 of that Act, or

        (ii) any enactment not falling within subparagraph (i);

that relates to such interference.][1]

4. *Power to provide for lawful interception*

(1) Conduct by any person ("the interceptor") consisting in the interception of a communication in the course of its transmission by means of a telecommunication system is authorised by this section if—

---

[1] s.3(5)(c)(i)–(ii) substituted for words by Wireless Telegraphy Act 2006 c. 36 Sch. 7 para. 22(3)(b)

(a) the interception is carried out for the purpose of obtaining information about the communications of a person who, or who the interceptor has reasonable grounds for believing, is in a country or territory outside the United Kingdom;

(b) the interception relates to the use of a telecommunications service provided to persons in that country or territory which is either—

    (i) a public telecommunications service; or

    (ii) a telecommunications service that would be a public telecommunications service if the persons to whom it is offered or provided were members of the public in a part of the United Kingdom;

(c) the person who provides that service (whether the interceptor or another person) is required by the law of that country or territory to carry out, secure or facilitate the interception in question;

(d) the situation is one in relation to which such further conditions as may be prescribed by regulations made by the Secretary of State are required to be satisfied before conduct may be treated as authorised by virtue of this subsection; and

(e) the conditions so prescribed are satisfied in relation to that situation.

(2) Subject to subsection (3), the Secretary of State may by regulations authorise any such conduct described in the regulations as appears to him to constitute a legitimate practice reasonably required for the purpose, in connection with the carrying on of any business, of monitoring or keeping a record of—

(a) communications by means of which transactions are entered into in the course of that business; or

(b) other communications relating to that business or taking place in the course of its being carried on.

(3) Nothing in any regulations under subsection (2) shall authorise the interception of any communication except in the course of its transmission using apparatus or services provided by or to the person carrying on the business for use wholly or partly in connection with that business.

(4) conduct taking place in a prison is authorised by this section if it is conduct in exercise of any power conferred by or under any rules made under section 47 of the Prison Act 1952, section 39 of the Prisons (Scotland) Act 1989 or section 13 of the Prison Act (Northern Ireland) 1953 (prison rules).

(5) Conduct taking place in any hospital premises where high security psychiatric services are provided is authorised by this section if it is conduct in pursuance of, and in accordance with, any direction given under section 8 of the National Health Service Act 2006, or section 19 or 23 of the National Health Service (Wales) Act 2006 (directions as to the carrying out of their functions by health bodies) to the body providing those services at those premises.

(6) Conduct taking place in a state hospital is authorised by this section if it is conduct in pursuance of, and in accordance with, any direction given to the State Hospitals Board for Scotland under section 2(5) of the National Health Service (Scotland) Act 1978 (regulations and directions as to the exercise of their functions by health boards) as applied by Article 5(1) of and the Schedule to The State Hospitals Board for Scotland Order 1995 (which applies certain provisions of that Act of 1978 to the State Hospitals Board).

(7) In this section references to a business include references to any activities of a government department, of any public authority or of any person or office holder on whom functions are conferred by or under any enactment.

(8) In this section—

"government department" includes any part of the Scottish Administration, a Northern Ireland department and [the Welsh Assembly Government][2];

"high security psychiatric services" has the same meaning as in the section 4 of the National Health Service Act 2006;

"hospital premises" has the same meaning as in *section 4(3)* of that Act; and

"state hospital" has the same meaning as in the National Health Service (Scotland) Act 1978.

(9) In this section "prison" means—

(a) any prison, young offender institution, young offenders centre or remand centre which is under the general superintendence of, or is provided by, the Secretary of State under the Prison Act 1952 or the Prison Act (Northern Ireland) 1953, or

(b) any prison, young offenders institution or remand centre which is under the general superintendence of the Scottish Ministers under the Prisons (Scotland) Act 1989, and includes any contracted out prison, within the meaning of Part IV of the Criminal Justice Act 1991 or section 106(4) of the Criminal Justice and Public Order Act 1994, and any legalised police cells within the meaning of section 14 of the Prisons (Scotland) Act 1989.

[. . .]

CHAPTER II

ACQUISITION AND DISCLOSURE OF COMMUNICATIONS DATA

21. *Lawful acquisition and disclosure of communications data*

(1) This Chapter applies to—

(a) any conduct in relation to a postal service or telecommunication system for obtaining communications data, other than conduct consisting in the interception of communications in the course of their transmission by means of such a service or system; and

(b) the disclosure to any person of communications data.

(2) Conduct to which this Chapter applies shall be lawful for all purposes if—

(a) it is conduct in which any person is authorised or required to engage by an authorisation or notice granted or given under this Chapter; and

(b) the conduct is in accordance with, or in pursuance of, the authorisation or requirement.

(3) A person shall not be subject to any civil liability in respect of any conduct of his which—

(a) is incidental to any conduct that is lawful by virtue of subsection (2); and

(b) is not itself conduct an authorisation or warrant for which is capable of being granted under a relevant enactment and might reasonably have been expected to have been sought in the case in question.

(4) In this Chapter "communications data" means any of the following—

(a) any traffic data comprised in or attached to a communication (whether by the sender or otherwise) for the purposes of any postal service or telecommunication system by means of which it is being or may be transmitted;

---

[2] words substituted by Government of Wales Act 2006 (Consequential Modifications and Transitional Provisions) Order 2007/1388 Sch. 1 para. 76(2)

(b) any information which includes none of the contents of a communication (apart from any information falling within paragraph (a)) and is about the use made by any person—

    (i) of any postal service or telecommunications service; or

    (ii) in connection with the provision to or use by any person of any telecommunications service, of any part of a telecommunication system;

(c) any information not falling within paragraph (a) or (b) that is held or obtained, in relation to persons to whom he provides the service, by a person providing a postal service or telecommunications service.

(5) In this section "relevant enactment" means—

(a) an enactment contained in this Act;

(b) section 5 of the Intelligence Services Act 1994 (warrants for the intelligence services); or

(c) an enactment contained in Part III of the Police Act 1997 (powers of the police and of customs officers).

(6) In this section "traffic data", in relation to any communication, means—

(a) any data identifying, or purporting to identify, any person, apparatus or location to or from which the communication is or may be transmitted,

(b) any data identifying or selecting, or purporting to identify or select, apparatus through which, or by means of which, the communication is or may be transmitted,

(c) any data comprising signals for the actuation of apparatus used for the purposes of a telecommunication system for effecting (in whole or in part) the transmission of any communication, and

(d) any data identifying the data or other data as data comprised in or attached to a particular communication.

but that expression includes data identifying a computer file or computer program access to which is obtained, or which is run, by means of the communication to the extent only that the file or program is identified by reference to the apparatus in which it is stored.

(7) In this section—

(a) references, in relation to traffic data comprising signals for the actuation of apparatus, to a telecommunication system by means of which a communication is being or may be transmitted include references to any telecommunication system in which that apparatus is comprised; and

(b) references to traffic data being attached to a communication include references to the data and the communication being logically associated with each other;

and in this section "data", in relation to a postal item, means anything written on the outside of the item.

22. *Obtaining and disclosing communications data*

(1) This section applies where a person designated for the purposes of this Chapter believes that it is necessary on grounds falling within subsection (2) to obtain any communications data.

(2) It is necessary on grounds falling within this subsection to obtain communications data if it is necessary—

(a) in the interests of national security;

(b) for the purpose of preventing or detecting crime or of preventing disorder;

(c) in the interests of the economic well-being of the United Kingdom;

(d) in the interests of public safety;

(e) for the purpose of protecting public health;

(f) for the purpose of assessing or collecting any tax, duty, levy or other imposition, contribution or charge payable to a government department;

(g) for the purpose, in an emergency, of preventing death or injury or any damage to a person's physical or mental health, or of mitigating any injury or damage to a person's physical or mental health; or

(h) for any purpose (not falling within paragraphs (a) to (g)) which is specified for the purposes of this subsection by an order made by the Secretary of State.

(3) Subject to subsection (5), the designated person may grant an authorisation for persons holding offices, ranks or positions with the same relevant public authority as the designated person to engage in any conduct to which this Chapter applies.

(4) Subject to subsection (5), where it appears to the designated person that a postal or telecommunications operator is or may be in possession of, or be capable of obtaining, any communications data, the designated person may, by notice to the postal or telecommunications operator, require the operator—

(a) if the operator is not already in possession of the data, to obtain the data; and

(b) in any case, to disclose all of the data in his possession or subsequently obtained by him.

(5) The designated person shall not grant an authorisation under subsection (3), or give a notice under subsection (4), unless he believes that obtaining the data in question by the conduct authorised or required by the authorisation or notice is proportionate to what is sought to be achieved by so obtaining the data.

(6) It shall be the duty of the postal or telecommunications operator to comply with the requirements of any notice given to him under subsection (4).

(7) A person who is under a duty by virtue of subsection (6) shall not be required to do anything in pursuance of that duty which it is not reasonably practicable for him to do.

(8) The duty imposed by subsection (6) shall be enforceable by civil proceedings by the Secretary of State for an injunction, or for specific performance of a statutory duty under section 45 of the Court of Session Act 1988, or for any other appropriate relief.

(9) The Secretary of State shall not make an order under subsection (2)(h) unless a draft of the order has been laid before Parliament and approved by a resolution of each House.

23. *Form and duration of authorisation and notices*

(1) An authorisation under section 22(3)—

(a) must be granted in writing or (if not in writing) in a manner that produces a record of its having been granted;

(b) must describe the conduct to which this Chapter applies that is authorised and the communications data in relation to which it is authorised;

(c) must specify the matters falling within section 22(2) by reference to which it is granted; and

(d) must specify the office, rank or position held by the person granting the authorisation.

(2) A notice under section 22(4) requiring communications data to be disclosed or to be obtained and disclosed—

(a) must be given in writing or (if not in writing) must be given in a manner that produces a record of its having been given;

(b) must describe the communications data to be obtained or disclosed under the notice;

(c) must specify the matters falling within section 22(2) by reference to which the notice is given;

(d) must specify the office, rank or position held by the person giving it; and

(e) must specify the manner in which any disclosure required by the notice is to be made.

(3) A notice under section 22(4) shall not require the disclosure of data to any person other than—

(a) the person giving the notice; or

(b) such other person as may be specified in or otherwise identified by, or in accordance with, the provisions of the notice;

but the provisions of the notice shall not specify or otherwise identify a person for the purposes of paragraph (b) unless he holds an office, rank or position with the same relevant public authority as the person giving the notice.

(4) An authorisation under section 22(3) or notice under section 22(4)—

(a) shall not authorise or require any data to be obtained after the end of the period of one month beginning with the date on which the authorisation is granted or the notice given; and

(b) in the case of a notice, shall not authorise or require any disclosure after the end of that period of any data not in the possession of, or obtained by, the postal or telecommunications operator at a time during that period.

(5) An authorisation under section 22(3) or notice under section 22(4) may be renewed at any time before the end of the period of one month applying (in accordance with subsection (4) or subsection (7)) to that authorisation or notice.

(6) A renewal of an authorisation under section 22(3) or of a notice under section 22(4) shall be by the grant or giving, in accordance with this section, of a further authorisation or notice.

(7) Subsection (4) shall have effect in relation to a renewed authorisation or renewal notice as if the period of one month mentioned in that subsection did not begin until the end of the period of one month applicable to the authorisation or notice that is current at the time of the renewal.

(8) Where a person who has given a notice under subsection (4) of section 22 is satisfied—

(a) that it is no longer necessary on grounds falling within subsection (2) of that section for the requirements of the notice to be complied with, or

(b) that the conduct required by the notice is no longer proportionate to what is sought to be achieved by obtaining communications data to which the notice relates,

he shall cancel the notice.

(9) The Secretary of State may by regulations provide for the person by whom any duty imposed by subsection (8) is to be performed in a case in which it would otherwise fall on a person who is no longer available to perform it; and regulations under this subsection may provide for the person on whom the duty is to fall to be a person appointed in accordance with the regulations.

24. *Arrangements for payments*

(1) It shall be the duty of the Secretary of State to ensure that such arrangements are in force as he thinks appropriate for requiring or authorising, in such cases as he thinks fit, the making to postal and telecommunications operators of appropriate contributions towards the costs incurred by them in complying with notices under section 22(4).

(2) For the purpose of complying with his duty under this section, the Secretary of State may make arrangements for payments to be made out of money provided by Parliament.

25. *Interpretation of Chapter II*

(1) In this Chapter—

"communications data" has the meaning given by section 21(4);

"designated" shall be construed in accordance with subsection (2);

"postal or telecommunications operator" means a person who provides a postal service or telecommunications service;

"relevant public authority" means (subject to subsection (4)) any of the following—

    (a) a police force;

    (b) the Serious Organised Crime Agency;

  [(ca) the Scottish Crime and Drug Enforcement Agency;][3]

    (d) the Commissioners of Customs and Excise;

    (e) the Commissioners of Inland Revenue;

    (f) any of the intelligence services;

    (g) any such public authority not falling within paragraphs (a) to (f) as may be specified for the purposes of this subsection by an order made by the Secretary of State.

(2) Subject to subsection (3), the persons designated for the purposes of this Chapter are the individuals holding such offices, ranks or positions with relevant public authorities as are prescribed for the purposes of this subsection by an order made by the Secretary of State.

(3) The Secretary of State may by order impose restrictions—

    (a) on the authorisations and notices under this Chapter that may be granted or given by any individual holding an office, rank or position with a specified public authority; and

    (b) on the circumstances in which, or the purposes for which, such authorisations may be granted or notices given by any such individual.

(3A) References in this Chapter to an individual holding an office or position with the Serious Organised Crime Agency include references to any member of the staff of that Agency.

(4) The Secretary of State may by order—

    (a) remove any person from the list of persons who are for the time being relevant public authorities for the purposes of this Chapter; and

---

[3] added by Police, Public Order and Criminal Justice (Scotland) Act 2006 (Consequential Provisions and Modifications) Order 2007/1098 Sch. 1(1) para. 4(5)

(b) make such consequential amendments, repeals or revocations in this or any other enactment as appear to him to be necessary or expedient.

(5) The Secretary of State shall not make an order under this section—

(a) that adds any person to the list of persons who are for the time being relevant public authorities for the purposes of this Chapter, or

(b) that by virtue of subsection (4)(b) amends or repeals any provision of an Act, unless a draft of the order has been laid before Parliament and approved by a resolution of each House.

Index